Edmund Spenser

The Works of
Edmund Spenser

*with an Introduction by Tim Cook,
and Bibliography*

Wordsworth Poetry Library

This edition published 1995 by Wordsworth Editions Ltd,
Cumberland House, Crib Street, Ware, Hertfordshire SG12 9ET.

Copyright © Wordsworth Editions 1995.

ISBN 1-85326-442-3

Printed and bound in Denmark by Nørhaven.

The paper in this book is produced from pure wood
pulp, without the use of chlorine or any other substance
harmful to the environment. The energy used in its
production consists almost entirely of hydroelectricity
and heat generated from waste materials, thereby
conserving fossil fuels and contributing little to the
greenhouse effect.

CONTENTS

INTRODUCTION

APART from Milton and Shakespeare, few poets have influenced English literature as much as Edmund Spenser. Indeed, until around 1900, these, with Chaucer, were regarded as the four supreme masters of English poetry. Now, however, though Chaucer, because of the approachability of his content, is still read, though often in translation, and Shakespeare has a vast international audience, Milton is regarded even by students of literature as difficult, if not irrelevant, and it is quite likely that recent graduates in English will not have read a single word of Spenser. To the ordinary poetry lover he is barely a name. Yet Milton, Pope and all the greatest poets of the Romantic period admired him and acknowledged their debt to him.

Spenser is believed to have been born in 1552, just six years before Queen Elizabeth I (whom he was going to celebrate, with reservations, in his great epic as Gloriana, the Faerie Queene) came to the throne and England became Protestant again. He had a sound Classical education at the Merchant Taylors' School in London under the distinguished teacher Richard Mulcaster and went on to Cambridge, the intellectual headquarters of Puritanism in England. After a brief period as a bishop's secretary, he entered the service of Lord Leicester, the Queen's favourite, having already had his first poems (some rather laboured translations) published. However, it was his set of pastoral poems, *The Shepheardes Kalender*, printed in 1579, that made his name.

The great Roman epic poet Virgil had launched his career in a similar way, and Spenser consciously followed his example. Virgil's *Eclogues* contain descriptions of shepherd life (modelled on the Greek poet Theocritus), intermingled with elegy, prophecy and references to current events. His Fourth Eclogue had seemed to foretell the birth of Christ and, as a result, he was almost seen as an honorary Christian. Later Italian poets, such as Petrarch, had used pastoral to comment covertly on religious and political matters. Spenser partly followed their example. His *Kalender* comprises shepherd monologues and dialogues with love and poetry as their subjects, set in a fairly realistically drawn rustic English environment ('Ianuarie', 'March', 'Iune', 'August', 'October', 'November', 'December') interspersed with satirical fables making coded comments on religious affairs from a Puritan point of view ('Februarie', 'Maye', 'Iulye', 'September') and one ('Aprill') enthusiastically celebrating in an elaborate lyric the virtues of the Queen.

Significantly, even at this early stage of his career, while celebrating

Elizabeth, Spenser is not afraid to criticise her policies. The good shepherd Algrind in 'Iulye' is almost certainly Bishop Grindal, a leading Puritan, and the dropping of a shellfish on his head by an eagle, the royal bird, would then refer to his dismissal by the Queen, while other politico- religious poems in the series warn of dangers from Rome and high church episcopacy. On the other hand, the charming fable of the Oak and the Briar in 'Februarie' seems to suggest that over-zealous Puritanism might destroy what was valuable in the old religion's legacy. This interpretation is consistent with Spenser's recognition of the dedication of the Catholic priesthood in his entertaining satire *Mother Hubberd's Tale*, admired by Dryden but virtually forgotten today, which was probably written early in his career, though published much later (see lines 447-454).

However, it was as a display of the poet's virtuosity and for its daringly innovative use of language, rather than for its content, that *The Shepheardes Kalender* made such an impact in 1579. Though much of the *Kalender* is written in the simple couplets Chaucer used, it contains, besides the elaborate Eliza ode already mentioned, a lyrical elegy for an unidentified woman friend of Leicester ('Lobbin' in pastoral code) mourned as 'Dido'. It also includes ('August') an example of a sestina, a difficult Renaissance form using the same seven words to conclude the seven lines of each stanza, a dialogue ('Iulye') in the old fourteen- syllabled line favoured by earlier Elizabethan poets, a lighter lyrical dialogue ('March') including a story about the mischievous love god Cupid, and a concluding lament ('December') in stately six-line stanzas.

For the whole sequence Spenser developed a special poetic language, based on Chaucer and on regional dialects, which must have seemed as original to his first readers as, say, the poems of Hardy or Gerard Manley Hopkins. Indeed two of his most distinguished contemporaries, Sir Philip Sidney and Ben Jonson, felt he had been too bold in his linguistic experiments.

Spenser's awareness that he was perhaps being too innovative for his readership is shown by his decision to provide a commentary, written by the so far unidentified 'E.K.' to explain his work, though scholars have felt that this raises as many questions as it answers. A modern parallel is the set of notes added by T.S. Eliot to *The Waste Land*.

The success of his pastorals brought Spenser the patronage of Sir Philip Sidney and employment on government service in Ireland, where he was the neighbour of another distinguished poet-politician, Sir Walter Raleigh, and worked on the great epic that had been foreshadowed in the discussion of the state of poetry in his 'October' eclogue, where Spenser is referred to as 'Colin'. The first three books of *The Faerie Queene* were published in 1591 during a visit to England and it was immediately acclaimed as a masterpiece. Spenser's intentions in writing it are set out in his letter to Raleigh, written in 1589 and printed at the end of the poem in this edition.

The aim of *The Faerie Queene*, we are told, was to 'fashion a gentleman or noble person in vertuous and gentle discipline'. It proposed to do this by showing the 'twelve morall vertues' in action in a set of stories, with each book devoted to a particular virtue. Unfortunately Spenser's early death in 1599, as a refugee from well justified rebellion in Ireland, prevented him from completing the plan, so that we are left with only six books and a long fragment of a seventh, the so-called 'Mutabilitie Cantos'. These are one of the greatest expressions of Spenser's myth-making power, ending with a characteristic meditation on change and death and a final affirmation of faith that forms a very moving and appropriate conclusion to the poet's career.

The six completed books are each based on the Arthurian idea of the knightly quest, with their heroes representing not so much the particular virtue being illustrated as the aspiration to that virtue. Each book dramatises a learning process and works on several different levels. There is the initial level of the straightforward adventure story, derived from medieval romances about knights, monsters, ogres and damsels in distress. Then there are the levels of moral, political, historical and religious significance, each of them intertwined with the others. Spenser's contemporaries were used to reading stories as allegories or 'dark conceits' (i.e. imaginative conceptions with hidden meanings), but even his contemporaries may not have worked out everything that was in his mind, and only scholars familiar with the complexities of Elizabethan politics, society and religion will be concerned with the more esoteric elements in the poem. Nevertheless, one has no need of this rare expertise to enjoy *The Faerie Queene*. It should appeal to anyone who loves poetry and is interested in the moral, psychological and religious questions that have preoccupied poets through the centuries.

There is the sheer craftmanship of the work, for a start. Spenser chose to write his poem as the Italian writers of romance epic, Ariosto and Tasso had done, in stanzas, but he substituted for the *ottava rima* they used (an eight line stanza with two alternating rhymes for the first six lines and a final couplet) a complex nine-line stanza with interlacing rhymes and a final longer line which he used for special effects. This gives his poem a predominantly slow and stately quality as it moves from stanza to stanza, although at times it is fully capable of speed and urgency, as when the Red Cross Knight disregards the urgent warnings of his lady Una in Book I, Canto I and is almost throttled by the female monster Error.

However, the medium is best adapted to great, carefully-structured set pieces: the procession of the Seven Deadly Sins in Canto IV of that opening book; the Cave of Mammon in Book II, Canto VII, with its echoes of the Classical underworld; the Bower of Blisse, imitated from Tasso but given a powerfully erotic quality that is entirely Spenserian, in the last canto of the same book; the Platonic Gardens of Adonis (another example of Spenser's philosophical myth-making), in Book III, Canto VI; the sinister Masque of Cupid in Canto XII; the Temple of Venus in Book IV, Canto X; and of course the great Mutabilitie Cantos themselves. These are perhaps the points at which Spenser's combination of evocative language and visionary imagination is at its most striking and memorable.

Although in epic one can scarcely expect the range and depth of characterisation one looks for in Elizabethan and Jacobean drama, or in the novel, there is plenty of variety and interest to be found in the people we meet on our way through the poem. There is the foolhardy, inexperienced Red Cross knight, in his inherited armour, separated from his lady, Una, the true faith, and deceived into an affair with the false one before recovering his spirits and strength in time to meet, as St George, the assault of the dragon. There are the treacherous magician Archimago and the dishevelled, skeletal figure of Despair, with his powerful suicide-inducing rhetoric. There is Book II's very human Sir Guyon, the knight of Temperance, seeking to learn self-mastery, who is erotically aroused by the watery striptease of two girls on his way to the Bower of Blisse and makes us feel the painful effort needed to resist the demands of desire as he responds reluctantly to the instructions of the humourless Palmer, representing the moral self, and overcomes the tempting sensuality of the witch Acrasia.

Books III and IV introduce us to Britomart, the energetic and attractively feminine champion of Chastity and fidelity in its positive aspects. She meets many challenges, ranging from a whole series of male knights to the giant Ollyphant and the enchanter Busyrane (the torturer of Amoret, the embodiment of vulnerable womanhood seen as the imprisoned object of male lust), on the way to her encounter with her ideal partner Artegall. Artegall himself becomes the human side of Justice in Book V, with the robot-like Talus representing the impersonal, even savage, severity with which the poet felt it necessary to crush Irish and other threats to Elizabethan power, while in the last completed sixth book there is the knight of Courtesy, Calidore, who temporarily and almost disastrously forgets his responsibilities and quest to enjoy life with his shepherdess love Pastorella. Other characters include the Diana- or Queen Elizabeth-like and sometimes ironically viewed Belphoebe, the seducer Paridell, and the comic Braggadochio, a blustering false knight deriving ultimately from Classical comedy.

In an age where our capacity to transform verbally created images into mentally visualised ones has been weakened by films and television, it is difficult to recreate the leisurely meditative process of reading Spenser and imagining his world as Milton, Keats, Byron, Wordsworth and countless ordinary readers did before 1900. His invented stanza, too, was admired and used by many important poets He is too easily seen as chief poet-propagandist of Queen Elizabeth's reign, and co-creator of her 'Gloriana' image. But we have seen that he began as a critic of aspects of the Elizabethan regime, and his Complaints volume, published in 1591 shows him still unafraid to speak his mind, within the limits imposed by contemporary censorship. His championship of the rejected policies favoured by his dead patrons, Leicester and Sidney, comes across clearly. It is significant that he borrowed his pen-name, Colin Clout, from an earlier satirist, John Skelton. If one reads *The Faerie Queene* carefully, it seems clear that although the Queen as symbol is the object of unalloyed praise, the Queen as human being is perhaps the most important of those 'gentle persons' the poem was designed to educate.

The Faerie Queene is undoubtedly the greatest and richest of Spenser's achievements, and *The Shepheardes Kalender* a remarkable early masterpiece. However he also gave us, in his *Fowre Hymnes*, a deeply felt statement of neo-Platonic theories of beauty and love; in *The Ruins of Time* and *Astrophell* powerful elegies on his patrons Leicester and Sidney; in *Mother Hubberd's Tale* a witty beast satire anticipating in its form the couplets of Dryden and Pope; in *Muiopotmos* an entertaining mock-epic, with possibly a hidden meaning, about the death of a butterfly trapped by a spider; in *Colin Clout's Come Home Again* an interesting examination of the state of England in the last quarter of Elizabeth's reign; in his *Amoretti* an unusual sonnet sequence, in that it was written to the girl whom the poet eventually married; in *Prothalamion* a great ode written in Classical style in honour of a great aristocratic wedding, and in his *Epithalamion* another, even finer, to celebrate his own wedding day in what is one of the most deeply felt and most skilfully constructed love poems in any language, whatever some may nowadays feel about the attitudes to women that it reveals.

Tim Cook
Kingston University

FURTHER READING

Introductory

C.S. Lewis, *English Literature in the Sixteenth Century* (1954), pp 347-39.
M. Evans, *English Poetry in the Sixteenth Century* (1967).
M. Evans, *Spenser's Anatomy of Heroism* (1970).
Peter Bayley, *Edmund Spenser, Prince of Poets* (1971).

More Specialised

N.J. Hoffman, *Spenser's Pastorals* (1977).
G. Hough, *A Preface to The Faerie Queene* (1962).
A. Fowler, *Edmund Spenser* (1977).
Anthea Hume, *Edmund Spenser, Protestant Poet* (1984).
R. Headlam Wells, *Spenser's 'Faerie Queene' and the cult of Elizabeth* (1983).
Simon Shepherd, *Spenser* (for a provocative critical theory based approach) (1989).

THE POETICAL WORKS

OF

EDMUND SPENSER

THE FAERIE
QVEENE.

Difpofed into twelue bookes,

Fashioning

XII. Morall vertues.

LONDON
Printed for VVilliam Ponfonbie.
1 5 9 6.

TO
THE MOST HIGH,
MIGHTIE
And
MAGNIFICENT
EMPRESSE RENOVV-
MED FOR PIETIE, VER-
TVE, AND ALL GRATIOVS
GOVERNMENT ELIZABETH BY
THE GRACE OF GOD QVEENE
OF ENGLAND FRAVNCE AND
IRELAND AND OF VIRGI-
NIA, DEFENDOVR OF THE
FAITH, &c.   HER MOST
HVMBLE SERVAVNT
EDMVND SPENSER
DOTH IN ALL HV-
MILITIE DEDI-
CATE, PRE-
SENT
AND CONSECRATE THESE
HIS LABOVRS TO LIVE
VVITH THE ETERNI-
TIE OF HER
FAME.

THE FIRST
BOOKE OF THE
FAERIE QVEENE.

Contayning

THE LEGENDE OF THE
KNIGHT OF THE RED CROSSE,

OR

OF HOLINESSE.

1

Lo I the man, whose Muse whilome did maske,
  As time her taught, in lowly Shepheards weeds,
  Am now enforst a far vnfitter taske,
  For trumpets sterne to chaunge mine Oaten
    reeds,
  And sing of Knights and Ladies gentle deeds;
  Whose prayses hauing slept in silence long,
  Me, all too meane, the sacred Muse areeds
  To blazon broad emongst her learned throng:
Fierce warres and faithfull loues shall moralize
    my song.

2

Helpe then, O holy Virgin chiefe of nine,
  Thy weaker Nouice to performe thy will,
  Lay forth out of thine euerlasting scryne
  The antique rolles, which there lye hidden still,
  Of Faerie knights and fairest *Tanaquill*,
  Whom that most noble Briton Prince so long
  Sought through the world, and suffered so
    much ill,
  That I must rue his vndeserued wrong:
O helpe thou my weake wit, and sharpen my
    dull tong.

3

And thou most dreaded impe of highest *Ioue*,
  Faire *Venus* sonne, that with thy cruell dart
  At that good knight so cunningly didst roue,
  That glorious fire it kindled in his hart,
  Lay now thy deadly Heben bow apart,
  And with thy mother milde come to mine ayde:
  Come both, and with you bring triumphant
    Mart,
  In loues and gentle iollities arrayd.
After his murdrous spoiles and bloudy rage
    allayd.

4

And with them eke, O Goddesse heauenly
    bright,
  Mirrour of grace and Maiestie diuine,
  Great Lady of the greatest Isle, whose light
  Like *Phœbus* lampe throughout the world doth
    shine,
  Shed thy faire beames into my feeble eyne,
  And raise my thoughts too humble and too vile,
  To thinke of that true glorious type of thine,
  The argument of mine afflicted stile:
The which to heare, vouchsafe, O dearest dred
    a-while.

Canto I.

The Patron of true Holinesse,
Foule Errour doth defeate :
Hypocrisie him to entrappe,
Doth to his home entreate.

I

A Gentle Knight was pricking on the plaine,
  Y cladd in mightie armes and siluer shielde,
  Wherein old dints of deepe wounds did re-
    maine,
  The cruell markes of many' a bloudy fielde ;
  Yet armes till that time did he neuer wield :
  His angry steede did chide his foming bitt,
  As much disdayning to the curbe to yield :
  Full iolly knight he seemd, and faire did sitt,
As one for knightly giusts and fierce encounters
  fitt.

2

But on his brest a bloudie Crosse he bore,
  The deare remembrance of his dying Lord,
  For whose sweete sake that glorious badge he
    wore,
  And dead as liuing euer him ador'd :
  Vpon his shield the like was also scor'd,
  For soueraine hope, which in his helpe he had:
  Right faithfull true he was in deede and word,
  But of his cheere did seeme too solemne sad ;
Yet nothing did he dread, but euer was ydrad.

3

Vpon a great aduenture he was bond,
  That greatest *Gloriana* to him gaue,
  That greatest Glorious Queene of *Faerie* lond,
  To winne him worship, and her grace to haue,
  Which of all earthly things he most did craue ;
  And euer as he rode, his hart did earne
  To proue his puissance in battell braue
  Vpon his foe, and his new force to learne ;
Vpon his foe, a Dragon horrible and stearne.

4

A louely Ladie rode him faire beside,
  Vpon a lowly Asse more white then snow,
  Yet she much whiter, but the same did hide
  Vnder a vele, that wimpled was full low,
  And ouer all a blacke stole she did throw,
  As one that inly mournd : so was she sad,
  And heauie sat vpon her palfrey slow :
  Seemed in heart some hidden care she had,
And by her in a line a milke white lambe she lad.

5

So pure an innocent, as that same lambe,
  She was in life and euery vertuous lore,
  And by descent from Royall lynage came
  Of ancient Kings and Queenes, that had of yore
  Their scepters stretcht from East to Westerne
    shore,
  And all the world in their subiection held ;
  Till that infernall feend with foule vprore
  Forwasted all their land, and them expeld :
Whom to auenge, she had this Knight from far
  compeld.

6

Behind her farre away a Dwarfe did lag,
  That lasie seemd in being euer last,
  Or wearied with bearing of her bag
  Of needments at his backe.   Thus as they past,
  The day with cloudes was suddeine ouercast,
  And angry *Ioue* an hideous storme of raine
  Did poure into his Lemans lap so fast,
  That euery wight to shrowd it did constrain,
And this faire couple eke to shroud themselues
  were fain.

7

Enforst to seeke some couert nigh at hand,
  A shadie groue not far away they spide,
  That promist ayde the tempest to withstand :
  Whose loftie trees yclad with sommers pride,
  Did spred so broad, that heauens light did hide,
  Not perceable with power of any starre :
  And all within were pathes and alleies wide,
  With footing worne, and leading inward farre :
Faire harbour that them seemes ; so in they
  entred arre.

8

And foorth they passe, with pleasure forward led,
  Ioying to heare the birdes sweete harmony,
  Which therein shrouded from the tempest dred,
  Seemd in their song to scorne the cruell sky.
  Much can they prayse the trees so straight and
    hy,
  The sayling Pine, the Cedar proud and tall,
  The vine-prop Elme, the Poplar neuer dry,
  The builder Oake, sole king of forrests all,
The Aspine good for staues, the Cypresse funerall.

9

The Laurell, meed of mightie Conquerours
  And Poets sage, the Firre that weepeth still,
  The Willow worne of forlorne Paramours,
  The Eugh obedient to the benders will,
  The Birch for shaftes, the Sallow for the mill,
  The Mirrhe sweete bleeding in the bitter wound,
  The warlike Beech, the Ash for nothing ill,
  The fruitfull Oliue, and the Platane round,
The caruer Holme, the Maple seeldom inward
  sound.

10

Led with delight, they thus beguile the way,
Vntill the blustring storme is ouerblowne ;
When weening to returne, whence they did
   stray,   [showne,
They cannot finde that path, which first was
But wander too and fro in wayes vnknowne,
Furthest from end then, when they neerest
   weene,   [their owne :
That makes them doubt, their wits be not
So many pathes, so many turnings seene,
That which of them to take, in diuerse doubt
   they been.

11

At last resoluing forward still to fare,
Till that some end they finde or in or out,
That path they take, that beaten seemd most
And like to lead the labyrinth about ; [bare,
Which when by tract they hunted had
   throughout,
At length it brought them to a hollow caue,
Amid the thickest woods. The Champion stout
Eftsoones dismounted from his courser braue,
And to the Dwarfe a while his needlesse spere
   he gaue.

12

Be well aware, quoth then that Ladie milde,
Least suddaine mischiefe ye too rash prouoke :
The danger hid, the place vnknowne and wilde,
Breedes dreadfull doubts : Oft fire is without
   smoke,
And perill without show : therefore your stroke
Sir knight with-hold, till further triall made.
Ah Ladie (said he) shame were to reuoke
The forward footing for an hidden shade :
Vertue giues her selfe light, through darkenesse
   for to wade.

13

Yea but (quoth she) the perill of this place
I better wot then you, though now too late
To wish you backe returne with foule disgrace,
Yet wisedome warnes, whilest foot is in the gate,
To stay the steppe, ere forced to retrate.
This is the wandring wood, this *Errours den*,
A monster vile, whom God and man does hate :
Therefore I read beware. Fly fly (quoth then
The fearefull Dwarfe :) this is no place for liuing
   men.

14

But full of fire and greedy hardiment,
The youthfull knight could not for ought be staide,
But forth vnto the darksome hole he went,
And looked in : his glistring armor made
A litle glooming light, much like a shade,
By which he saw the vgly monster plaine,
Halfe like a serpent horribly displaide,
But th'other halfe did womans shape retaine,
Most lothsom, filthie, foule, and full of vile disdaine.

15

And as she lay vpon the durtie ground,
Her huge long taile her den all ouerspred,
Yet was in knots and many boughtes vpwound,
Pointed with mortall sting. Of her there bred
A thousand yong ones, which she dayly fed,
Sucking vpon her poisonous dugs, eachone
Of sundry shapes, yet all ill fauored :
Soone as that vncouth light vpon them shone,
Into her mouth they crept, and suddain all
   were gone.

16

Their dam vpstart, out of her den effraide,
And rushed forth, hurling her hideous taile
About her cursed head, whose folds displaid
Were stretcht now forth at length without
   entraile.
She lookt about, and seeing one in mayle
Armed to point, sought backe to turne againe ;
For light she hated as the deadly bale,
Ay wont in desert darkenesse to remaine,
Where plaine none might her see, nor she see
   any plaine.

17

Which when the valiant Elfe perceiu'd, he lept
As Lyon fierce vpon the flying pray,
And with his trenchand blade her boldly kept
From turning backe, and forced her to stay :
Therewith enrag'd she loudly gan to bray,
And turning fierce, her speckled taile aduaunst,
Threatning her angry sting, him to dismay :
Who nought aghast, his mightie hand enhaunst :
The stroke down from her head vnto her
   shoulder glaunst.

18

Much daunted with that dint, her sence was dazd,
Yet kindling rage, her selfe she gathered round,
And all attonce her beastly body raizd
With doubled forces high aboue the ground :
Tho wrapping vp her wrethed sterne arownd,
Lept fierce vpon his shield, and her huge traine
All suddenly about his body wound,
That hand or foot to stirre he stroue in vaine :
God helpe the man so wrapt in *Errours* end-
   lesse traine.

19

His Lady sad to see his sore constraint,
Cride out, Now now Sir knight, shew what ye
   bee,
Add faith vnto your force, and be not faint :
Strangle her, else she sure will strangle thee.
That when he heard, in great perplexitie,
His gall did grate for griefe and high disdaine,
And knitting all his force got one hand free,
Wherewith he grypt her gorge with so great
   paine,
That soone to loose her wicked bands did her
   constraine.

20

Therewith she spewd out of her filthy maw
 A floud of poyson horrible and blacke,
 Full of great lumpes of flesh and gobbets raw,
 Which stunck so vildly, that it forst him slacke
 His grasping hold, and from her turne him backe:
 Her vomit full of bookes and papers was,
 With loathly frogs and toades, which eyes did
  lacke,
 And creeping sought way in the weedy gras :
Her filthy parbreake all the place defiled has.

21

As when old father *Nilus* gins to swell
 With timely pride aboue the *Aegyptian* vale,
 His fattie waues do fertile slime outwell,
 And ouerflow each plaine and lowly dale :
 But when his later spring gins to auale,
 Huge heapes of mudd he leaues, wherein there
  breed
 Ten thousand kindes of creatures, partly male
 And partly female of his fruitfull seed ;
Such vgly monstrous shapes elswhere may no
 man reed.

22

The same so sore annoyed has the knight,
 That welnigh choked with the deadly stinke,
 His forces faile, ne can no longer fight.
 Whose corage when the feend perceiu'd to
  shrinke,
 She poured forth out of her hellish sinke
 Her fruitfull cursed spawne of serpents small,
 Deformed monsters, fowle, and blacke as inke,
 Which swarming all about his legs did crall,
And him encombred sore, but could not hurt
 at all.

23

As gentle Shepheard in sweete euen-tide,
 When ruddy *Phœbus* gins to welke in west,
 High on an hill, his flocke to vewen wide,
 Markes which do byte their hasty supper best ;
 A cloud of combrous gnattes do him molest,
 All striuing to infixe their feeble stings,
 That from their noyance he no where can rest.
 But with his clownish hands their tender wings
He brusheth oft, and oft doth mar their mur-
 murings.

24

Thus ill bestedd, and fearefull more of shame,
 Then of the certaine perill he stood in,
 Halfe furious vnto his foe he came,
 Resolv'd in minde all suddenly to win,
 Or soone to lose, before he once would lin ;
 And strooke at her with more then manly force,
 That from her body full of filthie sin
 He raft her hatefull head without remorse ;
A streame of cole black bloud forth gushed
 from her corse.

25

Her scattred brood, soone as their Parent deare
 They saw so rudely falling to the ground,
 Groning full deadly, all with troublous feare,
 Gathred themselues about her body round,
 Weening their wonted entrance to haue found
 At her wide mouth : but being there withstood
 They flocked all about her bleeding wound,
 And sucked vp their dying mothers blood,
Making her death their life, and eke her hurt
 their good.

26

That detestable sight him much amazde,
 To see th'vnkindly Impes of heauen accurst,
 Deuoure their dam ; on whom while so he gazd,
 Hauing all satisfide their bloudy thurst,
 Their bellies swolne he saw with fulnesse burst,
 And bowels gushing forth : well worthy end
 Of such as drunke her life, the which them nurst;
 Now needeth him no lenger labour spend,
His foes haue slaine themselues, with whom he
 should contend.

27

His Ladie seeing all, that chaunst, from farre
 Approcht in hast to greet his victorie,
 And said, Faire knight, borne vnder happy
  starre,
 Who see your vanquisht foes before you lye ;
 Well worthy be you of that Armorie,
 Wherein ye haue great glory wonne this day,
 And proou'd your strength on a strong enimie,
 Your first aduenture : many such I pray,
And henceforth euer wish, that like succeed it
 may.

28

Then mounted he vpon his Steede againe,
 And with the Lady backward sought to wend ;
 That path he kept, which beaten was most
  plaine,
 Ne euer would to any by-way bend,
 But still did follow one vnto the end,
 The which at last out of the wood them
  brought.
 So forward on his way (with God to frend)
 He passed forth, and new aduenture sought ;
Long way he trauelled, before he heard of ought.

29

At length they chaunst to meet vpon the way
 An aged Sire, in long blacke weedes yclad,
 His feete all bare, his beard all hoarie gray,
 And by his belt his booke he hanging had ;
 Sober he seemde, and very sagely sad,
 And to the ground his eyes were lowly bent,
 Simple in shew, and voyde of malice bad,
 And all the way he prayed, as he went,
And often knockt his brest, as one that did
 repent.

30

He faire the knight saluted, louting low,
  Who faire him quited, as that courteous was :
  And after asked him, if he did know
  Of straunge aduentures, which abroad did pas.
  Ah my deare Sonne (quoth he) how should, alas,
  Silly old man, that liues in hidden cell,
  Bidding his beades all day for his trespas,
  Tydings of warre and worldly trouble tell ?
With holy father sits not with such things to
    mell.

31

But if of daunger which hereby doth dwell,
  And homebred euill ye desire to heare,
  Of a straunge man I can you tidings tell,
  That wasteth all this countrey farre and neare.
  Of such (said he) I chiefly do inquere,
  And shall you well reward to shew the place,
  In which that wicked wight his dayes doth
    weare :
  For to all knighthood it is foule disgrace,
That such a cursed creature liues so long a
    space.

32

Far hence (quoth he) in wastfull wildernesse
  His dwelling is, by which no liuing wight
  May euer passe, but thorough great distresse.
  Now (sayd the Lady) draweth toward night,
  And well I wote, that of your later fight
  Ye all forwearied be : for what so strong,
  But wanting rest will also want of might ?
  The Sunne that measures heauen all day long,
At night doth baite his steedes the *Ocean* waues
    emong.

33

Then with the Sunne take Sir, your timely rest,
  And with new day new worke at once begin :
  Vntroubled night they say giues counsell best.
  Right well Sir knight ye haue aduised bin,
  (Quoth then that aged man ;) the way to win
  Is wisely to aduise : now day is spent ;
  Therefore with me ye may take vp your In
  For this same night. The knight was well
    content :
So with that godly father to his home they
    went.

34

A little lowly Hermitage it was,
  Downe in a dale, hard by a forests side,
  Far from resort of people, that did pas
  In trauell to and froe : a little wyde
  There was an holy Chappell edifyde,
  Wherein the Hermite dewly wont to say
  His holy things each morne and euentyde :
  Thereby a Christall streame did gently play,
Which from a sacred fountaine welled forth
    alway.

35

Arriued there, the little house they fill,
  Ne looke for entertainement, where none was :
  Rest is their feast, and all things at their will ;
  The noblest mind the best contentment has.
  With faire discourse the euening so they pas :
  For that old man of pleasing wordes had store,
  And well could file his tongue as smooth as glas ;
  He told of Saintes and Popes, and euermore
He strowd an *Aue-Mary* after and before.

36

The drouping Night thus creepeth on them fast,
  And the sad humour loading their eye liddes,
  As messenger of *Morpheus* on them cast
  Sweet slombring deaw, the which to sleepe
    them biddes.
  Vnto their lodgings then his guestes he riddes :
  Where when all drownd in deadly sleepe he
    findes,
  He to his study goes, and there amiddes
  His Magick bookes and artes of sundry kindes,
He seekes out mighty charmes, to trouble sleepy
    mindes.

37

Then choosing out few wordes most horrible,
  (Let none them read) thereof did verses frame,
  With which and other spelles like terrible,
  He bad awake blacke *Plutoes* griesly Dame,
  And cursed heauen, and spake reprochfull shame
  Of highest God, the Lord of life and light ;
  A bold bad man, that dar'd to call by name
  Great *Gorgon*, Prince of darknesse and dead
    night,   [flight.
At which *Cocytus* quakes, and *Styx* is put to

38

And forth he cald out of deepe darknesse dred
  Legions of Sprights, the which like little flyes
  Fluttring about his euer damned hed,
  A-waite whereto their seruice he applyes,
  To aide his friends, or fray his enimies :
  Of those he chose out two, the falsest twoo,
  And fittest for to forge true-seeming lyes ;
  The one of them he gaue a message too,
The other by him selfe staide other worke to doo.

39

He making speedy way through spersed ayre,
  And through the world of waters wide and deepe,
  To *Morpheus* house doth hastily repaire.
  Amid the bowels of the earth full steepe,
  And low, where dawning day doth neuer peepe,
  His dwelling is ; there *Tethys* his wet bed
  Doth euer wash, and *Cynthia* still doth steepe
  In siluer deaw his euer-drouping hed,
Whiles sad Night ouer him her mantle black
    doth spred.

40

Whose double gates he findeth locked fast,
The one faire fram'd of burnisht Yuory,
The other all with siluer ouercast ;
And wakefull dogges before them farre do lye,
Watching to banish Care their enimy,
Who oft is wont to trouble gentle Sleepe.
By them the Sprite doth passe in quietly,
And vnto *Morpheus* comes, whom drowned
deepe   [keepe.
In drowsie fit he findes : of nothing he takes

41

And more, to lulle him in his slumber soft,
A trickling streame from high rocke tumbling
downe
And euer-drizling raine vpon the loft,   [sowne
Mixt with a murmuring winde, much like the
Of swarming Bees, did cast him in a swowne :
No other noyse, nor peoples troublous cryes,
As still are wont t'annoy the walled towne,
Might there be heard : but carelesse Quiet lyes,
Wrapt in eternall silence farre from enemyes.

42

The messenger approching to him spake,
But his wast wordes returnd to him in vaine :
So sound he slept, that nought mought him
awake.   [paine,
Then rudely he him thrust, and pusht with
Whereat he gan to stretch : but he againe
Shooke him so hard, that forced him to speake.
As one then in a dreame, whose dryer braine
Is tost with troubled sights and fancies weake,
He mumbled soft, but would not all his silence
breake.

43

The Sprite then gan more boldly him to wake,
And threatned vnto him the dreaded name
Of *Hecate* : whereat he gan to quake,
And lifting vp his lumpish head, with blame
Halfe angry asked him, for what he came.
Hither (quoth he) me *Archimago* sent,
He that the stubborne Sprites can wisely tame,
He bids thee to him send for his intent
A fit false dreame, that can delude the sleepers
sent.

44

The God obayde, and calling forth straight way
A diuerse dreame out of his prison darke,
Deliuered it to him, and downe did lay
His heauie head, deuoide of carefull carke,
Whose sences all were straight benumbd and
starke.
He backe returning by the Yuorie dore,
Remounted vp as light as chearefull Larke,
And on his litle winges the dreame he bore
In hast vnto his Lord, where he him left afore.

45

Who all this while with charmes and hidden
artes,
Had made a Lady of that other Spright,
And fram'd of liquid ayre her tender partes
So liuely, and so like in all mens sight,
That weaker sence it could haue rauisht quight :
The maker selfe for all his wondrous witt,
Was nigh beguiled with so goodly sight :
Her all in white he clad, and ouer it
Cast a blacke stole, most like to seeme for *Vna*
fit.

46

Now when that ydle dreame was to him brought,
Vnto that Elfin knight he bad him fly,
Where he slept soundly void of euill thought,
And with false shewes abuse his fantasy,
In sort as he him schooled priuily :
And that new creature borne without her dew,
Full of the makers guile, with vsage sly
He taught to imitate that Lady trew,
Whose semblance she did carrie vnder feigned
hew.

47

Thus well instructed, to their worke they hast,
And comming where the knight in slomber lay,
The one vpon his hardy head him plast,
And made him dreame of loues and lustfull play,
That nigh his manly hart did melt away,
Bathed in wanton blis and wicked ioy :
Then seemed him his Lady by him lay,
And to him playnd, how that false winged boy
Her chast hart had subdewd, to learne Dame
pleasures toy.

48

And she her selfe of beautie soueraigne Queene,
Faire *Venus* seemde vnto his bed to bring
Her, whom he waking euermore did weene
To be the chastest flowre, that ay did spring
On earthly braunch, the daughter of a king,
Now a loose Leman to vile seruice bound :
And eke the *Graces* seemed all to sing,
Hymen iô Hymen, dauncing all around,
Whilst freshest *Flora* her with Yuie girlond
crownd.

49

In this great passion of vnwonted lust,
Or wonted feare of doing ought amis,
He started vp, as seeming to mistrust
Some secret ill, or hidden foe of his :
Lo there before his face his Lady is,
Vnder blake stole hyding her bayted hooke,
And as halfe blushing offred him to kis,
With gentle blandishment and louely looke,
Most like that virgin true, which for her knight
him took.

50

All cleane dismayd to see so vncouth sight,
And halfe enraged at her shamelesse guise,
He thought haue slaine her in his fierce despight:
But hasty heat tempring with sufferance wise,
He stayde his hand, and gan himselfe aduise
To proue his sense, and tempt her faigned truth.
Wringing her hands in wemens pitteous wise,
Tho can she weepe, to stirre vp gentle ruth,
Both for her noble bloud, and for her tender
    youth.

51

And said, Ah Sir, my liege Lord and my loue,
Shall I accuse the hidden cruell fate,
And mightie causes wrought in heauen aboue,
Or the blind God, that doth me thus amate,
For hoped loue to winne me certaine hate?
Yet thus perforce he bids me do, or die.
Die is my dew: yet rew my wretched state
You, whom my hard auenging destinie
Hath made iudge of my life or death indiffer-
    ently.

52

Your owne deare sake forst me at first to leaue
My Fathers kingdome, There she stopt with
    teares;
Her swollen hart her speach seemd to bereaue,
And then againe begun, My weaker yeares
Captiu'd to fortune and frayle worldly feares,
Fly to your faith for succour and sure ayde:
Let me not dye in languor and long teares.
Why Dame (quoth he) what hath ye thus
    dismayd?
What frayes ye, that were wont to comfort me
    affrayd?

53

Loue of your selfe, she said, and deare constraint
Lets me not sleepe, but wast the wearie night
In secret anguish and vnpittied plaint,
Whiles you in carelesse sleepe are drowned
    quight.
Her doubtfull words made that redoubted knight
Suspect her truth: yet since no'vntruth he knew,
Her fawning loue with foule disdainefull spight
He would not shend, but said, Deare dame I rew,
That for my sake vnknowne such griefe vnto
    you grew.

54

Assure your selfe, it fell not all to ground;
For all so deare as life is to my hart,
I deeme your loue, and hold me to you bound;
Ne let vaine feares procure your needlesse smart,
Where cause is none, but to your rest depart.
Not all content, yet seemd she to appease
Her mournefull plaintes, beguiled of her art,
And fed with words, that could not chuse but
    please,
So slyding softly forth, she turnd as to her ease.

55

Long after lay he musing at her mood,
Much grieu'd to thinke that gentle Dame so light,
For whose defence he was to shed his blood.
At last dull wearinesse of former fight
Hauing yrockt a sleepe his irkesome spright,
That troublous dreame gan freshly tosse his
    braine,   [delight:
With bowres, and beds, and Ladies deare
But when he saw his labour all was vaine,
With that misformed spright he backe returnd
    againe.

Cant. II.

The guilefull great Enchaunter parts
The Redcrosse Knight from Truth:
Into whose stead faire falshood steps,
And workes him wofull ruth.

1

By this the Northerne wagoner had set
His seuenfold teme behind the stedfast starre,
That was in Ocean waues yet neuer wet,
But firme is fixt, and sendeth light from farre
To all, that in the wide deepe wandring arre:
And chearefull Chauntclere with his note shrill
Had warned once, that *Phœbus* fiery carre
In hast was climbing vp the Easterne hill,
Full enuious that night so long his roome did fill.

2

When those accursed messengers of hell,
That feigning dreame, and that faire-forged
    Spright
Came to their wicked maister, and gan tell
Their bootelesse paines, and ill succeeding
    night:
Who all in rage to see his skilfull might
Deluded so, gan threaten hellish paine
And sad *Proserpines* wrath, them to affright.
But when he saw his threatning was but vaine,
He cast about, and searcht his balefull bookes
    againe.

3

Eftsoones he tooke that miscreated faire,
And that false other Spright, on whom he spred
A seeming body of the subtile aire,
Like a young Squire, in loues and lusty-hed
His wanton dayes that euer loosely led,
Without regard of armes and dreaded fight:
Those two he tooke, and in a secret bed,
Couered with darknesse and misdeeming night,
Them both together laid, to ioy in vaine delight.

4

Forthwith he runnes with feigned faithfull hast
Vnto his guest, who after troublous sights
And dreames, gan now to take more sound
     repast,
Whom suddenly he wakes with fearefull frights,
As one aghast with feends or damned sprights,
And to him cals, Rise rise vnhappy Swaine,
That here wex old in sleepe, whiles wicked
     wights   [chaine ;
Haue knit themselues in *Venus* shamefull
Come see, where your false Lady doth her
     honour staine.

5

All in amaze he suddenly vp start
With sword in hand, and with the old man went ;
Who soone him brought into a secret part,
Where that false couple were full closely ment
In wanton lust and lewd embracement :
Which when he saw, he burnt with gealous fire,
The eye of reason was with rage yblent,
And would haue slaine them in his furious ire,
But hardly was restreined of that aged sire.

6

Returning to his bed in torment great,
And bitter anguish of his guiltie sight,
He could not rest, but did his stout heart eat,
And wast his inward gall with deepe despight,
Yrkesome of life, and too long lingring night.
At last faire *Hesperus* in highest skie
Had spent his lampe, and brought forth dawn-
     ing light
Then vp he rose, and clad him hastily ;
The Dwarfe him brought his steed : so both
     away do fly.

7

Now when the rosy-fingred Morning faire,
Weary of aged *Tithones* saffron bed,
Had spred her purple robe through deawy aire,
And the high hils *Titan* discoured,
The royall virgin shooke off drowsy-hed,
And rising forth out of her baser bowre,
Lookt for her knight, who far away was fled,
And for her Dwarfe, that wont to wait each
     houre ;
Then gan she waile and weepe, to see that woe-
     full stowre.

8

And after him she rode with so much speede
As her slow beast could make ; but all in vaine :
For him so far had borne his light-foot steede,
Pricked with wrath and fiery fierce disdaine,
That him to follow was but fruitlesse paine ;
Yet she her weary limbes would neuer rest,
But euery hill and dale, each wood and plaine
Did search, sore grieued in her gentle brest,
He so vngently left her, whom she loued best.

9

But subtill *Archimago*, when his guests
He saw diuided into double parts,
And *Vna* wandring in woods and forrests,
Th'end of his drift, he praisd his diuelish arts,
That had such might ouer true meaning harts ;
Yet rests not so, but other meanes doth make,
How he may worke vnto her further smarts :
For her he hated as the hissing snake,
And in her many troubles did most pleasure
     take.

10

He then deuisde himselfe how to disguise ;
For by his mightie science he could take
As many formes and shapes in seeming wise,
As euer *Proteus* to himselfe could make :
Sometime a fowle, sometime a fish in lake,
Now like a foxe, now like a dragon fell,
That of himselfe he oft for feare would quake,
And oft would flie away. O who can tell
The hidden power of herbes, and might of
     Magicke spell ?

11

But now seemde best, the person to put on
Of that good knight, his late beguiled guest :
In mighty armes he was yclad anon,
And siluer shield : vpon his coward brest
A bloudy crosse, and on his crauen crest
A bounch of haires discolourd diuersly :
Full iolly knight he seemde, and well addrest,
And when he sate vpon his courser free,
Saint George himself ye would haue deemed him
     to be.

12

But he the knight, whose semblaunt he did
     beare,
The true *Saint George* was wandred far away,
Still flying from his thoughts and gealous feare ;
Will was his guide, and griefe led him astray.
At last him chaunst to meete vpon the way
A faithlesse Sarazin all arm'd to point,
In whose great shield was writ with letters gay
Sans foy : full large of limbe and euery ioint
He was, and cared not for God or man a point.

13

He had a faire companion of his way,
A goodly Lady clad in scarlot red,
Purfled with gold and pearle of rich assay,
And like a *Persian* mitre on her hed
She wore, with crownes and owches garnished,
The which her lauish louers to her gaue ;
Her wanton palfrey all was ouerspred
With tinsell trappings, wouen like a waue,
Whose bridle rung with golden bels and bosses
     braue.

14

With faire disport and courting dalliaunce
  She intertainde her louer all the way :
  But when she saw the knight his speare
     aduaunce,
  She soone left off her mirth and wanton play,
  And bad her knight addresse him to the fray :
  His foe was nigh at hand. He prickt with pride
  And hope to winne his Ladies heart that day,
Forth spurred fast : adowne his coursers side
The red bloud trickling staind the way, as he
    did ride.

15

The knight of the *Redcrosse* when him he spide,
  Spurring so hote with rage dispiteous,
  Gan fairely couch his speare, and towards ride :
  Soone meete they both, both fell and furious,
  That daunted with their forces hideous,
  Their steeds do stagger, and amazed stand,
  And eke themselues too rudely rigorous,
Astonied with the stroke of their owne hand,
Do backe rebut, and each to other yeeldeth
    land.

16

As when two rams stird with ambitious pride,
  Fight for the rule of the rich fleeced flocke,
  Their horned fronts so fierce on either side
  Do meete, that with the terrour of the shocke
  Astonied both, stand sencelesse as a blocke,
  Forgetfull of the hanging victory :
  So stood these twaine, vnmoued as a rocke,
Both staring fierce, and holding idely
The broken reliques of their former cruelty.

17

The *Sarazin* sore daunted with the buffe
  Snatcheth his sword, and fiercely to him flies ;
  Who well it wards, and quyteth cuff with cuff :
  Each others equall puissaunce enuies,
  And through their iron sides with cruell spies
  Does seeke to perce : repining courage yields
  No foote to foe. The flashing fier flies
As from a forge out of their burning shields,
And streames of purple bloud new dies the
  ▼erdant fields.

18

Curse on that Crosse (quoth then the *Sarazin*)
  That keepes thy body from the bitter fit ;
  Dead long ygoe I wote thou haddest bin,
  Had not that charme from thee forwarned it :
  But yet I warne thee now assured sitt,
  And hide thy head. Therewith vpon his crest
  With rigour so outrageous he smitt,
That a large share it hewd out of the rest,
And glauncing downe his shield, from blame
  him fairely blest.

19

Who thereat wondrous wroth, the sleeping spark
  Of natiue vertue gan eftsoones reuiue,
  And at his haughtie helmet making mark,
  So hugely stroke, that it the steele did riue,
  And cleft his head. He tumbling downe aliue,
  With bloudy mouth his mother earth did kis,
  Greeting his graue : his grudging ghost did
    striue
With the fraile flesh ; at last it flitted is,
Whither the soules do fly of men, that liue amis.

20

The Lady when she saw her champion fall,
  Like the old ruines of a broken towre,
  Staid not to waile his woefull funerall,
  But from him fled away with all her powre ;
  Who after her as hastily gan scowre,
  Bidding the Dwarfe with him to bring away
  The *Sarazins* shield, signe of the conqueroure.
Her soone he ouertooke, and bad to stay,
For present cause was none of dread her to
    dismay.

21

She turning backe with ruefull countenaunce,
  Cride, Mercy mercy Sir vouchsafe to show
  On silly Dame, subiect to hard mischaunce,
  And to your mighty will. Her humblesse low
  In so ritch weedes and seeming glorious show,
  Did much emmoue his stout heroïcke heart,
  And said, Deare dame, your suddein ouer-
    throw
Much rueth me ; but now put feare apart,
And tell, both who ye be, and who that tooke
  your part.

22

Melting in teares, then gan she thus lament ;
  The wretched woman, whom vnhappy howre
  Hath now made thrall to your commandement,
  Before that angry heauens list to lowre,
  And fortune false betraide me to your powre
  Was, (O what now auaileth that I was !)
  Borne the sole daughter of an Emperour,
He that the wide West vnder his rule has,
And high hath set his throne, where *Tiberis*
  doth pas.

23

He in the first flowre of my freshest age,
  Betrothed me vnto the onely haire
  Of a most mighty king, most rich and sage ;
  Was neuer Prince so faithfull and so faire,
  Was neuer Prince so meeke and debonaire ;
  But ere my hoped day of spousall shone,
  My dearest Lord fell from high honours staire,
Into the hands of his accursed fone,
And cruelly was slaine, that shall I euer mone.

24

His blessed body spoild of liuely breath,
  Was afterward, I know not how, conuaid
  And fro me hid: of whose most innocent death
  When tidings came to me vnhappy maid,
  O how great sorrow my sad soule assaid.
Then forth I went his woefull corse to find,
  And many yeares throughout the world I straid,
  A virgin widow, whose deepe wounded mind
With loue, long time did languish as the striken
    hind.

25

At last it chaunced this proud *Sarazin*
  To meete me wandring, who perforce me led
  With him away, but yet could neuer win
  The Fort, that Ladies hold in soueraigne dread.
  There lies he now with foule dishonour dead,
Who whiles he liu'de, was called proud *Sans foy*,
  The eldest of three brethren, all three bred
  Of one bad sire, whose youngest is *Sans ioy*,
And twixt them both was borne the bloudy
    bold *Sans loy*.

26

In this sad plight, friendlesse, vnfortunate,
  Now miserable I *Fidessa* dwell,
  Crauing of you in pitty of my state,
  To do none ill, if please ye not do well.
  He in great passion all this while did dwell,
More busying his quicke eyes, her face to view,
  Then his dull eares, to heare what she did tell;
  And said, Faire Lady hart of flint would rew
The vndeserued woes and sorrowes, which ye
    shew.

27

Henceforth in safe assuraunce may ye rest,
  Hauing both found a new friend you to aid,
  And lost an old foe, that did you molest :
  Better new friend then an old foe is said.
  With chaunge of cheare the seeming simple
    maid
Let fall her eyen, as shamefast to the earth,
  And yeelding soft, in that she nought gain-said,
  So forth they rode, he feining seemely merth,
And she coy lookes : so dainty they say maketh
    derth.

28

Long time they thus together traueiled,
  Till weary of their way, they came at last,
  Where grew two goodly trees, that faire did
    spred
  Their armes abroad, with gray mosse ouercast,
  And their greene leaues trembling with euery
    blast,
Made a calme shadow far in compasse round :
  The fearefull Shepheard often there aghast
  Vnder them neuer sat, ne wont there sound
His mery oaten pipe, but shund th'vnlucky
    ground.

29

But this good knight soone as he them can spie,
  For the coole shade him thither hastly got :
  For golden *Phœbus* now ymounted hie,
  From fiery wheeles of his faire chariot
  Hurled his beame so scorching cruell hot,
That liuing creature mote it not abide ;
  And his new Lady it endured not.
  There they alight, in hope themselues to hide
From the fierce heat, and rest their weary limbs
    a tide.

30

Faire seemely pleasaunce each to other makes,
  With goodly purposes there as they sit :
  And in his falsed fancy he her takes
  To be the fairest wight, that liued yit ;
  Which to expresse, he bends his gentle wit,
And thinking of those braunches greene to frame
  A girlond for her dainty forehead fit,
  He pluckt a bough ; out of whose rift there came
Small drops of gory bloud, that trickled downe
    the same.

31

Therewith a piteous yelling voyce was heard,
  Crying, O spare with guilty hands to teare
  My tender sides in this rough rynd embard,
  But fly, ah fly far hence away, for feare
  Least to you hap, that happened to me heare,
And to this wretched Lady, my deare loue,
  O too deare loue, loue bought with death too
    deare.
Astond he stood, and vp his haire did houe
And with that suddein horror could no member
    moue.

32

At last whenas the dreadfull passion
  Was ouerpast, and manhood well awake,
  Yet musing at the straunge occasion,
  And doubting much his sence, he thus bespake ;
  What voyce of damned Ghost from *Limbo* lake,
Or guilefull spright wandring in empty aire,
  Both which fraile men do oftentimes mistake,
  Sends to my doubtfull eares these speaches rare,
And ruefull plaints, me bidding guiltlesse bloud
    to spare ?

33

Then groning deepe, Nor damned Ghost, (quoth
    he,)   [speake,
  Nor guilefull sprite to thee these wordes doth
  But once a man *Fradubio*, now a tree,
  Wretched man, wretched tree ; whose nature
    weake,
  A cruell witch her cursed will to wreake,
Hath thus transformd, and plast in open plaines,
  Where *Boreas* doth blow full bitter bleake,
  And scorching Sunne does dry my secret vaines:
For though a tree I seeme, yet cold and heat me
    paines.

34

Say, on *Fradubio* then, or man, or tree,
  Quoth then the knight, by whose mischieuous
    arts
  Art thou misshaped thus, as now I see ?
He oft finds med'cine, who his griefe imparts ;
But double griefs afflict concealing harts,
  As raging flames who striueth to suppresse.
  The author then (said he) of all my smarts,
Is one *Duessa* a false sorceresse,
That many errant knights hath brought to
    wretchednesse.

35

In prime of youthly yeares, when corage hot
  The fire of loue and ioy of cheualree
  First kindled in my brest, it was my lot
To loue this gentle Lady, whom ye see,
Now not a Lady, but a seeming tree ;
  With whom as once I rode accompanyde,
  Me chaunced of a knight encountred bee,
That had a like faire Lady by his syde,
Like a faire Lady, but did fowle *Duessa* hyde.

36

Whose forged beauty he did take in hand,
  All other Dames to haue exceeded farre ;
  I in defence of mine did likewise stand,
Mine, that did then shine as the Morning starre:
So both to battell fierce arraunged arre,
  In which his harder fortune was to fall
  Vnder my speare : such is the dye of warre :
His Lady left as a prise martiall,
Did yield her comely person, to be at my call.

37

So doubly lou'd of Ladies vnlike faire,
  Th'one seeming such, the other such indeede,
  One day in doubt I cast for to compare,
Whether in beauties glorie did exceede ;
A Rosy girlond was the victors meede :
  Both seemde to win, and both seemde won to
    bee,
So hard the discord was to be agreede.
Frælissa was as faire, as faire mote bee,
And euer false *Duessa* seemde as faire as shee.

38

The wicked witch now seeing all this while
  The doubtfull ballaunce equally to sway,
  What not by right, she cast to win by guile,
And by her hellish science raisd streight way
A foggy mist, that ouercast the day,
  And a dull blast, that breathing on her face,
  Dimmed her former beauties shining ray,
And with foule vgly forme did her disgrace :
Then was she faire alone, when none was faire
    in place.

39

Then cride she out, Fye, fye, deformed wight,
  Whose borrowed beautie now appeareth plaine
  To haue before bewitched all mens sight ;
O leaue her soone, or let her soone be slaine.
Her loathly visage viewing with disdaine,
  Eftsoones I thought her such, as she me told,
  And would haue kild her ; but with faigned
    paine,   [hold ;
The false witch did my wrathfull hand with-
So left her, where she now is turnd to treen
    mould.

40

Thens forth I tooke *Duessa* for my Dame,
  And in the witch vnweeting ioyd long time,
  Ne euer wist, but that she was the same,
Till on a day (that day is euery Prime,
When Witches wont do penance for their crime)
  I chaunst to see her in her proper hew,
  Bathing her selfe in origane and thyme :
A filthy foule old woman I did vew,
That euer to haue toucht her, I did deadly rew.

41

Her neather partes misshapen, monstruous,
  Were hidd in water, that I could not see,
  But they did seeme more foule and hideous,
Then womans shape man would beleeue to bee.
Thens forth from her most beastly companie
  I gan refraine, in minde to slip away,
  Soone as appeard safe opportunitie :
For danger great, if not assur'd decay
I saw before mine eyes, if I were knowne to
    stray.

42

The diuelish hag by chaunges of my cheare
  Perceiu'd my thought, and drownd in sleepie
    night,
  With wicked herbes and ointments did be-
    smeare   [might,
My bodie all, through charmes and magicke
That all my senses were bereaued quight :
  Then brought she me into this desert waste,
  And by my wretched louers side me pight,
Where now enclosd in wooden wals full faste,
Banisht from liuing wights, our wearie dayes
    we waste.

43

But how long time, said then the Elfin knight,
  Are you in this misformed house to dwell ?
We may not chaunge (quoth he) this euil pligh,
  Till we be bathed in a liuing well ;
  That is the terme prescribed by the spell.
O how, said he, mote I that well out find,
  That may restore you to your wonted well ?
Time and suffised fates to former kynd
Shall vs restore, none else from hence may vs
    vnbynd.

44

The false *Duessa*, now *Fidessa* hight,
Heard how in vaine *Fradubio* did lament,
And knew well all was true. But the good knight
Full of sad feare and ghastly dreriment,
When all this speech the liuing tree had spent,
The bleeding bough did thrust into the ground,
That from the bloud he might be innocent,
And with fresh clay did close the wooden wound:
Then turning to his Lady, dead with feare her found.

45

Her seeming dead he found with feigned feare,
As all vnweeting of that well she knew,
And paynd himselfe with busie care to reare
Her out of carelesse swowne. Her eylids blew
And dimmed sight with pale and deadly hew
At last she vp gan lift: with trembling cheare
Her vp he tooke, too simple and too trew,
And oft her kist. At length all passed feare,
He set her on her steede, and forward forth did beare.

Cant. III.

Forsaken Truth long seekes her loue,
And makes the Lyon mylde,
Marres blind Deuotions mart, and fals
In hand of leachour vylde.

I

Nought is there vnder heau'ns wide hollownesse,
That moues more deare compassion of mind,
Then beautie brought t'vnworthy wretchednesse
Through enuies snares or fortunes freakes [vnkind]
I, whether lately through her brightnesse blind,
Or through alleageance and fast fealtie,
Which I do owe vnto all woman kind,
Feele my heart perst with so great agonie,
When such I see, that all for pittie I could die.

2

And now it is empassioned so deepe,
For fairest *Vnaes* sake, of whom I sing,
That my fraile eyes these lines with teares do steepe,
To thinke how she through guilefull handeling,
Though true as touch, though daughter of a king,
Though faire as euer liuing wight was faire,
Though nor in word nor deede ill meriting,
Is from her knight diuorced in despaire
And her due loues deriu'd to that vile witches share.

3

Yet she most faithfull Ladie all this while
Forsaken, wofull, solitarie mayd
Farre from all peoples prease, as in exile,
In wildernesse and wastfull deserts strayd,
To seeke her knight; who subtilly betrayd
Through that late vision, which th'Enchaunter wrought,
Had her abandond. She of nought affrayd,
Through woods and wastnesse wide him daily sought;
Yet wished tydings none of him vnto her brought.

4

One day nigh wearie of the yrkesome way,
From her vnhastie beast she did alight,
And on the grasse her daintie limbes did lay
In secret shadow, farre from all mens sight:
From her faire head her fillet she vndight,
And laid her stole aside. Her angels face
As the great eye of heauen shyned bright,
And made a sunshine in the shadie place;
Did neuer mortall eye behold such heauenly grace.

5

It fortuned out of the thickest wood
A ramping Lyon rushed suddainly,
Hunting full greedie after saluage blood;
Soone as the royall virgin he did spy,
With gaping mouth at her ran greedily,
To haue attonce deuour'd her tender corse:
But to the pray when as he drew more ny,
His bloudie rage asswaged with remorse,
And with the sight amazd, forgat his furious forse.

6

In stead thereof he kist her wearie feet,
And lickt her lilly hands with fawning tong,
As he her wronged innocence did weet.
O how can beautie maister the most strong,
And simple truth subdue auenging wrong?
Whose yeelded pride and proud submission,
Still dreading death, when she had marked long,
Her hart gan melt in great compassion,
And drizling teares did shed for pure affection.

7

The Lyon Lord of euerie beast in field,
Quoth she, his princely puissance doth abate,
And mightie proud to humble weake does yield,
Forgetfull of the hungry rage, which late
Him prickt, in pittie of my sad estate:
But he my Lyon, and my noble Lord,
How does he find in cruell hart to hate
Her that him lou'd, and euer most adord,
As the God of my life? why hath he me abhord?

8

Redounding teares did choke th'end of her plaint,
  Which softly ecchoed from the neighbour wood;
  And sad to see her sorrowfull constraint
  The kingly beast vpon her gazing stood;
  With pittie calmd, downe fell his angry mood.
  At last in close hart shutting vp her paine,
  Arose the virgin borne of heauenly brood,
  And to her snowy Palfrey got againe,
To seeke her strayed Champion, if she might
  attaine.

9

The Lyon would not leaue her desolate,
  But with her went along, as a strong gard
  Of her chast person, and a faithfull mate
  Of her sad troubles and misfortunes hard:
  Still when she slept, he kept both watch and
    ward,
  And when she wakt, he waited diligent,
  With humble seruice to her will prepard:
  From her faire eyes he tooke commaundement,
And euer by her lookes conceiued her intent.

10

Long she thus traueiled through deserts wyde,
  By which she thought her wandring knight
    shold pas,
  Yet neuer shew of liuing wight espyde;
  Till that at length she found the troden gras,
  In which the tract of peoples footing was,
  Vnder the steepe foot of a mountaine hore;
  The same she followes, till at last she has
  A damzell spyde slow footing her before,
That on her shoulders sad a pot of water bore.

11

To whom approching she to her gan call,
  To weet, if dwelling place were nigh at hand;
  But the rude wench her answer'd nought at all,
  She could not heare, nor speake, nor vnderstand;
  Till seeing by her side the Lyon stand,
  With suddaine feare her pitcher downe she
    threw,
  And fled away: for neuer in that land
  Face of faire Ladie she before did vew,
And that dread Lyons looke her cast in deadly
  hew.

12

Full fast she fled, ne euer lookt behynd,
  As if her life vpon the wager lay,
  And home she came, whereas her mother blynd
  Sate in eternall night: nought could she say,
  But suddaine catching hold, did her dismay
  With quaking hands, and other signes of feare:
  Who full of ghastly fright and cold affray,
  Gan shut the dore. By this arriued there
Dame *Vna*, wearie Dame, and entrance did
  requere.

13

Which when none yeelded, her vnruly Page
  With his rude clawes the wicket open rent,
  And let her in; where of his cruell rage
  Nigh dead with feare, and faint astonishment,
  She found them both in darkesome corner pent;
  Where that old woman day and night did pray
  Vpon her beades deuoutly penitent;
  Nine hundred *Pater nosters* euery day,
And thrise nine hundred *Aues* she was wont to
  say.

14

And to augment her painefull pennance more,
  Thrise euery weeke in ashes she did sit,
  And next her wrinkled skin rough sackcloth
    wore,
  And thrise three times did fast from any bit:
  But now for feare her beads she did forget.
  Whose needlesse dread for to remoue away,
  Faire *Vna* framed words and count'nance fit:
  Which hardly doen, at length she gan them
    pray,
That in their cotage small, that night she rest
  her may.

15

The day is spent, and commeth drowsie night,
  When euery creature shrowded is in sleepe;
  Sad *Vna* downe her laies in wearie plight,
  And at her feet the Lyon watch doth keepe:
  In stead of rest, she does lament, and weepe
  For the late losse of her deare loued knight,
  And sighes, and grones, and euermore does
    steepe
  Her tender brest in bitter teares all night,
All night she thinks too long, and often lookes
  for light.

16

Now when *Aldeboran* was mounted hie
  Aboue the shynie *Cassiopeias* chaire,
  And all in deadly sleepe did drowned lie,
  One knocked at the dore, and in would fare;
  He knocked fast, and often curst, and sware,
  That readie entrance was not at his call:
  For on his backe a heauy load he bare
  Of nightly stelths and pillage seuerall,
Which he had got abroad by purchase criminall.

17

He was to weete a stout and sturdie thiefe,
  Wont to robbe Churches of their ornaments,
  And poore mens boxes of their due reliefe,
  Which giuen was to them for good intents;
  The holy Saints ot their rich vestiments
  He did disrobe, when all men carelesse slept,
  And spoild the Priests of their habiliments,
  Whiles none the holy things in safety kept;
Then he by cunning sleights in at the window
  crept.

18

And all that he by right or wrong could find,
  Vnto this house he brought, and did bestow
  Vpon the daughter of this woman blind,
Abessa daughter of *Corceca* slow,   [know,
  With whom he whoredome vsd, that few did
  And fed her fat with feast of offerings,
  And plentie, which in all the land did grow ;
Ne spared he to giue her gold and rings :
And now he to her brought part of his stolen
    things.

19

Thus long the dore with rage and threats he bet,
  Yet of those fearefull women none durst rize,
  The Lyon frayed them, him in to let :
He would no longer stay him to aduize,
  But open breakes the dore in furious wize,
  And entring is ; when that disdainfull beast
Encountring fierce, him suddaine doth surprize,
  And seizing cruell clawes on trembling brest,
Vnder his Lordly foot him proudly hath sup-
    prest.

20

Him booteth not resist, nor succour call,
  His bleeding hart is in the vengers hand,
  Whostreight him rent in thousand peeces small,
And quite dismembred hath : the thirstie land
  Drunke vp his life; his corse left on the strand.
  His fearefull friends weare out the wofull night,
Ne dare to weepe, nor seeme to vnderstand
  The heauie hap, which on them is alight,
Affraid, least to themselues the like mishappen
    might.

21

Now when broad day the world discouered has,
  Vp *Vna* rose, vp rose the Lyon eke,
  And on their former iourney forward pas,
In wayes vnknowne, her wandring knight to
    seeke,   [*Greeke*,
  With paines farre passing that long wandring
  That for his loue refused deitie ;
Such were the labours of this Lady meeke,
  Still seeking him, that from her still did flie,
Then furthest from her hope, when most she
    weened nie.

22

Soone as she parted thence, the fearefull twaine,
  That blind old woman and her daughter deare
  Came forth, and finding *Kirkrapine* there slaine,
For anguish great they gan to rend their heare,
  And beat their brests, and naked flesh to teare.
  And when they both had wept and wayld their
    fill,
Then forth they ranne like two amazed deare,
  Halfe mad through malice, and reuenging will,
To follow her, that was the causer of their ill.

23

Whom ouertaking, they gan loudly bray,
  With hollow howling, and lamenting cry,
  Shamefully at her rayling all the way,
And her accusing of dishonesty,
  That was the flowre of faith and chastity ;
  And still amidst her rayling, she did pray,
That plagues, and mischiefs, and long misery
  Might fall on her, and follow all the way,
And that in endlesse error she might euer stray.

24

But when she saw her prayers nought preuaile,
  She backe returned with some labour lost ;
  And in the way as she did weepe and waile,
A knight her met in mighty armes embost,
  Yet knight was not for all his bragging bost,
  But subtill *Archimag*, that *Vna* sought
By traynes into new troubles to haue tost :
  Of that old woman tydings he besought,
If that of such a Ladie she could tellen ought.

25

Therewith she gan her passion to renew,
  And cry, and curse, and raile, and rend her
    heare,
  Saying, that harlot she too lately knew,
That causd her shed so many a bitter teare,
  And so forth told the story of her feare :
  Much seemed he to mone her haplesse chaunce,
And after for that Ladie did inquere ;
  Which being taught, he forward gan aduaunce
His fair enchaunted steed, and eke his charmed
    launce.

26

Ere long he came, where *Vna* traueild slow,
  And that wilde Champion wayting her besyde :
  Whom seeing such, for dread he durst not show
Himselfe too nigh at hand, but turned wyde
  Vnto an hill; from whence when she him spyde,
  By his like seeming shield, her knight by narre
She weend it was, and towards him gan ryde :
  Approching nigh, she wist it was the same,
And with faire fearefull humblesse towards him
    shee came.

27

And weeping said, Ah my long lacked Lord,
  Where haue ye bene thus long out of my sight?
  Much feared I to haue bene quite abhord,
Or ought haue done, that ye displeasen might,
  That should as death vnto my deare hart light:
  For since mine eye your ioyous sight did mis,
My chearefull day is turnd to chearelesse night,
  And eke my night of death the shadow is ;
But welcome now my light, and shining lampe
    of blis.

28

He thereto meeting said, My dearest Dame,
 Farre be it from your thought, and fro my will,
 To thinke that knighthood I so much should
    shame,
 As you to leaue, that haue me loued still,
 And chose in Faery court of meere goodwill,
 Where noblest knights were to be found on earth:
 The earth shall sooner leaue her kindly skill
 To bring forth fruit, and make eternall derth,
 Then I leaue you, my liefe, yborne of heauenly
    berth.

29

And sooth to say, why I left you so long,
 Was for to seeke aduenture in strange place,
 Where *Archimago* said a felon strong
 To many knights did daily worke disgrace ;
 But knight he now shall neuer more deface :
 Good cause of mine excuse; that mote ye please
 Well to accept, and euermore embrace
 My faithfull seruice, that by land and seas
 Haue vowd you to defend, now then your plaint
    appease.

30

His louely words her seemd due recompence
 Of all her passed paines : one louing howre
 For many yeares of sorrow can dispence :
 A dram of sweet is worth a pound of sowre :
 She has forgot, how many a wofull stowre
 For him she late endur'd; she speakes no more
 Of past : true is, that true loue hath no powre
 To looken backe ; his eyes be fixt before.
 Before her stands her knight, for whom she
    toyld so sore.

31

Much like, as when the beaten marinere,
 That long hath wandred in the *Ocean* wide,
 Oft soust in swelling *Tethys* saltish teare,
 And long time hauing tand his tawney hide
 With blustring breath of heauen, that none
    can bide,
 And scorching flames of fierce *Orions* hound,
 Soone as the port from farre he has espide,
 His chearefull whistle merrily doth sound,
 And *Nereus* crownes with cups ; his mates him
    pledg around.

32

Such ioy made *Vna*, when her knight she found ;
 And eke th'enchaunter ioyous seemd no lesse,
 Then the glad marchant, that does vew from
    ground
 His ship farre come from watrie wildernesse,
 He hurles out vowes, and *Neptune* oft doth
    blesse :
 So forth they past, and all the way they spent
 Discoursing of her dreadfull late distresse,
 In which he askt her, what the Lyon ment :
 †Who told her all that fell in iourney as she went.

33

They had not ridden farre, when they might see
 One pricking towards them with hastie heat,
 Full strongly armd, and on a courser free,
 That through his fiercenesse fomed all with
    sweat,
 And the sharpe yron did for anger eat,
 When his hot ryder spurd his chauffed side ;
 His looke was sterne, and seemed still to threat
 Cruell reuenge, which he in hart did hyde,
 And on his shield *Sans loy* in bloudie lines was
    dyde.

34

When nigh he drew vnto this gentle payre
 And saw the Red-crosse, which the knight did
    beare,
 He burnt in fire, and gah eftsoones prepare
 Himselfe to battell with his couched speare.
 Loth was that other, and did faint through feare,
 To taste th'vntryed dint of deadly steele ;
 But yet his Lady did so well him cheare,
 That hope of new good hap he gan to feele ;
 So bent his speare, and spurnd his horse with
    yron heele.

35

But that proud Paynim forward came so fierce,
 And full of wrath, that with his sharp-head speare
 Through vainely crossed shield he quite did
    pierce,   [feare,
 And had his staggering steede not shrunke for
 Through shield and bodie eke he should him
    beare :
 Yet so great was the puissance of his push,
 That from his saddle quite he did him beare :
 He tombling rudely downe to ground did rush,
 And from his gored wound a well of bloud did
    gush.

36

Dismounting lightly from his loftie steed,
 He to him lept, in mind to reaue his life,
 And proudly said, Lo there the worthie meed
 Of him, that slew *Sansfoy* with bloudie knife ;
 Henceforth his ghost freed from repining strife,
 In peace may passen ouer *Lethe* lake,
 When mourning altars purgd with enemies life,
 The blacke infernall *Furies* doen aslake :
 Life from *Sansfoy* thou tookst, *Sansloy* shall
    from thee take.

37

Therewith in haste his helmet gan vnlace,
 Till *Vna* cride, O hold that heauie hand,
 Deare Sir, what euer that thou be in place :
 Enough is, that thy foe doth vanquisht stand
 Now at thy mercy : Mercie not withstand :
 For he is one the truest knight aliue,
 Though conquered now he lie on lowly land,
 And whilest him fortune fauourd, faire did thriue
 In bloudie field : therefore of life him not depriue.

38

Her piteous words might not abate his rage,
But rudely rending vp his helmet, would
Haue slaine him straight : but when he sees
   his age,
And hoarie head of *Archimago* old,
His hastie hand he doth amazed hold,
And halfe ashamed, wondred at the sight :
For the old man well knew he, though vntold,
In charmes and magicke to haue wondrous
   might,
Ne euer wont in field, ne in round lists to fight.

39

And said, Why *Archimago*, lucklesse syre,
What doe I see ? what hard mishap is this,
That hath thee hither brought to taste mine
   yre ?
Or thine the fault, or mine the error is,
In stead of foe to wound my friend amis ?
He answered nought, but in a traunce still lay,
And on those guilefull dazed eyes of his
The cloud of death did sit. Which doen away,
He left him lying so, ne would no lenger stay.

40

But to the virgin comes, who all this while
Amased stands, her selfe so mockt to see
By him, who has the guerdon of his guile,
For so misfeigning her true knight to bee :
Yet is she now in more perplexitie,
Left in the hand of that same Paynim bold,
From whom her booteth not at all to flie ;
Who by her cleanly garment catching hold,
Her from her Palfrey pluckt, her visage to
   behold.

41

But her fierce seruant full of kingly awe
And high disdaine, whenas his soueraine Dame
So rudely handled by her foe he sawe,
With gaping iawes full greedy at him came,
And ramping on his shield, did weene the same
Haue reft away with his sharpe rending clawes
But he was stout, and lust did now inflame
His corage more, that from his griping pawes
He hath his shield redeem'd, and foorth his swerd
   he drawes.

42

O then too weake and feeble was the forse
Of saluage beast, his puissance to withstand :
For he was strong, and of so mightie corse,
As euer wielded speare in warlike hand,
And feates of armes did wisely vnderstand.
Eftsoones he perced through his chaufed chest
With thrilling point of deadly yron brand,
And launcht his Lordly hart : with death opprest
He roar'd aloud, whiles life forsooke his stub-
   borne brest.

43

Who now is left to keepe the forlorne maid
From raging spoile of lawlesse victors will ?
Her faithfull gard remou'd, her hope dismaid,
Her selfe a yeelded pray to saue or spill.
He now Lord of the field, his pride to fill,
With foule reproches, and disdainfull spight
Her vildly entertaines, and will or nill,
Beares her away vpon his courser light :
Her prayers nought preuaile, his rage is more
   of might.

44

And all the way, with great lamenting paine,
And piteous plaints she filleth his dull eares,
That stony hart could riuen haue in twaine,
And all the way she wets with flowing teares :
But he enrag'd with rancor, nothing heares.
Her seruile beast yet would not leaue her so,
But followes her farre off, ne ought he feares,
To be partaker of her wandring woe,
More mild in beastly kind, then that her beastly
   foe.

Cant. IIII.

1

Young knight, what euer that dost armes pro-
   fesse,
And through long labours huntest after fame,
Beware of fraud, beware of ficklenesse,
In choice, and change of thy deare loued Dame,
Least thou of her beleeue too lightly blame,
And rash misweening doe thy hart remoue :
For vnto knight there is no greater shame,
Then lightnesse and inconstancie in loue ;
That doth this *Redcrosse* knights ensample
   plainly proue.

2

Who after that he had faire *Vna* lorne,
Through light misdeeming of her loialtie,
And false *Duessa* in her sted had borne,
Called *Fidess'*, and so supposd to bee ;
Long with her traueild, till at last they see
A goodly building, brauely garnished,
The house of mightie Prince it seemd to bee :
And towards it a broad high way that led,
All bare through peoples feet, which thither
   traueiled.

3

Great troupes of people traueild thitherward
  Both day and night, of each degree and place,
  But few returned, hauing scaped hard,
  With balefull beggerie, or foule disgrace,
  Which euer after in most wretched case,
  Like loathsome lazars, by the hedges lay.
  Thither *Duessa* bad him bend his pace:
  For she is wearie of the toilesome way,
And also nigh consumed is the lingring day.

4

A stately Pallace built of squared bricke,
  Which cunningly was without morter laid,
  Whose wals were high,but nothing strong; nor
    thick,
  And golden foile all ouer them displaid,
  That purest skye with brightnesse they dis-
    maid:
  High lifted vp were many loftie towres,
  And goodly galleries farre ouer laid,
  Full of faire windowes,and delightfull bowres;
And on the top a Diall told the timely howres.

5

It was a goodly heape for to behould,
  And spake the praises of the workmans wit;
  But full great pittie, that so faire a mould
  Did on so weake foundation euer sit:
  For on a sandie hill, that still did flit,
  And fall away, it mounted was full hie,
  That euery breath of heauen shaked it:
  And all the hinder parts, that few could spie,
Were ruinous and old, but painted cunningly.

6

Arriued there they passed in forth right;
  For still to all the gates stood open wide,
  Yet charge of them was to a Porter hight
  Cald *Maluenù*, who entrance none denide:
  Thence to the hall, which was on euery side
  With rich array and costly arras dight:
  Infinite sorts of people did abide
  There waiting long, to win the wished sight
Of her,that was the Lady of that Pallace bright.

7

By them they passe, all gazing on them round,
  And to the Presence mount: whose glorious
    vew
  Their frayle amazed senses did confound:
  In liuing Princes court none euer knew
  Such endlesse richesse,and so sumptuous shew;
  Ne *Persia* selfe, the nourse of pompous pride
  Like euer saw. And there a noble crew
  Of Lordes and Ladies stood on euery side,
Which with their presence faire, the place much
  beautifide.

8

High aboue all a cloth of State was spred,
  And a rich throne, as bright as sunny day,
  On which there sate most braue embellished
  With royall robes and gorgeous array,
  A mayden Queene, that shone as *Titans* ray,
  In glistring gold, and peerelesse pretious stone:
  Yet her bright blazing beautie did assay
  To dim the brightnesse of her glorious throne,
As enuying her selfe, that too exceeding shone.

9

Exceeding shone, like *Phœbus* fairest childe,
  That did presume his fathers firie wayne,
  And flaming mouthes of steedes vnwonted wilde
  Through highest heauen with weaker hand to
    rayne;
  Proud of such glory and aduancement vaine,
  While flashing beames do daze his feeble eyen,
  He leaues the welkin way most beaten plaine,
  And rapt with whirling wheeles, inflames the
    skyen,
With fire not made to burne, but fairely for to
  shyne.

10

So proud she shyned in her Princely state,
  Looking to heauen; for earth she did disdayne,
  And sitting high; for lowly she did hate:
  Lo vnderneath her scornefull feete, was layne
  A dreadfull Dragon with an hideous trayne,
  And in her hand she held a mirrhour bright,
  Wherein her face she often vewed fayne,
  And in her selfe-lou'd semblance tooke delight;
For she was wondrous faire,as any liuing wight.

11

Of griesly *Pluto* she the daughter was,
  And sad *Proserpina* the Queene of hell;
  Yet did she thinke her pearelesse worth to pas
  That parentage, with pride so did she swell,
  And thundring *Ioue*, that high in heauen doth
    dwell,
  And wield the world,she claymed for her syre,
  Or if that any else did *Ioue* excell:
  For to the highest she did still aspyre,
Or if ought higher were then that, did it desyre.

12

And proud *Lucifera* men did her call,   [be,
  That made her selfe a Queene, and crownd to
  Yet rightfull kingdome she had none at all,
  Ne heritage of natiue soueraintie,
  But did vsurpe with wrong and tyrannie
  Vpon the scepter, which she now did hold:
  Ne ruld her Realmes with lawes, but pollicie,
  And strong aduizement of six wisards old,
That with their counsels bad her kingdome did
  vphold.

13

Soone as the Elfin knight in presence came,
  And false *Duessa* seeming Lady faire,
  A gentle Husher, *Vanitie* by name   [paire :
Made rowme, and passage for them did pre-
So goodly brought them to the lowest staire
  Of her high throne, where they on humble knee
  Making obeyssance, did the cause declare,
Why they were come, her royall state to see,
To proue the wide report of her great Maiestee.

14

With loftie eyes, halfe loth to looke so low,
  She thanked them in her disdainefull wise,
  Ne other grace vouchsafed them to show
Of Princesse worthy, scarse them bad arise.
Her Lordes and Ladies all this while deuise
  Themselues to set ten forth to straungers sight:
  Some frounce their curled haire in courtly guise,
Some prancke their ruffes, and others trimly
  dight
Their gay attire: each others greater pride does
  spight.

15

Goodly they all that knight do entertaine,
  Right glad with him to haue increast their crew:
  But to *Duess'* each one himselfe did paine
All kindnesse and faire courtesie to shew ;
For in that court why lome her well they knew:
  Yet the stout Faerie mongst the middest crowd
  Thought all their glorie vaine in knightly vew,
And that great Princesse too exceeding prowd,
That to strange knight no better countenance
  allowd.

16

Suddein vpriseth from her stately place
  The royall Dame, and for her coche doth call :
  All hurtlen forth, and she with Princely pace,
As faire *Aurora* in her purple pall,
Out of the East the dawning day doth call :
  So forth she comes : her brightnesse brode
  doth blaze ;
The heapes of people thronging in the hall,
  Do ride each other, vpon her to gaze :
Her glorious glitterand light doth all mens eyes
  amaze.

17

So forth she comes, and to her coche does clyme,
  Adorned all with gold, and girlonds gay,
  That seemd as fresh as *Flora* in her prime,
And stroue to match, in royall rich array,
Great *Iunoes* golden chaire, the which they say
  The Gods stand gazing on, when she does ride
  To *Ioues* high house through heauens bras-
    paued way
Drawne of faire Pecocks, that excell in pride,
And full of *Argus* eyes their tailes dispredden
  wide.

18

But this was drawne of six vnequall beasts,
  On which her six sage Counsellours did ryde,
  Taught to obay their bestiall beheasts,
With like conditions to their kinds applyde :
Of which the first, that all the rest did guyde,
  Was sluggish *Idlenesse* the nourse of sin ;
  Vpon a slouthfull Asse he chose to ryde,
Arayd in habit blacke, and amis thin,
Like to an holy Monck, the seruice to begin.

19

And in his hand his Portesse still he bare,
  That much was worne, but therein little red,
  For of deuotion he had little care,
Still drownd in sleepe, and most of his dayes
  ded ;
Scarse could he once vphold his heauie hed,
  To looken, whether it were night or day :
  May seeme the wayne was very euill led,
When such an one had guiding of the way,
That knew not, whether right he went, or else
  astray.

20

From worldly cares himselfe he did esloyne,
  And greatly shunned manly exercise,
  From euery worke he chalenged essoyne,
For contemplation sake : yet otherwise,
His life he led in lawlesse riotise ;
  By which he grew to grieuous malady ;
  For in his lustlesse limbs through euill guise
A shaking feuer raignd continually :
Such one was *Idlenesse*, first of this company.

21

And by his side rode loathsome *Gluttony*,
  Deformed creature, on a filthie swyne,
  His belly was vp-blowne with luxury,
And eke with fatnesse swollen were his eyne,
And like a Crane his necke was long and fyne,
  With which he swallowd vp excessiue feast,
  For want whereof poore people oft did pyne ;
And all the way, most like a brutish beast,
He spued vp his gorge, that all did him deteast.

22

In greene vine leaues he was right fitly clad ;
  For other clothes he could not weare for heat,
  And on his head an yuie girland had,
From vnder which fast trickled downe the
  sweat :
Still as he rode, he somewhat still did eat,
  And in his hand did beare a bouzing can,
  Of which he supt so oft, that on his seat
His dronken corse he scarse vpholden can,
In shape and life more like a monster, then a
  man.

23

Vnfit he was for any worldly thing,
  And eke vnhable once to stirre or go,
  Not meet to be of counsell to a king,
  Whose mind in meat and drinke was drowned so,
  That from his friend he seldome knew his fo :
  Full of diseases was his carcas blew,
  And a dry dropsie through his flesh did flow :
  Which by misdiet daily greater grew :
Such one was *Gluttony*, the second of that crew.

24

And next to him rode lustfull *Lechery*,
  Vpon a bearded Goat, whose rugged haire,
  And whally eyes (the signe of gelosy,)
  Was like the person selfe, whom he did beare :
  Who rough, and blacke, and filthy did appeare,
  Vnseemely man to please faire Ladies eye ;
  Yet he of Ladies oft was loued deare,
  When fairer faces were bid standen by :
O who does know the bent of womens fantasy ?

25

In a greene gowne he clothed was full faire,
  Which vnderneath did hide his filthinesse,
  And in his hand a burning hart he bare,
  Full of vaine follies, and new fanglenesse :
  For he was false, and fraught with ficklenesse,
  And learned had to loue with secret lookes,
  And well could daunce, and sing with ruefulnesse,
  And fortunes tell, and read in louing bookes,
And thousand other wayes, to bait his fleshly hookes.

26

Inconstant man, that loued all he saw,
  And lusted after all, that he did loue,
  Ne would his looser life be tide to law,
  But ioyd weake wemens hearts to tempt and proue
  If from their loyall loues he might then moue ;
  Which lewdnesse fild him with reprochfull paine
  Of that fowle euill, which all men reproue,
  That rots the marrow, and consumes the braine :
Such one was *Lecherie*, the third of all this traine.

27

And greedy *Auarice* by him did ride,
  Vpon a Camell loaden all with gold ;
  Two iron coffers hong on either side,
  With precious mettall full, as they might hold,
  And in his lap an heape of coine he told ;
  For of his wicked pelfe his God he made,
  And vnto hell him selfe for money sold ;
  Accursed vsurie was all his trade,
And right and wrong ylike in equall ballaunce waide.

28

His life was nigh vnto deaths doore yplast,
  And thred-bare cote, and cobled shoes he ware,
  Ne scarse good morsell all his life did tast,
  But both from backe and belly still did spare,
  To fill his bags, and richesse to compare ;
  Yet chylde ne kinsman liuing had he none
  To leaue them to ; but thorough daily care
  To get, and nightly feare to lose his owne,
He led a wretched life vnto him selfe vnknowne.

29

Most wretched wight, whom nothing might suffise,
  Whose greedy lust did lacke in greatest store,
  Whose need had end, but no end couetise,
  Whose wealth was want, whose plenty made him pore,
  Who had enough, yet wished euer more ;
  A vile disease, and eke in foote and hand
  A grieuous gout tormented him full sore,
  That well he could not touch, nor go, nor stand:
Such one was *Auarice*, the fourth of this faire band.

30

And next to him malicious *Enuie* rode,
  Vpon a rauenous wolfe, and still did chaw
  Betweene his cankred teeth a venemous tode,
  That all the poison ran about his chaw ;
  But inwardly he chawed his owne maw
  At neighbours wealth, that made him euer sad;
  For death it was, when any good he saw,
  And wept, that cause of weeping none he had,
But when he heard of harme, he wexed wondrous glad.

31

All in a kirtle of discolourd say
  He clothed was, ypainted full of eyes ;
  And in his bosome secretly there lay
  An hatefull Snake, the which his taile vptyes
  In many folds, and mortall sting implyes.
  Still as he rode, he gnasht his teeth, to see
  Those heapes of gold with griple Couetyse,
  And grudged at the great felicitie
Of proud *Lucifera*, and his owne companie.

32

He hated all good workes and vertuous deeds,
  And him no lesse, that any like did vse,
  And who with gracious bread the hungry feeds,
  His almes for want of faith he doth accuse ;
  So euery good to bad he doth abuse :
  And eke the verse of famous Poets witt
  He does backebite, and spightfull poison spues
  From leprous mouth on all, that euer writt :
Such one vile *Enuie* was, that fifte in row did sitt.

33

And him beside rides fierce reuenging *Wrath*,
  Vpon a Lion, loth for to be led ;
  And in his hand a burning brond he hath,
  The which he brandisheth about his hed ;
  His eyes did hurle forth sparkles fiery red,
  And stared sterne on all, that him beheld,
  As ashes pale of hew and seeming ded ;
  And on his dagger still his hand he held,
Trembling through hasty rage, when choler in
    him sweld.

34

His ruffin raiment all was staind with blood,
  Which he had spilt, and all to rags yrent,
  Through vnaduized rashnesse woxen wood ;
  For of his hands he had no gouernement,
  Ne car'd for bloud in his auengement :
  But when the furious fit was ouerpast,
  His cruell facts he often would repent ;
  Yet wilfull man he neuer would forecast,
How many mischieues should ensue his heed-
    lesse hast.

35

Full many mischiefes follow cruell *Wrath* ;
  Abhorred bloudshed, and tumultuous strife,
  Vnmanly murder, and vnthrifty scath,
  Bitter despight, with rancours rusty knife,
  And fretting griefe the enemy of life ;
  All these, and many euils moe haunt ire,
  The swelling Splene, and Frenzy raging rife,
  The shaking Palsey, and Saint *Fraunces* fire :
Such one was *Wrath*, the last of this vngodly
    tire.

36

And after all, vpon the wagon beame
  Rode *Sathan*, with a smarting whip in hand,
  With which he forward lasht the laesie teme,
  So oft as *Slowth* still in the mire did stand.
  Huge routs of people did about them band,
  Showting for ioy, and still before their way
  A foggy mist had couered all the land ;
  And vnderneath their feet, all scattered lay
Dead sculs and bones of men, whose life had
    gone astray.

37

So forth they marchen in this goodly sort,
  To take the solace of the open aire,
  And in fresh flowring fields themselues to sport ;
  Emongst the rest rode that false Lady faire,
  The fowle *Duessa*, next vnto the chaire
  Of proud *Lucifera*, as one of the traine :
  But that good knight would not so nigh repaire,
  Him selfe estraunging from their ioyaunce
    vaine,
Whose fellowship seemd far vnfit for warlike
    swaine.

38

So hauing solaced themselues a space
  With pleasaunce of the breathing fields yfed,
  They backe returned to the Princely Place ;
  Whereas an errant knight in armes ycled,
  And heathnish shield, wherein with letters red
  Was writ *Sans ioy*, they new arriued find :
  Enflam'd with fury and fiers hardy-hed,
  ·He seemd in hart to harbour thoughts vnkind,
And nourish bloudy vengeaunce in his bitter
    mind.

39

Who when the shamed shield of slaine *Sans foy*
  He spide with that same Faery champions page,
  Bewraying him, that did of late destroy
  His eldest brother, burning all with rage
  He to him leapt, and that same enuious gage
  Of victors glory from him snatcht away :
  But th'Elfin knight, which ought that warlike
    wage,
  Disdaind to loose the meed he wonne in fray,
And him rencountring fierce, reskewd the noble
    pray.

40

Therewith they gan to hurtlen greedily,
  Redoubted battaile ready to darrayne,
  And clash their shields, and shake their swords
    on hy,   [traine ;
  That with their sturre they troubled all the
  Till that great Queene vpon eternall paine
  Of high displeasure, that ensewen might,
  Commaunded them their fury to refraine,
  And if that either to that shield had right,
In equall lists they should the morrow next it
    fight.

41

Ah dearest Dame, (quoth then the Paynim bold,)
  Pardon the errour of enraged wight,
  Whom great griefe made forget the raines to hold
  Of reasons rule, to see this recreant knight,
  No knight, but treachour full of false despight
  And shamefull treason, who through guile
    hath slayn
  The prowest knight, that euer field did fight,
  Euen stout *Sans foy* (O who can then refrayn ?)
Whose shield he beares renuerst, the more to
    heape disdayn.

42

And to augment the glorie of his guile,
  His dearest loue the faire *Fidessa* loe
  Is there possessed of the traytour vile,
  Who reapes the haruest sowen by his foe,
  Sowen in bloudy field, and bought with woe :
  That brothers hand shall dearely well requight
  So be, O Queene, you equall fauour showe.
  Him litle answerd th'angry Elfin knight ;
He neuer meant with words, but swords to
    plead his right.

43

But threw his gauntlet as a sacred pledge,
  His cause in combat the next day to try :
  So been they parted both, with harts on edge,
  To be aueng'd each on his enimy.
  That night they pas in ioy and iollity,
  Feasting and courting both in bowre and hall ;
  For Steward was excessiue *Gluttonie,*
  That of his plenty poured forth to all ;
Which doen, the Chamberlain *Slowth* did to rest
  them call.

44

Now whenas darkesome night had all displayd
  Her coleblacke curtein ouer brightest skye,
  The warlike youthes on dayntie couches layd,
  Did chace away sweet sleepe from sluggish eye,
  To muse on meanes of hoped victory.
  But whenas *Morpheus* had with leaden mace
  Arrested all that courtly company,
  Vp-rose *Duessa* from her resting place,
And to the Paynims lodging comes with silent
  pace.

45

Whom broad awake she finds, in troublous fit,
  Forecasting, how his foe he might annoy,
  And him amoues with speaches seeming fit :
  Ah deare *Sans ioy,* next dearest to *Sans foy,*
  Cause of my new griefe, cause of my new ioy,
  Ioyous, to see his ymage in mine eye,
  And greeu'd, to thinke how foe did him destroy,
  That was the flowre of grace and cheualrye ;
Lo his *Fidessa* to thy secret faith I flye.

46

With gentle wordes he can her fairely greet,
  And bad say on the secret of her hart.
  Then sighing soft, I learne that litle sweet
  Oft tempred is (quoth she) with muchell smart:
  For since my brest was launcht with louely
    dart
  Of deare *Sansfoy,* I neuer ioyed howre,
  But in eternall woes my weaker hart
  Haue wasted, louing him with all my powre,
And for his sake haue felt full many an heauie
  stowre.

47

At last when perils all I weened past,
  And hop'd to reape the crop of all my care,
  Into new woes vnweeting I was cast,
  By this false faytor, who vnworthy ware
  His worthy shield, whom he with guilefull snare
  Entrapped slew, and brought to shamefull graue.
  Me silly maid away with him he bare,
  And euer since hath kept in darksome caue,
For that I would not yeeld, that to *Sans-foy*
  I gaue.

48

But since faire Sunne hath sperst that lowring
    clowd,
  And to my loathed life now shewes some light,
  Vnder your beames I will me safely shrowd,
  From dreaded storme of his disdainfull spight:
  To you th'inheritance belongs by right
  Of brothers prayse, to you eke longs his loue.
  Let not his loue, let not his restlesse spright
  Be vnreueng'd, that calles to you aboue
From wandring *Stygian* shores, where it doth
  endlesse moue.

49

Thereto said he, Faire Dame be nought dismaid
  For sorrowes past ; their griefe is with them
    gone :
  Ne yet of present perill be affraid ;
  For needlesse feare did neuer vantage none,
  And helplesse hap it booteth not to mone.
  Dead is *Sans-foy,* his vitall paines are past,
  Though greeued ghost for vengeance deepe do
    grone :
He liues, that shall him pay his dewties last,
And guiltie Elfin bloud shall sacrifice in hast.

50

O but I feare the fickle freakes (quoth shee)
  Of fortune false, and oddes of armes in field.
  Why dame (quoth he) what oddes can euer bee,
  Where both do fight alike, to win or yield ?
  Yea but (quoth she) he beares a charmed shield,
  And eke enchaunted armes, that none can perce,
  Ne none can wound the man, that does them
    wield.
  Charmd or enchaunted (answerd he then ferce)
I no whit reck, ne you the like need to reherce.

51

But faire *Fidessa,* sithens fortunes guile,
  Or enimies powre hath now captiued you,
  Returne from whence ye came, and rest a while
  Till morrow next, that I the Elfe subdew,
  And with *Sans-foyes* dead dowry you endew.
  Ay me, that is a double death (she said)
  With proud foes sight my sorrow to renew :
  Where euer yet I be, my secrete aid
Shall follow you. So passing forth she him obaid.

Cant. V.

ᘏᕘᘏᕘᘏᕘᘏᕘᘏᕘᘏᕘᘏᕘᘏᕘᘏᕘᘏᕘᘏ

The faithfull knight in equall field
subdewes his faithlesse foe,
Whom false Duessa saues, and for
his cure to hell does goe.

ᘏᕘᘏᕘᘏᕘᘏᕘᘏᕘᘏᕘᘏᕘᘏᕘᘏᕘᘏᕘᘏ

1

The noble hart, that harbours vertuous thought,
And is with child of glorious great intent,
Can neuer rest, vntill it forth haue brought
Th'eternall brood of glorie excellent :
Such restlesse passion did all night torment
The flaming corage of that Faery knight,
Deuizing, how that doughtie turnament
With greatest honour he atchieuen might ;
Still did he wake, and still did watch for dawn-
    ing light.

2

At last the golden Orientall gate
Of greatest heauen gan to open faire,
And *Phœbus* fresh, as bridegrome to his mate,
Came dauncing forth, shaking his deawie haire:
And hurld his glistring beames through gloomy
    aire.   [streight way
Which when the wakeful Elfe perceiu'd,
He started vp, and did him selfe prepaire,
In sun-bright armes, and battailous array :
For with that Pagan proud he combat will that
    day.

3

And forth he comes into the commune hall,
Where earely waite him many a gazing eye,
To weet what end to straunger knights may fall.
There many Minstrales maken melody,
To driue away the dull melancholy,
And many Bardes, that to the trembling chord
Can tune their timely voyces cunningly,
And many Chroniclers, that can record
Old loues, and warres for Ladies doen by many
    a Lord.

4

Soone after comes the cruell Sarazin,
In wouen maile all armed warily,
And sternly lookes at him, who not a pin
Does care for looke of liuing creatures eye.
They bring them wines of *Greece* and *Araby*,
And daintie spices fetcht from furthest *Ynd*,
To kindle heat of corage priuily :
And in the wine a solemne oth they bynd
T'obserue the sacred lawes of armes, that are
    assynd.

5

At last forth comes that far renowmed Queene,
With royall pomp and Princely maiestie ;
She is ybrought vnto a paled greene,
And placed vnder stately canapee,
The warlike feates of both those knights to see.
On th'other side in all mens open vew
Duessa placed is, and on a tree
Sans-foy his shield is hangd with bloudy hew :
Both those the lawrell girlonds to the victor dew.

6

A shrilling trompet sownded from on hye,
And vnto battaill bad them selues addresse :
Their shining shieldes about their wrestes they
    tye,
And burning blades about their heads do blesse,
The instruments of wrath and heauinesse :
With greedy force each other doth assayle,
And strike so fiercely, that they do impresse
Deepe dinted furrowes in the battred mayle ;
The yron walles to ward their blowes are weake
    and fraile.

7

The Sarazin was stout, and wondrous strong,
And heaped blowes like yron hammers great :
For after bloud and vengeance he did long.
The knight was fiers, and full of youthly heat :
And doubled strokes, like dreaded thunders
    threat :
For all for prayse and honour he did fight.
Both stricken strike, and beaten both do beat,
That from their shields forth flyeth firie light,
And helmets hewen deepe, shew marks of
    eithers might.

8

So th'one for wrong, the other striues for right :
As when a Gryfon seized of his pray,
A Dragon fiers encountreth in his flight,
Through widest ayre making his ydle way,
That would his rightfull rauine rend away :
With hideous horrour both together smight,
And souce so sore, that they the heauens affray:
The wise Southsayer seeing so sad sight,
Th'amazed vulgar tels of warres and mortall
    fight.

9

So th'one for wrong, the other striues for right,
And each to deadly shame would driue his foe :
The cruell steele so greedily doth bight
In tender flesh, that streames of bloud down
    flow,   [show,
With which the armes, that earst so bright did
Into a pure vermillion now are dyde :
Great ruth in all the gazers harts did grow,
Seeing the gored woundes to gape so wyde,
That victory they dare not wish to either side.

10

At last the Paynim chaunst to cast his eye,
　His suddein eye, flaming with wrathfull fyre,
Vpon his brothers shield, which hong thereby :
　Therewith redoubled was his raging yre,
　And said, Ah wretched sonne of wofull syre,
Doest thou sit wayling by black *Stygian* lake,
　Whilest here thy shield is hangd for victors hyre,
　And sluggish german doest thy forces slake,
To after-send his foe, that him may ouertake ?

11

Goe caytiue Elfe, him quickly ouertake,
　And soone redeeme from his long wandring woe ;
Goe guiltie ghost, to him my message make,
　That I his shield haue quit from dying foe.
　Therewith vpon his crest he stroke him so,
That twise he reeled, readie twise to fall ;
　End of the doubtfull battell deemed tho
　The lookers on, and lowd to him gan call
The false *Duessa*, Thine the shield, and I, and
　all.

12

Soone as the Faerie heard his Ladie speake,
　Out of his swowning dreame he gan awake,
And quickning faith, that earst was woxen weake,
　The creeping deadly cold away did shake :
　Tho mou'd with wrath, and shame, and Ladies
　　sake,
Of all attonce he cast auengd to bee,
　And with so'exceeding furie at him strake,
　That forced him to stoupe vpon his knee ;
Had he not stouped so, he should haue clouen
　bee,

13

And to him said, Goe now proud Miscreant,
　Thy selfe thy message doe to german deare,
Alone he wandring thee too long doth want :
　Goe say, his foe thy shield with his doth beare.
　Therewith his heauie hand he high gan reare,
Him to haue slaine ; when loe a darkesome clowd
　Vpon him fell : he no where doth appeare,
　But vanisht is. The Elfe him cals alowd,
But answer none receiues : the darknes him
　does shrowd.

14

In haste *Duessa* from her place arose,
　And to him running said, O prowest knight,
That euer Ladie to her loue did chose,
　Let now abate the terror of your might,
　And quench the flame of furious despight,
And bloudie vengeance ; lo th'infernall powres
　Couering your foe with cloud of deadly night,
　Haue borne him hence to *Plutoes* balefull bowres.
The conquest yours, I yours, the shield, and
　glory yours.

15

Not all so satisfide, with greedie eye
　He sought all round about, his thirstie blade
To bath in bloud of faithlesse enemy ;
　Who all that while lay hid in secret shade :
　He standes amazed, how he thence should fade.
At last the trumpets Triumph sound on hie,
　And running Heralds humble homage made,
　Greeting him goodly with new victorie,
And to him brought the shield, the cause of
　enmitie.

16

Wherewith he goeth to that soueraine Queene,
　And falling her before on lowly knee,
To her makes present of his seruice seene :
　Which she accepts, with thankes, and goodly
　　gree,
Greatly aduauncing his gay cheualree.
　So marcheth home, and by her takes the knight,
Whom all the people follow with great glee,
　Shouting, and clapping all their hands on hight,
That all the aire it fils, and flyes to heauen
　bright.

17

Home is he brought, and laid in sumptuous bed :
　Where many skilfull leaches him abide,
To salue his hurts, that yet still freshly bled.
　In wine and oyle they wash his woundes wide,
　And softly can embalme on euery side.
And all the while, most heauenly melody
　About the bed sweet musicke did diuide,
　Him to beguile of griefe and agony :
And all the while *Duessa* wept full bitterly.

18

As when a wearie traueller that strayes
　By muddy shore of broad seuen-mouthed *Nile*,
Vnweeting of the perillous wandring wayes,
　Doth meet a cruell craftie Crocodile,
　Which in false griefe hyding his harmefull guile,
Doth weepe full sore, and sheddeth tender teares :
　The foolish man, that pitties all this while
　His mournefull plight, is swallowd vp vnwares,
Forgetfull of his owne, that mindes anothers
　cares.

19

So wept *Duessa* vntill euentide,
　That shyning lampes in *Ioues* high house were
　　light :
Then forth she rose, ne lenger would abide,
　But comes vnto the place, where th'Hethen
　　knight
In slombring swownd nigh voyd of vitall spright,
　Lay couer'd with inchaunted cloud all day :
Whom when she found, as she him left in plight,
　To wayle his woefull case she would not stay,
But to the easterne coast of heauen makes
　speedy way.

20

Where griesly *Night*, with visage deadly sad,
That *Phœbus* chearefull face durst neuer vew,
And in a foule blacke pitchie mantle clad,
She findes forth comming from her darkesome
    mew,
Where she all day did hide her hated hew.
Before the dore her yron charet stood,
Alreadie harnessed for iourney new ;
And coleblacke steedes yborne of hellish brood,
That on their rustie bits did champ, as they
    were wood.

21

Who when she saw *Duessa* sunny bright,
Adornd with gold and iewels shining cleare,
She greatly grew amazed at the sight,
And th'vnacquainted light began to feare :
For neuer did such brightnesse there appeare,
And would haue backe retyred to her caue,
Vntill the witches speech she gan to heare,
Saying, Yet O thou dreaded Dame, I craue
Abide, till I haue told the message, which I
    haue.

22

She stayd, and foorth *Duessa* gan proceede,
O thou most auncient Grandmother of all,
More old then *Ioue*, whom thou at first didst
    breede,
Or that great house of Gods cælestiall,
Which wast begot in *Dæmogorgons* hall,
And sawst the secrets of the world vnmade,
Why suffredst thou thy Nephewes deare to fall
With Elfin sword, most shamefully betrade ?
Lo where the stout *Sansioy* doth sleepe in
    deadly shade.

23

And him before, I saw with bitter eyes
The bold *Sansfoy* shrinke vnderneath his speare;
And now the pray of fowles in field he lyes,
Nor wayld of friends, nor laid on groning beare,
That whylome was to me too dearely deare.
O what of Gods then boots it to be borne,
If old *Aueugles* sonnes so euill heare ?
Or who shall not great *Nightes* children scorne,
When two of three her Nephews are so fowle
    forlorne.

24

Vp then, vp dreary Dame, of darknesse Queene,
Go gather vp the reliques of thy race,
Or else goe them auenge, and let be seene,
That dreaded *Night* in brightest day hath place,
And can the children of faire light deface.
Her feeling speeches some compassion moued
In hart, and chaunge in that great mothers face:
Yet pittie in her hart was neuer proued
Till then : for euermore she hated, neuer loued.

25

And said, Deare daughter rightly may I rew
The fall of famous children borne of mee,
And good successes, which their foes ensew :
But who can turne the streame of destinee,
Or breake the chayne of strong necessitee,
Which fast is tyde to *Ioues* eternall seat ?
The sonnes of Day he fauoureth, I see,
And by my ruines thinkes to make them great:
To make one great by others losse, is bad ex-
    cheat.

26

Yet shall they not escape so freely all ;
For some shall pay the price of others guilt :
And he the man that made *Sansfoy* to fall,
Shall with his owne bloud price that he hath spilt.
But what art thou, that telst of Nephews kilt ?
I that do seeme not I, *Duessa* am,
(Quoth she) how euer now in garments gilt,
And gorgeous gold arayd I to thee came ;
Duessa I, the daughter of Deceipt and Shame.

27

Then bowing downe her aged backe, she kist
The wicked witch, saying ; In that faire face
The false resemblance of Deceipt, I wist
Did closely lurke ; yet so true-seeming grace
It carried, that I scarse in darkesome place
Could it discerne, though I the mother bee
Of falshood, and root of *Duessaes* race.
O welcome child, whom I haue longd to see,
And now haue seene vnwares. Lo now I go
    with thee.

28

Then to her yron wagon she betakes,
And with her beares the fowle welfauourd witch:
Through mirkesome aire her readie way she
    makes.
Her twyfold Teme, of which two blacke as pitch,
And two were browne, yet each to each vnlich,
Did softly swim away, ne euer stampe,
Vnlesse she chaunst their stubborne mouths
    to twitch ;
Then foming tarre, their bridles they would
    champe,
And trampling the fine element, would fiercely
    rampe.

29

So well they sped, that they be come at length
Vnto the place, whereas the Paynim lay,
Deuoid of outward sense, and natiue strength,
Couerd with charmed cloud from vew of day,
And sight of men, since his late luckelesse fray.
His cruell wounds with cruddy bloud congealed,
They binden vp so wisely, as they may,
And handle softly, till they can be healed :
So lay him in her charet, close in night concealed.

30

And all the while she stood vpon the ground,
The wakefull dogs did neuer cease to bay,
As giuing warning of th'vnwonted sound,
With which her yron wheeles did them affray,
And her darke griesly looke them much dismay ;
The messenger of death, the ghastly Owle
With drearie shriekes did also her bewray ;
And hungry Wolues continually did howle,
At her abhorred face, so filthy and so fowle.

31

Thence turning backe in silence soft they stole,
And brought the heauie corse with easie pace
To yawning gulfe of deepe *Auernus* hole.
By that same hole an entrance darke and bace
With smoake and sulphure hiding all the place,
Descends to hell : there creature neuer past,
That backe returned without heauenly grace ;
But dreadfull *Furies*, which their chaines haue brast,
And damned sprights sent forth to make ill men aghast.

32

By that same way the direfull dames doe driue
Their mournefull charet, fild with rusty blood,
And downe to *Plutoes* house are come biliue :
Which passing through, on euery side them stood
The trembling ghosts with sad amazed mood,
Chattring their yron teeth, and staring wide
With stonie eyes ; and all the hellish brood
Of feends infernall flockt on euery side,
To gaze on earthly wight, that with the Night durst ride.

33

They pas the bitter waues of *Acheron*,
Where many soules sit wailing woefully,
And come to fiery flood of *Phlegeton*,
Whereas the damned ghosts in torments fry,
And with sharpe shrilling shriekes doe bootlesse cry,
Cursing high *Ioue*, the which them thither sent.
The house of endlesse paine is built thereby,
In which ten thousand sorts of punishment
The cursed creatures doe eternally torment.

34

Before the threshold dreadfull *Cerberus*
His three deformed heads did lay along,
Curled with thousand adders venemous,
And lilled forth his bloudie flaming tong :
At them he gan to reare his bristles strong,
And felly gnarre, vntill dayes enemy
Did him appease ; then downe his taile he hong
And suffered them to passen quietly :
For she in hell and heauen had power equally.

35

There was *Ixion* turned on a wheele,
For daring tempt the Queene of heauen to sin ;
And *Sisyphus* an huge round stone did reele
Against an hill, ne might from labour lin ;
There thirstie *Tantalus* hong by the chin ;
And *Tityus* fed a vulture on his maw ;
Typhœus ioynts were stretched on a gin,
Theseus condemned to endlesse slouth by law,
And fifty sisters water in leake vessels draw.

36

They all beholding worldly wights in place,
Leaue off their worke, vnmindfull of their smart,
To gaze on them ; who forth by them doe pace,
Till they be come vnto the furthest part :
Where was a Caue ywrought by wondrous art,
Deepe, darke, vneasie, dolefull, comfortlesse,
In which sad *Æsculapius* farre a part
Emprisond was in chaines remedilesse,
For that *Hippolytus* rent corse he did redresse.

37

Hippolytus a iolly huntsman was,
That wont in charet chace the foming Bore ;
He all his Peeres in beautie did surpas,
But Ladies loue as losse of time forbore :
His wanton stepdame loued him the more,
But when she saw her offred sweets refused
Her loue she turnd to hate, and him before
His father fierce of treason false accused,
And with her gealous termes his open eares abused.

38

Who all in rage his Sea-god syre besought,
Some cursed vengeance on his sonne to cast :
From surging gulf two monsters straight were brought,
With dread whereof his chasing steedes aghast,
Both charet swift and huntsman ouercast.
His goodly corps on ragged cliffs yrent,
Was quite dismembred, and his members chast
Scattered on euery mountaine, as he went,
That of *Hippolytus* was left no moniment.

39

His cruell stepdame seeing what was donne,
Her wicked dayes with wretched knife did end,
In death auowing th'innocence of her sonne.
Which hearing his rash Syre, began to rend
His haire, and hastie tongue, that did offend :
Tho gathering vp the relicks of his smart
By *Dianes* meanes, who was *Hippolyts* frend,
Them brought to *Æsculape*, that by his art
Did heale them all againe, and ioyned euery part.

40

Such wondrous science in mans wit to raine
When *Ioue* auizd, that could the dead reuiue,
And fates expired could renew againe,
Of endlesse life he might him not depriue,
But vnto hell did thrust him downe aliue,
With flashing thunderbolt ywounded sore :
Where long remaining, he did alwaies striue
Himselfe with salues to health for to restore,
And slake the heauenly fire, that raged euer-
       more.

41

There auncient Night arriuing, did alight
From her nigh wearie waine, and in her armes
To *Æsculapius* brought the wounded knight :
Whom hauing softly disarayd of armes,
Tho gan to him discouer all his harmes,
Beseeching him with prayer, and with praise,
If either salues, or oyles, or herbes, or charmes
A fordonne wight from dore of death mote
       raise,
He would at her request prolong her nephews
       daies.

42

Ah Dame (quoth he) thou temptest me in vaine,
To dare the thing, which daily yet I rew,
And the old cause of my continued paine
With like attempt to like end to renew.
Is not enough, that thrust from heauen dew
Here endlesse penance for one fault I pay,
But that redoubled crime with vengeance new
Thou biddest me to eeke ? Can Night defray
The wrath of thundring *Ioue*, that rules both
       night and day ?

43

Not so (quoth she) but sith that heauens king
From hope of heauen hath thee excluded
       quight,
Why fearest thou, that canst not hope for thing,
And fearest not, that more thee hurten might,
Now in the powre of euerlasting Night ?
Goe to then, O thou farre renowmed sonne
Of great *Apollo*, shew thy famous might
In medicine, that else hath to thee wonne
Great paines, and greater praise, both neuer to
       be donne.

44

Her words preuaild: And then the learned leach
His cunning hand gan to his wounds to lay,
And all things else, the which his art did teach:
Which hauing seene, from thence arose away
The mother of dread darknesse, and let stay
Aueugles sonne there in the leaches cure,
And backe returning tooke her wonted way,
To runne her timely race, whilst *Phœbus* pure
In westerne waues his wearie wagon did recure.

45

The false *Duessa* leauing noyous Night,
Returnd to stately pallace of dame Pride ;
Where when she came, she found the Faery
       knight
Departed thence, albe his woundes wide
Not throughly heald, vnreadie were to ride.
Good cause he had to hasten thence away :
For on a day his wary Dwarfe had spide,
Where in a dongeon deepe huge numbers lay
Of caytiue wretched thrals, that wayled night
       and day.

46

A ruefull sight, as could be seene with eie ;
Of whom he learned had in secret wise
The hidden cause of their captiuitie,
How mortgaging their liues to *Couetise*,
Through wastfull Pride, and wanton Riotise,
They were by law of that proud Tyrannesse
Prouokt with *Wrath*, and *Enuies* false surmise,
Condemned to that Dongeon mercilesse,
Where they should liue in woe, and die in
       wretchednesse.

47

There was that great proud king of *Babylon*,
That would compell all nations to adore,
And him as onely God to call vpon,
Till through celestiall doome throwne out of
       dore,
Into an Oxe he was transform'd of yore :
There also was king *Crœsus*, that enhaunst
His heart too high through his great richesstore ;
And proud *Antiochus*, the which aduaunst
His cursed hand gainst God, and on his altars
       daunst.

48

And them long time before, great *Nimrod* was,
That first the world with sword and fire warrayd;
And after him old *Ninus* farre did pas
In princely pompe, of all the world obayd ;
There also was that mightie Monarch layd
Low vnder all, yet aboue all in pride,
That name of natiue syre did fowle vpbrayd,
And would as *Ammons* sonne be magnifide,
Till scornd of God and man a shamefull death
       he dide.

49

All these together in one heape were throwne,
Like carkases of beasts in butchers stall.
And in another corner wide were strowne
The antique ruines of the *Romaines* fall :
Great *Romulus* the Grandsyre of them all,
Proud *Tarquin*, and too lordly *Lentulus*,
Stout *Scipio*, and stubborne *Hanniball*,
Ambitious *Sylla*, and sterne *Marius*,
High *Cæsar*, great *Pompey*, and fierce *Antonius*.

50

Amongst these mighty men were wemen mixt,
Proud wemen, vaine, forgetfull of their yoke:
The bold *Semiramis*, whose sides transfixt
With sonnes owne blade, her fowle reproches
  spoke ;
Faire *Sthenobœa*, that her selfe did choke
With wilfull cord, for wanting of her will ;
High minded *Cleopatra*, that with stroke
Of Aspes sting her selfe did stoutly kill :
And thousands moe the like, that did that
  dongeon fill.

51

Besides the endlesse routs of wretched thralles,
Which thither were assembled day by day,
From all the world after their wofull falles,
Through wicked pride, and wasted wealthes decay.
But most of all, which in that Dongeon lay
Fell from high Princes courts, or Ladies bowres,
Where they in idle pompe, or wanton play,
Consumed had their goods, and thriftlesse
  howres,
And lastly throwne themselues into these heauy
  stowres.

52

Whose case when as the carefull Dwarfe had tould,
And made ensample of their mournefull sight
Vnto his maister, he no lenger would
There dwell in perill of like painefull plight,
But early rose, and ere that dawning light
Discouered had the world to heauen wyde,
He by a priuie Posterne tooke his flight,
That of no enuious eyes he mote be spyde :
For doubtlesse death ensewd, if any him de-
  scryde.

53

Scarse could he footing find in that fowle way,
For many corses, like a great Lay-stall
Of murdred men which therein strowed lay,
Without remorse, or decent funerall :
Which all through that great Princesse pride
  did fall
And came to shamefull end.   And them beside
Forth ryding vnderneath the castell wall,
A donghill of dead carkases he spide,
The dreadfull spectacle of that sad house of
  Pride.

Cant. VI.

From lawlesse lust by wondrous grace
   fayre Vna is releast :
Whom saluage nation does adore,
   and learnes her wise beheast.

I

As when a ship, that flyes faire vnder saile,
An hidden rocke escaped hath vnwares,
That lay in waite her wrack for to bewaile,
The Marriner yet halfe amazed stares
At perill past, and yet in doubt ne dares
To ioy at his foole-happie ouersight :
So doubly is distrest twixt ioy and cares
The dreadlesse courage of this Elfin knight,
Hauing escapt so sad ensamples in his sight.

2

Yet sad he was that his too hastie speed
The faire *Duess'* had forst him leaue behind ;
And yet more sad, that *Vna* his deare dreed
Her truth had staind with treason so vnkind ;
Yet crime in her could neuer creature find,
But for his loue, and for her owne selfe sake,
She wandred had from one to other *Ynd*,
Him for to seeke, ne euer would forsake,
Till her vnwares the fierce *Sansloy* did ouertake.

3

Who after *Archimagoes* fowle defeat,
Led her away into a forrest wilde,
And turning wrathfull fire to lustfull heat,
With beastly sin thought her to haue defilde,
And made the vassall of his pleasures vilde.
Yet first he cast by treatie, and by traynes,
Her to perswade, that stubborne fort to yilde :
For greater conquest of hard loue he gaynes,
That workes it to his will, then he that it con-
  straines.

4

With fawning wordes he courted her a while,
And looking louely, and oft sighing sore,
Her constant hart did tempt with diuerse guile:
But wordes, and lookes, and sighes she did
  abhore,
As rocke of Diamond stedfast euermore.
Yet for to feed his fyrie lustfull eye,
He snatcht the vele, that hong her face before;
Then gan her beautie shine, as brightest skye,
And burnt his beastly hart t'efforce her
  chastitye.

5

So when he saw his flatt'ring arts to fayle,
  And subtile engines bet from batteree,
  With greedy force he gan the fort assayle,
  Whereof he weend possessed soone to bee,
  And win rich spoile of ransackt chastetee.
  Ah heauens, that do this hideous act behold,
  And heauenly virgin thus outraged see,
  How can ye vengeance iust so long withhold,
And hurle not flashing flames vpon that Pay-
    nim bold ?

6

The pitteous maiden carefull comfortlesse,
  Does throw out thrilling shriekes, and shriek-
    ing cryes,
  The last vaine helpe of womens great distresse,
  And with loud plaints importuneth the skyes,
  That molten starres do drop like weeping eyes;
  And *Phœbus* flying so most shamefull sight,
  His blushing face in foggy cloud implyes,
  And hides for shame. What wit of mortall wight
Can now deuise to quit a thrall from such a
    plight ?

7

Eternall prouidence exceeding thought,
  Where none appeares can make her selfe a way:
  A wondrous way it for this Lady wrought,
  From Lyons clawes to pluck the griped pray.
  Her shrill outcryes and shriekes so loud did
    bray,
  That all the woodes and forestes did resownd ;
  A troupe of *Faunes* and *Satyres* far away
Within the wood were dauncing in a rownd,
Whiles old *Syluanus* slept in shady arber sownd.

8

Who when they heard that pitteous strained voice,
  In hast forsooke their rurall meriment,
  And ran towards the far rebownded noyce,
  To weet, what wight so loudly did lament.
  Vnto the place they come incontinent :
  Whom when the raging Sarazin espide,
  A rude, misshapen, monstrous rablement,
  Whose like he neuer saw, he durst not bide,
But got his ready steed, and fast away gan ride.

9

The wyld woodgods arriued in the place,
  There find the virgin dolefull desolate,
  With ruffled rayments, and faire blubbred face,
  As her outrageous foe had left her late,
  And trembling yet through feare of former hate;
  All stand amazed at so vncouth sight,
  And gin to pittie her vnhappie state,
  All stand astonied at her beautie bright,
In their rude eyes vnworthie of so wofull plight.

10

She more amaz'd, in double dread doth dwell ;
  And euery tender part for feare does shake :
  As when a greedie Wolfe through hunger fell
  A seely Lambe farre from the flocke does take,
  Of whom he meanes his bloudie feast to make,
  A Lyon spyes fast running towards him,
  The innocent pray in hast he does forsake,
  Which quit from death yet quakes in euery lim
With chaunge of feare, to see the Lyon looke so
    grim.

11

Such fearefull fit assaid her trembling hart,
  Ne word to speake, ne ioynt to moue she had :
  The saluage nation feele her secret smart,
  And read her sorrow in her count'nance sad ;
  Their frowning forheads with rough hornes
    yclad,
  And rusticke horror all a side doe lay,
  And gently grenning, shew a semblance glad
  To comfort her, and feare to put away,
Their backward bent knees teach her humbly to
    obay.

12

The doubtfull Damzell dare not yet commit
  Her single person to their barbarous truth,
  But still twixt feare and hope amazd does sit,
  Late learnd what harme to hastie trust ensu'th,
  They in compassion of her tender youth,
  And wonder of her beautie soueraine,
  Are wonne with pitty and vnwonted ruth,
  And all prostrate vpon the lowly plaine,
Do kisse her feete, and fawne on her with
    count'nance faine.

13

Their harts she ghesseth by their humble guise,
  And yieldes her to extremitie of time ;
  So from the ground she fearelesse doth arise,
  And walketh forth without suspect of crime:
  They all as glad, as birdes of ioyous Prime,
  Thence lead her forth, about her dauncing round,
  Shouting, and singing all a shepheards ryme,
  And with greene braunches strowing all the
    ground,
Do worship her, as Queene, with oliue girlond
    cround.

14

And all the way their merry pipes they sound,
  That all the woods with doubled Eccho ring,
  And with their horned feet do weare the ground,
  Leaping like wanton kids in pleasant Spring.
  So towards old *Syluanus* they her bring ;
  Who with the noyse awaked, commeth out,
  To weet the cause, his weake steps gouerning,
  And aged limbs on Cypresse stadle stout,
And with an yuie twyne his wast is girt about.

15

Far off he wonders, what them makes so glad,
Or *Bacchus* merry fruit they did inuent,
Or *Cybeles* franticke rites haue made them mad;
They drawing nigh, vnto their God present
That flowre of faith and beautie excellent.
The God himselfe vewing that mirrhour rare,
Stood long amazd, and burnt in his intent;
His owne faire *Dryope* now he thinkes not faire,
And *Pholoe* fowle, when her to this he doth
compaire.

16

The woodborne people fall before her flat,
And worship her as Goddesse of the wood;
And old *Syluanus* selfe bethinkes not, what
To thinke of wight so faire, but gazing stood,
In doubt to deeme her borne of earthly brood;
Sometimes Dame *Venus* selfe he seemes to see,
But *Venus* neuer had so sober mood;
Sometimes *Diana* he her takes to bee,
But misseth bow, and shaftes, and buskins to
her knee.

17

By vew of her he ginneth to reuiue
His ancient loue, and dearest *Cyparisse*,
And calles to mind his pourtraiture aliue,
How faire he was, and yet not faire to this,
And how he slew with glauncing dart amisse
A gentle Hynd, the which the louely boy
Did loue as life, aboue all worldly blisse;
For griefe whereof the lad n'ould after ioy,
But pynd away in anguish and selfe-wild annoy.

18

The wooddy Nymphes, faire *Hamadryades*
Her to behold do thither runne apace,
And all the troupe of light-foot *Naiades*,
Flocke all about to see her louely face:
But when they vewed haue her heauenly grace,
They enuie her in their malitious mind,
And fly away for feare of fowle disgrace:
But all the *Satyres* scorne their woody kind,
And henceforth nothing faire, but her on earth
they find.

19

Glad of such lucke, the luckelesse lucky maid,
Did her content to please their feeble eyes,
And long time with that saluage people staid,
To gather breath in many miseries.
During which time her gentle wit she plyes,
To teach them truth, which worship her in
vaine,
And made her th'Image of Idolatryes;
But when their bootlesse zeale she did restraine
From her own worship, they her Asse would
worship fayn

20

It fortuned a noble warlike knight
By iust occasion to that forrest came,
To seeke his kindred, and the lignage right,
From whence he tooke his well deserued name:
He had in armes abroad wonne muchell fame,
And fild far landes with glorie of his might,
Plaine, faithfull, true, and enimy of shame,
And euer lou'd to fight for Ladies right,
But in vaine glorious frayes he litle did delight.

21

A Satyres sonne yborne in forrest wyld,
By straunge aduenture as it did betyde,
And there begotten of a Lady myld,
Faire *Thyamis* the daughter of *Labryde*,
That was in sacred bands of wedlocke tyde
To *Therion*, a loose vnruly swayne;
Who had more ioy to raunge the forrest wyde,
And chase the saluage beast with busie payne,
Then serue his Ladies loue, and wast in
pleasures vayne.

22

The forlorne mayd did with loues longing burne,
And could not lacke her louers company,
But to the wood she goes, to serue her turne,
And seeke her spouse, that from her still does fly,
And followes other game and venery:
A Satyre chaunst her wandring for to find,
And kindling coles of lust in brutish eye,
The loyall links of wedlocke did vnbind,
And made her person thrall vnto his beastly
kind.

23

So long in secret cabin there he held
Her captiue to his sensuall desire,
Till that with timely fruit her belly sweld,
And bore a boy vnto that saluage sire:
Then home he suffred her for to retire,
For ransome leauing him the late borne childe;
Whom till to ryper yeares he gan aspire,
He noursled vp in life and manners wilde,
Emongst wild beasts and woods, from lawes of
men exilde.

24

For all he taught the tender ymp, was but
To banish cowardize and bastard feare;
His trembling hand he would him force to put
Vpon the Lyon and the rugged Beare,
And from the she Beares teats her whelps to
teare;
And eke wyld roring Buls he would him make
To tame, and ryde their backes not made to
beare;
And the Robuckes in flight to ouertake,
That euery beast for feare of him did fly and quake.

25

Thereby so fearelesse, and so fell he grew,
That his owne sire and maister of his guise
Did often tremble at his horrid vew,
And oft for dread of hurt would him aduise,
The angry beasts not rashly to despise,
Nor too much to prouoke; for he would learne
The Lyon stoup to him in lowly wise,
(A lesson hard) and make the Libbard sterne
Leaue roaring, when in rage he for reuenge did earne.

26

And for to make his powre approued more,
Wyld beasts in yron yokes he would compell ;
The spotted Panther, and the tusked Bore,
The Pardale swift, and the Tigre cruell ;
The Antelope, and Wolfe both fierce and fell ;
And them constraine in equall teme to draw,
Such ioy he had, their stubborne harts to quell,
And sturdie courage tame with dreadfull aw,
That his beheast they feared, as a tyrans law.

27

His louing mother came vpon a day
Vnto the woods, to see her little sonne ;
And chaunst vnwares to meet him in the way,
After his sportes, and cruell pastime donne,
When after him a Lyonesse did runne,
That roaring all with rage, did lowd requere
Her children deare, whom he away had wonne:
The Lyon whelpes she saw how he did beare,
And lull in rugged armes, withouten childish feare.

28

The fearefull Dame all quaked at the sight,
And turning backe, gan fast to fly away,
Vntill with loue reuokt from vaine affright,
She hardly yet perswaded was to stay,
And then to him these womanish words gan say ;
Ah *Satyrane*, my dearling, and my ioy,
For loue of me leaue off this dreadfull play ;
To dally thus with death, is no fit toy,
Go find some other play-fellowes, mine own sweet boy.

29

In these and like delights of bloudy game
He trayned was, till ryper yeares he raught,
And there abode, whilst any beast of name
Walkt in that forest, whom he had not taught
To feare his force: and then his courage haught
Desird of forreine foemen to be knowne,
And far abroad for straunge aduentures sought:
In which his might was neuer ouerthrowne,
But through all Faery lond his famous worth was blown.

30

Yet euermore it was his manner faire,
After long labours and aduentures spent,
Vnto those natiue woods for to repaire,
To see his sire and ofspring auncient.
And now he thither came for like intent ;
Where he vnwares the fairest *Vna* found,
Straunge Lady, in so straunge habiliment,
Teaching the Satyres, which her sat around,
Trew sacred lore, which from her sweet lips did redound.

31

He wondred at her wisedome heauenly rare,
Whose like in womens wit he neuer knew ;
And when her curteous deeds he did compare,
Gan her admire, and her sad sorrowes rew,
Blaming of Fortune, which such troubles threw,
And ioyd to make proofe of her crueltie
On gentle Dame, so hurtlesse, and so trew :
Thenceforth he kept her goodly company,
And learnd her discipline of faith and veritie.

32

But she all vowd vnto the *Redcrosse* knight,
His wandring perill closely did lament,
Ne in this new acquaintaunce could delight,
But her deare heart with anguish did torment,
And all her wit in secret counsels spent,
How to escape. At last in priuie wise
To *Satyrane* she shewed her intent ;
Who glad to gain such fauour, gan deuise,
How with that pensiue Maid he best might thence arise.

33

So on a day when Satyres all were gone,
To do their seruice to *Syluanus* old,
The gentle virgin left behind alone
He led away with courage stout and bold.
Too late it was, to Satyres to be told,
Or euer hope recouer her againe :
In vaine he seekes that hauing cannot hold.
So fast he carried her with carefull paine,
That they the woods are past, and come now to the plaine.

34

The better part now of the lingring day,
They traueild had, when as they farre espide
A wearie wight forwandring by the way,
And towards him they gan in hast to ride,
To weet of newes, that did abroad betide,
Or tydings of her knight of the *Redcrosse*.
But he them spying, gan to turne aside,
For feare as seemd, or for some feigned losse ;
More greedy they of newes, fast towards him do cr sse.

35

A silly man, in simple weedes forworne,
  And soild with dust of the long dried way ;
His sandales were with toilesome trauell torne,
  And face all tand with scorching sunny ray,
  As he had traueild many a sommers day,
Through boyling sands of *Arabie* and *Ynde* ;
  And in his hand a *Iacobs* staffe, to stay
His wearie limbes vpon : and eke behind,
His scrip did hang, in which his needments he
    did bind.

36

The knight approching nigh, of him inquerd
  Tydings of warre, and of aduentures new ;
But warres, nor new aduentures none he herd.
  Then *Vna* gan to aske, if ought he knew,
  Or heard abroad of that her champion trew,
That in his armour bare a croslet red.
  Aye me, Deare dame (quoth he) well may I rew
To tell the sad sight, which mine eies haue red :
These eyes did see that knight both liuing and
    eke ded.

37

That cruell word her tender hart so thrild,
  That suddein cold did runne through euery
    vaine,
And stony horrour all her sences fild
  With dying fit, that downe she fell for paine.
  The knight her lightly reared vp againe,
And comforted with curteous kind reliefe :
  Then wonne from death, she bad him tellen plaine
The further processe of her hidden griefe ;
The lesser pangs can beare, who hath endur'd
    the chiefe.

38

Then gan the Pilgrim thus, I chaunst this day,
  This fatall day, that shall I euer rew,
To see two knights in trauell on my way
  (A sory sight) arraung'd in battell new, [hew:
  Both breathing vengeaunce, both of wrathfull
My fearefull flesh did tremble at their strife,
  To see their blades so greedily imbrew,
That drunke with bloud, yet thristed after life:
What more ? the *Redcrosse* knight was slaine
    with Paynim knife.

39

Ah dearest Lord (quoth she) how might that bee,
  And he the stoutest knight, that euer wonne ?
Ah dearest dame (quoth he) how might I see
  The thing, that might not be, and yet was
    donne ?
Where is (said *Satyrane*) that Paynims sonne,
  That him of life, and vs of ioy hath reft ?
Not far away (quoth he) he hence doth wonne
Foreby a fountaine, where I late him left
Wasning his bloudy wounds, that through the
    steele were cleft.

40

Therewith the knight thence marched forth in
    hast,
  Whiles *Vna* with huge heauinesse opprest,
Could not for sorrow follow him so fast ;
  And soone he came, as he the place had ghest,
  Whereas that *Pagan* proud him selfe did rest,
In secret shadow by a fountaine side :
  Euen he it was, that earst would haue supprest
Faire *Vna* : whom when *Satyrane* espide,
With fowle reprochfull words he boldly him
    defide.

41

And said, Arise thou cursed Miscreaunt, [train
  That hast with knightlesse guile and trecherous
Faire knighthood fowly shamed, and doest vaunt
  That good knight of the *Redcrosse* to haue slain:
  Arise, and with like treason now maintain
Thy guilty wrong, or else thee guilty yield.
  The *Sarazin* this hearing, rose amain,
And catching vp in hast his three square shield,
And shining helmet, soone him buckled to the
    field.

42

And drawing nigh him said, Ah misborne Elfe,
  In euill houre thy foes thee hither sent,
Anothers wrongs to wreake vpon thy selfe :
  Yet ill thou blamest me, for hauing blent
  My name with guile and traiterous intent ;
That *Redcrosse* knight, perdie, I neuer slew,
  But had he beene, where earst his armes were
    lent,
Th'enchaunter vaine his errour should not rew :
But thou his errour shalt, I hope now prouen
    trew.

43

Therewith they gan, both furious and fell,
  To thunder blowes, and fiersly to assaile
Each other bent his enimy to quell. [maile,
  That with their force they perst both plate and
  And made wide furrowes in their fleshes fraile,
That it would pitty any liuing eie. [raile :
  Large floods of bloud adowne their sides did
But floods of bloud could not them satisfie :
Both hungred after death : both chose to win,
    or die.

44

So long they fight, and fell reuenge pursue,
  That fainting each, themselues to breathen let,
And oft refreshed, battell oft renue :
  As when two Bores with rancling malice met,
  Their gory sides fresh bleeding fiercely fret,
Til breathlesse both them selues aside retire,
  Where foming wrath, their cruell tuskes they
    whet, [respire ;
And trample th'earth, the whiles they may
Then backe to fight againe, new breathed and
    entire.

45

So fiersly, when these knights had breathed once,
They gan to fight returne, increasing more
Their puissant force, and cruell rage attonce,
With heaped strokes more hugely, then before,
That with their drerie wounds and bloudy gore
They both deformed, scarsely could be known.
By this sad *Vna* fraught with anguish sore,
Led with their noise, which through the aire
     was thrown,
Arriu'd, where they in erth their fruitles bloud
     had sown.

46

Whom all so soone as that proud Sarazin
Espide, he gan reuiue the memory
Of his lewd lusts, and late attempted sin,
And left the doubtfull battell hastily,
To catch her, newly offred to his eie :
But *Satyrane* with strokes him turning, staid,
And sternely bad him other businesse plie,
Then hunt the steps of pure vnspotted Maid :
Wherewith he all enrag'd, these bitter speaches
     said.

47

O foolish faeries sonne, what furie mad
Hath thee incenst, to hast thy dolefull fate ?
Were it not better, I that Lady had,
Then that thou hadst repented it too late ?
Mostsencelessemanhe,thathimselfedothhate,
To loue another. Lo then for thine ayd
Here take thy louers token on thy pate.
So they to fight ; the whiles the royall Mayd
Fled farre away, of that proud Paynim sore
     afrayd.

48

But that false *Pilgrim*, which that leasing told,
Being in deed old *Archimage*, did stay
In secret shadow, all this to behold,
And much reioyced in their bloudy fray :
But when he saw the Damsell passe away
He left his stond, and her pursewd apace,
In hope to bring her to her last decay.
But for to tell her lamentable cace,
And eke this battels end, will need another
     place.

Cant. VII.

The Redcrosse knight is captiue made
By Gyaunt proud opprest,
Prince Arthur meets with Vna great-
ly with those newes distrest.

1

What man so wise, what earthly wit so ware,
As to descry the crafty cunning traine,
By which deceipt doth maske in visour faire,
And cast her colours dyed deepe in graine,
To seeme like Truth, whose shape she well can
     faine,
And fitting gestures to her purpose frame,
The guiltlesse man with guile to entertaine ?
Greatmaistresse of her art was that false Dame,
The false *Duessa*, cloked with *Fidessaes* name.

2

Who when returning from the drery *Night*,
She fownd not in that perilous house of *Pryde*,
Where she had left, the noble *Redcrosse* knight,
Her hoped pray, she would no lenger bide,
But forth she went, to seeke him far and wide.
Ere long she fownd, whereas he wearie sate,
To rest him selfe, foreby a fountaine side,
Disarmed all of yron-coted Plate,
And by his side his steed the grassy forage ate.

3

He feedes vpon the cooling shade, and bayes
His sweatie forehead in the breathing wind,
Which through the trembling leaues full gently
     playes
Wherein the cherefull birds of sundry kind
Do chaunt sweet musick, to delight his mind :
The Witch approching gan him fairely greet,
And with reproch of carelesnesse vnkind
Vpbrayd, for leauing her in place vnmeet,
With fowle words tempring faire, soure gall
     with hony sweet.

4

Vnkindnesse past, they gan of solace treat,
And bathe in pleasaunce of the ioyous shade,
Which shielded them against the boyling heat,
And with greene boughes decking a gloomy
     glade,
About the fountaine like a girlond made ;
Whose bubbling waue did euer freshly well,
Ne euer would through feruent sommer fade :
The sacred Nymph, which therein wont to dwell,
Was out of *Dianes* fauour, as it then befell.

5

The cause was this : one day when *Phœbe* fayre
  With all her band was following the chace,
  This Nymph, quite tyr'd with heat of scorching
  Sat downe to rest in middest of the race: [ayre
The goddesse wroth gan fowly her disgrace,
  And bad the waters, which from her did flow,
  Be such as she her selfe was then in place.
Thenceforth her waters waxed dull and slow,
And all that drunke thereof, did faint and feeble
    grow.

6

Hereof this gentle knight vnweeting was,
  And lying downe vpon the sandie graile,
  Drunke of the streame, as cleare as cristall glas;
Eftsoones his manly forces gan to faile,
  And mightie strong was turnd to feeble fraile.
  His chaunged powres at first themselues not felt,
Till crudled cold his corage gan assaile,
  And chearefull bloud in faintnesse chill did melt,
Which like a feuer fit through all his body swelt.

7

Yet goodly court he made still to his Dame,
  Pourd out in loosnesse on the grassy grownd,
  Both carelesse of his health, and of his fame :
Till at the last he heard a dreadfull sownd,
  Which through the wood loud bellowing, did
    rebownd,
That all the earth for terrour seemd to shake,
  And trees did tremble. Th'Elfe therewith
    astownd,
Vpstarted lightly from his looser make,
And his vnready weapons gan in hand to take.

8

But ere he could his armour on him dight,
  Or get his shield, his monstrous enimy
  With sturdie steps came stalking in his sight,
An hideous Geant horrible and hye,
  That with his talnesse seemd to threat the skye,
  The ground eke groned vnder him for dreed ;
His liuing like saw neuer liuing eye,
  Ne durst behold : his stature did exceed
The hight of three the tallest sonnes of mortall
    seed.

9

The greatest Earth his vncouth mother was,
  And blustring *Æolus* his boasted sire,
  Who with his breath, which through the world
    doth pas,
Her hollow womb did secretly inspire,
  And fild her hidden caues with stormie yre,
  That she conceiu'd; and trebling the dew time,
In which the wombes of women do expire,
  Brought forth this monstrous masse of earthly
    slime,   [crime.
Puft vp with emptie wind, and fild with sinfull

10

So growen great through arrogant delight
  Of th'high descent, whereof he was yborne,
  And through presumption of his matchlesse
    might,
All other powres and knighthood he did scorne.
  Such now he marcheth to this man forlorne,
  And left to losse : his stalking steps are stayde
Vpon a snaggy Oke, which he had torne
  Out of his mothers bowelles, and it made
His mortall mace, wherewith his foemen he
    dismayde.

11

That when the knight he spide, he gan aduance
  With huge force and insupportable mayne,
  And towardes him with dreadfull fury praunce ;
Who haplesse, and eke hopelesse, all in vaine
  Did to him pace, sad battaile to darrayne,
  Disarmd, disgrast, and inwardly dismayde,
And eke so faint in euery ioynt and vaine,
  Through that fraile fountaine, which him feeble
    made,
That scarsely could he weeld his bootlesse single
    blade.

12

The Geaunt strooke so maynly mercilesse,
  That could haue ouerthrowne a stony towre,
  And were not heauenly grace, that him did blesse,
He had beene pouldred all, as thin as flowre :
  But he was wary of that deadly stowre,
  And lightly lept from vnderneath the blow :
Yet so exceeding was the villeins powre,
  That with the wind it did him ouerthrow,
And all his sences stound, that still he lay full
    low.

13

As when that diuelish yron Engin wrought
  In deepest Hell, and framd by *Furies* skill,
  With windy Nitre and quick Sulphur fraught,
And ramd with bullet round, ordaind to kill,
  Conceiueth fire, the heauens it doth fill
  With thundring noyse, and all the ayre doth
    choke,
That none can breath, nor see, nor heare at will,
  Through smouldry cloud of duskish stincking
    smoke,
That th'onely breath him daunts, who hath escapt
    the stroke.

14

So daunted when the Geaunt saw the knight,
  His heauie hand he heaued vp on hye,
  And him to dust thought to haue battred quight,
Vntill *Duessa* loud to him gan crye ;
  O great *Orgoglio*, greatest vnder skye,
  O hold thy mortall hand for Ladies sake,
Hold for my sake, and do him not to dye,
  But vanquisht thine eternall bondslaue make,
And me thy worthy meed vnto thy Leman take.

15

He hearkned, and did stay from further harmes,
To gayne so goodly guerdon, as she spake :
So willingly she came into his armes,
Who her as willingly to grace did take,
And was possessed of his new found make.
Then vp he tooke the slombred sencelesse corse,
And ere he could out of his swowne awake,
Him to his castle brought with hastie forse,
And in a Dongeon deepe him threw without
    remorse.

16

From that day forth *Duessa* was his deare,
And highly honourd in his haughtie eye,
He gaue her gold and purple pall to weare,
And triple crowne set on her head full hye,
And her endowd with royall maiestye :
Then for to make her dreaded more of men,
And peoples harts with awfull terrour tye,
A monstrous beast ybred in filthy fen
He chose, which he had kept long time in dark-
    some den.

17

Such one it was, as that renowmed Snake
Which great *Alcides* in *Stremona* slew,
Long fostred in the filth of *Lerna* lake,
Whose many heads out budding euer new,
Did breed him endlesse labour to subdew :
But this same Monster much more vgly was ;
For seuen great heads out of his body grew,
An yron brest, and backe of scaly bras,
And all embrewd in bloud, his eyes did shine as
    glas.

18

His tayle was stretched out in wondrous length,
That to the house of heauenly gods it raught,
And with extorted powre, and borrow'd
    strength,
The euer-burning lamps from thence it brought,
And prowdly threw to ground, as things of
    nought ;
And vnderneath his filthy feet did tread
The sacred things, and holy heasts foretaught.
Vpon this dreadfull Beast with seuenfold head
He set the false *Duessa*, for more aw and dread.

19

The wofull Dwarfe, which saw his maisters fall,
Whiles he had keeping of his grasing steed,
And valiant knight become a caytiue thrall,
When all was past, tooke vp his forlorne weed,
His mightie armour, missing most at need ;
His siluer shield, now idle maisterlesse ;
His poynant speare, that many made to bleed,
The ruefull moniments of heauinesse,
And with them all departes, to tell his great
    distresse.

20

He had not trauaild long, when on the way
He wofull Ladie, wofull *Vna* met,
Fast flying from the Paynims greedy pray,
Whilest *Satyrane* him from pursuit did let :
Who when her eyes she on the Dwarfe had set,
And saw the signes, that deadly tydings spake,
She fell to ground for sorrowfull regret,
And liuely breath her sad brest did forsake,
Yet might her pitteous hart be seene to pant
    and quake.

21

The messenger of so vnhappie newes
Would faine haue dyde : dead was his hart
    within,
Yet outwardly some little comfort shewes :
At last recouering hart, he does begin
To rub her temples, and to chaufe her chin,
And euery tender part does tosse and turne :
So hardly he the flitted life does win,
Vnto her natiue prison to retourne :
Then gins her grieued ghost thus to lament and
    mourne.

22

Ye dreary instruments of dolefull sight,
That doe this deadly spectacle behold,
Why do ye lenger feed on loathed light,
Or liking find to gaze on earthly mould,
Sith cruell fates the carefull threeds vnfould,
The which my life and loue together tyde ?
Now let the stony dart of senselesse cold
Perce to my hart, and pas through euery side,
And let eternall night so sad sight fro me hide.

23

O lightsome day, the lampe of highest *Ioue*,
First made by him, mens wandring wayes to
    guyde,
When darknesse he in deepest dongeon droue,
Henceforth thy hated face for euer hyde,
And shut vp heauens windowes shyning wyde :
For earthly sight can nought but sorrow breed,
And late repentance, which shall long abyde,
Mine eyes no more on vanitie shall feed,
But seeled vp with death, shall haue their deadly
    meed.

24

Then downe againe she fell vnto the ground ;
But he her quickly reared vp againe :
Thrise did she sinke adowne in deadly swownd,
And thrise he her reviu'd with busie paine :
At last when life recouer'd had the raine,
And ouer-wrestled his strong enemie,
With foltring tong, and trembling euery vaine,
Tell on (quoth she) the wofull Tragedie,
The which these reliques sad present vnto mine
    eie.

25

Tempestuous fortune hath spent all her spight,
 And thrilling sorrow throwne his vtmost dart ;
Thy sad tongue cannot tell more heauy plight,
Then that I feele, and harbour in mine hart :
Who hath endur'd the whole, can beare each part.
 If death it be, it is not the first wound,
That launched hath my brest with bleeding
  smart.
 Begin, and end the bitter balefull stound ;
If lesse, then that I feare, more fauour I haue
  found.

26

Then gan the Dwarfe the whole discourse declare,
 The subtill traines of *Archimago* old ;
The wanton loues of false *Fidessa* faire,
Bought with the bloud of vanquisht Paynim
  bold :   [mould :
 The wretched payre transform'd to treen
The house of Pride, and perils round about ;
The combat, which he with *Sansioy* did hould ;
 The lucklesse conflict with the Gyant stout,
Wherein captiu'd, of life or death he stood in
  doubt.

27

She heard with patience all vnto the end,
 And stroue to maister sorrowfull assay,
Which greater grew, the more she did contend,
And almost rent her tender hart in tway ;
And loue fresh coles vnto her fire did lay :
 For greater loue, the greater is the losse.
Was neuer Ladie loued dearer day,
 Then she did loue the knight of the *Redcrosse* ;
For whose deare sake so many troubles her did
  tosse.

28

At last when feruent sorrow slaked was,
 She vp arose, resoluing him to find
Aliue or dead : and forward forth doth pas,
All as the Dwarfe the way to her assynd :
And euermore in constant carefull mind
 She fed her wound with fresh renewed bale ;
Long tost with stormes, and bet with bitter
  wind,
 High ouer hils, and low adowne the dale,
She wandred many a wood, and measurd many
  a vale.

29

At last she chaunced by good hap to meet
 A goodly knight, faire marching by the way
Together with his Squire, arayed meet :
His glitterand armour shined farre away,
Like glauncing light of *Phœbus* brightest ray ;
 From top to toe no place appeared bare,
That deadly dint of steele endanger may :
 Athwart his brest a bauldrick braue he ware,
That shynd, like twinkling stars, with stons
  most pretious rare.

30

And in the midst thereof one pretious stone
 Of wondrous worth, and eke of wondrous
  mights,
Shapt like a Ladies head, exceeding shone,
Like *Hesperus* emongst the lesser lights,
And stroue for to amaze the weaker sights ;
 Thereby his mortall blade full comely hong
In yuory sheath, ycaru'd with curious slights ;
 Whose hilts were burnisht gold, and handle
  strong
Of mother pearle, and buckled with a golden
  tong.

31

His haughtie helmet, horrid all with gold,
 Both glorious brightnesse, and great terrour
  bred ;
For all the crest a Dragon did enfold
With greedie pawes, and ouer all did spred
His golden wings : his dreadfull hideous hed
 Close couched on the beuer, seem'd to throw
From flaming mouth bright sparkles fierie red,
 That suddeine horror to faint harts did show ;
And scaly tayle was stretcht adowne his backe
  full low.

32

Vpon the top of all his loftie crest,
 A bunch of haires discolourd diuersly,
With sprincled pearle, and gold full richly drest,
Did shake, and seem'd to daunce for iollity,
Like to an Almond tree ymounted hye
 On top of greene *Selinis* all alone,
With blossomes braue bedecked daintily ;
 Whose tender locks do tremble euery one
At euery little breath, that vnder heauen is
  blowne.

33

His warlike shield all closely couer'd was,
 Ne might of mortall eye be euer seene ;
Not made of steele, nor of enduring bras,
Such earthly mettals soone consumed bene :
But all of Diamond perfect pure and cleene
 It framed was, one massie entire mould,
Hewen out of Adamant rocke with engines keene,
 That point of speare it neuer percen could,
Ne dint of direfull sword diuide the substance
  would.

34

The same to wight he neuer wont disclose,
 But when as monsters huge he would dismay,
Or daunt vnequall armies of his foes,
Or when the flying heauens he would affray ;
For so exceeding shone his glistring ray,
 That *Phœbus* golden face it did attaint,
As when a cloud his beames doth ouer-lay ;
 And siluer *Cynthia* wexed pale and faint,
As when her face is staynd with magicke arts
  constraint.

35

No magicke arts hereof had any might,
　Nor bloudie wordes of bold Enchaunters call,
　But all that was not such, as seemd in sight,
Before that shield did fade, and suddeine fall :
　And when him list the raskall routes appall,
Men into stones therewith he could transmew,
And stones to dust, and dust to nought at all ;
　And when him list the prouder lookes subdew,
He would them gazing blind, or turne to other
　　hew.

36

Ne let it seeme, that credence this exceedes,
　For he that made the same, was knowne right
　　well
To haue done much more admirable deedes.
It *Merlin* was, which whylome did excell
All liuing wightes in might of magicke spell :
　Both shield, and sword, and armour all he
　　wrought
For this young Prince, when first to armes he
　　fell ;
But when he dyde, the Faerie Queene it brought
To Faerie lond, where yet it may be seene, if
　　sought.

37

A gentle youth, his dearely loued Squire
　His speare of heben wood behind him bare,
Whose harmefull head, thrice heated in the fire,
Had riuen many a brest with pike head square;
　A goodly person, and could menage faire
His stubborne steed with curbed canon bit,
Who vnder him did trample as the aire,
　And chauft, that any on his backe should sit ;
The yron rowels into frothy fome he bit.

38

When as this knight nigh to the Ladie drew,
　With louely court he gan her entertaine ;
But when he heard her answeres loth, he knew
Some secret sorrow did her heart distraine :
　Which to allay, and calme her storming paine,
Faire feeling words he wisely gan display,
And for her humour fitting purpose faine,
　To tempt the cause it selfe for to bewray ;
Wherewith emmou'd, these bleeding words she
　　gan to say.

39

What worlds delight, or ioy of liuing speach
　Can heart, so plung'd in sea of sorrowes deepe,
And heaped with so huge misfortunes, reach ?
The carefull cold beginneth for to creepe,
　And in my heart his yron arrow steepe,
Soone as I thinke vpon my bitter bale :
Such helplesse harmes yts better hidden keepe,
　Then rip vp griefe, where it may not auaile,
My last left comfort is, my woes to weepe and
　　waile.

40

Ah Ladie deare, quoth then the gentle knight,
　Well may I weene, your griefe is wondrous great;
For wondrous great griefe groneth in my spright,
Whiles thus I heare you of your sorrowes treat.
　But wofull Ladie let me you intrete,
For to vnfold the anguish of your hart :
Mishaps are maistred by aduice discrete,
　And counsell mittigates the greatest smart ;
Found neuer helpe, who neuer would his hurts
　　impart.

41

O but (quoth she) great griefe will not be tould,
　And can more easily be thought, then said.
Right so ; (quoth he) but he, that neuer would,
Could neuer : will to might giues greatest aid.
　But griefe (quoth she) does greater grow displaid,
If then it find not helpe, and breedes despaire.
Despaire breedes not (quoth he) where faith is
　　staid.
No faith so fast (quoth she) but flesh does paire.
Flesh may empaire (quoth he) but reason can
　　repaire.

42

His goodly reason, and well guided speach
　So deepe did settle in her gratious thought,
That her perswaded to disclose the breach,
　Which loue and fortune in her heart had
　　wrought,　　　　　　　　　　　　[brought
And said ; Faire Sir, I hope good hap hath
You to inquire the secrets of my griefe,
　Or that your wisedome will direct my thought,
Or that your prowesse can me yield reliefe :
Then heare the storie sad, which I shall tell you
　　briefe.

43

The forlorne Maiden, whom your eyes haue seene
　The laughing stocke of fortunes mockeries,
Am th'only daughter of a King and Queene,
Whose parents deare, whilest equall destinies
　Did runne about, and their felicities
The fauourable heauens did not enuy,
Did spread their rule through all the territories,
　Which *Phison* and *Euphrates* floweth by,
And *Gehons* golden waues doe wash continually.

44

Till that their cruell cursed enemy,
　An huge great Dragon horrible in sight,
Bred in the loathly lakes of *Tartary*,
With murdrous rauine, and deuouring might
　Their kingdome spoild, and countrey wasted
　　quight :
Themselues, for feare into his iawes to fall,
He forst to castle strong to take their flight,
　Where fast embard in mightie brasen wall,
He has them now foure yeres besiegd to make
　　them thrall.

45

Full many knights aduenturous and stout
Haue enterprizd that Monster to subdew ;
From euery coast that heauen walks about,
Haue thither come the noble Martiall crew,
That famous hard atchieuements still pursew,
Yet neuer any could that girlond win,
But all still shronke, and still he greater grew:
All they for want of faith, or guilt of sin,
The pitteous pray of his fierce crueltie haue bin.

46

At last yledd with farre reported praise,
 Which flying fame throughout the world had
  spred,
 Of doughtie knights, whom Faery land did raise,
That noble order hight of Maidenhed,
Forthwith to court of *Gloriane* I sped,
Of *Gloriane* great Queene of glory bright,
Whose kingdomes seat *Cleopolis* is red,
There to obtaine some such redoubted knight,
That Parents deare from tyrants powre deliuer
  might.

47

It was my chance (my chance was faire and good)
 There for to find a fresh vnproued knight,
 Whose manly hands imbrew'd in guiltie blood
Had neuer bene, ne euer by his might
Had throwne to ground the vnregarded right :
Yet of his prowesse proofe he since hath made
(I witnesse am) in many a cruell fight ;
The groning ghosts of many one dismaide
Haue felt the bitter dint of his auenging blade.

48

And ye the forlorne reliques of his powre,
 His byting sword, and his deuouring speare,
 Which haue endured many a dreadfull stowre,
Can speake his prowesse, that did earst you
  beare,
And well could rule: now he hath left you heare,
To be the record of his ruefull losse,
And of my dolefull disauenturous deare :
O heauie record of the good *Redcrosse*,
Where haue you left your Lord, that could so
  well you tosse?

49

Well hoped I, and faire beginnings had,
 That he my captiue langour should redeeme,
 Till all vnweeting, an Enchaunter bad
His sence abusd, and made him to misdeeme
My loyalty, not such as it did seeme ;
That rather death desire, then such despight.
Be iudge ye heauens, that all things right
  esteeme,
How I him lou'd, and loue with all my might,
So thought I eke of him, and thinke I thought
  aright.

50

Thenceforth me desolate he quite forsooke,
 To wander, where wilde fortune would me lead,
 And other bywaies he himselfe betooke,
Where neuer foot of liuing wight did tread,
That brought not backe the balefull body dead;
In which him chaunced false *Duessa* meete,
Mine onely foe, mine onely deadly dread,
Who with her witchcraft and misseeming sweete,
Inueigled him to follow her desires vnmeete.

51

At last by subtill sleights she him betraid
 Vnto his foe, a Gyant huge and tall,
 Who him disarmed, dissolute, dismaid,
Vnwares surprised, and with mightie mall
The monster mercilesse him made to fall,
Whose fall did neuer foe before behold ;
And now in darkesome dungeon, wretched
  thrall,
Remedilesse, for aie he doth him hold ;
This is my cause of griefe, more great, then
  may be told.

52

Ere she had ended all, she gan to faint :
 But he her comforted and faire bespake,
 Certes, Madame, ye haue great cause of plaint,
That stoutest heart, I weene, could cause to
  quake.
But be of cheare, and comfort to you take :
For till I haue acquit your captiue knight,
Assure your selfe, I will you not forsake.
His chearefull words reuiu'd her chearelesse
  spright,   [euer right.
So forth they went, the Dwarfe them guiding

Cant. VIII.

⋘⋙⋘⋙⋘⋙⋘⋙⋘⋙⋘⋙⋘⋙

*Faire virgin to redeeme her deare
  brings Arthur to the fight :
Who slayes the Gyant, wounds the beast,
  and strips Duessa quight.*

⋘⋙⋘⋙⋘⋙⋘⋙⋘⋙⋘⋙⋘⋙

1

Ay me, how many perils doe enfold
The righteous man, to make him daily fall ?
Were not, that heauenly grace doth him vphold,
And stedfast truth acquite him out of all.
Her loue is firme, her care continuall,
So oft as he through his owne foolish pride,
Or weakenesse is to sinfull bands made thrall :
Else should this *Redcrosse* knight in bands
  haue dyde,   [thither guide.
For whose deliuerance she this Prince doth

2

They sadly traueild thus, vntill they came
  Nigh to a castle builded strong and hie:
  Then cryde the Dwarfe, lo yonder is the same,
  In which my Lord my liege doth lucklesse lie,
  Thrall to that Gyants hatefull tyrannie:
Therefore, deare Sir, your mightie powres assay.
  The noble knight alighted by and by
  From loftie steede, and bad the Ladie stay,
To see what end of fight should him befall that
  day.

3

So with the Squire, th'admirer of his might,
  He marched forth towards that castle wall;
  Whose gates he found fast shut, ne liuing wight
  To ward the same, nor answere commers call.
  Then tooke that Squire an horne of bugle small,
  Which hong adowne his side in twisted gold,
  And tassels gay. Wyde wonders ouer all
  Of that same hornes great vertues weren told,
Which had approued bene in vses manifold.

4

Was neuer wight, that heard that shrilling sound,
  But trembling feare did feele in euery vaine;
  Three miles it might be easie heard around,
  And Ecchoes three answerd it selfe againe:
  No false enchauntment, nor deceiptfull traine
  Might once abide the terror of that blast,
  But presently was voide and wholly vaine:
  No gate so strong, no locke so firme and fast,
But with that percing noise flew open quite, or
  brast.

5

The same before the Geants gate he blew,
  That all the castle quaked from the ground,
  And euery dore of freewill open flew.
  The Gyant selfe dismaied with that sownd,
  Where he with his *Duessa* dalliance fownd,
  In hast came rushing forth from inner bowre,
  With staring countenance sterne, as one
  astownd,   [stowre
And staggering steps, to weet, what suddein
  Had wrought that horror strange, and dar'd his
  dreaded powre.

6

And after him the proud *Duessa* came,
  High mounted on her manyheaded beast,
  And euery head with fyrie tongue did flame,
  And euery head was crowned on his creast,
  And bloudie mouthed with late cruell feast.
  That when the knight beheld, his mightie shild
  Vpon his manly arme he soone addrest,
  And at him fiercely flew, with courage fild,
And eger greedinesse through euery member
  thrild.

7

Therewith the Gyant buckled him to fight,
  Inflam'd with scornefull wrath and high disdaine,
  And lifting vp his dreadfull club on hight,
  All arm'd with ragged snubbes and knottie graine,
  Him thought at first encounter to haue slaine.
  But wise and warie was that noble Pere,
  And lightly leaping from so monstrous maine,
  Did faire auoide the violence him nere;
It booted nought, to thinke, such thunderbolts
  to beare.

8

Ne shame he thought to shunne so hideous
  might:
  The idle stroke, enforcing furious way,
  Missing the marke of his misaymed sight
  Did fall to ground, and with his heauie sway
  So deepely dinted in the driuen clay,
  That three yardes deepe a furrow vp did throw:
  The sad earth wounded with so sore assay,
  Did grone full grieuous vnderneath the blow,
And trembling with strange feare, did like an
  earthquake show.

9

As when almightie *Ioue* in wrathfull mood,
  To wreake the guilt of mortall sins is bent,
  Hurles forth his thundring dart with deadly food,
  Enrold in flames, and smouldring dreriment,
  Through riuen cloudes and molten firmament;
  The fierce threeforked engin making way,
  Both loftie towres and highest trees hath rent,
  And all that might his angrie passage stay,
And shooting in the earth, casts vp a mount of
  clay.

10

His boystrous club, so buried in the ground,
  He could not rearen vp againe so light,
  But that the knight him at auantage found,
  And whiles he stroue his combred clubbe to quight
  Out of the earth, with blade all burning bright
  He smote off his left arme, which like a blocke
  Did fall to ground, depriu'd of natiue might;
  Large streames of bloud out of the truncked
  stocke
Forth gushed, like fresh water streame from
  riuen rocke.

11

Dismaied with so desperate deadly wound,
  And eke impatient of vnwonted paine,
  He loudly brayd with beastly yelling sound,
  That all the fields rebellowed againe;
  As great a noyse, as when in Cymbrian plaine
  An heard of Bulles, whom kindly rage doth sting,
  Do for the milkie mothers want complaine,
  And fill the fields with troublous bellowing,
The neighbour woods around with hollow
  murmur ring.

12

That when his deare *Duessa* heard, and saw
  The euill stownd, that daungerd her estate,
  Vnto his aide she hastily did draw
Her dreadfull beast, who swolne with bloud of
    late
Came ramping forth with proud presumpteous
    gate,
  Andthreatnedall his heads like flaming brands.
  But him the Squire made quickly to retrate,
Encountring fierce with single sword in hand,
And twixt him and his Lord did like a bul-
    warke stand.

13

The proud *Duessa* full of wrathfull spight,
  And fierce disdaine, to be affronted so,
  Enforst her purple beast with all her might
That stop out of the way to ouerthroe,
Scorning the let of so vnequall foe :
  But nathemore would that courageous swayne
  To her yeeld passage, gainst his Lord to goe,
But with outrageous strokes did him restraine,
And with his bodie bard the way atwixt them
    twaine.

14

Then tooke the angrie witch her golden cup,
  Which still she bore, replete with magick artes ;
  Death and despeyre did many thereof sup,
And secret poyson through their inner parts,
Th'eternall bale of heauie wounded harts ;
  Which after charmes and some enchaunt-
    ments said,
  She lightly sprinkled on his weaker parts ;
Therewith his sturdie courage soone was quayd.
And all his senses were with suddeine dread
    dismayd.

15

So downe he fell before the cruell beast,
  Who on his necke his bloudie clawes did seize,
  That life nigh crusht out of his panting brest :
No powre he had to stirre, nor will to rize.
That when the carefull knight gan well auise,
  He lightly left the foe, with whom he fought,
  And to the beast gan turne his enterprise ;
For wondrous anguish in his hart it wrought,
To see his loued Squire into such thraldome
    brought.

16

And high aduauncing his bloud-thirstie blade,
  Stroke one of those deformed heads so sore,
  That of his puissance proud ensample made ;
His monstrous scalpe downe to his teeth it tore,
And that misformed shape mis-shaped more :
  A sea of bloud gusht from the gaping wound,
  That her gay garments staynd with filthy gore,
And ouerflowed all the field around ;
That ouer shoes in bloud he waded on the
    ground.

17

Thereat he roared for exceeding paine,
  That to haue heard, great horror would haue
    bred,   [traine,
  And scourging th'emptie ayre with his long
Through great impatience of his grieued hed
His gorgeous ryder from her loftie sted
  Wouldhauecastdowne,and trod in durtie myre,
  Had not the Gyant soone her succoured ;
Who all enrag'd with smart and franticke yre,
Came hurtling in full fierce, and forst the knight
    retyre.

18

The force, which wont in two to be disperst,
  In one alone left hand he now vnites,
  Which is through rage more strong then both
    were erst ;
With which his hideous club aloft he dites,
And at his foe with furious rigour smites,
  Thatstrongest Oake might seeme to ouerthrow :
  The stroke vpon his shield so heauie lites,
That to the ground it doubleth him full low :
What mortall wight could euer beare so mon-
    strous blow ?

19

And in his fall his shield, that couered was,
  Did loose his vele by chaunce, and open flew :
  The light whereof, that heauens light did pas,
Such blazing brightnesse through the aier threw,
That eye mote not the same endure to vew.
  Which when the Gyaunt spyde with staring eye,
  He downe let fall his arme, and soft withdrew
His weapon huge, that heaued was on hye
For to haue slaine the man, that on the ground
    did lye.

20

And eke the fruitfull-headed beast, amaz'd
  At flashing beames of that sunshiny shield,
  Became starke blind, and all his senses daz'd,
That downe he tumbled on the durtie field,
And seem'd himselfe as conquered to yield.
  Whom when his maistresse proud perceiu'd to fall,
  Whiles yet his feeble feet for faintnesse reeld,
Vnto the Gyant loudly she gan call,
O helpe *Orgoglio*, helpe, or else we perish all.

21

At her so pitteous cry was much amoou'd
  Her champion stout, and for to ayde his frend,
  Againe his wonted angry weapon proou'd :
But all in vaine : for he has read his end
In that bright shield, and all their forces spend
  Themselues in vaine : for since that glauncing
    sight,
  He hath no powre to hurt, nor to defend ;
As where th'Almighties lightning brond does light,
It dimmes the dazed eyen, and daunts the
    senses quight.

22

Whom when the Prince, to battell new addrest,
 And threatning high his dreadfull stroke did see,
His sparkling blade about his head he blest,
 And smote off quite his right leg by the knee,
 That downe he tombled ; as an aged tree,
High growing on the top of rocky clift,
 Whose hartstrings with keene steele nigh
  · hewen be,
 The mightie trunck halfe rent, with ragged rift
Doth roll adowne the rocks, and fall with feare-
  full drift.

23

Or as a Castle reared high and round,
 By subtile engins and malitious slight
Is vndermined from the lowest ground,
 And her foundation forst, and feebled quight,
 At last downe falles, and with her heaped hight
Her hastie ruine does more heauie make,
 And yields it selfe vnto the victours might ;
 Such was this Gyaunts fall, that seemd to shake
The stedfast globe of earth, as it for feare did
  quake.

24

The knight then lightly leaping to the pray,
 With mortall steele him smot againe so sore,
That headlesse his vnweldy bodie lay,
 All wallowd in his owne fowle bloudy gore,
 Which flowed from his wounds in wondrous
  store.
 But soone as breath out of his breast did pas,
That huge great body, which the Gyaunt bore,
 Was vanisht quite, and of that monstrous mas
Was nothing left, but like an emptie bladder
  was.

25

Whose grieuous fall, when false *Duessa* spide,
 Her golden cup she cast vnto the ground,
And crowned mitre rudely threw aside ;
 Such percing griefe her stubborne hart did
  wound,
 That she could not endure that dolefull stound,
But leauing all behind her, fled away :
 The light-foot Squire her quickly turnd around,
 And by hard meanes enforcing her to stay,
So brought vnto his Lord, as his deserued pray.

26

The royall Virgin, which beheld from farre,
 In pensiue plight, and sad perplexitie,
The whole atchieuement of this doubtfull warre,
 Came running fast to greet his victorie,
 With sober gladnesse, and myld modestie,
And with sweet ioyous cheare him thus bespake ;
 Faire braunch of noblesse, flowre of cheualrie,
 That with your worth the world amazed make,
How shall I quite the paines, ye suffer for my
  sake ?

27

And you fresh bud of vertue springing fast,
 Whom these sad eyes saw nigh vnto deaths
  dore,
What hath poore Virgin for such perill past,
 Wherewith you to reward ? Accept therefore
My simple selfe, and seruice euermore ;
 And he that high does sit, and all things see
With equall eyes, their merites to restore,
 Behold what ye this day haue done for mee,
And what I cannot quite, requite with vsuree.

28

But sith the heauens, and your faire handeling
 Haue made you maister of the field this day,
Your fortune maister eke with gouerning,
 And well begun end all so well, I pray,
 Ne let that wicked woman scape away ;
For she it is, that did my Lord bethrall,
 My dearest Lord, and deepe in dongeon lay,
 Where he his better dayes hath wasted all.
O heare, how piteous he to you for ayd does call.

29

Forthwith he gaue in charge vnto his Squire,
 That scarlot whore to keepen carefully ;
Whiles he himselfe with greedie great desire
 Into the Castle entred forcibly,
 Where liuing creature none he did espye ;
Then gan he lowdly through the house to call :
 But no man car'd to answere to his crye.
 There raignd a solemne silence ouer all,
Nor voice was heard, nor wight was seene in
  bowre or hall.

30

At last with creeping crooked pace forth came
 An old old man, with beard as white as
  snow,
That on a staffe his feeble steps did frame,
 And guide his wearie gate both too and fro :
 For his eye sight him failed long ygo,
And on his arme a bounch of keyes he bore,
 The which vnused rust did ouergrow :
 Those were the keyes of euery inner dore,
But he could not them vse, but kept them still
  in store.

31

But very vncouth sight was to behold,
 How he did fashion his vntoward pace,
For as he forward moou'd his footing old,
 So backward still was turnd his wrincled face,
 Vnlike to men, who euer as they trace,
Both feet and face one way are wont to lead.
 This was the auncient keeper of that place,
 And foster father of the Gyant dead ;
His name *Ignaro* did his nature right aread.

32

His reuerend haires and holy grauitie
  The knight much honord, as beseemed well,
  And gently askt, where all the people bee,
  Which in that stately building wont to dwell.
  Who answerd him full soft, he could not tell.
  Againe he askt, where that same knight was
    layd,
  Whom great *Orgoglio* with his puissaunce fell
  Had made his caytiue thrall ; againe he sayde,
He could not tell : ne euer other answere made.

33

Then asked he, which way he in might pas :
  He could not tell, againe he answered.
  Thereat the curteous knight displeased was,
  And said, Old sire, it seemes thou hast not red
  How ill it sits with that same siluer hed
  In vaine to mocke, or mockt in vaine to bee :
  But if thou be, as thou art pourtrahed
  With natures pen, in ages graue degree,
Aread in grauer wise, what I demaund of thee.

34

His answere likewise was, he could not tell.
  Whose sencelesse speach, and doted ignorance
  When as the noble Prince had marked well,
  He ghest his nature by his countenance,
  And calmd his wrath with goodly temperance.
  Then to him stepping, from his arme did reach
  Those keyes, and made himselfe free enterance.
  Each dore he opened without any breach ;
There was no barre to stop, nor foe him to
    empeach.

35

There all within full rich arayd he found,
  With royall arras and resplendent gold.
  And did with store of euery thing abound,
  That greatest Princes presence might behold.
  But all the floore (too filthy to be told)
  With bloud of guiltlesse babes, and innocents
    trew,   [fold,
  Which there were slaine, as sheepe out of the
  Defiled was, that dreadfull was to vew,
And sacred ashes ouer it was strowed new.

36

And there beside of marble stone was built
  An Altare, caru'd with cunning imagery,
  On which true Christians bloud was often spilt,
  And holy Martyrs often doen to dye,
  With cruell malice and strong tyranny :
  Whose blessed sprites from vnderneath the
    stone
  To God for vengeance cryde continually,
  And with great griefe were often heard to grone,
That hardest heart would bleede, to heare their
    piteous mone.

37

Through euery rowme he sought, and euery bowr,
  But no where could he find that wofull thrall :
  At last he came vnto an yron doore,
  That fast was lockt, but key found not at all
  Emongst that bounch, to open it withall ;
  But in the same a little grate was pight,
  Through which he sent his voyce, and lowd
    did call
With all his powre, to weet, if liuing wight
Were housed therewithin, whom he enlargen
    might.

38

Therewith an hollow, dreary, murmuring voyce
  These piteous plaints and dolours did resound ;
  O who is that, which brings me happy choyce
  Of death, that here lye dying euery stound,
  Yet liue perforce in balefull darkenesse bound?
  For now three Moones haue changed thrice
    their hew,   [ground,
  And haue beene thrice hid vnderneath the
  Since I the heauens chearefull face did vew,
O welcome thou, that doest of death bring
    tydings trew.

39

Which when that Champion heard, with perc-
    ing point
  Of pitty deare his hart was thrilled sore,
  And trembling horrour ran through euery ioynt,
  For ruth of gentle knight so fowle forlore :
  Which shaking off, he rent that yron dore,
  With furious force, and indignation fell ;
  Where entred in, his foot could find no flore,
  But all a deepe descent, as darke as hell,
That breathed euer forth a filthie banefull smell.

40

But neither darkenesse fowle, nor filthy bands,
  Nor noyous smell his purpose could withhold,
  (Entire affection hateth nicer hands)
  But that with constant zeale, and courage bold,
  After long paines and labours manifold,
  He found the meanes that Prisoner vp to reare;
  Whose feeble thighes, vnhable to vphold
  His pined corse, him scarse to light could beare,
A ruefull spectacle of death and ghastly drere.

41

His sad dull eyes deepe sunck in hollow pits,
  Could not endure th'vnwonted sunne to view ;
  His bare thin cheekes for want of better bits,
  And empty sides deceiued of their dew,
  Could make a stony hart his hap to rew ;
  His rawbone armes, whose mighty brawned bowrs
  Were wont to riue steele plates, and helmets hew,
  Were cleane consum'd, and all his vitall powres
Decayd, and all his flesh shronk vp like
    withered flowres.

42

Whom when his Lady saw, to him she ran
With hasty ioy : to see him made her glad,
And sad to view his visage pale and wan,
Who earst in flowres of freshest youth was clad.
Tho when her well of teares she wasted had,
She said, Ah dearest Lord, what euill starre
On you hath fround, and pourd his influence bad,
That of your selfe ye thus berobbed arre,
And this misseeming hew your manly looks
   doth marre ?

43

But welcome now my Lord, in wele or woe,
Whose presence I haue lackt too long a day ;
And fie on Fortune mine auowed foe,
Whose wrathfull wreakes them selues do now
   alay.
And for these wrongs shall treble penaunce pay
Of treble good : good growes of euils priefe.
The chearelesse man, whom sorrow did dismay,
Had no delight to treaten of his griefe ;
His long endured famine needed more reliefe.

44

Faire Lady, then said that victorious knight,
The things, that grieuous were to do, or beare,
Them to renew, I wote, breeds no delight ;
Best musicke breeds †delight in loathing eare :
But th'onely good, that growes of passed feare,
Is to be wise, and ware of like agein.
This dayes ensample hath this lesson deare
Deepe written in my heart with yron pen,
That blisse may not abide in state of mortall
   men.

45

Henceforth sir knight, take to you wonted
   strength,
And maister these mishaps with patient might ;
Loe where your foe lyes stretcht in monstrous
   length,
And loe that wicked woman in your sight,
The roote of all your care, and wretched plight,
Now in your powre, to let her liue, or dye.
To do her dye (quoth *Vna*) were despight,
And shame t'auenge so weake an enimy ;
But spoile her of her scarlot robe, and let her fly.

46

So as she bad, that witch they disaraid,
And robd of royall robes, and purple pall,
And ornaments that richly were displaid ;
Ne spared they to strip her naked all.
Then when they had despoild her tire and call,
Such as she was, their eyes might her behold,
That her misshaped parts did them appall,
A loathly, wrinckled hag, ill fauoured, old,
Whose secret filth good manners biddeth not be
   told.

47

Her craftie head was altogether bald,
And as in hate of honorable eld,
Was ouergrowne with scurfe and filthy scald ;
Her teeth out of her rotten gummes were feld,
And her sowre breath abhominably smeld ;
Her dried dugs, like bladders lacking wind,
Hong downe, and filthy matter from them weld ;
Her wrizled skin as rough, as maple rind,
So scabby was, that would haue loathd all
   womankind.

48

Her neather parts, the shame of all her kind,
My chaster Muse for shame doth blush to write ;
But at her rompe she growing had behind
A foxes taile, with dong all fowly dight ;
And eke her feete most monstrous were in sight ;
For one of them was like an Eagles claw,
With griping talaunts armd to greedy fight,
The other like a Beares vneuen paw :
More vgly shape yet neuer liuing creature saw.

49

Which when the knights beheld, amazd they
   were,
And wondred at so fowle deformed wight.
Such then (said *Vna*) as she seemeth here,
Such is the face of falshood, such the sight
Of fowle *Duessa*, when her borrowed light
Is laid away, and counterfesaunce knowne.
Thus when they had the witch disrobed quight,
And all her filthy feature open showne,
They let her goe at will, and wander wayes
   vnknowne.

50

She flying fast from heauens hated face,
   And from the world that her discouered wide,
Fled to the wastfull wildernesse apace,
   From liuing eyes her open shame to hide,
   And lurkt in rocks and caues long vnespide.
But that faire crew of knights, and *Vna* faire
   Did in that castle afterwards abide,
   To rest them selues, and weary powres repaire,
Where store they found of all, that dainty was and rare.

Cant. IX.

His loues and lignage Arthur tells :
The knights knit friendly bands :
Sir Treuisan flies from Despayre,
Whom Redcrosse knight withstands.

1

O goodly golden chaine, wherewith yfere
 The vertues linked are in louely wize :
And noble minds of yore allyed were,
 In braue poursuit of cheualrous emprize,
That none did others safety despize,
 Nor aid enuy to him, in need that stands,
 But friendly each did others prayse deuize
How to aduaunce with fauourable hands,
As this good Prince redeemd the *Redcrosse*
 knight from bands.

2

Who when their powres, empaird through
 labour long,
 With dew repast they had recured well,
And that weake captiue wight now wexed
 strong,
Them list no lenger there at leasure dwell,
 But forward fare, as their aduentures fell,
But ere they parted, *Vna* faire besought
 That straunger knight his name and nation tell ;
Least so great good, as he for her had wrought,
Should die vnknown, and buried be in thank-
 lesse thought.

3

Faire virgin (said the Prince) ye me require
 A thing without the compas of my wit :
For both the lignage and the certain Sire,
 From which I sprong, from me are hidden yit.
For all so soone as life did me admit
 Into this world, and shewed heauens light,
 From mothers pap I taken was vnfit :
And streight deliuered to a Faery knight,
To be vpbrought in gentle thewes and martiall
 might.

4

Vnto old *Timon* he me brought byliue,
 Old *Timon*, who in youthly yeares hath beene
In warlike feates th'expertest man aliue,
 And is the wisest now on earth I weene ;
His dwelling is low in a valley greene,
 Vnder the foot of *Rauran* mossy hore,
 From whence the riuer *Dee* as siluer cleene
His tombling billowes rolls with gentle rore :
There all my dayes he traind me vp in vertuous
 lore.

5

Thither the great Magicien *Merlin* came,
 As was his vse, ofttimes to visit me :
For he had charge my discipline to frame,
 And Tutours nouriture to ouersee.
Him oft and oft I askt in priuitie,
 Of what loines and what lignage I did spring :
 Whose aunswere bad me still assured bee,
That I was sonne and heire vnto a king,
As time in her iust terme the truth to light
 should bring.

6

Well worthy impe, said then the Lady gent,
 And Pupill fit for such a Tutours hand.
But what aduenture, or what high intent
 Hath brought you hither into Faery land,
Arcad Prince *Arthur*, crowne of Martiall band ?
 Full hard it is (quoth he) to read aright
 The course of heauenly cause, or vnderstand
The secret meaning of th'eternall might,
That rules mens wayes, and rules the thoughts of
 liuing wight.

7

For whither he through fatall deepe foresight
 Me hither sent, for cause to me vnghest,
Or that fresh bleeding wound, which day and
 night
Whilome doth rancle in my riuen brest,
 With forced fury following his behest,
Me hither brought by wayes yet neuer found,
 You to haue helpt I hold my selfe yet blest.
Ah curteous knight (quoth she) what secret
 wound
Could euer find, to grieue the gentlest hart on
 ground ?

8

Deare Dame (quoth he) you sleeping sparkes
 awake,
Which troubled once, into huge flames will grow,
 Ne euer will their feruent fury slake,
Till liuing moysture into smoke do flow,
 And wasted life do lye in ashes low.
Yet sithens silence lesseneth not my fire,
 But told it flames, and hidden it does glow,
I will reuele, what ye so much desire :
Ah Loue, lay downe thy bow, the whiles I may
 respire.

9

It was in freshest flowre of youthly yeares,
 When courage first does creepe in manly chest,
Then first the coale of kindly heat appeares
 To kindle loue in euery liuing brest ;
But me had warnd old *Timons* wise behest,
 Those creeping flames by reason to subdew,
 Before their rage grew to so great vnrest,
As miserable louers vse to rew,
Which still wex old in woe, whiles woe still
 wexeth new.

10

That idle name of loue, and louers life,
  As losse of time, and vertues enimy
  I euer scornd, and ioyd to stirre vp strife,
  In middest of their mournfull Tragedy,
  Ay wont to laugh, when them I heard to cry,
  And blow the fire, which them to ashes brent :
  Their God himselfe, grieu'd at my libertie,
  Shot many a dart at me with fiers intent,
But I them warded all with wary gouernment.

11

But all in vaine : no fort can be so strong,
  Ne fleshly brest can armed be so sound,
  But will at last be wonne with battrie long,
  Or vnawares at disauantage found ;
  Nothing is sure, that growes on earthly ground:
  And who most trustes in arme of fleshly might,
  And boasts, in beauties chaine not to be bound,
  Doth soonest fall in disauentrous fight,
And yeeldes his caytiue neck to victours most
    despight.

12

Ensample make of him your haplesse ioy,
  And of my selfe now mated, as ye see ;
  Whose prouder vaunt that proud auenging boy
  Did soone pluck downe, and curbd my libertie.
  For on a day prickt forth with iollitie
  Of looser life, and heat of hardiment,
  Raunging the forest wide on courser free,
  The fields, the floods, the heauens with one
    consent
Did seeme to laugh on me, and fauour mine
    intent.

13

For-wearied with my sports, I did alight
  From loftie steed, and downe to sleepe me layd;
  The verdant gras my couch did goodly dight,
  And pillow was my helmet faire displayd :
  Whiles euery sence the humour sweet embayd,
  And slombring soft my hart did steale away,
  Me seemed, by my side a royall Mayd
  Her daintie limbes full softly down did lay :
So faire a creature yet saw neuer sunny day.

14

Most goodly glee and louely blandishment
  She to me made, and bad me loue her deare,
  For dearely sure her loue was to me bent,
  As when iust time expired should appeare.
  But whether dreames delude, or true it were,
  Was neuer hart so rauisht with delight,
  Ne liuing man like words did euer heare,
  As she to me deliuered all that night ;
And at her parting said, She Queene of Faeries
    hight.

15

When I awoke, and found her place deuoyd,
  And nought but pressed gras, where she had lyen,
  I sorrowed all so much, as earst I ioyd,
  And washed all her place with watry eyen.
  From that day forth I lou'd that face diuine ;
  From that day forth I cast in carefull mind,
  To seeke her out with labour, and long tyne,
  And neuer vow to rest, till her I find,
Nine monethes I seeke in vaine yet ni'll that
    vow vnbind.

16

Thus as he spake, his visage wexed pale,
  And chaunge of hew great passion did bewray;
  Yet still he stroue to cloke his inward bale,
  And hide the smoke, that did his fire display,
  Till gentle *Vna* thus to him gan say ;
  O happy Queene of Faeries, that hast found
  Mongst many, one that with his prowesse may
  Defend thine honour, and thy foes confound :
True Loues are often sown, but seldom grow on
    ground.

17

Thine, O then, said the gentle *Redcrosse* knight,
  Next to that Ladies loue, shalbe the place,
  O fairest virgin, full of heauenly light,
  Whose wondrous faith, exceeding earthly race,
  Was firmest fixt in mine extremest case.
  And you, my Lord, the Patrone of my life,
  Of that great Queene may well gaine worthy
    grace :
  For onely worthy you through prowes priefe
Yf liuing man mote worthy be, to be her liefe.

18

So diuersly discoursing of their loues,
  The golden Sunne his glistring head gan shew,
  And sad remembraunce now the Prince amoues,
  With fresh desire his voyage to pursew :
  Als *Vna* earnd her traueill to renew.   [bynd,
  Then those two knights, fast friendship for to
  And loue establish each to other trew,
  Gaue goodly gifts, the signes of gratefull mynd,
And eke as pledges firme, right hands together
    ioynd.

19

Prince *Arthur* gaue a boxe of Diamond sure,
  Embowd with gold and gorgeous ornament,
  Wherein were closd few drops of liquor pure,
  Of wondrous worth, and vertue excellent,
  That any wound could heale incontinent :
  Which to requite, the *Redcrosse* knight him gaue
  A booke, wherein his Saueours testament
  Was writ with golden letters rich and braue ;
A worke of wondrous grace, and able soules to
    saue.

20

Thus beene they parted, *Arthur* on his way
  To seeke his loue, and th'other for to fight
  With *Vnaes* foe, that all her realme did pray.
  But she now weighing the decayed plight,
  And shrunken synewes of her chosen knight,
  Would not a while her forward course pursew,
  Ne bring him forth in face of dreadfull fight,
  Till he recouered had his former hew:
For him to be yet weake and wearie well she
    knew.

21

So as they traueild, lo they gan espy
  An armed knight towards them gallop fast,
  That seemed from some feared foe to fly,
  Or other griesly thing, that him agast.
  Still as he fled, his eye was backward cast,
  As if his feare still followed him behind;
  Als flew his steed, as he his bands had brast,
  And with his winged heeles did tread the
    wind,
As he had beene a fole of *Pegasus* his kind.

22

Nigh as he drew, they might perceiue his head
  To be vnarmd, and curld vncombed heares
  Vpstaring stiffe, dismayd with vncouth dread;
  Nor drop of bloud in all his face appeares
  Nor life in limbe: and to increase his feares,
  In fowle reproch of knighthoods faire degree,
  About his neck an hempen rope he weares,
  That with his glistring armes does ill agree;
But he of rope or armes has now no memoree.

23

The *Redcrosse* knight toward him crossed fast,
  To weet, what mister wight was so dismayd:
  There him he finds all sencelesse and aghast,
  That of him selfe he seemd to be afrayd;
  Whom hardly he from flying forward stayd,
  Till he these wordes to him deliuer might;
  Sir knight, aread who hath ye thus arayd,
  And eke from whom make ye this hasty flight:
For neuer knight I saw in such misseeming
    plight.

24

He answerd nought at all, but adding new
  Feare to his first amazment, staring wide
  With stony eyes, and hartlesse hollow hew,
  Astonisht stood, as one that had aspide
  Infernall furies, with their chaines vntide.
  Him yet againe, and yet againe bespake
  The gentle knight; who nought to him replide,
  But trembling euery ioynt did inly quake,
And foltring tongue at last these words seemd
    forth to shake.

25

For Gods deare loue, Sir knight, do me not stay;
  For loe he comes, he comes fast after mee.
  Eft looking backe would faine haue runne away;
  But he him forst to stay, and tellen free
  The secret cause of his perplexitie:
  Yet nathemore by his bold hartie speach,
  Could his bloud-frosen hart emboldned bee,
  But through his boldnesse rather feare did reach,
Yet forst, at last he made through silence
    suddein breach.

26

And am I now in safetie sure (quoth he)
  From him, that would haue forced me to dye?
  And is the point of death now turnd fro mee,
  That I may tell this haplesse history?
  Feare nought: (quoth he) no daunger now is nye.
  Then shall I you recount a ruefull cace,
  (Said he) the which with this vnlucky eye
  I late beheld, and had not greater grace
Me reft from it, had bene partaker of the place.

27

I lately chaunst (Would I had neuer chaunst)
  With a faire knight to keepen companee,
  Sir *Terwin* hight, that well himselfe aduaunst
  In all affaires, and was both bold and free,
  But not so happie as mote happie bee:
  He lou'd, as was his lot, a Ladie gent,
  That him againe lou'd in the least degree:
  For she was proud, and of too high intent,
And ioyd to see her louer languish and lament.

28

From whom returning sad and comfortlesse,
  As on the way together we did fare,
  We met that villen (God from him me blesse)
  That cursed wight, from whom I scapt why
    leare,
  A man of hell, that cals himselfe *Despaire*:
  Who first vs greets, and after faire areedes
  Of tydings strange, and of aduentures rare:
  So creeping close, as Snake in hidden weedes,
Inquireth of our states, and of our knightly
    deedes.

29

Which when he knew, and felt our feeble harts
  Embost with bale, and bitter byting griefe,
  Which loue had launched with his deadly darts,
  With wounding words and termes of foule
    repriefe
  He pluckt from vs all hope of due reliefe,
  That earst vs held in loue of lingring life;
  Then hopelesse hartlesse, gan the cunning thiefe
  Perswade vs die, to stint all further strife:
To me he lent this rope, to him a rustie knife.

30

With which sad instrument of hastie death,
  That wofull louer, loathing lenger light,
  A wide way made to let forth liuing breath.
But I more fearefull, or more luckie wight,
  Dismayd with that deformed dismall sight,
  Fled fast away, halfe dead with dying feare :
  Ne yet assur'd of life by you, Sir knight,
Whose like infirmitie like chaunce may beare :
But God you neuer let his charmed speeches
      heare.

31

How may a man (said he) with idle speach
  Be wonne, to spoyle the Castle of his health ?
I wote (quoth he) whom triall late did teach,
  That like would not for all this worldes wealth:
  His subtill tongue, like dropping honny,
      mealt'th
Into the hart, and searcheth euery vaine,
  That ere one be aware, by secret stealth
  His powre is reft, and weaknesse doth remaine.
O neuer Sir desire to try his guilefull traine.

32

Certes (said he) hence shall I neuer rest,
  Till I that treachours art haue heard and tride;
And you Sir knight, whose name mote I request,
  Of grace do me vnto his cabin guide.
  I that hight *Treuisan* (quoth he) will ride
Against my liking backe, to doe you grace :
  But nor for gold nor glee will I abide
By you, when ye arriue in that same place ;
For leuer had I die, then see his deadly face.

33

Ere long they come, where that same wicked wight
  His dwelling has, low in an hollow caue,
Farre vnderneath a craggie clift ypight,
  Darke, dolefull, drearie, like a greedie graue,
  That still for carrion carcases doth craue :
On top whereof aye dwelt the ghastly Owle,
  Shrieking his balefull note, which euer draue
Farre from that haunt all other chearefull fowle;
And all about it wandring ghostes did waile and
      howle.

34

And all about old stockes and stubs of trees,
  Whereon nor fruit, nor leafe was euer seene,
Did hang vpon the ragged rocky knees ;
  On which had many wretches hanged beene,
  Whose carcases were scattered on the greene,
And throwne about the cliffs. Arriued there,
  That bare-head knight for dread and dolefull
      teene,
Would faine haue fled, ne durst approchen neare,
But th'other forst him stay, and comforted in feare.

35

That darkesome caue they enter, where they find
  That cursed man, low sitting on the ground,
  Musing full sadly in his sullein mind ;
His griesie lockes, long growen, and vnbound,
  Disordred hong about his shoulders round,
  And hid his face; through which his hollow
      eyne
Lookt deadly dull, and stared as astound ;
  His raw-bone cheekes through penurie and pine,
Were shronke into his iawes, as he did neuer
      dine.

36

His garment nought but many ragged clouts,
  With thornes together pind and patched was,
  The which his naked sides he wrapt abouts ;
And him beside there lay vpon the gras
  A drearie corse, whose life away did pas,
  All wallowd in his owne yet luke-warme blood,
That from his wound yet welled fresh alas ;
  In which a rustie knife fast fixed stood,
And made an open passage for the gushing
      flood.

37

Which piteous spectacle, approuing trew
  The wofull tale that *Treuisan* had told,
When as the gentle *Redcrosse* knight did vew,
  With firie zeale he burnt in courage bold,
  Him to auenge, before his bloud were cold,
And to the villein said, Thou damned wight,
  The author of this fact, we here behold,
What iustice can but iudge against thee right,
With thine owne bloud to price his bloud, here
      shed in sight ?

38

What franticke fit (quoth he) hath thus distraught
  Thee, foolish man, so rash a doome to giue ?
  What iustice euer other iudgement taught,
But he should die, who merites not to liue ?
  None else to death this man despayring driue,
  But his owne guiltie mind deseruing death.
Is then vniust to each his due to giue ?
  Or let him die, that loatheth liuing breath ?
Or let him die at ease, that liueth here vneath ?

39

Who trauels by the wearie wandring way,
  To come vnto his wished home in haste,
And meetes a flood, that doth his passage stay,
  Is not great grace to helpe him ouer past,
  Or free his feet, that in the myre sticke fast ?
Most enuious man, that grieues at neighbours
      good,
And fond, that ioyest in the woe thou hast,
  Why wilt not let him passe, that long hath stood
Vpon the banke, yet wilt thy selfe not passe
      the flood ?

40

He there does now enioy eternall rest
And happie ease, which thou doest want and
And further from it daily wanderest:　　[craue,
What if some litle paine the passage haue,
That makes fraile flesh to feare the bitter waue?
Is not short paine well borne, that brings long ease,
And layes the soule to sleepe in quiet graue?
Sleepe after toyle, port after stormie seas,
Ease after warre, death after life does greatly
　　please.

41

The knight much wondred at his suddeine wit,
And said, The terme of life is limited,
Ne may a man prolong, nor shorten it;
The souldier may not moue from watchfull sted,
Nor leaue his stand, vntill his Captaine bed.
Who life did limit by almightie doome,
(Quoth he) knowes best the termes established;
And he, that points the Centonell his roome,
Doth license him depart at sound of morning
　　droome.

42

Is not his deed, what euer thing is donne,
In heauen and earth? did not he all create
To die againe? all ends that was begonne.
Their times in his eternall booke of fate
Are written sure, and haue their certaine date.
Who then can striue with strong necessitie,
That holds the world in his still chaunging state,
Or shunne the death ordaynd by destinie?
When houre of death is come, let none aske
　　whence, nor why.

43

The lenger life, I wote the greater sin,
The greater sin, the greater punishment:
All those great battels, which thou boasts to win,
Through strife, and bloud-shed, and auenge-
　　ment,
Now praysd, hereafter deare thou shalt repent:
For life must life, and bloud must bloud repay.
Is not enough thy euill life forespent?
For he, that once hath missed the right way,
The further he doth goe, the further he doth
　　stray.

44

Then do no further goe, no further stray,
But here lie downe, and to thy rest betake,
Th'ill to preuent, that life ensewen may.
For what hath life, that may it loued make,
And giues not rather cause it to forsake?
Feare, sicknesse, age, losse, labour, sorrow,
　　strife,　　　　　　　　　　　　[quake;
Paine, hunger, cold, that makes the hart to
And euer fickle fortune rageth rife,
All which, and thousands mo do make a loath-
　　some life.

45

Thou wretched man, of death hast greatest need,
If in true ballance thou wilt weigh thy state:
For neuer knight, that dared warlike deede,
More lucklesse disauentures did amate:
Witnesse the dongeon deepe, wherein of late
Thy life shut vp, for death so oft did call;
And though good lucke prolonged hath thy
　　date,
Yet death then, would the like mishaps forestall,
Into the which hereafter thou maiest happen
　　fall.

46

Why then doest thou, O man of sin, desire
To draw thy dayes forth to their last degree?
Is not the measure of thy sinfull hire
High heaped vp with huge iniquitie,
Against the day of wrath, to burden thee?
Is not enough, that to this Ladie milde
Thou falsed hast thy faith with periurie,
And sold thy selfe to serue *Duessa* vilde,
With whom in all abuse thou hast thy selfe
　　defilde?

47

Is not he iust, that all this doth behold
From highest heauen, and beares an equall eye?
Shall he thy sins vp in his knowledge fold,
And guiltie be of thine impietie?
Is not his law, Let euery sinner die:
Die shall all flesh? what then must needs be
　　donne,
Is it not better to doe willinglie,
Then linger, till the glasse be all out ronne?
Death is the end of woes: die soone, O faeries
　　sonne.

48

The knight was much enmoued with his speach,
That as a swords point through his hart did
　　perse,
And in his conscience made a secret breach,
Well knowing true all, that he did reherse
And to his fresh remembrance did reuerse
The vgly vew of his deformed crimes,
That all his manly powres it did disperse,
As he were charmed with inchaunted rimes,
That oftentimes he quakt, and fainted often-
　　times.

49

In which amazement, when the Miscreant
Perceiued him to wauer weake and fraile,
Whiles trembling horror did his conscience dant,
And hellish anguish did his soule assaile,
To driue him to despaire, and quite to quaile,
He shew'd him painted in a table plaine,
The damned ghosts, that doe in torments waile,
And thousand feends that doe them endlesse
　　paine　　　　　　　　　　　　[remaine.
With fire and brimstone, which for euer shall

50

The sight whereof so throughly him dismaid,
  That nought but death before his eyes he saw,
  And euer burning wrath before him laid,
  By righteous sentence of th'Almighties law:
  Then gan the villein him to ouercraw,
  And brought vnto him swords,ropes,poison,fire,
  And all that might him to perdition draw;
  And bad him choose,what death he would desire:
For death was due to him, that had prouokt
    Gods ire.

51

But when as none of them he saw him take,
  He to him raught a dagger sharpe and keene,
  And gaue it him in hand: his hand did quake,
  And trèmble like a leafe of Aspin greene,
  And troubled bloud through his pale face was
    seene
  To come, and goe with tydings from the hart,
  As it a running messenger had beene.
  At last resolu'd to worke his finall smart,
He lifted vp his hand, that backe againe did
    start.

52

Which when as *Vna* saw, through euery vaine
  The crudled cold ran to her well of life,
  As in a swowne: but soone reliu'd againe,
  Out of his hand she snatcht the cursed knife,
  And threw it to the ground, enraged rife,
  And to him said, Fie, fie, faint harted knight,
  What meanest thou by this reprochfull strife?
  Is this the battell, which thou vauntst to fight
With that fire-mouthed Dragon, horrible and
    bright?

53

Come, come away, fraile, feeble, fleshly wight,
  Ne let vaine words bewitch thy manly hart,
  Ne diuelish thoughts dismay thy constant
    spright.
  In heauenly mercies hast thou not a part?
  Why shouldst thou then despeire, that chosen
    art?
  Where iustice growes, there grows eke greater
    grace,   [smart,
  The which doth quench the brond of hellish
  And that accurst hand-writing doth deface.
Arise, Sir knight arise, and leaue this cursed
    place.

54

So vp he rose, and thence amounted streight.
  Which when the carle beheld,and saw his guest
  Would safe depart, for all his subtill sleight,
  He chose an halter from among the rest,
  And with it hung himselfe, vnbid vnblest.
  But death he could not worke himselfe thereby;
  For thousand times he so himselfe had drest,
  Yet nathelesse it could not doe him die,
Till he should die his last, that is eternally.

Cant. X.

ᴐᴇᴐᴇᴐᴇᴐᴇᴐᴇᴐᴇᴐᴇᴐᴇᴐᴇᴐᴇᴐᴇᴐᴇᴐᴇᴐᴇᴐᴇᴐᴇᴐ

Her faithfull knight faire Vna brings
  to house of Holinesse,
Where he is taught repentance, and
  the way to heauenly blesse.

ᴐᴇᴐᴇᴐᴇᴐᴇᴐᴇᴐᴇᴐᴇᴐᴇᴐᴇᴐᴇᴐᴇᴐᴇᴐᴇᴐᴇᴐᴇᴐᴇᴐ

I

What man is he, that boasts of fleshly might,
  And vaine assurance of mortality,
  Which all so soone, as it doth come to fight,
  Against spirituall foes, yeelds by and by,
  Or from the field most cowardly doth fly?
  Ne let the man ascribe it to his skill,
  That thorough grace hath gained victory.
  If any strength we haue, it is to ill,
But all the good is Gods, both power and eke
    will.

2

By that, which lately hapned, *Vna* saw,
  That this her knight was feeble, and too faint;
  And all his sinews woxen weake and raw,
  Through long enprisonment, and hard con-
    straint,
  Which he endured in his late restraint,
  That yet he was vnfit for bloudie fight:
  Therefore to cherish him with diets daint,
  She cast to bring him, where he chearen might,
Till he recouered had his late decayed plight.

3

There was an auntient house not farre away,
  Renowmd throughout the world for sacred lore,
  And pure vnspotted life: so well they say
  It gouernd was, and guided euermore,
  Through wisedome of a matrone graue and hore;
  Whose onely ioy was to relieue the needes
  Of wretched soules, and helpe the helpelesse
    pore:
  All night she spent in bidding of her bedes,
And all the day in doing good and godly deedes.

4

Dame *Cœlia* men did her call, as thought
  From heauen to come, or thither to arise,
  The mother of three daughters, well vpbrought
  In goodly thewes, and godly exercise:
  The eldest two most sober, chast, and wise,
  Fidelia and *Speranza* virgins were,
  Though spousd, yet wanting wedlocks solem-
    nize;
  But faire *Charissa* to a louely fere
Was lincked,and by him had many pledges dere.

5

Arriued there, the dore they find fast lockt ;
  For it was warely watched night and day,
  For feare of many foes : but when they knockt,
  The Porter opened vnto them streight way :
  He was an aged syre, all hory gray,
  With lookes full lowly cast, and gate full slow,
  Wont on a staffe his feeble steps to stay,
  Hight *Humiltà.* They passe in stouping low ;
For streight and narrow was the way, which he
    did show.

6

Each goodly thing is hardest to begin,
  But entred in a spacious court they see,
  Both plaine, and pleasant to be walked in,
  Where them does meete a francklin faire and
    free,
  And entertaines with comely courteous glee,
  His name was *Zele,* that him right well became,
  For in his speeches and behauiour hee
  Did labour liuely to expresse the same,
And gladly did them guide, till to the Hall they
    came.

7

There fairely them receiues a gentle Squire,
  Of milde demeanure, and rare courtesie,
  Right cleanly clad in comely sad attire ;
  In word and deede that shew'd great modestie,
  And knew his good to all of each degree,
  Hight *Reuerence.* He them with speeches meet
  Does faire entreat ; no courting nicetie,
  But simple true, and eke vnfained sweet,
As might become a Squire so great persons to
    greet.

8

And afterwards them to his Dame he leades,
  That aged Dame, the Ladie of the place :
  Who all this while was busie at her beades :
  Which doen, she vp arose with seemely grace,
  And toward them full matronely did pace.
  Where when that fairest *Vna* she beheld,
  Whom well she knew to spring from heauenly
    race,
  Her hart with ioy vnwonted inly sweld,
As feeling wondrous comfort in her weaker eld.

9

And her embracing said, O happie earth,
  Whereon thy innocent feet doe euer tread,
  Most vertuous virgin borne of heauenly berth,
  That to redeeme thy woefull parents head,
  From tyrans rage, and euer-dying dread,
  Hast wandred through the world now long a
    day ;
  Yet ceasest not thy wearie soles to lead,
  What grace hath thee now hither brought this
    way ?
Or doen thy feeble feet vnweeting hither stray ?

10

Strange thing it is an errant knight to see
  Here in this place, or any other wight,
  That hither turnes his steps. So few there bee,
  That chose the narrow path, or seeke the right :
  All keepe the broad high way, and take delight
  With many rather for to go astray,
  And be partakers of their euill plight,
  Then with a few to walke the rightest way ;
O foolish men, why haste ye to your owne
    decay ?

11

Thy selfe to see, and tyred limbs to rest,
  O matrone sage (quoth she) I hither came,
  And this good knight his way with me addrest,
  Led with thy prayses and broad-blazed fame,
  That vp to heauen is blowne. The auncient
    Dame
  Him goodly greeted in her modest guise,
  And entertaynd them both, as best became,
  With all the court'sies, that she could deuise,
Ne wanted ought, to shew her bounteous or
    wise.

12

Thus as they gan of sundry things deuise,
  Loe two most goodly virgins came in place,
  Ylinked arme in arme in louely wise,
  With countenance demure, and modest grace,
  They numbred euen steps and equall pace :
  Of which the eldest, that *Fidelia* hight,
  Like sunny beames threw from her Christall
    face,
  That could haue dazd the rash beholders sight,
And round about her head did shine like
    heauens light.

13

She was araied all in lilly white,
  And in her right hand bore a cup of gold,
  With wine and water fild vp to the hight,
  In which a Serpent did himselfe enfold,
  That horrour made to all, that did behold ;
  But she no whit did chaunge her constant mood :
  And in her other hand she fast did hold
  A booke, that was both signd and seald with
    blood,
Wherein darke things were writ, hard to be
    vnderstood.

14

Her younger sister, that *Speranza* hight,
  Was clad in blew, that her beseemed well ;
  Not all so chearefull seemed she of sight,
  As was her sister ; whether dread did dwell,
  Or anguish in her hart, is hard to tell :
  Vpon her arme a siluer anchor lay,
  Whereon she leaned euer, as befell :
  And euer vp to heauen, as she did pray,
Her stedfast eyes were bent, ne swarued other
    way.

15

They seeing *Vna*, towards her gan wend,
  Who them encounters with like courtesie ;
  Many kind speeches they betwene them spend,
  And greatly ioy each other well to see :
  Then to the knight with shamefast modestie
  They turne themselues, at *Vnaes* meeke request,
  And him salute with well beseeming glee ;
  Who faire them quites, as him beseemed best,
And goodly gan discourse of many a noble gest.

16

Then *Vna* thus ; But she your sister deare ;
  The deare *Charissa* where is she become ?
  Or wants she health, or busie is elsewhere ?
  Ah no, said they, but forth she may not come :
  For she of late is lightned of her wombe,
  And hath encreast the world with one sonne
    more,
  That her to see should be but troublesome.
  Indeede (quoth she) that should her trouble
    sore,
But thankt be God, and her encrease so euer-
    more.

17

Then said the aged *Cœlia*, Deare dame,
  And you good Sir, I wote that of your toyle,
  And labours long, through which ye hither came,
  Ye both forwearied be : therefore a whyle
  I read you rest, and to your bowres recoyle.
  Then called she a Groome, that forth him led
  Into a goodly lodge, and gan despoile
  Of puissant armes, and laid in easie bed ;
His name was meeke *Obedience* rightfully ared.

18

Now when their wearie limbes with kindly rest,
  And bodies were refresht with due repast,
  Faire *Vna* gan *Fidelia* faire request,
  To haue her knight into her schoolehouse plaste,
  That of her heauenly learning he might taste,
  And heare the wisedome of her words diuine.
  She graunted, and that knight so much agraste,
  That she him taught celestiall discipline,
And opened his dull eyes, that light mote in
    them shine.

19

And that her sacred Booke, with bloud ywrit,
  That none could read, except she did them
    teach,
  She vnto him disclosed euery whit,
  And heauenly documents thereout did preach,
  That weaker wit of man could neuer reach,
  Of God, of grace, of iustice, of free will,
  That wonder was to heare her goodly speach :
  For she was able, with her words to kill,
And raise againe to life the hart, that she did
  thrill.

20

And when she list poure out her larger spright,
  She would commaund the hastie Sunne to stay,
  Or backward turne his course from heauens
    hight ;   [may,
  Sometimes great hostes of men she could dis-
  Dry-shod to passe, she parts the flouds in tway ;
  And eke huge mountaines from their natiue seat
  She would commaund, themselues to beare away,
  And throw in raging sea with roaring threat.
Almightie God her gaue such powre, and puis-
    sance great.

21

The faithfull knight now grew in litle space,
  By hearing her, and by her sisters lore,
  To such perfection of all heauenly grace,
  That wretched world he gan for to abhore,
  And mortall life gan loath, as thing forlore,
  Greeu'd with remembrance of his wicked wayes,
  And prickt with anguish of his sinnes so sore,
  That he desirde to end his wretched dayes :
So much the dart of sinfull guilt the soule dis-
    mayes.

22

But wise *Speranza* gaue him comfort sweet,
  And taught him how to take assured hold
  Vpon her siluer anchor, as was meet ;
  Else had his sinnes so great, and manifold
  Made him forget all that *Fidelia* told.
  In this distressed doubtfull agonie,
  When him his dearest *Vna* did behold,
  Disdeining life, desiring leaue to die,
She found her selfe assayld with great per-
    plexitie.

23

And came to *Cœlia* to declare her smart,
  Who well acquainted with that commune plight,
  Which sinfull horror workes in wounded hart,
  Her wisely comforted all that she might,
  With goodly counsell and aduisement right ;
  And streightway sent with carefull diligence,
  To fetch a Leach, the which had great insight
  In that disease of grieued conscience,
And well could cure the same ; His name was
  Patience.

24

Who comming to that soule-diseased knight,
  Could hardly him intreat, to tell his griefe :
  Which knowne, and all that noyd his heauie
    spright
  Well searcht, eftsoones he gan apply reliefe
  Of salues and med'cines, which had passing
    priefe,
  And thereto added words of wondrous might :
  By which to ease he him recured briefe,
  And much asswag'd the passion of his plight,
That he his paine endur'd, as seeming now more
  light.

25

But yet the cause and root of all his ill,
  Inward corruption, and infected sin,
  Not purg'd nor heald, behind remained still,
  And festring sore did rankle yet within,
  Close creeping twixt the marrow and the skin.
  Which to extirpe, he laid him priuily
  Downe in a darkesome lowly place farre in,
  Whereas he meant his corrosiues to apply,
And with streight diet tame his stubborne
    malady,

26

In ashes and sackcloth he did array
  His daintie corse, proud humors to abate,
  And dieted with fasting euery day,
  The swelling of his wounds to mitigate,
  And made him pray both earely and eke late :
  And euer as superfluous flesh did rot
  Amendment readie still at hand did wayt,
  To pluck it out with pincers firie whot,
That soone in him was left no one corrupted iot.

27

And bitter *Penance* with an yron whip,
  Was wont him once to disple euery day :
  And sharpe *Remorse* his hart did pricke and
    nip,
  That drops of bloud thence like a well did play;
  And sad *Repentance* vsed to embay
  His bodie in salt water smarting sore,
  The filthy blots of sinne to wash away.
  So in short space they did to health restore
The man that would not liue, but earst lay at
    deathes dore.

28

In which his torment often was so great,
  That like a Lyon he would cry and rore,
  And rend his flesh, and his owne synewes eat.
  His owne deare *Vna* hearing euermore
  His ruefull shriekes and gronings, often tore
  Her guiltlesse garments, and her golden heare,
  For pitty of his paine and anguish sore ;
  Yet all with patience wisely she did beare ;
For well she wist, his crime could else be neuer
    cleare.

29

Whom thus recouer'd by wise Patience,
  And trew *Repentance* they to *Vna* brought :
  Who ioyous of his cured conscience,
  Him dearely kist, and fairely eke besought
  Himselfe to chearish, and consuming thought
  To put away out of his carefull brest.
  By this *Charissa*, late in child-bed brought,
  Was woxen strong, and left her fruitfull nest ;
To her faire *Vna* brought this vnacquainted
    guest.

30

She was a woman in her freshest age,
  Of wondrous beauty, and of bountie rare,
  With goodly grace and comely personage,
  That was on earth not easie to compare ;
  Full of great loue, but *Cupids* wanton snare
  As hell she hated, chast in worke and will ;
  Her necke and breasts were euer open bare,
  That ay thereof her babes might sucke their fill ;
The rest was all in yellow robes arayed still.

31

A multitude of babes about her hong,
  Playing their sports, that ioyd her to behold,
  Whom still she fed, whiles they were weake
    and young,
  But thrust them forth still, as they wexed old :
  And on her head she wore a tyre of gold,
  Adornd with gemmes and owches wondrous
    faire,
  Whose passing price vneath was to be told ;
  And by her side there sate a gentle paire
Of turtle doues, she sitting in an yuorie chaire.

32

The knight and *Vna* entring, faire her greet,
  And bid her ioy of that her happie brood ;
  Who them requites with court'sies seeming meet,
  And entertaines with friendly chearefull mood.
  Then *Vna* her besought, to be so good,
  As in her vertuous rules to schoole her knight,
  Now after all his torment well withstood,
  In that sad house of *Penaunce*, where his
    spright
Had past the paines of hell, and long enduring
    night.

33

She was right ioyous of her iust request,
  And taking by the hand that Faeries sonne,
  Gan him instruct in euery good behest,
  Of loue, and righteousnesse, and well to donne,
  And wrath, and hatred warely to shonne,
  That drew on men Gods hatred, and his wrath,
  And many soules in dolours had fordonne :
  In which when him she well instructed hath,
From thence to heauen she teacheth him the
    ready path.

34

Wherein his weaker wandring steps to guide,
  An auncient matrone she to her does call,
  Whose sober lookes her wisedome well descride :
  Her name was *Mercie*, well knowne ouer all,
  To be both gratious, and eke liberall :
  To whom the carefull charge of him she gaue,
  To lead aright, that he should neuer fall
  In all his wayes through this wide worldes waue,
That Mercy in the end his righteous soule might
    saue.

35

The godly Matrone by the hand him beares
  Forth from her presence, by a narrow way,
  Scattred with bushy thornes, and ragged
    breares,
  Which still before him she remou'd away,
  That nothing might his ready passage stay :
  And euer when his feet encombred were,
  Or gan to shrinke, or from the right to stray,
  She held him fast, and firmely did vpbeare,
As carefull Nourse her child from falling oft
    does reare.

36

Eftsoones vnto an holy Hospitall,
  That was fore by the way, she did him bring,
  In which seuen Bead-men that had vowed all
  Their life to seruice of high heauens king
  Did spend their dayes in doing godly thing :
  Their gates to all were open euermore,
  That by the wearie way were traueiling,
  And one sate wayting euer them before,
To call in commers-by, that needy were and
    pore.

37

The first of them that eldest was, and best,
  Of all the house had charge and gouernement,
  As Guardian and Steward of the rest :
  His office was to giue entertainement
  And lodging, vnto all that came, and went :
  Not vnto such, as could him feast againe,
  And double quite, for that he on them spent,
  But such, as want of harbour did constraine :
Those for Gods sake his dewty was to entertaine.

38

The second was as Almner of the place,
  His office was, the hungry for to feed,
  And thristy giue to drinke, a worke of grace :
  He feard not once him selfe to be in need,
  Ne car'd to hoord for those,whom he did breede :
  The grace of God he layd vp still in store,
  Which as a stocke he left vnto his seede ;
  He had enough, what need him care for more?
And had he lesse, yet some he would giue to the
    pore.

39

The third had of their wardrobe custodie,
  In which were not rich tyres, nor garments gay,
  The plumes of pride, and wings of vanitie,
  But clothes meet to keepe keene could away,
  And naked nature seemely to aray :
  With which bare wretched wights he dayly clad,
  The images of God in earthly clay ;
  And if that no spare cloths to giue he had,
His owne coate he would cut, and it distribute
    glad.

40

The fourth appointed by his office was,
  Poore prisoners to relieue with gratious ayd,
  And captiues to redeeme with price of bras,
  From Turkes and Sarazins, which them had stayd :
  And though they faultie were, yet well he wayd,
  That God to vs forgiueth euery howre   [layd,
  Much more then that, why they in bands were
  And he that harrowd hell with heauie stowre,
The faultie soules from thence brought to his
    heauenly bowre.

41

The fift had charge sicke persons to attend,
  And comfort those, in point of death which lay ;
  For them most needeth comfort in the end,
  When sin, and hell, and death do most dismay
  The feeble soule departing hence away.
  All is but lost, that liuing we bestow,
  If not well ended at our dying day.
  O man haue mind of that last bitter throw ;
For as the tree does fall, so lyes it euer low.

42

The sixt had charge of them now being dead,
  In seemely sort their corses to engraue,
  And deck with dainty flowres their bridall bed,
  That to their heauenly spouse both sweet and
    braue
  They might appeare, when he their soules
    shall saue.   [mould,
  The wondrous workemanship of Gods owne
  Whose face he made, all beasts to feare, and gaue
  All in his hand, euen dead we honour should.
Ah dearest God me graunt, I dead be not
    defould.

43

The seuenth now after death and buriall done,
  Had charge the tender Orphans of the dead
  And widowes ayd, least they should be vndone :
  In face of iudgement he their right would plead,
  Ne ought the powre of mighty men did dread
  In their defence, nor would for gold or fee
  Be wonne their rightfull causes downe to tread ;
  And when they stood in most necessitee,
He did supply their want, and gaue them euer
    free.

44

There when the Elfin knight arriued was,
  The first and chiefest of the seuen, whose care
  Was guests to welcome, towardes him did pas :
  Where seeing *Mercie,* that his steps vp bare,
  And alwayes led, to her with reuerence rare
  He humbly louted in meeke lowlinesse,
  And seemely welcome for her did prepare :
  For of their order she was Patronesse,
Albe *Charissa* were their chiefest founderesse.

45

There she awhile him stayes, him selfe to rest,
That to the rest more able he might bee :
During which time, in euery good behest
And godly worke of Almes and charitee
She him instructed with great industree ;
Shortly therein so perfect he became,
That from the first vnto the last degree,
His mortall life he learned had to frame
In holy righteousnesse, without rebuke or blame.

46

Thence forward by that painfull way they pas,
Forth to an hill, that was both steepe and hy ·
On top whereof a sacred chappell was,
And eke a litle Hermitage thereby,
Wherein an aged holy man did lye,
That day and night said his deuotion,
Ne other worldly busines did apply ;
His name was heauenly *Contemplation* ;
Of God and goodnesse was his meditation.

47

Great grace that old man to him giuen had ;
For God he often saw from heauens hight,
All were his earthly eyen both blunt and bad,
And through great age had lost their kindly
     sight,   [spright,
Yet wondrous quick and persant was his
As Eagles eye, that can behold the Sunne :
That hill they scale with all their powre and
     might,
That his frayle thighes nigh wearie and for-
     donne
Gan faile, but by her helpe the top at last he
     wonne.

48

There they do finde that godly aged Sire,
With snowy lockes adowne his shoulders shed,
As hoarie frost with spangles doth attire
The mossy braunches of an Oke halfe ded.
Each bone might through his body well be red,
And euery sinew seene through his long fast :
For nought he car'd his carcas long vnfed ;
His mind was full of spirituall repast,
And pyn'd his flesh, to keepe his body low and
     chast.

49

Who when these two approching he aspide,
At their first presence grew agrieued sore,
That forst him lay his heauenly thoughts aside ;
And had he not that Dame respected more,
Whom highly he did reuerence and adore,
He would not once haue moued for the knight.
They him saluted standing far afore ;
Who well them greeting, humbly did requight,
And asked, to what end they clomb that tedious
     height.

50

What end (quoth she) should cause vs take such
     paine,
But that same end, which euery liuing wight
Should make his marke, high heauen to attaine ?
Is not from hence the way, that leadeth right
To that most glorious house, that glistreth bright
With burning starres, and euerliuing fire,
Whereof the keyes are to thy hand behight
By wise *Fidelia* ? she doth thee require,
To shew it to this knight, according his desire.

51

Thrise happy man, said then the father graue,
Whose staggering steps thy steady hand doth
     lead,
And shewes the way, his sinfull soule to saue.
Who better can the way to heauen aread,
Then thou thy selfe, that was both borne and bred
In heauenly throne, where thousand Angels shine ?
Thou doest the prayers of the righteous sead
Present before the maiestie diuine,
And his auenging wrath to clemencie incline.

52

Yet since thou bidst, thy pleasure shalbe donne.
Then come thou man of earth, and see the way,
That neuer yet was seene of Faeries sonne,
That neuer leads the traueiler astray,
But after labours long, and sad delay,
Brings them to ioyous rest and endlesse blis.
But first thou must a season fast and pray,
Till from her bands the spright assoiled is,
And haue her strength recur'd from fraile in-
     firmitis.

53

That done, he leads him to the highest Mount ;
Such one, as that same mighty man of God,
That bloud-red billowes like a walled front
On either side disparted with his rod,
Till that his army dry-foot through them yod,
Dwelt fortie dayes vpon ; where writ in stone
With bloudy letters by the hand of God,
The bitter doome of death and balefull mone
He did receiue, whiles flashing fire about him
     shone.

54

Or like that sacred hill, whose head full hie,
Adornd with fruitfull Oliues all arownd,
Is, as it were for endlesse memory
Of that deare Lord, who oft thereon was fownd,
For euer with a flowring girlond crownd :
Or like that pleasaunt Mount, that is for ay
Through famous Poets verse each where re-
     nownd,
On which the thrise three learned Ladies play
Their heauenly notes, and make full many a
     louely lay.

55

From thence, far off he vnto him did shew
  A litle path, that was both steepe and long,
  Which to a goodly Citie led his vew ;
  Whose wals and towres were builded high and
      strong
Of perle and precious stone, that earthly tong
Cannot describe, nor wit of man can tell ;
Too high a ditty for my simple song ;
The Citie of the great king hight it well,
Wherein eternall peace and happinesse doth
      dwell.

56

As he thereon stood gazing, he might see
  The blessed Angels to and fro descend
  From highest heauen, in gladsome companee,
  And with great ioy into that Citie wend,
  As commonly as friend does with his frend.
Whereat he wondred much, and gan enquere,
What stately building durst so high extend
Her loftie towres vnto the starry sphere,
And what vnknowen nation there empeopled
      were.

57

Faire knight (quoth he) *Hierusalem* that is,
  The new *Hierusalem*, that God has built
  For those to dwell in, that are chosen his,
  His chosen people purg'd from sinfull guilt,
  With pretious bloud, which cruelly was spilt
On cursed tree, of that vnspotted lam,
That for the sinnes of all the world was kilt :
Now are they Saints all in that Citie sam,
More deare vnto their God, then younglings to
      their dam.

58

Till now, said then the knight, I weened well,
  That great *Cleopolis*, where I haue beene,
  In which that fairest *Faerie Queene* doth dwell,
  The fairest Citie was, that might be seene ;
  And that bright towre all built of christall cleene,
Panthea, seemd the brightest thing, that was :
But now by proofe all otherwise I weene ;
For this great Citie that does far surpas,
And this bright Angels towre quite dims that
      towre of glas.

59

Most trew, then said the holy aged man ;
  Yet is *Cleopolis* for earthly frame,
  The fairest peece, that eye beholden can :
  And well beseemes all knights of noble name,
  That couet in th'immortall booke of fame
To be eternized, that same to haunt,
And doen their seruice to that soueraigne Dame,
That glorie does to them for guerdon graunt :
For she is heauenly borne, and heauen may
      iustly vaunt.

60

And thou faire ymp, sprong out from English race,
  How euer now accompted Elfins sonne,
  Well worthy doest thy seruice for her grace,
  To aide a virgin desolate foredonne.
  But when thou famous victorie hast wonne,
And high emongst all knights hast hong thy
      shield,
Thenceforth the suit of earthly conquest shonne,
And wash thy hands from guilt of bloudy field:
For bloud can nought but sin, and wars but
      sorrowes yield.

61

Then seeke this path, that I to thee presage,
  Which after all to heauen shall thee send ;
  Then peaceably thy painefull pilgrimage
  To yonder same *Hierusalem* do bend,
  Where is for thee ordaind a blessed end :
For thou emongst those Saints, whom thou
      doest see,
Shalt be a Saint, and thine owne nations frend
And Patrone: thou Saint *George* shalt called bee,
Saint *George* of mery England, the signe of
      victoree.

62

Vnworthy wretch (quoth he) of so great grace,
  How dare I thinke such glory to attaine ?
  These that haue it attaind, were in like cace
  (Quoth he) as wretched, and liu'd in like paine.
  But deeds of armes must I at last be faine,
And Ladies loue to leaue so dearely bought ?
What need of armes, where peace doth ay
      remaine,
(Said he) and battailes none are to be fought ?
As for loose loues are vaine, and vanish into
      nought.

63

O let me not (quoth he) then turne againe
  Backe to the world, whose ioyes so fruitlesse
      are ;
  But let me here for aye in peace remaine,
  Or streight way on that last long voyage fare,
  That nothing may my present hope empare.
That may not be (said he) ne maist thou yit
Forgo that royall maides bequeathed care,
Who did her cause into thy hand commit,
Till from her cursed foe thou haue her freely
      quit.

64

Then shall I soone, (quoth he) so God me grace,
  Abet that virgins cause disconsolate,
  And shortly backe returne vnto this place,
  To walke this way in Pilgrims poore estate.
  But now aread, old father, why of late
Didst thou behight me borne of English blood,
Whom all a Faeries sonne doen nominate ?
That word shall I (said he) auouchen good,
Sith to thee is vnknowne the cradle of thy brood.

65

For well I wote, thou springst from ancient race
Of *Saxon* kings, that haue with mightie hand
And many bloudie battailes fought in place
High reard their royall throne in *Britane* land,
And vanquisht them, vnable to withstand:
From thence a Faerie thee vnweeting reft,
There as thou slepst in tender swadling band,
And her base Elfin brood there for thee left.
Such men do Chaungelings call, so chaungd by
Faeries theft.

66

Thence she thee brought into this Faerie lond,
And in an heaped furrow did thee hyde,
Where thee a Ploughman all vnweeting fond,
As he his toylesome teme that way did guyde,
And brought thee vp in ploughmans state
to byde,
Whereof *Georgos* he thee gaue to name ;
Till prickt with courage, and thy forces pryde,
To Faery court thou cam'st to seeke for fame,
And proue thy puissaunt armes, as seemes thee
best became.

67

O holy Sire (quoth he) how shall I quight
The many fauours I with thee haue found,
That hast my name and nation red aright,
And taught the way that does to heauen bound?
This said, adowne he looked to the ground,
To haue returnd, but dazed were his eyne,
Through passing brightnesse, which did quite
confound
His feeble sence, and too exceeding shyne.
So darke are earthly things compard to things
diuine.

68

At last whenas himselfe he gan to find,
To *Vna* back he cast him to retire ;
Who him awaited still with pensiue mind.
Great thankes and goodly meed to that good
syre,
He thence departing gaue for his paines hyre.
So came to *Vna*, who him ioyd to see,
And after litle rest, gan him desire,
Of her aduenture mindfull for to bee.
So leaue they take of *Cælia*, and her daughters
three.

Cant. XI.

The knight with that old Dragon fights
two dayes incessantly :
The third him ouerthrowes, and gayns
most glorious victory.

1

High time now gan it wex for *Vna* faire,
To thinke of those her captiue Parents deare,
And their forwasted kingdome to repaire :
Whereto whenas they now approched neare,
With hartie words her knight she gan to cheare,
And in her modest manner thus bespake ;
Deare knight, as deare, as euer knight was deare,
That all these sorrowes suffer for my sake,
High heauen behold the tedious toyle, ye for
me take.

2

Now are we come vnto my natiue soyle,
And to the place, where all our perils dwell ;
Here haunts that feend, and does his dayly
spoyle,
Therefore henceforth be at your keeping well,
And euer ready for your foeman fell.
The sparke of noble courage now awake,
And striue your excellent selfe to excell ;
That shall ye euermore renowmed make,
Aboue all knights on earth, that battèill
vndertake.

3

And pointing forth, lo yonder is (said she)
The brasen towre in which my parents deare
For dread of that huge feend emprisond be,
Whom I from far see on the walles appeare,
Whose sight my feeble soule doth greatly cheare:
And on the top of all I do espye
The watchman wayting tydings glad to heare,
That O my parents might I happily
Vnto you bring, to ease you of your misery.

4

With that they heard a roaring hideous sound,
That all the ayre with terrour filled wide,
And seemd vneath to shake the stedfast ground.
Eftsoones that dreadfull Dragon they espide,
Where stretcht he lay vpon the sunny side
Of a great hill, himselfe like a great hill.
But all so soone, as he from far descride
Those glistring armes, that heauen with light
did fill,
He rousd himselfe full blith, and hastned them
vntill.

5

Then bad the knight his Lady yede aloofe,
And to an hill her selfe with draw aside,
From whence she might behold that battailles
  proof
And eke be safe from daunger far descryde :
She him obayd, and turnd a little wyde.
Now O thou sacred Muse, most learned Dame,
Faire ympe of *Phœbus*, and his aged bride,
The Nourse of time, and euerlasting fame,
That warlike hands ennoblest with immortall
  name ;

6

O gently come into my feeble brest,
Come gently, but not with that mighty rage,
Wherewith the martiall troupes thou doest infest,
And harts of great Heroes doest enrage,
That nought their kindled courage may aswage,
Soone as thy dreadfull trompe begins to sownd ;
The God of warre with his fiers equipage
Thou doest awake, sleepe neuer he so sownd,
And scared nations doest with horrour sterne
  astownd.

7

Faire Goddesse lay that furious fit aside,
Till I of warres and bloudy *Mars* do sing,
And Briton fields with Sarazin bloud bedyde,
Twixt that great faery Queene and Paynim king,
That with their horrour heauen and earth did
  ring,
A worke of labour long, and endlesse prayse :
But now a while let downe that haughtie string,
And to my tunes thy second tenor rayse,
That I this man of God his godly armes may
  blaze.

8

By this the dreadfull Beast drew nigh to hand,
Halfe flying, and halfe footing in his hast,
That with his largenesse measured much land,
And made wide shadow vnder his huge wast ;
As mountaine doth the valley ouercast.
Approching nigh, he reared high afore
His body monstrous, horrible, and vast,
Which to increase his wondrous greatnesse more,
Was swolne with wrath, and poyson, and with
  bloudy gore.

9

And ouer, all with brasen scales was armd,
Like plated coate of steele, so couched neare,
That nought mote perce, ne might his corse be
  harmd
With dint of sword, nor push of pointed speare ;
Which as an Eagle, seeing pray appeare,
His aery plumes doth rouze, full rudely dight,
So shaked he, that horrour was to heare,
For as the clashing of an Armour bright,
Such noyse his rouzed scales did send vnto the
  knight.

10

His flaggy wings when forth he did display,
Were like two sayles, in which the hollow wynd
Is gathered full, and worketh speedy way :
And eke the pennes, that did his pineons bynd,
Were like mayne-yards, with flying canuas lynd,
With which whenas him list the ayre to beat,
And there by force vnwonted passage find,
The cloudes before him fled for terrour great,
And all the heauens stood still amazed with his
  threat.

11

His huge long tayle wound vp in hundred foldes,
Does ouerspred his long bras-scaly backe,
Whose wreathed boughts when euer he vn-
  foldes,
And thicke entangled knots adown does slacke,
Bespotted as with shields of red and blacke,
It sweepeth all the land behind him farre,
And of three furlongs does but litle lacke ;
And at the point two stings in-fixed arre,
Both deadly sharpe, that sharpest steele ex-
  ceeden farre.

12

But stings and sharpest steele did far exceed
The sharpnesse of his cruell rending clawes ;
Dead was it sure, as sure as death in deed,
What euer thing does touch his rauenous pawes,
Or what within his reach he euer drawes.
But his most hideous head my toung to tell
Does tremble : for his deepe deuouring iawes
Wide gaped, like the griesly mouth of hell,
Through which into his darke abisse all rauin fell.

13

And that more wondrous was, in either iaw
Threeranckes of yron teeth enraunged were,
In which yet trickling bloud and gobbets raw
Of late deuoured bodies did appeare,
That sight thereof bred cold congealed feare :
Which to increase, and all atonce to kill,
A cloud of smoothering smoke and sulphur seare
Out of his stinking gorge forth steemed still,
That all the ayre about with smoke and stench
  did fill.

14

His blazing eyes, like two bright shining shields,
Did burne with wrath, and sparkled liuing fyre ;
As two broad Beacons, set in open fields,
Send forth their flames farre off to euery shyre,
And warning giue, that enemies conspyre,
With fire and sword the region to inuade ;
So flam'd his eyne with rage and rancorous yre :
But farre within, as in a hollow glade,
Those glaring lampes were set, that made a
  dreadfull shade.

15

So dreadfully he towards him did pas,
  Forelifting vp aloft his speckled brest,
  And often bounding on the brused gras,
  As for great ioyance of his newcome guest.
Eftsoones he gan aduance his haughtie crest,
  As chauffed Bore his bristles doth vpreare,
  And shoke his scales to battell readie drest ;
That made the *Redcrosse* knight nigh quake
    for feare,
As bidding bold defiance to his foeman neare.

16

The knight gan fairely couch his steadie speare,
  And fiercely ran at him with rigorous might :
  The pointed steele arriuing rudely theare,
  His harder hide would neither perce, nor bight,
  But glauncing by forth passed forward right ;
Yet sore amoued with so puissant push,
  The wrathfull beast about him turned light,
And him so rudely passing by, did brush
With his long tayle, that horse and man to
    ground did rush.

17

Both horse and man vp lightly rose againe,
  And fresh encounter towards him addrest :
  But th'idle stroke yet backe recoyld in vaine,
  And found no place his deadly point to rest.
Exceeding rage enflam'd the furious beast,
  To be auenged of so great despight ;
  For neuer felt his imperceable brest
So wondrous force, from hand of liuing wight ;
Yet had he prou'd the powre of many a puis-
    sant knight.

18

Then with his wauing wings displayed wyde,
  Himselfe vp high he lifted from the ground,
  And with strong flight did forcibly diuide
  The yielding aire, which nigh too feeble found
  Her flitting partes, and element vnsound,
To beare so great a weight : he cutting way
  With his broad sayles, about him soared round :
At last low stouping with vnweldie sway,
Snatcht vp both horse and man, to beare them
    quite away.

19

Long he them bore aboue the subiect plaine,
  So farre as Ewghen bow a shaft may send,
  Till struggling strong did him at last con-
    straine,
To let them downe before his flightes end :
As hagard hauke presuming to contend
  With hardie fowle, aboue his hable might,
  His wearie pounces all in vaine doth spend,
To trusse the pray too heauie for his flight ;
Which comming downe to ground, does free it
    selfe by fight.

20

He so disseized of his gryping grosse,
  The knight his thrillant speare againe assayd
  In his bras-plated body to embosse,
  And three mens strength vnto the stroke he layd;
  Wherewith the stiffe beame quaked, as affrayd,
And glauncing from his scaly necke, did glyde
  Close vnder his left wing, then broad displayd.
The percing steele there wrought a wound full
    wyde,
That with the vncouth smart the Monster
    lowdly cryde.

21

He cryde, as raging seas are wont to rore,
  When wintry storme his wrathfull wreck does
    threat,
The rolling billowes beat the ragged shore,
  As they the earth would shoulder from her seat,
  And greedie gulfe does gape, as he would eat
His neighbour element in his reuenge :
  Then gin the blustring brethren boldly threat,
To moue the world from off his stedfast henge,
And boystrous battell make, each other to
    auenge.

22

The steely head stucke fast still in his flesh,
  Till with his cruell clawes he snatcht the wood,
  And quite a sunder broke. Forth flowed fresh
  A gushing riuer of blacke goarie blood,
  That drowned all the land, whereon he stood;
The streame thereof would driue a water-mill.
  Trebly augmented was his furious mood
With bitter sense of his deepe rooted ill,
That flames of fire he threw forth from his large
    nosethrill.

23

His hideous tayle then hurled he about,
  And therewith all enwrapt the nimble thyes
  Of his froth-fomy steed, whose courage stout
  Striuing to loose the knot, that fast him tyes,
  Himselfe in streighter bandes too rash implyes,
That to the ground he is perforce constraynd
  To throw his rider : who can quickly ryse
From off the earth, with durty bloud distaynd,
For that reprochfull fall right fowly he disdaynd.

24

And fiercely tooke his trenchand blade in hand,
  With which he stroke so furious and so fell,
  That nothing seemd the puissance could with-
    stand :
Vpon his crest the hardned yron fell,
  But his more hardned crest was armd so well,
  That deeper dint therein it would not make ;
Yet so extremely did the buffe him quell,
That from thenceforth he shund the like to
    take,   [forsake.
But when he saw them come, he did them still

25

The knight was wrath to see his stroke beguyld,
  And smote againe with more outrageous might;
  But backe againe the sparckling steele recoyld,
  And left not any marke, where it did light ;
  As if in Adamant rocke it had bene pight.
  The beast impatient of his smarting wound,
  And of so fierce and forcible despight,
  Thought with his wings to stye aboue the
    ground ;
But his late wounded wing vnseruiceable found.

26

Then full of griefe and anguish vehement,
  He lowdly brayd, that like was neuer heard,
  And from his wide deuouring ouen sent
  A flake of fire, that flashing in his beard,
  Him all amazd, and almost made affeard :
  The scorching flame sore swinged all his face,
  And through his armour all his bodie seard,
  That he could not endure so cruell cace,
But thought his armes to leaue, and helmet to
    vnlace.

27

Not that great Champion of the antique world,
  Whom famous Poetes verse so much doth vaunt,
  And hath for twelue huge labours high extold,
  So many furies and sharpe fits did haunt,
  When him the poysoned garment did enchaunt
  With *Centaures* bloud, and bloudie verses
    charm'd,
  As did this knight twelue thousand dolours
    daunt,   [arm'd,
  Whom fyrie steele now burnt, that earst him
That erst him goodly arm'd, now most of all
    him harm'd.

28

Faint, wearie, sore, emboyled, grieued, brent
  With heat, toyle, wounds, armes, smart, and
    inward fire
  That neuer man such mischiefes did torment ;
  Death better were, death did he oft desire,
  But death will neuer come, when needes require.
  Whom so dismayd when that his foe beheld,
  He cast to suffer him no more respire,
  But gan his sturdie sterne about to weld,
And him so strongly stroke, that to the ground
    him feld.

29

It fortuned (as faire it then befell)
  Behind his backe vnweeting, where he stood,
  Of auncient time there was a springing well,
  From which fast trickled forth a siluer flood,
  Full of great vertues, and for med'cine good.
  Whylome, before that cursed Dragon got
  That happie land, and all with innocent blood
  Defyld those sacred waues, it rightly hot
The well of life, ne yet his vertues had forgot.

30

For vnto life the dead it could restore,
  And guilt of sinfull crimes cleane wash away,
  Those that with sicknesse were infected sore,
  It could recure, and aged long decay
  Renew, as one were borne that very day.
  Both *Silo* this, and *Iordan* did excell,
  And th'English *Bath*, and eke the german *Spau*,
  Ne can *Cephise*, nor *Hebrus* match this well :
Into the same the knight backe ouerthrowen,
    fell.

31

Now gan the golden *Phœbus* for to steepe
  His fierie face in billowes of the west,
  And his faint steedes watred in Ocean deepe,
  Whiles from their iournall labours they did
    rest,
  When that infernall Monster, hauing kest
  His wearie foe into that liuing well,
  Can high aduance his broad discoloured brest,
  Aboue his wonted pitch, with countenance fell,
And clapt his yron wings, as victor he did
    dwell.

32

Which when his pensiue Ladie saw from farre,
  Great woe and sorrow did her soule assay,
  As weening that the sad end of the warre,
  And gan to highest God entirely pray,
  That feared chance from her to turne away ;
  With folded hands and knees full lowly bent
  All night she watcht, ne once adowne would lay
  Her daintie limbs in her sad dreriment,
But praying still did wake, and waking did
    lament.

33

The morrow next gan early to appeare,
  That *Titan* rose to runne his daily race ;
  But early ere the morrow next gan reare
  Out of the sea faire *Titans* deawy face,
  Vp rose the gentle virgin from her place,
  And looked all about, if she might spy
  Her loued knight to moue his manly pace :
For she had great doubt of his safety,
Since late she saw him fall before his enemy.

34

At last she saw, where he vpstarted braue
  Out of the well, wherein he drenched lay ;
  As Eagle fresh out of the Ocean waue,
  Where he hath left his plumes all hoary gray,
  And deckt himselfe with feathers youthly gay,
  Like *Eyas* hauke vp moũts vnto the skies,
  His newly budded pineons to assay,
  And marueiles at himselfe, still as he flies :
So new this new-borne knight to battell new
    did rise.

35

Whom when the damned feend so fresh did spy,
No wonder if he wondred at the sight,
And doubted, whether his late enemy
It were, or other new supplied knight.
He, now to proue his late renewed might,
High brandishing his bright deaw-burning
  blade,
Vpon his crested scalpe so sore did smite,
That to the scull a yawning wound it made:
The deadly dint his dulled senses all dismaid.

36

I wote not, whether the reuenging steele
Were hardned with that holy water dew,
Wherein he fell, or sharper edge did feele,
Or his baptized hands now greater grew;
Or other secret vertue did ensew;
Else neuer could the force of fleshly arme,
Ne molten mettall in his bloud embrew:
For till that stownd could neuer wight him
  harme,
By subtilty, nor slight, nor might, nor mighty
  charme.

37

The cruell wound enraged him so sore,
That loud he yelled for exceeding paine;
As hundred ramping Lyons seem'd to rore,
Whom rauenous hunger did thereto constraine:
Then gan he tosse aloft his stretched traine,
And therewith scourge the buxome aire so sore,
That to his force to yeelden it was faine;
Ne ought his sturdie strokes might stand afore,
That high trees ouerthrew, and rocks in peeces
  tore.

38

The same aduauncing high aboue his head,
With sharpe intended sting so rude him smot,
That to the earth him droue, as stricken dead,
Ne liuing wight would haue him life behot:
The mortall sting his angry needle shot
Quite through his shield, and in his shoulder
  seasd,
Where fast it stucke, ne would there out be got:
The griefe thereof him wondrous sore diseasd,
Ne might his ranckling paine with patience be
  appeasd.

39

But yet more mindfull of his honour deare,
Then of the grieuous smart, which him did wring,
From loathed soile he can him lightly reare,
And stroue to loose the farre infixed sting:
Which when in vaine he tryde with struggeling,
Inflam'd with wrath, his raging blade he heft,
And strooke so strongly, that the knotty string
Of his huge taile he quite a sunder cleft,
Fiue ioynts thereof he hewd, and but the stump
  him left.

40

Hart cannot thinke, what outrage, and what cryes,
With foule enfouldred smoake and flashing fire,
The hell-bred beast threw forth vnto the skyes,
That all was couered with darknesse dire:
Then fraught with rancour, and engorged ire,
He cast at once him to auenge for all,
And gathering vp himselfe out of the mire,
With his vneuen wings did fiercely fall
Vpon his sunne-bright shield, and gript it fast
  withall.

41

Much was the man encombred with his hold,
In feare to lose his weapon in his paw,
Ne wist yet, how his talants to vnfold;
Nor harder was from *Cerberus* greedie iaw
To plucke a bone, then from his cruell claw
To reaue by strength the griped gage away:
Thrise he assayd it from his foot to draw,
And thrise in vaine to draw it did assay,
It booted nought to thinke, to robbe him of his
  pray.

42

Tho when he saw no power might preuaile,
His trustie sword he cald to his last aid,
Wherewith he fiercely did his foe assaile,
And double blowes about him stoutly laid,
That glauncing fire out of the yron plaid;
As sparckles from the Anduile vse to fly,
When heauie hammers on the wedge are swaid;
Therewith at last he forst him to vnty
One of his grasping feete, him to defend thereby.

43

The other foot, fast fixed on his shield,
Whenas no strength, nor stroks mote him
  constraine
To loose, ne yet the warlike pledge to yield,
He smot thereat with all his might and maine,
That nought so wondrous puissance might
  sustaine;
Vpon the ioynt the lucky steele did light,
And made such way, that hewd it quite in
  twaine;
The paw yet missed not his minisht might,
But hong still on the shield, as it at first was
  pight.

44

For griefe thereof, and diuelish despight,
From his infernall fournace forth he threw
Huge flames, that dimmed all the heauens light,
Enrold in duskish smoke and brimstone blew;
As burning *Aetna* from his boyling stew
Doth belch out flames, and rockes in peeces broke,
And ragged ribs of mountaines molten new,
Enwrapt in coleblacke clouds and filthy smoke,
That all the land with stench, and heauen with
  horror choke.

45

The heate whereof, and harmefull pestilence
　So sore him noyd, that forst him to retire
　A little backward for his best defence,
To saue his bodie from the scorching fire,
Which he from hellish entrailes did expire.
It chaunst (eternall God that chaunce did guide)
　As he recoyled backward, in the mire
　His nigh forwearied feeble feet did slide,
And downe he fell, with dread of shame sore
　terrifide.

46

There grew a goodly tree him faire beside,
　Loaden with fruit and apples rosie red,
　As they in pure vermilion had beene dide,
Whereof great vertues ouer all were red:
For happie life to all, which thereon fed,
And life eke euerlasting did befall:
　Great God it planted in that blessed sted
　With his almightie hand, and did it call
The tree of life, the crime of our first fathers fall.

47

In all the world like was not to be found,
　Saue in that soile, where all good things did
　　grow,
And freely sprong out of the fruitfull ground,
As incorrupted Nature did them sow,
Till that dread Dragon all did ouerthrow.
Another like faire tree eke grew thereby,
　Whereof who so did eat, eftsoones did know
　Both good and ill: O mornefull memory:
That tree through one mans fault hath doen vs
　all to dy.

48

From that first tree forth flowd, as from a well,
　A trickling streame of Balme, most soueraine
And daintie deare, which on the ground still fell,
And ouerflowed all the fertill plaine,
As it had deawed bene with timely raine:
Life and long health that gratious ointment
　gaue,
　And deadly woundes could heale, and reare
　　againe
The senselesse corse appointed for the graue.
Into that same he fell: which did from death
　him saue.

49

For nigh thereto the euer damned beast
　Durst not approch, for he was deadly made,
　And all that life preserued, did detest:
Yet he it oft aduentur'd to inuade.
By this the drouping day-light gan to fade,
And yeeld his roome to sad succeeding night,
　Who with her sable mantle gan to shade
　The face of earth, and wayes of liuing wight,
And high her burning torch set vp in heauen
　bright.

50

When gentle *Vna* saw the second fall
　Of her deare knight, who wearie of long fight,
　And faint through losse of bloud, mou'd not at
　　all,
But lay as in a dreame of deepe delight,
Besmeard with pretious Balme, whose ver-
　tuous might
Did heale his wounds, and scorching heat alay,
　Againe she stricken was with sore affright,
　And for his safetie gan deuoutly pray;
And watch the noyous night, and wait for
　ioyous day.

51

The ioyous day gan early to appeare,
　And faire *Aurora* from the deawy bed
　Of aged *Tithone* gan her selfe to reare,
With rosie cheekes, for shame as blushing red;
Her golden lockes for haste were loosely shed
About her eares, when *Vna* her did marke
　Clymbe to her charet, all with flowers spred,
　From heauen high to chase the chearelesse darke;
With merry note her loud salutes the mounting
　larke.

52

Then freshly vp arose the doughtie knight,
　All healed of his hurts and woundes wide,
　And did himselfe to battell readie dight;
Whose early foe awaiting him beside
To haue deuourd, so soone as day he spyde,
When now he saw himselfe so freshly reare,
　As if late fight had nought him damnifyde,
　He woxe dismayd, and gan his fate to feare;
Nathlesse with wonted rage he him aduaunced
　neare.

53

And in his first encounter, gaping wide,
　He thought at once him to haue swallowd quight,
　And rusht vpon him with outragious pride;
Who him r'encountring fierce, as hauke in flight,
Perforce rebutted backe. The weapon bright
Taking aduantage of his open iaw,
　Ran through his mouth with so importune might,
　That deepe emperst his darksome hollow maw,
And back retyrd, his life bloud forth with all did
　draw.

54

So downe he fell, and forth his life did breath,
　That vanisht into smoke and cloudes swift;
　So downe he fell, that th'earth him vnderneath
Did grone, as feeble so great load to lift;
So downe he fell, as an huge rockie clift,
Whose false foundation waues haue washt away,
　With dreadfull poyse is from the mayneland rift,
　And rolling downe, great *Neptune* doth dismay;
So downe he fell, and like an heaped mountaine
　lay.

55

The knight himselfe euen trembled at his fall,
So huge and horrible a masse it seem'd;
And his deare Ladie, that beheld it all,
Durst not approch for dread, which she mis-
deem'd,
But yet at last, when as the direfull feend
She saw not stirre, off-shaking vaine affright,
She nigher drew, and saw that ioyous end:
Then God she praysd, and thankt her faithfull
knight,
That had atchieu'd so great a conquest by his
might.

Cant. XII.

Faire Vna to the Redcrosse knight
betrouthed is with ioy:
Though false Duessa it to barre
her false sleights doe imploy.

1

Behold I see the hauen nigh at hand,
To which I meane my wearie course to bend;
Vere the maine shete, and beare vp with the land,
The which afore is fairely to be kend,
And seemeth safe from stormes, that may offend;
There this faire virgin wearie of her way
Must landed be, now at her iourneyes end:
There eke my feeble barke a while may stay,
Till merry wind and weather call her thence
away.

2

Scarsely had *Phœbus* in the glooming East
Yet harnessed his firie-footed teeme,
Ne reard aboue the earth his flaming creast,
When the last deadly smoke aloft did steeme,
That signe of last outbreathed life did seeme
Vnto the watchman on the castle wall;
Who thereby dead that balefull Beast did deeme,
And to his Lord and Ladie lowd gan call,
To tell, how he had seene the Dragons fatall fall.

3

Vprose with hastie ioy, and feeble speed
That aged Sire, the Lord of all that land,
And looked forth, to weet, if true indeede
Those tydings were, as he did vnderstand,
Which whenas true by tryall he out fond,
He bad to open wyde his brazen gate,
Which long time had bene shut, and out of hond
Proclaymed ioy and peace through all his state;
For dead now was their foe, which them for-
rayed late.

4

Then gan triumphant Trompets sound on hie,
That sent to heauen the ecchoed report
Of their new ioy, and happie victorie
Gainst him, that had them long opprest with
And fast imprisoned in sieged fort.   [tort,
Then all the people, as in solemne feast,
To him assembled with one full consort,
Reioycing at the fall of that great beast,
From whose eternall bondage now they were
release.

5

Forth came that auncient Lord and aged Queene,
Arayd in antique robes downe to the ground,
And sad habiliments right well beseene;
A noble crew about them waited round
Of sage and sober Peres, all grauely gownd;
Whom farre before did march a goodly band
Of tall young men, all hable armes to sownd,
But now they laurell braunches bore in hand;
Glad signe of victorie and peace in all their land.

6

Vnto that doughtie Conquerour they came,
And him before themselues prostrating low,
Their Lord and Patrone loud did him proclame,
And at his feet their laurell boughes did throw.
Soone after them all dauncing on a row
The comely virgins came, with girlands dight,
As fresh as flowres in medow greene do grow,
When morning deaw vpon their leaues doth light:
And in their hands sweet Timbrels all vpheld on
hight.

7

And them before, the fry of children young
Their wanton sports and childish mirth did play,
And to the Maydens sounding tymbrels sung
In well attuned notes, a ioyous lay,
And made delightfull musicke all the way,
Vntill they came, where that faire virgin stood;
As faire *Diana* in fresh sommers day
Beholds her Nymphes, enraung'd in shadie wood,
Some wrestle, some do run, some bathe in
christall flood

8

So she beheld those maydens meriment
With chearefull vew; who when to her they
came,
Themselues to ground with gratious humblesse
And her ador'd by honorable name,   [bent,
Lifting to heauen her euerlasting fame:
Then on her head they set a girland greene,
And crowned her twixt earnest and twixt game;
Who in her selfe-resemblance well beseene,
Did seeme such, as she was, a goodly maiden
Queene.

9

And after, all the raskall many ran,
Heaped together in rude rablement,
To see the face of that victorious man:
Whom all admired, as from heauen sent,
And gazd vpon with gaping wonderment.
But when they came, where that dead Dragon lay,
Stretcht on the ground in monstrous large extent,
The sight with idle feare did them dismay,
Ne durst approch him nigh, to touch, or once assay.

10

Some feard, and fled; some feard and well it faynd;
One that would wiser seeme, then all the rest,
Warnd him not touch, for yet perhaps remaynd
Some lingring life within his hollow brest,
Or in his wombe might lurke some hidden nest
Of many Dragonets, his fruitfull seed;
Another said, that in his eyes did rest
Yet sparckling fire, and bad thereof take heed;
Another said, he saw him moue his eyes indeed.

11

One mother, when as her foolehardie chyld
Did come too neare, and with his talants play,
Halfe dead through feare, her litle babe reuyld,
And to her gossips gan in counsell say;
How can I tell, but that his talants may
Yet scratch my sonne, or rend his tender hand?
So diuersly themselues in vaine they fray;
Whiles some more bold, to measure him nigh stand,
To proue how many acres he did spread of land.

12

Thus flocked all the folke him round about,
The whiles that hoarie king, with all his traine,
Being arriued, where that champion stout
After his foes defeasance did remaine,
Him goodly greetes, and faire does entertaine,
With princely gifts of yuorie and gold,
And thousand thankes him yeelds for all his paine.
Then when his daughter deare he does behold,
Her dearely doth imbrace, and kisseth manifold.

13

And after to his Pallace he them brings,
With shaumes, and trompets, and with Clarions sweet;
And all the way the ioyous people sings,
And with their garments strowes the paued street:
Whence mounting vp, they find purueyance meet
Of all, that royall Princes court became,
And all the floore was vnderneath their feet
Bespred with costly scarlot of great name,
On which they lowly sit, and fitting purpose frame.

14

What needs me tell their feast and goodly guize,
In which was nothing riotous nor vaine?
What needs of daintie dishes to deuize,
Of comely seruices, or courtly trayne?
My narrow leaues cannot in them containe
The large discourse of royall Princes state.
Yet was their manner then but bare and plaine:
For th'antique world excesse and pride did hate;
Such proud luxurious pompe is swollen vp but late.

15

Then when with meates and drinkes of euery kinde
Their feruent appetites they quenched had,
That auncient Lord gan fit occasion finde,
Of straunge aduentures, and of perils sad,
Which in his trauell him befallen had,
For to demaund of his renowmed guest:
Who then with vtt'rance graue, and count'nance sad,
From point to point, as is before exprest,
Discourst his voyage long, according his request.

16

Great pleasure mixt with pittifull regard,
That godly King and Queene did passionate,
Whiles they his pittifull aduentures heard,
That oft they did lament his lucklesse state,
And often blame the too importune fate,
That heapd on him so many wrathfull wreakes:
For neuer gentle knight, as he of late,
So tossed was in fortunes cruell freakes;
And all the while salt teares bedeawd the hearers cheaks.

17

Then said that royall Pere in sober wise;
Deare Sonne, great beene the euils, which ye bore
From first to last in your late enterprise,
That I note, whether prayse, or pitty more:
For neuer liuing man, I weene, so sore
In sea of deadly daungers was distrest;
But since now safe ye seised haue the shore,
And well arriued are, (high God be blest)
Let vs deuize of ease and euerlasting rest.

18

Ah dearest Lord, said then that doughty knight,
Of ease or rest I may not yet deuize;
For by the faith, which I to armes haue plight,
I bounden am streight after this emprize,
As that your daughter can ye well aduize,
Backe to returne to that great Faerie Queene,
And her to serue six yeares in warlike wize,
Gainst that proud Paynim king, that workes her teene:
Therefore I ought craue pardon, till I there haue beene.

19

Vnhappie falles that hard necessitie,
 (Quoth he) the troubler of my happie peace,
 And vowed foe of my felicitie ;
 Ne I against the same can iustly preace :
 But since that band ye cannot now release,
 Nor doen vndo ; (for vowes may not be vaine)
 Soone as the terme of those six yeares shall
   cease,
 Ye then shall hither backe returne againe,
The marriage to accomplish vowd betwixt you
   twain.

20

Which for my part I couet to performe,
 In sort as through the world I did proclame,
 That who so kild that monster most deforme,
 And him in hardy battaile ouercame,
 Should haue mine onely daughter to his Dame,
 And of my kingdome heire apparaunt bee :
 Therefore since now to thee perteines the same,
 By dew desert of noble cheualree,
Both daughter and eke kingdome, lo I yield to
   thee.

21

Then forth he called that his daughter faire,
 The fairest *Vn'* his onely daughter deare,
 His onely daughter, and his onely heyre ;
 Who forth proceeding with sad sober cheare,
 As bright as doth the morning starre appeare
 Out of the East, with flaming lockes bedight,
 To tell that dawning day is drawing neare,
 And to the world does bring long wished light ;
So faire and fresh that Lady shewd her selfe in
   sight.

22

So faire and fresh, as freshest flowre in May ;
 For she had layd her mournefull stole aside,
 And widow-like sad wimple throwne away,
 Wherewith her heauenly beautie she did hide,
 Whiles on her wearie iourney she did ride ;
 And on her now a garment she did weare,
 All lilly white, withoutten spot, or pride,
 That seemd like silke and siluer wouen neare,
But neither silke nor siluer therein did appeare.

23

The blazing brightnesse of her beauties beame,
 And glorious light of her sunshyny face
 To tell, were as to striue against the streame.
 My ragged rimes are all too rude and bace,
 Her heauenly lineaments for to enchace.
 Ne wonder ; for her owne deare loued knight,
 All were she dayly with himselfe in place,
 Did wonder much at her celestiall sight :
Oft had he seene her faire, but neuer so faire
   dight.

24

So fairely dight, when she in presence came,
 She to her Sire made humble reuerence,
 And bowed low, that her right well became,
 And added grace vnto her excellence :
 Who with great wisedome, and graue eloquence
 Thus gan to say. But eare he thus had said,
 With flying speede, and seeming great pretence,
 Came running in, much like a man dismaid,
A Messenger with letters, which his message said.

25

All in the open hall amazed stood,
 At suddeinnesse of that vnwarie sight,
 And wondred at his breathlesse hastie mood.
 But he for nought would stay his passage right
 Till fast before the king he did alight ;
 Where falling flat, great humblesse he did make,
 And kist the ground, whereon his foot was pight:
 Then to his hands that writ he did betake,
Which he disclosing, red thus, as the paper
   spake.

26

To thee, most mighty king of *Eden* faire,
 Her greeting sends in these sad lines addrest,
 The wofull daughter, and forsaken heire
 Of that great Emperour of all the West ;
 And bids thee be aduized for the best,
 Ere thou thy daughter linck in holy band
 Of wedlocke to that new vnknowen guest :
 For he already plighted his right hand
Vnto another loue, and to another land.

27

To me sad mayd, or rather widow sad,
 He was affiaunced long time before,
 And sacred pledges he both gaue, and had,
 False erraunt knight, infamous, and forswore :
 Witnesse the burning Altars, which he swore,
 And guiltie heauens of his bold periury,
 Which though he hath polluted oft of yore,
 Yet I to them for iudgement iust do fly,
And them coniure t'auenge this shamefull iniury.

28

Therefore since mine he is, or free or bond,
 Or false or trew, or liuing or else dead,
 Withhold, O soueraine Prince, your hasty hond
 From knitting league with him, I you aread ;
 Ne weene my right with strength adowne to
   tread,
 Through weakenesse of my widowhed, or woe :
 For truth is strong, her rightfull cause to plead,
 And shall find friends, if need requireth soe,
So bids thee well to fare, Thy neither friend,
   nor foe, *Fidessa*.

SPENSER   D

29

When he these bitter byting words had red,
  The tydings straunge did him abashed make,
  That still he sate long time astonished
  As in great muse, ne word to creature spake.
  At last his solemne silence thus he brake,
  With doubtfull eyes fast fixed on his guest ;
  Redoubted knight, that for mine onely sake
  Thy life and honour late aduenturest,
Let nought be hid from me, that ought to be
    exprest.

30

What meane these bloudy vowes, and idle threats,
  Throwne out from womanish impatient mind ?
  What heauens ? what altars ? what enraged
    heates
  Here heaped vp with termes of loue vnkind,
  My conscience cleare with guilty bands would
    bind ?
  High God be witnesse, that I guiltlesse ame.
  But if your selfe, Sir knight, ye faultie find,
  Or wrapped be in loues of former Dame,
With crime do not it couer, but disclose the
    same.

31

To whom the *Redcrosse* knight this answere sent,
  My Lord, my King, be nought hereat dismayd,
  Till well ye wote by graue intendiment,
  What woman, and wherefore doth me vpbrayd
  With breach of loue, and loyalty betrayd.
  It was in my mishaps, as hitherward
  I lately traueild, that vnwares I strayd
  Out of my way, through perils straunge and
    hard ;
That day should faile me, ere I had them all
    declard.

32

There did I find, or rather I was found
  Of this false woman, that *Fidessa* hight,
  Fidessa hight the falsest Dame on ground,
  Most false *Duessa*, royall richly dight,
  That easie was t' inuegle weaker sight :
  Who by her wicked arts, and wylie skill,
  Too false and strong for earthly skill or might,
  Vnwares me wrought vnto her wicked will,
And to my foe betrayd, when least I feared ill.

33

Then stepped forth the goodly royall Mayd,
  And on the ground her selfe prostrating low,
  With sober countenaunce thus to him sayd ;
  O pardon me, my soueraigne Lord, to show
  The secret treasons, which of late I know
  To haue bene wroght by that false sorceresse.
  She onely she it is, that earst did throw
  This gentle knight into so great distresse,
That death him did awaite in dayly wretched-
    nesse.

34

And now it seemes, that she suborned hath
  This craftie messenger with letters vaine,
  To worke new woe and improuided scath,
  By breaking of the band betwixt vs twaine ;
  Wherein she vsed hath the practicke paine
  Of this false footman, clokt with simplenesse,
  Whom if ye please for to discouer plaine,
  Ye shall him *Archimago* find, I ghesse,
The falsest man aliue ; who tries shall find no
    lesse.

35

The king was greatly moued at her speach,
  And all with suddein indignation fraight,
  Bad on that Messenger rude hands to reach.
  Eftsoones the Gard, which on his state did
    wait,
  Attacht that faitor false, and bound him strait :
  Who seeming sorely chauffed at his band,
  As chained Beare, whom cruell dogs do bait,
  With idle force did faine them to withstand,
And often semblaunce made to scape out of
    their hand.

36

But they him layd full low in dungeon deepe,
  And bound him hand and foote with yron
    chains.
  And with continuall watch did warely keepe ;
  Who then would thinke, that by his subtile
    trains
  He could escape fowle death or deadly paines ?
  Thus when that Princes wrath was pacifide,
  He gan renew the late forbidden banes,
  And to the knight his daughter deare he tyde,
With sacred rites and vowes for euer to abyde.

37

His owne two hands the holy knots did knit,
  That none but death for euer can deuide ;
  His owne two hands, for such a turne most fit,
  The housling fire did kindle and prouide,
  And holy water thereon sprinckled wide ;
  At which the bushy Teade a groome did light,
  And sacred lampe in secret chamber hide,
  Where it should not be quenched day nor
    night,
For feare of euill fates, but burnen euer bright.

38

Then gan they sprinckle all the posts with wine,
  And made great feast to solemnize that day ;
  They all perfumde with frankencense diuine,
  And precious odours fetcht from far away,
  That all the house did sweat with great aray :
  And all the while sweete Musicke did apply
  Her curious skill, the warbling notes to play,
  To driue away the dull Melancholy ;
The whiles one sung a song of loue and iollity.

39

During the which there was an heauenly noise
Heard sound through all the Pallace pleasantly,
Like as it had bene many an Angels voice,
Singing before th'eternall maiesty,
In their trinall triplicities on hye ;
Yet wist no creature, whence that heauenly sweet
Proceeded, yet each one felt se retly
Himselfe thereby reft of his sences meet,
And rauished with rare impression in his sprite.

40

Great ioy was made that day of young and old,
And solemne feast proclaimd throughout the land,
That their exceeding merth may not be told :
Suffice it heare by signes to vnderstand
The vsuall ioyes at knitting of loues band.
Thrise happy man the knight himselfe did hold,
Possessed of his Ladies hart and hand,
And euer, when his eye did her behold,
His heart did seeme to melt in pleasures manifold.

41

Her ioyous presence and sweet company
In full content he there did long enioy,
Ne wicked enuie, ne vile gealosy
His deare delights were able to annoy :
Yet swimming in that sea of blisfull ioy,
He nought forgot, how he whilome had sworne,
In case he could that monstrous beast destroy,
Vnto his Farie Queene backe to returne :
The which he shortly did, and *Vna* left to mourne.

42

Now strike your sailes ye iolly Mariners,
For we be come vnto a quiet rode,
Where we must land some of our passengers,
And light this wearie vessell of her lode.
Here she a while may make her safe abode,
Till she repaired haue her tackles spent,
And wants supplide. And then againe abroad
On the long voyage whereto she is bent :
Well may she speede and fairely finish her intent.

FINIS LIB. I.

THE SECOND
BOOKE OF THE
FAERIE QVEENE.
Contayning,
THE LEGEND OF SIR GVYON.
OR
Of Temperaunce.

1

RIGHT well I wote most mighty Soueraine,
  That all this famous antique history,
  Of some th'aboundance of an idle braine
  Will iudged be, and painted forgery,
  Rather then matter of iust memory,
  Sith none, that breatheth liuing aire, does
      know,
  Where is that happy land of Faery,
  Which I so much do vaunt, yet no where
      show,
  But vouch antiquities, which no body can
      know.

2

But let that man with better sence aduize,
  That of the world least part to vs is red :
  And dayly how through hardy enterprize,
  Many great Regions are discouered,
  Which to late age were neuer mentioned.
  Who euer heard of th'Indian *Peru* ?
  Or who in venturous vessell measured
  The *Amazons* huge riuer now found trew ?
  Or fruitfullest *Virginia* who did euer vew ?

3

Yet all these were, when no man did them know ;
  Yet haue from wisest ages hidden beene :
  And later times things more vnknowne shall
      show.
  Why then should witlesse man so much mis-
      weene
  That nothing is, but that which he hath seene ?
  What if within the Moones faire shining spheare?
  What if in euery other starre vnseene
  Of other worldes he happily should heare ?
  He wonder would much more : yet such to
      some appeare.

4

Of Faerie lond yet if he more inquire,
  By certaine signes here set in sundry place
  He may it find ; ne let him then admire,
  But yield his sence to be too blunt and bace,
  That no'te without an hound fine footing trace
  And thou, O fairest Princesse vnder sky,
  In this faire mirrhour maist behold thy face,
  And thine owne realmes in lond of Faery,
  And in this antique Image thy great auncestry

5

The which O pardon me thus to enfold
In couert vele, and wrap in shadowes light,
That feeble eyes your glory may behold,
Which else could not endure those beames
        bright,
But would be dazled with exceeding light.
O pardon, and vouchsafe with patient eare
The braue aduentures of this Faery knight
The good Sir *Guyon* gratiously to heare,
In whom great rule of Temp'raunce goodly
        doth appeare.

Cant. I.

ᴄᴠᴄᴠᴄᴠᴄᴠᴄᴠᴄᴠᴄᴠᴄᴠᴄᴠᴄᴠᴄᴠᴄᴠᴄᴠᴄᴠᴄᴠ

Guyon by Archimage abusd,
   The Redcrosse knight awaytes,
Findes Mordant and Amauia slaine
   With pleasures poisoned baytes.

ᴄᴠᴄᴠᴄᴠᴄᴠᴄᴠᴄᴠᴄᴠᴄᴠᴄᴠᴄᴠᴄᴠᴄᴠᴄᴠᴄᴠᴄᴠ

1

That cunning Architect of cancred guile,
Whom Princes late displeasure left in bands,
For falsed letters and suborned wile,
Soone as the *Redcrosse* knight he vnderstands
To beene departed out of *Eden* lands,
To serue againe his soueraine Elfin Queene,
His artes he moues, and out of caytiues hands
Himselfe he frees by secret meanes vnseene;
His shackles emptie left, him selfe escaped
        cleene.

2

And forth he fares full of malicious mind,
To worken mischiefe and auenging woe,
Where euer he that godly knight may find,
His onely hart sore, and his onely foe,
Sith *Vna* now he algates must forgoe,
Whom his victorious hands did earst restore
To natiue crowne and kingdome late ygoe:
Where she enioyes sure peace for euermore,
As weather-beaten ship arriu'd on happie shore.

3

Him therefore now the obiect of his spight
And deadly food he makes: him to offend
By forged treason, or by open fight
He seekes, of all his drift the aymed end:
Thereto his subtile engins he does bend,
His practick wit, and his faire filed tong,
With thousand other sleights: for well he
        kend,
His credit now in doubtfull ballaunce hong;
For hardly could be hurt, who was already stong.

4

Still as he went, he craftie stales did lay,
With cunning traines him to entrap vnwares,
And priuie spials plast in all his way,
To weete what course he takes, and how he fares;
To ketch him at a vantage in his snares.
But now so wise and warie was the knight
By triall of his former harmes and cares,
That he describe, and shonned still his slight:
The fish that once was caught, new bait will
        hardly bite.

5

Nath'lesse th'Enchaunter would not spare his
        paine,
In hope to win occasion to his will;
Which when he long awaited had in vaine,
He chaungd his minde from one to other ill:
For to all good he enimy was still.
Vpon the way him fortuned to meet,
Faire marching vnderneath a shady hill,
A goodly knight, all armd in harnesse meete,
That from his head no place appeared to his
        feete.

6

His carriage was full comely and vpright,
His countenaunce demure and temperate,
But yet so sterne and terrible in sight,
That cheard his friends, and did his foes amate:
He was an Elfin borne of noble state,
And mickle worship in his natiue land;
Well could he tourney and in lists debate,
And knighthood tooke of good Sir *Huons* hand,
When with king *Oberon* he came to Faerie land.

7

Him als accompanyd vpon the way
A comely Palmer, clad in blacke attire,
Of ripest yeares, and haires all hoarie gray,
That with a staffe his feeble steps did stire,
Least his long way his aged limbes should tire:
And if by lookes one may the mind aread,
He seemd to be a sage and sober sire,
And euer with slow pace the knight did lead,
Who taught his trampling steed with equall
        steps to tread.

8

Such whenas *Archimago* them did view,
He weened well to worke some vncouth wile,
Eftsoones vntwisting his deceiptfull clew,
He gan to weaue a web of wicked guile,
And with faire countenance and flattring stile,
To them approching, thus the knight bespake:
Faire sonne of *Mars*, that seeke with warlike
        spoile,
And great atchieu'ments great your selfe to
        make,
Vouchsafe to stay your steed for humble misers
        sake.

9

he stayd his steed for humble misers sake,
And bad tell on the tenor of his plaint ;
Who feigning then in euery limbe to quake,
Through inward feare, and seeming pale and
faint
With piteous mone his percing speach gan paint;
Deare Lady how shall I declare thy cace,
Whom late I left in langourous constraint ?
Would God thy selfe now present were in place,
To tell this ruefull tale ; thy sight could win
thee grace.

10

Or rather would, O would it so had chaunst,
That you, most noble Sir, had present beene,
When that lewd ribauld with vile lust aduaunst
Layd first his filthy hands on virgin cleene,
To spoile her daintie corse so faire and sheene,
As on the earth, great mother of vs all,
With liuing eye more faire was neuer seene,
Of chastitie and honour virginall :
Witnesse ye heauens, whom she in vaine to
helpe did call.

11

How may it be,(said then the knight halfe wroth,)
That knight should knighthood euer so haue
shent ?   [troth,
None but that saw (quoth he) would weene for
How shamefully that Maid he did torment.
Her looser golden lockes he rudely rent,
And drew her on the ground, and his sharpe sword
Against her snowy brest he fiercely bent,
And threatned death with many a bloudie word ;
Toung hates to tell the rest, that eye to see
abhord.

12

Therewith amoued from his sober mood,
And liues he yet (said he) that wrought this act,
And doen the heauens afford him vitall food ?
He liues, (quoth he) and boasteth of the fact,
Ne yet hath any knight his courage crackt.
Where may that treachour then (said he) be
found,
Or by what meanes may I his footing tract ?
That shall I shew (said he) as sure, as hound
The stricken Deare doth chalenge by the bleed-
ing wound.

13

He staid not lenger talke, but with fierce ire
And zealous hast away is quickly gone
To seeke that knight, where him that craftie Squire
Suppos'd to be. They do arriue anone,
Where sate a gentle Lady all alone,
With garments rent, and haire dischenueled,
Wringing her hands, and making piteous mone;
Her swollen eyes were much disfigured,
And her faire face with teares was fowly
blubbered.

14

The knight approching nigh, thus to her said,
Faire Ladie, through foule sorrow ill bedight,
Great pittie is to see you thus dismaid,
And marre the blossome of your beautie bright:
For thy appease your griefe and heauie plight,
And tell the cause of your conceiued paine.
For if he liue, that hath you doen despight,
He shall you doe due recompence againe,
Or else his wrong with greater puissance main-
taine.

15

Which when she heard, as in despightfull wise,
She wilfully her sorrow did augment,
And offred hope of comfort did despise :
Her golden lockes most cruelly she rent,
And scratcht her face with ghastly dreriment,
Ne would she speake, ne see, ne yet be seene,
But hid her visage, and her head downe bent,
Either for grieuous shame, or for great teene,
As if her hart with sorrow had transfixed beene.

16

Till her that Squire bespake, Madame my liefe,
For Gods deare loue be not so wilfull bent,
But doe vouchsafe now to receiue reliefe,
The which good fortune doth to you present.
For what bootes it to weepe and to wayment,
When ill is chaunst, but doth the ill increase,
And the weake mind with double woe torment ?
When she her Squire heard speake, she gan
appease
Her voluntarie paine, and feele some secret ease.

17

Eftsoone she said, Ah gentle trustie Squire,
What comfort can I wofull wretch conceaue,
Or why should euer I henceforth desire
To see faire heauens face, and life not leaue,
Sith that false Traytour did my honour reaue?
False traytour certes (said the Faerie knight)
I read the man, that euer would deceaue
A gentle Ladie, or her wrong through might :
Death were too little paine for such a foule
despight.

18

But now, faire Ladie, comfort to you make,
And read, who hath ye wrought this shamefull
plight ;
That short reuenge the man may ouertake,
Where so he be, and soone vpon him light.
Certes (saide she) I wote not how he hight,
But vnder him a gray steede did he wield,
Whose sides with dapled circles weren dight ;
Vpright he rode, and in his siluer shield
He bore a bloudie Crosse, that quartred all the field.

19

Now by my head (said *Guyon*) much I muse,
  How that same knight should do so foule amis,
  Or euer gentle Damzell so abuse :
  For may I boldly say, he surely is
  A right good knight, and true of word ywis :
  I present was, and can it witnesse well,
  When armes he swore, and streight did
    enterpris
Th'aduenture of the *Errant damozell*,
In which he hath great glorie wonne, as I heare
  tell.

20

Nathlesse he shortly shall againe be tryde,
  And fairely quite him of th'imputed blame,
  Else be ye sure he dearely shall abyde,
  Or make you good amendment for the same :
  All wrongs haue mends, but no amends of
    shame.
Now therefore Ladie, rise out of your paine,
  And see the saluing of your blotted name.
Fullloth she seemd thereto, but yet did faine ;
For she was inly glad her purpose so to gaine.

21

Her purpose was not such, as she did faine,
  Ne yet her person such, as it was seene,
  But vnder simple shew and semblant plaine
  Lurckt false *Duessa* secretly vnseene,
  As a chast Virgin, that had wronged beene :
  So had false *Archimago* her disguisd,
  To cloke her guile with sorrow and sad teene ;
  And eke himselfe had craftily deuisd
To be her Squire, and do her seruice well aguisd.

22

Her late forlorne and naked he had found,
  Where she did wander in waste wildernesse,
  Lurking in rockes and caues farre vnder ground,
  And with greene mosse cou'ring her nakednesse,
  To hide her shame and loathly filthinesse ;
  Sith her Prince *Arthur* of proud ornaments
  And borrow'd beautie spoyld. Her nathelesse
  Th'enchaunter finding fit for his intents,
Did thus reuest, and deckt with due habili-
  ments.

23

For all he did, was to deceiue good knights,
  And draw them from pursuit of praise and fame,
  To slug in slouth and sensuall delights,
  And end their daies with irrenowmed shame.
  And now exceeding griefe him ouercame,
  To see the *Redcrosse* thus aduaunced hye ;
  Therefore this craftie engine he did frame,
  Against his praise to stirre vp enmitye
Of such, as vertues like mote vnto him allye.

24

So now he *Guyon* guides an vncouth way
  Through woods and mountaines, till they came
  Into a pleasant dale, that lowly lay [at last
  Betwixt two hils, whose high heads ouerplast,
  The valley did with coole shade ouercast,
  Through midst thereof a little riuer rold,
  By which there sate a knight with helme vnlast,
  Himselfe refreshing with the liquid cold,
After his trauell long, and labours manifold.

25

Loe yonder he, cryde *Archimage* alowd,
  That wrought the shamefull fact, which I did shew ;
  And now he doth himselfe in secret shrowd,
  To flie the vengeance for his outrage dew ;
  But vaine : for ye shall dearely do him rew,
  So God ye speed, and send you good successe ;
  Which we farre off will here abide to vew.
  So they him left, inflam'd with wrathfulnesse,
That streight against that knight his speare he
  did addresse.

26

Who seeing him from farre so fierce to pricke,
  His warlike armes about him gan embrace,
  And in the rest his readie speare did sticke ;
  Tho when as still he saw him towards pace,
  He gan rencounter him in equall race.
  They bene ymet, both readie to affrap,
  When suddenly that warriour gan abace
  His threatned speare, as if some new mishap
Had him betidde, or hidden daunger did entrap.

27

And cryde, Mercie Sir knight, and mercie Lord,
  For mine offence and heedlesse hardiment,
  That had almost committed crime abhord,
  And with reprochfull shame mine honour shent,
  Whiles cursed steele against that badge I bent,
  The sacred badge of my Redeemers death,
  Which on your shield is set for ornament :
  But his fierce foe with steede could stay vneath,
Who prickt with courage kene, did cruell
  battell breath.

28

But when he heard him speake, streight way he
    knew
  His error, and himselfe inclyning sayd ;
  Ah deare Sir *Guyon*, well becommeth you,
  But me behoueth rather to vpbrayd,
  Whose hastie hand so farre from reason strayd,
  That almost it did haynous violence
  On that faire image of that heauenly Mayd,
  That decks and armes your shield with faire
    defence :
Your court'sie takes on you anothers due offence.

29

So bene they both attone, and doen vpreare
  Their beuers bright, each other for to greete ;
  Goodly comportance each to other beare,
  And entertaine themselues with court'sies meet.
  Then said the *Redcrosse* knight, Now mote I weet,
  Sir *Guyon*, why with so fierce saliaunce,
  And fell intent ye did at earst me meet ;
  For sith I know your goodly gouernaunce,
Great cause, I weene, you guided, or some vn-
    couth chaunce.

30

Certes (said he) well mote I shame to tell
  The fond encheason, that me hither led.
  A false infamous faitour late befell
  Me for to meet, that seemed ill bested,
  And playnd of grieuous outrage, which he red
  A knight had wrought against a Ladie gent ;
  Which to auenge, he to this place me led,
  Where you he made the marke of his intent,
And now is fled ; foule shame him follow, where
    he went.

31

So can he turne his earnest vnto game,
  Through goodly handling and wise temperance.
  By this his aged guide in presence came ;
  Who soone as on that knight his eye did glance,
  Eft soones of him had perfect cognizance,
  Sith him in Faerie court he late auizd ;
  And said, Faire sonne, God giue you happie
    chance,
  And that deare Crosse vpon your shield deuizd,
Wherewith aboue all knights ye goodly seeme
    aguizd.

32

Ioy may you haue, and euerlasting fame,
  Of late most hard atchieu'ment by you donne,
  For which enrolled is your glorious name
  In heauenly Registers aboue the Sunne,
  Where you a Saint with Saints your seat haue
    wonne :   [marke,
  But wretched we, where ye haue left your
  Must now anew begin, like race to runne ;
  God guide thee, *Guyon*, well to end thy warke,
And to the wished hauen bring thy weary barke.

33

Palmer, (him answered the *Redcrosse* knight)
  His be the praise, that this atchieu'ment wrought,
  Who made my hand the organ of his might ;
  More then goodwill to me attribute nought :
  For all I did, I did but as I ought.
  But you, faire Sir, whose pageant next ensewes,
  Well mote yee thee, as well can wish your
    thought,
  That home ye may report thrise happie newes ;
For well ye worthie bene for worth and gentle
    thewes.

34

So courteous conge both did giue and take,
  With right hands plighted, pledges of good will.
  Then *Guyon* forward gan his voyage make,
  With his blacke Palmer, that him guided still.
  Still he him guided ouer dale and hill,
  And with his steedie staffe did point his way :
  His race with reason, and with words his will,
  From foule intemperance he oft did stay,
And suffred not in wrath his hastie steps to stray.

35

In this faire wize they traueild long yfere,
  Through many hard assayes, which did betide ;
  Of which he honour still away did beare,
  And spred his glorie through all countries wide.
  At last as chaunst them by a forest side
  To passe, for succour from the scorching ray,
  They heard a ruefull voice, that dearnly cride
  With percing shriekes, and many a dolefull lay ;
Which to attend, a while their forward steps
    they stay.

36

But if that carelesse heauens (quoth she) despise
  The doome of iust reuenge, and take delight
  To see sad pageants of mens miseries,
  As bound by them to liue in liues despight,
  Yet can they not warne death from wretched
    wight.   [to mee,
  Come then, come soone, come sweetest death
  And take away this long lent loathed light :
  Sharpe be thy wounds, but sweet the medi-
    cines bee,
That long captiued soules from wearie thral-
    dome free.

37

But thou, sweet Babe, whom frowning froward fate
  Hath made sad witnesse of thy fathers fall,
  Sith heauen thee deignes to hold in liuing state,
  Long maist thou liue, and better thriue withall,
  Then to thy lucklesse parents did befall :
  Liue thou, and to thy mother dead attest,
  That cleare she dide from blemish criminall ;
  Thy litle hands embrewd in bleeding brest
Loe I for pledges leaue. So giue me leaue to rest.

38

With that a deadly shrieke she forth did throw,
  That through the wood reecchoed againe,
  And after gaue a grone so deepe and low,
  That seemd her tender heart was rent in twaine,
  Or thrild with point of thorough piercing paine ;
  As gentle Hynd, whose sides with cruell steele
  Through launched, forth her bleeding life does
    raine,
  Whiles the sad pang approching she does feele,
Brayes out her latest breath, and vp her eyes
    doth seele.

39

Which when that warriour heard, dismounting
  straict
From his tall steed, he rusht into the thicke,
And soone arriued, where that sad pourtraict
Of death and dolour lay, halfe dead, halfe quicke,
In whose white alabaster brest did sticke
A cruell knife, that made a griesly wound,
From which forth gusht a streme of gorebloud
  thick,
That all her goodly garments staind around,
And into a deepe sanguine dide the grassie
  ground.

40

Pittifull spectacle of deadly smart,
  Beside a bubbling fountaine low she lay,
Which she increased with her bleeding hart,
And the cleane waues with purple gore did ray;
Als in her lap a louely babe did play
His cruell sport, in stead of sorrow dew ;
For in her streaming blood he did embay
His litle hands, and tender ioynts embrew ;
Pitifull spectacle, as euer eye did view.

41

Besides them both, vpon the soiled gras
  The dead corse of an armed knight was spred,
Whose armour all with bloud besprinckled was;
His ruddie lips did smile, and rosy red
Did paint his chearefull cheekes, yet being ded:
Seemd to haue beene a goodly personage,
Now in his freshest flowre of lustie hed,
Fit to inflame faire Lady with loues rage,
But that fiers fate did crop the blossome of
  his age.

42

Whom when the good Sir *Guyon* did behold,
  His hart gan wexe as starke, as marble stone,
And his fresh bloud did frieze with fearefull cold,
That all his senses seemd bereft attone :
At last his mightie ghost gan deepe to grone,
As Lyon grudging in his great disdaine,
Mournes inwardly, and makes to himselfe mone,
Till ruth and fraile affection did constraine
His stout courage to stoupe, and shew his in-
  ward paine.

43

Out of her gored wound the cruell steele
  He lightly snatcht, and did the floudgate stop
With his faire garment : then gan softly feele
Her feeble pulse, to proue if any drop
Of liuing bloud yet in her veynes did hop ;
Which when he felt to moue, he hoped faire
To call backe life to her forsaken shop ;
So well he did her deadly wounds repaire,
That at the last she gan to breath out liuing aire.

44

Which he perceiuing greatly gan reioice,
  And goodly counsell, that for wounded hart
Is meetest med'cine, tempred with sweet voice
Ay me, deare Lady, which the image art
Of ruefull pitie, and impatient smart,
What direfull chance, armd with reuenging fate,
Or cursed hand hath plaid this cruell part,
Thus fowle to hasten your vntimely date ;
Speake, O deare Lady speake : help neuer comes
  too late.

45

Therewith her dim eie-lids she vp gan rearc,
  On which the drery death did sit, as sad
As lump of lead, and made darke clouds appeare;
But when as him all in bright armour clad
Before her standing she espied had,
As one out of a deadly dreame affright,
She weakely started, yet she nothing drad :
Streight downe againe her selfe in great
  despight
She groueling threw to ground, as hating life
  and light.

46

The gentle knight her soone with carefull paine
  Vplifted light, and softly did vphold :
Thrise he her reard, and thrise she sunke againe,
Till he his armes about her sides gan fold,
And to her said ; Yet if the stony cold
Haue not all seized on your frozen hart,
Let one word fall that may your griefe vnfold,
And tell the secret of your mortall smart ;
He oft finds present helpe, who does his griefe
  impart.

47

Then casting vp a deadly looke, full low
  Shee sight from bottome of her wounded brest,
And after, many bitter throbs did throw
With lips full pale and foltring tongue opprest,
These words she breathed forth from riuen
  chest ;
Leaue, ah leaue off, what euer wight thou bee,
To let a wearie wretch from her dew rest,
And trouble dying soules tranquilitee.
Take not away now got, which none would giue
  to me.

48

Ah farre be it (said he) Deare dame fro mee,
  To hinder soule from her desired rest,
Or hold sad life in long captiuitee :
For all I seeke, is but to haue redrest
The bitter pangs, that doth your heart infest.
Tell then, O Lady tell, what fatall priefe
Hath with so huge misfortune you opprest ?
That I may cast to compasse your reliefe,
Or die with you in sorrow, and partake your griefe.

49

With feeble hands then stretched forth on hye,
As heauen accusing guiltie of her death,
And with dry drops congealed in her eye,
In these sad words she spent her vtmost breath:
Heare then, O man, the sorrowes that vneath
My tongue can tell, so farre all sense they pas :
Loe this dead corpse, that lies here vnderneath,
The gentlest knight, that euer on greene gras
Gay steed with spurs did pricke, the good Sir
   Mordant was.

50

Was, (ay the while, that he is not so now)
My Lord my loue; my deare Lord, my deare loue,
So long as heauens iust with equall brow
Vouchsafed to behold vs from aboue,
One day when him high courage did emmoue,
As wont ye knights to seeke aduentures wilde,
He pricked forth, his puissant force to proue,
Me then he left enwombed of this child,
This lucklesse child, whom thus ye see with
   bloud defild.

51

Him fortuned (hard fortune ye may ghesse)
To come, where vile *Acrasia* does wonne,
Acrasia a false enchaunteresse,
That many errant knights hath foule fordonne:
Within a wandring Island, that doth ronne
And stray in perilous gulfe, her dwelling is.;
Faire Sir, if euer there ye trauell, shonne
The cursed land where many wend amis,
And know it by the name ; it hight the *Bowre*
   of blis.

52

Her blisse is all in pleasure and delight,
Wherewith she makes her louers drunken mad,
And then with words and weedes of wondrous
   might,
On them she workes her will to vses bad :
My lifest Lord she thus beguiled had ;
For he was flesh : (all flesh doth frailtie breed.)
Whom when I heard to beene so ill bestad,
Weake wretch I wrapt my selfe in Palmers weed,
And cast to seeke him forth through daunger
   and great dreed.

53

Now had faire *Cynthia* by euen tournes
Full measured three quarters of her yeare,
And thrise three times had fild her crooked
   hornes,
Whenas my wombe her burdein would forbeare,
And bad me call *Lucina* to me neare.
Lucina came : a manchild forth I brought :
The woods, the Nymphes, my bowres, my
   midwiues weare,
Hard helpe at need. So deare thee babe I bought,
Yet nought too deare I deemd, while so my dear
   I sought.

54

Him so I sought, and so at last I found,
Where him that witch had thralled to her will,
In chaines of lust and lewd desires ybound,
And so transformed from his former skill,
That me he knew not, neither his owne ill ;
Till through wise handling and faire gouernance,
I him recured to a better will,
Purged from drugs of foule intemperance :
Then meanes I gan deuise for his deliuerance.

55

Which when the vile Enchaunteresse perceiu'd,
How that my Lord from her I would repriue,
With cup thus charmd, him parting she deceiu'd;
Sad verse, giue death to him that death does giue,
And losse of loue, to her that loues to liue,
So soone as Bacchus with the Nymphe does lincke :
So parted we and on our iourney driue,
Till comming to this well, he stoupt to drincke:
The charme fulfild, dead suddenly he downe did
   sincke.

56

Which when I wretch, Not one word more she sayd
But breaking off the end for want of breath,
And slyding soft, as downe to sleepe her layd,
And ended all her woe in quiet death.
That seeing good Sir *Guyon*, could vneath
From teares abstaine, for griefe his hart did
   grate,
And from so heauie sight his head did wreath,
Accusing fortune, and too cruell fate,
Which plunged had faire Ladie in so wretched
   state.

57

Then turning to his Palmer said, Old syre
Behold the image of mortalitie,
And feeble nature cloth'd with fleshly tyre,
When raging passion with fierce tyrannie
Robs reason of her due regalitie,
And makes it seruant to her basest part :
The strong it weakens with infirmitie,
And with bold furie armes the weakest hart ;
The strong through pleasure soonest falles, the
   weake through smart.

58

But temperance (said he) with golden squire
Betwixt them both can measure out a meane,
Neither to melt in pleasures whot desire,
Nor fry in hartlesse griefe and dolefull teene.
Thrise happie man, who fares them both
   atweene :
But sith this wretched woman ouercome
Of anguish, rather then of crime hath beene,
Reserue her cause to her eternall doome,
And in the meane vouchsafe her honorable
   toombe.

59

Palmer (quoth he) death is an equall doome
  To good and bad, the common Inne of rest ;
  But after death the tryall is to come,
  When best shall be to them, that liued best :
  But both alike, when death hath both supprest,
  Religious reuerence doth buriall teene,
  Which who so wants, wants so much of his rest :
  For all so great shame after death I weene,
As selfe to dyen bad, vnburied bad to beene.

60

So both agree their bodies to engraue ;
  The great earthes wombe they open to the sky,
  And with sad Cypresse seemely it embraue,
  Then couering with a clod their closed eye,
  They lay therein those corses tenderly,
  And bid them sleepe in euerlasting peace.
  But ere they did their vtmost obsequy,
  Sir *Guyon* more affection to increace,
Bynempt a sacred vow, which none should aye
    releace.

61

The dead knights sword out of his sheath he drew,
  With which he cut a locke of all their heare,
  Which medling with their bloud and earth, he
    threw
  Into the graue, and gan deuoutly sweare ;
  Such and such euill God on *Guyon* reare,
  And worse and worse young Orphane be thy paine,
  If I or thou dew vengeance doe forbeare,
  Till guiltie bloud her guerdon doe obtaine :
So shedding many teares, they closd the earth
    againe.

Cant. II.

Babes bloudie hands may not be clensd :
  the face of golden Meane.
Her sisters two Extremities
  striue her to banish cleane.

1

Thus when Sir *Guyon* with his faithfull guide
Had with due rites and dolorous lament
The end of their sad Tragedie vptyde,
The litle babe vp in his armes he hent ;
Who with sweet pleasance and bold blandish-
    ment
Gan smyle on them, that rather ought to weepe,
As carelesse of his woe, or innocent
Of that was doen, that ruth emperced deepe
In that knights heart, and wordes with bitter
    teares did steepe.

2

Ah lucklesse babe, borne vnder cruell starre,
  And in dead parents balefull ashes bred,
  Full litle weenest thou, what sorrowes are
  Left thee for portion of thy liuelihed,
  Poore Orphane in the wide world scattered,
  As budding braunch rent from the natiue tree,
  And throwen forth, till it be withered :
  Such is the state of men : thus enter wee
Into this life with woe, and end with miseree.

3

Then soft himselfe inclyning on his knee
  Downe to that well, did in the water weene
  (So loue does loath disdainfull nicitee)
  His guiltie hands from bloudie gore to cleene.
  He washt them oft and oft, yet nought they beene
  For all his washing cleaner. Still he stroue,
  Yet still the litle hands were bloudie seene ;
  The which him into great amaz'ment droue,
And into diuerse doubt his wauering wonder
    cloue.

4

He wist not whether blot of foule offence
  Might not be purgd with water nor with bath ;
  Or that high God, in lieu of innocence,
  Imprinted had that token of his wrath,
  To shew how sore bloudguiltinesse he hat'th ;
  Or that the charme and venim, which they
    druncke,
  Their bloud with secret filth infected hath,
  Being diffused through the senselesse truncke,
That through the great contagion direfull
    deadly stunck,

5

Whom thus at gaze, the Palmer gan to bord
  With goodly reason, and thus faire bespake ;
  Ye bene right hard amated, gratious Lord,
  And of your ignorance great maruell make,
  Whiles cause not well conceiued ye mistake.
  But know, that secret vertues are infusd
  In euery fountaine, and in euery lake,
  Which who hath skill them rightly to haue
    chusd,
To proofe of passing wonders hath full often vsd.

6

Of those some were so from their sourse indewd
  By great Dame Nature, from whose fruitfull pap
  Their welheads spring, and are with moisture
    deawd ;
  Which feedes each liuing plant with liquid sap,
  And filles with flowres faire *Floraes* painted lap :
  But other some by gift of later grace,
  Or by good prayers, or by other hap,
  Had vertue pourd into their waters bace,
And thenceforth were renowmd, and sought
    from place to place.

7

Such is this well, wrought by occasion straunge,
Which to her Nymph befell. Vpon a day,
As she the woods with bow and shafts did raunge,
The hartlesse Hind and Robucke to dismay,
Dan Faunus chaunst to meet her by the way,
And kindling fire at her faire burning eye,
Inflamed was to follow beauties chace,
And chaced her, that fast from him did fly ;
As Hind from her, so she fled from her enimy.

8

At last when fayling breath began to faint,
And saw no meanes to scape, of shame affrayd,
She set her downe to weepe for sore constraint,
And to *Diana* calling lowd for ayde,
Her deare besought, to let her dye a mayd.
The goddesse heard, and suddeine where she sate,
Welling out streames of teares, and quite
dismayd
With stony feare of that rude rustick mate,
Transformd her to a stone from stedfast virgins
state.

9

Lo now she is that stone, from whose two heads,
As from two weeping eyes, fresh streames do
flow,
Yet cold through feare, and old conceiued dreads ;
And yet the stone her semblance seemes to show,
Shapt like a maid, that such ye may her know ;
And yet her vertues in her water byde :
For it is chast and pure, as purest snow,
Ne lets her waues with any filth be dyde,
But euer like her selfe vnstained hath beene
tryde.

10

From thence it comes, that this babes bloudy
hand
May not be clensd with water of this well :
Ne certes Sir striue you it to withstand,
But let them still be bloudy, as befell,
That they his mothers innocence may tell,
As she bequeathd in her last testament ;
That as a sacred Symbole it may dwell
In her sonnes flesh, to minde reuengement,
And be for all chast Dames an endlesse moni-
ment.

11

He hearkned to his reason, and the childe
Vptaking, to the Palmer gaue to beare ;
But his sad fathers armes with bloud defilde,
An heauie load himselfe did lightly reare,
And turning to that place, in which whyleare
He left his loftie steed with golden sell,
And goodly gorgeous barbes, him found not
theare.
By other accident that earst befell,
He is conuaide, but how or where, here fits not tell.

12

Which when Sir *Guyon* saw, all were he wroth,
Yet algates mote he soft himselfe appease,
And fairely fare on foot, how euer loth ;
His double burden did him sore disease.
So long they traueiled with litle ease,
Till that at last they to a Castle came,
Built on a rocke adioyning to the seas ;
It was an auncient worke of antique fame,
And wondrous strong by nature, and by skilfull
frame.

13

Therein three sisters dwelt of sundry sort,
The children of one sire by mothers three ;
Who dying whylome did diuide this fort
To them by equall shares in equall fee :
But strifull minde, and diuerse qualitee
Drew them in parts, and each made others foe :
Still did they striue, and dayly disagree ;
The eldest did against the youngest goe,
And both against the middest meant to worken
woe.

14

Where when the knight arriu'd, he was right
well
Receiu'd, as knight of so much worth became,
Of second sister, who did far excell
The other two ; *Medina* was her name,
A sober sad, and comely curteous Dame ;
Who rich arayd, and yet in modest guize,
In goodly garments, that her well became,
Faire marching forth in honorable wize,
Him at the threshold met, and well did enter-
prize.

15

She led him vp into a goodly bowre,
And comely courted with meet modestie,
Ne in her speach, ne in her hauiour,
Was lightnesse seene, or looser vanitie,
But gratious womanhood, and grauitie,
Aboue the reason of her youthly yeares :
Her golden lockes she roundly did vptye
In breaded tramels, that no looser heares
Did out of order stray about her daintie eares.

16

Whilest she her selfe thus busily did frame,
Seemely to entertaine her new-come guest,
Newes hereof to her other sisters came,
Who all this while were at their wanton rest,
Accourting each her friend with lauish fest :
They were two knights of perelesse puissance,
And famous far abroad for warlike gest,
Which to these Ladies loue did countenaunce,
And to his mistresse each himselfe stroue to
aduaunce.

17

He that made loue vnto the eldest Dame,
  Was hight Sir *Huddibras*, an hardy man ;
  Yet not so good of deedes, as great of name,
  Which he by many rash aduentures wan,
  Since errant armes to sew he first began ;
  More huge in strength, then wise in workes he
    was,
  And reason with foole-hardize ouer ran ;
  Sterne melancholy did his courage pas,
And was for terrour more, all armd in shyning
    bras.

18

But he that lou'd the youngest, was *Sans-loy*,
  He that faire *Vna* late fowle outraged,
  The most vnruly, and the boldest boy,
  That euer warlike weapons menaged,
  And to all lawlesse lust encouraged,
  Through strong opinion of his matchlesse might:
  Ne ought he car'd, whom he endamaged
  By tortious wrong, or whom bereau'd of right.
He now this Ladies champion chose for loue to
    fight.

19

These two gay knights, vowd to so diuerse loues,
  Each other does enuie with deadly hate,
  And dayly warre against his foeman moues,
  In hope to win more fauour with his mate,
  And th'others pleasing seruice to abate,
  To magnifie his owne. But when they heard,
  How in that place straunge knight arriued late,
  Both knights and Ladies forth right angry far'd,
And fiercely vnto battell sterne themselues
    prepar'd.

20

But ere they could proceede vnto the place,
  Where he abode, themselues at discord fell,
  And cruell combat ioynd in middle space :
  With horrible assault, and furie fell,
  They heapt huge strokes, the scorned life to quell,
  That all on vprore from her settled seat
  The house was raysd, and all that in did dwell ;
  Seemd that lowde thunder with amazement
    great
Did rend the ratling skyes with flames of foul-
    dring heat.

21

The noyse thereof cald forth that straunger knight,
  To weet, what dreadfull thing was there in
    hand ;   [fight
  Where when as two braue knights in bloudy
  With deadly rancour he enraunged fond,
  His sunbroad shield about his wrest he bond,
  And shyning blade vnsheathd, with which he
    ran
  Vnto that stead, their strife to vnderstond ;
  And at his first arriuall, them began
With goodly meanes to pacifie, well as he can.

22

But they him spying, both with greedy forse
  Attonce vpon him ran, and him beset
  With strokes of mortall steele without remorse,
  And on his shield like yron sledges bet :
  As when a Beare and Tygre being met
  In cruell fight on lybicke Ocean wide,
  Espye a traueiler with feet surbet,
  Whom they in equall pray hope to deuide,
They stint their strife, and him assaile on euery
    side.

23

But he, not like a wearie traueilere,
  Their sharpe assault right boldly did rebut,
  And suffred not their blowes to byte him nere,
  But with redoubled buffes them backe did put :
  Whose grieued mindes, which choler did englut,
  Against themselues turning their wrathfull
    spight,
  Gan with new rage their shields to hew and cut ;
  But still when *Guyon* came to part their fight,
With heauie load on him they freshly gan to
    smight.

24

As a tall ship tossed in troublous seas,
  Whom raging windes threatning to make the pray
  Of the rough rockes, do diuersly disease,
  Meetes two contrary billowes by the way,
  That her on either side do sore assay,
  And boast to swallow her in greedy graue ;
  She scorning both their spights, does make
    wide way,
  And with her brest breaking the fomy waue,
Does ride on both their backs, and faire her
    selfe doth saue.

25

So boldly he him beares, and rusheth forth
  Betweene them both, by conduct of his blade.
  Wondrous great prowesse and heroick worth
  He shewd that day, and rare ensample made,
  When two so mighty warriours he dismade :
  Attonce he wards and strikes, he takes and
    payes,
  Now forst to yield, now forcing to inuade,
  Before, behind, and round about him layes.
So double was his paines, so double be his prayse.

26

Straunge sort of fight, three valiaunt knights to
    see
  Three combats ioyne in one, and to darraine
  A triple warre with triple enmitee,
  All for their Ladies froward loue to gaine,
  Which gotten was but hate. So loue does raine
  In stoutest minds, and maketh monstrous warre ;
  He maketh warre, he maketh peace againe,
  And yet his peace is but continuall iarre :
O miserable men, that to him subiect arre.

27

Whilst thus they mingled were in furious armes,
The faire *Medina* with her tresses torne,
And naked brest, in pitty of their harmes,
Emongst them ran, and falling them beforne,
Besought them by the womb, which them had
borne, [deare,
And by the loues, which were to them most
And by the knighthood, which they sure had
sworne,
Their deadly cruell discord to forbeare,
And to her iust conditions of faire peace to
heare.

28

But her two other sisters standing by,
Her lowd gainsaid, and both their champions
bad
Pursew the end of their strong enmity,
As euer of their loues they would be glad.
Yet she with pitthy words and counsell sad,
Still stroue their stubborne rages to reuoke,
That at the last suppressing fury mad,
They gan abstaine from dint of direfull stroke,
And hearken to the sober speaches, which she
spoke.

29

Ah puissaunt Lords, what cursed euill Spright,
Or fell *Erinnys*, in your noble harts
Her hellish brond hath kindled with despight,
And stird you vp to worke your wilfull smarts?
Is this the ioy of armes? be these the parts
Of glorious knighthood, after bloud to thrust,
And not regard dew right and iust desarts?
Vaine is the vaunt, and victory vniust,
That more to mighty hands, then rightfull cause
doth trust.

30

And were there rightfull cause of difference,
Yet were not better, faire it to accord,
Then with bloud guiltinesse to heape offence,
And mortall vengeaunce ioyne to crime abhord?
O fly from wrath, fly, O my liefest Lord :
Sad be the sights, and bitter fruits of warre,
And thousand furies wait on wrathfull sword ;
Ne ought the prayse of prowesse more doth marre,
Then fowle reuenging rage, and base conten-
tious iarre.

31

But louely concord, and most sacred peace
Doth nourish vertue, and fast friendship breeds;
Weake she makes strong, and strong thing does
increace,
Till it the pitch of highest prayse exceeds :
Braue be her warres, and honorable deeds,
By which she triumphes ouer ire and pride,
And winnes an Oliue girlond for her meeds :
Be therefore, O my deare Lords, pacifide,
And this misseeming discord meekely lay aside.

32

Her gracious wordes their rancour did appall,
And suncke so deepe into their boyling brests,
That downe they let their cruell weapons fall,
And lowly did abase their loftie crests
To her faire presence, and discrete behests.
Then she began a treatie to procure,
And stablish termes betwixt **doth** their requests,
That as a law for euer should endure ;
Which to obserue in word of knights they did
assure.

33

Which to confirme, and fast to bind their league,
After their wearie sweat and bloudy toile,
She them besought, during their quiet treague,
Into her lodging to repaire a while,
To rest themselues, and grace to reconcile.
They soone consent : so forth with her they
fare, [spoile
Where they are well receiu'd, and made to
Themselues of soiled armes, and to prepare
Their minds to pleasure, and their mouthes to
dainty fare.

34

And those two froward sisters, their faire loues
Came with them eke, all were they wondrous
loth,
And fained cheare, as for the time behoues,
But could not colour yet so well the troth,
But that their natures bad appeard in both :
For both did at their second sister grutch,
And inly grieue, as doth an hidden moth
The inner garment fret, not th'vtter touch ;
One thought their cheare too litle, th'other
thought too mutch.

35

Elissa (so the eldest hight) did deeme
Such entertainment base, ne ought would eat,
Ne ought would speake, but euermore did seeme
As discontent for want of merth or meat ;
No solace could her Paramour intreat
Her once to show, ne court, nor dalliance,
But with bent lowring browes, as she would
threat, [naunce,
She scould, and frownd with froward counte-
Vnworthy of faire Ladies comely gouernaunce.

36

But young *Perissa* was of other mind,
Full of disport, still laughing, loosely light,
And quite contrary to her sisters kind ;
No measure in her mood, no rule of right,
But poured out in pleasure and delight ;
In wine and meats she flowd aboue the bancke,
And in excesse exceeded her owne might ;
In sumptuous tire she ioyd her selfe to prancke,
But of her loue too lauish (litle haue she thancke.)

37

Fast by her side did sit the bold *Sans-loy*,
  Fit mate for such a mincing mineon,
  Who in her loosenesse tooke exceeding ioy ;
  Might not be found a franker franion,
  Of her lewd parts to make companion ;
But *Huddibras*, more like a Malecontent,
  Did see and grieue at his bold fashion ;
  Hardly could he endure his hardiment,
Yet still he sat, and inly did him selfe torment.

38

Betwixt them both the faire *Medina* sate
  With sober grace, and goodly carriage :
  With equall measure she did moderate
  The strong extremities of their outrage ;
  That forward paire she euer would asswage,
When they would striue dew reason to exceed ;
  But that same froward twaine would accourage,
  And of her plenty adde vnto their need :
So kept she them in order, and her selfe in heed.

39

Thus fairely she attempered her feast,
  And pleasd them all with meete satietie,
  At last when lust of meat and drinke was ceast,
  She *Guyon* deare besought of curtesie,
  To tell from whence he came through ieopardie,
And whither now on new aduenture bound.
  Who with bold grace, and comely grauitie,
  Drawing to him the eyes of all around,
From lofty siege began these words aloud to
    sound.

40

This thy demaund, O Lady, doth reuiue
  Fresh memory in me of that great Queene,
  Great and most glorious virgin Queene aliue,
  That with her soueraigne powre, and scepter
    shene
  All Faery lond does peaceably sustene.
In widest Ocean she her throne does reare,
  That ouer all the earth it may be seene ;
  As morning Sunne her beames dispredden
    cleare,
And in her face faire peace, and mercy doth
    appeare.

41

In her the richesse of all heauenly grace
  In chiefe degree are heaped vp on hye :
  And all that else this worlds enclosure bace
  Hath great or glorious in mortall eye,
  Adornes the person of her Maiestie ;
That men beholding so great excellence,
  And rare perfection in mortalitie,
  Do her adore with sacred reuerence,
As th'Idole of her makers great magnificence.

42

To her I homage and my seruice owe,
  In number of the noblest knights on ground,
  Mongst whom on me she deigned to bestowe
  Order of *Maydenhead*, the most renownd,
  That may this day in all the world be found :
An yearely solemne feast she wontes to make
  The day that first doth lead the yeare around :
  To which all knights of worth and courage bold
Resort, to heare of straunge aduentures to be
    told.

43

There this old Palmer shewed himselfe that day,
  And to that mighty Princesse did complaine
  Of grieuous mischiefes, which a wicked Fay
  Had wrought, and many whelmd in deadly
    paine,
  Whereof he crau'd redresse. My Soueraine,
Whose glory is in gracious deeds, and ioyes
  Throughout the world her mercy to maintaine,
  Eftsoones deuisd redresse for such annoyes ;
Me all vnfit for so great purpose she employes

44

Now hath faire *Phœbe* with her siluer face
  Thrise seene the shadowes of the neather world
  Sith last I left that honorable place,
  In which her royall presence is †introld ;
  Ne euer shall I rest in house nor hold,
Till I that false *Acrasia* haue wonne ;
  Of whose fowle deedes, too hideous to be told
  I witnesse am, and this their wretched sonne,
Whose wofull parents she hath wickedly for-
    donne.

45

Tell on, faire Sir, said she, that dolefull tale,
  From which sad ruth does seeme you to re-
    straine,
  That we may pitty such vnhappy bale,
  And learne from pleasures poyson to abstaine :
  Ill by ensample good doth often gayne.
Then forward he his purpose gan pursew,
  And told the storie of the mortall payne,
  Which *Mordant* and *Amauia* did rew ;
As with lamenting eyes him selfe did lately vew

46

Night was far spent, and now in *Ocean* deepe
  Orion, flying fast from hissing snake,
  His flaming head did hasten for to steepe,
  When of his pitteous tale he end did make ;
  Whilest with delight of that he wisely spake,
Those guestes beguiled, did beguile their eye
  Of kindly sleepe, that did them ouertake.
  At last when they had markt the chaunged
    skyes,   [rest him hyes
They wist their houre was spent ; then each to

Cant. III.

೧ಿೀ೧ಿಾ೧ಿೀ೧ಿೀ೧ಿೀ೧ಿೀ೧ಿೀ೧ಿೀ೧ಿೀ

*Vaine Braggadocchio getting Guyons
horse is made the scorne
Of knighthood trew, and is of fayre
Belphœbe fowle forlorne.*

೧ಿೀ೧ಿಾ೧ಿೀ೧ಿೀ೧ಿೀ೧ಿೀ೧ಿೀ೧ಿೀ೧ಿೀ

1

Soone as the morrow faire with purple beames
Disperst the shadowes of the mistie night,
And *Titan* playing on the eastern streames,
Gan cleare the deawy ayre with springing light,
Sir *Guyon* mindfull of his vow yplight,
Vprose from drowsie couch, and him addrest
Vnto the iourney which he had behight :
His puissaunt armes about his noble brest,
And many-folded shield he bound about his
    wrest.

2

Then taking *Congé* of that virgin pure,
The bloudy-handed babe vnto her truth
Did earnestly commit, and her coniure,
In vertuous lore to traine his tender youth,
And all that gentle noriture ensu'th :
And that so soone as ryper yeares he raught,
He might for memorie of that dayes ruth,
Be called *Ruddymane,* and thereby taught,
T'auenge his Parents death on them, that had
    it wrought.

3

So forth he far'd, as now befell, on foot,
Sith his good steed is lately from him gone ;
Patience perforce ; helpelesse what may it boot
To fret for anger, or for griefe to mone ?
His Palmer now shall foot no more alone :
So fortune wrought, as vnder greene woods syde
He lately heard that dying Lady grone,
He left his steed without, and speare besyde,
And rushed in on foot to ayd her, ere she dyde.

4

The whiles a losell wandring by the way,
One that to bountie neuer cast his mind,
Ne thought of honour euer did assay
His baser brest, but in his kestrell kind
A pleasing vaine of glory vaine did find,
To which his flowing toung, and troublous
    spright
Gaue him great ayd, and made him more
    inclind :
He that braue steed there finding ready dight,
Purloynd both steed and speare, and ran away
    full light.

5

Now gan his hart all swell in iollitie,
And of him selfe great hope and helpe con-
    ceiu'd,
That puffed vp with smoke of vanitie,
And with selfe-loued personage deceiu'd,
He gan to hope, of men to be receiu'd
For such, as he him thought, or faine would
    bee :
But for in court gay portaunce he perceiu'd,
And gallant shew to be in greatest gree,
Eftsoones to court he cast t'auaunce his first
    degree.

6

And by the way he chaunced to espy
One sitting idle on a sunny bancke,
To whom auaunting in great brauery,
As Peacocke, that his painted plumes doth
    prancke,
He smote his courser in the trembling flancke,
And to him threatned his hart-thrilling speare:
The seely man seeing him ryde so rancke,
And ayme at him, fell flat to ground for feare,
And crying Mercy lowd, his pitious hands gan
    reare.

7

Thereat the Scarcrow wexed wondrous prowd,
Through fortune of his first aduenture faire,
And with big thundring voyce reuyld him lowd;
Vile Caytiue, vassall of dread and despaire,
Vnworthie of the commune breathed aire,
Why liuest thou, dead dog, a lenger day,
And doest not vnto death thy selfe prepaire,
Dye, or thy selfe my captiue yield for ay ;
Great fauour I thee graunt, for aunswere thus
    to stay.

8

Hold, O deare Lord, hold your dead-doing hand,
Then loud he cryde, I am your humble thrall,
Ah wretch (quoth he) thy destinies withstand
My wrathfull will, and do for mercy call.
I giue thee life : therefore prostrated fall,
And kisse my stirrup ; that thy homage bee.
The Miser threw him selfe, as an Offall,
Streight at his foot in base humilitee,
And cleeped him his liege, to hold of him in fee.

9

So happy peace they made and faire accord :
Eftsoones this liege-man gan to wexe more bold,
And when he felt the folly of his Lord,
In his owne kind he gan him selfe vnfold :
For he was wylie witted, and growne old
In cunning sleights and practick knauery,
From that day forth he cast for to vphold
His idle humour with fine flattery,
And blow the bellowes to his swelling vanity.

10

Trompart fit man for *Braggadocchio*,
  To serue at court in view of vaunting eye ;
  Vaine-glorious man, when fluttring wind does
    blow
  In his light wings, is lifted vp to skye :
  The scorne of knighthood and trew cheualrye,
  To thinke without desert of gentle deed,
  And noble worth to be aduaunced hye :
  Such prayse is shame; but honour vertues meed
Doth beare the fairest flowre in honorable seed.

11

So forth they pas, a well consorted paire,
  Till that at length with *Archimage* they meet :
  Who seeing one that shone in armour faire,
  On goodly courser thundring with his feet,
  Eftsoones supposed him a person meet,
  Of his reuenge to make the instrument :
  For since the *Redcrosse* knight he earst did weet,
  To beene with *Guyon* knit in one consent,
The ill, which earst to him, he now to *Guyon* ment.

12

And comming close to *Trompart* gan inquere
  Of him, what mighty warriour that mote bee,
  That rode in golden sell with single spere,
  But wanted sword to wreake his enmitee.
  He is a great aduenturer, (said he)
  That hath his sword through hard assay forgone,
  And now hath vowd, till he auenged bee,
  Of that despight, neuer to wearen none ;
That speare is him enough to doen a thousand
    grone.

13

Th'enchaunter greatly ioyed in the vaunt,
  And weened well ere long his will to win,
  And both his foen with equall foyle to daunt.
  Tho to him louting lowly, did begin
  To plaine of wrongs, which had committed bin
  By *Guyon*, and by that false *Redcrosse* knight,
  Which two through treason and deceiptfull gin,
  Had slaine Sir *Mordant*, and his Lady bright :
That mote him honour win, to wreake so foule
    despight.

14

Therewith all suddeinly he seemd enraged,
  And threatned death with dreadfull counte-
    naunce,
  As if their liues had in his hand beene gaged ;
  And with stiffe force shaking his mortall launce,
  To let him weet his doughtie valiaunce,
  Thus said ; Old man, great sure shalbe thy
    meed,   [gcaunce
  If where those knights for feare of dew ven-
  Do lurke, thou certainly to me areed,
That I may wreake on them their hainous hate-
full deed.

15

Certes, my Lord, (said he) that shall I soone,
  And giue you eke good helpe to their decay,
  But mo:e I wisely you aduise to doon ;
  Giue no ods to your foes, but do puruay
  Your selfe of sword before that bloudy day :
  For they be two the prowest knights on ground,
  And oft approu'd in many hard assay,
  And eke of surest steele, that may be found,
Do arme your selfe against that day, them to
    confound.

16

Dotard (said he) let be thy deepe aduise ;
  Seemes that through many yeares thy wits
    thee faile,
  And that weake eld hath left thee nothing wise,
  Else neuer should thy iudgement be so fraile,
  To measure manhood by the sword or maile.
  Is not enough foure quarters of a man,
  Withouten sword or shield, an host to quaile ?
  Thou little wotest, what this right hand can :
Speake they, which haue beheld the battailes,
    which it wan.

17

The man was much abashed at his boast ;
  Yet well he wist, that who so would contend
  With either of those knights on euen coast,
  Should need of all his armes, him to defend ;
  Yet feared least his boldnesse should offend,
  When *Braggadocchio* said, Once I did sweare,
  When with one sword seuen knights I brought
    to end,
  Thence forth in battell neuer sword to beare,
But it were that, which noblest knight on earth
    doth weare.

18

Perdie Sir knight, said then th'enchaunter bliue,
  That shall I shortly purchase to your hond :
  For now the best and noblest knight aliue
  Prince *Arthur* is, that wonnes in Faerie lond :
  He hath a sword, that flames like burning brond,
  The same by my deuice I vndertake
  Shall by to morrow by thy side be fond.
  At which bold word that boaster gan to quake,
And wondred in his mind, what mote that
    monster make.

19

He stayd not for more bidding, but away
  Was suddein vanished out of his sight :
  The Northerne wind his wings did broad dis-
    play
  At his commaund, and reared him vp light
  From off the earth to take his aerie flight.
  They lookt about, but no where could espie
  Tract of his foot : then dead through great
    affright
They both nigh were, and each bad other flie :
Both fled attonce, ne euer backe returned eie.

20

Till that they come vnto a forrest greene,
In which they shrowd themselues from cause-
lesse feare ;   [beeｉe,
Yet feare them followes still, where so they
Each trembling leafe, and whistling wind they
heare,
As ghastly bug their haire on end does reare :
Yet both doe striue their fearfulnesse to faine.
At last they heard a horne, that shrilled cleare
Throughout the wood, that ecchoed againe,
And made the forrest ring, as it would riue in
twaine.

21

Eft through the thicke they heard one rudely rush;
With noyse whereof he from his loftie steed
Downe fell to ground, and crept into a bush,
To hide his coward head from dying dreed.
But *Trompart* stoutly stayd to taken heed
Of what might hap. Eftsoone there stepped forth
A goodly Ladie clad in hunters weed,
That seemd to be a woman of great worth,
And by her stately portance, borne of heauenly
birth.

22

Her face so faire as flesh it seemed not,
But heauenly pourtraict of bright Angels hew,
Cleare as the skie, withouten blame or blot,
Through goodly mixture of complexions dew ;
And in her cheekes the vermeill red did shew
Like roses in a bed of lillies shed,
The which ambrosiall odours from them threw,
And gazers sense with double pleasure fed,
Hable to heale the sicke, and to reuiue the ded.

23

In her faire eyes two liuing lamps did flame,
Kindled aboue at th'heauenly makers light,
And darted fyrie beames out of the same,
So passing persant, and so wondrous bright,
That quite bereau'd the rash beholders sight :
In them the blinded god his lustfull fire
To kindle oft assayd, but had no might ;
For with dredd Maiestie, and awfull ire,
She broke his wanton darts, and quenched base
desire.

24

Her iuorie forhead, full of bountie braue,
Like a broad table did it selfe dispred,
For Loue his loftie triumphes to engraue,
And write the battels of his great godhed :
All good and honour might therein be red :
For there their dwelling was.   And when she
spake,
Sweet words, like dropping honny she did shed,
And twixt the perles and rubins softly brake
A siluer sound, that heauenly musicke seemd to
make.

25

Vpon her eyelids many Graces sate,
Vnder the shadow of her euen browes,
Working belgards, and amorous retrate,
And euery one her with a grace endowes :
And euery one with meekenesse to her bowes.
So glorious mirrhour of celestiall grace,
And soueraine moniment of mortall vowes,
How shall fraile pen descriue her heauenly face,
For feare through want of skill her beautie to
disgrace ?

26

So faire, and thousand thousand times more faire
She seemd, when she presented was to sight,
And was yclad, for heat of scorching aire,
All in a silken Camus lylly whight,
Purfled vpon with many a folded plight,
Which all aboue besprinckled was throughout
With golden aygulets, that glistred bright,
Like twinckling starres, and all the skirt about
Was hemd with golden fringe.

27

Below her ham her weed did somewhat traine,
And her streight legs most brauely were embayld
In gilden buskins of costly Cordwaine,
All bard with golden bendes, which were entayld
With curious antickes, and full faire aumayld :
Before they fastned were vnder her knee
In a rich Iewell, and therein entrayld
The ends of all their knots, that none might see,
How they within their fouldings close enwrapped
bee.

28

Like two faire marble pillours they were seene,
Which doe the temple of the Gods support,
Whom all the people decke with girlands greene,
And honour in their festiuall resort ;
Those same with stately grace, and princely port
She taught to tread, when she her selfe would
grace,
But with the wooddie Nymphes when she did
play,
Or when the flying Libbard she did chace,
She could them nimbly moue, and after fly
apace.

29

And in her hand a sharpe bore-speare she held,
And at her backe a bow and quiuer gay,
Stuft with steele-headed darts, wherewith she
queld
The saluage beastes in her victorious play,
Knit with a golden bauldricke, which forelay
Athwart her snowy brest, and did diuide
Her daintie paps ; which like young fruit in
May
Now little gan to swell, and being tide,
Through her thin weed their places only signifide.

30

Her yellow lockes crisped, like golden wyre,
 About her shoulders weren loosely shed,
 And when the winde emongst them did inspyre,
 They waued like a penon wide dispred,
 And low behinde her backe were scattered :
 And whether art it were, or heedlesse hap,
 As through the flouring forrest rash she fled,
 In her rude haires sweet flowres themselues did lap,
And flourishing fresh leaues and blossomes did enwrap.

31

Such as *Diana* by the sandie shore
 Of swift *Eurotas*, or on *Cynthus* greene,
 Where allth Nymphes haue her vnwares forlore,
 Wandreth alone with bow and arrowes keene,
 To seeke her game : Or as that famous Queene
 Of *Amazons*, whom *Pyrrhus* did destroy,
 The day that first of *Priame* she was seene,
 Did shew her selfe in great triumphant ioy,
To succour the weake state of sad afflicted *Troy*.

32

Such when as hartlesse *Trompart* did her vew,
 He was dismayed in his coward mind,
 And doubted, whether he himselfe should shew,
 Or fly away, or bide alone behind :
 Both feare and hope he in her face did find,
 When she at last him spying thus bespake ;
 Hayle Groome ; didst not thou see a bleeding Hind, [strake?
 Whose right haunch earst my stedfast arrow
If thou didst, tell me, that I may her ouertake.

33

Wherewith reviu'd, this answere forth he threw ;
 O Goddesse, (for such I thee take to bee)
 For neither doth thy face terrestriall shew,
 Nor voyce sound mortall ; I auow to thee,
 Such wounded beast, as that, I did not see,
 Sith earst into this forrest wild I came.
 But mote thy goodlyhed forgiue it mee,
 To weet, which of the Gods I shall thee name,
That vnto thee due worship I may rightly frame.

34

To whom she thus ; but ere her words ensewed,
 Vnto the bush her eye did suddein glaunce,
 In which vaine *Braggadocchio* was mewed,
 And saw it stirre : she left her percing launce,
 And towards gan a deadly shaft aduaunce,
 In mind to ma k the beast. At which sad stowre,
 Trompart forth stept, to stay the mortall chaunce,
 Out crying, O what euer heauenly powre,
Or earthly wight thou be, withhold this deadly howre.

35

O stay thy hand, for yonder is no game
 For thy fierce arrowes, them to exercize,
 But loe my Lord, my liege, whose warlike name
 Is farre renowmd through many bold emprize ;
 And now in shade he shrowded yonder lies.
 She staid : with that he crauld out of his nest,
 Forth creeping on his caitiue hands and thies,
 And standing stoutly vp, his loftie crest
Did fiercely shake, and rowze, as comming late from rest.

36

As fearefull fowle, that long in secret caue
 For dread of soaring hauke her selfe hath hid,
 Not caring how, her silly life to saue,
 She her gay painted plumes disorderid,
 Seeing at last her selfe from daunger rid,
 Peepes foorth, and soone renewes her natiue pride ;
 She gins her feathers foule disfigured
 Proudly to prune, and set on euery side,
So shakes off shame, ne thinks how erst she did her hide.

37

So when her goodly visage he beheld,
 He gan himselfe to vaunt : but when he vewed
 Those deadly tooles, which in her hand she held,
 Soone into other fits he was transmewed,
 Till she to him her gratious speach renewed ;
 All haile, Sir knight, and well may thee befall,
 As all the like, which honour haue pursewed
 Through deedes of armes and prowesse martiall ;
All vertue merits praise, but such the most of all.

38

To whom he thus ; O fairest vnder skie,
 True be thy words, and worthy of thy praise,
 That warlike feats doest highest glorifie.
 Therein haue I spent all my youthly daies,
 And many battailes fought, and many fraies
 Throughout the world, wher so they might be found,
 Endeuouring my dreadded name to raise
 Aboue the Moone, that fame may it resound
In her eternall trompe, with laurell girland cround.

39

But what art thou, O Ladie, which doest raunge
 In this wilde forrest, where no pleasure is,
 And doest not it for ioyous court exchaunge,
 Emongst thine equall peres, where happie blis
 And all delight does raigne, much more then this ?
 There thou maist loue, and dearely loued bee,
 And swim in pleasure, which thou here does. mis;
 There maist thou best be seene, and best maist see :
The wood is fit for beasts, the court is fit for thee.

40

Who so in pompe of proud estate (quoth she)
  Does swim, and bathes himselfe in courtly blis,
  Does waste his dayes in darke obscuritee,
  And in obliuion euer buried is :
  Where ease abounds, yt's eath to doe amis ;
  But who his limbs with labours, and his mind
  Behaues with cares, cannot so easie mis.
Abroad in armes, at home in studious kind
Who seekes with painfull toile, shall honor
    soonest find.

41

In woods, in waues, in warres she wonts to dwell,
  And will be found with perill and with paine ;
  Ne can the man, that moulds in idle cell,
  Vnto her happie mansion attaine :
  Before her gate high God did Sweat ordaine,
  And wakefull watches euer to abide :
  But easie is the way, and passage plaine
To pleasures pallace ; it may soone be spide,
And day and night her dores to all stand open
    wide.

42

In Princes court, The rest she would haue said,
  But that the foolish man, fild with delight
  Of her sweet words, that all his sence dismaid,
  And with her wondrous beautie rauisht quight,
  Gan burne in filthy lust, and leaping light,
  Thought in his bastard armes her to embrace.
  With that she swaruing backe, her Iauelin
    bright
Against him bent, and fiercely did menace
So turned her about, and fled away apace.

43

Which when the Peasant saw, amazd he stood,
  And grieued at her flight ; yet durst he not
  Pursew her steps, through wild vnknowen wood ;
  Besides he feard her wrath, and threatned shot
  Whiles in the bush he lay, not yet forgot :
  Ne car'd he greatly for her presence vaine,
  But turning said to *Trompart*, What foule blot
Is this to knight, that Ladie should againe
Depart to woods vntoucht, and leaue so proud
    disdaine ?

44

Perdie (said *Trompart*) let her passe at will,
  Least by her presence daunger mote befall.
  For who can tell (and sure I feare it ill)
  But that she is some powre celestiall ?
  For whiles she spake, her great words did apall
  My feeble courage, and my hart oppresse,
  That yet I quake and tremble ouer all.
And I (said *Braggadocchio*) thought no lesse,
When first I heard her horne sound with such
    ghastlinesse.

45

For from my mothers wombe this grace I haue
  Me giuen by eternall destinie,
  That earthly thing may not my courage braue
  Dismay with feare, or cause one foot to flie,
  But either hellish feends, or powres on hie :
  Which was the cause, when earst that horne
    I heard,
  Weening it had beene thunder in the skie,
I hid my selfe from it, as one affeard ;
But when I other knew, my selfe I boldly reard.

46

But now for feare of worse, that may betide,
  Let vs soone hence depart. They soone agree ;
  So to his steed he got, and gan to ride,
  As one vnfit therefore, that all might see
  He had not trayned bene in cheualree.
  Which well that valiant courser did discerne;
  For he despysd to tread in dew degree,
But chaufd and fom'd, with courage fierce and
    sterne,
And to be easd of that base burden still did erne.

Cant. IIII.

Guyon does Furor bind in chaines,
    and stops Occasion :
Deliuers Phedon, and therefore
    by Strife is rayld vpon.

1

In braue pursuit of honorable deed,
  There is I know not what great difference
  Betweene the vulgar and the noble seed,
  Which vnto things of valorous pretence
  Seemes to be borne by natiue influence ;
  As feates of armes, and loue to entertaine,
  But chiefly skill to ride, seemes a science
Proper to gentle bloud ; some others faine
To menage steeds, as did this vaunter ; but in
    vaine.

2

But he the rightfull owner of that steed,
  Who well could menage and subdew his pride,
  The whiles on foot was forced for to yeed,
  With that blacke Palmer, his most trusty guide ;
  Who suffred not his wandring feet to slide.
  But when strong passion, or weake fleshlinesse
  Would from the right way seeke to draw him
    wide,
He would through temperance and stedfastnesse,
Teach him the weake to strengthen, and the
    strong suppresse.

3

It fortuned forth faring on his way,
  He saw from farre, or seemed for to see
  Some troublous vprore or contentious fray,
  Whereto he drew in haste it to agree.
  A mad man, or that feigned mad to bee,
  Drew by the haire along vpon the ground,
  A handsome stripling with great crueltee,
  Whom sore he bett, and gor'd with many a wound,
That cheekes with teares, and sides with bloud
    did all abound.

4

And him behind, a wicked Hag did stalke,
  In ragged robes, and filthy disaray,
  Her other leg was lame, that she no'te walke,
  But on a staffe her feeble steps did stay ;
  Her lockes, that loathly were and hoarie gray,
  Grew all afore, and loosely hong vnrold,
  But all behind was bald, and worne away,
  That none thereof could euer taken hold,
And eke her face ill fauourd, full of wrinckles
    old.

5

And euer as she went, her tongue did walke
  In foule reproch, and termes of vile despight,
  Prouoking him by her outrageous talke,
  To heape more vengeance on that wretched
    wight ;   [smite,
  Sometimes she raught him stones, wherwith to
  Sometimes her staffe, though it her one leg were,
  Withouten which she could not go vpright ;
  Ne any euill meanes she did forbeare,
That might him moue to wrath, and indignation
    reare.

6

The noble *Guyon* mou'd with great remorse,
  Approching, first the Hag did thrust away,
  And after adding more impetuous forse,
  His mightie hands did on the madman lay,
  And pluckt him backe ; who all on fire streight
  Against him turning all his fell intent, [way,
  With beastly brutish rage gan him assay,
  And smot, and bit, and kickt, and scratcht,
    and rent,
And did he wist not what in his auengement.

7

And sure he was a man of mickle might,
  Had he had gouernance, it well to guide :
  But when the franticke fit inflamd his spright,
  His force was vaine, and strooke more often wide,
  Then at the aymed marke, which he had eide :
  And oft himselfe he chaunst to hurt vnwares,
  Whilst reason blent through passion, nought
    descride,
  But as a blindfold Bull at randon fares,
And where he hits, nought knowes, and whom
    he hurts, nought cares.

8

His rude assault and rugged handeling
  Straunge seemed to the knight, that aye with foe
  In faire defence and goodly menaging
  Of armes was wont to fight, yet nathemoe
  Was he abashed now not fighting so,
  But more enfierced through his currish play,
  Him sternely grypt, and haling to and fro,
  To ouerthrow him strongly did assay,
But ouerthrew himselfe vnwares, and lower lay.

9

And being downe the villein sore did beat,
  And bruze with clownish fistes his manly face :
  And eke the Hag with many a bitter threat,
  Still cald vpon to kill him in the place.
  With whose reproch and odious menace
  The knight emboyling in his haughtie hart,
  Knit all his forces, and gan soone vnbrace
  His grasping hold : so lightly did vpstart,
And drew his deadly weapon, to maintaine his
    part.

10

Which when the Palmer saw, he loudly cryde,
  Not so, O *Guyon*, neuer thinke that so
  That Monster can be maistred or destroyd :
  He is not, ah, he is not such a foe,
  As steele can wound, or strength can ouerthroe.
  That same is *Furor*, cursed cruell wight,
  That vnto knighthood workes much shame
    and woe ;
And that same Hag, his aged mother, hight
Occasion, the root of all wrath and despight.

11

With her, who so will raging *Furor* tame,
  Must first begin, and well her amenage :
  First her restraine from her reprochfull blame
  And euill meanes, with which she doth enrage
  Her franticke sonne, and kindles his courage.
  Then when she is withdrawen, or strong with-
    stood,
  It's eath his idle furie to asswage,
  And calme the tempest of his passion wood ;
The bankes are ouerflowen, when stopped is the
    flood.

12

Therewith Sir *Guyon* left his first emprise,
  And turning to that woman, fast her hent
  By the hoare lockes, that hong before her eyes,
  And to the ground her threw : yet n'ould she
    stent
  Her bitter rayling and foule reuilement,
  But still prouokt her sonne to wreake her wrong;
  But nathelesse he did her still torment,
  And catching hold of her vngratious tong,
Thereon an yron lock did fasten firme and
    strong.

13

Then when as vse of speach was from her reft,
  With her two crooked handes she signes did
    make,
  And beckned him, the last helpe she had left :
  But he that last left helpe away did take,
  And both her hands fast bound vnto a stake,
  That she note stirre. Then gan her sonne to flie
  Full fast away, and did her quite forsake ;
  But *Guyon* after him in haste did hie,
And soone him ouertooke in sad perplexitie.

14

In his strong armes he stiffely him embraste,
  Who him gainstriuing, nought at all preuaild :
  For all his power was vtterly defaste,
  And furious fits at earst quite weren quaild :
  Oft he re'nforst, and oft his forces fayld,
  Yet yield he would not, nor his rancour slacke :
  Then him to ground he cast, and rudely hayld,
  And both his hands fast bound behind his backe,
And both his feet in fetters to an yron racke.

15

With hundred yron chaines he did him bind,
  And hundred knots that did him sore constraine :
  Yet his great yron teeth he still did grind,
  And grimly gnash, threatning reuenge in vaine ;
  His burning eyen, whom bloudie strakes did
    staine,
  Stared full wide, and threw forth sparkes of fire,
  And more for ranck despight, then for great
    paine,
  Shakt his long lockes, colourd like copper-wire,
And bit his tawny beard to shew his raging ire.

16

Thus when as *Guyon Furor* had captiu'd,
  Turning about he saw that wretched Squire,
  Whom that mad man of life nigh late depriu'd,
  Lying on ground, all soild with bloud and mire :
  Whom when as he perceiued to respire,
  He gan to comfort, and his wounds to dresse.
  Being at last recured, he gan inquire,
  What hard mishap him brought to such distresse,
And made that caitiues thral, the thral of
    wretchednesse.

17

With hart then throbbing, and with watry eyes,
  Faire Sir (quoth he) what man can shun the hap,
  That hidden lyes vnwares him to surpryse ?
  Misfortune waites aduantage to entrap
  The man most warie in her whelming lap.
  So me weake wretch, of many weakest one,
  Vnweeting, and vnware of such mishap,
  She brought to mischiefe through occasion,
Where this same wicked villein did me light vpon.

18

It was a faithlesse Squire, that was the sourse
  Of all my sorrow, and of these sad teares,
  With whom from tender dug of commune nourse,
  Attonce I was vpbrought, and eft when yeares
  More rype vs reason lent to chose our Peares,
  Our selues in league of vowed loue we knit :
  In which we long time without gealous feares,
  Or faultie thoughts continewd, as was fit ;
And for my part I vow, dissembled not a whit.

19

It was my fortune commune to that age,
  To loue a Ladie faire of great degree,
  The which was borne of noble parentage,
  And set in highest seat of dignitee,
  Yet seemd no lesse to loue, then loued to bee :
  Long I her seru'd, and found her faithfull still,
  Ne euer thing could cause vs disagree :
  Loue that two harts makes one, makes eke one
    will :
Each stroue to please, and others pleasure to
    fulfill.

20

My friend, hight *Philemon*, I did partake
  Of all my loue and all my priuitie ;
  Who greatly ioyous seemed for my sake,
  And gratious to that Ladie, as to mee,
  Ne euer wight, that mote so welcome bee,
  As he to her, withouten blot or blame,
  Ne euer thing, that she could thinke or see,
  But vnto him she would impart the same :
O wretched man, that would abuse so gentle
    Dame.

21

At last such grace I found, and meanes I wrought,
  That I that Ladie to my spouse had wonne ;
  Accord of friends, consent of parents sought,
  Affiance made, my happinesse begonne,
  There wanted nought but few rites to be donne,
  Which mariage make ; that day too farre did
    seeme :
  Most ioyous man, on whom the shining Sunne
  Did shew his face, my selfe I did esteeme,
And that my falser friend did no lesse ioyous
    deeme.

22

But ere that wished day his beame disclosd,
  He either enuying my toward good,
  Or of himselfe to treason ill disposd,
  One day vnto me came in friendly mood,
  And told for secret how he vnderstood
  That Ladie whom I had to me assynd,
  Had both distaind her honorable blood,
  And eke the faith, which she to me did bynd ;
And therfore wisht me stay, till I more truth
    should fynd.

23

The gnawing anguish and sharpe gelosy,
  Which his sad speech infixed in my brest,
  Ranckled so sore, and festred inwardly,
  That my engreeued mind could find no rest,
  Till that the truth thereof I did outwrest,
  And him besought by that same sacred band
  Betwixt vs both, to counsell me the best.
He then with solemne oath and plighted hand
Assur'd, ere long the truth to let me vnderstand.

24

Ere long with like againe he boorded mee,
  Saying, he now had boulted all the floure,
  And that it was a groome of base degree,
  Which of my loue was partner Paramoure :
  Who vsed in a darkesome inner bowre
  Her oft to meet : which better to approue,
  He promised to bring me at that howre,
  When I should see, that would me nearer moue,
And driue me to withdraw my blind abused loue.

25

This gracelesse man for furtherance of his guile,
  Did court the handmayd of my Lady deare,
  Who glad t'embosome his affection vile,
  Did all she might, more pleasing to appeare.
  One day to worke her to his will more neare,
  He woo'd her thus : *Pryene* (so she hight)
  What great despight doth fortune to thee beare,
  Thus lowly to abase thy beautie bright,
That it should not deface all others lesser light?

26

But if she had her least helpe to thee lent,
  T'adorne thy forme according thy desart,
  Their blazing pride thou wouldest soone haue
  blent,   [part ;
  And staynd their prayses with thy least good
  Ne should faire *Claribell* with all her art,
  Though she thy Lady be, approch thee neare :
  For proofe thereof, this euening, as thou art,
  Aray thy selfe in her most gorgeous geare,
That I may more delight in thy embracement
  deare.

27

The Maiden proud through prayse, and mad
  through loue
  Him hearkned to, and soone her selfe arayd,
  The whiles to me the treachour did remoue
  His craftie engin, and as he had sayd,
  Me leading, in a secret corner layd,
  The sad spectatour of my Tragedie ;   [playd,
  Where left, he went, and his owne false part
  Disguised like that groome of base degree,
Whom he had feignd th'abuser of my loue to bee.

28

Eftsoones he came vnto th'appointed place,
  And with him brought *Pryene*, rich arayd,
  In *Claribellaes* clothes. Her proper face
  I not descerned in that darkesome shade,
  But weend it was my loue, with whom he playd
  Ah God, what horrour and tormenting griefe
  My hart, my hands, mine eyes, and all assayd ?
  Me liefer were ten thousand deathes priefe,
Then wound of gealous worme, and shame of
  such repriefe.

29

I home returning, fraught with fowle despight,
  And chawing vengeance all the way I went,
  Soone as my loathed loue appeard in sight,
  With wrathfull hand I slew her innocent ;
  That after soone I dearely did lament :
  For when the cause of that outrageous deede
  Demaunded, I made plaine and euident,
  Her faultie Handmayd, which that bale did
  breede,
Confest, how *Philemon* her wrought to chaunge
  her weede.

30

Which when I heard, with horrible affright
  And hellish fury all enragd, I sought
  Vpon my selfe that vengeable despight
  To punish : yet it better first I thought,
  To wreake my wrath on him, that first it wrought.
  To *Philemon*, false faytour *Philemon*
  I cast to pay, that I so dearely bought ;
  Of deadly drugs I gaue him drinke anon,
And washt away his guilt with guiltie potion.

31

Thus heaping crime on crime, and griefe on griefe,
  To losse of loue adioyning losse of frend,
  I meant to purge both with a third mischiefe,
  And in my woes beginner it to end :
  That was *Pryene* ; she did first offend,
  She last should smart : with which cruell intent,
  When I at her my murdrous blade did bend,
  She fled away with ghastly dreriment,
And I pursewing my fell purpose, after went.

32

Feare gaue her wings, and rage enforst my flight ;
  Through woods and plaines so long I did her
  chace,
  Till this mad man, whom your victorious might
  Hath now fast bound, me met in middle space,
  As I her, so he me pursewd apace,
  And shortly ouertooke : I, breathing yre,
  Sore chauffed at my stay in such a cace,
  And with my heat kindled his cruell fyre ;
Which kindled once, his mother did more rage
  inspyre.

33

Betwixt them both, they haue me doen to dye,
Through wounds, and strokes, and stubborne
    handeling,
That death were better, then such agony,
As griefe and furie vnto me did bring ;
Of which in me yet stickes the mortall sting,
That during life will neuer be appeasd.
When he thus ended had his sorrowing,
Said *Guyon*, Squire, sore haue ye beene diseasd ;
But all your hurts may soone through temper-
    ance be easd.

34

Then gan the Palmer thus, Most wretched man,
That to affections does the bridle lend ;
In their beginning they are weake and wan,
But soone through suff'rance grew to fearefull
    end ;   [contend :
Whiles they are weake betimes with them
For when they once to perfect strength do grow,
Strong warres they make, and cruell battry bend
Gainst fort of Reason, it to ouerthrow :
Wrath, gelosie, griefe, loue this Squire haue
    layd thus low.

35

Wrath, gealosie, griefe, loue do thus expell :
Wrath is a fire, and gealosie a weede,
Griefe is a flood, and loue a monster fell ;
The fire of sparkes, the weede of little seede,
The flood of drops, the Monster filth did breede :
But sparks, seed, drops, and filth do thus delay ;
The sparks soone quench, the springing seed
    outweed,
The drops dry vp, and filth wipe cleane away :
So shall wrath, gealosie, griefe, loue dye and
    decay.

36

Vnlucky Squire (said *Guyon*) sith thou hast
Falne into mischiefe through intemperaunce,
Henceforth take heede of that thou now hast past,
And guide thy wayes with warie gouernaunce,
Least worse betide thee by some later chaunce.
But read how art thou nam'd, and of what kin.
Phedon I hight (quoth he) and do aduaunce
Mine auncestry from famous *Coradin*,
Who first to rayse our house to honour did begin.

37

Thus as he spake, lo far away they spyde
A varlet running towards hastily,
Whose flying feet so fast their way applyde,
That round about a cloud of dust did fly,
Which mingled all with sweate, did dim his eye.
He soone approched, panting, breathlesse, whot,
And all so soyld, that none could him descry ;
His countenaunce was bold, and bashed not
For *Guyons* lookes, but scornefull eyglaunce at
    him shot.

38

Behind his backe he bore a brasen shield,
On which was drawen faire, in colours fit,
A flaming fire in midst of bloudy field,
And round about the wreath this word was writ,
Burnt I do burne. Right well beseemed it,
To be the shield of some redoubted knight ;
And in his hand two darts exceeding flit,
And deadly sharpe he held, whose heads were
    dight
In poyson and in bloud, of malice and despight.

39

When he in presence came, to *Guyon* first
He boldly spake, Sir knight, if knight thou bee,
Abandon this forestalled place at erst,
For feare of further harme, I counsell thee,
Or bide the chaunce at thine owne ieoperdie.
The knight at his great boldnesse wondered,
And though he scornd his idle vanitie,
Yet mildly him to purpose answered ;
For not to grow of nought he it coniectured.

40

Varlet, this place most dew to me I deeme,
Yielded by him, that held it forcibly.
But whence should come that harme, which
    thou doest seeme
To threat to him, that minds his chaunce t'abye?
Perdy (said he) here comes, and is hard by
A knight of wondrous powre, and great assay,
That neuer yet encountred enemy,
But did him deadly daunt, or fowle dismay ;
Ne thou for better hope, if thou his presence stay.

41

How hight he then (said *Guyon*) and from
    whence ?
Pyrochles is his name, renowmed farre
For his bold feats and hardy confidence,
Full oft approu'd in many a cruell warre,
The brother of *Cymochles*, both which arre
The sonnes of old *Acrates* and *Despight*,
Acrates sonne of *Phlegeton* and *Iarre* ;
But *Phlegeton* is sonne of *Herebus* and *Night* ;
But *Herebus* sonne of *Aeternitie* is hight.

42

So from immortall race he does proceede,
That mortall hands may not withstand his
    might,
Drad for his derring do, and bloudy deed ;
For all in bloud and spoile is his delight.
His am I *Atin*, his in wrong and right,
That matter make for him to worke vpon
And stirre him vp to strife and cruell fight.
Fly therefore, fly this fearefull stead anon,
Least thy foolhardize worke thy sad confusion.

43

His be that care, whom most it doth concerne,
(Said he) but whither with such hasty flight
Art thou now bound ? for well mote I discerne
Great cause, that carries thee so swift and light.
My Lord (quoth he) me sent, and streight behight
To seeke *Occasion*, where so she bee :
For he is all disposd to bloudy fight,
And breathes out wrath and hainous crueltie ;
Hard is his hap, that first fals in his leopardie.

44

Madman (said then the Palmer) that does seeke
Occasion to wrath, and cause of strife ;
She comes vnsought, and shonned followes eke.
Happy, who can abstaine, when Rancour rife
Kindles Reuenge, and threats his rusty knife ;
Woe neuer wants, where euery cause is caught,
And rash *Occasion* makes vnquiet life.
Then loe, where bound she sits, whom thou
   hast sought,
(Said *Guyon*,) let that message to thy Lord be
   brought.

45

That when the varlet heard and saw, streight
   way
He wexed wondrous wroth, and said, Vile knight,
That knights and knighthood doest with
   shame vpbray,
And shewst th'ensample of thy childish might,
With silly weake old woman thus to fight.
Great glory and gay spoile sure hast thou got,
And stoutly prou'd thy puissaunce here in sight ;
That shall *Pyrochles* well requite, I wot,
And with thy bloud abolish so reprochfull blot.

46

With that one of his thrillant darts he threw,
Headed with ire and vengeable despight ;
The quiuering steele his aymed end well knew,
And to his brest it selfe intended right :
But he was warie, and ere it empight
In the meant marke, aduaunst his shield
   atweene,
On which it seizing, no way enter might,
But backe rebounding, left the forckhead keene ;
Eftsoones he fled away, and might no where be
   seene.

Cant. V.

Pyrochles does with Guyon fight,
And Furors chayne vnbinds :
Of whom sore hurt, for his reuenge
Atin Cymochles finds.

1

Who euer doth to temperaunce apply
His stedfast life, and all his actions frame,
Trust me, shall find no greater enimy,
Then stubborne perturbation, to the same ;
To which right well the wise do giue that name,
For it the goodly peace of stayed mindes
Does ouerthrow, and troublous warre proclame :
His owne woes authour, who so bound it findes,
As did *Pyrochles*, and it wilfully vnbindes.

2

After that varlets flight, it was not long,
Ere on the plaine fast pricking *Guyon* spide
One in bright armes embatteiled full strong,
That as the Sunny beames do glaunce and glide
Vpon the trembling waue, so shined bright,
And round about him threw forth sparkling fire,
That seemd him to enflame on euery side :
His steed was bloudy red, and fomed ire,
When with the maistring spur he did him
   roughly stire.

3

Approching nigh, he neuer stayd to greete,
Ne chaffar words, prowd courage to prouoke,
But prickt so fiers, that vnderneath his feete
The smouldring dust did round about him
   smoke,
Both horse and man nigh able for to choke ;
And fairly couching his steele-headed speare,
Him first saluted with a sturdy stroke ;
It booted nought Sir *Guyon* comming neare
To thinke, such hideous puissaunce on foot to
   beare.

4

But lightly shunned it, and passing by,
With his bright blade did smite at him so fell,
That the sharpe steele arriuing forcibly
On his broad shield, bit not, but glauncing fell
On his horse necke before the quilted sell
And from the head the body sundred quight.
So him dismounted low, he did compell
On foot with him to matchen equall fight ;
The truncked beast fast bleeding, did him fowly
   dight.

5

Sore bruzed with the fall, he slow vprose,
  And all enraged, thus him loudly shent ;
  Disleall knight, whose coward courage chose
  To wreake it selfe on beast all innocent,
  And shund the marke, at which it should be
        ment,   [hood fraile ;
  Thereby thine armes seeme strong, but man-
  So hast thou oft with guile thine honour blent ;
  But litle may such guile thee now auaile,
If wonted force and fortune do not much me faile.

6

With that he drew his flaming sword, and strooke
  At him so fiercely, that the vpper marge
  Of his seuenfolded shield away it tooke,
  And glauncing on his helmet, made a large
  And open gash therein : were not his targe,
  That broke the violence of his intent,
  The weary soule from thence it would discharge ;
  Nathelesse so sore a buff to him it lent,
That made him reele, and to his brest his beuer
        bent.

7

Exceeding wroth was *Guyon* at that blow,
  And much ashamd, that stroke of liuing arme
  Should him dismay, and make him stoup so low,
  Though otherwise it did him litle harme :
  Tho hurling high his yron braced arme,
  He smote so manly on his shoulder plate,
  That all his left side it did quite disarme ;
  Yet there the steele stayd not, but inly bate
Deepe in his flesh, and opened wide a red flood-
        gate.

8

Deadly dismayd, with horrour of that dint
  Pyrochles was, and grieued eke entyre ;
  Yet nathemore did it his fury stint,
  But added flame vnto his former fire,
  That welnigh molt his hart in raging yre,
  Ne thenceforth his approued skill, to ward,
  Or strike, or hurtle round in warlike gyre,
  Remembred he, ne car'd for his saufgard,
But rudely rag'd, and like a cruell Tygre far'd.

9

He hewd, and lasht, and foynd, and thundred
        blowes,
  And euery way did seeke into his life,
  Ne plate, ne male could ward so mighty throwes,
  But yielded passage to his cruell knife.
  But *Guyon*, in the heat of all his strife,
  Was warie wise, and closely did awayt
  Auauntage, whilest his foe did rage most rife ;
  Sometimes a thwart, sometimes he strooke him
        strayt,
And falsed oft his blowes, t'illude him with such
        bayt.

10

Like as a Lyon, whose imperiall powre
  A prowd rebellious Vnicorne defies,
  T'auoide the rash assault and wrathfull stowre
  Of his fiers foe, him to a tree applies,
  And when him running in full course he spies,
  He slips aside ; the whiles that furious beast
  His precious horne, sought of his enimies,
  Strikes in the stocke, ne thence can be releast,
But to the mighty victour yields a bounteous
        feast.

11

With such faire slight him *Guyon* often faild,
  Till at the last all breathlesse, wearie, faint
  Him spying, with fresh onset he assaild,
  And kindling new his courage seeming queint,
  Strooke him so hugely, that through great
        constraint
  He made him stoup perforce vnto his knee,
  And do vnwilling worship to the Saint,
  That on his shield depainted he did see ;
Such homage till that instant neuer learned hee.

12

Whom *Guyon* seeing stoup, pursewed fast
  The present offer of faire victory,
  And soone his dreadfull blade about he cast,
  Wherewith he smote his haughty crest so hye,)
  That streight on ground made him full low to
        lye ;
  Then on his brest his victour foote he thrust,
  With that he cryde, Mercy, do me not dye,
  Ne deeme thy force by fortunes doome vniust,
That hath (maugre her spight) thus low me laid
        in dust.

13

Eftsoones his cruell hand Sir *Guyon* stayd,
  Tempring the passion with aduizement slow,
  And maistring might on enimy dismayd :
  For th'equall dye of warre he well did know ;
  Then to him said, Liue and allegaunce owe,
  To him that giues thee life and libertie,
  And henceforth by this dayes ensample trow,
  That hasty wroth, and heedlesse hazardrie
Do breede repentaunce late, and lasting in-
        famie.

14

So vp he let him rise, who with grim looke
  And count'naunce sterne vpstanding, gan to
        grind
  His grated teeth for great disdeigne, and shooke
  His sandy lockes, long hanging downe behind,
  Knotted in bloud and dust, for griefe of mind,
  That he in ods of armes was conquered ;
  Yet in himselfe some comfort he did find,
  That him so noble knight had maistered,
Whose bounty more then might, yet both he
        wondered.

15

Which *Guyon* marking said, Be nought agrieu'd,
Sir knight, that thus ye now subdewed arre :
Was neuer man, who most conquestes at chieu'd,
But sometimes had the worse, and lost by warre,
Yet shortly gaynd, that losse exceeded farre :
Losse is no shame, nor to be lesse then foe,
But to be lesser, then himselfe, doth marre
Both loosers lot, and victours prayse alsoe.
Vaine others ouerthrowes, who selfe doth ouer-
throwe.

16

Fly, O *Pyrochles*, fly the dreadfull warre,
That in thy selfe thy lesser parts do moue,
Outrageous anger, and woe-working iarre,
Direfull impatience, and hart murdring loue ;
Those, those thy foes, those warriours farre moue,
Which thee to endlesse bale captiued lead.
But sith in might thou didst my mercy proue,
Of curtesie to me the cause aread,
That thee against me drew with so impetuous
dread.

17

Dreadlesse (said he) that shall I soone declare :
It was complaind, that thou hadst done great
tort
Vnto an aged woman, poore and bare,
And thralled her in chaines with strong effort,
Voide of all succour and needfull comfort :
That ill beseemes thee, such as I thee see,
To worke such shame. Therefore I thee exhort,
To chaunge thy will, and set *Occasion* free,
And to her captiue sonne yield his first libertee.

18

Thereat Sir *Guyon* smilde, And is that all
(Said he) that thee so sore displeased hath ?
Great mercy sure, for to enlarge a thrall,
Whose freedome shall thee turne to greatest
scath.   [wrath :
Nath'lesse now quench thy whot emboyling
Loe there they be ; to thee I yield them free.
Thereat he wondrous glad, out of the path
Did lightly leape, where he them bound did see,
And gan to breake the bands of their captiuitee.

19

Soone as *Occasion* felt her selfe vntyde,
Before her sonne could well assoyled bee,
She to her vse returnd, and streight defyde
Both *Guyon* and *Pyrochles* : th'one (said shee)
Bycause he wonne ; the other because hee
Was wonne : So matter did she make of
nought,
To stirre vp strife, and do them disagree :
But soone as *Furor* was enlargd, she sought
To kindle his quencht fire, and thousand causes
wrought.

20

It was not long, ere she inflam'd him so,
That he would algates with *Pyrochles* fight,
And his redeemer chalengd for his foe,
Because he had not well mainteind his right,
But yielded had to that same straunger knight :
Now gan *Pyrochles* wex as wood, as hee,
And him affronted with impatient might :
So both together fiers engrasped bee,
Whiles *Guyon* standing by, their vncouth strife
does see.

21

Him all that while *Occasion* did prouoke
Against *Pyrochles*, and new matter framed
Vpon the old, him stirring to be wroke
Of his late wrongs, in which she oft him blamed
For suffering such abuse, as knighthood shamed,
And him dishabled quite. But he was wise
Ne would with vaine occasions be inflamed ;
Yet others she more vrgent did deuise :
Yet nothing could him to impatience entise.

22

Their fell contention still increased more,
And more thereby increased *Furors* might,
That he his foe has hurt, and wounded sore,
And him in bloud and durt deformed quight.
His mother eke, more to augment his spight,
Now brought to him a flaming fire brond,
Which she in *Stygian* lake, ay burning bright,
Had kindled : that she gaue into his hond,
That armd with fire, more hardly he mote him
withstond.

23

Tho gan that villein wex so fiers and strong,
That nothing might sustaine his furious forse ;
He cast him downe to ground, and all along
Drew him through durt and myre without
remorse,
And fowly battered his comely corse,
That *Guyon* much disdeignd so loathly sight.
At last he was compeld to cry perforse,
Helpe, O Sir *Guyon*, helpe most noble knight,
To rid a wretched man from hands of hellish
wight.

24

The knight was greatly moued at his plaint,
And gan him dight to succour his distresse,
Till that the Palmer, by his graue restraint,
Him stayd from yielding pitifull redresse ;
And said, Deare sonne, thy causelesse ruth
represse,
Ne let thy stout hart melt in pitty vayne :
He that his sorrow sought through wilfulnesse,
And his foe fettred would release agayne,
Deserues to tast his follies fruit, repented payne.

25

Guyon obayd ; So him away he drew
From needlesse trouble of renewing fight
Already fought, his voyage to pursew.
But rash *Pyrochles* varlet, *Atin* hight,
When late he saw his Lord in heauy plight,
Vnder Sir *Guyons* puissaunt stroke to fall,
Him deeming dead, as then he seemd in sight,
Fled fast away, to tell his funerall
Vnto his brother, whom *Cymochles* men did call.

26

He was a man of rare redoubted might,
Famous throughout the world for warlike prayse,
And glorious spoiles, purchast in perilous fight:
Full many doughtie knights he in his dayes
Had doen to death, subdewde in equall frayes,
Whose carkases, for terrour of his name,
Of fowles and beastes he made the piteous prayes,
And hong their conquered armes for more defame
On gallow trees, in honour of his dearest Dame.

27

His dearest Dame is that Enchaunteresse,
The vile *Acrasia*, that with vaine delightes,
And idle pleasures in her *Bowre* of *Blisse*,
Does charme her louers, and the feeble sprightes
Can call out of the bodies of fraile wightes :
Whom then she does transforme to monstrous hewes,
And horribly misshapes with vgly sightes,
Captiu'd eternally in yron mewes,
And darksom dens, where *Titan* his face neuer shewes.

28

There *Atin* found *Cymochles* soiourning,
To serue his Lemans loue : for he, by kind,
Was giuen all to lust and loose liuing,
When euer his fiers hands he free mote find :
And now he has pourd out his idle mind
In daintie delices, and lauish ioyes,
Hauing his warlike weapons cast behind,
And flowes in pleasures, and vaine pleasing toyes,
Mingled emongst loose Ladies and lasciuious boyes.

29

And ouer him, art striuing to compaire
With nature, did an Arber greene dispred,
Framed of wanton Yuie, flouring faire,
Through which the fragrant Eglantine did spred
His pricking armes, entrayld with roses red,
Which daintie odours round about them threw,
And all within with flowres was garnished,
That when myld *Zephyrus* emongst them blew,
Did breath out bounteous smels, and painted colors shew.

30

And fast beside, there trickled softly downe
A gentle streame, whose murmuring waue did play
Emongst the pumy stones, and made a sowne,
To lull him soft a sleepe, that by it lay ;
The wearie Traueiler, wandring that way,
Therein did often quench his thristy heat,
And then by it his wearie limbes display,
Whiles creeping slomber made him to forget
His former paine, and wypt away his toylsom sweat.

31

And on the other side a pleasaunt groue
Was shot vp high, full of the stately tree,
That dedicated is t'*Olympicke Ioue*,
And to his sonne *Alcides*, whenas hee
Gaynd in *Nemea* goodly victoree ;
Therein the mery birds of euery sort
Chaunted alowd their chearefull harmonie :
And made emongst themselues a sweet consort,
That quickned the dull spright with musicall comfort.

32

There he him found all carelesly displayd,
In secret shadow from the sunny ray,
On a sweet bed of lillies softly layd,
Amidst a flocke of Damzels fresh and gay,
That round about him dissolute did play
Their wanton follies, and light meriment ;
Euery of which did loosely disaray
Her vpper parts of meet habiliments,
And shewd them naked, deckt with many ornaments.

33

And euery of them stroue, with most delights,
Him to aggrate, and greatest pleasures shew ;
Some framd faire lookes, glancing like euening lights,
Others sweet words, dropping like honny dew ;
Some bathed kisses, and did soft embrew
The sugred licour through his melting lips :
One boastes her beautie, and does yeeld to vew
Her daintie limbes aboue her tender hips ;
Another her out boastes, and all for tryall strips.

34

He, like an Adder. lurking in the weeds,
His wandring thought in deepe desire does steepe,
And his fraile eye with spoyle of beautie feedes ;
Sometimes he falsely faines himselfe to sleepe,
Whiles through their lids his wanton eies do peepe,
To steale a snatch of amorous conceipt,
Whereby close fire into his heart does creepe :
So, them deceiues, deceiu'd in his deceipt,
Made drunke with drugs of deare voluptuous receipt.

35

Atin arriuing there, when him he spide,
Thus in still waues of deepe delight to wade,
Fiercely approching, to him lowdly cride,
Cymochles; oh no, but *Cymochles* shade,
In which that manly person late did fade,
What is become of great *Acrates* sonne ?
Or where hath he hong vp his mortall blade,
That hath so many haughtie conquests wonne ?
Is all his force forlorne, and all his glory donne ?

36

Then pricking him with his sharpe-pointed dart,
He said ; Vp, up, thou womanish weake
     knight,
That here in Ladies lap entombed art,
Vnmindfull of thy praise and prowest might,
And weetlesse eke of lately wrought despight,
Whiles sad *Pyrochles* lies on senselesse ground,
And groneth out his vtmost grudging spright,
Through many a stroke, and many a stream-
     ing wound,
Calling thy helpe in vaine, that here in ioyes art
     dround.

37

Suddeinly out of his delightfull dreame
The man awoke, and would haue questiond
     more ;
But he would not endure that wofull theame
For to dilate at large, but vrged sore
With percing words, and pittifull implore,
Him hastie to arise. As one affright
With hellish feends, or *Furies* mad vprore,
He then vprose, inflam'd with fell despight,
And called for his armes ; for he would algates
     fight.

38

They bene ybrought; he quickly does him dight,
And lightly mounted, passeth on his way,
Ne Ladies loues, ne sweete entreaties might
Appease his heat, or hastie passage stay ;
For he has vowd, to beene aueng'd that day,
(That day it selfe him seemed all too long :)
On him, that did *Pyrochles* deare dismay :
So proudly pricketh on his courser strong,
And *Atin* aie him pricks with spurs of shame
     and wrong.

Cant. VI.

സ്സ/സ്സ/സ്സ/സ്സ/സ്സ/സ്സ/സ്സ/സ്സ/സ്സ

*Guyon is of immodest Mcrth
    led into loose desire,
Fights with Cymochles, whiles his bro-
    ther burnes in furious fire.*

സ്സ/സ്സ/സ്സ/സ്സ/സ്സ/സ്സ/സ്സ/സ്സ/സ്സ

1

A Harder lesson, to learne Continence
In ioyous pleasure, then in grieuous paine :
For sweetnesse doth allure the weaker sence
So strongly, that vneathes it can refraine
From that, which feeble nature couets faine ;
But griefe and wrath, that be her enemies,
And foes of life, she better can restraine ;
Yet vertue vaunts in both their victories,
And *Guyon* in them all shewes goodly maisteries.

2

Whom bold *Cymochles* trauelling to find,
With cruell purpose bent to wreake on him
The wrath, which *Atin* kindled in his mind,
Came to a riuer, by whose vtmost brim
Wayting to passe, he saw whereas did swim
A long the shore, as swift as glaunce of eye,
A litle Gondelay, bedecked trim
With boughes and arbours wouen cunningly,
That like a litle forrest seemed outwardly.

3

And therein sate a Ladie fresh and faire,
Making sweet solace to her selfe alone ;
Sometimes she sung, as loud as larke in aire,
Sometimes she laught, that nigh her breth was
     gone,
Yet was there not with her else any one,
That might to her moue cause of meriment :
Matter of merth enough, though there were none,
She could deuise, and thousand waies inuent,
To feede her foolish humour, and vaine iolli-
     ment.

4

Which when farre off *Cymochles* heard, and saw,
He loudly cald to such, as were a bord,
The little barke vnto the shore to draw,
And him to ferrie ouer that deepe ford :
The merry marriner vnto his word
Soone hearkned, and her painted bote
     streightway   [Lord
Turnd to the shore, where that same warlike
She in receiu'd ; but *Atin* by no way
She would admit, albe the knight her much did
     pray.

5

Eftsoones her shallow ship away did slide,
More swift, then swallow sheres the liquid skie,
Withouten oare or Pilot it to guide,
Or winged canuas with the wind to flie,
Only she turn'd a pin, and by and by
It cut away vpon the yielding waue,
Ne cared she her course for to apply :
For it was taught the way, which she would
          haue,
And both from rocks and flats it selfe could
          wisely saue.

6

And all the way, the wanton Damzell found
New merth, her passenger to entertaine :
For she in pleasant purpose did abound,
And greatly ioyed merry tales to faine,
Of which a store-house did with her remaine,
Yet seemed, nothing well they her became ;
For all her words she drownd with laughter
          vaine,
And wanted grace in vtt'ring of the same,
That turned all her pleasance to a scoffing game.

7

And other whiles vaine toyes she would deuize
As her fantasticke wit did most delight,
Sometimes her head she fondly would aguize
With gaudie girlonds, or fresh flowrets dight
About her necke, or rings of rushes plight ;
Sometimes to doe him laugh, she would assay
To laugh at shaking of the leaues light,
Or to behold the water worke, and play
About her litle frigot, therein making way.

8

Her light behauiour, and loose dalliaunce
Gaue wondrous great contentment to the
          knight,
That of his way he had no souenaunce,
Nor care of vow'd reuenge, and cruell fight,
But to weake wench did yeeld his martiall
          might.
So easie was to quench his flamed mind
With one sweet drop of sensuall delight,
So easie is, t'appease the stormie wind
Of malice in the calme of pleasant womankind.

9

Diuerse discourses in their way they spent,
Mongst which *Cymochles* of her questioned,
Both what she was, and what that vsage ment,
Which in her cot she daily practised.
Vaine man (said she) that wouldest be reckoned
A straunger in thy home, and ignoraunt
Of *Phædria* (for so my name is red)
Of *Phædria*, thine owne fellow seruaunt :
For thou to serue *Acrasia* thy selfe doest vaunt.

10

In this wide Inland sea, that hight by name
The *Idle lake*, my wandring ship I row,
That knowes her port, and thither sailes by a yme,
Ne care, ne feare I, how the wind do blow,
Or whether swift I wend, or whether slow :
Both slow and swift a like do serue my tourne,
Ne swelling *Neptune,* ne loud thundring *Ioue*
Can chaunge my cheare, or make me euer mourne;
My litle boat can safely passe this perilous
          bourne.

11

Whiles thus she talked, and whiles thus she toyd,
They were farre past the passage, which he spake,
And come vnto an Island, waste and voyd,
That floted in the midst of that great lake,
There her small Gondelay her port did make,
And that gay paire issuing on the shore
Disburdned her. Their way they forward take
Into the land, that lay them faire before,
Whose pleasaunce she him shew'd, and plentifull
          great store.

12

It was a chosen plot of fertile land,
Emongst wide waues set, like a litle nest,
As if it had by Natures cunning hand
Bene choisely picked out from all the rest,
And laid forth for ensample of the best :
No daintie flowre or herbe, that growes on ground,
No arboret with painted blossomes drest,
And smelling sweet, but there it might be found
To bud out faire, and her sweet smels throw all
          around.

13

No tree, whose braunches did not brauely spring;
No braunch, whereon a fine bird did not sit :
No bird, but did her shrill notes sweetly sing ;
No song but did containe a louely dit :
Trees, braunches, birds, and songs were
          framed fit,
For to allure fraile mind to carelesse ease.
Carelesse the man soone woxe, and his weake wit
Was ouercome of thing, that did him please ;
So pleased, did his wrathfull purpose faire
          appease.

14

Thus when she had his eyes and senses fed
With false delights, and fild with pleasures vaine,
Into a shadie dale she soft him led,
And laid him downe vpon a grassie plaine ;
And her sweet selfe without dread, or disdaine,
She set beside, laying his head disarm'd
In her loose lap, it softly to sustaine,
Where soone he slumbred, fearing not be harm'd,
The whiles with a loud lay she thus him sweetly
          charm'd.

15

Behold, O man, that toilesome paines doest take,
The flowres, the fields, and all that pleasant
    growes,
How they themselues doe thine ensample make,
Whiles nothing enuious nature them forth
    throwes
Out of her fruitfull lap; how, no man knowes,
They spring, they bud, they blossome fresh
    and faire,   [showes;
And deck the world with their rich pompous
Yet no man for them taketh paines or care,
Yet no man to them can his carefull paines
    compare.

16

The lilly, Ladie of the flowring field,
The Flowre-deluce, her louely Paramoure,
Bid thee to them thy fruitlesse labours yield,
And soone leaue off this toylesome wearie stoure;
Loe loe how braue she decks her bounteous
    boure,
With silken curtens and gold couerlets,
Therein to shrowd her sumptuous Belamoure,
Yet neither spinnes nor cardes, ne cares nor frets,
But to her mother Nature all her care she lets.

17

Why then dost thou, O man, that of them all
Art Lord, and eke of nature Soueraine,
Wilfully make thy selfe a wretched thrall,
And wast thy ioyous houres in needlesse paine,
Seeking for daunger and aduentures vaine?
What bootes it all to haue, and nothing vse?
Who shall him rew, that swimming in the maine,
Will die for thirst, and water doth refuse?
Refuse such fruitlesse toile, and present plea-
    sures chuse.

18

By this she had him lulled fast a sleepe,
That of no worldly thing he care did take;
Then she with liquors strong his eyes did steepe,
That nothing should him hastily awake:
So she him left, and did her selfe betake
Vnto her boat againe, with which she cleft
The slouthfull waue of that great griesly lake;
Soone she that Island farre behind her left,
And now is come to that same place, where first
    she weft.

19

By this time was the worthy *Guyon* brought
Vnto the other side of that wide strond,
Where she was rowing, and for passage sought:
Him needed not long call, she soone to hond
Her ferry brought, where him she byding fond,
With his sad guide; himselfe she tooke a boord,
But the *Blacke Palmer* suffred still to stond,
Ne would for price, or prayers once affoord,
To ferry that old man ouer the perlous foord.

20

Guyon was loath to leaue his guide behind,
Yet being entred, might not backe retyre;
For the flit barke, obaying to her mind,
Forth launched quickly, as she did desire,
Ne gaue him leaue to bid that aged sire
Adieu, but nimbly ran her wonted course
Through the dull billowes thicke as troubled
    mire,   [forse,
Whom neither wind out of their seat could
Nor timely tides did driue out of their sluggish
    sourse.

21

And by the way, as was her wonted guize,
Her merry fit she freshly gan to reare,
And did of ioy and iollitie deuize,
Her selfe to cherish, and her guest to cheare:
The knight was courteous, and did not forbeare
Her honest merth and pleasaunce to partake;
But when he saw her toy, and gibe, and geare,
And passe the bonds of modest merimake,
Her dalliance he despisd, and follies did forsake.

22

Yet she still followed her former stile,
And said, and did all that mote him delight,
Till they arriued in that pleasant Ile,
Where sleeping late she left her other knight.
But when as *Guyon* of that land had sight,
He wist himselfe amisse, and angry said;
Ah Dame, perdie ye haue not doen me right,
Thus to mislead me, whiles I you obaid:
Me litle needed from my right way to haue straid.

23

Faire Sir (quoth she) be not displeasd at all;
Who fares on sea, may not commaund his way,
Ne wind and weather at his pleasure call:
The sea is wide, and easie for to stray;
The wind vnstable, and doth neuer stay.
But here a while ye may in safety rest,
Till season serue new passage to assay;
Better safe port, then be in seas distrest.
Therewith she laught, and did her earnest end
    in iest.

24

But he halfe discontent, mote nathelesse
Himselfe appease, and issewd forth on shore:
The ioyes whereof, and happie fruitfulnesse,
Such as he saw, she gan him lay before,
And all though pleasant, yet she made much
    more: [spring,
The fields did laugh, the flowres did freshly
The trees did bud, and earely blossomes bore,
And all the quire of birds did sweetly sing,
And told that gardins pleasures in their caroling

25

And she more sweet, then any bird on bough,
Would oftentimes emongst them beare a part.
And striue to passe (as she could well enough)
Their natiue musicke by her skilfull art :
So did she all, that might his constant hart
Withdraw from thought of warlike enterprize,
And drowne in dissolute delights apart.
Where noyse of armes, or vew of martiall guize
Might not reuiue desire of knightly exercize.

26

But he was wise, and warie of her will,
And euer held his hand vpon his hart :
Yet would not seeme so rude, and thewed ill,
As to despise so courteous seeming part,
That gentle Ladie did to him impart,
But fairely tempring fond desire subdewd,
And euer her desired to depart.
She list not heare, but her disports poursewd,
And euer bad him stay, till time the tide renewd.

27

And now by this, *Cymochles* howre was spent,
That he awoke out of his idle dreme,
And shaking off his drowzie dreriment,
Gan him auize, how ill did him beseeme,
In slouthfull sleepe his molten hart to steme,
And quench the brond of his conceiued ire.
Tho vp he started, stird with shame extreme,
Ne staied for his Damzell to inquire,
But marched to the strond, there passage to require.

28

And in the way he with Sir *Guyon* met,
Accompanyde with *Phædria* the faire,
Eftsoones he gan to rage, and inly fret,
Crying, Let be that Ladie debonaire,
Thou recreant knight, and soone thy selfe prepaire
To battell, if thou meane her loue to gaine :
Loe, loe alreadie, how the fowles in aire
Doe flocke, awaiting shortly to obtaine
Thy carcasse for their pray, the guerdon of thy paine.

29

And therewithall he fiercely at him flew,
And with importune outrage him assayld ;
Who soone prepard to field, his sword forth drew,
And him with equall value counteruayld :
Their mightie strokes their habereons dismayld,
And naked made each others manly spalles ;
The mortall steele despiteously entayld
Deepe in their flesh, quite through the yron walles,   [falles.
That a large purple streme adown their giambeux

30

Cymochles, that had neuer met before
So puissant foe, with enuious despight
His proud presumed force increased more,
Disdeigning to be held so long in fight ;
Sir *Guyon* grudging not so much his might,
As those vnknightly rayli\ gs, which he spoke,
With wrathfull fire his courage kindled bright,
Thereof deuising shortly to be wroke,
And doubling all his powres, redoubled euery stroke.

31

Both of them high attonce their hands enhaunst,
And both attonce their huge blowes downe did sway ;
Cymochles sword on *Guyons* shield yglaunst,
And thereof nigh one quarter sheard away ;
But *Guyons* angry blade so fierce did play
On th'others helmet, which as *Titan* shone,
That quite it cloue his plumed crest in tway,
And bared all his head vnto the bone ;
Wherewith astonisht, still he stood, as senselesse stone.

32

Still as he stood, faire *Phædria*, that beheld
That deadly daunger, soone atweene them ran;
And at their feet her selfe most humbly feld,
Crying with pitteous voice, and count'nance wan ;
Ah well away, most noble Lords, how can
Your cruell eyes endure so pitteous sight,
To shed your liues on ground ? wo worth the man,
That first did teach the cursed steele to bight
In his owne flesh, and make way to the liuing spright.

33

If euer loue of Ladie did empierce
Your yron brestes, or pittie could find place,
Withhold your bloudie hands from battell fierce,
And sith for me ye fight, to me this grace
Both yeeld, to stay your deadly strife a space.
They stayd a while : and forth she gan proceed :
Most wretched woman, and of wicked race,
That am the author of this hainous deed,
And cause of death betweene two doughtie knights doe breed.

34

But if for me ye fight, or me will serue,
Not this rude kind of battell, nor these armes
Are meet, the which doe men in bale to sterue,
And dolefull sorrow heape with deadly harmes:
Such cruell game my scarmoges disarmes :
Another warre, and other weapons I
Doe loue, where loue does giue his sweet alarmes,
Without bloudshed, and where the enemy
Does yeeld vnto his foe a pleasant victory.

35

Debatefull strife, and cruell enmitie
The famous name of knighthood fowly shend ;
But louely peace, and gentle amitie,
And in Amours the passing houres to spend,
The mightie martiall hands doe most commend:
Of loue they euer greater glory bore,
Then of their armes : *Mars* is *Cupidoes* frend,
And is for *Venus* loues renowmed more,
Then all his wars and spoiles, the which he did
    of yore.

36

Therewith she sweetly smyld. They though
    full bent
To proue extremities of bloudie fight,
Yet at her speach their rages gan relent,
And calme the sea of their tempestuous spight,
Such powre haue pleasing words : such is the
    might
Of courteous clemencie in gentle hart.
Now after all was ceast, the Faery knight
Besought that Damzell suffer him depart,
And yield him readie passage to that other part.

37

She no lesse glad, then he desirous was
Of his departure thence ; for of her ioy
And vaine delight she saw he light did pas,
A foe of folly and immodest toy,
Still solemne sad, or still disdainfull coy,
Delighting all in armes and cruell warre,
That her sweet peace and pleasures did annoy,
Troubled with terrour and vnquiet iarre,
That she well pleased was thence to amoue him
    farre.

38

Tho him she brought abord, and her swift bote
Forthwith directed to that further strand ;
The which on the dull waues did lightly flote
And soone arriued on the shallow sand,
Where gladsome *Guyon* salied forth to land,
And to that Damzell thankes gaue for reward.
Vpon that shore he spied *Atin* stand,
There by his maister left, when late he far'd
In *Phædrias* flit barke ouer that perlous shard.

39

Well could he him remember, sith of late
He with *Pyrochles* sharp debatement made ;
Streight gan he him reuile, and bitter rate,
As shepheards curre, that in darke euenings
    shade
Hath tracted forth some saluage beastes trade;
Vile Miscreant (said he) whither doest thou flie
The shame and death, which will thee soone
    inuade ?
What coward hand shall doe thee next to die,
That art thus foully fled from famous enemie ?

40

With that he stiffely shooke his steelehead dart:
But sober *Guyon*, hearing him so raile,
Though somewhat moued in his mightie hart,
Yet with strong reason maistred passion fraile,
And passed fairely forth. He turning taile,
Backe to the strond retyrd, and there still stayd,
Awaiting passage, which him late did faile ;
The whiles *Cymochles* with that wanton mayd
The hastie heat of his auowd reuenge delayd.

41

Whylest there the varlet stood, he saw from farre
An armed knight, that towards him fast ran,
He ran on foot, as if in lucklesse warre
His forlorne steed from him the victour wan ;
He seemed breathlesse, hartlesse, faint, and
    wan,
And all his armour sprinckled was with bloud,
And soyld with durtie gore, that no man can
Discerne the hew thereof. He neuer stood,
But bent his hastie course towards the idle flood.

42

The varlet saw, when to the flood he came,
How without stop or stay he fiercely lept,
And deepe him selfe beducked in the same,
That in the lake his loftie crest was steept,
Ne of his safetie seemed care he kept,
But with his raging armes he rudely flasht
The waues about, and all his armour swept,
That all the bloud and filth away was washt,
Yet still he bet the water, and the billowes dasht.

43

Atin drew nigh, to weet what it mote bee ;
For much he wondred at that vncouth sight ;
Whom should he, but his owne deare Lord,
    there see,
His owne deare Lord *Pyrochles*, in sad plight,
Readie to drowne himselfe for fell despight.
Harrow now out, and well away, he cryde,
What dismall day hath lent this cursed light,
To see my Lord so deadly damnifyde ?
Pyrochles, O *Pyrochles*, what is thee betyde ?

44

I burne, I burne, I burne, then loud he cryde,
O how I burne with implacable fire,
Yet nought can quench mine inly flaming syde,
Nor sea of licour cold, nor lake of mire,
Nothing but death can doe me to respire.
Ah be it (said he) from *Pyrochles* farre
After pursewing death once to require,
Or think, that ought those puissant hands may
    marre :
Death is for wretches borne vnder vnhappie
    starre.

45

Perdie, then is it fit for me (said he)
That am, I weene, most wretched man aliue,
Burning in flames, yet no flames can I see,
And dying daily, daily yet reuiue :
O *Atin*, helpe to me last death to giue.
The varlet at his plaint was grieued so sore,
That his deepe wounded hart in two did riue,
And his owne health remembring now no more,
Did follow that ensample, which he blam'd afore.

46

Into the lake he lept, his Lord to ayd,
(So Loue the dread of daunger doth despise)
And of him catching hold him strongly stayd
From drowning. But more happie he, then wise
Of that seas nature did him not auise.
The waues thereof so slow and sluggish were,
Engrost with mud, which did them foule agrise,
That euery weightie thing they did vpbeare,
Ne ought mote euer sinke downe to the bottome
    there.

47

Whiles thus they strugled in that idle waue,
And stroue in vaine, the one himselfe to drowne,
The other both from drowning for to saue,
Lo, to that shore one in an auncient gowne,
Whose hoarie locks great grauitie did crowne,
Holding in hand a goodly arming sword,
By fortune came, led with the troublous sowne :
Where drenched deepe he found in that dull ford
The carefull seruant, striuing with his raging
    Lord.

48

Him *Atin* spying, knew right well of yore,
And loudly cald, Helpe helpe, O *Archimage* ;
To saue my Lord, in wretched plight forlore ;
Helpe with thy hand, or with thy counsell sage :
Weake hands, but counsell is most strong in age.
Him when the old man saw, he wondred sore,
To see *Pyrochles* there so rudely rage :
Yet sithens helpe, he saw, he needed more
Then pittie, he in hast approched to the shore.

49

And cald, *Pyrochles*, what is this, I see ?
What hellish furie hath at earst thee hent ?
Furious euer I thee knew to bee,
Yet neuer in this straunge astonishment.
These flames, these flames (he cryde) do me
    torment.
What flames (quoth he) when I thee present see,
In daunger rather to be drent, then brent ?
Harrow, the flames, which me consume (said
    hee)
Ne can be quencht, within my secret bowels bee.

50

That cursed man, that cruell feend of hell,
Furor, oh *Furor* hath me thus bedight :
His deadly wounds within my liuers swell,
And his whot fire burnes in mine entrails bright,
Kindled through his infernall brond of spight,
Sith late with him I batteil vaine would boste ;
That now I weene *Ioues* dreaded thunder light
Does scorch not halfe so sore, nor damned ghoste
In flaming *Phlegeton* does not so felly roste.

51

Which when as *Archimago* heard, his griefe
He knew right well, and him attonce disarmd :
Then searcht his secret wounds, and made a
    priefe
Of euery place, that was with brusing harmd,
Or with the hidden fire too inly warmd.
Which done, he balmes and herbes thereto
    applyde,
And euermore with mighty spels them charmd,
That in short space he has them qualifyde,
And him restor'd to health, that would haue
    algates dyde.

Cant. VII.

Guyon findes Mammon in a delue,
Sunning his threasure hore :
Is by him tempted, and led downe,
To see his secret store.

1

As Pilot well expert in perilous waue,
That to a stedfast starre his course hath bent,
When foggy mistes, or cloudy tempests haue
The faithfull light of that faire lampe yblent,
And couer'd heauen with hideous dreriment,
Vpon his card and compas firmes his eye,
The maisters of his long experiment,
And to them does the steddy helme apply,
Bidding his winged vessell fairely forward fly :

2

So *Guyon* hauing lost his trusty guide,
Late left beyond that *Ydle lake*, proceedes
Yet on his way, of none accompanide ;
And euermore himselfe with comfort feedes,
Of his owne vertues, and prayse-worthy deedes.
So long he yode, yet no aduenture found,
Which fame of her shrill trompet worthy reedes :
For still he traueild through wide wastfull
    ground,   [around.
That nought but desert wildernesse shew'd all

3

At last he came vnto a gloomy glade,   [light,
  Couer'd with boughes and shrubs from heauens
  Whereas he sitting found in secret shade
  An vncouth, saluage, and vnciuile wight,
  Of griesly hew, and fowle ill fauour'd sight ;
  His face with smoke was tand, and eyes were
    bleard,
  His head and beard with sout were ill bedight,
  His cole-blacke hands did seeme to haue beene
    seard
In smithes fire-spitting forge, and nayles like
    clawes appeard.

4

His yron coate all ouergrowne with rust,
  Was vnderneath enueloped with gold,
  Whose glistring glosse darkned with filthy dust,
  Well yet appeared, to haue beene of old
  A worke of rich entayle, and curious mould,
  Wouen with antickes and wild Imagery :
  And in his lap a masse of coyne he told,
  And turned vpsidowne, to feede his eye
And couetous desire with his huge threasury.

5

And round about him lay on euery side
  Great heapes of gold, that neuer could be spent:
  Of which some were rude owre, not purifide
  Of *Mulcibers* deuouring element ;
  Some others were new driuen, and distent
  Into great Ingoes, and to wedges square ;
  Some in round plates withouten moniment ;
  But most were sta npt, and in their metall bare
The antique shapes of kings and kesars straunge
    and rare.

6

Soone as he *Guyon* saw, in great affright
  And hast he rose, for to remoue aside
  Those pretious hils from straungers enuious
    sight,   [wide,
  And downe them poured through an hole full
  Into the hollow earth, them there to hide.
  But *Guyon* lightly to him leaping, stayd
  His hand, that trembled, as one terrifyde ;
  And though him selfe were at the sight dismayd,
Yet him perforce restraynd, and to him doubt-
    full sayd.

7

What art thou man, (if man at all thou art)
  That here in desert hast thine habitaunce,
  And these rich heapes of wealth doest hide apart
  From the worldes eye, and from her right vsaunce?
  Thereat with staring eyes fixed askaunce,
  In great disdaine, he answerd ; Hardy Elfe,
  That darest vew my direfull countenaunce,
  I read thee rash, and heedlesse of thy selfe,
To trouble my still seate, and heapes of pretious
    pelfe.

8

God of the world and worldlings I me call,
  Great *Mammon*, greatest god below the skye,
  That of my plenty poure out vnto all,
  And vnto none my graces do enuye :
  Riches, renowme, and principality,
  Honour, estate, and all this worldes good,
  For which men swinck and sweat incessantly,
  Fro me do flow into an ample flood,
And in the hollow earth haue their eternall
    brood.

9

Wherefore if me thou deigne to serue and sew,
  At thy commaund lo all these mountaines bee ;
  Or if to thy great mind, or greedy vew
  All these may not suffise, there shall to thee
  Ten times so much be numbred francke and free.
  Mammon (said he) thy godheades vaunt is vaine,
  And idle offers of thy golden fee ;
  To them, that couet such eye-glutting gaine,
Proffer thy giftes, and fitter seruaunts entertaine.

10

Me ill besits, that in der-doing armes,
  And honours suit my vowed dayes do spend,
  Vntothy bounteous baytes, and pleasing charmes,
  With which weake men thou witchest, to attend:
  Regard of worldly mucke doth fowly blend,
  And low abase the high heroicke spright,
  That ioyes for crownes and kingdomes to con-
    tend ;   [delight ·
  Faire shields, gay steedes, bright armes be my
Those be the riches fit for an aduent'rous knight.

11

Vaine glorious Elfe (said he) doest not thou weet,
  That money can thy wantes at will supply ?
  Sheilds, steeds, and armes, and all things for
    thee meet
  It can puruay in twinckling of an eye ;
  And crownes and kingdomes to thee multiply.
  Do not I kings create, and throw the crowne
  Sometimes to him, that low in dust doth ly ?
  And him that raignd, into his rowme thrust
    downe,
  And whom I lust, do heape with glory and
    renowne ?

12

All otherwise (said he) I riches read,
  And deeme them roote of all disquietnesse ;
  First got with guile, and then preseru'd with
    dread,
  And after spent with pride and lauishnesse,
  Leauing behind them griefe and heauinesse.
  Infinite mischiefes of them do arize,
  Strife, and debate, bloudshed, and bitternesse,
  Outrageous wrong, and hellish couetize,
That noble heart as great dishonour do th despize.

13

Ne thine be kingdomes, ne the scepters thine ;
But realmes and rulers thou doest both con-
        found,
And loyall truth to treason doest incline ;
Witnesse the guiltlesse bloud pourd oft on
        ground,
The crowned often slaine, the slayer cround,
The sacred Diademe in peeces rent,
And purple robe gored with many a wound ;
Castles surprizd, great cities sackt and brent :
So mak'st thou kings, and gaynest wrongfull
        gouernement.

14

Long were to tell the troublous stormes, that tosse
The priuate state, and make the life vnsweet:
Who swelling sayles in Caspian sea doth crosse,
And in frayle wood on *Adrian* gulfe doth fleet,
Doth not, I weene, so many euils meet.
Then *Mammon* wexing wroth, And why then,
        said,
Are mortall men so fond and vndiscreet,
So euill thing to seeke vnto their ayd,
And hauing not complaine, and hauing it
        vpbraid ?

15

Indeede (quoth he) through fowle intemperaunce,
Frayle men are oft captiu'd to couetise :
But would they thinke, with how small
        allowaunce
Vntroubled Nature doth her selfe suff.se,
Such superfluities they would despise,
Which with sad cares empeach our natiue ioyes:
At the well head the purest streames arise :
But mucky filth his braunching armes annoyes,
And with vncomely weedes the gentle waue
        accloyes.

16

The antique world, in his first flowring youth,
Found no defect in his Creatours grace,
But with glad thankes, and vnreproued truth,
The gifts of soueraigne bountie did embrace :
Like Angels life was then mens happy cace ;
But later ages pride, like corn-fed steed,
Abusd her plenty, and fat swolne encreace
To all licentious lust, and gan exceed [need.
The measure of her meane, and naturall first

17

Then gan a cursed hand the quiet wombe
Of his great Grandmother with steele to wound,
And the hid treasures in her sacred tombe,
With Sacrilege to dig. Therein he found
Fountaines of gold and siluer to abound,
Of which the matter of his huge desire
And pompous pride eftsoones he did compound;
Then auarice gan through his veines inspire
His greedy flames, and kindled life-deuouring fire.

18

Sonne (said he then) let be thy bitter scorne,
And leaue the rudenesse of that antique age
To them, that liu'd therein in state forlorne ;
Thou that doest liue in later times, must wage
Thy workes for wealth, and life for gold engage.
If then thee list my offred grace to vse,
Take what thou please of all this surplusage ;
If thee list not, leaue haue thou to refuse :
But thing refused, do not afterward accuse.

19

Me list not (said the Elfin knight) receaue
Thing offred, till I know it well be got,
Ne wote I, but thou didst these goods bereaue
From rightfull owner by vnrighteous lot,
Or that bloud guiltinesse or guile them blot.
Perdy (quoth he) yet neuer eye did vew,
Ne toung did tell, ne hand these handled not,
But safe I haue them kept in secret mew,
From heauens sight, and powre of all which
        them pursew.

20

What secret place (quoth he) can safely hold
So huge a masse, and hide from heauens eye ?
Or where least thou thy wonne, that so much gold
Thou canst preserue from wrong and robbery?
Come thou (quoth he) and see. So by and by
Through that thicke couert he him led, and
        found
A darkesome way, which no man could descry,
That deepe descended through the hollow
        ground,
And was with dread and horrour compassed
        around.

21

At length they came into a larger space,
That stretcht it selfe into an ample plaine,
Through which a beaten broad high way did
        trace,
That streight did lead to *Plutoes* griesly raine :
By that wayes side, there sate infernall Payne,
And fast beside him sat tumultuous Strife :
The one in hand an yron whip did straine,
The other brandished a bloudy knife,
And both did gnash their teeth, and both did
        threaten life.

22

On thother side in one consort there sate,
Cruell Reuenge, and rancorous Despight,
Disloyall Treason, and hart-burning Hate,
But gnawing Gealosie out of their sight
Sitting alone, his bitter lips did bight,
And trembling Feare still to and fro did fly,
And found no place, where safe he shroud him
        might,
Lamenting Sorrow did in darkenesse lye,
And Shame his vgly face did hide from liuing eye.

23

And ouer them sad Horrour with grim hew,
Did alwayes sore, beating his yron wings ;
And after him Owles and Night-rauens flew.
The hatefull messengers of heauy things,
Of death and dolour telling sad tidings ;
Whiles sad *Celeno*, sitting on a clift,
A song of bale and bitter sorrow sings,
That hart of flint a sunder could haue rift :
Which hauing ended, after him she flyeth swift.

24

All these before the gates of *Pluto* lay,
By whom they passing, spake vnto them
   nought.
But th'Elfin knight with wonder all the way
Did feed his eyes, and fild his inner thought.
At last him to a litle dore he brought,
That to the gate of Hell, which gaped wide,
Was next adioyning, ne them parted ought :
Betwixt them both was but a litle stride,
That did the house of Richesse from hell-mouth
   diuide.

25

Before the dore sat selfe-consuming Care,
Day and night keeping wary watch and ward,
For feare least Force or Fraud should vnaware
Breake in, and spoile the treasure there in gard :
Ne would he suffer Sleepe once thither-ward
Approch, albe his drowsie den were next ;
For next to death is Sleepe to be compard :
Therefore his house is vnto his annext ;
Here Sleep, there Richesse, and Hel-gate them
   both betwext.

26

So soone as *Mammon* there arriu'd, the dore
To him did open, and affoorded way ;
Him followed eke Sir *Guyon* euermore,
Ne darkenesse him, ne daunger might dismay.
Soone as he entred was, the dore streight way
Did shut, and from behind it forth there lept
An vgly feend, more fowle then dismall day,
The which with monstrous stalke behind him
   stept,
And euer as he went, dew watch vpon him kept.

27

Well hoped he, ere long that hardy guest,
If euer couetous hand, or lustfull eye,
Or lips he layd on thing, that likt him best,
Or euer sleepe his eye-strings did vntye,
Should be his pray. And therefore still on hye
He ouer him did hold his cruell clawes,
Threatning with greedy gripe to do him dye
And rend in peeces with his rauenous pawes,
If euer he transgrest the fatall *Stygian* lawes.

28

That houses forme within was rude and strong,
Like an huge caue, hewne out of rocky clift,
From whose rough vaut the ragged breaches
   hong,
Embost with massy gold of glorious gift,
And with rich metall loaded euery rift,
That heauy ruine they did seeme to threat ;
And ouer them *Arachne* high did lift
Her cunning web, and spred her subtile net,
Enwrapped in fowle smoke and clouds more
   blacke then Iet.

29

Both roofe, and floore, and wals were all of gold,
But ouergrowne with dust and old decay,
And hid in darkenesse, that none could behold
The hew thereof : for vew of chearefull day
Did neuer in that house it selfe display,
But a faint shadow of vncertain light ;
Such as a lamp, whose life does fade away :
Or as the Moone cloathed with clowdy night,
Does shew to him, that walkes in feare and sad
   affright.

30

In all that rowme was nothing to be seene,
But huge great yron chests and coffers strong,
All bard with double bends, that none could
   weene
Them to efforce by violence or wrong ;
On euery side they placed were along.
But all the ground with sculs was scattered,
And dead mens bones, which round about were
   flong,
Whose liues, it seemed, whilome there were
   shed,
And their vile carcases now left vnburied.

31

They forward passe, ne *Guyon* yet spoke word,
Till that they came vnto an yron dore,
Which to them opened of his owne accord,
And shewd of richesse such exceeding store,
As eye of man did neuer see before ;
Ne euer could within one place be found,
Though all the wealth, which is, or was of yore,
Could gathered be through all the world around,
And that aboue were added to that vnder
   ground.

32

The charge thereof vnto a couetous Spright
Commaunded was, who thereby did attend,
And warily awaited day and night,
From other couetous feends it to defend,
Who it to rob and ransacke did intend.
Then *Mammon* turning to that warriour, said ;
Loe here the worldes blis, loe here the end,
To which all men do ayme, rich to be made :
Such grace now to be happy, is before thee laid.

33

Certes (said he) I n'ill thine offred grace,
Ne to be made so happy do intend :
Another blis before mine eyes I place,
Another happinesse, another end.
  To them, that list, these base regardes I lend:
But I in armes, and in atchieuements braue,
Do rather choose my flitting houres to spend,
And to be Lord of those, that riches haue,
Then them to haue my selfe, and be their seruile
  sclaue.

34

Thereat the feend his gnashing teeth did grate,
And grieu'd, so long to lacke his greedy pray;
For well he weened, that so glorious bayte
Would tempt his guest, to take thereof assay:
  Had he so doen, he had him snatcht away,
More light then Culuer in the Faulcons fist.
Eternall God thee saue from such decay.
But whenas *Mammon* saw his purpose mist,
Him to entrap vnwares another way he wist.

35

Thence forward he him led, and shortly brought
Vnto another rowme, whose dore forthright,
To him did open, as it had beene taught :
Therein an hundred raunges weren pight,
  And hundred fornaces all burning bright ;
By euery fornace many feends did bide,
Deformed creatures, horrible in sight,
And euery feend his busie paines applide,
To melt the golden metall, ready to be tride.

36

One with great bellowes gathered filling aire,
And with forst wind the fewell did inflame ;
Another did the dying bronds repaire
With yron toungs, and sprinckled oft the same
  With liquid waues, fiers *Vulcans* rage to tame,
Who maistring them, renewd his former heat;
Some scumd the drosse, that from the metall
  came ;
Some stird the molten owre with ladles great ;
And euery one did swincke, and euery one did
  sweat.

37

But when as earthly wight they present saw,
Glistring in armes and battailous aray,
From their whot worke they did themselues
  withdraw
To wonder at the sight : for till that day,
  They neuer creature saw, that came that way.
Their staring eyes sparckling with feruent fire,
And vgly shapes did nigh the man dismay,
That were it not for shame, he would retire,
Till that him thus bespake their soueraigne
  Lord and sire.

38

Behold, thou Faeries sonne, with mortall eye,
That liuing eye before did neuer see :
The thing, that thou didst craue so earnestly,
To weet, whence all the wealth late shewd by mee,
  Proceeded, lo now is reueald to thee.
Here is the fountaine of the worldes good :
Now therefore, if thou wilt enriched bee,
Auise thee well, and chaunge thy wilfull mood,
Least thou perhaps hereafter wish, and be
  withstood.

39

Suffise it then, thou Money God (quoth hee)
That all thine idle offers I refuse.
All that I need I haue ; what needeth mee
To couet more, then I haue cause to vse ?
  With such vaine shewes thy worldlings vile
    abuse :
But giue me leaue to follow mine emprise.
Mammon was much displeasd, yet no'te he chuse,
But beare the rigour of his bold mesprise,
And thence him forward led, him further to
  entise.

40

He brought him through a darksome narrow
  strait,
To a broad gate, all built of beaten gold :
The gate was open, but therein did wait
A sturdy villein, striding stiffe and bold,
  As if that highest God defie he would ;
In his right hand an yron club he held,
But he himselfe was all of golden mould,
Yet had both life and sence, and well could weld
That cursed weapon, when his cruell foes he
  queld.

41

Disdayne he called was, and did disdaine
To be so cald, and who so did him call :
Sterne was his looke, and full of stomacke vaine,
His portaunce terrible, and stature tall,
  Far passing th'hight of men terrestriall ;
Like an huge Gyant of the *Titans* race,
That made him scorne all creatures great and
  small,
And with his pride all others powre deface :
More fit amongst blacke fiendes, then men to
  haue his place.

42

Soone as those glitterand armes he did espye,
That with their brightnesse made that dark-
  nesse light,
His harmefull club he gan to hurtle hye,
And threaten batteill to the Faery knight ;
  Who likewise gan himselfe to batteill dight,
Till *Mammon* did his hasty hand withhold,
And counseld him abstaine from perilous fight:
For nothing might abash the villein bold,
Ne mortall steele emperce his miscreated mould.

43

So hauing him with reason pacifide,
  And the fiers Carle commaunding to forbeare.
He brought him in. The rowme was large and
    wide,
  As it some Gyeld or solemne Temple weare :
Many great golden pillours did vpbeare
  The massy roofe, and riches huge sustayne,
And euery pillour decked was full deare
  With crownes and Diademes, and titles vaine.
Which mortall Princes wore, whiles they on earth
    did rayne.

44

A route of people there assembled were,
  Of euery sort and nation vnder skye,
Which with great vprore preaced to draw nere
  To th'vpper part, where was aduaunced hye
A stately siege of soueraigne maiestye ;
  And thereon sat a woman gorgeous gay,
And richly clad in robes of royaltye,
  That neuer earthly Prince in such aray
His glory did enhaunce, and pompous pride
    display.

45

Her face right wondrous faire did seeme to bee,
  That her broad beauties beam great brightnes
    threw   [see :
Through the dim shade, that all men might it
  Yet was not that same her owne natiue hew,
But wrought by art and counterfetted shew,
  Thereby more louers vnto her to call ;
Nath'lesse most heauenly faire in deed and vew
  She by creation was, till she did fall ;
Thenceforth she sought for helps, to cloke her
    crime withall.

46

There, as in glistring glory she did sit,
  She held a great gold chaine ylincked well,
Whose vpper end to highest heauen was knit,
  And lower part did reach to lowest Hell ;
And all that preace did round about her swell,
  To catchen hold of that long chaine, thereby
To clime aloft, and others to excell :
  That was *Ambition*, rash desire to sty,
And euery lincke thereof a step of dignity.

47

Some thought to raise themselues to high degree,
  By riches and vnrighteous reward,
Some by close shouldring, some by flatteree ;
  Others through friends, others for base regard ;
And all by wrong wayes for themselues prepard.
  Those that were vp themselues, kept others low,
Those that were low themselues, held others
    hard,
  Ne suffred them to rise or greater grow,
But euery one did striue his fellow downe to
    throw.

48

Which whenas *Guyon* saw, he gan inquire,
  What meant that preace about that Ladies
    throne,
And what she was that did so high aspire.
  Him *Mammon* answered ; That goodly one,
Whom all that folke with such contention,
  Do flocke about, my deare, my daughter is ;
Honour and dignitie from her alone
  Deriued are, and all this worldes blis
For which ye men do striue : few get, but many
    mis.

49

And faire *Philotime* she rightly hight,
  The fairest wight that wonneth vnder skye,
But that this darksome neather world her light
  Doth dim with horrour and deformitie,
Worthy of heauen and hye felicitie,
  From whence the gods haue her for enuy thrust :
But sith thou hast found fauour in mine eye,
  Thy spouse I will her make, if that thou lust,
That she may thee aduance for workes and
    merites iust.

50

Gramercy *Mammon* (said the gentle knight)
  For so great grace and offred high estate ;
But I, that am fraile flesh and earthly wight,
  Vnworthy match for such immortall mate
My selfe well wote, and mine vnequall fate ;
  And were I not, yet is my trouth yplight,
And loue auowd to other Lady late,
  That to remoue the same I haue no might :
To chaunge loue causelesse is reproch to warlike
    knight.

51

Mammon emmoued was with inward wrath ;
  Yet forcing it to faine, him forth thence led
Through grisly shadowes by a beaten path,
  Into a gardin goodly garnished
With hearbs and fruits, whose kinds mote not
    be red :
  Not such, as earth out of her fruitfull woomb
Throwes forth to men, sweet and well sauoured,
  But direfull deadly blacke both leafe and bloom,
Fit to adorne the dead, and decke the drery
    toombe.

52

There mournfull *Cypresse* grew in greatest store,
  And trees of bitter *Gall*, and *Heben* sad,
Dead sleeping *Poppy*, and blacke *Hellebore*,
  Cold *Coloquintida*, and *Tetra* mad,
Mortall *Samnitis*, and *Cicuta* bad,
  With which th'vniust *Atheniens* made to dy
Wise *Socrates*, who thereof quaffing glad
  Pourd out his life, and last Philosophy
To the faire *Critias* his dearest Belamy.

53

The *Gardin* of *Proserpina* this hight ;
  And in the midst thereof a siluer seat,
  With a thicke Arber goodly ouer dight,
  In which she often vsd from open heat
  Her selfe to shroud, and pleasures to entreat.
Next thereunto did grow a goodly tree,
  With braunches broad dispred and body great,
  Clothe I with leaues, that none the wood mote see
And loaden all with fruit as thicke as it might
  bee.

54

Their fruit were golden apples glistring bright,
  That goodly was their glory to behold,
  On earth like neuer grew, ne liuing wight
  Like euer saw, but they from hence were sold :
  For those, which *Hercules* with conquest bold
Got from great *Atlas* daughters, hence began,
  And planted there, did bring forth fruit of gold :
  And those with which th'*Eubœan* young man
  wan
Swift *Atalanta*, when through craft he her out
  ran.

55

Here also sprong that goodly golden fruit,
  With which *Acontius* got his louer trew,
  Whom he had long time sought with fruitlesse
  suit :
  Here eke that famous golden Apple grew,
  The which emongst the gods false *Ate* threw ;
For which th'*Idæan* Ladies disagreed,
  Till partiall *Paris* dempt it *Venus* dew,
  And had of her, faire *Helen* for his meed,
That many noble *Greekes* and *Troians* made to
  bleed.

56

The warlike Elfe much wondred at this tree,
  So fa'rean lgreat, that shadowed all the ground,
  And his broad braunches, laden with rich fee.
  Did stretch themselues without the vtmost bound
  Of this great gardin, compast with a mound,
Which ouer-hanging, they themselues did steepe,
  In a blacke flood which flow'd about it round ;
  That is the riuer of *Cocytus* deepe,
In which full many soules do endlesse waile and
  weepe.

57

Which to behold, he clomb vp to the banke,
  And looking downe, saw many damned wights,
  In those sad waues, which direfull deadly stanke,
  Plonged continually of cruell Sprights,
  That with their pitteous cryes, and yelling
  shrights,
They made the further shore resounden wide :
  Emongst the rest of those same ruefull sights,
  One cursed creature he by chaunce espide,
That drenched lay full deepe, vnder the Garden
  side.

58

Deepe was he drenched to the vpmost chin,
  Yet gaped still, as coueting to drinke
  Of the cold liquor, which he waded in,
  And stretching forth his hand, did often thinke
  To reach the fruit, which grew vpon the brincke :
But both the fruit from hand, and floud from
  mouth
  Did flie abacke, and made him vainely swinke :
  The whiles he steru'd with hunger and with
  drouth
He daily dyde, yet neuer throughly dyen couth.

59

The knight him seeing labour so in vaine,
  Askt who he was, and what he ment thereby :
  Who groning deepe, thus answerd him againe ;
  Most cursed of all creatures vnder skye,
  Lo *Tantalus*, I here torn.ented lye :
Of whom high *Ioue* wont whylome feasted bee,
  Lo here I now for want of food doe dye :
  But if that thou be such, as I thee see,
Of grace I pray thee, giue to eat and drinke to
  mee.

60

Nay, nay, thou greedie *Tantalus* (quoth he)
  Abide the fortune of thy present fate,
  And vnto all that liue in high degree,
  Ensample be of mind intemperate,
  To teach them how to vse their present state.
Then gan the cursed wretch aloud to cry,
  Accusing highest *Ioue* and gods ingrate,
  And eke blaspheming heauen bitterly,
As authour of vniustice, there to let him dye.

61

He lookt a little further, and espyde
  Another wretch, whose carkasse deepe was
  drent
  Within the riuer, which the same did hyde :
  But both his hands most filthy feculent,
  Aboue the water were on high extent,
And faynd to wash themselues incessantly ;
  Yet nothing cleaner were for such intent,
  But rather fowler seemed to the eye ;
So lost his labour vaine and idle industry.

62

The knight him calling, asked who he was,
  Who lifting vp his head, him answerd thus :
  I *Pilate* am the falsest Iudge, alas,
  And most vniust, that by vnrighteous
  And wicked doome, to Iewes despiteous
Deliuered vp the Lord of life to die,
  And did acquite a murdrer felonous ;
  The whiles my hands I washt in puritie,
The whiles my soule was soyld with foule
  iniquitie.

63

Infinite moe, tormented in like paine
  He there beheld, too long here to be told:
  Ne *Mammon* would there let him long remaine,
  For terrour of the tortures manifold,
  In which the damned soules he did behold,
  But roughly him bespake. Thou fearefull foole,
  Why takest not of that same fruit of gold,
  Ne sittest downe on that same siluer stoole,
To rest thy wearie person, in the shadow coole.

64

All which he did, to doe him deadly fall
  In frayle intemperance through sinfull bayt;
  To which if he inclined had at all,
  That dreadfull feend, which did behind him
    wayt,
  Would him haue rent in thousand peeces strayt:
  But he was warie wise in all his way,
  And well perceiued his deceiptfull sleight,
  Ne suffred lust his safetie to betray;
So goodly did beguile the Guyler of the pray.

65

And now he has so long remained there,
  That vitall powres gan wexe both weake and
    wan,
  For want of food, and sleepe, which two vpbeare,
  Like mightie pillours, this fraile life of man,
  That none without the same enduren can.
  For now three dayes of men were full out-
    wrought,
  Since he this hardie enterprize began:
  For thy great *Mammon* fairely he besought,
Into the world to guide him backe, as he him
    brought.

66

The God, though loth, yet was constraind t'obay,
  For lenger time, then that, no liuing wight
  Below the earth, might suffred be to stay:
  So backe againe, him brought to liuing light.
  But all so soone as his enfeebled spright
  Gan sucke this vitall aire into his brest,
  As ouercome with too exceeding might,
  The life did flit away out of her nest,
And all his senses were with deadly fit opprest.

Cant. VIII.

Sir Guyon laid in swowne is by
Acrates sonnes despoyld,
Whom Arthur soone hath reskewed
And Paynim brethren foyld.

1

And is there care in heauen? and is there loue
  In heauenly spirits to these creatures bace,
  That may compassion of their euils moue?
  There is: else much more wretched were the cace
  Of men, then beasts. But O th'exceeding grace
  Of highest God, that loues his creatures so,
  And all his workes with mercy doth embrace,
  That blessed Angels, he sends to and fro,
To serue to wicked man, to serue his wicked foe.

2

How oft do they, their siluer bowers leaue,
  To come to succour vs, that succour want?
  How oft do they with golden pineons, cleaue
  The flitting skyes, like flying Pursuiuant,
  Against foule feends to aide vs millitant?
  They for vs fight, they watch and dewly ward,
  And their bright Squadrons round about vs
    plant,
  And all for loue, and nothing for reward:
O why should heauenly God to men haue such
    regard?

3

During the while, that *Guyon* did abide
  In *Mammons* house, the Palmer, whom why leare
  That wanton Mayd of passage had denide,
  By further search had passage found elsewhere,
  And being on his way, approched neare,
  Where *Guyon* lay in traunce, when suddenly
  He heard a voice, that called loud and cleare,
  Come hither, come hither, O come hastily;
That all the fields resounded with the ruefull cry.

4

The Palmer lent his eare vnto the noyce,
  To weet, who called so importunely:
  Againe he heard a more efforced voyce,
  That bad him come in haste. He by and by
  His feeble feet directed to the cry;
  Which to that shadie delue him brought at last,
  Where *Mammon* earst did sunne his threasury:
  There the good *Guyon* he found slumbring fast
In senselesse dreame; which sight at first him
    sore aghast.

5

Beside his head there sate a faire young man,
  Of wondrous beautie, and of freshest yeares,
  Whose tender bud to blossome new began,
  And flourish faire aboue his equall peares ;
  His snowy front curled with golden heares,
  Like *Phœbus* face adornd with sunny rayes,
  Diuinely shone, and two sharpe winged sheares,
  Decked with diuerse plumes, like painted Iayes,
Were fixed at his backe, to cut his ayerie wayes.

6

Like as *Cupido* on *Idæan* hill,
  When hauing laid his cruell bow away,
  And mortall arrowes, wherewith he doth fill
  The world with murdrous spoiles and bloudie
      pray,
  With his faire mother he him dights to play,
  And with his goodly sisters. *Graces* three ;
  The Goddesse pleased with his wanton play,
  Suffers her selfe through sleepe beguild to bee,
The whiles the other Ladies mind their merry
      glee.

7

Whom when the Palmer saw, abasht he was
  Through fear and wonder, that he nought
      could say,
  Till him the child bespoke, Long lackt, alas,
  Hath bene thy faithfull aide in hard assay,
  Whiles deadly fit thy pupill doth dismay ;
  Behold this heauie sight, thou reuerend Sire,
  But dread of death and dolour doe away ;
  For life ere long shall to her home retire,
And he that breathlesse seemes, shal corage bold
      respire.

8

The charge, which God doth vnto me arret,
  Of his deare safetie, I to thee commend ;
  Yet will I not forgoe, ne yet forget
  The care thereof my selfe vnto the end,
  But euermore him succour, and defend
  Against his foe and mine : watch thou I pray ;
  For euill is at hand him to offend.
  So hauing said, eftsoones he gan display
His painted nimble wings, and vanisht quite
      away.

9

The Palmer seeing his left empty place,
  And his slow eyes beguiled of their sight,
  Woxe sore affraid, and standing still a space,
  Gaz'd after him, as fowle escapt by flight ;
  At last him turning to his charge behight,
  With trembling hand his troubled pulse gan try ;
  Where finding life not yet dislodged quight,
  He much reioyst, and courd it tenderly,
As chicken newly hatcht, from dreaded destiny.

10

At last he spide, where towards him did pace
  Two Paynim knights, all armd as bright as skie,
  And them beside an aged Sire did trace,
  And farre before a light-foot Page did flie,
  That breathed strife and troublous enmitie ;
  Those were the two sonnes of *Acrates* old,
  Who meeting earst with *Archimago* slie,
  Foreby that idle strond, of him were told,
That he, which earst them combatted, was
      Guyon bold.

11

Which to auenge on him they dearely vowd,
  Where euer that on ground they mote him fynd ;
  False *Archimage* prouokt their courage prowd,
  And stryfull *Atin* in their stubborne mynd
  Coles of contention and whot vengeance tynd.
  Now bene they come, whereas the Palmer sate,
  Keeping that slombred corse to him assynd ;
  Well knew they both his person, sith of late
With him in bloudie armes they rashly did
      debate.

12

Whom when *Pyrochles* saw, inflam'd with rage,
  That sire he foule bespake, Thou dotard vile,
  That with thy brutenesse shendst thy comely age,
  Abandone soone, I read, the caitiue spoile
  Of that same outcast carkasse, that erewhile
  Made it selfe famous through false trechery,
  And crownd his cowardcrest with knightlystile ;
  Loe where he now inglorious doth lye,
To proue he liued ill, that did thus foully dye.

13

To whom the Palmer fearelesse answered ;
  Certes, Sir knight, ye bene too much to blame,
  Thus for to blot the honour of the dead,
  And with foule cowardize his carkasse shame,
  Whose liuing hands immortalizd his name.
  Vile is the vengeance on the ashes cold,
  And enuie base, to barke at sleeping fame :
  Was neuer wight, that treason of him told ;
Your selfe his prowesse prou'd and found him
      fiers and bold.

14

Then said *Cymochles* ; Palmer, thou doest dote,
  Ne canst of prowesse, ne of knighthood deeme,
  Saue as thou seest or hearst. But well I wote,
  That of his puissance tryall made extreeme ;
  Yet gold all is not, that doth golden seeme,
  Ne all good knights, that shake well speare and
      shield :
  The worth of all men by their end esteeme,
  And then due praise, or due reproch them
      yield ;   [on field.
Bad therefore I him deeme, that thus lies dead

15

Good or bad (gan his brother fierce reply)
What doe I recke, sith that he dyde entire ?
Or what doth his bad death now satisfy
The greedy hunger of reuenging ire,
Sith wrathfull hand wrought not her owne desire?
Yet since no way is left to wreake my spight,
I will him reaue of armes, the victors hire,
And of that shield, more worthy of good knight;
For why should a dead dog be deckt in armour
        bright ?

16

Faire Sir, said then the Palmer suppliaunt,
For knighthoods loue, do not so foule a deed,
Ne blame your honour with so shamefull vaunt
Of vile reuenge. To spoile the dead of weed
Is sacrilege, and doth all sinnes exceed ;
But leaue these relicks of his liuing might,
To decke his herce, and trap his tomb-blacke
        steed.   [dight,
What herce or steed (said he) should he haue
But be entombed in the rauen or the kight ?

17

With that, rude hand vpon his shield he laid,
And th'other brother gan his helme vnlace,
Both fiercely bent to haue him disaraid ;
Till that they spide, where towards them did pace
An armed knight, of bold and bounteous grace,
Whose squire bore after him an heben launce,
And couerd shield. Well kend him so farre space
Th'enchaunter by his armes and amenaunce,
When vnder him he saw his Lybian steed to
        praunce.

18

And to those brethren said, Rise rise by liue,
And vnto battell doe your selues addresse ;
For yonder comes the prowest knight aliue,
Prince *Arthur*, flowre of grace and nobilesse,
That hath to Paynim knights wrought great
        distresse,
And thousand Sar'zins foully donne to dye.
That word so deepe did in their harts impresse,
That both eftsoones vpstarted furiously,
And gan themselues prepare to battell greedily.

19

But fierce *Pyrochles*, lacking his owne sword,
The want thereof now greatly gan to plaine,
And *Archimage* besought, him that afford,
Which he had brought for *Braggadocchio* vaine.
So would I (said th'enchaunter) glad and faine
Beteeme to you this sword, you to defend,
Or ought that else your honour might maintaine,
But that this weapons powre I well haue kend,
To be contrarie to the worke, which ye intend.

20

For that same knights owne sword this is of yore,
Which *Merlin* made by his almightie art
For that his noursling, when he knighthoods swore,
Therewith to doen his foes eternall smart.
The metall first he mixt with *Medæwart*,
That no enchauntment from his dint might saue;
Then it in flames of *Aetna* wrought apart,
And seuen times dipped in the bitter waue
Of hellish *Styx*, which hidden vertue to it gaue.

21

The vertue is, that neither steele, nor stone
The stroke thereof from entrance may defend ;
Ne euer may be vsed by his fone,
Ne forst his rightfull owner to offend,
Ne euer will it breake, ne euer bend.
Wherefore *Morddure* it rightfully is hight.
In vaine therefore, *Pyrochles*, should I lend
The same to thee, against his lord to fight,
For sure it would deceiue thy labour, and thy
        might.

22

Foolish old man, said then the Pagan wroth,
That weenest wôrds or charmes may force
        withstond :
Soone shalt thou see, and then beleeue for troth,
That I can carue with this inchaunted brond
His Lords owne flesh. Therewith out of his hond
That vertuous steele he rudely snatcht away,
And *Guyons* shield about his wrest he bond ;
So readie dight, fierce battaile to assay,
And match his brother proud in battailous array.

23

By this that straunger knight in presence came,
And goodly salued them ; who nought againe
Him answered, as courtesie became,
But with sterne lookes, and stomachous disdaine,
Gaue signes of grudge and discontentment vaine:
Then turning to the Palmer, he gan spy
Where at his feete, with sorrowfull demaine
And deadly hew, an armed corse did lye,
In whose dead face he red great magnanimity.

24

Said he then to the Palmer, Reuerend syre,
What great misfortune hath betidd this knight?
Or did his life her fatall date expyre,
Or did he fall by treason, or by fight ?
How euer, sure I rew his pitteous plight.
Not one, nor other, (said the Palmer graue)
Hath him befalne, but cloudes of deadly night
A while his heauie eylids couer'd haue,
And all his senses drowned in deepe senselesse
        waue.

25

Which, those his cruell foes, that stand hereby,
Making aduantage, to reuenge their spight,
Would him disarme, and treaten shamefully,
Vnworthy vsage of redoubted knight.
But you, faire Sir, whose honorable sight
Doth promise hope of helpe, and timely grace,
Mote I beseech to succour his sad plight,
And by your powre protect his feeble cace.
First praise of knighthood is, foule outrage to
     deface.

26

Palmer, (said he) no knight so rude, I weene,
As to doen outrage to a sleeping ghost :
Ne was there euer noble courage scene,
That in aduauntage would his puissance bost:
Honour is least, where oddes appeareth most.
May be, that better reason will asswage
The rash reuengers heat. Words well dispost
Haue secret powre, t'appease inflamed rage :
If not, leaue vnto me thy knights last patronage.

27

Tho turning to those brethren, thus bespoke,
Ye warlike payre, whose valorous great might
It seemes, iust wrongs to vengeance doe prouoke,
To wreake your wrath on this dead seeming
     knight,
Mote ought allay the storme of your despight,
And settle patience in so furious heat ?
Not to debate the chalenge of your right,
But for this carkasse pardon I entreat,
Whom fortune hath alreadie laid in lowest seat.

28

To whom *Cymochles* said ; For what art thou,
That mak'st thy selfe his dayes-man, to prolong
The vengeance prest? Or who shall let me now,
On this vile bodie from to wreake my wrong,
And make his carkasse as the outcast dong ?
Why should not that dead carrion satisfie
The guilt, which if he liued had thus long,
His life for due reuenge should deare abie ?
The trespasse still doth liue, albe the person die

29

Indeed (then said the Prince) the euill donne
Dyes not, when breath the bodie first doth leaue,
But from the grandsyre to the Nephewes sonne,
And all his seed the curse doth often cleaue,
Till vengeance vtterly the guilt bereaue :
So streightly God doth iudge. But gentle
     knight,
That doth against the dead his hand vpreare,
His honour staines with rancour and despight,
And great disparagment makes to his former
     might.

30

Pyrochles gan reply the second time,
And to him said, Now felon sure I read,
How that thou art partaker of his crime :
Therefore by *Termagaunt* thou shalt be dead.
With that his hand, more sad then lomp of lead,
Vplifting high, he weened with *Morddure*,
His owne good sword *Morddure*, to cleaue his
     head.
The faithfull steele such treason no'uld endure,
But swaruing from the marke, his Lords life did
     assure.

31

Yet was the force so furious and so fell,
That horse and man it made to reele aside ;
Nath'lesse the Prince would not forsake his sell:
For well of yore he learned had to ride,
But full of anger fiercely to him cride ;
False traitour miscreant, thou broken hast
The law of armes, to strike foe vndefide.
But thou thy treasons fruit, I hope, shalt taste
Right sowre, and feele the law, the which thou
     hast defast.

32

With that his balefull speare he fiercely bent
Against the Pagans brest, and therewith thought
His cursed life out of her lodge haue rent :
But ere the point arriued, where it ought,
That seuen-fold shield, which he from *Guyon*
     brought
He cast betwene toward the bitter stound :
Through all those foldes the steele head passage
     wrought   ground
And through his shoulder pierst ; wherwith to
He groueling fell, all gored in his gushing wound.

33

Which when his brother saw, fraught with great
     griefe
And wrath, he to him leaped furiously,
And fowly said, By *Mahoune*, cursed thiefe,
That direfull stroke thou dearely shalt aby.
Then hurling vp his harmefull blade on hye,
Smote him so hugely on his haughtie crest,
That from his saddle forced him to fly :
Else mote it needes downe to his manly brest
Haue cleft his head in twaine, and life thence
     dispossest.

34

Now was the Prince in daungerous distresse,
Wanting his sword, when he on oot should fight :
His single speare could doe him small redresse,
Against two foes of so exceeding might,
The least of which was match for any knight.
And now the other, whom he earst did daunt,
Had reard himselfe againe to cruell fight,
Three times more furious, and more puissaunt,
Vnmindfull of his wound, of his fate ignoraunt

35

So both attonce him charge on either side,
  With hideous strokes, and importable powre,
  That forced him his ground to trauerse wide,
  And wisely watch to ward that deadly stowre:
  For in his shield, as thicke as stormie showre,
  Their strokes did raine, yet did he neuer quaile,
  Ne backward shrinke, but as a stedfast towre,
  Whom foe with double battry doth assaile,
Them on her bulwarke beares, and bids them
    nought auaile.

36

So stoutly he withstood their strong assay,
  Till that at last, when he aduantage spyde,
  His poinant speare he thrust with puissant sway
  At proud *Cymochles*, whiles his sh eld was wyde,
  That through his thigh the mortall steele did
    gryde:
  He swaruing with the force, within his flesh
  Did breake the launce, and let the head abyde:
  Out of the wound the red bloud flowed fresh,
That vnderneath his feet soone made a purple
    plesh.

37

Horribly then he gan to rage, and rayle,
  Cursing his Gods, and himselfe damning deepe:
  Als when his brother saw the red bloud rayle
  Adowne so fast, and all his armour steepe,
  For very felnesse lowd he gan to weepe,
  And said, Caytiue, cursse on thy cruell hond,
  That twise hath sped; yet shall it not thee keepe
  From the third brunt of this my fatall brond:
Loe where the dreadfull Death behind thy backe
    doth stond.

38

With that he strooke, and th'other strooke withall,
  That nothing seem'd mote beare so monstrous
    might:
  The one vpon his couered shield did fall,
  And glauncing downe would not his owner byte:
  But th'other did vpon his troncheon smyte,
  Which hewing quite a sunder, further way
  It made, and on his hacqueton did lyte,
  The which diuiding with importune sway,
It seizd in his right side, and there the dint did
    stay.

39

Wyde was the wound, and a large lukewarme flood,
  Red as the Rose, thence gushed grieuously;
  That when the Paynim spyde the streaming
    blood,
  Gaue him great hart, and hope of victory.
  On th'other side, in huge perplexity,
  The Prince now stood, hauing his weapon broke;
  Nought could he hurt, but still at ward did ly:
  Yet with his troncheon he so rudely stroke
Cymochles twise, that twise him forst his foot
    reuoke.

40

Whom when the Palmer saw in such distresse,
  Sir *Guyons* sword he rightly to him raught,
  And said; Faire Son, great God thy right
    hand blesse,
  To vse that sword so wisely as it ought.
  Glad was the knight, and with fresh courage
    fraught,
  When as againe he armed felt his hond;
  Then like a Lion, which hath long time saught
  His robbed whelpes, and at the last them fond
Emongst the shepheard swaynes, then wexeth
    wood and yond.

41

So fierce he laid about him, and dealt blowes
  On either side, that neither mayle could hold,
  Ne shield defend the thunder of his throwes:
  Now to *Pyrochles* many strokes he told;
  Eft to *Cymochles* twise so many fold:
  Then backe againe turning his busie hond,
  Them both attonce compeld with courage bold,
  To yield wide way to his hart-thrilling brond;
And though they both stood stiffe, yet could
    not both withstond.

42

As saluage Bull, whom two fierce mastiues bayt,
  When rancour doth with rage him once engore,
  Forgets with warie ward them to awayt,
  But with his dreadfull hornes them driues afore,
  Or flings aloft, or treads downe in the flore,
  Breathing out wrath, and bellowing disdaine,
  That all the forrest quakes to heare him rore:
  So rag'd Prince *Arthur* twixt his foemen twaine,
That neither could his mightie puissance sustaine.

43

But euer at *Pyrochles* when he smit,
  Who *Guyons* shield cast euer him before,
  Whereon the Faery Queenes pourtract was writ,
  His hand relented, and the stroke forbore,
  And his deare hart the picture gan adore,
  Which oft the Paynim sau'd from deadly stowre.
  But him henceforth the same can saue no more;
  For now arriued is his fatall howre,
That no'te auoyded be by earthly skill or powre.

44

For when *Cymochles* saw the fowle reproch,
  Which them appeached, prickt with guilty shame,
  And inward griefe, he fiercely gan approch,
  Resolu'd to put away that loathly blame,
  Or dye with honour and desert of fame;
  And on the hauberk stroke the Prince so sore,
  That quite disparted all the linked frame,
  And pierced to the skin, but bit no more,
Yet made him twise to reele, that neuer moou'd
    afore.

45

Whereat renfierst with wrath and sharpe regret,
 He stroke so hugely with his borrowd blade,
 That it empierst the Pagans burganet,
 And cleauing the hard steele, did deepe inuade
 Into his head, and cruell passage made
 Quite through his braine. He tombling downe
    on ground,
 Breathd out his ghost, which to th'infernall
    shade
 Fast flying, there eternall torment found,
For all the sinnes, wherewith his lewd life did
    abound.

46

Which when his german saw, the stony feare
 Ran to his hart, and all his sence dismayd,
 Ne thenceforth life ne courage did appeare,
 But as a man, whom hellish feends haue frayd,
 Long tremblingstill he stood: at last thus sayd;
 Traytour what hast thou doen? how euer may
 Thy cursed hand so cruelly haue swayd
 Against that knight: Harrow and well away,
After so wicked deed whyliu'st thou lenger day?

47

With that all desperate as loathing light,
 And with reuenge desiring soone to dye,
 Assembling all his force and vtmost might,
 With his owne sword he fierce at him did flye,
 And strooke, and foynd, and lasht outrageously,
 Withouten reason or regard. Well knew
 The Prince, with patience and sufferaunce sly
 So hasty heat soone cooled to subdew:
Tho when this breathlesse woxe, that batteil
    gan renew.

48

As when a windy tempest bloweth hye,
 That nothing may withstand his stormy stowre,
 The cloudes, as things affrayd, before him flye;
 But all so soone as his outrageous powre
 Is layd, they fiercely then begin to shoure,
 And as in scorne of his spent stormy spight,
 Now all attonce their malice forth do poure;
 So did Prince *Arthur* beare himselfe in fight,
And suffred rash *Pyrochles* wast his idle might.

49

At last when as the Sarazin perceiu'd,
 How that straunge sword refusd, to serue his
    need,   [deceiu'd,
 But when he stroke most strong, the dint
 He flong it from him, and deuoyd of dreed,
 Vpon him lightly leaping without heed,
 Twixt his two mighty armes engrasped fast,
 Thinking to ouerthrow and downe him tred:
 But him in strength and skill the Prince surpast,
And through his nimble sleight did vnder him
    down cast.

50

Nought booted it the Paynim then to striue
 For as a Bittur in the Eagles claw,
 That may not hope by flight to scape aliue,
 Still waites for death with dread and trembling
    aw;
 So he now subiect to the victours law,
 Did not once moue, nor vpward cast his eye.
 For vile disdaine and rancour, which did gnaw
 His hart in twaine with sad melancholy,
As one that loathed life, and yet despisd to dye

51

But full of Princely bounty and great mind,
 The Conquerour nought cared him to slay,
 But casting wrongs and all reuenge behind
 More glory thought to giue life, then decay,
 And said, Paynim, this is thy dismall day;
 Yet if thou wilt renounce thy miscreaunce,
 And my trew liegeman yield thy selfe for ay
 Life will I graunt thee for thy valiaunce,
And all thy wrongs will wipe out of my souen
    aunce.

52

Foole (said the Pagan) I thy gift defye,
 But vse thy fortune, as it doth befall,
 And say, that I not ouercome do dye,
 But in despight of life, for death do call.
 Wroth was the Prince, and sory yet withall
 That he so wilfully refused grace;
 Yet sith his fate so cruelly did fall,
 His shining Helmet he gan soone vnlace,
And left his headlesse body bleeding all the
    place.

53

By this Sir *Guyon* from his traunce awakt,
 Life hauing maistered her sencelesse foe;
 And looking vp, when as his shield he lakt,
 And sword saw not, he wexed wondrous woe:
 But when the Palmer, whom he long ygoe
 Had lost, he by him spide, right glad he grew,
 And said, Deare sir, whom wandring to and fro
 I long haue lackt, I ioy thy face to vew;
Firme is thy faith, whom daunger neuer fro me
    drew.

54

But read what wicked hand hath robbed mee
 Of my good sword and shield? The Palmer glad,
 With so fresh hew vprising him to see,
 Him answered; Faire sonne, be no whit sad
 For want of weapons, they shall soone be had.
 So gan he to discourse the whole debate,
 Which that straunge knight for him sustained
    had,
 And those two Sarazins confounded late,
Whose carcases on ground were horribly pros-
    trate.

55

Which when he heard, and saw the tokens trew,
 His hart with great affection was embayd,
 And to the Prince bowing with reuerence dew.
 As to the Patrone of his life, thus sayd ;
 My Lord, my liege, by whose most gratious ayd
 I liue this day, and see my foes subdewd,
 What may suffise, to be for meede repayd
 Of so great graces, as ye haue me shewd,
But to be euer bound

56

To whom the Infant thus, Faire Sir, what need
 Good turnes be counted, as a seruile bond,
 To bind their doers, to receiue their meede ?
 Are not all knights by oath bound, to with-
  stond
 Oppressours powre by armes and puissant
  hond ?
 Suffise, that I haue done my dew in place.
 So goodly purpose they together fond,
 Of kindnesse and of curteous aggrace ;
The whiles false *Archimage* and *Atin* fled apace.

Cant. IX.

ᘓᘓᘓᘓᘓᘓᘓᘓᘓᘓᘓᘓᘓᘓᘓ

The house of Temperance, in which
doth sober Alma dwell,
Besiegd of many foes, whom straunger
knightes to flight compell.

ᘓᘓᘓᘓᘓᘓᘓᘓᘓᘓᘓᘓᘓᘓ

I

Of all Gods workes, which do this world adorne,
 There is no one more faire and excellent,
 Then is mans body both for powre and forme,
 Whiles it is kept in sober gouernment ;
 But none then it, more fowle and indecent,
 Distempred through misrule and passions bace :
 It growes a Monster, and incontinent
 Doth loose his dignitie and natiue grace.
Behold, who list, both one and other in this
 place.

2

After the Paynim brethren conquer'd were,
 The *Briton* Prince recou'ring his stolne sword,
 And *Guyon* his lost shield, they both yfere
 Forth passed on their way in faire accord,
 Till him the Prince with gentle court did bord ;
 Sir knight, mote I of you this curt'sie read,
 To weet why on your shield so goodly scord
 Beare ye the picture of that Ladies head ?
Full liuely is the semblaunt, though the sub-
 stance dead.

3

Faire Sir (said he) if in that picture dead
 Such life ye read, and vertue in vaine shew,
 What mote ye weene, if the trew liuely-head
 Of that most glorious visage ye did vew ?
 But if the beautie of her mind ye knew,
 That is her bountie, and imperiall powre,
 Thousand times fairer then her mortall hew,
 O how great wonder would your thoughts
  deuoure,
And infinite desire into your spirite poure !

4

She is the mighty Queene of *Faerie*,
 Whose faire retrait I in my shield do beare ;
 She is the flowre of grace and chastitie,
 Throughout the world renowmed far and neare,
 My liefe, my liege, my Soueraigne, my deare,
 Whose glory shineth as the morning starre,
 And with her light the earth enlumines cleare;
 Far reach her mercies, and her prayses farre,
As well in state of peace, as puissaunce in warre.

5

Thrise happy man, (said then the *Briton* knight)
 Whom gracious lot, and thy great valiaunce
 Haue made the esouldier of that Princesse brigl.t,
 Which with her bounty and glad countenance
 Doth blesse her seruants, and them high
  aduaunce.
 How may straunge knight hope euer to aspire,
 By faithfull seruice, and meet amenance,
 Vnto such blisse ? sufficient were that hire
For losse of thousand liues, to dye at her desire.

6

Said *Guyon*, Noble Lord, what meed so great,
 Or grace of earthly Prince so soueraine,
 But by your wondrous worth and warlike feat
 Ye well may hope, and easely attaine ?
 But were your will, her sold to entertaine,
 And numbred be mongst knights of *Maydenhed*,
 Great guerdon, well I wote, should you remaine,
 And in her fauour high be reckoned,
As *Arthegall*, and *Sophy* now beene honored.

7

Certes (then said the Prince) I God auow,
 That sith I armes and knighthood first did
  plight,
 My whole desire hath beene, and yet is now,
 To serue that Queene with all my powre and
  might.
 Now hath the Sunne with his lamp-burning light,
 Walkt round about the world, and I no lesse,
 Sith of that Goddesse I haue sought the sight,
 Yet no where can her find : such happinesse
Heauen doth to me enuy, and fortune fauourlesse.

8

Fortune, the foe of famous cheuisaunce
Seldome (said *Guyon*) yields to vertue aide.
But in her way throwes mischiefe and mis-
  chaunce,
Whereby her course is stopt, and passage staid.
But you, faire Sir, be not herewith dismaid,
But constant keepe the way, in which ye stand;
Which were it not, that I am else delaid
With hard aduenture, which I haue in hand,
I labour would to guide you through all Faery
  land.

9

Gramercy Sir (said he) but mote I weete,
What straunge aduenture do ye now pursew ?
Perhaps my succour, or aduizement meete
Mote stead you much your purpose to subdew.
Then gan Sir *Guyon* all the story shew
Of false *Acrasia*, and her wicked wiles,
Which to auenge, the Palmer him forth drew
From Faery court. So talked they, the whiles
They wasted had much way, and measurd many
  miles.

10

And now faire *Phœbus* gan decline in hast
His weary wagon to the Westerne vale,
Whenas they spide a goodly castle, plast
Foreby a riuer in a pleasaunt dale,
Which choosing for that euenings hospitale,
They thither marcht : but when they came in
  sight,
And from their sweaty Coursers did auale,
They found the gates fast barred long ere night,
And euery loup fast lockt, as fearing foes
  despight.

11

Which when they saw, they weene lfowlereproch
Was to them doen, their entrance to forstall,
Till that the Squire gan nigher to approch ;
And wind his horne vnder the castle wall,
That with the noise it shooke, as it would fall :
Eftsoones forth looked from the highest spire
The watch, and lowd vnto the knights did call,
To weete, what they so rudely did require.
Who gently answered, They entrance did desire.

12

Fly fly, good knights, (said he) fly fast away
If that your liues ye loue, as meete ye should ;
Fly fast and saue your selues from neare decay,
Here may ye not haue entraunce, though we
  would :
We would and would againe if that we could ;
But thousand enemies about vs raue,
And with long siege vs in this castle hould :
Seuen yeares this wize they vs besieged haue,
And many good knights slaine, that haue vs
  sought to saue.

13

Thus as he spoke, loe with outragious cry
A thousand villeins round about them swarmd
Out of the rockes and caues adioyning nye,
Vile caytiue wretches, ragged, rude, deformd,
All threatning death, all in straunge manner
  armd,
Some with vnweldy clubs, some with long speares,
Some rusty kniues, some staues in fire warm'd.
Sterne was their looke, like wild aṁazed steares,
Staring with hollow eyes, and stiffe vpstanding
  heares.

14

Fiersly at first those knights they did assaile,
And droue them to recoile : but when againe
They gaue fresh charge, their forces gan to faile,
Vnhable their encounter to sustaine ;
For with such puissaunce and impetuous maine
Those Champions broke on them, that forst
  them fly,   [swaine
Like scattered Sheepe, whenas the Shepheards
A Lyon and a Tigre doth espye,
With greedy pace forth rushing from the forest
  nye.

15

A while they fled, but soone returnd againe
With greater fury, then before was found ;
And euermore their cruell Capitaine
Sought with his raskall routs t'enclose them
  round,
And ouerrun to tread them to the ground.
But soone the knights with their bright-burn-
  ing blades   [found,
Broke their rude troupes, and orders did con-
Hewing and slashing at their idle shades ;
For though they bodies seeme, yet substance
  from them fades.

16

As when a swarme of Gnats at euentide
Out of the fennes of Allan do arise,
Their murmuring small trompets sounden wide,
Whiles in the aire their clustring army flies,
That as a cloud doth seeme to dim the skies ;
Ne man nor beast may rest, or take repast,
For their sharpe wounds, and noyous iniuries,
Till the fierce Northerne wind with blustring blast
Doth blow them quite away, and in the *Ocean*
  cast.

17

Thus when they had that troublous rout disperst,
Vnto the castle gate they come againe,
And entraunce crau'd, which was denied erst.
Now when report of that their perilous paine,
And combrous conflict, which they did sustaine,
Came to the Ladies eare, which there did dwell,
She forth issewed with a goodly traine
Of Squires and Ladies equipaged well,
And entertained them right fairely, as befell

18

Alma she called was, a virgin bright ;
  That had not yet felt *Cupides* wanton rage,
  Yet was she woo'd of many a gentle knight,
  And many a Lord of noble parentage,
  That sought with her to lincke in marriage :
  For she was faire, as faire mote euer bee,
  And in the flowre now of her freshest age ;
  Yet full of grace and goodly modestee,
That euen heauen reioyced her sweete face to
  see.

19

In robe of lilly white she was arayd,
  That from her shoulder to her heele downe raught,
  The traine whereof loos · far behind her strayd,
  Braunched with gol.l and pearle, most richly
    wrought,
  And borne of two faire Damsels, which were
    taught
That seruice well. Her yellow golden heare
  Was trimly wouen, and in tresses wrought,
  Ne other tyre she on her head did weare,
But crowned with a garland of sweete Rosiere.

20

Goodly she entertaind those noble knights,
  And brought them vp into her castle hall ;
  Where gentle court and gracious delight
  She to them made, with mildnesse virginall,
  Shewing her selfe both wise and liberall :
  There when they rested had a season dew,
  They her besought of fauour speciall,
  Of that faire Castle to affoord them vew ;
She graunt:d, and them leading forth, the
  same did shew.

21

First she them led vp to the Castle wall,
  That was so high, as foe might not it clime,
  And all so faire, and fensible withall,
  Not built of bricke, ne yet of stone and lime,
  But of thing like to that *Ægyptian* slime,
  Whereof king *Nine* whilome built *Babell* towre;
  But O great pitty, that no lenger time
  So goodly workemanship should not endure :
Soone it must turne to earth ; no earthly thing
  is sure.

22

The frame thereof seemd partly circulare,
  And part triangulare, O worke diuine ;
  Those two the first and last proportions are,
  The one imperfect, mortall, fœminine ;
  Th'other immortall, perfect, masculine,
  And twixt them both a quadrate was the base
  Proportioned equally by seuen and nine ;
  Nine was the circle set in heauens place,
All which compacted made a goodly diapase.

23

Therein two gates were placed seemly well :
  The one before, by which all in did pas,
  Did th'other far in workmanship excell ;
  For not of wood, nor of enduring bras,
  But of more worthy substance fram'd it was;
  Doubly disparted, it did locke and close,
  That when it locked, none might thorough pas,
  And when it opened, no man might it close,
Still open to their friends, and closed to their
  foes.

24

Of hewen stone the porch was fairely wrought,
  Stone more of valew, and more smooth and
    fine,
  Then Iet or Marble far from Ireland brought ;
  Ouer the which was cast a wandring vine,
  Enchaced with a wanton yuie twine.
  And ouer it a faire Portcullis hong,
  Which to the gate directly did incline,
  With comely compasse, and compacture strong,
Neither vnseemely short, nor yet exceeding
  long.

25

Within the Barbican a Porter sate,
  Day and night duely keeping watch and ward,
  Nor wight, nor word mote passe out of the gate,
  But in good order, and with dew regard ;
  Vtterers of secrets he from thence debard,
  Bablers of folly, and blazers of crime.
  His larumbell might lowd and wide be hard,
  When cause requird, but neuer out of time ;
Early and late it rong, at euening and at prime.

26

And round about the porch on euery side
  Twise sixteen warders sat, all armed bright
  In glistring steele, and strongly fortifide :
  Tall yeomen seemed they, and of great might,
  And were enraunged ready, still for fight.
  By them as *Alma* passed with her guestes,
  They did obeysaunce, as beseemed right,
  And then againe returned to their restes :
The Porter eke to her did lout with humble
  gestes.

27

Thence she them brought into a stately Hall,
  Wherein were many tables faire dispred,
  And ready dight with drapets festiuall,
  Against the viaundes should be ministred,
  At th'upper end there sate, yclad in red
  Downe to the ground, a comely personage,
  That in his hand a white rod menaged,
  He Steward was hight *Diet* ; rype of age,
And in demeanure sober, and in counsell sage.

28

And through the Hall there walked to and fro
A iolly yeoman, Marshall of the same,
Whose name was *Appetite* ; he did bestow
Both guestes and meate, when euer in they
   came,
And knew them how to order without blame,
As him the Steward bad. They both attone
Did dewty to their Lady, as became ;
Who passing by, forth led her guestes anone
Into the kitchin rowme, ne spard for nicenesse
   none.

29

It was a vaut ybuilt for great dispence,
With many raunges reard along the wall ;
And one great chimney, whose long tonnell
   thence
The smoke forth threw. And in the midst of all
There placed was a caudron wide and tall,
Vpon a mighty furnace, burning whot,
More whot, then *Aetn'*, or flaming *Mongiball*:
For day and night it brent, ne ceased not,
So long as any thing it in the caudron got.

30

But to delay the heat, least by mischaunce
It might breake out, and set the whole on fire,
There added was by goodly ordinaunce,
An huge great paire of bellowes, which did styre
Continually, and cooling breath inspyre.
About the Caudron many Cookes accoyld,
With hookes and ladles, as need did require ;
The whiles the viandes in the vessell boyld
They did about their businesse sweat, and sorely
   toyld.

31

The maister Cooke was cald *Concoction*,
A carefull man, and full of comely guise :
The kitchin Clerke, that hight *Digestion*,
Did order all th'Achates in seemely wise,
And set them forth, as well he could deuise.
The rest had seuerall offices assird,
Some to remoue the scum, as it did rise ;
Others to beare the same away did mind ;
And others it to vse according to his kind.

32

But all the liquour, which was fowle and wast,
Not good nor seruiceable else for ought,
They in another great round vessell plast,
Till by a conduit pipe it thence were brought :
And all the rest, that noyous was, and nought,
By secret wayes, that none might it espy,
Was close conuaid, and to th back-gate brought,
That cleped was *Port Esquiline*, whereby
It was auoided quite, and throwne out priuily.

33

Which goodly order, and great workmans skill
Whenas those knights beheld, with rare delight,
And gazing wonder they their minds did fill;
For neuer had they seene so straunge a sight.
Thence backe againe faire *Alma* led them right,
And soone into a goodly Parlour brought,
That was with royall arras richly dight,
In which was nothing pourtrahed, nor wrought,
Not wrought, nor pourtrahed, but easie to be
   thought.

34

And in the midst thereof vpon the floure,
A louely beuy of faire Ladies sate,
Courted of many a iolly Paramoure,
The which them did in modest wise amate,
And eachone sought his Lady to aggrate :
And eke emongst them litle *Cupid* playd
His wanton sports, being returned late
From his fierce warres, and hauing from him layd
His cruell bow, wherewith he thousands hath
   dismayd.

35

Diuerse delights they found them selues to
   please ;
Some song in sweet consort, some laught for ioy,
Some plaid with strawes, some idly sat at ease;
But other some could not abide to toy,
All pleasaunce was to them griefe and annoy:
This frownd, that faund, the third for shame
   did blush,
Another seemed enuious, or coy,
Another in her teeth did gnaw a rush :
But at these straungers presence euery one did
   hush.

36

Soone as the gracious *Alma* came in place
They all attonce out of their seates arose,
And to her homage made, with humble grace :
Whom when the knights beheld, they gan dispose
Themselues to court, and each a Damsell chose:
The Prince by chaunce did on a Lady light,
That was right faire and fresh as morning rose,
But somwhat sad, and solemne eke in sight,
As if some pensiue thought constraind her
   gentle spright.

37

In a long purple pall, whose skirt with gold
Was fretted all about, she was arayd ;
And in her hand a Poplar braunch did hold:
To whom the Prince in curteous manner said,
Gentle Madame, why beene ye thus dismaid,
And your faire beautie do with sadnesse spill ?
Liues any, that you hath thus ill apaid ?
Or doen you loue, or doen you lacke your will?
What euer be the cause, it sure beseemes you ill.

38

Faire Sir, (said she halfe in disdainefull wise.)
How is it, that this mood in me ye blame,
And in your selfe do not the same aduise ?
Him ill beseemes, anothers fault to name,
That may vnwares be blotted with the same :
Pensiue I yeeld I am, and sad in mind,
Through great desire of glory and of fame ;
Ne ought I weene are ye therein behind,
That haue twelue moneths sought one, yet no
     where can her find.

39

The Prince was inly moued at her speach,
Well weeting trew, what she had rashly told ;
Yet with faire semblaunt sought to hide the
     breach,
Which chaunge of colour did perforce vnfold,
Now seeming flaming whot, now stony cold.
Tho turning soft aside, he did inquire,
What wight she was, that Poplar braunch did
     hold :
It answered was, her name was *Prays-desire*,
That by well doing sought to honour to aspire.

40

The whiles, the *Faerie* knight did entertaine
Another Damsell of that gentle crew,
That was right faire, and modest of demaine,
But that too oft she chaung'd her natiue hew :
Straunge was her tyre, and all her garment blew,
Close round about her tuckt with many a plight :
Vpon her fist the bird, which shonneth vew,
And keepes in couerts close from liuing wight,
Did sit, as yet ashamd, how rude *Pan* did her
     dight.

41

So long as *Guyon* with her commoned,
Vnto the ground she cast her modest eye,
And euer and anone with rosie red
The bashfull bloud her snowy cheekes did dye,
That her became, as polisht yuory,
Which cunning Craftesmans hand hath ouerlayd
With faire vermilion or pure Castory.
Great wonder had the knight, to see the mayd
So straungely passioned, and to her gently sayd,

42

Faire Damzell, seemeth, by your troubled cheare,
That either me too bold ye weene, this wise
You to molest, or other ill to feare
That in the secret of your hart close lyes,
From whence it doth, as cloud from sea arise.
If it be I, of pardon I you pray ;
But if ought else that I mote not deuise,
I will, if please you it discure, assay,
To ease you of that ill, so wisely as I may.

43

She answerd nought, but more abasht for shame,
Held downe her head, the whiles her louely face
The flashing bloud with blushing did inflame,
And the strong passion mard her modest grace,
That *Guyon* meruayld at her vncouth cace :
Till *Alma* him bespake, Why wonder yee
Faire Sir at that, which ye so much embrace ?
She is the fountaine of your modestee ;
You shamefast are, but *Shamefastnesse* it selfe
     is shee.

44

Thereat the Elfe did blush in priuitee,
And turnd his face away ; but she the same
Dissembled faire, and faynd to ouersee.
Thus they awhile with court and goodly game,
Themselues did solace each one with his Dame,
Till that great Ladie thence away them sought,
To vew her castles other wondrous frame.
Vp to a stately Turret she them brought,
Ascending by ten steps of Alablaster wrought.

45

That Turrets frame most admirable was,
Like highest heauen compassed around,
And lifted high aboue this earthly masse,
Which it suruew'd, as hils doen lower ground ;
But not on ground mote like to this be found,
Not that, which antique *Cadmus* whylome built
In *Thebes*, which *Alexander* did confound ;
Nor that proud towre of *Troy*, though richly
     guilt,
From which young *Hectors* bloud by cruell
     Greekes was spilt.

46

The roofe hereof was arched ouer head,
And deckt with flowers and herbars daintily ;
Two goodly Beacons, set in watches stead,
Therein gaue light, and flam'd continually :
For they of liuing fire most subtilly
Were made, and set in siluer sockets bright,
Couer'd with lids deuiz'd of substance sly,
That readily they shut and open might.
O who can tell the prayses of that makers might !

47

Ne can I tell, ne can I stay to tell
This parts great workmanship, and wondrous
     powre,
That all this other worlds worke doth excell,
And likest is vnto that heauenly towre,
That God hath built for his owne blessed bowre.
Therein were diuerse roomes, and diuerse stages,
But three the chiefest, and of greatest powre,
In which there dwelt three honorable sages,
The wisest men, I weene, that liued in their ages

48

Not he, whom *Greece*, the Nourse of all good arts,
By *Phœbus* doome, the wisest thought aliue,
Might be compar'd to these by many parts:
Nor that sage *Pylian* syre, which did suruiue
Three ages, such as mortall men contriue,
By whose aduise old *Priams* cittie fell,
With these in praise of pollicies mote striue.
These three in these three roomes did sundry dwell,
And counselled faire *Alma*, how to gouerne well.

49

The first of them could things to come foresee:
The next could of things present best aduize;
The third things past could keepe in memoree,
So that no time, nor reason could arize,
But that the same could one of these comprize.
For thy the first did in the forepart sit,
That nought mote hinder his quicke preiudize:
He had a sharpe foresight, and working wit,
That neuer idle was, ne once could rest a whit.

50

His chamber was dispainted all within,
With sundry colours, in the which were writ
Infinite shapes of things dispersed thin;
Some such as in the world were neuer yit,
Ne can deuized be of mortall wit;
Some daily seene, and knowen by their names,
Such as in idle fantasies doe flit:
Infernall Hags, *Centaurs*, feendes, *Hippodames*,
Apes, Lions, Ægles, Owles, fooles, louers, children, Dames.

51

And all the chamber filled was with flyes,
Which buzzed all about, and made such sound,
That they encombred all mens eares and eyes,
Like many swarmes of Bees assembled round,
After their hiues with honny do abound:
All those were idle thoughts and fantasies,
Deuices, dreames, opinions vnsound,
Shewes, visions, sooth-sayes, and prophesies;
And all that fained is, as leasings, tales, and lies.

52

Emongst them all sate he, which wonned there,
That hight *Phantastes* by his nature trew;
A man of yeares yet fresh, as mote appere,
Of swarth complexion, and of crabbed hew,
That him full of melancholy did shew;
Bent hollow beetle browes, sharpe staring eyes,
That mad or foolish seemd: one by his vew
Mote deeme him borne with ill disposed skyes,
When oblique *Saturne* sate in the house of agonyes.

53

Whom *Alma* hauing shewed to her guestes,
Thence brought them to the second roome,
  whose wals
Were painted faire with memorable gestes,
Of famous Wisards, and with picturals
Of Magistrates, of courts, of tribunals,
Of commen wealthes, of states, of pollicy,
Of lawes, of iudgements, and of decretals;
All artes, all science, all Philosophy,
And all that in the world was aye thought wittily.

54

Of those that roome was full, and them among
There sate a man of ripe and perfect age,
Who did them meditate all his life long,
That through continuall practise and vsage,
He now was growne right wise, and wondrous
  sage.
Great pleasure had those stranger knights, to see
His goodly reason, and graue personage,
That his disciples both desir'd to bee;
But *Alma* thence them led to th'hindmost roome
  of three.

55

That chamber seemed ruinous and old,
And therefore was remoued farre behind,
Yet were the wals, that did the same vphold,
Right firme and strong, though somewhat they
  declind;
And therein sate an old oldman, halfe blind,
And all decrepit in his feeble corse,
Yet liuely vigour rested in his mind,
And recompenst him with a better scorse:
Weake body well is chang'd for minds redoubled
  forse.

56

This man of infinite remembrance was,
And things foregone through many ages held,
Which he recorded still, as they did pas,
Ne suffred them to perish through long eld,
As all things else, the which this world doth weld,
But laid them vp in his immortall scrine,
Where they for euer incorrupted dweld:
The warres he well remembred of king *Nine*,
Of old *Assaracus*, and *Inachus* diuine.

57

The yeares of *Nestor* nothing were to his,
Ne yet *Mathusalem*, though longest liu'd;
For he remembred both their infancies:
Ne wonder then, if that he were depriu'd
Of natiue strength now, that he them suruiu'd.
His chamber all was hangd about with rolles,
And old records from auncient times deriu'd,
Some made in books, some in long parchment
  scrolles,   [holes.
That were all worme-eaten, and full of canker

58

Amidst them all he in a chaire was set,
  Tossing and turning them withouten end ;
  But for he was vnhable them to fet,
  A litle boy did on him still attend,
  To reach, when euer he for ought did send ;
  And oft when things were lost, or laid amis,
  That boy them sought, and vnto him did lend.
  Therefore he *Anamnestes* cleped is,
And that old man *Eumnestes*, by their propertis.

59

The knights there entring, did him reuerence
    dew
  And wondred at his endlesse exercise,
  Then as they gan his Librarie to vew,
  And antique Registers for to auise,
  There chaunced to the Princes hand to rize,
  An auncient booke, hight *Briton moniments*,
  That of this lands first conquest did deuize,
  And old diuision into Regiments,
Till it reduced was to one mans gouernments.

60

Sir *Guyon* chaunst eke on another booke,
  That hight *Antiquitie* of *Faerie* lond,
  In which when as he greedily did looke,
  Th'off-spring of Elues and Faries there he fond,
  As it deliuered was from hond to hond :
  Whereat they burning both with feruent fire,
  Their countries auncestry to vnderstond,
  Crau'd leaue of *Alma*, and that aged sire,
To read those bookes; who gladly graunted their
    desire.

Cant. X.

A chronicle of Briton kings,
    from Brute to Vthers rayne.
And rolles of Elfin Emperours,
    till time of Gloriane.

1

Who now shall giue vnto me words and sound,
  Equall vnto this haughtie enterprise ?
  Or who shall lend me wings, with which from
    ground
My lowly verse may loftily arise,
  And lift it selfe vnto the highest skies ?
  More ample spirit, then hitherto was wount,
  Here needes me, whiles the famous auncestries
  Of my most dreaded Soueraigne I recount,
By which all earthly Princes she doth farre
    surmount.

2

Ne vnder Sunne, that shines so wide and faire,
  Whence all that liues, does borrow life and light,
  Liues ought, that to her linage may compaire,
  Which though from earth it be deriued right,
  Yet doth it selfe stretch forth to heauens hight,
  And all the world with wonder ouerspred ;
  A labour huge, exceeding farre my might :
  How shall fraile pen, with feare disparaged,
Conceiue such soueraine glory, and great
    bountihed ?

3

Argument worthy of *Mæonian* quill,
  Or rather worthy of great *Phæbus* rote,
  Whereon the ruines of great *Ossa* hill,
  And triumphes of *Phlegræan Ioue* he wrote,
  That all the Gods admird his loftie note.
  But if some relish of that heauenly lay
  His learned daughters would to me report,
  To decke my song withall, I would assay,
Thy name, O soueraine Queene, to blazon farre
    away.

4

Thy name O soueraine Queene, thy realme and
    race,
  From this renowmed Prince deriued arre,
  Who mightily vpheld that royall mace,
  Which now thou bear'st, to thee descended farre
  From mightie kings and conquerours in warre,
  Thy fathers and great Grandfathers of old,
  Whose noble deedes aboue the Northerne starre
  Immortall fame for euer hath enrold ;
As in that old mans booke they were in order
    told.

5

The land, which warlike Britons now possesse,
  And therein haue their mightie empire raysd,
  In antique times was saluage wildernesse,
  Vnpeopled, vnmanurd, vnprou'd, vnpraysd,
  Ne was it Island then, ne was it paysd
  Amid the *Ocean* waues, ne was it sought
  Of marchants farre, for profits therein praysd,
  But was all desolate, and of some thought
By sea to haue bene from the *Celticke* mayn-
    land brought.

6

Ne did it then deserue a name to haue,
  Till that the venturous Mariner that way
  Learning his ship from those white rocks to saue,
  Which all along the Southerne sea-coast lay,
  Threatning vnheedie wrecke and rash decay,
  For safeties sake that same his sea-marke made,
  And namd it *Albion*. But later day
  Finding in it fit ports for fishers trade,
Gan more the same frequent, and further to
    inuade.

7

But farre in land a saluage nation dwelt,
  Of hideous Giants, and halfe beastly men,
  That neuer tasted grace, nor goodnesse felt,
  But like wild beasts lurking in loathsome den,
  And flying fast as Roebucke through the fen,
  All naked without shame, or care of cold,
  By hunting and by spoiling liued then ;
  Of stature huge, and eke of courage bold,
That sonnes of men amazd their sternnesse to
    behold.

8

But whence they sprong, or how they were begot,
  Vneath is to assure ; vneath to wene
  That monstrous error, which doth some assot,
  That *Dioclesians* fiftie daughters shene
  Into this land by chaunce haue driuen bene,
  Where companing with feends and filthy
    Sprights,
  Through vaine illusion of their lust vnclene,
  They brought forth Giants and such dreadfull
    wights,
As farre exceeded men in their immeasurd
    mights.

9

They held this land, and with their filthinesse
  Polluted this same gentle soyle long time :
  That their owne mother loathd their beastli-
    nesse,
  And gan abhorre her broods vnkindly crime,
  All were they borne of her owne natiue slime,
  Vntill that *Brutus* anciently deriu'd
  From royall stocke of old *Assaracs* line,
  Driuen by fatall error, here arriu'd,
And them of their vniust possession depriu'd.

10

But ere he had established his throne,
  And spred his empire to the vtmost shore,
  He fought great battels with his saluage fone ;
  In which he them defeated euermore,
  And many Giants left on groning flore ;
  That well can witnesse yet vnto this day
  The westerne Hogh, besprincled with the gore
  Of mightie *Goëmot*, whom in stout fray
Corineus conquered, and cruelly did slay.

11

And eke that ample Pit, yet farre renownd,
  For the large leape, which *Debon* did compell
  Coulin to make, being eight lugs of grownd ;
  Into the which returning backe, he fell,
  But those three monstrous stones doe most excell
  Which that huge sonne of hideous *Albion*,
  Whose father *Hercules* in Fraunce did quell,
  Great *Godmer* threw, in fierce contention,
At bold *Canutus* ; but of him was slaine anon.

12

In meed of these great conquests by them got,
  Corineus had that Prouince vtmost west,
  To him assigned for his worthy lot,
  Which of his name and memorable gest
  He called *Cornewaile*, yet so called best :
  And *Debons* shayre was, that is *Deuonshyre* :
  But *Canute* had his portion from the rest,
  The which he cald *Canutium*, for his hyre ;
Now *Cantium*, which Kent we commenly inquire.

13

Thus *Brute* this Realme vnto his rule subdewd,
  And raigned long in great felicitie,
  Lou'd of his friends, and of his foes eschewd,
  He left three sonnes, his famous progeny,
  Borne of faire *Inogene* of *Italy* ;
  Mongst whom he parted his imperiall state,
  And *Locrine* left chiefe Lord of *Britany*.
  At last ripe age bad him surrender late
His life, and long good fortune vnto finall fate.

14

Locrine was left the soueraine Lord of all ;
  But *Albanact* had all the Northrene part,
  Which of himselfe *Albania* he did call ;
  And *Camber* did possesse the Westerne quart,
  Which *Seuerne* now from *Logris* doth depart :
  And each his portion peaceably enioyd,
  Ne was there outward breach, nor grudge in hart,
  That once their quiet gouernment annoyd,
But each his paines to others profit still employd.

15

Vntill a nation straung, with visage swart,
  And courage fierce, that all men did affray,
  Which through the world then swarmd in euery
    part,
  And ouerflow'd all countries farre away,
  Like *Noyes* great flood, with their importune
    sway,
  This land inuaded with like violence,
  And did themselues through all the North
    display :
  Vntill that *Locrine* for his Realmes defence,
Did head against them make, and strong muni-
    fience.

16

He them encountred, a confused rout,
  Foreby the Riuer, that whylome was hight
  The auncient *Abus*, where with courage stout
  He them defeated in victorious fight,
  And chaste so fiercely after fearfull flight,
  That forst their Chieftaine, for his safeties sake,
  (Their Chieftaine *Humber* named was aright)
  Vnto the mightie streame him to betake,
Where he an end of battell, and of life did make.

17

The king returned proud of victorie,
  And insolent wox through vnwonted ease,
  That shortly he forgot the ieopardie,
  Which in his land he lately did appease,
  And fell to vaine voluptuous disease :
  He lou'd faire Ladie *Estrild*, lewdly lou'd,
  Whose wanton pleasures him too much did
    please,
  That quite his hart from *Guendolene* remou'd,
From *Guendolene* his wife, though alwaies faith-
    full prou'd.

18

The noble daughter of *Corineus*
  Would not endure to be so vile disdaind,
  But gathering force, and courage valorous,
  Encountred him in battell well ordaind,
  In which him vanquisht she to fly constraind :
  But she so fast pursewd, that him she tooke,
  And threw in bands, where he till death remaind;
  Als his faire Leman, flying through a brooke,
She ouerhent, nought moued with her piteous
    looke.

19

But both her selfe, and eke her daughter deare,
  Begotten by her kingly Paramoure,
  The faire *Sabrina* almost dead with feare,
  She there attached, farre from all succoure ;
  The one she slew in that impatient stoure,
  But the sad virgin innocent of all,
  Adowne the rolling riuer she did poure,
  Which of her name now *Seuerne* men do call :
Such was the end, that to disloyall loue did fall.

20

Then for her sonne, which she to *Locrin* bore,
  Madan was young, vnmeet the rule to sway,
  In her owne hand the crowne she kept in store,
  Till ryper yeares he raught, and stronger stay :
  During which time her powre she did display
  Through all this realme, the glorie of her sex,
  And first taught men a woman to obay :
  But when her sonne to mans estate did wex,
She it surrendred, ne her selfe would lenger vex.

21

Tho *Madan* raignd, vnworthie of his race
  For with all shame that sacred throne he fild :
  Next *Memprise*, as vnworthy of that place,
  In which being consorted with *Manild*,
  For thirst of single kingdome him he kild.
  But *Ebranck* salued both their infamies
  With noble deedes, and warreyd on *Brunchild*
  In *Henault*, where yet of his victories
Braue moniments remaine, which yet that land
    enuies.

22

An happie man in his first dayes he was,
  And happie father of faire progeny :
  For all so many weekes as the yeare has,
  So many children he did multiply ;
  Of which were twentie sonnes, which did apply
  Their minds to praise, and cheualrous desire:
  Those germans did subdew all Germany,
  Of whom it hight ; but in the end their Sire
With foule repulse from Fraunce was forced to
    retire.

23

Which blot his sonne succeeding in his seat,
  The second *Brute*, the second both in name,
  And eke in semblance of his puissance great,
  Right well recur'd, and did away that blame
  With recompence of euerlasting fame.
  He with his victour sword first opened
  The bowels of wide Fraunce, a forlorne Dame,
  And taught her first how to be conquered ;
Since which, with sundrie spoiles she hath beene
    ransacked.

24

Let *Scaldis* tell, and let tell *Hania*,
  And let the marsh of *Estham bruges* tell,
  What colour were their waters that same day,
  And all the moore twixt *Eluersham* and *Dell*,
  With bloud of *Henalois*, which therein fell.
  How oft that day did sad *Brunchildis* see
  The greene shield dyde in dolorous vermell ?
  That not *Scuith guiridh* it mote seeme to bee,
But rather *y Scuith gogh*, signe of sad crueltee.

25

His sonne king *Leill* by fathers labour long,
  Enioyd an heritage of lasting peace,
  And built *Cairleill*, and built *Cairleon* strong.
  Next *Huddibras* his realme did not encrease,
  But taught the land from wearie warres to cease.
  Whose footsteps *Bladud* following, in arts
  Exceld at *Athens* all the learned preace,
  From whence he brought them to these
    saluage parts,
And with sweet science mollifide their stub-
    borne harts.

26

Ensample of his wondrous faculty,
  Behold the boyling Bathes at *Cairbadon*,
  Which seeth with secret fire eternally,
  And in their entrails, full of quicke Brimston,
  Nourish the flames which they are warm'd vpon,
  That to their people wealth they forth do well,
  And health to euery forreine nation :
  Yet he at last contending to excell
The reach of men, through flight into fond
    mischief fell.

27

Next him king *Leyr* in happie peace long raind,
  But had no issue male him to succeed,
  But three faire daughters, which were well
    vptraind,
In all that seemed fit for kingly seed :
Mongst whom his realme he equally decreed
To haue diuided. Tho when feeble age
Nigh to his vtmost date he saw proceed,
He ca'd his daughters ; and with speeches sag ·
Inquyrd, which of them most did loue her
    parentage.

28

The eldest *Gonorill* gan to protest,
  That she much more then her own life himlou'd:
And *Regan* greater loue to him profest,
  Then all the world, when euer it were proou'd ;
But *Cordeill* said she lou'd him, as behoou'd :
Whose simple answere, wanting colours faire
To paint it forth, him to displeasance moou'd,
That in his crowne he counted her no haire,
But twixt the other twaine his kingdome whole
    did shaire.

29

So wedded th'one to *Maglan* king of Scots,
  And th'other to the king of *Cambria*,
And twixt them shayrd his realme by equall lots:
  But without dowre the wise *Cordelia*
Was sent to *Aganip* of *Celtica*.
Their aged Syre, thus eased of his crowne,
A priuate life led in *Albania*,
With *Gonorill*, long had in great renowne,
That nought him grieu'd to bene from rule
    deposed downe.

30

But true it is, that when the oyle is spent,
  The light goes out, and weeke is throwne away ;
So when he had resigned his regiment,
  His daughter gan despise his drouping day,
And wearie waxe of his continuall stay.
Tho to his daughter *Regan* he repayrd,
Who him at first well vsed euery way ;
But when of his departure she despayrd,
Her bountie she abated, and his cheare empayrd.

31

The wretched man gan then auise too late,
  That loue is not, where most it is profest,
Too truely tryde in his extreamest state ;
  At l st resolu'd likewise to proue the rest,
He to *Cordelia* him selfe addrest,
Who with entire affection him receau'd,
As for her Syre and king her seemed best ;
And after all an army strong she leau'd,
To war on those, which him had of his realme
    bereau'd.

32

So to his crowne she him restor'd againe,
  In which he dyde, made ripe for death by eld,
And after wild, it should to her remaine :
Who peaceably the same long time did weld :
And all mens harts in dew obedience held :
Till that her sisters children, woxen strong
Through proud ambition, against her rebeld,
And ouercommen kept in prison long,
Till wearie of that wretched life, her selfe she
    hong.

33

Then gan the bloudie brethren both to raine :
  But fierce *Cundah* gan shortly to enuie
His brother *Morgan*, prickt with proud disdaine,
To haue a pere in part of soueraintie, ·
And kindling coles of cruell enmitie,
Raisd warre, and him in battell ouerthrew :
Whence as he to those woodie hils did flie,
Which hight of him *Glamorgan*, there him slew:
Then did he raigne alone, when he none equall
    knew.

34

His sonne *Riuallo* his dead roome did supply,
  In whose sad time bloud did from heauen raine:
Next great *Gurgustus*, then faire *Cæcily*
In constant peace their kingdomes did containe,
After whom *Lago*, and *Kinmarke* did raine,
And *Gorbogud*, till farre in yeares he grew :
Then his ambitious sonnes vnto them twaine
Arraught the rule, and from their father drew,
Stout *Ferrex* and sterne *Porrex* him in prison
    threw.

35

But O, the greedy thirst of roya'l crowne,
  That knowes no kinred, nor regardes no right,
Stird *Porrex* vp to put his brother downe ;
Who vnto him assembling forraine might,
Made warre on him, and fell him selfe in fight :
Whose death t'auenge, his mother mercilesse,
Most mercilesse of women, *Wyden* hight,
Her other sonne fast sleeping did oppresse,
And with most cruell hand him murdred pitti-
    lesse.

36

Here ended *Brutus* sacred progenie,
  Which had seuen hundred yeares this scepter
    borne,
With high renowme, and great felicitie ;
The noble braunch from th'antique stocke was
    torne
Through discord, and the royall throne forlorne:
Thenceforth this Realme was into factions rent,
Whilest each of *Brutus* boasted to be borne,
That in the end was left no moniment
Of *Brutus*, nor of Britons glory auncient.

37

Then vp arose a man of matchlesse might,
And wondrous wit to menage high affaires,
Who stird with pitty of the stressed plight
Of this sad Realme, cut into sundry shaires
By such, as claymd themselues *Brutes* rightfull
    haires,
Gathered the Princes of the people loose,
To taken counsell of their common cares ;
Who with his wisedom won, him streight did
    choose
Their king, and swore him fealty to win or loose.

38

Then made he head against his enimies,
And *Ymner* slew, of *Logris* miscreate ;
Then *Ruddoc* and proud *Stater*, both allyes,
This of *Albanie* newly nominate,
And that of *Cambry* king confirmed late,
He ouerthrew through his owne valiaunce ;
Whose countreis he redus'd to quiet state,
And shortly brought to ciuill gouernaunce,
Now one, which earst were many, made through
    variaunce.

39

Then made he sacred lawes, which some men say
Were vnto him reueald in vision,
By which he freed the Traueilers high way,
The Churches part, and Ploughmans portion,
Restraining stealth, and strong extortion ;
The gracious *Numa* of great *Britanie* :
For till his dayes, the chiefe dominion
By strength was wielded without pollicie ;
Therefore he first wore crowne of gold for dignitie.

40

Donwallo dyde (for what may liue for ay ?)
And left two sonnes, of pearelesse prowesse both;
That sacked *Rome* too dearely did assay,
The recompence of their periured oth,
And ransackt *Greece* well tryde, when they were
    wroth ;
Besides subiected *Fraunce*, and *Germany*,
Which yet their prayses speake, all be they loth,
And inly tremble at the memory
Of *Brennus* and *Bellinus*, kings of Britany.

41

Next them did *Gurgunt*, great *Bellinus* sonne
In rule succeede, and eke in fathers prayse ;
He Easterland subdewd, and Danmarke wonne,
And of them both did foy and tribute raise,
The which was dew in his dead fathers dayes :
He also gaue to fugitiues of *Spayne*,
Whom he at sea found wandring from their
    A seate in *Ireland* safely to remayne,   [wayes,
Which they should hold of him, as subiect to
    Britayne.

42

After him raigned *Guitheline* his hayre,
The iustest man and trewest in his dayes,
Who had to wife Dame *Mertia* the fayre,
A woman worthy of immortall prayse,
Which for this Realme found many goodly layes,
And wholesome Statutes to her husband
    brought ;
Her many deemd to haue beene of the *Fayes*,
As was *Aegerie*, that *Numa* tought ;
Those yet of her be *Mertian* lawes both nam'd
    and thought.

43

Her sonne *Sisillus* after her did rayne,
And then *Kimarus*, and then *Danius* ;
Next whom *Morindus* did the crowne sustaine,
Who, had he not with wrath outrageous,
And cruell rancour dim'd his valorous
And mightie deeds, should matched haue the
    best :
As well in that same field victorious
Against the forreine *Morands* he exprest ;
Yet liues his memorie, though carcas sleepe in
    rest.

44

Fiue sonnes he left begotten of one wife,
All which successiuely by turnes did raine ;
First *Gorboman* a man of vertuous life ;
Next *Archigald*, who for his proud disdaine,
Deposed was from Princedome soueraine,
And pitteous *Elidure* put in his sted ;
Who shortly it to him restord againe,
Till by his death he it recouered ;
But *Peridure* and *Vigent* him disthronized.

45

In wretched prison long he did remaine,
Till they outraigned had their vtmost date,
And then therein reseized was againe,
And ruled long with honorable state,
Till he surrendred Realme and life to fate.
Then all the sonnes of these fiue brethren raynd
By dew successe, and all their Nephewes late,
Euen thrise eleuen descents the crowne retaynd,
Till aged *Hely* by dew heritage it gaynd.

46

He had two sonnes, whose eldest called *Lud*
Left of his life most famous memory,
And endlesse moniments of his great good :
The ruin'd wals he did reædifye
Of *Troynouant*, gainst force of enimy,
And built that gate, which of his name is hight,
By which he lyes entombed solemnly.
He left two sonnes, too young to rule aright,
Androgeus and *Tenantius*, pictures of his might.

47
Whilst they were young, *Cassibalane* their Eme
Was by the people chosen in their sted,
Who on him tooke the royall Diademe,
And goodly well long time it gouerned,
Till the prowd *Romanes* him disquieted,
And warlike *Cæsar*, tempted with the name
Of this sweet Island, neuer conquered,
And enuying the Britons blazed fame,
(O hideous hunger of dominion) hither came.

48
Yet twise they were repulsed backe againe,
And twise renforst, backe to their ships to fly,
The whiles with bloud they all the shore did
    staine,
And the gray *Ocean* into purple dy :
Ne had they footing found at last perdie,
Had not *Androgeus*, false to natiue soyle,
And enuious of Vncles soueraintie,
Betrayd his contrey vnto forreine spoyle :
Nought else, but treason, from the first this land
    did foyle.

49
So by him *Cæsar* got the victory,
Through great bloudshed,and many a sad assay,
In which him selfe was charged heauily
Of hardy *Nennius*, whom he yet did slay,
But lost his sword, yet to be seene this day.
Thenceforth this land was tributarie made
T'ambitious *Rome*, and did their rule obay,
Till *Arthur* all that reckoning defrayd ;
Yet oft the Briton kings against them strongly
    swayd.

50
Next him *Tenantius* raigned, then *Kimbeline*,
What time th'eternall Lord in fleshly slime
Enwombed was, from wretched *Adams* line
To purge away the guilt of sinfull crime :
O ioyous memorie of happy time,
That heauenly grace so plenteously displayd ;
(O too high ditty for my simple rime.)
Soone after this the *Romanes* him warrayd ;
For that their tribute he refusd to let be payd.

51
Good *Claudius*, that next was Emperour,
An army brought,and with him battell fought,
In which the king was by a Treachetour
Disguised slaine, ere any thereof thought :
Yet ceased not the bloudy fight for ought ;
For *Aruirage* his brothers place supplide,
Both in his armes, and crowne, and by that
    draught
Did driue the *Romanes* to the weaker side,
That they to peace agreed. So all was pacifide.

52
Was neuer king more highly magnifide,
Nor dred of *Romanes*, then was *Aruirage*,
For which the Emperour to him allide
His daughter *Genuiss*' in marriage :
Yet shortly he renounst the vassalage
Of *Rome* againe, who hither hastly sent
Vespasian, that with great spoile and rage
Forwasted all, till *Genuissa* gent
Perswaded him to ceasse,and her Lord to relent.

53
He dyde ; and him succeeded *Marius*,
Who ioyd his dayes in great tranquillity,
Then *Coyll*, and after him good *Lucius*,
That first receiued Christianitie,
The sacred pledge of Christes Euangely ;
Yet true it is, that long before that day
Hither came *Ioseph* of *Arimathy*,
Who brought with him the holy grayle. (they say)
And preacht the truth, but since it greatly did
    decay.

54
This good king shortly without issew dide,
Whereof great trouble in the kingdome grew,
That did her selfe in sundry parts diuide,
And with her powre her owne selfe ouerthrew.
Whilest *Romanes* dayly did the weake subdew :
Which seeing stout *Bunduca*, vp arose,
And taking armes, the *Britons* to her drew ;
With whom she marched streight against her
    foes,
And them vnwares besides the *Seuerne* did
    enclose.

55
There she with them a cruell battell tride,
Not with so good successe, as she deseru'd ;
By reason that the Captaines on her side,
Corrupted by *Paulinus*, from her sweru'd :
Yet such, as were through former flight pre-
    seru'd,
Gathering againe, her Host she did renew,
And with fresh courage on the victour seru'd :
But being all defeated, saue a few,
Rather then fly,or be captiu'd her selfe she slew.

56
O famous moniment of womens prayse,
Matchable either to *Semiramis*,
Whom antique history so high doth raise,
Or to *Hypsiphil*' or to *Thomiris* :
Her Host two hundred thousand numbred is ;
Who whiles good fortune fauoured her might,
Triumphed oft against her enimis ,
And yet though ouercome in haplesse fight,
She triumphed on death, in enemies despight.

57

Her reliques *Fulgent* hauing gathered,
Fought with *Seuerus*, and him ouerthrew ;
Yet in the chace was slaine of them, that fled :
So made them victours, whom he did subdew.
Then gan *Carausius* tirannize anew,
And gainst the *Romanes* bent their proper powre,
But him *Allectus* treacherously slew,
And took on him the robe of Emperoure :
Nath'lesse the same enioyed but short happy howre :

58

For *Asclepiodate* him ouercame,
And left inglorious on the vanquisht playne,
Without or robe, or rag, to hide his shame.
Then afterwards he in his stead did rayne ;
But shortly was by *Coyll* in battell slaine :
Who after long debate, since *Lucies* time,
Was of the *Britons* first crownd Soueraine :
Then gan this Realme renewe her passed prime :
He of his name *Coylchester* built of stone and lime.

59

Which when the *Romanes* heard, they hither sent
Constantius, a man of mickle might,
With whom king *Coyll* made an agreement,
And to him gaue for wife his daughter bright,
Faire *Helena*, the fairest liuing wight ;
Who in all godly thewes, and goodly prayse
Did far excell, but was most famous hight
For skill in Musicke of all in her dayes,
Aswell in curious instruments, as cunning layes.

60

Of whom he did great *Constantine* beget,
Who afterward was Emperour of *Rome* ;
To which whiles absent he his mind did set,
Octauius here lept into his roome,
And it vsurped by vnrighteous doome :
But he his title iustifide by might,
Slaying *Traherne*, and hauing ouercome
The *Romane* legion in dreadfull fight :
So settled he his kingdome, and confirmd his right.

61

But wanting issew male, his daughter deare
He gaue in wedlocke to *Maximian*,
And him with her made of his kingdome heyre,
Who soone by meanes thereof the Empire wan.
Till murdred by the friends of *Gratian* ;
Then gan the Hunnes and Picts inuade this land,
During the raigne of *Maximinian* ;
Who dying left none heire them to withstand,
But that they ouerran all parts with easie hand.

62

The weary *Britons*, whose war-hable youth
Was by *Maximian* lately led away,
With wretched miseries, and woefull ruth,
Were to those Pagans made an open pray,
And dayly spectacle of sad decay :
Whom *Romane* warres, which now foure hundred yeares,
And more had wasted, could no whit dismay ;
Till by consent of Commons and of Peares,
Tney crownd the second *Constantine* with ioyous teares,

63

Who hauing oft in battell vanquished
Those spoilefull Picts, and swarming Easterlings,
Long time in peace his Realme established,
Yet oft annoyd with sundry bordragings
Of neighbour Scots, and forrein Scatterlings,
With which the world in those dayes abound:
Which to outbarre, with painefull pyonings
From sea to sea he heapt a mightie mound,
Which from *Alcluid* to *Panwell* did that border bound.

64

Three sonnes he dying left, all vnder age ;
By meanes whereof, their vncle *Vortigere*
Vsurpt the crowne, during their pupillage ;
Which th' Infants tutors gathering to feare,
Them closely into *Armorick* did beare :
For dread of whom, and for those Picts annoyes,
He sent to *Germanie*, straunge aid to reare,
From whence eftsoones arriued here three hoyes
Of *Saxons*, whom he for his safetie imployes.

65

Two brethren were their Capitains, which hight
Hengist and *Horsus*, well approu'd in warre,
And both of them men of renowmed might ;
Who making vantage of their ciuill iarre,
And of those forrein rs, which came from farre,
Grew great, and got large portions of land,
That in the Realme ere long they strong er arre,
Then they which sought at first their helping hand,
And *Vortiger* enforst the kingdome to aband.

66

But by the helpe of *Vortimere* his sonne,
He is againe vnto his rule restord,
And *Hengist* seeming sad, for that was donne,
Receiu d is to grace and new accord,
Through his faire daughters face, and flattring word ;
Soone after which, three hundred Lordes he slew
Of British bloud, all sitting at his bord ;
Whose dolefull moniments who list to rew,
Th'eternall markes of treason may at *Stonheng* vew.

67

By this the sonnes of *Constantine*, which fled,
Ambrose and *Vther* did ripe years attaine,
And here arriuing, strongly challenged
The crowne, which *Vortiger* did long detaine:
Who flying from his guilt, by them was slaine,
And *Hengist* eke soone brought to shamefull
death.
Thenceforth *Aurelius* peaceably did rayne,
Till that through poyson stopped was his breath;
So now entombed lyes at Stoneheng by the
heath.

68

After him *Vther*, which *Pendragon* hight,
Succeding There abruptly it did end,
Without full point, or other Cesure right,
As if the rest some wicked hand did rend,
Or th'Authour selfe could not at least attend
To finish it: that so vntimely breach
The Prince him selfe halfe seemeth to offend,
Yet secret pleasure did offence empeach,
And wonder of antiquitie long stopt his speach.

69

At last quite rauisht with delight, to heare
The royall Ofspring of his natiue land,
Cryde out, Deare countrey, O how dearely deare
Ought thy remembraunce, and perpetuall band
Be to thy foster Childe, that from thy hand
Did commun breath and nouriture receaue?
How brutish is it not to vnderstand,
How much to her we owe, that all vs gaue,
That gaue vnto vs all, what euer good we haue.

70

But *Guyon* all this while his booke did read,
Ne yet has ended: for it was a great
And ample volume, that doth far excead
My leasure, so long leaues here to repeat:
It told, how first *Prometheus* did create
A man, of many partes from beasts deriued,
And then stole fire from heauen, to animate
His worke, for which he was by *Ioue* depriued
Of life him selfe, and hart-strings of an Ægle
riued.

71

That man so made, he call d *Elfe*, to weet
Quick, the first authour of all Elfin kind:
Who wandring through the world with wearie
feet,
Did in the gardins of *Adonis* find
A goodly creature, whom he deemd in mind
To be no earthly wight, but either Spright,
Or Angell, th'authour of all woman kind;
Therefore a *Fay* he her according hight,
Of whom all *Faeryes* spring, and fetch their
lignage right.

72

Of these a mightie people shortly grew,
And puissaunt kings, which all the world
warrayd,
And to them selues all Nations did subdew:
The first and eldest, which that scepter swayd,
Was *Elfin*; him all *India* obayd,
And all that now *America* men call:
Next him was noble *Elfinan*, who layd
Cleopolis foundation first of all:
But *Elfiline* enclosd it with a golden wall.

73

His sonne was *Elfinell*, who ouercame
The wicked *Gobbelines* in bloudy field:
But *Elfant* was of most renowmed fame,
Who all of Christall did *Panthea* build:
Then *Elfar*, who two brethren gyants kild,
The one of which had two heads, th'other three:
Then *Elfinor*, who was in Magick skild;
He built by art vpon the glassy See
A bridge of bras, whose sound heauens thunder
seem'd to bee.

74

He left three sonnes, the which in order raynd,
And all their Ofspring, in their dew descents,
Euen seuen hundred Princes, which maintaynd
With mightie deedes their sundry gouernments;
That were too long their infinite contents
Here to record, ne much materiall:
Yet should they be most famous moniments,
And braue ensample, both of martiall,
And ciuill rule to kings and states imperiall.

75

After all these *Elficleos* did rayne,
The wise *Elficleos* in great Maiestie,
Who mightily that scepter did sustayne,
And with rich spoiles and famous victorie,
Did high aduaunce the crowne of *Faery*:
He left two sonnes, of which faire *Elferon*
The eldest brother did vntimely dy;
Whose emptie place the mightie *Oberon*
Doubly supplide, in spousall, and dominion.

76

Great was his power and glorie ouer all,
Which him before, that sacred seate d d fill,
That yet remaines his wide memoriall:
He dying left the fairest *Tanaquill*,
Him to succeede therein, by his last will:
Fairer and nobler liueth none this howre,
Ne like in grace, ne like in learned skill;
Therefore they *Glorian* call that glorious flowre
Long mayst thou *Glorian* liue, in glory and
great powre.

77

Beguild thus with delight of nouelties,
And naturall desire of countreys state,
So long they red in those antiquities,
That how the time was fled, they quite forgate,
Till gentle *Alma* seeing it so late,
Perforce their studies broke, and them besought
To thinke, how supper did them long awaite.
So halfe vnwilling from their bookes them brought,
And fairely feasted, as so noble knights she ought.

Cant. XI.

The enimies of Temperaunce
besiege her dwelling place :
Prince Arthur them repelles, and fowle
Maleger doth deface.

1

What warre so cruell, or what siege so sore,
As that, which strong affections do apply
Against the fort of reason euermore
To bring the soule into captiuitie :
Their force is fiercer through infirmitie
Of the fraile flesh, relenting to their rage,
And exercise most bitter tyranny
Vpon the parts, brought into their bondage :
No wretchednesse is like to sinfull vellenage.

2

But in a body, which doth freely yeeld
His partes to reasons rule obedient,
And letteth her that ought the scepter weeld,
All happy peace and goodly gouernment
Is setled there in sure establishment ;
There *Alma* like a virgin Queene most bright,
Doth florish in all beautie excellent :
And to her guestes doth bounteous banket dight,
Attempred goodly well for health and for delight.

3

Early before the Morne with cremosin ray,
The windowes of bright heauen opened had,
Through which into the world the dawning day
Might looke, that maketh euery creature glad,
Vprose Sir *Guyon*, in bright armour clad,
And to his purposd iourney him prepar'd :
With him the Palmer eke in habit sad,
Him selfe addrest to that aduenture hard :
So to the riuers side they both together far'd.

4

Where them awaited ready at the ford
The *Ferriman*, as *Alma* had behight,
With his well rigged boate : They go abord,
And he eftsoones gan launch his barke forthright.
Ere long they rowed were quite out of sight,
And fast the land behind them fled away.
But let them pas, whiles wind and weather right
Doserue their turnes : here I a while must stay,
To see a cruell fight doen by the Prince this day.

5

For all so soone, as *Guyon* thence was gon
Vpon his voyage with his trustie guide,
That wicked band of villeins fresh begon
That castle to assaile on euery side,
And lay strong siege about it far and wide.
So huge and infinite their numbers were,
That all the land they vnder them did hide ;
So fowle and vgly, that exceeding feare
Their visages imprest, when they approched neare.

6

Them in twelue troupes their Captain did dispart
And round about in fittest steades did place,
Where each might best offend his proper part,
And his contrary obiect most deface,
As euery one seem'd meetest in that cace.
Seuen of the same against the Castle gate,
In strong entrenchments he did closely place,
Which with incessaunt force and endlesse hate,
They battred day and night, and entraunce did awate.

7

The other fiue, fiue sundry wayes he set,
Against the fiue great Bulwarkes of that pile,
And vnto each a Bulwarke did arret,
T'assayle with open force or hidden guile,
In hope thereof to win victorious spoile.
They all that charge did feruently apply,
With greedie malice and importune toyle,
And planted there their huge artillery,
With which they dayly made most dreadfull battery.

8

The first troupe was a monstrous rablement
Of fowle misshapen wights, of which some were
Headed like Owles, with beckes vncomely bent,
Others like Dogs, others like Gryphons dreare,
And some had wings, and some had clawes to teare,
And euery one of them had Lynces eyes,
And euery one did bow and arrowes beare :
All those were lawlesse lustes, corrupt enuies,
And couetous aspectes, all cruell enimies.

9

Those same against the bulwarke of the *Sight*
Did lay strong siege, and battailous assault,
Ne once did yield it respit day nor night,
But soone as *Titan* gan his head exault,
And soone againe as he his light with hault,
Their wicked engins they against it bent :
That is each thing, by which the eyes may fault,
But two then all more huge and violent,
Beautie, and money, they that Bulwarke
    sorely rent.

10

The second Bulwarke was the *Hearing* sence,
  Gainst which the second troupe dessignment
    makes ;
Deformed creatures, in straunge difference,
Some hauing heads like Harts, some like to
    Snakes,
Some like wild Bores late rouzd out of the brakes;
Slaunderous reproches, and fowle infamies,
Leasings, backbytings, and vaine-glorious
    crakes,
Bad counsels, prayses, and false flatteries.
All those against that fort did bend their
    batteries.

11

Likewise that same third Fort, that is the *Smell*
Of that third troupe was cruelly assayd :
Whose hideous shapes were like to feends of hell,
Some like to hounds, some like to Apes, dismayd,
Some like to Puttockes, all in plumes arayd :
All shap't according their conditions,
For by those vgly formes weren pourtrayd,
Foolish delights and fond abusions,
Which do that sence besiege with light illusions.

12

And that fourth band, which cruell battry bent,
Against the fourth Bulwarke, that is the *Tast*,
Was as the rest, a grysie rablement,
Some mouth'd like greedy Oystriges, some fast
Like loathly Toades, some fashioned in the wast
Like swine ; for so deformd is luxury,
Surfeat, misdiet, and vnthriftie wast,
Vaine feasts, and idle superfluity :
All those this sences Fort assayle incessantly.

13

But the fift troupe most horrible of hew,
And fierce of force, was dreadfull to report :
For some like Snailes, some did like spyders shew,
And some like vgly Vrchins thicke and short :
Cruelly they assayled that fift Fort,
Armed with darts of sensuall delight,
With stings of carnall lust, and strong effort
Of feeling pleasures, with which day and night
Against that same fift bulwarke they continued
    fight.

14

Thus these twelue troupes with dreadfull puissance
Against that Castle restlesse siege did lay,
And euermore their hideous Ordinance
Vpon the Bulwarkes cruelly did play,
That now it gan to threaten neare decay :
And euermore their wicked Capitaine
Prouoked them the breaches to assay,
Somtimes with threats, somtimes with hope
    of gaine,
Which by the ransack of that peece they should
    attaine.

15

On th'other side, th'assieged Castles ward
Their stedfast stonds did mightily maintaine,
And many bold repulse, and many hard
Atchieuement wrought with perill and with
    paine,
That goodly frame from ruine to sustaine :
And those two brethren Giants did defend
The walles so stoutly with their sturdie maine,
That neuer entrance any durst pretend,
But they to direfull death their groning ghosts
    did send.

16

The noble virgin, Ladie of the place,
Was much dismayed with that dreadfull sight ·
For neuer was she in so euill cace,
Till that the Prince seeing her wofull plight,
Gan her recomfort from so sad affright,
Offring his seruice, and his dearest life
For her defence, against that Carle to fight,
Which was their chiefe and th'author of that
    strife :
She him remercied as the Patrone of her life.

17

Eftsoones himselfe in glitterand armes he dight,
And his well proued weapons to him hent ;
So taking courteous conge he behight,
Those gates to be vnbar'd, and forth he went.
Faire mote he thee, the prowest and most gent,
That euer brandished bright steele on hye :
Whom soone as that vnruly rablement,
With his gay Squire issuing did espy,
They reard a most outrageous dreadfull yelling
    cry.

18

And therewith all attonce at him let fly
Their fluttring arrowes, thicke as flakes of snow,
And round about him flocke impetuously,
Like a great water flood, that tombling low
From the high mountaines, threats to ouerflow
With suddein fury all the fertile plaine,
And the sad husbandmans long hope doth throw
A downe the streame, and all his vowes make
    vaine,   [sustaine
Nor bounds nor banks his headlong ruine may

19

Vpon his shield their heaped hayle he bore,
  And with his sword disperst the raskall flockes,
  Which fled a sunder, and him fell before,
  As withered leaues drop from their dried
      stockes,   [locks ;
When the wroth Western wind does reaue their
  And vnder neath him his courageous steed,
  The fierce *Spumador* trode them downe like docks,
  The fierce *Spumador* borne of heauenly seed :
Such as *Laomedon* of *Phœbus* race did breed.

20

Which suddeine horrour and confused cry,
  When as their Captaine heard, in haste he yode,
  The cause to weet, and fault to remedy ;
  Vpon a Tygre swift and fierce he rode,
  That as the winde ran vnderneath his lode,
  Whiles his long legs nigh raught vnto the ground;
  Full large he was of limbe, and shoulders brode,
  But of such subtile substance and vnsound,
That like a ghost he seem'd, whose graue-
     clothes were vnbound.

21

And in his hand a bended bow was seene,
  And many arrowes vnder his right side,
  All deadly daungerous, all cruell keene,
  Headed with flint, and feathers bloudie dide,
  Such as the *Indians* in their quiuers hide ;
  Those could he well direct and streight as line,
  And bid them strike the marke, which he had
    eyde,
  Ne was there salue, ne was there medicine,
That mote recure their wounds : so inly they
    did tine.

22

As pale and wan as ashes was his looke,
  His bodie leane and meagre as a rake,
  And skin all withered like a dryed rooke,
  Thereto as cold and drery as a Snake,
  That seem'd to tremble euermore, and quake :
  All in a canuas thin he was bedight,
  And girded with a belt of twisted brake,
  Vpon his head he wore an Helmet light,
Made of a dead mans skull, that seem'd a
    ghastly sight.

23

Maleger was his name, and after him,
  There follow'd fast at hand two wicked Hags,
  With hoarie lockes all loose, and visage grim ;
  Their feet vnshod, their bodies wrapt in rags,
  And both as swift on foot, as chased Stags ;
  And yet the one her other legge had lame,
  Which with a staffe, all full of litle snags
  She did support, and *Impotence* her name :
But th'other was *Impatience*, arm'd with raging
    flame.

24

Soone as the Carle from farre the Prince espyde,
  Glittering in armes and warlike ornament.
  His Beast he felly prickt on either syde,
  And his mischieuous bow full readie bent
  With which at him a cruell shaft he sent :
  But he was warie, and it warded well
  Vpon his shield, that it no further went,
  But to the ground the idle quarrell fell :
Then he another and another did expell.

25

Which to preuent, the Prince his mortall speare
  Soone to him raught, and fierce at him did
    ride,
  To be auenged of that shot whyleare :
  But he was not so hardie to abide
  That bitter stownd, but turning quicke aside
  His light-foot beast, fled fast away for feare :
  Whom to pursue, the Infant after hide,
  So fast as his good Courser could him beare,
But labour lost it was, to weene approch him
    neare.

26

For as the winged wind his Tigre fled,
  That vew of eye could scarse him ouertake,
  Ne scarse his feet on ground were seene to tred ;
  Through hils and dales he speedie way did
    make,
  Ne hedge ne ditch his readie passage brake,
  And in his flight the villein turn'd his face,
  (As wonts the *Tartar* by the *Caspian* lake,
  When as the *Russian* him in fight does chace)
Vnto his Tygres taile, and shot at him apace.

27

Apace he shot, and yet he fled apace,
  Still as the greedy knight nigh to him drew,
  And oftentimes he would relent his pace,
  That him his foe more fiercely should pursew :
  Who when his vncouth manner he did vew,
  He gan auize to follow him no more,
  But keepe his standing, and his shafte eschew,
  Vntill he quite had spent his perlous store,
And then assayle him fresh, ere he could shift
    for more.

28

But that lame Hag, still as abroad he strew
  His wicked arrowes, gathered them againe,
  And to him brought, fresh battell to renew :
  Which he espying, cast her to restraine
  From yielding succour to that cursed Swaine,
  And her attaching, thought her hands to tye ;
  But soone as him dismounted on the plaine,
  That other Hag did farre away espy
Birding her sister, she to him ran hastily.

29

And catching hold of him, as downe he lent,
Him backward ouerthrew, and downe him stayd
With their rude hands and griesly graplement,
Till that the villein comming to their ayd,
Vpon him fell, and lode vpon him layd ;
Full litle wanted, but he had him slaine,
And of the battell balefull end had made,
Had not his gentle Squire beheld his paine,
And commen to his reskew, ere his bitter bane.

30

So greatest and most glorious thing on ground
May often need the helpe of weaker hand ;
So feeble is mans state, and life vnsound,
That in assurance it may neuer stand,
Till it dissolued be from earthly band.
Proofe be thou Prince, the prowest man aliue,
And noblest borne of all in *Britayne* land ;
Yet thee fierce Fortune did so nearely driue,
That had not grace thee blest, thou shouldest
     not suruiue.

31

The Squire arriuing, fiercely in his armes
Snatcht first the one, and then the other Iade,
His chiefest lets and authors of his harmes,
And them perforce withhel. with threatned blade,
Least that his Lord they should behind inuade ;
The whiles the Prince prickt with reprochfull
     shame,
As one awakt out of long slombring shade,
Reuiuing thought of glorie and of fame,
Vnited all his powres to purge himselfe from
     blame.

32

Like as a fire, the which in hollow caue
Hath long bene vnderkept, and downe supprest,
With murmurous disdaine doth inly raue,
And grudge, in so streight prison to be prest,
At last breakes forth with furious vnrest,
And striues to mount vnto his natiue seat ;
All that did earst it hinder and molest,
It now deuoures with flames and scorching heat,
And carries into smoake with rage and horror
     great.

33

So mightily the *Briton* Prince him rouzd
Out of his hold, and broke his caitiue bands,
And as a Beare whom angry curres haue touzd,
Hauing off shakt them, and escapt their hands,
Becomes more fell, and all that him withstands
Treads downe and ouerthrowes. Now had
     the Carle
Alighted from his Tigre, and his hands
Discharged of his bow and deadly quar'le,
To seize vpon his foe flat lying on the marle.

34

Which now him turnd to disauantage deare ;
For neither can he fly, nor other harme,
But trust vnto his strength and manhood meare,
Sith now he is farre from his monstrous swarme,
And of his weapons did himselfe disarme.
The knight yet wrothfull for his late disgrace,
Fiercely aduaunst his valorous right arme,
And him so sore smote with his yron mace,
That groueling to the ground he fell, and fild
     his place.

35

Well weened he, that field was then his owne,
And all his labour brought to happie end,
When suddein vp the villein ouerthrowne,
Out of his swowne arose, fresh to contend,
And gan himselfe to second battell bend,
As hurt he had not bene. Thereby there lay
An huge great stone, which stood vpon one end,
And had not bene remoued many a day ;
Some land-marke seem'd to be, or signe of
     sundry way.

36

The same he snatcht, and with exceeding sway
Threw at his foe, who was right well aware
To shunne the engin of his meant decay ;
It booted not to thinke that throw to beare,
But ground he gaue, and lightly leapt areare :
Eft fierce returning, as a Faulcon faire
That once hath failed of her souse full neare,
Remounts againe into the open aire,
And vnto better fortune doth her selfe prepare.

37

So braue returning, with his brandisht blade,
He to the Carle himselfe againe addrest,
And strooke at him so sternely, that he made
An open passage through his riuen brest,
That halfe the steele behind his back did rest ;
Which drawing backe, he looked euermore
When the hart bloud should gush out of his
     chest,
Or his dead corse should fall vpon the flore ;
But his dead corse vpon the flore fell nathemore.

38

Ne drop of bloud appeared shed to bee,
All were the wounde so wide and wonderous,
That through his carkasse one might plainely see :
Halfe in a maze with horror hideous,
And halfe in rage, to be deluded thus,
Againe through both the sides he strooke him
     quight,
That made his spright to grone full piteous :
Yet nathemore forth fled his groning spright,
But freshly as at first, prepard himselfe to fight.

SPENSER   F

39

Thereat he smitten was with great affright,
  And trembling terror did his hart apall,
  Ne wist he, what to thinke of that same sight,
  Ne what to say, ne what to doe at all ;
  He doubted, least it were some magicall
  Illusion, that did beguile his sense,
  Or wandring ghost, that wanted funerall,
  Or aerie spirit vnder false pretence,
Or hellish feend raysd vp through diuelish
    science.

40

His wonder farre exceeded reasons reach,
  That he began to doubt his dazeled sight,
  And oft of error did himselfe appeach :
  Flesh without bloud, a person without spright,
  Wounds without hurt, a bodie without might,
  That could doe harme, yet could not harmed
    bee,
  That could not die, yet seem'd a mortall wight,
  That was most strong in most infirmitee ;
Like did he neuer heare, like did he neuer see.

41

A while he stood in this astonishment,
  Yet would he not for all his great dismay
  Giue ouer to effect his first intent,
  And th'vtmost meanes of victorie assay,
  Or th'vtmost issew of his owne decay.
  His owne good sword *Morddure*, that neuer
    fayld
  At need, till now, he lightly threw away,
  And his bright shield, that nought him now
    auayld,
And with his naked hands him forcibly assayld.

42

Twixt his two mightie armes him vp he snatcht,
  And crusht his carkasse so against his brest,
  That the disdainfull soule he thence dispatcht,
  And th'idle breath all vtterly exprest :
  Tho when he felt him dead, a downe he kest
  The lumpish corse vnto the senselesse grownd ;
  Adowne he kest it with so puissant wrest,
  That backe againe it did aloft rebownd,
And gaue against his mother earth a gronefull
    sownd.

43

As when *Ioues* harnesse-bearing Bird from hie
  Stoupes at a flying heron with proud disdaine,
  The stone-dead quarrey fals so forcibile.
  That it rebounds against the lowly plaine,
  A second fall redoubling backe againe.
  Then thought the Prince all perill sure was past,
  And that he victor onely did remaine :
  No sooner thought, then that the Carle as fast
Gan heap huge strokes on him as ere he downe
    was cast.

44

Nigh his wits end then woxe th'amazed knight,
  And thought his labour lost and trauell vaine,
  Against this lifelesse shadow so to fight :
  Yet life he saw, and felt his mightie maine,
  That whiles he marueild still, did still him paine:
  For thy he gan some other wayes aduize,
  How to take life from that dead-liuing swaine,
  Whom still he marked freshly to arize
From th'earth, and from her wombe new spirits
    to reprize.

45

He then remembred well, that had bene sayd,
  How th'Earth his mother was, and first him bore;
  She eke so often, as his life decayd,
  Did life with vsury to him restore,
  And raysd him vp much stronger then before,
  So soone as he vnto her wombe did fall ;
  Therefore to ground he would him cast no more,
  Ne him commit to graue terrestriall,
But beare him farre from hope of succour vsuall.

46

Tho vp he caught him twixt his puissant hands,
  And hauing scruzd out of his carrion corse
  The lothfull life, now loosd from sinfull bands,
  Vpon his shoulders carried him perforse
  Aboue three furlongs, taking his full course,
  Vntill he came vnto a standing lake ;
  Him thereinto he threw without remorse,
  Ne stird, till hope of life did him forsake ;
So end of that Carles dayes, and his owne paines
    did make.

47

Which when those wicked Hags from farre
    did spy,
  Like two mad dogs they ran about the lands,
  And th'one of them with dreadfull yelling cry,
  Throwing away her broken chaines and bands,
  And hauing quencht her burning fier brands,
  Hedlong her selfe did cast into that lake ;
  But *Impotence* with her owne wilfull hands,
  One of *Malegers* cursed darts did take,
So riu'd her trembling hart, and wicked end
    did make.

48

Thus now alone he conquerour remaines ;
  Tho comming to his Squire, that kept his steed,
  Thought to haue mounted, but his feeble vaines
  Him faild thereto, and serued not his need,
  Through losse of bloud, which from his wounds
    did bleed,
  That he began to faint, and life decay :
  But his good Squire him helping vp with speed,
  With stedfast hand vpon his horse did stay,
And led him to the Castle by the beaten way.

49

Where many Groomes and Squiers readie were,
To take him from his steed full tenderly,
And eke the fairest *Alma* met him there
With balme and wine and costly spicery,
To comfort him in his infirmity ;
Eftsoones she causd him vp to be conuayd,
And of his armes despoyled easily,
In sumptuous bed she made him to be layd,
And all the while his wounds were dressing, by
    him stayd.

Cant. XII.

Guyon, by Palmers gouernance,
    passing through perils great,
Doth ouerthrow the Bowre of blisse,
    and Acrasie defeat.

1

Now gins this goodly frame of Temperance
Fairely to rise, and her adorned hed
To pricke of highest praise forth to aduance,
Formerly grounded, and fast setteled
On firme foundation of true bountihed ;
And this braue knight, that for that vertue
    fights,
Now comes to point of that same perilous sted,
Where Pleasure dwelles in sensuall delights,
Mongst thousand dangers, and ten thousand
    magick mights.

2

Two dayes now in that sea he sayled has,
Ne euer land beheld, ne liuing wight,
Ne ought saue perill, still as he did pas :
Tho when appeared the third *Morrow* bright,
Vpon the waues to spred her trembling light,
An hideous roaring farre away they heard,
That all their senses filled with affright,
And streight they saw the raging surges reard
Vp to the skyes, that them of drowning made
    affeard.

3

Said then the Boteman, Palmer stere aright,
And keepe an euen course ; for yonder way
We needes must passe (God do vs well ac-
    quight,)
That is the *Gulfe of Greedinesse*. they say,
That deepe engorgeth all this worldes pray :
Which hauing swallowd vp excessiuely,
He soone in vomit vp againe doth lay,
And belcheth forth his superfluity,
That all the seas for feare do seeme away to fly.

4

On th'other side an hideous Rocke is pight,
Of mightie *Magnes* stone, whose craggie clift
Depending from on high, dreadfull to sight,
Ouer the waues his rugged armes doth lift,
And threatneth downe to throw his ragged r.ft
On who so commeth nigh ; yet nigh it drawes
All passengers, that none from it can shift :
For whiles they fly that Gulfes deuouring iawes,
They on this rock are rent, and sunck in help-
    lesse wawes.

5

Forward they passe, and strongly he them rowes,
Vntill they nigh vnto that Gulfe arriue,
Where streame more violent and greedy growes:
Then he with all his puissance doth striue
To strike his oares, and mightily doth driue
The hollow vessell through the threatfull waue,
Which gaping wide, to swallow them aliue,
In th'huge abysse of his engulfing graue,
Doth rore at them in vaine, and with great
    terror raue.

6

They passing by, that griesly mouth did see,
Sucking the seas into his entralles deepe,
That seem'd more horrible then hell to bee,
Or that darke dreadfull hole of *Tartare* steepe,
Through which the damned ghosts doen often
    creepe
Backe to the world, bad liuers to torment :
But nought that falles into this direfull deepe,
Ne that approcheth nigh the wide descent,
May backe returne, but is condemned to be
    drent.

7

On th'other side, they saw that perilous Rocke,
Threatning it selfe on them to ruinate,
On whose sharpe clifts the ribs of vessels broke,
And shiuered ships, which had bene wrecked late,
Yet stuck, with carkasses exanimate
Of such, as hauing all their substance spent
In wanton ioyes, and lustes intemperate,
Did afterwards make shipwracke violent,
Both of their life, and fame for euer fowly blent.

8

For thy, this hight *The Rocke* of vile *Reproch*,
A daungerous and detestable place,
To which nor fish nor fowle did once approch,
But yelling Meawes, with Seagulles hoarse and
    bace,
And Cormoyrants, with birds of rauenous race,
Which still sate waiting on that wastfull clift,
For spoyle of wretches, whose vnhappie cace,
After lost credite and consumed thrift,
At last them driuen hath to this despairefull drift.

9

The Palmer seeing them in safetie past,
  Thus said ; Behold th'ensamples in our sights,
  Of lustfull luxurie and thriftlesse wast :
  What now is left of miserable wights,
  Which spent their looser daies in lewd delights,
  But shame and sad reproch, here to be red,
  By these rent reliques, speaking their ill plights?
  Let all that liue, hereby be counselled,
To shunne *Rocke of Reproch*, and it as death to
  dred.

10

So forth they rowed, and that *Ferryman*
  With his stiffe oares did brush the sea so strong,
  That the hoare waters from his frigot ran,
  And the light bubbles daunced all along,
  Whiles the salt brine out of the billowes sprong.
  At last farre off they many Islands spy,
  On euery side floting the floods emong :
  Then said the knight, Loe I the land descry,
Therefore old Syre thy course do thereunto
  apply.

11

That may not be, said then the *Ferryman*
  Least we vnweeting hap to be fordonne :
  For those same Islands, seeming now and than,
  Are not firme lande, nor any certein wonne,
  But straggling plots, which to and fro do ronne
  In the wide waters : therefore are they hight
  The *wandring Islands*. Therefore doe them
  shonne ;
  For they haue oft drawne many a wandring
  wight
Into most deadly daunger and distressed plight.

12

Yet well they seeme to him, that farre doth vew,
  Both faire and fruitfull, and the ground dispred
  With grassie greene of delectable hew,
  And the tall trees with leaues apparelled,
  Are deckt with blossomes dyde in white and red,
  That mote the passengers thereto allure ;
  But whosoeuer once hath fastened
  His foot thereon, may neuer it recure,
But wandreth euer more vncertein and vnsure.

13

As th'Isle of *Delos* whylome men report
  Amid th' *Aegaean* sea long time did stray,
  Ne made for shipping any certaine port,
  Till that *Latona* traueiling that way,
  Flying from *Iunoes* wrath and hard assay,
  Of her faire twins was there deliuered,
  Which afterwards did rule the night and day ;
  Thenceforth it firmely was established,
And for *Apolloes* honor highly herried.

14

They to him hearken, as beseemeth meete,
  And passe on forward : so their way does ly,
  That one of those same Islands, which doe fleet
  In the wide sea, they needes must passen by,
  Which seemd so sweet and pleasant to the eye,
  That it would tempt a man to touchen there :
  Vpon the banck they sitting did espy
  A daintie damzell, dressing of her heare,
By whom a litle skippet floting did appeare.

15

She them espying, loud to them can call,
  Bidding them nigher draw vnto the shore ;
  For she had cause to busie them withall ;
  And therewith loudly laught : But nathemore
  Would they once turne, but kept on as afore :
  Which when she saw, she left her lockes vn-
  dight,
  And running to her boat withouten ore
  From the departing land it launched light,
And after them did driue with all her power and
  might.

16

Whom ouertaking, she in merry sort
  Them gan to bord, and purpose diuersly,
  Now faining dalliance and wanton sport,
  Now throwing forth lewd words immodestly ;
  Till that the Palmer gan full bitterly
  Her to rebuke, for being loose and light
  Which not abiding, but more scornefully
  Scoffing at him, that did her iustly wite,
She turnd her bote about, and from them rowed
  quite.

17

That was the wanton *Phaedria*, which late
  Did ferry him ouer the *Idle lake* :
  Whom nought regarding, they kept on their
  gate,
  And all her vaine allurements did forsake,
  When them the wary Boateman thus bespake;
  Here now behoueth vs well to auyse,
  And of our safetie good heede to take ;
  For here before a perlous passage lyes,
Where many Mermayds haunt, making false
  melodies.

18

But by the way, there is a great Quicksand,
  And a whirlepoole of hidden ieopardy,
  Therefore, Sir Palmer, keepe an euen hand ;
  For twixt them both the narrow way doth ly
  Scarse had he said, when hard at hand they spy
  That quicksand nigh with water couered :
  But by the checked waue they did descry
  It plaine, and by the sea discoloured :
It called was the quicksand of *Vnthriftyhed*.

19

They passing by, a goodly Ship did see,
  Laden from far with precious merchandize,
  And brauely furnished, as ship might bee,
  Which through great disauenture, or mesprize,
  Her selfe had runne into that hazardize;
  Whose mariners and merchants with much toyle,
  Labour'd in vaine, to haue recur'd their prize,
  And the rich wares to saue from pitteous spoyle,
But neither toyle nor trauell might her backe
  recoyle.

20

On th'other side they see that perilous Poole,
  That called was the *Whirlepoole of decay*,
  In which full many had with haplesse doole
  Beene suncke, of whom no memorie did stay:
  Whose circled waters rapt with whirling sway,
  Like to a restlesse wheele, still running round,
  Did couet, as they passed by that way,
  To draw their boate within the vtmost bound
Of his wide *Labyrinth*, and then to haue them
  dround.

21

But th'heedfull Boateman strongly forth did
  stretch
  His brawnie armes, and all his body straine,
  That th'vtmost sandy breach they shortly fetch,
  Whiles the dred daunger does behind remaine.
  Suddeine they see from midst of all the Maine,
  The surging waters like a mountaine rise,
  And the great sea puft vp with proud disdaine,
  To swell aboue the measure of his guise,
As threatning to deuoure all, that his powre
  despise.

22

The waues come rolling, and the billowes rore
  Outragiously, as they enraged were,
  Or wrathfull *Neptune* did them driue before
  His whirling charet, for exceeding feare:
  For not one puffe of wind there did appeare,
  That all the three thereat woxe much afrayd,
  Vnweeting, what such horrour straunge did reare.
  Eftsoones they saw an hideous hoast arrayd,
Of huge Sea monsters, such as liuing sence
  dismayd.

23

Most vgly shapes, and horrible aspects,
  Such as Dame Nature selfe mote feare to see,
  Or shame, that euer should so fowle defects
  From her most cunning hand escaped bee;
  All dreadfull pourtraicts of deformitee:
  Spring-headed *Hydraes*, and sea-shouldring
  Whales,
  Great whirlpooles, which all fishes make to flee,
  Bright Scolopendraes, arm'd with siluer scales,
Mighty *Monoceros*, with immeasured tayles.

24

The dreadfull Fish, that hath deseru'd the name
  Of Death, and like him lookes in dreadfull hew,
  The griesly Wasserman, that makes his game
  The flying ships with swiftnesse to pursew,
  The horrible Sea-satyre, that doth shew
  His fearefull face in time of greatest storme,
  Huge *Ziffius*, whom Mariners eschew
  No lesse, then rockes, (as trauellers informe,)
And greedy *Rosmarines* with visages deforme.

25

All these, and thousand thousands many more,
  And more deformed Monsters thousand fold,
  With dreadfull noise, and hollow rombling rore,
  Came rushing in the fomy waues enrold,
  Which seem'd to fly for feare, them to behold:
  Ne wonder, if these did the knight appall;
  For all that here on earth we dreadfull hold,
  Be but as bugs to fearen babes withall,
Compared to the creatures in the seas entrall.

26

Feare nought, (then said the Palmer well auiz'd;)
  For these same Monsters are not these in deed,
  But are into these fearefull shapes disguiz'd
  By that same wicked witch, to worke vs dreed,
  And draw from on this iourney to proceede.
  Tho lifting vp his vertuous staffe on hye,
  He smote the sea, which calmed was with speed,
  And all that dreadfull Armie fast gan flye
Into great *Tethys* bosome, where they hidden
  lye.

27

Quit from that daunger, forth their course they
  kept,
  And as they went, they heard a ruefull cry
  Of one, that wayld and pittifully wept,
  That through the sea the resounding plaints
  did fly:
  At last they in an Island did espy
  A seemely Maiden, sitting by the shore,
  That with great sorrow and sad agony,
  Seemed some great misfortune to deplore,
And lowd to them for succour called euermore.

28

Which *Guyon* hearing, streight his Palmer bad,
  To stere the boate towards that dolefull Mayd,
  That he might know, and ease her sorrow sad:
  Who him auizing better, to him sayd;
  Faire Sir, be not displeasd, if disobayd:
  For ill it were to hearken to her cry;
  For she is inly nothing ill apayd,
  But onely womanish fine forgery,
Your stubborne hart t'affect with fraile infirmity.

29

To which when she your courage hath inclind
  Through foolish pitty, then her guilefull bayt
She will embosome deeper in your mind,
  And for your ruine at the last awayt.
  The knight was ruled, and the Boateman strayt
Held on his course with stayed stedfastnesse,
  Ne euer shruncke, ne euer sought to bayt
His tyred armes for toylesome wearinesse,
But with his oares did sweepe the watry wilder-
  nesse.

30

And now they nigh approched to the sted,
  Where as those Mermayds dwelt : it was a still
And calmy bay, on th'one side sheltered
  With the brode shadow of an hoarie hill,
  On th'other side an high rocke toured still,
  That twixt them both a pleasaunt port they
    made,
  And did like an halfe Theatre fulfill :
There those fiue sisters had continuall trade,
And vsd to bath themselues in that deceiptfull
  shade.

31

They were faire Ladies, till they fondly striu'd
  With th'*Heliconian* maides for maistery ;
Of whom they ouer-comen, were depriu'd
  Of their proud beautie, and th'one moyity
  Transform'd to fish, for their bold surquedry,
  But th'vpper halfe their hew retained still,
  And their sweet skill in wonted melody ;
Which euer after they abusd to ill,
T'allure weake trauellers, whom gotten they
  did kill.

32

So now to *Guyon*, as he passed by,
  Their pleasaunt tunes they sweetly thus
    applide ;
O thou faire sonne of gentle Faery,
  That art in mighty armes most magnifide
  Aboue all knights, that euer battell tride,
  O turne thy rudder hither-ward a while :
  Here may thy storme-bet vessell safely ride ;
This is the Port of rest from troublous toyle,
The worlds sweet In, from paine and weari-
  some turmoyle.

33

With that the rolling sea resounding soft,
  In his big base them fitly answered,
And on the rocke the waues breaking aloft,
  A solemne Meane vnto them measured,
  The whiles sweet *Zephirus* lowd whisteled
  His treble, a straunge kinde of harmony ;
  Which *Guyons* senses softly tickeled,
That he the boateman bad row easily,
And let him heare some part of their rare melody.

34

But him the Palmer from that vanity,
  With temperate aduice discounselled,
That they it past, and shortly gan descry
  The land, to which their course they leueled ;
  When suddeinly a grosse fog ouer spred
With his dull vapour all that desert has,
  And heauens chearefull face enueloped,
That all things one, and one as nothing was,
And this great Vniuerse seemd one confused
  mas.

35

Thereat they greatly were dismayd, ne wist
  How to direct their way in darkenesse wide,
But feard to wander in that wastfull mist,
  For tombling into mischiefe vnespide.
  Worse is the daunger hidden, then describe.
Suddeinly an innumerable flight
  Of harmefuil fowles about them fluttering, cride,
And with their wicked wings them oft did smight,
And sore annoyed, groping in that griesly night.

36

Euen all the nation of vnfortunate
  And fatall birds about them flocked were,
Such as by nature men abhorre and hate,
  The ill-faste Owle, deaths dreadfull messengere,
  The hoars Night-rauen, trump of dolefull drere,
  The lether-winged Bat, dayes enimy,
  The ruefull Strich, still waiting on the bere,
The Whistler shrill, that who so heares, doth dy,
The hellish Harpies, prophets of sad destiny.

37

All those, and all that else does horrour breed,
  About them flew, and fild their sayles with feare:
Yet stayd they not, but forward did proceed,
  Whiles th'one did row, and th'other stifly
    steare ;
Till that at last the weather gan to cleare,
  And the faire land it selfe did plainly show.
  Said then the Palmer, Lo where does appeare
The sacred soile, where all our perils grow ;
Therefore, Sir knight, your ready armes about
  you throw.

38

He hearkned, and his armes about him tooke,
  The whiles the nimble boate so well her sped,
That with her crooked keele the land she strooke,
  Then forth the noble *Guyon* sallied,
  And his sage Palmer, that him gouerned ;
  But th'other by his boate behind did stay.
  They marched fairly forth, of nought ydred,
Both firmely armd for euery hard assay,
With constancy and care, gainst daunger and
  dismay.

39

Ere long they heard an hideous bellowing
  Of many beasts, that roard outrageously,
  As if that hungers point, or *Venus* sting
  Had them enraged with fell surquedry;
  Yet nought they feard, but past on hardily,
  Vntill they came in vew of those wild beasts:
  Who all attonce, gaping full greedily,
  And rearing fiercely their vpstarting crests,
Ran towards, to deuoure those vnexpected guests.

40

But soone as they approcht with deadly threat,
  The Palmer ouer them his staffe vpheld,
  His mighty staffe, that could all charmes defeat:
  Eftsoones their stubborne courages were queld,
  And high aduaunced crests downe meekely feld,
  In stead of fraying, they them selues did feare,
  And trembled, as them passing they beheld:
  Such wondrous powre did in that staffe appeare,
All monsters to subdew to him, that did it beare.

41

Of that same wood it fram'd was cunningly,
  Of which *Caduceus* whilome was made,
  Caduceus the rod of *Mercury*,
  With which he wonts the *Stygian* realmes inuade,
  Through ghastly horrour, and eternall shade;
  Th' infernall feends with it he can asswage,
  And *Orcus* tame, whom nothing can perswade,
  And rule the *Furyes*, when they most do rage:
Such vertue in his staffe had eke this Palmer sage.

42

Thence passing forth, they shortly do arriue,
  Whereas the Bowre of *Blisse* was situate;
  A place pickt out by choice of best aliue,
  That natures worke by art can imitate:
  In which what euer in this worldly state
  Is sweet, and pleasing vnto liuing sense,
  Or that may dayntiest fantasie aggrate,
  Was poured forth with plentifull dispence,
And made there to abound with lauish affluence.

43

Goodly it was enclosed round about,
  Aswell their entred guestes to keepe within,
  As those vnruly beasts to hold without;
  Yet was the fence thereof but weake and thin;
  Nought feard their force, that fortilage to win,
  But wisedomes powre, and temperaunces might,
  By which the mightiest things efforced bin:
  And eke the gate was wrought of substaunce light,
Rather for pleasure, then for battery or fight.

44

Yt framed was of precious yuory,
  That seemd a worke of admirable wit;
  And therein all the famous history
  Of *Iason* and *Medæa* was ywrit;
  Her mighty charmes, her furious louing fit,
  His goodly conquest of the golden fleece,
  His falsed faith, and loue too lightly flit,
  The wondred *Argo*, which in venturous peece
First through the *Euxine* seas bore all the flowr of *Greece*.

45

Ye might haue seene the frothy billowes fry
  Vnder the ship, as thorough them she went,
  That seemd the waues were into yuory,
  Or yuory into the waues were sent;
  And other where the snowy substaunce sprent
  With vermell, like the boyes bloud therein shed,
  A piteous spectacle did represent,
  And otherwhiles with gold besprinkeled;
Yt seemd th'enchaunted flame, which did *Creüsa* wed.

46

All this, and more might in that goodly gate
  Be red; that euer open stood to all,
  Which thither came: but in the Porch there sate
  A comely personage of stature tall,
  And semblaunce pleasing, more then naturall,
  That trauellers to him seemd to entize;
  His looser garment to the ground did fall,
  And flew about his heeles in wanton wize,
Not fit for speedy pace, or manly exercize.

47

They in that place him *Genius* did call:
  Not that celestiall powre, to whom the care
  Of life, and generation of all
  That liues, pertaines in charge particulare,
  Who wondrous things concerning our welfare,
  And straunge phantomes doth let vs oft forsee,
  And oft of secret ill bids vs beware:
  That is our Selfe, whom though we do not see,
Yet each doth in him selfe it well perceiue to bee.

48

Therefore a God him sage Antiquity
  Did wisely make, and good *Agdistes* call:
  But this same was to that quite contrary,
  The foe of life, that good enuyes to all,
  That secretly doth vs procure to fall,
  Through guilefull semblaunts, which he makes vs see.
  He of this Gardin had the gouernall,
  And Pleasures porter was deuizd to bee,
Holding a staffe in hand for more formalitee.

49

With diuerse flowres he daintily was deckt,
  And strowed round about, and by his side
  A mighty Mazer bowle of wine was set,
  As if it had to him bene sacrifide ;
  Wherewith all new-come guests he gratifide :
  So did he eke Sir *Guyon* passing by :
  But he his idle curtesie defide,
  And ouerthrew his bowle disdainfully ;
And broke his staffe, with which he charmed semblants sly.

50

Thus being entred, they behold around
  A large and spacious plaine, on euery side
  Strowed with pleasauns, whose faire grassy ground
  Mantled with greene, and goodly beautifide
  With all the ornaments of *Floraes* pride,
  Wherewith her mother Art, as halfe in scorne
  Of niggard Nature, like a pompous bride
  Did decke her, and too lauishly adorne,
When forth from virgin bowre she comes in th'early morne.

51

Thereto the Heauens alwayes Iouiall,
  Lookt on them louely, still in stedfast state,
  Ne suffred storme nor frost on them to fall,
  Their tender buds or leaues to violate,
  Nor scorching heat, nor cold intemperate
  T'afflict the creatures, which therein did dwell,
  But the milde aire with season moderate
  Gently attempred, and disposd so well,
That still it breathed forth sweet spirit and holesome smell.

52

More sweet and holesome, then the pleasaunt hill
  Of *Rhodope*, on which the Nimphe, that bore
  A gyaunt babe, her selfe for griefe did kill ;
  Or the Thessalian *Tempe*, where of yore
  Faire *Daphne Phœbus* hart with loue did gore ;
  Or *Ida*, where the Gods lou'd to repaire,
  When euer they their heauenly bowres forlore ;
  Or sweet *Parnasse*, the haunt of Muses faire ;
Or *Eden* selfe, if ought with *Eden* mote compaire.

53

Much wondred *Guyon* at the faire aspect
  Of that sweet place, yet suffred no delight
  To sincke into his sence, nor mind affect,
  But passed forth, and lookt still forward right,
  Bridling his will, and maistering his might :
  Till that he came vnto another gate ;
  No gate, but like one, being goodly dight
  With boughes and braunches, which did broad dilate
Their clasping armes, in wanton wreathings intricate.

54

So fashioned a Porch with rare deuice,
  Archt ouer head with an embracing vine,
  Whose bounches hanging downe, seemd to entice
  All passers by, to tast their lushious wine,
  And did themselues into their hands incline,
  As freely offering to be gathered :
  Some deepe empurpled as the *Hyacint*,
  Some as the Rubine, laughing sweetly red,
Some like faire Emeraudes, not yet well ripened.

55

And them amongst, some were of burnisht gold,
  So made by art, to beautifie the rest,
  Which did themselues emongst the leaues enfold,
  As lurking from the vew of couetous guest,
  That the weake bowes, with so rich load opprest,
  Did bow adowne, as ouer-burdened.
  Vnder that Porch a comely dame did rest,
  Clad in faire weedes, but fowle disordered,
And garments loose, that seemd vnmeet for womanhed.

56

In her left hand a Cup of gold she held,
  And with her right the riper fruit did reach,
  Whose sappy liquor, that with fulnesse sweld,
  Into her cup she scruzd, with daintie breach
  Of her fine fingers, without fowle empeach,
  That so faire wine-presse made the wine more sweet :
  Thereof she vsd to giue to drinke to each,
  Whom passing by she happened to meet :
It was her guise, all Straungers goodly so to greet.

57

So she to *Guyon* offred it to tast ;
  Who taking it out of her tender hond,
  The cup to ground did violently cast,
  That all in peeces it was broken fond,
  And with the liquor stained all the lond :
  Whereat *Excesse* exceedingly was wroth,
  Yet no'te the same amend, ne yet withstond,
  But suffered him to passe, all were she loth ;
Who nought regarding her displeasure forward goth.

58

There the most daintie Paradise on ground,
  It selfe doth offer to his sober eye,
  In which all pleasures plenteously abound,
  And none does others happinesse enuye :
  The painted flowres, the trees vpshooting hye,
  The dales for shade, the hilles for breathing space,
  The trembling groues, the Christall running by ;
  And that, which all faire workes doth most aggrace,
The art, which all that wrought, appeared in no place.

59

One would haue thought, (so cunningly, the rude,
  And scorned parts were mingled with the fine,)
  That nature had for wantonesse ensude
  Art, and that Art at nature did repine ;
  So striuing each th' other to vndermine,
  Each did the others worke more beautifie ;
  So difft'ring both in willes, agreed in fine :
  So all agreed through sweete diuersitie,
This Gardin to adorne with all varietie.

60

And in the midst of all, a fountaine stood,
  Of richest substaunce, that on earth might bee,
  So pure and shiny, that the siluer flood
  Through euery channell running one might see ;
  Most goodly it with curious imageree
  Was ouer-wrought, and shapes of naked boyes,
  Of which some seemd with liuely iollitee,
  To fly about, playing their wanton toyes,
Whilest others did them selues embay in liquid
  ioyes.

61

And ouer all, of purest gold was spred,
  A trayle of yuie in his natiue hew :
  For the rich mettall was so coloured,
  That wight, who did not well auis'd it vew,
  Would surely deeme it to be yuie trew :
  Low his lasciuious armes adown did creepe,
  That themselues dipping in the siluer dew,
  Their fleecy flowres they tenderly did steepe,
Which drops of Christall seemd for wantones to
  weepe.

62

Infinit streames continually did well
  Out of this fountaine, sweet and faire to see,
  The which into an ample lauer fell,
  And shortly grew to so great quantitie,
  That like a little lake it seemd to bee ;
  Whose depth exceeded not three cubits hight,
  That through the waues one might the bottom
    see,
  All pau'd beneath with Iaspar shining bright,
That seemd the fountaine in that sea did sayle
  vpright.

63

And all the margent round about was set,
  With shady Laurell trees, thence to defend
  The sunny beames, which on the billowes bet,
  And those which therein bathed, mote offend.
  As *Guyon* hapned by the same to wend,
  Two naked Damzelles he therein espyde,
  Which therein bathing, seemed to contend,
  And wrestle wantonly, ne car'd to hyde,
Their dainty parts from vew of any, which
  them eyde.

64

Sometimes the one would lift the other quight
  Aboue the waters, and then downe againe
  Her plong, as ouer maistered by might,
  Where both awhile would couered remaine,
  And each the other from to rise restraine ;
  The whiles their snowy limbes, as through a vele,
  So through the Christall waues appeared plaine :
  Then suddeinly both would themselues vnhele,
And th'amarous sweet spoiles to greedy eyes
  reuele.

65

As that faire Starre, the messenger of morne,
  His deawy face out of the sea doth reare :
  Or as the *Cyprian* goddesse, newly borne
  Of th'Oceans fruitfull froth, did first appeare :
  Such seemed they, and so their yellow heare
  Christalline humour dropped downe apace.
  Whom such when *Guyon* saw, he drew him neare,
  And somewhat gan relent his earnest pace,
His stubborne brest gan secret pleasaunce to
  embrace.

66

The wanton Maidens him espying, stood
  Gazing a while at his vnwonted guise ;
  Then th'one her selfe low ducked in the flood,
  Abasht, that her a straunger did a vise :
  But th'other rather higher did arise,
  And her two lilly paps aloft displayd,
  And all, that might his melting hart entise
  To her delights, she vnto him bewrayd :
The rest hid vnderneath, him more desirous
  made.

67

With that, the other likewise vp arose,
  And her faire lockes, which formerly were bownd
  Vp in one knot, she low adowne did lose :
  Which flowing long and thick, her cloth'd
    arownd,
  And th'yuorie in golden mantle gownd :
  So that faire spectacle from him was reft,
  Yet that, which reft it, no lesse faire was fownd :
  So hid in lockes and waues from lookers theft,
Nought but her louely face she for his looking
  left.

68

Withall she laughed, and she blusht withall,
  That blushing to her laughter gaue more grace,
  And laughter to her blushing, as did fall :
  Now when they spide the knight to slacke his
    pace,
  Them to behold, and in his sparkling face
  The secret signes of kindled lust appeare,
  Their wanton meriments they did encreace,
  And to him beckned, to approch more neare,
And shewd him many sights, that courage cold
  could reare.

69

On which when gazing him the Palmer saw,
  He much rebukt those wandring eyes of his,
  And counseld well, him forward thence did
    draw.
Now are they come nigh to the *Bowre of blis*
Of her fond fauorites so nam'd amis :
When thus the Palmer ; Now Sir, well auise ;
For here the end of all our trauell is :
Here wonnes *Acrasia*, whom we must surprise,
Else she will slip away, and all our drift despise.

70

Eftsoones they heard a most melodious sound,
  Of all that mote delight a daintie eare,
  Such as attonce might not on liuing ground,
  Saue in this Paradise, be heard elswhere :
  Right hard it was, for wight, which did it heare,
  To read, what manner musicke that mote bee :
  For all that pleasing is to liuing eare,
  Was there consorted in one harmonee,
Birdes, voyces, instruments, windes, waters, all
    agree.

71

The ioyous birdes shrouded in chearefull shade,
  Their notes vnto the voyce attempred sweet ;
  Th'Angelicall soft trembling voyces made
  To th'instruments diuine respondence meet :
  The siluer sounding instruments did meet
  With the base murmure of the waters fall :
  The waters fall with difference discreet,
  Now soft, now loud, vnto the wind did call :
The gentle warbling wind low answered to all.

72

There, whence that Musick seemed heard to bee,
  Was the faire Witch her selfe now solacing,
  With a new Louer, whom through sorceree
  And witchcraft, she from farre did thither bring :
  There she had him now layd a slombering,
  In secret shade, after long wanton ioyes :
  Whilst round about them pleasauntly did sing
  Many faire Ladies, and lasciuious boyes,
That euer mixt their song with light licentious
    toyes.

73

And all that while, right ouer him she hong,
  With her false eyes fast fixed in his sight,
  As seeking medicine, whence she was stong,
  Or greedily depasturing delight :
  And oft inclining downe with kisses light,
  For feare of waking him, his lips bedewd,
  And through his humid eyes did sucke his
    spright,
  Quite molten into lust and pleasure lewd ;
Wherewith she sighed soft, as if his case she rewd.

74

The whiles some one did chaunt this louely lay ;
  Ah see, who so faire thing doest faine to see,
  In springing flowre the image of thy day ;
  Ah see the Virgin Rose, how sweetly shee
  Doth first peepe forth with bashfull modestee,
  That fairer seemes, the lesse ye see her may ;
  Lo see soone after, how more bold and free
  Her bared bosome she doth broad display ;
Loe see soone after, how she fades, and falles
    away.

75

So passeth, in the passing of a day,
  Of mortall life the leafe, the bud, the flowre,
  Ne more doth flourish after first decay,
  That earst was sought to decke both bed and
    bowre,
  Of many a Ladie, and many a Paramowre :
  Gather therefore the Rose, whilest yet is prime,
  For soone comes age, that will her pride deflowre :
  Gather the Rose of loue, whilest yet is time,
Whilest louing thou mayst loued be with equall
    crime.

76

He ceast, and then gan all the quire of birdes
  Their diuerse notes t'attune vnto his lay,
  As in approuance of his pleasing words.
  The constant paire heard all, that he did say,
  Yet swarued not, but kept their forward way,
  Through many couert groues, and thickets close,
  In which they creeping did at last display
  That wanton Ladie, with her louer lose,
Whose sleepie head she in her lap did soft dispose.

77

Vpon a bed of Roses she was layd,
  As faint through heat, or dight to pleasant sin,
  And was arayd, or rather disarayd,
  All in a vele of silke and siluer thin,
  That hid no whit her alablaster skin,
  But rather shewd more white, if more might bee :
  More subtile web *Arachne* cannot spin,
  Nor the fine nets, which oft we wouen see
Of scorched deaw, do not in th'aire more lightly
    flee.

78

Her snowy brest was bare to readie spoyle
  Of hungry eies, which n'ote therewith be fild,
  And yet through languour of her late sweet toyle,
  Few drops, more cleare then Nectar, forth
    distild,
  That like pure Orient perles adowne it trild
  And her faire eyes sweet smyling in delight,
  Moystened their fierie beames, with which she
    thrild
  Fraile harts, yet quenched not ; like starry light
Which sparckling on the silent waues, does
    seeme more bright.

79

The young man sleeping by her, seemd to bee
  Some goodly swayne of honorable place,
  That certes it great pittie was to see
  Him his nobilitie so foule deface ;
  A sweet regard, and amiable grace,
  Mixed with manly sternnesse did appeare
  Yet sleeping, in his well proportiond face,
  And on his tender lips the downy heare
Did now but freshly spring, and silken blos-
   somes beare.

80

His warlike armes, the idle instruments
  Of sleeping praise, were hong vpon a tree,
  And his braue shield, full of old moniments,
  Was fowly ra'st, that none the signes might see ;
  Ne for them, ne for honour cared hee,
  Ne ought, that did to his aduauncement tend,
  But in lewd loues, and wastfull luxuree,
  His dayes, his goods, his bodie he did spend :
O horrible enchantment, that him so did blend.

81

The noble Elfe, and carefull Palmer drew
  So nigh them, minding nought, but lustfull game,
  That suddein forth they on them rusht, and
   threw
  A subtile net, which onely for the same
  The skilfull Palmer formally did frame.
  So held them vnder fast, the whiles the rest
  Fled all away for feare of fowler shame.
  The faire Enchauntresse, so vnwares opprest,
Tryde all her arts, and all her sleights, thence
   out to wrest.

82

And eke her louer stroue : but all in vaine ;
  For that same net so cunningly was wound,
  That neither guile, nor force might it distraine.
  They tooke them both, and both them strongly
   bound   [found :
  In captiue bandes, which there they readie
  But her in chaines of adamant he tyde ;
  For nothing else might keepe her safe and
   sound ;
But *Verdant* (so he hight) he soone vntyde,
And counsell sage in steed thereof to him applyde.

83

But all those pleasant bowres and Pallace braue,
  Guyon broke downe, with rigour pittilesse ;
  Ne ought their goodly workmanship might saue
  Them from the tempest of his wrathfulnesse,
  But that their blisse he turn'd to balefulnesse :
  Their groues he feld, their gardins did deface,
  Their arbers spoyle, their Cabinets suppresse,
  Their banket houses burne, their buildings race,
And of the fairest late, now made the fowlest
   place.

84

Then led they her away, and eke that knight
  They with them led, both sorrowfull and sad :
  The way they came, the same retourn'd they right,
  Till they arriued, where they lately had   [mad.
  Charm'd those wild-beasts, that rag'd with furie
  Which now awaking, fierce at them gan fly,
  As in their mistresse reskew, whom they lad ;
  But them the Palmer soone did pacify.
Then *Guyon* askt, what meant those beastes,
   which there did ly.

85

Said he, These seeming beasts are men indeed,
  Whom this Enchauntresse hath transformed
   thus,
  Whylome her louers, which her lusts did feed,
  Now turned into figures hideous,
  According to their mindes like monstruous.
  Sad end (quoth he) of life intemperate,
  And mournefull meed of ioyes delicious :
  But Palmer, if it mote thee so aggrate,
Let them returned be vnto their former state.

86

Streight way he with his vertuous staffe them
   strooke,
  And streight of beasts they comely men became ;
  Yet being men they did vnmanly looke,
  And stared ghastly, some for inward shame,
  And some for wrath, to see their captiue Dame :
  But one aboue the rest in speciall,
  That had an hog beene late, hight *Grille* by name,
  Repined greatly, and did him miscall,
That had from hoggish forme him brought to
   naturall.

87

Said *Guyon*, See the mind of beastly man,
  That hath so soone forgot the excellence
  Of his creation, when he life began,
  That now he chooseth, with vile difference,
  To be a beast, and lacke intelligence.
  To whom the Palmer thus, The donghill kind
  Delights in filth and foule incontinence :
  Let Grill be *Grill*, and haue his hoggish mind,
But let vs hence depart, whilest wether serues and wind.

THE THIRD

BOOKE OF THE

FAERIE QVEENE.

Contayning,

THE LEGEND OF BRITOMARTIS.

OR

Of Chastitie.

1

It falls me here to write of Chastity,
  That fairest vertue, farre aboue the rest ;
  For which what needs me fetch from *Faery*
Forreine ensamples, it to haue exprest ?
Sith it is shrined in my Soueraines brest,
And form'd so liuely in each perfect part,
That to all Ladies, which haue it profest,
Need but behold the pourtraict of her hart,
If pourtrayd it might be by any liuing art.

2

But liuing art may not least part expresse,
  Nor life-resembling pencill it can paint,
  All were it *Zeuxis* or *Praxiteles* :
His dædale hand would faile, and greatly
  faint,
And her perfections with his error taint :
Ne Poets wit, that passeth Painter farre
In picturing the parts of beautie daint,
So hard a workmanship aduenture darre,
For fear through want of words her excellence
  to marre.

3

How then shall I, Apprentice of the skill,
  That whylome in diuinest wits did raine,
  Presume so high to stretch mine humble
    quill ?
Yet now my lucklesse lot doth me constraine
Hereto perforce. But O dred Soueraine
Thus farre forth pardon, sith that choicest
  wit
Cannot your glorious pourtraict figure plaine
That I in colourd showes may shadow it,
And antique praises vnto present persons fit.

4

But if in liuing colours, and right hew,
  Your selfe you couet to see pictured,
  Who can it doe more liuely, or more trew,
Then that sweet verse, with *Nectar* sprinckeled,
In which a gracious seruant pictured
His *Cynthia*, his heauens fairest light ?
That with his melting sweetnesse rauished,
And with the wonder of her beames bright,
My senses lulled are in slomber of delight.

5

But let that same delitious Poet lend
A little leaue vnto a rusticke Muse
To sing his mistresse prayse, and let him mend,
If ought amis her liking may abuse :
Ne let his fairest *Cynthia* refuse,
In mirrours more then one her selfe to see,
But either *Gloriana* let her chuse,
Or in *Belphœbe* fashioned to bee :
In th'one her rule, in th'other her rare chastitee.

Cant. I.

Guyon encountreth Britomart,
faire Florimell is chaced :
Duessaes traines and Malecastaes
champions are defaced.

1

The famous Briton Prince and Faerie knight,
After long wayes and perilous paines endured,
Hauing their wearie limbes to perfect plight
Restord, and sory wounds right well recured,
Of the faire *Alma* greatly were procured,
To make there lenger soiourne and abode ;
But when thereto they might not be allured,
From seeking praise, and deeds of armes abrode,
They courteous conge tooke, and forth together
    yode.

2

But the captiu'd *Acrasia* he sent,
Because of trauell long, a nigher way,
With a strong gard, all reskew to preuent,
And her to Faerie court safe to conuay,
That her for witnesse of his hard assay,
Vnto his *Faerie* Queene he might present :
But he him selfe betooke another way,
To make more triall of his hardiment,
And seeke aduentures, as he with Prince *Arthur*
    went.

3

Long so they trauelled through wastefull wayes,
Where daungers dwelt, and perils most did
    wonne,
To hunt for glorie and renowmed praise ;
Full many Countries they did ouerronne,
From the vprising to the setting Sunne,
And many hard aduentures did atchieue ;
Of all the which they honour euer wonne,
Seeking the weake oppressed to relieue,
And to recouer right for such, as wrong did
    grieue.

4

At last as through an open plaine they yode,
They spide a knight, that towards pricked faire,
And him beside an aged Squire there rode,
That seem'd to couch vnder his shield three-
    square,
As if that age bad him that burden spare,
And yield it those, that stouter could it wield :
He them espying, gan himselfe prepare,
And on his arme addresse his goodly shield
That bore a Lion passant in a golden field.

5

Which seeing good Sir *Guyon*, deare besought
The Prince of grace, to let him runne that turne.
He graunted : then the Faery quickly raught
His poinant speare, and sharpely gan to spurne
His fomy steed, whose fierie feete did burne
The verdant grasse, as he thereon did tread ;
Ne did the other backe his foot returne,
But fiercely forward came withouten dread,
And bent his dreadfull speare against the others
    head.

6

They bene ymet, and both their points arriued,
But *Guyon* droue so furious and fell,
That seem'd both shield and plate it would
    haue riued ;
Nathelesse it bore his foe not from his sell,
But made him stagger, as he were not well :
But *Guyon* selfe, ere well he was aware,
Nigh a speares length behind his crouper fell,
Yet in his fall so well him selfe he bare,
That mischieuous mischance his life and limbes
    did spare.

7

Great shame and sorrow of that fall he tooke ;
For neuer yet, sith warlike armes he bore,
And shiuering speare in bloudie field first shooke,
He found himselfe dishonored so sore.
Ah gentlest knight, that euer armour bore,
Let not thee grieue dismounted to haue beene,
And brought to ground, that neuer wast before ;
For not thy fault, but secret powre vnseene,
That speare enchaunted was, which layd thee
    on the greene.

8

But weenedst thou what wight thee ouerthrew,
Much greater griefe and shamefuller regret
For thy hard fortune then thou wouldst renew,
That of a single damzell thou wert met
On equall plaine, and there so hard beset ;
Euen the famous *Britomart* it was,
Whom straunge aduenture did from *Britaine* fet,
To seeke her louer (loue farre sought alas,)
Whose image she had seene in *Venus* looking
    glas.

9

Full of disdainefull wrath, he fierce vprose,
 For to reuenge that foule reprochfull shame,
 And snatching his bright sword began to close
 With her on foot, and stoutly forward came;
 Die rather would he, then endure that same.
 Which when his Palmer saw, he gan to feare
 His toward perill and vntoward blame,
 Which by that new rencounter he should reare:
For death sate on the point of that enchaunted
 speare.

10

And hasting towards him gan faire perswade,
 Not to prouoke misfortune, nor to weene
 His speares default to mend with cruell blade ;
 For by his mightie Science he had seene
 The secret vertue of that weapon keene,
 That mortall puissance mote not withstond :
 Nothing on earth mote alwaies happie beene.
 Great hazard were it, and aduenture fond,
To loose long gotten honour with one euill hond.

11

By such good meanes he him discounselled,
 From prosecuting his reuenging rage ;
 And eke the Prince like treaty handeled,
 His wrathfull will with reason to asswage,
 And laid the blame, not to his carriage,
 But to his starting steed, that swaru'd asyde,
 And to the ill purueyance of his page,
 That had his furnitures not firmely tyde :
So is his angry courage fairely pacifyde.

12

Thus reconcilement was betweene them knit,
 Through goodly temperance, and affection
 chaste,
 And either vowd with all their power and wit,
 To let not others honour be defaste,
 Of friend or foe, who euer it embrace,
 Ne armes to beare against the others syde :
 In which accord the Prince was also plaste,
 And with that golden chaine of concord tyde.
So goodly all agreed, they forth yfere did ryde.

13

O goodly vsage of those antique times,
 In which the sword was seruant vnto right ;
 When not for malice and contentious crimes,
 But all for praise, and proofe of manly might,
 The martiall brood accustomed to fight :
 Then honour was the meed of victorie,
 And yet the vanquished had no despight :
 Let later age that noble vse enuie,
Vile rancour to auoid, and cruell surquedrie.

14

Long they thus trauelled in friendly wise,
 Through countries waste, and eke well edifyde
 Seeking aduentures hard, to exercise
 Their puissance, whylome full dernely tryde
 At length they came into a forrest wyde,
 Whose hideous horror and sad trembling sound
 Full griesly seem'd: Therein they long did ryde
 Yet tract of liuing creatures none they found
Saue Beares, Lions, and Buls, which romed
 them around.

15

All suddenly out of the thickest brush,
 Vpon a milk-white Palfrey all alone,
 A goodly Ladie did foreby them rush,
 Whose face did seeme as cleare as Christall
 stone,
 And eke through feare as white as whales bone:
 Her garments all were wrought of beaten gold
 And all her steed with tinsell trappings shone
 Which fled so fast, that nothing mote him hold
And scarse them leasure gaue, her passing to
 behold.

16

Still as she fled, her eye she backward threw,
 As fearing euill, that pursewd her fast ;
 And her faire yellow locks behind her flew,
 Loosely disperst with puffe of euery blast :
 All as a blazing starre doth farre outcast
 His hearie beames, and flaming lockes dispred
 At sight whereof the people stand aghast :
 But the sage wisard telles, as he has red,
That it importunes death and dolefull drerihed

17

So as they gazed after her a while,
 Lo where a griesly Foster forth did rush,
 Breathing out beastly lust her to defile :
 His tyreling iade he fiercely forth did push,
 Through thicke and thin, both ouer banke and
 bush
 In hope her to attaine by hooke or crooke,
 That from his gorie sides the bloud did gush :
 Large were his limbes, and terrible his looke
And in his clownish hand a sharp bore speare he
 shooke.

18

Which outrage when those gentle knights did see,
 Full of great enuie and fell gealosy,
 They stayd not to auise, who first should bee
 But all spurd after fast, as they mote fly,
 To reskew her from shamefull villany.
 The Prince and *Guyon* equally byliue
 Her selfe pursewd, in hope to win thereby
 Most goodly meede, the fairest Dame aliue :
But after the foule foster *Timias* did striue.

19

The whiles faire *Britomart*, whose constant mind,
Would not so lightly follow beauties chace,
Ne reckt of Ladies Loue, did stay behind,
And them awayted there a certaine space,
To weet if they would turne backe to that place:
But when she saw them gone, she forward went,
As lay her iourney, through that perlous Pace,
With stedfast courage and stout hardiment ;
Ne euill thing she fear'd, ne euill thing she ment.

20

At last as nigh out of the wood she came,
A stately Castle farre away she spyde,
To which her steps directly she did frame.
That Castle was most goodly edifyde,
And plaste for pleasure nigh that forrest syde :
But faire before the gate a spatious plaine,
Mantled with greene, it selfe did spredden wyde,
On which she saw sixe knights, that did darraine
Fierce battell against one, with cruell might and
maine.

21

Mainly they all attonce vpon him laid,
And sore beset on euery side around,
That nigh he breathlesse grew, yet nought
dismaid,
Ne euer to them yielded foot of ground
All had he lost much bloud through many a
wound,
But stoutly dealt his blowes, and euery way
To which he turned in his wrathfull stound,
Made them recoile, and fly from dred decay,
That none of all the sixe before, him durst assay.

22

Like dastard Curres, that hauing at a bay
The saluage beast embost in wearie chace,
Dare not aduenture on the stubborne pray,
Ne byte before, but rome from place to place,
To get a snatch, when turned is his face.
In such distresse and doubtfull ieopardy,
When *Britomart* him saw, she ran a pace
Vnto his reskew, and with earnest cry,
Bad those same sixe forbeare that single enimy.

23

But to her cry they list not lenden eare,
Ne ought the more their mightie strokes sur-
ceasse,
But gathering him round about more neare,
Their direfull rancour rather did encreasse ;
Till that she rushing through the thickest preasse,
Perforce disparted their compacted gyre,
And soone compeld to hearken vnto peace :
Tho gan she myldly of them to inquyre
The cause of their dissention and outrageous yre.

24

Whereto that single knight did answere frame ;
These sixe would me enforce by oddes of might,
To chaunge my liefe, and loue another Dame,
That death me liefer were, then such despight,
So vnto wrong to yield my wrested right :
For I loue one, the truest one on ground,
Ne list me chaunge; she th'*Errant Damzell* hight,
For whose deare sake full many a bitter stownd,
I haue endur'd, and tasted many a bloudy
wound.

25

Certes (said she) then bene ye sixe to blame,
To weene your wrong by force to iustifie :
For knight to leaue his Ladie were great shame,
That faithfull is, and better were to die.
All losse is lesse, and lesse the infamie,
Then losse of loue to him, that loues but one ;
Ne may loue be compeld by maisterie ;
For soone as maisterie comes, sweet loue anone
Taketh his nimble wings, and soone away is gone.

26

Then spake one of those sixe, There dwelleth here
Within this castle wall a Ladie faire,
Whose soueraine beautie hath no liuing perc,
Thereto so bounteous and so debonaire,
That neuer any mote with her compaire.
She hath ordaind this law, which we approue,
That euery knight, which doth this way repaire,
In case he haue no Ladie, nor no loue,
Shall doe vnto her seruice neuer to remoue.

27

But if he haue a Ladie or a Loue,
Then must he her forgoe with foule defame,
Or else with vs by dint of sword approue,
That she is fairer, then our fairest Dame,
As did this knight, before ye hither came.
Perdie (said *Britomart*) the choise is hard :
But what reward had he, that ouercame ?
He should aduaunced be to high regard,
(Said they) and haue our Ladies loue for his
reward.

28

Therefore aread Sir, if thou haue a loue.
Loue haue I sure, (quoth she) but Lady none ;
Yet will I not fro mine owne loue remoue,
Ne to your Lady will I seruice done,
But wreake your wrongs wrought to this
knight alone,
And proue his cause. With that her mortall
speare
She mightily auentred towards one,
And downe him smot, ere well aware he weare,
Then to the next she rode, and downe the next
did beare.

29

Ne did she stay, till three on ground she layd
That none of them himselfe could reare againe,
The fourth was by that other knight dismayd,
All were he wearie of his former paine,
That now there do but two of six remaine ;
Which two did yield, before she did them smight.
Ah (said she then) now may ye all see plaine,
That truth is strong, and trew loue most of
might,   [fight.
That for his trusty seruaunts doth so strongly

30

Too well we see, (said they) and proue too well
Our faul..yw..akn..sse, an.l your matchlesse might:
For thy, faire Sir, yours be the Damozell,
Which by her owne law to your lot doth light,
And we your liege men faith vnto you plight.
So vnderneath her feet their swords they mard,
And after her besought, well as they might,
To enter in, and reape the dew reward :
She graunted, and then in they all together far'd.

31

Long were it to describe the goodly frame,
And stately port of *Castle Ioyeous*,
(For so that Castle hight l y commune name)
Where they were entertaind with curteous
And comely glee of many gracious
Faire Ladies, and of many a gentle knight,
Who through a Chamber long and spacious,
Eftsoones them brought vnto their Ladies sight,
That of them cleeped was the *Lady of delight*.

32

But for to tell the sumptuous aray
Of that great chamber, should be labour lost :
For liuing wit, I weene, cannot display
The royall riches and exceeding cost,
Of euery pillour and of euery post ;
Which all of purest bullion framed were,
And with great pearles and pretious stones
embost,
That the bright glister of their beames cleare
Did sparckle forth great light, and glorious did
appeare.

33

These straunger knights through passing, forth
were led
Into an inner rowme, whose royaltee
And rich purueyance might vneath be red ;
Mote Princes place beseeme so deckt to bee.
Which stately manner when as they did see,
The image of superfluous riotize,
Exceeding much the state of meane degree,
They greatly wondred, whence so sumptuous
guize   [deuize.
Might be maintaynd, and each gan diuersely

34

The wals were round about apparelled
With costly clothes of *Arras* and of *Toure*,
In which with cunning hand was pourtrahed
The loue of *Venus* and her Paramoure
The faire *Adonis*, turned to a flowre,
A worke of rare deuice, and wondrous wit.
First did it shew the bitter balefull stowre,
Which her assayd with many a feruent fit,
When first her tender hart was with his beautie
smit.

35

Then with what sleights and sweet allurements she
Entyst the Boy, as well that art she knew,
And wooed him her Paramoure to be ;
Now making girlonds of each flowre that grew,
To crowne his golden lockes with honour dew ;
Now leading him into a secret shade
From his Beauperes, and from bright heauens
vew,
Where him to sleepe she gently would perswade,
Or bathe him in a fountaine by some couert
glade.

36

And whilst he slept, she ouer him would spred
Her mantle, colour'd like the starry skyes,
And her soft arme lay vnderneath his hed,
And with ambrosiall kisses bathe his eyes ;
And whilest he bath'd, with her two crafty spyes,
She secretly would search each daintie lim,
And throw into the well sweet Rosemaryes,
And fragrant violets, and Pances trim,
And euer with sweet Nectar she did sprinkle him.

37

So did she steale his heedelesse hart away,
And ioyd his loue in secret vnespyde.
But for she saw him bent to cruell play,
To hunt the saluage beast in forrest wyde,
Dreadfull of daunger, that mote him betyde,
She oft and oft aduiz'd him to refraine
From chase of greater beasts, whose brutish pryde
Mote breede him scath vnwares: but all in vaine;
For who can shun the chaunce, that dest'ny
doth ordaine ?

38

Lo, where beyond he lyeth languishing,
Deadly engored of a great wild Bore,
And by his side the Goddesse groueling
Makes for him endlesse mone, and euermore
With her soft garment wipes away the gore,
Which staines his snowy skin with hatefull hew:
But when she saw no helpe might him restore,
Him to a dainty flowre she did transmew,
Which in that cloth was wrought, as if it liuely
grew.

39

So was that chamber clad in goodly wize,
  And round about it many beds were dight,
  As whilome was the antique worldes guize,
  Some for vntimely ease, some for delight,
  As pleased them to vse, that vse it might :
  And all was full of Damzels, and of Squires,
  Dauncing and reueling both day and night,
  And swimming deepe in sensuall desires,
And *Cupid* still emongst them kindled lustfull fires.

40

And all the while sweet Musicke did diuide
  Her looser notes with *Lydian* harmony ;
  And all the while sweet birdes thereto applide
  Their daintie layes and dulcet melody,
  Ay caroling of loue and iollity,
  That wonder was to heare their trim consort.
  Which when those knights beheld, with scornefull eye,
  They sdeigned such lasciuious disport,
And loath'd the loose demeanure of that wanton sort.

41

Thence they were brought to that great Ladies vew,
  Whom they found sitting on a sumptuous bed,
  That glistred all with gold and glorious shew,
  As the proud *Persian* Queenes accustomed :
  She seemd a woman of great bountihed,
  And of rare beautie, sauing that askaunce
  Her wanton eyes, ill signes of womanhed,
  Did roll too lightly, and too often glaunce,
Without regard of grace, or comely amenaunce.

42

Long worke it were, and needlesse to deuize
  Their goodly entertainement and great glee :
  She caused them be led in curteous wize
  Into a bowre, disarmed for to bee,
  And cheared well with wine and spiceree :
  The *Redcrosse* Knight was soone disarmed there,
  But the braue Mayd would not disarmed bee,
  But one'y vented vp her vmbriere,
And so did let her goodly visage to appere.

43

As when faire *Cynthia*, in darkesome night,
  Is in a noyous cloud enueloped,
  Where she may find the substaunce thin and light,   [hed
  Breakes forth her siluer beames, and her bright
  Discouers to the world discomfited ;
  Of the poore traueller, that went astray,
  With thousand blessings she is heried ;
  Such was the beautie and the shining ray,
With which faire *Britomart* gaue light vnto the day.

44

And eke those six, which lately with her fought,
  Now were disarmd, and did them selues present
  Vnto her vew, and company vnsoght ;
  For they all seemed curteous and gent,
  And all sixe brethren, borne of one parent,
  Which had them traynd in all ciuilitee,
  And goodly taught to tilt and turnament ;
  Now were they liegemen to this Lady free,
And her knights seruice ought, to hold of her in fee.

45

The first of them by name *Gardante* hight,
  A iolly person, and of comely vew ;
  The second was *Parlante*, a bold knight,
  And next to him *Iocante* did ensew ;
  Basciante did him selfe most curteous shew ;
  But fierce *Bacchante* seemd too fell and keene ;
  And yet in armes *Noctante* greater grew :
  All were faire knights, and goodly well beseene,
But to faire *Britomart* they all but shadowes beene.

46

For she was full of amiable grace,
  And manly terrour mixed therewithall,
  That as the one stird vp affections bace,
  So th'other did mens rash desires apall,
  And hold them backe, that would in errour fall ;
  As he, that hath espide a vermeill Rose,
  To which sharpe thornes and breres the way forstall,
Dare not for dread his hardy hand expose,
But wishing it far off, his idle wish doth lose.

47

Whom when the Lady saw so faire a wight,
  All ignoraunt of her contrary sex,
  (For she her weend a fresh and lusty knight)
  She greatly gan enamoured to wex,
  And with vaine thoughts her falsed fancy vex:
  Her fickle hart conceiued hasty fire,
  Like sparkes of fire, which fall in sclender flex,
  That shortly brent into extreme desire,
And ransackt all her veines with passion entire.

48

Eftsoones she grew to great impatience
  And into termes of open outrage brust,
  That plaine discouered her incontinence,
  Ne reckt she, who her meaning did mistrust ;
  For she was giuen all to fleshly lust,
  And poured forth in sensuall delight,
  That all regard of shame she had discust,
  And meet respect of honour put to flight :
So shamelesse beauty soone becomes a loathly sight.

49

Faire Ladies, that to loue captiued arre,
  And chaste desires do nourish in your mind,
Let not her fault your sweet affections marre,
Ne blot the bounty of all womankind ;
  'Mongst thousands good one wanton Dame to
    find :
Emongst the Roses grow some wicked weeds ;
For this was not to loue, but lust inclind ;
  For loue does alwayes bring forth bounteous
    deeds,
And in each gentle hart desire of honour breeds.

50

Nought so of loue this looser Dame did skill,
  But as a coale to kindle fleshly flame,
Giuing the bridle to her wanton will,
  And treading vnder foote her honest name :
Such loue is hate, and such desire is shame.
  Still did she roue at her with crafty glaunce
Of her false eyes, that at her hart did ayme,
  And told her meaning in her countenaunce ;
But *Britomart* dissembled it with ignoraunce.

51

Supper was shortly dight and downe they sat,
  Where they were serued with all sumptuous fare,
Whiles fruitfull *Ceres*, and *Lyæus* fat
  Pourd out their plenty, without spight or spare :
Nought wanted there, that dainty was and rare ;
  And aye the cups their bancks did ouerflow,
And aye betweene the cups, she did prepare
  Way to her loue, and secret darts did throw ;
But *Britomart* would not such guilfull message
    know.

52

So when they slaked had the feruent heat
  Of appetite with meates of euery sort,
The Lady did faire *Britomart* entreat,
  Her to disarme, and with delightfull sport
To loose her warlike limbs and strong effort,
  But when she mote not thereunto be wonne,
(For she her sexe vnder that straunge purport
  Did vse to hide, and plaine apparaunce shonne :)
In plainer wise to tell her grieuaunce she be-
    gonne.

53

And all attonce discouered her desire
  With sighes, and sobs, and plaints, and
    piteous griefe,
The outward sparkes of her in burning fire ;
  Which spent in vaine, at last she told her briefe,
That but if she did lend her short reliefe,
  And do her comfort, she mote algates dye.
But the chaste damzell, that had neuer priefe
  Of such malengine and fine forgerie,
Did easily beleeue her strong extremitie.

54

Full easie was for her to haue beliefe,
  Who by self-feeling of her feeble sexe,
And by long triall of the inward griefe,
  Wherewith imperious loue her hart did vexe,
Could iudge what paines do louing harts
    perplexe.
Who meanes no guile, be guiled soonest shall,
  And to faire semblaunce doth light faith annexe ;
The bird, that knowes not the false fowlers call,
Into his hidden net full easily doth fall.

55

For thy she would not in discourteise wise,
  Scorne the faire offer of good will profest ;
For great rebuke it is, loue to despise,
  Or rudely sdeigne a gentle harts request ;
But with faire countenaunce, as beseemed best,
  Her entertaynd ; nath'lesse she inly deemd
Her loue too light, to wooe a wandring guest :
  Which she misconstruing, thereby esteemd
That from like inward fire that outward smoke
    had steemd.

56

Therewith a while she her flit fancy fed,
  Till she mote winne fit time for her desire,
But yet her wound still inward freshly bled,
  And through her bones the false instilled fire
Did spred it selfe, and venime close inspire.
  Tho were the tables taken all away,
And euery knight, and euery gentle Squire
  Gan choose his dame with *Basciomani* gay,
With whom he meant to make his sport and
    courtly play.

57

Some fell to daunce, some fell to hazardry,
  Some to make loue, some to make meriment,
As diuerse wits to diuers things apply ;
  And all the while faire *Malecasta* bent
Her crafty engins to her close intent.
  By this th'eternall lampes, wherewith high *Ioue*
Doth light the lower world, were halfe yspent,
  And the moist daughters of huge *Atlas* stroue
Into the *Ocean* deepe to driue their weary droue.

58

High time it seemed then for euery wight
  Them to betake vnto their kindly rest ;
Eftsoones long waxen torches weren light,
  Vnto their bowres to guiden euery guest :
Tho when the Britonesse saw all the rest
  Auoided quite, she gan her selfe despoile,
And safe commit to her soft fethered nest,
  Where through long watch, and late dayes
    weary toile,
She soundly slept, and carefull thoughts did
    quite assoile.

59

Now whenas all the world in silence deepe
Yshrowded was, and euery mortall wight
Was drowned in the depth of deadly sleepe,
Faire *Malecasta*, whose engrieued spright
Could find no rest in such perplexed plight,
Lightly arose out of her wearie bed,
And vnder the blacke vele of guilty Night,
Her with a scarlot mantle couered,
That was with gold and Ermines faire enueloped.

60

Then panting soft, and trembling euerie ioynt,
Her fearfull feete towards the bowres she moued;
Where she for secret purpose did appoynt
To lodge the warlike mayd vnwisely loued,
And to her bed approching, first she prooued,
Whether she slept or wakt, with her soft hand
She softly felt, if any member mooued,
And lent her wary eare to vnderstand,
If any puffe of breath, or signe of sence she fond.

61

Which whenas none she fond, with easie shift,
For feare least her vnwares she should abrayd,
Th'embroderd quilt she lightly vp did lift,
And by her side her selfe she softly layd,
Of euery finest fingers touch affrayd;
Ne any noise she made, ne word she spake,
But inly sigh'd.   At last the royall Mayd
Out of her quiet slomber did awake,
And chaungd her weary side, the better ease to
    take.

62

Where feeling one close couched by her side,
She lightly lept out of her filed bed,
And to her weapon ran, in minde to gride
The loathed leachour. But the Dame halfe ded
Through suddein feare and ghastly drerihed,
Did shrieke alowd, that through the house it
    rong,
And the whole family therewith adred,
Rashly out of their rouzed couches sprong,
And to the troubled chamber all in armes did
    throng.

63

And those six Knights that Ladies Champions,
And eke the *Redcrosse* knight ran to the stownd,
Halfe armd and halfe vnarmd, with the mattons:
Where when confusedly they came, they fownd
Their Lady lying on the sencelesse grownd;
On th'other side, they saw the warlike Mayd
All in her snow-white smocke, with locks
    vnbownd,
Threatning the point of her auenging blade,
That with so troublous terrour they were all
    dismayde.

64

About their Lady first they flockt arownd,
Whom hauing laid in comfortable couch,
Shortly they reard out of her frosen swownd;
And afterwards they gan with fowle reproch
To stirre vp strife, and troublous contecke broch:
But by ensample of the last dayes losse,
None of them rashly durst to her approch,
Ne in so glorious spoile themselues embosse;
Her succourd eke the Champion of the bloudy
    Crosse.

65

But one of those sixe knights, *Gardante* hight,
Drew out a deadly bow and arrow keene,
Which forth he sent with felonous despight,
And fell intent against the virgin sheene:
The mortall steele stayd not, till it was seene
To gore her side, yet was the wound not deepe,
But lightly rased her soft silken skin,
That drops of purple bloud thereout did weepe,
Which did her lilly smock with staines of ver-
    meil steepe.

66

Wherewith enrag'd she fiercely at them flew,
And with her flaming sword about her layd,
That none of them foule mischiefe could eschew,
But with her dreadfull strokes were all dismayd:
Here, there, and euery where about her swayd
Her wrathfull steele, that none mote it abide;
And eke the *Redcrosse* knight gaue her good
    aid,
Ay ioyning foot to foot, and side to side,
That in short space their foes they haue quite
    terrifide.

67

Tho whenas all were put to shamefull flight,
The noble *Britomartis* her arayd,
And her bright armes about her body dight:
For nothing would she lenger there be stayd,
Where so loose life, and so vngentle trade
Was vsd of Knights and Ladies seeming gent:
So earely ere the grosse Earthes gryesy shade
Was all disperst out of the firmament,
They tooke their steeds, and forth vpon their iourney went.

Cant. II.

The Redcrosse knight to Britomart
describeth Artegall :
The wondrous myrrhour, by which she
in loue with him did fall.

1

Here haue I cause, in men iust blame to find,
That in their proper prayse too partiall bee,
And not indifferent to woman kind,
To whom no share in armes and cheualrie
They do impart, ne maken memorie
Of their braue gestes and prowesse martiall ;
Scarse do they spare to one or two or three,
Rowme in their writs; yet the same writing small
Does all their deeds deface, and dims their
    glories all.

2

But by record of antique times I find,
That women wont in warres to beare most sway,
And to all great exploits them selues inclind :
Of which they still the girlond bore away,
Till enuious Men fearing their rules decay,
Gan coyne streight lawes to curb their liberty ;
Yet sith they warlike armes haue layd away,
They haue exceld in artes and pollicy,
That now we foolish men that prayse gin eke
    t'enuy.

3

Of warlike puissaunce in ages spent,
Be thou faire *Britomart*, whose prayse I write,
But of all wisedome be thou precedent,
O soueraigne Queene, whose prayse I would
    endite,
Endite I would as dewtie doth excite ;
But ah my rimes too rude and rugged arre,
When in so high an obiect they do lite,
And striuing, fit to make, I feare do marre :
Thy selfe thy prayses tell, and make them
    knowen farre.

4

She trauelling with *Guyon* by the way,
Of sundry things faire purpose gan to find,
T'abridg their iourney long, and lingring day ;
Mongst which it fell into that Faeries mind,
To aske this Briton Mayd, what vncouth wind,
Brought her into those parts, and what inquest
Made her dissemble her disguised kind :
¹ aire Lady she him seemd, like Lady drest,
But fairest knight aliue, when armed was her
brest.

5

Thereat she sighing softly, had no powre
To speake a while, ne ready answere make,
But with hart-thrilling throbs and bitter
    stowr,,
As if she had a feuer fit, did quake,
And euery daintie limbe with horrour shake ;
And euer and anone the rosy red,
Flasht through her face, as it had been a flake
Of lightning, through bright heauen fulmined ;
At last the passion past she thus him answered.

6

Faire Sir, I let you weete, that from the howre
I taken was from nourses tender pap,
I haue beene trained vp in warlike stowre,
To tossen speare and shield, and to affrap
The warlike ryder to his most mishap ;
Sithence I loathed haue my life to lead,
As Ladies wont, in pleasures wanton lap,
To finger the fine needle and nyce thread ;
Me leuer were with point of foemans speare be
    dead.

7

All my delight on deedes of armes is set,
To hunt out perils and aduentures hard,
By sea, by land, where so they may be met,
Onely for honour and for high regard,
Without respect of richesse or reward.
For such intent into these parts I came,
Withouten compasse, or withouten card,
Far fro my natiue soyle, that is by name
The greater *Britaine*, here to seeke for prayse
and fame.

8

Fame blazed hath, that here in Faery lond
Do many famous Knightes and Ladies wonne,
And many straunge aduentures to be fond,
Of which great worth and worship may be
    wonne ;
Which I to proue, this voyage haue begonne.
But mote I weet of you, right curteous knight,
Tydings of one, that hath vnto me donne
Late foule dishonour and reprochfull spight,
The which I seeke to wreake, and *Arthegall* he
hight.

9

The word gone out, she backe againe would call,
As her repenting so to haue missayd,
But that he it vp-taking ere the fall,
Her shortly answer d ; Faire martiall Mayd
Certes ye misauised beene, t'vpbrayd
A gentle knight with so vnknightly blame :
For weet ye well of all, that euer playd
At tilt or tourney, or like warlike game,
The noble *Arthegall* hath euer borne the name.

10

For thy great wonder were it, if such shame
  Should euer enter in his bounteous thought,
  Or euer do, that mote deseruen blame :
  The noble courage neuer weeneth ought,
  That may vnworthy of it selfe be thought.
  Therefore, faire Damzell, be ye well aware,
  Least that too farre ye haue your sorrow
      sought :
  You and your countrey both I wish welfare,
And honour both; for each of other worthy are.

11

The royall Mayd woxe inly wondrous glad,
  To heare her Loue so highly magnifide,
  And ioyd that euer she affixed had,
  Her hart on knight so goodly glorifide,
  How euer finely she it faind to hide :
  The louing mother, that nine monethes did
      beare,
  In the deare closet of her painefull side,
  Her tender babe, it seeing safe appeare,
Doth not so much reioyce, as she reioyced theare.

12

But to occasion him to further talke,
  To feed her humour with his pleasing stile,
  Her list in strifull termes with him to balke,
  And thus replide, How euer, Sir, ye file
  Your curteous tongue, his prayses to compile,
  It ill beseemes a knight of gentle sort,
  Such as ye haue him boasted, to beguile
  A simple mayd, and worke so haynous tort,
In shame of knighthood, as I largely can report.

13

Let be therefore my vengeaunce to disswade,
  And read, where I that faytour false may find.
  Ah, but if reason faire might you perswade,
  To slake your wrath, and mollifie your mind,
  (Said he) perhaps ye should it better find :
  For hardy thing it is, to weene by might,
  That man to hard conditions to bind,
  Or euer hope to match in equall fight,
Whose prowesse paragon saw neuer liuing wight.

14

Ne soothlich is it easie for to read,
  Where now on earth, or how he may be found ;
  For he ne wonneth in one certaine stead,
  But restlesse walketh all the world around,
  Ay doing things, that to his fame redound,
  Defending Ladies cause, and Orphans right,
  Where so he heares, that any doth confound
  Them comfortlesse, through tyranny or might;
So is his soueraine honour raisde to heauens
      hight.

15

His feeling words her feeble sence much pleased,
  And softly suncke into her molten hart ;
  Hart that is inly hurt, is greatly eased
  With hope of thing, that may allegge his smart;
  For pleasing words are like to Magick art,
  That doth the charmed Snake in slomber lay :
  Such secret ease felt gentle *Britomart*,
  Yet list the same efforce with faind gainesay ;
So dischord oft in Musick makes the sweeter lay.

16

And said, Sir knight, these idle termes forbeare,
  And sith it is vneath to find his haunt,
  Tell me some markes, by which he may appeare,
  If chaunce I him encounter parauaunt ;
  For perdie one shall other slay, or daunt :
  What shape, what shield, what armes, what
      steed, what sted,
  And what so else his person most may vaunt ?
  All which the *Redcrosse* knight to point ared,
And him in euery part before her fashioned.

17

Yet him in euery part before she knew,
  How euer list her now her knowledge faine,
  Sith him whilome in *Britaine* she did vew,
  To her reuealed in a mirrhour plaine,
  Whereof did grow her first engraffed paine ;
  Whose root and stalke so bitter yet did tast,
  That but the fruit more sweetnesse did containe,
  Her wretched dayes in dolour she mote wast,
And yield the pray of loue to lothsome death at
      last.

18

By strange occasion she did him behold,
  And much more strangely gan to loue his sight,
  As it in bookes hath written bene of old.
  In *Deheubarth* that now South-wales is hight,
  What time king *Ryence* raign'd, and dealed right,
  The great Magitian *Merlin* had deuiz'd,
  By his deepe science, and hell-dreaded might,
  A looking glasse, right wondrously aguiz'd,
Whose vertues through the wyde world soone
      were solemniz'd.

19

It vertue had, to shew in perfect sight,
  What euer thing was in the world contaynd,
  Betwixt the lowest earth and heauens hight,
  So that it to the looker appertaynd,
  What euer foe had wrought, or frend had faynd,
  Therein discouered was, ne ought mote pas,
  Ne ought in secret from the same remaynd ;
  For thy it round and hollow shaped was,
Like to the world it selfe, and seem'd a world of
      glas.

20

Who wonders not, that reades so wonderous
    worke ?
But who does wonder, that has red the Towre,
Wherein th'Ægyptian *Phao* long did lurke
From all mens vew, that none might her
    discoure,
Yet she might all men vew out of her bowre ?
Great *Ptolomæe* it for his lemans sake
Ybuilded all of glasse, by Magicke powre,
And also it impregnable did make ;
Yet when his loue was false, he with a peaze it
    brake.

21

Such was the glassie globe that *Merlin* made,
And gaue vnto king *Ryence* for his gard,
That neuer foes his kingdome might inuade,
But he it knew at home before he hard
Tydings thereof, and so them still debar'd.
It was a famous Present for a Prince,
And worthy worke of infinite reward,
That treasons could bewray, and foes conuince ;
Happie this Realme, had it remained euer since.

22

One day it fortuned, faire *Britomart*
Into her fathers closet to repayre ;
For nothing he from her reseru'd apart,
Being his onely daughter and his hayre :
Where when she had espyde that mirrhour fayre,
Her selfe a while therein she vewd in vaine ;
Tho her auizing of the vertues rare,
Which thereof spoken were, she gan againe
Her to bethinke of, that mote to her selfe per-
    taine.

23

But as it falleth, in the gentlest harts
Imperious Loue hath highest set his throne,
And tyrannizeth in the bitter smarts
Of them, that to him buxome are and prone :
So thought this Mayd (as maydens vse to done)
Whom fortune for her husband would allot,
Not that she lusted after any one ;
For she was pure from blame of sinfull blot,
Yet wist her life at last must lincke in that
    same knot.

24

Eftsoones there was presented to her eye
A comely knight, all arm'd in complete wize,
Through whose bright ventayle lifted vp on hye
His manly face, that did his foes agrize,
And friends to termes of gentle truce entize,
Lookt foorth, as *Phœbus* face out of the east,
Betwixt two shadie mountaines doth arize ;
Portly his person was, and much increast
Through his Heroicke grace, and honorable gest.

25

His crest was couered with a couchant Hound,
And all his armour seem'd of antique mould,
But wondrous massie and assured sound,
And round about yfretted all with gold,
In which there written was with cyphers old,
Achilles armes, which Arthegall did win.
And on his shield enueloped seuenfold
He bore a crowned litle Ermilin,
That deckt the azure field with her faire poul-
    dred skin.

26

The Damzell well did vew his personage,
And liked well, ne further fastned not,
But went her way ; ne her vnguilty age
Did weene, vnwares, that her vnlucky lot
Lay hidden in the bottome of the pot ;
Of hurt vnwist most daunger doth redound :
But the false Archer, which that arrow shot
So slyly, that she did not feele the wound,
Did smyle full smoothly at her weetlesse wofull
    stound.

27

Thenceforth the feather in her loftie crest,
Ruffed of loue, gan lowly to auaile,
And her proud portance, and her princely gest,
With which she earst tryumphed, now did quaile :
Sad, solemne, sowre, and full of fancies fraile
She woxe ; yet wist she neither how, nor why,
She wist not, silly Mayd, what she did aile,
Yet wist, she was not well at ease perdy,
Yet thought it was not loue, but some melan-
    choly.

28

So soone as Night had with her pallid hew
Defast the beautie of the shining sky,
And reft from men the worlds desired vew,
She with her Nourse adowne to sleepe did lye ;
But sleepe full farre away from her did fly :
In stead thereof sad sighes, and sorrowes deepe
Kept watch and ward about her warily,
That nought she did but wayle, and often steepe
Her daintie couch with teares, which closely she
    did weepe.

29

And if that any drop of slombring rest
Did chaunce to still into her wearie spright,
When feeble nature felt her selfe opprest,
Streight way with dreames, and with fantas-
    ticke sight
Of dreadfull things the same was put to flight,
That oft out of her bed she did astart,
As one with vew of ghastly feends affright :
Tho gan she to renew her former smart,
And thinke of that faire visage, written in her
    hart.

30

One night, when she was tost with such vnrest,
  Her aged Nurse, whose name was *Glauce* hight,
  Feeling her leape out of her loathed nest,
  Betwixt her feeble armes her quickly keight,
  And downe againe in her warme bed her dight;
  Ah my deare daughter, ah my dearest dread,
  What vncouth fit (said she) what euill plight
  Hath thee opprest, and with sad drearyhead
Chaunged thy liuely cheare, and liuing made thee dead?

31

For not of nought these suddeine ghastly feares
  All night afflict thy naturall repose,
  And all the day, when as thine equall peares
  Their fit disports with faire delight doe chose,
  Thou in dull corners doest thy selfe inclose,
  Ne tastest Princes pleasures, ne doest spred
  Abroad thy fresh youthes fairest flowre, but lose
  Both leafe and fruit, both too vntimely shed,
As one in wilfull bale for euer buried.

32

The time, that mortall men their weary cares
  Do lay away, and all wilde beastes do rest,
  And euery riuer eke his course forbeares,
  Then doth this wicked euill thee infest,
  And riue with thousand throbs thy thrilled brest;
  Like an huge *Aetn'* of deepe engulfed griefe,
  Sorrow is heaped in thy hollow chest,
  Whence forth it breakes in sighes and anguish rife,
As smoke and sulphure mingled with confused strife.

33

Aye me, how much I feare, least loue it bee ;
  But if that loue it be, as sure I read
  By knowen signes and passions, which I see,
  Be it worthy of thy race and royall sead,
  Then I auow by this most sacred head
  Of my deare foster child, to ease thy griefe,
  And win thy will : Therefore away doe dread ;
  For death nor daunger from thy dew reliefe
Shall me debarre, tell me therefore my liefest liefe.

34

So hauing said, her twixt her armes twaine
  She straightly straynd, and colled tenderly,
  And euery trembling ioynt, and euery vaine
  She softly felt, and rubbed busily,
  To doe the frosen cold away to fly ;
  And her faire deawy eies with kisses deare
  She oft did bath, and oft againe did dry ;
  And euer her importund, not to feare
To let the secret of her hart to her appeare.

35

The Damzell pauzd, and then thus fearefully;
  Ah Nurse, what needeth thee to eke my paine?
  Is not enough, that I alone doe dye,
  But it must doubled be with death of twaine ?
  For nought for me but death there doth remaine.
  O daughter deare (said she) despaire no whit ;
  For neuer sore, but might a salue obtaine :
  That blinded God, which hath ye blindly smit,
Another arrow hath your louers hart to hit.

36

But mine is not (quoth she) like others wound ;
  For which no reason can find remedy.
  Was neuer such, but mote the like be found,
  (Said she) and though no reason may apply
  Salue to your sore, yet loue can higher stye,
  Then reasons reach, and oft hath wonders donne.
  But neither God of loue, nor God of sky
  Can doe (said she) that, which cannot be donne.
Things oft impossible (quoth she) seeme, ere begonne.

37

These idle words (said she) doe nought asswage
  My stubborne smart, but more annoyance breed,
  For no no vsuall fire, no vsuall rage
  It is, O Nurse, which on my life doth feed,
  And suckes the bloud, which from my hart doth bleed.
  But since thy faithfull zeale lets me not hyde
  My crime, (if crime it be) I will it reed.
  Nor Prince, nor pere it is, whose loue hath gryde
My feeble brest of late, and launched this wound wyde.

38

Nor man it is, nor other liuing wight ;
  For then some hope I might vnto me draw,
  But th'only shade and semblant of a knight,
  Whose shape or person yet I neuer saw,
  Hath me subiected to loues cruell law :
  The same one day, as me misfortune led,
  I in my fathers wondrous mirrhour saw,
  And pleased with that seeming goodly-hed,
Vnwares the hidden hooke with baite I swallowed.

39

Sithens it hath infixed faster hold
  Within my bleeding bowels, and so sore
  Now ranckleth in this same fraile fleshly mould,
  That all mine entrailes flow with poysnous gore,
  And th'vlcer groweth daily more and more ;
  Ne can my running sore find remedie,
  Other then my hard fortune to deplore,
  And languish as the leafe falne from the tree,
Till death make one end of my dayes and miserie.

40

Daughter (said she) what need ye be dismayd,
Or why make ye such Monster of your mind ?
Of much more vncouth thing I was affrayd ;
Of filthy lust, contrarie vnto kind :
But this affection nothing straunge I find ;
For who with reason can you aye reproue,
To loue the semblant pleasing most your mind,
And yield your heart, whence ye cannot re-
moue ?
No guilt in you, but in the tyranny of loue.

41

Not so th'*Arabian Myrrhe* did set her mind ;
Nor so did *Biblis* spend her pining hart,
But lou d their natiue flesh against all kind,
And to their purpose vsed wicked art :
Yet playd *Pasiphaë* a more monstrous part,
That lou'd a Bull, and learnd a beast to bee ;
Such shamefull lusts who loaths not, which
depart
From course of nature and of modestie?
Sweet loue such lewdnes bands from his faire
companie.

42

But thine my Deare (welfare thy heart my deare)
Though strange beginning had, yet fixed is
On one, that worthy may perhaps appeare ;
And certes seemes bestowed not amis :
Ioy thereof haue thou and eternall blis.
With that vpleaning on her elbow weake,
Her alablaster brest she soft did kis,
Which all that while she felt to pant and quake,
As it an Earth-quake were ; at last she thus
bespake.

43

Beldame, your words doe worke me litle ease;
For though my loue be not so lewdly bent,
As those ye blame, yet may it nought appease
My raging smart, ne ought my flame relent,
But rather doth my helpelesse griefe augment
For they, how euer shamefull and vnkind,
Yet did possesse their horrible intent :
Short end of sorrowes they thereby did find ;
So was their fortune good, though wicked were
their mind.

44

But wicked fortune mine, though mind be good,
Can haue no end, nor hope of my desire,
But feed on shadowes, whiles I die for food,
And like a shadow wexe, whiles with entire
Affection, I doe langui h and expire.
I fonder, then *Cephisus* foolish child,
Who hauing vewed in a fountaine shere
His face, was with the loue thereof beguild ;
I fonder loue a shade, the bodie farre exild.

45

Nought like (quoth she) for that same wretched
boy
Was of himselfe the idle Paramoure :
Both loue and louer, without hope of ioy,
For which he faded to a watry flowre.
But better fortune thine, and better howre,
Which lou'st the shadow of a warlike knight ;
No shadow, but a bodie hath in powre :
That bodie, wheresoeuer that it light,
May learned be by cyphers, or by Magicke
might.

46

But if thou may with reason yet represse
The growing euill, ere it strength haue got,
And thee abandon wholly doe possesse,
Against it strongly striue, and yield thee not,
Till thou in open field adowne be smot.
But if the passion mayster thy fraile might,
So that needs loue or death must be thy lot,
Then I auow to thee, by wrong or right
To compasse thy desire, and find that loued
knight.

47

Her chearefull words much cheard the feeble
spright
Of the sicke virgin, that her downe she layd
In her warme bed to sleepe, if that she might;
And the old-woman carefully displayd
The clothes about her round with busie ayd;
So that at last a little creeping sleepe
Surprisd her sense : She therewith well apayd,
The drunken lampe downe in the oyle did steepe,
And set her by to watch, and set her by to
weepe.

48

Earely the morrow next, before that day
His ioyous face did to the world reueale,
They both vprose and tooke their readie way
Vnto the Church, their prayers to appeale,
With great deuotion, and with litle zeale :
For the faire Damzell from the holy herse
Her loue-sicke hart to other thoughts did steale;
And that old Dame said many an idle verse,
Out of her daughters hart fond fancies to
reuerse.

49

Returned home, the royall Infant fell
Into her former fit ; for why, no powre
Nor guidance of her selfe in her did dwell.
Put th'aged Nurse her calling to her bowre,
Had gathered Rew, and Sauine, and the flowre
Of *Camphora*, and Calamint, and Dill,
All which she in a earthen Pot did poure,
And to the brim with Colt wood did it fill,
And many drops of milke and bloud through it
did spill.

50

Then taking thrise three haires from off her head,
Them trebly breaded in a threefold lace,
And round about the pots mouth, bound the
   thread,
And after hauing whispered a space
Certaine sad words, with hollow voice and bace,
She to the virgin said, thrise said she it ;
Come daughter come, come ; spit vpon my face,
Spit thrise vpon me, thrise vpon me spit ;
Th'vneuen number for this businesse is most fit.

51

That sayd, her round about she from her turnd,
She turned her contrarie to the Sunne,
Thrise she her turnd contrary, and returnd,
All contrary, for she the right did shunne,
And euer what she did, was streight vndonne.
So thought she to vndoe her daughters loue :
But loue, that is in gentle brest begonne,
No idle charmes so lightly may remoue,
That well can witnesse, who by triall it does
   proue.

52

Ne ought it mote the noble Mayd auayle,
Ne slake the furie of her cruell flame,
But that she still did waste, and still did wayle,
That through long languour, and hart-burning
   brame
She shortly like a pyned ghost became,
Which long hath waited by the Stygian strond.
That when old *Glauce* saw, for feare least blame
Of her miscarriage should in her be fond,
She wist not how t'amend, nor how it to with-
stond.

Cant. III.

Merlin bewrayes to Britomart,
the state of Artegall.
And shewes the famous Progeny
which from them springen shall.

1

Most sacred fire, that burnest mightily
In liuing brests, ykindled first aboue,
Emongst th'eternall spheres and lamping sky,
And thence pourd into men, which men call Loue;
Not that same, which doth base affections moue
In brutish minds, and filthy lust inflame,
But that sweet fit, that doth true beautie loue,
And choseth vertue for his dearest Dame,
Whence spring all noble deeds and neuer dying
fame :

2

Well did Antiquitie a God thee deeme,
That ouer mortall minds hast so gre..t might,
To order them, as best to thee doth seeme,
And all their actions to direct aright ;
The fatall purpose of diuine foresight,
Thou doest effect in destined descents,
Through deepe impression of thy secret might,
And stirredst vp th'Heroes high intents,
Which the late world admyres for wondrous
   moniments.

3

But thy dread darts in none doe triumph more,
Ne brauer proofe in any, of thy powre
Shew'dst thou, then in this royall Maid of yore,
Making her seeke an vnknowne Paramoure,
From the worlds end, through many a bitter
   stowre :   [rayse
From whose two loynes thou afterwards did
Most famous fruits of matrimoniall bowre,
Which through the earth haue spred their
   liuing prayse,
That fame in trompe of gold eternally displayes.

4

Begin then, O my dearest sacred Dame,
Daughter of *Phœbus* and of *Memorie*,
That doest ennoble with immortall name
The warlike Worthies, from antiquitie,
In thy great volume of Eternitie :
Begin, O *Clio*, and recount from hence
My glorious Soueraines goodly auncestrie,
Till that by dew degrees and long protense,
Thou haue it lastly brought vnto her Excellence.

5

Full many wayes within her troubled mind,
Old *Glauce* cast, to cure this Ladies griefe :
Full many waies she sought, but none could find,
Nor herbes, nor charmes, nor counsell, that is
   chiefe
And choisest med'cine for sicke harts reliefe :
For thy great care she tooke, and greater feare,
Least that it should her turne to foule repriefe,
And sore reproch, when so her father deare
Should of his dearest daughters hard misfortune
   heare.

6

At last she her auisd, that he, which made
That mirrhour, wherein the sicke Damosell
So straungely vewed her straunge louers shade,
To weet, the learned *Merlin*, well could tell,
Vnder what coast of heauen the man did dwell,
And by what meanes his loue might best be
   wrought :
For though beyond the *Africk Ismaell*
Or th'Indian *Peru* he were, she thought
Him forth through infinite endeuour to haue
   sought.

7

Forthwith themselues disguising both in straunge
And base attyre, that none might them bewray,
To *Maridunum*, that is now by chaunge
Of name *Cayr-Merdin* cald, they tooke their
way:
There the wise *Merlin* whylome wont (they say)
To make his wonne, low vnderneath the ground,
In a deepe delue, farre from the vew of day,
That of no liuing wight he mote be found,
When so he counseld with his sprights encom-
past round.

8

And if thou euer happen that same way
To trauell, goe to see that dreadfull place:
It is an hideous hollow caue (they say)
Vnder a rocke that lyes a little space
From the swift *Barry*, tombling downe apace,
Emongst the woodie hilles of *Dyneuowre*:
But dare thou not, I charge, in any cace,
To enter into that same balefull Bowre,
For fear the cruell Feends should thee vnwares
deuowre.

9

But standing high aloft, low lay thine eare,
And there such ghastly noise of yron chaines,
And brasen Caudrons thou shalt rombling heare,
Which thousand sprights with long enduring
paines
Doe tosse, that it will stonne thy feeble braines,
And oftentimes great grones, and grieuous
stounds,
When too huge toile and labour them constraines:
And oftentimes loud strokes, and ringing sounds
From vnder that deepe Rocke most horribly
rebounds.

10

The cause some say is this: A litle while
Before that *Merlin* dyde, he did intend,
A brasen wall in compas to compile
About *Cairmardin*, and did it commend
Vnto these Sprights, to bring to perfect end.
During which worke the Ladie of the Lake,
Whom long he lou'd, for him in hast did send,
Who thereby forst his workemen to forsake,
Them bound till his returne, their labour not to
slake.

11

In the meane time through that false Ladies traine,
He was surprisd, and buried vnder beare,
Ne euer to his worke returnd againe:
Nath'lesse those feends may not their worke
forbeare,
So greatly his commaundement they feare,
But there doe toyle and trauell day and night,
Vntill that brasen wall they vp doe reare:
For *Merlin* had in Magicke more insight,
Then euer him before or after liuing wight.

12

For he by words could call out of the sky
Both Sunne and Moone, and make them him
obay:
The land to sea, and sea to maineland dry,
And darkesome night he eke could turne to day:
Huge hostes of men he could alone dismay,
And hostes of men of meanest things could
frame,
When so him list his enimies to fray:
That to this day for terror of his fame,
The feends do quake, when any him to them
does name.

13

And sooth, men say that he was not the sonne
Of mortall Syre, or other liuing wight,
But wondrously begotten, and begonne
By false illusion of a guilefull Spright,
On a faire Ladie Nonne, that whilome hight
Matilda, daughter to *Pubidius*,
Who was the Lord of *Mathrauall* by right,
And coosen vnto king *Ambrosius*:
Whence he indued was with skill so maruellous.

14

They here ariuing, staid a while without,
Ne durst aduenture rashly in to wend,
But of their first intent gan make new dout
For dread of daunger, which it might portend:
Vntill the hardie Mayd (with loue to frend)
First entering, the dreadfull Mage there found
Deepe busied bout worke of wondrous end,
And writing strange characters in the ground,
With which the stubborn feends he to his seruice
bound.

15

He nought was moued at their entrance bold:
For of their comming well he wist afore,
Yet list them bid their businesse to vnfold,
As if ought in this world in secret store
Were from him hidden, or vnknowne of yore.
Then *Glauce* thus, Let not it thee offend,
That we thus rashly through thy darkesome
dore,
Vnwares haue prest: for either fatall end,
Or other mightie cause vs two did hither send.

16

He bad tell on; And then she thus began.
Now haue three Moones with borrow'd
brothers light,   [wan,
Thrice shined faire, and thrice seem'd dim and
Sith a sore euill, which this virgin bright
Tormenteth, and doth plonge in dolefull plight,
First rooting tooke; but what thing it mote bee,
Or whence it sprong, I cannot read aright:
But this I read, that but if remedee
Thou her afford, full shortly I her dead shall see.

17

Therewith th'Enchaunter softly gan to smyle
At her smooth speeches, weeting inly well,
That she to him dissembled womanish guyle,
And to her said, Beldame, by that ye tell,
More need of leach-craft hath your Damozell,
Then of my skill: who helpe may haue else-
    where,
In vaine seekes wonders out of Magicke spell.
Th'old woman wox half blanck, those words to
    heare;
And yet was loth to let her purpose plaine
    appeare.

18

And to him said, If any leaches skill,
Or other learned meanes could haue redrest
This my deare daughters deepe engraffed ill,
Certes I should be loth thee to molest:
But this sad euill, which doth her infest,
Doth course of naturall cause farre exceed,
And housed is within her hollow brest,
That either scemes some cursed witches deed,
Or euill spright, that in her doth such torment
    breed.

19

The wisard could no lenger beare her bord,
But brusting forth in laughter, to her sayd;
Glauce, what needs this colourable word,
To cloke the cause, that hath it selfe bewrayd?
Ne ye faire *Britomartis,* thus arayd,
More hidden are, then Sunne in cloudy vele;
Whom thy good fortune, hauing fate obayd,
Hath hither brought, for succour to appele:
The which the powres to thee are pleased to
    reuele.

20

The doubtfull Mayd, seeing her selfe descryde,
Was all abasht, and her pure yuory
Into a cleare Carnation suddeine dyde;
As faire *Aurora* rising hastily,
Doth by her blushing tell, that she did lye
All night in old *Tithonus* frosen bed,
Whereof she seemes ashamed inwardly.
But her old Nourse was nought dishartened,
But vauntage made of that, which *Merlin* had
    ared.

21

And sayd, Sith then thou knowest all our griefe,
(For what doest not thou know?) of grace I
    pray,
Pitty our plaint, and yield vs meet reliefe.
With that the Prophet still awhile did stay,
And then his spirite thus gan forth display;
Most noble Virgin, that by fatall lore
Hast learn'd to loue, let no whit thee dismay
The hard begin, that meets thee in the dore,
And with sharpe fits thy tender hart oppresseth
    sore.

22

For so must all things excellent begin,
And eke enrooted deepe must be that Tree,
Whose big embodied braunches shall not lin,
Till they to heauens hight forth stretched bee.
For from thy wombe a famous Progenie
Shall spring, out of the auncient *Troian* blood,
Which shall reuiue the sleeping memorie
Of those same antique Peres the heauens brood,
Which *Greeke* and *Asian* riuers stained with
    their blood.

23

Renowmed kings, and sacred Emperours,
Thy fruitfull Ofspring, shall from thee descend;
Braue Captaines, and most mighty warriours,
That shall their conquests through all lands
    extend,
And their decayed kingdomes shall amend:
The feeble Britons, broken with long warre,
They shall vpreare, and mightily defend
Against their forrein foe, that comes from farre,
Till vniuersall peace compound all ciuill iarre.

24

It was not, *Britomart,* thy wandring eye,
Glauncing vnwares in charmed looking glas,
But the streight course of heauenly destiny,
Led with eternall prouidence, that has
Guided thy glaunce, to bring his will to pas:
Ne is thy fate, ne is thy fortune ill,
To loue the prowest knight, that euer was.
Therefore submit thy wayes vnto his will,
And do by all dew meanes thy destiny fulfill.

25

But read (said *Glauce*) thou Magitian
What meanes shall she out seeke, or what
    wayes take?
How shall she know, how shall she find the
    man?
Or what needs her to toyle, sith fates can make
Way for themselues, their purpose to partake?
Then *Merlin* thus; Indeed the fates are firme,
And may not shrinck, though all the world do
    shake:
Yet ought mens good endeuours them confirme,
And guide the heauenly causes to their con-
    stant terme.

26

The man whom heauens haue ordaynd to bee
The spouse of *Britomart,* is *Arthegall:*
He wonneth in the land of *Fayeree,*
Yet is no *Fary* borne, ne sib at all
To Elfes, but sprong of seed terrestriall,
And whilome by false *Faries* stolne away,
Whiles yet in infant cradle he did crall;
Ne other to himselfe is knowne this day,
But that he by an Elfe was gotten of a *Fay.*

27

But sooth he is the sonne of *Gorlois*,
And brother vnto *Cador* Cornish king,
And for his warlike feates renowmed is,
From where the day out of the sea doth spring,
Vntill the closure of the Euening.
From thence, him firmely bound with faithfull
  band,
To this his natiue soyle thou backe shalt bring,
Strongly to aide his countrey, to withstand
The powre of forrein Paynims, which inuade
  thy land.

28

Great aid thereto his mighty puissaunce,
And dreaded name shall giue in that sad day :
Where also proofe of thy prow valiaunce
Thou then shalt make, t' increase thy louers pray.
Long time ye both in armes shall beare great sway,
Till thy wombes burden thee from them do call,
And his last fate him from thee take away,
Too rathe cut off by practise criminall
Of secret foes, that him shall make in mischiefe
  fall.

29

With thee yet shall he leaue for memory
Of his late puissaunce, his Image dead,
That liuing him in all actiuity
To thee shall represent. He from the head
Of his coosin *Constantius* without dread
Shall take the crowne, that was his fathers right,
And therewith crowne himselfe in th' others stead:
Then shall he issew forth with dreadfull might,
Against his Saxon foes in bloudy field to fight.

30

Like as a Lyon, that in drowsie caue
Hath long time slept, himselfe so shall he shake,
And comming forth, shall spred his banner braue
Ouer the troubled South, that it shall make
The warlike *Mertians* for feare to quake :
Thrise shall he fight with them, and twise shall
  win,
But the third time shall faire accordaunce make:
And if he then with victorie can lin,
He shall his dayes with peace bring to his earthly
  In.

31

His sonne, hight *Vortipore*, shall him succeede
In kingdome, but not in felicity ;
Yet shall he long time warre with happy speed,
And with great honour many battels try :
But at the last to th' importunity
Of froward fortune shall be forst to yield.
But his sonne *Malgo* shall full mightily
Auenge his fathers losse, with speare and shield,
And his proud foes discomfit in victorious field.

32

Behold the man, and tell me *Britomart*,
If ay more goodly creature thou didst see ;
How like a Gyaunt in each manly part
Beares he himselfe with portly maiestee,
That one of th' old *Heroes* seemes to bee :
He the six Islands, comprouinciall
In auncient times vnto great Britainee,
Shall to the same reduce, and to him call
Their sundry kings to do their homage seuerall.

33

All which his sonne *Careticus* awhile
Shall well defend, and *Saxons* powre suppresse
Vntill a straunger king from vnknowne soyl
Arriuing, him with multitude oppresse ;
Great *Gormond*, hauing with huge mightinesse
Ireland subdewd, and therein fixt his throne,
Like a swift Otter, fell through emptinesse,
Shall ouerswim the sea with many one
Of his Norueyses, to assist the Britons fone.

34

He in his furie all shall ouerrunne,
And holy Church with faithlesse hands deface,
That thy sad people vtterly fordonne,
Shall to the vtmost mountaines fly apace :
Was neuer so great wast in any place,
Nor so fowle outrage doen by liuing men :
For all thy Cities they shall sacke and race,
And the greene grasse, that groweth, they
  shall bren,
That euen the wild beast shall dy in starued den.

35

Whiles thus thy Britons do in languour pine,
Proud *Etheldred* shall from the North arise,
Seruing th' ambitious will of *Augustine*,
And passing *Dee* with hardy enterprise,
Shall backe repulse the valiaunt *Brockwell* twise.
And *Bangor* with massacred Martyrs fill ;
But the third time shall rew his foolhardise :
For *Cadwan* pittying his peoples ill,
Shall stoutly him defeat, and thousand *Saxons*
  kill.

36

But after him, *Cadwallin* mightily
On his sonne *Edwin* all those wrongs shall wreake;
Ne shall auaile the wicked sorcery
Of false *Pellite*, his purposes to breake,
But him shall slay, and on a gallowes bleake
Shall giue th' enchaunter his vnhappy hire ;
Then shall the Britons, late dismayd and weake,
From their long vassalage gin to respire,
And on their Paynim foes auenge theirranckled
  ire.

37

Ne shall he yet his wrath so mitigate,
  Till both the sonnes of *Edwin* he haue slaine,
  Offricke and *Osricke*, twinnes vnfortunate,
  Both slaine in battell vpon Layburne plaine,
  Together with the king of *Louthiane*,
  Hight *Adin*, and the king of *Orkeny*,
  Both ioynt partakers of their fatall paine :
  But *Penda*, fearefull of like desteny,
Shall yield him selfe his liegeman, and sweare
    fealty.

38

Him shall he make his fatall Instrument,
  T'afflict the other *Saxons* vnsubdewd ;
  He marching forth with fury insolent
  Against the good king *Oswald*, who indewd
  With heauenly powre, and by Angels rcskewd,
  All holding crosses in their hands on hye,
  Shall him defeate withouten bloud imbrewd :
  Of which, that field for endlesse memory,
Shall *Heuenfield* be cald to all posterity.

39

Where at *Cadwallin* wroth, shall forth issew,
  And an huge hoste into Northumber lead,
  With which he godly *Oswald* shall subdew,
  And crowne with martyrdome his sacred
    head.
  Whose brother *Oswin*, daunted with like dread,
  With price of siluer shall his kingdome buy,
  And *Penda*, seeking him adowne to tread,
  Shall tread adowne, and do him fowly dye,
But shall with gifts his Lord *Cadwallin* pacify.

40

Then shall *Cadwallin* dye, and then the raine
  Of *Britons* eke with him attonce shall dye ;
  Ne shall the good *Cadwallader* with paine,
  Or powre, be hable it to remedy,
  When the full time prefixt by destiny,
  Shalbe expird of *Britons* regiment.
  For heauen it selfe shall their successe enuy,
  And them with plagues and murrins pestilent
Consume, till all their warlike puissaunce be
    spent.

41

Yet after all these sorrowes, and huge hills
  Of dying people, during eight yeares space,
  Cadwallader not yielding to his ills,
  From *Armoricke*, where long in wretched
    cace
  He liu'd, returning to his natiue place,
  Shalbe by vision staid from his intent :
  For th'heauens haue decreed, to displace
  The *Britons*, for their sinnes dew punishment,
And to the *Saxons* ouer-giue their gouernment.

42

Then woe, and woe, and euerlasting woe,
  Be to the Briton babe, that shalbe borne,
  To liue in thraldome of his fathers foe ;
  Late King, now captiue, late Lord, now forlorne,
  The worlds reproch, the cruell victors scorne,
  Banisht from Princely bowre to wastfull wood :
  O who shall helpe me to lament, and mourne
  The royall seed, the antique *Troian* blood,
Whose Empire lenger here, then euer any stood.

43

The Damzell was full deepe empassioned,
  Both for his griefe, and for her peoples sake,
  Whose future woes so plaine he fashioned,
  And sighing sore, at length him thus bespake ,
  Ah but will heauens fury neuer slake,
  Nor vengeaunce huge relent it selfe at last ?
  Will not long misery late mercy make,
  But shall their name for euer be defast,
And quite from of the earth their memory be
    rast ?

44

Nay but the terme (said he) is limited,
  That in this thraldome *Britons* shall abide,
  And the iust reuolution measured,
  That they as Straungers shalbe notifide.
  For twise foure hundreth yeares shalbe supplide.
  Ere they to former rule restor'd shalbee,
  And their importune fates all satisfide :
  Yet during this their most obscuritee,
Their beames shall oft breake forth, that men
    them faire may see.

45

For *Rhodoricke*, whose surname shalbe Great,
  Shall of him selfe a braue ensample shew,
  That Saxon kings his friendship shall intreat ;
  And *Howell Dha* shall goodly well indew
  The saluage minds with skill of iust and trew ;
  Then *Griffyth Conan* also shall vp reare
  His dreaded head, and the old sparkes renew
  Of natiue courage, that his foes shall feare,
Least backe againe the kingdome he from them
    should beare.

46

Ne shall the Saxons selues all peaceably
  Enioy the crowne, which they from Britons
    wonne
  First ill, and after ruled wickedly :
  For ere two hundred yeares be full outronne,
  There shall a Rauen far from rising Sunne,
  With his wide wings vpon them fiercely fly,
  And bid his faithlesse chickens ouerronne
  The fruitfull plaines, and with fell cruelty,
In their auenge, tread downe the victours sur-
    quedry.

47

Yet shall a third both these, and thine subdew ;
There shall a Lyon from the sea-bord wood
Of *Neustria* come roring, with a crew
Of hungry whelpes, his battailous bold brood,
Whose clawes were newly dipt in cruddy blood,
That from the Daniske Tyrants head shall rend
Th'vsurped crowne, as if that he were wood,
And the spoile of the countrey conquered
Emongst his young ones shall diuide with
    bountyhed.

48

Tho when the terme is full accomplishid,
There shall a sparke of fire, which hath long-
    while
Bene in his ashes raked vp, and hid,
Be freshly kindled in the fruitfull Ile
Of *Mona*, where it lurked in exile ;   [flame,
Which shall breake forth into bright burning
And reach into the house, that beares the stile
Of royall maiesty and soueraigne name ;
So shall the Briton bloud their crowne againe
    reclame.

49

Thenceforth eternall vnion shall be made
Betweene the nations different afore,
And sacred Peace shall louingly perswade
The warlike minds, to learne her goodly lore,
And ciuile armes to exercise no more :
Then shall a royall virgin raine, which shall
Stretch her white rod ouer the *Belgicke* shore,
And the great Castle smite so sore with all,
That it shall make him shake, and shortly
    learne to fall.

50

But yet the end is not. There *Merlin* stayd,
As ouercomen of the spirites powre,
Or other ghastly spectacle dismayd,
That secretly he saw, yet note discoure :
Which suddein fit, and halfe extatick stoure
When the two fearefull women saw, they grew
Greatly confused in behauioure ;
At last the fury past, to former hew
Hee turnd againe, and chearefull looks (as earst)
    did shew.

51

Then, when them selues they well instructed had
Of all, that needed them to be inquird,
They both conceiuing hope of comfort glad,
With lighter hearts vnto their home retird ;
Where they in secret counsell close conspird,
How to effect so hard an enterprize,
And to possesse the purpose they desird :
Now this, now that twixt them they did deuise,
And diuerse plots did frame, to maske in strange
    disguise.

52

At last the Nourse in her foolhardy wit
Conceiu'd a bold deuise, and thus bespake ;
Daughter, I deeme that counsell aye most fit,
That of the time doth dew aduauntage take ;
Ye see that good king *Vther* now doth make
Strong warre vpon the Paynim brethren, hight
Octa and *Oza*, whom he lately brake
Beside *Cayr Verolame*, in victorious fight,
That now all *Britanie* doth burne in armes
    bright.

53

That therefore nought our passage may empeach,
Let vs in feigned armes our selues disguize,
And our weake hands (whom need new
    strength shall teach)
The dreadfull speare and shield to exercize :
Ne certes daughter that same warlike wize
I weene, would you misseeme ; for ye bene tall,
And large of limbe, t'atchieue an hard emprize,
Ne ought ye want, but skill, which practize
    small
Will bring, and shortly make you a mayd
    Martiall.

54

And sooth, it ought your courage much inflame,
To heare so often, in that royall hous,
From whence to none inferiour ye came,
Bards tell of many women valorous
Which haue full many feats aduenturous
Performd, in paragone of proudest men :
The bold *Bunduca*, whose victorious
Exploits made *Rome* to quake, stout *Guendolen*,
Renowmed *Martia*, and redoubted *Emmilen*.

55

And that, which more then all the rest may sway,
Late dayes ensample, which these eyes beheld,
In the last field before *Meneuia*
Which *Vther* with those forrein Pagans held,
I saw a *Saxon* Virgin, the which feld
Great *Vlfin* thrise vpon the bloudy plaine,
And had not *Carados* her hand withheld
From rash reuenge, she had him surely slaine,
Yet *Carados* himselfe from her escapt with paine.

56

Ah read, (quoth *Britomart*) how is she hight ?
Faire *Angela* (quoth she) men do her call,
No whit lesse faire, then terrible in fight :
She hath the leading of a Martiall
And mighty people, dreaded more then all
The other *Saxons*, which do for her sake
And loue, themselues of her name *Angles* call.
Therefore faire Infant her ensample make
Vnto thy selfe, and equall courage to thee take.

57

Her harty words so deepe into the mynd
Of the young Damzell sunke, that great desire
Of warlike armes in her forthwith they tynd,
And generous stout courage did inspire,
That she resolu'd, vnweeting to her Sire,
Aduent'rous knighthood on her selfe to don,
And counseld with her Nourse, her Maides attire
To turne into a massy habergeon,
And bad her all things put in readinesse anon.

58

Th'old woman nought, that needed, did omit ;
But all things did conueniently puruay :
It fortuned (so time their turne did fit)
A band of Britons ryding on forray
Few dayes before, had gotten a great pray
Of Saxon goods, emongst the which was seene
A goodly Armour, and full rich aray,
Which long'd to *Angela*, the Saxon Queene,
All fretted round with gold, and goodly well
　beseene.

59

The same, with all the other ornaments,
King *Ryence* caused to be hanged hy
In his chiefe Church, for endlesse moniments
Of his successe and gladfull victory :
Of which her selfe auising readily,
In th'euening late old *Glauce* thither led
Faire *Britomart*, and that same Armory
Downe taking, her therein appareled,
Well as she might, and with braue bauldrick
　garnished.

60

Beside those armes there stood a mighty speare,
Which *Bladud* made by Magick art of yore,
And vsd the same in battell aye to beare ;
Sith which it had bin here preseru'd in store,
For his great vertues proued long afore :
For neuer wight so fast in sell could sit,
But him perforce vnto the ground it bore :
Both speare she tooke, and shield, which hong
　by it :
Both speare and shield of great powre, for her
　purpose fit.

61

Thus when she had the virgin all arayd,
Another harnesse, which did hang thereby,
About her selfe she dight, that the young Mayd
She might in equall armes accompany,
And as her Squire attend her carefully :
Tho to their ready Steeds they clombe full
　light,
And through back wayes, that none might
　them espy,
Couered with secret cloud of silent night,
Themselues they forth conuayd, and passed
　forward right.

62

Ne rested they, till that to Faery lond
They came, as *Merlin* them directed late :
Where meeting with this *Redcrosse* knight, she
Of diuerse things discourses to dilate,　[fond
But most of *Arthegall*, and his estate.
At last their wayes so fell, that they mote part:
Then each to other well affectionate,
Friendship professed with vnfained hart,
The *Redcrosse* knight diuerst, but forth rode
　Britomart.

Cant. IIII.

╰∽╯∽╯∽╯∽╯∽╯∽╯∽╯∽╯∽╯∽╯∽╯∽╯∽

Bold Marinell of Britomart,
Is throwne on the Rich strond :
Faire Florimell of Arthur is
Long followed, but not fond.

╰∽╯∽╯∽╯∽╯∽╯∽╯∽╯∽╯∽╯∽╯∽╯∽╯∽

1

Where is the Antique glory now become,
That whilome wont in women to appeare ?
Where be the braue atchieuements doen by
　some ?
Where be the battels, where the shield and
　speare,
And all the conquests, which them high did reare,
That matter made for famous Poets verse,
And boastfull men so oft abasht to heare ?
Bene they all dead, and laid in dolefull herse ?
Or doen they onely sleepe, and shall againe
　reuerse ?

2

If they be dead, then woe is me therefore :
But if they sleepe, O let them soone awake :
For all too long I burne with enuy sore,
To heare the warlike feates, which *Homere* spake
Of bold *Penthesilee*, which made a lake
Of *Greekish* bloud so oft in *Troian* plaine ;
But when I read, how stout *Debora* strake
Proud *Sisera*, and how *Camill'* hath slaine
The huge *Orsilochus*, I swell with great disdaine.

3

Yet these, and all that else had puissaunce,
Cannot with noble *Britomart* compare,
Aswell for glory of great valiaunce,
As for pure chastitie and vertue rare,
That all her goodly deeds do well declare.
Well worthy stock, from which the branches
　sprong,
That in late yeares so faire a blossome bare,
As thee, O Queene, the matter of my song,
Whose lignage from this Lady I deriue along.

4

Who when through speaches with the *Redcrosse*
        knight,
She learned had th'estate of *Arthegall*,
And in each point her selfe informd aright,
A friendly league of loue perpetuall
She with him bound, and *Congé* tooke withall.
Then he forth on his iourney did proceede,
To seeke aduentures, which mote him befall,
And win him worship through his warlike deed,
Which alwayes of his paines he made the chiefest
        meed.

5

But *Britomart* kept on her former course,
Ne euer dofte her armes, but all the way
Grew pensiue through that amorous discourse,
By which the *Redcrosse* knight did earst display
Her louers shape, and cheualrous aray ;
A thousand thoughts she fashioned in her mind,
And in her feigning fancie did pourtray
Him such, as fittest she for loue could find,
Wise, warlike, personable, curteous, and kind.

6

With such selfe-pleasing thoughts her wound
        she fed,
And thought so to beguile her grieuous smart ;
But so her smart was much more grieuous bred,
And the deepe wound more deepe engord her
        hart,
That nought but death her dolour mote depart.
So forth she rode without repose or rest,
Searching all lands and each remotest part,
Following the guidance of her blinded guest,
Till that to the sea-coast at length she her
        addrest.

7

There she alighted from her light-foot beast,
And sitting downe vpon the rocky shore,
Bad her old Squire vnlace her lofty creast ;
Tho hauing vewd a while the surges hore,
That gainst the craggy clifts did loudly rore,
And in their raging surquedry disdaynd,
That the fast earth affronted them so sore,
And their deuouring couetize restraynd,
Thereat she sighed deepe, and after thus com-
        playnd.

8

Huge sea of sorrow, and tempestuous griefe,
Wherein my feeble barke is tossed long,
Far from the hoped hauen of reliefe,
Why do thy cruell billowes beat so strong,
And thy moyst mountaines each on others throng,
Threatning to swallow vp my fearefull life ?
O do thy cruell wrath and spightfull wrong
At length allay, and stint thy stormy strife,
Which in these troubled bowels raignes, and
        rageth rife.

9

For else my feeble vessell crazd, and crackt
Through thy strong buffets and outrageous
        blowes,
Cannot endure, but needs it must be wrackt
On the rough rocks, or on the sandy shallowes,
The whiles that loue it steres, and fortune rowes ;
Loue my lewd Pilot hath a restlesse mind
And fortune Boteswaine no assuraunce knowes,
But saile withouten starres gainst tide and
        wind :
How can they other do, sith both are bold and
        blind ?

10

Thou God of winds, that raignest in the seas,
That raignest also in the Continent,
At last blow vp some gentle gale of ease,
The which may bring my ship, ere it be rent,
Vnto the gladsome port of her intent :
Then when I shall my selfe in safety see,
A table for eternall moniment
Of thy great grace, and my great ieopardee,
Great *Neptune*, I auow to hallow vnto thee.

11

Then sighing softly sore, and inly deepe,
She shut vp all her plaint in priuy griefe ;
For her great courage would not let her weepe,
Till that old *Glauce* gan with sharpe repriefe,
Her to restraine, and giue her good reliefe,
Through hope of those, which *Merlin* had her
        told
Should of her name and nation be chiefe,
And fetch their being from the sacred mould
Of her immortall wombe, to be in heauen enrold.

12

Thus as she her recomforted, she spyde,
Where farre away one all in armour bright,
With hastie gallop towards her did ryde ;
Her dolour soone she ceast, and on her dight
Her Helmet, to her Courser mounting light :
Her former sorrow into suddein wrath,
Both coosen passions of distroubled spright,
Conuerting, forth she beates the dustie path ;
Loue and despight attonce her courage kindled
        hath.

13

As when a foggy mist hath ouercast
The face of heauen, and the cleare aire engrost,
The world in darkenesse dwels, till that at last
The watry Southwinde from the seabord cost
Vpblowing, doth disperse the vapour lo'st,
And poures it selfe forth in a stormy showre ;
So the faire *Britomart* hauing disclo'st
Her clowdy care into a wrathfull stowre,
The mist of griefe dissolu'd, did into vengeance
        powre.

14

Eftsoones her goodly shield addressing faire,
That mortall speare she in her hand did take,
And vnto battell did her selfe prepaire.
The knight approching, sternely her bespake ;
Sir knight, that doest thy voyage rashly make
By this forbidden way in my despight,
Ne doest by others death ensample take,
I read thee soone retyre, whiles thou hast might,
Least afterwards it be too late to take thy flight.

15

Ythrild with deepe disdaine of his proud threat,
She shortly thus ; Fly they, that need to fly ;
Words fearen babes. I meane not thee entreat
To passe ; but maugre thee will passe or dy.
Ne lenger stayd for th'other to reply,
But with sharpe speare the rest made dearly
    knowne.
Strongly the straunge knight ran, and sturdily
Strooke her full on the brest, that made her
    downe
Decline her head, and touch her crouper with
    her crowne.

16

But she againe him in the shield did smite
With so fierce furie and great puissaunce,
That through his threesquare scuchin percing
    quite,
And through his mayled hauberque, by mis-
    chaunce   [glaunce ;
The wicked steele through his left side did
Him so transfixed she before her bore
Beyond his croupe, the length of all her launce,
Till sadly soucing on the sandie shore,
He tombled on a heape, and wallowd in his
    gore.

17

Like as the sacred Oxe, that carelesse stands,
With gilden hornes, and flowry girlonds crownd,
Proud of his dying honor and deare bands,
Whiles th'altars fume with frankincense arownd,
All suddenly with mortall stroke astownd,
Doth groueling fall, and with his streaming gore
Distaines the pillours, and the holy grownd,
And the faire flowres, that decked him afore ;
So fell proud *Marinell* vpon the pretious shore.

18

The martiall Mayd stayd not him to lament,
But forward rode, and kept her readie way
Along the strond, which as she ouer-went,
She saw bestrowed all with rich aray
Of pearles and pretious stones of great assay,
And all the grauell mixt with golden owre ;
Whereat she wondred much, but would not stay
For gold, or perles, or pretious stones an howre,
But them despised all ; for all was in her powre.

19

Whiles thus he lay in deadly stonishment,
Tydings hereof came to his mothers eare :
His mother was the blacke-browd *Cymoent,*
The daughter of great *Nereus*, which did beare
This warlike sonne vnto an earthly peare,
The famous *Dumarin ;* who on a day
Finding the Nymph a sleepe in secret wheare,
As he by chaunce did wander that same way,
Was taken with her loue, and by her closely lay.

20

There he this knight of her begot, whom borne
She of his father *Marinell* did name,
And in a rocky caue as wight forlorne,
Long time she fostred vp, till he became
A mightie man at armes, and mickle fame
Did get through great aduentures by him donne :
For neuer man he suffred by that same
Rich strond to trauell, whereas he did wonne,
But that he must do battell with the Sea-
    nymphes sonne.

21

An hundred knights of honorable name
He had subdew'd, and them his vassals made,
That through all Farie lond his noble fame
Now blazed was, and feare did all inuade,
That none durst passen through that perilous
    glade.
And to aduance his name and glorie more,
Her Sea-god syre she dearely did perswade,
T'endow her sonne with threasure and richstore,
Boue all the sonnes, that were of earthly
    wombes ybore.

22

The God did graunt his daughters deare demaund,
To doen his Nephew in all riches flow ;
Eftsoones his heaped waues he did commaund,
Out of their hollow bosome forth to throw
All the huge threasure, which the sea below
Had in his greedie gulfe deuoured deepe,
And him enriched through the ouerthrow
And wreckes of many wretches, which did weepe,
And often waile their wealth, which they from
    them did keepe.

23

Shortly vpon that shore there heaped was,
Exceeding riches and all pretious things.
The spoyle of all the world, that it did pas
The wealth of th'East, and pompe of *Persian*
    kings ;
Gold, amber, yuorie, perles, owches, rings,
And all that else was pretious and deare,
The sea vnto him voluntary brings,
That shortly he a great Lord did appeare,
As was in all the lond of Faery, or elsewheare.

SPENSER   G

24

Thereto he was a doughtie dreaded knight,
  Tryde often to the scath of many deare,
  That none in equall armes him matchen
    might,
  The which his mother seeing, gan to feare
  Least his too haughtie hardines might reare
  Some hard mishap, in hazard of his life :
  For thy she oft him counseld to forbeare
  The bloudie battell, and to stirre vp strife,
But after all his warre, to rest his wearie knife.

25

And for his more assurance, she inquir'd
  One day of *Proteus* by his mightie spell,
  (For *Proteus* was with prophecie inspir'd)
  Her deare sonnes destinie to her to tell,
  And the sad end of his sweet *Marinell.*
  Who through foresight of his eternall skill,
  Bad her from womankind to keepe him well :
  For of a woman he should haue much ill,
A virgin strange and stout him should dismay,
    or kill.

26

For thy she gaue him warning euery day,
  The loue of women not to entertaine ;
  A lesson too too hard for liuing clay,
  From loue in course of nature to refraine :
  Yet he his mothers lore did well retaine,
  And euer from faire Ladies loue did fly ;
  Yet many Ladies faire did oft complaine,
  That they for loue of him would algates dy :
Dy, who so list for him, he was loues enimy.

27

But ah, who can deceiue his destiny,
  Or weene by warning to auoyd his fate ?
  That when he sleepes in most security,
  And safest seemes, him soonest doth amate,
  And findeth dew effect or soone or late.
  So feeble is the powre of fleshly arme,
  His mother bad him womens loue to hate,
  For she of womans force did feare no harme ;
So weening to haue arm'd him, she did quite
    disarme.

28

This was that woman, this that deadly wound,
  That *Proteus* prophecide should him dismay,
  The which his mother vainely did expound,
  To be hart-wounding loue, which should assay
  To bring her sonne vnto his last decay.
  So tickle be the termes of mortall state,
  And full of subtile sophismes, which do play
  With double senses, and with false debate,
T'approue the vnknowen purpose of eternall
    fate.

29

Too true the famous *Marinell* it fownd,
  Who through late triall, on that wealthy Strond
  Inglorious now lies in senselesse swownd,
  Through heauy stroke of *Britomartis* hond.
  Which when his mother deare did vnderstond,
  And heauy tydings heard, whereas she playd
  Amongst her watry sisters by a pond,
  Gathering sweet daffadillyes, to haue made
Gay girlonds, from the Sun their forheads faire
    to shade ;

30

Eftsoones both flowres and girlonds farre away
  She flong, and her faire deawy lockes yrent,
  To sorrow huge she turnd her former play,
  And gamesom merth to grieuous dreriment :
  She threw her selfe downe on the Continent,
  Ne word did speake, but lay as in a swowne,
  Whiles all her sisters did for her lament,
  With yelling outcries, and with shrieking sowne ;
And euery one did teare her girlond from her
    crowne.

31

Soone as she vp out of her deadly fit
  Arose, she bad her charet to be brought,
  And all her sisters, that with her did sit,
  Bad eke attonce their charets to be sought ;
  Tho full of bitter griefe and pensiue thought,
  She to her wagon clombe ; clombe all the rest,
  And forth together went, with sorrow fraught.
  The waues obedient to their beheast,
Them yielded readie passage, and their rage
    surceast.

32

Great *Neptune* stood amazed at their sight,
  Whiles on his broad round backe they softly slid
  And eke himselfe mournd at their mournfull
    plight,
  Yet wist not what their wailing ment, yet did
  For great compassion of their sorrow, bid
  His mightie waters to them buxome bee :
  Eftsoones the roaring billowes still abid,
  And all the griesly Monsters of the See
Stood gaping at their gate, and wondred them
    to see.

33

A teme of Dolphins raunged in aray,
  Drew the smooth charet of sad *Cymoent* ;
  They were all taught by *Triton*, to obay
  To the long raynes, at her commaundement :
  As swift as swallowes, on the waues they went,
  That their broad flaggie finnes no fome did reare,
  Ne bubbling roundell they behind them sent ;
  The rest of other fishes drawen weare,
Which with their finny oars the swelling sea did
    sheare.

34

Soone as they bene arriu'd vpon the brim
　Of the *Rich strond*, their charets they forlore,
　And let their temed fishes softly swim
　Along the margent of the fomy shore,　[sore
　Least they their finnes should bruze, and surbate
　Their tender feet vpon the stony ground :
　And comming to the place, where all in gore
　And cruddy bloud enwallowed they found
The lucklesse *Marinell*, lying in deadly swound ;

35

His mother swowned thrise, and the third time
　Could scarce recouered be out of her paine ;
　Had she not bene deuoyd of mortall slime,
　She should not then haue bene reliu'd againe,
　But soone as life recouered had the raine,
　She made so piteous mone and deare wayment,
　That the hard rocks could scarse from teares
　refraine,
　And all her sister Nymphes with one consent
Supplide her sobbing breaches with sad com-
　plement.

36

Deare image of my selfe (she said) that is,
　The wretched sonne of wretched mother borne,
　Is this thine high aduauncement, O is this
　Th'immortall name, with which thee yet vn-
　borne
　Thy Gransire *Nereus* promist to adorne ?
　Now lyest thou of life and honor reft ;
　Now lyest thou a lumpe of earth forlorne,
　Ne of thy late life memory is left,
Ne can thy irreuocable destiny be weft ?

37

Fond *Proteus*, father of false prophecis,
　And they more fond, that credit to thee giue,
　Not this the worke of womans hand ywis,
　That so deepe wound through these deare
　members driue.
　I feared loue : but they that loue do liue,
　But they that die, doe neither loue nor hate.
　Nath'lesse to thee thy folly I forgiue,
　And to my selfe, and to accursed fate
The guilt I doe ascribe : deare wisedome bought
　too late.

38

O what auailes it of immortall seed
　To beene ybred and neuer borne to die ?
　Farre better I it deeme to die with speed,
　Then waste in woe and wailefull miserie.
　Who dyes the vtmost dolour doth abye,
　But who that liues, is left to waile his losse :
　So life is losse, and death felicitie.
　Sad life worse then glad death : and greater
　crosse　　　　　　　　　　　　　　[engrosse.
To see friends graue, then dead the graue selfe to

39

But if the heauens did his dayes enuie,
　And my short blisse maligne, yet mote they well
　Thus much afford me, ere that he did die
　That the dim eyes of my deare *Marinell*
　I mote haue closed, and him bed farewell,
　Sith other offices for mother meet
　They would not graunt.
　Yet maulgre them farewell, my sweetest sweet ;
Farewell my sweetest sonne, sith we no more
　shall meet.

40

Thus when they all had sorrowed their fill,
　They softly gan to search his griesly wound :
　And that they might him handle more at will,
　They him disarm'd, and spredding on the ground
　Their watchet mantles frindgd with siluer round,
　They softly wipt away the gelly blood
　From th'orifice ; which hauing well vpbound,
　They pourd in soueraine balme, and Nectar
　good,
Good both for earthly med'cine, and for
　heauenly food.

41

Tho when the lilly handed *Liagore*,
　(This *Liagore* whylome had learned skill
　In leaches craft, by great *Appolloes* lore,
　Sith her whylome vpon high *Pindus* hill,
　He loued, and at last her wombe did fill
　With heauenly seed, whereof wise *Pæon* sprong)
　Did feele his pulse, she knew their staied still
　Some litle life his feeble sprites emong ;
Which to his mother told, despeire she from her
　flong.

42

Tho vp him taking in their tender hands,
　They easily vnto her charet beare :
　Her teme at her commaundement quiet stands,
　Whiles they the corse into her wagon reare,
　And strow with flowres the lamentable beare :
　Then all the rest into their coches clim,
　And through the brackish waues their passage
　sheare ;
　Vpon great *Neptunes* necke they softly swim,
And to her watry chamber swiftly carry him.

43

Deepe in the bottome of the sea, her bowre
　Is built of hollow billowes heaped hye,
　Like to thicke cloudes, that threat a stormy
　showre,
　And vauted all within, like to the sky,
　In which the Gods do dwell eternally :
　There they him laid in easie couch well dight ;
　And sent in haste for *Tryphon*, to apply
　Salues to his wounds, and medicines of might :
For *Tryphon* of sea gods the soueraine leach is
　hight.

44

The whiles the *Nymphes* sit all about him round,
Lamenting his mishap and heauy plight ;
And oft his mother vewing his wide wound,
Cursed the hand, that did so deadly smight
Her dearest sonne, her dearest harts delight.
But none of all those curses ouertooke
The warlike Maid, th'ensample of that might,
But fairely well she thriu'd, and well did brooke
Her noble deeds, ne her right course for ought
forsooke.

45

Yet did false *Archimage* her still pursew,
To bring to passe his mischieuous intent,
Now that he had her singled from the crew
Of courteous knights, the Prince, and Faery gent,
Whom late in chace of beautie excellent
She left, pursewing that same foster strong ;
Of whose foule outrage they impatient,
And full of fiery zeale, him followed long,
To reskew her from shame, and to reuenge her
wrong.

46

Through thick and thin, through mountaines
and through plains,
Those two great champions did attonce pursew
The fearefull damzell, with incessant paines :
Who from them fled, as light-foot hare from vew
Of hunter swift, and sent of houndes trew.
At last they came vnto a double way,
Where, doubtfull which to take, her to reskew,
Themselues they did dispart, each to assay,
Whether more happie were, to win so goodly
pray.

47

But *Timias*, the Princes gentle Squire,
That Ladies loue vnto his Lord forlent,
And with proud enuy, and indignant ire,
After that wicked foster fiercely went.
So beene they three three sundry wayes ybent.
But fairest fortune to the Prince befell,
Whose chaunce it was, that soone he did repent,
To take that way, in which that Damozell
Was fled afore, affraid of him, as feend of hell.

48

At last of her farre off he gained vew :
Then gan he freshly pricke his fomy steed,
And euer as he nigher to her drew,
So euermore he did increase his speed,
And of each turning still kept warie heed :
Aloud to her he oftentimes did call,
To doe away vaine doubt, and needlesse dreed:
Full myld to her he spake, and oft let fall
Many meeke wordes, to stay and comfort her
withall.

49

But nothing might relent her hastie flight ;
So deepe the deadly feare of that foule swaine
Was earst impressed in her gentle spright :
Like as a fearefull Doue, which through the raine,
Of the wide aire her way does cut amaine,
Hauing farre off espyde a Tassell gent,
Which after her his nimble wings doth straine,
Doubleth her haste for feare to be for-hent,
And with her pineons cleaues the liquid firma-
ment.

50

With no lesse haste, and eke with no lesse dreed,
That fearefull Ladie fled from him, that ment
To her no euill thought, nor euill deed ;
Yet former feare of being fowly shent,
Carried her forward with her first intent :
And though oft looking backward, well she
vewd,
Her selfe freed from that foster insolent,
And that it was a knight, which now her sewd,
Yet she no lesse the knight feard, then that
villein rude.

51

His vncouth shield and straunge armes her
dismayd,
Whose like in Faery lond were seldome seene,
That fast she from him fled, no lesse affrayd,
Then of wilde beastes if she had chased beene :
Yet he her follow'd still with courage keene,
So long that now the golden *Hesperus*
Was mounted high in top of heauen sheene,
And warnd his other brethren ioyeous,
To light their blessed lamps in *Ioues* eternall
hous.

52

All suddenly dim woxe the dampish ayre,
And griesly shadowes couered heauen bright,
That now with thousand starres was decked
fayre ;
Which when the Prince beheld, a lothfull sight,
And that perforce, for want of lenger light,
He mote surcease his suit, and lose the hope
Of his long labour, he gan fowly wyte
His wicked fortune, that had turnd aslope,
And cursed night, that reft from him so goodly
scope.

53

Tho when her wayes he could no more descry,
But to and fro at disauenture strayd ;
Like as a ship, whose Lodestarre suddenly
Couered with cloudes, her Pilot hath dismayd ;
His wearisome pursuit perforce he stayd,
And from his loftie steed dismounting low,
Did let him forage. Downe himselfe he layd
Vpon the grassie ground, to sleepe a throw ;
The cold earth was his couch, the hard steele
his pillow.

54

But gentle Sleepe enuyde him any rest ;
In stead thereof sad sorrow, and disdaine
Of his hard hap did vexe his noble brest,
And thousand fancies bet his idle braine
With their light wings, the sights of semblants
    vaine :
Oft did he wish, that Lady faire mote bee
His Faery Queene, for whom he did complaine:
Or that his Faery Queene were such, as shee :
And euer hastie Night he blamed bitterlie.

55

Night thou foule Mother of annoyance sad,
Sister of heauie death, and nourse of woe,
Which wast begot in heauen, but for thy bad
And brutish shape thrust downe to hell below,
Where by the grim floud of *Cocytus* slow
Thy dwelling is, in *Herebus* blacke hous,
(Blacke *Herebus* thy husband is the foe
Of all the Gods) where thou vngratious,
Halfe of thy dayes doest lead in horrour hideous.

56

What had th'eternall Maker need of thee,
The world in his continuall course to keepe,
That doest all things deface, ne lettest see
The beautie of his worke ?   Indeed in sleepe
The slouthfull bodie, that doth loue to steepe
His lustlesse limbes, and drowne his baser mind,
Doth praise thee oft, and oft from *Stygian* deepe
Calles thee, his goddesse in his error blind,
And great Dame Natures handmaide, chearing
    euery kind.

57

But well I wote, that to an heauy hart
Thou art the root and nurse of bitter cares,
Breeder of new, renewer of old smarts :
In stead of rest thou lendest rayling teares,
In stead of sleepe thou sendest troublous feares,
And dreadfull visions, in the which aliue
The drearie image of sad death appeares :
So from the wearie spirit thou doest driue
Desired rest, and men of happinesse depriue.

58

Vnder thy mantle blacke there hidden lye,
Light-shonning theft, and traiterous intent,
Abhorred bloudshed, and vile felony,
Shamefull deceipt, and daunger imminent ;
Foule horror, and eke hellish dreriment :
All these I wote in thy protection bee,
And light doe shonne, for feare of being shent :
For light ylike is loth'd of them and thee,
And all that lewdnesse loue, doe hate the light
    to see.

59

For day discouers all dishonest wayes,
And sheweth each thing, as it is indeed :
The prayses of high God he faire displayes
And his large bountie rightly doth areed.
Dayes dearest children be the blessed seed,
Which darknesse shall subdew, and heauen
    win:
Truth is his daughter ; he her first did breed,
Most sacred virgin, without spot of sin.
Our life is day, but death with darknesse doth
    begin.

60

O when will day then turne to me againe,
And bring with him his long expected light ?
O *Titan*, haste to reare thy ioyous waine :
Speed thee to spred abroad thy beames bright,
And chase away this too long lingring night,
Chase her away, from whence she came, to hell.
She, she it is, that hath me done despight :
There let her with the damned spirits dwell,
And yeeld her roome to day, that can it gouerne
    well.

61

Thus did the Prince that wearie night outweare,
In restlesse anguish and vnquiet paine :
And earely, ere the morrow did vpreare
His deawy head out of the *Ocean* maine,
He vp arose, as halfe in great disdaine,
And clombe vnto his steed. So forth he went,
With heauie looke and lumpish pace, that
    plaine
In him bewraid great grudge and maltalent
His steed eke seem'd t'apply his steps to his
    intent.

Cant. V.

∽∽∽∽∽∽∽∽∽∽∽∽∽∽∽∽∽

Prince Arthur heares of Florimell :
three fosters Timias wound,
Belphebe finds him almost dead,
and reareth out of sownd.

∽∽∽∽∽∽∽∽∽∽∽∽∽∽∽∽∽

1

Wonder it is to see, in diuerse minds,
How diuersly loue doth his pageants play,
And shewes his powre in variable kinds :
The baser wit, whose idle thoughts alway
Are wont to cleaue vnto the lowly clay,
It stirreth vp to sensuall desire,
And in lewd slouth to wast his carelesse day :
But in braue sprite it kindles goodly fire,
That to all high desert and honour doth aspire.

2

Ne suffereth it vncomely idlenesse,
In his free thought to build her sluggish nest :
Ne suffereth it thought of vngentlenesse,
Euer to creepe into his noble brest,
But to the highest and the worthiest
Lifteth it vp, that else would lowly fall :
It lets not fall, it lets it not to rest :
It lets not scarse this Prince to breath at all,
But to his first poursuit him forward still doth
call.

3

Who long time wandred through the forrest
wyde,
To finde some issue thence, till that at last
He met a Dwarfe, that seemed terrifyde
With some late perill, which he hardly past,
Or other accident, which him aghast ;
Of whom he asked, whence he lately came,
And whither now he trauelled so fast :
Forsore heswat, and running through that same
Thicke forest, was bescratcht, and both his feet
nigh lame.

4

Panting for breath, and almost out of hart,
The Dwarfe him answerd, Sir, ill mote I stay
To tell the same. I lately did depart
From Faery court, where I haue many a day
Serued a gentle Lady of great sway,
And high accompt through out all Elfin land,
Who lately left the same, and tooke this way :
Her now I seeke, and if ye vnderstand
Which way she fared hath, good Sir tell out of
hand.

5

What mister wight (said he) and how arayd ?
Royally clad (quoth he) in cloth of gold,
As meetest may beseeme a noble mayd ;
Her faire lockes in rich circlet be enrold,
A fairer wight did neuer Sunne behold,
And on a Palfrey rides more white then snow,
Yet she her selfe is whiter manifold :
The surest signe, whereby ye may her know,
Is, that she is the fairest wight aliue, I trow.

6

Now certes swaine (said he) such one I weene,
Fast flying through this forest from her fo,
A foule ill fauoured foster, I haue seene ;
Her selfe, well as I might, I reskewd tho,
But could not stay : so fast she did foregoe,
Carried away with wings of speedy feare.
Ah dearest God (quoth he) that is great woe,
And wondrous ruth to all, that shall it heare.
But can ye read Sir, how I may her find, or
where ?

7

Perdy me leuer were to weeten that,
(Said he) then ransome of the richest knight,
Or all the good that euer yet I gat :
But froward fortune, and too forward Night
Such happinesse did, maulgre, to me spight,
And fro me reft both life and light attone.
But Dwarfe aread, what is that Lady bright,
That through this forest wandreth thus alone ;
For of her errour straunge I haue great ruth and
mone.

8

That Lady is (quoth he) where so she bee,
The bountiest virgin, and most debonaire,
That euer liuing eye I weene did see ;
Liues none this day, that may with her compare
In stedfast chastitie and vertue rare,
The goodly ornaments of beautie bright ;
And is ycleped *Florimell* the faire,
Faire *Florimell* belou'd of many a knight,
Yet she loues none but one, that *Marinell* is
hight.

9

A Sea-nymphes sonne, that *Marinell* is hight,
Of my deare Dame is loued dearely well ;
In other none, but him, she sets delight,
All her delight is set on *Marinell* ;
But he sets nought at all by *Florimell* :
For Ladies loue his mother long ygoe
Did him, they say, forwarne through sacred
spell.
But fame now flies, that of a forreine foe
He is yslaine, which is the ground of all our woe.

10

Fiue dayes there be, since he (they say) was
slaine,
And foure, since *Florimell* the Court for-went,
And vowed neuer to returne againe,
Till him aliue or dead she did inuent.
Therefore, faire Sir, for loue of knighthood gent,
And honour of trew Ladies, if ye may
By your good counsell, or bold hardiment,
Or succour her, or me direct the way ;
Do one, or other good, I you most humbly pray.

11

So may ye gaine to you full great renowme,
Of all good Ladies through the world so wide,
And haply in her hart find highest rowme,
Of whom ye seeke to be most magnifide :
At least eternall meede shall you abide.
To whom the Prince ; Dwarfe, comfort to thee
take,
For till thou tidings learne, what her betide,
I here auow thee neuer to forsake.
Ill weares he armes, that nill them vse for Ladies
sake.

12

So with the Dwarfe he backe return'd againe,
  To seeke his Lady, where he mote her find ;
  But by the way he greatly gan complaine
  The want of his good Squire late left behind,
  For whom he wondrous pensiue grew in mind,
  For doubt of daunger, which mote him betide ;
  For him he loued aboue all mankind,
  Hauing him trew and faithfull euer tride,
And bold, as euer Squire that waited by knights
    side.

13

Who all this while full hardly was assayd
  Of deadly daunger, which to him betid ;
  For whiles his Lord pursewd that noble Mayd,
  After that foster fowle he fiercely rid,
  To bene auenged of the shame, he did
  To that faire Damzell : Him he chaced long
  Through the thicke woods, wherein he would
    haue hid
  His shamefull head from his auengement strong,
And oft him threatned death for his outrageous
    wrong.

14

Nathlesse the villen sped him selfe so well,
  Whether through swiftnesse of his speedy beast,
  Or knowledge of those woods, where he did
    dwell,
  That shortly he from daunger was releast,
  And out of sight escaped at the least ;
  Yet not escaped from the dew reward
  Of his bad deeds, which dayly he increast,
  Ne ceased not, till him oppressed hard
The heauy plague, that for such leachours is
    prepard.

15

For soone as he was vanisht out of sight,
  His coward courage gan emboldned bee,
  And cast t'auenge him of that fowle despight,
  Which he had borne of his bold enimee.
  Tho to his brethren came : for they were three
  Vngratious children of one gracelesse sire,
  And vnto them complained, how that he
  Had vsed bene of that foolehardy Squire ;
So them with bitter words he stird to bloudy ire.

16

Forthwith themselues with their sad instruments
  Of spoyle and murder they gan arme byliue,
  And with him forth into the forest went,
  To wreake the wrath, which he did earst reuiue
  In their sterne brests, on him which late did
    driue
  Their brother to reproch and shamefull flight :
  For they had vow'd, that neuer he aliue
  Out of that forest should escape their might ;
Vile rancour their rude harts had fild with such
    despight.

17

Within that wood there was a couert glade,
  Foreby a narrow foord, to them well knowne,
  Through which it was vneath for wight to wade ;
  And now by fortune it was ouerflowne :
  By that same way they knew that Squire vn-
    knowne
  Mote algates passe ; for thy themselues they set
  There in await, with thicke woods ouer growne,
  And all the while their malice they did whet
With cruell threats, his passage through the ford
    to let.

18

It fortuned, as they deuized had,
  The gentle Squire came ryding that same way,
  Vnweeting of their wile and treason bad,
  And through the ford to passen did assay ;
  But that fierce foster, which late fled away,
  Stoutly forth stepping on the further shore,
  Him boldly bad his passage there to stay,
  Till he had made amends, and full restore
For all the damage, which he had him doen afore.

19

With that at him a quiu'ring dart he threw,
  With so fell force and villeinous despighte,
  That through his haberieon the forkehead flew,
  And through the linked mayles empierced quite,
  But had no powre in his soft flesh to bite :
  That stroke the hardy Squire did sore displease,
  But more that him he could not come to smite ;
  For by no meanes the high banke he could sease,
But labour'd long in that deepe ford with vaine
    disease.

20

And still the foster with his long bore-speare
  Him kept from landing at his wished will ;
  Anone one sent out of the thicket neare
  A cruell shaft, headed with deadly ill,
  And fethered with an vnlucky quill ;
  The wicked steele stayd not, till it did light
  In his left thigh, and deepely did it thrill :
  Exceeding griefe that wound in him empight,
But more that with his foes he could not come
    to fight.

21

At last through wrath and vengeaunce making
    way,
  He on the bancke arriu'd with mickle paine,
  Where the third brother him did sore assay,
  And droue at him with all his might and maine
  A forrest bill, which both his hands did straine;
  But warily he did auoide the blow,
  And with his speare requited him againe,
  That both his sides were thrilled with the
    throw,
And a large streame of bloud out of the wound
    did flow.

22

He tombling downe, with gnashing teeth did
    bite
The bitter earth, and bad to let him in
Into the balefull house of endlesse night,
Where wicked ghosts do waile their former sin.
Tho gan the battell freshly to begin ;
For nathemore for that spectacle bad,
Did th'other two their cruell vengeaunce blin,
But both attonce on both sides him bestad,
And load vpon him layd, his life for to haue had.

23

Tho when that villain he auiz'd, which late
Affrighted had the fairest *Florimell,*
Full of fiers fury, and indignant hate,
To him he turned, and with rigour fell
Smote him so rudely on the Pannikell,
That to the chin he cleft his head in twaine :
Downe on the ground his carkas groueling fell;
His sinfull soule with desperate disdaine,
Out of her fleshly ferme fled to the place of paine.

24

That seeing now the onely last of three,
Who with that wicked shaft him wounded had,
Trembling with horrour, as that did foresee
The fearefull end of his auengement sad,
Through which he follow should his brethren
    bad,
His bootelesse bow in feeble hand vpcaught,
And therewith shot an arrow at the lad ;
Which faintly fluttring, scarce his helmet
    raught,
And glauncing fell to ground, but him annoyed
    naught.

25

With that he would haue fled into the wood ;
But *Timias* him lightly ouerhent,
Right as he entring was into the flood,
And strooke at him with force so violent,
That headlesse him into the foord he sent :
The carkas with the streame was carried downe,
But th'head fell backeward on the Continent.
So mischief fel vpon the meaners crowne :
They three be dead with shame, the Squire liues
    with renowne.

26

He liues, but takes small ioy of his renowne ;
For of that cruell wound he bled so sore,
That from his steed he fell in deadly swowne ;
Yet still the bloud forth gusht in so great store,
That he lay wallowd all in his owne gore.
Now God thee keepe, thou gentlest Squire aliue,
Else shall thy louing Lord thee see no more,
But both of comfort him thou shalt depriue,
And eke thy selfe of honour, which thou didst
    atchiue.

27

Prouidence heauenly passeth liuing thought,
And doth for wretched mens reliefe make way ;
For loe great grace or fortune thither brought
Comfort to him, that comfortlesse now lay.
In those same woods, ye well remember may,
How that a noble hunteresse did wonne,
She, that base *Braggadochio* did affray,
And made him fast out of the forrest runne ;
Belphœbe was her name, as faire as *Phœbus*
    sunne.

28

She on a day, as she pursewd the chace
Of some wild east, which with her arrowes
    keene
She wounded had, the same along did trace
By tract of bloud, which she had freshly seene,
To haue besprinckled all the grassy greene ;
By the great persue, which she there perceau'd,
Well hoped she the beast engor'd had beene,
And made more hast, the life to haue bereau'd :
But ah, her expectation greatly was deceau'd.

29

Shortly she came, whereas that woefull Squire
With bloud deformed, lay in deadly swownd :
In whose faire eyes, like lamps of quenched fire,
The Christall humour stood congealed rownd ;
His locks, like faded leaues fallen to grownd,
Knotted with bloud, in bounches rudely ran,
And his sweete lips, on which before thatstownd
The bud of youth to blossome faire began,
Spoild of their rosie red, were woxen pale and
    wan.

30

Saw neuer liuing eye more heauy sight,
That could haue made a rocke of stone to rew,
Or riue in twaine : which when that Lady bright
Besides all hope with melting eyes did vew,
All suddeinly abasht she chaunged hew,
And with sterne horrour backward gan to start :
But when she better him beheld, she grew
Full of soft passion and vnwonted smart :
The point of pitty perced through her tender
    hart.

31

Meekely she bowed downe, to weete if life
Yet in his frosen members did remaine,
And feeling by his pulses beating rife,
That the weake soule her seat did yet retaine,
She cast to comfort him with busie paine :
His double folded necke she reard vpright,
And rubd his temples, and each trembling
    vaine ;
His mayled haberieon she did vndight,
And from his head his heauy burganet did light

32

Into the woods thenceforth in hast she went,
To seeke for hearbes, that mote him remedy ;
For she of hearbes had great intendiment,
Taught of the Nymphe, which from her infancy
Her nourced had in trew Nobility :
There, whether it diuine *Tobacco* were,
Or *Panachæa*, or *Polygony*,
She found, and brought it to her patient deare
Who al this while lay bleeding out his hart-
bloud neare.

33

The soueraigne weede betwixt two marbles plaine
She pownded small, and did in peeces bruze,
And then atweene her lilly handes twaine,
Into his wound the iuyce thereof did scruze,
And round about, as she could well it vze,
The flesh therewith she suppled and did steepe,
T'abate all spasme, and soke the swelling bruze,
And after hauing searcht the intuse deepe,
She with her scarfe did bind the wound from
cold to keepe.

34

By this he had sweete life recur'd againe,
And groning inly deepe, at last his eyes,
His watry eyes, drizling like deawy raine,
He vp gan lift toward the azure skies,
From whence descend all hopelesse remedies :
Therewith he sigh'd, and turning him aside,
The goodly Mayd full of diuinities,
And gifts of heauenly grace he by him spide,
Her bow and gilden quiuer lying him beside.

35

Mercy deare Lord (said he) what grace is this,
That thou hast shewed to me sinfull wight,
To send thine Angell from her bowre of blis,
To comfort me in my distressed plight ?
Angell, or Goddesse do I call thee right ?
What seruice may I do vnto thee meete,
That hast from darkenesse me returnd to light,
And with thy heauenly salues and med'cines
sweete,
Hast drest my sinfull wounds ?   I kisse thy
blessed feete.

36

Thereat she blushing said, Ah gentle Squire,
Nor Goddesse I, nor Angell, but the Mayd,
And daughter of a woody Nymphe, desire
No seruice, but thy safety and ayd ;
Which if thou gaine, I shalbe well apayd.
We mortall wights whose liues and fortunes bee
To commun accidents still open layd,
Are bound with commun bond of frailtee,
To succour wretched wights, whom we captiued
see.

37

By this her Damzels, which the former chace
Had vndertaken after her, arriu'd,
As did *Belphœbe*, in the bloudy place,
And thereby deemd the beast had bene depriu'd
Of life, whom late their Ladies arrow ryu'd :
For thy the bloudy tract they follow fast,
And euery one to runne the swiftest stryu'd ;
But two of them the rest far ouerpast,
And where their Lady was, arriued at the last.

38

Where when they saw that goodly boy, with
blood
Defowled, and their Lady dresse his wownd,
They wondred much, and shortly vnderstood,
How him in deadly case their Lady fownd,
And reskewed out of the heauy stownd.
Eftsoones his warlike courser, which was strayd
Farre in the woods, whiles that he lay in
swownd,   [stayd,
She made those Damzels search, which being
They did him set thereon, and forth with them
conuayd.

39

Into that forest farre they thence him led,
Where was their dwelling, in a pleasant glade,
With mountaines round about enuironed,
And mighty woods, which did the valley shade,
And like a stately Theatre it made,
Spreading it selfe into a spatious plaine.
And in the midst a little riuer plaide
Emongst the pumy stones, which seemd to plaine
With gentle murmure, that his course they did
restraine.

40

Beside the same a dainty place there lay,
Planted with mirtle trees and laurels greene,
In which the birds song many a louely lay
Of gods high prayse, and of their loues sweet
teene,
As it an earthly Paradize had beene :
In whose enclosed shadow there was pight
A faire Pauilion, scarcely to be seene,
The which was all within most richly dight,
That greatest Princes liuing it mote well delight.

41

Thither they brought that wounded Squire, and
layd
In easie couch his feeble limbes to rest,
He rested him a while, and then the Mayd
His ready wound with better salues new drest ;
Dayly she dressed him, and did the best
His grieuous hurt to garish, that she might,
That shortly she his dolour hath redrest,
And his foule sore reduced to faire plight :
It she reduced, but himselfe destroyed quigh'

42

O foolish Physick, and vnfruitfull paine,
  That heales vp one and makes another wound:
  She his hurt thigh to him recur'd againe,
  But hurt his hart, the which before was sound,
  Through an vnwary dart, which did rebound
  From her faire eyes and gracious countenaunce.
  What bootes it him from death to be vnbound,
  To be captiued in endlesse duraunce
Of sorrow and despaire without aleggeaunce ?

43

Still as his wound did gather, and grow hole,
  So still his hart woxe sore, and health decayd :
  Madnesse to saue a part, and lose the whole.
  Still whenas he beheld the heauenly Mayd,
  Whiles dayly plaisters to his wound she layd,
  So still his Malady the more increast,
  The whiles her matchlesse beautie him dismayd.
  Ah God, what other could he do at least,
But loue so faire a Lady, that his life releast ?

44

Long while he stroue in his courageous brest,
  With reason dew the passion to subdew,
  And loue for to dislodge out of his nest :
  Still when her excellencies he did vew,
  Her soueraigne bounty, and celestiall hew,
  The same to loue he strongly was constraind :
  But when his meane estate he did reuew,
  He from such hardy boldnesse was restraind,
And of his lucklesse lot and cruell loue thus
  plaind.

45

Vnthankfull wretch (said he) is this the meed,
  With which her soueraigne mercy thou doest
    quight ?
  Thy life she saued by her gracious deed,
  But thou doest weene with villeinous despight,
  To blot her honour, and her heauenly light.
  Dye rather, dye, then so disloyally
  Deeme of her high desert, or seeme so light :
  Faire death it is to shonne more shame, to dy :
Dye rather, dy, then euer loue disloyally.

46

But if to loue disloyalty it bee,
  Shall I then hate her, that from deathes dore
  Me brought? ah farre be such reproch fro mee.
  What can I lesse do, then her loue therefore,
  Sith I her dew reward cannot restore ?
  Dye rather, dye, and dying do her serue,
  Dying her serue, and liuing her adore ;
  Thy life she gaue, thy life she doth deserue :
Dye rather, dye, then euer from her seruice
  swerue.

47

But foolish boy, what bootes thy seruice bace
  To her, to whom the heauens do serue and sew?
  Thou a meane Squire, of meeke and lowly place,
  She heauenly borne, and of celestiall hew.
  How then ? of all loue taketh equall vew :
  And doth not highest God vouchsafe to take
  The loue and seruice of the basest crew ?
  If she will not, dye meekly for her sake ;
Dye rather, dye, then euer so faire loue forsake.

48

Thus warreid he long time against his will,
  Till that through weaknesse he was forst at last,
  To yield himselfe vnto the mighty ill :
  Which as a victour proud, gan ransack fast
  His inward parts, and all his entrayles wast,
  That neither bloud in face, nor life in hart
  It left, but both did quite drye vp, and blast ;
  As percing leuin, which the inner part
Of euery thing consumes, and calcineth by art.

49

Which seeing faire *Belphœbe* gan to feare,
  Least that his wound were inly well not healed,
  Or that the wicked steele empoysned were :
  Litle she weend, that loue he close concealed ;
  Yet still he wasted, as the snow congealed,
  When the bright sunne his beams thereon
    doth beat ;
  Yet neuer he his hart to her reuealed,
  But rather chose to dye for sorrow great,
Then with dishonorable termes her to entreat.

50

She gracious Lady, yet no paines did spare,
  To do him ease, or do him remedy :
  Many Restoratiues of vertues rare,
  And costly Cordialles she did apply,
  To mitigate his stubborne mallady :
  But that sweet Cordiall, which can restore
  A loue-sick hart, she did to him enuy ;
  To him, and to all th'vnworthy world forlore
She did enuy that soueraigne salue, in secret
  store.

51

That dainty Rose, the daughter of her Morne,
  More deare then life she tendered, whose flowre
  The girlond of her honour did adorne :
  Ne suffred she the Middayes scorching powre,
  Ne the sharp Northerne wind thereon to
    showre,
  But lapped vp her silken leaues most chaire,
  When so the froward skye began to lowre :
  But soone as calmed was the Christall aire,
She did it faire dispred, and let to florish faire.

52

Eternall God in his almighty powre,
 To make ensample of his heauenly grace,
 In Paradize whilome did plant this flowre,
 Whence he it fetcht out of her natiue place,
 And did in stocke of earthly flesh enrace,
 That mortall men her glory should admire :
 In gentle Ladies brest, and bounteous race
 Of woman kind it fairest flowre doth spire,
And beareth fruit of honour and all chast desire.

53

Faire ympes of beautie, whose bright shining
 beames
 Adorne the world with like to heauenly light,
 And to your willes both royalties and Realmes
 Subdew, through conquest of your wondrous
 might,
 With this faire flowre your goodly girlonds
 dight,
 Of chastity and vertue virginall,
 That shall embellish more your beautie bright,
And crowne your heades with heauenly coronall,
Such as the Angels weare before Gods tribunall.

54

To youre faire selues a faire ensample frame,
 Of this faire virgin, this *Belphœbe* faire,
 To whom in perfect loue, and spotlesse fame
 Of chastitie, none liuing may compaire :
 Ne poysnous Enuy iustly can empaire
 The prayse of her fresh flowring Maidenhead ;
 For thy she standeth on the highest staire
 Of th'honorable stage of womanhead,
That Ladies all may follow her ensample dead.

55

In so great prayse of stedfast chastity,
 Nathlesse she was so curteous and kind,
 Tempred with grace, and goodly modesty,
 That seemed those two vertues stroue to find
 The higher place in her Heroick mind :
 So striuing each did other more augment,
 And both encrease the prayse of woman kind,
 And both encrease her beautie excellent ;
So all did make in her a perfect complement.

Cant. VI.

cxcxcxcxcxcxcxcxcxcxcxcxcxcxcxcx

The birth of faire Belphœbe and
Of Amoret is told.
The Gardins of Adonis fraught
With pleasures manifold.

cxcxcxcxcxcxcxcxcxcxcxcxcxcx

1

Well may I weene, faire Ladies, all this while
 Ye wonder, how this noble Damozell
 So great perfections did in her compile,
 Sith that in saluage forests she did dwell,
 So farre from court and royall Citadell,
 The great schoolmistresse of all curtesy :
 Seemeth that such wild woods should far expell
 All ciuill vsage and gentility,
And gentle sprite deforme with rude rusticity.

2

But to this faire *Belphœbe* in her berth
 The heauens so fauourable were and free,
 Looking with myld aspect vpon the earth,
 In th'*Horoscope* of her natiuitee,
 That all the gifts of grace and chastitee
 On her they poured forth of plenteous horne ;
 Ioue laught on *Venus* from his soueraigne see,
 And *Phœbus* with faire beames did her adorne,
And all the *Graces* rockt her cradle being borne.

3

Her berth was of the wombe of Morning dew,
 And her conception of the ioyous Prime,
 And all her whole creation did her shew
 Pure and vnspotted from all loathly crime,
 That is ingenerate in fleshly slime.
 So was this virgin borne, so was she bred,
 So was she trayned vp from time to time,
 In all chast vertue, and true bounti-hed
Till to her dew perfection she was ripened.

4

Her mother was the faire *Chrysogonee*,
 The daughter of *Amphisa*, who by race
 A Faerie was, yborne of high degree,
 She bore *Belphœbe*, she bore in like cace
 Faire *Amoretta* in the second place :
 These two were twinnes, and twixt them two
 did share
 The heritage of all celestiall grace.
 That all the rest it seem'd they robbed bare
Of bountie, and of beautie, and all vertues
 rare.

5

It were a goodly storie, to declare,
By what straunge accident faire *Chrysogone*
Conceiu'd these infants, and how them she bare,
In this wild forrest wandring all alone,
After she had nine moneths fulfild and gone :
For not as other wemens commune brood,
They were enwombed in the sacred throne
Of her chaste bodie, nor with commune food,
As other wemens babes, they sucked vitall
blood.

6

But wondrously they were begot, and bred
Through influence of th'heauens fruitfull ray,
As it in antique bookes is mentioned.
It was vpon a Sommers shynie day,
When *Titan* faire his beames did display,
In a fresh fountaine, farre from all mens vew,
She bath'd her brest, the boyling heat t' allay;
She bath'd with roses red, and violets blew,
And all the sweetest flowres, that in the forrest
grew.

7

Till faint through irkesome wearinesse, adowne
Vpon the grassie ground her selfe she layd
To sleepe, the whiles a gentle slombring swowne
Vpon her fell all naked bare displayd,
The sunne-beames bright vpon her body playd,
Being through former bathing mollifide,
And pierst into her wombe, where they embayd
With so sweet sence and secret power vnspide,
That in her pregnant flesh they shortly fructifide.

8

Miraculous may seeme to him, that reades
So straunge ensample of conception ;
But reason teacheth that the fruitfull seades
Of all things liuing, through impression
Of the sunbeames in moyst complexion,
Doe life conceiue and quickned are by kynd :
So after *Nilus* invndation,
Infinite shapes of creatures men do fynd,
Informed in the mud, on which the Sunne hath
shynd.

9

Great father he of generation
Is rightly cald, th'author of life and light ;
And his faire sister for creation
Ministreth matter fit, which tempred right
With heate and humour, breedes the liuing
wight.
So sprong these twinnes in wombe of *Chrysogone*,
Yet wist she nought thereof, but sore affright,
Wondred to see her belly so vpblone,
Which still increast, till she her terme had full
outgone.

10

Whereof conceiuing shame and foule disgrace,
Albe her guiltlesse conscience her cleard,
She fled into the wildernesse a space,
Till that vnweeldy burden she had reard,
And shund dishonor, which as death she feard:
Where wearie of long trauell, downe to rest
Her selfe she set, and comfortably cheard ;
There a sad cloud of sleepe her ouerkest,
And seized euery sense with sorrow sore opprest.

11

It fortuned, faire *Venus* hauing lost
Her little sonne, the winged god of loue,
Who for some light displeasure, which him crost,
Was from her fled, as flit as ayerie Doue,
And left her blisfull bowre of ioy aboue,
(So from her often he had fled away,
When she for ought him sharpely did reproue,
And wandred in the world in strange aray,
Disguiz'd in thousand shapes, that none might
him bewray.)

12

Him for to seeke, she left her heauenly hous,
The house of goodly formes and faire aspects,
Whence all the world deriues the glorious
Features of beautie, and all shapes select,
With which high God his workmanship hath
deckt ;
And searched euery way, through which his
wings
Had borne him, or his tract she mote detect :
She promist kisses sweet, and sweeter things
Vnto the man, that of him tydings to her brings.

13

First she him sought in Court, where most he vsed
Why lome to haunt, but there she found him not;
But many there she found, which sore accused
His falsehood, and with foule infamous blot
His cruell deedes and wicked wyles did spot :
Ladies and Lords she euery where mote heare
Complayning, how with his empoysned shot
Their wofull harts he wounded had whyleare,
And so had left them languishing twixt hope
and feare.

14

She then the Citties sought from gate to gate,
And euery one did aske, did he him see ;
And euery one her answerd, that too late
He had him seene, and felt the crueltie
Of his sharpe darts and whot artillerie ;
And euery one threw forth reproches rife
Of his mischieuous deedes, and said, That hee
Was the disturber of all ciuill life,
The enimy of peace, and author of all strife.

15

Then in the countrey she abroad him sought,
  And in the rurall cottages inquired,
  Where also many plaints to her were brought,
  How he their heedlesse harts with loue had fyred,
  And his false venim through their veines
    inspyred ;
  And eke the gentle shepheard swaynes, which
    sat
  Keeping their fleecie flockes, as they were hyred,
  She sweetly heard complaine, both how and what
Her sonne had to them doen ; yet she did smile
    thereat.

16

But when in none of all these she him got,
  She gan auize, where else he mote him hyde :
  At last she her bethought, that she had not
  Yet sought the saluage woods and forrests wyde,
  In which full many louely Nymphes abyde,
  Mongst whom might be, that he did closely lye,
  Or that the loue of some of them him tyde :
  For thy she thither cast her course t'apply,
To search the secret haunts of *Dianes* company.

17

Shortly vnto the wastefull woods she came,
  Whereas she found the Goddesse with her crew,
  After late chace of their embrewed game,
  Sitting beside a fountaine in a rew,
  Some of them washing with the liquid dew
  From off their dainty limbes the dustie sweat,
  And soyle which did deforme their liuely hew ;
  Others lay shaded from the scorching heat ;
The rest vpon her person gaue attendance great.

18

She hauing hong vpon a bough on high
  Her bow and painted quiuer, had vnlaste
  Her siluer buskins from her nimble thigh,
  And her lancke loynes vngirt, and brests vn-
    braste,
  After her heat the breathing cold to taste :
  Her golden lockes, that late in tresses bright
  Embreaded were for hindring of her haste,
  Now loose about her shoulders hong vndight,
And were with sweet *Ambrosia* all besprinckled
    light.

19

Soone as she *Venus* saw behind her backe,
  She was asham'd to be so loose surprized,
  And woxe halfe wroth against her damzels slacke,
  That had not her thereof before auized,
  But suffred her so carelesly disguized
  Be ouertaken. Soone her garments loose
  Vpgath'ring, in her bosome she comprized,
  Well as she might, and to the Goddesse rose,
Whiles all her Nymphes did like a girlond her
    enclose.

20

Goodly she gan faire *Cytherea* greet,
  And shortly asked her, what cause her brought
  Into that wildernesse for her vnmeet,
  From her sweete bowres, and beds with
    pleasures fraught :
  That suddein change she strange aduentur
    thought.
  To whom halfe weeping, she thus answered,
  That she her dearest sonne *Cupido* sought,
  Who in his frowardnesse from her was fled ;
That she repented sore, to haue him angered.

21

Thereat *Diana* gan to smile, in scorne
  Of her vaine plaint, and to her scoffing sayd ;
  Great pittie sure, that ye be so forlorne
  Of your gay sonne, that giues ye so good ayd
  To your disports : ill mote ye bene apayd.
  But she was more engrieued, and replide ;
  Faire sister, ill beseemes it to vpbrayd
  A dolefull heart with so disdainfull pride ;
The like that mine, may be your paine another
    tide.

22

As you in woods and wanton wildernesse
  Your glory set, to chace the saluage beasts,
  So my delight is all in ioyfulnesse,
  In beds, in bowres, in banckets, and in feasts :
  And ill becomes you with your loftie creasts,
  To scorne the ioy, that *Ioue* is glad to seeke ;
  We both are bound to follow heauens beheasts,
  And tend our charges with obeisance meeke :
Spare, gentle sister, with reproch my paine to
    eeke.

23

And tell me, if that ye my sonne haue heard,
  To lurke emongst your Nymphes in secret wize ;
  Or keepe their cabins : much I am affeard,
  Least he like one of them him selfe disguize,
  And turne his arrowes to their exercize :
  So may he long himselfe full easie hide :
  For he is faire and fresh in face and guize,
  As any Nymph (let not it be enuyde.)
So saying euery Nymph full narrowly she eyde.

24

But *Phœbe* therewith sore was angered,
  And sharply said ; Goe Dame, goe seeke your
    boy,
  Where you him lately left, in *Mars* his bed ;
  He comes not here, we scorne his foolish ioy,
  Ne lend we leisure to his idle toy :
  But if I catch him in this company,
  By *Stygian* lake I vow, whose sad annoy
  The Gods doe dread, he dearely shall abye :
Ile clip his wanton wings, that he no more shall
    fly.

25

Whom when as *Venus* saw so sore displeased,
She inly sory was, and gan relent,
What she had said: so her she soone appeased,
With sugred words and gentle blandishment,
Which as a fountaine from her sweet lips went,
And welled goodly forth, that in short space
She was well pleasd, and forth her damzels sent,
Through all the woods, to search from place to
place,
If any tract of him or tydings they mote trace.

26

To search the God of loue, her Nymphes she sent
Throughout the wandring forrest euery where:
And after them her selfe eke with her went
To seeke the fugitiue, both farre and nere,
So long they sought, till they arriued were
In that same shadie couert, whereas lay
Faire *Crysogone* in slombry traunce whilere :
Who in her sleepe (a wondrous thing to say)
Vnwares had borne two babes, as faire as spring-
ing day.

27

Vnwares she them conceiu'd, vnwares she bore :
She bore withouten paine, that she conceiued
Withouten pleasure : ne her need implore
Lucinaes aide : which when they both per-
ceiued,
They were through wonder nigh of sense
bereaued,
And gazing each on other, nought bespake :
At last they both agreed, her seeming grieued
Out of her heauy swowne not to awake,
But from her louing side the tender babes to take.

28

Vp they them tooke, each one a babe vptooke,
And with them carried, to be fostered ;
Dame *Phœbe* to a Nymph her babe betooke,
To be vpbrought in perfect Maydenhed,
And of her selfe her name *Belphœbe* red :
But *Venus* hers thence farre away conuayd,
To be vpbrought in goodly womanhed,
And in her litle loues stead, which was strayd,
Her *Amoretta* cald, to comfort her dismayd.

29

She brought her to her ioyous Paradize,
Where most she wonnes, when she on earth
does dwel.
So faire a place, as Nature can deuize :
Whether in *Paphos*, or *Cytheron* hill,
Or it in *Gnidus* be, I wote not well ;
But well I wote by tryall, that this same
All other pleasant places doth excell,
And called is by her lost louers name,
The *Gardin* of *Adonis*, farre renowmd by fame.

30

In that same Gardin all the goodly flowres,
Wherewith dame Nature doth her beautifie,
And decks the girlonds of her paramoures,
Are fetcht : there is the first seminarie
Of all things, that are borne to liue and die,
According to their kindes. Long worke it were,
Here to account the endlesse progenie
Of all the weedes, that bud and blossome there ;
But so much as doth need, must needs be
counted here.

31

It sited was in fruitfull soyle of old,
And girt in with two walles on either side ;
The one of yron, the other of bright gold,
That none might thorough breake, nor ouer-
stride :
And double gates it had, which opened wide,
By which both in and out men moten pas ;
Th'one faire and fresh, the other old and dride:
Old *Genius* the porter of them was,
Old *Genius*, the which a double nature has.

32

He letteth in, he letteth out to wend,
All that to come into the world desire ;
A thousand thousand naked babes attend
About him day and night, which doe require,
That he with fleshly weedes would them attire:
Such as him list, such as eternall fate
Ordained hath, he clothes with sinfull mire,
And sendeth forth to liue in mortall state,
Till they againe returne backe by the hinder gate.

33

After that they againe returned beene,
They in that Gardin planted be againe ;
And grow afresh, as they had neuer seene
Fleshly corruption, nor mortall paine.
Some thousand yeares so doen they there
remaine ;
And then of him are clad with other hew,
Or sent into the chaungefull world againe,
Till thither they returne, where first they grew:
So like a wheele around they runne from old to
new.

34

Ne needs there Gardiner to set, or sow,
To plant or prune : for of their owne accord
All things, as they created were, doe grow,
And yet remember well the mightie word,
Which first was spoken by th'Almightie lord,
That bad them to increase and multiply :
Ne doe they need with water of the ford,
Or of the clouds to moysten their roots dry ;
For in themselues eternall moisture they imply.

35

Infinite shapes of creatures there are bred,
And vncouth formes, which none yet euer knew,
And euery sort is in a sundry bed
Set by it selfe, andranckt in comely rew :
Some fit for reasonable soules t'indew,
Some made for beasts, some made for birds to
     weare,
And all the fruitfull spawne of fishes hew
In endlesse rancks along enraunged were,
That seem'd the *Ocean* could not containe them
     there.

36

Daily they grow, and daily forth are sent
Into the world, it to replenish more ;
Yet is the stocke not lessened, nor spent,
But still remaines in euerlasting store,
As it at first created was of yore.
For in the wide wombe of the world there lyes,
In hatefull darkenesse and in deepe horrore,
An huge eternall *Chaos*, which supplyes
The substances of natures fruitfull progenyes.

37

All things from thence doe their first being fetch,
And borrow matter, whereof they are made,
Which when as forme and feature it does ketch,
Becomes a bodie, and doth then inuade
The state of life, out of the griesly shade.
That substance is eterne, and bideth so,
Ne when the life decayes, and forme does fade,
Doth it consume, and into nothing go,
But chaunged is, and often altred to and fro.

38

The substance is not chaunged, nor altered,
But th'onely forme and outward fashion ;
For euery substance is conditioned
To change her hew, and sundry formes to don,
Meet for her temper and complexion :
For formes are variable and decay,
By course of kind, and by occasion ;
And that faire flowre of beautie fades away,
As doth the lilly fresh before the sunny ray.

39

Great enimy to it, and to all the rest,
That in the *Gardin* of *Adonis* springs,
Is wicked *Time*, who with his scyth addrest,
Does mow the flowring herbes and goodly
     things,
And all their glory to the ground downe flings,
Where they doe wither, and are fowly mard :
He flyes about, and with his flaggy wings
Beates downe both leaues and buds without
     regard,
Ne euer pittie may relent his malice hard.

40

Yet pittie often did the gods relent,
To see so faire things mard, and spoyled quight :
And their great mother *Venus* did lament
The losse of her deare brood, her deare delight :
Her hart was pierst with pittie at the sight,
When walking through the Gardin, them she
     spyde,
Yet no'te she find redresse for such despight.
For all that liues, is subiect to that law :
All things decay in time, and to their end do
     draw.

41

But were it not, that *Time* their troubler is,
All that in this delightfull Gardin growes,
Should happie be, and haue immortall blis :
For here all plentie, and all pleasure flowes,
And sweet loue gentle fits emongst them throwes,
Without fell rancor, or fond gealosie ;
Franckly each paramour his leman knowes,
Each bird his mate, ne any does enuie
Their goodly meriment, and gay felicitie.

42

There is continuall spring, and haruest there
Continuall, both meeting at one time : [beare,
For both the boughes doe laughing blossomes
And with fresh colours decke the wanton Prime,
And eke attonce the heauy trees they clime,
Which seeme to labour vnder their fruits lode :
The whiles the ioyous birdes make their pastime
Emongst the shadie leaues, their sweet abode,
And their true loues without suspition tell
     abrode.

43

Right in the middest of that Paradise,
There stood a stately Mount, on whose round top
A gloomy groue of mirtle trees did rise, [lop,
Whose shadie boughes sharpe steele did neuer
Nor wicked beasts their tender buds did crop,
But like a girlond compassed the hight,
And from their fruitfull sides sweet gum did
     drop,
That all the ground with precious deaw bedight,
Threw forth most dainty odours, and most
     sweet delight.

44

And in the thickest couert of that shade,
There was a pleasant arbour, not by art,
But of the trees owne inclination made,
Which knitting their rancke braunches part to
     part,
With wanton yuie twyne entrayld athwart,
And Eglantine, and Caprifole emong,
Fashiond aboue within their inmost part,
That nether *Phœbus* beams could through
     them throng,   [wrong.
Nor *Aeolus* sharp blast could worke them any

45

And all about grew euery sort of flowre,
  To which sad louers were transformd of yore ;
  Fresh *Hyacinthus*, *Phœbus* paramoure,
  And dearest loue,
  Foolish *Narcisse*, that likes the watry shore,
  Sad *Amaranthus*, made a flowre but late,
  Sad *Amaranthus*, in whose purple gore
  Me seemes I see *Amintas* wretched fate,
To whom sweet Poets verse hath giuen endlesse
    date.

46

There wont faire *Venus* often to enioy
  Her deare *Adonis* ioyous company,
  And reape sweet pleasure of the wanton boy ;
  There yet, some say, in secret he does ly,
  Lapped in flowres and pretious spycery,
  By her hid from the world, and from the skill
  Of *Stygian* Gods, which doe her loue enuy ;
  But she her selfe, when euer that she will,
Possesseth him, and of his sweetnesse takes her
    fill.

47

And sooth it seemes they say : for he may not
  For euer die, and euer buried bee
  In balefull night, where all things are forgot ;
  All be he subiect to mortalitie,
  Yet is eterne in mutabilitie,
  And by succession made perpetuall,
  Transformed oft, and chaunged diuerslie :
  For him the Father of all formes they call ;
Therefore needs mote he liue, that liuing giues
    to all.

48

There now he liueth in eternall blis,
  Ioying his goddesse, and of her enioyd :
  Ne feareth he henceforth that foe of his,
  Which with his cruell tuske him deadly cloyd :
  For that wilde Bore, the which him once an-
    noyd,
  She firmely hath emprisoned for ay,
  That her sweet loue his malice mote auoyd,
  In a strong rocky Caue, which is they say,
Hewen vnderneath that Mount, that none him
    losen may.

49

There now he liues in euerlasting ioy,
  With many of the Gods in company,
  Which thither haunt, and with the winged boy
  Sporting himselfe in safe felicity :
  Who when he hath with spoiles and cruelty
  Ransackt the world, and in the wofull harts
  Of many wretches set his triumphes hye,
  Thither resorts, and laying his sad darts
Aside, with faire *Adonis* playes his wanton
    parts.

50

And his true loue faire *Psyche* with him playes,
  Faire *Psyche* to him lately reconcyld,
  After long troubles and vnmeet vpbrayes,
  With which his mother *Venus* her reuyld,
  And eke himselfe her cruelly exyld :
  But now in stedfast loue and happy state
  She with him liues, and hath him borne a chyld,
  Pleasure, that doth both gods and men aggrate,
Pleasure, the daughter of *Cupid* and *Psyche* late.

51

Hither great *Venus* brought this infant faire,
  The younger daughter of *Chrysogonee*,
  And vnto *Psyche* with great trust and care
  Committed her, yfostered to bee,
  And trained vp in true feminitee :
  Who no lesse carefully her tendered,
  Then her owne daughter *Pleasure*, to whom shee
  Made her companion, and her lessoned
In all the lore of loue, and goodly womanhead.

52

In which when she to perfect ripenesse grew,
  Of grace and beautie noble Paragone,
  She brought her forth into the worldes vew,
  To be th'ensample of true loue alone,
  And Lodestarre of all chaste affectione,
  To all faire Ladies, that doe liue on ground.
  To Faery court she came, where many one
  Admyrd her goodly haueour, and found
His feeble hart wide launched with loues cruell
    wound.

53

But she to none of them her loue did cast,
  Saue to the noble knight Sir *Scudamore*,
  To whom her louing hart she linked fast
  In faithfull loue, t'abide for euermore,
  And for his dearest sake endured sore,
  Sore trouble of an hainous enimy ;
  Who her would forced haue to haue forlore
  Her former loue, and stedfast loialty,
As ye may elsewhere read that ruefull history.

54

But well I weene, ye first desire to learne,
  What end vnto that fearefull Damozell,
  Which fled so fast from that same foster
    stearne,
  Whom with his brethren *Timias* slew, befell :
  That was to weet, the goodly *Florimell* ;
  Who wandring for to seeke her louer deare,
  Her louer deare, her dearest *Marinell*,
  Into misfortune fell, as ye did heare,
And from Prince *Arthur* fled with wings of idle
    feare.

Cant. VII.

๛๛๛๛๛๛๛๛๛๛๛๛๛๛๛๛๛

The witches sonne loues Florimell :
she flyes, he faines to die.
Satyrane saues the Squire of Dames
from Gyants tyrannie.

๛๛๛๛๛๛๛๛๛๛๛๛๛๛๛๛๛

1

Like as an Hynd forth singled from the heard,
  That hath escaped from a rauenous beast,
  Yet flyes away of her owne feet affeard,
  And euery leafe, that shaketh with the least
  Murmure of winde, her terror hath encreast ;
So fled faire *Florimell* from her vaine feare,
  Long after she from perill was releast :
Each shade she saw, and each noyse she did heare,
Did seeme to be the same, which she escapt whyleare.

2

All that same euening she in flying spent,
  And all that night her course continewed :
  Ne did she let dull sleepe once to relent,
  Nor wearinesse to slacke her hast, but fled
  Euer alike, as if her former dred
  Were hard behind, her readie to arrest :
  And her white Palfrey hauing conquered
The maistring raines out of her weary wrest,
Perforce her carried, where euer he thought best.

3

So long as breath, and hable puissance
  Did natiue courage vnto him supply,
  His pace he freshly forward did aduaunce,
  And carried her beyond all ieopardy,
  But nought that wanteth rest, can long aby.
  He hauing through incessant trauell spent
  His force, at last perforce a downe did ly,
  Ne foot could further moue : The Lady gent
Thereat was suddein strooke with great astonishment.

4

And forst t'alight, on foot mote algates fare,
  A traueller vnwonted to such way :
  Need teacheth her this lesson hard and rare,
  That fortune all in equall launce doth sway,
  And mortall miseries doth make her play.
  So long she trauelled, till at length she came
  To an hilles side, which did to her bewray
  A little valley, subiect to the same,
All couerd with thick woods, that quite it ouercame.

5

Through the tops of the high trees she did descry
  A litle smoke, whose vapour thin and light,
  Reeking aloft, vprolled to the sky :
  Which, chearefull signe did send vnto her sight,
  That in the same did wonne some liuing wight.
  Eftsoones her steps she thereunto applyde,
  And came at last in weary wretched plight
  Vnto the place, to which her hope did guyde,
To find some refuge there, and rest her weary syde.

6

There in a gloomy hollow glen she found
  A little cottage, built of stickes and reedes
  In homely wize, and wald with sods around,
  In which a witch did dwell, in loathly weedes,
  And wilfull want, all carelesse of her needes ;
  So choosing solitarie to abide,
  Far from all neighbours, that her deuilish deedes
  And hellish arts from people she might hide,
And hurt far off vnknowne, whom euer she enuide.

7

The Damzell there arriuing entred in ;
  Where sitting on the flore the Hag she found,
  Busie (as seem'd) about some wicked gin :
  Who soone as she beheld that suddein stound,
  Lightly vpstarted from the dustie ground,
  And with fell looke and hollow deadly gaze
  Stared on her awhile, as one astound,
  Ne had one word to speake, for great amaze,
But shewd by outward signes, that dread her sence did daze.

8

At last turning her feare to foolish wrath,
  She askt, what deuill had her thither brought,
  And who she was, and what vnwonted path
  Had guided her, vnwelcomed, vnsought ?
  To which the Damzell full of doubtfull thought,
  Her mildly answer'd ; Beldame be not wroth
  With silly Virgin by aduenture brought
  Vnto your dwelling, ignorant and loth,
That craue but rowme to rest, while tempest ouerblo'th.

9

With that adowne out of her Christall eyne
  Few trickling teares she softly forth let fall,
  That like two Orient pearles, did purely shyne
  Vpon her snowy cheeke ; and therewithall
  She sighed soft, that none so bestiall,
  Nor saluage hart, but ruth of her sad plight
  Would make to melt, or pitteously appall ;
  And that vile Hag, all were her whole delight
In mischiefe, was much moued at so pitteous sight.

10

And gan recomfort her in her rude wyse,
With womanish compassion of her plaint,
Wiping the teares from her suffused eyes,
And bidding her sit downe, to rest her faint
And wearie limbs a while. She nothing quaint
Nor s'deignfull of so homely fashion,
Sith brought she was now to so hard constraint,
Sate downe vpon the dusty ground anon,
As glad of that small rest, as Bird of tempest gon.

11

Tho gan she gather vp her garments rent,
And her loose lockes to dight in order dew,
With golden wreath and gorgeous ornament;
Whom such whenas the wicked Hag did vew,
She was astonisht at her heauenly hew,
And doubted her to deeme an earthly wight,
But or some Goddesse, or of *Dianes* crew,
And thought her to adore with humble spright;
T'adore thing so diuine as beauty, were but right.

12

This wicked woman had a wicked sonne,
The comfort of her age and weary dayes,
A laesie loord, for nothing good to donne,
But stretched forth in idlenesse alwayes,
Ne euer cast his mind to couet prayse,
Or ply him selfe to any honest trade,
But all the day before the sunny rayes
He vs'd to slug, or sleepe in slothfull shade:
Such laesinesse both lewd and poore attonce
him made.

13

He comming home at vndertime, there found
The fairest creature, that he euer saw,
Sitting beside his mother on the ground;
The sight whereof did greatly him adaw,
And his base thought with terrour and with aw
So inly smot, that as one, which had gazed
On the bright Sunne vnwares, doth soone
withdraw
His feeble eyne, with too much brightnesse
dazed,
So stared he on her, and stood long while amazed.

14

Softly at last he gan his mother aske,
What mister wight that was, and whence
deriued,
That in so straunge disguizement there did
maske,
And by what accident she there arriued:
But she, as one nigh of her wits depriued,
With nought but ghastly lookes him answered,
Like to a ghost, that lately is reuiued
From *Stygian* shores, where late it wandered;
So both at her, and each at other wondered.

15

But the faire Virgin was so meeke and mild,
That she to them vouchsafed to embace
Her goodly port, and to their senses vild,
Her gentle speach applide, that in short space
She grew familiare in that desert place.
During which time, the Chorle through her so
kind
And curteise vse conceiu'd affection bace,
And cast to loue her in his brutish mind;
No loue, but brutish lust, that was so beastly
tind.

16

Closely the wicked flame his bowels brent,
And shortly grew into outrageous fire;
Yet had he not the hart, nor hardiment,
As vnto her to vtter his desire;
His caytiue thought durst not so high aspire,
But with soft sighes, and louely semblaunces,
He ween'd that his affection entire
She should aread; many resemblaunces
To her he made, and many kind remembraunces.

17

Oft from the forrest wildings he did bring,
Whose sides empurpled were with smiling red,
And oft young birds, which he had taught tosing
His mistresse prayses, sweetly caroled,
Girlonds of flowres sometimes for her faire hed
He fine would dight; sometimes the squirell wild
He brought to her in bands, as conquered
To be her thrall, his fellow seruant vild;
All which, she of him tooke with countenance
meeke and mild.

18

But past awhile, when she fit season saw
To leaue that desert mansion, she cast
In secret wize her selfe thence to withdraw,
For feare of mischiefe, which she did forecast
Might be by the witch or that her sonne com-
past:
Her wearie Palfrey closely, as she might,
Now well recouered after long repast,
In his proud furnitures she freshly dight,
His late miswandred wayes now to remeasure
right.

19

And earely ere the dawning day appeard,
She forth issewed, and on her iourney went;
She went in perill, of each noyse affeard,
And of each shade, that did it selfe present;
For still she feared to be ouerhent,
Of that vile hag, or her vnciuile sonne.
Who when too late awaking, well they kent,
That their faire guest was gone, they both
begonne   [vndonne
To make exceeding mone, as they had bene

20

But that lewd louer did the most lament
For her depart, that euer man did heare ;
He knockt his brest with desperate intent,
And scratcht his face, and with his teeth did teare
His rugged flesh, and rent his ragged heare :
That his sad mother seeing his sore plight,
Was greatly woe begon, and gan to feare,
Least his fraile senses were emperisht quight,
And loue to frenzy turnd, sith loue is franticke
  hight.

21

All wayes she sought, him to restore to plight,
With herbs, with charms, with counsell, and
  with teares,
But tears, nor charms, nor herbs, nor counsell
  might
Asswage the fury, which his entrails teares :
So strong is passion, that no reason heares.
Tho when all other helpes she saw to faile,
She turnd her selfe backe to her wicked leares
And by her deuilish arts thought to preuaile,
To bring her backe againe, or worke her finall
  bale.

22

Eftsoones out of her hidden caue she cald
An hideous beast, of horrible aspect,
That could the stoutest courage haue appald ;
Monstrous mishapt, and all his backe was spect
With thousand spots of colours queint elect,
Thereto so swift, that it all beasts did pas :
Like neuer yet did liuing eye detect ;
But likest it to an *Hyena* was,
That feeds on womens flesh, as others feede on
  gras.

23

It forth she cald, and gaue it streight in charge,
Through thicke and thin her to pursew apace,
Ne once to stay to rest, or breath at large,
Till her he had attaind, and brought in place,
Or quite deuourd her beauties scornefull grace.
The Monster swift as word, that from her went,
Went forth in hast, and did her footing trace
So sure and swiftly, through his perfect sent,
And passing speede, that shortly he her ouerhent.

24

Whom when the fearefull Damzell nigh espide,
No need to bid her fast away to flie ;
That vgly shape so sore her terrifide,
That it she shund no lesse, then dread to die,
And her flit Palfrey did so well apply
His nimble feet to her conceiued feare,
That whilest his breath did strength to him
  supply,
From perill free he her away did beare :
But when his force gan faile, his pace gan wex
  areare.

25

Which whenas she perceiu'd, she was dismayd
At that same last extremitie full sore,
And of her safetie greatly grew afrayd ;
And now she gan approch to the sea shore.
As it befell, that she could flie no more,
But yield her selfe to spoile of greedinesse.
Lightly she leaped, as a wight forlore,
From her dull horse, in desperate distresse,
And to her feet betooke her doubtfull sickernesse.

26

Not halfe so fast the wicked *Myrrha* fled
From dread of her reuenging fathers hond :
Nor halfe so fast to saue her maidenhed,
Fled fearefull *Daphne* on th'*Ægæan* strond,
As *Florimell* fled from that Monster yond,
To reach the sea, ere she of him were raught :
For in the sea to drowne her selfe she fond,
Rather then of the tyrant to be caught :
Thereto feare gaue her wings, and neede her
  courage taught.

27

It fortuned (high God did so ordaine)
As she arriued on the roring shore,
In minde to leape into the mighty maine,
A little boate lay houing her before,
In which there slept a fisher old and pore,
The whiles his nets were drying on the sand :
Into the same she leapt, and with the ore
Did thrust the shallop from the floting strand :
So safetie found at sea, which she found not at
  land.

28

The Monster ready on the pray to sease,
Was of his forward hope deceiued quight ;
Ne durst assay to wade the perlous seas,
But greedily long gaping at the sight,
At last in vaine was forst to turne his flight,
And tell the idle tidings to his Dame :
Yet to auenge his deuilish despight,
He set vpon her Palfrey tired lame,
And slew him cruelly, ere any reskew came.

29

And after hauing him embowelled,
To fill his hellish gorge, it chaunst a knight
To passe that way, as forth he trauelled ;
It was a goodly Swaine, and of great might,
As euer man that bloudy field did fight ;
But in vaine sheows, that wont yong knights
  bewitch,
And courtly seruices tooke no delight,
But rather ioyd to be, then seemen sich :
For both to be and seeme to him was labour lich.

30

It was to weete the good Sir *Satyrane*,
  That raungd abroad to seeke aduentures wilde,
  As was his wont in forrest, and in plaine ;
  He was all armd in rugged steele vnfilde,
  As in the smoky forge it was compilde,
  And in his Scutchin bore a Satyres hed :
  He comming present, where the Monster vilde
  Vpon that milke-white Palfreyes carkas fed,
Vnto his reskew ran, and greedily him sped.

31

There well perceiu'd he, that it was the horse,
  Whereon faire *Florimell* was wont to ride,
  That of that feend was rent without remorse :
  Much feared he, least ought did ill betide
  To that faire Mayd, the flowre of womens pride ;
  For her he dearely loued, and in all
  His famous conquests highly magnifide :
  Besides her golden girdle, which did fall
From her in flight, he found, that did him sore apall.

32

Full of sad feare, and doubtfull agony,
  Fiercely he flew vpon that wicked feend,
  And with huge strokes, and cruell battery
  Him forst to leaue his pray, for to attend
  Him selfe from deadly daunger to defend :
  Full many wounds in his corrupted flesh
  He did engraue, and muchell bloud did spend,
  Yet might not do him dye, but aye more fresh
And fierce he still appeard, the more he did him thresh.

33

He wist not, how him to despoile of life,
  Ne how to win the wished victory,
  Sith him he saw still stronger grow through strife,
  And him selfe weaker through infirmity ;
  Greatly he grew enrag'd, and furiously
  Hurling his sword away, he lightly lept
  Vpon the beast, that with great cruelty
  Rored, and raged to be vnder-kept :
Yet he perforce him held, and strokes vpon him hept.

34

As he that striues to stop a suddein flood,
  And in strong banckes his violence enclose,
  Forceth it swell aboue his wonted mood,
  And largely ouerflow the fruitfull plaine,
  That all the countrey seemes to be a Maine,
  And the rich furrowes flote, all quite fordonne :
  The wofull husbandman doth lowd complaine,
  To see his whole yeares labour lost so soone,
For which to God he made so many an idle boone.

35

So him he held, and did through might amate:
  So long he held him, and him bet so long,
  That at the last his fiercenesse gan abate,
  And meekely stoup vnto the victour strong :
  Who to auenge the implacable wrong,
  Which he supposed donne to *Florimell*,
  Sought by all meanes his dolour to prolong,
  Sith dint of steele his carcas could not quell:
His maker with her charmes had framed him so well.

36

The golden ribband, which that virgin wore
  About her sclender wast, he tooke in hand,
  And with it bound the beast, that lowd did rore
  For great despight of that vnwonted band,
  Yet dared not his victour to withstand,
  But trembled like a lambe, fled from the pray,
  And all the way him followd on the strand,
  As he had long bene learned to obay ;
Yet neuer learned her such seruice, till that day.

37

Thus as he led the Beast along the way,
  He spide far off a mighty Giauntesse,
  Fast flying on a Courser dapled gray,
  From a bold knight, that with great hardinesse
  Her hard pursewd, and sought for to suppresse ;
  She bore before her lap a dolefull Squire,
  Lying athwart her horse in great distresse,
  Fast bounden hand and foote with cords of wire,
Whom she did meane to make the thrall of her desire.

38

Which whenas *Satyrane* beheld, in hast
  He left his captiue Beast at liberty,
  And crost the nearest way, by which he cast
  Her to encounter, ere she passed by :
  But she the way shund nathemore for thy,
  But forward gallopt fast ; which when he spyde,
  His mighty speare he couched warily,
  And at her ran : she hauing him descryde,
Her selfe to fight addrest, and threw her lode aside.

39

Like as a Goshauke, that in foote doth beare
  A trembling Culuer, hauing spide on hight
  An Egle, that with plumy wings doth sheare
  The subtile ayre, stouping with all his might,
  The quarrey throwes to ground with fell despight,
  And to the battell doth her selfe prepare :
  So ran the Geauntesse vnto the fight ;
  Her firie eyes with furious sparkes did stare,
And with blasphemous bannes high God in peeces tare.

40

She caught in hand an huge great yron mace,
Wherewith she many had of life depriued,
But ere the stroke could seize his aymed place,
His speare amids her sun-broad shield arriued;
Yet nathemore the steele a sunder riued,
All were the beame in bignesse like a mast,
Ne her out of the stedfast sadle driued,
But glauncing on the tempred mettall, brast
In thousand shiuers, and so forth beside her past.

41

Her Steed did stagger with that puissaunt strooke;
But she no more was moued with that might,
Then it had lighted on an aged Oke ;
Or on the marble Pillour, that is pight
Vpon the top of Mount *Olympus* hight,
For the braue youthly Champions to assay,
With burning charet wheeles it nigh to smite :
But who that smites it, mars his ioyous play,
And is the spectacle of ruinous decay.

42

Yet therewith sore enrag'd, with sterne regard
Her dreadfull weapon she to him addrest,
Which on his helmet martelled so hard,
That made him low incline his lofty crest,
And bowd his battred visour to his brest :
Wherewith he was so stund, that he n'ote ryde,
But reeled to and fro from East to West :
Which when his cruel enimy espyde,
She lightly vnto him adioyned side to syde ;

43

And on his collar laying puissant hand,
Out of his wauering seat him pluckt perforse,
Perforse him pluckt, vnable to withstand,
Or helpe himselfe, and laying thwart her horse,
In loathly wise like to a carion corse,
She bore him fast away. Which when the knight,
That her pursewed, saw, with great remorse
He neare was touched in his noble spright,
And gan encrease his speed, as she encreast her flight.

44

Whom when as nigh approching she espyde,
She threw away her burden angrily ;
For she list not the battell to abide,
But made her selfe more light, away to fly :
Yet her the hardy knight pursewd so nye, .
That almost in the backe he oft her strake :
But still when him at hand she did espy,
She turnd, and semblaunce of faire fight did make ;
But when he stayd, to flight againe she did her take.

45

By this the good Sir *Satyrane* gan wake
Out of his dreame, that did him long entraunce,
And seeing none in place, he gan to make
Exceeding mone, and curst that cruell chaunce,
Which reft from him so faire a cheuisaunce :
At length he spide, whereas that wofull Squire,
Whom he had reskewed from captiuaunce
Of his strong foe, lay tombled in the myre,
Vnable to arise, or foot or hand to styre.

46

To whom approching, well he mote perceiue
In that foule plight a comely personage,
And louely face, made fit for to deceiue
Fraile Ladies hart with loues consuming rage,
Now in the blossome of his freshest age :
He reard him vp, and loosd his yron bands,
And after gan inquire his parentage,
And how he fell into that Gyaunts hands,
And who that was, which chaced her along the lands.

47

Then trembling yet through feare, the Squire bespake,
That Geauntesse *Argante* is behight,
A daughter of the *Titans* which did make
Warre against heauen, and heaped hils on hight,
To scale the skyes, and put *Ioue* from his right :
Her sire *Typhœus* was, who mad through merth,
And drunke with bloud of men, slaine by his might,
Through incest, her of his owne mother Earth
Whilome begot, being but halfe twin of that berth.

48

For at that berth another Babe she bore,
To weet the mighty *Ollyphant*, that wrought
Great wreake to many errant knights of yore,
And many hath to foule confusion brought.
These twinnes, men say, (a thing far passing thought)
Whiles in their mothers wombe enclosd they were,
Ere they into the lightsome world were brought,
In fleshly lust were mingled both yfere,
And in that monstrous wise did to the world appere.

49

So liu'd they euer after in like sin,
Gainst natures law, and good behauioure :
But greatest shame was to that maiden twin,
Who not content so fowly to deuoure
Her natiue flesh, and staine her brothers bowre,
Did wallow in all other fleshly myre,
And suffred beasts her body to deflowre :
So whot she burned in that lustfull fyre,
Yet all that might not slake her sensuall desyre.

50

But ouer all the countrey she did raunge,
To seeke young men, to quench her flaming
thrust,
And feed her fancy with delightfull chaunge:
Whom so she fittest finds to serue her lust,
Through her maine strength, in which she
most doth trust,
She with her brings into a secret Ile,
Where in eternall bondage dye he must,
Or be the vassall of her pleasures vile,
And in all shamefull sort him selfe with her defile.

51

Me seely wretch she so at vauntage caught,
After she long in waite for me did lye,
And meant vnto her prison to haue brought,
Her lothsome pleasure there to satisfye;
That thousand deathes me leuer were to dye,
Then breake the vow, that to faire *Columbell*
I plighted haue, and yet keepe stedfastly:
As for my name, it mistreth not to tell;
Call me the *Squyre of Dames*, that me beseemeth
well.

52

But that bold knight, whom ye pursuing saw
That Geauntesse, is not such, as she seemed,
But a faire virgin, that in martiall law,
And deedes of armes aboue all Dames is deemed,
And aboue many knights is eke esteemed,
For her great worth; She *Palladine* is hight:
She you from death, you me from dread re-
deemed.
Ne any may that Monster match in fight,
But she, or such as she, that is so chaste a wight.

53

Her well beseemes that Quest (quoth *Satyrane*)
But read, thou *Squyre of Dames*, what vow is this,
Which thou vpon thy selfe hast lately ta'ne?
That shall I you recount (quoth he) ywis,
So be ye pleasd to pardon all amis.
That gentle Lady, whom I loue and serue,
After long suit and weary seruicis,
Did aske me, how I could her loue deserue,
And how she might be sure, that I would neuer
swerue.

54

I glad by any meanes her grace to gaine,
Bad her commaund my life to saue, or spill.
Eftsoones she bad me, with incessaunt paine
To wander through the world abroad at will,
And euery where, where with my power or skill
I might do seruice vnto gentle Dames,
That I the same should faithfully fulfill,
And at the twelue monethes end should bring
their names   [games.
And pledges; as the spoiles of my victorious

55

So well I to faire Ladies seruice did,
And found such fauour in their louing hartes,
That ere the yeare his course had compassid,
Three hundred pledges for my good desartes,
And thrise three hundred thanks for my good
partes
I with me brought, and did to her present:
Which when she saw, more bent to eke my
smartes,
Then to reward my trusty true intent,
She gan for me deuise a grieuous punishment.

56

To weet, that I my trauell should resume,
And with like labour walke the world around,
Ne euer to her presence should presume,
Till I so many other Dames had found,
The which, for all the suit I could propound,
Would me refuse their pledges to afford,
But did abide for euer chast and sound.
Ah gentle Squire (quoth he) tell at one word,
How many foundst thou such to put in thy
record?

57

In deed Sir knight (said he) one word may tell
All, that I euer found so wisely stayd;
For onely three they were disposd so well,
And yet three yeares I now abroad haue strayd,
To find them out. Mote I (then laughing sayd
The knight) inquire of thee, what were those
three,
The which thy proffred curtesie denayd?
Or ill they seemed sure auizd to bee,
Or brutishly brought vp, that neu'r did fashions
see.

58

The first which then refused me (said hee)
Certes was but a common Courtisane,
Yet flat refusd to haue a do with mee,
Because I could not giue her many a Iane.
(Thereat full hartely laughed *Satyrane*)
The second was an holy Nunne to chose,
Which would not let me be her Chappellane,
Because she knew, she said, I would disclose
Her counsell, if she should her trust in me repose.

59

The third a Damzell was of low degree,
Whom I in country cottage found by chaunce;
Full little weened I, that chastitee
Had lodging in so meane a maintenaunce,
Yet was she faire, and in her countenance
Dwelt simple truth in seemely fashion.
Long thus I woo'd her with dew obseruance,
In hope vnto my pleasure to haue won;
But was as farre at last, as when I first begon.

60

Safe her, I neuer any woman found,
  That chastity did for it selfe embrace,
  But were for other causes firme and sound ;
Either for want of handsome time and place,
Or else for feare of shame and fowle disgrace.
Thus am I hopelesse euer to attaine
My Ladies loue, in such a desperate case,
But all my dayes am like to wast in vaine,
Seeking to match the chaste with th'vnchaste
  Ladies traine.

61

Perdy, (said *Satyrane*) thou *Squire of Dames*,
  Great labour fondly hast thou hent in hand,
To get small thankes, and therewith many
  blames,
That may emongst *Alcides* labours stand.
Thence backe returning to the former land,
Where late he left the Beast, he ouercame,
He found him not ; for he had broke his band,
And was return'd againe vnto his Dame,
To tell what tydings of faire *Florimell* became.

Cant. VIII.

The Witch creates a snowy Lady,
  like to Florimell,
Who wrongd by Carle by Proteus sau'd,
  is sought by Paridell.

1

So oft as I this history record,
  My hart doth melt with meere compassion,
To thinke, how causelesse of her owne accord
This gentle Damzell, whom I write vpon,
Should plonged be in such affliction,
Without all hope of comfort or reliefe,
That sure I weene, the hardest hart of stone,
Would hardly find to aggrauate her griefe ;
For misery craues rather mercie, then repriefe.

2

But that accursed Hag, her hostesse late,
  Had so enranckled her malitious hart,
That she desyrd th'abridgement of her fate,
Or long enlargement of her painefull smart.
Now when the Beast, which by her wicked art
Late forth she sent, she backe returning spyde,
Tyde with her broken girdle, it a part
Of her rich spoyles, whom he had earst destroyd,
She weend, and wondrous gladnesse to her hart
  applyde.

3

And with it running hast'ly to her sonne,
  Thought with that sight him much to haue
  reliued ;
Who thereby deeming sure the thing as donne
His former griefe with furie fresh reuiued,
Much more then earst, and would haue algates
  riued
The hart out of his brest : for sith her ded
He surely dempt, himselfe he thought depriued
Quite of all hope, wherewith he long had fed
His foolish maladie, and long time had misled.

4

With thought whereof, exceeding mad he grew,
  And in his rage his mother would haue slaine,
Had she not fled into a secret mew,
Where she was wont her Sprights to entertaine
The maisters of her art : there was she faine
To call them all in order to her ayde,
And them coniure vpon eternall paine,
To counsell her so carefully dismayd,
How she might heale her sonne, whose senses
  were decayd.

5

By their aduise, and her owne wicked wit,
  She there deuiz'd a wondrous worke to frame,
Whose like on earth was neuer framed yit,
That euen Nature selfe enuide the same,
And grudg'd to see the counterfet should shame
The thing it selfe. In hand she boldly tooke
To make another like the former Dame,
Another *Florimell*, in shape and looke
So liuely and so like, that many it mistooke.

6

The substance, whereof she the bodie made,
  Was purest snow in massie mould congeald,
Which she had gathered in a shadie glade
Of the *Riphœan* hils, to her reueald
By errant Sprights, but from all men conceald:
The same she tempred with fine Mercury,
And virgin wex, that neuer yet was seald,
And mingled them with perfect vermily,
That like a liuely sanguine it seem'd to the eye.

7

In stead of eyes two burning lampes she set
  In siluer sockets, shyning like the skyes,
And a quicke mouing Spirit did arret
To stirre and roll them, like a womans eyes :
In stead of yellow lockes she did deuise,
With golden wyre to weaue her curled head ;
Yet golden wyre was not so yellow thrise
As *Florimells* faire haire : and in the stead
Of life, she put a Spright to rule the carkasse dead.

8

A wicked Spright yfraught with fawning guile,
And faire resemblance aboue all the rest,
Which with the Prince of Darknesse fell some-
  while,
From heauens blisse and euerlasting rest ;
Him needed not instruct, which way were best
Himselfe to fashion likest *Florimell*,
Ne how to speake, ne how to vse his gest,
For he in counterfeisance did excell,
And all the wyles of wemens wits knew passing
  well.

9

Him shaped thus, she deckt in garments gay,
Which *Florimell* had left behind her late,
That who so then her saw, would surely say,
It was her selfe, whom it did imitate,
Or fairer then her selfe, if ought algate
Might fairer be. And then she forth her
  brought
Vnto her sonne, that lay in feeble state ;
Who seeing her gan streight vpstart, and
  thought
She was the Lady selfe, whom he so long had
  sought.

10

Tho fast her clipping twixt his armes twaine,
Extremely ioyed in so happie sight,
And soone forgot his former sickly paine ;
But she, the more to seeme such as she hight,
Coyly rebutted his embracement light ;
Yet still with gentle countenaunce retained,
Enough to hold a foole in vaine delight :
Him long she so with shadowes entertained,
As her Creatresse had in charge to her ordained.

11

Till on a day, as he disposed was
To walke the woods with that his Idole faire,
Her to disport, and idle time to pas,
In th'open freshnesse of the gentle aire,
A knight that way there chaunced to repaire ;
Yet knight he was not, but a boastfull swaine,
That deedes of armes had euer in despaire,
Proud *Braggadocchio*, that in vaunting vaine
His glory did repose, and credit did maintaine.

12

He seeing with that Chorle so faire a wight,
Decked with many a costly ornament,
Much merueiled thereat, as well he might,
And thought that match a fowle disparagement:
His bloudie speare eftsoones he boldly bent
Against the silly clowne, who dead through feare,
Fell streight to ground in great astonishment;
Villein (said he) this Ladie is my deare,
Dy, if thou it gainesay : I will away her beare.

13

The fearefull Chorle durst not gainesay, nor dooe,
But trembling stood, and yielded him the pray ;
Who finding litle leasure her to wooe,
On *Tromparts* steed her mounted without stay,
And without reskew led her quite away.
Proud man himselfe then *Braggadocchio* deemed,
And next to none, after that happie day,
Being possessed of that spoyle, which seemed
The fairest wight on ground, and most of men
  esteemed.

14

But when he saw himselfe free from poursute,
He gan make gentle purpose to his Dame,
With termes of loue and lewdnesse dissolute ;
For he could well his glozing speaches frame
To such vaine vses, that him best became :
But she thereto would lend but light regard,
As seeming sory, that she euer came
Into his powre, that vsed her so hard,
To reaue her honor, which she more then life
  prefard.

15

Thus as they two of kindnesse treated long,
There them by chaunce encountred on the way
An armed knight, vpon a courser strong,
Whose trampling feet vpon the hollow lay
Seemed to thunder, and did nigh affray
That Capons courage : yet he looked grim,
And fain'd to cheare his Ladie in dismay ;
Who seem'd for feare to quake in euery lim,
And her to saue from outrage, meekely prayed
  him.

16

Fiercely that stranger forward came, and nigh
Approching, with bold words and bitter threat,
Bad that same boaster, as he mote, on high
To leaue to him that Lady for excheat,
Or bide him battell without further treat.
That challenge did too peremptory seeme,
And fild his senses with abashment great ;
Yet seeing nigh him icopardy extreme,
He it dissembled well, and light seem'd to
  esteeme.

17

Saying, Thou foolish knight, that weenst with
  words
To steale away, that I with blowes haue wonne,
And brought throgh points of many perilous
  swords :
But if thee list to see thy Courser ronne,
Or proue thy selfe, this sad encounter shonne,
And seeke else without hazard of thy hed.
At those proud words that other knight be-
  gonne
To wexe exceeding wroth, and him ared
To turne his steede about, or sure he should be
  ded

18

Sith then (said *Braggadocchio*) needes thou wilt
Thy dayes abridge, through proofe of puissance,
Turne we our steedes, that both in equall tilt
May meet againe, and each take happie chance.
This said, they both a furlongs mountenance
Retyrd their steeds, to ronne in euen race :
But *Braggadocchio* with his bloudie lance
Once hauing turnd, no more returnd his face,
But left his loue to losse, and fled himselfe apace.

19

The knight him seeing fly, had no regard
Him to poursew, but to the Ladie rode,
And hauing her from *Trompart* lightly reard,
Vpon his Courser set the louely lode,
And with her fled away without abode.
Well weened he, that fairest *Florimell*
It was, with whom in company he yode,
And so her selfe did alwaies to him tell ;
So made him thinke him selfe in heauen, that
was in hell.

20

But *Florimell* her selfe was farre away,
Driuen to great distresse by Fortune straunge,
And taught the carefull Mariner to play,
Sith late mischaunce had her compeld to
chaunge
The land for sea, at randon there to raunge :
Yet there that cruell Queene auengeresse,
Not satisfide so farre her to estraunge
From courtly blisse and wonted happinesse,
Did heape on her new waues of weary wretched-
nesse.

21

For being fled into the fishers bote,
For refuge from the Monsters crueltie,
Long so she on the mightie maine did flote,
And with the tide droue forward careleslie ;
For th'aire was milde, and cleared was the skie,
And all his windes *Dan Aeolus* did keepe,
From stirring vp their stormy enmitie,
As pittying to see her waile and weepe ;
But all the while the fisher did securely sleepe.

22

At last when droncke with drowsinesse, he woke,
And saw his drouer driue along the streame,
He was dismayd, and thrise his breast he stroke,
For maruell of that accident extreame ;
But when he saw that blazing beauties beame,
Which with rare light his bote did beautifie,
He marueild more, and thought he yet did
dreame
Not well awakt, or that some extasie
Assotted had his sense, or dazed was his eie.

23

But when her well auizing, he perceiued
To be no vision, nor fantasticke sight,
Great comfort of her presence he conceiued,
And felt in his old courage new delight
To gin awake, and stirre his frozen spright :
Tho rudely askt her, how she thither came.
Ah (said she) father, I note read aright,
What hard misfortune brought me to the same ;
Yet am I glad that here I now in safety am.

24

But thou good man, sith farre in sea we bee,
And the great waters gin apace to swell,
That now no more we can the maine-land see,
Haue care, I pray, to guide the cock-bote well,
Least worse on sea then vs on land befell.
Thereat th'old man did nought but fondly grin,
And said, his boat the way could wisely tell :
But his deceiptfull eyes did neuer lin,
To looke on her faire face, and marke her snowy
skin.

25

The sight whereof in his congealed flesh,
Infixt such secret sting of greedy lust,
That the drie withered stocke it gan refresh,
And kindled heat, that soone in flame forth
brust :
The driest wood is soonest burnt to dust.
Rudely to her he lept, and his rough hand
Where ill became him, rashly would haue thrust,
But she with angry scorne him did withstond,
And shamefully reproued for his rudenesse fond.

26

But he, that neuer good nor maners knew,
Her sharpe rebuke full litle did esteeme ;
Hard is to teach an old horse amble trew.
The inward smoke, that did before but steeme,
Broke into open fire and rage extreme,
And now he strength gan adde vnto his will,
Forcing to doe, that did him fowle misseeme :
Beastly he threw her downe, ne car'd to spill
Her garments gay with scales of fish, that all did
fill.

27

The silly virgin stroue him to withstand,
All that she might, and him in vaine reuild :
She struggled strongly both with foot and hand,
To saue her honor from that villaine vild,
And cride to heauen, from humane helpe exild.
O ye braue knights, that boast this Ladies loue,
Where be ye now, when she is nigh defild
Of filthy wretch ? well may shee you reproue
Of falshood or of slouth, when most it may
behoue.

28

But if that thou, Sir *Satyran*, didst weete,
Or thou, Sir *Peridure*, her sorie state,
How soone would yee assemble many a fleete,
To fetch from sea, that ye at land lost late ;
Towres, Cities, Kingdomes ye would ruinate,
In your auengement and dispiteous rage,
Ne ought your burning fury mote abate ;
But if Sir *Calidore* could it presage,
No liuing creature could his cruelty asswage.

29

But sith that none of all her knights is nye,
See how the heauens of voluntary grace,
And soueraine fauour towards chastity,
Doe succour send to her distressed cace :
So much high God doth innocence embrace.
It fortuned, whilest thus she stifly stroue,
And the wide sea importuned long space
With shrilling shriekes, *Proteus* abroad did roue,
Along the fomy waues driuing his finny droue.

30

Proteus is Shepheard of the seas of yore,
And hath the charge of *Neptunes* mightie heard ;
An aged sire with head all frory hore,
And sprinckled frost vpon his deawy beard :
Who when those pittifull outcries he heard,
Through all the seas so ruefully resound,
His charet swift in haste he thither steard,
Which with a teeme of scaly *Phocas* bound
Was drawne vpon the waues, that fomed him
     around.

31

And comming to that Fishers wandring bote,
That went at will, withouten carde or sayle,
He therein saw that yrkesome sight, which smote
Deepe indignation and compassion frayle
Into his hart attonce : streight did he hayle
The greedy villein from his hoped pray,
Of which he now did very litle fayle,
And with his staffe, that driues his Heard astray,
Him bet so sore, that life and sense did much
     dismay.

32

The whiles the pitteous Ladie vp did ryse,
Ruffled and fowly raid with filthy soyle,
And blubbred face with teares of her faire eyes :
Her heart nigh broken was with weary toyle,
To saue her selfe from that outrageous spoyle,
But when she looked vp, to weet, what wight
Had her from so infamous fact assoyld,
For shame, but more for feare of his grim sight,
Downe in her lap she hid her face, and loudly
     shright.

33

Her selfe not saued yet from daunger dred
She thought, but chaung'd from one to other
     feare ;
Like as a fearefull Partridge, that is fled
From the sharpe Hauke, which her attached
     neare,
And fals to ground, to seeke for succour theare,
Whereas the hungry Spaniels she does spy,
With greedy iawes her readie for to teare ;
In such distresse and sad perplexity
Was *Florimell*, when *Proteus* she did see thereby.

34

But he endeuoured with speeches milde
Her to recomfort, and accourage bold,
Bidding her feare no more her foeman vilde,
Nor doubt himselfe ; and who he was, her told.
Yet all that could not from affright her hold,
Ne to recomfort her at all preuayld ;
For her faint heart was with the frozen cold
Benumbd so inly, that her wits nigh fayld,
And all her senses with abashment quite were
     quayld.

35

Her vp betwixt his rugged hands he reard,
And with his frory lips full softly kist,
Whiles the cold ysickles from his rough beard,
Dropped adowne vpon her yuorie brest :
Yet he himselfe so busily addrest,
That her out of astonishment he wrought,
And out of that same fishers filthy nest
Remouing her, into his charet brought,
And there with many gentle termes her faire
     besought.

36

But that old leachour, which with bold assault
That beautie durst presume to violate,
He cast to punish for his hainous fault ;
Then tooke he him yet trembling sith of late,
And tyde behind his charet, to aggrate
The virgin, whom he had abusde so sore :
So drag'd him through the waues in scornefull
     state,
And after cast him vp, vpon the shore ;
But *Florimell* with him vnto his bowre he bore.

37

His bowre is in the bottome of the maine,
Vnder a mightie rocke, gainst which do raue
The roaring billowes in their proud disdaine,
That with the angry working of the waue,
Therein is eaten out an hollow caue,   [keene
That seemes rough Masons hand with engines
Had long while laboured it to engraue :
There was his wonne, ne liuing wight was seene,
Saue one old *Nymph*, hight *Panope* to keepe it
     cleane.

38

Thither he brought the sory *Florimell*,
And entertaind her the best he might
And *Panope* her entertaind eke well,
As an immortall mote a mortall wight,
To winne her liking vnto his delight :
With flattering words he sweetly wooed her,
And offered faire gifts t'allure her sight,
But she both offers and the offerer
Despysde, and all the fawning of the flatterer.

39

Daily he tempted her with this or that,
And neuer suffred her to be at rest :
But euermore she him refused flat,
And all his fained kindnesse did detest,
So firmely she had sealed vp her brest.
Sometimes he boasted, that a God he hight :
But she a mortall creature loued best :
Then he would make himselfe a mortall wight;
But then she said she lou'd none, but a Faerie
    knight.

40

Then like a Faerie knight himselfe he drest ;
For euery shape on him he could endew :
Then like a king he was to her exprest,
And offred kingdomes vnto her in vew,
To be his Leman and his Ladie trew :
But when all this he nothing saw preuaile,
With harder meanes he cast her to subdew,
And with sharpe threates her often did assaile,
So thinking for to make her stubborne courage
    quaile.

41

To dreadfull shapes he did himselfe transforme,
Now like a Gyant, now like to a feend,
Then like a Centaure, then like to a storme,
Raging within the waues : thereby he weend
Her will to win vnto his wished end.
But when with feare, nor fauour, nor with all
He else could doe, he saw himselfe esteemd,
Downe in a Dongeon deepe he let her fall,
And threatned there to make her his eternall
    thrall.

42

Eternall thraldome was to her more liefe,
Then losse of chastitie, or chaunge of loue :
Die had she rather in tormenting griefe,
Then any should of falsenesse her reproue,
Or loosenesse, that she lightly did remoue.
Most vertuous virgin, glory be thy meed,
And crowne of heauenly praise with Saints aboue,
Where most sweet hymmes of this thy famous
    deed
Are still emongst them song, that far my rymes
    exceed.

43

Fit song of Angels caroled to bee ;
But yet what so my feeble Muse can frame,
Shall be t'aduance thy goodly chastitee,
And to enroll thy memorable name,
In th'heart of euery honourable Dame,
That they thy vertuous deedes may imitate,
And be partakers of thy endlesse fame.
It yrkes me, leaue thee in this wofull state,
To tell of *Satyrane*, where I him left of late.

44

Who hauing ended with that *Squire of Dames*
A long discourse of his aduentures vaine,
The which himselfe, then Ladies more defames,
And finding not th' *Hyena* to be slaine,
With that same *Squire*, returned backe againe
To his first way. And as they forward went,
They spyde a knight faire pricking on the plaine,
As if he were on some aduenture bent,
And in his port appeared manly hardiment.

45

Sir *Satyrane* him towards did addresse,
To weet, what wight he was, and what his
    quest :
And comming nigh, eftsoones he gan to gesse
Both by the burning hart, which on his brest
He bare, and by the colours in his crest,
That *Paridell* it was. Tho to him yode,
And him saluting, as beseemed best,
Gan first inquire of tydings farre abrode ;
And afterwardes, on what aduenture now he
    rode.

46

Who thereto answering, said ; The tydings bad,
Which now in Faerie court all men do tell,
Which turned hath great mirth, to mourning
    sad,
Is the late ruine of proud *Marinell*,
And suddein parture of faire *Florimell*,
To find him forth : and after her are gone
All the braue knights, that doen in armes excell,
To sauegard her, ywandred all alone ;
Emongst the rest my lot (vnworthy) is to be one.

47

Ah gentle knight (said then Sir *Satyrane*)
Thy labour all is lost, I greatly dread,
That hast a thanklesse seruice on thee ta'ne,
And offrest sacrifice vnto the dead :
For dead, I surely doubt, thou maist aread
Henceforth for euer *Florimell* to be,
That all the noble knights of *Maydenhead*,
Which her ador'd, may sore repent with me,
And all faire Ladies may for euer sory be.

48

Which words when *Paridell* had heard, his hew
  Gan greatly chaunge, and seem'd dismayd to
  bee ;
  Then said, Faire Sir, how may I weene it trew,
  That ye doe tell in such vncertaintee ?
  Or speake ye of report, or did ye see   [sore ?
  Iust cause of dread, that makes ye doubt so
  For perdie else how mote it euer bee,
  That euer hand should dare for to engore
Her noble bloud ? the heauens such crueltie
  abhore.

49

These eyes did see, that they will euer rew
  T'haue seene, (quoth he) when as a monstrous
  beast
  The Palfrey, whereon she did trauell, slew,
  And of his bowels made his bloudie feast :
  Which speaking token sheweth at the least
  Her certaine losse, if not her sure decay :
  Besides, that more suspition encreast,
  I found her golden girdle cast astray,
Distaynd with durt and bloud, as relique of the
  pray.

50

Aye me, (said *Paridell*) the signes be sad,
  And but God turne the same to good soothsay,
  That Ladies safetie is sore to be drad :
  Yet will I not forsake my forward way,
  Till triall doe more certaine truth bewray.
  Faire Sir (quoth he) well may it you succeed,
  Ne long shall *Satyrane* behind you stay,
  But to the rest, which in this Quest proceed
My labour adde, and be partake of their speed.

51

Ye noble knights (said then the *Squire of Dames*)
  Well may ye speed in so praiseworthy paine :
  But sith the Sunne now ginnes to slake his
  beames,
  In deawy vapours of the westerne maine,
  And lose the teme out of his weary waine,
  Mote not mislike you also to abate
  Your zealous hast, till morrow next againe
Both light of heauen, and strength of men relate :
Which if ye please, to yonder castle turne your
  gate.

52

That counsell pleased well ; so all yfere
  Forth marched to a Castle them before,
  Where soone arriuing, they restrained were
  Of readie entrance. which ought euermore
  To errant knights be commun : wondrous sore
  Thereat displeasd they were, till that young
  Squire
Gan them informe the cause, why that same dore
  Was shut to all, which lodging did desire :
The which to let you weet. will further time require.

Cant. IX.

1

Redoubted knights, and honorable Dames,
  To whom I leuell all my labours end,
  Right sore I feare, least with vnworthy blames
  This odious argument my rimes should shend,
  Or ought your goodly patience offend,
  Whiles of a wanton Lady I do write,
  Which with her loose incontinence doth blend
  The shyning glory of your soueraigne light,
And knighthood fowle defaced by a faithlesse
  knight.

2

But neuer let th'ensample of the bad
  Offend the good : for good by paragone
  Of euill, may more notably be rad,
  As white seemes fairer, macht with blacke at tone;
  Ne all are shamed by the fault of one :
  For lo in heauen, whereas all goodnesse is,
  Emongst the Angels, a whole legione
  Of wicked Sprights did fall from happy blis ;
What wonder then, if one of women all did mis?

3

Then listen Lordings, if ye list to weet
  The cause, why *Satyrane* and *Paridell*
  Mote not be entertaynd, as seemed meet,
  Into that Castle (as that Squire does tell.)
  Therein a cancred crabbed Carle does dwell,
  That has no skill of Court nor courtesie,
  Ne cares, what men say of him ill or well ;
  For all his dayes he drownes in priuitie,
Yet has full large to liue, and spend at libertie.

4

But all his mind is set on mucky pelfe,
  To hoord vp heapes of euill gotten masse,
  For which he others wrongs, and wreckes him-
  selfe ;
  Yet is he lincked to a louely lasse,
  Whose beauty doth her bounty far surpasse,
  The which to him both far vnequall yeares,
  And also far vnlike conditions has ;
  For she does ioy to play emongst her peares,
And to be free from hard restraint and gealous
  feares.

5

But he is old, and withered like hay,
  Vnfit faire Ladies seruice to supply ;
  The priuie guilt whereof makes him alway
  Suspect her truth, and keepe continuall spy
  Vpon her with his other blincked eye ;
  Ne suffreth he resort of liuing wight
  Approch to her, ne keepe her company,
  But in close bowre her mewes from all mens
    sight,
Depriu'd of kindly ioy and naturall delight.

6

Malbecco he, and *Hellenore* she hight,
  Vnfitly yokt together in one teeme,
  That is the cause, why neuer any knight
  Is suffred here to enter, but he seeme
  Such, as no doubt of him he neede misdeeme.
  Thereat Sir *Satyrane* gan smile, and say ;
  Extremely mad the man I surely deeme,
  That weenes with watch and hard restraint to
    stay
A womans will, which is disposd to go astray.

7

In vaine he feares that, which he cannot shonne :
  For who wotes not, that womans subtiltyes
  Can guilen *Argus*, when she list misdonne ?
  It is not yron bandes, nor hundred eyes,
  Nor brasen walls, nor many wakefull spyes,
  That can withhold her wilfull wandring feet ;
  But fast good will with gentle curtesyes,
  And timely seruice to her pleasures meet
May her perhaps containe, that else would
    algates fleet.

8

Then is he not more mad (said *Paridell*)
  That hath himselfe vnto such seruice sold,
  In dolefull thraldome all his dayes to dwell ?
  For sure a foole I do him firmely hold,
  That loues his fetters, though they were of gold.
  But why do we deuise of others ill,
  Whiles thus we suffer this same dotard old,
  To keepe vs out, in scorne of his owne will,
And rather do not ransack all, and him selfe kill?

9

Nay let vs first (said *Satyrane*) entreat
  The man by gentle meanes, to let vs in,
  And afterwardes affray with cruell threat,
  Ere that we to efforce it do begin :
  Then if all fayle, we will by force it win,
  And eke reward the wretch for his mesprise,
  As may be worthy of his haynous sin.
  That counsell pleasd : then *Paridell* did rise,
And to the Castle gate approcht in quiet wise.

10

Whereat soft knocking, entrance he desyrd.
  The good man selfe, which then the Porter
    playd,
  Him answered, that all were now retyrd
  Vnto their rest, and all the keyes conuayd
  Vnto their maister, who in bed was layd,
  That none him durst awake out of his dreme ;
  And therefore them of patience gently prayd.
  Then *Paridell* began to chaunge his theme,
And threatned him with force and punishment
    extreme.

11

But all in vaine ; for nought mote him relent,
  And now so long before the wicket fast
  They wayted, that the night was forward spent,
  And the faire welkin fowly ouercast,
  Gan blowen vp a bitter stormy blast,
  With shoure and hayle so horrible and dred,
  That this faire many were compeld at last,
  To fly for succour to a little shed,
The which beside the gate for swine was ordered.

12

It fortuned, soone after they were gone,
  Another knight, whom tempest thither brought,
  Came to that Castle, and with earnest mone,
  Like as the rest, late entrance deare besought ;
  But like so as the rest he prayd for nought,
  For flatly he of entrance was refusd,
  Sorely thereat he was displeasd, and thought
  How to auenge himselfe so sore abusd,
And euermore the Carle of curtesie accusd.

13

But to auoyde th'intollerable stowre,
  He was compeld to seeke some refuge neare,
  And to that shed, to shrowd him from the
    showre,
  He came, which full of guests he found whyleare,
  So as he was not let to enter there :
  Whereat he gan to wex exceeding wroth,
  And swore, that he would lodge with them yfere,
  Or them dislodge, all were they liefe or loth ;
And so defide them each, and so defide them
    both.

14

Both were full loth to leaue that needfull tent,
  And both full loth in darkenesse to debate ;
  Yet both full liefe him lodging to haue lent,
  And both full liefe his boasting to abate ;
  But chiefly *Paridell* his hart did grate,
  To heare him threaten so despightfully,
  As if he did a dogge to kenell rate,
  That durst not barke ; and rather had he dy,
Then when he was defide, in coward corner ly.

15

Tho hastily remounting to his steed,
  He forth issew'd ; like as a boistrous wind,
  Which in th'earthes hollow caues hath long bin
    hid,
  And shut vp fast within her prisons blind,
  Makes the huge element against her kind
  To moue, and tremble as it were agast,
  Vntill that it an issew forth may find ;
  Then forth it breakes, and with his furious blast
Confounds both land and seas, and skyes doth
    ouercast.

16

Their steel-hed speares they strongly coucht,
    and met
  Together with impetuous rage and forse,
  That with the terrour of their fierce affret,
  They rudely droue to ground both man and horse,
  That each awhile lay like a sencelesse corse.
  But *Paridell* sore brused with the blow,
  Could not arise, the counterchaunge to scorse,
  Till that young Squire him reared from below ;
Then drew he his bright sword, and gan about
    him throw.

17

But *Satyrane* forth stepping, did them stay
  And with faire treatie pacifide their ire,
  Then when they were accorded from the fray,
  Against that Castles Lord they gan conspire,
  To heape on him dew vengeaunce for his hire.
  They bene agreed, and to the gates they goe
  To burne the same with vnquenchable fire,
  And that vncurteous Carle their commune foe
To do fowle death to dye, or wrap in grieuous
    woe.

18

Malbecco seeing them resolu'd in deed
  To flame the gates, and hearing them to call
  For fire in earnest, ran with fearefull speed,
  And to them calling from the castle wall,
  Besought them humbly, him to beare with all,
  As ignoraunt of seruants bad abuse,
  And slacke attendaunce vnto straungers call.
  The knights were willing all things to excuse,
Though nought beleu'd, and entraunce late did
    not refuse.

19

They bene ybrought into a comely bowre,
  And seru'd of all things that mote needfull bee ;
  Yet secretly their hoste did on them lowre,
  And welcomde more for feare, then charitee ;
  But they dissembled, what they did not see,
  And welcomed themselues. Each gan vndight
  Their garments wet, and weary armour free,
  To dry them selues by *Vulcanes* flaming light,
And eke their lately bruzed parts to bring in plight.

20

And eke that straunger knight emongst the rest
  Was for like need enforst to disaray :
  Tho whenas vailed was her loftie crest, ✓
  Her golden locks, that were in tramels gay
  Vpbounden, did them selues adowne display,
  And raught vnto her heeles ; like sunny beames,
  That in a cloud their light did long time stay,
  Their vapour vaded, shew their golden gleames,
And through the persant aire shoote forth their
    azure streames.

21

She also dofte her heauy haberieon,
  Which the faire feature of her limbs did hyde,
  And her well plighted frock, which she did won
  To tucke about her short, when she did ryde,
  She low let fall, that flowd from her lanck syde
  Downe to her foot, with carelesse modestee.
  Then of them all she plainly was espyde,
  To be a woman wight, vnwist to bee,
The fairest woman wight, that euer eye did see.

22

Like as *Minerua*, being late returnd
  From slaughter of the Giaunts conquered ;
  Where proud *Encelade*, whose wide nosethrils
    burnd
  With breathed flames, like to a furnace red,
  Transfixed with the speare, downe tombled ded
  From top of *Hemus*, by him heaped hye ;
  Hath loosd her helmet from her lofty hed,
  And her *Gorgonian* shield gins to vntye
From her left arme, to rest in glorious victorye.

23

Which whenas they beheld, they smitten were
  With great amazement of so wondrous sight.
  And each on other, and they all on her
  Stood gazing, as if suddein great affright
  Had them surprised. At last auizing right,
  Her goodly personage and glorious hew,
  Which they so much mistooke, they tooke delight
  In their first errour, and yet still anew
With wonder of her beauty fed their hungry vew.

24

Yet note their hungry vew be satisfide,
  But seeing still the more desir'd to see,
  And euer firmely fixed did abide
  In contemplation of diuinitie :
  But most they meruaild at her cheualree,
  And noble prowesse, which they had approued,
  That much they faynd to know, who she mote
    bee ;
  Yet none of all them her thereof amoued,
Yet euery one her likte, and euery one her loued.

25

And *Paridell* though partly discontent
    With his late fall, and fowle indignity,
    Yet was soone wonne his malice to relent,
    Through gracious regard of her faire eye,
    And knightly worth, which he too late did try,
    Yet tried did adore. Supper was dight ;
    Then they *Malbecco* prayd of curtesy,
    That of his Lady they might haue the sight,
And company at meat, to do them more delight.

26

But he to shift their curious request,
    Gan causen, why she could not come in place ;
    Her crased health, her late recourse to rest,
    And humid euening ill for sicke folkes cace :
    But none of those excuses could take place ;
    Ne would they eate, till she in presence came.
    She came in presence with right comely grace,
    And fairely them saluted, as became,
And shewd her selfe in all a gentle curteous
    Dame.

27

They sate to meat, and *Satyrane* his chaunce
    Was her before, and *Paridell* besyde ;
    But he him selfe sate looking still askaunce,
    Gainst *Britomart*, and euer closely eyde
    Sir *Satyrane*, that glaunces might not glyde :
    But his blind eye, that syded *Paridell*,
    All his demeasnure from his sight did hyde :
    On her faire face so did he feede his fill,
And sent close messages of loue to her at will.

28

And euer and anone, when none was ware,
    With speaking lookes, that close embassage
        bore,
    He rou'd at her, and told his secret care :
    For all that art he learned had of yore.
    Ne was she ignoraunt of that lewd lore,
    But in his eye his meaning wisely red,
    And with the like him answerd euermore :
    She sent at him one firie dart, whose hed
Empoisned was with priuy lust, and gealous dred.

29

He from that deadly throw made no defence.
    But to the wound his weake hart opened wyde ;
    The wicked engine through false influence,
    Past through his eyes, and secretly did glyde
    Into his hart, which it did sorely gryde.
    But nothing new to him was that same paine,
    Ne paine at all ; for he so oft had tryde
    The powre thereof, and lou'd so oft in vaine,
That thing of course he counted, loue to enter-
    taine.

30

Thenceforth to her he sought to intimate
    His inward griefe, by meanes to him well
        knowne,
    Now *Bacchus* fruit out of the siluer plate
    He on the table dasht, as ouerthrowne,
    Or of the fruitfull liquor ouerflowne,
    And by the dauncing bubbles did diuine,
    Or therein write to let his loue be showne ;
    Which well she red out of the learned line,
A sacrament prophane in mistery of wine.

31

And when so of his hand the pledge she raught,
    The guilty cup she fained to mistake,
    And in her lap did shed her idle draught,
    Shewing desire her inward flame to slake :
    By such close signes they secret way did make
    Vnto their wils, and one eyes watch escape ;
    Two eyes him needeth, for to watch and wake,
    Who louers will deceiue. Thus was the ape,
By their faire handling, put into *Malbeccoes* cape.

32

Now when of meats and drinks they had their fill,
    Purpose was moued by that gentle Dame,
    Vnto those knights aduenturous, to tell
    Of deeds of armes, which vnto them became,
    And euery one his kindred, and his name.
    Then *Paridell*, in whom a kindly pryde
    Of gracious speach, and skill his words to frame
    Abounded, being glad of so fit tyde
Him to commend to her, thus spake, of all well
    eyde.

33

Troy, that art now nought, but an idle name,
    And in thine ashes buried low dost lie,
    Though whilome far much greater then thy
        fame,
    Before that angry Gods, and cruell skye
    Vpon thee heapt a direfull destinie,
    What boots it boast thy glorious descent,
    And fetch from heauen thy great Genealogie,
    Sith all thy worthy prayses being blent,
Their of-spring hath embaste, and later glory
    shent.

34

Most famous Worthy of the world, by whome
    That warre was kindled, which did *Troy* inflame,
    And stately towres of *Ilion* whilome
    Brought vnto balefull ruine, was by name
    Sir *Paris* far renowmd through noble fame,
    Who through great prowesse and bold hardi-
        nesse,
    From *Lacedæmon* fetcht the fairest Dame,
    That euer *Greece* did boast, or knight possesse,
Whom *Venus* to him gaue for meed of worthi-
    nesse.

35

Faire *Helene,* flowre of beautie excellent,
And girlond of the mighty Conquerours,
That madest many Ladies deare lament
The heauie losse of their braue Paramours,
Which they far off beheld from *Troian* toures,
And saw the fieldes of faire *Scamander* strowne
With carcases of noble warrioures,
Whose fruitlesse liues were vnder furrow sowne,
And *Xanthus* sandy bankes with bloud all ouer-flowne.

36

From him my linage I deriue aright,
Who long before the ten yeares siege of *Troy,*
Whiles yet on *Ida* he a shepheard hight,
On faire *Oenone* got a louely boy,
Whom for remembraunce of her passed ioy,
She of his Father *Parius* did name ;
Who, after *Greekes* did *Priams* realme destroy,
Gathred the *Troian* reliques sau'd from flame,
And with them sayling thence, to th'Isle of *Paros* came.

37

That was by him cald *Paros,* which before
Hight *Nausa,* there he many yeares did raine,
And built *Nausicle* by the *Pontick* shore,
The which he dying left next in remaine
To *Paridas* his sonne.
From whom I *Paridell* by kin descend ;
But for faire Ladies loue, and glories gaine,
My natiue soile haue left, my dayes to spend
In sewing deeds of armes, my liues and labours end.

38

Whenas the noble *Britomart* heard tell
Of *Troian* warres, and *Priams* Citie sackt,
The ruefull story of Sir *Paridell,*
She was empassiond at that piteous act,
With zelous enuy of Greekes cruell fact,
Against that nation, from whose race of old
She heard, that she was lineally extract :
For noble *Britons* sprong from *Troians* bold,
And *Troynouant* was built of old *Troyes* ashes cold.

39

Then sighing soft awhile, at last she thus :
O lamentable fall of famous towne,
Which raignd so many yeares victorious,
And of all *Asie* bore the soueraigne crowne,
In one sad night consumd, and throwen downe :
What stony hart, that heares thy haplesse fate,
Is not empierst with deepe compassiowne,
And makes ensample of mans wretched state,
That floures so fresh at morne, and fades at euening late ?

40

Behold, Sir, how your pitifull complaint
Hath found another partner of your payne :
For nothing may impresse so deare constraint,
As countries cause, and commune foes disdayne.
But if it should not grieue you, backe agayne
To turne your course, I would to heare desyre,
What to *Aeneas* fell ; sith that men sayne
He was not in the Cities wofull fyre
Consum'd, but did him selfe to saietie retyre.

41

Anchyses sonne begot of *Venus* faire,
(Said he,) out of the flames for safegard fled,
And with a remnant did to sea repaire,
Where he through fatall errour long was led
Full many yeares, and weetlesse wandered
From shore to shore, emongst the Lybicke sands,
Ere rest he found. Much there he suffered,
And many perils past in forreine lands,
To saue his people sad from victours vengefull hands.

42

At last in *Latium* he did arriue,
Where he with cruell warre was entertaind
Of th'inland folke, which sought him backe to driue,
Till he with old *Latinus* was constraind,
To contract wedlock : (so the fates ordaind.)
Wedlock contract in bloud, and eke in blood
Accomplished, that many deare complaind :
The riuall slaine, the victour through the flood
Escaped hardly, hardly praisd his wedlock good.

43

Yet after all, he victour did suruiue,
And with *Latinus* did the kingdome part.
But after, when both nations gan to striue,
Into their names the title to conuart,
His sonne *Iülus* did from thence depart,
With all the warlike youth of *Troians* bloud,
And in long *Alba* plast his throne apart,
Where faire it florished, and long time stoud,
Till *Romulus* renewing it, to *Rome* remoud.

44

There there (said *Britomart*) a fresh appeard
The glory of the later world to spring,
And *Troy* againe out of her dust was reard,
To sit in second seat of soueraigne king,
Of all the world vnder her gouerning.
But a third kingdome yet is to arise,
Out of the *Troians* scattered of-spring,
That in all glory and great enterprise,
Both first and second *Troy* shall dare to equalise.

45

It *Troynouant* is hight, that with the waues
Of wealthy *Thamis* washed is along,
Vpon whose stubborne neck, whereat he raues
With roring rage, and sore himselfe does throng,
That all men feare to tempt his billowes strong,
She fastned hath her foot, which standes so hy,
That it a wonder of the world is song
In forreine landes, and all which passen by,
Beholding it from far, do thinke it threates the skye.

46

The *Troian Brute* did first that Citie found,
And Hygate made the meare thereof by West,
And *Ouert* gate by North : that is the bound
Toward the land ; two riuers bound the rest.
So huge a scope at first him seemed best,
To be the compasse of his kingdomes seat :
So huge a mind could not in lesser rest,
Ne in small meares containe his glory great,
That *Albion* had conquered first by warlike feat.

47

Ah fairest Lady knight, (said *Paridell*)
Pardon I pray my heedlesse ouersight,
Who had forgot, that whilome I heard tell
From aged *Mnemon* ; for my wits bene light.
Indeed he said (if I remember right,)
That of the antique *Troian* stocke, there grew
Another plant, that raught to wondrous hight,
And far abroad his mighty branches threw,
Into the vtmost Angle of the world he knew.

48

For that same *Brute*, whom much he did aduaunce
In all his speach, was *Syluius* his sonne,
Whom hauing slaine, through luckles arrowes glaunce
He fled for feare of that he had misdonne,
Or else for shame, so fowle reproch to shonne,
And with him led to sea an youthly trayne,
Where wearie wandring they long time did wonne,
And many fortunes prou'd in th'*Ocean* mayne,
And great aduentures found, that now were long to sayne.

49

At last by fatall course they driuen were
Into an Island spatious and brode,
The furthest North, that did to them appeare .
Which after rest they seeking far abrode,
Found it the fittest soyle for their abode,
Fruitfull of all things fit for liuing foode,
But wholy wast, and void of peoples trode,
Saue an huge nation of the Geaunts broode,
That fed on liuing flesh, and druncke mens vitall blood.

50

Whom he through wearie wars and labours long,
Subdewd with losse of many *Britons* bold :
In which the great *Goemagot* of strong
Corineus, and *Coulin* of *Debon* old
Were ouerthrowne, and layd on th'earth full cold,
Which quaked vnder their so hideous masse,
A famous history to be enrold
In euerlasting moniments of brasse,
That all the antique Worthies merits far did passe.

51

His worke great *Troynouant*, his worke is eke
Faire *Lincolne*, both renowmed far away,
That who from East to West will endlong seeke,
Cannot two fairer Cities find this day,
Except *Cleopolis :* so heard I say
Old *Mnemon*. Therefore Sir, I greet you well
Your countrey kin, and you entirely pray
Of pardon for the strife, which late befell
Betwixt vs both vnknowne. So ended *Paridell*.

52

But all the while, that he these speaches spent,
Vpon his lips hong faire Dame *Hellenore*,
With vigilant regard, and dew attent,
Fashioning worlds of fancies euermore
In her fraile wit, that now her quite forlore :
The whiles vnwares away her wondring eye,
And greedy eares her weake hart from her bore :
Which he perceiuing, euer priuily
In speaking, many false belgardes at her let fly.

53

So long these knights discoursed diuersly,
Of straunge affaires, and noble hardiment,
Which they had past with mickle ieopardy,
That now the humid night was farforth spent,
And heauenly lampes were halfendeale ybrent :
Which th'old man seeing well, who too long thought
Euery discourse and euery argument,
Which by the houres he measured, besought
Them go to rest. So all vnto their bowres were brought.

Cant. X.

இஇஇஇஇஇஇஇஇஇஇஇஇஇஇஇஇ

Paridell rapeth Hellenore
Malbecco her pursewes :
Findes emongst Satyres, whence with him
To turne she doth refuse.

இஇஇஇஇஇஇஇஇஇஇஇஇஇஇஇஇ

1

The morow next, so soone as *Phœbus* Lamp
Bewrayed had the world with early light,
And fresh *Aurora* had the shady damp
Out of the goodly heauen amoued quight,
Faire *Britomart* and that same *Faerie* knight
Vprose, forth on their iourney for to wend :
But *Paridell* complaynd, that his late fight
With *Britomart*, so sore did him offend,
That ryde he could not, till his hurts he did
     amend.

2

So forth they far'd, but he behind them stayd,
Maulgre his host, who grudged grieuously,
To house a guest, that would be needes obayd,
And of his owne him left not liberty :
Might wanting measure moueth surquedry.
Two things he feared, but the third was death ;
That fierce youngmans vnruly maistery ;
His money, which he lou'd as liuing breath ;
And his faire wife, whom honest long he kept
     vneath.

3

But patience perforce he must abie,
What fortune and his fate on him will lay,
Fond is the feare, that findes no remedie ;
Yet warily he watcheth euery way,
By which he feareth euill happen may :
So th'euill thinkes by watching to preuent ;
Ne doth he suffer her, nor night, nor day,
Out of his sight her selfe once to absent.
So doth he punish her and eke himselfe torment.

4

But *Paridell* kept better watch, then hee,
A fit occasion for his turne to find :
False loue, why do men say, thou canst
     not see,
And in their foolish fancie feigne thee blind,
That with thy charmes the sharpest sight doest
     bind,
And to thy will abuse ? Thou walkest free.
And seest euery secret of the mind ;
Thou seest all, yet none at all sees thee ;
All that is by the working of thy Deitee.

5

So perfect in that art was *Paridell*,
That he *Malbeccoes* halfen eye did wyle,
His halfen eye he wiled wondrous well,
And *Hellenors* both eyes did eke beguyle,
Both eyes and hart attonce, during the whyle
That he there soiourned his wounds to heale ;
That *Cupid* selfe it seeing, close did smyle,
To weet how he her loue away did steale,
And bad, that none their ioyous treason should
     reueale.

6

The learned louer lost no time nor tyde,
That least auantage mote to him afford,
Yet bore so faire a saile, that none espyde
His secret drift, till he her layd abord.
When so in open place, and commune bord,
He fortun'd her to meet, with commune speach
He courted her, yet bayted euery word,
That his vngentle hoste n'ote him appeach
Of vile vngentlenesse, or hospitages breach.

7

But when apart (if euer her apart)
He found, then his false engins fast he plyde,
And all the sleights vnbosomd in his hart ;
He sigh'd, he sobd, he swownd, he perdy dyde,
And cast himselfe on ground her fast besyde :
Tho when againe he him bethought to liue,
He wept, and wayld, and false laments belyde,
Saying, but if she Mercie would him giue
That he mote algates dye, yet did his death
     forgiue.

8

And otherwhiles with amorous delights,
And pleasing toyes he would her entertaine.
Now singing sweetly, to surprise her sprights,
Now making layes of loue and louers paine,
Bransles, Ballads, virelayes, and verses vaine :
Oft purposes, oft riddles he deuysd,
And thousands like, which flowed in his
     braine,
With which he fed her fancie, and entysd
To take to his new loue, and leaue her old
     despysd.

9

And euery where he might, and euery while
He did her seruice dewtifull, and sewed
At hand with humble pride, and pleasing guile,
So closely yet, that none but she it vewed,
Who well perceiued all, and all indewed.
Thus finely did he his false nets dispred,
With which he many weake harts had sub-
     dewed
Of yore, and many had ylike misled :
What wonder then, if she were likewise carried ?

10

No fort so sensible, no wals so strong,
  But that continuall battery will riue,
  Or daily siege through dispuruayance long,
  And lacke of reskewes will to parley driue ;
  And Peece, that vnto parley eare will giue,
  Will shortly yeeld it selfe, and will be made
  The vassall of the victors will byliue :
  That stratageme had oftentimes assayd
This crafty Paramoure, and now it plaine dis-
    playd.

11

For through his traines he her intrapped hath,
  That she her loue and hart hath wholy sold
  To him, without regard of gaine, or scath,
  Or care of credite, or of husband old,
  Whom she hath vow'd to dub a faire Cucquold.
  Nought wants but time and place, which
    shortly shee
  Deuized hath, and to her louer told.
  It pleased well. So well they both agree ;
So readie rype to ill, ill wemens counsels bee.

12

Darke was the Euening, fit for louers stealth,
  When chaunst *Malbecco* busie be elsewhere,
  She to his closet went, where all his wealth
  Lay hid : thereof she countlesse summes did
    reare,
  The which she meant away with her to beare ;
  The rest she fyr'd for sport, or for despight ;
  As *Hellene*, when she saw aloft appeare
  The *Troiane* flames, and reach to heauens hight
Did clap her hands, and ioyed at that dolefull
    sight.

13

This second *Hellene*, faire Dame *Hellenore*,
  The whiles her husband ranne with sory haste,
  To quench the flames, which she hadtyn'd before,
  Laught at his foolish labour spent in waste ;
  And ranne into her louers armes right fast ;
  Where streight embraced, she to him did cry,
  And call aloud for helpe, ere helpe were past ;
  For loe that Guest would beare her forcibly,
And meant to rauish her, that rather had to dy.

14

The wretched man hearing her call for ayd,
  And readie seeing him with her to fly,
  In his disquiet mind was much dismayd :
  But when againe he backward cast his eye,
  And saw the wicked fire so furiously
  Consume his hart, and scorch his Idoles face,
  He was therewith distressed diuersly,
  Ne wist he how to turne, nor to what place ;
Was neuer wretched man in such a wofull cace.

15

Ay when to him she cryde, to her he turnd,
  And left the fire ; loue money ouercame :
  But when he marked, how his money burnd,
  He left his wife ; money did loue disclame :
  Both was he loth to loose his loued Dame,
  And loth to leaue his liefest pelfe behind,
  Yet sith he n'ote saue both, he sau'd that same,
  Which was the dearest to his donghill mind,
The God of his desire, the ioy of misers blind.

16

Thus whilest all things in troublous vprore were,
  And all men busie to suppresse the flame,
  The louing couple need no reskew feare,
  But leasure had, and libertie to frame
  Their purpost flight, free from all mens reclame ;
  And Night, the patronesse of loue-stealth faire,
  Gaue them safe conduct, till to end they came :
  So bene they gone yfeare, a wanton paire
Of louers loosely knit, where list them to repaire.

17

Soone as the cruell flames yslaked were,
  Malbecco seeing, how his losse did lye,
  Out of the flames, which he had quencht
    whylere
  Into huge waues of griefe and gealosye
  Full deepe emplonged was, and drowned nye,
  Twixt inward doole and felonous despight ;
  He rau'd, he wept, he stampt, he lowd did cry,
  And all the passions, that in man may light,
Did him attonce oppresse, and vex his caytiue
    spright.

18

Long thus he chawd the cud of inward griefe,
  And did consume his gall with anguish sore,
  Still when he mused on his late mischiefe,
  Then still the smart thereof increased more,
  And seem'd more grieuous, then it was before :
  At last when sorrow he saw booted nought,
  Ne griefe might not his loue to him restore,
  He gan deuise, how her he reskew mought,
Ten thousand wayes he cast in his confused
    thought.

19

At last resoluing, like a pilgrim pore,
  To search her forth, where so she might be fond,
  And bearing with him treasure in close store,
  The rest he leaues in ground : So takes in hond
  To seeke her endlong, both by sea and lond.
  Long he her sought, he sought her farre and
    nere,
  And euery where that he mote vnderstond,
  Of knights and ladies any meetings were,
And of eachone he met, he tydings did inquere.

20

But all in vaine, his woman was too wise,
  Euer to come into his clouch againe,
  And he too simple euer to surprise
  The iolly *Paridell*, for all his paine.
  One day, as he forpassed by the plaine
  With weary pace, he farre away espide
  A couple, seeming well to be his twaine,
  Which houed close vnder a forrest side,
As if they lay in wait, or else themselues did hide.

21

Well weened he, that those the same mote bee,
  And as he better did their shape auize,
  Him seemed more their manner did agree ;
  For th'one was armed all in warlike wize,
  Whom, to be *Paridell* he did deuize ;
  And th'other all yclad in garments light,
  Discolour'd like to womanish disguise,
  He did resemble to his Ladie bright ;
And euer his faint hart much earned at the sight.

22

And euer faine he towards them would goe,
  But yet durst not for dread approchen nie,
  But stood aloofe, vnweeting what to doe ;
  Till that prickt forth with loues extremitie,
  That is the father of foule gealosy,
  He closely nearer crept, the truth to weet :
  But, as he nigher drew, he easily
  Might scerne, that it was not his sweetest sweet,
Ne yet her Belamour, the partner of his sheet.

23

But it was scornefull *Braggadocchio*,
  That with his seruant *Trompart* houerd there,
  Sith late he fled from his too earnest foe :
  Whom such when as *Malbecco* spyed clere,
  He turned backe, and would haue fled arere ;
  Till *Trompart* ronning hastily, him did stay,
  And bad before his soueraine Lord appere :
  That was him loth, yet durst he not gainesay,
And comming him before, low louted on the lay.

24

The Boaster at him sternely bent his browe,
  As if he could haue kild him with his looke,
  That to the ground him meekely made to bowe,
  And awfull terror deepe into him strooke,
  That euery member of his bodie quooke.
  Said he, Thou man of nought, what doest thou
    here,
  Vnfitly furnisht with thy bag and booke,
  Where I expected one with shield and spere,
To proue some deedes of armes vpon an equall
    pere.

25

The wretched man at his imperious speach,
  Was all abasht, and low prostrating, said ;
  Good Sir, let not my rudenesse be no breach
  Vnto your patience, ne be ill ypaid ;
  For I vnwares this way by fortune straid,
  A silly Pilgrim driuen to distresse,
  That seeke a Lady, There he suddein staid,
  And did the rest with grieuous sighes suppresse,
While teares stood in his eies, few drops of
    bitternesse.

26

What Ladie, man ? (said *Trompart*) take good
    hart,
  And tell thy griefe, if any hidden lye ;
  Was neuer better time to shew thy smart,
  Then now, that noble succour is thee by,
  That is the whole worlds commune remedy.
  That chearefull word his weake hart much did
    cheare,
  And with vaine hope his spirits faint supply,
  That bold he said ; O most redoubted Pere,
Vouchsafe with mild regard a wretches cace to
    heare.

27

Then sighing sore, It is not long (said hee)
  Sith I enioyd the gentlest Dame aliue ;
  Of whom a knight, no knight at all perdee,
  But shame of all, that doe for honor striue,
  By treacherous deceipt did me depriue ;
  Through open outrage he her bore away,
  And with fowle force vnto his will did driue,
  Which all good knights, that armes do beare
    this day,
Are bound for to reuenge, and punish if they may.

28

And you most noble Lord, that can and dare
  Redresse the wrong of miserable wight,
  Cannot employ your most victorious speare
  In better quarrell, then defence of right,
  And for a Ladie gainst a faithlesse knight ;
  So shall your glory be aduaunced much,
  And all faire Ladies magnifie your might,
  And eke my selfe, albe I simple such,
Your worthy paine shall well reward with
    guerdon rich.

29

With that out of his bouget forth he drew
  Great store of treasure, therewith him to tempt ;
  But he on it lookt scornefully askew,
  As much disdeigning to be so misdempt,
  Or a war-monger to be basely nempt ;
  And said ; Thy offers base I greatly loth,
  And eke thy words vncourteous and vnkempt ;
  I tread in dust thee and thy money both,
That, were it not for shame, So turned from him
    wroth.

30

But *Trompart*, that his maisters humor knew,
In lofty lookes to hide an humble mind,
Was inly tickled with that golden vew,
And in his eare him rounded close behind :
Yet stoupt he not, but lay still in the wind,
Waiting aduauntage on the pray to sease ;
Till *Trompart* lowly to the ground inclind,
Besought him his great courage to appease,
And pardon simple man, that rash did him
   displease.

31

Bigge looking like a doughtie Doucepere,
At last he thus ; Thou clod of vilest clay,
I pardon yield, and with thy rudenesse beare ;
But weete henceforth, that all that golden pray,
And all that else the vaine world vaunten may,
I loath as doung, ne deeme my dew reward :
Fame is my meed, and glory vertues pray.
But minds of mortall men are muchell mard,
And mou'd amisse with massie mucks vnmeet
   regard.

32

And more, I graunt to thy great miserie
Gratious respect, thy wife shall backe be sent,
And that vile knight, who euer that he bee,
Which hath thy Lady reft, and knighthood shent,
By *Sanglamort* my sword, whose deadly dent
The bloud hath of so many thousands shed,
I sweare, ere long shall dearely it repent ;
Ne he twixt heauen and earth shall hide his hed,
But soone he shall be found, and shortly doen
   be ded.

33

The foolish man thereat woxe wondrous blith,
As if the word so spoken, were halfe donne,
And humbly thankcd him a thousand sith,
That had from death to life him newly wonne.
Tho forth the Boaster marching, braue begonne
His stolen steed to thunder furiously,
As if he heauen and hell would ouerronn
And all the world confound with cruelty,
That much *Malbecco* ioyed in his iollity.

34

Thus long they three together traueiled,
   Through many a wood, and many an vncouth
      way,
To seeke his wife, that was farre wandered :
But those two sought nought, but the present
   pray,
To weete the treasure, which he did bewray,
On which their cies and harts were wholly set,
With purpose, how they might it best betray ;
For sith the houre, that first he did them let
The same behold, therewith their keene desires
   were whet.

35

It fortuned as they together far'd,
They spide, where *Paridell* came pricking fast
Vpon the plaine, the which himselfe prepar'd
To giust with that braue straunger knight a cast,
As on aduenture by the way he past :
Alone he rode without his *Paragone* ;
For hauing filcht her bels, her vp he cast
To the wide world, and let her fly alone,
He nould be clogd. So had he serued many one.

36

The gentle Lady, loose at randon left,   [wide
The greene-wood long did walke, and wander
At wilde aduenture, like a forlorne weft,
Till on a day the *Satyres* her espide
Straying alone withouten groome or guide ;
Her vp they tooke, and with them home her led,
With them as housewife euer to abide,
To milk their gotes, and make them cheese
   and bred,
And euery one as commune good her handeled.

37

That shortly she *Malbecco* has forgot,
And eke Sir *Paridell*, all were he deare ;
Who from her went to seeke another lot,
And now by fortune was arriued here,
Where those two guilers with *Malbecco* were :
Soone as the oldman saw Sir *Paridell*,
He fainted, and was almost dead with feare,
Ne word he had to speake, his griefe to tell,
But to him louted low, and greeted goodly well.

38

And after asked him for *Hellenore*,
I take no keepe of her (said *Paridell*)
She wonneth in the forrest there before.
So forth he rode, as his aduenture fell ;
The whiles the Boaster from his loftie sell
Faynd to alight, something amisse to mend ;
But the fresh Swayne would not his leasure dwell,
But went his way ; whom when he passed kend,
He vp remounted light, and after faind to wend.

39

Perdy nay (said *Malbecco*) shall ye not :
But let him passe as lightly, as he came :
For litle good of him is to be got,
And mickle perill to be put to shame.
But let vs go to seeke my dearest Dame,
Whom he hath left in yonder forrest wyld :
For of her safety in great doubt I am,
Least saluage beastes her person haue despoyld:
Then all the world is lost, and we in vaine haue
   toyld.

40

They all agree, and forward them addrest :
Ah but (said craftie *Trompart*) weete ye well,
That yonder in that wastefull wildernesse
Huge monsters haunt, and many dangers dwell ;
Dragons, and Minotaures, and feendes of hell,
And many wilde woodmen, which robbe and rend
All trauellers ; therefore aduise ye well,
Before ye enterprise that way to wend :
One may his iourney bring too soone to euill end.

41

Malbecco stopt in great astonishment,
And with pale eyes fast fixed on the rest,
Their counsell crau'd, in daunger imminent.
Said *Trompart*, You that are the most opprest
With burden of great treasure, I thinke best
Here for to stay in safetie behind ;
My Lord and I will search the wide forrest.
That counsell pleased not *Malbeccoes* mind ;
For he was much affraid, himselfe alone to find.

42

Then is it best (said he) that ye doe leaue
Your treasure here in some securitie,
Either fast closed in some hollow greaue,
Or buried in the ground from ieopardie,
Till we returne againe in safetie :
As for vs two, least doubt of vs ye haue,
Hence farre away we will blindfolded lie,
Ne priuie be vnto your treasures graue.
It pleased : so he did. Then they march forward braue.

43

Now when amid the thickest woods they were,
They heard a noyse of many bagpipes shrill,
And shrieking Hububs them approching nere,
Which all the forrest did with horror fill :
That dreadtull sound the boasters hart did thrill,
With such amazement, that in haste he fled,
Ne euer looked backe for good or ill,
And after him eke fearefull *Trompart* sped ;
The old man could not fly, but fell to ground halfe ded.

44

Yet afterwards close creeping, as he might,
He in a bush did hide his fearefull hed,
The iolly *Satyres* full of fresh delight,
Came dauncing forth, and with them nimbly led
Faire *Hellenore*, with girlonds all bespred,
Whom their May-lady they had newly made :
She proud of that new honour, which they red,
And of their louely fellowship full glade,
Daunst liuely, and her face did with a Lawrell shade.

45

The silly man that in the thicket lay
Saw all this goodly sport, and grieued sore,
Yet durst he not against it doe or say,
But did his hart with bitter thoughts engore,
To see th'vnkindnesse of his *Hellenore*.
All day they daunced with great lustihed,
And with their horned feet the greene grasse wore,
The whiles their Gotes vpon the brouzes fed,
Till drouping *Phœbus* gan to hide his golden hed.

46

Tho vp they gan their merry pypes to trusse,
And all their goodly heards did gather round,
But euery *Satyre* first did giue a busse
To *Hellenore* : so busses did abound.
Now gan the humid vapour shed the ground
With perly deaw, and th'Earthes gloomy shade
Did dim the better brightnesse of the welkin round,
That euery bird and beast awarned made,
To shrowd themselues, whiles sleepe their senses did inuade.

47

Which when *Malbecco* saw, out of his bush
Vpon his hands and feete he crept full light,
And like a Gote emongst the Gotes did rush,
That through the helpe of his faire hornes on hight,
And misty dampe of misconceiuing night,
And eke through likenesse of his gotish beard,
He did the better counterfeite aright :
So home he marcht emongst the horned heard,
That none of all the *Satyres* him espyde or heard.

48

At night, when all they went to sleepe, he vewd,
Whereas his louely wife emongst them lay,
Embraced of a *Satyre* rough and rude,
Who all the night did minde his ioyous play :
Nine times he heard him come aloft ere day,
That all his hart with gealosie did swell ;
But yet that nights ensample did bewray,
That not for nought his wife them loued so well,
When one so oft a night did ring his matins bell.

49

So closely as he could, he to them crept,
When wearie of their sport to sleepe they fell,
And to his wife, that now full soundly slept,
He whispered in her eare, and did her tell,
That it was he, which by her side did dwell,
And therefore prayd her wake, to heare him plaine.
As one out of a dreame not waked well,
She turned her, and returned backe againe :
Yet her for to awake he did the more constraine.

50

At last with irkesome trouble she abrayd ;
  And then perceiuing, that it was indeed
  Her old *Malbecco*, which did her vpbrayd,
  With loosenesse of her loue, and loathly deed,
  She was astonisht with exceeding dreed,
  And would haue wakt the *Satyre* by her syde ;
  But he her prayd, for mercy, or for meed,
  To saue his life, ne let him be descryde,
But hearken to his lore, and all his counsell hyde.

51

Tho gan he her perswade, to leaue that lewd
  And loathsome life, of God and man abhord,
  And home returne, where all should be renewd
  With perfect peace, and bandes of fresh accord,
  And she receiu'd againe to bed and bord,
  As if no trespasse euer had bene donne :
  But she it all refused at one word,
  And by no meanes would to his will be wonne,
But chose emongst the iolly *Satyres* still to
    wonne.

52

He wooed her, till day spring he espyde ;
  But all in vaine : and then turnd to the heard,
  Who butted him with hornes on euery syde,
  And trode downe in the durt, where his hore
    beard
  Was fowly dight, and he of death afeard.
  Early before the heauens fairest light
  Out of the ruddy East was fully reard,
  The heardes out of their foldes were loosed
    quight,
And he emongst the rest crept forth in sory
    plight.

53

So soone as he the Prison dore did pas,
  He ran as fast, as both his feete could beare,
  And neuer looked, who behind him was,
  Ne scarsely who before : like as a Beare
  That creeping close, amongst the hiues to reare
  An hony combe, the wakefull dogs espy,
  And him assayling, sore his carkasse teare,
  That hardly he with life away does fly,
Ne stayes, till safe himselfe he see from ieopardy.

54

Ne stayd he, till he came vnto the place,
  Where late his treasure he entombed had,
  Where when he found it not (for *Trompart* bace
  Had it purloyned for his maister bad :)
  With extreme fury he became quite mad,
  And ran away, ran with himselfe away :
  That who so straungely had him seene bestad,
  With vpstart haire, and staring eyes dismay,
From Limbo lake him late escaped sure would say.

55

High ouer hilles and ouer dales he fled,
  As if the wind him on his winges had borne,
  Ne banck nor bush could stay him, when he sped
  His nimble feet, as treading still on thorne :
  Griefe, and despight, and gealosie, and scorne
  Did all the way him follow hard behind,
  And he himselfe himselfe loath'd so forlorne,
  So shamefully forlorne of womankind ;
That as a Snake, still lurked in his wounded
    mind.

56

Still fled he forward, looking backward still,
  Ne stayd his flight, nor fearefull agony,
  Till that he came vnto a rockie hill,
  Ouer the sea, suspended dreadfully,
  That liuing creature it would terrify,
  To looke adowne, or vpward to the hight :
  From thence he threw himselfe dispiteously,
  All desperate of his fore-damned spright,
That seem'd no helpe for him was left in liuing
    sight.

57

But through long anguish, and selfe-murdring
    thought
  He was so wasted and forpined quight,
  That all his substance was consum'd to nought,
  And nothing left, but like an aery Spright,
  That on the rockes he fell so flit and light,
  That he thereby receiu'd no hurt at all,
  But chaunced on a craggy cliff to light ;
  Whence he with crooked clawes so long did crall,
That at the last he found a caue with entrance
    small.

58

Into the same he creepes, and thenceforth there
  Resolu'd to build his balefull mansion,
  In drery darkenesse, and continuall feare
  Of that rockes fall, which euer and anon
  Threates with huge ruine him to fall vpon,
  That he dare neuer sleepe, but that one eye
  Still ope he keepes for that occasion ;
  Ne euer rests he in tranquillity,
The roring billowes beat his bowre so boystrously.

59

Ne euer is he wont on ought to feed,
  But toades and frogs, his pasture poysonous,
  Which in his cold complexion do breed
  A filthy bloud, or humour rancorous,
  Matter of doubt and dread suspitious,
  That doth with curelesse care consume the hart,
  Corrupts the stomacke with gall vitious,
  Croscuts the liuer with internall smart,
And doth transfixe the soule with deathes
    eternall dart.

60

Yet can he neuer dye, but dying liues,
　And doth himselfe with sorrow new sustaine,
　That death and life attonce vnto him giues.
　And painefull pleasure turnes to pleasing paine.
　There dwels he euer, miserable swaine,
　Hatefull both to him selfe, and euery wight;
　Where he through priuy griefe, and horrour
　　vaine,
Is woxen so deform'd, that he has quight
Forgot he was a man, and *Gealosie* is hight.

Cant. XI.

Britomart chaceth Ollyphant,
　findes Scudamour distrest :
Assayes the house of Busyrane,
　where Loues spoyles are exprest.

I

O hatefull hellish Snake, what furie furst
　Brought thee from balefull house of *Proserpine*,
　Where in her bosome she thee long had nurst,
　And fostred vp with bitter milke of tine,
　Fowle Gealosie, that turnest loue diuine
　To ioylesse dread, and mak'st the louing hart
　With hatefull thoughts to languish and to pine,
　And feed it selfe with selfe-consuming smart ?
Of all the passions in the mind thou vilest art.

2

O let him far be banished away,
　And in his stead let Loue for euer dwell,
　Sweet Loue, that doth his golden wings embay
　In blessed Nectar, and pure Pleasures well,
　Vntroubled of vile feare, or bitter fell.
　And ye faire Ladies, that your kingdomes make
　In th'harts of men, them gouerne wisely well,
　And of faire *Britomart* ensample take,
That was as trew in loue, as Turtle to her make.

3

Who with Sir *Satyrane*, as earst ye red,
　Forth ryding from *Malbeccoes* hostlesse hous,
　Far off aspyde a young man, the which fled
　From an huge Geaunt, that with hideous
　And hatefull outrage long him chaced thus ;
　It was that *Ollyphant*, the brother deare
　Of that *Argante* vile and vitious,
　From whom the *Squire of Dames* was reft
　　whylere ;
This all as bad as she, and worse, if worse ought
　were.

4

For as the sister did in feminine
　And filthy lust exceede all woman kind,
　So he surpassed his sex masculine,
　In beastly vse that I did euer find ;
　Whom when as *Britomart* beheld behind
　The fearefull boy so greedily pursew,
　She was emmoued in her noble mind,
　T'employ her puissaunce to his reskew,
And pricked fiercely forward, where she him did
　vew.

5

Ne was Sir *Satyrane* her far behinde,
　But with like fiercenesse did ensew the chace :
　Whom when the Gyaunt saw, he soone resinde
　His former suit, and from them fled apace ;
　They after both, and boldly bad him bace,
　And each did striue the other to out-goe,
　But he them both outran a wondrous space,
　For he was long, and swift as any Roe,
And now made better speed, t'escape his feared
　foe.

6

It was not *Satyrane*, whom he did feare,
　But *Britomart* the flowre of chastity ;
　For he the powre of chast hands might not
　　beare,
　But alwayes did their dread encounter fly
　And now so fast his feet he did apply,
　That he has gotten to a forrest neare,
　Where he is shrowded in security.
The wood they enter, and search euery where,
They searched diuersely, so both diuided were.

7

Faire *Britomart* so long him followed,
　That she at last came to a fountaine sheare,
　By which there lay a knight all wallowed
　Vpon the grassy ground, and by him neare
　His haberieon, his helmet, and his speare ;
　A little off, his shield was rudely throwne,
　On which the winged boy in colours cleare
　Depeincted was, full easie to be knowne,
And he thereby, where euer it in field was
　showne.

8

His face vpon the ground did groueling ly,
　As if he had bene slombring in the shade,
　That the braue Mayd would not for courtesy,
　Out of his quiet slomber him abrade,
　Nor seeme too suddeinly him to inuade :
　Still as she stood, she heard with grieuous
　　throb
　Him grone, as if his hart were peeces made,
　And with most painefull pangs to sigh and sob,
That pitty did the Virgins hart of patience rob.

9

At last forth breaking into bitter plaintes
  He said ; O soueraigne Lord that sit'st on hye,
  And raignst in blis emongst thy blessed Saintes,
  How suffrest thou such shamefull cruelty,
  So long vnwreaked of thine enimy ?
  Or hast thou, Lord, of good mens cause no heed?
  Or doth thy iustice sleepe, and silent ly ?
  What booteth then the good and righteous deed,
If goodnesse find no grace, nor righteousnesse
  no meed ?

10

If good find grace, and righteousnesse reward,
  Why then is *Amoret* in caytiue band,
  Sith that more bounteous creature neuer far'd
  On foot, vpon the face of liuing land ?
  Or if that heauenly iustice may withstand
  The wrongfull outrage of vnrighteous men,
  Why then is *Busirane* with wicked hand
  Suffred, these seuen monethes day in secret den
My Lady and my loue so cruelly to pen ?

11

My Lady and my loue is cruelly pend
  In dolefull darkenesse from the vew of day,
  Whilest deadly torments do her chast brest
    rend,
  And the sharpe steele doth riue her hart in tway,
  All for she *Scudamore* will not denay.
  Yet thou vile man, vile *Scudamore* art sound,
  Ne canst her ayde, ne canst her foe dismay ;
  Vnworthy wretch to tread vpon the ground,
For whom so faire a Lady feeles so sore a
    wound.

12

There an huge heape of singultes did oppresse
  His strugling soule, and swelling throbs em-
    peach
  His foltring toung with pangs of drerinesse,
  Choking the remnant of his plaintife speach,
  As if his dayes were come to their last reach.
  Which when she heard, and saw the ghastly fit,
  Threatning into his life to make a breach,
  Both with great ruth and terrour she was smit,
Fearing least from her cage the wearie soule
    would flit.

13

Tho stooping downe she him amoued light ;
  Who therewith somewhat starting, vp gan looke,
  And seeing him behind a straunger knight,
  Whereas no liuing creature he mistooke,
  With great indignaunce he that sight forsooke,
  And downe againe himselfe disdainefully
  Abiecting, th'earth with his faire forhead
    strooke :
  Which the bold Virgin seeing, gan apply
Fit medcine to his griefe, and spake thus
  courtesly.

14

Ah gentle knight, whose deepe conceiued griefe
  Well seemes t'exceede the powre of patience,
  Yet if that heauenly grace some good reliefe
  You send, submit you to high prouidence,
  And euer in your noble hart prepense,
  That all the sorrow in the world is lesse,
  Then vertues might, and values confidence,
  For who nill bide the burden of distresse,
Must not here thinke to liue : for life is
  wretchednesse.

15

Therefore, faire Sir, do comfort to you take,
  And freely read, what wicked felon so
  Hath outrag'd you, and thrald your gentle make.
  Perhaps this hand may helpe to ease your woe,
  And wreake your sorrow on your cruell foe,
  At least it faire endeuour will apply.
  Those feeling wordes so neare the quicke did
    goe,
  That vp his head he reared easily,
And leaning on his elbow, these few wordes let
  fly.

16

What boots it plaine, that cannot be redrest,
  And sow vaine sorrow in a fruitlesse eare,
  Sith powre of hand, nor skill of learned brest,
  Ne worldly price cannot redeeme my deare,
  Out of her thraldome and continuall feare ?
  For he the tyraunt, which her hath in ward
  By strong enchauntments and blacke Magicke
    leare,
  Hath in a dungeon deepe her close embard,
And many dreadfull feends hath pointed to her
  gard.

17

There he tormenteth her most terribly,
  And day and night afflicts with mortall paine,
  Because to yield him loue she doth deny,
  Once to me yold, not to be yold againe :
  But yet by torture he would her constraine
  Loue to conceiue in her disdainfull brest ;
  Till so she do, she must in doole remaine,
  Ne may by liuing meanes be thence relest :
What boots it then to plaine, that cannot be
  redrest ?

18

With this sad hersall of his heauy stresse,
  The warlike Damzell was empassiond sore,
  And said ; Sir knight, your cause is nothing lesse,
  Then is your sorrow, certes if not more ;
  For nothing so much pitty doth implore,
  As gentle Ladies helplesse misery.
  But yet, if please ye listen to my lore,
  I will with proofe of last extremity,
Deliuer her fro thence, or with her for you dy.

19

Ah gentlest knight aliue, (said *Scudamore*)
What huge heroicke magnanimity
Dwels in thy bounteous brest ? what couldst
thou more,
If she were thine, and thou as now am I ?
O spare thy happy dayes, and them apply
To better boot, but let me dye, that ought ;
More is more losse : one is enough to dy.
Life is not lost, (said she) for which is bought
Endlesse renowm, that more then death is to be
sought.

20

Thus she at length perswaded him to rise,
And with her wend, to see what new successe
Mote him befall vpon new enterprise ;
His armes, which he had vowed to disprofesse,
She gathered vp and did about him dresse,
And his forwandred steed vnto him got :
So forth they both yfere make their progresse,
And march not past the mountenaunce of a shot,
Till they arriu'd, whereas their purpose they did
plot.

21

There they dismounting, drew their weapons bold
And stoutly came vnto the Castle gate ;
Whereas no gate they found, them to withhold,
Nor ward to wait at morne and euening late,
But in the Porch, that did them sore amate,
A flaming fire, ymixt with smouldry smoke,
And stinking Sulphure, that with griesly hate
And dreadfull horrour did all entraunce choke,
Enforced them their forward footing to reuoke.

22

Greatly thereat was *Britomart* dismayd,
Ne in that stownd wist, how her selfe to beare;
For daunger vaine it were, to haue assay'd
That cruell element, which all things feare,
Ne none can suffer to approchen neare :
And turning backe to *Scudamour*, thus sayd ;
What monstrous enmity prouoke we heare,
Foolhardy as th'Earthes children, the which
made
Battell against the Gods ? so we a God inuade.

23

Daunger without discretion to attempt,
Inglorious and beastlike is : therefore Sir
knight,
Aread what course of you is safest dempt,
And how we with our foe may come to fight,
This is (quoth he) the dolorous despight,
Which earst to you I playnd : for neither may
This fire be quencht by any wit or might,
Ne yet by any meanes remou'd away,
So mighty be th'enchauntments, which the
same do stay.

24

What is there else, but cease these fruitlesse
paines,
And leaue me to my former languishing ?
Faire *Amoret* must dwell in wicked chaines,
And *Scudamore* here dye with sorrowing.
Perdy not so ; (said she) for shamefull thing
It were t'abandon noble cheuisaunce,
For shew of perill, without venturing :
Rather let try extremities of chaunce,
Then enterprised prayse for dread to disauaunce.

25

Therewith resolu'd to proue her vtmost might,
Her ample shield she threw before her face,
And her swords point directing forward right,
Assayld the flame, the which eftsoones gaue
place,
And did it selfe diuide with equall space,
That through she passed ; as a thunder bolt
Perceth the yielding ayre, and doth displace
The soring clouds into sad showres ymolt ;
So to her yold the flames, and did their force
reuolt.

26

Whom whenas *Scudamour* saw past the fire,
Safe and vntoucht, he likewise gan assay,
With greedy will, and enuious desire,
And bad the stubborne flames to yield him
way :
But cruell *Mulciber* would not obay
His threatfull pride, but did the more augment
His mighty rage, and with imperious sway
Him forst (maulgre) his fiercenesse to relent,
And backe retire, all scorcht and pitifully brent.

27

With huge impatience he inly swelt,
More for great sorrow, that he could not pas,
Then for the burning torment, which he felt,
That with fell woodnesse he effierced was,
And wilfully him throwing on the gras,
Did beat and bounse his head and brest full sore ;
The whiles the Championesse now entred has
The vtmost rowme, and past the formest dore,
The vtmost rowme, abounding with all precious
store.

28

For round about, the wals yclothed were
With goodly arras of great maiesty,
Wouen with gold and silke so close and nere,
That the rich metall lurked priuily,
As faining to be hid from enuious eye ;
Yet here, and there, and euery where vnwares
It shewd it selfe, and shone vnwillingly ;
Like a discolourd Snake, whose hidden snares
Through the greene gras his long bright bur-
nisht backe declares.

29

And in those Tapets weren fashioned
Many faire pourtraicts, and many a faire feate,
And all of loue, and all of lusty-hed,
As seemed by their semblaunt did entreat;
And eke all *Cupids* warres they did repeate,
And cruell battels, which he whilome fought
Gainst all the Gods, to make his empire great;
Besides the huge massacres, which he wrought
On mighty kings and kesars, into thraldome
  brought.

30

Therein was writ, how often thundring *Ioue*
Had felt the point of his hart-percing dart,
And leauing heauens kingdome, here did roue
In straunge disguize, to slake his scalding
  smart;
Now like a Ram, faire *Helle* to peruart,
Now like a Bull, *Europa* to withdraw:
Ah, how the fearefull Ladies tender hart
Did liuely seeme to tremble, when she saw
The huge seas vnder her t'obay her seruaunts
  law.

31

Soone after that into a golden showre
Him selfe he chaung'd faire *Danaë* to vew,
And through the roofe of her strong brasen
  towre
Did raine into her lap an hony dew,
The whiles her foolish garde, that little knew
Of such deceipt, kept th'yron dore fast bard,
And watcht, that none should enter nor issew;
Vaine was the watch, and bootlesse all the
  ward,
Whenas the God to golden hew him selfe trans-
  fard.

32

Then was he turnd into a snowy Swan,
To win faire *Leda* to his louely trade:
O wondrous skill, and sweet wit of the man,
That her in daffadillies sleeping made,
From scorching heat her daintie limbes to shade:
Whiles the proud Bird ruffing his fethers wyde,
And brushing his faire brest, did her inuade:
She slept, yet twixt her eyelids closely spyde,
How towards her he rusht, and smiled at his
  pryde.

33

Then shewd it, how the *Thebane Semelee*
Deceiu'd of gealous *Iuno*, did require
To see him in his soueraigne maiestee,
Armd with his thunderbolts and lightning fire,
Whence dearely she with death bought her
  desire.
But faire *Alcmena* better match did make,
Ioying his loue in likenesse more entire;
Three nights in one, they say, that for her sake
He then did put, her pleasures lenger to partake.

34

Twise was he seene in soaring Eagles shape,
And with wide wings to beat the buxome ayre,
Once, when he with *Asterie* did scape,
Againe, when as the *Troiane* boy so faire
He snatcht from *Ida* hill, and with him bare:
Wondrous delight it was, there to behould,
How the rude Shepheards after him did stare,
Trembling through feare, least down he fallen
  should,
And often to him calling, to take surer hould.

35

In *Satyres* shape *Antiopa* he snatcht:
And like a fire, when he *Aegin'* assayd:
A shepheard, when *Mnemosyne* he catcht:
And like a Serpent to the *Thracian* mayd.
Whiles thus on earth great *Ioue* these page-
  aunts playd,
The winged boy did thrust into his throne,
And scoffing, thus vnto his mother sayd,
Lo now the heauens obey to me alone,
And take me for their *Ioue*, whiles *Ioue* to earth
  is gone.

36

And thou, faire *Phœbus*, in thy colours bright
Wast there enwouen, and the sad distresse,
In which that boy thee plonged, for despight,
That thou bewray'dst his mothers wantonnesse,
When she with *Mars* was meynt in ioyfulnesse:
For thy he thrild thee with a leaden dart,
To loue faire *Daphne*, which thee loued lesse:
Lesse she thee lou'd, then was thy iust desart,
Yet was thy loue her death, and her death was
  thy smart.

37

So louedst thou the lusty *Hyacinct*,
So louedst thou the faire *Coronis* deare:
Yet both are of thy haplesse hand extinct,
Yet both in flowres do liue, and loue thee beare,
The one a Paunce, the other a sweet breare:
For griefe whereof, ye mote haue liuely seene
The God himselfe rending his golden heare,
And breaking quite his gyrlond euer greene,
With other signes of sorrow and impatient teene.

38

Both for those two, and for his owne deare
  sonne,
The sonne of *Climene* he did repent,
Who bold to guide the charet of the Sunne,
Himselfe in thousand peeces fondly rent,
And all the world with flashing fier brent;
So like, that all the walles did seeme to flame.
Yet cruell *Cupid*, not herewith content,
Forst him eftsoones to follow other game,
And loue a Shepheards daughter for his dearest
• Dame.

39

He loued *Isse* for his dearest Dame,
And for her sake her cattell fed a while,
And for her sake a cowheard vile became,
The seruant of *Admetus* cowheard vile,
Whiles that from heauen he suffered exile.
Long were to tell each other louely fit,
Now like a Lyon, hunting after spoile,
Now like a Stag, now like a faulcon flit :
All which in that faire arras was most liuely writ.

40

Next vnto him was *Neptune* pictured,
In his diuine resemblance wondrous lyke :
His face was rugged, and his hoarie hed
Dropped with brackish deaw ; his three-forkt
Pyke   [stryke
He stearnly shooke, and therewith fierce did
The raging billowes, that on euery syde
They trembling stood, and made a long broad
dyke,
That his swift charet might haue passage wyde,
Which foure great *Hippodames* did draw in
temewise tyde.

41

His sea-horses did seeme to snort amayne,
And from their nosethrilles blow the brynie
streame,   [agayne,
hat made the sparckling waues to smoke
and flame with gold, but the white fomy creame,
Did shine with siluer, and shoot forth his beame.
The God himselfe did pensiue seeme and sad,
And hong adowne his head, as he did dreame :
For priuy loue his brest empierced had,
Ne ought but deare *Bisaltis* ay could make him
glad.

42

He loued eke *Iphimedia* deare,
And *Aeolus* faire daughter *Arne* hight,
For whom he turnd him selfe into a Steare,
And fed on fodder, to beguile her sight.
Also to win *Deucalions* daughter bright,
He turnd him selfe into a Dolphin fayre ;
And like a winged horse he tooke his flight,
To snaky-locke *Medusa* to repayre,
On whom he got faire *Pegasus,* that flitteth in
the ayre.

43

Next *Saturne* was, (but who would euer weene,
That sullein *Saturne* euer weend to loue ?
Yet loue is sullein, and *Saturnlike* seene,
As he did for *Erigone* it proue,)
That to a *Centaure* did him selfe transmoue.
So proou'd it eke that gracious God of wine,
When for to compasse *Philliras* hard loue,
He turnd himselfe into a fruitfull vine,
And into her faire bosome made his grapes
decline.

44

Long were to tell the amorous assayes,
And gentle pangues, with which he maked meeke
The mighty *Mars,* to learne his wanton playes :
How oft for *Venus,* and how often eek
For many other Nymphes he sore did shreek,
With womanish tcares, and with vnwarlike
Priuily moystenirg nis horrid cheek. [smarts,
There was he painted full of burning darts,
And many wide woundes launched through his
inner parts.

45

Ne did he spare (so cruell was the Elfe)
His owne deare mother, (ah why should he so?)
Ne did he spare sometime to pricke himselfe,
That he might tast the sweet consuming woe,
Which he had wrought to many others moe.
But to declare the mournfull Tragedyes,
And spoiles, wherewith he all the ground did
strow,
More eath to number, with how many eyes
High heauen beholds sad louers nightly
theeuereyes.

46

Kings Queenes, Lords Ladies, Knights and
Damzels gent
Were heap'd together with the vulgar sort,
And mingled with the raskall rablement,
Without respect of person or of port,
To shew Dan *Cupids* powre and great effort :
And round about a border was entrayld,
Of broken bowes and arrowes shiuered short,
And a long bloudy riuer through them rayld,
So liuely and so like, that liuing sence it fayld.

47

And at the vpper end of that faire rowme,
There was an Altar built of pretious stone,
Of passing valew, and of great renowme,
On which there stood an Image all alone,
Of massy gold, which with his owne light shone ;
And wings it had with sundry colours dight,
More sundry colours, then the proud *Pauone*
Beares in his boasted fan, or *Iris* bright,
When her discolourd bow she spreds through
heauen bright.

48

Blindfold he was, and in his cruell fist
A mortall bow and arrowes keene did hold,
With which he shot at randon, when him list,
Some headed with sad lead, some with pure
gold ;
(Ah man beware, how thou those darts behold)
A wounded Dragon vnder him did ly,
Whose hideous tayle his left foot did enfold,
And with a shaft was shot through either eye,
That no man forth might draw, ne no man
remedye.

49

And vnderneath his feet was written thus,
　Vnto the Victor of the Gods this bee :
And all the people in that ample hous
　Did to that image bow their humble knee,
　And oft committed fowle Idolatree.
That wondrous sight faire *Britomart* amazed,
　Ne seeing could her wonder satisfie,
　But euermore and more vpon it gazed,
The whiles the passing brightnes her fraile sences dazed.

50

Tho as she backward cast her busie eye,
　To search each secret of that goodly sted,
　Ouer the dore thus written she did spye
Be bold : she oft and oft it ouer-red,
　Yet could not find what sence it figured :
But what so were therein or writ or ment,
　She was no whit thereby discouraged
　From prosecuting of her first intent,
But forward with bold steps into the next roome went.

51

Much fairer, then the former, was that roome,
　And richlier by many partes arayd :
For not with arras made in painefull loome,
　But with pure gold it all was ouerlayd,
　Wrought with wilde Antickes, which their follies playd,
In the rich metall, as they liuing were :
　A thousand monstrous formes therein were made,
　Such as false loue doth oft vpon him weare,
For loue in thousand monstrous formes doth oft appeare.

52

And all about, the glistring walles were hong
　With warlike spoiles, and with victorious prayes,
Of mighty Conquerours and Captaines strong,
　Which were whilome captiued in their dayes
　To cruell loue, and wrought their owne decayes :
Their swerds and speres were broke, and hauberques rent ;
　And their proud girlonds of tryumphant bayes
　Troden in dust with fury insolent,
To shew the victors might and mercilesse intent.

53

The warlike Mayde beholding earnestly
　The goodly ordinance of this rich place,
Did greatly wonder, ne could satisfie
　Her greedy eyes with gazing a long space,
　But more she meruaild that no footings trace,
Nor wight appear'd, but wastefull emptinesse,
　And solemne silence ouer all that place :
　Straunge thing it seem'd, that none was to possesse　　　[fulnesse.
So rich purueyance, ne them keepe with care-

54

And as she lookt about, she did behold,
　How ouer that same dore was likewise writ.
Be bold, be bold, and euery where *Be bold,*
　That much she muz'd, yet could not construe it
　By any ridling skill, or commune wit.
At last she spyde at that roomes vpper end,
　Another yron dore, on which was writ,
　Be not too bold ; whereto though she did bend
Her earnest mind, yet wist not what it might intend.

55

Thus she there waited vntill euentyde,
　Yet liuing creature none she saw appeare :
And now sad shadowes gan the world to hyde,
　From mortall vew, and wrap in darkenesse dreare ;
　Yet nould she d'off her weary armes, for feare
Of secret daunger, ne let sleepe oppresse
　Her heauy eyes with natures burdein deare,
　But drew her selfe aside in sickernesse,
And her welpointed weapons did about her dresse.

Cant. XII.

∞∞∞∞∞∞∞∞∞∞∞∞∞∞∞∞∞∞∞∞

The maske of Cupid, and th'enchaunted
　　Chamber are displayd.
Whence Britomart redeemes faire
　　Amoret, through charmes decayd.

∞∞∞∞∞∞∞∞∞∞∞∞∞∞∞∞∞∞∞∞

1

Tho when as chearelesse Night ycouered had
　Faire heauen with an vniuersall cloud,
That euery wight dismayd with darknesse sad,
　In silence and in sleepe themselues did shroud,
　She heard a shrilling Trompet sound aloud,
Signe of nigh battell, or got victory ;
　Nought therewith daunted was her courage proud,
　But rather stird to cruell enmity,
Expecting euer, when some foe she might descry.

2

With that, an hideous storme of winde arose,
　With dreadfull thunder and lightning atwixt,
And an earth-quake, as if it streight would lose
　The worlds foundations from his centre fixt ;
　A direfull stench of smoke and sulphure mixt
Ensewd, whose noyance fild the fearefull sted,
　From the fourth houre of night vntill the sixt ;
　Yet the bold *Britonesse* was nought ydred,
Though much emmou'd, but stedfast still perseuered.

3

All suddenly a stormy whirlwind blew
  Throughout the house, that clapped euery dore,
  With which that yron wicket open flew,
  As it with mightie leuers had bene tore :
  And forth issewd, as on the ready flore
  Of some Theatre, a graue personage,
  That in his hand a branch of laurell bore,
  With comely haueour and count'nance sage,
Yclad in costly garments, fit for tragicke Stage.

4

Proceeding to the midst, he still did stand,
  As if in mind he somewhat had to say,
  And to the vulgar beckning with his hand,
  In signe of silence, as to heare a play,
  By liuely actions he gan bewray
  Some argument of matter passioned ;
  Which doen, he backe retyred soft away,
  And passing by, his name discouered,
Ease, on his robe in golden letters cyphered.

5

The noble Mayd, still standing all this vewd,
  And merueild at his strange intendiment ;
  With that a ioyous fellowship issewd
  Of Minstrals, making goodly meriment,
  With wanton Bardes, and Rymers impudent,
  All which together sung full chearefully
  A lay of loues delight, with sweet concent :
  After whom marcht a iolly company,
In manner of a maske, enranged orderly.

6

The whiles a most delitious harmony,
  In full straunge notes was sweetly heard to
    sound,
  That the rare sweetnesse of the melody
  The feeble senses wholly did confound,
  And the fraile soule in deepe delight nigh dround:
  And when it ceast, shrill trompets loud did bray,
  That their report did farre away rebound,
  And when they ceast, it gan againe to play,
The whiles the maskers marched forth in trim
  aray.

7

The first was *Fancy*, like a louely boy,
  Of rare aspect, and beautie without peare ;
  Matchable either to that ympe of *Troy*,
  Whom *Ioue* did loue, and chose his cup to beare,
  Or that same daintie lad, which was so deare
  To great *Alcides*, that when as he dyde,
  He wailed womanlike with many a teare,
  And euery wood, and euery valley wyde
He fild with *Hylas* name ; the Nymphes eke
  Hylas cryde.

8

His garment neither was of silke nor say,
  But painted plumes, in goodly order dight,
  Like as the sunburnt *Indians* do aray
  Their tawney bodies, in their proudest plight :
  As those same plumes, so seemd he vaine and
    light,
  That by his gate might easily appeare ;
  For still he far'd as dauncing in delight,
  And in his hand a windy fan did beare,
That in the idle aire he mou'd still here and there.

9

And him beside marcht amorous *Desyre*,
  Whose seemd of riper yeares, then th'other Swaine,
  Yet was that other swayne this elders syre,
  And gaue him being, commune to them twaine :
  His garment was disguised very vaine,
  And his embrodered Bonet sat awry ;
  Twixt both his hands few sparkes he close did
    straine,
  Which still he blew, and kindled busily,
That soone they life conceiu'd, and forth in
  flames did fly.

10

Next after him went *Doubt*, who was yclad
  In a discolour'd cote, of straunge disguyse,
  That at his backe a brode Capuccio had,
  And sleeues dependant *Albanese*-wyse :
  He lookt askew with his mistrustfull eyes,
  And nicely trode, as thornes lay in his way,
  Or that the flore to shrinke he did auyse,
  And on a broken reed he still did stay
His feeble steps, which shrunke, when hard
  theron he lay.

11

With him went *Daunger*, cloth'd in ragged weed,
  Made of Beares skin, that him more dreadfull
    made,
  Yet his owne face was dreadfull, ne did need
  Straunge horrour, to deforme his griesly shade :
  A net in th'one hand, and a rustie blade
  In th'other was, this Mischiefe, that Mishap ;
  With th'one his foes he threatned to inuade,
  With th'other he his friends ment to enwrap :
For whom he could not kill, he practizd to
  entrap.

12

Next him was *Feare*, all arm'd from top to toe,
  Yet thought himselfe not safe enough thereby,
  But feard each shadow mouing to and fro,
  And his owne armes when glittering he did spy,
  Or clashing heard, he fast away did fly,
  As ashes pale of hew, and wingyheeld ;
  And euermore on daunger fixt his eye,
  Gainst whom he alwaies bent a brasen shield,
Which his right hand vnarmed fearefully did
  wield.

13

With him went *Hope* in rancke, a handsome
  Mayd,
Of chearefull looke and louely to behold ;
In silken samite she was light arayd,
And her faire lockes were wouen vp in gold ;
She alway smyld, and in her hand did hold
An holy water Sprinckle, dipt in deowe,
With which she sprinckled fauours manifold,
On whom she list, and did great liking sheowe,
Great liking vnto many, but true loue to feowe.

14

And after them *Dissemblance*, and *Suspect*
Marcht in one rancke, yet a vnequall paire :
For she was gentle, and of milde aspect,
Courteous to all, and seeming debonaire,
Goodly adorned, and exceeding faire :
Yet was that all but painted, and purloynd,
And her bright browes were deckt with bor-
  rowed haire :
Her deedes were forged, and her words false
  coynd,
And alwaies in her hand two clewes of silke she
  twynd.

15

But he was foule, ill fauoured, and grim,
Vnder his eyebrowes looking still askaunce ;
And euer as *Dissemblance* laught on him,
He lowrd on her with daungerous eyeglaunce ;
Shewing his nature in his countenance ;
His rolling eyes did neuer rest in place,
But walkt each where, for feare of hid mis-
  chaunce,
Holding a lattice still before his face,
Through which he still did peepe, as forward he
  did pace.

16

Next him went *Griefe*, and *Fury* matcht yfere ;
Griefe all in sable sorrowfully clad,
Downe hanging his dull head with heauy chere,
Yet inly being more, then seeming sad :
A paire of Pincers in his hand he had,
With which he pinched people to the hart,
That from thenceforth a wretched life they lad,
In wilfull languor and consuming smart,
Dying each day with inward wounds of dolours
  dart.

17

But *Fury* was full ill appareiled
In rags, that naked nigh she did appeare,
With ghastly lookes and dreadfull drerihed ;
For from her backe her garments she did teare,
And from her head oft rent her snarled heare :
In her right hand a firebrand she did tosse
About her head, still roming here and there ;
As a dismayed Deare in chace embost,
Forgetfull of his safety, hath his right way lost.

18

After them went *Displeasure* and *Pleasance*,
He looking lompish and full sullein sad,
And hanging downe his heauy countenance ;
She chearefull fresh and full of ioyance glad,
As if no sorrow she ne felt ne drad ;
That euill matched paire they seemd to bee
An angry Waspe th'one in a viall had
Th'other in hers an hony-lady Bee ;
Thus marched these sixe couples forth in faire
  degree.

19

After all these there marcht a most faire Dame,
Led of two grysie villeins, th'one *Despight*,
The other cleped *Cruelty* by name :
She dolefull Lady, like a dreary Spright,
Cald by strong charmes out of eternall night,
Had deathes owne image figurd in her face,
Full of sad signes, fearefull to liuing sight ;
Yet in that horror shewd a seemely grace,
And with her feeble feet did moue a comely pace.

20

Her brest all naked, as net iuory,
Without adorne of gold or siluer bright,
Wherewith the Craftesman wonts it beautify,
Of her dew honour was despoyled quight,
And a wide wound therein (O ruefull sight)
Entrenched deepe with knife accursed keene,
Yet freshly bleeding forth her fainting spright,
(The worke of cruell hand) was to be seene,
That dyde in sanguine red her skin all snowy
  cleene.

21

At that wide orifice her trembling hart
Was drawne forth, and in siluer basin layd,
Quite through transfixed with a deadly dart,
And in her bloud yet steeming fresh embayd :
And those two villeins, which her steps vpstayd,
When her weake feete could scarcely her sus-
  taine,
And fading vitall powers gan to fade,
Her forward still with torture did constraine,
And euermore encreased her consuming paine.

22

Next after her the winged God himselfe
Came riding on a Lion rauenous,
Taught to obay the menage of that Elfe,
That man and beast with powre imperious
Subdeweth to his kingdome tyrannous :
His blindfold eyes he bad a while vnbind,
That his proud spoyle of that same dolorous
Faire Dame he might behold in perfect kind :
Which seene, he much reioyced in his cruell
  mind.

23

Of which full proud, himselfe vp rearing hye,
  He looked round about with sterne disdaine ;
  And did suruay his goodly company :
  And marshalling the euill ordered traine,
  With that the darts which his right hand did
    straine,
  Full dreadfully he shooke that all did quake,
  And clapt on hie his coulourd winges twaine,
  That all his many it affraide did make :
Tho blinding him againe, his way he forth did
    take.

24

Behinde him was *Reproch, Repentance, Shame* ;
  Reproch the first, *Shame* next, *Repent* behind:
  Repentance feeble, sorrowfull, and lame:
  Reproch despightfull, carelesse, and vnkind ;
  Shame most ill fauourd, bestiall, and blind :
  Shame lowrd, *Repentance* sigh'd, *Reproch* did
    scould ;   [twind,
  Reproch sharpe stings, *Repentance* whips en-
  Shame burning brond-yrons in her hand did hold:
All three to each vnlike, yet all made in one
    mould.

25

And after them a rude confused rout
  Of persons flockt, whose names is hard to read:
  Emongst them was sterne *Strife*, and *Anger*
  Vnquiet *Care*, and fond *Vnthriftihead*, [stout,
  Lewd *Losse of Time*, and *Sorrow* seeming dead,
  Inconstant *Chaunge*, and false *Disloyaltie*,
  Consuming *Riotise*, and guilty *Dread*
  Of heauenly vengeance, faint *Infirmitie*,
Vile *Pouertie*, and lastly *Death* with infamie.

26

There were full many moe like maladies,
  Whose names and natures I note readen well;
  So many moe, as there be phantasies
  In wauering wemens wit, that none can tell,
  Or paines in loue, or punishments in hell ;
  All which disguized marcht in masking wise,
  About the chamber with that Damozell,
  And then returnéd, hauing marched thrise,
Into the inner roome, from whence they first did
    rise.

27

So soone as they were in, the dore streight way
  Fast locked, driuen with that stormy blast,
  Which first it opened ; and bore all away.
  Then the braue Maid, which all this while was
    plast
  In secret shade, and saw both first and last,
  Issewed forth, and went vnto the dore,
  To enter in, but found it locked fast :
  It vaine she thought with rigorous vprore
For to efforce, when charmes had closed it afore.

28

Where force might not auaile, there sleights and
    art
  She cast to vse, both fit for hard emprize ;
  For thy from that same roome not to depart
  Till morrow next, she did her selfe auize,
  When that same Maskeagaine should forth arize.
  The morrow next appeard with ioyous cheare,
  Calling men to their daily exercize,
  Then she, as morrow fresh, her selfe did reare
Out of her secret stand, that day for to out
    weare.

29

All that day she outwore in wandering,
  And gazing on that Chambers ornament,
  Till that againe the second euening
  Her couered with her sable vestiment,
  Wherewith the worlds faire beautie she hath
    blent :
  Then when the second watch was almost past,
  That brasen dore flew open, and in went
  Bold *Britomart*, as she had late forecast,
Neither of idle shewes, nor of false charmes
    aghast.

30

So soone as she was entred, round about
  She cast her eies, to see what was become
  Of all those persons, which she saw without :
  But lo, they streight were vanisht all and some,
  Ne liuing wight she saw in all that roome,
  Saue that same woefull Ladie, both whose hands
  Were bounden fast, that did her ill become,
  And her small wast girt round with yron bands,
Vnto a brasen pillour, by the which she stands.

31

And her before the vile Enchaunter sate,
  Figuring straunge characters of his art,
  With liuing bloud he those characters wrate,
  Dreadfully dropping from her dying hart,
  Seeming transfixed with a cruell dart,
  And all perforce to make her him to loue.
  Ah who can loue the worker of her smart ?
  A thousand charmes he formerly did proue ;
Yet thousand charmes could not her stedfast
    heart remoue.

32

Soone as that virgin knight he saw in place,
  His wicked bookes in hast he ouerthrew,
  Not caring his long labours to deface,
  And fiercely ronning to that Lady trew,
  A murdrous knife out of his pocket drew,
  The which he thought, for villeinous despight,
  In her tormented bodie to embrew :
  But the stout Damzell to him leaping light,
His cursed hand withheld, and maistered his
    might.

33

From her, to whom his fury first he ment,
  The wicked weapon rashly he did wrest,
  And turning to her selfe his fell intent,
  Vnwares it strooke into her snowie chest,
  That little drops empurpled her faire brest.
  Exceeding wroth therewith the virgin grew,
  Albe the wound were nothing deepe imprest,
  And fiercely forth her mortall blade she drew,
To giue him the reward for such vile outrage dew.

34

So mightily she smote him, that to ground
  He fell halfe dead; next stroke him should
    haue slaine,
  Had not the Lady, which by him stood bound,
  Dernely vnto her called to abstaine,
  From doing him to dy. For else her paine
  Should be remedilesse, sith none but hee,
  Which wrought it, could the same recure againe.
  Therewith she stayd her hand, loth stayd to bee;
For life she him enuyde, and long'd reuenge to
    see.

35

And to him said, Thou wicked man, whose meed
  For so huge mischiefe, and vile villany
  Is death, or if that ought do death exceed,
  Be sure, that nought may saue thee from to dy,
  But if that thou this Dame doe presently
  Restore vnto her health, and former state;
  This doe and liue, else die vndoubtedly.
  He glad of life, that lookt for death but late,
Did yield himselfe right willing to prolong his
    date.

36

And rising vp, gan streight to ouerlooke
  Those cursed leaues, his charmes backe to
    reuerse;
  Full dreadfull things out of that balefull booke
  He red, and measur'd many a sad verse,
  That horror gan the virgins hart to perse,
  And her faire locks vp stared stiffe on end,
  Hearing him those same bloudy lines reherse;
  And all the while he red, she did extend
Her sword high ouer him, if ought he did offend.

37

Anon she gan perceiue the house to quake,
  And all the dores to rattle round about;
  Yet all that did not her dismaied make,
  Nor slacke her threatfull hand for daungers
    dout,
  But still with stedfast eye and courage stout
  Abode, to weet what end would come of all.
  At last that mightie chaine, which round about
  Her tender waste was wound, adowne gan fall,
And that great brasen pillour broke in peeces
    small.

38

The cruell steele, which thrild her dying hart,
  Fell softly forth, as of his owne accord,
  And the wyde wound, which lately did dispart
  Her bleeding brest, and riuen bowels gor'd,
  Was closed vp, as it had not bene bor'd,
  And euery part to safety full sound,
  As she were neuer hurt, was soone restor'd:
  Tho when she felt her selfe to be vnbound,
And perfect hole, prostrate she fell vnto the
    ground.

39

Before faire *Britomart*, she fell prostrate,
  Saying, Ah noble knight, what worthy meed
  Can wretched Lady, quit from wofull state,
  Yield you in liew of this your gratious deed?
  Your vertue selfe her owne reward shall breed,
  Euen immortall praise, and glory wyde,
  Which I your vassall, by your prowesse freed,
  Shall through the world make to be notifyde,
And goodly well aduance, that goodly well was
    tryde.

40

But *Britomart* vprearing her from ground,
  Said, Gentle Dame, reward enough I weene
  For many labours more, then I haue found,
  This, that in safety now I haue you seene,
  And meane of your deliuerance haue beene:
  Henceforth faire Lady comfort to you take,
  And put away remembrance of late teene;
  In stead thereof know, that your louing Make,
Hath no lesse griefe endured for your gentle sake.

41

She much was cheard to heare him mentiond,
  Whom of all liuing wights she loued best.
  Then laid the noble Championesse strong hond
  Vpon th'enchaunter, which had her distrest
  So sore, and with foule outrages opprest:
  With that great chaine, wherewith not long ygo
  He bound that pitteous Lady prisoner, now
    relest,
  Himselfe she bound, more worthy to be so,
And captiue with her led to wretchednesse and
    wo.

42

Returning backe, those goodly roomes, which
    erst
  She saw so rich and royally arayd,
  Now vanisht vtterly, and cleane subuerst
  She found, and all their glory quite decayd,
  That sight of such a chaunge her much dismayd.
  Thence forth descending to that perlous Porch,
  Those dreadfull flames she also found delayd,
  And quenched quite, like a consumed torch,
That erst all entrers wont so cruelly to scorch.

43

More easie issew now, then entrance late
  She found: for now that fained dreadfull flame,
  Which chokt the porch of that enchaunted gate,
  And passage bard to all, that thither came,
  Was vanisht quite, as it were not the same,
  And gaue her leaue at pleasure forth to passe.
  Th'Enchaunter selfe, which all that fraud did frame,
  To haue efforst the loue of that faire lasse,
Seeing his worke now wasted deepe engrieued was.

44

But when the victoresse arriued there,
  Where late she left the pensife *Scudamore*,
  With her owne trusty Squire, both full of feare,
  Neither of them she found where she them lore:
  Thereat her noble hart was stonisht sore ;
  But most faire *Amoret,* whose gentle spright
  Now gan to feede on hope, which she before
  Conceiued had, to see her owne deare knight,
Being thereof beguyld was fild with new affright.

45

But he sad man, when he had long in drede
  Awayted there for *Britomarts* returne,
  Yet saw her not nor signe of her good speed,
  His expectation to despaire did turne,
  Misdeeming sure that her those flames did burne ;
  And therefore gan aduize with her old Squire,
  Who her deare nourslings losse no lesse did mourne,
  Thence to depart for further aide t'enquire :
Where let them wend at will, whilest here I doe respire.

Stanzas 43-45 *were first inserted in the* 1596 *quarto, displacing the following stanzas which concluded Book III in the first edition.*

At last she came vnto the place, where late
  She left Sir *Scudamour* in great distresse,
  Twixt dolour and despight halfe desperate,
  Of his loues succour, of his owne redresse,
  And of the hardie *Britomarts* successe :
  There on the cold earth him now thrown she found,
  In wilfull anguish, and dead heauinesse,
  And to him cald ; whose voices knowen sound
Soon as he heard, himself he reared light from ground.

There did he see, that most on earth him ioyd,
  His dearest loue, the comfort of his dayes,
  Whose too long absence him had sore annoyd
  And wearied his life with dull delayes :
  Straight he vpstarted from the loathed layes,
  And to her ran with hasty egernesse,
  Like as a Deare, that greedily embayes
  In the coole soile, after long thirstinesse,
Which he in chace endured hath, now nigh breath-lesse.

Lightly he clipt her twixt his armes twaine,
  And streightly did embrace her body bright,
  Her body, late the prison of sad paine,
  Now the sweet lodge of loue and deare delight :
  But she faire Lady ouercommen quight
  Of huge affection, did in pleasure melt,
  And in sweete rauishment pourd out her spright :
  No word they spake, nor earthly thing they felt,
But like two senceles stocks in long embracement dwelt.

Had ye them seene, ye would haue surely thought,
  That they had beene that faire *Hermaphrodite,*
  Which that rich *Romane* of white marble wrought,
  And in his costly Bath causd to bee site :
  So seemd those two, as growne together quite,
  That *Britomart* halfe enuying their blesse,
  Was much empassiond in her gentle sprite,
  And to her selfe oft wisht like happinesse,
In vaine she wisht, that fate n'ould let her yet possesse.

Thus doe those louers with sweet counteruayle,
  Each other of loues bitter fruit despoile.
  But now my teme begins to faint and fayle,
  All woxen weary of their iournall toyle :
  Therefore I will their sweatie yokes assoyle
  At this same furrowes end, till a new day :
  And ye faire Swayns, after your long turmoyle,
  Now cease your worke, and at your pleasure play;
Now cease your worke ; to morrow is an holy day.

THE SECOND

PART OF THE

FAERIE QVEENE.

Containing

THE FOVRTH,
FIFTH, AND
SIXTH BOOKES.

By Ed. Spenſer

Imprinted at London for VVilliam
Ponſonby. 1596

THE FOVRTH

BOOKE OF THE

FAERIE QVEENE.

Containing

The Legend of CAMBEL and TELAMOND,

OR

OF FRIENDSHIP.

1

The rugged forhead that with graue foresight
 Welds kingdomes causes, and affaires of state,
 My looser rimes (I wote) doth sharply wite,
 For praising loue, as I haue done of late,
 And magnifying louers deare debate ;
 By which fraile youth is oft to follie led,
 Through false allurement of that pleasing
  baite,
 That better were in vertues discipled,
Then with vaine poemes weeds to haue their
  fancies fed.

2

Such ones ill iudge of loue, that cannot loue,
 Ne in their frosen hearts feele kindly flame :
 For thy they ought not thing vnknowne
  reproue,
 Ne naturall affection faultlesse blame,
 For fault of few that haue abusd the same.
 For it of honor and all vertue is
 The roote, and brings forth glorious flowres
  of fame,
 That crowne true louers with immortall blis,
The meed of them that loue, and do not liue
  amisse.

3

Which who so list looke backe to former ages,
 And call to count the things that then were
  donne,
 Shall find, that all the workes of those wise
  sages,
 And braue exploits which great Heroes wonne,
 In loue were either ended or begunne :
 Witnesse the tather of Philosophie,
 Which to his *Critias*, shaded oft from sunne,
 Of loue full manie lessons did apply,
The which these Stoicke censours cannot well
  deny.

4

To such therefore I do not sing at all,
 But to that sacred Saint my soueraigne
  Queene,
 In whose chast breast all bountie naturall,
 And treasures of true loue enlocked beene,
 Boue all her sexe that euer yet was seene ;
 To her I sing of loue, that loueth best,
 And best is lou'd of all aliue I weene :
 To her this song most fitly is addrest,
The Queene of loue, and Prince of peace from
  heauen blest.

5

Which that she may the better deigne to heare,
  Do thou dred infant, *Venus* dearling doue,
  From her high spirit chase imperious feare,
  And vse of awfull Maiestie romoue :
  In sted thereof with drops of melting loue,
  Deawd with ambrosiall kisses, by thee gotten
  From thy sweete smyling mother from aboue,
  Sprinckle her heart, and haughtie courages soften,
That she may hearke to loue, and reade this
    lesson often.

Cant. I.

CXCXCXCXCXCXCXCXCXCXCXCXCXCXCX

> *Fayre Britomart saues Amoret,*
>   *Duessa discord breedes*
> *Twixt Scudamour and Blandamour :*
>   *Their fight and warlike deedes.*

CXCXCXCXCXCXCXCXCXCXCXCXCXCXCX

1

Of louers sad calamities of old,
  Full many piteous stories doe remaine,
  But none more piteous euer was ytold,
  Then that of *Amorets* hart-binding chaine,
  And this of *Florimels* vnworthie paine :
  The deare compassion of whose bitter fit
  My softened heart so sorely doth constraine,
That I with teares full oft doe pittie it,
And oftentimes doe wish it neuer had bene writ.

2

For from the time that *Scudamour* her bought
  In perilous fight, she neuer ioyed day,
  A perilous fight when he with force her brought
  From twentie Knights, that did him all assay :
  Yet fairely well he did them all dismay :
  And with great glorie both the shield of loue,
  And eke the Ladie selfe he brought away,
  Whom hauing wedded as did him behoue,
A new vnknowen mischiefe did from him re-
    moue.

3

For that same vile Enchauntour *Busyran*,
  The very selfe same day that she was wedded,
  Amidst the bridale feast, whilest euery man
  Surcharg'd with wine, were heedlesse and ill
    hedded,
  All bent to mirth before the bride was bedded,
  Brought in that mask of loue which late was
    showen :
  And there the Ladie ill of friends bestedded,
  By way of sport, as oft in maskes is knowen,
Conueyed quite away to liuing wight vnknowen.

4

Seuen moneths he so her kept in bitter smart,
  Because his sinfull lust she would not serue,
  Vntill such time as noble *Britomart*
  Released her, that else was like to sterue,
  Through cruell knife that her deare heart did
    kerue.
  And now she is with her vpon the way,
  Marching in louely wise, that could deserue
  No spot of blame, though spite did oft assay
To blot her with dishonor of so faire a pray.

5

Yet should it be a pleasant tale, to tell
  The diuerse vsage and demeanure daint,
  That each to other made, as oft befell.
  For *Amoret* right fearefull was and faint,
  Lest she with blame her honor should attaint,
  That euerie word did tremble as she spake,
  And euerie looke was coy, and wondrous quaint,
  And euerie limbe that touched her did quake :
Yet could she not but curteous countenance to
    her make.

6

For well she wist, as true it was indeed,
  That her liues Lord and patrone of her health
  Right well deserued as his duefull meed,
  Her loue, her seruice, and her vtmost wealth.
  All is his iustly, that all freely dealth :
  Nathlesse her honor dearer then her life,
  She sought to saue, as thing reseru'd from stealth;
  Die had she leuer with Enchanters knife,
Then to be false in loue, profest a virgine wife.

7

Thereto her feare was made so much the greater
  Through fine abusion of that Briton mayd :
  Who for to hide her fained sex the better,
  And maske her wounded mind, both did and
    sayd
  Full many things so doubtfull to be wayd,
  That well she wist not what by them to gesse,
  For other whiles to her she purpos made
  Of loue, and otherwhiles of lustfulnesse,
That much she feard his mind would grow to
    some excesse.

8

His will she feard ; for him she surely thought
  To be a man, such as indeed he seemed,
  And much the more, by that he lately wrought,
  When her from deadly thraldome he redeemed,
  For which no seruice she too much esteemed,
  Yet dread of shame, and doubt of fowle dishonor
  Made her not yeeld so much, as due she deemed,
  Yet *Britomart* attended duly on her,
As well became a knight, and did to her all honor.

9

It so befell one euening, that they came
Vnto a Castell, lodged there to bee,
Where many a knight, and many a louely Dame
Was then assembled, deeds of armes to see :
Amongst all which was none more faire then
   shee,
That many of them mou'd to eye her sore.
The custome of that place was such, that hee
Which had no loue nor lemman there in store,
Should either winne him one, or lye without
   the dore.

10

Amongst the rest there was a iolly knight,
Who being asked for his loue, auow'd
That fairest *Amoret* was his by right,
And offred that to iustifie alowd.
The warlike virgine seeing his so prowd
And boastfull chalenge, wexed inlie wroth,
But for the present did her anger shrowd ;
And sayd, her loue to lose she was full loth,
But either he should neither of them haue, or
   both.

11

So foorth they went, and both together giusted ;
But that same younker soone was ouerthrowne,
And made repent, that he had rashly lusted
For thing vnlawfull, that was not his owne :
Yet since he seemed valiant, though vnknowne,
She that no lesse was courteous then stout,
Cast how to salue, that both the custome showne
Were kept, and yet that Knight not locked out,
That seem'd full hard t'accord two things so
   far in dout.

12

The Seneschall was cal'd to deeme the right,
Whom she requir'd, that first fayre *Amoret*
Might be to her allow'd, as to a Knight,
That did her win and free from chalenge set :
Which straight to her was yeelded without let.
Then since that strange Knights loue from
   him was quitted,
She claim'd that to her selfe, as Ladies det,
He as a Knight might iustly be admitted ;
So none should be out shut, sith all of loues
   were fitted.

13

With that her glistring helmet she vnlaced ;
Which dofт, her golden lockes, that were vp
   bound
Still in a knot, vnto her heeles downe traced,
And like a silken veile in compasse round
About her backe and all her bodie wound :
Like as the shining skie in summers night,
What time the dayes with scorching heat abound,
Is creasted all with lines of firie light,
That it prodigious seemes in common peoples
   sight.

14

Such when those Knights and Ladies all about
Beheld her, all were with amazement smit,
And euery one gan grow in secret dout
Of this and that, according to each wit :
Some thought that some enchantment faygned
   it ;
Some, that *Bellona* in that warlike wise
To them appear'd, with shield and armour fit ;
Some, that it was a maske of strange disguise :
So diuersely each one did sundrie doubts deuise.

15

But that young Knight, which through her
   gentle deed
Was to that goodly fellowship restor'd,
Ten thousand thankes did yeeld her for her
   meed,
And doubly ouercommen, her ador'd :
So did they all their former strife accord ;
And eke fayre *Amoret* now freed from feare,
More franke affection did to her afford,
And to her bed, which she was wont forbeare,
Now freely drew, and found right safe assurance
   theare.

16

Where all that night they of their loues did treat,
And hard aduentures twixt themselues alone,
That each the other gan with passion great,
And griefull pittie priuately bemone.
The morow next so soone as *Titan* shone,
They both vprose, and to their waies them dight :
Long wandred they, yet neuer met with none,
That to their willes could them direct aright,
Or to them tydings tell, that mote their harts
   delight.

17

Lo thus they rode, till at the last they spide
Two armed Knights, that toward them did pace,
And ech of them had ryding by his side
A Ladie, seeming in so farre a space,
But Ladies none they were, albee in face
And outward shew faire semblance they did
   beare ;
For vnder maske of beautie and good grace,
Vile treason and fowle falshood hidden were,
That mote to none but to the warie wise appeare.

18

The one of them the false *Duessa* hight,
That now had chang'd her former wonted hew:
For she could d'on so manie shapes in sight,
As euer could Cameleon colours new ;
So could she forge all colours, saue the trew.
The other no whit better was then shee,
But that such as she was, she plaine did shew ;
Yet otherwise much worse, if worse might bee,
And dayly more offensiue vnto each degree.

19

Her name was *Ate*, mother of debate,
  And all dissention, which doth dayly grow
  Amongst fraile men, that many a publike state
  And many a priuate oft doth ouerthrow.
  Her false *Duessa* who full well did know,
  To be most fit to trouble noble knights,
  Which hunt for honor, raised from below,
  Out of the dwellings of the damned sprights,
Where she in darknes wastes her cursed daies
    and nights.

20

Hard by the gates of hell her dwelling is,
  There whereas all the plagues and harmes
    abound,
  Which punish wicked men, that walke amisse :
  It is a darksome delue farre vnder ground,
  With thornes and barren brakes enuirond
    round,
  That none the same may easily out win ;
  Yet many waies to enter may be found,
  But none to issue forth when one is in :
For discord harder is to end then to begin.

21

And all within the riuen walls were hung
  With ragged monuments of times forepast,
  All which the sad effects of discord sung :
  There were rent robes, and broken scepters plast,
  Altars defyl'd, and holy things defast,
  Disshiuered speares, and shields ytorne in
    twaine,
  Great cities ransackt, and strong castles rast,
  Nations captiued, and huge armies slaine :
Of all which ruines there some relicks did
    remaine.

22

There was the signe of antique Babylon,
  Of fatall Thebes, of Rome that raigned long,
  Of sacred Salem, and sad Ilion,
  For memorie of which on high there hong
  The golden Apple, cause of all their wrong,
  For which the three faire Goddesses did striue :
  There also was the name of *Nimrod* strong,
  Of *Alexander*, and his Princes fiue,
Which shar'd to them the spoiles that he had
    got aliue.

23

And there the relicks of the drunken fray,
  The which amongst the *Lapithees* befell,
  And of the bloodie feast, which sent away
  So many *Centaures* drunken soules to hell,
  That vnder great *Alcides* furie fell :
  And of the dreadfull discord, which did driue
  The noble *Argonauts* to outrage fell,
  That each of life sought others to depriue,
All mindlesse of the Golden fleece, which made
    them striue.

24

And eke of priuate persons many moe,
  That were too long a worke to count them all ;
  Some of sworne friends, that did their faith
    forgoe ;
  Some of borne brethren, prov'd vnnaturall ;
  Some of deare louers, foes perpetuall :
  Witnesse their broken bandes there to be seene,
  Their girlonds rent, their bowres despoyled all ;
  The moniments whereof there byding beene,
As plaine as at the first, when they were fresh
    and greene.

25

Such was her house within ; but all without,
  The barren ground was full of wicked weedes,
  Which she her selfe had sowen all about,
  Now growen great, at first of little seedes,
  The seedes of euill wordes, and factious deedes ;
  Which when to ripenesse due they growen arre,
  Bring foorth an infinite increase, that breedes
  Tumultuous trouble and contentious iarre,
The which most often end in bloudshed and
    in warre.

26

And those same cursed seedes doe also serue
  To her for bread, and yeeld her liuing food :
  For life it is to her, when others sterue
  Through mischieuous debate, and deadly feood,
  That she may sucke their life, and drinke their
    blood,
  With which she from her childhood had bene fed.
  For she at first was borne of hellish brood,
  And by infernall furies nourished,
That by her monstrous shape might easily
    be red.

27

Her face most fowle and filthy was to see,
  With squinted eyes contrarie wayes intended,
  And loathly mouth, vnmeete a mouth to bee,
  That nought but gall and venim comprehended,
  And wicked wordes that God and man offended :
  Her lying tongue was in two parts diuided,
  And both the parts did speake, and both
    contended ;
  And as her tongue, so was her hart discided,
That neuer thoght one thing, but doubly stil
    was guided.

28

Als as she double spake, so heard she double,
  With matchlesse eares deformed and distort,
  Fild with false rumors and seditious trouble,
  Bred in assemblies of the vulgar sort,
  That still are led with euery light report.
  And as her eares so eke her feet were odde,
  And much vnlike, th'one long, the other short,
  And both misplast ; that when th'one for-
    ward yode,
The other backe retired, and contrarie trode.

29

Likewise vnequall were her handes twaine,
  That one did reach, the other pusht away,
  That one did make, the other mard againe,
  And sought to bring all things vnto decay ;
  Whereby great riches gathered manie a day,
  She in short space did often bring to nought,
  And their possessours often did dismay.
For all her studie was and all her thought,
How she might ouerthrow the things that Con-
    cord wrought.

30

So much her malice did her might surpas,
  That euen th'Almightie selfe she did maligne,
  Because to man so mercifull he was,
  And vnto all his creatures so benigne,
  Sith she her selfe was of his grace indigne :
  For all this worlds faire workmanship she tride,
  Vnto his last confusion to bring,
  And that great golden chaine quite to diuide,
With which it blessed Concord hath together
    tide.

31

Such was that hag, which with *Duessa* roade,
  And seruing her in her malitious vse,
  To hurt good knights, was as it were her baude,
  To sell her borrowed beautie to abuse.
  For though like withered tree, that wanteth
    iuyce,
  She old and crooked were, yet now of late,
  As fresh and fragrant as the floure deluce
  She was become, by chaunge of her estate,
And made full goodly ioyance to her new found
    mate

32

Her mate he was a iollie youthfull knight,
  That bore great sway in armes and chiualrie,
  And was indeed a man of mickle might :
  His name was *Blandamour*, that did descrie
  His fickle mind full of inconstancie.
  And now himselfe he fitted had right well,
  With two companions of like qualitie,
  Faithlesse *Duessa*, and false *Paridell*,
That whether were more false, full hard it is
    to tell.

33

Now when this gallant with his goodly crew,
  From farre espide the famous *Britomart*,
  Like knight aduenturous in outward vew,
  With his faire paragon, his conquests part,
  Approching nigh, eftsoones his wanton hart
  Was tickled with delight, and iesting sayd ;
  Lo there Sir *Paridel*, for your desart,
  Good lucke presents you with yond louely
    mayd,
For pitie that ye want a fellow for your ayd.

34

By that the louely paire drew nigh to hond :
  Whom when as *Paridel* more plaine beheld,
  Albee in heart he like affection fond,
  Yet mindfull how he late by one was feld,
  That did those armes and that same scutchion
    weld,
  He had small lust to buy his loue so deare,
  But answerd, Sir him wise I neuer held,
  That hauing once escaped perill neare,
Would afterwards afresh the sleeping euill reare.

35

This knight too late his manhood and his might,
  I did assay, that me right dearely cost,
  Ne list I for reuenge prouoke new fight,
  Ne for light Ladies loue, that soone is lost.
  The hot-spurre youth so scorning to be crost,
  Take then to you this Dame of mine (quoth hee)
  And I without your perill or your cost,
  Will chalenge yond same other for my fee :
So forth he fiercely prickt, that one him scarce
    could see.

36

The warlike Britonesse her soone addrest,
  And with such vncouth welcome did receaue
  Her fayned Paramour, her forced guest,
  That being forst his saddle soone to leaue,
  Him selfe he did of his new loue deceaue :
  And made him selfe th'ensample of his follie.
  Which done, she passed forth not taking leaue,
  And left him now as sad, as whilome iollie,
Well warned to beware with whom he dar'd
    to dallie.

37

Which when his other companie beheld,
  They to his succour ran with readie ayd :
  And finding him vnable once to weld,
  They reared him on horsebacke, and vpstayd,
  Till on his way they had him forth conuayd :
  And all the way with wondrous griefe of mynd,
  And shame, he shewd him selfe to be dismayd,
  More for the loue which he had left behynd,
Then that which he had to Sir *Paridel* resynd.

38

Nathlesse he forth did march well as he might,
  And made good semblance to his companie,
  Dissembling his disease and euill plight ;
  Till ere long they chaunced to espie
  Two other knights, that towards them did ply
  With speedie course, as bent to charge them
    new.
  Whom when as *Blandamour* approching nie,
  Perceiu'd to be such as they seemd in vew,
He was full wo, and gan his former griefe renew.

39

For th'one of them he perfectly describe,
To be Sir *Scudamour*, by that he bore
The God of loue, with wings displayed wide,
Whom mortally he hated euermore,
Both for his worth, that all men did adore,
And eke because his loue he wonne by right :
Which when he thought, it grieued him full
      sore,
That through the bruses of his former fight,
He now vnable was to wreake his old despight.

40

For thy he thus to *Paridel* bespake,
Faire Sir, of friendship let me now you pray,
That as I late aduentured for your sake,
The hurts whereof me now from battell stay,
Ye will me now with like good turne repay,
And iustifie my cause on yonder knight.
Ah Sir (said *Paridel*) do not dismay
Your selfe for this, my selfe will for you fight,
As ye haue done for me : the left hand rubs
      the right.

41

With that he put his spurres vnto his steed,
With speare in rest, and toward him did fare,
Like shaft out of a bow preuenting speed.
But *Scudamour* was shortly well aware
Of his approch, and gan him selfe prepare
Him to receiue with entertainment meete.
So furiously they met, that either bare
The other downe vnder their horses feete,
That what of them became, themselues did
      scarsly weete.

42

As when two billowes in the Irish sowndes,
Forcibly driuen with contrarie tydes
Do meete together, each abacke rebowndes
With roaring rage ; and dashing on all sides,
That filleth all the sea with fome, diuydes
The doubtfull current i ito diuers wayes :
So fell those two in spirht of both their prydes,
But *Scudamour* himselfe did soone vprayse,
And mounting light his foe for lying long
      vpbrayes.

43

Who rolled on an heape lay still in swound,
All carelesse of his taunt and bitter rayle
Till that the rest him seeing lie on ground,
Ran hastily, to weete what did him ayle.
Where finding that the breath gan him to fayle,
With busie care they stroue him to awake,
And doft his helmet, and vndid his mayle :
So much they did, that at the last they brake
His slomber, yet so mazed, that he nothing
      spake.

44

Which when as *Blandamour* beheld, he sayd,
False faitour *Scudamour*, that hast by slight
And foule aduantage this good Knight dismayd,
A Knight much better then thy selfe behight,
Well falles it thee that I am not in plight
This day, to wreake the dammage by thee donne:
Such is thy wont, that still when any Knight
Is weakned, then thou doest him ouerronne :
So hast thou to thy selfe false honour often
      wonne.

45

He little answer'd, but in manly heart
His mightie indignation did forbeare,
Which was not yet so secret, but some part
Thereof did in his frouning face appeare :
Like as a gloomie cloud, the which doth beare
An hideous storme, is by the Northerne blast
Quite ouerblowne, yet doth not passe so cleare,
But that it all the skie doth ouercast
With darknes dred, and threatens all the world
      to wast.

46

Ah gentle knight, then false *Duessa* sayd,
Why do ye striue for Ladies loue so sore,
Whose chiefe desire is loue and friendly aid
Mongst gentle Knights to nourish euermore?
Ne be ye wroth Sir *Scudamour* therefore,
That she your loue list loue another knight,
Ne do your selfe dislike a whit the more ;
For Loue is free, and led with selfe delight,
Ne will enforced be with maisterdome or might.

47

So false *Duessa*, but vile *Ate* thus ;
Both foolish knights, I can but laugh at both,
That striue and storme with stirre outrageous,
For her that each of you alike doth loth,
And loues another, with whom now she goth
In louely wise, and sleepes, and sports, and
      playes ;
Whilest both you here with many a cursed oth,
Sweare she is yours, and stirre vp bloudie frayes,
To win a willow bough, whilest other weares
      the bayes.

48

Vile hag (sayd *Scudamour*) why dost thou lye ?
And falsly seekst a vertuous wight to shame ?
Fond knight (sayd she) the thing that with
      this eye
I saw, why should I doubt to tell the same ?
Then tell (quoth *Blandamour*) and feare no
      blame,
Tell what thou saw'st, maulgre who so it heares.
I saw (quoth she) a stranger knight, whose name
I wote not well, but in his shield he beares
(That well I wote) the heads of many broken
      spleares.

49

I saw him haue your *Amoret* at will,
I saw him kisse, I saw him her embrace,
I saw him sleepe with her all night his fill,
All manie nights, and manie by in place,
That present were to testifie the case.
Which when as *Scudamour* did heare, his heart
Was thrild within ward griefe, as when in chace
The Parthian strikes a stag with shiuering dart,
The beast astonisht stands in middest of his smart.

50

So stood Sir *Scudamour*, when this he heard,
Ne word he had to speake for great dismay,
But lookt on *Glauce* grim, who woxe afeard
Of outrage for the words, which she heard say,
Albee vntrue she wist them by assay.
But *Blandamour*, whenas he did espie
His chaunge of cheere, that anguish did bewray,
He woxe full blithe, as he had got thereby,
And gan thereat to triumph without victorie.

51

Lo recreant (sayd he) the fruitlesse end
Of thy vaine boast, and spoile of loue misgotten,
Whereby the name of knight-hood thou dost shend,
And all true louers with dishonor blotten,
All things not rooted well, will soone be rotten.
Fy fy false knight (then false *Duessa* cryde)
Vnworthy life that loue with guile hast gotten,
Be thou, where euer thou do go or ryde,
Loathed of ladies all, and of all knights defyde.

52

But *Scudamour* for passing great despight
Staid not to answer, scarcely did refraine,
But that in all those knights and ladies sight,
He for reuenge had guiltlesse *Glauce* slaine :
But being past, he thus began amaine ;
False traitour squire, false squire, of falsest knight,   [abstaine,
Why doth mine hand from thine auenge
Whose Lord hath done my loue this foule despight ?
Why do I not it wreake, on thee now in my might ?

53

Discourteous, disloyall *Britomart*,
Vntrue to God, and vnto man vniust,
What vengeance due can equall thy desart,
That hast with shamefull spot of sinfull lust
Defil'd the pledge committed to thy trust ?
Let vgly shame and endlesse infamy
Colour thy name with foule reproaches rust.
Yet thou false Squire his fault shalt deare aby,
And with thy punishment his penance shalt supply.

54

The aged Dame him seeing so enraged,
Was dead with feare, nathlesse as neede required,
His flaming furie sought to haue assuaged
With sober words, that sufferance desired,
Till time the tryall of her truth expyred :
And euermore sought *Britomart* to cleare.
But he the more with furious rage was fyred,
And thrise his hand to kill her did vpreare,
And thrise he drew it backe : so did at last forbeare.

Cant. II.

Blandamour winnes false Florimell,
Paridell for her striues,
They are accorded : Agape
doth lengthen her sonnes liues.

1

Firebrand of hell first tynd in Phlegeton,
By thousand furies, and from thence out throwen
Into this world, to worke confusion,
And set it all on fire by force vnknowen,
Is wicked discord, whose small sparkes once blowen
None but a God or godlike man can slake ;
Such as was *Orpheus*, that when strife was growen
Amongst those famous ympes of Greece, did take
His siluer Harpe in hand, and shortly friends them make.

2

Or such as that celestiall Psalmist was,
That when the wicked feend his Lord tormented,
With heauenly notes, that did all other pas,
The outrage of his furious fit relented.
Such Musicke is wise words with time concented,
To moderate stiffe minds, disposd to striue :
Such as that prudent Romane well inuented,
What time his people into partes did riue,
Them reconcyld againe, and to their homes did driue.

3

Such vs'd wise *Glauce* to that wrathfull knight,
To calme the tempest of his troubled thought :
Yet *Blandamour* with termes of foule despight,
And *Paridell* her scornd, and set at nought,
As old and crooked and not good for ought.
Both they vnwise, and warelesse of the euill,
That by themselues vnto themselues is wrought,
Through that false witch, and that foule aged dreuill,
The one a feend, the other an incarnate deuill.

4

With whom as they thus rode accompanide,
  They were encountred of a lustie Knight,
  That had a goodly Ladie by his side,
  To whom he made great dalliance and delight.
  It was to weete the bold Sir *Ferraugh* hight,
  He that from *Braggadocchio* whilome reft
  The snowy *Florimell*, whose beautie bright
  Made him seeme happie for so glorious theft ;
Yet was it in due triall but a wandring weft.

5

Which when as *Blandamour*, whose fancie light
  Was alwaies flitting as the wauering wind,
  After each beautie, that appeard in sight,
  Beheld, eftsoones it prickt his wanton mind
  With sting of lust, that reasons eye did blind,
  That to Sir *Paridell* these words he sent ;
  Sir knight why ride ye dumpish thus behind,
  Since so good fortune doth to you present
So fayre a spoyle, to make you ioyous meriment?

6

But *Paridell* that had too late a tryall
  Of the bad issue of his counsell vaine,
  List not to hearke, but made this faire denyall ;
  Last turne was mine, well proued to my paine,
  This now be yours, God send you better gaine.
  Whose scoffed words he taking halfe in scorne,
  Fiercely forth prickt his steed as in disdaine,
  Against that Knight, ere he him well could torne :
By meanes whereof he hath him lightly ouerborne.

7

Who with the sudden stroke astonisht sore,
  Vpon the ground a while in slomber lay ;
  The whiles his loue away the other bore,
  And shewing her, did *Paridell* vpbray :
  Lo sluggish Knight the victors happie pray :
  So fortune friends the bold : whom *Paridell*
  Seeing so faire indeede, as he did say,
  His hart with secret enuie gan to swell,
And inly grudge at him, that he had sped so well.

8

Nathlesse proud man himselfe the other deemed,
  Hauing so peerelesse paragon ygot :
  For sure the fayrest *Florimell* him seemed,
  To him was fallen for his happie lot,
  Whose like aliue on earth he weened not :
  Therefore he her did court, did serue, did wooe,
  With humblest suit that he imagine mot,
  And all things did deuise, and all things dooe,
That might her loue prepare, and liking win thereto.

9

She in regard thereof him recompenst
  With golden words, and goodly countenance,
  And such fond fauours sparingly dispenst :
  Sometimes him blessing with a light eye-glance,
  And coy lookes tempring with loose dalliance ;
  Sometimes estranging him in sterner wise,
  That hauing cast him in a foolish trance,
  He seemed brought to bed in Paradise,
And prou'd himselfe most foole, in what he seem'd most wise.

10

So great a mistresse of her art she was,
  And perfectly practiz'd in womans craft,
  That though therein himselfe he thought to pas,
  And by his false allurements wylie draft
  Had thousand women of their loue beraft,
  Yet now he was surpriz'd : for that false spright,
  Which that same witch had in this forme engraft,
  Was so expert in euery subtile slight,
That it could ouerreach the wisest earthly wight.

11

Yet he to her did dayly seruice more,
  And dayly more deceiued was thereby ;
  Yet *Paridell* him enuied therefore,
  As seeming plast in sole felicity :
  So blind is lust, false colours to descry.
  But *Ate* soone discouering his desire,
  And finding now fit opportunity
  To stirre vp strife, twixt loue and spight and ire,
Did priuily put coles vnto his secret fire.

12

By sundry meanes thereto she prickt him forth,
  Now with remembrance of those spightfull speaches,
  Now with opinion of his owne more worth,
  Now with recounting of like former breaches
  Made in their friendship, as that Hag him teaches :
  And euer when his passion is allayd,
  She it reuiues and new occasion reaches :
  That on a time as they together way'd,
He made him open chalenge, and thus boldly sayd.

13

Too boastfull *Blandamour*, too long I beare
  The open wrongs, thou doest me day by day ;
  Well know'st thou, when we friendship first did sweare,
  The couenant was, that euery spoyle or pray
  Should equally be shard betwixt vs tway :
  Where is my part then of this Ladie bright,
  Whom to thy selfe thou takest quite away ?
  Render therefore therein to me my right,
Or answere for thy wrong, as shall fall out in fight.

14

Exceeding wroth thereat was *Blandamour*,
And gan this bitter answere to him make ;
Too foolish *Paridell*, that fayrest floure
Wouldst gather faine, and yet no paines wouldst
But not so easie will I her forsake ;   [take:
This hand her wonne, this hand shall her defend.
With that they gan their shiuering speares to
shake,
And deadly points at eithers breast to bend,
Forgetfull each to haue bene euer others frend.

15

Their firie Steedes with so vntamed forse
Did beare them both to fell auenges end,
That both their speares with pitilesse remorse,
Through shield and mayle, and haberieon did
wend,
And in their flesh a griesly passage rend,
That with the furie of their owne affret,
Each other horse and man to ground did send;
Where lying still a while, both did forget
The perilous present stownd, in which their liues
were set.

16

As when two warlike Brigandines at sea,
With murdrous weapons arm'd to cruell fight,
Doe meete together on the watry lea,
They stemme ech other with so fell despight,
That with the shocke of their owne heedlesse
might,
Their wooden ribs are shaken nigh a sonder ;
They which from shore behold the dreadfull sight
Of flashing fire, and heare the ordenance thondcr,
Do greatly stand amaz'd at such vnwonted
wonder.

17

At length they both vpstarted in amaze,
As men awaked rashly out of dreme ;
And round about themselues a while did gaze,
Till seeing her, that *Florimell* did seme,
In doubt to whom she victorie should deeme,
Therewith their dulled sprights they edgd anew,
And drawing both theirswordswithrageextreme,
Like two mad mastiffes each on other flew,
And shields did share, and mailes did rash, and
helmes did hew.

18

So furiously each other did assayle
As if their soules they would attonce haue rent
Out of their brests, that streames of bloud did rayle
Adowne, as if their springs of life were spent ;
That all the ground with purple bloud was sprent,
And all their armours staynd with bloudie gore,
Yet scarcely once to breath would they relent,
So mortall was their malice and so sore,
Become of fayned friendship which they vow'd
afore.

19

And that which is for Ladies most besitting,
To stint all strife, and foster friendly peace,
Was from those Dames so farre and so vn-
fitting,
As that in stead of praying them surcease,
They did much more their cruelty encrease ;
Bidding them fight for honour of their loue,
And rather die then Ladies cause release.
With which vaine termes so much they did
them moue,
That both resolu'd the last extremities to proue.

20

There they I weene would fight vntill this day,
Had not a Squire, euen he the Squire of Dames,
By great aduenture trauelled that way ;
Who seeing both bent to so bloudy games,
And both of old well knowing by their names,
Drew nigh, to weete the cause of their debate :
And first laide on those Ladies thousand blames,
That did not seeke t'appease their deadly hate,
But gazed on their harmes, not pittying their
estate.

21

And then those Knights he humbly did beseech,
To stay their hands, till he a while had spoken:
Who lookt a little vp at that his speech,
Yet would not let their battell so be broken,
Both greedie fiers on other to be wroken.
Yet he to them so earnestly did call,
And them coniur'd by some wellknowen token,
That they at last their wrothfull hands let fall,
Content to heare him speake, and glad to rest
withall.

22

First he desir'd their cause of strife to see :
They said, it was for loue of *Florimell*.
Ah gentle knights (quoth he) how may that bee,
And she so farre astray, as none can tell.
Fond Squire, full angry then sayd *Paridell*,
Seest not the Ladie there before thy face ?
He looked backe, and her aduizing well,
Weend as he said, by that her outward grace,
That fayrest *Florimell* was present there in place.

23

Glad man was he to see that ioyous sight,
For none aliue but ioy'd in *Florimell*,
And lowly to her lowting thus behight ;
Fayrest of faire, that fairenesse doest excell,
This happie day I haue to greete you well,
In which you safe I see, whom thousand late
Misdoubted lost through mischiefe that befell;
Long may you liue in health and happie state.
She litle answer'd him, but lightly did aggrate.

24

Then turning to those Knights, he gan a new ;
And you Sir *Blandamour* and *Paridell*,
That for this Ladie present in your vew,
Haue rays'd this cruell warre and outrage fell,
Certes me seemes bene not aduised well,
But rather ought in friendship for her sake
To ioyne your force, their forces to repell,
That seeke perforce her from you both to take,
And of your gotten spoyle their owne triumph
    to make.

25

Thereat Sir *Blandamour* with countenance sterne,
All full of wrath, thus fiercely him bespake ;
A read thou Squire, that I the man may learne,
That dare fro me thinke *Florimell* to take.
Not one (quoth he) but many doe partake
Herein, as thus.   It lately so befell,
That *Satyran* a girdle did vptake,
Well knowne to appertaine to *Florimell*,
Which for her sake he wore, as him beseemed
    well.

26

But when as she her selfe was lost and gone,
Full many knights, that loued her like deare,
Thereat did greatly grudge, that he alone
That lost faire Ladies ornament should weare,
And gan therefore close spight to him to beare :
Which he to shun, and stop vile enuies sting,
Hath lately caus'd to be proclaim'd each where
A solemne feast, with publike turneying,
To which all knights with them their Ladies are
    to bring.

27

And of them all she that is fayrest found,
Shall haue that golden girdle for reward,
And of those Knights who is most stout on
    ground,
Shall to that fairest Ladie be prefard.
Since therefore she her selfe is now your ward,
To you that ornament of hers pertaines,
Against all those, that chalenge it to gard,
And saue her honour with your ventrous paines ;
That shall you win more glory, then ye here find
    gaines.

28

When they the reason of his words had hard,
They gan abate the rancour of their rage,
And with their honours and their loues regard,
The furious flames of malice to asswage.
Tho each to other did his faith engage,
Like faithfull friends thenceforth to ioyne in one
With all their force, and battell strong to wage
Gainst all those knights, as their professed fone,
That chaleng'd ought in *Florimell*, saue they
    alone.

29

So well accorded forth they rode together
In friendly sort, that lasted but a while ;
And of all old dislikes they made faire weather,
Yet all was forg'd and spred with golden foyle,
That vnder it hidde hate and hollow guyle.
Ne certes can that friendship long endure,
How euer gay and goodly be the style,
That doth ill cause or euill end enure :
For vertue is the band, that bindeth harts most
    sure.

30

Thus as they marched all in close disguise
Of fayned loue, they chaunst to ouertake
Two knights, that lincked rode in louely wise,
As if they secret counsels did partake ;
And each not farre behinde him had his make,
To weete, two Ladies of most goodly hew,
That twixt themselues did gentle purpose make,
Vnmindfull both of that discordfull crew,
The which with speedie pace did after them
    pursew.

31

Who as they now approched nigh at hand,
Deeming them doughtie as they did appeare,
They sent that Squire afore, to vnderstand,
What mote they be : who viewing them more
    neare
Returned readie newes, that those same weare
Two of the prowest Knights in Faery lond ;
And those two Ladies their two louers deare,
Couragious *Cambell*, and stout *Triamond*,
With *Canacee* and *Cambine* linckt in louely bond.

32

Whylome as antique stories tellen vs,
Those two were foes the fellonest on ground,
And battell made the dreddest daungerous,
That euer shrilling trumpet did resound ;
Though now their acts be no where to be found,
As that renowmed Poet them compyled,
With warlike numbers and Heroicke sound,
Dan *Chaucer*, well of English vndefyled,
On Fames eternall beadroll worthie to be fyled.

33

But wicked Time that all good thoughts doth
    waste,
And workes of noblest wits to nought out
    weare,
That famous moniment hath quite defaste,
And robd the world of threasure endlesse deare,
The which mote haue enriched all vs heare.
O cursed Eld the cankerworme of writs,
How may these rimes, so rude as doth appeare,
Hope to endure, sith workes of heauenly wits
Are quite deuourd, and brought to nought by
    little bits ?

34

Then pardon, O most sacred happie spirit,
That I thy labours lost may thus reuiue,
And steale from thee the meede of thy due
    merit,
That none durst euer whilest thou wast aliue,
And being dead in vaine yet many striue :
Ne dare I like, but through infusion sweete
Of thine owne spirit, which doth in me suruiue,
I follow here the footing of thy feete,
That with thy meaning so I may the rather meete.

35

Cambelloes sister was fayre *Canacee*,
That was the learnedst Ladie in her dayes,
Well seene in eucrie science that mote bee,
And euery secret worke of natures wayes,
In wittie riddles, and in wise soothsayes,
In power of herbes, and tunes of beasts and
    burds ;
And, that augmented all her other prayse,
She modest was in all her deedes and words,
And wondrous chast of life, yet lou'd of Knights
    and Lords.

36

Full many Lords, and many Knights her loued,
Yet she to none of them her liking lent,
Ne euer was with fond affection moued,
But rul'd her thoughts with goodly gouerne-
    ment,
For dread of blame and honours blemishment ;
And eke vnto her lookes a law she made,
That none of them once out of order went,
But like to warie Centonels well stayd,
Still watcht on euery side, of secret foes affrayd.

37

So much the more as she refusd to loue,
So much the more she loued was and sought,
That oftentimes vnquiet strife did moue
Amongst her louers, and great quarrels wrought,
That oft for her in bloudie armes they fought,
Which whenas *Cambell*, that was stout and wise,
Perceiu'd would breede great mischiefe, he
    bethought
How to preuent the perill that mote rise,
And turne both him and her to honour in this
    wise.

38

One day, when all that troupe of warlike wooers
Assembled were, to weet whose she should bee,
All mightie men and dreadfull derring dooers,
(The harder it to make them well agree)
Amongst them all this end he did decree ;
That of them all, which loue to her did make,
They by consent should chose the stoutest three,
That with himselfe should combat for her sake,
And of them all the victour should his sister take.

39

Bold was the chalenge, as himselfe was bold,
And courage full of haughtie hardiment,
Approued oft in perils manifold,
Which he atchieu'd to his great ornament :
But yet his sisters skill vnto him lent
Most confidence and hope of happie speed,
Conceiued by a ring, which she him sent,
That mongst the manie vertues, which we reed,
Had power to staunch al wounds, that mortally
    did bleed.

40

Well was that rings great vertue knowen to all,
That dread thereof, and his redoubted might
Did all that youthly rout so much appall,
That none of them durst vndertake the fight ;
More wise they weend to make of loue delight,
Then life to hazard for faire Ladies looke,
And yet vncertaine by such outward sight,
Though for her sake they all that perill tooke,
Whether she would them loue, or in her liking
    brooke.

41

Amongst those knights there were three
    brethren bold,
Three bolder brethren neuer were yborne,
Borne of one mother in one happie mold,
Borne at one burden in one happie morne,
Thrise happie mother, and thrise happie morne,
That bore three such, three such not to be fond ;
Her name was *Agape* whose children werne
All three as one, the first hight *Priamond*,
The second *Dyamond*, the youngest *Triamond*.

42

Stout *Priamond*, but not so strong to strike,
Strong *Diamond*, but not so stout a knight,
But *Triamond* was stout and strong alike :
On horsebacke vsed *Triamond* to fight,
And *Priamond* on foote had more delight,
But horse and foote knew *Diamond* to wield :
With curtaxe vsed *Diamond* to smite,
And *Triamond* to handle speare and shield,
But speare and curtaxe both vsd *Priamond* in
    field.

43

These three did loue each other dearely well,
And with so firme affection were allyde,
As if but one soule in them all did dwell,
Which did her powre into three parts diuyde ;
Like three faire branches budding farre and wide,
That from one roote deriu'd their vitall sap :
And like that roote that doth her life diuide,
Their mother was, and had full blessed hap,
These three so noble babes to bring forth at one
    clap.

44

Their mother was a Fay, and had the skill
　Of secret things, and all the powres of nature,
　Which she by art could vse vnto her will,
　And to her seruice bind each liuing creature,
　Through secret vnderstanding of their feature.
Thereto she was right faire, when so her face
　She list discouer, and of goodly stature ;
　But she as Fayes are wont, in priuie place
Did spend her dayes, and lov'd in forests wyld
　　to space.

45

There on a day a noble youthly knight
　Seeking aduentures in the saluage wood,
　Did by great fortune get of her the sight,
　As she sate carelesse by a cristall flood,
　Combing her golden lockes, as seemd her good :
And vnawares vpon her laying hold,
　That stroue in vaine him long to haue with-
　　stood,
　Oppressed her, and there (as it is told)
Got these three louely babes, that prov'd three
　　champions bold.

46

Which she with her long fostred in that wood,
　Till that to ripenesse of mans state they grew :
　Then shewing forth signes of their fathers blood,
　They loued armes, and knighthood did ensew,
　Seeking aduentures, where they anie knew.
Which when their mother saw, she gan to dout
　Their safetie, least by searching daungers new,
　And rash prouoking perils all about,
Their days mote be abridged through their
　　corage stout.

47

Therefore desirous th'end of all their dayes
　To know, and them t'enlarge with long extent,
　By wondrous skill, and many hidden wayes,
　To the three fatall sisters house she went.
　Farre vnder ground from tract of liuing went,
Downe in the bottome of the deepe *Abysse*,
　Where *Demogorgon* in dull darkenesse pent,
　Farre from the view of Gods and heauens blis,
The hideous *Chaos* keepes, their dreadfull dwell-
　　ing is.

48

There she them found, all sitting round about
　The direfull distaffe standing in the mid,
　And with vnwearied fingers drawing out
　The lines of life, from liuing knowledge hid.
　Sad *Clotho* held the rocke, the whiles the thrid
By griesly *Lachesis* was spun with paine,
　That cruell *Atropos* eftsoones vndid,
　With cursed knife cutting the twist in twaine :
Most wretched men, whose dayes depend on
　　thrids so vaine.

49

She them saluting, there by them sate still,
　Beholding how the thrids of life they span :
　And when at last she had beheld her fill,
　Trembling in heart, and looking pale and wan,
　Her cause of comming she to tell began.
To whom fierce *Atropos*, Bold Fay, that durst
　Come see the secret of the life of man,
　Well worthie thou to be of *Ioue* accurst,
And eke thy childrens thrids to be a sunder
　　burst.

50

Whereat she sore affrayd, yet her besought
　To graunt her boone, and rigour to abate,
　That she might see her childrens thrids forth
　　brought,
　And know the measure of their vtmost date,
　To them ordained by eternall fate.
Which *Clotho* graunting, shewed her the same :
　That when she saw, it did her much amate,
　To see their thrids so thin, as spiders frame,
And eke so short, that seemd their ends out
　　shortly came.

51

She then began them humbly to intreate,
　To draw them longer out, and better twine,
　That so their liues might be prolonged late.
　But *Lachesis* thereat gan to repine,
　And sayd, Fond dame that deem'st of things
　　diuine
As of humane, that they may altred bee,
　And chaung'd at pleasure for those impes of
　　thine.
　Not so ; for what the Fates do once decree,
Not all the gods can chaunge, nor *Ioue* him self
　　can free.

52

Then since (quoth she) the terme of each mans life
　For nought may lessened nor enlarged bee,
　Graunt this, that when ye shred with fatall knife
　His line, which is the eldest of the three,
　Which is of them the shortest, as I see,
Eftsoones his life mav passe into the next ;
　And when the next shall likewise ended bee,
　That both their liues may likewise be annext
Vnto the third, that his may so be trebly wext.

53

They graunted it ; and then that carefull Fay
　Departed thence with full contented mynd ;
　And comming home, in warlike fresh aray
　Them found all three according to their kynd ;
　But vnto them what destinie was assynd,
Or how their liues were eekt, she did not tell ;
　But euermore, when she fit time could fynd,
　She warned them to tend their safeties well,
And loue each other deare, what euer them befell.

54

So did they surely during all their dayes,
And neuer discord did amongst them fall :
Which much augmented all their other praise.
And now t'increase affection naturall,
In loue of *Canacee* they ioyned all :
Vpon which ground this same great battell grew,
Great matter growing of beginning small ;
The which for length I will not here pursew,
But rather will reserue it for a Canto new.

Cant. III.

The battell twixt three brethren with
Cambell for Canacee :
Cambina with true friendships bond
doth their long strife agree.

1

O why doe wretched men so much desire,
To draw their dayes vnto the vtmost date,
And doe not rather wish them soone expire,
Knowing the miserie of their estate,
And thousand perills which them still awate,
Tossing them like a boate amid the mayne,
That euery houre they knocke at deathes gate ?
And he that happie seemes and least in payne,
Yet is as nigh his end, as he that most doth
playne.

2

Therefore this Fay I hold but fond and vaine,
The which in seeking for her children three
Long life, thereby did more prolong their
paine.
Yet whilest they liued none did euer see
More happie creatures, then they seem'd to
bee,
Nor more ennobled for their courtesie,
That made them dearely lou'd of each degree ;
Ne more renowmed for their cheualrie,
That made them dreaded much of all men farre
and nie.

3

These three that hardie chalenge tooke in hand,
For *Canacee* with *Cambell* for to fight :
The day was set, that all might vnderstand,
And pledges pawnd the same to keepe a right,
That day, the dreddest day that liuing wight
Did euer see vpon this world to shine,
So soone as heauens window shewed light,
These warlike Champions all in armour shine,
Assembled were in field, the chalenge to define.

4

The field with listes was all about enclos'd,
To barre the prease of people farre away ;
And at th'one side sixe iudges were dispos'd,
To view and deeme the deedes of armes that
day ;
And on the other side in fresh aray,
Favre *Canacee* vpon a stately stage
Was set, to see the fortune of that fray,
And to be seene, as his most worthie wage,
That could her purchase with his liues aduen
tur'd gage.

5

Then entred *Cambell* first into the list,
With stately steps, and fearelesse countenance
As if the conquest his he surely wist.
Soone after did the brethren three aduance,
In braue aray and goodly amenance,
With scutchins gilt and banners broad displayd :
And marching thrise in warlike ordinance,
Thrise lowted lowly to the noble Mayd,
The whiles shril trompets and loud clarions
sweetly playd.

6

Which doen the doughty chalenger came forth,
All arm'd to point his chalenge to abet :
Gainst whom Sir *Priamond* with equall worth,
And equall armes himselfe did forward set.
A trompet blew ; they both together met,
With dreadfull force, and furious intent,
Carelesse of perill in their fiers affret,
As if that life to losse they had forelent,
And cared not to spare, that should be shortly
spent.

7

Right practicke was Sir *Priamond* in fight,
And throughly skild in vse of shield and speare
Ne lesse approued was *Cambelloes* might,
Ne lesse his skill in weapons did appeare,
That hard it was to weene which harder were.
Full many mightie strokes on either side
Were sent, that seemd death in them to beare,
But they were both so watchfull and well eyde,
That they auoyded were, and vainely by did
slyde.

8

Yet one of many was so strongly bent
By *Priamond*, that with vnluckie glaunce
Through *Cambels* shoulder it vnwarely went,
That forced him his shield to disaduaunce :
Much was he grieued with that gracelesse
chaunce,
Yet from the wound no drop of bloud there fell,
But wondrous paine, that did the more en
haunce
His haughtie courage to aduengement fell :
Smart daunts not mighty harts, but makes
them more to swell.

SPENSER   I

9

With that his poynant speare he fierce auentred,
With doubled force close vnderneath his shield,
That through the mayles into his thigh it
  entred,
And there arresting, readie way did yield,
For bloud to gush forth on the grassie field;
That he for paine himselfe n'ote right vpreare,
But too and fro in great amazement reel'd,
Like an old Oke whose pith and sap is seare,
At puffe of euery storme doth stagger here and
  theare.

10

Whom so dismayd when *Cambell* had espide,
Againe he droue at him with double might,
That nought mote stay the steele, till in his
  side
The mortall point most cruelly empight :
Where fast infixed, whilest he sought by slight
It forth to wrest, the staffe a sunder brake,
And left the head behind: with which despight
He all enrag'd, his shiuering speare did shake,
And charging him afresh thus felly him bespake.

11

Lo faitour there thy meede vnto thee take,
The meede of thy mischalenge and abet:
Not for thine owne, but for thy sisters sake,
Haue I thus long thy life vnto thee let :
But to forbeare doth not forgiue the det.
The wicked weapon heard his wrathfull vow,
And passing forth with furious affret,
Pierst through his beuer quite into his brow,
That with the force it backward forced him
  to bow.

12

Therewith a sunder in the midst it brast,
And in his hand nought but the troncheon left,
The other halfe behind yet sticking fast,
Out of his headpeece *Cambell* fiercely reft,
And with such furie backe at him it heft,
That making way vnto his dearest life,
His weasand pipe it through his gorget cleft:
Thence streames of purple bloud issuing rife,
Let forth his wearie ghost and made an end of
  strife.

13

His wearie ghost assoyld from fleshly band,
Did not as others wont, directly fly
Vnto her rest in Plutoes griesly land,
Ne into ayre did vanish presently,
Ne chaunged was into a starre in sky :
But through traduction was eftsoones deriued,
Like as his mother prayd the Destinie,
Into his other brethren, that suruiued,
In whom he liu'd a new, of former life depriued.

14

Whom when on ground his brother next beheld
Though sad and sorie for so heauy sight,
Yet leaue vnto his sorrow did not yeeld,
But rather stird to vengeance and despight,
Through secret feeling of his generous spright
Rusht fiercely forth, the battell to renew,
As in reuersion of his brothers right;
And chalenging the Virgin as his dew.
His foe was soone addrest: the trompets freshly
  blew.

15

With that they both together fiercely met,
As if that each ment other to deuoure ;
And with their axes both so sorely bet,
That neither plate nor mayle, whereas their
  powre   [stowre
They felt, could once sustaine the hideous
But riued were like rotten wood a sunder,
Whilest through their rifts the ruddie bloud
  did showre
And fire did flash, like lightning after thunder
That fild the lookers on attonce with ruth and
  wonder.

16

As when two Tygers prickt with hungers rage,
Haue by good fortune found some beasts
  fresh spoyle,
On which they weene their famine to asswage,
And gaine a feastfull guerdon of their toyle,
Both falling out doe stirre vp strifefull broyle,
And cruell battell twixt thems lues doe make
Whiles neither lets the other touch the soyle,
But either sdeignes with other to partake :
So cruelly these Knights stroue for that Ladies
  sake.

17

Full many strokes, that mortally were ment,
The whiles were enterchaunged twixt them two:
Yet they were all with so good wariment
Or warded, or auoyded and let goe,
That still the life stood fearelesse of her foe :
Till *Diamond* disdeigning long delay
Of doubtfull fortune waueri ng to and fro,
Resolu'd to end it one or other way;
And heau'd his murdrous axe at him with
  mighty sway.

18

The dreadfull stroke in case it had arriued,
Where it was ment, (so deadly it was ment)
The soule had sure out of his bodie riued,
And stinted all the strife incontinent.
But *Cambels* fate that fortune did preuent :
For seeing it at hand, he swaru'd asyde,
And so gaue way vnto his fell intent :
Who missing of the marke which he had eyde,
Was with the force nigh feld whilst his right
  foot did slyde.

19

As when a Vulture greedie of his pray,
Through hunger long, that hart to him doth lend,
Strikes at an Heron with all his bodies sway,
That from his force seemes nought may it defend;
The warie fowle that spies him toward bend
His dreadfull souse, auoydes it shunning light,
And maketh him his wing in vaine to spend;
That with the weight of his owne weeldlesse
    might,
He fall'th nigh to ground, and scarse recouereth
    flight.

20

Which faire aduenture when *Cambello* spide,
Full lightly, ere himselfe he could recower,
From daungers dread to ward his naked side,
He can let driue at him with all his power,
And with his axe him smote in euill hower,
That from his shoulders quite his head he reft :
The headlesse tronke, as heedlesse of that stower,
Stood still a while, and his fast footing kept,
Till feeling life to fayle, he fell, and deadly slept.

21

They which that piteous spectacle beheld,
Were much amaz'd the headlesse tronke to see
Stand vp so long, and weapon vaine to weld,
Vnweeting of the Fates diuine decree,
For lifes succession in those brethren three.
For notwithstanding that one soule was reft,
Yet, had the bodie not dismembred bee,
It would haue liued, and reuiued eft ;
But finding no fit seat, the lifelesse corse it left.

22

It left ; but that same soule, which therein dwelt,
Str ight entri g into *Triamond*, him fild
With double life, and griefe, which when he felt,
As one whose inner parts had bene ythrild
With point of steele, that close his hartbloud
    spild,
He lightly lept out of his place of rest,
And rushi g forth into the emptie field,
Agai st *Cambello* fiercely him addrest;
Who him affronting soone to fight was readie
    prest.

23

Well mote ye wonder how that noble Knight,
After he had so often wounded beene,
Could stand on foot, now to renew the fight.
But had ye then him forth aduauncing seene,
Some newborne wight ye would him surely
    weene :
So fresh he seemed and so fierce in sight;
Like as a Snake, whom wearie winters teene
Hath worne to nought, now feeling sommers
    might.   [dight.
Casts off his ragged skin and freshly doth him

24

All was through vertue of the ring he wore,
The which not onely did not from him let
One drop of bloud to fall, but did restore
His weakned powers, and dulled spirits whet,
Through working of the stone therein yset.
Else how could one of equall might with most,
Against so many no lesse mightie met,
Once thinke to match three such on equall cost,
Three such as able were to match a puissant
    host.

25

Yet nought thereof was *Triamond* adredde,
Ne desperate of glorious victorie,
But sharpely him assayld, and sore bestedde,
With heapes of strokes, which he at him let
    flie,
As thicke as hayle forth poured from the skie:
He stroke, he soust, he foynd, he hewd, he
    lasht,
And did his yron brond so fast applie,
That from the same the fierie sparkles flasht,
As fast as water-sprinkles gainst a rocke are
    dasht.

26

Much was *Cambello* daunted with his blowes.
So thicke they fell, and forcibly were sent,
That he was forst from daunger of the throwes
Backe to retire, and somewhat to relent,
Till th'heat of his fierce furie he had spent:
Which when for want of breath gan to abate,
He then afresh with new encouragement
Did him assayle, and mightily amate,
As fast as forward erst, now backward to retrate.

27

Like as the tide that comes fro th'Ocean mayne,
Flowes vp the Shenan with contrarie forse,
And ouerruling him in his owne rayne,
Driues backe the current of his kindly course,
And makes it seeme to haue some other sourse:
But when the floud is spent, then backe againe
His borrowed waters forst to redisbourse,
He sends the sea his owne with double gaine,
And tribute eke withall, as to his Soueraine.

28

Thus did the battell varie to and fro,
With diuerse fortune doubtfull to be deemed :
Now this the better had, now had his fo ;
Then he halfe vanquisht, then the other seemed,
Yet victors both them selues alwayes esteemed.
And all the while the disentrayled blood
Adowne their sides like litle riuers stremed,
That with the wasting of his vitall flood,
Sir *Triamond* at last full faint and feeble stood.

29

But *Cambell* still more strong and greater grew,
Ne felt his blood to wast, ne powres emperisht,
Through that rings vertue, that with vigour new,
Still when as he enfeebled was, him cherisht,
And all his wounds, and all his bruses guarisht,
Like as a withered tree through husbands toyle
Is often seene full freshly to haue florisht,
And fruitfull apples to haue borne awhile,
As fresh as when it first was planted in the soyle.

30

Through which a duantage, in his strength he rose,
And smote the other with so wondrous might,
That through the seame, which did his hauberk close,
Into his throate and life it pierced quight,
That downe he fell as dead in all mens sight:
Yet dead he was not, yet he sure did die,
As all men do, that lose the liuing spright:
So did one soule out of his bodie flie
Vnto her natiue home from mortall miserie.

31

But nathelesse whilst all the lookers on
Him dead behight, as he to all appeard,
All vnawares he started vp anon,
As one that had out of a dreame bene reard,
And fresh assayld his foe, who halfe affeard
Of th'vncouth sight, as he some ghost had seene,
Stood still amaz'd, holding his idle sweard;
Till hauing often by him stricken beene,
He forced was to strike, and saue him selfe
     from teene.

32

Yet from thenceforth more warily he fought,
As one in feare the Stygian gods t'offend,
Ne followd on so fast, but rather sought
Him selfe to saue, and daunger to defend,
Then life and labour both in vaine to spend,
Which *Triamond* perceiuing, weened sure
He gan to faint, toward the battels end,
And that he should not long on foote endure,
A signe which did to him the victorie assure.

33

Whereof full blith, eftsoones his mightie hand
He heav'd on high, in mind with that same blow
To make an end of all that did withstand:
Which *Cambell* seeing come, was nothing slow
Him selfe to saue from that so deadly throw ;
And at that instant reaching forth his sweard
Close vnderneath his shield, that scarce did show,
Stroke him, as he his hand to strike vpreard,
In th'arm-pit full, that through both sides the
     wound appeard.

34

Yet still that direfull stroke kept on his way,
And falling heauie on *Cambelloes* crest,
Strooke him so hugely, that in swowne he lay,
And in his head an hideous wound imprest :
And sure had it not happily found rest
Vpon the brim of his brode plated shield,
It would haue cleft his braine downe to his brest.
So both at once fell dead vpon the field,
And each to other seemd the victorie to yield.

35

Which when as all the lookers on beheld,
They weened sure the warre was at an end,
And Iudges rose, and Marshals of the field
Broke vp the listes, their armes away to rend;
And *Canacee* gan wayle her dearest frend.
All suddenly they both vpstarted light,
The one out of the swownd, which him did blend,
The other breathing now another spright,
And fiercely each assayling, gan afresh to fight.

36

Long while they then continued in that wize,
As if but then the battell had begonne :
Strokes, wounds, wards, weapons, all they did
     despise,
Ne either car'd to ward, or perill shonne,
Desirous both to haue the battell donne ;
Ne either cared life to saue or spill,
Ne which of them did winne, ne which were
     wonne,
So wearie both of fighting had their fill,
That life it selfe seemd loathsome, and long
     safetie ill.

37

Whilst thus the case in doubtfull ballance hong,
Vnsure to whether side it would incline,
And all mens eyes and hearts, which there among
Stood gazing, filled were with rufull tine,
And secret feare, to see their fatall fine, .
All suddenly they heard a troublous noyes,
That seemd some perilous tumult to desine,
Confusd with womens cries, and shouts of boyes,
Such as the troubled Theaters oftimes annoyes.

38

Thereat the Champions both stood still a space,
To weeten what that sudden clamour ment ;
Lo where they spyde with speedie whirling pace,
One in a charet of straunge furniment,
Towards them driuing like a storme out sent.
The charet decked was in wondrous wize,
With gold and many a gorgeous ornament,
After the Persian Monarks antique guize,
Such as the maker selfe could best by art deuize.

39

And drawne it was (that wonder is to tell)
Of two grim lyons, taken from the wood,
In which their powre all others did excell ;
Now made forget their former cruell mood,
T'obey their riders hest, as seemed good.
And therein sate a Ladie passing faire
And bright, that seemed borne of Angels brood,
And with her beautie bountie did compare,
Whether of them in her should haue the greater
    share.

40

Thereto she learned was in Magicke leare,
And all the artes, that subtill wits discouer,
Hauing therein bene trained many a yeare,
And well instructed by the Fay her mother,
That in the same she farre exceld all other.
Who vnderstanding by her mightie art,
Of th'euill plight, in which her dearest brother
Now stood, came forth in hast to take his part,
And pacifie the strife, which causd so deadly
    smart.

41

And as she passed through th'vnruly preace
Of people, thronging thicke her to behold,
Her angrie teame breaking their bonds of peace,
Great heapes of them, like sheepe in narrow
    fold,
For hast did ouer-runne, in dust enrould,
That thorough rude confusion of the rout,
Some fearing shriekt, some being harmed hould,
Some laught for sport, some did for wonder
    shout,
And some that would seeme wise, their wonder
    turnd to dout.

42

In her right hand a rod of peace shee bore,
About the which two Serpents weren wound.
Entrayled mutually in louely lore,
And by the tailes together firmely bound,
And both were with one oliue garland crownd,
Like to the rod which *Maias* sonne doth wield,
Wherewith the hellish fiends he doth confound.
And in her other hand a cup she hild,
The which was with Nepenthe to the brim
    vpfild.

43

Nepenthe is a drinck of souerayne grace,
Deuized by the Gods, for to asswage
Harts grief, and bitter gall away to chace,
Which stirs vp anguish and contentious rage :
In stead thereof sweet peace and quiet age
It doth establish in the troubled mynd.
Few men, but such as sober are and sage,
Are by the Gods to drinck thereof assynd ;
But such as drinck, eternall happinesse do fynd.

44

Such famous men, such worthies of the earth,
As *Ioue* will haue aduaunced to the skie,
And there made gods, though borne of mortall
    berth,
For their high merits and great dignitie,
Are wont, before they may to heauen flie,
To drincke hereof, whereby all cares forepast
Are washt away quite from their memorie.
So did those olde Heroes hereof taste,
Before that they in blisse amongst the Gods
    were plaste.

45

Much more of price and of more gratious powre
Is this, then that same water of Ardenne,
The which *Rinaldo* drunck in happie howre,
Described by that famous Tuscane penne :
For that had might to change the hearts of men
Fro loue to hate, a change of euill choise :
But this doth hatred make in loue to brenne
And heauy heart with comfort doth reioyce.
Who would not to this vertue rather yeeld his
    voice ?

46

At last arriuing by the listes side,
Shee with her rod did softly smite the raile,
Which straight flew ope, and gaue her way to ride.
Eftsoones out of her Coch she gan auaile,
And pacing fairely forth, did bid all haile,
First to her brother, whom she loued deare,
That so to see him made her heart to quaile :
And next to *Cambell*, whose sad ruefull cheare
Made her to change her hew, and hidden loue
    t'appeare.

47

They lightly her requit (for small delight
They had as then her long to entertaine,)
And eft them turned both againe to fight,
Which when she saw, downe on the bloudy plaine
Her selfe she threw, and teares gan shed amaine ;
Amongst her teares immixing prayers meeke,
And with her prayers reasons to restraine
From blouddy strife, and blessed peace to seeke,
By all that vnto them was deare, did them
    beseeke.

48

But when as all might nought with them preuaile,
Shee smote them lightly with her powrefull wand.
Then suddenly as if their hearts did faile,
Their wrathfull blades downe fell out of their
    hand,
And they like men astonisht still did stand.
Thus whilest their minds were doubtfully dis-
    traught,
And mighty spirites bound with mightier band,
Her golden cup to them for drinke she raught,
Whereof full glad for thirst, ech drunk an harty
    draught.

49

Of which so soone as they once tasted had,
  Wonder it is that sudden change to see:
Instead of strokes, each other kissed glad,
  And louely haulst from feare of treason free,
  And plighted hands for euer friends to be.
When all men saw this sudden change of things,
  So mortall foes so friendly to agree,
For passing ioy, which so great maruaile
    brings,
They all gan shout aloud, that all the heauen
    rings.

50

All which, when gentle *Canacee* beheld,
  In hast she from her lofty chaire descended,
To weet what sudden tidings was befeld:
  Where when she saw that cruell war so ended,
  And deadly foes so faithfully affrended,
In louely wise she gan that Lady greet,
  Which had so great dismay so well amended,
  And entertaining her with curt'sies meet,
Profest to her true friendship and affection
    sweet.

51

Thus when they all accorded goodly were,
  The trumpets sounded, and they all arose,
Thence to depart with glee and gladsome chere.
  Those warlike champions both together chose,
  Homeward to march, themselues there to
    repose,
And wise *Cambina* taking by her side
  Faire *Canacee*, as fresh as morning rose,
Vnto her Coch remounting, home did ride,
Admir'd of all the people, and much glorifide.

52

Where making ioyous feast theire daies they
    spent
In perfect loue, deuoide of hatefull strife,
  Allide with bands of mutuall couplement;
For *Triamond* had *Canacee* to wife,
  With whom he ledd a long and happie life;
  And *Cambel* tooke *Cambina* to his fere,
The which as life were each to other liefe.
  So all alike did loue, and loued were,
That since their days such louers were not found
    elswhere.

Cant. IIII.

Satyrane makes a Turneyment
   For loue of Florimell:
Britomart winnes the prize from all,
   And Artegall doth quell.

I

It often fals, (as here it earst befell)
  That mortall foes doe turne to faithfull frends,
And friends profest are chaungd to foemen fell:
  The cause of both, of both their minds depends,
  And th'end of both likewise of both their ends.
For enmitie, that of no ill proceeds,
  But of occasion, with th'occasion ends;
And friendship, which a faint affection breeds
Without regard of good, dyes like ill grounded
    seeds.

2

That well (me seemes) appeares, by that of late
  Twixt *Cambell* and Sir *Triamond* befell,
As els by this, that now a new debate
  Stird vp twixt *Scudamour* and *Paridell*,
  The which by course befals me here to tell:
Who hauing those two other Knights espide
  Marching afore, as ye remember well,
Sent forth their Squire to haue them both descride,
And eke those masked Ladies riding them
    beside.

3

Who backe returning, told as he had seene,
  That they were doughtie knights of dreaded
    name;
  And those two Ladies, their two loues vnseene;
And therefore wisht them without blot or blame,
  To let them passe at will, for dread of shame.
But *Blandamour* full of vainglorious spright,
  And rather stird by his discordfull Dame,
Vpon them gladly would haue prov'd his might,
But that he yet was sore of his late lucklesse
    fight.

4

Yet nigh approching, he them fowle bespake,
  Disgracing them, him selfe thereby to grace,
As was his wont, so weening way to make
  To Ladies loue, where so he came in place,
  And with lewd termes their louers to deface.
Whose sharpe prouokem̃nt them incenst so sore,
  That both were bent t'auenge his vsage base,
And gan their shields addresse themselues afore:
For euill deedes may better then bad words be
    bore.

5

But faire *Cambina* with perswasions myld,
Did mitigate the fiercenesse of their mode,
That for the present they were reconcyld,
And gan to treate of deeds of armes abrode,
And strange aduentures, all the way they rode:
Amongst the which they told, as then befell,
Of that great turney, which was blazed brode,
For that rich girdle of faire *Florimell*,
The prize of her, which did in beautie most excell.

6

To which folke-mote they all with one consent,
Sith each of them his Ladie had him by,
Whose beautie each of them thought excellent,
Agreed to trauell, and their fortunes try.
So as they passed forth, they did espy
One in bright armes, with ready speare in rest,
That toward them his course seem'd to apply,
Gainst whom Sir *Paridell* himselfe addrest,
Him weening, ere he nigh approcht to haue represt.

7

Which th'other seeing, gan his course relent,
And vaunted speare eftsoones to disaduaunce,
As if he naught but peace and pleasure ment,
Now falne into their fellowship by chance,
Whereat they shewed curteous countenaunce.
So as he rode with them accompanide,
His rouing eie did on the Lady glaunce,
Which *Blandamour* had riding by his side
Whom sure he weend, that he some wher tofore had eide.

8

It was to weete that snowy *Florimell*,
Which *Ferrau* late from *Braggadochio* wonne,
Whom he now seeing, her remembred well,
How hauing reft her from the witches sonne,
He soone her lost: wherefore he now begunne
To challenge her anew, as his owne prize,
Whom formerly he had in battell wonne,
And proffer made by force her to reprize,
Which scornefull offer, *Blandamour* gan soone despize.

9

And said, Sir Knight, sith ye this Lady clame,
Whom he that hath, were loth to lose so light,
(For so to lose a Lady, were great shame)
Yee shall her winne, as I haue done in fight:
And lo shee shall be placed here in sight,
Together with this Hag beside her set,
That who so winnes her, may her haue by right:
But he shall haue the Hag that is ybet,
And with her alwaies ride, till he another get.

10

That offer pleased all the company,
So *Florimell* with *Ate* forth was brought,
At which they all gan laugh full merrily :
But *Braggadochio* said, he neuer thought
For such an Hag, that seemed worse then nought,
His person to emperill so in fight.
But if to match that Lady they had sought
Another like, that were like faire and bright,
His life he then would spend to iustifie his right.

11

At which his vaine excuse they all gan smile,
As scorning his vnmanly cowardize :
And *Florimell* him fowly gan reuile,
That for her sake refus'd to enterprize
The battell, offred in so knightly wize.
And *Ate* eke prouokt him priuily,
With loue of her, and shame of such mesprize,
But naught he car'd for friend or enemy,
For in base mind nor friendship dwels nor enmity.

12

But *Cambell* thus did shut vp all in iest,
Braue Knights and Ladies, certes ye doe wrong
To stirre vp strife, when most vs needeth rest,
That we may vs reserue both fresh and strong,
Against the Turneiment which is not long.
When who so list to fight, may fight his fill,
Till then your challerges ye may prolong;
And then it shall be tried, if ye will,
Whether shall haue the Hag, or hold the Lady still.

13

They all agreed, so turning all to game,
And pleasaunt bord, they past forth on their way,
And all that while, where so they rode or came,
That masked Mock-knight was their sport and play.
Till that at length vpon th'appointed day,
Vnto the place of turneyment they came ;
Where they before them found in fresh aray
Manie a braue knight, and manie a daintie dame
Assembled, for to get the honour of that game.

14

There this faire crewe arriuing, did diuide
Them selues asunder : *Blandamour* with those
Of his, on th'one ; the rest on th'other side.
But boastfull *Braggadocchio* rather chose,
For glorie vaine their fellowship to lose,
That men on him the more might gaze alone.
The rest them selues in troupes did else dispose,
Like as it seemed best to euery one ;
The knights in couples marcht, with ladies linckt attone.

15

Then first of all forth came Sir *Satyrane*,
Bearing that precious relicke in an arke
Of gold, that bad eyes might it not prophane :
Which drawing softly forth out of the darke,
He open shewd, that all men it mote marke.
A gorgeous girdle, curiously embost
With pearle and precious stone, worth many a
    marke ;
Yet did the workmanship farre passe the cost:
It was the same, which lately *Florimel* had lost.

16

That same aloft he hong in open vew,
To be the prize of beautie and of might ;
The which eftsoones discouered, to it drew
The eyes of all, allur'd with close delight,
And hearts quite robbed with so glorious sight,
That all men threw out vowes and wishes vaine.
Thrise happie Ladie, and thrise happie knight,
Them seemd that could so goodly riches gaine,
So worthie of the perill, worthy of the paine.

17

Then tooke the bold Sir *Satyrane* in hand
An huge great speare, such as he wont to wield,
And vauncing forth from all the other band
Of knights, addrest his maiden-headed shield,
Shewing him selfe all ready for the field.
Gainst whom there singled from the other side
A Painim knight, that well in armes was skild,
And had in many a battell oft bene tride,
Hight *Bruncheual* the bold, who fiersly forth did
    ride.

18

So furiously they both together met,
That neither could the others force sustaine :
As two fierce Buls, that striue the rule to get
Of all the heard, meete with so hideous maine,
That both rebutted, tumble on the plaine :
So these two champions to the ground were feld,
Where in a maze they both did long remaine,
And in their hands their idle troncheons held,
Which neither able were to wag, or once to weld.

19

Which when the noble *Ferramont* espide,
He pricked forth in ayd of *Satyran* ;
And him against Sir *Blandamour* did ride
With all the strength and stifnesse that he can.
But the more strong and stiffely that he ran,
So much more sorely to the ground he fell,
That on an heape were tumbled horse and man.
Vnto whose rescue forth rode *Paridell* ;
But him likewise with that same speare he eke
    did quell.

20

Which *Braggadocchio* seeing, had no will
To hasten greatly to his parties ayd,
Albee his turne were next ; but stood there still,
As one that seemed doubtfull or dismayd.
But *Triamond* halfe wroth to see him staid,
Sternly stept forth, and raught away his speare,
With which so sore he *Ferramont* assaid,
That horse and man to ground he quite did
    beare,
That neither could in hast themselues againe
    vpreare.

21

Which to auenge, Sir *Deuon* him did dight,
But with no better fortune then the rest :
For him likewise he quickly downe did smight,
And after him Sir *Douglas* him addrest,
And after him Sir *Paliumord* forth prest,
But none of them against his strokes could
    stand,
But all the more, the more his praise increst,
For either they were left vppon the land,
Or went away sore wounded of his haplesse hand.

22

And now by this, Sir *Satyrane* abraid,
Out of the swowne, in which too long he lay
And looking round about, like one dismaid,
When as he saw the mercilesse affray,
Which doughty *Triamond* had wrought that
    day,
Vnto the noble Knights of Maidenhead,
His mighty heart did almost rend in tway,
For very gall, that rather wholly dead
Himselfe he wisht haue beene, then in so bad a
    stead.

23

Eftsoones he gan to gather vp around
His weapons, which lay scattered all abrode,
And as it fell, his steed he ready found.
On whom remounting, fiercely forth he rode,
Like sparke of fire that from the anduile glode,
There where he saw the valiant *Triamond*
Chasing, and laying on them heauy lode.
That none his force were able to withstand,
So dreadfull were his strokes, so deadly was his
    hond.

24

With that at him his beamlike speare he aimed,
And thereto all his power and might applide :
The wicked steele for mischiefe first ordained,
And hauing now misfortune got for guide,
Staid not, till it arriued in his side,
And therein made a very griesly wound,
That streames of bloud his armour all bedide.
Much was he daunted with that direfull stound,
That scarse he him vpheld from falling in a
    sound.

25

Yet as he might, himselfe he soft withdrew
Out of the field, that none perceiu'd it plaine,
Then gan the part of Chalengers anew
To range the field, and victorlike to raine,
That none against them battell durst maintaine.
By that the gloomy euening on them fell,
That forced them from fighting to refraine,
And trumpets sound to cease did them compell,
So *Satyrane* that day was iudg'd to beare the
    bell.

26

The morrow next the Turney gan anew,
And with the first the hardy *Satyrane*
Appear'd in place, with all his noble crew,
On th'other side, full many a warlike swaine,
Assembled were, that glorious prize to gaine.
But mongst them all, was not Sir *Triamond*,
Vnable he new battell to darraine,
Through grieuaunce of his late receiued wound,
That doubly did him grieue, when so himselfe
    he found.

27

Which *Cambell* seeing, though he could not salue,
Ne done vndoe, yet for to salue his name,
And purchase honour in his friends behalue,
This goodly counterfesaunce he did frame.
The shield and armes well knowne to be the
    same,
Which *Triamond* had worne, vnwares to wight,
And to his friend vnwist, for doubt of blame,
If he misdid, he on himselfe did dight,
That none could him discerne, and so went
    forth to fight.

28

There *Satyrane* Lord of the field he found,
Triumphing in great ioy and iolity;
Gainst whom noneable was to stand on ground;
That much he gan his glorie to enuy,
And cast t'auenge his friends indignity.
A mightie speare eftsoones at him he bent ;
Who seeing him come on so furiously,
Met him mid-way with equall hardiment,
That forcibly to ground they both together went.

29

They vp againe them selues can lightly reare,
And to their tryed swords them selues betake :
With which they wrought such wondrous
    maruels there,
That all the rest it did amazed make,
Ne any dar'd their perill to partake ;
Now cuffling close, now chacing to and fro,
Now hurtling round aduantage for to take :
As two wild Boares together grapling go,
Chauning and foming choler each against his fo.

30

So as they courst, and turneyd here and theare,
It chaunst Sir *Satyrane* his steed at last,
Whether through foundring or through sodein
    feare
To stumble, that his rider nigh he cast;
Which vauntage *Cambell* did pursue so fast,
That ere him selfe he had recouered well.
So sore he sowst him on the compast creast,
That forced him to leaue his loftie sell,
And rudely tumbling downe vnder his horse
    feete fell.

31

Lightly *Cambello* leapt downe from his steed,
For to haue rent his shield and armes away,
That whylome wont to be the victors meed ;
When all vnwares he felt an hideous sway
Of many swords, that lode on him did lay.
An hundred knights had him enclosed round,
To rescue *Satyrane* out of his pray ;
All which at once huge strokes on him did
    pound,
In hope to take him prisoner, where he stood on
    ground.

32

He with their multitude was nought dismayd,
But with stout courage turnd vpon them all,
And with his brondiron round about him layd;
Of which he dealt large almes, as did befall :
Like as a Lion that by chaunce doth fall
Into the hunters toile, doth rage and rore,
In royall heart disdaining to be thrall.
But all in vaine: for what might one do more?
They haue him taken captiue, though it grieue
    him sore.

33

Whereof when newes to *Triamond* was brought,
There as he lay, his wound he soone forgot,
And starting vp, streight for his armour sought:
In vaine he sought; for there he found it not;
Cambello it away before had got :
Cambelloes armes therefore he on him threw,
And lightly i sewd forth to take his lot.
There he in troupe found all that warlike crew,
Leading his friend away, full sorie to his vew.

34

Into the thickest of that knightly preasse
He thrust, and smote downe all that was
    betweene,
Caried with feruent zeale, ne did he ceasse,
Till that he came, where he had *Cambell* scene,
Like captive thral two other Knights atweene,
There he amongst them cruell hauocke makes,
That they which lead him, soone enforced beene
To let him loose, to saue their proper stakes,
Who being freed, from one a weapon fiercely
    takes.

35

With that he driues at them with dreadfull might,
  Both in remembrance of his friends late harme,
  And in reuengement of his owne despight,
  So both together giue a new allarme,
  As if but now the battell wexed warme.
As when two greedy Wolues doe breake by force
  Into an heard, farre from the husband farme,
  They spoile and rauine without all remorse,
So did these two through all the field their foes enforce.

36

Fiercely they followd on their bolde emprize,
  Till trumpets sound did warne them all to rest;
  Then all with one consent did yeeld the prize
  To *Triamond* and *Cambell* as the best.
  But *Triamond* to *Cambell* it relest.
And *Cambell* it to *Triamond* transferd;
  Each labouring t'aduance the others gest,
  And make his praise before his owne preferd :
So that the doome was to another day differd.

37

The last day came, when all those knightes againe
  Assembled were their deedes of armes to shew.
  Full many deedes that day were shewed plaine:
  But *Satyrane* boue all the other crew,
  His wondrous worth declared in all mens view.
For from the first he to the last endured,
  And though some while Fortune from him withdrew,
  Yet euermore his honour he recured,
And with vnwearied powre his party still assured.

38

Ne was there Knight that euer thought of armes,
  But that his vtmost prowesse there made knowen,   [harmes,
  That by their many wounds, and carelesse
  By shiuered speares, and swords all vnder strowen,
By scattered shields was easie to be showen.
  There might ye see loose steeds at random ronne,
  Whose luckelesse riders late were ouerthrowen ;
  And squiers make hast to helpe their Lords fordonne,
But still the Knights of Maidenhead the better wonne.

39

Till that there entred on the other side,   [reed,
  A straunger knight, from whence no man could
  In quyent disguise, full hard to be describe.
  For all his armour was like saluage weed,
  With woody mosse bedight, and all his steed
With oaken leaues attrapt, that seemed fit
  For saluage wight, and thereto well agreed
  His word, which on his ragged shield was writ,
Saluagesse sans finesse, shewing secret wit.

40

He at his first incomming, charg'd his spere
  At him, that first appeared in his sight :
  That was to weet, the stout Sir *Sangliere*,
  Who well was knowen to be a valiant Knight,
  Approued oft in many a perlous fight.
Him at the first encounter downe he smote,
  And ouerbore beyond his crouper quight,
  And after him another Knight, that hote
Sir *Brianor*, so sore, that none him life behote.

41

Then ere his hand he reard, he ouerthrew
  Seuen Knights one after other as they came :
  And when his speare was brust, his sword he drew,
  The instrument of wrath, and with the same
  Far'd like a lyon in his bloodie game,
Hewing, and slashing shields, and helmets bright,
  And beating downe, what euer nigh him came,
  That euery one gan shun his dreadfull sight,
No lesse then death it selfe, in daungerous affright.

42

Much wondred all men, what, or whence he came,
  That did amongst the troupes so tyrannize ;
  And each of other gan inquire his name.
  But when they could not learne it by no wize,
  Most answerable to his wyld disguize
It seemed, him to terme the saluage knight.
  But certes his right name was otherwize,
  Though knowne to few, that *Arthegall* he hight,
The doughtiest knight that liv'd that day, and most of might.

43

Thus was Sir *Satyrane* with all his band
  By his sole manhood and atchieuement stout
  Dismayd, that none of them in field durst stand,
  But beaten were, and chased all about.
  So he continued all that day throughout,
Till euening, that the Sunne gan downward bend.
  Then rushed forth out of the thickest rout
  A stranger knight, that did his glorie shend :
So nought may be esteemed happie till the end.

44

He at his entrance charg'd his powrefull speare
  At *Artegall*, in middest of his pryde,
  And therewith smote him on his Vmbriere
  So sore, that tombling backe, he downe did slyde
  Ouer his horses taile aboue a stryde ;
Whence litle lust he had to rise againe.
  Which *Cambell* seeing, much the same enuyde,
  And ran at him with all his might and maine ;
But shortly was likewise seene lying on the plaine.

45

Whereat full inly wroth was *Triamond*,
And cast t'auenge the shame doen to his freend:
But by his friend himselfe eke soone he fond,
In no lesse neede of helpe, then him he weend.
All which when *Blandamour* from end to end
Beheld, he woxe therewith displeased sore,
And thought in mind it shortly to amend:
His speare he feutred, and at him it bore;
But with no better fortune, then the rest afore.

46

Full many others at him likewise ran:
But all of them likewise dismounted were,
Ne certes wonder; for no powre of man
Could bide the force of that enchaunted speare,
The which this famous *Britomart* did beare;
With which she wondrous deeds of arms
   atchieued,
And ouerthrew, what euer came her neare,
That all those stranger knights full sore
   agrieued,
And that late weaker band of chalengers relieued.

47

Like as in sommers day when raging heat
Doth burne the earth, and boyled riuers drie,
That all brute beasts forst to refraine fro meat,
Doe hunt for shade, where shrowded they may
   lie,
And missing it, faine from themselues to flie;
All trauellers tormented are with paine:
A watry cloud doth ouercast the skie,
And poureth forth a sudden shoure of raine,
That all the wretched world recomforteth againe.

48

So did the warlike *Britomart* restore
The prize, to knights of Maydenhead that day,
Which else was like to haue bene lost, and bore
The prayse of prowesse from them all away.
Then shrilling trompets loudly gan to bray,
And bad them leaue their labours and long toyle,
To ioyous feast and other gentle play,
Where beauties prize shold win that pretious
   spoyle:
Where I with sound of trompe will also rest a
   whyle.

Cant. V.

The Ladies for the girdle striue
of famous Florimell :
Scudamour comming to Cares house,
doth sleepe from him expell.

1

It hath bene through all ages euer seene,
That with the praise of armes and cheualrie,
The prize of beautie still hath ioyned beene;
And that for reasons speciall priuitie:
For either doth on other much relie.
For he me seemes most fit the faire to serue,
That can her best defend from villenie;
And she most fit his seruice doth deserue,
That fairest is and from her faith will neuer
   swerue.

2

So fitly now here commeth next in place,
After the proofe of prowesse ended well,
The controuerse of beauties soueraine grace;
In which to her that doth the most excell,
Shall fall the girdle of faire *Florimell*:
That many wish to win for glorie vaine,
And not for vertuous vse, which some doe
   tell
That glorious belt did in it selfe containe,
Which Ladies ought to loue, and seeke for to
   obtaine.

3

That girdle gaue the vertue of chast loue,
And wiuehood true, to all that did it
   beare;
But whosoeuer contrarie doth proue,
Might not the same about her middle weare,
But it would loose, or else a sunder teare.
Whilome it was (as Faeries wont report)
Dame *Venus* girdle, by her steemed deare,
What time she vsd to liue in wiuely sort;
But layd aside, when so she vsd her looser sport.

4

Her husband *Vulcan* whylome for her sake,
When first he loued her with heart entire,
This pretious ornament they say did make,
And wrought in *Lemno* with vnquenched fire:
And afterwards did for her loues first hire,
Giue it to her, for euer to remaine,
Therewith to bind lasciuious desire,
And loose affections streightly to restraine;
Which vertue it for euer after did retaine.

5

The same one day, when she her selfe disposd
To visite her beloued Paramoure,
The God of warre, she from her middle loosd,
And left behind her in her secret bowre,
On *Acidalian* mount, where many an howre
She with the pleasant *Graces* wont to play.
There *Florimell* in her first ages flowre
Was fostered by those *Graces*, (as they say)
And brought with her from thence that goodly
belt away.

6

That goodly belt was *Cestus* hight by name,
And as her life by her esteemed deare.
No wonder then, if that to winne the same
So many Ladies sought, as shall appeare ;
For peärelesse she was thought, that did it beare.
And now by this their feast all being ended,
The iudges which thereto selected were,
Into the Martian field adowne descended,
To deeme this doutfull case, for which they all
contended.

7

But first was question made, which of those
Knights
That lately turneyd, had the wager wonne :
There was it iudged by those worthie wights,
That *Satyrane* the first day best had donne :
For he last ended, hauing first begonne.
The second was to *Triamond* behight,
For that he sau'd the victour from fordonne :
For *Cambell* victour was in all mens sight,
Till by mishap he in his foemens hand did light.

8

The third dayes prize vnto that straunger Knight,
Whom all men term'd Knight of the Hebene
speare,
To *Britomart* was giuen by good right ;
For that with puissant stroke she downe did
beare
The *Saluage* Knight, that victour was whileare,
And all the rest, which had the best afore,
And to the last vnconquer'd did appeare ;
For last is deemed best. To her therefore
The fayrest Ladie was adiudgd for Paramore.

9

But thereat greatly grudged *Arthegall*,
And much repynd, that both of victors meede,
And eke of honour she did him forestall.
Yet mote he not withstand, what was decreede ;
But inly thought of that despightfull deede
Fit time t'awaite auenged for to bee.
This being ended thus, and all agreed,
Then next ensew'd the Paragon to see
Of beauties praise, and yeeld the fayrest her due
fee.

10

Then first *Cambello* brought vnto their view
His faire *Cambina*, couered with a veale ;
Which being once withdrawne, most perfect hew
And passing beautie did eftsoones reueale,
That able was weake harts away to steale
Next did Sir *Triamond* vnto their sight
The face of his deare *Canacee* vnheale ;
Whose beauties beame eftsoones did shine so
bright,
That daz'd the eyes of all, as with exceeding
light.

11

And after her did *Paridell* produce
His false *Duessa*, that she might be seene,
Who with her forged beautie did seduce
The hearts of some, that fairest her did weene ;
As diuerse wits affected diuers beene.
Then did Sir *Ferramont* vnto them shew
His *Lucida*, that was full faire and sheene,
And after these an hundred Ladies moe
Appear'd in place, the which each other did
outgoe.

12

All which who so dare thinke for to enchace,
Him needeth sure a golden pen I weene,
To tell the feature of each goodly face.
For since the day that they created beene,
So many heauenly faces were not seene
Assembled in one place : ne he that thought
For *Chian* folke to pourtraict beauties Queene,
By view of all the fairest to him brought,
So many faire did see, as here he might haue
sought.

13

At last the most redoubted *Britonesse*,
Her louely *Amoret* did open shew ;
Whose face discouered, plainely did expresse
The heauenly pourtraict of bright Angels hew.
Well weened all, which her that time did vew,
That she should surely beare the bell away,
Till *Blandamour*, who thought he had the trew
And very *Florimell*, did her display :
The sight of whom once seene did all the rest
dismay.

14

For all afore that seemed fayre and bright,
Now base and contemptible did appeare,
Compar'd to her, that shone as Phebes light,
Amongst the lesser starres in euening cleare.
All that her saw with wonder rauisht weare,
And weend no mortall creature she should bee,
But some celestiall shape, that flesh did beare :
Yet all were glad there *Florimell* to see :
Yet thought that *Florimell* was not so faire as
shee.

15

As guilefull Goldsmith that by secret skill,
With golden foyle doth finely ouer spred
Some baser metall, which commend he will
Vnto the vulgar for good gold insted,
He much more goodly glosse thereon doth shed,
To hide his falshood, then if it were trew :
So hard, this Idole was to be ared,
That *Florimell* her selfe in all mens vew
She seem'd to passe : so forged things do fairest
    shew.

16

Then was that golden belt by doome of all
Graunted to her, as to the fayrest Dame.
Which being brought, about her middle small
They thought to gird, as best it her became ;
But by no meanes they could it thereto
    frame.
For euer as they fastned it, it loos'd
And fell away, as feeling secret blame.
Full oft about her wast she it enclos'd ;
And it as oft was from about her wast disclos'd.

17

That all men wondred at the vncouth sight,
And each one thought, as to their fancies came.
But she her selfe did thinke it doen for spight,
And touched was with secret wrath and shame
Therewith, as thing deuiz'd her to defame.
Then many other Ladies likewise tride,
About their tender loynes to knit the same ;
But it would not on none of them abide,
But when they thought it fast, eftsoones it was
    vntide.

18

Which when that scornefull *Squire of Dames* did
    vew,
He lowdly gan to laugh, and thus to iest ;
Alas for pittie that so faire a crew,
As like can not be seene from East to West,
Cannot find one this girdle to inuest.
Fie on the man, that did it first inuent,
To shame vs all with this, *Vngirt vnblest*.
Let neuer Ladie to his loue assent,
That hath this day so many so vnmanly shent.

19

Thereat all Knights gan laugh, and Ladies lowre :
Till that at last the gentle *Amoret*
Likewise assayd, to proue that girdles powre ;
And hauing it about her middle set,
Did find it fit, withouten breach or let.
Whereat the rest gan greatly to enuie :
But *Florimell* exceedingly did fret,
And snatching from her hand halfe angrily
The belt againe, about her bodie gan it tie.

20

Yet nathemore would it her bodie fit ;
Yet nathelesse to her, as her dew right,
It yeelded was by them, that iudged it :
And she her selfe adiudged to the Knight,
That bore the Hebene speare, as wonne in fight.
But *Britomart* would not thereto assent,
Ne her owne *Amoret* forgoe so light
For that strange Dame, whose beauties won-
    derment
She lesse esteem'd, then th'others vertuous
    gouernment.

21

Whom when the rest did see her to refuse,
They were full glad, in hope themselues to get
    her :
Yet at her choice they all did greatly muse.
But after that the Iudges did arret her
Vnto the second best, that lou'd her better ;
That was the *Saluage* Knight : but he was gone
In great displeasure, that he could not get her.
Then was she iudged *Triamond* his one ;
But *Triamond* lou'd *Canacee*, and other none.

22

Tho vnto *Satyran* she was adiudged,
Who was right glad to gaine so goodly meed :
But *Blandamour* thereat full greatly grudged,
And litle prays'd his labours euill speed,
That for to winne the saddle, lost the steed.
Ne lesse thereat did *Paridell* complaine,
And thought t'appeale from that, which was
    decreed,
To single combat with Sir *Satyrane*.
Thereto him *Ate* stird, new discord to maintaine.

23

And eke with these, full many other Knights
She through her wicked working did incense,
Her to demaund, and chalenge as their rights,
Deserued for their perils recompense.
Amongst the rest with boastfull vaine pretense
Stept *Braggadochio* forth, and as his thrall
Her claym'd, by him in battell wonne long sens :
Whereto her selfe he did to witnesse call ;
Who being askt, accordingly confessed all.

24

Thereat exceeding wroth was *Satyran* ;
And wroth with *Satyran* was *Blandamour* ;
And wroth with *Blandamour* was *Eriuan* ;
And at them both Sir *Paridell* did loure.
So all together stird vp strifull stoure,
And readie were new battell to darraine.
Each one profest to be her paramoure,
And vow'd with speare and shield it to main-
    taine ;   [restraine.
Ne Iudges powre, ne reasons rule mote them

25

Which troublous stirre when *Satyrane* auiz'd,
He gan to cast how to appease the same,
And to accord them all, this meanes deuiz'd :
First in the midst to set that fayrest Dame,
To whom each one his chalenge should disclame,
And he himselfe his right would eke releasse :
Then looke to whom she voluntarie came,
He should without disturbance her possesse :
Sweete is the loue that comes alone with will-
     ingnesse.

26

They all agreed, and then that snowy Mayd
Was in the middest plast among them all ;
All on her gazing wisht, and vowd, and prayd,
And to the Queene of beautie close did call,
That she vnto their portion might befall.
Then when she long had lookt vpon each one,
As though she wished to haue pleasd them all,
At last to *Braggadochio* selfe alone
She came of her accord, in spight of all his fone.

27

Which when they all beheld they chaft and rag'd,
And woxe nigh mad for very harts despight,
That from reuenge their willes they scarse
     asswag'd :
Some thought from him her to haue reft by
     might ;
Some proffer made with him for her to fight.
But he nought car'd for all that they could say :
For he their words as wind esteemed light.
Yet not fit place he thought it there to stay,
But secretly from thence that night her bore
     away.

28

They which remaynd, so soone as they perceiu'd,
That she was gone, departed thence with speed,
And follow'd them, in mind her to haue reau'd
From wight vnworthie of so noble meed.
In which poursuit how each one did succeede,
Shall else be told in order, as it fell.
But now of *Britomart* it here doth neede,
The hard aduentures and strange haps to tell ;
Since with the rest she went not after *Florimell*.

29

For soone as she them saw to discord set,
Her list no longer in that place abide;
But taking with her louely *Amoret*,
Vpon her first aduenture forth did ride,
To seeke her lou'd, making blind loue her guide.
Vnluckie Mayd to seeke her enemie,
Vnluckie Mayd to seeke him farre and wide,
Whom, when he was vnto her selfe most nie,
She through his late disguizement could him
     not descrie.

30

So much the more her griefe, the more her toyle
Yet neither toyle nor griefe she once did spare
In seeking him, that should her paine assoyle
Whereto great comfort in her sad misfare
Was *Amoret*, companion of her care :
Who likewise sought her louer long miswent
The gentle *Scudamour*, whose hart whileare
That stryfull hag with gealous discontent
Had fild, that he to fell reueng was fully bent.

31

Bent to reuenge on blamelesse *Britomart*
The crime, which cursed *Ate* kindled earst,
The which like tpornes did pricke his gealous hart
And through his soule like poysned arrow perst,
That by no reason it might be reuerst ;
For ought that *Glauce* could or doe or say.
For aye the more that she the same reherst,
The more it gauld, and grieu'd him night and day,
That nought but dire reuenge his anger mote
     defray.

32

So as they trauelled, the drouping night
Couered with cloudie storme and bitter showre,
That dreadfull seem'd to euery liuing wight,
Vpon them fell, before her timely howre ;
That forced them to seeke some couert bowre,
Where they might hide their heads in quiet rest,
And shrowd their persons from that stormie
     stowre.
Not farre away, not meete for any guest
They spide a little cottage, like some poore
     mans nest.

33

Vnder a steepe hilles side it placed was,
There where the mouldred earth had cav'd
     the banke ;
And fast beside a little brooke did pas
Of muddie water, that like puddle stanke,
By which few crooked sallowes grew in ranke :
Whereto approaching nigh, th y heard the sound
Of many yron hammers beating ranke,
And answering their wearie turnes around,
That seemed some blacksmith dwelt in that
     desert ground.

34

There entring in, they found the goodman selfe,
Full busily vnto his worke ybent ;
Who was to weet a wretched wearish elfe,
With hollow eyes and rawbone cheekes forspent,
As if he had in prison long bene pent :
Full blacke and griesly did his face appeare,
Besmeard with smoke that nigh his eye-sight
     blent ;
With rugged beard, and hoarie shagged heare,
The which he neuer wont to combe, or comely
     sheare.

35

Rude was his garment, and to rags all rent,
Ne better had he, ne for better cared :
With blistred hands emongst the cinders brent,
And fingers filthie, with long nayles vnpared,
Right fit to rend the food, on which he fared.
His name was *Care*; a blacksmith by his trade,
That neither day nor night from working spared,
But to small purpose yron wedges made :
Those be vnquiet thoughts, that carefull minds inuade.

36

In which his worke he had sixe seruants prest,
About the Andvile standing euermore,
With huge great hammers, that did neuer rest
From heaping stroakes, which thereon soused sore :
All sixe strong groomes, but one then other more ;
For by degrees they all were disagreed ;
So likewise did the hammers which they bore,
Like belles in greatnesse orderly succeed,
That he which was the last, the first did farre exceede.

37

He like a monstrous Gyant seem'd in sight,
Farre passing *Bronteus*, or *Pyracmon* great,
The which in *Lipari* doe day and night
Frame thunderbolts for *Ioues* auengefull threate.
So dreadfully he did the anduile beat,
That seem'd to dust he shortly would it driue :
So huge his hammer and so fierce his heat,
That seem'd a rocke of Diamond it could riue,
And rend a sunder quite, if he thereto list striue.

38

Sir *Scudamour* there entring, much admired
The manner of their worke and wearie paine ;
And hauing long beheld, at last enquired
The cause and end thereof: but all in vaine ;
For they for nought would from their worke refraine,
Ne let his speeches come vnto their eare.
And eke the breathfull bellowes blew amaine,
Like to the Northren winde, that none could heare :   [bellowes weare.
Those *Pensifenesse* did moue ; and *Sighes* the

39

Which when that warriour saw, he said no more,
But in his armour layd him downe to rest :
To rest he layd him downe vpon the flore,
(Why lome for ventrous Knights the bedding best)
And thought his wearie limbs to haue redrest.
And that old aged Dame, his faithfull Squire,
Her feeble ioynts layd eke a downe to rest ;
That needed much her weake age to desire,
After so long a trauell, which them both did tire.

40

There lay Sir *Scudamour* long while expecting,
When gentle sleepe his heauie eyes would close ;
Oft chaunging sides, and oft new place electing,
Where better seem'd he mote himselfe repose ;
And oft in wrath he thence againe vprose ;
And oft in wrath he layd him downe againe.
But wheresoeuer he did himselfe dispose,
He by no meanes could wished ease obtaine :
So euery place seem'd painefull, and ech changing vaine.

41

And euermore, when he to sleepe did thinke,
The hammers sound his senses did molest ;
And euermore, when he began to winke,
The bellowes noyse disturb'd his quiet rest,
Ne suffred sleepe to settle in his brest.
And all the night the dogs did barke and howle
About the house, at sent of stranger guest :
And now the crowing Cocke, and now the Owle
Lowde shriking him afflicted to the very sowle.

42

And if by fortune any litle nap
Vpon his heauie eye-lids chaunst to fall,
Eftsoones one of those villeins him did rap
Vpon his headpeece with his yron mall ;
That he was soone awaked therewithall,
And lightly started vp as one affrayd ;
Or as if one him suddenly did call.
So oftentimes he out of sleepe abrayd,
And then lay musing long, on that him ill apayd.

43

So long he muzed, and so long he lay,
That at the last his wearie sprite opprest
With fleshly weaknesse, which no creature may
Long time resist, gaue place to kindly rest,
That all his senses did full soone arrest :
Yet in his soundest sleepe, his dayly feare
His ydle braine gan busily molest,
And made him dreame those two disloyall were :
The things that day most minds, at night doe most appeare.

44

With that, the wicked carle the maister Smith
A paire of redwhot yron tongs did take
Out of the burning cinders, and therewith
Vnder his side him nipt, that forst to wake,
He felt his hart for very paine to quake,
And started vp auenged for to be
On him, the which his quiet slomber brake :
Yet looking round about him none could see ;
Yet did the smart remaine, though he himselfe did flee.

45

In such disquiet, and hartfretting payne,
  He all that night, that too long night did passe.
And now the day out of the Ocean mayne
Began to peepe aboue this earthly masse,
With pearly dew sprinkling the morning
    grasse :
Then vp he rose like heauie lumpe of lead,
That in his face, as in a looking glasse,
The signes of anguish one mote plainely read,
And ghesse the man to be dismayd with gealous
    dread.

46

Vnto his lofty steede he clombe anone,
  And forth vpon his former voiage fared,
And with him eke that aged Squire attone ;
Who whatsoeuer perill was prepared,
Both equall paines and equall perill shared :
The end whereof and daungerous euent
Shall for another canticle be spared.
But here my wearie teeme nigh ouer spent
Shall breath it selfe awhile, after so long a went.

Cant. VI.

Both Scudamour and Arthegall
Doe fight with Britomart,
He sees her face ; doth fall in loue,
and soone from her depart.

1

What equall torment to the griefe of mind,
  And pyning anguish hid in gentle hart,
That inly feeds it selfe with thoughts vnkind,
And nourisheth her owne consuming smart ?
What medicine can any Leaches art
Yeeld such a sore, that doth her grieuance hide,
And will to none her maladie impart ?
Such was the wound that *Scudamour* did gride;
For which *Dan Phebus* selfe cannot a salue
    prouide.

2

Who hauing left that restlesse house of *Care*,
  The next day, as he on his way did ride,
Full of melancholie and sad misfare,
Through misconceipt; all vnawares espide
An armed Knight vnder a forrest side,
Sitting in shade beside his grazing steede ;
Who soone as them approaching he descride,
Gan towards them to pricke with eger speede,
That seem'd he was full bent to some mis-
    chieuous deede.

3

Which *Scudamour* perceiuing, forth issewed
  To haue rencountred him in equall race ;
But soone as th'other nigh approaching, vewed
The armes he bore, his speare he gan abase,
And voide his course : at which so suddain case
He wondred much. But th'other thus can say ;
Ah gentle *Scudamour*, vnto your grace
I me submit, and you of pardon pray,
That almost had against you trespassed this day

4

Whereto thus *Scudamour*, Small harme it were
  For any knight, vpon a ventrous knight
Without displeasance for to proue his spere.
But reade you Sir, sith ye my name haue hight,
What is your owne, that I mote you requite.
Certes (sayd he) ye mote as now excuse
Me from discouering you my name aright :
For time yet serues that I the same refuse,
But call ye me the *Saluage Knight*, as others vse.

5

Then this, Sir *Saluage Knight* (quoth he) areede;
  Or doe you here within this forrest wonne,
That seemeth well to answere to your weede?
Or haue ye it for some occasion donne ?
That rather seemes, sith knowen armes ye
    shonne.
This other day (sayd he) a stranger knight
Shame and dishonour hath vnto me donne ;
On whom I waite to wreake that foule despight,
When euer he this way shall passe by day or
    night.

6

Shame be his meede (quoth he) that meaneth
    shame.
  But what is he, by whom ye shamed were ?
A stranger knight, sayd he, vnknowne by name,
But knowne by fame, and by an Hebene speare,
With which he all that met him, downe did beare.
He in an open Turney lately held,
Fro me the honour of that game did reare ;
And hauing me all wearie earst, downe feld,
The fayrest Ladie reft, and euer since withheld.

7

When *Scudamour* heard mention of that speare,
  He wist right well, that it was *Britomart*,
The which from him his fairest loue did beare.
Tho gan he swell in euery inner part,
For fell despight, and gnaw his gealous hart,
That thus he sharply sayd; Now by my head,
Yet is not this the first vnknightly part,
Which that same knight, whom by his launce
    I read,
Hath doen to noble knights, that many makes
    him dread.

8

For lately he my loue hath fro me reft,
  And eke defiled with foule villanie
The sacred pledge, which in his faith was left,
  In shame of knighthood and fidelitie ;
  The which ere long full deare he shall abie.
And if to that auenge by you decreed
This hand may helpe, or succour ought supplie,
  It shall not fayle, when so ye shall it need.
So both to wreake their wrathes on *Britomart* agreed.

9

Whiles thus they communed, lo farre away
  A Knight soft ryding towards them they spyde,
Attyr'd in forraine armes and straunge aray :
  Whom when they nigh approcht, they plaine descryde
  To be the same, for whom they did abyde.
Sayd then Sir *Scudamour*, Sir *Saluage* knight
Let me this craue, sith first I was defyde,
  That first I may that wrong to him requite :
And if I hap to fayle, you shall recure my right.

10

Which being yeelded, he his threatfull speare
  Gan fewter, and against her fiercely ran.
Who soone as she him saw approaching neare
  With so fell rage, her selfe she lightly gan
  To dight, to welcome him, well as she can :
But entertaind him in so rude a wise,
That to the ground she smote both horse and man ;
  Whence neither greatly hasted to arise,
But on their common harmes together did deuise.

11

But *Artegall* beholding his mischaunce,
  New matter added to his former fire ;
And eft auentring his steeleheaded launce,
  Against her rode, full of despiteous ire,
  That nought but spoyle and vengeance did require.
But to himselfe his felonous intent
Returning, disappointed his desire,
  Whiles vnawares his saddle he forwent,
And found himselfe on ground in great amazement.

12

Lightly he started vp out of that stound,
  And snatching forth his direfull deadly blade,
Did leape to her, as doth an eger hound
  Thrust to an Hynd within some couert glade,
  Whom without perill he cannot inuade.
With such fell greedines he her assayled,
That though she mounted were, yet he her made
  To giue him ground, (so much his force preuayld)
And shun his mightie strokes, gainst which no armes auayled.

13

So as they coursed here and there, it chaunst
  That in her wheeling round, behind her crest
So sorely he her strooke, that thence it glaunst
  Adowne her backe, the which it fairely blest
  From foule mischance ; ne did it euer rest,
Till on her horses hinder parts it fell ;
  Where byting deepe, so deadly it imprest,
That quite it chynd his backe behind the sell.
And to alight on foote her algates did compell.

14

Like as the lightning brond from riuen skie,
  Throwne out by angry *Ioue* in his vengeance,
With dreadfull force falles on some steeple hie ;
  Which battring, downe it on the church doth glance,
  And teares it all with terrible mischance.
Yet she no whit dismayd, her steed forsooke,
  And casting from her that enchaunted lance,
Vnto her sword and shield her soone betooke ;
  And therewithall at him right furiously she strooke.

15

So furiously she strooke in her first heat,
  Whiles with long fight on foot he breathlesse was,
That she him forced backward to retreat,
  And yeeld vnto her weapon way to pas :
  Whose raging rigour neither steele nor bras
Could stay, but to the tender flesh it went,
  And pour'd the purple bloud forth on the gras ;
That all his mayle yriv'd, and plates yrent.
Shew'd all his bodie bare vnto the cruell dent.

16

At length when as he saw her hastie heat
  Abate, and panting breath begin to fayle,
He through long sufferance growing now more great,
  Rose in his strength, and gan her fresh assayle,
  Heaping huge strokes, as thicke as showre of [hayle.
And lashing dreadfully at euery part,
  As if he thought her soule to disentrayle.
Ah cruell hand, and thrise more cruell hart,
That workst such wrecke on her, to whom thou dearest art.

17

What yron courage euer could endure,
  To worke such outrage on so faire a creature ?
And in his madnesse thinke with hands impure
  To spoyle so goodly workmanship of nature,
  The maker selfe resembling in her feature ?
Certes some hellish furie, or some feend
  This mischiefe framd, for their first loues defeature.
To bath their hands in bloud of dearest freend.
Thereby to make their loues beginning, their liues end.

18

Thus long they trac'd, and trauerst to and fro,
  Sometimes pursewing, and sometimes pursewed,
  Still as aduantage they espyde thereto:
  But toward th'end Sir *Arthegall* renewed
  His strength still more, but she still more
      decrewed.
At last his lucklesse hand he heau'd on hie,
  Hauing his forces all in one accrewed,
  And therewith stroke at her so hideouslie,
That seemed nought but death mote be her
      destinie.

19

The wicked stroke vpon her helmet chaunst,
  And with the force, which in it selfe it bore,
  Her ventayle shard away, and thence forth
      glaunst
A downe in vaine, ne harm'd her any more.
  With that her angels face, vnseene afore,
  Like to the ruddie morne appeard in sight,
  Deawed with siluer drops, through sweating sore,
  But somewhat redder, then beseem'd aright,
Through toylesome heate and labour of her
      weary fight.

20

And round about the same, her yellow heare
  Hauing through stirring loosd their wonted band,
  Like to a golden border did appeare,
  Framed in goldsmithes forge with cunning hand:
  Yet goldsmithes cunning could not vnderstand
  To frame such subtile wire, so shinie cleare.
  For it did glister like the golden sand,
  The which *Pactolus* with his waters shere,
Throwes forth vpon the riuage round about
      him nere.

21

And as his hand he vp againe did reare,
  Thinking to worke on her his vtmost wracke,
  His powrelesse arme benumbd with secret feare
  From his reuengefull purpose shronke abacke,
  And cruell sword out of his fingers slacke
  Fell downe to ground, as if the steele had sence,
  And felt some ruth, or sence his hand did lacke,
  Or both of them did thinke, obedience
To doe to so diuine a beauties excellence.

22

And he himselfe long gazing thereupon,
  At last fell humbly downe vpon his knee,
  And of his wonder made religion,
  Weening some heauenly goddesse he did see,
  Or else vnweeting, what it else might bee ;
  And pardon her besought his errour frayle,
  That had done outrage in so high degree :
  Whilest trembling horrour did his sense
      assayle,
And made ech member quake, and manly hart
      to quayle.

23

Nathelesse she full of wrath for that late stroke,
  All that long while vpheld her wrathfull hand,
  With fell intent, on him to bene ywroke,
  And looking sterne, still ouer him did stand,
  Threatning to strike, vnlesse he would with-
      stand :
And bad him rise, or surely he should die.
  But die or liue for nought he would vpstand
  But her of pardon prayd more earnestlie,
Or wreake on him her will for so great iniurie.

24

Which when as *Scudamour*, who now abrayd,
  Beheld, whereas he stood not farre aside,
  He was therewith right wondrously dismayd,
  And drawing nigh, when as he plaine descride
  That peerelesse paterne of Dame natures pride,
  And heauenly image of perfection,
  He blest himselfe, as one sore terrifide,
  And turning his feare to faint deuotion,
Did worship her as some celestiall vision.

25

But *Glauce*, seeing all that chaunced there,
  Well weeting how their errour to assoyle,
  Full glad of so good end, to them drew nere,
  And her salewd with seemely belaccoyle,
  Ioyous to see her safe after long toyle.
  Then her besought, as she to her was deare,
  To graunt vnto those warriours truce a whyle ;
  Which yeelded, they their beuers vp did reare,
And shew'd themselues to her, such as indeed
      they were.

26

When *Britomart* with sharpe auizefull eye
  Beheld the louely face of *Artegall*,
  Tempred with sternesse and stout maiestie,
  She gan eftsoones it to her mind to call,
  To be the same which in her fathers hall
  Long since in that enchaunted glasse she saw.
  Therewith her wrathfull courage gan appall,
  And haughtie spirits meekely to adaw,
That her enhaunced hand she downe can soft
      withdraw.

27

Yet she it forst to haue againe vpheld,
  As fayning choler, which was turn'd to cold :
  But euer when his visage she beheld,
  Her hand fell downe, and would no longer hold
  The wrathfull weapon gainst his countnance
      bold :
But when in vaine to fight she oft assayd,
  She arm'd her tongue, and thought at him to
      scold ;
Nathlesse her tongue not to her will obayd,
But brought forth speeches myld, when she
      would haue missayd.

28

But *Scudamour* now woxen inly glad,
  That all his gealous fear: he false had found,
And how that Hag his loue abused had
  With breach of faith and loyaltie vnsound,
  The which long time his grieued hart did wound,
He thus bespake ; Certes Sir *Artegall*,
  I ioy to see you lout so low on ground,
And now become to liue a Ladies thrall,
That whylome in your minde wont to despise
  them all.

29

Soone as she heard the name of *Artegall*,
  Her hart did leape, and all her hart-strings
    tremble,
For sudden ioy, and secret feare withall,
  And all her vitall powres with motion nimble,
  To succour it, themselues gan there assemble,
That by the swift recourse of flushing blood
  Right plaine appeard, though she it would
    dissemble,
And fayned still her former angry mood,
Thinking to hide the depth by troubling of the
    flood.

30

When *Glauce* thus gan wisely all vpknit ;
  Ye gentle Knights, whom fortune here hath
    To be spectators of this vncouth fit, [brought,
  Which secret fate hath in this Ladie wrought,
  Against the course of kind, ne meruaile nought,
Ne thenceforth feare the thing that hethertoo
  Hath troubled both your mindes with idle
    thought,
Fearing least she your loues away should woo,
Feared in vaine, sith meanes ye see there wants
    theretoo.

31

And you Sir *Artegall*, the saluage knight,
  Henceforth may not disdaine. that womans hand
Hath conquered you anew in second fight :
  For whylome they haue conquerd sea and land,
  And heauen it selfe, that nought may them
    withstand.
Ne henceforth be rebellious vnto loue,
  That is the crowne of knighthood, and the band
Of noble minds deriued from aboue,
Which being knit with vertue, neuer will
  remoue.

32

And you faire Ladie knight, my dearest Dame,
  Relent the rigour of your wrathfull will,
Whose fire were better turn'd to other flame ;
  And wiping out remembrance of all ill,
  Graunt him your grace, but so that he fulfill
The penance, which ye shall to him empart :
  For louers heauen must passe by sorrowes hell.
Thereat full inly blushed *Britomart* ;
But *Artegall* close smyling ioy'd in secret hart.

33

Yet durst he not make loue so suddenly,
  Ne thinke th'affection of her hart to draw
From one to other so quite contrary :
  Besides her modest countenance he saw
  So goodly graue, and full of princely aw,
That it his ranging fancie did refraine,
  And looser thoughts to lawfull bounds with-
    draw ;
Whereby the passion grew more fierce and faine,
Like to a stubborne steede whom strong hand
  would restraine.

34

But *Scudamour* whose hart twixt doubtfull feare
  And feeble hope hung all this while suspence,
Desiring of his *Amoret* to heare
  Some gladfull newes and sure intelligence,
  Her thus bespake ; But Sir without offence
Mote I request you tydings of my loue,
  My *Amoret*, sith you her freed fro thence,
Where she captiued long, great woes did proue;
That where ye left, I may her seeke, as doth
  behoue.

35

To whom thus *Britomart*, Certes Sir knight,
  What is of her become, or whether reft,
I can not vnto you aread a right.
  For from that time I from enchaunters theft
  Her freed, in which ye her all hopelesse left,
I her preseru'd from perill and from feare,
  And euermore from villenie her kept :
Ne euer was there wight to me more deare
Then she, ne vnto whom I more true loue did
  beare.

36

Till on a day as through a desert wyld
  We trauelled, both wearie of the way
We did alight, and sate in shadow myld ;
  Where fearelesse I to sleepe me downe did lay.
  But when as I did out of sleepe abray,
I found her not, where I her left whyleare,
  But thought she wandred was, or gone astray.
I cal'd her loud, I sought her farre and neare ;
But no where could her find, nor tydings of her
  heare.

37

When *Scudamour* those heauie tydings heard,
  His hart was thrild with point of deadly feare;
Ne in his face or bloud or life appeard,
  But senselesse stood, like to a mazed steare,
  That yet of mortall stroke the stound doth beare.
Till *Glauce* thus; Faire Sir, be nought dismayd
  With needelesse dread, till certaintie ye heare:
For yet she may be safe though somewhat
    strayd ;
Its best to hope the best, though of the worst
  affrayd.

38

Nathlesse he hardly of her chearefull speech
Did comfort take, or in his troubled sight
Shew'd change of better cheare : so sore a
   breach
That sudden newes had made into his spright;
Till *Britomart* him fairely thus behight ;
Great cause of sorrow certes Sir ye haue :
But comfort take : for by this heauens light
I vow, you dead or liuing not to leaue,
Till I her find, and wreake on him that her did
   reaue.

39

Therewith he rested, and well pleased was.
So peace being confirm'd amongst them all,
They tooke their steeds, and forward thence
   did pas
Vnto some resting place, which mote befall,
All being guided by Sir *Artegall.*
Where goodly solace was vnto them made,
And dayly feasting both in bowre and hall,
Vntill that they their wounds well healed had,
And wearie limmes recur'd after late vsage bad.

40

In all which time, Sir *Artegall* made way
Vnto the loue of noble *Britomart,*
And with meeke seruice and much suit did lay
Continuall siege vnto her gentle hart,
Which being whylome launcht with louely dart,
More eath was new impression to receiue,
How euer she her paynd with womanish art
To hide her wound, that none might it
   perceiue :
Vaine is the art that seekes it selfe for to
   deceiue.

41

So well he woo'd her, and so well he wrought her,
With faire entreatie and sweet blandishment,
That at the length vnto a bay he brought her,
So as she to his speeches was content
To lend an eare, and softly to relent.
At last through many vowes which forth he
   pour'd,
And many othes, she yeelded her consent
To be his loue, and take him for her Lord,
Till they with mariage meet might finish that
   accord.

42

Tho when they had long time there taken rest,
Sir *Artegall,* who all this while was bound
Vpon an hard aduenture yet in quest,
Fit time for him thence to depart it found,
To follow that, which he did long propound ;
And vnto her his congee came to take.
But her therewith full sore displeasd he found,
And loth to leaue her late betrothed make,
Her dearest loue full loth so shortly to forsake.

43

Yet he with strong perswasions her asswaged,
And wonne her will to suffer him depart ;
For which his faith with her he fast engaged,
And thousand vowes from bottome of his hart,
That all so soone as he by wit or art
Could that atchieue, whereto he did aspire,
He vnto her would speedily reuert :
No longer space thereto he did desire,
But till the horned moone three courses did
   expire.

44

With which she for the present was appeased,
And yeelded leaue, how euer malcontent
She inly were, and in her mind displeased.
So early in the morrow next he went
Forth on his way, to which he was ybent.
Ne wight him to attend, or way to guide,
As whylome was the custome ancient
Mongst Knights, when on aduentures they did
   ride,
Saue that she algates him a while accompanide.

45

And by the way she sundry purpose found
Of this or that, the time for to delay,
And of the perils whereto he was bound,
The feare whereof seem'd much her to affray :
But all she did was but to weare out day.
Full oftentimes she leaue of him did take ;
And eft againe deuiz'd some what to say,
Which she forgot, whereby excuse to make :
So loth she was his companie for to forsake.

46

At last when all her speeches she had spent,
And new occasion fayld her more to find,
She left him to his fortunes gouernment,
And backe returned with right heauie mind,
To *Scudamour,* who she had left behind,
With whom she went to seeke faire *Amoret,*
Her second care, though in another kind ;
For vertues onely sake, which doth beget
True loue and faithfull friendship, she by her
   did set.

47

Backe to that desert forrest they retyred,
Where sorie *Britomart* had lost her late ;
There they her sought, and euery where in-
   quired,
Where they might tydings get of her estate ;
Yet found they none. But by what haplesse
   fate,
Or hard misfortune she was thence conuayd,
And stolne away from her beloued mate,
Were long to tell ; therefore I here will stay
Vntill another tyde, that I it finish may.

Cant. VII.

CACACACACACACACACACACACACACA

Amoret rapt by greedie lust
Belphebe saues from dread,
The Squire her loues, and being blam'd
his dayes in dole doth lead.

CACACACACACACACACACACACACACA

1

Great God of loue, that with thy cruell dart
Doest conquer greatest conquerors on ground,
And setst thy kingdome in the captiue harts
Of Kings and Keasars, to thy seruice bound,
What glorie, or what guerdon hast thou found
In feeble Ladies tyranning so sore ;
And adding anguish to the bitter wound,
With which their liues thou lanchedst long
        afore,
By heaping stormes of trouble on them daily
    more ?

2

So whylome didst thou to faire *Florimell* ;
And so and so to noble *Britomart* :
So doest thou now to her, of whom I tell,
The louely *Amoret*, whose gentle hart
Thou martyrest with sorow and with smart,
In saluage forrests, and in deserts wide,
With Beares and Tygers taking heauie part,
Withouten comfort, and withouten guide,
That pittie is to heare the perils, which she tride.

3

So soone as she with that braue Britonesse
Had left that Turneyment for beauties prise,
They trauel'd long, that now for wearinesse,
Both of the way, and warlike exercise,
Both through a forest ryding did deuise
T'alight, and rest their wearie limbs awhile.
There heauie sleepe the eye-lids did surprise
Of *Britomart* after long tedious toyle,
That did her passed paines in quiet rest assoyle.

4

The whiles faire *Amoret*, of nought affeard,
  Walkt through the wood, for pleasure, or for
    need ;
When suddenly behind her backe she heard
One rushing forth out of the thickest weed,
That ere she backe could turne to taken heed,
Had vnawares her snatched vp from ground.
Feebly she shriekt, but so feebly indeed,
That *Britomart* heard not the shrilling sound,
There where through weary trauel she lay
    sleeping sound.

5

It was to weet a wilde and saluage man,
  Yet was no man, but onely like in shape
  And eke in stature higher by a span,
  All ouergrowne with haire, that could awhape
An hardy hart, and his wide mouth did gape
With huge great teeth, like to a tusked Bore :
For he liu'd all on rauin and on rape
Of men and beasts ; and fed on fleshly gore,
The signe whereof yet stain'd his bloudy lips
    afore

6

His neather lip was not like man nor beast,
  But like a wide deepe poke, downe hanging low,
  In which he wont the relickes of his feast,
  And cruell spoyle, which he had spard, to stow :
And ouer it his huge great nose did grow,
Full dreadfully empurpled all with bloud ;
And downe both sides two wide long eares did
    glow,   [stood,
And raught downe to his waste, when vp he
More great then th'eares of Elephants by *Indus*
    flood.

7

His wast was with a wreath of yuie greene
Engirt about, ne other garment wore :
For all his haire was like a garment seene ;
And in his hand a tall young oake he bore,
Whose knottie snags were sharpned all afore,
And beath'd in fire for steele to be in sted.
But whence he was, or of what wombe ybore,
Of beasts, or of the earth, I haue not red :
But certes was with milke of Wolues and Tygres
    fed.

8

This vgly creature in his armes her snatcht,
And through the forrest bore her quite away,
With briers and bushes all to rent and scratcht ;
Ne care he had, ne pittie of the pray,
Which many a knight had sought so many a day.
He stayed not, but in his armes her bearing
Ran, till he came to th'end of all his way,
Vnto his caue farre from all peoples hearing,
And there he threw her in, nought feeling, ne
    nought fearing.

9

For she deare Ladie all the way was dead,
  Whilest he in armes her bore ; but when she felt
Her selfe downe soust, she waked out of dread
Streight into griefe, that her deare hart nigh
    swelt,
And eft gan into tender teares to melt.
Then when she lookt about. and nothing found
But darknesse and dread horrour, where she
    dwelt,
She almost fell againe into a swound,
Ne wist whether aboue she were, or vnder
    ground.

10

With that she heard some one close by her side
Sighing and sobbing sore, as if the paine
Her tender hart in peeces would diuide :
Which she long listning, softly askt againe
What mister wight it was that so did plaine ?
To whom thus aunswer'd was : Ah wretched wight
That seekes to know anothers griefe in vaine,
Vnweeting of thine owne like haplesse plight :
Selfe to forget to mind another, is ouersight.

11

Aye me (said she) where am I, or with whom ?
Emong the liuing, or emong the dead ?
What shall of me vnhappy maid become ?
Shall death be th'end, or ought else worse,
aread.
Vnhappy mayd (then answerd she) whose dread
Vntride, is lesse then when thou shalt it try :
Death is to him, that wretched life doth lead,
Both grace and gaine ; but he in hell doth lie,
That liues a loathed life, and wishing cannot die.

12

This dismall day hath thee a caytiue made,
And vassall to the vilest wretch aliue,
Whose cursed vsage and vngodly trade
The heauens abhorre, and into darkenesse driue.
For on the spoile of women he doth liue,
Whose bodies chast, when euer in his powre
He may them catch, vnable to gainestriue,
He with his shamefull lust doth first deflowre,
And afterwards themselues doth cruelly deuoure.

13

Now twenty daies, by which the sonnes of men
Diuide their works, haue past through heuen
sheene,
Since I was brought into this dolefull den ;
During which space these sory eies haue seen
Seauen women by him slaine, and eaten clene.
And now no more for him but I alone,
And this old woman here remaining beene ;
Till thou cam'st hither to augment our mone,
And of vs three to morrow he will sure eate one.

14

Ah dreadfull tidings which thou doest declare,
(Quoth she) of all that euer hath bene knowen :
Full many great calamities and rare
This feeble brest endured hath, but none
Equall to this, where euer I haue gone.
But what are you, whom like vnlucky lot
Hath linckt with me in the same chaine attone ?
To tell (quoth she) that which ye see, needs not ;
A wofull wretched maid, of God and man forgot.

15

But what I was, it irkes me to reherse ;
Daughter vnto a Lord of high degree ;
That ioyd in happy peace, till fates peruerse
With guilefull loue did secretly agree,
To ouerthrow my state and dignitie.
It was my lot to loue a gentle swaine,
Yet was he but a Squire of low degree ;
Yet was he meet, vnlesse mine eye did faine,
By any Ladies side for Leman to haue laine.

16

But for his meannesse and disparagement,
My Sire, who me too dearely well did loue,
Vnto my choise by no meanes would assent,
But often did my folly fowle reproue.
Yet nothing could my fixed mind remoue,
But whether willed or nilled friend or foe,
I me resolu'd the vtmost end to proue,
And rather then my loue abandon so,
Both sire, and friends, and all for euer to forgo.

17

Thenceforth I sought by secret meanes to worke
Time to my will, and from his wrathfull sight
To hide th'intent, which in my heart did lurke,
Till I thereto had all things ready dight.
So on a day vnweeting vnto wight,
I with that Squire agreede away to flit,
And in a priuy place, betwixt vs hight,
Within a groue appointed him to meete ;
To which I boldly came vpon my feeble feete.

18

But ah vnhappy houre me thither brought :
For in that place where I him thought to find,
There was I found, contrary to my thought,
Of this accursed Carle of hellish kind,
The shame of men, and plague of womankind,
Who trussing me, as Eagle doth his pray,
Me hether brought with him, as swift as wind,
Where yet vntouched till this present day,
I rest his wretched thrall, the sad *Æmylia.*

19

Ah sad *Æmylia* (then sayd *Amoret,*)
Thy ruefull plight I pitty as mine owne.
But read to me, by what deuise or wit,
Hast thou in all this time, from him vnknowne
Thine honor sau'd, though into thraldome
throwne.
Through helpe (quoth she) of this old woman
here
I haue so done, as she to me hath showne.
For euer when he burnt in lustfull fire,
She in my stead supplide his bestiall desire.

20

Thus of their euils as they did discourse,
    And each did other much bewaile and mone ;
    Loe where the villaine selfe, their sorrowes
        sourse,
    Came to the caue, and rolling thence the stone,
    Which wont to stop the mouth thereof, that
        none
    Might issue forth, came rudely rushing in,
    And spredding ouer all the flore alone,
    Gan dight him selfe vnto his wonted sinne :
Which ended, then his bloudy banket should
        beginne.

21

Which when as fearefull *Amoret* perceiued,
    She staid not the vtmost end thereof to try,
    But like a ghastly Gelt, whose wits are reau~d,
    Ran forth in hast with hideous outcry,
    For horrour of his shamefull villany.
    But after her full lightly he vprose,
    And her pursu'd as fast as she did flie :
    Full fast she flies, and farre afore him goes,
Ne feeles the thorns and thickets pricke her
        tender toes.

22

Nor hedge, nor ditch, nor hill, nor dales hestaies,
    But ouerleapes them all, like Robucke light,
    And through the thickest makes her nighest
        waies ;
    And euermore when with regardfull sight
    She looking backe, espies that griesly wight
    Approching nigh, she gins to mend her pace,
    And makes her feare a spur to hast her flight :
    More swift then *Myrrh*' or *Daphne* in her race,
Or any of the Thracian Nimphes in saluage chase.

23

Long so she fled, and so he follow'd long ;
    Ne liuing aide for her on earth appeares,
    But if the heauens helpe to redresse her wrong,
    Moued with pity of her plenteous teares.
    It fortuned *Belphebe* with her peares
    The woody Nimphs, and with that louely boy,
    Was hunting then the Libbards and the Beares,
    In these wild woods, as was her wonted ioy,
To banish sloth, that oft doth noble mindes
        annoy.

24

It so befell, as oft it fals in chace,
    That each of them from other sundred were,
    And that same gentle Squire arriu'd in place,
    Where this same cursed caytiue did appeare,
    Pursuing that faire Lady full of feare,
    And now he her quite ouertaken had :
    And now he her away with him did beare
    Vnder his arme, as seeming wondrous glad,
That by his grenning laughter mote farre off be
        rad.

25

Which drery sight the gentle Squire espying,
    Doth hast to crosse him by the nearest way,
    Led with that wofull Ladies piteous crying,
    And him assailes with all the might he may,
    Yet will not he the louely spoile downe lay,
    But with his craggy club in his right hand,
    Defends him selfe, and saues his gotten pray.
    Yet had it bene right hard him to withstand,
But that he was full light and nimble on the land.

26

Thereto the villaine vsed craft in fight ;
    For euer when the Squire his iauelin shooke,
    He held the Lady forth before him right,
    And with her body, as a buckler, broke
    The puissance of his intended stroke.
    And if it chaunst, (as needs it must in fight)
    Whilest he on him was greedy to be wroke,
    That any little blow on her did light,
Then would he laugh aloud, and gather great
        delight.

27

Which subtill sleight did him encumber much,
    And made him oft, when he would strike, for-
        beare ;
    For hardly could he come the carle to touch,
    But that he her must hurt, or hazard neare
    Yet he his hand so carefully did beare,
    That at the last he did himselfe attaine,
    And therein left the pike head of his speare.
    A streame of coleblacke bloud thence gusht
        amaine,
That all her silken garments did with bloud be-
        staine.

28

With that he threw her rudely on the flore,
    And laying both his hands vpon his glaue,
    With dreadfull strokes let driue at him so sore,
    That forst him flie abacke, himselfe to saue :
    Yet he therewith so felly still did raue,
    That scarse the Squire his hand could once
        vpreare,
    But for aduantage ground vnto him gaue,
    Tracing and trauersing, now here, now there ;
For bootlesse thing it was to think such blowes
        to beare.

29

Whilest thus in battell they embusied were,
    Belphebe raunging in that forrest wide,
    The hideous noise of their huge strokes did
        heare,
    And drew thereto, making her eare her guide.
    Whom when that theefe approching nigh espide,
    With bow in hand, and arrowes ready bent,
    He by his former combate would not bide,
    But fled away with ghastly dreriment,
Well knowing her to be his deaths sole instrument.

30

Whom seeing flie, she speedily poursewed
With winged feete, as nimble as the winde,
And euer in her bow she ready shewed
The arrow, to his deadly marke desynde.
As when *Latonaes* daughter cruell kynde,
In vengement of her mothers great disgrace,
With fell despight her cruell arrowes tynde
Gainst wofull *Niobes* vnhappy race,
That all the gods did mone her miserable case.

31

So well she sped her and so far she ventred,
That ere vnto his hellish den he raught,
Euen as he ready was there to haue entred,
She sent an arrow forth with mighty draught,
That in the very dore him ouercaught,
And in his nape arriuing, through it thrild
His greedy throte, therewith in two distraught,
That all his vitall spirites thereby spild,
And all his hairy brest with gory bloud was fild.

32

Whom when on ground she groueling saw to
rowle,
She ran in hast his life to haue bereft:
But ere she could him reach, the sinfull sowle
Hauing his carrion corse quite sencelesse left,
Was fled to hell, surcharg'd with spoile and theft.
Yet ouer him she there long gazing stood,
And oft admir'd his monstrous shape, and oft
His mighty limbs, whilest all with filthy bloud
The place there ouerflowne, seemd like a
sodaine flood.

33

Thence forth she past into his dreadfull den,
Where nought but darkesome drerinesse she
found,
Ne creature saw, but hearkned now and then
Some litle whispering, and soft groning sound.
With that she askt, what ghosts there vnder
ground
Lay hid in horrour of eternall night?
And bad them, if so be they were not bound,
To come and shew themselues before the light,
Now freed from feare and danger of that dismall
wight.

34

Then forth the sad *Æmylia* issewed,
Yet trembling euery ioynt through former
feare;
And after her the Hag, there with her mewed,
A foule and lothsome creature did appeare;
A leman fit for such a louer deare.
That mou'd *Belphebe* her no lesse to hate,
Then for to rue the others heauy cheare;
Of whom she gan enquire of her estate.
Who all to her at large, as hapned, did relate.

35

Thence she them brought toward the place,
where late
She left the gentle Squire with *Amoret*:
There she him found by that new louely mate.
Who lay the whiles in swoune, full sadly set,
From her faire eyes wiping the deawy wet,
Which softly stild, and kissing them atweene,
And handling soft the hurts, which she did get.
For of that Carle she sorely bruz'd had beene,
Als of his owne rash hand one wound was to be
seene.

36

Which when she saw, with sodaine glauncing eye,
Her noble heart with sight thereof was fild
With deepe disdaine, and great indignity,
That in her wrath she thought them both haue
thrild,
With that selfe arrow, whi.h the Carle had kild:
Yet held her wrathfull hand from vengeance
sore,
But drawing nigh, ere he her well beheld;
Is this the faith, she said, and said no more,
But turnd her face, and fled away for euermore.

37

He seeing her depart, arose vp light,
Right sore agrieued at her sharpe reproofe,
And follow'd fast: but when he came in sight,
He durst not nigh approch, but kept aloofe,
For dread of her displeasures vtmost proofe.
And euermore, when he did grace entreat,
And framed speaches fit for his behoofe,
Her mortall arrowes she at him did threat,
And forst him backe with fowle dishonor to
retreat.

38

At last when long he follow'd had in vaine,
Yet found no ease of griefe, nor hope of grace,
Vnto those woods he turned backe againe,
Full of sad anguish, and in heauy case:
And finding there fit solitary place
For wofull wight, chose out a gloomy glade,
Where bright eye mote see bright heauens face,
For mossy trees, which couered all with shade
And sad melancholy: there he his cabin made.

39

His wonted warlike weapons all he broke,
And threw away, with vow to vse no more,
Ne thenceforth euer strike in battell stroke,
Ne euer word to speake to woman more;
But in that wildernesse, of men forlore,
And of the wicked world forgotten quight,
His hard mishap in dolor to deplore,
And wast his wretched daies in wofull plight:
So on him selfe to wreake his follies owne
despight.

40

And eke his garment, to be thereto meet,
  He wilfully did cut and shape anew ;
And his faire lockes, that wont with ointment
    sweet
To be embaulm'd, and sweat out dainty dew,
He let to grow and griesly to concrew,
Vncomb'd, vncurl'd, and carelesly vnshed ;
That in short time his face they ouergrew,
And ouer all his shoulders did dispred,
That who he whilome was, vneath was to be red.

41

There he continued in this carefull plight,
  Wretchedly wearing out his youthly yeares,
Through wilfull penury consumed quight,
That like a pined ghost he soone appeares.
For other food then that wilde forrest beares,
Ne other drinke there did he euer tast,
Then running water, tempred with his teares,
The more his weakened body so to wast :
That out of all mens knowledge he was worne
  at last.

42

For on a day, by fortune as it fell,
  His owne deare Lord Prince *Arthure* came
    that way,
Seeking aduentures, where he mote heare tell ;
And as he through the wandring wood did stray,
Hauing espide this Cabin far away,
He to it drew, to weet who there did wonne ;
Weening therein some holy Hermit lay,
That did resort of sinfull people shonne ;
Or else some woodman shrowded there from
    scorching sunne.

43

Arriuing there, he found this wretched man,
  Spending his daies in dolour and despaire,
And through long fasting woxen pale and wan,
All ouergrowen with rude and rugged haire ;
That albeit his owne deare Squire he were,
Yet he him knew not, ne auiz'd at all,
But like strange wight, whom he had seene no
    where,
Saluting him, gan into speach to fall,
And pitty much his plight, that liu'd like outcast
    thrall.

44

But to his speach he aunswered no whit,
  But stood still mute, as if he had beene dum,
Ne signe of sence did shew, ne common wit,
As one with griefe and anguishe ouercum,
And vnto euery thing did aunswere mum :
And euer when the Prince vnto him spake,
He louted lowly, as did him becum,
And humble homage did vnto him make,
Midst sorrow shewing ioyous semblance for his
    sake.

45

At which his vncouth guise and vsage quaint
  The Prince did wonder much, yet could not
    ghesse
The cause of that his sorrowfull constraint ;
Yet weend by secret signes of manlinesse,
Which close appeard in that rude brutishnesse,
That he whilome some gentle swaine had beene,
Traind vp in feats of armes and knightlinesse;
Which he obseru'd, by that he him had seene
To weld his naked sword, and try the edges
    keene.

46

And eke by that he saw on euery tree,
  How he the name of one engrauen had,
Which likly was his liefest loue to be,
For whom he now so sorely was bestad ;
Which was by him *BELPHEBE* rightly rad.
Yet who was that *Belphebe*, he ne wist ;
Yet saw he often how he wexed glad,
When he it heard, and how the ground he kist,
Wherein it written was, and how himselfe he
    blist :

47

Tho when he long had marked his demeanor,
  And saw that all he said and did, was vaine,
Ne ought mote make him change his wonted
    tenor,
Ne ought mote ease or mitigate his paine,
He left him there in languor to remaine,
Till time for him should remedy prouide,
And him restore to former grace againe.
Which for it is too long here to abide,
I will deferre the end vntill another tide.

Cant. VIII.

The gentle Squire recouers grace,
  Sclaunder her guests doth staine :
Corflambo chaseth Placidas,
  And is by Arthure slaine.

I

Well said the wiseman, now prou'd true by this,
  Which to this gentle Squire did happen late,
That the displeasure of the mighty is
Then death it selfe more dread and desperate.
For naught the same may calme ne mitigate,
Till time the tempest doe thereof delay
With sufferaunce soft, which rigour can abate,
And haue the sterne remembrance wypt away
Of bitter thoughts, which deepe therein infixed
    lay.

2

Like as it fell to this vnhappy boy,
  Whose tender heart the faire *Belphebe* had
  With one sterne looke so daunted, that no ioy
  In all his life, which afterwards he lad,
  He euer tasted, but with penaunce sad
  And pensiue sorrow pind and wore away,
  Ne euer laught, ne once shew'd countenance
    glad ;
  But alwaies wept and wailed night and day,
As blasted bloosme through heat doth languish
    and decay ;

3

Till on a day, as in his wonted wise
  His doole he made, there chaunst a turtle Doue
  To come, where he his dolors did deuise,
  That likewise late had lost her dearest loue,
  Which losse her made like passion also proue.
  Who seeing his sad plight, her tender heart
  With deare compassion deeply did emmoue,
  That she gan mone his vndeserued smart,
And with her dolefull accent beare with him a
    part.

4

Shee sitting by him as on ground he lay,
  Her mournefull notes full piteously did frame,
  And thereof made a lamentable lay,
  So sensibly compyld, that in the same
  Him seemed oft he heard his owne right name.
  With that he forth would poure so plenteous
    teares,
  And beat his breast vnworthy of such blame,
  And knocke his head, and rend his rugged
    heares,
That could haue perst the hearts of Tigres and
  of Beares.

5

Thus long this gentle bird to him did vse,
  Without n dread of perill to r paire
  Vnto his wonne, and with her mournefull muse
  Him to recomfort in his greatest care
  That much did ease his mourning and misfare:
  And euery day for guerdon of her song,
  He part of his small feast to her would share ;
That at the last of all his woe and wrong
Companion she became, and so continued long.

6

Vpon a day as she him sate beside,
  By chance he certaine miniments forth drew,
  Which yet with him as relickes did abide
  Of all the bounty, which *Belphebe* threw
  On him, whilst goodly grace she did him shew:
  Amongst the rest a iewell rich he found,
  That was a Ruby of right perfect hew,
  Shap'd like a heart, yet bleeding of the wound,
And with a litle golden chaine about it bound.

7

The same he tooke, and with a riband new,
  In which his Ladies colours were, did bind
  About the turtles necke, that with the vew
  Did greatly solace his engrieued mind.
  All vnawares the bird, when she did find
  Her selfe so deckt, her nimble wings displaid,
  And flew away, as lightly as the wind :
  Which sodaine accident him much dismaid,
And looking after long, did marke which way
    she straid.

8

But when as long he looked had in vaine,
  Yet saw her forward still to make her flight,
  His weary eie returnd to him againe,
  Full of discomfort and disquiet plight,
  That both his iuell he had lost so light,
  And eke his deare companion of his care.
  But that sweet bird departing, flew forth right
  Through the wide region of the wastfull aire,
Vntill she came where wonned his *Belphebe* faire.

9

There found she her (as then it did betide)
  Sitting in couert shade of arbors sweet,
  After late weary toile, which she had tride
  In saluage chase, to rest as seem'd her meet.
  There she alighting, fell before her feet,
  And gan to her her mournfull plaint to make,
  As was her wont, thinking to let her weet
  The great tormenting griefe, that for her
    sake
Her gentle Squire through her displeasure did
  pertake.

10

She her beholding with attentiue eye,
  At length did marke about her purple brest
  That precious iuell, which she formerly
  Had knowne right well with colourd ribbands
    drest :
  Therewith she rose in hast, and her addrest
  With ready hand it to haue reft away.
  But the swift bird obayd not her behest,
  But swaru'd aside, and there againe did stay :
She follow'd her, and thought againe it to assay.

11

And euer when she nigh approcht, the Doue
  Would flit a litle forward, and then stay,
  Till she drew neare, and then againe remoue ;
  So tempting her still to pursue the pray,
  And still from her escaping soft away :
  Till that at length into that forrest wide,
  She drew her far, and led with slow delay.
  In th'end she her vnto that place did guide,
Whereas that wofull man in languor did abide.

12

Eftsoones she flew vnto his fearelesse hand,
  And there a piteous ditty new deuiz'd,
  As if she would haue made him vnderstand,
  His sorrowes cause to be of her despis'd.
  Whom when she saw in wretched weedes
      disguiz'd,
  With heary glib deform'd, and meiger face,
  Like ghost late risen from his graue agryz'd,
  She knew him not, but pittied much his case,
And wisht it were in her to doe him any grace.

13

He her beholding, at her feet downe fell,
  And kist the ground on which her sole did tread,
  And washt the same with water, which did well
  From his moist eies, and like two streames
      procead,
  Yet spake no word, whereby she might aread
  What mister wight he was, or what he ment,
  But as one daunted with her presence dread,
  Onely few ruefull lookes vnto her sent,
As messengers of his true meaning and intent.

14

Yet nathemore his meaning she ared,
  But wondred much at his so selcouth case,
  And by his persons secret seemlyhed
  Well weend, that he had beene some man of
      place,
  Before misfortune did his hew deface
  That being mou'd with ruth she thus bespake.
  Ah wofull man, what heauens hard disgrace,
  Or wrath of cruell wight on thee ywrake ?
Or selfe disliked life doth thee thus wretched
      make ?

15

If heauen, then none may it redresse or blame,
  Sith to his powre we all are subiect borne :
  If wrathfull wight, then fowle rebuke and shame
  Be theirs, that haue so cruell thee forlorne ;
  But if through inward griefe or wilfull scorne
  Of life it be, then better doe aduise.
  For he whose daies in wilfull woe are worne,
  The grace of his Creator doth despise,
That will not vse his gifts for thanklesse
      nigardise.

16

When so he heard her say, eftsoones he brake
  His sodaine silence, which he long had pent,
  And sighing inly deepe, her thus bespake ;
  Then haue they all themselues against me bent :
  For heauen, first author of my languishment,
  Enuying my too great felicity,
  Did closely with a cruell one consent,
  To cloud my daies in dolefull misery,
And make me loath this life, still longing for
      to die.

17

Ne any but your selfe, O dearest dred, [wight
  Hath done this wrong, to wreake on worthlesse
  Your high displesure, through misdeeming bred:
  That when your pleasure is to deeme aright,
  Ye may redresse, and me restore to light.
  Which sory words her mightie hart did mate
  With mild regard, to see his ruefull plight,
  That her inburning wrath she gan abate,
And him receiu'd againe to former fauours state.

18

In which he long time afterwards did lead ·
  An happie life with grace and good accord,
  Fearlesse of fortunes chaunge or enuies dread,
  And eke all mindlesse of his owne deare Lord
  The noble Prince, who neuer heard one word
  Of tydings, what did vnto him betide,
  Or what good fortune did to him afford,
  But through the endlesse world did wander wide,
Him seeking euermore, yet no where him
      descride.

19

Till on a day as through that wood he rode,
  He chaunst to come where those two Ladies late,
  Æmylia and Amoret abode,
  Both in full sad and sorrowfull estate ;
  The one right feeble through the euill rate
  Of food, which in her duresse she had found :
  The other almost dead and desperate
  Through her late hurts, and through that
      haplesse wound,
With which the Squire in her defence her sore
      astound.

20

Whom when the Prince beheld, he gan to rew
  The euill case in which those Ladies lay ;
  But most was moued at the piteous vew
  Of Amoret. so neare vnto decay,
  That her great daunger did him much dismay.
  Eftsoones that pretious liquour forth he drew,
  Which he in store about him kept alway,
  And with few drops thereof did softly dew
Her wounds, that vnto strength restor'd her her
      soone anew.

21

Tho when they both recouered were right well,
  He gan of them inquire, what euill guide
  Them thether brought, and how their harmes
      befell.
  To whom they told all, that did them betide,
  And how from thraldome vile they were vntide
  Of that same wicked Carle, by Virgins hond ;
  Whose bloudie corse they shew'd him there
      beside,
  And eke his caue, in which they both were bond:
At which he wondred much, when all those
      signes he fond.

22

And euermore he greatly did desire
  To know, what Virgin did them thence vnbind;
  And oft of them did earnestly inquire,
  Where was her won, and how he mote her find.
  But when as nought according to his mind
  He could outlearne, he them from ground did
    reare:
  No seruice lothsome to a gentle kind;
  And on his warlike beast them both did beare,
Himselfe by them on foot, to succour them
    from feare.

23

So when that forrest they had passed well,
  A litle cotage farre away they spide,
  To which they drew, ere night vpon them fell;
  And entring in, found none therein abide,
  But one old woman sitting there beside,
  Vpon the ground in ragged rude attyre,
  With filthy lockes about her scattered wide,
  Gnawing her nayles for felnesse and for yre,
And there out sucking venime to her parts
    entyre.

24

A foule and loathly creature sure in sight,
  And in conditions to be loath'd no lesse:
  For she was stuft with rancour and despight
  Vp to the throat, that oft with bitternesse
  It forth would breake, and gush in great
    excesse,
  Pouring out streames of poyson and of gall
  Gainst all, that truth or vertue doe professe,
  Whom she with leasings lewdly did miscall,
And wickedly backbite: Her name men
  Sclaunder call.

25

Her nature is all goodnesse to abuse,
  And causelesse crimes continually to frame,
  With which she guiltlesse persons may accuse,
  And steale away the crowne of their good name;
  Ne euer Knight so bold, ne euer Dame
  So chast and loyall liu'd, but she would striue
  With forged cause them falsely to defame;
  Ne euer thing so well was doen aliue,
But she with blame would blot, and of due
    praise depriue.

26

Her words were not, as common words are ment,
  T'expresse the meaning of the inward mind,
  But noysome breath, and poysnous spirit sent
  From inward parts, with cancred malice lind,
  And breathed forth with blast of bitter wind;
  Which passing through the eares, would
    pierce the hart,
  And wound the soule it selfe with griefe vnkind:
  For like the stings of Aspes, that kill with smart,
Her spightfull words did pricke, and wound the
    inner part.

27

Such was that Hag, vnmeet to host such guests,
  Whom greatest Princes court would welcome
    fayne,
  But neede, that answers not to all requests,
  Bad them not looke for better entertayne;
  And eke that age despysed nicenesse vaine,
  Enur'd to hardnesse and to homely fare,
  Which them to warlike discipline did trayne,
  And manly limbs endur'd with litle care
Against all hard mishaps and fortunelesse
    misfare.

28

Then all that euening welcommed with cold,
  And chearelesse hunger, they together spent;
  Yet found no fault, but that the Hag did scold
  And rayle at them with grudgefull discontent,
  For lodging there without her owne consent:
  Yet they endured all with patience milde,
  And vnto rest themselues all onely lent,
  Regardlesse of that queane so base and vilde,
To be vniustly blamd, and bitterly reuilde.

29

Here well I weene, when as these rimes be red
  With misregard, that some rash witted wight,
  Whose looser thought will lightly be misled,
  These gentle Ladies will misdeeme too light,
  For thus conuersing with this noble Knight;
  Sith now of dayes such temperance is rare
  And hard to finde, that heat of youthfull
    spright
  For ought will from his greedie pleasure spare,
More hard for hungry steed t'abstaine from
    pleasant lare.

30

But antique age yet in the infancie
  Of time, did liue then like an innocent,
  In simple truth and blamelesse chastitie,
  Ne then of guile had made experiment,
  But voide of vile and treacherous intent,
  Held vertue for it selfe in soueraine awe:
  Then loyall loue had royall regiment,
  And each vnto his lust did make a lawe,
From all forbidden things his liking to withdraw.

31

The Lyon there did with the Lambe consort,
  And eke the Doue sate by the Faulcons side,
  Ne each of other feared fraud or tort,
  But did in safe securitie abide,
  Withouten perill of the stronger pride:
  But when the world woxe old, it woxe warre
    old
  (Whereof it hight) and hauing shortly tride
  The traines of wit, in wickednesse woxe bold,
And dared of all sinnes the secrets to vnfold.

32

Then beautie, which was made to represent
  The great Creatours owne resemblance bright,
  Vnto abuse of lawlesse lust was lent,
  And made the baite of bestiall delight :
  Then faire grew foule, and foule grew faire in
    sight,
  And that which wont to vanquish God and man,
Was made the vassall of the victors might ;
  Then did her glorious flowre wex dead and wan,
Despisd and troden downe of all that ouerran.

33

And now it is so vtterly decayd,
  That any bud thereof doth scarse remaine, [ayd,
  But if few plants preseru'd through heauenly
  In Princes Court doe hap to sprout againe,
  Dew'd with her drops of bountie Soueraine,
  Which from that goodly glorious flowre proceed,
  Sprung of the auncient stocke of Princes straine,
  Now th'onely remnant of that royall breed,
Whose noble kind at first was sure of heauenly
    seed.

34

Tho soone as day discouered heauens face
  To sinfull men with darknes ouercight,
  This gentle crew gan from their eye-lids chace
  The drowzie humour of the dampish night,
  And did thems lues vnto their iourney dight.
  So forth they yode, and forward softly paced,
  That them to view had bene an vncouth sight ;
  How all the way the Prince on footpace traced,
The Ladies both on horse, together fast
    embraced.

35

Soone as they thence departed were afore,
  That shamefull Hag, the slaunder of her sexe,
  Them follow'd fast, and them reuiled sore,
  Him calling theefe, them whores ; that much
    did vexe
  His noble hart ; thereto she did annexe
  False crimes and facts, such as they neuer ment,
  That those two Ladies much asham'd did wexe :
  The more did she pursue her lewd intent,
And rayl'd and rag'd, till she had all her poyson
    spent.

36

At last when they were passed out of sight,
  Yet she did not her spightfull speach forbeare,
  But after them did barke, and still backbite,
  Though there were none her hatefull words
    to heare :
  Like as a curre doth felly bite and teare
  The stone, which passed straunger at him threw;
  So she them seeing past the reach of eare,
  Against the stones and trees did rayle anew,
Till she had duld the sting, which in her tongs
    end grew.

37

They passing forth kept on their readie way,
  With easie steps so soft as foot could stry'de,
  Both for great feeblesse, which did oft assay
  Faire *Amoret*, that scarcely she could ryde,
  And eke through heauie armes, which sore
    annoyd
  The Prince on foot, not wonted so to fare ;
  Whose steadie hand was faine his steede to guyde,
  And all the way from trotting hard to spare,
So was his toyle the more, the more that was
    his care.

38

At length they spide, where towards them with
    speed
  A Squire came gallopping, as he would flie :
  Bearing a litle Dwarfe before his steed,
  That all the way full loud for aide did crie,
  That seem'd his shrikes would rend the
    brasen skie :
  Whom after did a mightie man pursew,
  Ryding vpon a Dromedare on hie,
  Of stature huge, and horrible of hew,
That would haue maz'd a man his dreadfull
    face to vew.

39

For from his fearefull eyes two fierie beames,
  More sharpe then points of needles did proceede,
  Shooting forth farre away two flaming streames,
  Full of sad powre, that poysonous bale did breede
  To all, that on him lookt without good heed,
  And secretly his enemies did slay :
  Like as the Basiliske of serpents seede,
  From powrefull eyes close venim doth conuay
Into the lookers hart, and killeth farre away.

40

He all the way did rage at that same Squire,
  And after him full many threatnings threw,
  With curses vaine in his auengefull ire :
  But none of them (so fast away he flew)
  Him ouertooke, before he came in vew.
  Where when he saw the Prince in armour bright,
  He cald to him aloud, his case to rew,
  And rescue him through succour of his might,
From that his cruell foe, that him pursewd in
    sight.

41

Eftsoones the Prince tooke downe those Ladies
    twaine
  From loftie steede, and mounting in their stead
  Came to that Squire, yet trembling euery vaine :
  Of whom he gan enquire his cause of dread ;
  Who as he gan the same to him aread,
  Loe hard behind his backe his foe was prest,
  With dreadfull weapon aymed at his head,
  That vnto death had doen him vnredrest,
Had not the noble Prince his readie stroke represt.

42

Who thrusting boldly twixt him and the blow,
The burden of the deadly brunt did beare
Vpon his shield, which lightly he did throw
Ouer his head, before the harme came neare.
Nathlesse it fell with so despiteous dreare
And heauie sway, that hard vnto his crowne
The shield it droue, and did the couering reare,
Therewith both Squire and dwarfe did tomble
    downe
Vnto the earth, and lay long while in senselesse
    swowne.

43

Whereat the Prince full wrath, his strong right
    hand
In full auengement heaued vp on hie,
And stroke the Pagan with his steely brand
So sore, that to his saddle bow thereby
He bowed low, and so a while did lie :
And sure had not his massie yron mace
Betwixt him and his hurt bene happily,
It would haue cleft him to the girding place,
Yet as it was, it did astonish him long space.

44

But when he to himselfe returnd againe,
All full of rage he gan to curse and sweare,
And vow by *Mahoune* that he should be slaine.
With that his murdrous mace he vp did reare,
That seemed nought the souse thereof could
    beare,
And therewith smote at him with all his might.
But ere that it to him approched neare,
The royall child with readie quicke foresight,
Did shun the proofe thereof and it auoyded
    light.

45

But ere his hand he could recure againe,
To ward his bodie from the balefull stound,
He smote at him with all his might and maine,
So furiously, that ere he wist, he found
His head before him tombling on the ground.
The whiles his babling tongue did yet blaspheme
And curse his God, that did him so confound ;
The whiles his life ran foorth in bloudie streame,
His soule descended downe into the Stygian
    reame.

46

Which when that Squire beheld, he woxe full glad
To see his foe br ath out his spright in vaine :
But that sam dwarfe right ories em u and sad,
And howld aloud to see his Lord there slaine,
And rent his haire and scratcht his face for
    paine.
Then gan the Prince at leasure to inquire
Of all the accident, there hapned plaine,
And what he was, whose eyes did flam with fire ;
All which was thus to him declared by that Squire.

47

This mightie man (quoth he) whom you haue
    slaine,
Of an huge Geauntesse whylome was bred ;
And by his strength rule to himselfe did gaine
Of many Nations into thraldome led,
And mightie kingdomes of his force adred ;
Whom yet he conquer'd not by bloudie fight,
Ne hostes of men with banners brode dispred,
But by the powre of his infectious sight,
With which he killed all, that came within his
    might.

48

Ne was he euer vanquished afore,
But euer vanquisht all, with whom he fought ;
Ne was there man so strong, but he downe bore,
Ne woman yet so faire, but he her brought
Vnto his bay, and captiued her thought.
For most of strength and beautie his desire
Was spoyle to make, and wast them vnto nought,
By casting secret flakes of lustfull fire
From his false eyes, into their harts and parts
    entire.

49

Therefore *Corflambo* was he cald aright,
Though namelesse there his bodie now doth lie,
Yet hath he left one daughter that is hight
The faire *Pœana* ; who seemes outwardly
So faire, as euer yet saw liuing eie :
And were her vertue like her beautie bright,
She were as faire as any vnder skie.
But ah she giuen is to vaine delight,
And eke too loose of life, and eke of loue too
    light.

50

So as it fell there was a gentle Squire,
That lou'd a Ladie of high parentage,
But for his meane degree might not aspire
To match so high, her friends with counsell sage,
Disuaded her from such a disparage.
But she, whose hart to loue was wholly lent,
Out of his hands could not redeeme her gage
But firmly following her first intent,
Resolu'd with him to wend, gainst all her friends
    consent.

51

So twixt themselues they pointed time and place,
To which when he according did repaire,
An hard mishap and disauentrous case
Him chaunst ; in stead of his *Æmylia* faire
This Gyants sonne, that lies there on the laire
An headlesse heape, him vnawares there
    caught,
And all dismayd through mercilesse despaire,
Him wretched thrall vnto his dongeon brought,
Where he remaines, of all vnsuccour'd and
    vnsought.

52

This Gyants daughter came vpon a day
  Vnto the prison in her ioyous glee,
  To view the thrals, which there in bondage
    lay :
  Amongst the rest she chaunced there to see
  This louely swaine the Squire of low degree ;
  To whom she did her liking lightly cast,
  And wooed him her paramour to bee :
  From day to day she woo'd and prayd him fast,
And for his loue him promist libertie at last.

53

He though affide vnto a former loue,
  To whom his faith he firmely ment to hold,
  Yet seeing not how thence he mote remoue,
  But by that meanes, which fortune did vnfold,
  Her graunted loue, but with affection cold
  To win her grace his libertie to get.
  Yet she him still detaines in captiue hold,
  Fearing least if she should him freely set,
He would her shortly leaue, and former loue
    forget.

54

Yet so much fauour she to him hath hight,
  Aboue the rest, that he sometimes may space
  And walke about her gardens of delight,
  Hauing a keeper still with him in place,
  Which keeper is this Dwarfe, her dearling base,
  To whom the keyes of euery prison dore
  By her committed be, of speciall grace,
  And at his will may whom he list restore,
And whom he list r serue, to be afflicted more.

55

Whereof when tydi gs came vnto mine eare,
  Full inly sorie for the feruent zeal ,
  Which I to him as to my soule did beare ;
  I thether went where I did long conceale
  My selfe, till that the Dwarfe did me r ueale,
  And told his Dame, her Squire of low degree
  Did secretly out of her prison steale ;
  For me he did mistake that Squire to bee ;
For neuer two so like did liuing creature see.

56

Then was I taken and before her brought,
  Who through the likenesse of my outward hew,
  Being likewise beguild in her thought,
  Gan blame me much for being so vntrew,
  To seeke by flight her fellowship t'eschew,
  That lou'd me deare, as dearest thing aliue.
  Thence she commaunded me to prison new ;
  Whereof I glad did not gainesay nor striue,
But suffred that same Dwarfe me to her don-
    geon driue.

57

There did I finde mine onely faithfull frend
  In heauy plight and sad perplexitie ;
  Whereof I sorie, yet my selfe did bend,
  Him to recomfort with my companie.
  But him the more agreeu d I found thereby :
  For all his ioy, he said, in that distresse
  Was mine and his *Æmylias* libertie.
  Æmylia well he lou'd, as I mote ghesse ;
Yet greater loue to me then her he did professe.

58

But I with better reason him auiz'd,
  And shew'd him how through error and
    mis-thought
  Of our like persons eath to be disguiz'd,
  Or his exchange, or freedome might be
    wrought.
  Whereto full loth was he, ne would for ought
  Consent, that I who stood all fearelesse free,
  Should wilfully be into thraldome brought,
  Till fortune did perforce it so decree.
Yet ouerrul'd at last, he did to me agree.

59

The morrow next about the wonted howre,
  The Dwarfe cald at the doore of *Amyas*,
  To come forthwith vnto his Ladi s bowre.
  In steed of whom forth came I *Placidas*.
  And vndiscerned. forth with him did pas.
  There with great ioyance and with gladsome
    glee,
  Of faire *Pœana* I receiued was,
  And oft imbrast, as if that I were hee,
And with kind words accoyd, vowing great
    loue to mee.

60

Which I, that was not bent to former loue,
  As was my friend, that had her long refusd,
  Did well accept, as well it did behoue,
  And to the present neede it wisely vsd.
  My former hardnesse first I faire excusd ;
  And after promist large amends to make.
  With such smooth termes her error I abusd,
  To my friends good, more then for mine owne
    sake,
For whose sole libertie I loue and life did stake.

61

Thenceforth I found more fauour at her hand,
  That to her Dwarfe, which had me in his charge,
  She bad to lighten my too heauie band,
  And graunt more scope to me to walke at large.
  So on a day as by the flowrie marge
  Of a fresh streame I with that Elfe did play,
  Finding no meanes how I might vs enlarge,
  But if that Dwarfe I could with me conuay,
I lightly snatcht him vp, and with me bore away.

62

Thereat he shriekt aloud, that with his cry
The Tyrant selfe came forth with yelling bray,
And me pursew'd ; but nathemore would I
Forgoe the purchase of my gotten pray,
But haue perforce him hether brought away.
Thus as they talked, loe where nigh at hand
Those Ladies two yet doubtfull through dismay
In presence came, desirous t'vnderstand
Tydings of all, which there had hapned on the
    land.

63

Where soone as sad *Æmylia* did espie
Her captiue louers friend, young *Placidas* ;
All mindlesse of her wonted modestie,
She to him ran, and him with streight embras
Enfolding said, And liues yet *Amyas* ?
He liues (quoth he) and his *Æmylia* loues.
Then lesse (said she) by all the woe I pas,
With which my weaker patience fortune proues.
But what mishap thus long him fro my selfe
    remoues ?

64

Then gan he all this storie to renew,
And tell the course of his captiuitie ;
That her deare hart full deepely made to rew,
And sigh full sore, to heare the miserie,
In which so long he mercilesse did lie.
Then after many teares and sorrowes spent,
She deare besought the Prince of remedie :
Who thereto did with readie will consent,
And well perform'd, as shall appeare by his
    euent.

Cant. IX.

&ctext;&ctext;&ctext;&ctext;&ctext;&ctext;&ctext;&ctext;&ctext;&ctext;&ctext;&ctext;&ctext;&ctext;&ctext;

The Squire of low degree releast
Pœana takes to wife :
Britomart fightes with many Knights,
Prince Arthur stints their strife.

&ctext;&ctext;&ctext;&ctext;&ctext;&ctext;&ctext;&ctext;&ctext;&ctext;&ctext;&ctext;&ctext;&ctext;&ctext;

1.

Hard is the doubt, and difficult to deeme,
When all three kinds of loue together meet,
And doe dispart the hart with powre extreme,
Whether shall weigh the balance downe ; to
    weet
The deare affection vnto kindred sweet,
Or raging fire of loue to woman kind,
Or zeale of friends combynd with vertues meet.
But of them all the band of vertuous mind
Me seemes the gentle hart should most assured
    bind.

2

For naturall affection soone doth cesse,
And quenched is with *Cupids* greater flame :
But faithfull friendship doth them both
    suppresse,
And them with may string discipline doth tame,
Through thoughts aspyring to eternall fame.
For as the soule doth rule the earthly masse,
And all the seruice of the bodie frame,
So loue of soule doth loue of bodie passe,
No lesse then perfect gold surmounts the meanest
    brasse.

3

All which who list by tryall to assay,
Shall in this storie find approued plaine ;
In which these Squires true friendship more
    did sway,
Then either care of parents could refraine,
Or loue of fairest Ladie could constraine.
For though *Pœana* were as faire as morne,
Yet did this trustie Squire with proud disdaine
For his friends sake her offred fauours scorne,
And she her selfe her syre, of whom she was
    yborne.

4

Now after that Prince *Arthur* graunted had,
To yeeld strong succour to that gentle swayne,
Who now long time had lyen in prison sad,
He gan aduise how best he mote darrayne
That enterprize, for greatest glories gayne.
That headlesse tyrants tronke he reard from
    ground,
And hauing ympt the head to it agayne,
Vpon his vsuall beast it firmely bound,
And made it so to ride, as it aliue was found.

5

Then did he take that chaced Squire, and layd
Before the ryder, as he captiue were,   [ayd,
And made his Dwarfe, though with vnwilling
To guide the beast, that did his maister beare,
Till to his castle they approched neare.   [ward
Whom when the watch, that kept continuall
Saw comming home ; all voide of doubtfull feare,
He running downe, the gate to him vnbard ;
Whom straight the Prince ensuing, in together
    far'd.

6

There he did find in her delitious boure
The faire *Pœana* playing on a Rote,
Complayning of her cruell Paramoure,
And singing all her sorrow to the note,
As she had learned readily by rote.
That with the sweetnesse of her rare delight,
The Prince halfe rapt, began on her to dote :
Till better him bethinking of the right,
He her vnwares attacht, and captiue held by
    might.

7

Whence being forth produc'd, when she perceiued
Her owne deare sire, she cald to him for aide.
But when of him no aunswere she receiued,
But saw him sencelesse by the Squire vpstaide,
She weened well, that then she was betraide :
Then gan she loudly cry, and weepe, and waile,
And that same Squire of treason to vpbraide.
But all in vaine, her plaints might not preuaile,
Ne none there was to reskue her, ne none to
    baile.

8

Then tooke he that same Dwarfe, and him com-
To open vnto him the prison dore,   [peld
And forth to bring those thrals, which there
    he held.
Thence forth were brought to him aboue a score
Of Knights and Squires to him vnknowne afore:
All which he did from bitter bondage free,
And vnto former liberty restore.
Amongst the rest, that Squire of low degree
Came forth full weake and wan, not like him
    selfe to bee.

9

Whom soone as faire *Æmylia* beheld,
And *Placidas*, they both vnto him ran,
And him embracing fast betwixt them held,
Striuing to comfort him all that they can,
And kissing oft his visage pale and wan.
That faire *Pœana* them beholding both,
Gan both enuy, and bitterly to ban ;
Through iealous passion weeping inly wroth,
To see the sight perforce, that both her eyes
    were loth.

10

But when a while they had together beene,
And diuersly conferred of their case,
She, though full oft she both of them had seene
   sunder, yet not euer in one place,
Began to doubt, when she them saw embrace,
Which was the captiue Squire she lou'd so deare,
Deceiued through great likenesse of their face,
For they so like in person did appeare,
That she vneath discerned, whether whether
    weare.

11

And eke the Prince, when as he them auized,
Their like resemblaunce much admired there,
And mazd how nature had so well disguized
Her worke, and counterfet her selfe so nere,
As if that by one patterne seene somewhere,
She had them made a paragone to be,
Or whether it through skill, or errour were.
Thus gazing long, at them much wondred he,
So did the other knights and Squires, which him
    did see.

12

Then gan they ransacke that same Castle strong,
In which he found great store of hoorded
   threasure,
The which that tyrant gathered had by wrong
And tortious powre, without respect or measure.
Vpon all which the Briton Prince made seasure,
And afterwards continu'd there a while,
To rest him selfe, and solace in soft pleasure
Those weaker Ladies after weary toile ;
To whom he did diuide part of his purchast
    spoile.

13

And for more ioy, that captiue Lady faire
The faire *Pœana* he enlarged free ;
And by the rest did set in sumptuous chaire,
To feast and frollicke ; nathemore would she
Shew gladsome countenaunce nor pleasaunt
   glee :
But grieued was for losse both of her sire,
And eke of Lordship, with both land and fee :
But most she touched was with griefe entire,
For losse of her new loue, the hope of her desire.

14

But her the Prince through his well wonted grace
To better termes of myldnesse did entreat,
From that fowle rudenesse, which did her deface;
And that same bitter corsiue, which did eat
Her tender heart, and made refraine from meat,
He with good thewes and speaches well applyde,
Did mollifie, and calme her raging heat.
For though she were most faire, and goodly
   dyde,
Yet she it all did mar with cruelty and pride.

15

And for to shut vp all in friendly loue,
Sith loue was first the ground of all her griefe,
That trusty Squire he wisely well did moue
Not to despise that dame, which lou'd him liefe,
Till he had made of her some better priefe,
But to accept her to his wedded wife.
Thereto he offred for to make him chiefe
Of all her land and lordship during life :
He yeelded, and her tooke ; so stinted all their
    strife.

16

From that day forth in peace and ioyous blis,
They liu'd together long without debate,
Ne priuate iarre, ne spite of enemis
Could shake the safe assuraunce of their state.
And she whom Nature did so faire create,
That she mote match the fairest of her daies,
Yet with lewd loues and lust intemperate
Had it defaste ; thenceforth reformd her waies,
That all men much admyrde her change, and
    spake her praise.

17

Thus when the Prince had perfectly compylde
These paires of friends in peace and setled rest,
Him selfe, whose minde did trauell as with
    chylde,
Of his old loue, conceau'd in secret brest,
Resolued to pursue his former quest ;
And taking leaue of all, with him did beare
Faire *Amoret*, whom Fortune by bequest
Had left in his protection whileare,
Exchanged out of one into an other feare.

18

Feare of her safety did her not constraine,
For well she wist now in a mighty hond,
Her person late in perill, did remaine,
Who able was all daungers to withstond.
But now in feare of shame she more did stond,
Seeing her selfe all soly succourlesse,
Left in the victors powre, like vassall bond ;
Whose will her weakenesse could no way represse,
In case his burning lust should breake into
    excesse.

19

But cause of feare sure had she none at all
Of him, who goodly learned had of yore
The course of loose affection to forstall,
And lawlesse lust to rule with reasons lore
That all the while he by his side her bore,
She was as safe as in a Sanctuary ;
Thus many miles they two together wore,
To seeke their loues dispersed diuersly,
Yet neither shewed to other their hearts priuity.

20

At length they came, whereas a troupe of Knights
They saw together skirmishing, as seemed :
Sixe they were all, all full of fell despight,
But foure of them the battell best beseemed,
That which of them was best, mote not be
    deemed.
Those foure were they, from whom false *Flori-*
    mell
By *Braggadochio* lately was redeemed.
To weet, sterne *Druon*, and lewd *Claribell*,
Loue-lauish *Blandamour*, and lustfull *Paridell*.

21

Druons delight was all in single life,
And vnto Ladies loue would lend no leasure :
The more was *Claribell* enraged rife
With feruent flames, and loued out of measure :
So eke lou'd *Blandamour*, but yet at pleasure
Would change his liking, and new Lemans proue :
But *Paridell* of loue did make no threasure,
But lusted after all, that him did moue.
So diuersly these foure disposed were to loue.

22

But those two other which beside them stoode
Were *Britomart*, and gentle *Scudamour*,
Who all the while beheld their wrathfull moode,
And wondred at their impacable stoure,
Whose like they neuer saw till that same houre :
So dreadfull strokes each did at other driue,
And laid on load with all their might and powre,
As if that euery dint the ghost would riue
Out of their wretched corses, and their liues
    depriue.

23

As when *Dan Æolus* in great displeasure,
For losse of his deare loue by *Neptune* hent,
Sends forth the winds out of his hidden
    threasure,
Vpon the sea to wreake his fell intent ;
They breaking forth with rude vnruliment,
From all foure parts of heauen doe rage full sore,
And tosse the deepes, and teare the firmament,
And all the world confound with wide vprore,
As if in stead thereof they *Chaos* would restore.

24

Cause of their discord, and so fell debate,
Was for the loue of that same snowy maid,
Whome they had lost in Turneyment of late,
And seeking long, to weet which way she straid,
Met here together, where through lewd vpbraide
Of *Ate* and *Duessa* they fell out,
And each one taking part in others aide,
This cruell conflict raised thereabout,
Whose dangerous successe depended yet in dout.

25

For sometimes *Paridell* and *Blandamour*
The better had, and bet the others backe,
Eftsoones the others did the field recoure,
And on their foes did worke full cruell wracke :
Yet neither would their fiendlike fury slacke,
But euermore their malice did augment ;
Till that vneath they forced were for lacke
Of breath, their raging rigour to relent,
And rest themselues for to recouer spirits spent.

26

There gan they change their sides, and new
    parts take ;
For *Paridell* did take to *Druons* side,
For old despight, which now forth newly brake
Gainst *Blandamour*, whom alwaies he enuide
And *Blandamour* to *Claribell* relide.
So all afresh gan former fight renew.
As when two Barkes, this caried with the tide,
That with the wind, contrary courses sew,
If wind and tide doe change, their courses
    change anew.

27

Thenceforth they much more furiously gan fare,
As if but then the battell had begonne,
Ne helmets bright,ne hawberks strong did spare,
That through the clifts the vermeil bloud out
    sponne,
And all adowne their riuen sides did ronne.
Such mortall malice, wonder was to see
In friends profest,and so great outrage donne:
But sooth is said, and tride in each degree,
Faint friends when they fall out, most cruell
    fomen bee.

28

Thus they long while continued in fight,
    Till *Scudamour*, and that same Briton maide,
By fortune in that place did chance to light:
Whomsooneas they with wrathfull eie bewraide,
They gan remember of the fowle vpbraide,
The which that Britonesse had to them donne,
In that late Turney for the snowy maide;
Where she had them both shamefully fordonne,
And eke the famous prize of beauty from them
    wonne.

29

Eftsoones all burning with a fresh desire
    Of fell reuenge, in their malicious mood
They from them selues gan turne their furious
    ire,
And cruell blades yet steeming with whot bloud,
Against those two let driue, as they were wood:
Who wondring much at that so sodaine fit,
Yet nought dismayd, them stoutly well with-
    stood;
Ne yeelded foote, ne once abacke did flit,
But being doubly smitten likewise doubly smit.

30

The warlike Dame was on her part assaid,
    Of *Claribell* and *Blandamour* attone;
And *Paridell* and *Druon* fiercely laid
At *Scudamour*, both his professed fone.
Foure charged two, and two surcharged one;
Yet did those two them selues so brauely beare,
That the other litle gained by the lone,
But with their owne repayed duely weare,
And vsury withall: such gaine was gotten deare.

31

Full oftentimes did *Britomart* assay
    To speake to them,and some emparlance moue;
But they for nought their cruell hands would
    stay,
Ne lend an eare to ought, that might behoue,
As when an eager mastiffe once doth proue
The tast of bloud of some engored beast,
No words may rate, nor rigour him remoue
From greedy hold of that his blouddy feast:
So litle did they hearken to her sweet beheast.

32

Whom when the Briton Prince a farre beheld
    With ods of so vnequall match opprest,
His mighty heart with indignation sweld,
And inward grudge fild his heroicke brest:
Eftsoones him selfe he to their aide addrest,
And thrusting fierce into the thickest preace,
Diuided them, how euer loth to rest,
And would them faine from battell to surceasse,
With gentle words perswading them to friendly
    peace.

33

But they so farre from peace or patience were,
    That all at once at him gan fiercely flie,
And lay on load,as they him downe would beare;
Like to a storme, which houers vnder skie
Long here and there,and round about doth stie,
At length breakes downe in raine, and haile,
    and sleet,
First from one coast, till nought thereof be drie;
And then another, till that likewise fleet;
And so from side to side till all the world it weet.

34

But now their forces greatly were decayd,
    The Prince yet being fresh vntoucht afore;
Who them with speaches milde gan first
    disswade
From such foule outrage,and them long forbore:
Till seeing them through suffrance hartned more,
Him selfe he bent their furies to abate,
And layd at them so sharpely and so sore,
That shortly them compelled to retrate,
And being brought in daunger,to relent too late.

35

But now his courage being throughly fired,
    He ment to make them know their follies prise,
Had not those two him instantly desired
T'asswage his wrath,and pardon their mesprise.
At whose request he gan him selfe aduise
To stay his hand, and of a truce to treat
In milder tearmes, as list them to deuise:
Mongst which the cause of their so cruell heat
He did them aske, who all that passed gan
    repeat.

36

And told at large how that same errant Knight,
    To weet faire *Britomart*, them late had foyled
In open turney, and by wrongfull fight
Both of their publicke praise had them de-
    spoyled,
And also of their priuate loues beguyled,
Of two full hard to read the harder theft.
But she that wrongfull challenge sooneassoyled,
And shew'd that she had not that Lady reft,
(As they supposd) but her had to her liking left.

37

To whom the Prince thus goodly well replied ;
Certes sir Knight, ye seemen much to blame,
To rip vp wrong, that battell once hath tried ;
Wherein the honor both of Armes ye shame,
And eke the loue of Ladies foule defame ;
To whom the world this franchise euer yeelded,
That of their loues choise they might freedom clame,
And in that right should by all knights be shielded :
Gainst which me seemes this war ye wrongfully haue wielded.

38

And yet (quoth she) a greater wrong remaines :
For I thereby my former loue haue lost,
Whom seeking euer since with endlesse paines,
Hath me much sorrow and much trauell cost ;
Aye me to see that gentle maide so tost.
But *Scudamour* then sighing deepe, thus saide,
Certes her losse ought me to sorrow most,
Whose right she is, where euer she be straide,
Through many perils wonne, and many fortunes waide.

39

For from the first that I her loue profest,
Vnto this houre, this present lucklesse howre,
I neuer ioyed happinesse nor rest,
But thus turmoild from one to other stowre,
I wast my life, and doe my daies deuowre
In wretched anguishe and incessant woe,
Passing the measure of my feeble powre,
That liuing thus, a wretch and louing so,
I neither can my loue, ne yet my life forgo.

40

Then good sir *Claribell* him thus bespake,
Now were it not sir *Scudamour* to you
Dislikefull paine, so sad a taske to take,
Mote we entreat you, sith this gentle crew
Is now so well accorded all anew ;
That as we ride together on our way,
Ye will recount to vs in order dew
All that aduenture, which ye did assay
For that faire Ladies loue: past perils well apay.

41

So gan the rest him likewise to require,
But *Britomart* did him importune hard,
To take on him that paine: whose great desire
He glad to satisfie, him selfe prepar'd
To tell through what misfortune he had far'd,
In that atchieuement, as to him befell.
And all those daungers vnto them declar'd,
Which sith they cannot in this Canto well
Comprised be, I will them in another tell.

Cant. X.

Scudamour doth his conquest tell,
Of vertuous Amoret :
Great Venus Temple is describ'd,
And louers life forth set.

I

True he it said, what euer man it sayd,
That loue with gall and hony doth abound,
But if the one be with the other wayd,
For euery dram of hony therein found,
A pound of gall doth ouer it redound.
That I too true by triall haue approued :
For since the day that first with deadly wound
My heart was launcht, and learned to haue loued,
I neuer ioyed howre, but still with care was moued.

2

And yet such grace is giuen them from aboue,
That all the cares and euill which they meet,
May nought at all their setled mindes remoue,
But seeme gainst common sence to them most sweet ;
As bosting in their martyrdome vnmeet.
So all that euer yet I haue endured,
I count as naught, and tread downe vnder feet,
Since of my loue at length I rest assured,
That to disloyalty she will not be allured.

3

Long were to tell the trauell and long toile,
Through which this shield of loue I late haue wonne,
And purchased this peerelesse beauties spoile,
That harder may be ended, then begonne.
But since ye so desire, your will be donne.
Then hearke ye gentle knights and Ladies free,
My hard mishaps, that ye may learne to shonne ;
For though sweet loue to conquer glorious bee,
Yet is the paine thereof much greater then the fee.

4

What time the fame of this renowmed prise
Flew first abroad, and all mens eares possest,
I hauing armes then taken, gan auise
To winne me honour by some noble gest,
And purchase me some place amongst the best.
I boldly thought (so young mens thoughts are bold)
That this same braue emprize for me did rest,
And that both shield and she whom I behold,
Might be my lucky lot ; sith all by lot we hold.

5

So on that hard aduenture forth I went,
   And to the place of perill shortly came.
   That was a temple faire and auncient,
   Which of great mother *Venus* bare the name,
   And farre renowmed through exceeding fame ;
   Much more then that, which was in *Paphos*
     built,
   Or that in *Cyprus*, both long since this same,
   Though all the pillours of the one were guilt,
And all the others pauement were with yuory
   spilt.

6

And it was seated in an Island strong,
   Abounding all with delices most rare,
   And wall'd by nature gainst inuaders wrong,
   That none mote haue accesse, nor inward fare,
   But by one way, that passage did prepare.
   It was a bridge ybuilt in goodly wize,
   With curious Corbes and pendants grauen faire,
   And arched all with porches, did arize
On stately pillours, fram'd after the Doricke
   guize.

7

And for defence thereof, on th'other end
   There reared was a castle faire and strong,
   That warded all which in or out did wend,
   And flancked both the bridges sides along,
   Gainst all that would it faine to force or wrong.
   And therein wonned twenty valiant Knights ;
   All twenty tride in warres experience long ;
   Whose office was, against all manner wights
By all meanes to maintaine that castels ancient
   rights.

8

Before that Castle was an open plaine,
   And in the midst thereof a piller placed ;
   On which this shield, of many sought in vaine,
   The shield of Loue, whose guerdon me hath
     graced,
   Was hangd on high with golden ribbands laced ;
   And in the marble stone was written this,
   With golden letters goodly well enchaced,
   Blessed the man that well can vse his blis :
Whose euer be the shield, faire Amoret be his.

9

Which when I red, my heart did inly earne,
   And pant with hope of that aduentures hap :
   Ne stayed further newes thereof to learne,
   But with my speare vpon the shield did rap,
   That all the castle ringed with the clap.
   Streight forth issewd a Knight all arm'd to
     proofe,
   And brauely mounted to his most mishap
Who staying nought to question from aloofe,
Ran fierce at me, that fire glaunst from his
   horses hoofe.

10

Whom boldly I encountred (as I could)
   And by good fortune shortly him vnseated.
   Eftsoones out sprung two more of equall
     mould ;
   But I them both with equall hap defeated :
   So all the twenty I likewise entreated,
   And left them groning there vpon the plaine.
   Then preacing to the pillour I repeated
   The read thereof for guerdon of my paine,
And taking downe the shield, with me did it
   retaine.

11

So forth without impediment I past,
   Till to the Bridges vtter gate I came :
   The which I found sure lockt and chained fast.
   I knockt, but no man aunswred me by name ;
   I cald, but no man answerd to my clame.
   Yet I perseuer'd still to knocke and call,
   Till at the last I spide within the same,
   Where one stood peeping through a creuisse small,
To whom I cald aloud, halfe angry therewithall.

12

That was to weet the Porter of the place,
   Vnto whose trust the charge thereof was lent :
   His name was *Doubt,* that had a double face,
   Th'one forward looking, th'other backeward
     bent,
   Therein resembling *Ianus* auncient,
   Which hath in charge the ingate of the yeare :
   And euermore his eyes about him went,
   As if some proued perill he did feare,
Or did misdoubt some ill, whose cause did not
   appeare.

13

On th'one side he, on th'other sate *Delay*,
   Behinde the gate, that none her might espy
   Whose manner was all passengers to stay,
   And entertaine with her occasions sly,
   Through which some lost great hope vnheedily,
   Which neuer they recouer might againe ;
   And others quite excluded forth, did ly
   Long languishing there in vnpittied paine,
And seeking often entraunce, afterwards in
   vaine.

14

Me when as he had priuily espide,
   Bearing the shield which I had conquerd late,
   He kend it streight, and to me opened wide.
   So in I past, and streight he closd the gate.
   But being in, *Delay* in close awaite
   Caught hold on me, and thought my steps to
     stay,
   Feigning full many a fond excuse to prate,
   And time to steale, the threasure of mans day,
Whose smallest minute lost, no riches render
   may.

15

But by no meanes my way I would forslow,
  For ought that euer she could doe or say,
  But from my lofty steede dismounting low,
  Past forth on foote, beholding all the way
  The goodly workes, and stones of rich assay,
  Cast into sundry shapes by wondrous skill,
  That like on earth no where I recken may:
  And vnderneath, the riuer rolling still
With murmure soft, that seem'd to serue the
      workmans will.

16

Thence forth I passed to the second gate,
  The *Gate of good desert*, whose goodly pride
  And costly frame, were long here to relate.
  The same to all stoode alwaies open wide:
  But in the Porch did euermore abide
  An hideous Giant, dreadfull to behold,
  That stopt the entraunce with his spacious
      stride,
  And with the terrour of his countenance bold
Full many did affray, that else faine enter would.

17

His name was *Daunger* dreaded ouer all,
  Who day and night did watch and duely ward,
  From fearefull cowards, entrance to forstall,
  And faint-heart-fooles, whom shew of perill hard
  Could terrifie from Fortunes faire adward:
  For oftentimes faint hearts at first espiall
  Of his grim face, were from approaching scard;
  Vnworthy they of grace, whom one deniall
Excludes from fairest hope, withouten further
      triall.

18

Yet many doughty warriours, often tride
  In greater perils to be stout and bold,
  Durst not the sternnesse of his looke abide,
  But soone as they his countenance did behold,
  Began to faint, and feele their corage cold.
  Againe some other, that in hard assaies
  Were cowards knowne, and litle count did hold,
  Either through gifts, or guile, or such like waies,
Crept in by stouping low, or stealing of the kaies.

19

But I though meanest man of many moe,
  Yet much disdaining vnto him to lout,
  Or creepe betweene his legs, so in to goe,
  Resolu'd him to assault with manhood stout,
  And either beat him in, or driue him out.
  Eftsoones aduauncing that enchaunted shield,
  With all my might I gan to lay about:
  Which when he saw, the glaiue which he did
      wield
He gan forthwith t'auale, and way vnto me yield.

20

So as I entred, I did backeward looke,
  For feare of harme, that might lie hidden there;
  And loe his hindparts, whereof heed I tooke,
  Much more deformed fearefull vgly were.
  Then all his former parts did earst appere.
  For hatred, murther, treason, and despight,
  With many moe lay in ambushment there,
  Awayting to entrap the warelesse wight,
Which did not them preuent with vigilant
      foresight.

21

Thus hauing past all perill, I was come
  Within the compasse of that Islands space;
  The which did seeme vnto my simple doome
  The onely pleasant and delightfull place,
  That euer troden was of footings trace.
  For all that nature by her mother wit
  Could frame in earth, and forme of substance
      base,
  Was there, and all that nature did omit,
Art playing second natures part, supplyed it.

22

No tree, that is of count, in greenewood growes,
  From lowest Iuniper to Ceder tall,
  No flowre in field, that daintie odour throwes,
  And deckes his branch with blossomes ouer all,
  But there was planted, or grew naturall:
  Nor sense of man so coy and curious nice,
  But there mote find to please it selfe withall;
  Nor hart could wish for any queint deuice,
But there it present was, and did fraile sense
      entice.

23

In such luxurious plentie of all pleasure,
  It seem'd a second paradise to ghesse,
  So lauishly enricht with natures threasure,
  That if the happie soules, which doe possesse
  Th'Elysian fields, and liue in lasting blesse,
  Should happen this with liuing eye to see,
  They soone would loath their lesser happinesse,
  And wish to life return'd againe to bee,
That in this ioyous place they mote haue
      ioyance free.

24

Fresh shadowes, fit to shroud from sunny ray;
  Faire lawnds, to take the sunne in season dew;
  Sweet springs, in which a thousand Nymphs
      did play;
  Soft rombling brookes, that gentle slomber drew;
  High reared mounts, the lands about to vew;
  Low looking dales, disloignd from common gaze;
  Delightfull bowres, to solace louers trew;
  False Labyrinthes, fond runners eyes to daze;
All which by nature made did nature selfe amaze.

25

And all without were walkes and alleyes dight
  With diuers trees, enrang'd in euen rankes ;
And here and there were pleasant arbors pight,
  And shadie seates, and sundry flowring bankes,
  To sit and rest the walkers wearie shankes,
And therein thousand payres of louers walkt,
  Praysing their god, and yeelding him great
    thankes,
Ne euer ought but of their true loues talkt,
Ne euer for rebuke or blame of any balkt.

26

All these together by themselues did sport
  Their spotlesse pleasures, and sweet loues con-
    tent.
But farre away from these, another sort
Of louers lincked in true harts consent ;
  Which loued not as these, for like intent,
But on chast vertue grounded their desire,
  Farre from all fraud, or fayned blandishment ;
Which in their spirits kindling zealous fire,
Braue thoughts and noble deedes did euermore
    aspire.

27

Such were great *Hercules,* and *Hylas* deare ;
Trew *Ionathan,* and *Dauid* trustie tryde ;
  Stout *Theseus,* and *Pirithous* his feare ;
Pylades and *Orestes* by his syde ;
  Myld *Titus* and *Gesippus* without pryde ;
Damon and *Pythias* whom death could not seuer:
  All these and all that euer had bene tyde
In bands of friendship, there did liue for euer,
Whose liues although decay'd, yet loues decayed
    neuer.

28

Which when as I, that neuer tasted blis,
  Nor happie howre, beheld with gazefull eye,
I thought there was none other heauen then this;
  And gan their endlesse happinesse enuye,
  That being free from feare and gealosye,
Might frankely there their loues desire possesse ;
  Whilest I through paines and perlous ieopardie,
Was forst to seeke my lifes deare patronesse :
Much dearer be the things, which come through
    hard distresse.

29

Yet all those sights, and all that else I saw,
  Might not my steps withhold, but that forth-
    right
Vnto that purposd place I did me draw,
  Where as my loue was lodged day and night :
The temple of great *Venus,* that is hight
The Queene of beautie, and of loue the mother,
  There worshipped of euery liuing wight ;
Whose goodly workmanship farre past all other
That euer were on earth, all were they set
    together.

30

Not that same famous Temple of *Diane,*
  Whose hight all *Ephesus* did ouersee,
And which all *Asia* sought with vowes prophane,
  One of the worlds seuen wonders sayd to bee,
  Might match with this by many a degree :
Nor that, which that wise King of *Iurie* framed,
  With endlesse cost, to be th'Almighties see ;
Nor all that else through all the world is named
To all the heathen Gods, might like to this be
    clamed.

31

I much admyring that so goodly frame,
  Vnto the porch approcht, which open stood ;
But therein sate an amiable Dame,
  That seem'd to be of very sober mood,
  And in her semblant shewed great womanhood :
Strange was her tyre ; for on her head a crowne
  She wore much like vnto a Danisk hood,
Poudred with pearle and stone, and all her gowne
Enwouen was with gold, that raught full low a
    downe.

32

On either side of her, two young men stood,
  Both strongly arm'd, as fearing one another :
Yet were they brethren both of halfe the blood,
  Begotten by two fathers of one mother,
  Though of contrarie natures each to other :
The one of them hight *Loue,* the other *Hate,*
  Hate was the elder, *Loue* the younger brother :
Yet was the younger stronger in his state
Then th'elder, and him maystred still in all
    debate.

33

Nathlesse that Dame so well them tempred both,
  That she them forced hand to ioyne in hand,
Albe that *Hatred* was thereto full loth,
  And turn'd his face away, as he did stand,
  Vnwilling to behold that louely band.
Yet she was of such grace and vertuous might,
  That her commaundment he could not with-
    stand,
But bit his lip for felonous despight,
And gnasht his yron tuskes at that displeasing
    sight.

34

Concord she cleeped was in common reed,
  Mother of blessed *Peace,* and *Friendship* trew ;
They both her twins, both borne of heauenly
    seed,
  And she her selfe likewise diuinely grew ;
  The which right well her workes diuine did shew :
For strength, and wealth, and happinesse she
    lends,
  And strife, and warre, and anger does subdew :
Of litle much, of foes she maketh frends,
And to afflicted minds sweet rest and quiet
    sends.

35

By her the heauen is in his course contained,
   And all the world in state vnmoued stands,
   As their Almightie maker first ordained,
   And bound them with inuiolable bands;
Else would the waters ouerflow the lands,
   And fire deuoure the ayre, and hell them quight,
   But that she holds them with her blessed hands.
She is the nourse of pleasure and delight,
And vnto *Venus* grace the gate doth open right.

36

By her I entring halfe dismayed was,
   But she in gentle wise me entertayned,
   And twixt her selfe and *Loue* did let me pas;
   But *Hatred* would my entrance haue re-
     strayned,
And with his club me threatned to haue brayned,
   Had not the Ladie with her powrefull speach
   Him from his wicked will vneath refrayned;
And th'other eke his malice did empeach,
Till I was throughly past the perill of his reach.

37

Into the inmost Temple thus I came,
   Which fuming all with frankensence I found,
   And odours rising from the altars flame.
   Vpon an hundred marble pillors round
The roofe vp high was reared from the ground,
   All deckt with crownes, and chaynes, and
     girlands gay,
   And thousand pretious gifts worth many
     a pound,
The which sad louers for their vowes did pay;
And all the ground was strow'd with flowres, as
    fresh as May.

38

An hundred Altars round about were set,
   All flaming with their sacrifices fire,
   That with the steme thereof the Temple swet,
   Which rould in clouds to heauen did aspire,
And in them bore true louers vowes entire:
   And eke an hundred brasen caudrons bright,
   To bath in ioy and amorous desire,
Euery of which was to a damzell hight;
For all the Priests were damzels, in soft linnen
    dight.

39

Right in the midst the Goddesse selfe did stand
   Vpon an altar of some costly masse,
   Whose substance was vneath to vnderstand:
   For neither pretious stone, nor durefull brasse,
Nor shining gold, nor mouldring clay it was;
   But much more rare and pretious to esteeme,
   Pure in aspect, and like to christall glasse,
Yet glasse was not, if one did rightly deeme,
But being faire and brickle, likest glasse did
    seeme.

40

But it in shape and beautie did excell
   All other Idoles, which the heathen adore,
   Farre passing that, which by surpassing skill
   Phidias did make in *Paphos* Isle of yore,
With which that wretched Greeke, that life
    forlore,
   Did fall in loue: yet this much fairer shined,
   But couered with a slender veile afore;
And both her feete and legs together twyned
Were with a snake, whose head and tail were
    fast combyned.   41

The cause why she was couered with a vele,
   Was hard to know, for that her Priests the same
   From peoples knowledge labour'd to concele.
   But sooth it was not sure for womanish shame,
Nor any blemish, which the worke mote blame;
   But for, they say, she hath both kinds in one,
   Both male and female, both vnder one name:
She syre and mother is her selfe alone,
Begets and eke conceiues, ne needeth other none.

42

And all about her necke and shoulders flew
   A flocke of litle loues, and sports, and ioyes,
   With nimble wings of gold and purple hew;
   Whose shapes seem'd not like to terrestriall
    boyes,
But like to Angels playing heauenly toyes;
   The whilest their eldest brother was away,
   Cupid their eldest brother; he enioyes
The wide kingdome of loue with Lordly sway,
And to his law compels all creatures to obay.

43

And all about her altar scattered lay
   Great sorts of louers piteously complayning,
   Some of their losse, some of their loues delay,
   Some of their pride, some paragons disdayning,
Some fearing fraud, some fraudulently fayning,
   As euery one had cause of good or ill.
   Amongst the rest some one through loues
    constrayning,
Tormented sore, could not containe it still,
But thus brake forth, that all the temple it
    did fill.   44

Great *Venus*, Queene of beautie and of grace,
   The ioy of Gods and men, that vnder skie
   Doest fayrest shine, and most adorne thy place,
   That with thy smyling looke doest pacifie
The raging seas, and makst the stormes to flie;
   Thee goddesse, thee the winds, the clouds
    doe feare,
   And when thou spredst thy mantle forth on hie,
The waters play and pleasant lands appeare,
And heauens laugh, and al the world shews
    ioyous cheare.

45

Then doth the dædale earth throw forth to thee
　Out of her fruitfull lap aboundant flowres,
　And then all liuing wights, soone as they see
　The spring breake forth out of his lusty bowres,
　They all doe learne to play the Paramours ;
　First doe the merry birds, thy prety pages
　Priuily pricked with thy lustfull powres,
　Chirpe loud to thee out of their leauy cages,
And thee their mother call to coole their kindly
　　rages.

46

Then doe the saluage beasts begin to play
　Their pleasant friskes, and loath their wonted
　　food ;
　The Lyons rore, the Tygres loudly bray,
　The raging Buls rebellow through the wood,
　And breaking forth, dare tempt the deepest
　　flood,
　To come where thou doest draw them with
　　desire :
　So all things else, that nourish vitall blood,
　Soone as with fury thou doest them inspire,
In generation seeke to quench their inward fire.

47

So all the world by thee at first was made,
　And dayly yet thou doest the same repayre :
　Ne ought on earth that merry is and glad,
　Ne ought on earth that louely is and fayre,
　But thou the same for pleasure didst prepayre.
　Thou art the root of all that ioyous is,
　Great God of men and women, queene of th'ayre,
　Mother of laughter, and welspring of blisse,
O graunt that of my loue at last I may not misse.

48

So did he say : but I with murmure soft,
　That none might heare the sorrow of my hart,
　Yet inly groning deepe and sighing oft,
　Besought her to graunt ease vnto my smart,
　And to my wound her gratious help impart.
　Whilest thus I spake, behold with happy eye
　I spyde, where at the Idoles feet apart
　A beuie of fayre damzels close did lye,
Wayting when as the Antheme should be sung
　　on hye.

49

The first of them did seeme of ryper yeares,
　And grauer countenance then all the rest ;
　Yet all the rest were eke her equall peares,
　Yet vnto her obayed all the best.
　Her name was *Womanhood*, that she exprest
　By her sad semblant and demeanure wyse :
　For stedfast still her eyes did fixed rest,
　Ne rov'd at randon after gazers guyse,
Whose luring baytes oftimes doe heedlesse
　harts entyse.

50

And next to her sate goodly *Shamefastnesse*,
　Ne euer durst her eyes from ground vpreare,
　Ne euer once did looke vp from her desse,
　As if some blame of euill she did feare,
　That in her cheekes made roses oft appeare :
　And her against sweet *Cherefulnesse* was placed,
　Whose eyes like twinkling stars in euening
　　cleare,
　Were deckt with smyles, that all sad humors
　　chaced,
And darted forth delights, the which her goodly
　graced.

51

And next to her sate sober *Modestie*,
　Holding her hand vpon her gentle hart ;
　And her against sate comely *Curtesie*,
　That vnto euery person knew her part ;
　And her before was seated ouerthwart
　Soft *Silence*, and submisse *Obedience*,
　Both linckt together neuer to dispart,
　Both gifts of God not gotten but from thence,
Both girlonds of his Saints against their foes
　offence.

52

Thus sate they all a round in seemely rate :
　And in the midst of them a goodly mayd,
　Euen in the lap of *Womanhood* there sate,
　The which was all in lilly white arayd,
　With siluer streames amongst the linnen
　　stray'd ;
　Like to the Morne, when first her shyning face
　Hath to the gloomy world it selfe bewray'd,
　That same was fayrest *Amoret* in place,
Shyning with beauties light, and heauenly
　vertues grace.

53

Whom soone as I beheld, my hart gan throb,
　And wade in doubt, what best were to be donne :
　For sacrilege me seem'd the Church to rob,
　And folly seem'd to leaue the thing vndonne,
　Which with so strong attempt I had begonne.
　Tho shaking off all doubt and shamefast feare,
　Which Ladies loue I heard had neuer wonne
　Mongst men of worth, I to her stepped neare,
And by the lilly hand her labour'd vp to reare.

54

Thereat that formost matrone me did blame,
　And sharpe rebuke, for being ouer bold ;
　Saying it was to Knight vnseemely shame,
　Vpon a recluse Virgin to lay hold,
　That vnto *Venus* seruices was sold.
　To whom I thus, Nay but it fitteth best,
　For *Cupids* man with *Venus* mayd to hold,
　For ill your goddesse seruices are drest
By virgins, and her sacrifices let to rest

55

With that my shield I forth to her did show,
  Which all that while I closely had conceald;
  On which when *Cupid* with his killing bow
  And cruell shafts emblazond she beheld,
  At sight thereof she was with terror queld,
  And said no more: but I which all that
    while
  The pledge of faith, her hand engaged held,
  Like warie Hynd within the weedie soyle,
For no intreatie would forgoe so glorious spoyle.

56

And euermore vpon the Goddesse face
  Mine eye was fixt, for feare of her offence,
  Whom when I saw with amiable grace
  To laugh at me, and fauour my pretence,
  I was emboldned with more confidence,
  And nought for nicenesse nor for enuy sparing,
  In presence of them all forth led her thence,
  All looking on, and like astonisht staring,
Yet to lay hand on her, not one of all them
    daring.

57

She often prayd, and often me besought,
  Sometime with tender teares to let her goe,
  Sometime with witching smyles: but yet for
    nought,
  That euer she to me could say or doe,
  Could she her wished freedome fro me wooe;
  But forth I led her through the Temple
    gate,
  By which I hardly past with much adoe:
  But that same Ladie which me friended late
In entrance, did me also friend in my retrate.

58

No lesse did *Daunger* threaten me with dread,
  When as he saw me, maugre all his powre,
  That glorious spoyle of beautie with me lead,
  Then *Cerberus*, when *Orpheus* did recoure
  His Leman from the Stygian Princes boure.
  But euermore my shield did me defend,
  Against the storme of euery dreadfull stoure:
  Thus safely with my loue I thence did wend.
So ended he his tale, where I this Canto end.

Cant. XI.

Marinells former wound is heald,
  he comes to Proteus hall,
Where Thames doth the Medway wedd,
  and feasts the Sea-gods all.

1

Bvt ah for pittie that I haue thus long
  Left a fayre Ladie languishing in payne:
  Now well away, that I haue doen such wrong
  To let faire *Florimell* in bands remayne,
  In bands of loue, and in sad thraldomes chayne:
  From which vnlesse some heauenly powre her
  By miracle, not yet appearing playne, [free
  She lenger yet is like captiu'd to bee:
That euen to thinke thereof, it inly pitties mee.

2

Here neede you to remember, how erewhile
  Vnlouely *Proteus*, missing to his mind
  That Virgins loue to win by wit or wile,
  Her threw into a dongeon deepe and blind,
  And there in chaynes her cruelly did bind,
  In hope thereby her to his bent to draw:
  For when as neither gifts nor graces kind
  Her constant mind could moue at all he saw,
He thought her to compell by crueltie and awe.

3

Deepe in the bottome of an huge great rocke
  The dongeon was, in which her bound he left,
  That neither yron barres, nor brasen locke
  Did neede to gard from force, or secret theft
  Of all her louers, which would her haue reft.
  For wall'd it was with waues, which rag'd
    and ror'd
  As they the cliffe in peeces would haue cleft;
  Besides ten thousand monsters foule abhor'd
Did waite about it, gaping griesly all begor'd.

4

And in the midst thereof did horror dwell,
  And darkenesse dredd, that neuer viewed day
  Like to the balefull house of lowest hell,
  In which old *Styx* her aged bones alway,
  Old *Styx* the Grandame of the Gods, doth lay.
  There did this lucklesse mayd seuen months
    abide,
  Ne euer euening saw, ne mornings ray,
  Ne euer from the day the night descride,
But thought it all one night, that did no houres
    diuide.

5

And all this was for loue of *Marinell*,
  Who her despysd (ah who would her despyse?)
  And wemens loue did from his hart expell,
  And all those ioyes that weake mankind entyse.
  Nathlesse his pride full dearely he did pryse;
  For of a womans hand it was ywroke,
  That of the wound he yet in languor lyes,
  Ne can be cured of that cruell stroke
Which *Britomart* him gaue, when he did her prouoke.

6

Yet farre and neare the Nymph his mother sought,
  And many salues did to his sore applie,
  And many herbes did vse. But when as nought
  She saw could ease his rankling maladie,
  At last to *Tryphon* she for helpe did hie,
  (This *Tryphon* is the seagods surgeon hight)
  Whom she besought to find some remedie:
  And for his paines a whistle him behight
That of a fishes shell was wrought with rare delight.

7

So well that Leach did hearke to her request,
  And did so well employ his carefull paine,
  That in short space his hurts he had redrest,
  And him restor'd to healthfull state againe:
  In which he long time after did remaine
  There with the Nymph his mother, like her thrall;
  Who sore against his will did him retaine,
  For feare of perill, which to him mote fall,
Through his too ventrous prowesse proued ouer all.

8

It fortun'd then, a solemne feast was there
  To all the Sea-gods and their fruitfull seede,
  In honour of the spousalls, which then were
  Betwixt the *Medway* and the *Thames* agreed.
  Long had the *Thames* (as we in records reed)
  Before that day her wooed to his bed;
  But the proud Nymph would for no worldly meed,
  Nor no entreatie to his loue be led;
Till now at last relenting, she to him was wed.

9

So both agreed, that this their bridale feast
  Should for the Gods in *Proteus* house be made;
  To which they all repayr'd, both most and least,
  Aswell which in the mightie Ocean trade,
  As that in riuers swim, or brookes doe wade.
  All which not if an hundred tongues to tell,
  And hundred mouthes, and voice of brasse I had,
  And endlesse memorie, that mote excell,
In order as they came, could I recount them well.

10

Helpe therefore, O thou sacred imp of *Ioue*,
  The noursling of Dame *Memorie* his deare,
  To whom those rolles, layd vp in heauen aboue,
  And records of antiquitie appeare,
  To which no wit of man may comen neare;
  Helpe me to tell the names of all those floods,
  And all those Nymphes, which then assembled were
  To that great banquet of the watry Gods,
And all their sundry kinds, and all their hid abodes.

11

First came great *Neptune* with his threeforkt mace,
  That rules the Seas, and makes them rise or fall;
  His dewy lockes did drop with brine apace,
  Vnder his Diademe imperiall:
  And by his side his Queene with coronall,
  Faire *Amphitrite*, most diuinely faire,
  Whose yuorie shoulders weren couered all,
  As with a robe, with her owne siluer haire,
And deckt with pearles, which th' Indian seas for her prepaire.

12

These marched farre afore the other crew;
  And all the way before them as they went,
  Triton his trompet shrill before them blew,
  For goodly triumph and great iollyment,
  That made the rockes to roare, as they were rent.
  And after them the royall issue came,
  Which of them sprung by lineall descent:
  First the Sea-gods, which to themselues doe clame
The powre to rule the billowes, and the waues to tame.

13

Phorcys, the father of that fatall brood,
  By whom those old Heroes wonne such fame;
  And *Glaucus*, that wise southsayes vnderstood;
  And tragicke *Inoes* sonne, the which became
  A God of seas through his mad mothers blame,
  Now hight *Palemon*, and is saylers frend;
  Great *Brontes*, and *Astræus*, that did shame
  Himselfe with incest of his kin vnkend;
And huge *Orion*, that doth tempests still portend.

14

The rich *Cteatus*, and *Eurytus* long;
  Neleus and *Pelias* louely brethren both;
  Mightie *Chrysaor*, and *Caïcus* strong;
  Eurypulus, that calmes the waters wroth;
  And faire *Euphœmus*, that vpon them goth
  As on the ground, without dismay or dread:
  Fierce *Eryx*, and *Alebius* that know'th
  The waters depth, and doth their bottome tread;
And sad *Asopus*, comely with his hoarie head.

15

There also some most famous founders were
Of puissant Nations, which the world possest;
Yet sonnes of *Neptune*, now assembled here:
Ancient *Ogyges*, euen th' aundentest,
And *Inachus* renowmd aboue the rest;
Phœnix, and *Aon*, and *Pelasgus* old,
Great *Belus*, *Phœax*, and *Agenor* best;
And mightie *Albion*, father of the bold
And warlike people, which the *Britaine* Islands hold.

16

For *Albion* the sonne of *Neptune* was,
Who for the proofe of his great puissance,
Out of his *Albion* did on dry-foot pas
Into old *Gall*, that now is cleeped *France*,
To fight with *Hercules*, that did aduance
To vanquish all the world with matchlesse might,
And there his mortall part by great mischance
Was slaine: but that which is th'immortall spright
Liues still: and to this feast with *Neptunes* seed was dight.

17

But what doe I their names seeke to reherse,
Which all the world haue with their issue fild?
How can they all in this so narrow verse
Contayned be, and in small compasse hild?
Let them record them, that are better skild,
And know the moniments of passed times:
Onely what needeth, shall be here fulfild,
T'expresse some part of that great equipage,
Which from great *Neptune* do deriue their parentage.

18

Next came the aged *Ocean*, and his Dame,
Old *Tethys*, th'oldest two of all the rest,
For all the rest of those two parents came,
Which afterward both sea and land possest:
Of all which *Nereus* th'eldest, and the best,
Did first proceed, then which none more vpright,
Ne more sincere in word and deed profest;
Most voide of guile, most free from fowle despight,
Doing him selfe, and teaching others to doe right.

19

Thereto he was expert in prophecies,
And could the ledden of the Gods vnfold,
Through which, when *Paris* brought his famous
The faire Tindarid lasse, he him fortold, [prise
That her all *Greece* with many a champion bold
Should fetch againe, and finally destroy
Proud *Priams* towne. So wise is *Nereus* old,
And so well skild; nathlesse he takes great ioy
Oft-times amongst the wanton Nymphs to sport and toy.

20

And after him the famous riuers came,
Which doe the earth enrich and beautifie:
The fertile Nile, which creatures new doth frame; [the skie;
Long Rhodanus, whose sourse springs from
Faire Ister, flowing from the mountaines hie;
Diuine Scamander, purpled yet with blood
Of Greekes and Troians, which therein did die;
Pactolus glistring with his golden flood,
And Tygris fierce, whose streames of none may be withstood.

21

Great Ganges, and immortall Euphrates,
Deepe Indus, and Mæander intricate,
Slow Peneus, and tempestuous Phasides,
Swift Rhene, and Alpheus still immaculate:
Ooraxes, feared for great *Cyrus* fate;
Tybris, renowned for the Romaines fame,
Rich Oranochy, though but knowen late;
And that huge Riuer, which doth beare his name
Of warlike Amazons, which doe possesse the same.

22

Ioy on those warlike women, which so long
Can from all men so rich a kingdome hold;
And shame on you, O men, which boast your strong [and bold.
And valiant hearts, in thoughts lesse hard
Yet quaile in conquest of that land of gold.
But this to you, O Britons, most pertaines,
To whom the right hereof it selfe hath sold:
The which for sparing litle cost or paines,
Loose so immortall glory, and so endlesse gaines.

23

Then was there heard a most celestiall sound,
Of dainty musicke, which did next ensew
Before the spouse: that was *Arion* crownd:
Who playing on his harpe, vnto him drew
The eares and hearts of all that goodly crew,
That euen yet the Dolphin, which him bore
Through the Ægæan seas from Pirates vew,
Stood still by him astonisht at his lore,
And all the raging seas for ioy forgot to rore.

24

So went he playing on the watery plaine.
Soone after whom the louely Bridegroome came,
The noble Thamis, with all his goodly traine,
But him before there went, as best became,
His auncient parents, namely th'auncient Thame.
But much more aged was his wife then he,
The Ouze, whom men doe Isis rightly name;
Full weake and crooked creature seemed shee,
And almost blind through eld, that scarce her way could see.

25

Therefore on either side she was sustained
  Of two smal grooms, which by their names
    were hight
  The *Churne*, and *Charwell*, two small streames,
    which pained
  Them selues her footing to direct aright,
  Whichfayledoft through faint andfeebleplight:
  But *Thame* was stronger, and of better stay;
  Yet seem'd full aged by his outward sight,
  With head all hoary, and his beard all gray,
Deawed with siluer drops, that trickled downe
    alway.

26

And eke he somewhat seem'd to stoupe afore
  With bowed backe, by reason of the lode,
  And auncient heauy burden, which he bore
  Of that faire City, wherein make abode
  So many learned impes, that shoote abrode,
  And with their braunches spred all Britany,
  No lesse then do her elder sisters broode.
  Ioy to you both, ye double noursery
Of Arts, but Oxford thine doth *Thame* most
    glorify.

27

But he their sonne full fresh and iolly was,
  All decked in a robe of watchet hew,
  On which the waues, glittering like Christall
    glas,
  So cunningly enwouen were. that few
  Could weenen, whether they were false or trew.
  And on his head like to a Coronet
  He wore, that seemed strange to common vew,
  In which were many towres and castels set,
That it encompast round as with a golden fret.

28

Like as the mother of the Gods, they say,
  In her great iron charet wonts to ride,
  When to *Ioues* pallace she doth take her way:
  Old *Cybele*, arayd with pompous pride,
  Wearing a Diademe embattild wide
  With hundred turrets, like a Turribant.
  With such an one was Thamis beautifide;
  That was to weet the famous Troynouant,
In which her kingdomes throne is chiefly resiant.

29

And round about him many a pretty Page
  Attended duely, ready to obay;
  All little Riuers, which owe vassallage
  To him, as to their Lord, and tribute pay:
  The chaulky Kenet, and the Thetis gray,
  The morish Cole, and the soft sliding Breane,
  The wanton Lee, that oft doth loose his way,
  And the still Darent, in whose waters cleane
Ten thousand fishes play, and decke his
    pleasant streame.

30

Then came his neighbour flouds, which nigh
    him dwell
  And water all the English soile throughout;
  They all on him this day attended well;
  And with meet seruice waited him about:
  Ne none disdained low to him to lout:
  No not the stately Seuerne grudg'd at all,
  Ne storming Humber, though he looked stout;
  But both him honor'd as their principall,
And let their swelling waters low before him fall.

31

There was the speedy Tamar, which deuides
  The Cornish and the Deuonish confines;
  Through both whose borders swiftly downe
    it glides,   [declines:
  And meeting Plim, to Plimmouth thence
  And Dart, nigh chockt with sands of tinny
    mines.
  But Auon marched in more stately path,
  Proud of his Adamants, with which he shines
  And glisters wide, as als' of wondrous Bath,
And Bristow faire, which on his waues he
    builded hath.

32

And there came Stoure with terrible aspect,
  Bearing his sixe deformed heads on hye,
  That doth his course through Blandford plains
    direct,
  And washeth Winborne meades in season drye.
  Next him went Wylibourne with passage slye,
  That of his wylinesse his name doth take,
  And of him selfe doth name the shire thereby:
  And Mole, that like a nousling Mole doth make
His way still vnder ground, till Thamis he
    ouertake.

33

Then came the Rother, decked all with woods
  Like a wood God, and flowing fast to Rhy:
  And Sture, that parteth with his pleasant floods
  The Easterne Saxons from the Southerne ny.
  And Clare, and Harwitch both doth beautify:
  Him follow'd Yar, soft washing Norwitch wall,
  And with him brought a present ioyfully
  Of his owne fish vnto their festiuall,
Whose like none else could shew, the which they
    Ruffins call.

34

Next these the plenteous Ouse came far from land,
  By many a city, and by many a towne,
  And many riuers taking vnder hand
  Into his waters, as he passeth downe,   [Rowne.
  The Cle, the Were, the Grant, the Sture, the
  Thence doth by Huntingdon and Cambridge flit,
  My mother Cambridge, whom as with a Crowne
  He doth adorne, and is adorn'd of it
With many a gentle Muse, and many a learned wit.

35

And after him the fatall Welland went,
That if old sawes proue true (which God forbid)
Shall drowne all Holland with his excrement,
And shall see Stamford, though now homely hid,
Then shine in learning, more then euer did
Cambridge or Oxford, Englands goodly beames.
And next to him the Nene downe softly slid;
And bounteous Trent, that in himselfe enseames
Both thirty sorts of fish, and thirty sundry streames.

36

Next these came Tyne, along whose stony bancke
That Romaine Monarch built a brasen wall,
Which mote the feebled Britons strongly flancke
Against the Picts, that swarmed ouer all,
Which yet thereof Gualseuer they doe call:
And Twede the limit betwixt Logris land
And Albany: And Eden though but small,
Yet often stainde with bloud of many a band
Of Scots and English both, that tyned on his strand.

37

Then came those sixe sad brethren, like forlorne,
That whilome were (as antique fathers tell)
Sixe valiant Knights, of one faire Nymphe yborne,
Which did in noble deedes of armes excell,
And wonned there, where now Yorke people dwell;
Still Vre, swift Werfe, and Oze the most of might,
High Swale, vnquiet Nide, and troublous Skell;
All whom a Scythian king, that Humber hight,
Slew cruelly, and in the riuer drowned quight.

38

But past not long, ere *Brutus* warlicke sonne
Locrinus them aueng'd, and the same date,
Which the proud Humber vnto them had donne,
By equall dome repayd on his owne pate:
For in the selfe same riuer, where he late
Had drenched them, he drowned him againe;
And nam'd the riuer of his wretched fate;
Whose bad condition yet it doth retaine,
Oft tossed with his stormes, which therein still remaine.

39

These after, came the stony shallow Lone,
That to old Loncaster his name doth lend;
And following Dee, which Britons long ygone
Did call diuine, that doth by Chester tend;
And Conway which out of his streame doth send
Plenty of pearles to decke his dames withall,
And Lindus that his pikes doth most commend,
Of which the auncient Lincolne men doe call;
All these together marched toward *Proteus* hall.

40

Ne thence the Irishe Riuers absent were,
Sith no lesse famous then the rest they bee,
And ioyne in neighbourhood of kingdome nere,
Why should they not likewise in loue agree,
And ioy likewise this solemne day to see?
They saw it all, and present were in place;
Though I them all according their degree,
Cannot recount, nor tell their hidden race,
Nor read the saluage cuntreis, thorough which they pace.

41

There was the Liffy rolling downe the lea,
The sandy Slane, the stony Aubrian,
The spacious Shenan spreading like a sea,
The pleasant Boyne, the fishy fruitfull Ban,
Swift Awniduff, which of the English man
Is cal'de Blacke water, and the Liffar deep,
Sad Trowis, that once his people ouerran,
Strong Allo tombling from Slewlogher steep,
And Mulla mine, whose waues I whilom taught to weep.

42

And there the three renowmed brethren were,
Which that great Gyant *Blomius* begot,
Of the faire Nimph *Rheusa* wandring there.
One day, as she to shunne the season whot,
Vnder Slewbloome in shady groue was got,
This Gyant found her, and by force deflowr'd,
Whereof conceiuing, she in time forth brought
These three faire sons, which being thence forth powrd
In three great riuers ran, and many countreis scowrd.

43

The first, the gentle Shure that making way
By sweet Clonmell, adornes rich Waterford;
The next, the stubborne Newre, whose waters gray
By faire Kilkenny and Rosseponte boord,
The third, the goodly Barow, which doth hoord
Great heapes of Salmons in his deepe bosome:
All which long sundred, doe at last accord
To ioyne in one, ere to the sea they come,
So flowing all from one, all one at last become.

44

There also was the wide embayed Mayre,
The pleasaunt Bandon crownd with many a wood,
The spreading Lee, that like an Island fayre
Encloseth Corke with his deuided flood;
And balefull Oure, late staind with English blood:
With many more, whose names no tongue can tell.
All which that day in order seemly good
Did on the Thamis attend, and waited well
To doe their duefull seruice, as to them befell.

45

Then came the Bride, the louely *Medua* came,
  Clad in a vesture of vnknowen geare,
  And vncouth fashion, yet her well became ;
  That seem'd like siluer, sprinckled here and
    theare
  With glittering spangs, that did like starres
    appeare,
  And wau'd vpon, like water Chamelot,
  To hide the metall, which yet euery where
  Bewrayd it selfe, to let men plainely wot,
It was no mortall worke, that seem'd and yet
    was not.

46

Her goodly lockes adowne her backe did flow
  Vnto her waste, with flowres bescattered,
  The which ambrosiall odours forth did throw
  To all about, and all her shoulders spred
  As a new spring ; and likewise on her hed
  A Chapelet of sundry flowers she wore,
  From vnder which the deawy humour shed,
  Did tricle downe her haire, like to the hore
Congealed litle drops, which doe the morne adore.

47

On her two pretty handmaides did attend,
  One cald the *Theise*, the other cald the *Crane* ;
  Which on her waited, things amisse to mend,
  And both behind vpheld her spredding traine ;
  Vnder the which, her feet appeared plaine,
  Her siluer feet, faire washt against this day :
  And her before there paced Pages twaine,
  Both clad in colours like, and like array,
The *Doune* and eke the *Frith*, both which pre-
    pard her way.

48

And after these the Sea Nymphs marched all,
  All goodly damzels, deckt with long greene
    haire,
  Whom of their sire *Nereides* men call,
  All which the Oceans daughter to him bare
  The gray eyde *Doris* : all which fifty are ;
  All which she there on her attending had.
  Swift *Proto*, milde *Eucrate*, *Thetis* faire,
  Soft *Spio*, sweete *Eudore*, *Sao* sad,
Light *Doto*, wanton *Glauce*, and *Galene* glad.

49

White hand *Eunica*, proud *Dynamene*,
  Ioyous *Thalia*, goodly *Amphitrite*,
  Louely *Pasithee*, kinde *Eulimene*,
  Light foote *Cymothoe*, and sweete *Melite*,
  Fairest *Pherusa*, *Phao* lilly white,
  Wondred *Agaue*, *Poris*, and *Nesæa*,
  With *Erato* that doth in loue delite,
  And *Panopæ*, and wise *Protomedæa*,
And snowy neckd *Doris*, and milkewhite
    Galathæa.

50

Speedy *Hippothoe*, and chaste *Actea*,
  Large *Lisianassa*, and *Pronæa* sage,
  Euagore, and light *Pontoporea*,
  And she, that with her least word can asswage
  The surging seas, when they do sorest rage,
  Cymodoce, and stout *Autonoe*,
  And *Neso*, and *Eione* well in age,
  And seeming still to smile, *Glauconome*,
And she that hight of many heastes *Polynome*.

51

Fresh *Alimeda*, deckt with girlond greene ;
  Hyponeo, with salt bedewed wrests
  Laomedia, like the christall sheene ;
  Liagore, much praisd for wise behests ;
  And *Psamathe*, for her brode snowy brests ;
  Cymo, *Eupompe*, and *Themiste* iust ;
  And she that vertue loues and vice detests
  Euarna, and *Menippe* true in trust,
And *Nemertea* learned well to rule her lust.

52

All these the daughters of old *Nereus* were,
  Which haue the sea in charge to them assinde,
  To rule his tides, and surges to vprere,
  To bring forth stormes, or fast them to
    vpbinde,
  And sailers saue from wreckes of wrathfull
    winde.
  And yet besides three thousand more there were
  Of th'Oceans seede, but *Ioues* and *Phœbus*
    kinde ;
  The which in floods and fountaines doe appere,
And all mankinde do nourish with their waters
    clere.

53

The which, more eath it were for mortall wight,
  To tell the sands, or count the starres on hye,
  Or ought more hard, then thinke to reckon right.
  But well I wote, that these which I descry,
  Were present at this great solemnity :
  And there amongst the rest, the mother was
  Of luckelesse *Marinell Cymodoce*.
  Which, for my Muse her selfe now tyred has,
  Vnto an other Canto I will ouerpas.

Cant. XII.

c/xc/xc/xc/xc/xc/xc/xc/xc/xc/xc/xc/xc/xc/xc/xc/o

Marin for loue of Florimell,
In languor wastes his life :
The Nymph his mother getteth her,
And giues to him for wife.

c/xc/xc/xc/xc/xc/xc/xc/xc/xc/xc/xc/xc/xc/xc/xc/o

1

O what an endlesse worke haue I in hand,
  To count the seas abundant progeny,
  Whose fruitfull seede farre passeth those in
    land,
  And also those which wonne in th'azure sky ?
  For much more eath to tell the starres on hy,
  Albe they endlesse seeme in estimation,
  Then to recount the Seas posterity :
So fertile be the flouds in generation,
So huge their numbers, and so numberlesse
    their nation.

2

Therefore the antique wisards well inuented,
  That *Venus* of the fomy sea was bred ;
  For that the seas by her are most augmented.
  Witnesse th'exceeding fry, which there are fed,
  And wondrous sholes, which may of none be red.
  Then blame me not, if I haue err'd in count
  Of Gods, of Nymphs, of riuers yet vnred :
  For though their numbers do much more sur-
    mount,
Yet all those same were there, which erst I did
    recount.

3

All those were there, and many other more,
  Whose names and nations were too long to tell,
  That *Proteus* house they fild euen to the dore ;
  Yet were they all in order, as befell,
  According their degrees disposed well.
  Amongst the rest, was faire *Cymodoce*,
  The mother of vnlucky *Marinell*,
  Who thither with her came, to learne and see
The manner of the Gods when they at banquet be.

4

But for he was halfe mortall, being bred
  Of mortall sire, though of immortall wombe,
  He might not with immortall food be fed,
  Ne with th'eternall Gods to bancket come ;
  But walkt abrode, and round about did rome,
  To view the building of that vncouth place,
  That seem'd vnlike vnto his earthly home :
  Where, as he to and fro by chaunce did trace,
There vnto him betid a disauentrous case.

5

Vnder the hanging of an hideous clieffe,
  He heard the lamentable voice of one,
  That piteously complaind her carefull grieffe,
  Which neuer she before disclosd to none,
  But to her selfe her sorrow did bemone,
  So feelingly her case she did complaine,
  That ruth it moued in the rocky stone,
  And made it seeme to feele her grieuous paine,
And oft to grone with billowes beating from the
    maine.

6

Though vaine I see my sorrowes to vnfold,
  And count my cares, when none is nigh to heare,
  Yet hoping griefe may lessen being told,
  I will them tell though vnto no man neare :
  For heauen that vnto all lends equall eare,
  Is farre from hearing of my heauy plight ;
  And lowest hell, to which I lie most neare,
  Cares not what euils hap to wretched wight ;
And greedy seas doe in the spoile of life delight.

7

Yet loe the seas I see by often beating,
  Doe pearce the rockes, and hardest marble
    weares ;
  But his hard rocky hart for no entreating
  Will yeeld, but when my piteous plaints he
    heares,
  Is hardned more with my aboundant teares.
  Yet though he neuer list to me relent,
  But let me waste in woe my wretched yeares,
  Yet will I neuer of my loue repent,
But ioy that for his sake I suffer prisonment.

8

And when my weary ghost with griefe outworne,
  By timely death shall winne her wished rest,
  Let then this plaint vnto his eares be borne,
  That blame it is to him, that armes profest,
  To let her die, whom he might haue redrest.
  There did she pause, inforced to giue place
  Vnto the passion, that her heart opprest,
  And after she had wept and wail'd a space,
She gan afresh thus to renew her wretched case.

9

Ye Gods of seas, if any Gods at all
  Haue care of right, or ruth of wretches wrong,
  By one or other way me woefull thrall,
  Deliuer hence out of this dungeon strong,
  In which I daily dying am too long.
  And if ye deeme me death for louing one,
  That loues not me, then doe it not prolong,
  But let me die and end my daies attone,
And let him liue vnlou'd, or loue him selfe alone.

10

But if that life ye vnto me decree,
 Then let mee liue, as louers ought to do,
 And of my lifes deare loue beloued be :
 And if he shall through pride your doome vndo,
 Do you by duresse him compell thereto,
 And in this prison put him here with me :
 One prison fittest is to hold vs two :
So had I rather to be thrall, then free ;
Such thraldome or such freedome let it surely be.

11

But O vaine iudgement, and conditions vaine,
 The which the prisoner points vnto the free,
 The whiles I him condemne, and deeme his paine,
 He where he list goes loose, and laughes at me.
 So euer loose, so euer happy be.
 But where so loose or happy that thou art,
 Know *Marinell* that all this is for thee.
With that she wept and wail'd, as if her hart
Would quite haue burst through great abundance of her smart.

12

All which complaint when *Marinell* had heard,
 And vnderstood the cause of all her care
 To come of him, for vsing her so hard,
 His stubborne heart, that neuer felt misfare
 Was toucht with soft remorse and pitty rare ;
 That euen for griefe of minde he oft did grone,
 And inly wish, that in his powre it weare
Her to redresse : but since he meanes found none
He could no more but her great misery bemone.

13

Thus whilst his stony heart with tender ruth
 Was toucht, and mighty courage mollifide,
 Dame *Venus* sonne that tameth stubborne youth
 With iron bit, and maketh him abide,
 Till like a victor on his backe he ride,
 Into his mouth his maystring bridle threw,
 That made him stoupe, till he did him bestride :
Then gan he make him tread his steps anew,
And learne to loue, by learning louers paines to rew.

14

Now gan he in his grieued minde deuise,
 How from that dungeon he might her enlarge :
 Some while he thought, by faire and humble wise
 To *Proteus* selfe to sue for her discharge :
 But then he fear'd his mothers former charge
 Gainst womens loue, long giuen him in vaine.
 Then gan he thinke, perforce with sword and targe
Her forth to fetch, and *Proteus* to constraine :
But soone he gan such folly to forthinke againe.

15

Then did he cast to steale her thence away,
 And with him beare, where none of her might know.
 But all in vaine : for why he found no way
 To enter in, or issue forth below :
 For all about that rocke the sea did flow.
 And though vnto his will she giuen were,
 Yet without ship or bote her thence to row,
 He wist not how her thence away to bere ;
And daunger well he wist long to continue there.

16

At last when as no meanes he could inuent,
 Backe to him selfe he gan returne the blame,
 That was the author of her punishment ;
 And with vile curses, and reprochfull shame
 To damne him selfe by euery euill name ;
 And deeme vnworthy or of loue or life
 That had despisde so chast and faire a dame,
Which him had sought through trouble and long strife ;
Yet had refusde a God that her had sought to wife.

17

In this sad plight he walked here and there,
 And romed round about the rocke in vaine,
 As he had lost him selfe, he wist not where ;
 Oft listening if he mote her heare againe ;
 And still bemoning her vnworthy paine.
 Like as an Hynde whose calfe is falne vnwares
 Into some pit, where she him heares complaine,
An hundred times about the pit side fares,
Right sorrowfully mourning her bereaued cares.

18

And now by this the feast was throughly ended,
 And euery one gan homeward to resort.
 Which seeing *Marinell*, was sore offended,
 That his departure thence should be so short,
 And leaue his loue in that sea-walled fort.
 Yet durst he not his mother disobay,
 But her attending in full seemly sort,
Did march amongst the many all the way :
And all the way did inly mourne, like one astray.

19

Being returned to his mothers bowre,
 In solitary silence far from wight,
 He gan record the lamentable stowre,
 In which his wretched loue lay day and night,
 For his deare sake, that ill deseru'd that plight :
 The thought whereof empierst his hart so deepe,
 That of no worldly thing he tooke delight ;
Ne dayly food did take, ne nightly sleepe,
But pyn'd, and mourn'd, and languisht, and alone did weepe.

20

That in short space his wonted chearefull hew
Gan fade, and liuely spirits deaded quight :
His cheeke bones raw, and eie-pits hollow grew,
And brawne yarmes had lost their knowen might,
That nothing like himselfe he seem d in sight.
Ere long so weake of limbe, and sicke of loue
He woxe, that lenger he note stand vpright,
But to his bed was brought, and layd aboue,
Like ruefull ghost, vnable once to stirre or moue.

21

Which when his mother saw, she in her mind
Was troubled sore, ne wist well what to weene :
Ne could by search nor any meanes out find
The secret cause and nature of his teene,
Whereby she might apply some medicine ;
But weeping day and night, did him attend,
And mourn'd to see her losse before her eyne,
Which grieu'd her more, that she it could not
    mend :
To see an helpelesse euill, double griefe doth lend.

22

Nought could she read the roote of his disease,
Ne weene what mister maladie it is,
Whereby to seeke some meanes it to appease.
Most did she thinke, but most she thought amis,
That that same former fatall wound of his
Whyleare by *Tryphon* was not throughly healed,
But closely rankled vnder th'orifis :
Least did she thinke, that which he most con-
    cealed,
That loue it was, which in his hart lay vn-
    reuealed.

23

Therefore to *Tryphon* she againe doth hast,
And him doth chyde as false and fraudulent,
That fayld the trust, which she in him had plast,
To cure her sonne, as he his faith had lent :
Who now was falne into new languishment
Of his old hurt, which was not throughly cured.
So backe he came vnto her patient,
Where searching euery part, her well assured,
That it was no old sore, which his new paine
    procured.

24

But that it was some other maladie,
Or griefe vnknowne, which he could not discerne :
So left he her withouten remedie.   [earne,
Then gan her heart to faint, and quake, and
And inly troubled was, the truth to learne.
Vnto himselfe she came, and him besought,
Now with faire speches, now with threatnings
    sterne,
If ought lay hidden in his grieued thought,
It to reueale : who still her answered, there was
    nought.

25

Nathlesse she rested not so satisfide,
But leauing watry gods, as booting nought,
Vnto the shinie heauen in haste she hide,
And thence *Apollo* King of Leaches brought.
Apollo came ; who soone as he had sought
Through his disease, did by and by out find,
That he did languish of some inward thought,
The which afflicted his engrieued mind ;
Which loue he red to be, that leads each liuing
    kind.

26

Which when he had vnto his mother told,
She gan thereat to fret, and greatly grieue.
And comming to her sonne, gan first to scold,
And chyde at him, that made her misbelieue :
But afterwards she gan him soft to shrieue,
And wooe with faire intreatie, to disclose,
Which of the Nymphes his heart so sore did
    mieue.
For sure she weend it was some one of those,
Which he had lately seene, that for his loue he
    chose.

27

Now lesse she feared that same fatall read,
That warned him of womens loue beware :
Which being ment of mortall creatures sead,
For loue of Nymphes she thought she need not
    care,
But promist him, what euer wight she weare,
That she her loue to him would shortly gaine :
So he her told : but soone as she did heare
That *Florimell* it was, which wrought his paine,
She gan a fresh to chafe, and grieue in euery
    vaine.

28

Yet since she saw the streight extremitie,
In which his life vnluckily was layd,
It was no time to scan the prophecie,
Whether old *Proteus* true or false had sayd,
That his decay should happen by a mayd.
It's late in death of daunger to aduize,
Or loue forbid him, that is life denayd :
But rather gan in troubled mind deuize,
How she that Ladies libertie might enterprize.

29

To *Proteus* selfe to sew she thought it vaine,
Who was the root and worker of her woe :
Nor vnto any meaner to complaine,
But vnto great king *Neptune* selfe did goe,
And on her knee before him falling lowe,
Made humble suit vnto his Maiestie,
To graunt to her, her sonnes life, which his foe
A cruell Tyrant had presumpteouslie
By wicked doome condemn'd, a wretched death
    to die.

30

To whom God *Neptune* softly smyling, thus ;
  Daughter me seemes of double wrong ye plaine,
  Gainst one that hath both wronged you, and vs :
  For death t'adward I ween'd did appertaine
  To none, but to the seas sole Soueraine.
Read therefore who it is, which this hath wrought,
  And for what cause ; the truth discouer plaine.
  For neuer wight so euill did or thought,
But would some rightfull cause pretend, though rightly nought.

31

To whom she answerd, Then it is by name
  Proteus, that hath ordayn'd my sonne to die ;
  For that a waift, the which by fortune came
  Vpon your seas, he claym'd as propertie :
  And yet nor his, nor his in equitie,
  But yours the waift by high prerogatiue.
  Therefore I humbly craue your Maiestie,
  It to repleuie, and my sonne repriue :
So shall you by one gift saue all vs three aliue.

32

He graunted it : and streight his warrant made,
  Vnder the Sea-gods seale autenticall,
  Commaunding *Proteus* straight t'enlarge the mayd,
  Which wandring on his seas imperiall,
  He lately tooke, and sithence kept as thrall.
  Which she receiuing with meete thankefulnesse,
  Departed straight to *Proteus* therewithall :
  Who reading it with inward loathfulnesse,
Was grieued to restore the pledge, he did possesse.

33

Yet durst he not the warrant to withstand,
  But vnto her deliuered *Florimell*.
  Whom she receiuing by the lilly hand,
  Admyr'd her beautie much, as she mote well :
  For she all liuing creatures did excell ;
  And was right ioyous, that she gotten had
  So faire a wife for her sonne *Marinell*.
So home with her she streight the virgin lad,
And shewed her to him, then being sore bestad.

34

Who soone as he beheld that angels face,
  Adorn'd with all diuine perfection,
  His cheared heart eftsoones away gan chace
  Sad death, reuiued with her sweet inspection,
  And feeble spirit inly felt refection ;
  As withered weed through cruell winters tine,
  That feeles the warmth of sunny beames reflection,
  Liftes vp his head, that did before decline
And gins to spread his leafe before the faire sunshine.

35

Right so himselfe did *Marinell* vpreare,
  When he in place his dearest loue did spy ;
  And though his limbs could not his bodie beare,
  Ne former strength returne so suddenly,
  Yet chearefull signes he shewed outwardly.
  Ne lesse was she in secret hart affected,
  But that she masked it with modestie,
  For feare she should of lightnesse be detected :
Which to another place I leaue to be perfected.

THE FIFTH
BOOKE OF THE
FAERIE QVEENE.

Contayning,

THE LEGEND OF ARTEGALL,

OR

OF IVSTICE.

1

So oft as I with state of present time,
  The image of the antique world compare,
  When as mans age was in his freshest prime,
  And the first blossome of faire vertue bare,
  Such oddes I finde twixt those, and these which are,
  As that, through long continuance of his course,
  Me seemes the world is runne quite out of square,
  From the first point of his appointed sourse,
And being once amisse growes daily wourse and wourse.

2

For from the golden age, that first was named,
  It's now at earst become a stonie one ;
  And men themselues, the which at first were framed
  Of earthly mould, and form'd of flesh and bone,
  Are now transformed into hardest stone :
  Such as behind their backs (so backward bred)
  Were throwne by *Pyrrha* and *Deucalione* :
  And if then those may any worse be red,
They into that ere long will be degendered.

3

Let none then blame me, if in discipline
  Of vertue and of ciuill vses lore,
  I doe not forme them to the common line
  Of present dayes, which are corrupted sore,
  But to the antique vse, which was of yore,
  When good was onely for it selfe desyred,
  And all men sought their owne, and none no more ;
  When Iustice was not for most meed outhyred,
But simple Truth did rayne, and was of all admyred.

4

For that which all men then did vertue call,
  Is now cald vice ; and that which vice was hight,
  Is now hight vertue, and so vs'd of all :
  Right now is wrong, and wrong that was is right,
  As all things else in time are chaunged quight.
  Ne wonder ; for the heauens reuolution
  Is wandred farre from where it first was pight,
  And so doe make contrarie constitution
Of all this lower world, toward his dissolution.

5

For who so list into the heauens looke,
 And search the courses of the rowling spheares,
 Shall find that from the point, where they first
   tooke
 Their setting forth, in these few thousand yeares
 They all are wandred much; that plaine
   appeares.
 For that same golden fleecy Ram, which bore
 Phrixus and *Helle* from their stepdames feares,
 Hath now forgot, where he was plast of yore,
And shouldred hath the Bull, which fayre
   Europa bore.

6

And eke the Bull hath with his bow-bent horne
 So hardly butted those two twinnes of *Ioue*,
 That they haue crusht the Crab, and quite him
 Into the great *Nemæan* lions groue.   [borne
 So now all range, and doe at randon roue
 Out of their proper places farre away,
 And all this world with them amisse doe moue,
 And all his creatures from their course astray,
Till they arriue at their last ruinous decay.

7

Ne is that same great glorious lampe of light,
 That doth enlumine all these lesser fyres,
 In better case, ne keepes his course more right,
 But is miscaried with the other Spheres.
 For since the terme of fourteene hundred yeres,
 That learned *Ptolomæe* his hight did take,
 He is declyned from that marke of theirs,
 Nigh thirtie minutes to the Southerne lake ;
That makes me feare in time he will vs quite
   forsake.

8

And if to those Ægyptian wisards old,
 Which in Star-read were wont haue best insight,
 Faith may be giuen, it is by them told,
 That since the time they first tooke the Sunnes
   hight,
 Foure times his place he shifted hath in sight,
 And twice hath risen, where he now doth West,
 And wested twice, where he ought rise aright.
 But most is *Mars* amisse of all the rest,
And next to him old *Saturne*, that was wont be
   best.

9

For during *Saturnes* ancient raigne it's sayd,
 That all the world with goodnesse did abound:
 All loued vertue, no man was affrayd
 Of force, ne fraud in wight was to be found :
 No warre was knowne, no dreadfull trompets
   sound,
 Peace vniuersall rayn'd mongst men and beasts,
 And all things freely grew out of the ground:
 Iustice sate high ador'd with solemne feasts,
And to all people did diuide her dred beheasts.

10

Most sacred vertue she of all the rest,
 Resembling God in his imperiall might ;
 Whose soueraine powre is herein most exprest,
 That both to good and bad he dealeth right,
 And all his workes with Iustice hath bedight.
 That powre he also doth to Princes lend,
 And makes them like himselfe in glorious sight,
 To sit in his owne seate, his cause to end,
And rule his people right, as he doth recom-
   mend.

11

Dread Soueraygne Goddesse, that doest highest sit
 In seate of iudgement, in th'Almighties stead,
 And with magnificke might and wondrous wit
 Doest to thy people righteous doome aread,
 That furthest Nations filles with awfull dread,
 Pardon the boldnesse of thy basest thrall,
 That dare discourse of so diuine a read,
 As thy great iustice praysed ouer all :
The instrument whereof loe here thy *Artegall*.

Cant. I.

ᘓᘓᘓᘓᘓᘓᘓᘓᘓᘓᘓᘓᘓᘓᘓᘓᘓᘓᘓ

Artegall trayn'd in Iustice lore
Irenaes quest pursewed,
He doeth auenge on Sanglier
his Ladies bloud embrewed.

ᘓᘓᘓᘓᘓᘓᘓᘓᘓᘓᘓᘓᘓᘓᘓᘓᘓᘓᘓ

1

Though vertue then were held in highest price,
 In those old times, of which I doe intreat,
 Yet then likewise the wicked seede of vice
 Began to spring which shortly grew full great,
 And with their boughes the gentle plants did
   beat.
 But euermore some of the vertuous race
 Rose vp, inspired with heroicke heat,
 That cropt the branches of the sient base,
And with strong hand their fruitfull ranckness
   did deface.

2

Such first was *Bacchus*, that with furious might
 All th'East before vntam'd did ouerronne,
 And wrong repressed, and establisht right,
 Which lawlesse men had formerly fordonne.
 There Iustice first her princely rule begonne.
 Next *Hercules* his like ensample shewed,
 Who all the West with equall conquest wonne,
 And monstrous tyrants with his club subdewed;
The club of Iustice dread, with kingly powre
   endewed.

3

And such was he, of whom I haue to tell,
The Champion of true Iustice *Artegall*,
Whom (as ye lately mote remember well)
An hard aduenture, which did then befall,
Into redoubted perill forth did call;
That was to succour a distressed Dame,
Whom a strong tyrant did vniustly thrall,
And from the heritage, which she did clame,
Did with strong hand withhold : *Grantorto* was
  his name.

4

Wherefore the Lady, which *Irena* hight,
Did to the Faery Queene her way addresse,
To whom complayning her afflicted plight,
She her besought of gratious redresse.
That soueraine Queene, that mightie Em-
  peresse,
Whose glorie is to aide all suppliants pore,
And of weake Princes to be Patronesse,
Chose *Artegall* to right her to restore :
For that to her he seem'd best skild in righteous
  lore.

5

For *Artegall* in iustice was vpbrought
Euen from the cradle of his infancie,
And all the depth of rightfull doome was taught
By faire *Astræa*, with great industrie,
Whilest here on earth she liued mortallie.
For till the world from his perfection fell
Into all filth and foule iniquitie,
Astræa here mongst earthly men did dwell,
And in the rules of iustice them instructed well.

6

Whiles through the world she walked in this sort,
Vpon a day she found this gentle childe,
Amongst his peres playing his childish sport:
Whom seeing fit, and with no crime defilde,
She did allure with gifts and speaches milde,
To wend with her. So thence him farre she
Into a caue from companie exilde,   [brought
In which she noursled him, till yeares he raught,
And all the discipline of iustice there him taught.

7

There she him taught to weigh both right and
  wrong
In equall ballance with due recompence,
And equitie to measure out along,
According to the line of conscience,
When so it needs with rigour to dispence.
Of all the which, for want there of mankind,
She caused him to make experience
Vpon wyld beasts, which she in woods did find,
With wrongfull powre oppressing others of
  their kind.

8

Thus she him trayned, and thus she him taught
In all the skill of deeming wrong and right,
Vntill the ripenesse of mans yeares he raught ;
That euen wilde beasts did feare his awfull sight,
And men admyr'd his ouerruling might ;
Ne any liu'd on ground, that durst withstand
His dreadfull heast, much lesse him match in
  fight,
Or bide the horror of his wreakfull hand,
When so he list in wrath lift vp his steely brand.

9

Which steely brand, to make him dreaded more,
She gaue vnto him, gotten by her slight
And earnest search, where it was kept in store
In *Ioues* eternall house, vnwist of wight,
Since he himselfe it vs'd in that great fight
Against the *Titans*, that whylome rebelled
Gainst highest heauen ; *Chrysaor* it was hight ;
Chrysaor that all other swords excelled,
Well prou'd in that same day, when *Ioue* those
  Gyants quelled.

10

For of most perfect metall it was made,
Tempred with Adamant amongst the same,
And garnisht all with gold vpon the blade
In goodly wise, whereof it tooke his name,
And was of no lesse vertue, then of fame.
For there no substance was so firme and hard,
But it would pierce or cleaue, where so it came ;
Ne any armour could his dint out ward,
But wheresoeuer it did light, it throughly shard.

11

Now when the world with sinne gan to abound,
Astræa loathing lenger here to space
Mongst wicked men, in whom no truth she found,
Return'd to heauen, whence she deriu'd her
  race ;
Where she hath now an euerlasting place,
Mongst those twelue signes, which nightly we
  doe see   [chace ;
The heauens bright-shining baudricke to en-
And is the *Virgin*, sixt in her degree,
And next her selfe her righteous ballance hang-
  ing bee.

12

But when she parted hence, she left her groome
An yron man, which did on her attend
Alwayes, to execute her stedfast doome,
And willed him with *Artegall* to wend,
And doe what euer thing he did intend.
His name was *Talus*, made of yron mould,
Immoueable, resistlesse, without end.
Who in his hand an yron flale did hould,
With which he thresht out falshood, and did
  truth vnfould.

13

He now went with him in this new inquest,
  Him for to aide, if aide he chaunst to neede,
Against that cruell Tyrant, which opprest
The faire *Irena* with his foule misdeede,
And kept the crowne in which she should
    succeed.
And now together on their way they bin,
When as they saw a Squire in squallid weed,
Lamenting sore his sorowfull sad tyne,
With many bitter teares shed from his blubbred
    eyne.

14

To whom as they approched, they espide
  A sorie sight, as euer seene with eye ;
An headlesse Ladie lying him beside,
In her owne blood all wallow'd wofully,
That her gay clothes did in discolour die.
Much was he moued at that ruefull sight ;
  And flam'd with zeale of vengeance inwardly,
He askt, who had that Dame so fouly dight ;
Or whether his owne hand, or whether other
    wight ?

15

Ah woe is me, and well away (quoth hee)
  Bursting forth teares, like springs out of a banke,
That euer I this dismall day did see :
Full farre was I from thinking such a pranke ;
Yet litle losse it were, and mickle thanke,
If I should graunt that I haue doen the same,
  That I mote drinke the cup, whereof she dranke :
But that I should die guiltie of the blame,
The which another did, who now is fled with
    shame.

16

Who was it then (sayd *Artegall*) that wrought?
  And why ? doe it declare vnto me trew.
A knight (said he) if knight he may be thought,
That did his hand in Ladies bloud embrew,
And for no cause, but as I shall you shew.
This day as I in solace sate hereby
  With a fayre loue, whose losse I now do rew,
There came this knight, hauing in companie
This lucklesse Ladie, which now here doth
    headlesse lie.

17

He, whether mine seem'd fayrer in his eye,
  Or that he wexed weary of his owne,
Would change with me ; but I did it denye ;
So did the Ladies both, as may be knowne,
But he, whose spirit was with pride vpblowne,
Would not so rest contented with his right,
  But hauing from his courser her downe throwne,
Fro me reft mine away by lawlesse might,
And on his steed her set, to beare her out of
    sight.

18

Which when his Ladie saw, she follow'd fast,
  And on him catching hold, gan loud to crie
Not so to leaue her, nor away to cast,
But rather of his hand besought to die.
With that his sword he drew all wrathfully,
And at one stroke cropt off her head with scorne,
  In that same place, whereas it now doth lie.
So he my loue away with him hath borne,
And left me here, both his and mine own loue
    to morne.

19

Aread (sayd he) which way then did he make ?
  And by what markes may he be knowne againe?
To hope (quoth he) him soone to ouertake,
That hence so long departed, is but vaine :
But yet he pricked ouer yonder plaine,
And as I marked, bore vpon his shield,
  By which it's easie him to know againe,
A broken sword within a bloodie field ;
Expressing well his nature, which the same did
    wield.

20

No sooner sayd, but streight he after sent
  His yron page, who him pursew'd so light,
As that it seem'd aboue the ground he went :
For he was swift as swallow in her flight,
And strong as Lyon in his Lordly might.
It was not long, before he ouertooke
  Sir *Sanglier* ; (so cleeped was that Knight)
Whom at the first he ghessed by his looke,
And by the other markes, which of his shield he
    tooke.

2

He bad him stay, and backe with him retire ;
  Who full of scorne to be commaunded so,
The Lady to alight did eft require,
Whilest he reformed that vnciuill fo :
And streight at him with all his force did go.
Who mou'd no more therewith, then when a
    rocke
Is lightly stricken with some stones throw ;
But to him leaping, lent him such a knocke,
That on the ground he layd him like a sence-
    lesse blocke.

22

But ere he could him selfe recure againe,
  Him in his iron paw he seized had ;
That when he wak't out of his warelesse paine,
He found him selfe, vnwist, so ill bestad,
That lim he could not wag. Thence he him lad,
Bound like a beast appointed to the stall :
  The sight whereof the Lady sore adrad,
And fain'd to fly for feare of being thrall ;
But he her quickly stayd, and forst to wend
    withall.

23

When to the place they came, where *Artegall*
By that same carefull Squire did then abide,
He gently gan him to demaund of all,
That did betwixt him and that Squire betide.
Who with sterne countenance and indignant pride
Did aunswere, that of all he guiltlesse stood,
And his accuser thereuppon defide :
For neither he did shed that Ladies bloud,
Nor tooke away his loue, but his owne proper good.

24

Well did the Squire perceiue him selfe too weake,
To aunswere his defiaunce in the field,
And rather chose his challenge off to breake,
Then to approue his right with speare and shield.
And rather guilty chose him selfe to yield.
But *Artegall* by signes perceiuing plaine,
That he it was not, which that Lady kild,
But that strange Knight, the fairer loue to gaine,
Did cast about by sleight the truth thereout to straine.

25

And sayd, Now sure this doubtfull causes right
Can hardly but by Sacrament be tride,
Or else by ordele, or by blooddy fight ;
That ill perhaps mote fall to either side.
But if ye please, that I your cause decide,
Perhaps I may all further quarrell end,
So ye will sweare my iudgement to abide.
Thereto they both did franckly condiscend,
And to his doome with listfull eares did both attend.

26

Sith then (sayd he) ye both the dead deny,
And both the liuing Lady claime your right,
Let both the dead and liuing equally
Deuided be betwixt you here in sight,
And each of either take his share aright.
But looke who does dissent from this my read,
He for a twelue moneths day shall in despight
Beare for his penaunce that same Ladies head;
To witnesse to the world, that she by him is dead.

27

Well pleased with that doome was *Sangliere*,
And offred streight the Lady to be slaine.
But that same Squire, to whom she was more dere,
When as he saw she should be cut in twaine,
Did yield, she rather should with him remaine
Aliue, then to him selfe be shared dead ;
And rather then his loue should suffer paine,
He chose with shame to beare that Ladies head.
True loue despiseth shame, when life is cald in dread.

28

Whom when so willing *Artegall* perceaued ;
Not so thou Squire, (he sayd) but thine I deeme
The liuing Lady, which from thee he reaued :
For worthy thou of her doest rightly seeme.
And you, Sir Knight, that loue so light esteeme,
As that ye would for little leaue the same,
Take here your owne, that doth you best beseeme,
And with it beare the burden of defame ;
Your owne dead Ladies head, to tell abrode your shame.

29

But *Sangliere* disdained much his doome,
And sternly gan repine at his beheast ;
Ne would for ought obay, as did become,
To beare that Ladies head before his breast,
Vntill that *Talus* had his pride represt,
And forced him, maulgre, it vp to reare.
Who when he saw it bootelesse to resist,
He tooke it vp, and thence with him did beare,
As rated Spaniell takes his burden vp for feare.

30

Much did that Squire Sir *Artegall* adore,
For his great iustice, held in high regard ;
And as his Squire him offred euermore
To serue, for want of other meete reward,
And wend with him on his aduenture hard.
But he thereto would by no meanes consent ;
But leauing him forth on his iourney far'd :
Ne wight with him but onely *Talus* went.
They two enough t'encounter an whole Regiment.

Cant. II.

Artegall heares of Florimell,
Does with the Pagan fight :
Him slaies, drownes Lady Munera,
Does race her castle quight.

1

Nought is more honorable to a knight,
Ne better doth beseeme braue cheualry,
Then to defend the feeble in their right,
And wrong redresse in such as wend awry.
Whilome those great Heroes got thereby
Their greatest glory, for their rightfull deedes,
And place deserued with the Gods on hy.
Herein the noblesse of this knight exceedes,
Who now to perils great for iustice sake proceedes.

2

To which as he now was vppon the way,
  He chaunst to meet a Dwarfe in hasty course ;
  Whom he requir'd his forward hast to stay,
  Till he of tidings mote with him discourse.
  Loth was the Dwarfe, yet did he stay perforse,
  And gan of sundry newes his store to tell,
  As to his memory they had recourse :
  But chiefely of the fairest *Florimell*,
How she was found againe, and spousde to
  Marinell.

3

For this was *Dony*, *Florimels* owne Dwarfe,
  Whom hauing lost (as ye haue heard whyleare)
  And finding in the way the scattred scarfe,
  The fortune of her life long time did feare.
  But of her health when *Artegall* did heare,
  And safe returne, he was full inly glad,
  And askt him where, and when her bridale
    cheare
  Should be solemniz'd : for if time he had,
He would be there, and honor to her spousall ad.

4

Within three daies (quoth hee) as I do here,
  It will be at the Castle of the strond ;
  What time if naught me let, I will be there
  To doe her seruice, so as I am bond.
  But in my way a little here beyond
  A cursed cruell Sarazin doth wonne,
  That keepes a Bridges passage by strong hond,
  And many errant Knights hath there fordonne ;
That makes all men for feare that passage for
  to shonne.

5

What mister wight (quoth he) and how far
    hence
  Is he, that doth to trauellers such harmes ?
  He is (said he) a man of great defence ;
  Expert in battell and in deedes of armes ;
  And more emboldned by the wicked charmes,
  With which his daughter doth him still support ;
  Hauing great Lordships got and goodly farmes,
  Through strong oppression of his powre extort ;
By which he stil them holds, and keepes with
  strong effort.

6

And dayly he his wrongs encreaseth more,
  For neuer wight he lets to passe that way,
  Ouer his Bridge, albee he rich or poore,
  But he him makes his passage-penny pay :
  Else he doth hold him backe or beat away.
  Thereto he hath a groome of euill guize,
  Whose scalp is bare, that bondage doth bewray,
  Which pols and pils the poore in piteous wize ;
But he him selfe vppon the rich doth tyrannize.

7

His name is hight *Pollente*, rightly so
  For that he is so puissant and strong,
  That with his powre he all doth ouergo,
  And makes them subiect to his mighty wrong ;
  And some by sleight he eke doth vnderfong.
  For on a Bridge he custometh to fight,
  Which is but narrow, but exceeding long ;
  And in the same are many trap fals pight,
Through which the rider downe doth fall
  through ouersight.

8

And vnderneath the same a riuer flowes,
  That is both swift and dangerous deepe withall ;
  Into the which whom so he ouerthrowes,
  All destitute of helpe doth headlong fall,
  But he him selfe, through practise vsuall,
  Leapes forth into the floud, and there assaies
  His foe confused through his sodaine fall,
  That horse and man he equally dismaies,
And either both them drownes, or trayter-
  ously slaies.

9

Then doth he take the spoile of them at will,
  And to his daughter brings, that dwels thereby :
  Who all that comes doth take, and therewith
    fill
  The coffers of her wicked threasury :
  Which she with wrongs hath heaped vp so hy,
  That many Princes she in wealth exceedes,
  And purchast all the countrey lying ny
  With the reuenue of her plenteous meedes,
Her name is *Munera*, agreeing with her deedes.

10

Thereto she is full faire, and rich attired,
  With golden hands and siluer feete beside,
  That many Lords haue her to wife desired :
  But she them all despiseth for great pride.
  Now by my life (sayd he) and God to guide,
  None other way will I this day betake,
  But by that Bridge, whereas he doth abide :
  Therefore me thither lead. No more he spake,
But thitherward forthright his ready way did
  make.

11

Vnto the place he came within a while,
  Where on the Bridge he ready armed saw
  The Sarazin, awayting for some spoile.
  Who as they to the passage gan to draw,
  A villaine to them came with scull all raw,
  That passage money did of them require,
  According to the custome of their law.
  To whom he aunswerd wroth, Loe there thy
    hire ;
And with that word him strooke, that streight
  he did expire.

12

Which when the Pagan saw, he wexed wroth,
  And streight him selfe vnto the fight addrest,
  Ne was Sir *Artegall* behinde : so both
  Together ran with ready speares in rest.
  Right in the midst, whereas they brest to brest
  Should meete, a trap was letten downe to fall
  Into the floud: streight leapt the Carle vnblest,
  Well weening that his foe was falne withall :
But he was well aware, and leapt before his fall.

13

There being both together in the floud,
  They each at other tyrannously flew ;
  Ne ought the water cooled their whot bloud,
  But rather in them kindled choler new.
  But there the Paynim, who that vse well knew
  To fight in water, great aduantage had,
  That oftentimes him nigh he ouerthrew :
  And eke the courser, whereuppon he rad,
Could swim like to a fish, whiles he his backe bestrad.

14

Which oddes when as Sir *Artegall* espide,
  He saw no way, but close with him in hast ;
  And to him driuing strongly downe the tide,
  Vppon his iron coller griped fast,
  That with the straint his wesand nigh he brast.
  There they together stroue and struggled long,
  Either the other from his steede to cast ;
  Ne euer *Artegall* his griple strong
For any thing wold slacke, but still vppon him hong.

15

As when a Dolphin and a Sele are met,
  In the wide champian of the Ocean plaine :
  With cruell chaufe their courages they whet,
  The maysterdome of each by force to gaine,
  And dreadfull battaile twixt them do darraine:
  They snuf, they snort, they bounce, they rage, they rore,
  That all the sea disturbed with their traine,
  Doth frie with fome aboue the surges hore.
Such was betwixt these two the troublesome vprore.

16

So *Artegall* at length him forst forsake
  His horses backe, for dread of being drownd,
  And to his handy swimming him betake.
  Eftsoones him selfe he from his hold vnbownd,
  And then no ods at all in him he fownd :
  For *Artegall* in swimming skilfull was,
  And durst the depth of any water sownd.
  So ought each Knight, that vse of perill has,
In swimming be expert through waters force to pas.

17

Then very doubtfull was the warres euent,
  Vncertaine whether had the better side :
  For both were skild in that experiment,
  And both in armes well traind and throughly tride.
  But *Artegall* was better breath'd beside,
  And towards th'end, grew greater in his might,
  That his faint foe no longer could abide
  His puissance, ne beare him selfe vpright,
But from the water to the land betooke his flight.

18

But *Artegall* pursewd him still so neare,
  With bright Chrysaor in his cruell hand,
  That as his head he gan a litle reare
  Aboue the brincke, to tread vpon the land,
  He smote it off, that tumbling on the strand
  It bit the earth for very fell despight,
  And gnashed with his teeth, as if he band
  High God, whose goodnesse he despaired quight,
Or curst the hand, which did that vengeance on him dight.

19

His corps was carried downe along the Lee,
  Whose waters with his filthy bloud it stayned :
  But his blasphemous head, that all might see,
  He pitcht vpon a pole on high ordayned ;
  Where many years it afterwards remayned,
  To be a mirrour to all mighty men,
  In whose right hands great power is contayned,
  That none of them the feeble ouerren,
But alwaies doe their powre within iust compasse pen.

20

That done, vnto the Castle he did wend,
  In which the Paynims daughter did abide,
  Guarded of many which did her defend :
  Of whom her entrance sought, but was denide,
  And with reprochfull blasphemy defide,
  Beaten with stones downe from the battilment,
  That he was forced to withdraw aside ;
  And bad his seruant *Talus* to inuent
Which way he enter might, without endangerment.

21

Eftsoones his Page drew to the Castle gate,
  And with his iron flale at it let flie,
  That all the warders it did sore amate,
  The which erewhile spake so reprochfully,
  And made them stoupe, that looked earst so hie.
  Yet still he bet, and bounst vppon the dore,
  And thundred strokes thereon so hideouslie,
  That all the peece he shaked from the flore,
And filled all the house with feare and great vprore.

22

With noise whereof the Lady forth appeared
Vppon the Castle wall, and when she saw
The daungerous state, in which she stood, she
The sad effect of her neare ouerthrow; [feared
And gan entreat that iron man below,
To cease his outrage, and him faire besought,
Sith neither force of stones which they did throw,
Nor powr of charms, which she against him
wrought,
Might otherwise preuaile, or make him cease
for ought.

23

But when as yet she saw him to proceede,
Vnmou'd with praiers, or with piteous thought,
She ment him to corrupt with goodly meede ;
And causde great sackes with endlesse riches
Vnto the battilment to be vpbrought, [fraught,
And powred forth ouer the Castle wall,
That she might win some time, though dearly
bought
Whilest he to gathering of the gold did fall.
But he was nothing mou'd, nor tempted there-
withall.

24

But still continu'd his assault the more,
And layd on load with his huge yron flaile,
That at the length he has yrent the dore,
And made way for his maister to assaile.
Who being entred, nought did then auaile
For wight, against this powre themselues to reare:
Each one did flie ; their hearts began to faile,
And hid them selues in corners here and there ;
And eke their dame halfe dead did hide her self
for feare.

25

Long they her sought, yet no where could they
finde her,
That sure they ween'd she was escapt away :
But *Talus*, that could like a lime hound wind e her,
And all things secrete wisely could bewray,
At length found out, whereas she hidden lay
Vnder an heape of gold. Thence he her drew
By the faire lockes, and fowly did array,
Withouten pitty of her goodly hew,
That *Artegall* him selfe her seemelesse plight
did rew.

26

Yet for no pitty would he change the course
Of Iustice, which in *Talus* hand did lye ;
Who rudely hayld her forth without remorse,
Still holding vp her suppliant hands on hye,
And kneeling at his feete submissiuely.
But he her suppliant hands, those hands of gold,
And eke her feete, those feete of siluer trye,
Which sought vnrighteousnesse, and iustice sold,
Chopt off, and nayld on high, that all might
them behold.

27

Her selfe then tooke he by the sclender wast,
In vaine loud crying, and into the flood
Ouer the Castle wall adowne her cast,
And there her drowned in the durty mud :
But the streame washt away her guilty blood.
Thereafter all that mucky pelfe he tooke,
The spoile of peoples euill gotten good,
The which her sire had scrap't by hooke and
crooke,
And burning all to ashes, powr'd it downe the
brooke.

28

And lastly all that Castle quite he raced,
Euen from the sole of his foundation,
And all the hewen stones thereof defaced,
That there mote be no hope of reparation,
Nor memory thereof to any nation.
All which when *Talus* throughly had per-
fourmed,
Sir *Artegall* vndid the euill fashion,
And wicked customes of that Bridge refourmed.
Which done, vnto his former iourney he re-
tourned.

29

In which they measur'd mickle weary way,
Till that at length nigh to the sea they drew ;
By which as they did trauell on a day,
They saw before them, far as they could vew,
Full many people gathered in a crew ;
Whose great assembly they did much admire.
For neuer there the like resort they knew.
So towardes them they coasted, to enquire
What thing so many nations met, did there
desire.

30

There they beheld a mighty Gyant stand
Vpon a rocke, and holding forth on hie
An huge great paire of ballance in his hand,
With which he boasted in his surquedrie,
That all the world he would weigh equallie,
If ought he had the same to counterpoys.
For want whereof he weighed vanity,
And fild his ballaunce full of idle toys :
Yet was admired much of fooles, women, and
boys.

31

He sayd that he would all the earth vptake,
And all the sea, deuided each from either :
So would he of the fire one ballaunce make,
And one of th'ayre, without or wind, or wether·
Then would he ballaunce heauen and hell to-
gether,
And all that did within them all containe
Of all whose weight, he would not misse a fether
And looke what surplus did of each remaine,
He would to his owne part restore the same
againe.

32
For why, he sayd they all vnequall were,
And had encroched vppon others share,
Like as the sea (which plaine he shewed there)
Had worne the earth, so did the fire the aire,
So all the rest did others parts empaire.
And so were realmes and nations run awry.
All which he vndertooke for to repaire,
In sort as they were formed aunciently ;
And all things would reduce vnto equality.

33
Therefore the vulgar did about him flocke,
And cluster thicke vnto his leasings vaine,
Like foolish flies about an hony crocke,
In hope by him great benefite to gaine,
And vncontrolled freedome to obtaine.
All which when *Artegall* did see, and heare,
How he mis-led the simple peoples traine,
In sdeignfull wize he drew vnto him neare,
And thus vnto him spake, without regard or feare.

34
Thou that presum st to weigh the world anew,
And all things to an equall to restore,
In stead of right me seemes great wrong dost shew,
And far aboue thy forces pitch to sore
For ere thou limit what is lesse or more
In euery thing, thou oughtest first to know,
What was the poyse of euery part of yore :
And looke then how much it doth ouerflow,
Or faile thereof, so much is more then iust to trow.

35
For at the first they all created were
In goodly measure, by their Makers might,
And weighed out in ballaunces so nere,
That not a dram was missing of their right,
The earth was in the middle centre pight,
In which it doth immoueable abide,
Hemd in with waters like a wall in sight ;
And they with aire, that not a drop can slide :
Al which the heauens containe, and in their courses guide.

36
Such heauenly iustice doth among them raine,
That euery one doe know their certaine bound,
In which they doe these many yeares remaine,
And mongst them al no change hath yet beene found.
But if thou now shouldst weigh them new in pound,
We are not sure they would so long remaine :
All change is perillous, and all chaunce vnsound.
Therefore leaue off to weigh them all againe,
Till we may be assur'd they shall their course retaine.

37
Thou foolishe Elfe (said then the Gyant wroth)
Seest not, how badly all things present bee,
And each estate quite out of order goth ?
The sea it selfe doest thou not plainely see
Encroch vppon the land there vnder thee ;
And th'earth it selfe how daily its increast,
By all that dying to it turned be ?
Were it not good that wrong were then surceast,
And from the most, that some were giuen to the least ?

38
Therefore I will throw downe these mountaines hie,
And make them leuell with the lowly plaine :
These towring rocks, which reach vnto the skie,
I will thrust downe into the deepest maine,
And as they were, them equalize againe.
Tyrants that make men subiect to their law,
I will suppresse, that they no more may raine ;
And Lordings curbe, that commons ouer-aw ;
And all the wealth of rich men to the poore will draw.

39
Of things vnseene how canst thou deeme aright,
Then answered the righteous *Artegall*,
Sith thou misdeem'st so much of things in sight?
What though the sea with waues continuall
Doe eate the earth, it is no more at all :
Ne is the earth the lesse, or loseth ought,
For whatsoeuer from one place doth fall,
Is with the tide vnto an other brought :
For there is nothing lost, that may be found, if sought.

40
Likewise the earth is not augmented more,
By all that dying into it doe fade.
For of the earth they formed were of yore.
How euer gay their blossome or their blade
Doe flourish now, they into dust shall vade.
What wrong then is it, if that when they die,
They turne to that, whereof they first were made ?
All in the powre of their great Maker lie :
All creatures must obey the voice of the most hie.

41
They liue, they die, like as he doth ordaine,
Ne euer any asketh reason why.
The hils doe not the lowly dales disdaine ;
The dales doe not the lofty hills enuy.
He maketh Kings to sit in souerainty ;
He maketh subiects to their powre obay ;
He pulleth downe, he setteth vp on hy ;
He giues to this, from that he takes away.
For all we haue is his : what he list doe, he may.

42

What euer thing is done, by him is donne,
Ne any may his mighty will withstand ;
Ne any may his soueraine power shonne,
Ne loose that he hath bound with stedfast band.
In vaine therefore doest thou now take in hand,
To call to count, or weigh his workes anew,
Whose counsels depth thou canst not vnderstand,
Sith of things subiect to thy daily vew
Thou doest not know the causes, nor their
    courses dew.

43

For take thy ballaunce, if thou be so wise,
And weigh the winde, that vnder heauen doth
    blow ;
Or weigh the light, that in the East doth rise;
Or weigh the thought, that from mans mind
    doth flow.
But if the weight of these thou canst not show,
Weigh but one word which from thy lips doth fall.
For how canst thou those greater secrets know,
That doest not know the least thing of them all ?
Ill can he rule the great, that cannot reach the
    small.

44

Therewith the Gyant much abashed sayd ;
That he of little things made reckoning light,
Yet the least word that euer could be layd
Within his ballaunce, he could way aright.
Which is (sayd he) more heauy then in weight,
The right or wrong, the false or else the trew ?
He answered, that he would try it streight,
So he the words into his ballaunce threw,
But streight the winged words out of his
    ballaunce flew.

45

Wroth wext he then, and sayd, that words were
    light,
Ne would within his ballaunce well abide.
But he could iustly weigh the wrong or right.
Well then, sayd *Artegall*, let it be tride.
First in one ballance set the true aside.
He did so first ; and then the false he layd
In th'other scale ; but still it downe did slide,
And by no meane could in the weight be stayd,
For by no meanes the false will with the truth be
    wayd.

46

Now take the right likewise, sayd *Artegale*,
And counterpeise the same with so much wrong.
So first the right he put into one scale ;
And then the Gyant stroue with puissance strong
To fill the other scale with so much wrong.
But all the wrongs that he therein could lay,
Might not it peise ; yet did he labour long,
And swat, and chauf'd, and proued euery way :
Yet all the wrongs could not a little right
    downe way.

47

Which when he saw, he greatly grew in rage,
And almost would his balances haue broken :
But *Artegall* him fairely gan asswage,
And said ; Be not vpon thy balance wroken :
For they doe nought but right or wrong be-
    token ;
But in the mind the doome of right must bee ;
And so likewise of words, the which be spoken,
The eare must be the ballance, to decree
And iudge, whether with truth or falshood they
    agree.

48

But set the truth and set the right aside,
For they with wrong or falshood will not fare ;
And put two wrongs together to be tride,
Or else two falses, of each equall share ;
And then together doe them both compare.
For truth is one, and right is euer one.
So did he, and then plaine it did appeare,
Whether of them the greater were attone.
But right sate in the middest of the beame
    alone.

49

But he the right from thence did thrust away,
For it was not the right, which he did seeke ;
But rather stroue extremities to way,
Th'one to diminish, th'other for to eeke:
For of the meane he greatly did misleeke.
Whom when so lewdly minded *Talus* found,
Approching nigh vnto him cheeke by cheeke,
He shouldered him from off the higher ground,
And down the rock him throwing, in the sea
    him dround.

50

Like as a ship, whom cruell tempest driues
Vpon a rocke with horrible dismay,
Her shattered ribs in thousand peeces riues,
And spoyling all her geares and goodly ray,
Does make her selfe misfortunes piteous pray.
So downe the cliffe the wretched Gyant
    tumbled ;
His battred ballances in peeces lay,
His timbered bones all broken rudely rumbled,
So was the high aspyring with huge ruine
    humbled.

51

That when the people, which had there about
Long wayted, saw his sudden desolation,
They gan to gather in tumultuous rout,
And mutining, to stirre vp ciuill faction,
For certaine losse of so great expectation.
For well they hoped to haue got great good,
And wondrous riches by his innouation.
Therefore resoluing to reuenge his blood,
They rose in armes, and all in battell order stood.

52

Which lawlesse multitude him comming too
In warlike wise, when *Artegall* did vew,
He much was troubled, ne wist what to doo.
For loth he was his noble hands t'embrew
In the base blood of such a rascall crew ;
And otherwise, if that he should retire,
He fear'd least they with shame would him
pursew.
Therefore he *Talus* to them sent, t'inquire
The cause of their array, and truce for to desire.

53

But soone as they him nigh approching spide,
They gan with all their weapons him assay,
And rudely stroke at him on euery side :
Yet nought they could him hurt, ne ought
dismay.
But when at them he with his flaile gan lay,
He like a swarme of flyes them ouerthrew ;
Ne any of them durst come in his way,
But here and there before his presence flew,
And hid themselues in holes and bushes from
his vew.

54

As when a Faulcon hath with nimble flight
Flowne at a flush of Ducks, foreby the brooke,
The trembling foule dismayd with dreadfull
sight
Of death, the which them almost ouertooke,
Doe hide themselues from her astonying looke,
Amongst the flags and couert round about.
When *Talus* saw they all the field forsooke
And none appear'd of all that raskall rout,
To *Artegall* he turn'd, and went with him
throughout.

Cant. III.

ഗ്രഗ്രഗ്രഗ്രഗ്രഗ്രഗ്രഗ്രഗ്രഗ്രഗ്ര

The spousals of faire Florimell,
where turney many knights :
There Braggadochio is vncas'd
in all the Ladies sights.

ഗ്രഗ്രഗ്രഗ്രഗ്രഗ്രഗ്രഗ്രഗ്രഗ്രഗ്ര

I

After long stormes and tempests ouerblowne,
The sunne at length his ioyous face doth cleare:
So when as fortune all her spight hath showne,
Some blisfull houres at last must needes appeare ;
Else should afflicted wights oftimes despeire.
So comes it now to *Florimell* by tourne,
After long sorrowes suffered whyleare,
In which captiu'd she many moneths did mourne,
To tast of ioy, and to wont pleasures to retourne.

2

Who being freed from *Proteus* cruell band
By *Marinell*, was vnto him affide,
And by him brought againe to Faerie land ;
Where he her spous'd, and made his ioyous bride.
The time and place was blazed farre and wide ;
And solemne feasts and giusts ordain'd there-
fore.
To which there did resort from euery side
Of Lords and Ladies infinite great store ;
Ne any Knight was absent, that braue courage
bore.

3

To tell the glorie of the feast that day,
The goodly seruice, the deuicefull sights,
The bridegromes state, the brides most rich
aray,
The pride of Ladies, and the worth of knights,
The royall banquets, and the rare delights
Were worke fit for an Herauld, not for me :
But for so much as to my lot here lights,
That with this present treatise doth agree,
True vertue to aduance, shall here recounted bee.

4

When all men had with full satietie
Of meates and drinkes their appetites suffiz'd,
To deedes of armes and proofe of cheualrie
They gan themselues addresse, full rich aguiz'd,
As each one had his furnitures deuiz'd.
And first of all issu'd Sir *Marinell*,
And with him sixe knights more, which enter-
priz'd
To chalenge all in right of *Florimell*,
And to maintaine, that she all others did excell.

5

The first of them was hight Sir *Orimont*,
A noble Knight, and tride in hard assayes :
The second had to name Sir *Bellisont*,
But second vnto none in prowesse prayse ;
The third was *Brunell*, famous in his dayes ;
The fourth *Ecastor*, of exceeding might ;
The fift *Armeddan*, skild in louely layes ;
The sixt was *Lansack*, a redoubted Knight :
All sixe well seene in armes, and prou'd in many
a fight.

6

And them against came all that list to giust,
From euery coast and countrie vnder sunne :
None was debard, but all had leaue that lust.
The trompets sound ; then all together ronne.
Full many deedes of armes that day were donne,
And many knights vnhorst, and many wounded
As fortune fell ; yet litle lost or wonne :
But all that day the greatest prayse redounded
To *Marinell*, whose name the Heralds loud
resounded.

7

The second day, so soone as morrow light
Appear'd in heauen, into the field they came,
And there all day continew'd cruell fight,
With diuers fortune fit for such a game,
In which all stroue with perill to winne fame.
Yet whether side was victor, note be ghest :
But at the last the trompets did proclame
That *Marinell* that day deserued best.
So they disparted were, and all men went to rest.

8

The third day came, that should due tryall lend
Of all the rest, and then this warlike crew
Together met, of all to make an end.
There *Marinell* great deeds of armes did shew ;
And through the thickest like a Lyon flew,
Rashing off helmes, and ryuing plates a sonder,
That euery one his daunger did eschew.
So terribly his dreadfull strokes did thonder,
That all men stood amaz'd, and at his might did
  wonder.

9

But what on earth can alwayes happie stand ?
The greater prowesse greater perils find.
So farre he past amongst his enemies band,
That they haue him enclosed so behind,
As by no meanes he can himselfe outwind.
And now perforce they haue him prisoner taken;
And now they doe with captiue bands him bind;
And now they lead him thence, of all forsaken,
Vnlesse some succour had in time him ouertaken.

10

It fortun'd whylest they were thus ill beset,
Sir *Artegall* into the Tilt-yard came,
With *Braggadochio*, whom he lately met
Vpon the way, with that his snowy Dame.
Where when he vnderstood by common fame,
What euill hap to *Marinell* betid,
He much was mou'd at so vnworthie shame,
And streight that boaster prayd, with whom
  he rid,
To change his shield with him, to be the better hid.

11

So forth he went, and soone them ouer hent,
Where they were leading *Marinell* away,
Whom he assayld with dreadlesse hardiment,
And forst the burden of their prize to stay.
They were an hundred knights of that array ;
Of which th'one halfe vpon himselfe did set,
The other stayd behind to gard the pray.
But he ere long the former fiftie bet ;
And from the other fiftie soone the prisoner
  fet.

12

So backe he brought Sir *Marinell* againe ;
Whom hauing quickly arm'd againe anew,
They both together ioyned might and maine,
To set afresh on all the other crew.
Whom with sore hauocke soone they ouerthrew,
And chaced quite out of the field, that none
Against them durst his head to perill shew.
So were they left Lords of the field alone :
So *Marinell* by him was rescu'd from his fone.

13

Which when he had perform'd, then backe againe
To *Braggadochio* did his shield restore :
Who all this while behind him did remaine,
Keeping there close with him in pretious store
That his false Ladie, as ye heard afore.
Then did the trompets sound, and Iudges rose,
And all these knights, which that day armour
  bore,
Came to the open hall, to listen whose
The honour of the prize should be adiudg'd by
  those.

14

And thether also came in open sight
Fayre *Florimell*, into the common hall,
To greet his guerdon vnto euery knight,
And best to him, to whom the best should fall.
Then for that stranger knight they loud did call,
To whom that day they should the girlond yield
Who came not forth, but for Sir *Artegall*
Came *Braggadochio*, and did shew his shield,
Which bore the Sunne brode blazed in a golden
  field.

15

The sight whereof did all with gladnesse fill :
So vnto him they did addeeme the prise
Of all that Tryumph. Then the trompets shrill
Don *Braggadochios* name resounded thrise :
So courage lent a cloke to cowardise.
And then to him came fayrest *Florimell*,
And goodly gan to greet his braue emprise,
And thousand thankes him yeeld, that had so
  well
Approu'd that day, that she all others did excell.

16

To whom the boaster, that all knights did blot,
With proud disdaine did scornefull answere
  make ;
That what he did that day, he did it not
For her, but for his owne deare Ladies sake,
Whom on his perill he did vndertake,
Both her and eke all others to excell :
And further did vncomely speaches crake.
Much did his words the gentle Ladie quell,
And turn'd aside for shame to heare, what he
  did tell.

17

Then forth he brought his snowy *Florimele*,
Whom *Trompart* had in keeping there beside,
Couered from peoples gazement with a vele.
Whom when discouered they had throughly eide,
With great amazement they were stupefide ;
And said, that surely *Florimell* it was,
Or if it were not *Florimell* so tride,
That *Florimell* her selfe she then did pas.
So feeble skill of perfect things the vulgar has.

18

Which when as *Marinell* beheld likewise,
He was therewith exceedingly dismayd ;
Ne wist he what to thinke, or to deuise,
But like as one, whom feends had made affrayd,
He long astonisht stood, ne ought he sayd,
Ne ought he did, but with fast fixed eies
He gazed still vpon that snowy mayd ;
Whom euer as he did the more auize,
The more to be true *Florimell* he did surmize.

19

As when two sunnes appeare in the azure skye,
Mounted in *Phœbus* charet fierie bright,
Both darting forth faire beames to each mans eye,
And both adorn'd with lampes of flaming light,
All that behold so strange prodigious sight,
Not knowing natures worke, nor what to weene,
Are rapt with wonder, and with rare affright.
So stood Sir *Marinell*, when he had seene
The semblant of this false by his faire beauties
  Queene.

20

All which when *Artegall*, who all this while
Stood in the preasse close couered, well aduewed,
And saw that boasters pride and gracelesse
  guile,
He could no longer beare, but forth issewed,
And vnto all himselfe there open shewed,
And to the boaster said ; Thou losell base,
That hast with borrowed plumes thy selfe
  endewed,
And others worth with leasings doest deface,
When they are all restor'd, thou shalt rest in
  disgrace.

21

That shield, which thou doest beare, was it indeed,
Which this dayes honour sau'd to *Marinell* ;
But not that arme, nor thou the man I reed,
Which didst that seruice vnto *Florimell*.
For proofe shew forth thy sword, and let it tell,
What strokes, what dreadfull stoure it stird
  this day :
Or shew the wounds, which vnto thee befell ;
Or shew the sweat, with which thou diddest
  sway
So sharpe a battell, that so many did dismay.

22

But this the sword, which wrought those cruell
  stounds,
And this the arme, the which that shield did
  beare,   [wounds]
And these the signes, (so shewed forth his
By which that glorie gotten doth appeare.
As for this Ladie, which he sheweth here,
Is not (I wager) *Florimell* at all ;
But some fayre Franion, fit for such a fere,
That by misfortune in his hand did fall.
For proofe whereof, he bad them *Florimell*
  forth call.

23

So forth the noble Ladie was ybrought,
Adorn'd with honor and all comely grace :
Whereto her bashfull shamefastnesse ywrought
A great increase in her faire blushing face ;
As roses did with lillies interlace.
For of those words, the which that boaster
  threw,
She inly yet conceiued great disgrace.
Whom when as all the people such did vew,
They shouted loud, and signes of gladnesse all
  did shew.

24

Then did he set her by that snowy one
Like the true saint beside the image set,
Of both their beauties to make paragone,
And triall, whether should the honor get.
Streight way so soone as both together met,
Th'enchaunted Damzell vanisht into nought:
Her snowy substance melted as with heat,
Ne of that goodly hew remayned ought,
But th'emptie girdle, which about her wast was
  wrought.

25

As when the daughter of *Thaumantes* faire,
Hath in a watry cloud displayd wide
Her goodly bow, which paints the liquid ayre ;
That all men wonder at her colours pride ;
All suddenly, ere one can looke aside,
The glorious picture vanisheth away,
Ne any token doth thereof abide :
So did this Ladies goodly forme decay,
And into nothing goe, ere one could it bewray.

26

Which when as all that present were, beheld,
They stricken were with great astonishment,
And their faint harts with senselesse horrour
  queld,
To see the thing, that seem'd so excellent,
So stolen from their fancies wonderment ;
That what of it became, none vnderstood.
And *Braggadochio* selfe with dreriment
So daunted was in his despeyring mood,
That like a lifelesse corse immoueable he stood.

27

But *Artegall* that golden belt vptooke,
  The which of all her spoyle was onely left ;
  Which was not hers, as many it mistooke,
  But *Florimells* owne girdle, from her reft,
  While she was flying, like a weary weft,
  From that foule monster, which did her compell
  To perils great ; which he vnbuckling eft,
  Presented to the fayrest *Florimell* ;
Who round about her tender wast it fitted well.

28

Full many Ladies often had assayd,
  About their middles that faire belt to knit ;
  And many a one suppos'd to be a mayd :
  Yet it to none of all their loynes would fit,
  Till *Florimell* about her fastned it.
  Such power it had, that to no womans wast
  By any skill or labour it would sit,
  Vnlesse that she were continent and chast,
But it would lose or breake, that many had disgrast.

29

Whilest thus they busied were bout *Florimell*,
  And boastfull *Braggadochio* to defame,
  Sir *Guyon* as by fortune then befell,
  Forth from the thickest preasse of people came,
  His owne good steed, which he had stolne, to clame ;
  And th'one hand seizing on his golden bit,
  With th'other drew his sword : for with the same
  He ment the thiefe there deadly to haue smit :
And had he not bene held, he nought had fayld of it.

30

Thereof great hurly burly moued was
  Throughout the hall, for that same warlike horse.
  For *Braggadochio* would not let him pas ;
  And *Guyon* would him algates haue perforse,
  Or it approue vpon his carrion corse.
  Which troublous stirre when *Artegall* perceiued,
  He nigh them drew to stay th'auengers forse,
  And gan inquire, how was that steed bereaued,
Whether by might extort, or else by slight deceaued.

31

Who all that piteous storie, which befell
  About that wofull couple, which were slaine,
  And their young bloodie babe to him gan tell ;
  With whom whiles he did in the wood remaine,
  His horse purloyned was by subtill traine :
  For which he chalenged the thiefe to fight.
  But he for nought could him thereto constraine.
  For as the death he hated such despight,
And rather had to lose, then trie in armes his right.

32

Which *Artegall* well hearing, though no more
  By law of armes there neede ones right to trie,
  As was the wont of warlike knights of yore,
  Then that his foe should him the field denie,
  Yet further right by tokens to descrie,
  He askt, what priuie tokens he did beare.
  If that (said *Guyon*) may you satisfie,
  Within his mouth a blacke spot doth appeare,
Shapt like a horses shoe, who list to seeke it there.

33

Whereof to make due tryall, one did take
  The horse in hand, within his mouth to looke :
  But with his heeles so sorely he him strake,
  That all his ribs he quite in peeces broke,
  That neuer word from that day forth he spoke.
  Another that would seeme to haue more wit,
  Him by the bright embrodered hedstall tooke :
  But by the shoulder him so sore he bit,
That he him maymed quite, and all his shoulder split.

34

Ne he his mouth would open vnto wight,
  Vntill that *Guyon* selfe vnto him spake,
  And called *Brigadore* (so was he hight)
  Whose voice so soone as he did vndertake,
  Eftsoones he stood as still as any stake,
  And suffred all his secret marke to see :
  And when as he him nam'd, for ioy he brake
  His bands, and follow'd him with gladfull glee,
And friskt, and flong aloft, and louted low on knee.

35

Thereby Sir *Artegall* did plaine areed,
  That vnto him the horse belong'd, and sayd ;
  Lo there Sir *Guyon*, take to you the steed,
  As he with golden saddle is arayd ;
  And let that losell, plainely now displayd,
  Hence fare on foot, till he an horse haue gayned.
  But the proud boaster gan his doome vpbrayd,
  And him reuil'd, and rated, and disdayned,
That iudgement so vniust against him had ordayned.

36

Much was the knight incenst with his lewd word,
  To haue reuenged that his villeny ;
  And thrise did lay his hand vpon his sword,
  To haue him slaine, or dearely doen aby.
  But *Guyon* did his choler pacify,
  Saying, Sir knight, it would dishonour bee
  To you, that are our iudge of equity,
  To wreake your wrath on such a carle as hee :
It's punishment enough, that all his shame doe see.

SPENSER.   L

37

So did he mitigate Sir *Artegall*,
But *Talus* by the backe the boaster hent,
And drawing him out of the open hall,
Vpon him did inflict this punishment.
First he his beard did shaue, and fowly shent :
Then from him reft his shield, and it renuerst,
And blotted out his armes with falshood blent,
And himselfe baffuld, and his armes vnherst,
And broke his sword in twaine, and all his
    armour sperst.

38

The whiles his guilefull groome was fled away :
But vaine it was to thinke from him to flie.
Who ouertaking him did disaray,
And all his face deform'd with infamie,
And out of court him scourged openly.
So ought all faytours, that true knighthood
    shame,
And armes dishonour with base villanie,
From all braue knights be banisht with defame :
For oft their lewdnes blotteth good deserts
    with blame.

39

Now when these counterfeits were thus vncased
Out of the foreside of their forgerie,
And in the sight of all men cleane disgraced,
All gan to iest and gibe full merilie
At the remembrance of their knauerie.
Ladies can laugh at Ladies, Knights at Knights,
To thinke with how great vaunt of brauerie
He them abused, through his subtill slights,
And what a glorious shew he made in all their
    sights.

40

There leaue we them in pleasure and repast,
Spending their ioyous dayes and gladfull nights,
And taking vsurie of time forepast,
With all deare delices and rare delights,
Fit for such Ladies and such louely knights :
And turne we here to this faire furrowes end
Our wearie yokes, to gather fresher sprights,
That when as time to *Artegall* shall tend,
We on his first aduenture may him forward send.

Cant. IIII.

Artegall dealeth right betwixt
two brethren that doe striue,
Saues Terpine from the gallow tree,
and doth from death repriue.

1

Who so vpon him selfe will take the skill
True Iustice vnto people to diuide,
Had neede haue mightie hands, for to fulfill
That, which he doth with righteous doome
    decide,
And for to maister wrong and puissant pride.
For vaine it is to deeme of things aright,
And makes wrong doers iustice to deride,
Vnlesse it be perform'd with dreadlesse might.
For powre is the right hand of Iustice truely hight.

2

Therefore whylome to knights of great emprise
The charge of Iustice giuen was in trust,
That they might execute her iudgements wise,
And with their might beat downe licentious lust,
Which proudly did impugne her sentence iust.
Whereof no brauer president this day
Remaines on earth, preseru'd from yron rust
Of rude obliuion, and long times decay,
Then this of *Artegall*, which here we haue to say.

3

Who hauing lately left that louely payre,
Enlincked fast in wedlockes loyall bond,
Bold *Marinell* with *Florimell* the fayre,
With whom great feast and goodly glee he fond,
Departed from the Castle of the strond,
To follow his aduentures first intent,
Which long agoe he taken had in hond :
Ne wight with him for his assistance went,
But that great yron groome, his gard and
    gouernment.

4

With whom as he did passe by the sea shore,
He chaunst to come, whereas two comely
    Squires,
Both brethren, whom one wombe together bore,
But stirred vp with different desires,
Together stroue, and kindled wrathfull fires :
And them beside two seemely damzels stood,
By all meanes seeking to asswage their ires,
Now with faire words ; but words did little good,
Now with sharpe threats ; but threats the more
    increast their mood.

5

And there before them stood a Coffer strong,
  Fast bound on euery side with iron bands,
  But seeming to haue suffred mickle wrong,
  Either by being wreckt vppon the sands,
  Or being carried farre from forraine lands.
Seem'd that for it these Squires at ods did fall,
And bent against them selues their cruell hands.
But euermore, those Damzels did forestall
Their furious encounter, and their fiercenesse
    pall.

6

But firmely fixt they were, with dint of sword,
  And battailes doubtfull proofe their rights
    to try,
  Ne other end their fury would afford,
  But what to them Fortune would iustify.
  So stood they both in readinesse thereby,
  To ioyne the combate with cruell intent ;
  When *Artegall* arriuing happily,
Did stay a while their greedy bickerment,
Till he had questioned the cause of their dissent.

7

To whom the elder did this aunswere frame ;
  Then weete ye Sir, that we two brethren be,
  To whom our sire, *Milesio* by name,
  Did equally bequeath his lands in fee,
  Two Ilands, which ye there before you see
  Not farre in sea ; of which the one appeares
  But like a little Mount of small degree ;
  Yet was as great and wide ere many yeares,
As that same other Isle, that greater bredth now
    beares.

8

But tract of time, that all things doth decay,
  And this deuouring Sea, that naught doth spare,
  The most part of my land hath washt away,
  And throwne it vp vnto my brothers share :
  So his encreased, but mine did empaire.
  Before which time I lou'd, as was my lot,
  That further mayd, hight *Phillera* the faire,
  With whom a goodly doure I should haue got,
And should haue ioyned bene to her in wedlocks
    knot.

9

Then did my younger brother *Amidas*
  Loue that same other Damzell, *Lucy* bright,
  To whom but little dowre allotted was ;
  Her vertue was the dowre, that did delight.
  What better dowre can to a dame be hight ?
  But now when *Philtra* saw my lands decay,
  And former liuelod fayle, she left me quight,
  And to my brother did ellope streight way :
Who taking her from me, his owne loue left
    astray.

10

She seeing then her selfe forsaken so,
  Through dolorous despaire, which she con-
    ceyued,
  Into the Sea her selfe did headlong throw,
  Thinking to haue her griefe by death bereaued.
  But see how much her purpose was deceaued.
  Whilest thus amidst the billowes beating of her
  Twixt life and death, long to and fro she weaued,
  She chaunst vnwares to light vppon this coffer,
Which to her in that daunger hope of life did
    offer.

11

The wretched mayd that earst desir'd to die,
  When as the paine of death she tasted had,
  And but halfe seene his vgly visnomie,
  Gan to repent, that she had beene so mad,
  For any death to chaunge life though most bad
  And catching hold of this Sea-beaten chest,
  The lucky Pylot of her passage sad,
  After long tossing in the seas distrest,
Her weary barke at last vppon mine Isle did rest.

12

Where I by chaunce then wandring on the shore,
  Did her espy, and through my good endeuour
  From dreadfull mouth of death, which threa-
    tned sore
  Her to haue swallow'd vp, did helpe to saue her.
  She then in recompence of that great fauour,
  Which I on her bestowed, bestowed on me
  The portion of that good, which Fortune gaue
    her,
  Together with her selfe in dowry free ;
Both goodly portions, but of both the better she.

13

Yet in this coffer, which she with her brought,
  Great threasure sithence we did finde contained;
  Which as our owne we tooke, and so it thought.
  But this same other Damzell since hath fained,
  That to her selfe that threasure appertained ;
  And that she did transport the same by sea,
  To bring it to her husband new ordained,
  But suffred cruell shipwracke by the way.
But whether it be so or no, I can not say.

14

But whether it indeede be so or no,
  This doe I say, that what so good or ill
  Or God or Fortune vnto me did throw,
  Not wronging any other by my will,
  I hold mine owne, and so will hold it still.
  And though my land he first did winne away,
  And then my loue (though now it little skill,)
  Yet my good lucke he shall not likewise pray ;
But I will it defend, whilest euer that I may.

15

So hauing sayd, tne younger did ensew ;
Full true it is, what so about our land
My brother here declared hath to you :
But not for it this ods twixt vs doth stand,
But for this threasure throwne vppon his strand;
Which well I proue, this maides, with whom I fastned hand,
To be this maides, with whom I fastned hand,
Known by good markes, and perfect good espiall,
Therefore it ought be rendred her without
deniall.

16

When they thus ended had, the Knight began ;
Certes your strife were easie to accord,
Would ye remit it to some righteous man.
Vnto your selfe, said they, we giue our word,
To bide what iudgement ye shall vs afford.
Then for assuraunce to my doome to stand,
Vnder my foote let each lay downe his sword,
And then you shall my sentence vnderstand.
So each of them layd downe his sword out of his
hand.

17

Then *Artegall* thus to the younger sayd ; .
Now tell me *Amidas*, if that ye may,
Your brothers land the which the sea hath layd
Vnto your part, and pluckt from his away,
By what good right doe you withhold this day?
What other right (quoth he) should you esteeme,
But that the sea it to my share did lay ?
Your right is good (sayd he) and so I deeme,
That what the sea vnto you sent, your own
should seeme.

18

Then turning to the elder thus he sayd ;
Now *Bracidas* let this likewise be showne.
Your brothers threasure, which from him is
strayd,
Being the dowry of his wife well knowne,
By what right doe you claime to be your owne ?
What other right (quoth he) should you esteeme,
But that the sea hath it vnto me throwne ?
Your right is good (sayd he) and so I deeme,
That what the sea vnto you sent, your own
should seeme.

19

For equall right in equall things doth stand,
For what the mighty Sea hath once possest,
And plucked quite from all possessors hand,
Whether by rage of waues, that neuer rest,
Or else by wracke, that wretches hath distrest,
He may dispose by his imperiall might,
As thing at randon left, to whom he list.
So *Amidas*, the land was yours first hight,
And so the threasure yours is *Bracidas* by right.

20

When he his sentence thus pronounced had,
Both *Amidas* and *Philtra* were displeased ;
But *Bracidas* and *Lucy* were right glad,
And on the threasure by that iudgement seased.
So was their discord by this doome appeased,
And each one had his right. Then *Artegall*
When as their sharpe contention he had ceased,
Departed on his way, as did befall,
To follow his old quest, the which him forth did
call.

21

So as he trauelled vppon the way,
He chaunst to come, where happily he spide
A rout of many people farre away ;
To whom his course he hastily applide,
To weete the cause of their assemblaunce wide.
To whom when he approched neare in sight,
(An vncouth sight) he plainely then descride
To be a troupe of women warlike dight,
With weapons in their hands, as ready for to
fight.

22

And in the midst of thcm he saw a Knight,
With both his hands behinde him pinnoed hard,
And round about his necke an halter tight,
As ready for the gallow tree prepard :
His face was couered, and his head was bar'd,
That who he was, vneath was to descry ;
And with full heauy heart with them he far'd,
Grieu'd to the soule, and groning inwardly,
That he of womens hands so base a death should
dy.

23

But they like tyrants, mercilesse the more,
Reioyced at his miserable case,
And him reuiled, and reproched sore
With bitter taunts, and termes of vile disgrace.
Now when as *Artegall* arriu'd in place,
Did aske, what cause brought that man to
decay,
They round about him gan to swarme apace,
Meaning on him their cruell hands to lay,
And to haue wrought vnwares some villanous
assay.

24

But he was soone aware of their ill minde,
And drawing backe deceiued their intent ;
Yet though him selfe did shame on womankinde
His mighty hand to shend, he *Talus* sent
To wrecke on them their follies hardyment :
Who with few sowces of his yron flaile,
Dispersed all their troupe incontinent,
And sent them home to tell a piteous tale,
Of their vaine prowesse, turned to their proper
bale.

25

But that same wretched man, ordaynd to die,
They left behind them, glad to be so quit :
Him *Talus* tooke out of perplexitie,
And horrour of fowle death for Knight vnfit,
Who more then losse of life ydreaded it ;
And him restoring vnto liuing light,
So brought vnto his Lord, where he did sit,
Beholding all that womanish weake fight ;
Whom soone as he beheld, he knew, and thus
   behight.

26

Sir *Terpine*, haplesse man, what make you here?
Or haue you lost your selfe, and your discretion,
That euer in this wretched case ye were ?
Or haue ye yeelded you to proude oppression
Of womens powre, that boast of mens subiec-
Or else what other deadly dismall day [tion ?
Is falne on you, by heauens hard direction,
That ye were runne so fondly far astray,
As for to lead your selfe vnto your owne decay ?

27

Much was the man confounded in his mind,
Partly with shame, and partly with dismay,
That all astonisht he him selfe did find,
And little had for his excuse to say,
But onely thus ; Most haplesse well ye may
Me iustly terme, that to this shame am brought,
And made the scorne of Knighthod this same
   day.
But who can scape, what his owne fate hath
   wrought ?
The worke of heauens will surpasseth humaine
   thought.

28

Right true : but faulty men vse oftentimes
To attribute their folly vnto fate,
And lay on heauen the guilt of their owne crimes.
But tell, Sir *Terpin*, ne let you amate
Your misery, how fell ye in this state.
Then sith ye needs (quoth he) will know my
   shame,
And all the ill, which chaunst to me of late,
I shortly will to you rehearse the same,
In hope ye will not turne misfortune to my
   blame.

29

Being desirous (as all Knights are woont)
Through hard aduentures deedes of armes to try,
And after fame and honour for to hunt,
I heard report that farre abrode did fly,
That a proud Amazon did late defy
All the braue Knights, that hold of Maidenhead,
And vnto them wrought all the villany,
That she could forge in her malicious head,
Which some hath put to shame, and many done
   be dead.

30

The cause, they say, of this her cruell hate,
Is for the sake of *Bellodant* the bold,
To whom she bore most feruent loue of late,
And wooed him by all the waies she could :
But when she saw at last, that he ne would
For ought or nought be wonne vnto her will,
She turn'd her loue to hatred manifold,
And for his sake vow'd to doe all the ill
Which she could doe to Knights, which now she
   doth fulfill.

31

For all those Knights, the which by force or guile
She doth subdue, she fowly doth entreate.
First she doth them of warlike armes despoile,
And cloth in womens weedes : And then with
   threat
Doth them compell to worke, to earne their
   meat,
To spin, to card, to sew, to wash, to wring ;
Ne doth she giue them other thing to eat,
But bread and water, or like feeble thing,
Them to disable from reuenge aduenturing.

32

But if through stout disdaine of manly mind,
Any her proud obseruaunce will withstand,
Vppon that gibbet, which is there behind,
She causeth them be hang'd vp out of hand ;
In which condition I right now did stand.
For being ouercome by her in fight,
And put to that base seruice of her band,
I rather chose to die in liues despight,
Then lead that shamefull life, vnworthy of
   a Knight.

33

How hight that Amazon (sayd *Artegall*) ?
And where, and how far hence does she abide ?
Her name (quoth he) they *Radigund* doe call,
A Princesse of great powre, and greater pride,
And Queene of Amazons, in armes well tride,
And sundry battels, which she hath atchieued
With great successe, that her hath glorifide,
And made her famous, more then is belieued ;
Ne would I it haue ween'd, had I not late it
   prieued.

34

Now sure (said he) and by the faith that I
To Maydenhead and noble knighthood owe,
I will not rest, till I her might doe trie,
And venge the shame, that she to Knights doth
   show.
Therefore Sir *Terpin* from you lightly throw
This squalid weede, the patterne of dispaire,
And wend with me, that ye may see and know,
How Fortune will your ruin'd name repaire,
And knights of Maidenhead, whose praise she
   would empaire.

35

With that, like one that hopelesse was repryu'd
From deathes dore, at which he latcly lay,
Those yron fetters, wherewith he was gyu'd,
The badges of reproch, he threw away,
And nimbly did him dight to guide the way
Vnto the dwelling of that Amazone.
Which was from thence not past a mile or tway:
A goodly citty and a mighty one,
The which of her owne name she called *Radegone.*

36

Where they arriuing, by the watchmen were
Descried streight, who all the citty warned,
How that three warlike persons did appeare,
Of which the one him seem'd a Knight all armed,
And th'other two well likely to haue harmed.
Eftsoones the people all to harnesse ran,
And like a sort of Bees in clusters swarmed:
Ere long their Queene her selfe, halfe like a man
Came forth into the rout, and them t'array
began.

37

And now the Knights being arriued neare,
Did beat vppon the gates to enter in,
And at the Porter, skorning them so few,
Threw many threats, if they the towne did win,
To teare his flesh in peeces for his sin.
Which when as *Radigund* there comming heard,
Her heart for rage did grate, and teeth did grin:
She bad that streight the gates should be vnbard,
And to them way to make, with weapons well
prepard.

38

Soone as the gates were open to them set,
They pressed forward, entraunce to haue made.
But in the middle way they were ymet
With a sharpe showre of arrowes, which them
staid,
And better bad aduise, ere they assaid
Vnknowen perill of bold womens pride.
Then all that rout vppon them rudely laid,
And heaped strokes so fast on euery side,
And arrowes haild so thicke, that they could
not abide.

39

But *Radigund* her selfe, when she espide
Sir *Terpin,* from her direfull doome acquit,
So cruell doale amongst her maides diuide,
T'auenge that shame, they did on him commit,
All sodainely enflam'd with furious fit,
Like a fell Lionesse at him she flew,
And on his head-peece him so fiercely smit,
That to the ground him quite she ouerthrew,
Dismayd so with the stroke, that he no colours
knew.

40

Soone as she saw him on the ground to grouell,
She lightly to him leapt, and in his necke
Her proud foote setting, at his head did leuell,
Weening at once her wrath on him to wreake,
And his contempt, that did her iudg'ment
breake.
As when a Beare hath seiz'd her cruell clawes
Vppon the carkasse of some beast too weake,
Proudly stands ouer, and a while doth pause,
To heare the piteous beast pleading her plaintiffe
cause.

41

Whom when as *Artegall* in that distresse
By chaunce beheld, he left the bloudy slaughter,
In which he swam, and ranne to his redresse.
There her assayling fiercely fresh, he raught her
Such an huge stroke, that it of sence distraught
And had she not it warded warily,   [her:
It had depriu'd her mother of a daughter.
Nathlesse for all the powre she did apply,
It made her stagger oft, and stare with ghastly
eye.

42

Like to an Eagle in his kingly pride,
Soring through his wide Empire of the aire,
To weather his brode sailes, by chaunce hath
spide
A Goshauke, which hath seized for her share
Vppon some fowle, that should her feast prepare;
With dreadfull force he flies at her byliue,
That with his souce, which none enduren dare,
Her from the quarrey he away doth driue,
And from her griping pounce the greedy prey
doth riue.

43

But soone as she her sence recouer'd had,
She fiercely towards him her selfe gan dight,
Through vengeful wrath and sdeignfull pride
half mad:
For neuer had she suffred such despight.
But ere she could ioyne hand with him to fight,
Her warlike maides about her flockt so fast,
That they disparted them, maugre their might,
And with their troupes did far a sunder cast:
But mongst the rest the fight did vntill euening
last.

44

And euery while that mighty yron man,
With his strange weapon, neuer wont in warre,
Them sorely vext, and courst, and ouerran,
And broke their bowes, and did their shooting
marre,
That none of all the many once did darre
Him to assault, nor once approach him nie,
But like a sort of sheepe dispersed farre
For dread of their deuouring enemie,   [flie.
Through all the fields and vallies did before him

45

But when as daies faire shinie-beame, yclowded
With fearefull shadowes of deformed night,
Warn'd man and beast in quiet rest be shrowded,
Bold *Radigund* with sound of trumpe on hight,
Causd all her people to surcease from fight,
And gathering them vnto her citties gate,
Made them all enter in before her sight,
And all the wounded, and the weake in state,
To be conuayed in, ere she would once retrate.

46

When thus the field was voided all away,
And all things quieted, the Elfin Knight
Weary of toile and trauell of that day,
Causd his pauilion to be richly pight
Before the city gate, in open sight ;
Where he him selfe did rest in safety,
Together with sir *Terpin* all that night :
But *Talus* vsde in times of ieopardy
To keepe a nightly watch, for dread of treachery.

47

But *Radigund* full of heart-gnawing griefe,
For the rebuke, which she sustain'd that day,
Could take no rest, ne would receiue reliefe,
But tossed in her troublous minde, what way
She mote reuenge that blot, which on her
    lay.
There she resolu'd her selfe in single fight
To try her Fortune, and his force assay,
Rather then see her people spoiled quight,
As she had seene that day a disauenterous sight.

48

She called forth to her a trusty mayd,
Whom she thought fittest for that businesse,
Her name was *Clarin*, and thus to her sayd ;
Goe damzell quickly, doe thy selfe addresse,
To doe the message, which I shall expresse.
Goe thou vnto that stranger Faery Knight,
Who yesterday droue vs to such distresse,
Tell, that to morrow I with him wil fight,
And try in equall field, whether hath greater
    might.

49

But these conditions doe to him propound.
That if I vanquishe him, he shall obay
My law, and euer to my lore be bound,
And so will I, if me he vanquish may ;
What euer he shall like to doe or say :
Goe streight, and take with thee, to witnesse it,
Sixe of thy fellowes of the best array,
And beare with you both wine and iuncates fit,
And bid him eate, henceforth he oft shall
    hungry sit.

50

The Damzell streight obayd, and putting all
In readinesse, forth to the Towne-gate went,
Where sounding loud a Trumpet from the wall,
Vnto those warlike Knights she warning sent.
Then *Talus* forth issuing from the tent,
Vnto the wall his way did fearelesse take,
To weeten what that trumpets sounding ment :
Where that same Damzell lowdly him bespake,
And shew'd, that with his Lord she would
    emparlaunce make.

51

So he them streight conducted to his Lord,
Who, as he could, them goodly well did greete,
Till they had told their message word by word :
Which he accepting well, as he could weete,
Them fairely entertaynd with curt'sies meete,
And gaue them gifts and things of deare delight.
So backe againe they homeward turnd their
    feete.
But *Artegall* him selfe to rest did dight,
That he mote fresher be against the next daies
    fight.

Cant. V

Artegall fights with Radigund
And is subdewd by guile :
He is by her emprisoned,
But wrought by Clarins wile.

I

So soone as day forth dawning from the East,
Nights humid curtaine from the heauens with-
    drew,
And earely calling forth both man and beast,
Comaunded them their daily workes renew,
These noble warriors, mindefull to pursew
The last daies purpose of their vowed fight,
Them selues thereto preparde in order dew ;
The Knight, as best was seeming for a Knight,
And th'Amazon, as best it likt her selfe to dight

2

All in a Camis light of purple silke
Wouen vppon with siluer, subtly wrought,
And quilted vppon sattin white as milke,
Trayld with ribbands diuersly distraught
Like as the workeman had their courses taught :
Which was short tucked for light motion
Vp to her ham, but when she list, it raught
Downe to her lowest heele, and thereuppon
She wore for her defence a mayled habergeon.

3

And on her legs she painted buskins wore,
　Basted with bends of gold on euery side,
　And mailes betweene, and laced close afore :
Vppon her thigh her Cemitare was tide,
　With an embrodered belt of mickell pride ;
　And on her shoulder hung her shield, bedeckt
Vppon the bosse with stones, that shined wide,
　As the faire Moone in her most full aspect,
That to the Moone it mote be like in each respect.

4

So forth she came out of the citty gate,
　With stately port and proud magnificence,
　Guarded with many damzels, that did waite
Vppon her person for her sure defence,
　Playing on shaumes and trumpets, that from
　　hence
Their sound did reach vnto the heauens hight.
　So forth into the field she marched thence,
　Where was a rich Pauilion ready pight,
Her to receiue, till time they should begin the
　fight.

5

Then forth came *Artegall* out of his tent,
　All arm'd to point, and first the Lists did enter :
　Soone after eke came she, with fell intent,
And countenaunce fierce, as hauing fully bent
　her,
　That battels vtmost triall to aduenter.
The Lists were closed fast, to barre the rout
　From rudely pressing to the middle center ;
　Which in great heapes them circled all about,
Wayting, how Fortune would resolue that daun-
　gerous dout.

6

The Trumpets sounded, and the field began ;
　With bitter strokes it both began, and ended.
　She at the first encounter on him ran
With furious rage, as if she had intended
　Out of his breast the very heart haue rended :
　But he that had like tempests often tride,
From that first flaw him selfe right well
　defended.
　The more she rag'd, the more he did abide ;
She hewd, she foynd, she lasht, she laid on euery
　side.

7

Yet still her blowes he bore, and her forbore,
　Weening at last to win aduantage new ;
　Yet still her crueltie increased more,
And though powre faild, her courage did accrew,
　Which fayling he gan fiercely her pursew.
　Like as a Smith that to his cunning feat
The stubborne mettall seeketh to subdew,
　Soone as he feeles it mollifide with heat,
With his great yron sledge doth strongly on it
　beat.

8

So did Sir *Artegall* vpon her lay,
　As if she had an yron anduile beene,
　That flakes of fire, bright as the sunny ray,
Out of her steely armes were flashing seene,
　That all on fire ye would her surely weene.
　But with her shield so well her selfe she warded,
From the dread daunger of his weapon keene,
　That all that while her life she safely garded :
But he that helpe from her against her will dis-
　carded.

9

For with his trenchant blade at the next blow
　Halfe of her shield he shared quite away,
　That halfe her side it selfe did naked show,
And thenceforth vnto daunger opened way.
　Much was she moued with the mightie sway
　Of that sad stroke, that halfe enrag'd she grew,
And like a greedie Beare vnto her pray,
　With her sharpe Cemitare at him she flew,
That glauncing downe his thigh, the purple bloud
　forth drew.

10

Thereat she gan to triumph with great boast,
　And to vpbrayd that chaunce, which him
　　misfell,
As if the prize she gotten had almost,
　With spightfull speaches, fitting with her well ;
　That his great hart gan inwardly to swell
With indignation, at her vaunting vaine,
　And at her strooke with puissance fearefull fell ;
　Yet with her shield she warded it againe,
That shattered all to peeces round about the
　plaine.

11

Hauing her thus disarmed of her shield,
　Vpon her helmet he againe her strooke,
　That downe she fell vpon the grassie field,
In sencelesse swoune, as if her life forsooke,
　And pangs of death her spirit ouertooke.
　Whom when he saw before his foote prostrated,
He to her lept with deadly dreadfull looke,
　And her sunshynie helmet soone vnlaced,
Thinking at once both head and helmet to haue
　raced.

12

But when as he discouered had her face,
　He saw his senses straunge astonishment,
　A miracle of natures goodly grace,
In her faire visage voide of ornament,
　But bath'd in bloud and sweat together ment ;
　Which in the rudenesse of that euill plight,
Bewrayd the signes of feature excellent :
　Like as the Moone in foggie winters night,
Doth seeme to be her selfe, though darkned be
　her light.

13

At sight thereof his cruell minded hart
  Empierced was with pittifull regard,
  That his sharpe sword he threw from him apart,
  Cursing his hand that had that visage mard :
  No hand so cruell, nor no hart so hard,
  But ruth of beautie will it mollifie.
  By this vpstarting from her swoune, she star'd
  A while about her with confused eye ;
Like one that from his dreame is waked sud-
   denlye.

14

Soone as the knight she there by her did spy,
  Standing with emptie hands all weaponlesse,
  With fresh assault vpon him she did fly,
  And gan renew her former cruelnesse :
  And though he still retyr'd, yet nathelesse
  With huge redoubled strokes she on him layd ;
  And more increast her outrage mercilesse,
  The more that he with meeke intreatie prayd,
Her wrathful hand from greedy vengeance to
   haue stayd.

15

Like as a Puttocke hauing spyde in sight
  A gentle Faulcon sitting on an hill,
  Whose other wing, now made vnmeete for flight,
  Was lately broken by some fortune ill ;
  The foolish Kyte, led with licentious will,
  Doth beat vpon the gentle bird in vaine,
  With many idle stoups her troubling still :
  Euen so did *Radigund* with bootlesse paine
Annoy this noble Knight, and sorely him con-
   straine.

16

Nought could he do, but shun the dred despight
  Of her fierce wrath, and backward still retyre,
  And with his single shield, well as he might,
  Beare off the burden of her raging yre ;
  And euermore he gently did desyre,
  To stay her stroks, and he himselfe would yield :
  Yet nould she hearke, ne let him once respyre,
  Till he to her deliuered had his shield,
And to her mercie him submitted in plaine field.

17

So was he ouercome, not ouercome,
  But to her yeelded of his owne accord ;
  Yet was he iustly damned by the doome
  Of his owne mouth, that spake so warelesse
   word,
  To be her thrall, and seruice her afford.
  For though that he first victorie obtayned,
  Yet after by abandoning his sword,
  He wilfull lost, that he before attayned.
No fayrer conquest, then that with goodwill is
   gayned.

18

Tho with her sword on him she flatling strooke,
  In signe of true subiection to her powre,
  And as her vassall him to thraldome tooke.
  But *Terpine* borne to'a more vnhappy howre,
  As he, on whom the lucklesse starres did lowre,
  She causd to be attacht, and forthwith led
  Vnto the crooke t'abide the balefull stowre,
  From which he lately had through reskew fled.
Where he full shamefully was hanged by the hed.

19

But when they thought on *Talus* hands to lay,
  He with his yron flaile amongst them thondred,
  That they were fayne to let him scape away,
  Glad from his companie to be so sondred ;
  Whose presence all their troups so much en-
   combred
  That th'heapes of those, which he did wound
   and slay,   [bred :
  Besides the rest dismayd, might not be nom-
  Yet all that while he would not once assay,
To reskew his owne Lord, but thought it iust
   t'obay.

20

Then tooke the Amazon this noble knight,
  Left to her will by his owne wilfull blame,
  And caused him to be disarmed quight,
  Of all the ornaments of knightly name,
  With which whylome he gotten had great fame :
  In stead whereof she made him to be dight
  In womans weedes, that is to manhood shame,
  And put before his lap a napron white,
In stead of Curiets and bases fit for fight.

21

So being clad, she brought him from the field,
  In which he had bene trayned many a day,
  Into a long large chamber, which was sield
  With moniments of many knights decay,
  By her subdewed in victorious fray :
  Amongst the which she causd his warlike armes
  Be hang'd on high, that mote his shame bewray ;
  And broke his sword, for feare of further harmes.
With which he wont to stirre vp battailous
   alarmes.

22

There entred in, he round about him saw
  Many braue knights, whose names right well he
   knew,
  There bound t'obay that Amazons proud law,
  Spinning and carding all in comely rew,
  That his bigge hart loth'd so vncomely vew.
  But they were forst through penurie and pyne,
  To doe those workes, to them appointed dew :
  For nought was giuen them to sup or dyne,
But what their hands could earne by twisting
   linnen twyne.

23

Amongst them all she placed him most low,
  And in his hand a distaffe to him gaue,
  That he thereon should spin both flax and tow;
  A sordid office for a mind so braue.
  So hard it is to be a womans slaue.
  Yet he it tooke in his owne selfes despight,
  And thereto did himselfe right well behaue,
  Her to obay, sith he his faith had plight,
Her vassall to become, if she him wonne in fight.

24

Who had him seene, imagine mote thereby,
  That whylome hath of *Hercules* bene told,
  How for *Iolas* sake he did apply
  His mightie hands, the distaffe vile to hold,
  For his huge club, which had subdew'd of old
  So many monsters, which the world annoyed;
  His Lyons skin chaungd to a pall of gold,
  In which forgetting warres, he onely ioyed
In combats of sweet loue, and with his mistresse toyed.

25

Such is the crueltie of womenkynd,
  When they haue shaken off the shamefast band,
  With which wise Nature did them strongly bynd,
  T'obay the heasts of mans well ruling hand,
  That then all rule and reason they withstand,
  To purchase a licentious libertie.
  But vertuous women wisely vnderstand,
  That they were borne to base humilitie,
Vnlesse the heauens them lift to lawfull soueraintie.

26

Thus there there long while continu'd *Artegall*,
  Seruing proud *Radigund* with true subiection;
  How euer his noble heart did gall,
  T'obay a womans tyrannous direction,
  That might haue had of life or death election:
  But hauing chosen, now he might not chaunge.
  During which time, the warlike Amazon,
  Whose wandring fancie after lust did raunge,
Gan cast a secret liking to this captiue straunge.

27

Which long concealing in her couert brest,
  She chaw'd the cud of louers carefull plight;
  Yet could it not so thoroughly digest,
  Being fast fixed in her wounded spright,
  But it tormented her both day and night:
  Yet would she not thereto yeeld free accord,
  To serue the lowly vassall of her might,
  And of her seruant make her soueraynе Lord:
So great her pride, that she such basenesse much abhord.

28

So much the greater still her anguish grew,
  Through stubborne handling of her loue-sicke hart;
  And still the more she stroue it to subdew,
  The more she still augmented her owne smart,
  And wyder made the wound of th'hidden dart.
  At last when long she struggled had in vaine,
  She gan to stoupe, and her proud mind conuert
  To meeke obeysance of loues mightie raine,
And him entreat for grace, that had procur'd her paine.

29

Vnto her selfe in secret she did call
  Her nearest handmayd, whom she most did trust,
  And to her said; *Clarinda* whom of all
  I trust a liue, sith I thee fostred first;
  Now is the time, that I vntimely must
  Thereof make tryall, in my greatest need:
  It is so hapned, that the heauens vniust,
  Spighting my happie freedome, haue agreed,
To thrall my looser life, or my last bale to breed.

30

With that she turn'd her head, as halfe abashed,
  To hide the blush which in her visage rose,
  And through her eyes like sudden lightning flashed,
  Decking her cheeke with a vermilion rose:
  But soone she did her countenance compose,
  And to her turning, thus began againe;
  This griefes deepe wound I would to thee disclose,
  Thereto compelled through hart-murdring paine,
But dread of shame my doubtfull lips doth still restraine.

31

Ah my deare dread (said then the faithfull Mayd)
  Can dread of ought your dreadlesse hart withhold,
  That many hath with dread of death dismayd,
  And dare euen deathes most dreadfull face behold?
  Say on my souerayne Ladie, and be bold;
  Doth not your handmayds life at your foot lie?
  Therewith much comforted, she gan vnfold
  The cause of her conceiued maladie,
As one that would confesse, yet faine would it denie.

32

Clarin (sayd she) thou seest yond Fayry Knight,
  Whom not my valour, but his owne braue mind
  Subiected hath to my vnequall might;
  What right is it, that he should thraldome find,
  For lending life to me a wretch vnkind;
  That for such good him recompence with ill?
  Therefore I cast, how I may him vnbind,
  And by his freedome get his free goodwill;
Yet so, as bound to me he may continue still.

33

Bound vnto me, but not with such hard bands
Of strong compulsion, and streight violence,
As now in miserable state he stands ;
But with sweet loue and sure beneuolence,
Voide of malitious mind, or foule offence.
To which if thou canst win him any way,
Without discouerie of my thoughts pretence,
Both goodly meede of him it purchase may,
And eke with gratefull seruice me right wellapay.

34

Which that thou mayst the better bring to pas,
Loe here this ring, which shall thy warrant bee,
And token true to old *Eumenias*,
From time to time, when thou it best shalt see,
That in and out thou mayst haue passage free.
Goe now, *Clarinda*, well thy wits aduise,
And all thy forces gather vnto thee :
Armies of louely lookes, and speeches wise,
With which thou canst euen *Ioue* himselfe to
    loue entise.

35

The trustie Mayd, conceiuing her intent,
Did with sure promise of her good indeuour,
Giue her great comfort, and some harts content.
So from her parting, she thenceforth did labour
By all the meanes she might, to curry fauour
With th'Elfin Knight, her Ladies best beloued ;
With daily shew of courteous kind behauiour,
Euen at the markewhite of his hart she roued,
And with wide glauncing words, one day she thus
    him proued.

36

Vnhappie Knight, vpon whose hopelesse state
Fortune enuying good, hath felly frowned,
And cruell heauens haue heapt an heauy fate ;
I rew that thus thy better dayes are drowned
In sad despaire, and all thy senses swowned
In stupid sorow, sith thy iuster merit
Might else haue with felicitie bene crowned :
Looke vp at last, and wake thy dulled spirit,
To thinke how this long death thou mightest
    disinherit.

37

Much did he maruell at her vncouth speach,
Whose hidden drift he could not well perceiue ;
And gan to doubt, least she him sought
    t'appeach
Of treason, or some guilefull traine did weaue,
Through which she might his wretched life
    bereaue.
Both which to barre, he with this answere met
    her ;
Faire Damzell, that with ruth (as I perceaue)
Of my mishaps, art mou'd to wish me better,
For such your kind regard, I can but rest your
    detter.

38

Yet weet ye well, that to a courage great
It is no lesse beseeming well, to beare
The storme of fortunes frowne, or heauens
    threat,
Then in the sunshine of her countenance cleare
Timely to ioy, and carrie comely cheare.
For though this cloud haue now me ouercast,
Yet doe I not of better times despeyre ;
And, though (vnlike) they should for euer last,
Yet in my truthes assurance I rest fixed fast.

39

But what so stonie mind (she then replyde)
But if in his owne powre occasion lay,
Would to his hope a windowe open wyde,
And to his fortunes helpe make readie way ?
Vnworthy sure (quoth he) of better day,
That will not take the offer of good hope,
And eke pursew, if he attaine it may.
Which speaches she applying to the scope
Of her intent, this further purpose to him shope.

40

Then why doest not, thou ill aduized man,
Make meanes to win thy libertie forlorne,
And try if thou by faire entreatie, can
Moue *Radigund ?* who though she still haue
    worne
Her dayes in warre, yet (weet thou) was not
    borne
Of Beares and Tygres, nor so saluage mynded,
As that, albe all loue of men she scorne,
She yet forgets, that she of men was kynded :
And sooth oft seene, that proudest harts base loue
    hath blynded.

41

Certes *Clarinda*, not of cancred will,
(Sayd he) nor obstinate disdainefull mind,
I haue forbore this duetie to fulfill :
For well I may this weene, by that I fynd,
That she a Queene, and come of Princely kynd,
Both worthie is for to be sewd vnto,
Chiefely by him, whose life her law doth bynd,
And eke of powre her owne doome to vndo,
And als' of princely grace to be inclyn'd thereto.

42

But want of meanes hath bene mine onely let,
From seeking fauour, where it doth abound ;
Which if I might by your good office get,
I to your selfe should rest for euer bound,
And readie to deserue, what grace I found.
She feeling him thus bite vpon the bayt,
Yet doubting least his hold was but vnsound,
And not well fastened, would not strike him
    strayt,
But drew him on with hope, fit leasure to awayt.

43

But foolish Mayd, whyl, s heedlesse of the hooke,
　She thus oft times was beating off and on,
　Through slipperie footing, fell into the brooke,
　And there was caught to her confusion.
　For seeking thus to salue the Amazon,
　She wounded was with her deceipts owne dart,
　And gan thenceforth to cast affection,
　Conceiued close in her beguiled hart,
To *Artegall*, through pittie of his causelesse smart.

44

Yet durst she not disclose her fancies wound,
　Ne to himselfe, for doubt of being sdayned,
　Ne yet to any other wight on ground,
　For feare her mistresse shold haue knowledge
　　gayned,
　But to her selfe it secretly retayned,
　Within the closet of her couert brest:
　The more thereby her tender hart was payned.
　Yet to awayt fit time she weened best,
And fairely did dissemble her sad thoughts
　　vnrest.

45

One day her Ladie, calling her apart,
　Gan to demaund of her some tydings good,
　Touching her loues successe, her lingring smart.
　Therewith she gan at first to change her mood,
　As one adaw'd, and halfe confused stood;
　But quickly she it ouerpast, so soone
　As she her face had wypt, to fresh her blood:
　Tho gan she tell her all, that she had donne,
And all the wayes she sought, his loue for to
　　haue wonne.

46

But sayd, that he was obstinate and sterne,
　Scorning her offers and conditions vaine;
　Ne would be taught with any termes, to lerne
　So fond a lesson, as to loue againe.
　Die rather would he in penurious paine,
　And his abridged dayes in dolour wast,
　Then his foes loue or liking entertaine:
　His resolution was both first and last,
His bodie was her thrall, his hart was freely plast.

47

Which when the cruell Amazon perceiued,
　She gan to storme, and rage, and rend her gall,
　For very fell despight, which she conceiued,
　To be so scorned of a base borne thrall,
　Whose life did lie in her least eye-lids fall;
　Of which she vow'd with many a cursed threat,
　That she therefore would him ere long forstall.
　Nathlesse when calmed was her furious heat,
She chang'd that threatfull mood, and mildly
　　gan entreat.

48

What now is left *Clarinda*? what remaines,
　That we may compasse th. s our enterprize?
　Great shame to lose so long employed paines,
　And greater shame t'abide so great misprize,
　With which he dares our offers thus despize.
　Yet that his guilt the greater may appeare,
　And more my gratious mercie by this wize,
　I will a while with his first folly beare,
Till thou haue tride againe, and tempted him
　more neare.

49

Say, and do all, that may thereto preuaile;
　Leaue nought vnpromist, that may him per-
　　swade,
　Life, freedome, grace, and gifts of great auaile,
　With which the Gods themselues are mylder
　　made:
　Thereto adde art, euen womens witty trade,
　The art of mightie words, that men can charme;
　With which in case thou canst him not inuade,
　Let him feele hardnesse of thy heauie arme:
Who will not stoupe with good, shall be made
　stoupe with harme.

50

Some of his diet doe from him withdraw;
　For I him find to be too proudly fed.
　Giue him more labour, and with streighter law,
　That he with worke may be forwearied.
　Let him lodge hard, and lie in strawen bed,
　That may pull downe the courage of his pride;
　And lay vpon him, for his greater dread,
　Cold yron chaines, with which let him be tide;
And let, what euer he desires, be him denide.

51

When thou hast all this doen, then bring me
　newes
　Of his demeane: thenceforth not like a louer,
　But like a rebell stout I will him vse.
　For I resolue this siege not to giue ouer,
　Till I the conquest of my will recouer.
　So she departed, full of griefe and sdaine,
　Which inly did to great impatience moue her.
　But the false mayden shortly turn'd againe
Vnto the prison, where her hart did thrall
　remaine.

52

There all her subtill nets she did vnfold,
　And all the engins of her wit display;
　In which she meant him warelesse to enfold,
　And of his innocence to make her pray.
　So cunningly she wrought her craf. s assay,
　That both her Ladie, and her selfe withall,
　And eke the knight attonce she did betray:
But most the knight, whom she with guilefull call
Did cast for to allure, into her trap to fall.

53

As a bad Nurse, which fayning to receiue
In her owne mouth the food, ment for her chyld,
Withholdes it to her selfe, and doeth deceiue
The infant, so for want of nourture spoyld :
Euen so *Clarinda* her owne Dame beguyld,
And turn'd the trust, which was in her affyde,
To feeding of her priuate fire, which boyld
Her inward brest, and in her entrayles fryde,
The more that she it sought to couer and to hyde.

54

For comming to this knight, she purpose fayned,
How earnest suit she earst for him had made
Vnto her Queene, his freedome to haue gayned;
But by no meanes could her thereto perswade :
But that in stead thereof, she sternely bade
His miserie to be augmented more,
And many yron bands on him to lade.
All which nathlesse she for his loue forbore :
So praying him t'accept her seruice euermore.

55

And more then that, she promist that she would,
In case she might finde fauour in his eye,
Deuize how to enlarge him out of hould.
The Fayrie glad to gaine his libertie,
Can yeeld great thankes for such her curtesie,
And with faire words, fit for the time and place,
To feede the humour of her maladie,
Promist, if she would free him from that case,
He wold by all good means he might, deserue
    such grace.

56

So daily he faire semblant did her shew,
Yet neuer meant he in his noble mind,
To his owne absent loue to be vntrew :
Ne euer did deceiptfull *Clarin* find
In her false hart, his bondage to vnbind ;
But rather how he mote him faster tye.
Therefore vnto her mistresse most vnkind
She daily told, her loue he did defye,
And him she told, her Dame his freedome did
    denye.

57

Yet thus much friendship she to him did show,
That his scarse diet somewhat was amended,
And his worke lessened, that his loue mote
    grow :
Yet to her Dame him still she discommended,
That she with him mote be the more offended.
Thus he long while in thraldome there re-
    maynd,
Of both beloued well, but litle frended ;
Vntill his owne true loue his freedome gayned,
Which in an other Canto will be best contayned.

Cant. VI.

Talus brings newes to Britomart,
  of Artegals mishap,
She goes to seeke him, Dolon meetes,
  who seekes her to entrap.

1

Some men, I wote, will deeme in *Artegall*
Great weaknesse, and report of him much ill,
For yeelding so himselfe a wretched thrall,
To th'insolent commaund of womens will ;
That all his former praise doth fowly spill.
But he the man, that say or doe so dare,
Be well aduiz'd, that he stand stedfast still :
For neuer yet was wight so well aware,
But he at first or last was trapt in womens snare.

2

Yet in the streightnesse of that captiue state,
This gentle knight himselfe so well behaued,
That notwithstanding all the subtill bait,
With which those Amazons his loue still
    craued,
To his owne loue his loialtie he saued :
Whose character in th'Adamantine mould
Of his true hart so firmely was engraued,
That no new loues impression euer could
Bereaue it thence : such blot his honour
    blemish should.

3

Yet his owne loue, the noble *Britomart*,
Scarse so conceiued in her iealous thought,
What time sad tydings of his balefull smart
In womans bondage, *Talus* to her brought ;
Brought in vntimely houre, ere it was sought.
For after that the vtmost date, assynde
For his returne, she waited had for nought,
She gan to cast in her misdoubtfull mynde
A thousand feares, that loue-sicke fancies faine
    to fynde.

4

Sometime she feared, least some hard mishap
Had him misfalne in his aduenturous quest ;
Sometime least his false foe did him entrap
In traytrous traine, or had vnwares opprest :
But most she did her troubled mynd molest,
And secretly afflict with iealous feare,
Least some new loue had him from her possest;
Yet loth she was, since she no ill did heare,
To thinke of him so ill : yet could she not for-
    beare.

5

One while she blam'd her selfe ; another whyle
  She him condemn'd, as trustlesse and vntrew :
  And then, her griefe with errour to beguyle,
  She fayn'd to count the time againe anew,
  As if before she had not counted trew.
For houres but dayes ; for weekes, that passed
    were,
  She told but moneths, to make them seeme
    more few :
Yet when she reckned them, still drawing neare,
Each houre did seeme a moneth, and euery moneth
    a yeare.

6

But when as yet she saw him not returne,
  She thought to send some one to seeke him out;
  But none she found so fit to serue that turne,
  As her owne selfe, to ease her selfe of dout.
  Now she deuiz'd amongst the warlike rout
Of errant Knights, to seeke her errant Knight ;
  And then againe resolu'd to hunt him out
Amongst loose Ladies, lapped in delight :
And then both Knights enuide, and Ladies eke
    did spight.

7

One day, when as she long had sought for ease
  In euery place, and euery place thought best,
  Yet found no place, that could her liking please,
  She to a window came, that opened West,
  Towards which coast her loue his way addrest.
There looking forth, shee in her heart did find
  Many vaine fancies, working her vnrest ;
  And sent her winged thoughts, more swift
    then wind,
To beare vnto her loue the message of her mind.

8

There as she looked long, at last she spide
  One comming towards her with hasty speede :
  Well weend she then, ere him she plaine descride,
  That it was one sent from her loue indeede.
  Who when he nigh approcht, shee mote arede
That it was *Talus*, *Artegall* his groome ;
  Whereat her heart was fild with hope and drede;
Ne would she stay, till he in place could come,
But ran to meete him forth, to know his tidings
    somme.

9

Euen in the dore him meeting, she begun ;
  And where is he thy Lord, and how far hence ?
  Declare at once ; and hath he lost or wun ?
  The yron man, albe he wanted sence
  And sorrowes feeling, yet with conscience
Of his ill newes, did inly chill and quake,
  And stood still mute, as one in great suspence,
As if that by his silence he would make
Her rather reade his meaning, then him selfe
    it spake.

10

Till she againe thus sayd ; *Talus* be bold,
  And tell what euer it be, good or bad,
  That from thy tongue thy hearts intent doth
    hold.
To whom he thus at length. The tidings sad,
  That I would hide, will needs, I see, be rad.
My Lord, your loue, by hard mishap doth lie
  In wretched bondage, wofully bestad.
Ay me (quoth she) what wicked destinie ?
And is he vanquisht by his tyrant enemy ?

11

Not by that Tyrant, his intended foe ;
  But by a Tyrannesse (he then replide,)
  That him captiued hath in haplesse woe.
  Cease thou bad newes-man, badly doest thou
    hide
Thy maisters shame, in harlots bondage tide.
The rest my selfe too readily can spell.
  With that in rage she turn'd from him aside,
Forcing in vaine the rest to her to tell,
And to her chamber went like solitary cell.

12

There she began to make her monefull plaint
  Against her Knight, for being so vntrew ;
  And him to touch with falshoods fowle attaint,
  That all his other honour ouerthrew.
  Oft did she blame her selfe, and often rew,
For yeelding to a straungers loue so light,
  Whose life and manners straunges he neuer knew;
And euermore she did him sharpely twight
For breach of faith to her, which he had firmely
    plight.

13

And then she in her wrathfull will did cast,
  How to reuenge that blot of honour blent ;
  To fight with him, and goodly die her last :
  And then againe she did her selfe torment,
  Inflicting on her selfe his punishment.
A while she walkt, and chauft ; a while she threw
  Her selfe vppon her bed, and did lament :
Yet did she not lament with loude alew,
As women wont, but with deepe sighes, and
    singults few.

14

Like as a wayward childe, whose sounder sleepe
  Is broken with some fearefull dreames affright,
  With froward will doth set him selfe to weepe ;
  Ne can be stild for all his nurses might,
  But kicks, and squals, and shriekes for fell
    despight :
Now scratching her, and her loose locks mis-
    using ;
Now seeking darkenesse, and now seeking light,
  Then crauing sucke, and then the sucke refusing :
Such was this Ladies fit, in her loues fond accusing.

15

But when she had with such vnquiet fits
  Her selfe there close afflicted long in vaine,
  Yet found no easement in her troubled wits,
  She vnto *Talus* forth return'd againe,
  By change of place seeking to ease her paine ;
  And gan enquire of him, with mylder mood,
  The certaine cause of *Artegals* detaine ;
And what he did, and in what state he stood,
And whether he did woo, or whether he were
  woo'd.

16

Ah wellaway (sayd then the yron man,)
  That he is not the while in state to woo ;
  But lies in wretched thraldome, weake and wan,
  Not by strong hand compelled thereunto,
  But his owne doome, that none can now vndoo.
  Sayd I not then (quoth shee) erwhile aright,
  That this is things compacte betwixt you two,
  Me to deceiue of faith vnto me plight,
Since that he was not forst, nor ouercome in
  fight ?

17

With that he gan at large to her dilate
  The whole discourse of his captiuance sad,
  In sort as ye haue heard the same of late.
  All which when she with hard enduraunce had
  Heard to the end, she was right sore bestad,
  With sodaine stounds of wrath and griefe
  attone :
  Ne would abide, till she had aunswere made,
But streight her selfe did dight, and armor don;
And mounting to her steede, bad *Talus* guide
  her on.

18

So forth she rode vppon her ready way,
  To seeke her Knight, as *Talus* her did guide :
  Sadly she rode, and neuer word did say,
  Nor good nor bad, ne euer lookt aside,
  But still right downe, and in her thought did
  hide
  The felnesse of her heart, right fully bent
  To fierce auengement of that womans pride,
  Which had her Lord in his base prison pent,
And so great honour with so fowle reproch had
  blent.

19

So as she thus melancholicke did ride,
  Chawing the cud of griefe and inward paine,
  She chaunst to meete toward the euen-tide
  A Knight, that softly paced on the plaine,
  As if him selfe to solace he were faine.
  Well shot in yeares he seem'd, and rather bent
  To peace, then needlesse trouble to constraine.
  As well by view of that his vestiment,
As by his modest semblant, that no euill ment.

20

He comming neare, gan gently her salute,
  With curteous words, in the most comely wize;
  Who though desirous rather to rest mute,
  Then termes to entertaine of common guize,
  Yet rather then she kindnesse would despize,
  She would her selfe displease, so him requite.
  Then gan the other further to deuize
Of things abrode, as next to hand did light,
And many things demaund, to which she
  answer'd light.

21

For little lust had she to talke of ought,
  Or ought to heare, that mote delightfull bee ;
  Her minde was whole possessed of one thought,
  That gaue none other place. Which when as hee
  By outward signes, (as well he might) did see,
  He list no lenger to vse lothfull speach,
  But her besought to take it well in gree,
  Sith shady dampe had dimd the heauens reach,
To lodge with him that night, vnles good cause
  empeach.

22

The Championesse, now seeing night at dore,
  Was glad to yeeld vnto his good request :
  And with him went without gaine-saying more.
  Not farre away, but little wide by West,
  His dwelling was, to which he him addrest
  Where soone arriuing they receiued were
  In seemely wise, as them beseemed best :
  For he their host them goodly well did cheare,
And talk't of pleasant things, the night away
  to weare.

23

Thus passing th'euening well, till time of rest,
  Then *Britomart* vnto a bowre was brought ;
  Where groomes awayted her to haue vndrest.
  But she ne would vndressed be for ought,
  Nedoffe her armes, though he her much besought.
  For she had vow'd, she sayd, not to forgo
  Those warlike weedes, till she reuenge had
  wrought
Of a late wrong vppon a mortall foe ;
Which she would sure performe, betide her wele
  or wo.

24

Which when their Host perceiu'd, right dis-
  content
  In minde he grew, for feare least by that art
  He should his purpose misse, which close he ment :
  Yet taking leaue of her, he did depart.
  There all that night remained *Britomart*,
  Restlesse, recomfortlesse, with heart deepe
  grieued,
  Not suffering the least twinckling sleepe to start
Into her eye, which th'heart mote haue relieued,
But if the least appear'd, her eyes she streight
  reprieued.

25

Ye guilty eyes {sayd she) the which with guyle
My heart at first betrayd, will ye betray
My life now to, for which a little whyle
Ye will not watch? false watches, wellaway,
I wote when ye did watch both night and day
Vnto your losse: and now needes will ye
    sleepe?
Now ye haue made my heart to wake alway,
Now will ye sleepe? ah wake, and rather weepe,
To thinke of your nights want, that should yee
    waking keepe.

26

Thus did she watch, and weare the weary night
In wayfull plaints, that none was to appease;
Now walking soft, now sitting still vpright,
As sundry chaunge her seemed best to ease.
Ne lesse did *Talus* suffer sleepe to seaze
His eye-lids sad, but watcht continually,
Lying without her dore in great disease;
Like to a Spaniell wayting carefully
Least any should betray his Lady treacherously.

27

What time the natiue Belman of the night,
The bird, that warned *Peter* of his fall,
First rings his siluer Bell t'each sleepy wight,
That should their mindes vp to deuotion call,
She heard a wondrous noise below the hall.
All sodainely the bed, where she should lie,
By a false trap was let adowne to fall
Into a lower roome, and by and by
The loft was raysd againe, that no man could
    it spie.

28

With sight whereof she was dismayd right sore,
Perceiuing well the treason, which was ment:
Yet stirred not at all for doubt of more,
But kept her place with courage confident,
Wayting what would ensue of that euent.
It was not long, before she heard the sound
Of armed men, comming with close intent
Towards her chamber; at which dreadfull
    stound
She quickly caught her sword, and shield about
    her bound.

29

With that there came vnto her chamber dore
Two Knights, all armed ready for to fight,
And after them full many other more,
A raskall rout, with weapons rudely dight.
Whom soone as *Talus* spide by glims of night,
He started vp, there where on ground he lay,
And in his hand his thresher ready keight.
They seeing that, let driue at him streight way,
And round about him preace in riotous aray.

30

But soone as he began to lay about
With his rude yron flaile, they gan to flie,
Both armed Knights, and eke vnarmed rout:
Yet *Talus* after them apace did plie,
Where euer in the darke he could them spie:
That here and there like scattred sheepe they
    lay.
Then backe returning, where his Dame did lie,
He to her told the story of that fray,
And all that treason there intended did bewray.

31

Wherewith though wondrous wroth, and inly
    burning,
To be auenged for so fowle a deede,
Yet being forst to abide the daies returning,
She there remain'd, but with right wary heede,
Least any more such practise should proceede.
Now mote ye know (that which to *Britomart*
Vnknowen was) whence all this did proceede,
And for what cause so great mischieuous smart
Was ment to her, that neuer euill ment in hart.

32

The goodman of this house was *Dolon* hight,
A man of subtill wit and wicked minde,
That whilome in his youth had bene a Knight,
And armes had borne, but little good could
    finde,
And much lesse honour by that warlike kinde
Of life: for he was nothing valorous,
But with slie shiftes and wiles did vnderminde
All noble Knights, which were aduenturous,
And many brought to shame by treason
    treacherous.

33

He had three sonnes, all three like fathers sonnes,
Like treacherous, like full of fraud and guile,
Of all that on this earthly compasse wonnes:
The eldest of the which was slaine erewhile
By *Artegall*, through his owne guilty wile;
His name was *Guizor*, whose vntimely fate
For to auenge, full many treasons vile
His father *Dolon* had deuiz'd of late
With these his wicked sons, and shewd his
    cankred hate.

34

For sure he weend, that this his present guest
Was *Artegall*, by many tokens plaine;
But chiefly by that yron page he ghest,
Which still was wont with *Artegall* remaine:
And therefore ment him surely to haue slaine.
But by Gods grace, and her good heedinesse,
She was preserued from their traytrous traine.
Thus she all night wore out in watchfulnesse,
Ne suffred slothfull sleepe her eyelids to oppresse.

35

The morrow next, so soone as dawning houre
  Discouered had the light to liuing eye,
  She forth yssew'd out of her loathed bowre,
  With full intent t'auenge that villany,
  On that vilde man, and all his family.
And comming down to seeke them, where they
    wond,
  Nor sire, nor sonnes, nor any could she spie :
  Each rowme she sought, but them all empty fond:
They all were fled for feare, but whether, nether
    kond.

36

She saw it vaine to make there lenger stay,
  But tooke her steede, and thereon mounting light,
  Gan her addresse vnto her former way.
  She had not rid the mountenance of a flight,
  But that she saw there present in her sight,
  Those two false brethren, on that perillous
    Bridge,
  On which *Pollente* with *Artegall* did fight.
Streight was the passage like a ploughed ridge,
That if two met, the one mote needes fall ouer
    the lidge.

37

There they did thinke them selues on her to
    wreake :
  Who as she nigh vnto them drew, the one
  These vile reproches gan vnto her speake ;
  Thou recreant false traytor, that with lone
  Of armes hast knighthood stolne, yet Knight
    art none,
  No more shall now the darkenesse of the night
  Defend thee from the vengeance of thy fone,
  But with thy bloud thou shalt appease the spright
Of *Guizor*, by thee slaine, and murdred by thy
    slight.

38

Strange were the words in *Britomartis* eare ;
  Yet stayd she not for them, but forward fared,
  Till to the perillous Bridge she came, and there
  Talus desir'd, that he might haue prepared
  The way to her, and those two losels scared.
  But she thereat was wroth, that for despight
  The glauncing sparkles through her beuer glared,
  And from her eies did flash out fiery light,
Like coles, that through a siluer Censer sparkle
    bright.

39

She stayd not to aduise which way to take ;
  But putting spurres vnto her fiery beast,
  Thorough the midst of them she way did make.
  The one of them, which most her wrath increast,
  Vppon her speare she bore before her breast,
  Till to the Bridges further end she past,
  Where falling downe, his challenge she releast :
  The other ouer side the Bridge she cast
Into the riuer, where he drunke his deadly last.

40

As when the flashing Leuin haps to light
  Vppon two stubborne oakes, which stand so
    neare,
  That way betwixt them none appeares in sight ;
  The Engin fiercely flying forth, doth teare
  Th'one from the earth, and through the aire
    doth beare ;
  The other it with force doth ouerthrow,
  Vppon one side, and from his rootes doth reare.
So did the Championesse those two there strow,
And to their sire their carcasses left to bestow.

Cant. VII.

Britomart comes to Isis Church,
  Where shee strange visions sees :
  She fights with Radigund, her slaies,
  And Artegall thence frees.

1

Nought is on earth more sacred or diuine,
  That Gods and men doe equally adore,
  Then this same vertue, that doth right define :
  For th'heuens themselues, whence mortal men
    implore
  Right in their wrongs, are rul'd by righteous lore
  Of highest Ioue, who doth true iustice deale
  To his inferiour Gods, and euermore [weale :
  Therewith containes his heauenly Common-
The skill whereof to Princes hearts he doth
    reueale.

2

Well therefore did the antique world inuent,
  That Iustice was a God of soueraine grace,
  And altars vnto him, and temples lent,
  And heauenly honours in the highest place ;
  Calling him great *Osyris*, of the race
  Of th'old Ægyptian Kings, that whylome were ;
  With fayned colours shading a true case :
  For that *Osyris*, whilest he liued here,
The iustest man aliue, and truest did appeare.

3

His wife was *Isis*, whom they likewise made
  A Goddesse of great powre and souerainty,
  And in her person cunningly did shade
  That part of Iustice, which is Equity,
  Whereof I haue to treat here presently.
  Vnto whose temple when as *Britomart*
  Arriued, shee with great humility
  Did enter in, ne would that night depart ;
But *Talus* mote not be admitted to her part.

4

There she receiued was in goodly wize
  Of many Priests, which duely did attend
  Vppon the rites and daily sacrifize,
  All clad in linnen robes with siluer hemd;
  And on their heads with long locks comely
    kemd,
  They wore rich Mitres shaped like the Moone,
  To shew that *Isis* doth the Moone portend;
  Like as *Osyris* signifies the Sunne.
For that they both like race in equall iustice
    runne.

5

The Championesse them greeting, as she could,
  Was thence by them into the Temple led;
  Whose goodly building when she did behould,
  Borne vppon stately pillours, all dispred
  With shining gold, and arched ouer hed,
  She wondred at the workemans passing skill,
  Whose like before she neuer saw nor red;
  And thereuppon long while stood gazing still,
But thought, that she thereon could neuer gaze
    her fill.

6

Thence forth vnto the Idoll they her brought,
  The which was framed all of siluer fine,
  So well as could with cunning hand be wrought,
  And clothed all in garments made of line,
  Hemd all about with fringe of siluer twine.
  Vppon her head she wore a Crowne of gold,
  To shew that she had powre in things diuine;
  And at her feete a Crocodile was rold,
That with her wreathed taile her middle did
    enfold.

7

One foote was set vppon the Crocodile,
  And on the ground the other fast did stand,
  So meaning to suppresse both forged guile,
  And open force: and in her other hand
  She stretched forth a long white sclender wand.
  Such was the Goddesse; whom when *Britomart*
  Had long beheld, her selfe vppon the land
  She did prostrate, and with right humble hart,
Vnto her selfe her silent prayers did impart.

8

To which the Idoll as it were inclining,
  Her wand did moue with amiable looke,
  By outward shew her inward sence desining.
  Who well perceiuing how her wand she shooke,
  It as a token of good fortune tooke.
  By this the day with dampe was ouercast,
  And ioyous light the house of *Ioue* forsooke:
  Which when she saw, her helmet she vnlaste,
And by the altars side her selfe to slumber
    plaste.

9

For other beds the Priests there vsed none,
  But on their mother Earths deare lap did lie,
  And bake their sides vppon the cold hard stone,
  T'enure them selues to sufferaunce thereby
  And proud rebellious flesh to mortify.
  For by the vow of their religion
  They tied were to stedfast chastity,
  And continence of life, that all forgon,
They mote the better tend to their deuotion.

10

Therefore they mote not taste of fleshly food,
  Ne feed on ought, the which doth bloud con-
    taine,
  Ne drinke of wine, for wine they say is blood,
  Euen the bloud of Gyants, which were slaine,
  By thundring Ioue in the Phlegrean plaine.
  For which the earth (as they the story tell)
  Wroth with the Gods, which to perpetuall paine
  Had damn'd her sonnes, which gainst them did
    rebell,
With inward griefe and malice did against
    them swell.

11

And of their vitall bloud, the which was shed
  Into her pregnant bosome, forth she brought
  The fruitfull vine, whose liquor blouddy red
  Hauing the mindes of men with fury fraught,
  Mote in them stirre vp old rebellious thought,
  To make new warre against the Gods againe:
  Such is the powre of that same fruit, that nought
  The fell contagion may thereof restraine,
Ne within reasons rule, her madding mood
    containe.

12

There did the warlike Maide her selfe repose,
  Vnder the wings of *Isis* all that night,
  And with sweete rest her heauy eyes did close,
  After that long daies toile and weary plight.
  Where whilest her earthly parts with soft delight
  Of sencelesse sleepe did deeply drowned lie,
  There did appeare vnto her heauenly spright
  A wondrous vision, which did close implie
The course of all her fortune and posteritie.

13

Her seem'd, as she was doing sacrifize
  To *Isis*, deckt with Mitre on her hed,
  And linnen stole after those Priestes guize,
  All sodainely she saw transfigured
  Her linnen stole to robe of scarlet red,
  And Moone-like Mitre to a Crowne of gold,
  That euen she her selfe much wondered
  At such a chaunge, and ioyed to behold
Her selfe, adorn'd with gems and iewels manifold.

14

And in the midst of her felicity,
  An hideous tempest seemed from below,
  To rise through all the Temple sodainely,
  That from the Altar all about did blow
  The holy fire, and all the embers strow
  Vppon the ground, which kindled priuily,
  Into outragious flames vnwares did grow,
  That all the Temple put in ieopardy
Of flaming, and her selfe in great perplexity.

15

With that the Crocodile, which sleeping lay
  Vnder the Idols feete in fearelesse bowre,
  Seem'd to awake in horrible dismay,
  As being troubld with that stormy stowre ;
  And gaping greedy wide, did streight deuoure
  Both flames and tempest : with which growen
  great,
  And swolne with pride of his owne peerelesse
  powre,
  He gan to threaten her likewise to eat ;
But that the Goddesse with her rod him backe
  did beat.

16

Tho turning all his pride to humblesse meeke,
  Him selfe before her feete he lowly threw,
  And gan for grace and loue of her to seeke :
  Which she accepting, he so neare her drew,
  That of his game she soone enwombed grew,
  And forth did bring a Lion of great might ;
  That shortly did all other beasts subdew.
  With that she waked, full of fearefull fright,
And doubtfully dismayd through that so vn-
  couth sight.

17

So thereuppon long while she musing lay,
  With thousand thoughts feeding her fantasie,
  Vntill she spide the lampe of lightsome day,
  Vp-lifted in the porch of heauen hie.
  Then vp she rose fraught with melancholy,
  And forth into the lower parts did pas ;
  Whereas the Priestes she found full busily
  About their holy things for morrow Mas :
Whom she saluting faire, faire resaluted was.

18

But by the change of her vnchearefull looke,
  They might perceiue, she was not well in plight;
  Or that some pensiuenesse to heart she tooke.
  Therefore thus one of them, who seem'd in sight
  To be the greatest, and the grauest wight,
  To her bespake ; Sir Knight it seemes to me,
  That thorough euill rest of this last night,
  Or ill apayd, or much dismayd ye be,
That by your change of cheare is easie for to see.

19

Certes (sayd she) sith ye so well haue spide
  The troublous passion of my pensiue mind,
  I will not seeke the same from you to hide,
  But will my cares vnfolde, in hope to find
  Your aide, to guide me out of errour blind.
  Say on (quoth he) the secret of your hart :
  For by the holy vow, which me doth bind,
  I am adiur'd, best counsell to impart
To all, that shall require my comfort in their
  smart.

20

Then gan she to declare the whole discourse
  Of all that vision, which to her appeard,
  As well as to her minde it had recourse.
  All which when he vnto the end had heard,
  Like to a weake faint-hearted man he fared,
  Through great astonishment of that strange
  sight ;
  And with long locks vp-standing, stifly stared
  Like one adawed with some dreadfull spright.
So fild with heauenly fury, thus he her behight.

21

Magnificke Virgin, that in queint disguise
  Of British armes doest maske thy royall blood,
  So to pursue a perillous emprize,
  How couldst thou weene, through that dis-
  guized hood,
  To hide thy state from being vnderstood ?
  Can from th'immortall Gods ought hidden bee?
  They doe thy linage, and thy Lordly brood ;
  They doe thy sire, lamenting sore for thee ;
They doe thy loue, forlorne in womens thral-
  dome see.

22

The end whereof, and all the long euent,
  They doe to thee in this same dreame discouer.
  For that same Crocodile doth represent
  The righteous Knight, that is thy faithfull
  Like to *Osyris* in all iust endeuer.   [louer,
  For that same Crocodile *Osyris* is,
  That vnder *Isis* feete doth sleepe for euer :
  To shew that clemence oft in things amis,
Restraines those sterne behests, and cruell
  doomes of his.

23

That Knight shall all the troublous stormes
  asswage,
  And raging flames, that many foes shall reare,
  To hinder thee from the iust heritage   [deare.
  Of thy sires Crowne, and from thy countrey
  Then shalt thou take him to thy loued fere,
  And ioyne in equall portion of thy realme.
  And afterwards a sonne to him shalt beare,
  That Lion-like shall shew his powre extreame:
So blesse thee God, and giue thee ioyance of
  thy dreame.

24

All which when she vnto the end had heard,
　She much was eased in her troublous thought,
　And on those Priests bestowed rich reward :
　And royall gifts of gold and siluer wrought,
　She for a present to their Goddesse brought.
Then taking leaue of them, she forward went,
　To seeke her loue, where he was to be sought ;
　Ne rested till she came without relent
Vnto the land of Amazons, as she was bent.

25

Whereof when newes to *Radigund* was brought,
　Not with amaze, as women wonted bee,
　She was confused in her troublous thought,
　But fild with courage and with ioyous glee,
　As glad to heare of armes, the which now she
　Had long surceast, she bad to open bold,
　That she the face of her new foe might see.
　But when they of that yron man had told,
Which late her folke had slaine, she bad them
　forth to hold.

26

So there without the gate (as seemed best)
　She caused her Pauilion be pight ;
　In which stout *Britomart* her selfe did rest,
　Whiles *Talus* watched at the dore all night.
All night likewise, they of the towne in fright,
　Vppon their wall good watch and ward did
　keepe.
The morrow next, so soone as dawning light
　Bad doe away the dampe of drouzie sleepe,
The warlike Amazon out of her bowre did peepe.

27

And caused streight a Trumpet loud to shrill,
　To warne her foe to battell soone be prest :
　Who long before awoke (for she ful ill
　Could sleepe all night, that in vnquiet brest
　Did closely harbour such a iealous guest)
　Was to the battell whilome ready dight.
　Eftsoones that warriouresse with haughty crest
　Did forth issue, all ready for the fight :
On th'other side her foe appeared soone in sight.

28

But ere they reared hand, the Amazone
　Began the streight conditions to propound,
　With which she vsed still to tye her fone ;
　To serue her so, as she the rest had bound.
　Which when the other heard, she sternly frownd
　For high disdaine of such indignity,
　And would no lenger treat, but bad them
　sound.
For her no other termes should euer tie
Then what prescribed were by lawes of cheualrie.

29

The Trumpets sound, and they together run
　With greedy rage, and with their faulchins
　smot ;
Ne either sought the others strokes to shun,
　But through great fury both their skill forgot,
　And practicke vse in armes : ne spared not
　Their dainty parts, which nature had created
　So faire and tender, without staine or spot,
　For other vses, then they them translated :
Which they now hackt and hewd, as if such vse
　they hated.

30

As when a Tygre and a Lionesse
　Are met at spoyling of some hungry pray,
　Both challenge it with equall greedinesse :
　But first the Tygre clawes thereon did lay ;
　And therefore loth to loose her right away,
　Doth in defence thereof full stoutly stond :
　To which the Lion strongly doth gainesay,
　That she to hunt the beast first tooke in hond ;
And therefore ought it haue, where euer she it
　fond.

31

Full fiercely layde the Amazon about,
　And dealt her blowes vnmercifully sore .
　Which *Britomart* withstood with courage stout,
　And them repaide againe with double more.
So long they fought, that all the grassie flore
　Was fild with bloud, which from their sides
　did flow,
And gushed through their armes, that all in gore
　They trode, and on the ground their liues did
　strow,
Like fruitles seede, of which vntimely death
　should grow.

32

At last proud *Radigund* with fell despight,
　Hauing by chaunce espide aduantage neare,
　Let driue at her with all her dreadfull might,
　And thus vpbrayding said ; This token beare
　Vnto the man, whom thou doest loue so deare ;
　And tell him for his sake thy life thou gauest.
　Which spitefull words she sore engrieu'd to heare,
　Thus answer'd ; Lewdly thou my loue deprauest,
Who shortly must repent that now so vainely
　brauest.

33

Nath'lesse that stroke so cruell passage found,
　That glauncing on her shoulder plate, it bit
　Vnto the bone, and made a griesly wound,
　That she her shield through raging smart of it
　Could scarse vphold ; yet soone she it requit.
　For hauing force increast through furious paine,
　She her so rudely on the helmet smit,
　That it empierced to the very braine,
And her proud person low prostrated on the
　plaine.

34

Where being layd, the wrothfull Britonesse
Stayd not, till she came to her selfe againe,
But in reuenge both of her loues distresse,
And her late vile reproch, though vaunted
   vaine,
And also of her wound, which sore did paine,
She with one stroke both head and helmet cleft.
Which dreadfull sight, when all her warlike
   traine
There present saw, each one of sence bereft,
Fled fast into the towne, and her sole victor left.

35

But yet so fast they could not home retrate,
  But that swift *Talus* did the formost win ;
And pressing through the preace vnto the gate,
Pelmell with them attonce did enter in.
There then a piteous slaughter did begin :
For all that euer came within his reach,
He with his yron flaile did thresh so thin,
That he no worke at all left for the leach :
Like to an hideous storme, which nothing may
  empeach.

36

And now by this the noble Conqueresse
Her selfe came in, her glory to partake ;
Where though reuengefull vow she did professe,
Yet when she saw the heapes, which he did
  make,
Of slaughtred carkasses, her heart did quake
For very ruth, which did it almost riue,
That she his fury willed him to slake :
For else he sure had left not one aliue,
But all in his reuenge of spirite would depriue.

37

Tho when she had his execution stayd,
  She for that yron prison did enquire,
In which her wretched loue was captiue layd :
Which breaking open with indignant ire,
She entred into all the partes entire.
Where when she saw that lothly vncouth sight,
Of men disguiz'd in womanishe attire,
Her heart gan grudge, for very deepe despight
Of so vnmanly maske, in misery misdight.

38

At last when as to her owne Loue she came,
Whom like disguize no lesse deformed had,
At sight thereof abasht with secrete shame,
She turnd her head aside, as nothing glad,
To haue beheld a spectacle so bad :
And then too well beleeu'd, that which tofore
Iealous suspect as true vntruely drad,
Which vaine conceipt now nourishing no more,
She sought with ruth to salue his sad mis-
  fortunes sore.

39

Not so great wonder and astonishment,
Did the most chast *Penelope* possesse,
To see her Lord, that was reported drent,
And dead long since in dolorous distresse,
Come home to her in piteous wretchednesse,
After long trauell of full twenty yeares,
That she knew not his fauours likelynesse,
For many scarres and many hoary heares,
But stood long staring on him, mongst vncer-
  taine feares.

40

Ah my deare Lord, what sight is this (quoth she)
What May-game hath misfortune made of you ?
Where is that dreadfull manly looke ? where be
Those mighty palmes, the which ye wont t'em-
  brew
In bloud of Kings, and great hoastes to subdew?
Could ought on earth so wondrous change haue
  wrought,
As to haue robde you of that manly hew ?
Could so great courage stouped haue to ought?
Then farewell fleshly force ; I see thy pride is
  nought.

41

Thenceforth she streight into a bowre him brought,
And causd him those vncomely weedes vndight;
And in their steede for other rayment sought,
Whereof there was great store, and armors
  bright,
Which had bene reft from many a noble Knight;
Whom that proud Amazon subdewed had,
Whilest Fortune fauourd her successe in fight,
In which when as she him anew had clad,
She was reuiu'd, and ioyd much in his sem-
  blance glad.

42

So there a while they afterwards remained,
Him to refresh, and her late wounds to heale :
During which space she there as Princess rained,
And changing all that forme of common weale,
The liberty of women did repeale,
Which they had long vsurpt; and them restoring
To mens subiection, did true Iustice deale :
That all they as a Goddesse her adoring,
Her wisedome did admire, and hearkned to her
  loring.

43

For all those Knights, which long in captiue shade
Had shrowded bene, she did from thraldome
And magistrates of all that city made, [free;
And gaue to them great liuing and large fee :
And that they should for euer faithfull bee,
Made them sweare fealty to *Artegall*.
Who when him selfe now well recur'd did see,
He purposd to proceed, what so be fall,
Vppon his first aduenture, which him forth
  did call.

44

Full sad and sorrowfull was *Britomart*
For his departure, her new cause of griefe ;
Yet wisely moderated her owne smart,
Seeing his honor, which she tendred chiefe,
Consisted much in that aduentures priefe.
The care whereof, and hope of his successe
Gaue vnto her great comfort and reliefe,
That womanish complaints she did represse,
And tempred for the time her present heaui-
   nesse.

45

There she continu'd for a certaine space,
Till through his want her woe did more increase:
Then hoping that the change of aire and place
Would change her paine, and sorrow somewhat
   ease,
She parted thence, her anguish to appease.
Meane while her noble Lord sir *Artegall*
Went on his way, ne euer howre did cease,
Till he redeemed had that Lady thrall :
That for another Canto will more fitly fall.

Cant. VIII.

❧❧❧❧❧❧❧❧❧❧❧❧❧❧❧❧

Prince Arthure and Sir Artegall,
   Free Samient from feare :
They slay the Souldan, driue his wife,
   Adicia to despaire.

❧❧❧❧❧❧❧❧❧❧❧❧❧❧❧❧

I

Nought vnder heauen so strongly doth allure
The sence of man, and all his minde possesse,
As beauties louely baite, that doth procure
Great warriours oft their rigour to represse,
And mighty hands forget their manlinesse ;
Drawne with the powre of an heart-robbing eye,
And wrapt in fetters of a golden tresse,
That can with melting pleasaunce mollifye
Their hardned hearts, enur'd to blood and
   cruelty.

2

So whylome learnd that mighty Iewish swaine,
Each of whose lockes did match a man in might,
To lay his spoiles before his lemans traine :
So also did that great Oetean Knight
For his loues sake his Lions skin vndight :
And so did warlike *Antony* neglect
The worlds whole rule for *Cleopatras* sight.
Such wondrous powre hath wemens faire aspect,
To captiue men, and make them all the world
   reiect.

3

Yet could it not sterne *Artegall* retaine,
Nor hold from suite of his auowed quest,
Which he had vndertane to *Gloriane* ;
But left his loue, albe her strong request,
Faire *Britomart* in languor and vnrest,
And rode him selfe vppon his first intent :
Ne day nor night did euer idly rest ;
Ne wight but onely *Talus* with him went,
The true guide of his way and vertuous gouern-
   ment.

4

So trauelling, he chaunst far off to heed
A Damzell, flying on a palfrey fast
Before two Knights, that after her did speed
With all their powre, and her full fiercely chast
In hope to haue her ouerhent at last :
Yet fled she fast, and both them farre outwent,
Carried with wings of feare, like fowle aghast,
With locks all loose, and rayment all to rent ;
And euer as she rode, her eye was backeward
   bent.

5

Soone after these he saw another Knight,
That after those two former rode apace,
With speare in rest, and prickt with all his
   might :
So ran they all, as they had bene at bace,
They being chased, that did others chase.
At length he saw the hindmost ouertake
One of those two, and force him turne his face ;
How euer loth he were his way to slake,
Yet mote he algates now abide, and answere
   make.

6

But th'other still pursu'd the fearefull Mayd ;
Who still from him as fast away did flie,
Ne once for ought her speedy passage stayd,
Till that at length she did before her spie
Sir *Artegall*, to whom she streight did hie
With gladfull hast, in hope of him to get
Succour against her greedy enimy :
Who seeing her approch gan forward set,
To saue her from her feare, and him from force
   to let.

7

But he like hound full greedy of his pray,
Being impatient of impediment,
Continu'd still his course, and by the way
Thought with his speare him quight haue
   ouerwent.
So both together ylike felly bent,
Like fiercely met. But *Artegall* was stronger,
And better skild in Tilt and Turnament,
And bore him quite out of his saddle, longer
Then two speares length ; So mischiefe ouer-
   matcht the wronger.

8

And in his fall misfortune him mistooke ;
  For on his head vnhappily he pight,
  That his owne waight his necke asunder broke,
  And left there dead. Meane while the other
      Knight
Defeated had the other faytour quight,
  And all his bowels in his body brast :
  Whom leauing there in that dispiteous plight,
  He ran still on, thinking to follow fast
His other fellow Pagan, which before him past.

9

In stead of whom finding there ready prest
  Sir *Artegall*, without discretion
He at him ran, with ready speare in rest :
  Who seeing him come still so fiercely on,
  Against him made againe. So both anon
Together met, and strongly either strooke
  And broke their speares ; yet neither has forgon
  His horses backe, yet to and fro long shooke,
And tottred like two towres, which through
    a tempest quooke.

10

But when againe they had recouered sence,
  They drew their swords, in mind to make amends
For what their speares had fayld of their pretence.
  Which when the Damzell, who those deadly ends
  Of both her foes had seene, and now her frends
For her beginning a more fearefull fray,
  She to them runnes in hast, and her haire rends,
  Crying to them their cruell hands to stay,
Vntill they both doe heare, what she to them
    will say.

11

They stayd their hands, when she thus gan to
    speake ;
  Ah gentle Knights, what meane ye thus vnwise
Vpon your selues anothers wrong to wreake ?
  I am the wrong'd, whom ye did enterprise
Both to redresse, and both redrest likewise :
  Witnesse the Paynims both, whom ye may see
There dead on ground. What doe ye then deuise
  Of more reuenge ? if more, then I am shee,
Which was the roote of all, end your reuenge on
    mee.

12

Whom when they heard so say, they lookt about,
  To weete if it were true, as she had told ;
Where when they saw their foes dead out of
    doubt,   [hold,
Eftsoones they gan their wrothfull hands to
  And Ventailes reare, each other to behold.
  Tho when as *Artegall* did *Arthure* vew,
So faire a creature, and so wondrous bold,
  He much admired both his heart and hew,
And touched with intire affection, nigh him drew.

13

Saying, Sir Knight, of pardon I you pray,
  That all vnweeting haue you wrong'd thus sore,
Suffring my hand against my heart to stray :
  Which if ye please forgiue, I will therefore
Yeeld for amends my selfe yours euermore,
  Or what so penaunce shall by you be red.
To whom the Prince ; Certes me needeth more
  To craue the same, whom errour so misled,
As that I did mistake the liuing for the ded.

14

But sith ye please, that both our blames shall die,
  Amends may for the trespasse soone be made,
Since neither is endamadg'd much thereby.
  So can they both them selues full eath perswade
To faire accordaunce, and both faults to shade,
  Either embracing other louingly,
And swearing faith to either on his blade,
  Neuer thenceforth to nourish enmity,
But either others cause to maintaine mutually.

15

Then *Artegall* gan of the Prince enquire,
  What were those knights, which there on
    ground were layd,
And had receiu'd their follies worthy hire,
  And for what cause they chased so that Mayd.
Certes I wote not well (the Prince then sayd)
  But by aduenture found them faring so,
As by the way vnweetingly I strayd,
  And lo the Damzell selfe, whence all did grow,
Of whom we may at will the whole occasion
    know.

16

Then they that Damzell called to them nie,
  And asked her, what were those two her fone,
From whom she earst so fast away did flie ;
  And what was she her selfe so woe begone,
And for what cause pursu'd of them attone.
  To whom she thus ; Then wote ye well, that I
Doe serue a Queene, that not far hence doth
    wone,
  A Princesse of great powre and maiestie,
Famous through all the world, and honor'd
    far and nie.

17

Her name *Mercilla* most men vse to call ;
  That is a mayden Queene of high renowne,
For her great bounty knowen ouer all,
  And soueraine grace, with which her royall
    crowne
She doth support, and strongly beateth downe
  The malice of her foes, which her enuy,
And at her happinesse do fret and frowne :
  Yet she her selfe the more doth magnify,
And euen to her foes her mercies multiply.

18

Mongst many which maligne her happy state,
  There is a mighty man, which wonnes here by
  That with most fell despight and deadly hate,
  Seekes to subuert her Crowne and dignity,
  And all his powre doth thereunto apply :
  And her good Knights, of which so braue
    a band
  Serues her, as any Princesse vnder sky,
  He either spoiles, if they against him stand,
Or to his part allures, and bribeth vnder hand.

19

Ne him sufficeth all the wrong and ill,
  Which he vnto her people does each day,
  But that he seekes by traytrous traines to
    spill
  Her person, and her sacred selfe to slay :
  That O ye heauens defend, and turne away
  From her, vnto the miscreant him selfe,
  That neither hath religion nor fay,
  But makes his God of his vngodly pelfe,
And Idols serues : so let his Idols serue the Elfe.

20

To all which cruell tyranny they say,
  He is prouokt, and stird vp day and night
  By his bad wife, that hight *Adicia*,
  Who counsels him through confidence of might,
  To breake all bonds of law, and rules of right.
  For she her selfe professeth mortall foe
  To Iustice, and against her still doth fight,
  Working to all, that loue her, deadly woe,
And making all her Knights and people to doe so.

21

Which my liege Lady seeing, thought it best,
  With that his wife in friendly wise to deale,
  For stint of strife, and stablishment of rest
  Both to her selfe, and to her common weale,
  And all forepast displeasures to repeale.
  So me in message vnto her she sent,
  To treat with her by way of enterdeale,
  Of finall peace and faire attonement,
Which might concluded be by mutuall consent.

22

All times haue wont safe passage to afford
  To messengers, that come for causes iust :
  But this proude Dame disdayning all accord,
  Not onely into bitter termes forth brust,
  Reuiling me, and rayling as she lust,
  But lastly to make proofe of vtmost shame.
  Me like a dog she out of dores did thrust,
  Miscalling me by many a bitter name,
That neuer did her ill, ne once deserued blame.

23

And lastly, that no shame might wanting be,
  When I was gone, soone after me she sent
  These two false Knights, whom there ye lying see,
  To be by them dishonoured and shent :
  But thankt be God, and your good hardiment,
  They haue the price of their owne folly payd.
  So said this Damzell, that hight *Samient*,
  And to those knights, for their so noble ayd,
Her selfe most gratefull shew'd, and heaped
    thanks repayd.

24

But they now hauing throughly heard, and seene
  Al those great wrongs, the which that mayd
    complained
  To haue bene done against her Lady Queene,
  By that proud dame, which her so much dis-
    dained,   [fained,
  Were moued much thereat, and twixt them
  With all their force to worke a uengement strong
  Vppon the Souldan selfe, which it mayntained,
  And on his Lady, th'author of that wrong,
And vppon all those Knights, that did to her
    belong.

25

But thinking best by counterfet disguise
  To their deseigne to make the easier way,
  They did this complot twixt them selues deuise,
  First, that sir *Artegall* should him array,
  Like one of those two Knights, which dead there
  And then that Damzell, the sad *Samient*, [lay.
  Should as his purchast prize with him conuay
  Vnto the Souldans court, her to present
Vnto his scornefull Lady, that for her had sent.

26

So as they had deuiz'd, sir *Artegall*
  Him clad in th'armour of a Pagan knight,
  And taking with him, as his vanquisht thrall,
  That Damzell, led her to the Souldans right.
  Where soone as his proud wife of her had sight,
  Forth of her window as she looking lay,
  She weened streight, it was her Paynim Knight,
  Which brought that Damzell, as his purchast
    pray ;
And sent to him a Page, that mote direct his
    way.

27

Who bringing them to their appointed place,
  Offred his seruice to disarme the Knight ;
  But he refusing him to let vnlace,
  For doubt to be discouered by his sight,
  Kept himselfe still in his straunge armour dight.
  Soone after whom the Prince arriued there,
  And sending to the Souldan in despight
  A bold defyance, did of him requere
That Damzell, whom he held as wrongfull
    prisonere.

28

Wherewith the Souldan all with furie fraught,
  Swearing, and banning most blasphemously,
  Commaunded straight his armour to be brought,
  And mounting straight vpon a charret hye,
  With yron wheeles and hookes arm'd dread-
    fully,
  And drawne of cruell steedes, which he had fed
  With flesh of men, whom through fell tyranny
  He slaughtred had, and ere they were halfe ded,
Their bodies to his beasts for prouender did
    spred.

29

So forth he came all in a cote of plate,
  Burnisht with bloudie rust, whiles on the greene
  The Briton Prince him readie did awayte,
  In glistering armes right goodly well beseene,
  That shone as bright, as doth the heauen
    sheene ;
  And by his stirrup *Talus* did attend,
  Playing his pages part, as he had beene
  Before directed by his Lord ; to th'end
He should his flaile to finall execution bend.

30

Thus goe they both together to their geare,
  With like fierce minds, but meanings different :
  For the proud Souldan with presumpteous
    cheare,
  And countenance sublime and insolent,
  Sought onely slaughter and auengement :
  But the braue Prince for honour and for right,
  Gainst tortious powre and lawlesse regiment,
  In the behalfe of wronged weake did fight :
More in his causes truth he trusted then in
    might.

31

Like to the *Thracian* Tyrant, who they say
  Vnto his horses gaue his guests for meat,
  Till he himselfe was made their greedie pray,
  And torne in peeces by *Alcides* great.
  So thought the Souldan in his follies threat,
  Either the Prince in peeces to haue torne
  With his sharpe wheeles, in his first rages heat,
  Or vnder his fierce horses feet haue borne
And trampled downe in dust his thoughts dis-
    dained scorne.

32

But the bold child that perill well espying,
  If he too rashly to his charet drew,
  Gaue way vnto his horses speedie flying,
  And their resistlesse rigour did eschew.
  Yet as he passed by, the Pagan threw
  A shiuering dart with so impetuous force,
  That had he not it shun'd with heedfull vew,
  It had himselfe transfixed, or his horse,
Or made them both one masse withouten more
    remorse

33

Oft drew the Prince vnto his charret nigh,
  In hope some stroke to fasten on him neare :
  But he was mounted in his seat so high,
  And his wingfooted coursers him did beare
  So fast away, that ere his readie speare
  He could aduance, he farre was gone and past.
  Yet still he him did follow euery where,
  And followed was of him likewise full fast ;
So long as in his steedes the flaming breath did
    last.

34

Againe the Pagan threw another dart,
  Of which he had with him abundant store,
  On euery side of his embatteld cart,
  And of all other weapons lesse or more,
  Which warlike vses had deuiz'd of yore.
  The wicked shaft guyded through th'ayrie wyde,
  By some bad spirit, that it to mischiefe bore,
  Stayd not, till through his curat it did glyde,
And made a griesly wound in his enriuen side.

35

Much was he grieued with that haplesse throe,
  That opened had the welspring of his blood ;
  But much the more that to his hatefull foe
  He mote not come, to wreake his wrathfull
    mood.
  That made him raue, like to a Lyon wood,
  Which being wounded of the huntsmans hand
  Can not come neare him in the couert wood,
  Where he with boughes hath built his shady
    stand,
And fenst himselfe about with many a flaming
    brand.

36

Still when he sought t'approch vnto him ny,
  His charret wheeles about him whirled round,
  And made him backe againe as fast to fly ;
  And eke his steedes like to an hungry hound,
  That hunting after game hath carrion found,
  So cruelly did him pursew and chace,
  That his good steed, all were he much renound
  For noble courage, and for hardie race,
Durst not endure their sight, but fled from
    place to place.

37

Thus long they trast, and trauerst to and fro,
  Seeking by euery way to make some breach,
  Yet could the Prince not nigh vnto him goe,
  That one sure stroke he might vnto him reach,
  Whereby his strengthes assay he might him
    teach.
  At last from his victorious shield he drew
  The vaile, which did his powrefull light empeach ;
  And comming full before his horses vew,
As they vpon him prest, it plaine to them did
    shew.

38

Like lightening flash, that hath the gazer burned,
So did the sight thereof their sense dismay,
That backe againe vpon themselues they turned,
And with their ryder ranne perforce away:
Ne could the Souldan them from flying stay,
With raynes, or wonted rule, as well he knew.
Nought feared they, what he could do, or say,
But th'onely feare, that was before their vew;
From which like mazed deare, dismayfully they
flew.

39

Fast did they fly, as them their feete could beare,
High ouer hilles, and lowly ouer dales,
As they were follow'd of their former feare.
In vaine the Pagan bannes, and sweares, and
rayles,
And backe with both his hands vnto him hayles
The resty raynes, regarded now no more:
He to them calles and speakes, yet nought
auayles;
They heare him not, they haue forgot his lore,
But go, which way they list, their guide they
haue forlore.

40

As when the firie-mouthed steeds, which drew
The Sunnes bright wayne to *Phaetons* decay,
Soone as they did the monstrous Scorpion vew,
With vgly craples crawling in their way,
The dreadfull sight did them so sore affray,
That their well knowen courses they forwent,
And leading th'euer-burning lampe astray,
This lower world nigh all to ashes brent,
And left their scorched path yet in the firma-
ment.

41

Such was the furie of these head-strong steeds,
Soone as the infants sunlike shield they saw,
That all obedience both to words and deeds
They quite forgot, and scornd all former law;
Through woods, and rocks, and mountaines
they did draw
The yron charet, and the wheeles did teare,
And tost the Paynim, without feare or awe;
From side to side they tost him here and there,
Crying to them in vaine, that nould his crying
heare.

42

Yet still the Prince pursew'd him close behind,
Oft making offer him to smite, but found
No easie meanes according to his mind.
At last they haue all ouerthrowne to ground
Quite topside turuey, and the pagan hound
Amongst the yron hookes and graples keene,
Torne all to rags, and rent with many a wound,
That no whole peece of him was to be seene,
But scattred all about, and strow'd vpon the
greene.

43

Like as the cursed sonne of *Theseus*,
That following his chace in dewy morne,
To fly his stepdames loues outrageous,
Of his owne steedes was all to peeces torne,
And his faire limbs left in the woods forlorne;
That for his sake *Diana* did lament, [mourne.
And all the wooddy Nymphes did wayle and
So was this Souldan rapt and all to rent,
That of his shape appear'd no litle moniment.

44

Onely his shield and armour, which there lay,
Though nothing whole, but all to brusd and
broken,
He vp did take, and with him brought away,
That mote remaine for an eternall token
To all, mongst whom this storie should be
spoken,
How worthily, by heauens high decree,
Iustice that day of wrong her selfe had wroken,
That all men which that spectacle did see,
By like ensample mote for euer warned bee.

45

So on a tree, before the Tyrants dore,
He caused them be hung in all mens sight,
To be a moniment for euermore.
Which when his Ladie from the castles hight
Beheld, it much appalld her troubled spright:
Yet not, as women wont in dolefull fit,
She was dismayd, or faynted through affright,
But gatherd vnto her her troubled wit,
And gan eftsoones deuize to be aueng'd for it.

46

Streight downe she ranne, like an enraged cow,
That is berobbed of her youngling dere,
With knife in hand, and fatally did vow,
To wreake her on that mayden messengere,
Whom she had causd be kept as prisonere,
By *Artegall*, misween'd for her owne Knight,
That brought her backe.   And comming
present there,
She at her ran with all her force and might,
All flaming with reuenge and furious despight.

47

Like raging *Ino*, when with knife in hand
She threw her husbands murdred infant out,
Or fell *Medea*, when on *Colchicke* strand
Her brothers bones she scattered all about;
Or as that madding mother, mongst the rout
Of *Bacchus* Priests her owne deare flesh did
teare.
Yet neither *Ino*, nor *Medea* stout,
Nor all the *Mœnades* so furious were, [there.
As this bold woman, when she saw that Damzell

48

But *Artegall* being thereof aware,
Did stay her cruell hand, ere she her raught,
And as she did her selfe to strike prepare,
Out of her fist the wicked weapon caught:
With that like one enfelon'd or distraught,
She forth did rome, whether her rage her bore,
With franticke passion, and with furie fraught;
And breaking forth out at a posterne dore,
Vnto the wyld wood ranne, her dolours to deplore.

49

As a mad bytch, when as the franticke fit
Her burning tongue with rage inflamed hath,
Doth runne at randon, and with furious bit
Snatching at euery thing, doth wreake her wrath
On man and beast, that commeth in her path.
There they doe say, that she transformed was
Into a Tygre, and that Tygres scath
In crueltie and outrage she did pas,
To proue her surname true, that she imposed has.

50

Then *Artegall* himselfe discouering plaine,
Did issue forth gainst all that warlike rout
Of knights and armed men, which did maintaine
That Ladies part, and to the Souldan lout:
All which he did assault with courage stout,
All were they nigh an hundred knights of name,
And like wyld Goates them chaced all about,
Flying from place to place with cowheard shame,
So that with finall force them all he ouercame.

51

Then caused he the gates be opened wyde,
And there the Prince, as victour of that day,
With tryumph entertayn'd and gloriiyde,
Presenting him with all the rich array,
And roiall pompe, which there long hidden lay,
Purchast through lawlesse powre and tortious wrong
Of that proud Souldan, whom he earst did slay.
So both for rest there hauing stayd not long,
Marcht with that mayd, fit matter for another song.

Cant. IX.

cxcxcxcxcxcxcxcxcxcxcxcxcxcxcxcs

Arthur and Artegall catch Guyle
whom Talus doth dismay,
They to Mercillaes pallace come,
and see her rich array.

cxcxcxcxcxcxcxcxcxcxcxcxcxcxcxcs

1

What Tygre, or what other saluage wight
Is so exceeding furious and fell,
As wrong, when it hath arm'd it selfe with might?
Not fit mongst men, that doe with reason mell,
But mongst wyld beasts and saluage woods to dwell;
Where still the stronger doth the weake deuoure,
And they that most in boldnesse doe excell,
Are dreadded most, and feared for their powre
Fit for *Adicia*, there to build her wicked bowi

2

There let her wonne farre from resort of men,
Where righteous *Artegall* her late exyled
There let her euer keepe her damned den,
Where none may be with her lewd parts defyled,
Nor none but beasts may be of her despoyled:
And turne we to the noble Prince, where late
We did him leaue, after that he had foyled
The cruell Souldan, and with dreadfull fate
Had vtterly subuerted his vnrighteous state.

3

Where hauing with Sir *Artegall* a space
Well solast in that Souldans late delight,
They both resoluing now to leaue the place,
Both it and all the wealth therein behight
Vnto that Damzell in her Ladies right,
And so would haue departed on their way.
But she them woo'd by all the meanes she might,
And earnestly besought, to wend that day
With her, to see her Ladie thence not farre away.

4

By whose entreatie both they ouercommen,
Agree to goe with her, and by the way,
(As often falles) of sundry things did commen.
Mongst which that Damzell did to them bewray
A straunge aduenture, which not farre thence lay;
To weet a wicked villaine, bold and stout,
Which wonned in a rocke not farre away,
That robbed all the countrie there about,
And brought the pillage home, whence none could get it out.

5

Thereto both his owne wylie wit, (she sayd)
And eke the fastnesse of his dwelling place,
Both vnassaylable, gaue him great ayde :
For he so crafty was to forge and face,
So light of hand, and nymble of his pace,
So smooth of tongue, and subtile in his tale,
That could deceiue one looking in his face ;
Therefore by name *Malengin* they him call,
Well knowen by his feates, and famous ouer all.

6

Through these his slights he many doth con-
    found,
And eke the rocke, in which he wonts to dwell,
Is wondrous strong, and hewen farre vnder
    ground
A dreadfull depth, how deepe no man can tell ;
But some doe say, it goeth downe to hell.
And all within, it full of wyndings is, [smell
And hidden wayes, that scarse an hound by
Can follow out those false footsteps of his,
Ne none can backe returne, that once are gone
    amis.

7

Which when those knights had heard, their
    harts gan earne,
To vnderstand that villeins dwelling place,
And greatly it desir'd of her to learne,
And by which way they towards it should trace.
Were not (sayd she) that it should let your pace
Towards my Ladies presence by you ment,
I would you guyde directly to the place.
Then let not that (said they) stay your intent ;
For neither will one foot, till we that carle haue
    hent.

8

So forth they past, till they approched ny
Vnto the rocke, where was the villains won,
Which when the Damzell neare at hand did spy,
She warn'd the knights thereof: who thereupon
Gan to aduize, what best were to be done.
So both agreed, to send that mayd afore,
Where she might sit nigh to the den alone,
Wayling, and raysing pittifull vprore,
As if she did some great calamitie deplore.

9

With noyse whereof when as the caytiue carle
Should issue forth, in hope to find some spoyle,
They in awayt would closely him ensnarle,
Ere to his den he backward could recoyle,
And so would hope him easily to foyle.
The Damzell straight went, as she was directed,
Vnto the rocke, and there vpon the soyle
Hauing her selfe in wretched wize abiected,
Gan weepe and wayle, as if great griefe had her
    affected.

10

The cry whereof entring the hollow caue,
Eftsoones brought forth the villaine, as they
    ment,
With hope of her some wishfull boot to haue.
Full dreadfull wight he was, as euer went
Vpon the earth, with hollow eyes deepe pent,
And long curld locks, that downe his shoulders
    shagged,
And on his backe an vncouth vestiment
Made of straunge stuffe, but all to worne and
    ragged,
And vnderneath his breech was all to torne and
    iagged.

11

And in his hand an huge long staffe he held,
Whose top was arm'd with many an yron hooke,
Fit to catch hold of all that he could weld,
Or in the compasse of his clouches tooke ;
And euer round about he cast his looke.
Als at his backe a great wyde net he bore,
With which he seldome fished at the brooke,
But vsd to fish for fooles on the dry shore,
Of which he in faire weather wont to take great
    store.

12

Him when the damzell saw fast by her side,
So vgly creature, she was nigh dismayd,
And now for helpe aloud in earnest cride.
But when the villaine saw her so affrayd,
He gan with guilefull words her to perswade,
To banish feare, and with *Sardonian* smyle
Laughing on her, his false intent to shade,
Gan forth to lay his bayte her to beguyle,
That from her self vnwares he might her steale
    the whyle.

13

Like as the fouler on his guilefull pype
Charmes to the birds full many a pleasant lay,
That they the whiles may take lesse heedie
    keepe,
How he his nets doth for their ruine lay :
So did the villaine to her prate and play,
And many pleasant trickes before her show,
To turne her eyes from his intent away :
For he in slights and iugling feates did flow,
And of legierdemayne the mysteries did know.

14

To which whilest she lent her intentiue mind,
He suddenly his net vpon her threw,
That ouersprad her like a puffe of wind ;
And snatching her soone vp, ere well she knew,
Ran with her fast away vnto his mew,
Crying for helpe aloud.   But when as ny
He came vnto his caue, and there did vew
The armed knights stopping his passage by,
He threw his burden downe, and fast away did fly.

15

But *Artegall* him after did pursew,
The whiles the Prince there kept the entrance
  still:
Vp to the rocke he ran, and thereon flew
Like a wyld Gote, leaping from hill to hill,
And dauncing on the craggy cliffes at will;
That deadly daunger seem'd in all mens sight,
To tempt such steps, where footing was so ill:
Ne ought auayled for the armed knight,
To thinke to follow him, that was so swift and
  light.

16

Which when he saw, his yron man he sent,
To follow him; for he was swift in chace.
He him pursewd, where euer that he went,
Both ouer rockes, and hilles, and euery place,
Where so he fled, he followd him apace:
So that he shortly forst him to forsake
The hight, and downe descend vnto the base.
There he him courst a fresh, and soone did make
To leaue his proper forme, and other shape to
  take.

17

Into a Foxe himselfe he first did tourne;
But he him hunted like a Foxe full fast:
Then to a bush himselfe he did transforme,
But he the bush did beat, till that at last
Into a bird it chaung'd, and from him past,
Flying from tree to tree, from wand to wand:
But he then stones at it so long did cast,
That like a stone it fell vpon the land,
But he then tooke it vp, and held fast in his
  hand.

18

So he it brought with him vnto the knights,
And to his Lord Sir *Artegall* it lent,
Warning him hold it fast, for feare of slights.
Who whilest in hand it gryping hard he hent,
Into a Hedgehogge all vnwares it went,
And prickt him so, that he away it threw.
Then gan it runne away incontinent,
Being returned to his former hew:
But *Talus* soone him ouertooke, and backward
  drew.

19

But when as he would to a snake againe
Haue turn'd hir selfe, he with his yron flayle
Gan driue at him, with so huge might and maine,
That all his bones, as small as sandy grayle
He broke, and did his bowels disentrayle;
Crying in vaine for helpe, when helpe was past.
So did deceipt the selfe deceiuer fayle,
There they him left a carrion outcast;
For beasts and foules to feede vpon for their
  repast.

20

Thence forth they passed with that gentle Mayd,
To see her Ladie, as they did agree.
To which when she approched, thus she sayd:
Loe now, right noble knights, arriu'd ye bee
Nigh to the place, which ye desir'd to see:
There shall ye see my souerayne Lady Queene
Most sacred wight, most debonayre and free,
That euer yet vpon this earth was seene,
Or that with Diademe hath euer crowned beene.

21

The gentle knights reioyced much to heare
The prayses of that Prince so manifold,
And passing litle further, commen were,
Where they a stately pallace did behold,
Of pompous show, much more then she had told;
With many towres, and tarras mounted hye,
And all their tops bright glistering with gold,
That seemed to outshine the dimmed skye,
And with their brightnesse daz'd the straunge
  beholders eye.

22

There they alighting, by that Damzell were
Directed in, and shewed all the sight:
Whose porch, that most magnificke did appeare,
Stood open wyde to all men day and night;
Yet warded well by one of mickle might,
That sate thereby, with gyantlike resemblance,
To keepe out guyle, and malice, and despight,
That vnder shew oftimes of fayned semblance,
Are wont in Princes courts to worke great scath
  and hindrance.

23

His name was *Awe*; by whom they passing in
Went vp the hall, that was a large wyde roome,
All full of people making troublous din,
And wondrous noyse, as if that there were
  some,
Which vnto them was dealing righteous doome.
By whom they passing, through the thickest
  preasse,
The marshall of the hall to them did come;
His name hight *Order*, who commaunding peace,
Them guyded through the throng, that did
  their clamors ceasse.

24

They ceast their clamors vpon them to gaze;
Whom seeing all in armour bright as day,
Straunge there to see, it did them much amaze,
And with vnwonted terror halfe affray,
For neuer saw they there the like array,
Ne euer was the name of warre there spoken,
But ioyous peace and quietnesse alway,
Dealing iust iudgements, that mote not be
  broken
For any brybes, or threates of any to be wroken.

25

There as they entred at the Scriene, they saw
  Some one, whose tongue was for his trespasse
  Nayld to a post, adiudged so by law :   [vyle
  For that therewith he falsely did reuyle,
  And foule blaspheme that Queene for forged
    guyle,
  Both with bold speaches, which he blazed had,
  And with lewd poems, which he did compyle ;
  For the bold title of a Poet bad
He on himselfe had ta'en, and rayling rymes had
    sprad.

26

Thus there he stood, whylest high ouer his head,
  There written was the purport of his sin,
  In cyphersstrange, that few could rightly read,
  BON FONT: but *bon* that once had written bin,
  Was raced out, and *Mal* was now put in.
  So now *Malfont* was plainely to be red ;
  Eyther for th'euill, which he did therein,
  Or that he likened was to a welhed
Of euill words, and wicked sclaunders by him
    shed.

27

They passing by, were guyded by degree
  Vnto the presence of that gratious Queene :
  Who sate on high, that she might all men see,
  And might of all men royally be seene,
  Vpon a throne of gold full bright and sheene,
  Adorned all with gemmes of endlesse price,
  As either might for wealth haue gotten bene,
  Or could be fram d by workmans rare deuice ;
And all embost with Lyons and with Flour-
    delice.

28

All ouer her a cloth of state was spred,
  Not of rich tissew, nor of cloth of gold,
  Nor of ought else, that may be richest red,
  But like a cloud, as likest may be told,
  That her brode spreading wings did wyde vnfold;
  Whose skirts were bordred with bright sunny
    beams,
  Glistring like gold, amongst the plights enrold,
  And here and there shooting forth siluer streames,
Mongst which crept litle Angels through the glit-
    tering gleames.

29

Seemed those litle Angels did vphold
  The cloth of state, and on their purpled wings
  Did beare the pendants, through their nim-
    blesse bold :
  Besides a thousand more of such, as sings
  Hymnes to high God, and carols heauenly things,
  Encompassed the throne, on which she sate :
  She Angel-like, the heyre of ancient kings
  And mightie Conquerors, in royall state,
Whylest kings and kesars at her feet did them
    prostrate.

30

Thus she did sit in souerayne Maiestie,
  Holding a Scepter in her royall hand,
  The sacred pledge of peace and clemencie,
  With which high God had blest her happie land,
  Maugre so many foes, which did withstand.
  But at her feet her sword was likewise layde,
  Whose long rest rusted the bright steely brand ;
  Yet when as foes enforst, or friends sought
    ayde,
She could it sternely draw, that all the world
    dismayde.

31

And round about, before her feet there sate
  A beuie of faire Virgins clad in white,
  That goodly seem'd t'adorne her royall state,
  All louely daughters of high *Ioue*, that hight
  Litæ, by him begot in loues delight,
  Vpon the righteous *Themis* : those they say
  Vpon *Ioues* iudgement seat wayt day and night,
  And when in wrath he threats the worlds decay,
They doe his anger calme, and cruell vengeance
    stay.

32

They also doe by his diuine permission
  Vpon the thrones of mortall Princes tend,
  And often treat for pardon and remission
  To suppliants, through frayltie which offend.
  Those did vpon *Mercillaes* throne attend :
  Iust *Dice*, wise *Eunomie*, myld *Eirene*,
  And them amongst, her glorie to commend,
  Sate goodly *Temperance* in garments clene,
And sacred *Reuerence*, yborne of heauenly
    strene.

33

Thus did she sit in royall rich estate,
  Admyr'd of many, honoured of all,
  Whylest vnderneath her feete, there as she sate,
  An huge great Lyon lay, that mote appall
  An hardie courage, like captiued thrall,
  With a strong yron chaine and coller bound,
  That once he could not moue, nor quich at all ;
  Yet did he murmure with rebellious sound,
And softly royne, when saluage choler gan
    redound.

34

So sitting high in dreaded souerayntie,
  Those two strange knights were to her pre-
    sence brought ;
  Who bowing low before her Maiestie,
  Did to her myld obeysance, as they ought,
  And meekest boone, that they imagine mought.
  To whom she eke inclyning her withall,
  As a faire stoupe of her high soaring thought,
  A chearefull countenance on them let fall,
Yet tempred with some maiestie imperiall.

35

As the bright sunne, what time his fierie teme
  Towards the westerne brim begins to draw,
  Gins to abate the brightnesse of his beme,
  And feruour of his flames somewhat adaw :
  So did this mightie Ladie, when she saw
  Those two strange knights such homage to her
    make,
  Bate somewhat of that Maiestie and awe,
  That whylome wont to doe so many quake,
And with more myld aspect those two to
    entertake.

36

Now at that instant, as occasion fell,
  When these two stranger knights arriu'd in place,
  She was about affaires of common wele,
  Dealing of Iustice with indifferent grace,
  And hearing pleas of people meane and base.
  Mongst which as then, there was for to be heard
  The tryall of a great and weightie case,
  Which on both sides was then debating hard :
But at the sight of these, those were a while
    debard.

37

But after all her princely entertayne,
  To th'hearing of that former cause in hand,
  Her selfe eftsoones she gan conuert againe ;
  Which that those knights likewise mote vnder-
    stand,
  And witnesse forth aright in forrain land,
  Taking them vp vnto her stately throne,
  Where they mote heare the matter throughly
    scand
On either part, she placed th'one on th'one,
The other on the other side, and neare them
    none.

38

Then was there brought, as prisoner to the barre,
  A Ladie of great countenance and place,
  But that she it with foule abuse did marre ;
  Yet did appeare rare beautie in her face,
  But blotted with condition vile and base,
  That all her other honour did obscure,
  And titles of nobilitie deface :
  Yet in that wretched semblant, she did sure
The peoples great compassion vnto her allure.

39

Then vp arose a person of deepe reach,
  And rare in-sight, hard matters to reuele ;
  That well could charme his tongue, and time
    his speach
  To all assayes ; his name was called *Zele* :
  He gan that Ladie strongly to appele
  Of many haynous crymes, by her enured,
  And with sharpe reasons rang her such a pele,
  That those, whom she to pitie had allured,
He now t'abhorre and loath her person had
    procured.

40

First gan he tell, how this that seem'd so faire
  And royally arayd, *Duessa* hight
  That false *Duessa*, which had wrought great
    care,
  And mickle mischiefe vnto many a knight,
  By her beguyled, and confounded quight :
  But not for those she now in question came,
  Though also those mote question'd be aright,
  But for vyld treasons, and outrageous shame,
Which she against the dred *Mercilla* oft did
    frame.

41

For she whylome (as ye mote yet right well
  Remember) had her counsels false conspyred,
  With faithlesse *Blandamour* and *Paridell*,
  (Both two her paramours, both by her hyred,
  And both with hope of shadowes vaine inspyred,)
  And with them practiz'd, how for to depryue
  Mercilla of her crowne, by her aspyred,
  That she might it vnto her selfe deryue,
And tryumph in their blood, whom she to death
    did dryue.

42

But through high heauens grace, which fauour
    not
  The wicked driftes of trayterous desynes,
  Gainst loiall Princes, all this cursed plot,
  Ere proofe it tooke, discouered was betymes,
  And th'actours won the meede meet for their
    crymes.
  Such be the meede of all. that by such mene
  Vnto the type of kingdomes titl. clymes.
  But false *Duessa* now vntitled Queene,
Was brought to her sad doome, as here was to
    be seene.

43

Strongly did *Zele* her haynous fact enforce,
  And many other crimes of foule defame
  Against her brought, to banish all remorse,
  And aggrauate the horror of her blame.
  And with him to make part against her, came
  Many graue persons, that against her pled ;
  First was a sage old Syre, that had to name
  The *Kingdomes care*. with a white siluer hed,
That many high regards and reasons gainst
    her red.

44

Then gan *Authority* her to appose
  With peremptorie powre, that made all mute ;
  And then the law of *Nations* gainst her rose,
  And reasons brought, that no man could refute ;
  Next gan *Religion* gainst her to impute
  High Gods beheast, and powre of holy lawes ;
  Then gan the Peoples cry and Commons sute,
  Importune care of their owne publicke cause ;
And lastly *Iustice* charged her with breach of
    lawes.

45

But then for her, on the contrarie part,
  Rose many aduocates for her to plead :
First there came *Pittie*, with full tender hart,
  And with her ioyn'd *Regard* of womanhead ;
And then came *Daunger* threatning hidden
    dread,
  And high alliance vnto forren powre ;
Then came *Nobilitie* of birth, that bread
  Great ruth through her misfortunes tragicke
    stowre ;
And lastly *Griefe* did plead, and many teares
    forth powre.

46

With the neare touch whereof in tender hart
  The Briton Prince was sore empassionate,
And woxe inclined much vnto her part,
  Through the sad terror of so dreadfull fate,
  And wretched ruine of so high estate,
That for great ruth his courage gan relent.
  Which when as *Zele* perceiued to abate,
He gan his earnest feruour to augment,
And many fearefull obiects to them to present.

47

He gan t'efforce the euidence anew,
  And new accusements to produce in place :
He brought forth that old hag of hellish hew,
  The cursed *Ate*, brought her face to face,
  Who priuie was, and partie in the case :
She, glad of spoyle and ruinous decay,
  Did her appeach, and to her more disgrace,
The plot of all her practise did display,
And all her traynes, and all her treasons forth
    did lay.

48

Then brought he forth, with griesly grim aspect,
  Abhorred *Murder*, who with bloudie knyfe
Yet dropping fresh in hand did her detect,
  And there with guiltie bloudshed charged ryfe :
Then brought he forth *Sedition*, breeding stryfe
  In troublous wits, and mutinous vprore :
Then brought he forth *Incontinence* of lyfe,
  Euen foule *Adulterie* her face before,
And lewd *Impietie*, that her accused sore.

49

All which when as the Prince had heard and
    seene,
  His former fancies ruth he gan repent,
And from her partie eftsoones was drawne
    cleene.
But *Artegall* with constant firme intent,
  For zeale of Iustice was against her bent.
So was she guiltie deemed of them all.
  Then *Zele* began to vrge her punishment,
And to their Queene for iudgement loudly call,
Vnto *Mercilla* myld for Iustice gainst the thrall.

50

But she, whose Princely breast was touched nere
  With piteous ruth of her so wretched plight,
Though plaine she saw by all, that she did
    heare,
That she of death was guiltie found by right,
  Yet would not let iust vengeance on her light ;
But rather let in stead thereof to fall
  Few perling drops from her faire lampes of light;
The which she couering with her purple pall
Would haue the passion hid, and vp arose
    withall.

Cant. X.

*Prince Arthur takes the enterprize
  for Belge for to fight.
Gerioneos Seneschall
  he slayes in Belges right.*

1

Some Clarkes doe doubt in their deuicefull art,
  Whether this heauenly thing, whereof I treat,
To weeten *Mercie*, be of Iustice part,
  Or drawne forth from her by diuine extreate.
  This well I wote, that sure she is as great,
And meriteth to haue as high a place,
  Sith in th'Almighties euerlasting seat
She first was bred, and borne of heauenly race ;
From thence pour'd down on men, by influence
    of grace.

2

For if that Vertue be of so great might,
  Which from iust verdict will for nothing start,
But to preserue inuiolated right,
  Oft spilles the principall, to saue the part ;
So much more then is that of powre and art,
  That seekes to saue the subiect of her skill,
Yet neuer doth from doome of right depart :
  As it is greater prayse to saue, then spill,
And better to reforme, then to cut off the ill.

3

Who then can thee, *Mercilla*, throughly prayse,
  That herein doest all earthly Princes pas ?
What heauenly Muse shall thy great honour
    rayse
Vp to the skies, whence first deriu'd it was,
  And now on earth it selfe enlarged has,
From th'vtmost brinke of the *Armericke* shore,
  Vnto the margent of the *Molucas* ?
Those Nations farre thy iustice doe adore :
But thine owne people do thy mercy prayse
    much more.

4

Much more it praysed was of those two knights ;
  The noble Prince, and righteous *Artegall*,
  When they had seene and heard her doome
    a rights
  Against *Duessa*, damned by them all ;
  But by her tempred without griefe or gall,
  Till strong constraint did her thereto enforce.
And yet euen then ruing her wilfull fall,
  With more then needfull naturall remorse,
And yeelding the last honour to her wretched
    corse.

5

During all which, those knights continu'd there,
  Both doing and receiuing curtesies,
  Of that great Ladie, who with goodly chere
  Them entertayn'd, fit for their dignities,
  Approuing dayly to their noble eyes
  Royall examples of her mercies rare,
  And worthie paterns of her clemencies ;
  Which till this day mongst many liuing are,
Who them to their posterities doe still declare.

6

Amongst the rest, which in that space befell,
  There came two Springals of full tender yeares,
  Farre thence from forrein land, where they
    did dwell,
  To seeke for succour of her and of her Peares,
  With humble prayers and intreatfull teares ;
  Sent by their mother, who a widow was,
  Wrapt in great dolours and in deadly feares,
By a strong Tyrant, who inuaded has
Her land, and slaine her children ruefully alas.

7

Her name was *Belge*, who in former age
  A Ladie of great worth and wealth had beene,
  And mother of a frutefull heritage,   [seene
  Euen seuenteene goodly sonnes ; which who had
  In their first flowre, before this fatall teene
  Them ouertooke, and their faire blossomes
    blasted,
  More happie mother would her surely weene,
  Then famous *Niobe*, before she tasted
Latonaes childrens wrath, that all her issue
    wasted.

8

But this fell Tyrant, through his tortious powre,
  Had left her now but fiue of all that brood :
  For twelue of them he did by times deuoure,
  And to his Idols sacrifice their blood,
  Whylest he of none was stopped, nor withstood.
  For soothly he was one of matchlesse might,
  Of horrible aspect, and dreadfull mood,
  And had three bodies in one wast empight,
And th'armes and legs of three, to succour him
    in fight.

9

And sooth they say, that he was borne and bred
  Of Gyants race, the sonne of *Geryon*,
  He that whylome in Spaine so sore was dred,
  For his huge powre and great oppression,
  Which brought that land to his subiection,
  Through his three bodies powre, in one com-
    bynd ;
  And eke all strangers in that region
  Arryuing, to his kyne for food assynd ;
The fayrest kyne aliue, but of the fiercest kynd.

10

For they were all, they say, of purple hew,
  Kept by a cowheard, hight *Eurytion*,
  A cruell carle, the which all strangers slew,
  Ne day nor night did sleepe, t'attend them on,
  But walkt about them euer and anone,
  With his two headed dogge, that *Orthrus* hight ;
  Orthrus begotten by great *Typhaon*,
  And foule *Echidna*, in the house of night ;
But *Hercules* them all did ouercome in fight.

11

His sonne was this, *Geryoneo* hight,
  Who after that his monstrous father fell
  Vnder *Alcides* club, streight tooke his flight
  From that sad land, where he his syre did
    quell,
  And came to this, where *Belge* then did dwell,
  And flourish in all wealth and happinesse,
  Being then new made widow (as befell)
  After her Noble husbands late decesse ;
Which gaue beginning to her woe and wretched-
    nesse.

12

Then this bold Tyrant, of her widowhed
  Taking aduantage, and her yet fresh woes,
  Himselfe and seruice to her offered,
  Her to defend against all forrein foes,
  That should their powre against her right
    oppose.
  Whereof she glad, now needing strong defence,
  Him entertayn'd, and did her champion chose :
Which long he vsd with carefull diligence,
The better to confirme her fearelesse confidence.

13

By meanes whereof, she did at last commit
  All to his hands, and gaue him soueraine powre
  To doe, what euer he thought good or fit.
  Which hauing got, he gan forth from that
    howre
  To stirre vp strife, and many a Tragicke stowre,
  Giuing her dearest children one by one
  Vnto a dreadfull Monster to deuoure,
  And setting vp an Idole of his owne,
The image of his monstrous parent *Geryone*.

14

So tyrannizing, and oppressing all,
  The woefull widow had no meanes now left,
  But vnto gratious great *Mercilla* call
  For ayde, against that cruell Tyrants theft,
  Ere all her children he from her had reft.
  Therefore these two, her eldest sonnes she sent,
  To seeke for succour of this Ladies gieft :
  To whom their sute they humbly did present,
In th'hearing of full many Knights and Ladies
  gent.

15

Amongst the which then fortuned to bee
  The noble Briton Prince, with his braue Peare;
  Who when he none of all those knights did see
  Hastily bent, that enterprise to heare,
  Nor vndertake the same, for cowheard feare,
  He stepped forth with courage bold and great,
  Admyr'd of all the rest in presence there,
  And humbly gan that mightie Queene entreat,
To graunt him that aduenture for his former
  feat.

16

She gladly graunted it : then he straight way
  Himselfe vnto his iourney gan prepare,
  And all his armours readie dight that day,
  That nought the morrow next mote stay his
  fare.
  The morrow next appear'd, with purple hayre
  Yet dropping fresh out of the *Indian* fount,
  And bringing light into the heauens fayre,
  When he was readie to his steede to mount,
Vnto his way, which now was all his care and
  count.

17

Then taking humble leaue of that great Queene,
  Who gaue him roiall giftes and riches rare,
  As tokens of her thankefull mind beseene,
  And leauing *Artegall* to his owne care,
  Vpon his voyage forth he gan to fare,
  With those two gentle youthes, which him did
  guide,
  And all his way before him still prepare.
  Ne after him did *Artegall* abide,
But on his first aduenture forward forth did ride.

18

It was not long, till that the Prince arriued
  Within the land, where dwelt that Ladie sad,
  Whereof that Tyrant had her now depriued,
  And into moores and marshes banisht had,
  Out of the pleasant soyle, and citties glad,
  In which she wont to harbour happily :
  But now his cruelty so sore she drad,
  That to those fennes for fastnesse she did fly,
And there her selfe did hyde from his hard
  tyranny.

19

There he her found in sorrow and dismay,
  All solitarie without liuing wight;
  For all her other children, through affray,
  Had hid themselues, or taken further flight :
  And eke her selfe through sudden strange
  affright,
  When one in armes she saw, began to fly ;
  But when her owne two sonnes she had in sight,
  She gan take hart, and looke vp ioyfully :
For well she wist this knight came, succour to
  supply.

20

And running vnto them with greedy ioyes,
  Fell straight about their neckes, as they did
  kneele,
  And bursting forth in teares ; Ah my sweet boyes,
  (Sayd she) yet now I gin new life to feele,
  And feeble spirits, that gan faint and reele,
  Now rise againe, at this your ioyous sight.
  Alreadie seemes that fortunes headlong wheele
  Begins to turne, and sunne to shine more bright,
Then it was wont, through comfort of this noble
  knight.

21

Then turning vnto him ; And you Sir knight
  (Said she) that taken haue this toylesome paine
  For wretched woman, miserable wight,
  May you in heauen immortall guerdon gaine
  For so great trauell, as you doe sustaine :
  For other meede may hope for none of mee,
  To whom nought else, but bare life doth remaine,
  And that so wretched one, as ye do see
Is liker lingring death, then loathed life to bee.

22

Much was he moued with her piteous plight,
  And low dismounting from his loftie steede,
  Gan to recomfort her all that he might,
  Seeking to driue away deepe rooted dreede,
  With hope of helpe in that her greatest neede.
  So thence he wished her with him to wend,
  Vnto some place, where they mote rest and feede,
  And she take comfort, which God now did send :
Good hart in euils doth the euils much amend.

23

Ay me (sayd she) and whether shall I goe ?
  Are not all places full of forraine powres ?
  My pallaces possessed of my foe,
  My cities sackt, and their sky-threating towres
  Raced, and made smooth fields now full of flowres?
  Onely these marishes, and myrie bogs,
  In which the fearefull ewftes do build their
  bowres,
  Yeeld me an hostry mongst the croking frogs,
And harbour here in safety from those rauenous
  dogs.

24

Nathlesse (said he) deare Ladie with me goe,
  Someplace shall vs receiue, and harbour yield;
  If not, we will it force, maugre your foe,
  And purchase it to vs with speare and shield :
  And if all fayle, yet farewell open field :
  The earth to all her creatures lodging lends.
  Withsuch his chearefull speaches he doth wield
Her mind so well, that to his will she bends
And bynding vp her locks and weeds, forth with
  him wends.

25

They came vnto a Citie farre vp land,
  The which whylome that Ladies owne had
    bene ;
  But now by force extort out of her hand,
  By her strong foe, who had defaced cleene
  Herstatelytowres,andbuildingssunnysheene;
  Shut vp her hauen, mard her marchants trade,
  Robbed her people, that full rich had beene,
  And in her necke a Castle huge had made,
The which did her commaund, without needing
  perswade.

26

That Castle was the strength of all that state,
  Vntill that statebystrength waspulled downe,
  And that same citie, so now ruinate,
  Had bene the keye of all that kingdomes
    crowne ;
  Both goodly Castle, and both goodly Towne,
  Till that th'offended heauens list to lowre
  Vpon their blisse, and balefull fortune frowne,
When those gainst states and kingdomes do
  coniure,
Who then can thinke their hedlong ruine to
  recure.

27

But he had brought it now in seruile bond,
  And made it beare the yoke of inquisition,
  Stryuing long time in vaine it to withstond ;
  Yet glad at last to make most base submission,
  And life enioy for any composition.
  So now he hath new lawes and orders new
  Imposd on it, with many a hard condition,
  And forced it, the honour that is dew
To God, to doe vnto his Idole most vntrew.

28

To him he hath, before this Castle greene,
  Built a faire Chappell, and an Altar framed
  Of costly Iuory, full rich beseene,
  On which that cursed Idole farre proclamed,
  He hath set vp, and him his God hath named,
  Offring to him in sinfull sacrifice
  The flesh of men, to Gods owne likenesse
    framed,
  Andpowringforththeir bloud in brutishe wize,
That any yron eyes to see it would agrize.

29

And for more horror and more crueltie,
  Vnder that cursed Idols altar stone
  An hideous monster doth in darknesse lie,
  Whose dreadfull shape was neuer seene of none
  That liues on earth ; but vnto those alone
  The which vnto him sacrificed bee.
  Those he deuoures, they say, both flesh and bone:
  What else they haue, is all the Tyrants fee;
So that no whit of them remayning one may see.

30

There eke he placed a strong garrisone,
  And set a Seneschall of dreaded might,
  That by his powre oppressed euery one,
  And vanquished all ventrous knights in fight ;
  Towhom he wont shew all the shame he might,
  After that them in battell he had wonne.
  To which when now they gan approch in sight,
  The Ladie counseld him the place to shonne,
Whereas so many knights had fouly bene
  fordonne.

31

Her fearefull speaches nought he did regard,
  But ryding streight vnder the Castle wall,
  Called aloud vnto the watchfull ward,
  Which there did wayte, willing them forth to call
  Into the field their Tyrants Seneschall.
  Towhomwhentydingsthereofcame,hestreight
  Cals for his armes, and arming him withall,
  Eftsoones forth pricked proudly in his might,
And gan with courage fierce addresse him to
  the fight.

32

They both encounter in the middle plaine,
  And their sharpe speares doe both together
    smite
  Amid their shields, with so huge might and
    maine,
  That seem'd their soules they wold haue ryuen
    quight
  Out of their breasts, with furious despight.
  Yet could the Seneschals no entrance find
  Into the Princes shield, where it empight ;
  So pure the mettall was, and well refynd,
But shiuered all about, and scattered in the
  wynd.

33

Not so the Princes, but with restlesse force,
  Into his shield it readie passage found,
  Both through his haberieon, and eke his corse:
  Which tombling downe vpon the senselesse
    ground,
  Gaue leaue vntohisghost from thraldome bound,
  To wander in the griesly shades of night.
  Theredid the Prince him leaue in deadly swound,
  And thence vnto the castle marched right,
To see if entrance there as yet obtaine he might.

34

But as he nigher drew, three knights he spyde,
 All arm'd to point, issuing forth a pace,
 Which towards him with all their powre did ryde,
 And meeting him right in the middle race,
 Did all their speares attonce on him enchace.
 As three great Culuerings for battrie bent,
 And leueld all against one certaine place,
 Doe all attonce their thunders rage forth rent,
That makes the wals to stagger with astonish-
      ment.

35

So all attonce they on the Prince did thonder ;
 Who from his saddle swarued nought asyde,
 Ne to their force gaue way, that was great wonder,
 But like a bulwarke, firmely did abyde,
 Rebutting him, which in the midst did ryde,
 With so huge rigour, that his mortall speare
 Past through his shield, and pierst through
      either syde,
 That downe he fell vppon his mother deare,
And powred forth his wretched life in deadly
      dreare.

36

Whom when his other fellowes saw, they fled
 As fast as feete could carry them away ;
 And after them the Prince as swiftly sped,
 To be aueng'd of their vnknightly play. [stay,
 There whilest they entring, th'one did th'other
 The hindmost in the gate he ouerhent,
 And as he pressed in, him there did slay :
 His carkasse tumbling on the threshold, sent
His groning soule vnto her place of punishment.

37

The other which was entred, laboured fast
 To sperre the gate; but that same lumpe of clay,
 Whose grudging ghost was thereout fled and past,
 Right in the middest of the threshold lay,
 That it the Posterne did from closing stay :
 The whiles the Prince hard preased in betweene,
 And entraunce wonne. Streight th'other fled
      away,
 And ran into the Hall, where he did weene
Him selfe to saue : but he there slew him at the
      skreene.

38

Then all the rest which in that Castle were,
 Seeing that sad ensample them before,
 Durst not abide, but fled away for feare,
 And them conuayd out at a Posterne dore.
 Long sought the Prince, but when he found
      no more
 T'oppose against his powre, he forth issued
 Vnto that Lady, where he her had lore,
 And her gan cheare, with what she there had
      vewed,   [shewed.
And what she had not seene, within vnto her

39

Who with right humble thankes him goodly
      greeting,
 For so great prowesse, as he there had proued,
 Much greater then was euer in her weeting,
 With great admiraunce inwardly was moued,
 And honourd him, with all that her hehoued.
 Thenceforth into that Castle he her led,
 With her two sonnes, right deare of her beloued,
 Where all that night them selues they cherished,
And from her balefull minde all care he banished.

Cant. XI.

Prince Arthure ouercomes the great
   Gerioneo in fight :
Doth slay the Monster, and restore
   Belge vnto her right.

1

It often fals in course of common life,
 That right long time is ouerborne of wrong,
 Through auarice, or powre, or guile, or strife,
 That weakens her, and makes her party strong:
 But Iustice, though her dome she doe prolong,
 Yet at the last she will her owne cause right.
 As by sad *Belge* seemes, whose wrongs though
      long
 She suffred, yet at length she did requight,
And sent redresse thereof by this braue Briton
      Knight.

2

Whereof when newes was to that Tyrant brought,
 How that the Lady *Belge* now had found
 A Champion, that had with his Champion fought,
 And laid his Seneschall low on the ground,
 And eke him selfe did threaten to confound,
 He gan to burne in rage, and friese in feare,
 Doubting sad end of principle vnsound :
 Yet sith he heard but one, that did appeare,
He did him selfe encourage, and take better
      cheare.

3

Nathelesse him selfe he armed all in hast,
 And forth he far'd with all his many bad,
 Ne stayed step, till that he came at last
 Vnto the Castle, which they conquerd had.
 There with huge terrour, to be more ydrad,
 He sternely marcht before the Castle gate,
 And with bold vaunts, and ydle threatning bad
 Deliuer him his owne, ere yet too late,
To which they had no right, nor any wrongfull
      state.

4

The Prince staid not his aunswere to deuize,
But opening streight the Sparre, forth to him
came,
Full nobly mounted in right warlike wize ;
And asked him, if that he were the same,
Who all that wrong vnto that wofull Dame
So long had done, and from her natiue land
Exiled her, that all the world spake shame.
He boldly aunswerd him, he there did stand
That would his doings iustifie with his owne
hand.

5

With that so furiously at him he flew,
As if he would haue ouerrun him streight,
And with his huge great yron axe gan hew
So hideously vppon his armour bright,
As he to peeces would haue chopt it quight :
That the bold Prince was forced foote to giue
To his first rage, and yeeld to his despight ;
The whilest at him so dreadfully he driue,
That seem'd a marble rocke asunder could
haue riue.

6

Thereto a great aduauntage eke he has
Through his three double hands thrise
multiplyde,
Besides the double strength, which in them was:
For stil when fit occasion did betyde,
He could his weapon shift from side to syde,
From hand to hand, and with such nimblesse
sly
Could wield about, that ere it were espide,
The wicked stroke did wound his enemy,
Behinde, beside, before, as he it list apply.

7

Which vncouth vse when as the Prince perceiued,
He gan to watch the wielding of his hand,
Least by such slight he were vnwares deceiued;
And euer ere he saw the stroke to land,
He would it meete, and warily withstand.
One time, when he his weapon faynd to shift,
As he was wont, and chang'd from hand to hand,
He met him with a counterstroke so swift,
That quite smit off his arme, as he it vp did lift.

8

Therewith, all fraught with fury and disdaine,
He brayd aloud for very fell despight,
And sodainely t'auenge him selfe againe,
Gan into one assemble all the might
Of all his hands, and heaued them on hight,
Thinking to pay him with that one for all :
But the sad steele seizd not, where it was hight,
Vppon the childe, but somewhat short did fall,
And lighting on his horses head, him quite did
mall.

9

Downe streight to ground fell his astonisht steed,
And eke to th'earth his burden with him bare :
But he him selfe full lightly from him freed,
And gan him selfe to fight on foote prepare.
Whereof when as the Gyant was aware,
He wox right blyth, as he had got thereby,
And laught so loud, that all his teeth wide bare
One might haue seene enraung'd disorderly,
Like to a rancke of piles, that pitched are awry.

10

Eftsoones againe his axe he raught on hie,
Ere he were throughly buckled to his geare,
And can let driue at him so dreadfullie,
That had he chaunced not his shield to reare,
Ere that huge stroke arriued on him neare,
He had him surely clouen quite in twaine.
But th'Adamantine shield, which he did beare,
So well was tempred, that for all his maine,
It would no passage yeeld vnto his purpose
vaine.

11

Yet was the stroke so forcibly applide,
That made him stagger with vncertaine sway,
As if he would haue tottered to one side.
Wherewith full wroth, he fiercely gan assay,
That curt'sie with like kindnesse to repay ;
And smote at him with so importune might,
That two more of his armes did fall away,
Like fruitlesse braunches, which the hatchets
slight
Hath pruned from the natiue tree, and cropped
quight.

12

With that all mad and furious he grew,
Like a fell mastiffe through enraging heat,
And curst, and band, and blasphemies forth
threw,
Against his Gods, and fire to them did threat,
And hell vnto him selfe with horrour great.
Thenceforth he car'd no more, which way he
strooke,
Nor where it light, but gan to chaufe and sweat,
And gnasht his teeth, and his head at him shooke,
And sternely him beheld with grim and ghastly
looke.

13

Nought fear'd the childe his lookes, ne yet his
threats,
But onely wexed now the more aware, [threats,
To saue him selfe from those his furious heats,
And watch aduauntage, how to worke his care :
The which good Fortune to him offred faire.
For as he in his rage him ouerstrooke,
He ere he could his weapon backe repaire,
His side all bare and naked ouertooke,
And with his mortal steel quite throgh the body
strooke.

14

Through all three bodies he him strooke attonce;
That all the three attonce fell on the plaine :
Else should he thrise haue needed, for the nonce
Them to haue stricken, and thrise to haue
    slaine.
So now all three one sencelesse lumpe remaine,
Enwallow'd in his owne blacke bloudy gore,
And byting th'earth for very deaths disdaine ;
Who with a cloud of night him couering, bore
Downe to the house of dole, his daies there to
    deplore.

15

Which when the Lady from the Castle saw,
Where she with her two sonnes did looking
    stand,
She towards him in hast her selfe did draw,
To greet him the good fortune of his hand :
And all the people both of towne and land,
Which there stood gazing from the Citties wall
Vppon these warriours, greedy t'vnderstand,
To whether should the victory befall,
Now when they saw it falne, they eke him greeted
    all.

16

But *Belge* with her sonnes prostrated low
Before his feete, in all that peoples sight,
Mongst ioyes mixing some tears, mongst wele,
    some wo
Him thus bespake ; O most redoubted Knight,
The which hast me, of all most wretched wight,
That earst was dead, restor'd to life againe,
And these weake impes replanted by thy might;
What guerdon can I giue thee for thy paine,
But euen that which thou sauedst, thine still
    to remaine ?

17

He tooke her vp forby the lilly hand,
And her recomforted the best he might,
Saying ; Deare Lady, deedes ought not be scand
By th'authors manhood, nor the doers might,
But by their trueth and by the causes right :
That same is it, which fought for you this day.
What other meed then need me to requight,
But that which yeeldeth vertues meed alway ?
That is the vertue selfe, which her reward doth
    pay.

18

She humbly thankt him for that wondrous grace,
And further sayd ; Ah Sir, but mote ye please,
Sith ye thus farre haue tendred my poore case,
As from my chiefest foe me to release,
That your victorious arme will not yet cease,
Till ye haue rooted all the relickes out
Of that vilde race, and stablished my peace.
What is there else (sayd he) left of their rout?
Declare it boldly Dame, and doe not stand in
    dout.

19

Then wote you, Sir, that in this Church hereby,
There stands an Idole of great note and name,
The which this Gyant reared first on hie,
And of his owne vaine fancies thought did frame:
To whom for endlesse horrour of his shame,
He offred vp for daily sacrifize
My children and my people, burnt in flame ;
With all the tortures, that he could deuize,
The more t'aggrate his God with such his
    blouddy guize.

20

And vnderneath this Idoll there doth lie
An hideous monster, that doth it defend,
And feedes on all the carkasses, that die
In sacrifize vnto that cursed feend :
Whose vgly shape none euer saw, nor kend ;
That euer scap'd : for of a man they say
It has the voice, that speaches forth doth send,
Euen blasphemous words, which she doth bray
Out of her poysnous entrails, fraught with
    dire decay.

21

Which when the Prince heard tell, his heart
    gan earne
For great desire, that Monster to assay,
And prayd the place of her abode to learne.
Which being shew'd, he gan him selfe streight
    way
Thereto addresse, and his bright shield display.
So to the Church he came, where it was told,
The Monster vnderneath the Altar lay ;
There he that Idoll saw of massy gold
Most richly made, but there no Monster did
    behold.

22

Vpon the Image with his naked blade
Three times, as in defiance, there he strooke ;
And the third time out of an hidden shade,
There forth issewd, from vnder th'Altars
    smooke,
A dreadfull feend, with fowle deformed looke,
That stretcht it selfe, as it had long lyen still ;
And her long taile and fethers strongly shooke,
That all the Temple did with terrour fill ;
Yet him nought terrifide, that feared nothing ill.

23

An huge great Beast it was, when it in length
Was stretched forth, that nigh fild all the place,
And seem'd to be of infinite great strength ;
Horrible, hideous, and of hellish race,
Borne of the brooding of *Echidna* base,
Or other like infernall furies kinde :
For of a Mayd she had the outward face,
To hide the horrour, which did lurke behinde,
The better to beguile, whom she so fond did
    finde.

24

Thereto the body of a dog she had,
Full of fell rauin and fierce greedinesse ;
A Lions clawes, with powre and rigour clad,
To rend and teare, what so she can oppresse;
A Dragons taile, whose sting without redresse
Full deadly wounds, where so it is empight ;
And Eagles wings, for scope and speedinesse,
That nothing may escape her reaching might,
Whereto she euer list to make her hardy flight.

25

Much like in foulnesse and deformity
Vnto that Monster, whom the Theban Knight,
The father of that fatall progeny,
Made kill her selfe for very hearts despight,
That he had red her Riddle, which no wight
Could euer loose, but suffred deadly doole.
So also did this Monster vse like slight
To many a one, which came vnto her schoole,
Whom she did put to death, deceiued like
a foole.

26

She comming forth, when as she first beheld
The armed Prince, with shields so blazing bright,
Her ready to assaile, was greatly queld,
And much dismayd with that dismayfull sight,
That backe she would haue turnd for great
affright.
But he gan her with courage fierce assay,
That forst her turne againe in her despight,
To saue her selfe, least that he did her slay :
And sure he had her slaine, had she not turnd
her way.

27

Tho when she saw, that she was forst to fight,
She flew at him, like to an hellish feend,
And on his shield tooke hold with all her might,
As if that it she would in peeces rend,
Or reaue out of the hand, that did it hend.
Strongly he stroue out of her greedy gripe
To loose his shield, and long while did contend :
But when he could not quite it, with one stripe
Her Lions clawes he from her feete away did
wipe.

28

With that aloude she gan to bray and yell,
And fowle blasphemous speaches forth did
cast,
And bitter curses, horrible to tell,
That euen the Temple, wherein she was plast,
Did quake to heare, and nigh asunder brast.
Tho with her huge long taile she at him strooke,
That made him stagger, and stand halfe agast
With trembling ioynts, as he for terrour
shooke ;
Who nought was terrifide, but greater courage
tooke.

29

As when the Mast of some well timbred hulke
Is with the blast of some outragious storme
Blowne downe, it shakes the bottome of the
bulke,
And makes her ribs to cracke, as they were
torne,
Whilest still she stands as stonisht and for-
lorne :
So was he stound with stroke of her huge taile.
But ere that it she backe againe had borne,
He with his sword it strooke, that without faile
He ioynted it, and mard the swinging of her
flaile.

30

Then gan she cry much louder then afore,
That all the people there without it heard,
And *Belge* selfe was therewith stonied sore,
As if the onely sound thereof she feard.
But then the feend her selfe more fiercely reard
Vppon her wide great wings, and strongly flew
With all her body at his head and beard,
That had he not foreseene with heedfull vew,
And thrown his shield atween, she had him
done to rew.

31

But as she prest on him with heauy sway,
Vnder her wombe his fatall sword he thrust,
And for her entrailes made an open way,
To issue forth ; the which once being brust,
Like to a great Mill damb forth fiercely gusht,
And powred out of her infernall sinke
Most vgly filth, and poyson therewith rusht,
That him nigh choked with the deadly stinke :
Such loathly matter were small lust to speake,
or thinke.

32

Then downe to ground fell that deformed Masse,
Breathing out clouds of sulphure fowle and
blacke,
In which a puddle of contagion was,
More loathd then *Lerna*, or then *Stygian* lake,
That any man would nigh awhaped make.
Whom when he saw on ground, he was full glad,
And streight went forth his gladnesse to partake
With *Belge*, who watcht all this while full sad,
Wayting what end would be of that same
daunger drad.

33

Whom when she saw so ioyously come forth,
She gan reioyce, and shew triumphant chere,
Lauding and praysing his renowmed worth,
By all the names that honorable were.
Then in he brought her, and her shewed there
The present of his paines, that Monsters spoyle,
And eke that Idoll deem'd so costly dere ;
Whom he did all to peeces breake and foyle
In filthy durt, and left so in the loathely soyle.

34

Then all the people, which beheld that day,
  Gan shout aloud, that vnto heauen it rong ;
  And all the damzels of that towne in ray,
  Came dauncing forth, and ioyous carrols song :
  So him they led through all their streetes along,
  Crowned with girlonds of immortall baies,
  And all the vulgar did about them throng,
  To see the man, whose euerlasting praise
They all were bound to all posterities to raise.

35

There he with *Belge* did a while remaine,
  Making great feast and ioyous merriment,
  Vntill he had her settled in her raine,
  With safe assuraunce and establishment.
  Then to his first emprize his mind he lent,
  Full loath to *Belge*, and to all the rest :
  Of whom yet taking leaue, thenceforth he
     went
And to his former iourney him addrest,
On which long way he rode, ne euer day did rest.

36

But turne we now to noble *Artegall* ;
  Who hauing left *Mercilla*, streight way went
  On his first quest, the which him forth did call,
  To weet to worke *Irenaes* franchisement,
  And eke *Grantortoes* worthy punishment.
  So forth he fared as his manner was,
  With onely *Talus* wayting diligent,
  Through many perils and much way did pas,
Till nigh vnto the place at length approcht
     he has.

37

There as he traueld by the way, he met
  An aged wight, wayfaring all alone,
  Who through his yeares longsince aside had set
  The vse of armes, and battell quite forgone :
  To whom as he approcht, he knew anone,
  That it was he which whilome did attend
  On faire *Irene* in her affliction,
  When first to Faery court he saw her wend,
Vnto his soueraine Queene her suite for to
     commend.

38

Whom by his name saluting, thus he gan ;
  Haile good Sir *Sergis*, truest Knight aliue,
  Well tride in all thy Ladies troubles than,
  When her that Tyrant did of Crowne depriue,
  What new ocasion doth thee hither driue,
  Whiles she alone is left, and thou here found ?
  Or is she thrall, or doth she not suruiue ?
  To whom he thus ; She liueth sure and sound,
But by that Tyrant is in wretched thraldome
     bound.

39

For she presuming on th'appointed tyde,
  In which ye promist, as ye were a Knight,
  To meete her at the saluage Ilands syde,
  And then and there for triall of her right
  With her vnrighteous enemy to fight,
  Did thither come, where she afrayd of nought,
  By guilefull treason and by subtill slight
  Surprized was, and to *Grantorto* brought,
Who her imprisond hath, and her life often
     sought.

40

And now he hath to her prefixt a day,
  By which if that no champion doe appeare,
  Which will her cause in battailous array
  Against him iustifie, and proue her cleare
  Of all those crimes, that he gainst her doth
     reare,
  She death shall by. Those tidings sad
  Did much abash Sir *Artegall* to heare,
  And grieued sore, that through his fault she
     had
Fallen into that Tyrants hand and vsage bad.

41

Then thus replide ; Now sure and by my life,
  Too much am I to blame for that faire Maide,
  That haue her drawne to all this troublous
     strife,
  Through promise to afford her timely aide,
  Which by default I haue not yet defraide.
  But witnesse vnto me, ye heauens, that know
  How cleare I am from blame of this vpbraide :
  For ye into like thraldome me did throw,
And kept from complishing the faith, which
     I did owe.

42

But now aread, Sir *Sergis*, how long space,
  Hath he her lent, a Champion to prouide ?
  Ten daies (quoth he) he graunted hath of grace,
  For that he weeneth well, before that tide
  None can haue tidings to assist her side.
  For all the shores, which to the sea accoste,
  He day and night doth ward both far and wide,
  That none can there arriue without an hoste :
So her he deemes already but a damned ghoste.

43

Now turne againe (Sir *Artegall* then sayd)
  For if I liue till those ten daies haue end,
  Assure your selfe, Sir Knight, she shall haue
     ayd,
  Though I this dearest life for her doe spend :
  So backeward he attone with him did wend.
  Tho as they rode together on their way,
  A rout of people they before them kend,
  Flocking together in confusde array,
As if that there were some tumultuous affray.

44

To which as they approcht, the cause to know,
  They saw a Knight in daungerous distresse
Of a rude rout him chasing to and fro,
  That sought with lawlesse powre him to
    oppresse,
And bring in bondage of their brutishnesse :
  And farre away, amid their rakehell bands,
  They spide a Lady left all succourlesse,
Crying, and holding vp her wretched hands
To him for aide, who long in vaine their rage
    withstands.

45

Yet still he striues, ne any perill spares,
  To reskue her from their rude violence,
And like a Lion wood amongst them fares,
  Dealing his dreadfull blowes with large dis-
    pence,
  Gainst which the pallid death findes no defence.
But all in vaine, their numbers are so great,
  That naught may boot to banishe them from
    thence :
For soone as he their outrage backe doth beat,
They turne afresh, and oft renew their former
    threat.

46

And now they doe so sharpely him assay,
  That they his shield in peeces battred haue,
And forced him to throw it quite away,
  Fro dangers dread his doubtfull life to saue ;
  Albe that it most safety to him gaue,
And much did magnifie his noble name.
  For from the day that he thus did it leaue,
Amongst all Knights he blotted was with blame,
And counted but a recreant Knight, with endles
    shame.

47

Whom when they thus distressed did behold,
  They drew vnto his aide ; but that rude rout
Them also gan assaile with outrage bold,
  And forced them, how euer strong and stout
They were, as well approu'd in many a doubt,
  Backe to recule ; vntill that yron man
With his huge flaile began to lay about,
  From whose sterne presence they diffused ran,
Like scattred chaffe, the which the wind away
    doth fan.

48

So when that Knight from perill cleare was freed,
  He drawing neare, began to greete them faire,
And yeeld great thankes for their so goodly deed,
  In sauing him from daungerous despaire
Of those, which sought his life for to empaire.
  Of whom Sir *Artegall* gan then enquire
The whole occasion of his late misfare,
  And who he was, and what those villaines were,
The which with mortall malice him pursu'd so
    nere.

49

To whom he thus ; My name is *Burbon* hight,
  Well knowne, and far renowmed heretofore,
Vntill late mischiefe did vppon me light,
  That all my former praise hath blemisht sore ;
  And that faire Lady, which in that vprore
Ye with those caytiues saw, *Flourdelis* hight,
  Is mine owne loue, though me she haue forlore,
Whether withheld from me by wrongfull might,
Or with her owne good will, I cannot read
    aright.

50

But sure to me her faith she first did plight,
  To be my loue, and take me for her Lord,
Till that a Tyrant, which *Grandtorto* hight,
  With golden giftes and many a guilefull word
  Entyced her, to him for to accord.
O who may not with gifts and words be
    tempted ?
  Sith which she hath me euer since abhord,
And to my foe hath guilefully consented :
Ay me, that euer guyle in wemen was inuented.

51

And now he hath this troupe of villains sent,
  By open force to fetch her quite away :
Gainst whom my selfe I long in vaine haue
    bent,
  To rescue her, and daily meanes assay,
  Yet rescue her thence by no meanes I may :
For they doe me with multitude oppresse,
  And with vnequall might doe ouerlay,
That oft I driuen am to great distresse,
And forced to forgoe th'attempt remedilesse.

52

But why haue ye (said *Artegall*) forborne
  Your owne good shield in daungerous dismay ?
That is the greatest shame and foulest scorne,
  Which vnto any knight behappen may
To loose the badge, that should his deedes
    display.
  To whom Sir *Burbon*, blushing halfe for shame,
That shall I vnto you (quoth he) bewray ;
  Least ye therefore mote happily me blame,
And deeme it doen of will, that through inforce-
    ment came.

53

True is, that I at first was dubbed knight
  By a good knight, the knight of the *Redcrosse* ;
Who when he gaue me armes, in field to fight,
  Gaue me a shield, in which he did endosse
His deare Redeemers badge vpon the bosse :
  The same longwhile I bore, and therewithall
Fought many battels without wound or losse ;
  Therewith *Grandtorto* selfe I did appall,
And made him oftentimes in field before me fall.

54

But for that many did that shield enuie,
    And cruell enemies increased more ;
    To stint all strife and troublous enmitie,
    That bloudie scutchin being battered sore,
    I layd aside, and haue of late forbore,
    Hoping thereby to haue my loue obtayned :
    Yet can I not my loue haue nathemore ;
    For she by force is still fro me detayned,
And with corruptfull brybes is to vntruth
    mis-trayned.

55

To whom thus *Artegall* ; Certes Sir knight,
    Hard is the case, the which ye doe complaine ;
    Yet not so hard (for nought so hard may light,
    That it to such a streight mote you constraine)
    As to abandon, that which doth containe
    Your honours stile, that is your warlike shield.
    All perill ought be lesse, and lesse all paine
    Then losse of fame in disauentrous field ;
Dye rather, then doe ought, that mote dis-
    honour yield.

56

Not so ; (quoth he) for yet when time doth
    serue,
    My former shield I may resume againe :
    To temporize is not from truth to swerue,
    Ne for aduantage terme to entertaine,
    When as necessitie doth it constraine.
    Fie on such forgerie (said *Artegall*)
    Vnder one hood to shadow faces twaine.
    Knights ought be true, and truth is one in all :
Of all things to dissemble fouly may befall.

57

Yet let me you of courtesie request,
    (Said *Burbon*) to assist me now at need
    Against these pesants, which haue me opprest,
    And forced me to so infamous deed,
    That yet my loue may from their hands be
    freed.
    Sir *Artegall*, albe he earst did wyte
    His wauering mind, yet to his aide agreed,
    And buckling him eftsoones vnto the fight,
Did set vpon those troupes with all his powre
    and might.

58

Who flocking round about them, as a swarme
    Of flyes vpon a birchen bough doth cluster,
    Did them assault with terrible allarme,
    And ouer all the fields themselues did muster,
    With bils and glayues making a dreadfull
    luster ;
    That forst at first those knights backe to retyre :
    As when the wrathfull *Boreas* doth bluster,
    Nought may abide the tempest of his yre,
Both man and beast doe fly, and succour doe
    inquyre.

59

But when as ouerblowen was that brunt,
    Those knights began a fresh them to assayle,
    And all about the fields like Squirrels hunt ;
    But chiefly *Talus* with his yron flayle,
    Gainst which no flight nor rescue mote auayle,
    Made cruell hauocke of the baser crew,
    And chaced them both ouer hill and dale :
    The raskall manie soone they ouerthrew,
But the two knights themselues their captains
    did subdew.

60

At last they came whereas that Ladie bode,
    Whom now her keepers had forsaken quight,
    To saue themselues, and scattered were abrode :
    Her halfe dismayd they found in doubtfull
        plight,
    As neither glad nor sorie for their sight ;
    Yet wondrous faire she was, and richly clad
    In roiall robes, and many Iewels dight,
    But that those villens through their vsage bad
Them fouly rent, and shamefully defaced had.

61

But *Burbon* streight dismounting from his steed,
    Vnto her ran with greedie great desyre,
    And catching her fast by her ragged weed,
    Would haue embraced her with hart entyre,
    But she backstarting with disdainefull yre,
    Bad him auaunt, ne would vnto his lore
    Allured be, for prayer nor for meed.
    Whom when those knights so froward and
    forlore
Beheld, they her rebuked and vpbrayded sore.

62

Sayd *Artegall* ; What foule disgrace is this,
    To so faire Ladie, as ye seeme in sight,
    To blot your beautie, that vnblemisht is,
    With so foule blame, as breach of faith once
        plight,
    Or change of loue for any worlds delight ?
    Is ought on earth so pretious or deare,
    As prayse and honour ? Or is ought so bright
    And beautifull, as glories beames appeare,
Whose goodly light then *Phebus* lampe doth shine
    more cleare ?

63

Why then will ye, fond Dame, attempted bee
    Vnto a strangers loue so lightly placed,
    For guiftes of gold, or any worldly glee
    To leaue the loue, that ye before embraced,
    And let your fame with falshood be defaced ?
    Fie on the pelfe, for which good name is sold,
    And honour with indignitie debased :
    Dearer is loue then life, and fame then gold ;
But dearer then them both, your faith once
    plighted hold.

64

Much was the Ladie in her gentle mind
Abasht at his rebuke, that bit her neare,
Ne ought to answere thereunto did find ;
But hanging downe her head with heauie cheare,
Stood long amaz'd, as she amated weare.
Which *Burbon* seeing, her againe assayd,
And clasping twixt his armes, her vp did reare
Vpon his steede, whiles she no whit gainesayd,
So bore her quite away, nor well nor ill apayd.

65

Nathlesse the yron man did still pursew
That raskall many with vnpittied spoyle,
Ne ceassed not, till all their scattred crew
Into the sea he droue quite from that soyle,
The which they troubled had with great
    turmoyle.
But *Artegall* seeing his cruell deed,
Commaunded him from slaughter to recoyle,
And to his voyage gan againe proceed :
For that the terme approching fast, required
    speed

Cant. XII.

Artegall doth Sir Burbon aide,
And blames for changing shield :
He with the great Grantorto fights,
And slaieth him in field.

I

O sacred hunger of ambitious mindes,
And impotent desire of men to raine,
Whom neither dread of God, that deuils bindes,
Nor lawes of men, that common weales con-
    taine,
Nor bands of nature, that wilde beastes
    restraine,
Can keepe from outrage, and from doing wrong,
Where they may hope a kingdome to obtaine.
No faith so firme, no trust can be so strong,
No loue so lasting then, that may enduren long.

2

Witnesse may *Burbon* be, whom all the bands,
Which may a Knight assure, had surely bound,
Vntill the loue of Lordship and of lands
Made him become most faithlesse and vnsound :
And witnesse be *Gerioneo* found,
Who for like cause faire *Belge* did oppresse,
And right and wrong most cruelly confound :
And so be now *Grantorto*, who no lesse
Then all the rest burst out to all outragiousnesse.

3

Gainst whom Sir *Artegall*, long hauing since
Taken in hand th'exploit, being thereto
Appointed by that mightie Faerie Prince,
Great *Gloriane*, that Tyrant to fordoo,
Through other great aduentures hethertoo
Had it forslackt.   But now time drawing ny,
To him assynd, her high beheast to doo,
To the sea shore he gan his way apply,
To weete if shipping readie he mote there descry.

4

Tho when they came to the sea coast, they found
A ship all readie (as good fortune fell)
To put to sea, with whom they did compound,
To passe them ouer, where them list to tell :
The winde and weather serued them so well,
That in one day they with the coast did fall ;
Whereas they readie found them to repell,
Great hostes of men in order martiall,
Which them forbad to land, and footing did
    forstall.

5

But nathemore would they from land refraine,
But when as nigh vnto the shore they drew,
That foot of man might sound the bottome
    plaine,
Talus into the sea did forth issew,
Though darts from shore and stones they at
    him threw ;
And wading through the waues with stedfast
    sway,
Maugre the might of all those troupes in vew,
Did win the shore, whence he them chast away,
And made to fly, like doues, whom the Eagle
    doth affray.

6

The whyles Sir *Artegall*, with that old knight
Did forth descend, there being none them neare,
And forward marched to a towne in sight.
By this came tydings to the Tyrants eare,
By those, which earst did fly away for feare
Of their arriuall : wherewith troubled sore,
He all his forces streight to him did reare,
And forth issuing with his scouts afore,
Meant them to haue incountred, ere they left
    the shore.

7

But ere he marched farre, he with them met,
And fiercely charged them with all his force ;
But *Talus* sternely did vpon them set,
And brusht, and battred them without remorse,
That on the ground he left full many a corse ;
Ne any able was him to withstand,
But he them ouerthrew both man and horse,
That they lay scattred ouer all the land,
As thicke as doth the seede after the sowers
    hand.

8

Till *Artegall* him seeing so to rage,
  Willd him to stay, and signe of truce did make:
  To which all harkning, did a while asswage
  Their forces furie, and their terror slake ;
  Till he an Herauld cald, and to him spake,
  Willing him wend vnto the Tyrant streight,
  And tell him that not for such slaughters sake
  He thether came, but for to trie the right
Of fayre *Irenaes* cause with him in single fight.

9

And willed him for to reclayme with speed
  His scattred people, ere they all were slaine,
  And time and place conuenient to areed,
  In which they two the combat might darraine.
  Which message when *Grantorto* heard, full
    fayne
  And glad he was the slaughter so to stay,
  And pointed for the combat twixt them twayne
  The morrow next, ne gaue him longer day.
So sounded the retraite, and drew his folke
    away.

10

That night Sir *Artegall* did cause his tent
  There to be pitched on the open plaine ;
  For he had giuen streight commaundement,
  That none should dare him once to entertaine :
  Which none durst breake, though many would
    right faine
  For fayre *Irena*, whom they loued deare.
  But yet old *Sergis* did so well him paine,
  That from close friends, that dar'd not to
    appeare,
He all things did puruay, which for them need-
    full weare.

11

The morrow next, that was the dismall day,
  Appointed for *Irenas* death before,
  So soone as it did to the world display
  His chearefull face, and light to men restore,
  The heauy Mayd, to whom none tydings bore
  Of *Artegalls* arryuall, her to free,
  Lookt vp with eyes full sad and hart full sore;
  Weening her lifes last howre then neare to bee,
Sith no redemption nigh she did nor heare nor
    see.

12

Then vp she rose, and on her selfe did dight
  Most squalid garments, fit for such a day,
  And with dull countenance, and with dolefull
    spright,
  She forth was brought in sorrowfull dismay,
  For to receiue the doome of her decay.
  But comming to the place, and finding there
  Sir *Artegall*, in battailous array
  Wayting his foe, it did her dead hart cheare,
And new life to her lent, in midst of deadly feare.

13

Like as a tender Rose in open plaine,
  That with vntimely drought nigh withered was,
  And hung the head, soone as few drops of raine
  Thereon distill, and deaw her daintie face,
  Gins to looke vp, and with fresh wonted grace
  Dispreds the glorie of her leaues gay ;
  Such was *Irenas* countenance, such her case,
  When *Artegall* she saw in that array,
There wayting for the Tyrant, till it was farre
    day.

14

Who came at length, with proud presumpteous
    gate,
  Into the field, as if he fearelesse were,
  All armed in a cote of yron plate,
  Of great defence to ward the deadly feare,
  And on his head a steele cap he did weare
  Of colour rustie browne, but sure and strong ;
  And in his hand a huge Polaxe did beare,
  Whose steale was yron studded, but not long,
With which he wont to fight, to iustifie his
    wrong.

15

Of stature huge and hideous he was,
  Like to a Giant for his monstrous hight,
  And did in strength most sorts of men surpas,
  Ne euer any found his match in might ;
  Thereto he had great skill in single fight :
  His face was vgly, and his countenance sterne,
  That could haue frayd one with the very sight,
  And gaped like a gulfe, when he did gerne,
That whether man or monster one could scarse
    discerne.

16

Soone as he did within the listes appeare,
  With dreadfull looke he *Artegall* beheld,
  As if he would haue daunted him with feare,
  And grinning griesly, did against him weld
  His deadly weapon, which in hand he held.
  But th'Elfin swayne, that oft had seene like
    sight,
  Was with his ghastly count'nance nothing queld,
  But gan him streight to buckle to the fight,
And cast his shield about, to be in readie plight.

17

The trompets sound, and they together goe,
  With dreadfull terror, and with fell intent ;
  And their huge strokes full daungerously bestow,
  To doe most dammage, where as most they
    ment.
  But with such force and furie violent,
  The tyrant thundred his thicke blowes so fast,
  That through the yron walles their way they
    rent,
  And euen to the vitall parts they past,
Ne ought could them endure, but all they cleft
    or brast.

18

Which cruell outrage when as *Artegall*
Did well auize, thenceforth with warie heed
He shund his strokes, where euer they did fall,
And way did giue vnto their gracelesse speed :
As when a skilfull Marriner doth reed
A storme approching, that doth perill threat,
He will not bide the daunger of such dread,
But strikes his sayles, and vereth his mainsheat,
And lends vnto it leaue the emptie ayre to beat.

19

So did the Faerie knight himselfe abeare,
And stouped oft his head from shame to shield ;
No shame to stoupe, ones head more high to
reare,
And much to gaine, a litle for to yield ;
So stoutest knights doen oftentimes in field.
But still the tyrant sternely at him layd,
And did his yron axe so nimbly wield,
That many wounds into his flesh it made,
And with his burdenous blowes him sore did
ouerlade.

20

Yet when as fit aduantage he did spy,
The whiles the cursed felon high did reare
His cruell hand, to smite him mortally,
Vnder his stroke he to him stepping neare,
Right in the flanke him strooke with deadly
dreare,
That the gore bloud thence gushing grieuously,
Did vnderneath him like a pond appeare,
And all his armour did with purple dye ;
Thereat he brayed loud, and yelled dreadfully.

21

Yet the huge stroke, which he before intended,
Kept on his course, as he did it direct,
And with such monstrous poise adowne
descended,
That seemed nought could him from death
protect :
But he it well did ward with wise respect,
And twixt him and the blow his shield did cast,
Which thereon seizing, tooke no great effect,
But byting deepe therein did sticke so fast,
That by no meanes it backe againe he forth
could wrast.

22

Long while he tug'd and stroue, to get it out,
And all his powre applyed thereunto,
That he therewith the knight drew all about :
Nathlesse, for all that euer he could doe,
His axe he could not from his shield vndoe:
Which *Artegall* perceiuing, strooke no more,
But loosing soone his shield, did it forgoe,
And whiles he combred was therewith so sore,
He gan at him let driue more fiercely then afore.

23

So well he him pursew'd, that at the last,
He stroke him with *Chrysaor* on the hed,
That with the souse thereof full sore aghast,
He staggered to and fro in doubtfull sted.
Againe whiles he him saw so ill bested,
He did him smite with all his might and maine,
That falling on his mother earth he fed :
Whom when he saw prostrated on the plaine,
He lightly reft his head, to ease him of his paine.

24

Which when the people round about him saw,
They shouted all for ioy of his successe,
Glad to be quit from that proud Tyrants awe,
Which with strong powre did them long time
oppresse ;
And running all with greedie ioyfulnesse
To faire *Irena*, at her feet did fall,
And her adored with due humblenesse,
As their true Liege and Princesse naturall ;
And eke her champions glorie sounded ouer all.

25

Who streight her leading with meete maiestie
Vnto the pallace, where their kings did rayne,
Did her therein establish peaceablie,
And to her kingdomes seat restore agayne ;
And all such persons, as did late maintayne
That Tyrants part, with close or open ayde,
He sorely punished with heauie payne ;
That in short space, whiles there with her he
stayd,
Not one was left, that durst her once haue
disobayd.

26

During which time, that he did there remaine,
His studie was true Iustice how to deale,
And day and night employ'd his busie paine
How to reforme that ragged common-weale :
And that same yron man which could reueale
All hidden crimes, through all that realme he
sent,
To search out those, that vsd to rob and steale,
Or did rebell gainst lawfull gouernment ;
On whom he did inflict most grieuous punish-
ment.

27

But ere he could reforme it thoroughly,
He through occasion called was away,
To Faerie Court, that of necessity
His course of Iustice he was forst to stay,
And *Talus* to reuoke from the right way,
In which he was that Realme for to redresse.
But enuies cloud still dimmeth vertues ray.
So hauing freed *Irena* from distresse,
He tooke his leaue of her, there left in heauinesse

28

Tho as he backe returned from that land,
  And there arriu'd againe, whence forth he set,
  He had not passed farre vpon the strand,
  When as two old ill fauour'd Hags he met,
  By the way side being together set,
  Two griesly creatures ; and, to that their faces
  Most foule and filthie were, their garments yet
  Being all rag d and tatter'd, their disgraces
Did much the more augment, and made most
    vgly cases.

29

The one of them, that elder did appeare,
  With her dull eyes did seeme to looke askew,
  That her mis-shape much helpt ; and her
    foule heare
Hung loose and loathsomely : Thereto her hew
  Was wan and leane, that all her teeth arew,
  And all her bones might through her cheekes
    be red ;
  Her lips were like raw lether, pale and blew,
  And as she spake, therewith she slauered ;
Yet spake she seldom, but thought more, the
    lesse she sed.

30

Her hands were foule and durtie, neuer washt
  In all her life, with long nayles ouer raught,
  Like puttocks clawes : with th'one of which
    she scracht
Her cursed head, although it itched naught ;
  The other held a snake with venime fraught,
  On which she fed, and gnawed hungrily,
  As if that long she had not eaten ought ;
  That round about her iawes one might descry
The bloudie gore and poyson dropping loth-
    somely.

31

Her name was *Enuie*, knowen well thereby ;
  Whose nature is to grieue, and grudge at all,
  That euer she sees doen prays-worthily,
  Whose sight to her is greatest crosse, may fall,
  And worketh so, that makes her eat her gall.
  For when she wanteth other thing to eat,
  She feedes on her owne maw vnnaturall,
  And of her owne foule entrayles makes her
    meat ;
Meat fit for such a monsters monsterous dyeat.

32

And if she hapt of any good to heare,
  That had to any happily betid,
  Then would she inly fret, and grieue, and teare
  Her flesh for felnesse, which she inward hid :
  But if she heard of ill, that any did,
  Or harme, that any had, then would she make
  Great cheare, like one vnto a banquet bid ;
  And in anothers losse great pleasure take,
As she had got thereby, and gayned a great stake.

33

The other nothing better was, then shee ;
  Agreeing in bad will and cancred kynd,
  But in bad maner they did disagree :
  For what so *Enuie* good or bad did fynd,
  She did conceale, and murder her owne mynd ;
  But this, what euer euill she conceiued,
  Did spred abroad, and throw in th'open wynd.
  Yet this in all her words might be perceiued,
That all she sought, was mens good name to
    haue bereaued.

34

For what soeuer good by any sayd,
  Or doen she heard, she would streightwayes
    inuent,
  How to depraue, or slaunderously vpbrayd,
  Or to misconstrue of a mans intent,
  And turne to ill the thing, that well was ment.
  Therefore she vsed often to resort,
  To common haunts, and companies frequent,
  To hearke what any one did good report,
To blot the same with blame, or wrest in wicked
    sort.

35

And if that any ill she heard of any,
  She would it eeke, and make much worse by
    telling,
  And take great ioy to publish it to many,
  That euery matter worse was for her melling.
  Her name was hight *Detraction*, and her
    dwelling
Was neare to *Enuie*, euen her neighbour next ;
  A wicked hag, and *Enuy* selfe excelling
  In mischiefe : for her selfe she onely vext ;
But this same both her selfe, and others eke
    perplext.

36

Her face was vgly, and her mouth distort,
  Foming with poyson round about her gils,
  In which her cursed tongue full sharpe and short
  Appear'd like Aspis sting, that closely kils,
  Or cruelly does wound, whom so she wils :
  A distaffe in her other hand she had,
  Vpon the which she litle spinnes, but spils,
  And faynes to weaue false tales and leasings bad,
To throw amongst the good, which others had
    disprad.

37

These two now had themselues combynd in one,
  And linckt together gainst Sir *Artegall*,
  For whom they wayted as his mortall fone,
  How they might make him into mischiefe fall,
  For freeing from their snares *Irena* thrall,
  Besides vnto themselues they gotten had
  A monster, which the *Blatant beast* men call,
  A dreadfull feend of gods and men ydrad,
Whom they by slights allur'd, and to their
    purpose lad.

38

Such were these Hags, and so vnhandsome
   drest :
Who when they nigh approching, had espyde
Sir *Artegall* return'd from his late quest,
They both arose, and at him loudly cryde,
As it had bene two shepheards curres, had
   scryde
A rauenous Wolfe amongst the scattered
   flockes.
And *Enuie* first, as she that first him eyde,
Towards him runs, and with rude flaring
   lockes
About her eares, does beat her brest, and
   forhead knockes.

39

Then from her mouth the gobbet she does take,
The which whyleare she was so greedily
Deuouring, euen that halfe-gnawen snake,
And at him throwes it most despightfully.
The cursed Serpent, though she hungrily
Earst chawd thereon, yet was not all so dead,
But that some life remayned secretly,
And as he past afore withouten dread,
Bit him behind, that long the marke was to be
   read.

40

Then th'other comming neare, gan him reuile,
And fouly rayle, with all she could inuent ;
Saying, that he had with vnmanly guile,
And foule abusion both his honour blent,
And that bright sword, the sword of Iustice
   lent,
Had stayned with reprochfull crueltie,
In guiltlesse blood of many an innocent :
As for *Grandtorto*, him with treacherie
And traynes hauing surpriz'd, he fouly did
   to die.

41

Thereto the Blatant beast by them set on
At him began aloud to barke and bay,
With bitter rage and fell contention,
That all the woods and rockes nigh to that way,
Began to quake and tremble with dismay ;
And all the aire rebellowed againe.
So dreadfully his hundred tongues did bray,
And euermore those hags them selues did paine,
To sharpen him, and their owne cursed tongs
   did straine.

42

And still among most bitter wordes they spake,
Most shamefull, most vnrighteous, most
   vntrew,
That they the mildest man aliue would make
Forget his patience, and yeeld vengeaunce dew
To her, that so false sclaunders at him threw.
And more to make them pierce and wound
   more deepe,
She with the sting, which in her vile tongue
   grew,
Did sharpen them, and in fresh poyson steepe :
Yet he past on, and seem'd of them to take no
   keepe.

43

But *Talus* hearing her so lewdly raile,
And speake so ill of him, that well deserued,
Would her haue chastiz'd with his yron flaile,
If her Sir *Artegall* had not preserued,
And him forbidden, who his heast obserued.
So much the more at him still did she scold,
And stones did cast, yet he for nought would
   swerue
From his right course, but still the way did
   hold
To Faery Court, where what him fell shall else
   be told.

THE SIXTE
BOOKE OF THE
FAERIE QVEENE.

Contayning

THE LEGEND OF S. CALIDORE
OR
OF COVRTESIE.

1

THE waies, through which my weary steps I
   guyde,
In this delightfull land of Faery,
Are so exceeding spacious and wyde,
And sprinckled with such sweet variety,
Of all that pleasant is to eare or eye,
That I nigh rauisht with rare thoughts delight,
My tedious trauell doe forget thereby ;
And when I gin to feele decay of might,
It strength to me supplies, and chears my dulled
   spright.

2

Such secret comfort, and such heauenly
   pleasures,
Ye sacred imps, that on *Parnasso* dwell,
And there the keeping haue of learnings
   threasures,
Which doe all worldly riches farre excell,
Into the mindes of mortall men doe well,
And goodly fury into them infuse ;
Guyde ye my footing, and conduct me well
In these strange waies, where neuer foote
   did vse,
Ne none can find, but who was taught them by
   the Muse.

3

Reuele to me the sacred noursery
Of vertue, which with you doth there re-
   maine,
Where it in siluer bowre does hidden ly
From view of men, and wicked worlds dis-
   daine.
Since it at first was by the Gods with paine
Planted in earth, being deriu'd at furst
From heauenly seedes of bounty soueraine,
And by them long with carefull labour
   nurst,
Till it to ripenesse grew, and forth to honour
   burst.

4

Amongst them all growes not a fayrer flowre,
Then is the bloosme of comely courtesie,
Which though it on a lowly stalke doe bowre,
Yet brancheth forth in braue nobilitie,
And spreds it selfe through all ciuilitie :
Of which though present age doe plenteous
   seeme,
Yet being matcht with plaine Antiquitie,
Ye will them all but fayned showes esteeme,
Which carry colours faire, that feeble eies
   misdeeme.

5

But in the triall of true curtesie,
  Its now so farre from that, which then it was,
  That it indeed is nought but forgerie,
  Fashion'd to please the eies of them, that pas,
  Which see not perfect things but in a glas :
  Yet is that glasse so gay, that it can blynd
  The wisest sight, to thinke gold that is bras.
  But vertues seat is deepe within the mynd,
And not in outward shows, but inward thoughts
        defynd.

6

But where shall I in all Antiquity
  So faire a patterne finde, where may be seene
  The goodly praise of Princely curtesie,
  As in your selfe, O soueraine Lady Queene,
  In whose pure minde, as in a mirrour sheene,
  It showes, and with her brightnesse doth
        inflame
  The eyes of all, which thereon fixed beene ;
  But meriteth indeede an higher name :
Yet so from low to high vplifted is your name.

7

Then pardon me, most dreaded Soueraine,
  That from your selfe I doe this vertue bring,
  And to your selfe doe it returne againe :
  So from the Ocean all riuers spring,
  And tribute backe repay as to their King.
  Right so from you all goodly vertues well
  Into the rest, which round about you ring,
  Faire Lords and Ladies, which about you dwell,
And doe adorne your Court, where courtesies
        excell.

Cant. I.

∞∞∞∞∞∞∞∞∞∞∞∞∞∞∞∞∞∞∞

  Calidore saues from Maleffort,
    A Damzell vsed vylde :
  Doth vanquish Crudor, and doth make
    Briana wexe more mylde.

∞∞∞∞∞∞∞∞∞∞∞∞∞∞∞∞∞∞∞

1

Of Court it seemes, men Courtesie doe call,
  For that it there most vseth to abound ;
  And well beseemeth that in Princes hall
  That vertue should be plentifully found,
  Which of all goodly manners is the ground,
  And roote of ciuill conuersation.
  Right so in Faery court it did redound,
  Where curteous Knights and Ladies most
        did won
Of all on earth, and made a matchlesse paragon.

2

But mongst them all was none more courteous
        Knight,
  Then *Calidore*, beloued ouer all,
  In whom it seemes, that gentlenesse of spright
  And manners mylde were planted naturall ;
  To which he adding comely guize withall,
  And gracious speach, did steale mens hearts
        away.
  Nathlesse thereto he was full stout and tall,
  And well approu'd in batteilous affray,
That him did much renowme, and far his fame
        display.

3

Ne was there Knight, ne was there Lady found
  In Faery court, but him did deare embrace,
  For his faire vsage and conditions sound,
  The which in all mens liking gayned place,
  And with the greatest purchast greatest grace :
  Which he could wisely vse, and well apply,
  To please the best, and th'euill to embase.
  For he loathd leasing, and base flattery,
And loued simple truth and stedfast honesty.

4

And now he was in trauell on his way,
  Vppon an hard aduenture sore bestad,
  Whenas by chaunce he met vppon a day
  With *Artegall*, returning yet halfe sad
  From his late conquest, which he gotten had.
  Who whenas each of other had a sight,
  They knew them selues, and both their
        persons rad :
  When *Calidore* thus first ; Haile noblest
        Knight
Of all this day on ground, that breathen liuing
        spright.

5

Now tell, if please you, of the good successe,
  Which ye haue had in your late enterprize.
  To whom Sir *Artegall* gan to expresse
  His whole exploite, and valorous emprize,
  In order as it did to him arize.
  Now happy man (sayd then Sir *Calidore*)
  Which haue so goodly, as ye can deuize,
  Atchieu'd so hard a quest, as few before ;
That shall you most renowmed make for
        euermore.

6

But where ye ended haue, now I begin
  To tread an endlesse trace, withouten guyde,
  Or good direction, how to enter in,
  Or how to issue forth in waies vntryde,
  In perils strange, in labours long and wide,
  In which although good Fortune me befall,
  Yet shall it not by none be testifyde.
  What is that quest (quoth then Sir *Artegall*)
That you into such perils presently doth call ?

7

The Blattant Beast (quoth he) I doe pursew,
 And through the world incessantly doe chase,
 Till I him ouertake, or else subdew :
 Yet know I not or how, or in what place
 To find him out, yet still I forward trace.
 What is that Blattant Beast ? (then he
  replide.)
 It is a Monster bred of hellishe race,
 (Then answerd he) which often hath annoyd
Good Knights and Ladies true, and many else
  destroyd.

8

Of *Cerberus* whilome he was begot,
 And fell *Chimæra* in her darkesome den,
 Through fowle commixture of his filthy blot ;
 Where he was fostred long in *Stygian* fen,
 Till he to perfect ripenesse grew, and then
 Into this wicked world he forth was sent,
 To be the plague and scourge of wretched men :
 Whom with vile tongue and venemous intent
He sore doth wound, and bite, and cruelly
  torment.

9

Then since the saluage Island I did leaue,
 Sayd *Artegall*, I such a Beast did see,
 The which did seeme a thousand tongues to
  haue,
 That all in spight and malice did agree,
 With which he bayd and loudly barkt at mee,
 As if that he attonce would me deuoure.
 But I that knew my selfe from perill free,
 Did nought regard his malice nor his powre,
But he the more his wicked poyson forth did
  poure.

10

That surely is that Beast (saide *Calidore*)
 Which I pursue, of whom I am right glad
 To heare these tidings, which of none afore
 Through all my weary trauell I haue had :
 Yet now some hope your words vnto me add.
 Now God you speed (quoth then Sir *Artegall*)
 And keepe your body from the daunger drad :
 For ye haue much adoe to deale withall.
So both tooke goodly leaue, and parted seuerall.

11

Sir *Calidore* thence trauelled not long,
 When as by chaunce a comely Squire he found,
 That thorough some more mighty enemies
  wrong,
 Both hand and foote vnto a tree was bound :
 Who seeing him from farre, with piteous sound
 Of his shrill cries him called to his aide.
 To whom approching, in that painefull stound
 When he him saw, for no demaunds he staide,
But first him losde, and afterwards thus to him
  saide.

12

Vnhappy Squire, what hard mishap thee brought
 Into this bay of perill and disgrace ?
 What cruell hand thy wretched thraldome
  wrought,
 And thee captyued in this shamefull place ?
 To whom he answerd thus ; My haplesse case
 Is not occasiond through my misdesert,
 But through misfortune, which did me abase
 Vnto this shame, and my young hope subuert,
Ere that I in her guilefull traines was well
  expert.

13

Not farre from hence, vppon yond rocky hill,
 Hard by a streight there stands a castle strong,
 Which doth obserue a custome lewd and ill,
 And it hath long mayntaind with mighty wrong :
 For may no Knight nor Lady passe along
 That way, (and yet they needs must passe
  that way,)
 By reason of the streight, and rocks among,
 But they that Ladies lockes doe shaue away,
And that knights berd for toll, which they for
  passage pay.

14

A shamefull vse as euer I did heare,
 Sayd *Calidore*, and to be ouerthrowne.
 But by what meanes did they at first it reare,
 And for what cause, tell if thou haue it knowne.
 Sayd then that Squire : The Lady which doth
  owne
 This Castle, is by name *Briana* hight.
 Then which a prouder Lady liueth none :
 She long time hath deare lou'd a doughty
  Knight,
And sought to win his loue by all the meanes
  she might.

15

His name is *Crudor*, who through high disdaine
 And proud despight of his selfe pleasing mynd,
 Refused hath to yeeld her loue againe,
 Vntill a Mantle she for him doe fynd,
 With beards of Knights and locks of Ladies lynd.
 Which to prouide, she hath this Castle dight,
 And therein hath a Seneschall assynd,
 Cald *Maleffort*, a man of mickle might,
Who executes her wicked will, with worse
  despight.

16

He this same day, as I that way did come
 With a faire Damzell, my beloued deare,
 In execution of her lawlesse doome,
 Did set vppon vs flying both for feare :
 For little bootes against him hand to reare.
 Me first he tooke, vnhable to withstond ;
 And whiles he her pursued euery where,
 Till his returne vnto this tree he bond :
Ne wote I surely, whether her he yet haue fond.

17

Thus whiles they spake, they heard a ruefull
    shrieke
Of one loud crying, which they streight way
    ghest,
That it was she, the which for helpe did seeke.
Tho looking vp vnto the cry to lest,
They saw that Carle from farre, with hand vnblest
Hayling that mayden by the yellow heare,
That all her garments from her snowy brest,
And from her head her lockes he nigh did teare,
Ne would he spare for pitty, nor refraine for
    feare.

18

Which haynous sight when *Calidore* beheld,
Eftsoones he loosd that Squire, and so him left,
With hearts dismay and inward dolour queld,
For to pursue that villaine, which had reft
That piteous spoile by so iniurious theft.
Whom ouertaking, loude to him he cryde ;
Leaue faytor quickely that misgotten weft
To him, that hath it better iustifyde,
And turne thee soone to him, of whom thou art
    defyde.

19

Who hearkning to that voice, him selfe vpreard,
And seeing him so fiercely towardes make,
Against him stoutly ran, as nought afeard,
But rather more enrag'd for those words sake ;
And with sterne count'naunce thus vnto him
    spake.
Art thou the caytiue, that defyest me,
And for this Mayd, whose party thou doest take,
Wilt giue thy beard, though it but little bee ?
Yet shall it not her lockes for raunsome fro me
    free.

20

With that he fiercely at him flew, and layd
On hideous strokes with most importune might,
That oft he made him stagger as vnstayd,
And oft recuile to shunne his sharpe desp'ght.
But *Calidore*, that was well skild in fight,
Him long forbore, and still his spirite spar'd,
Lying in waite, how him he damadge might.
But when he felt him shrinke, and come to
    ward,
He greater grew, and gan to driue at him more
    hard.

21

Like as a water streame, whose swelling sourse
Shall driue a Mill, within strong banckes is pent,
And long restrayned of his ready course ;
So soone as passage is vnto him lent,
Breakes forth, and makes his way more violent.
Such was the fury of Sir *Calidore*,
When once he felt his foeman to relent ;
He fiercely him pursu'd, and pressed sore,
Who as he still decayd, so he encreased more

22

The heauy burden of whose dreadfull might
When as the Carle no longer could sustaine,
His heart gan faint, and streight he tooke his
    flight
Toward the Castle, where if need constraine,
His hope of refuge vsed to remaine.
Whom *Calidore* perceiuing fast to flie,
He him pursu'd and chaced through the plaine,
That he for dread of death gan loude to crie
Vnto the ward, to open to him hastilie.

23

They from the wall him seeing so aghast,
The gate soone opened to receiue him in,
But *Calidore* did follow him so fast,
That euen in the Porch he him did win,
And cleft his head asunder to his chin.
The carkasse tumbling downe within the dore,
Did choke the entraunce with a lumpe of sin,
That it could not be shut, whilest *Calidore*
Did enter in, and slew the Porter on the flore

24

With that the rest, the which the Castle kept,
About him flockt, and hard at him did lay ;
But he them all from him full lightly swept,
As doth a Steare, in heat of sommers day,
With his long taile the bryzes brush away.
Thence passing forth, into the hall he came,
Where of the Lady selfe in sad dismay
He was ymett, who with vncomely shame
Gan him salute, and fowle vpbrayd with faulty
    blame.

25

False traytor Knight, (sayd she) no Knight at
    all,
But scorne of armes that hast with guilty hand
Murdred my men, and slaine my Seneschall ;
Now comest thou to rob my house vnmand,
And spoile my selfe, that can not thee with-
    stand ?
Yet doubt thou not, but that some better
    Knight
Then thou, that shall thy treason vnderstand,
Will it auenge, and pay thee with thy right :
And if none do, yet shame shal thee with shame
    requight.

26

Much was the Knight abashed at that word ;
Yet answerd thus ; Not vnto me the shame,
But to the shamefull doer it afford.
Bloud is no blemish ; for it is no blame
To punish those, that doe deserue the same ;
But they that breake bands of ciuilitie,
And wicked customes make, those doe defame
Both noble armes and gentle curtesie.
No greater shame to man then inhumanitie.

27

Then doe your selfe, for dread of shame, forgoe
  This euill manner, which ye here maintaine,
  And doe in stead thereof mild curt'sie showe
To all, that passe.   That shall you glory gaine
More then his loue, which thus ye seeke t'obtaine.
  Wherewith all full of wrath, she thus replyde ;
Vile recreant, know that I doe much disdaine
Thy courteous lore, that doest my loue deride,
Who scornes thy ydle scoffe, and bids thee be
    defyde.

28

To take defiaunce at a Ladies word
  (Quoth he) I hold it no indignity ;
But were he here, that would it with his sword
Abett, perhaps he mote it deare aby.
  Cowherd (quoth she) were not, that thou
    wouldst fly,
Ere he doe come, he should be soone in place.
If I doe so, (sayd he) then liberty
I leaue to you, for aye me to disgrace
With all those shames, that erst ye spake me
    to deface.

29

With that a Dwarfe she cald to her in hast,
  And taking from her hand a ring of gould,
A priuy token, which betweene them past,
Bad him to flie with all the speed he could,
  To *Crudor*, and desire him that he would
Vouchsafe to reskue her against a Knight,
Who through strong powre had now her self
    in hould,
Hauing late slaine her Seneschall in fight,
And all her people murdred with outragious
    might.

30

The Dwarfe his way did hast, and went all night;
  But *Calidore* did with her there abyde
The comming of that so much threatned Knight,
  Where that discourteous Dame with scornfull
    pryde,
And fowle entreaty him indignifyde,
That yron heart it hardly could sustaine :
  Yet he, that could his wrath full wisely guyde,
Did well endure her womanish disdaine,
And did him selfe from fraile impatience re-
    fraine.

31

The morrow next, before the lampe of light
  Aboue the earth vpreard his flaming head,
The Dwarfe, which bore that message to her
    knight,
Brought aunswere backe, that ere he tasted bread,
He would her succour, and aliue or dead
  Her foe deliuer vp into her hand :
Therefore he wild her doe away all dread ;
And that of him she mote assured stand,
He sent to her his basenet, as a faithfull band.

32

Thereof full blyth the Lady streight became,
  And gan t'augment her bitternesse much more
Yet no whit more appalled for the same,
  Ne ought dismayed was Sir *Calidore*,
But rather did more chearefull seeme therefore.
  And hauing soone his armes about him dight,
Did issue forth, to meete his foe afore ;
Where long he stayed not, when as a Knight
He spide come pricking on with al his powre
    and might.

33

Well weend he streight, that he should be the
    same,
Which tooke in hand her quarrell to maintaine ;
Ne stayd to aske if it were he by name,
  But coucht his speare, and ran at him amaine.
They bene ymett in middest of the plaine,
  With so fell fury, and dispiteous forse,
That neither could the others stroke sustaine,
But rudely rowld to ground both man and
    horse,
Neither of other taking pitty nor remorse.

34

But *Calidore* vprose againe full light,
  Whiles yet his foe lay fast in sencelesse sound,
Yet would he not him hurt, although he might :
  For shame he weend a sleeping wight to wound.
But when *Briana* saw that drery stound,
  There where she stood vppon the Castle wall,
She deem'd him sure to haue bene dead on
    ground,
And made such piteous mourning therewith all,
That from the battlements she ready seem'd
    to fall.

35

Nathlesse at length him selfe he did vpreare
  In lustlesse wise, as if against his will,
Ere he had slept his fill, he wakened were,
  And gan to stretch his limbs ; which feeling ill
Of his late fall, a while he rested still :
  But when he saw his foe before in vew,
He shooke off luskishnesse, and courage chill
Kindling a fresh, gan battell to renew,
To proue if better foote then horsebacke would
    ensew.

36

There then began a fearefull cruell fray
  Betwixt them two, for maystery of might.
For both were wondrous practicke in that play,
  And passing well expert in single fight,
And both inflam'd with furious despight :
  Which as it still encreast, so still increast
Their cruell strokes and terrible affright ;
Ne once for ruth their rigour they releast,
Ne once to breath a while their angers tempest
    ceast.

37

Thus long they trac'd and trauerst to and fro,
  And tryde all waies, how each mote entrance
  make
Into the life of his malignant foe ;
They hew'd their helmes, and plates asunder
  brake,
As they had potshares bene ; for nought mote
  slake
Their greedy vengeaunces, but goary blood,
That at the last like to a purple lake
Of bloudy gore congeal'd about them stood,
Which from their riuen sides forth gushed like
  a flood.

38

At length it chaunst, that both their hands on hie
At once did heaue, with all their powre and might,
Thinking the vtmost of their force to trie,
And proue the finall fortune of the fight :
But *Calidore*, that was more quicke of sight,
And nimbler handed, then his enemie,
Preuented him before his stroke could light,
And on the helmet smote him formerlie,
That made him stoupe to ground with meeke
  humilitie.

39

And ere he could recouer foot againe,
  He following that faire aduantage fast,
  His stroke redoubled with such might and
  maine,
That him vpon the ground he groueling cast ;
And leaping to him light, would haue vnlast
His Helme, to make vnto his vengeance way.
Who seeing, in what daunger he was plast,
Cryde out, Ah mercie Sir, doe me not slay,
But saue my life, which lot before your foot
  doth lay.

40

With that his mortall hand a while he stayd,
  And hauing somewhat calm'd his wrathfull heat
  With goodly patience, thus he to him sayd ;
And is the boast of that proud Ladies threat,
That menaced me from the field to beat,
Now brought to this ? By this now may ye learne,
Strangers no more so rudely to intreat,
But put away proud looke, and vsage sterne,
The which shal nought to you but foule dis-
  honor yearne.

41

For nothing is more blamefull to a knight,
  That court'sie doth as well as armes professe,
  How euer strong and fortunate in fight,
Then the reproch of pride and cruelnesse.
In vaine he seeketh others to suppresse,
Who hath not learnd him selfe first to subdew :
All flesh is frayle, and full of ficklenesse,
Subiect to fortunes chance, still chaunging new;
What haps to day to me, to morrow may to you.

42

Who will not mercie vnto others shew,
  How can he mercy euer hope to haue ?
  To pay each with his owne is right and dew.
Yet since ye mercie now doe need to craue,
I will it graunt, your hopelesse life to saue ;
With these conditions, which I will propound :
First, that ye better shall your selfe behaue
Vnto all errant knights, whereso on ground ;
Next that ye Ladies ayde in euery stead and
  stound.

43

The wretched man, that all this while did dwell
  In dread of death, his heasts did gladly heare,
  And promist to performe his precept well,
And whatsoeuer else he would requere.
So suffring him to rise, he made him sweare
By his owne sword, and by the crosse thereon,
To take *Briana* for his louing fere,
Withouten dowre or composition ;
But to release his former foule condition.

44

All which accepting, and with faithfull oth
  Bynding himselfe most firmely to obay,
  He vp arose, how euer liefe or loth,
And swore to him true fealtie for aye.
Then forth he cald from sorrowfull dismay
The sad *Briana*, which all this beheld :
Who comming forth yet full of late affray,
Sir *Calidore* vpcheard, and to her teld
All this accord, to which he *Crudor* had compeld.

45

Whereof she now more glad, then sory earst,
  All ouercome with infinite affect,
  For his exceeding courtesie, that pearst
Her stubborne hart with inward deepe effect,
Before his feet her selfe she did proiect,
And him adoring as her liues deare Lord,
With all due thankes, and dutifull respect,
Her selfe acknowledg'd bound for that accord,
By which he had to her both life and loue
  restord.

46

So all returning to the Castle glad,
  Most ioyfully she them did entertaine,
  Where goodly glee and feast to them she made,
To shew her thankefull mind and meaning
  faine,
By all the meanes she mote it best explaine:
And after all, vnto Sir *Calidore*
She freely gaue that Castle for his paine,
And her selfe bound to him for euermore ;
So wondrously now chaung'd, from that she
  was afore.

47

But *Calidore* himselfe would not retaine
Nor land nor fee. for hyre of his good deede,
But gaue them streight vnto that Squire againe,
Whom from her Seneschall he lately freed,
And to his damzell as their rightfull meed,
For recompence of all their former wrong :
There he remaind with them right well agreed,
Till of his wounds he wexed hole and strong,
And then to his first quest he passed forth along.

Cant. II.

Calidore sees young Tristram slay
A proud discourteous knight,
He makes him Squire, and of him learnes
his state and present plight.

I

What vertue is so fitting for a knight,
Or for a Ladie, whom a knight should loue,
As Curtesie, to bzare themselues aright
To all ot each degree, as doth behoue ?
For whether they be placed high aboue,
Or low beneath, yet ought they well to know
Their good, that none them rightly may
  reproue
Of rudenesse, for not yeelding what they owe :
Great skill it is such duties timely to bestow.

2

Thereto great helpe dame Nature selfe doth lend:
For some so goodly gratious are by kind,
That euery action doth them much commend,
And in the eyes of men great liking find ;
Which others, that haue greater skill in mind,
Though they enforce themselues, cannot attaine.
For euerie thing, to which one is inclin'd,
Doth best become, and greatest grace doth
  gaine :
Yet praise likewise deserue good thewes, enforst
  with paine.

3

That well in courteous *Calidore* appeares,
Whose euery deed and word, that he did say,
Was like enchantment, that through both the
  eyes,
And both the eares did steale the hart away.
He now againe is on his former way,
To follow his first quest, when as he spyde
A tall young man from thence not farre away,
Fighting on foot, as well he him descryde,
Against an armed knight, that did on horse-
  backe ryde.

4

And them beside a Ladie faire he saw,
Standing alone on foot. in foule array :
To whom himselfe he hastily did draw,
To weet the cause of so vncomely fray,
And to depart them, if so be he may.
But ere he came in place, that youth had kild
That armed knight. that low on ground he lay ;
Which when he saw. his hart was inly child
With great amazement, and his thought with
  wonder fild.

5

Him stedfastly he markt, and saw to bee
A goodly youth of amiable grace,
Yet but a slender slip, that scarse did see
Yet seuenteene yeares. but tall and faire of face
That sure he deem'd him borne ot noble race.
All in a woodmans iacket he was clad
Of Lincolne greene, belayd with siluer lace ;
And on his head an hood with aglets sprad,
And by his side his hunters horne he hanging
  had.

6

Buskins he wore of costliest cordwayne,
Pinckt vpon gold, and paled part per part,
As then the guize was for each gentle swayne ;
In his right hand he held a trembling dart,
Whose fellow he before had sent apart ;
And in his left he held a sharpe borespeare,
With which he wont to launch the saluage hart
Of many a Lyon, and of many a Beare
That first vnto his hand in chase did happen
  neare.

7

Whom *Calidore* a while well hauing vewed,
At length bespake ; What meanes this,
  gentle swaine ?
Why hath thy hand too bold it selfe embrewed
In blood of knight, the which by thee is slaine,
By thee no knight ; which armes impugneth
  plaine ?
Certes (said he) loth were I to haue broken
The law of armes ; yet breake it should againe,
Rather then let my selfe of wight be stroken,
So long as these two armes were able to be
  wroken.

8

For not I him, as this his Ladie here
May witnesse well, did offer first to wrong,
Ne surely thus vnarm'd I likely were ;
But he me first, through pride and puissance
  strong
Assayld, not knowing what to armes doth long.
Perdie great blame, (then said Sir *Calidore*)
For armed knight a wight vnarm'd to wrong.
But then aread, thou gentle chyld, wherefore
Betwixt you two began this strife and sterne
  vprore.

9
That shall I sooth (said he) to you declare.
I whose vnryper yeares are yet vnfit
For thing of weight, or worke of greater care,
Doe spend my dayes,and bend my carelesse wit
To saluage chace, where I thereon may hit
In all this forrest, and wyld wooddie raine :
Where, as this day I was enraunging it,
I chaunst to meete this knight, who there lyes
      slaine,
Together with this Ladie, passing on the plaine.

10
The knight, as ye did see, on horsebacke was,
And this his Ladie, (that him ill became,)
On her faire feet by his horse side did pas
Through thicke and thin, vnfit for any Dame,
Yet not content, more to increase his shame,
When so she lagged, as she needs mote so,
He with his speare, that was to him great blame,
Would thumpe her forward,and inforce to goe,
Weeping to him in vaine, and making piteous
      woe.

11
Which when I saw, as they me passed by,
Much was I moued in indignant mind,
And gan to blame him for such cruelty
Towards a Ladie, whom with vsage kind
He rather should haue taken vp behind.
Wherewith he wroth,and full of proud disdaine,
Tooke in foule scorne, that I such fault did find,
And me in lieu thereof reuil'd againe,
Threatning to chastize me, as doth t'a chyld
      pertaine.

12
Which I no lesse disdayning, backe returned
His scornefull taunts vnto his teeth againe,
That he streight way with haughtie choler
      burned,   [twaine ;
And with his speare strooke me one stroke or
Which I enforst to beare though to my paine,
Cast to requite, and with a slender dart,
Fellow of this I beare, throwne not in vaine,
Strooke him, as seemeth, vnderneath the hart,
That through the wound his spirit shortly did
      depart.

13
Much did Sir *Calidore* admyre his speach
Tempred so well, but more admyr'd the stroke
That through the mayles had made so strong
      a breach
Into his hart, and had so sternely wroke
His wrath on him, that first occasion broke.
Yet rested not, but further gan inquire
Of that same Ladie, whether what he spoke,
Were soothly so, and that th'vnrighteous ire
Of her owne knight, had giuen him his owne
      due hire.

14
Of all which, when as she could nought deny,
But cleard that stripling of th'imputed blame,
Sayd then Sir *Calidore*; Neither will I [clame:
Him charge with guilt, but rather doe quite
For what he spake, for you he spake it, Dame :
And what he did, he did him selfe to saue :
Against both which that knight wrought
      knightlesse shame.
For knights and all men this by nature haue,
Towards all womenkind them kindly to behaue.

5
But sith that he is gone irreuocable,
Please it you Ladie, to vs to aread,
What cause could make him so dishonourable,
To driue you so on foot vnfit to tread,
And lackey by him, gainst all womanhead ?
Certes Sir knight (sayd she) full loth I were
To rayse a lyuing blame against the dead :
But since it me concernes, my selfe to clere,
I will the truth discouer,as it chaunst whylere.

16
This day, as he and I together roade
Vpon our way, to which we weren bent,
We chaunst to come foreby a couert glade
Within a wood, whereas a Ladie gent
Sate with a knight in ioyous iolliment
Of their franke loues, free from all gealous spyes:
Faire was the Ladie sure, that mote content
An hart, not carried with too curious eyes,
And vnto him did shew all louely courtesyes.

17
Whom when my knight did see so louely faire,
He inly gan her louer to enuy,
And wish, that he part of his spoyle might share.
Whereto when as my presence he did spy
To be a let, he bad me by and by
For to alight : but when as I was loth,
My loues owne part to leaue so suddenly,
He with strong hand down from his steed me
      throw'th,
And with presumpteous powre against that
      knight streight go'th.

18
Vnarm'd all was the knight, as then more meete
For Ladies seruice, and for loues delight,
Then fearing any foeman there to meete :
Whereof he taking oddes, streight bids him dight
Himselfe to yeeld his loue, or else to fight.
Whereat the other starting vp dismayd,
Yet boldly answer'd, as he rightly might ;
To leaue his loue he should be ill apayd,
In which he had good right gaynst all, that it
      gainesayd.

19

Yet since he was not presently in plight
  Her to defend, or his to iustifie,
  He him requested, as he was a knight,
  To lend him day his better right to trie,
  Or stay till he his armes, which were thereby,
  Might lightly fetch. But he was fierce and
  whot,
  Ne time would giue, nor any termes aby,
  But at him flew, and with his speare him smot;
From which to thinke to saue himselfe, it booted
  not.

20

Meane while his Ladie, which this outrage saw,
  Whilest they together for the quarrey stroue,
  Into the couert did her selfe withdraw,
  And closely hid her selfe within the groue.
  My knight hers soone, as seemes, to daunger
  droue
  And left sore wounded : but when her he mist,
  He woxe halfe mad, and in that rage gan roue
  And range through all the wood, where so he
  wist
She hidden was, and sought her so long, as
  him list.

21

But when as her he by no meanes could find,
  After long search and chauff, he turned backe
  Vnto the place, where me he left behind :
  There gan he me to curse and ban, for lacke
  Of that faire bootie, and with bitter wracke
  To wreake on me the guilt of his owne wrong.
  Of all which I yet glad to beare the packe,
  Stroue to appease him, and perswaded long:
But still his passion grew more violent and
  strong.

22

Then as it were t'auenge his wrath on mee,
  When forward we should fare, he flat refused
  To take me vp (as this young man did see)
  Vpon his steed, for no iust cause accused,
  But forst to trot on foot, and foule misused,
  Pounching me with the butt end of his speare,
  In vaine complayning, to be so abused.
  For he regarded neither playnt nor teare,
But more enforst my paine, the more my plaints
  to heare.

23

So passed we, till this young man vs met,
  And being moou'd with pittie of my plight,
  Spake, as was meet, for ease of my regret :
  Whereof befell, what now is in your sight.
  Now sure (then said Sir *Calidore*) and right
  Me seemes, that him befell by his owne fault :
  Who euer thinkes through confidence of might,
  Or through support of count'nance proud
  and hault
Towrong theweaker,oftfallesinhisowneassault.

24

Then turning backe vnto that gentle boy,
  Which had himselfe so stoutly well acquit ;
  Seeing his face so louely sterne and coy,
  And hearing th'answeres of his pregnant wit,
  He praysd it much, and much admyred it ;
  That sure he weend him borne of noble blood,
  With whom those graces did so goodly fit :
  And when he long had him beholding stood,
He burst into these words, as to him seemed
  good.

25

Faire gentle swayne, and yet as stout as fayre,
  That in these woods amongst the Nymphs
  dost wonne,
  Which daily may to thy sweete lookes repayre,
  As they are wont vnto *Latonaes* sonne,
  After his chace on woodie *Cynthus* donne :
  Well may I certes such an one thee read,
  As by thy worth thou worthily hast wonne,
  Or surely borne of some Heroicke sead,
That in thy face appeares and gratious goodly-
  head.

26

But should it not displease thee it to tell ;
  (Vnlesse thou in these woods thy selfe conceale,
  For loue amongst the woodie Gods to dwell;)
  I would thy selfe require thee to reueale,
  For deare affection and vnfayned zeale,
  Which to thy noble personage I beare,
  And wish thee grow in worship and great
  weale.
  For since the day that armes I first did reare,
I neuer saw in any greater hope appeare.

27

To whom then thus the noble youth ; May be
  Sir knight, that by discouering my estate,
  Harme may arise vnweeting vnto me ;
  Nathelesse, sith ye so courteous seemed late,
  To you I will not feare it to relate.
  Then wote ye that I am a Briton borne,
  Sonne of a King, how euer thorough fate
  Or fortune I my countrie haue forlorne,
And lost the crowne, which should my head by
  right adorne.

28

And *Tristram* is my name, the onely heire
  Of good king *Meliogras* which did rayne
  In Cornewale, till that he through liues
  despeire
  Vntimely dyde, before I did attaine
  Ripe yeares of reason, my right to maintaine.
  After whose death, his brother seeing mee
  An infant, weake a kingdome to sustaine,
  Vpon him tooke the roiall high degree,
And sent me, where him list, instructed for to
  bee.

29

The widow Queene my mother, which then hight
Faire *Emiline*, conceiuing then great feare
Of my fraile safetie, resting in the might
Of him, that did the kingly Scepter beare,
Whose gealous dread induring not a peare,
Is wont to cut off all, that doubt may breed,
Thought best away me to remoue somewhere
Into some forrein land, where as no need
Of dreaded daunger might his doubtfull humor
    feed.

30

So taking counsell of a wise man red,
She was by him aduiz'd, to send me quight
Out of the countrie, wherein I was bred,
The which the fertile *Lionesse* is hight,
Into the land of *Faerie*, where no wight
Should weet of me, nor worke me any wrong.
To whose wise read she hearkning, sent me
    streight
Into this land, where I haue wond thus long,
Since I was ten yeares old, now growen to
    stature strong.

31

All which my daies I haue not lewdly spent,
Nor spilt the blossome of my tender yeares
In ydlesse, but as was conuenient,
Haue trayned bene with many noble feres
In gentle thewes, and such like seemely leres.
Mongst which my most delight hath alwaies
    been,
To hunt the saluage chace amongst my peres,
Of all that raungeth in the forrest greene ;
Of which none is to me vnknowne, that eu'r was
    seene.

32

Ne is there hauke, which mantleth her on pearch,
Whether high towring, or accoasting low,
But I the measure of her flight doe search,
And all her pray, and all her diet know.
Such be our ioyes, which in these forrests grow :
Onely the vse of armes, which most I ioy,
And fitteth most for noble swayne to know,
I haue not tasted yet, yet past a boy,
And being now high time these strong ioynts to
    imploy.

33

Therefore, good Sir, sith now occasion fit
Doth fall, whose like hereafter seldome may,
Let me this craue, vnworthy though of it,
That ye will make me Squire without delay,
That from henceforth in batteilous array
I may beare armes, and learne to vse them
    right ;
The rather since that fortune hath this day
Giuen to me the spoile of this dead knight,
These goodly gilden armes, which I haue won
    in fight.

34

All which when well Sir *Calidore* had heard,
Him much more now, then earst he gan admire,
For the rare hope which in his yeares appear'd,
And thus replide ; Faire chyld, the high desire
To loue of armes, which in you doth aspire,
I may not certes without blame denie ;
But rather wish, that some more noble hire,
(Though none more noble then is cheualrie,)
I had, you to reward with greater dignitie.

35

There him he causd to kneele, and made to
    sweare
Faith to his knight, and truth to Ladies all,
And neuer to be recreant, for feare
Of perill, or of ought that might befall :
So he him dubbed, and his Squire did call.
Fullglad and ioyous then young *Tristram* grew,
Like as a flowre, whose silken leaues small,
Long shut vp in the bud from heauens vew,
At length breakes forth, and brode displayes his
    smyling hew.

36

Thus when they long had treated to and fro,
And *Calidore* betooke him to depart,
Chyld *Tristram* prayd, that he with him
    might goe
On his aduenture, vowing not to start,
But wayt on him in euery place and part.
Whereat Sir *Calidore* did much delight,
And greatly ioy'd at his so noble hart,
In hope he sure would proue a doughtie
    knight :
Yet for the time this answere he to him behight.

37

Glad would I surely be, thou courteous Squire
To haue thy presence in my present quest,
That mote thy kindled courage set on fire,
And flame forth honour in thy noble brest :
But I am bound by vow, which I profest
To my dread Soueraine, when I it assayd,
That in atchieuement of her high behest,
I should no creature ioyne vnto mine ayde,
For thy I may not graunt, that ye so greatly
    prayde.

38

But since this Ladie is all desolate,
And needeth safegard now vpon her way,
Ye may doe well in this her needfull state
To succour her, from daunger of dismay ;
That thankfull guerdon may to you repay.
The noble ympe of such new seruice fayne,
It gladly did accept, as he did say.
So taking courteous leaue, they parted twayne,
And *Calidore* forth passed to his former payne.

39

But *Tristram* then despoyling that dead knight
Of all those goodly implements of prayse,
Long fed his greedie eyes with the faire sight
Of the bright mettall, shyning like Sunne rayes;
Handling and turning them a thousand wayes.
And after hauing them vpon him dight,
He tooke that Ladie, and her vp did rayse
Vpon the steed of her owne late dead knight,
So with her marched forth, as she did him
behight.

40

There to their fortune leaue we them awhile,
And turne we backe to good Sir *Calidore*;
Who ere he thence had traueild many a mile,
Came to the place, whereas ye heard afore
This knight, whom *Tristram* slew, had
wounded sore
Another knight in his despiteous pryde;
There he that knight found lying on the flore,
With many wounds full perilous and wyde,
That all his garments, and the grasse in ver-
meill dyde.

41

And there beside him sate vpon the ground
His wofull Ladie, piteously complayning
With loud laments that most vnluckie stound,
And her sad selfe with carefull hand constrayning
To wype his wounds, and ease their bitter
payning.
Which sorie sight when *Calidore* did vew
With heauie eyne, from teares vneath refrayning,
His mightie hart their mournefull case can rew,
And for their better comfort to them nigher
drew.

42

Then speaking to the Ladie, thus he sayd:
Ye dolefull Dame, let not your griefe empeach
To tell, what cruell hand hath thus arayd
This knight vnarm'd, with so vnknightly breach
Of armes, that if I yet him nigh may reach,
I may auenge him of so foule despight.
The Ladie hearing his so courteous speach,
Gan reare her eyes as to the chearefull light,
And from her sory hart few heauie words forth
sight.

43

In which she shew'd, how that discourteous knight
(Whom *Tristram* slew) them in that shadow
found,
Ioying together in vnblam'd delight,
And him vnarm'd, as now he lay on ground,
Charg'd with his speare and mortally did wound,
Withouten cause, but onely her to reaue
From him, to whom she was for euer bound:
Yet when she fled into that couert greaue,
He her not finding, both them thus nigh dead
did leaue.

44

When *Calidore* this ruefull storie had
Well vnderstood, he gan of her demand,
What manner wight he was, and how yclad,
Which had this outrage wrought with wicked
hand.
She then, like as she best could vnderstand,
Him thus describ'd, to be of stature large,
Clad all in gilden armes, with azure band
Quartred athwart, and bearing in his targe
A Ladie on rough waues, row'd in a sommer
barge.

45

Then gan Sir *Calidore* to ghesse streight way
By many signes, which she described had,
That this was he, whom *Tristram* earst did slay,
And to her said; Dame be no longer sad:
For he, that hath your Knight so ill bestad,
Is now him selfe in much more wretched plight;
These eyes him saw vpon the cold earth sprad,
The meede of his desert for that despight,
Which to your selfe he wrought, and to your
loued knight.

46

Therefore faire Lady lay aside this griefe,
Which ye haue gathered to your gentle hart,
For that displeasure; and thinke what reliefe
Were best deuise for this your louers smart,
And how ye may him hence, and to what part
Conuay to be recur'd. She thankt him deare,
Both for that newes he did to her impart,
And for the courteous care, which he did beare
Both to her loue, and to her selfe in that sad
dreare.

47

Yet could she not deuise by any wit,
How thence she might conuay him to some place.
For him to trouble she it thought vnfit,
That was a straunger to her wretched case;
And him to beare, she thought it thing too base.
Which when as he perceiu'd, he thus bespake;
Faire Lady let it not you seeme disgrace,
To beare this burden on your dainty backe;
My selfe will beare a part, coportion of your
packe.

48

So off he did his shield, and downeward layd
Vpon the ground, like to an hollow beare;
And powring balme, which he had long puruayd,
Into his wounds, him vp thereon did reare,
And twixt them both with parted paines did
beare,
Twixt life and death, not knowing what was
donne.
Thence they him carried to a Castle neare,
In which a worthy auncient Knight did wonne
Where what ensu'd, shall in next Canto be
begonne.

Cant. III.

ᘓᘐᘓᘐᘓᘐᘓᘐᘓᘐᘓᘐᘓᘐᘓᘐᘓᘐ

Calidore brings Priscilla home,
Pursues the Blatant Beast :
Saues Serena whilest Calepine
By Turpine is opprest.

ᘓᘐᘓᘐᘓᘐᘓᘐᘓᘐᘓᘐᘓᘐᘓᘐᘓᘐ

1

True is, that whilome that good Poet sayd,
The gentle minde by gentle deeds is knowne.
For a man by nothing is so well bewrayd,
As by his manners, in which plaine is showne
Of what degree and what race he is growne.
For seldome seene, a trotting Stalion get
An ambling Colt, that is his proper owne :
So seldome seene, that one in basenesse set
Doth noble courage shew, with curteous manners met.

2

But euermore contrary hath bene tryde,
That gentle bloud will gentle manners breed ;
As well may be in *Calidore* descryde,
By late ensample of that courteous deed,
Done to that wounded Knight in his great need,
Whom on his backe he bore, till he him brought
Vnto the Castle where they had decreed.
There of the Knight, the which that Castle ought,
To make abode that night he greatly was besought.

3

He was to weete a man of full ripe yeares,
That in his youth had beene of mickle might,
And borne great sway in armes amongst his peares :
But now weake age had dimd his candle light.
Yet was he courteous still to euery wight,
And loued all that did to armes incline,
And was the father of that wounded Knight,
Whom *Calidore* thus carried on his chine,
And *Aldus* was his name, and his sonnes *Aladine*.

4

Who when he saw his sonne so ill bedight,
With bleeding wounds, brought home vpon a Beare,
By a faire Lady, and a straunger Knight,
Was inly touched with compassion deare,
And deare affection so dolefull dreare,
That he these words burst forth ; Ah sory boy,
Is this the hope that to my hoary heare
Thou brings ? aie me, is this the timely ioy,
Which I expected long, now turnd to sad annoy ?

5

Such is the weakenesse of all mortall hope ;
So tickle is the state of earthly things,
That ere they come vnto their aymed scope,
They fall too short of our fraile reckonings,
And bring vs bale and bitter sorrowings,
In stead of comfort, which we should embrace:
This is the state of Keasars and of Kings.
Let none therefore, that is in meaner place,
Too greatly grieue at any his vnlucky case.

6

So well and wisely did that good old Knight
Temper his griefe, and turned it to cheare,
To cheare his guests, whom he had stayd that night,
And make their welcome to them well appeare:
That to Sir *Calidore* was easie geare ;
But that faire Lady would be cheard for nought,
But sigh'd and sorrow'd for her louer deare,
And inly did afflict her pensiue thought,
With thinking to what case her name should now be brought.

7

For she was daughter to a noble Lord,
Which dwelt thereby, who sought her to affy
To a great pere ; but she did disaccord,
Ne could her liking to his loue apply,
But lou'd this fresh young Knight, who dwelt her ny,
The lusty *Aladine*, though meaner borne,
And of lesse liuelood and hability,
Yet full of valour, the which did adorne
His meanesse much, and make her th'others riches scorne.

8

So hauing both found fit occasion,
They met together in that luckelesse glade ;
Where that proud Knight in his presumption
The gentle *Aladine* did earst inuade,
Being vnarm'd, and set in secret shade.
Whereof she now bethinking, gan t'aduize,
How great a hazard she at earst had made
Of her good fame, and further gan deuize,
How she the blame might salue with coloured disguize.

9

But *Calidore* with all good courtesie
Fain'd her to frolicke, and to put away
The pensiue fit of her melancholie ;
And that old Knight by all meanes did assay,
To make them both as merry as he may.
So they the euening past, till time of rest,
When *Calidore* in seemly good array
Vnto his bowre was brought, and there vndrest,
Did sleepe all night through weary trauell of his quest.

10

But faire *Priscilla* (so that Lady hight)
  Would to no bed, nor take no kindely sleepe,
  But by her wounded loue did watch all night,
  And all the night for bitter anguish weepe,
  And with her teares his wounds did wash and
    steepe.
  So wellshe washt them, and so wellshe wacht him,
  That of the deadly swound, in which full deepe
  He drenched was, she at the length dispacht him,
And droue away the stound, which mortally
  attacht him.

11

The morrow next, when day gan to vplooke,
  He also gan vplooke with drery eye,
  Like one that out of deadly dreame awooke:
  Where when he saw his faire *Priscilla* by,
  He deepely sigh'd, and groaned inwardly,
  To thinke of this ill state, in which she stood,
  To which she for his sake had weetingly
  Now brought her selfe, and blam'd her noble
    blood:
For first, next after life, he tendered her good.

12

Which she perceiuing, did with plenteous teares
  His care more then her owne compassionate,
  Forgetfull of her owne, to minde his feares:
  So both conspiring, gan to intimate
  Each others griefe with zeale affectionate,
  And twixt them twaine with equall care to cast,
  How to saue whole her hazarded estate;
  For which the onely helpe now left them last
Seem'd to be *Calidore*: all other helpes were
  past

13

Him they did deeme, as sure to them he seemed,
  A courteous Knight, and full of faithfull trust:
  Therefore to him their cause they best esteemed
  Whole to commit, and to his dealing iust.
  Earely, so soone as *Titans* beames forth brust
  Through the thicke clouds, in which they
    steeped lay
  All night in darkenesse, duld with yron rust,
  Calidore rising vp as fresh as day,
Gan freshly him addresse vnto his former way.

14

But first him seemed fit, that wounded Knight
  To visite, after this nights perillous passe,
  And to salute him, if he were in plight,
  And eke that Lady his faire louely lasse.
  There he him found much better then he was,
  And moued speach to him of things of course,
  The anguish of his paine to ouerpasse:
  Mongst which he namely did to him discourse,
Of former daies mishap, his sorrowes wicked
  sourse.

15

Of which occasion *Aldine* taking hold,
  Gan breake to him the fortunes of his loue,
  And all his disaduentures to vnfold;
  That *Calidore* it dearly deepe did moue.
  In th'end his kyndly courtesie to proue,
  He him by all the bands of loue besought,
  And as it mote a faithfull friend behoue,
  To safeconduct his loue, and not for ought
To leaue, till to her fathers house he had her
  brought.

16

Sir *Calidore* his faith thereto did plight,
  It to performe: so after little stay,
  That she her selfe had to the iourney dight,
  He passed forth with her in faire array,
  Fearelesse, who ought did thinke, or ought did
    say,
  Sith his own thought he knew most cleare
    from wite.
  So as they past together on their way,
  He can deuize this counter-cast of slight,
To giue faire colour to that Ladies cause in
  sight.

17

Streight to the carkasse of that Knight he went,
  The cause of all this euill, who was slaine
  The day before by iust auengement
  Of noble *Tristram*, where it did remaine:
  There he the necke thereof did cut in twaine,
  And tooke with him the head, the signe of
    shame.
  So forth he passed thorough that daies paine,
  Till to that Ladies fathers house he came,
Most pensiue man, through feare, what of his
  childe became.

18

There he arriuing boldly, did present
  The fearefull Lady to her father deare,
  Most perfect pure, and guiltlesse innocent
  Of blame, as he did on his Knighthood sweare,
  Since first he saw her, and did free from feare
  Of a discourteous Knight, who her had reft,
  And by outragious force away did beare:
  Witnesse thereof he shew'd his head there left,
And wretched life forlorne for vengement of his
  theft.

19

Most ioyfull man her sire was her to see,
  And heare th'aduenture of her late mischaunce;
  And thousand thankes to *Calidore* for fee
  Of his large paines in her deliueraunce
  Did yeeld; Ne lesse the Lady did aduaunce.
  Thus hauing her restored trustily,
  As he had vow'd, some small continuaunce
  He there did make, and then most carefully
Vnto his first exploite he did him selfe apply.

20

So as he was pursuing of his quest
  He chaunst to come whereas a iolly Knight,
  In couert shade him selfe did safely rest,
  To solace with his Lady in delight :
  His warlike armes he had from him vndight :
  For that him selfe he thought from daunger
    free,
And far from enuious eyes that mote him spight.
  And eke the Lady was full faire to see,
And courteous withall, becomming her degree.

21

To whom Sir *Calidore* approaching nye,
  Ere they were well aware of liuing wight
  Them much abasht, but more him selfe
    thereby,
  That he so rudely did vppon them light,
  And troubled had their quiet loues delight.
  Yet since it was his fortune, not his fault,
  Him selfe thereof he labour'd to acquite,
  And pardon crau'd for his so rash default,
That he gainst courtesie so fowly did default.

22

With which his gentle words and goodly wit
  He soone allayd that Knights conceiu'd
    displeasure,
  That he besought him downe by him to sit,
  That they mote treat of things abrode at
    leasure ;
  And of aduentures, which had in his measure
  Of so long waies to him befallen late.
So downe he sate, and with delightfull pleasure
  His long aduentures gan to him relate,
Which he endured had through daungerous
    debate.

23

Of which whilest they discoursed both together,
  The faire *Serena* (so his Lady hight)
  Allur'd with myldnesse of the gentle wether,
  And pleasaunce of the place, the which was dight
  With diuers flowres distinct with rare delight,
  Wandred about the fields, as liking led
  Her wauering lust after her wandring sight,
  To make a garland to adorne her hed,
Without suspect of ill or daungers hidden dred.

24

All sodainely out of the forrest nere
  The Blatant Beast forth rushing vnaware,
  Caught her thus loosely wandring here and there,
  And in his wide great mouth away her bare,
  Crying aloud in vaine, to shew her sad misfare
  Vnto the Knights, and calling oft for ayde,
  Who with the horrour of her haplesse care
  Hastily starting vp, like men dismayde,
Ran after fast to reskue the distressed mayde.

25

The Beast with their pursuit incited more,
  Into the wood was bearing her apace
  For to haue spoyled her, when *Calidore*
  Who was more light of foote and swift in chace,
  Him ouertooke in middest of his race :
  And fiercely charging him with all his might,
  Forst to forgoe his pray there in the place,
  And to betake him selfe to fearefull flight ;
For he durst not abide with *Calidore* to fight.

26

Who nathelesse, when he the Lady saw
  There left on ground, though in full euill plight,
  Yet knowing that her Knight now neare did
    draw,
  Staide not to succour her in that affright,
  But follow'd fast the Monster in his flight :
  Through woods and hils he follow'd him so fast,
  That he nould let him breath nor gather spright,
  But forst him gape and gaspe, with dread
    aghast,
As if his lungs and lites were nigh a sunder brast.

27

And now by this Sir *Calepine*, so hight,
  Came to the place, where he his Lady found
  In dolorous dismay and deadly plight,
  All in gore bloud there tumbled on the ground,
  Hauing both sides through grypt with griesly
    wound.
  His weapons soone from him he threw away,
  And stouping downe to her in drery swound,
  Vprear'd her from the ground whereon she lay,
And in his tender armes her forced vp to stay.

28

So well he did his busie paines apply,
  That the faint sprite he did reuoke againe,
  To her fraile mansion of mortality.
  Then vp he tooke her twixt his armes twaine,
  And setting on his steede, her did sustaine
  With carefull hands soft footing her beside,
  Till to some place of rest they mote attaine,
  Where she in safe assuraunce mote abide,
Till she recured were of those her woundes wide.

29

Now when as *Phœbus* with his fiery waine
  Vnto his Inne began to draw apace ;
  Tho wexing weary of that toylesome paine,
  In trauelling on foote so long a space,
  Not wont on foote with heauy armes to trace,
  Downe in a dale forby a riuers syde,
  He chaunst to spie a faire and stately place,
  To which he meant his weary steps to guyde,
In hope there for his loue some succour to
    prouyde.

30

But comming to the riuers side, he found
  That hardly passable on foote it was:
  Therefore there still he stood as in a stound,
  Ne wist which way he through the foord mote pas.
  Thus whilest he was in this distressed case,
  Deuising what to doe, he nigh espyde
  An armed Knight approaching to the place,
  With a faire Lady lincked by his syde,
The which themselues prepard thorough the foord to ride.

31

Whom *Calepine* saluting (as became)
  Besought of courtesie in that his neede,
  For safe conducting of his sickely Dame,
  Through that same perillous foord with better heede,
  To take him vp behinde vpon his steed.
  To whom that other did this taunt returne.
  Perdy thou peasant Knight, mightst rightly reed
  Me then to be full base and euill borne,
If I would beare behinde a burden of such scorne.

32

But as thou hast thy steed forlorne with shame,
  So fare on foote till thou another gayne,
  And let thy Lady likewise doe the same.
  Or beare her on thy backe with pleasing payne,
  And proue thy manhood on the billowes vayne.
  With which rude speach his Lady much displeased,
  Did him reproue, yet could him not restrayne,
  And would on her owne Palfrey him haue eased,
For pitty of his Dame, whom she saw so diseased.

33

Sir *Calepine* her thanckt, yet inly wroth
  Against her Knight, her gentlenesse refused,
  And carelesly into the riuer goth,
  As in despight to be so fowle abused
  Of a rude churle, whom often he accused
  Of fowle discourtesie, vnfit for Knight;
  And strongly wading through the waues vnused,
  With speare in th'one hand, stayd him selfe vpright,
With th'other staide his Lady vp with steddy might.

34

And all the while, that same discourteous Knight,
  Stood on the further bancke beholding him,
  At whose calamity, for more despight
  He laught, and mockt to see him like to swim.
  But when as *Calepine* came to the brim,
  And saw his carriage past that perill well, [grim,
  Looking at that same Carle with count'nance
  His heart with vengeaunce inwardly did swell,
And forth at last did breake in speaches sharpe and fell.

35

Vnknightly Knight, the blemish of that name,
  And blot of all that armes vppon them take,
  Which is the badge of honour and of fame,
  Loe I defie thee, and here challenge make,
  That thou for euer doe those armes forsake,
  And be for euer held a recreant Knight,
  Vnlesse thou dare for thy deare Ladies sake,
  And for thine owne defence on foote alight,
To iustifie thy fault gainst me in equall fight.

36

The dastard, that did heare him selfe defyde,
  Seem'd not to weigh his threatfull words at all,
  But laught them out, as if his greater pryde
  Did scorne the challenge of so base a thrall:
  Or had no courage, or else had no gall.
  So much the more was *Calepine* offended,
  That him to no reuenge he forth could call,
  But both his challenge and him selfe contemned,
Ne cared as a coward so to be condemned.

37

But he nought weighing what he sayd or did,
  Turned his steede about another way,
  And with his Lady to the Castle rid,
  Where was his won; ne did the other stay,
  But after went directly as he may,
  For his sicke charge some harbour there to seeke,
  Where he arriuing with the fall of day,
  Drew to the gate, and there with prayers meeke,
And myld entreaty lodging did for her beseeke.

38

But the rude Porter that no manners had,
  Did shut the gate against him in his face,
  And entraunce boldly vnto him forbad.
  Nathelesse the Knight now in so needy case,
  Gan him entreat euen with submission base,
  And humbly praid to let them in that night:
  Who to him aunswer'd, that there was no place
  Of lodging fit for any errant Knight,
Vnlesse that with his Lord he formerly did fight.

39

Full loth am I (quoth he) as now at earst,
  When day is spent, and rest vs needeth most,
  And that this Lady, both whose sides are pearst
  With wounds, is ready to forgo the ghost:
  Ne would I gladly combate with mine host,
  That should to me such curtesie afford,
  Vnlesse that I were thereunto enforst.
  But yet aread to me, how hight thy Lord,
That doth thus strongly ward the Castle of the ford.

40

His name (quoth ne) if that thou list to learne,
Is hight Sir *Turpine*, one of mickle might,
And manhood rare, but terrible and stearne
In all assaies to euery errant Knight,
Because of one, that wrought him fowle despight.
Ill seemes (sayd he) if he so valiaunt be,
That he should be so sterne to stranger wight:
For seldome yet did liuing creature see,
That curtesie and manhood euer disagree.

41

But go thy waies to him, and fro me say,
That here is at his gate an errant Knight,
That house-rome craues, yet would be loth
　　t'assay
The proofe of battell, now in doubtfull night,
Or curtesie with rudenesse to requite:
Yet if he needes will fight, craue leaue till morne,
And tell withall, the lamentable plight,
In which this Lady languisheth forlorne,
That pitty craues, as he of woman was yborne.

42

The groome went streight way in, and to his Lord
Declar'd the message, which that Knight did
　　moue;
Who sitting with his Lady then at bord,
Not onely did not his demaund approue,
But both himselfe reuil'd, and eke his loue;
Albe his Lady, that *Blandina* hight,
Him of vngentle vsage did reproue
And earnestly entreated that they might
Finde fauour to be lodged there for that same
　　night.

43

Yet would he not perswaded be for ought,
Ne from his currish will awhit reclame.
Which answer when the groome returning,
To *Calepine*, his heart did inly flame [brought
With wrathfull fury for so foule a shame,
That he could not thereof auenged bee:
But most for pitty of his dearest Dame,
Whom now in deadly daunger he did see;
Yet had no meanes to comfort, nor procure
　　her glee.

44

But all in vaine; for why, no remedy
He saw, the present mischiefe to redresse,
But th'vtmost end perforce for to aby,
Which that nights fortune would for him
　　addresse.
So downe he tooke his Lady in distresse,
And layd her vnderneath a bush to sleepe,
Couer'd with cold, and wrapt in wretchednesse,
Whiles he him selfe all night did nought but
　　weepe,
And wary watch about her for her safegard keepe.

45

The morrow next, so soone as ioyous day
Did shew it selfe in sunny beames bedight,
Serena full of dolorous dismay,
Twixt darkenesse dread, and hope of liuing
　　light,
Vprear'd her head to see that chearefull sight.
Then *Calepine*, how euer inly wroth,
And greedy to auenge that vile despight,
Yet for the feeble Ladies sake, full loth
To make there lenger stay, forth on his iourney
　　goth.

46

He goth on foote all armed by her side,
Vpstaying still her selfe vppon her steede,
Being vnhable else alone to ride;
So sore her sides, so much her wounds did bleede:
Till that at length, in his extreamest neede,
He chaunst far off an armed Knight to spy,
Pursuing him apace with greedy speede,
Whom well he wist to be some enemy,
That meant to make aduantage of his misery.

47

Whereiore he stayd, till that he nearer drew
To weet what issue would thereof betyde,
Tho whenas he approched nigh in vew,
By certaine signes he plainely him descryde,
To be the man, that with such scornefull pryde
Had him abusde, and shamed yesterday;
Therefore misdoubting, least he should
　　misguyde
His former malice to some new assay,
He cast to keepe him selfe so safely as he may.

48

By this the other came in place likewise,
And couching close his speare and all his powre,
As bent to some malicious enterprise,
He bad him stand, t'abide the bitter stoure
Of his sore vengeaunce, or to make auoure
Of the lewd words and deedes, which he had
　　done:
With that ran at him, as he would deuoure
His life at once; who nought could do, but shun
The perill of his pride, or else be ouerrun.

49

Yet he him still pursew'd from place to place,
With full intent him cruelly to kill,
And like a wilde goate round about did chace,
Flying the fury of his bloudy will.
But his best succour and refuge was still
Behinde his Ladies backe, who to him cryde,
And called oft with prayers loud and shrill,
As euer he to Lady was affyde, [fyde
To spare her Knight, and rest with reason paci-

50

But he the more thereby enraged was,
  And with more eager felnesse him pursew'd,
  So that at length, after long weary chace,
  Hauing by chaunce a close aduantage vew'd,
  He ouer raught him, hauing long eschew'd
  His violence in vaine, and with his spere
  Strooke through his shoulder, that the blood
    ensew'd
In great aboundance, as a well it were,
That forth out of an hill fresh gushing did
  appere.

51

Yet ceast he not for all that cruell wound,
  But chaste him still, for all his Ladies cry,
  Not satisfyde till on the fatall ground
  He saw his life powrd forth dispiteously :
  The which was certes in great ieopardy,
  Hadnotawondrouschauncehisreskuewrought,
  And saued from his cruell villany.
Such chaunces oft exceed all humaine thought:
That in another Canto shall to end be brought.

Cant. IIII.

CXCXCXCXCXCXCXCXCXCXCXCXCXCXCXCX

Calepine by a saluage man
  from Turpine reskewed is,
  And whylest an Infant from a Beare
  he saues, his loue doth misse.

CXCXCXCXCXCXCXCXCXCXCXCXCXCXCXCX

1

Like as a ship with dreadfull storme long tost,
  Hauing spent all her mastes and her ground-
    hold,
  Now farre from harbour likely to be lost,
  At last some fisher barke doth neare behold,
  That giueth comfort to her courage cold.
  Such was the state of this most courteous knight
  Being oppressed by that faytour bold,
That he remayned in most perilous plight,
And his sad Ladie left in pitifull affright.

2

Till that by fortune, passing all foresight,
  A saluage man, which in those woods did wonne,
  Drawne with that Ladies loud and piteous
    shright,
  Toward the same incessantly did ronne,
  To vnderstand what there was to be donne.
  There he this most discourteous crauen found,
  As fiercely yet, as when he first begonne,
Chasing the gentle *Calepine* around, [wound.
Ne sparing him the more for all his grieuous

3

The saluage man, that neuer till this houre
  Did taste of pittie, neither gentlesse knew,
  Seeing his sharpe assault and cruell stoure
  Was much emmoued at his perils vew,
  That euen his ruder hart began to rew,
  And feele compassion of his euill plight,
  Against his foe that did him so pursew :
From whom he meant to free him, if he might,
And him auenge of that so villenous despight.

4

Yet armes or weapon had he none to fight,
  Ne knew the vse of warlike instruments,
  Saue such as sudden rage him lent to smite,
  But naked without needfull vestiments,
  To clad his corpse with meete habiliments,
  He cared not for dint of sword nor speere,
  No more then for the stroke of strawes or bents:
For from his mothers wombe, which him did
  beare,
He was invulnerable made by Magicke leare.

5

He stayed not t'aduize, which way were best
  His foe t'assayle, or how himselfe to gard,
  But with fierce fury and with force infest
  Vpon him ran ; who being well prepard,
  His first assault full warily did ward,
  And with the push of his sharp-pointed speare
  Full on the breast him strooke, so strong and
    hard,
That forst him backe recoyle, and reele areare ;
Yet in his bodie made no wound nor bloud
  appeare.

6

With that the wyld man more enraged grew,
  Like to a Tygre that hath mist his pray,
  And with mad mood againe vpon him flew,
  Regarding neither speare, that mote him slay,
  Nor his fierce steed, that mote him much dismay,
  The saluage nation doth all dread despize :
  Tho on his shield he griple hold did lay,
And held the same so hard, that by no wize
He could him force to loose, or leaue his
  enterprize.

7

Long did he wrest and wring it to and fro,
  And euery way did try, but all in vaine :
  For he would not his greedie grype forgoe,
  But hayld and puld with all his might and maine,
  That from his steed him nigh he drew againe.
  Who hauing now no vse of his long speare,
  So nigh at hand, nor force his shield to straine,
Both speare and shield, as things that need-
  lesse were,
He quite forsooke, and fled himselfe away for
  feare.

8

But after him the wyld man ran apace,
  And him pursewed with importune speed
  (For he was swift as any Bucke in chace)
  And had he not in his extreamest need,
  Bene helped through the swiftnesse of his steed,
  He had him ouertaken in his flight.
  Who euer, as he saw him nigh succeed,
  Gan cry aloud with horrible affright,
And shrieked out, a thing vncomely for a knight.

9

But when the Saluage saw his labour vaine,
  In following of him, that fled so fast,
  He wearie woxe, and backe return'd againe
  With speede vnto the place, whereas he last
  Had left that couple, nere their vtmost cast.
  There he that knight full sorely bleeding found,
  And eke the Ladie fearefully aghast,
  Both for the perill of the present stound,
And also for the sharpnesse of her rankling
  wound.

10

For though she were right glad, so rid to bee
  From that vile lozell, which her late offended,
  Yet now no lesse encombrance she did see,
  And perill by this saluage man pretended;
  Gainst whom she saw no meanes to be
    defended,
  By reason that her knight was wounded sore.
  Therefore her selfe she wholy recommended
  To Gods sole grace, whom she did oft implore,
To send her succour, being of all hope forlore.

11

But the wyld man, contrarie to her feare,
  Came to her creeping like a fawning hound,
  And by rude tokens made to her appeare
  His deepe compassion of her dolefull stound,
  Kissing his hands, and crouching to the ground;
  For other language had he none nor speach,
  But a soft murmure, and confused sound
  Of senselesse words, which nature did him
    teach,
T'expresse his passions, which his reason did
  empeach.

12

And comming likewise to the wounded knight,
  When he beheld the streames of purple blood
  Yet flowing fresh, as moued with the sight,
  He made great mone after his saluage mood,
  And running streight into the thickest wood,
  A certaine herbe from thence vnto him brought.
  Whose vertue he by vse well vnderstood:
  The iuyce whereof into his wound he wrought,
And stopt the bleeding straight, ere he it
  staunched thought.

13

Then taking vp that Recreants shield and speare,
  Which earst he left, he signes vnto them made,
  With him to wend vnto his wonning neare:
  To which he easily did them perswade.
  Farre in the forrest by a hollow glade, [brode
  Couered with mossie shrubs, which spredding
  Did vnderneath them make a gloomy shade;
  Where foot of liuing creature neuer trode,
Ne scarse wyld beasts durst come, there was this
  wights abode.

14

Thether he brought these vnacquainted guests;
  To whom faire semblance, as he could, he shewed
  By signes, by lookes, and all his other gests.
  But the bare ground, with hoarie mosse
    bestrowed,
  Must be their bed, their pillow was vnsowed,
  And the frutes of the forrest was their feast:
  For their bad Stuard neither plough'd nor sowed,
  Ne fed on flesh, ne euer of wyld beast
Did taste the bloud, obaying natures first
  beheast.

15

Yet howsoeuer base and meane it were,
  They tooke it well, and thanked God for all,
  Which had them freed from that deadly feare,
  And sau'd from being to that caytiue thrall.
  Here they of force (as fortune now did fall)
  Compelled were themselues a while to rest,
  Glad of that easement, though it were but small;
  That hauing there their wounds awhile redrest,
They mote the abler be to passe vnto the rest.

16

During which time, that wyld man did apply
  His best endeuour, and his daily paine,
  In seeking all the woods both farre and nye
  For herbes to dresse their wounds; still
    seeming faine,
  When ought he did, that did their lyking gaine.
  So as ere long he had that knightes wound
  Recured well, and made him whole againe:
  But that same Ladies hurts no herbe he found,
Which could redresse, for it was inwardly
  vnsound.

17

Now when as *Calepine* was woxen strong,
  Vpon a day he cast abrode to wend,
  To take the ayre, and heare the thrushes song,
  Vnarm'd, as fearing neither foe nor frend,
  And without sword his person to defend.
  There him befell, vnlooked for before,
  An hard aduenture with vnhappie end,
  A cruell Beare, the which an infant bore
Betwixt his bloodie iawes, besprinckled all with
  gore.

18

The litle babe did loudly scrike and squall,
  And all the woods with piteous plaints did fill,
  As if his cry did meane for helpe to call
To *Calepine*, whose eares those shrieches shrill
Percing his hart with pities point did thrill ;
  That after him he ran with zealous haste,
  To rescue th'infant, ere he did him kill :
Whom though he saw now somewhat ouerpast,
Yet by the cry he follow'd, and pursewed fast.

19

Well then him chaunst his heauy armes to want,
  Whose burden mote empeach his needfull speed,
  And hinder him from libertie to pant :
For hauing long time, as his daily weed,
Them wont to weare, and wend on foot for need,
  Now wanting them he felt himselfe so light,
  That like an Hauke, which feeling her selfe freed
From bels and iesses, which did let her flight,
Him seem'd his feet did fly, and in their speed delight.

20

So well he sped him, that the wearie Beare
  Ere long he ouertooke, and forst to stay,
  And without weapon him assayling neare,
Compeld him soone the spoyle adowne to lay.
Wherewith the beast enrag'd to loose his pray,
  Vpon him turned, and with greedie force
  And furie, to be crossed in his way,
Gaping full wyde, did thinke without remorse
To be aueng'd on him, and to deuoure his corse.

21

But the bold knight no whit thereat dismayd,
  But catching vp in hand a ragged stone,
  Which lay thereby (so fortune him did ayde)
Vpon him ran, and thrust it all attone
Into his gaping throte, that made him grone
  And gaspe for breath, that he nigh choked was,
  Being vnable to digest that bone ;
Ne could it vpward come, nor downward passe,
Ne could he brooke the coldnesse of the stony masse.

22

Whom when as he thus combred did behold,
  Struying in vaine that nigh his bowels brast,
  He with him closd, and laying mightie hold
Vpon his throte, did gripe his gorge so fast,
That wanting breath, him downe to ground he cast ;
  And then oppressing him with vrgent paine,
  Ere long enforst to breath his vtmost blast,
Gnashing his cruell teeth at him in vaine,
And threatning his sharpe clawes, now wanting powre to straine.

23

Then tooke he vp betwixt his armes twaine
  The litle babe, sweet relickes of his pray ;
  Whom pitying to heare so sore complaine,
From his soft eyes the teares he wypt away,
And from his face the filth that did it ray,
  And euery litle limbe he searcht around,
  And euery part, that vnder sweathbands lay,
Least that the beasts sharpe teeth had any wound
Made in his tender flesh, but whole them all he found.

24

So hauing all his bands againe vptyde,
  He with him thought backe to returne againe :
  But when he lookt about on euery syde,
To weet which way were best to entertaine,
To bring him to the place, where he would faine,
  He could no path nor tract of foot descry,
  Ne by inquirie learne, nor ghesse by ayme.
For nought but woods and forrests farre and nye,
That all about did close the compasse of his eye.

25

Much was he then encombred, ne could tell
  Which way to take : now West he went a while,
  Then North ; then neither, but as fortune fell.
So vp and downe he wandred many a mile,
With wearie trauell and vncertaine toile,
  Yet nought the nearer to his iourneys end ;
  And euermore his louely litle spoile
Crying for food, did greatly him offend.
So all that day in wandring vainely he did spend.

26

At last about the setting of the Sunne,
  Him selfe out of the forest he did wynd,
  And by good fortune the plaine champion wonne :
Where looking all about, where he mote fynd
Some place of succour to content his mynd,
  At length he heard vnder the forrests syde
  A voice, that seemed of some woman kynd,
Which to her selfe lamenting loudly cryde,
And oft complayn'd of fate, and fortune oft defyde.

27

To whom approching, when as she perceiued
  A stranger wight in place, her plaint she stayd,
  As if she doubted to haue bene deceiued,
Or loth to let her sorrowes be bewrayd.
Whom when as *Calepine* saw so dismayd,
  He to her drew, and with faire blandishment
  Her chearing vp, thus gently to her sayd ;
What be you wofull Dame, which thus lament,
And for what cause declare, so mote ye not repent.

28

To whom she thus, What need me Sir to tell,
  That which your selfe haue earst ared so right?
  A wofull dame ye haue me termed well;
  So much more wofull, as my wofull plight
Cannot redressed be by liuing wight.
Nathlesse (quoth he) if need doe not you bynd,
Doe it disclose, to ease your grieued spright:
Oftimes it haps, that sorrowes of the mynd
Find remedie vnsought, which seeking cannot
    fynd

29

Then thus began the lamentable Dame;
  Sith then ye needs will know the griefe I
    hoord,
  I am th'vnfortunate *Matilde* by name,
  The wife of bold Sir *Bruin*, who is Lord
Of all this land, late conquer'd by his sword
From a great Gyant, called *Cormoraunt*;
Whom he did ouerthrow by yonder foord,
And in three battailes did so deadly daunt,
That he dare not returnefor all his daily vaunt.

30

So is my Lord now seiz'd of all the land,
  As in his fee, with peaceable estate,
  And quietly doth hold it in his hand,
  Ne any dares with him for it debate.
But to these happie fortunes, cruell fate
Hath ioyn'd one euill, which doth ouerthrow
All these our ioyes, and all our blisse abate;
And like in time to further ill to grow,
And all this land with endlesse losse to ouerflow.

31

For th'heauens enuying our prosperitie,
  Haue not vouchsaft to graunt vnto vs twaine
  The gladfull blessing of posteritie,
  Which we might see after our selues remaine
In th'heritage of our vnhappie paine:
So that for want of heires it to defend,
All is in time like to returne againe
To that foule feend, who dayly doth attend
To leape into the same after our liues end.

32

But most my Lord is grieued herewithall,
  And makes exceeding mone, when he does
    thinke
  That all this land vnto his foe shall fall,
  For which he long in vaine did sweat and
    swinke,
That now the same he greatly doth forthinke.
Yet was it sayd, there should to him a sonne
Be gotten, not begotten, which should drinke
And dry vp all the water, which doth ronne
In the next brooke, by whom that feend shold
    be fordonne

33

Well hop't he then, when this was propheside,
  That from his sides some noble chyld should rize,
  The which through fame should farre be
    magnifide,
  And this proud gyant should with braue emprize
Quite ouerthrow, who now ginnes to despize
The good Sir *Bruin*, growing farre in yeares;
Who thinkes from me his sorrow all doth rize.
Lo this my cause of griefe to you appeares;
For which I thus doe mourne, and poure forth
    ceaselesse teares.

34

Which when he heard, he inly touched was
  With tender ruth for her vnworthy griefe,
  And when he had deuized of her case,
  He gan in mind conceiue a fit reliefe
For all her paine, if please her make the priefe.
And hauing cheared Her, thus said; Faire Dame,
In euils counsell is the comfort chiefe,
Which though I be not wise enough to frame,
Yet as I well it meane, vouchsafe it without
    blame.

35

If that the cause of this your languishment
  Be lacke of children, to supply your place,
  Lo how good fortune doth to you present
  This litle babe, of sweete and louely face,
And spotlesse spirit, in which ye may enchace
What euer formes ye list thereto apply,
Being now soft and fit them to embrace;
Whether ye list him traine in cheualry,
Or noursle vp in lore of learn'd Philosophy.

36

And certes it hath oftentimes bene seene,
  That of the like, whose linage was vnknowne,
  More braue and noble knights haue raysed
    beene,
  As their victorious deedes haue often showen,
Being with fame through many Nations blowen,
Then those, which haue bene dandled in the lap.
Therefore some thought, that those braue
    imps were sowen
Here by the Gods, and fed with heauenly sap,
That made them grow so high t'all honorable
    hap.

37

The Ladie hearkning to his sensefull speach,
  Found nothing that he said, vnmeet nor geason,
  Hauing oft seene it tryde, as he did teach.
  Therefore inclyning to his goodly reason,
Agreeing well both with the place and season,
She gladly did of that same babe accept,
As of her owne by liuerey and seisin,
And hauing ouer it a litle wept,
She bore it thence, and euer as her owne it kept.

38

Right glad was *Calepine* to be so rid
Of his young charge, whereof he skilled nought:
Ne she lesse glad; for she so wisely did,
And with her husband vnder hand so wrought,
That when that infant vnto him she brought,
She made him thinke it surely was his owne,
And it in goodly thewes so well vpbrought,
That it became a famous knight well knowne
And did right noble deedes, the which elswhere
  are showne.

39

But *Calepine*, now being left alone
Vnder the greenewoods side in sorie plight,
Withouten armes or steede to ride vpon,
Or house to hide his head from heauens spight,
Albe that Dame by all the meanes she might,
Him oft desired home with her to wend,
And offred him, his courtesie to requite,
Both horse and armes, and what so else to
  lend,
Yet he them all refusd, though thankt her as
  a frend.

40

And for exceeding griefe which inly grew,
That he his loue so lucklesse now had lost,
On the cold ground, maugre himselfe he threw,
For fell despight, to be so sorely crost;
And there all night himselfe in anguish tost,
Vowing, that neuer he in bed againe
His limbes would rest, ne lig in ease embost,
Till that his Ladies sight he mote attaine,
Or vnderstand, that she in safetie did remaine.

Cant. V.

The saluage serues Matilda well
till she Prince Arthure fynd,
Who her together with his Squyre
with th'Hermit leaues behynd.

1

O what an easie thing is to descry
The gentle bloud, how euer it be wrapt
In sad misfortunes foule deformity,
And wretched sorrowes, which haue often hapt?
For howsoeuer it may grow mis-shapt,
Like this wyld man, being vndisciplynd,
That to all vertue it may seeme vnapt,
Yet will it shew some sparkes of gentle mynd,
And at the last breake forth in his owne proper
  kynd.

2

That plainely may in this wyld man be red,
Who though he were still in this desert wood,
Mongst saluage beasts, both rudely borne
  and bred,
Ne euer saw faire guize, ne learned good,
Yet shewd some token of his gentle blood,
By gentle vsage of that wretched Dame.
For certes he was borne of noble blood,
How euer by hard hap he hether came;
As ye may know, when time shall be to tell
  the same.

3

Who when as now long time he lacked had
The good Sir *Calepine*, that farre was strayd,
Did wexe exceeding sorrowfull and sad,
As he of some misfortune were afrayd:
And leauing there this Ladie all dismayd,
Went forth streightway into the forrest wyde,
To seeke, if she perchance a sleepe were layd,
Or what so else were vnto him betyde:
He sought him farre and neare, yet him no where
  he spyde.

4

Tho backe returning to that sorie Dame,
He shewed semblant of exceeding mone,
By speaking signes, as he them best could frame;
Now wringing both his wretched hands in one,
Now beating his hard head vpon a stone,
That ruth it was to see him so lament.
By which she well perceiuing, what was done,
Gan teare her hayre, and all her garments rent,
And beat her breast, and piteously her selfe
  torment.

5

Vpon the ground her selfe she fiercely threw,
Regardlesse of her wounds, yet bleeding rife,
That with their bloud did all the flore imbrew,
As if her breast new launcht with murdrous
  knife,
Would streight di lodge the wretched wearie
  life.
There she long groueling, and deepe groning
As if her vitall powers were at strife   [lay,
With stronger death, and feared their decay,
Such were this Ladies pangs and dolorous assay.

6

Whom when the Saluage saw so sore distrest,
He reared her vp from the bloudie ground,
And sought by all the meanes, that he could best
Her to recure out of that stony swound,
And staunch the bleeding of her dreary wound.
Yet nould she be recomforted for nought,
Ne cease her sorrow and impatient stound,
But day and night did vexe her carefull thought,
And euer more and more her owne affliction
  wrought.

7

At length, when as no hope of his retourne
She saw now left, she cast to leaue the place,
And wend abrode, though feeble and forlorne,
To seeke some comfort in that sorie case.
His steede now strong through rest so long
    a space,
Well as she could, she got, and did bedight,
And being thereon mounted, forth did pace,
Withouten guide, her to conduct aright,
Or gard her to defend from bold oppressors
    might.

8

Whom when her Host saw readie to depart,
He would not suffer her alone to fare,
But gan himselfe addresse to take her part.
Those warlike armes, which *Calepine* whyleare
Had left behind, he gan eftsoones prepare,
And put them all about himselfe vnfit,
His shield, his helmet, and his curats bare.
But without sword vpon his thigh to sit :
Sir *Calepine* himselfe away had hidden it.

9

So forth they traueld an vneuen payre,
That mote to all men seeme an vncouth sight ;
A saluage man matcht with a Ladie fayre,
That rather seem'd the conquest of his might,
Gotten by spoyle, then purchaced aright.
But he did her attend most carefully,
And faithfully did serue both day and night,
Withouten thought of shame or villeny,
Ne euer shewed signe of foule disloyalty.

10

Vpon a day as on their way they went,
It chaunst some furniture about her steed
To be disordred by some accident :
Which to redresse, she did th'assistance need
Of this her groome, which he by signes did
    reede,
And streight his combrous armes aside did lay
Vpon the ground, withouten doubt or dreed,
And in his homely wize began to assay
T'amend what was amisse, and put in right aray.

11

Bout which whilest he was busied thus hard,
Lo where a knight together with his squire,
All arm'd to point came ryding thetherward,
Which seemed by their portance and attire,
To be two errant knights, that did inquire
After aduentures, where they mote them get.
Those were to weet (if that ye it require)
Prince *Arthur* and young *Timias*, which met
By straunge occasion, that here needs forth be
    set.

12

After that *Timias* had againe recured
The fauour of *Belphebe*, (as ye heard)
And of her grace did stand againe assured,
To happie blisse he was full high vprear'd,
Nether of enuy, nor of chaunge afeard,
Though many foes did him maligne therefore,
And with vniust detraction him did beard ;
Yet he himselfe so well and wisely bore,
That in her soueraine lyking he dwelt euermore.

13

But of them all, which did his ruine seeke
Three mightie enemies did him most despight,
Three mightie ones, and cruell minded eeke.
That him not onely sought by open might
To ouerthrow, but to supplant by slight.
The first of them by name was cald *Despetto*,
Exceeding all the rest in powre and hight ;
The second not so strong but wise, *Decetto* ;
The third nor strong nor wise, but spightfullest
    Defetto.

14

Oftimes their sundry powres they did employ,
And seuerall deceipts, but all in vaine :
For neither they by force could him destroy,
Ne yet entrap in treasons subtill traine.
Therefore conspiring all together plaine,
They did their counsels now in one compound :
Where singled forces faile, conioynd may
    gaine.
The *Blatant Beast* the fittest meanes they found,
To worke his vtter shame, and throughly him
    confound.

15

Vpon a day as they the time did waite,
When he did raunge the wood for saluage game,
They sent that *Blatant Beast* to be a baite,
To draw him from his deare beloued dame,
Vnwares into the daunger of defame.
For well they wist, that Squire to be so bold,
That no one beast in forrest wylde or tame,
Met him in chase, but he it challenge would,
And plucke the pray oftimes out of their greedy
    hould.

16

The hardy boy, as they deuised had,
Seeing the vgly Monster passing by,
Vpon him set, of perill nought adrad,
Ne skilfull of the vncouth ieopardy ;
And charged him so fierce and furiously,
That his great force vnable to endure,
He forced was to turne from him and fly :
Yet ere he fled, he with his tooth impure
Him heedlesse bit, the whiles he was thereof
    secure.

17

Securely he did after him pursew,
  Thinking by speed to ouertake his flight ;
  Who through thicke woods and brakes and
    briers him drew,
  To weary him the more, and waste his spight,
  So that he now has almost spent his spright.
Till that at length vnto a woody glade
  He came, whose couert stopt his further sight,
  There his three foes shrowded in guilefull shade,
Out of their ambush broke, and gan him to
    inuade.

18

Sharpely they all attonce did him assaile,
  Burning with inward rancour and despight,
  And heaped strokes did round about him haile
  With so huge force, that seemed nothing might
  Beare off their blowes, from percing thorough
    quite.
Yet he them all so warily did ward,
  That none of them in his soft flesh did bite,
  And all the while his backe for best safegard,
He lent against a tree, that backeward onset
  bard.

19

Like a wylde Bull, that being at a bay,
  Is bayted of a mastiffe, and a hound,
  And a curre-dog ; that doe him sharpe assay
  On euery side, and beat about him round ;
  But most that curre barking with bitter sownd,
  And creeping still behinde, doth him incomber,
  That in his chauffe he digs the trampled ground,
  And threats his horns, and bellowes like the
    thonder,
So did that Squire his foes disperse, and driue
  asonder.

20

Him well behoued so ; for his three foes
  Sought to encompasse him on euery side,
  And dangerously did round about enclose.
  But most of all *Defetto* him annoyde,
  Creeping behinde him still to haue destroyde :
  So did *Decetto* eke him circumuent,
  But stout *Despetto* in his greater pryde,
  Did front him face to face against him bent,
Yet he them all withstood, and often made relent.

21

Till that at length nigh tyrd with former chace,
  And weary now with carefull keeping ward,
  He gan to shrinke, and somewhat to giue place,
  Full like ere long to haue escaped hard ;
  When as vnwares he in the forrest heard
  A trampling steede, that with his neighing fast
  Did warne his rider be vppon his gard ;
  With noise whereof the Squire now nigh aghast,
Reuiued was, and sad dispaire away did cast.

22

Eftsoones he spide a Knight approching nye,
  Who seeing one in so great daunger set
  Mongst many foes, him selfe did faster hye ;
  To reskue him, and his weake part abet,
  For pitty so to see him ouerset.
Whom soone as his three enemies did vew,
  They fled, and fast into the wood did get :
  Him booted not to thinke them to pursew,
The couert was so thicke, that did no passage
  shew.

23

Then turning to that swaine, him well he knew
  To be his *Timias*, his owne true Squire,
  Whereof exceeding glad, he to him drew,
  And him embracing twixt his armes entire,
  Him thus bespake ; My liefe, my lifes desire,
  Why haue ye me alone thus long yleft ?
  Tell me what worlds despight, or heauens yre
  Hath you thus long away from me bereft ?
Where haue ye all this while bin wandring,
  where bene weft ?

24

With that he sighed deepe for inward tyne :
  To whom the Squire nought aunswered againe,
  But shedding few soft teares from tender eyne,
  His deare affect with silence did restraine,
  And shut vp all his plaint in priuy paine.
  There they awhile some gracious speaches spent,
  As to them seemed fit time to entertaine.
  After all which vp to their steedes they went,
And forth together rode a comely couplement.

25

So now they be arriued both in sight
  Of this wyld man, whom they full busie found
  About the sad *Serena* things to dight,
  With those braue armours lying on the ground,
  That seem'd the spoile of some right well
    renownd.
  Which when that Squire beheld, he to them
    stept,
  Thinking to take them from that hylding hound :
  But he it seeing, lightly to him lept,
And sternely with strong hand it from his
  handling kept.

26

Gnashing his grinded teeth with griesly looke,
  And sparkling fire out of his furious eyne,
  Him with his fist vnwares on th'head he strooke,
  That made him downe vnto the earth encline ;
  Whence soone vpstarting much he gan repine,
  And laying hand vpon his wrathfull blade,
  Thought therewithall forthwith him to haue
    slaine,
  Who it perceiuing, hand vpon him layd,
And greedily him griping, his auengement stayd.

27

With that aloude the faire *Serena* cryde
  Vnto the Knight, them to dispart in twaine:
Who to them stepping did them soone diuide,
And did from further violence restraine,
Albe the wyld-man hardly would refraine.
Then gan the Prince, of her for to demand,
What and from whence she was, and by what
     traine
She fell into that saluage villaines hand,
And whether free with him she now were, or in
  band.

28

To whom she thus ; I am, as now ye see,
  The wretchedst Dame, that liue this day on
     ground,
Who both in minde, the which most grieueth me,
And body haue receiu'd a mortall wound,
That hath me driuen to this drery stound.
I was erewhile, the loue of *Calepine*,
Who whether he aliue be to be found,
Or by some deadly chaunce be done to pine,
Since I him lately lost, vneath is to define.

29

In saluage forrest I him lost of late,
  Where I had surely long ere this bene dead,
Or else remained in most wretched state,
Had not this wylde man in that wofull stead
Kept, and deliuered me from deadly dread.
In such a saluage wight, of brutish kynd,
Amongst wilde beastes in desert forrests bred,
It is most straunge and wonderfull to fynd
So milde humanity, and perfect gentle mynd.

30

Let me therefore this fauour for him finde,
  That ye will not your wrath vpon him wreake,
Sith he cannot expresse his simple minde,
Ne yours conceiue, ne but by tokens speake :
Small praise to proue your powre on wight so
  weake.
With such faire words she did their heate asswage,
And the strong course of their displeasure breake,
That they to pitty turnd their former rage,
And each sought to supply the office of her page.

31

So hauing all things well about her dight,
  She on her way cast forward to proceede,
And they her forth conducted, where they might
Finde harbour fit to comfort her great neede.
For now her wounds corruption gan to breed ;
And eke this Squire, who likewise wounded was
Of that same Monster late, for lacke of heed,
Now gan to faint, and further could not pas
Through feeblenesse, which all his limbes op-
  pressed has.

32

So forth they rode together all in troupe,
  To seeke some place, the which mote yeeld some
     ease
To these sicke twaine, that now began to droupe,
And all the way the Prince sought to appease
The bitter anguish of their sharpe disease,
By all the courteous meanes he could inuent,
Somewhile with merry purpose fit to please,
And otherwhile with good encouragement,
To make them to endure the pains, did them
  torment.

33

Mongst which, *Serena* did to him relate
  The foule discourt'sies and vnknightly parts,
Which *Turpine* had vnto her shewed late,
Without compassion of her cruell smarts,
Although *Blandina* did with all her arts
Him otherwise perswade, all that she might ;
Yet he of malice, without her desarts,
Not onely her excluded late at night,
But also trayterously did wound her weary
  Knight.

34

Wherewith the Prince sore moued, there auoud,
  That soone as he returned backe againe,
He would auenge th'abuses of that proud
And shamefull Knight, of whom she did com-
     plaine.
This wize did they each other entertaine,
To passe the tedious trauell of the way ;
Till towards night they came vnto a plaine,
By which a little Hermitage there lay,
Far from all neighbourhood, the which annoy
  it may.

35

And nigh thereto a little Chappell stoode,
  Which being all with Yuy ouerspred,
Deckt all the roofe, and shadowing the roode,
Seem'd like a groue faire braunched ouer hed :
Therein the Hermite, which his life here led
In streight obseruaunce of religious vow,
Was wont his howres and holy things to bed ;
And therein he likewise was praying now,
Whenas these Knights arriu'd, they wist not
  where nor how.

36

They stayd not there, but streight way in did
  pas.
Whom when the Hermite present saw in place,
From his deuotion streight he troubled was ;
Which breaking off he toward them did pace,
With stayed steps, and graue beseeming grace:
For well it seem'd, that whilome he had beene
Some goodly person, and of gentle race,
That could his good to all, and well did weene,
How each to entertaine with curt'sie well
  beseene.

37

And soothly it was sayd by common fame,
So long as age enabled him thereto,
That he had bene a man of mickle name,
Renowmed much in armes and derring doe :
But being aged now and weary to
Of warres delight, and worlds contentious toyle,
The name of knighthood he did disauow,
And hanging vp his armes and warlike spoyle,
From all this worlds incombraunce did himselfe
    assoyle.

38

He thence them led into his Hermitage,
Letting their steedes to graze vpon the greene :
Small was his house, and like a little cage,
For his owne turne, yet inly neate and clene,
Deckt with greene boughes, and flowers gay
    beseene.
Therein he them full faire did entertaine
Not with such forged showes, as fitter beene
For courting fooles, that curtesies would faine,
But with entire affection and appearaunce
    plaine.

39

Yet was their fare but homely, such as hee
Did vse, his feeble body to sustaine ;
The which full gladly they did take in glee,
Such as it was, ne did of want complaine,
But being well suffiz'd, them rested faine.
But faire *Serene* all night could take no rest,
Ne yet that gentle Squire, for grieuous paine
Of their late woundes, the which the *Blatant Beast*
Had giuen them, whose griefe through suf-
    fraunce sore increast.

40

So all that night they past in great disease,
Till that the morning, bringing earely light
To guide mens labours, brought them also ease,
And some asswagement of their painefull plight.
Then vp they rose, and gan them selues to dight
Vnto their iourney ; but that Squire and Dame
So faint and feeble were, that they ne might
Endure to trauell, nor one foote to frame :
Their hearts were sicke, their sides were sore,
    their feete were lame.

41

Therefore the Prince, whom great affaires in mynd
Would not permit, to make there lenger stay,
Was forced there to leaue them both behynd,
In that good Hermits charge, whom he did pray
To tend them well. So forth he went his way,
And with him eke the saluage, that whyleare
Seeing his royall vsage and array,
Was greatly growne in loue of that braue pere,
Would needes depart, as shall declared be else-
    where.

Cant. VI.

The Hermite heales both Squire and dame
    Of their sore maladies :
He Turpine doth defeate, and shame
    For his late villanies.

1

No wound, which warlike hand of enemy
Inflicts with dint of sword, so sore doth light,
As doth the poysnous sting, which infamy
Infixeth in the name of noble wight :
For by no art, nor any leaches might
It euer can recured be againe ;
Ne all the skill, which that immortall spright
Of *Podalyrius* did in it retaine,
Can remedy such hurts ; such hurts are hellish
    paine.

2

Such were the wounds, the which that *Blatant
    Beast*
Made in the bodies of that Squire and Dame ;
And being such, were now much more increast,
For want of taking heede vnto the same,
That now corrupt and curelesse they became.
Howbe that carefull Hermite did his best,
With many kindes of medicines meete, to tame
The poysnous humour, which did most infest
Their ranckling wour.ds, and euery day them
    duely drest.

3

For he right well in Leaches craft was seene,
And through the long experience of his dayes,
Which had in many fortunes tossed beene,
And past through many perillous assayes,
He knew the diuerse went of mortall wayes,
And in the mindes of men had great insight ;
Which with sage counsell, when they went
    astray,
He could enforme, and them reduce aright,
And al the passions heale, which wound the
    weaker spright.

4

For whylome he had bene a doughty Knight,
As any one, that liued in his daies,
And proued oft in many perillous fight,
Of which he grace and glory wonne alwaies,
And in all battels bore away the baies.
But being now attacht with timely age,
And weary of this worlds vnquiet waies,
He tooke him selfe vnto this Hermitage,
In which he liu'd alone, like carelesse bird in
    cage.

5

One day, as he was searching of their wounds,
  He found that they had festred priuily,
  Andranckling inward with vnruly stounds,
  The inner parts now gan to putrify,
  That quite they seem'd past helpe of surgery,
  And rather needed to be disciplinde
  With holesome reede of sad sobriety,
To rule the stubborne rage of passion blinde :
Giue salues to euery sore, but counsell to the
   minde.

6

So taking them apart into his cell,
  He to that point fit speaches gan to frame,
  As he the art of words knew wondrous well,
  And eke could doe, as well as say the same,
  And thus he to them sayd ; Faire daughter
   Dame,
  And you faire sonne, which here thus long now
   lie
  In piteous languor, since ye hither came,
  In vaine of me ye hope for remedie,
And I likewise in vaine doe salues to you applie.

7

For in your selfe your onely helpe doth lie,
  To heale your selues, and must proceed alone
  From your owne will, to cure your maladie.
  Who can him cure, that will be cur'd of none ?
  If therefore health ye seeke, obserue this one.
  First learne your outward sences to refraine
  From things, that stirre vp fraile affection ;
  Your eies, your eares, your tongue, your talk
   restraine
From that they most affect, and in due termes
   containe.

8

For from those outward sences ill affected,
  The seede of all this euill first doth spring,
  Which at the first before it had infected,
  Mote easie be supprest with little thing :
  But being growen strong, it forth doth bring
  Sorrow, and anguish, and impatient paine
  In th'inner parts, and lastly scattering
  Contagious poyson close through euery vaine,
It neuer rests, till it haue wrought his finall bane.

9

For that beastes teeth, which wounded you
   tofore,
  Are so exceeding venemous and keene,
  Made all of rusty yron, ranckling sore,
  That where they bite, it booteth not to weene
  With salue, or antidote, or other mene
  It euer to amend : ne maruaile ought ;
  For that same beast was bred of hellish strene,
  And long in darksome *Stygian* den vpbrought,
Begot of foule *Echidna*, as in bookes is taught.

10

Echidna is a Monster direfull dred,
  Whom Gods doe hate, and heauens abhor to see ;
  So hideous is her shape, so huge her hed,
  That euen the hellish fiends affrighted bee
  At sight thereof, and from her presence flee :
  Yet did her face and former parts professe
  A faire young Mayden, full of comely glee ;
  But all her hinder parts did plaine expresse
A monstrous Dragon, full of fearefull vglinesse

11

To her the Gods, for her so dreadfull face,
  In fearefull darkenesse, furthest from the skie,
  And from the earth, appointed haue her place,
  Mongst rocks and caues, where she enrold doth
   lie
  In hideous horrour and obscurity,
  Wasting the strength of her immortall age.
  There did *Typhaon* with her company,
  Cruell *Typhaon*, whose tempestuous rage
Make th'heauens tremble oft, and him with
   vowes asswage.

12

Of that commixtion they did then beget
  This hellish Dog, that hight the *Blatant Beast* ;
  A wicked Monster, that his tongue doth whet
  Gainst all, both good and bad, both most and
   least,
  And poures his poysnous gall forth to infest
  The noblest wights with notable defame :
  Ne euer Knight, that bore so lofty creast,
  Ne euer Lady of so honest name,
But he them spotted with reproch, or secrete
   shame.

13

In vaine therefore it were, with medicine
  To goe about to salue such kynd of sore,
  That rather needes wise read and discipline,
  Then outward salues, that may augment it
   more.
  Aye me (sayd then *Serena* sighing sore)
  What hope of helpe doth then for vs remaine,
  If that no salues may vs to health restore ?
  But sith we need good counsell (sayd the swaine)
Aread good sire, some counsell, that may vs
   sustaine.

14

The best (sayd he) that I can you aduize,
  Is to auoide the occasion of the ill :
  For when the cause, whence euill doth arize,
  Remoued is, th'effect surceaseth still.
  Abstaine from pleasure, and restraine your will,
  Subdue desire, and bridle loose delight,
  Vse scanted diet, and forbeare your fill,
  Shun secresie, and talke in open sight :
So shall you soone repaire your present euill
   plight.

15

Thus hauing sayd, his sickely patients
  Did gladly hearken to his graue beheast,
  And kept so well his wise commaundements,
That in short space their malady was ceast,
And eke the biting of that harmefull Beast
  Was throughly heal'd. Tho when they did
    perceaue
Their wounds recur'd, and forces reincreast,
  Of that good Hermite both they tooke their
    leaue,
And went both on their way, ne ech would other
    leaue.

16

But each the other vow'd t'accompany,
  The Lady, for that she was much in dred,
  Now left alone in great extremity,
The Squire, for that he courteous was indeed,
Would not her leaue alone in her great need.
  So both together trauel'd, till they met
  With a faire Mayden clad in mourning weed,
Vpon a mangy iade vnmeetely set,
And a lewd foole her leading thorough dry and
    wet.

17

But by what meanes that shame to her befell,
  And how thereof her selfe she did acquite,
  I must a while forbeare to you to tell ;
Till that, as comes by course, I doe recite,
What fortune to the Briton Prince did lite,
  Pursuing that proud Knight, the which
    whileare
Wrought to Sir *Calidore* so foule despight ;
  And eke his Lady, though she sickely were,
So lewdly had abusde, as ye did lately heare.

18

The Prince according to the former token,
  Which faire *Serene* to him deliuered had,
  Pursu'd him streight, in mynd to bene ywroken
Of all the vile demeane, and vsage bad,
With which he had those two so ill bestad :
  Ne wight with him on that aduenture went,
  But that wyldeman, whom though he oft forbad,
Yet for no bidding, nor for being shent,
Would he restrayned be from his attendement.

19

Arriuing there, as did by chaunce befall,
  He found the gate wyde ope, and in he rode,
  Ne stayd, till that he came into the hall :
Where soft dismounting like a weary lode,
Vpon the ground with feeble feete he trode,
  As he vnable were for very neede   ·
  To moue one foote, but there must make
    abode ;
The whiles the saluage man did take his steede,
And in some stable neare did set him vp to feede.

20

Ere long to him a homely groome there came,
  That in rude wise him asked, what he was,
  That durst so boldly, without let or shame,
Into his Lords forbidden hall to passe.
To whom the Prince, him fayning to embase,
  Mylde answer made ; he was an errant Knight,
  The which was fall'n into this feeble case,
Through many wounds, which lately he in fight
Receiued had, and prayd to pitty his ill plight.

21

But he, the more outrageous and bold,
  Sternely did bid him quickely thence auaunt,
  Or deare aby, for why his Lord of old
Did hate all errant Knights, which there did
    haunt,
Ne lodging would to any of them graunt,
  And therefore lightly bad him packe away,
  Not sparing him with bitter words to taunt ;
And therewithall rude hand on him did lay,
To thrust him out of dore, doing his worst assay.

22

Which when the Saluage comming now in place,
  Beheld, eftsoones he all enraged grew,
  And running streight vpon that villaine base,
Like a fell Lion at him fiercely flew,
  And with his teeth and nailes, in present vew,
  Him rudely rent, and all to peeces tore :
So miserably him all helpelesse slew,
  That with the noise, whilest he did loudly rore,
The people of the house rose forth in great
    vprore.

23

Who when on ground they saw their fellow
    slaine,
  And that same Knight and Saluage standing by,
  Vpon them two they fell with might and maine,
And on them layd so huge and horribly,
As if they would haue slaine them presently.
  But the bold Prince defended him so well,
  And their assault withstood so mightily,
That maugre all their might, he did repell,
And beat them back, whilest many vnderneath
    him fell.

24

Yet he them still so sharpely did pursew,
  That few of them he left aliue, which fled,
  Those euill tidings to their Lord to shew.
Who hearing how his people badly sped,
  Came forth in hast : where when as with the dead
  He saw the ground all strow'd, and that same
    Knight
And saluage with their bloud fresh steeming red,
  He woxe nigh mad with wrath and fell despight,
And with reprochfull words him thus bespake
    on hight.

25

Art thou he, traytor, that with treason vile,
  Hast slaine my men in this vnmanly maner,
  And now triumphest in the piteous spoile
  Of these poore folk, whose soules with black
    dishonor
  And foule defame doe decke thy bloudy baner?
The meede whereof shall shortly be thy shame,
And wretched end, which still attendeth on her.
  With that him selfe to battell he did frame;
So did his forty yeomen, which there with him
    came.

26

With dreadfull force they all did him assaile,
  And round about with boystrous strokes
    oppresse,
  That on his shield did rattle like to haile
  In a great tempest; that in such distresse,
  He wist not to which side him to addresse.
  And euermore that crauen cowherd Knight
  Was at his backe with heartlesse heedinesse,
  Wayting if he vnwares him murther might:
For cowardize doth still in villany delight.

27

Whereof whenas the Prince was well aware,
  He to him turnd with furious intent,
  And him against his powre gan to prepare;
  Like a fierce Bull, that being busie bent
  To fight with many foes about him ment,
  Feeling some curre behinde his heeles to bite,
  Turnes him about with fell auengement;
  So likewise turnde the Prince vpon the Knight,
And layd at him amaine with all his wil! and
    might.

28

Who when he once his dreadfull strokes had
    tasted,
  Durst not the furie of his force abyde,
  But turn'd abacke, and to retyre him hasted
  Through the thick prease, there thinking him
    to hyde.
                              [eyde,
  But when the Prince had once him plainely
  He foot by foot him followed alway,
  Ne would him suffer once to shrinke asyde
  But ioyning close, huge lode at him did lay:
Who flying still did ward, and warding fly away.

29

But when his foe he still so eger saw,
  Vnto his heeles himselfe he did betake,
  Hoping vnto some refuge to withdraw:
  Ne would the Prince him euer foot forsake,
  Where so he went, but after him did make.
  He fled from roome to roome, from place to place,
  Why lest euery ioynt for dread of death did quake,
  Still looking after him, that did him chace;
That made him euermore increase his speedie pace.

30

At last he vp into the chamber came,
  Whereas his loue was sitting all alone,
  Wayting what tydings of her folke became.
  There did the Prince him ouertake anone,
  Crying in vaine to her, him to bemone;
  And with his sword him on the head did smyte,
  That to the ground he fell in senselesse swone:
  Yet whether thwart or flatly it did lyte,
The tempred steele did not into his braynepan
    byte.

31

Which when the Ladie saw, with great affright
  She starting vp, began to shrieke aloud,
  And with her garment couering him from sight,
  Seem'd vnder her protection him to shroud;
  And falling lowly at his feet, her bowd
  Vpon her knee, intreating him for grace,
  And often him besought, and prayd, and vowd;
  That with the ruth of her so wretched case,
He stayd his second strooke, and did his hand
    abase.

32

Her weed she then withdrawing, did him
    discouer,
  Who now come to himselfe, yet would not rize,
  But still did lie as dead, and quake, and quiuer,
  That euen the Prince his basenesse did despize,
  And eke his Dame him seeing in such guize,
  Gan him recomfort, and from ground to reare.
  Who rising vp at last in ghastly wize,
  Like troubled ghost did dreadfully appeare,
As one that had no life him left through former
    feare.

33

Whom when the Prince so deadly saw dismayd,
  He for such basenesse shamefully him shent,
  And with sharpe words did bitterly vpbrayd;
  Vile cowheard dogge, now doe I much repent,
  That euer I this life vnto thee lent,
  Whereof thou caytiue so vnworthie art;
  That both thy loue, for lacke of hardiment,
  And eke thy selfe, for want of manly hart,
And eke all knights hast shamed with this knight-
    lesse part.

34

Yet further hast thou heaped shame to shame,
  And crime to crime, by this thy cowheard feare.
  For first it was to thee reprochfull blame,
  To erect this wicked custome, which I heare,
  Gainst errant Knights and Ladies thou dost
    reare;
  Whom when thou mayst, thou dost of arms
    despoile,
  Or of their vpper garment, which they weare:
  Yet doest thou not with manhood, but with
    guile
Maintaine this euill vse, thy foes thereby to foile.

35

And lastly in approuance of thy wrong,
  To shew such faintnesse and foule cowardize,
  Is greatest shame: for oft it falles, that strong
And valiant knights doe rashly enterprize,
  Either for fame, or else for exercize,
A wrongfull quarrell to maintaine by fight;
  Yet haue, through prowesse and their braue
    emprize,
Gotten great worship in this worldes sight.
For greater force there needs to maintaine
  wrong, then right.

36

Yet since thy life vnto this Ladie fayre
  I giuen haue, liue in reproch and scorne;
  Ne euer armes, ne euer knighthood dare
Hence to professe: for shame is to adorne
With so braue badges one so basely borne;
  But onely breath sith that I did forgiue.
So hauing from his crauen bodie torne
Those goodly armes, he them away did giue
And onely suffred him this wretched life to liue.

37

There whilest he thus was setling things aboue,
Atwene that Ladie myld and recreant knight,
To whom his life he graunted for her loue,
He gan bethinke him, in what perilous plight
He had behynd him left that saluage wight,
  Amongst so many foes, whom sure he thought
By this quite slaine in so vnequall fight:
Therefore descending backe in haste, he sought
if yet he were aliue, or to destruction brought.

38

There he him found enuironed about
  With slaughtred bodies, which his hand had
    slaine,
And laying yet a fresh with courage stout
Vpon the rest, that did aliue remaine;
  Whom he likewise right sorely did constraine,
Like scattred sheepe, to seeke for safetie,
  After he gotten had with busie paine
Some of their weapons, which thereby did lie,
With which he layd about, and made them fast
  to flie.

39

Whom when the Prince so felly saw to rage,
  Approching to him neare, his hand he stayd,
And sought, by making signes, him to asswage:
Who them perceiuing, streight to him obayd,
  As to his Lord, and downe his weapons layd,
As if he long had to his heasts bene trayned.
  Thence he him brought away, and vp conuayd
Into the chamber, where that Dame remayned
With her vnworthy knight, who ill him enter-
  tayned.

40

Whom when the Saluage saw from daunger free,
  Sitting beside his Ladie there at ease,
He well remembred, that the same was hee,
Which lately sought his Lord for to displease:
  Tho all in rage, he on him streight did seaze,
As if he would in peeces him haue rent;
  And were not, that the Prince did him appeaze,
He had not left one limbe of him vnrent:
But streight he held his hand at his commaunde-
  ment.

41

Thus hauing all things well in peace ordayned,
  The Prince himselfe there all that night did
    rest,
Where him *Blandina* fayrely entertayned,
With all the courteous glee and goodly feast,
  The which for him she could imagine best.
For well she knew the wayes to win good will
  Of euery wight, that were not too infest,
And how to please the minds of good and ill,
Through tempering of her words and lookes by
  wondrous skill.

42

Yet were her words and lookes but false and
  fayned,
  To some hid end to make more easie way,
Or to allure such fondlings, whom she trayned
Into her trap vnto their owne decay:
  Thereto, when needed, she could weepe and
    pray,
And when her listed, she could fawne and flatter;
  Now smyling smoothly, like to sommers day,
Now glooming sadly, so to cloke her matter
Yet were her words but wynd, and all her teares
  but water.

43

Whether such grace were giuen her by kynd,
  As women wont their guilefull wits to guyde;
  Or learn'd the art to please, I doe not fynd.
This well I wote, that she so well applyde
  Her pleasing tongue, that soone she pacifyde
The wrathfull Prince, and wrought her hus-
    bands peace.
  Who nathelesse not therewith satisfyde,
His rancorous despight did not releasse,
Ne secretly from thought of fell reuenge sur-
  ceasse.

44

For all that night, the whyles the Prince did rest
  In carelesse couch, not weeting what was ment,
He watcht in close awayt with weapons prest,
Willing to worke his villenous intent
  On him, that had so shamefully him shent:
Yet durst he not for very cowardize
  Effect the same, why lest all the night was spent.
The morrow next the Prince did early rize,
And passed forth, to follow his first enterprise.

Cant. VII.

Turpine is baffuld, his two knights
doe gaine their treasons meed,
Fayre Mirabellaes punishment
for loues disdaine decreed.

1

Like as the gentle hart it selfe bewrayes,
In doing gentle deedes with franke delight,
Euen so the baser mind it selfe displayes,
In cancred malice and reuengefull spight.
For to maligne, t'enuie, t'vse shifting slight,
Be arguments of a vile donghill mind,
Which what it dare not doe by open might,
To worke by wicked treason wayes doth find,
By such discourteous deeds discouering his base
    kind.

2

That well appeares in this discourteous knight,
The coward *Turpine*, whereof now I treat ;
Who notwithstanding that in former fight
He of the Prince his life receiued late,
Yet in his mind malitious and ingrate
He gan deuize, to be aueng'd anew
For all that shame, which kindled inward hate.
Therefore so soone as he was out of vew,
Himselfe in hast he arm'd, and did him fast
    pursew.

3

Well did he tract his steps, as he did ryde,
Yet would not neare approch in daungers eye,
But kept aloofe for dread to be descryde,
Vntill fit time and place he mote espy,
Where he mote worke him scath and villeny.
At last he met two knights to him vnknowne,
The which were armed both agreeably,
And both combynd, what euer chaunce were
    blowne,
Betwixt them to diuide, and each to make his
    owne.

4

To whom false *Turpine* comming courteously,
To cloke the mischiefe, which he inly ment,
Gan to complaine of great discourtesie,
Which a straunge knight, that neare afore him
    went,
Had done to him, and his deare Ladie shent :
Which if they would afford him ayde at need
For to auenge, in time conuenient,
They should accomplish both a knightly deed,
And for their paines obtaine of him a goodly
    meed.

5

The knights beleeu'd, that all he sayd, was trew,
And being fresh and full of youthly spright,
Were glad to heare of that aduenture new,
In which they mote make triall of their might,
Which neuer yet they had approu'd in fight ;
And eke desirous of the ofired meed,
Said then the one of them ; Where is that wight,
The which hath doen to thee this wrongfull deed,
That we may it auenge, and punish him with
    speed ?

6

He rides (said *Turpine*) there not farre afore,
With a wyld man soft footing by his syde,
That if ye list to haste a litle more,
Ye may him ouertake in timely tyde.
Eftsoones they pricked forth with forward pryde,
And ere that litle while they ridden had,
The gentle Prince not farre away they spyde,
Ryding a softly pace witn portance sad,
Deuizing of his loue more, then of daunger drad.

7

Then one of them aloud vnto him cryde,
Bidding him turne againe, false traytour knight,
Foule womanwronger, for he him defyde.
With that they both at once with equall spight
Did bend their speares, and both with equall
    might   [marke,
Against him ran ; but th'one did misse his
And being carried with his force forthright,
Glaunst swiftly by ; like to that heauenly sparke,
Which glyding through the ayre lights all the
    heauens darke.

8

But th'other ayming better, did him smite
Full in the shield, with so impetuous powre,
That all his launce in peeces shiuered quite,
And scattered all about, fell on the flowre.
But the stout Prince, with much more steddy
    stowre
Full on his beuer did him strike so sore,
That the cold steele through piercing, did deuowre
His vitall breath, and to the ground him bore,
Where still he bathed lay in his owne bloody gore.

9

As when a cast of Faulcons make their flight
At an Herneshaw, that lyes aloft on wing,
The whyles they strike at him with heedlesse
    might,
The warie foule his bill doth backward wring ;
On which the first, whose force her first doth bring,
Her selfe quite through the bodie doth engore,
And falleth downe to ground like senselesse thing,
But th'other not so swift, as she before,
Fayles of her souse, and passing by doth hurt
    no more.

10

By this the other, which was passed by,
Himselfe recouering, was return'd to fight ;
Where when he saw his fellow lifelesse ly,
He much was daunted with so dismall sight ;
Yet nought abating of his former spight,
Let driue at him with so malitious mynd,
As if he would haue passed through him quight :
But the steele-head no stedfast hold could fynd,
But glauncing by, deceiu'd him of that he
    desynd.

11

Not so the Prince : for his well learned speare
Tooke surer hould, and from his horses backe
Aboue a launces length him forth did beare,
And gainst the cold hard earth so sore him
    strake,
That all his bones in peeces nigh he brake.
Where seeing him so lie, he left his steed,
And to him leaping, vengeance thought to take
Of him, for all his former follies meed,
With flaming sword in hand his terror more to
    breed.

12

The fearefull swayne beholding death so nie,
Cryde out aloud for mercie him to saue ;
In lieu whereof he would to him descrie,
Great treason to him meant, his life to reaue.
The Prince soone hearkned, and his life forgaue.
Then thus said he, There is a straunger knight,
The which for promise of great meed, vs draue
To this attempt, to wreake his hid despight,
For that himselfe thereto did want sufficient
    might.

13

The Prince much mused at such villenie,
And sayd ; Now sure ye well haue earn'd your
    meed,
For th'one is dead, and th'other soone shall die,
Vnlesse to me thou hether bring with speed
The wretch, that hyr'd you to this wicked deed.
He glad of life, and willing eke to wreake
The guilt on him, which did this mischiefe
    breed,
Swore by his sword, that neither day nor weeke
He would surceasse, but him, where so he were,
    would seeke.

14

So vp he rose, and forth streight way he went
Backe to the place, where *Turpine* late he lore ;
There he him found in great astonishment,
To see him so bedight with bloodie gore,
And griesiy wounds that him appalled sore.
Yet thus at length he said, How now Sir knight?
What meaneth this, which here I see before ?
How fortuneth this foule vncomely plight,
So different from that, which earst ye seem'd in
    sight ?

15

Perdie (said he) in euill houre it fell,
That euer I for meed did vndertake
So hard a taske, as life for hyre to sell ;
The which I earst aduentur'd for your sake.
Witnesse the wounds, and this wyde bloudie lake,
Which ye may see yet all about me steeme.
Therefore now yeeld, as ye did promise make,
My due reward, the which right well I deeme
I yearned haue, that life so dearely did redeeme.

16

But where then is (quoth he halfe wrothfully)
Where is the bootie, which therefore I bought,
That cursed caytiue, my strong enemy,
That recreant knight, whose hated life I sought?
And where is eke your friend, which halfe it ought?
He lyes (said he) vpon the cold bare ground,
Slayne of that errant knight, with whom he
    fought ;
Whom afterwards my selfe with many a wound
Did slay againe, as ye may see there in the
    stound.

17

Thereof false *Turpin* was full glad and faine,
And needs with him streight to the place
    would ryde,
Where he himselfe might see his foeman slaine ;
For else his feare could not be satisfyde.
So as they rode, he saw the way all dyde
With streames of bloud ; which tracting by
    the traile,
Ere long they came, whereas in euill tyde
That other swayne, like ashes deadly pale,
Lay in the lap of death, rewing his wretched
    bale.

18

Much did the Crauen seeme to mone his case,
That for his sake his deare life had forgone ;
And him bewayling with affection base,
Did counterfeit kind pittie, where was none :
For wheres no courage, theres no ruth nor mone.
Thence passing forth, not farre away he found,
Whereas the Prince himselfe lay all alone,
Loosely displayd vpon the grassie ground,
Possessed of sweete sleepe, that luld him soft in
    swound.

19

Wearie of trauell in his former fight,
He there in shade himselfe had layd to rest,
Hauing his armes and warlike things vndight,
Fearelesse of foes that mote his peace molest ;
The whyles his saluage page, that wont be prest,
Was wandred in the wood another way,
To doe some thing, that seemed to him best,
The whyles his Lord in siluer slomber lay,
Like to the Euening starre adorn'd with deawy
    ray.

20

Whom when as *Turpin* saw so loosely layd,
He weened well, that he in deed was dead,
Like as that other knight to him had sayd:
But when he nigh approcht, he mote aread
Plaine signes in him of life and liuelihead.
Whereat much grieu'd against that straunger knight,
That him too light of credence did mislead,
He would haue backe retyred from that sight,
That was to him on earth the deadliest despight.

21

But that same knight would not once let him start,
But plainely gan to him declare the case
Of all his mischiefe, and late lucklesse smart;
How both he and his fellow there in place
Were vanquished, and put to foule disgrace,
And how that he in lieu of life him lent,
Had vow'd vnto the victor, him to trace
And follow through the world, where so he went,
Till that he him deliuered to his punishment.

22

He therewith much abashed and affrayd,
Began to tremble euery limbe and vaine;
And softly whispering him, entyrely prayd,
T'aduize him better, then by such a traine
Him to betray vnto a straunger swaine:
Yet rather counseld him contrarywize,
Sith he likewise did wrong by him sustaine,
To ioyne with him and vengeance to deuize,
Whylest time did offer meanes him sleeping to surprize.

23

Nathelesse for all his speach, the gentle knight
Would not be tempted to such villenie,
Regarding more his faith, which he did plight,
All were it to his mortall enemie,
Then to entrap him by false treacherie:
Great shame in lieges blood to be embrew'd.
Thus whylest they were debating diuerslie,
The Saluage forth out of the wood issew'd
Backe to the place, whereas his Lord he sleeping vew'd.

24

There when he saw those two so neare him stand,
He doubted much what mote their meaning bee,
And throwing downe his load out of his hand,
To weet great store of forrest frute, which hee
Had for his food late gathered from the tree,
Himselfe vnto his weapon he betooke,
That was an oaken plant, which lately hee
Rent by the root; which he so sternely shooke,
That like an hazell wand, it quiuered and quooke.

25

Whereat the Prince awaking, when he spyde
The traytour *Turpin* with that other knight,
He started vp, and snatching neare his syde
His trustie sword, the seruant of his might,
Like a fell Lyon leaped to him light,
And his left hand vpon his collar layd.
Therewith the cowheard deaded with affright,
Fell flat to ground, ne word vnto him sayd,
But holding vp his hands, with silence mercie prayd.

26

But he so full of indignation was,
That to his prayer nought he would incline,
But as he lay vpon the humbled gras,
His foot he set on his vile necke, in signe
Of seruile yoke, that nobler harts repine.
Then letting him arise like abiect thrall,
He gan to him obiect his haynous crime,
And to reuile, and rate, and recreant call,
And lastly to despoyle of knightly bannerall.

27

And after all, for greater infamie,
He by the heeles him hung vpon a tree,
And baffuld so, that all which passed by,
The picture of his punishment might see,
And by the like ensample warned bee,
How euer they through treason doe trespasse.
But turne we now backe to that Ladie free,
Whom late we left ryding vpon an Asse,
Led by a Carle and foole, which by her side did passe.

28

She was a Ladie of great dignitie
And lifted vp to honorable place,
Famous through all the land of Faerie,
Though of meane parentage and kindred base,
Yet deckt with wondrous giftes of natures grace,
That all men did her person much admire,
And praise the feature of her goodly face,
The beames whereof did kindle louely fire
In th'harts of many a knight, and many a gentle squire.

29

But she thereof grew proud and insolent,
That none she worthie thought to be her fere,
But scornd them all, that loue vnto her ment,
Yet was she lou'd of many a worthy pere,
Vnworthy she to be belou'd so dere,
That could not weigh of worthinesse aright.
For beautie is more glorious bright and clere,
The more it is admir'd of many a wight,
And noblest she, that serued is of noblest knight.

30

But this coy Damzell thought contrariwize,
    That such proud looks would make her
        praysed more ;
And that the more she did all loue despize,
    The more would wretched louers her adore.
What cared she, who sighed for her sore,
    Or who did wayle or watch the wearie night ?
Let them that list, their lucklesse lot deplore ;
    She was borne free, not bound to any wight,
And so would euer liue, and loue her owne
        delight.

31

Through such her stubborne stifnesse, and hard
        hart,
    Many a wretch, for want of remedie,
Did languish long in lifeconsuming smart,
    And at the last through dreary dolour die :
Whylest she, the Ladie of her libertie,
    Did boast her beautie had such soueraine
        might,
That with the onely twinckle of her eye,
    She could or saue, or spill, whom she would
        hight.
What could the Gods doe more, but doe it more
        aright ?

32

But loe the Gods, that mortall follies vew,
    Did worthily reuenge this maydens pride ;
And nought regarding her so goodly hew,
    Did laugh at her, that many did deride,
Whilest she did weepe, of no man mercifide.
    For on a day, when *Cupid* kept his court,
As he is wont at each Saint Valentide,
    Vnto the which all louers doe resort,
That of their loues successe they there may make
        report ;

33

It fortun'd then, that when the roules were red,
    In which the names of all loues folke were fyled,
That many there were missing, which were ded,
    Or kept in bands, or from their loues exyled,
Or by some other violence despoyled,
    Which when as *Cupid* heard, he wexed wroth,
And doubting to be wronged, or beguyled,
    He bad his eyes to be vnblindfold both,
That he might see his men, and muster them by
        oth.

34

Then found he many missing of his crew,
    Which wont doe suit and seruice to his might ;
Of whom what was becomen, no man knew.
    Therefore a Iurie was impaneld streight,
T'enquire of them, whether by force, or sleight,
    Or their owne guilt, they were away conuayd.
To whom foule *Infamie*, and fell *Despight*
    Gaue euidence, that they were all betrayd,
And murdred cruelly by a rebellious Mayd.

35

Fayre *Mirabella* was her name, whereby
    Of all those crymes she there incited was :
All which when *Cupid* heard, he by and by
    In great displeasure, wild a *Capias*
Should issue forth, t'attach that scornefull lasse.
    The warrant straight was made, and there-
        withall
A Baylieffe errant forth in post did passe,
    Whom they by name there *Portamore* did call ;
He which doth summon louers to loues iudge-
        ment hall.

36

The damzell was attacht, and shortly brought
    Vnto the barre, whereas she was arrayned :
But she thereto nould plead, nor answere ought
    Euen for stubborne pride, which her restrayned
So iudgement past, as is by law ordayned
    In cases like, which when at last she saw,
Her stubborne hart, which loue before disdayned,
    Gan stoupe, and falling downe with humble awe,
Cryde mercie, to abate the extremitie of law.

37

The sonne of *Venus* who is myld by kynd,
    But where he is prouokt with peeuishnesse,
Vnto her prayers piteously enclynd,
    And did the rigour of his doome represse ;
Yet not so freely, but that nathelesse
    He vnto her a penance did impose,
Which was, that through this worlds wyde
        wildernes
    She wander should in companie of those,
Till she had sau'd so many loues, as she did lose.

38

So now she had bene wandring two whole yeares
    Throughout the world, in this vncomely case,
Wasting her goodly hew in heauie teares,
    And her good dayes in dolorous disgrace :
Yet had she not in all these two yeares space,
    Saued but two, yet in two yeares before,
Through her dispiteous pride, whilest loue
        lackt place,
    She had destroyed two and twenty more.
Aie me, how could her loue make half amends
        therefore ?

39

And now she was vppon the weary way,
    When as the gentle Squire, with faire *Serene*,
Met her in such misseeming foule array ;
    The whiles that mighty man did her demeane
With all the euill termes and cruell meane,
    That he could make ; And eeke that angry foole
Which follow'd her, with cursed hands vncleane
    Whipping her horse, did with his smarting toole
Oft whip her dainty selfe, and much augment
        her doole.

40

Ne ought it mote auaile her to entreat
  The one or th'other, better her to vse:
  For both so wilfull were and obstinate,
  That all her piteous plaint they did refuse,
  And rather did the more her beate and bruse.
  But most the former villaine, which did lead
  Her tyreling iade, was bent her to abuse ;
Who though she were with wearinesse nigh
    dead,
Yet would not let her lite, nor rest a little stead.

41

For he was sterne, and terrible by nature,
  And eeke of person huge and hideous,
  Exceeding much the measure of mans stature,
  And rather like a Gyant monstruous.
  For sooth he was descended of the hous
  Of those old Gyants, which did warres darraine
  Against the heauen in order battailous,
  And sib to great *Orgolio*, which was slaine
By *Arthure*, when as *Vnas* Knight he did
    maintaine.

42

His lookes were dreadfull, and his fiery eies
  Like two great Beacons, glared bright and wyde,
  Glauncing askew, as if his enemies
  He scorned in his ouerweening pryde ;
  And stalking stately like a Crane, did stryde
  At euery step vppon the tiptoes hie,
  And all the way he went, on euery syde
  He gaz'd about, and stared horriblie,
As if he with his lookes would all men terrifie.

43

He wore no armour, ne for none did care,
  As no whit dreading any liuing wight ;
  But in a Iacket quilted richly rare
  Vpon checklaton he was straungely dight,
  And on his head a roll of linnen plight,
  Like to the Mores of Malaber he wore ;
  With which his locks, as blacke as pitchy night,
  Were bound about, and voyded from before,
And in his hand a mighty yron club he bore.

44

This was *Disdaine*, who led that Ladies horse
  Through thick and thin, through mountains
    and through plains,
  Compelling her, wher she would not, by force,
  Haling her palfrey by the hempen raines.
  But that same foole, which most increast her
    paines,
Was *Scorne*, who hauing in his hand a whip,
  Her therewith yirks, and still when she com-
    plaines,
  The more he laughes, and does her closely quip,
To see her sore lament, and bite her tender lip.

45

Whose cruell handling when that Squire beheld,
  And saw those villaines her so vildely vse,
  His gentle heart with indignation sweld,
  And could no lenger beare so great abuse,
  As such a Lady so to beate and bruse ;
  But to him stepping, such a stroke him lent,
  That forst him th'halter from his hand to loose,
  And maugre all his might, backe to relent ;
Else had he surely there bene slaine, or fowly
    shent.

46

The villaine, wroth for greeting him so sore,
  Gathered him selfe together soone againe,
  And with his yron batton, which he bore,
  Let driue at him so dreadfully amaine,
  That for his safety he did him constraine
  To giue him ground, and shift to euery side,
  Rather then once his burden to sustaine :
  For bootelesse thing him seemed, to abide
So mighty blowes, or proue the puissaunce of
    his pride.

47

Like as a Mastiffe hauing at a bay
  A saluage Bull, whose cruell hornes doe threat
  Desperate daunger, if he them assay,
  Traceth his ground, and round about doth
    beat,
  To spy where he may some aduauntage get ;
  The whiles the beast doth rage and loudly rore :
  So did the Squire, the whiles the Carle did fret,
  And fume in his disdainefull mynd the more,
And oftentimes by Turmagant and Mahound
    swore.

48

Nathelesse so sharpely still he him pursewd,
  That at aduantage him at last he tooke,
  When his foote slipt (that slip he dearely rewd,)
  And with his yron club to ground him strooke ;
  Where still he lay, ne out of swoune awooke,
  Till heauy hand the Carle vpon him layd,
  And bound him fast : Tho when he vp did
    looke,
  And saw him selfe captiu d, he was dismayd,
Ne powre had to withstand, ne hope of any ayd.

49

Then vp he made him rise, and forward fare,
  Led in a rope, which both his hands did bynd ;
  Ne ought that foole for pitty did him spare,
  But with his whip him following behynd,
  Him often scourg'd, and forst his feete to fynd ;
  And other whiles with bitter mockes and mowes
  He would him scorne, that to his gentle mynd
  Was much more grieuous, then the others
    blowes :
Words sharpely wound, but greatest griefe of
    scorning growes.

50.

The faire *Serena*, when she saw him fall
 Vnder that villaines club, then surely thought
 That slaine he was, or made a wretched thrall,
 And fled away with all the speede she mought,
 To seeke for safety, which long time she
  sought :
 And past through many perils by the way,
 Ere she againe to *Calepine* was brought ;
 The which discourse as now I must delay,
 Till *Mirabellaes* fortunes I doe further say.

Cant. VIII.

Prince Arthure ouercomes Disdaine,
 Quites Mirabell from dreed :
 Serena found of Saluages,
 By Calepine is freed.

1

Ye gentle Ladies, in whose soueraine powre
 Loue hath the glory of his kingdome left,
 And th'hearts of men, as your eternall dowre,
 In yron chaines, of liberty bereft,
 Deliuered hath into your hands by gift ;
 Be well aware, how ye the same doe vse,
 That pride doe not to tyranny you lift ;
 Least if men you of cruelty accuse,
 He from you take that chiefedome, which ye
  doe abuse.

2

And as ye soft and tender are by kynde,
 Adornd with goodly gifts of beauties grace,
 So be ye soft and tender eeke in mynde ;
 But cruelty and hardnesse from you chace,
 That all your other praises will deface,
 And from you turne the loue of men to hate.
 Ensample take of *Mirabellaes* case,
 Who from the high degree of happy state,
 Fell into wretched woes, which she repented
  late.

3

Who after thraldome of the gentle Squire,
 Which she beheld with lamentable eye,
 Was touched with compassion entire,
 And much lamented his calamity,
 That for her sake fell into misery :
 Which booted nought for prayers, nor for
  threat
 To hope for to release or mollify ;
 For aye the more, that she did them entreat,
 The more they him misust, and cruelly did beat.

4

So as they forward on their way did pas,
 Him still reuiling and afflicting sore,
 They met Prince *Arthure* with Sir *Enias*,
 (That was that courteous Knight, whom he
  before
 Hauing subdew'd, yet did to life restore,)
 To whom as they approcht, they gan augment
 Their cruelty, and him to punish more,
 Scourging and haling him more vehement ;
 As if it them should grieue to see his punishment.

5

The Squire him selfe when as he saw his Lord,
 The witnesse of his wretchednesse, in place,
 Was much asham'd, that with an hempen cord
 He like a dog was led in captiue case,
 And did his head for bashfulnesse abase,
 As loth to see, or to be seene at all :
 Shame would be hid. But whenas *Enias*
 Beheld two such, of two such villaines thrall,
 His manly mynde was much emmoued there-
  withall.

6

And to the Prince thus sayd ; See you Sir
  Knight,
 The greatest shame that euer eye yet saw ?
 Yond Lady and her Squire with foule despight
 Abusde, against all reason and all law,
 Without regard of pitty or of awe.
 See how they doe that Squire beat and reuile ;
 See how they doe the Lady hale and draw.
 But if ye please to lend me leaue a while,
 I will them soone acquite, and both of blame
  assoile.

7

The Prince assented, and then he streight way
 Dismounting light, his shield about him threw,
 With which approching, thus he gan to say ;
 Abide ye caytiue treachetours vntrew,
 That haue with treason thralled vnto you
 These two, vnworthy of your wretched bands ;
 And now your crime with cruelty pursew.
 Abide, and from them lay your loathly hands ;
 Or else abide the death, that hard before you
  stands.

8

The villaine stayd not aunswer to inuent,
 But with his yron club preparing way,
 His mindes sad message backe vnto him sent ;
 The which descended with such dreadfull sway,
 That seemed nought the course thereof could
  stay :
 No more then lightening from the lofty sky.
 Ne list the Knight the powre thereof assay,
 Whose doome was death, but lightly slipping
  by,
 Vnwares defrauded his intended destiny.

9

And to requite him with the like againe,
  With his sharpe sword he fiercely at him flew,
  And strooke so strongly, that the Carle with paine
Saued him selfe, but that he there him slew :
Yet sau'd not so, but that the bloud it drew,
  And gaue his foe good hope of victory.
  Who therewith flesht, vpon him set anew,
And with the second stroke, thought certainely
To haue supplyde the first, and paide the vsury.

10

But Fortune aunswerd not vnto his call ;
  For as his hand was heaued vp on hight,
  The villaine met him in the middle fall,
And with his club bet backe his brondyron bright
So forcibly, that with his owne hands might
  Rebeaten backe vpon him selfe againe,
  He driuen was to ground in selfe despight ;
From whence ere he recouery could gaine,
He in his necke had set his foote with fell disdaine.

11

With that the foole, which did that end awayte,
  Came running in, and whilest on ground he lay,
  Laide heauy hands on him, and held so strayte,
That downe he kept him with his scornefull sway,
So as he could not weld him any way.
  The whiles that other villaine went about
  Him to haue bound, and thrald without delay ;
The whiles the foole did him reuile and flout,
Threatning to yoke them two and tame their corage stout.

12

As when a sturdy ploughman with his hynde
  By strength haue ouerthrowne a stubborne steare,
  They downe him hold, and fast with cords do bynde,
Till they him force the buxome yoke to beare :
So did these two this Knight oft tug and teare.
  Which when the Prince beheld, there standing by,
  He left his lofty steede to aide him neare,
And buckling soone him selfe, gan fiercely fly
Vppon that Carle, to saue his friend from ieopardy.

13

The villaine leauing him vnto his mate
  To be captiu'd, and handled as he list,
  Himselfe addrest vnto this new debate,
And with his club him all about so blist,
That he which way to turne him scarcely wist :
  Sometimes aloft he layd, sometimes alow ;
  Now here, now there, and oft him neare he mist ;
So doubtfully, that hardly one could know
Whether more wary were to giue or ward the blow.

14

But yet the Prince so well enured was
  With such huge strokes, approued oft in fight,
  That way to them he gaue forth right to pas.
Ne would endure the daunger of their might,
But wayt aduantage, when they downe did light.
  At last the caytiue after long discourse,
  When all his strokes he saw auoyded quite,
Resolued in one t'assemble all his force,
And make one end of him without ruth or remorse.

15

His dreadfull hand he heaued vp aloft,
  And with his dreadfull instrument of yre,
  Thought sure haue pownded him to powder soft,
Or deepe emboweld in the earth entyre :
But Fortune did not with his will conspire.
  For ere his stroke attayned his intent,
  The noble childe preuenting his desire,
Vnder his club with wary boldnesse went,
And smote him on the knee, that neuer yet was bent.

16

It neuer yet was bent, ne bent it now,
  Albe the stroke so strong and puissant were,
  That seem'd a marble pillour it could bow,
But all that leg, which did his body beare,
It crackt throughout, yet did no bloud appeare ;
  So as it was vnable to support
  So huge a burden on such broken geare,
But fell to ground, like to a lumpe of durt,
Whence he assayd to rise, but could not for his hurt.

17

Eftsoones the Prince to him full nimbly stept,
  And least he should recouer foote againe,
  His head meant from his shoulders to haue swept.
Which when the Lady saw, she cryde amaine ;
Stay stay, Sir Knight, for loue of God abstaine,
  From that vnwares ye weetlesse doe intend ;
  Slay not that Carle, though worthy to be slaine :
For more on him doth then him selfe depend ;
My life will by his death haue lamentable end.

18

He staide his hand according her desire,
  Yet nathemore him suffred to arize ;
  But still suppressing gan of her inquire,
What meaning mote those vncouth words comprize,
That in that villaines health her safety lies :
  That, were no might in man, nor heart in Knights,
  Which durst her dreaded reskue enterprize,
Yet heauens them selues, that fauour feeble rights,
Would for it selfe redresse, and punish such despights.

19

Then bursting forth in teares, which gushed fast
  Like many water streames, a while she stayd ;
  Till the sharpe passion being ouerpast,
  Her tongue to her restord, then thus she sayd ;
  Nor heauens, nor men can me most wretched
      mayd
  Deliuer from the doome of my desart,
  The which the God of loue hath on me layd,
  And damned to endure this direfull smart,
For penaunce of my proud and hard rebellious
    hart.

20

In prime of youthly yeares, when first the flowre
  Of beauty gan to bud, and bloosme delight,
  And nature me endu'd with plenteous dowre,
  Of all her gifts, that pleasde each liuing sight,
  I was belou'd of many a gentle Knight,
  And sude and sought with all the seruice dew
  Full many a one for me deepe groand and sight,
  And to the dore of death for sorrow drew,
Complayning out on me, that would not on
    them rew.

21

But let them loue that list, or liue or die ;
  Me list not die for any louers doole :
  Ne list me leaue my loued libertie,
  To pitty him that list to play the foole :
  To loue my selfe I learned had in schoole.
  Thus I triumphed long in louers paine,
  And sitting carelesse on the scorners stoole,
  Did laugh at those that did lament and plaine :
But all is now repayd with interest againe.

22

For loe the winged God, that woundeth harts,
  Causde me be called to accompt therefore,
  And for reuengement of those wrongfull
    smarts,
  Which I to others did inflict afore,
  Addeem'd me to endure this penaunce sore ;
  That in this wize, and this vnmeete array,
  With these two lewd companions, and no more,
  Disdaine and *Scorne,* I through the world
    should stray,
Till I haue sau'd so many, as I earst did slay.

23

Certes (sayd then the Prince) the God is iust,
  That taketh vengeaunce of his peoples spoile.
  For were no law in loue, but all that lust,
  Might them oppresse, and painefully turmoile,
  His kingdome would continue but a while.
  But tell me Lady, wherefore doe you beare
  This bottle thus before you with such toile,
  And eeke this wallet at your backe arreare,
That for these Carles to carry much more comely
    were ?

24

Here in this bottle (sayd the sory Mayd)
  I put the teares of my contrition,
  Till to the brim I haue it full defrayd :
  And in this bag which I behinde me don,
  I put repentaunce for things past and gon.
  Yet is the bottle leake, and bag so torne,
  That all which I put in, fals out anon ;
  And is behinde me trodden downe of *Scorne,*
Who mocketh all my paine, and laughs the
    more I mourn.

25

The Infant hearkned wisely to her tale,
  And wondred much at *Cupids* iudg'ment wise,
  That could so meekly make proud hearts auale,
  And wreake him selfe on them, that him despise.
  Then suffred he *Disdaine* vp to arise,
  Who was not able vp him selfe to reare, [prise,
  By meanes his leg through his late luckelesse
  Was crackt in twaine, but by his foolish feare
Was holpen vp, who him supported standing
    neare.

26

But being vp, he lookt againe aloft,
  As if he neuer had receiued fall ;
  And with sterne eye-browes stared at him oft,
  As if he would haue daunted him withall :
  And standing on his tiptoes, to seeme tall,
  Downe on his golden feete he often gazed,
  As if such pride the other could apall ;
  Who was so far from being ought amazed,
That he his lookes despised, and his boast
    dispraized.

27

Then turning backe vnto that captiue thrall,
  Who all this while stood there beside them
    bound,
  Vnwilling to be knowne, or seene at all,
  He from those bands weend him to haue
    vnwound.
  But when approching neare, he plainely found,
  It was his owne true groome, the gentle Squire,
  He thereat wext exceedingly astound,
  And him did oft embrace, and oft admire,
Ne could with seeing satisfie his great desire.

28

Meane while the Saluage man, when he beheld
  That huge great foole oppressing th'other
    Knight,
  Whom with his weight vnweldy downe he held,
  He flew vpon him, like a greedy kight
  Vnto some carrion offered to his sight, [teeth
  And downe him plucking, with his nayles and
  Gan him to hale, and teare, and scratch, and bite;
  And from him taking his owne whip, therewith
So sore him scourgeth, that the bloud downe
    followeth.

29

And sure I weene, had not the Ladies cry
Procur'd the Prince his cruell hand to stay,
He would with whipping, him haue done to dye:
But being checkt, he did abstaine streight way,
And let him rise. Then thus the Prince gan
    say ;
Now Lady sith your fortunes thus dispose,
That if ye list haue liberty, ye may,
Vnto your selfe I freely leaue to chose,
Whether I shall you leaue, or from these villaines
    lose.

30

Ah nay Sir Knight (sayd she) it may not be,
But that I needes must by all meanes fulfill
This penaunce, which enioyned is to me,
Least vnto me betide a greater ill ;
Yet no lesse thankes to you for your good will.
So humbly taking leaue, she turnd aside,
But *Arthure* with the rest, went onward still
On his first quest, in which did him betide
A great aduenture, which did him from them
    deuide.

31

But first it falleth me by course to tell
Of faire *Serena*, who as earst you heard,
When first the gentle Squire at variaunce fell
With those two Carles, fled fast away, afeard
Of villany to be to her inferd :
So fresh the image of her former dread,
Yet dwelling in her eye, to her appeard,
That euery foote did tremble, which did tread,
And euery body two, and two she foure did
    read.

32

Through hils and dales, through bushes and
    through breres
Long thus she fled, till that at last she thought
Her selfe now past the perill of her feares.
Then looking round about, and seeing nought,
Which doubt of daunger to her offer mought,
She from her palfrey lighted on the plaine,
And sitting downe, her selfe a while bethought
Of her long trauell and turmoyling paine ;
And often did of loue, and oft of lucke com-
    plaine.

33

And euermore she blamed *Calepine*,
The good Sir *Calepine*, her owne true Knight,
As th'onely author of her wofull tine :
For being of his loue to her so light,
As her to leaue in such a piteous plight.
Yet neuer Turtle truer to his make,
Then he was tride vnto his Lady bright
Who all this while endured for her sake,
Great perill of his life, and restlesse paines did take.

34

Tho when as all her plaints she had displayd,
And well disburdened her engrieued brest,
Vpon the grasse her selfe adowne she layd ;
Where being tyrde with trauell, and opprest
With sorrow, she betooke her selfe to rest.
There whilest in *Morpheus* bosome safe she lay,
Fearelesse of ought, that mote her peace molest,
False Fortune did her safety betray,
Vnto a straunge mischaunce, that menac'd her
    decay.

35

In these wylde deserts, where she now abode,
There dwelt a saluage nation, which did liue
Of stealth and spoile, and making nightly rode
Into their neighbours borders ; ne did giue
Them selues to any trade, as for to driue
The painefull plough, or cattell for to breed,
Or by aduentrous marchandize to thriue ;
But on the labours of poore men to feed,
And serue their owne necessities with others
    need.

36

Thereto they vsde one most accursed order,
To eate the flesh of men, whom they mote fynde,
And straungers to deuoure, which on their border
Were brought by errour, or by wreckfull wynde.
A monstrous cruelty gainst course of kynde.
They towards euening wandring euery way,
To seeke for booty, came by fortune blynde,
Whereas this Lady, like a sheepe astray,
Now drowned in the depth of sleepe all feare-
    lesse lay.

37

Soone as they spide her, Lord what gladfull glee
They made amongst them selues ; but when
    her face
Like the faire yuory shining they did see,
Each gan his fellow solace and embrace,
For ioy of such good hap by heauenly grace.
Then gan they to deuize what course to take :
Whether to slay her there vpon the place,
Or suffer her out of her sleepe to wake,
And then her eate attonce ; or many meales to
    make.

38

The best aduizement was of bad, to let her
Sleepe out her fill, without encomberment :
For sleepe they sayd would make her battill
    better.
Then when she wakt, they all gaue one consent,
That since by grace of God she there was sent,
Vnto their God they would her sacrifize,
Whose share, her guiltlesse bloud they would
    present,
But of her dainty flesh they did deuize
To make a common feast, and feed with gur-
    mandize.

39

So round about her they them selues did place
Vpon the grasse, and diuersely dispose,
As each thought best to spend the lingring space.
Some with their eyes the daintest morsels chose;
Some praise her paps, some praise her lips and
nose ;
Some whet their kniues, and strip their elboes
bare :
The Priest him selfe a garland doth compose
Of finest flowres, and with full busie care
His bloudy vessels wash, and holy fire prepare.

40

The Damzell wakes, then all attonce vpstart,
And round about her flocke, like many flies,
Whooping, and hallowing on euery part,
As if they would haue rent the brasen skies.
Which when she sees with ghastly griefful eies,
Her heart does quake, and deadly pallid hew
Benumbes her cheekes : Then out aloud she
cries,
Where none is nigh to heare, that will her rew,
And rends her golden locks, and snowy brests
embrew.

41

But all bootes not : they hands vpon her lay ;
And first they spoile her of her iewels deare,
And afterwards of all her rich array ;
The which amongst them they in peeces teare,
And of the pray each one a part doth beare.
Now being naked, to their sordid eyes
The goodly threasures of nature appeare :
Which as they view with lustfull fantasyes,
Each wisheth to him selfe, and to the rest
enuyes.

42

Her yuorie necke, her alablaster brest,
Her paps, which like white silken pillowes were,
For loue in soft delight thereon to rest ;
Her tender sides, her bellie white and clere,
Which like an Altar did it selfe vprere,
To offer sacrifice diuine thereon ;
Her goodly thighes, whose glorie did appeare
Like a triumphall Arch, and thereupon
The spoiles of Princes hang'd, which were in
battel won.

43

Those daintie parts, the dearlings of delight,
Which mote not be prophan'd of common eyes,
Those villeins vew'd with loose lasciuious sight,
And closely tempted with their craftie spyes ;
And some of them gan mongst themselues deuize,
Thereof by force to take their beastly pleasure.
But them the Priest rebuking, did aduize
To dare not to pollute so sacred threasure,
Vow'd to the gods : religion held euen theeues
in measure.

44

So being stayd, they her from thence directed
Vnto a litie groue not farre asyde,
In which an altar shortly they erected,
To slay her on. And now the Euentyde
His brode black wings had through the heauens
wyde
By this dispred, that was the tyme ordayned
For such a dismall deed, their guilt to hyde :
Of few greene turfes an altar soone they fayned,
And deckt it all with flowres, which they nigh
hand obtayned.

45

Tho when as all things readie were aright,
The Damzell was before the altar set,
Being alreadie dead with fearefull fright.
To whom the Priest with naked armes full net
Approching nigh, and murdrous knife well
whet,
Gan mutter close a certaine secret charme,
With other diuelish ceremonies met :
Which doen he gan aloft t'aduance his arme,
Whereat they shouted all, and made a loud
alarme.

46

Then gan the bagpypes and the hornes to shrill,
And shrieke aloud, that with the peoples voyce
Confused, did the ayre with terror fill,
And made the wood to tremble at the noyce :
The whyles she wayld, the more they did
reioyce.
Now mote ye vnderstand that to this groue
Sir *Calepine* by chaunce, more then by choyce,
The selfe same euening fortune hether droue,
As he to seeke *Serena* through the woods did
roue.

47

Long had he sought her, and through many a
soyle
Had traueld still on foot in heauie armes,
Ne ought was tyred with his endlesse toyles,
Ne ought was feared of his certaine harmes :
And now all weetlesse of the wretched stormes,
In which his loue was lost, he slept full fast,
Till being waked with these loud alarmes,
He lightly started vp like one aghast,
And catching vp his arms streight to the noise
forth past.

48

There by th'vncertaine glims of starry night,
And by the twinkling of their sacred fire,
He mote perceiue a litle dawning sight
Of all, which there was doing in that quire :
Mongst whom a woman spoyld of all attire
He spyde, lamenting her vnluckie strife,
And groning sore from grieued hart entire,
Eftsoones he saw one with a naked knife
Readie to launch her brest, and let out loued life.

49

With that he thrusts into the thickest throng,
And euen as his right hand adowne descends,
He him preuenting, layes on earth along,
And sacrifizeth to th'infernall feends.
Then to the rest his wrathfull hand he bends,
Of whom he makes such hauocke and such hew,
That swarmes of damned soules to hell he sends:
The rest that scape his sword and death eschew,
Fly like a flocke of doues before a Faulcons vew.

50

From them returning to that Ladie backe,
Whom by the Altar he doth sitting find,
Yet fearing death, and next to death the lacke
Of clothes to couer, what they ought by kind,
He first her hands beginneth to vnbind ;
And then to question of her present woe ;
And afterwards to cheare with speaches kind.
But she for nought that he could say or doe,
One word durst speake, or answere him a whit thereto.

51

So inward shame of her vncomely case
She did conceiue, through care of womanhood,
That though the night did couer her disgrace,
Yet she in so vnwomanly a mood,
Would not bewray the state in which she stood.
So all that night to him vnknowen she past.
But day, that doth discouer bad and good,
Ensewing, made her knowen to him at last :
The end whereof Ile keepe vntill another cast.

Cant. IX.

సిసిసిసిసిసిసిసిసిసిసిసిసిసి

Calidore hosies with Meliboe
and loues fayre Pastorell ;
Coridon enuies him, yet he
for ill rewards him well.

సిసిసిసిసిసిసిసిసిసిసిసిసిసి

1

Now turne againe my teme thou iolly swayne,
Backe to the furrow which I lately left ;
I lately left a furrow, one or twayne
Vnplough'd, the which my coulter hath not cleft :
Yet seem'd the soyle both fayre and frutefull eft,
As I it past, that were too great a shame,
That so rich frute should be from vs bereft ;
Besides the great dishonour and defame,
Which should befall to *Calidores* immortall name.

2

Great trauell hath the gentle *Calidore*
And toyle endured, sith I left him last
Sewing the *Blatant beast,* which I forbore
To finish then, for other present hast.
Full many pathes and perils he hath past,
Through hils, through dales, throgh forests, and throgh plaines
In that same quest which fortune on him cast,
Which he atchieued to his owne great gaines,
Reaping eternall glorie of his restlesse paines.

3

So sharply he the Monster did pursew,
That day nor night he suffred him to rest,
Ne rested he himselfe but natures dew,
For dread of daunger, not to be redrest,
If he for slouth forslackt so famous quest.
Him first from court he to the citties coursed,
And from the citties to the townes him prest,
And from the townes into the countrie forsed,
And from the country back to priuate farmes he scorsed.

4

From thence into the open fields he fled,
Whereas the Heardes were keeping of their neat,
And shepheards singing to their flockes, that fed,
Layes of sweete loue and youthes delightfull heat :
Him thether eke for all his fearefull threat
He followed fast, and chaced him so nie,
That to the folds, where sheepe at night doe seat,
And to the litle cots, where shepherds lie
In winters wrathfull time, he forced him to flie.

5

There on a day as he pursew'd the chace,
He chaunst to spy a sort of shepheard groomes,
Playing on pypes, and caroling apace,
The whyles their beasts there in the budded broomes
Beside them fed, and nipt the tender bloomes :
For other worldly wealth they cared nought.
To whom Sir *Calidore* yet sweating comes,
And them to tell him courteously besought,
If such a beast they saw, which he had thether brought.

6

They answer'd him, that no such beast they saw,
Nor any wicked feend, that mote offend
Their happie flockes, nor daunger to them draw :
But if that such there were (as none they kend)
They prayd high God him farre from them to send.
Then one of them him seeing so to sweat,
After his rusticke wise, that well he weend,
Offred him drinke, to quench his thirstie heat,
And if he hungry were, him offred eke to eat.

7

The knight was nothing nice, where was no need,
And tooke their gentle offer: so adowne
They prayd him sit, and gaue him for to feed
Such homely what, as serues the simple clowne,
That doth despise the dainties of the towne.
Tho hauing fed his fill, he there besyde
Saw a faire damzell, which did weare a crowne
Of sundry flowres, with silken ribbands tyde,
Yclad in home-made greene that her owne hands
  had dyde.

8

Vpon a litle hillocke she was placed
Higher then all the rest, and round about
Enuiron'd with a girland, goodly graced,
Of louely lasses, and them all without
The lustie shepheard swaynes sate in a rout,
The which did pype and sing her prayses dew,
And oft reioyce, and oft for wonder shout,
As if some miracle of heauenly hew
Were downe to them descended in that earthly
  vew.

9

And soothly sure she was full fayre of face,
And perfectly well shapt in euery lim,
Which she did more augment with modest grace,
And comely carriage of her count'nance trim,
That all the rest like lesser lamps did dim:
Who her admiring as some heauenly wight,
Did for their soueraine goddesse her esteeme,
And caroling her name both day and night,
The fayrest *Pastorella* her by name did hight.

10

Ne was there heard, ne was there shepheards
  swayne
But her did honour, and eke many a one
Burnt in her loue, and with sweet pleasing payne
Full many a night for her did sigh and grone:
But most of all the shepheard *Coridon*
For her did languish, and his deare life spend;
Yet neither she for him, nor other none
Did care a whit, ne any liking lend:
Though meane her lot, yet higher did her mind
  ascend.

11

Her whyles Sir *Calidore* there vewed well,
And markt her rare demeanure, which him
  seemed
So farre the meane of shepheards to excell,
As that he in his mind her worthy deemed,
To be a Princes Paragone esteemed,
He was vnwares surprisd in subtile bands
Of the blynd boy, ne thence could be redeemed
By any skill out of his cruell hands,
Caught like the bird, which gazing still on others
  stands.

12

So stood he still long gazing thereupon,
Ne any will had thence to moue away,
Although his quest were farre afore him gon;
But after he had fed, yet did he stay,
And sate there still, vntill the flying day
Was farre forth spent, discoursing diuersly
Of sundry things, as fell, to worke delay;
And euermore his speach he did apply
To th'heards, but meant them to the damzels
  fantazy.

13

By this the moystie night approching fast,
Her deawy humour gan on th'earth to shed,
That warn'd the shepheards to their homes to
  hast
Their tender flocks, now being fully fed,
For feare of wetting them before their bed;
Then came to them a good old aged syre,
Whose siluer lockes bedeckt his beard and hed,
With shepheards hooke in hand, and fit attyre,
That wild the damzell rise; the day did now
  expyre.

14

He was to weet by common voice esteemed
The father of the fayrest *Pastorell*,
And of her selfe in very deede so deemed;
Yet was not so, but as old stories tell
Found her by fortune, which to him befell,
In th'open fields an Infant left alone,
And taking vp brought home, and noursed well
As his owne chyld; for other he had none,
That she in tract of time accompted was his
  owne.

15

She at his bidding meekely did arise,
And streight vnto her litle flocke did fare:
Then all the rest about her rose likewise,
And each his sundrie sheepe with seuerall care
Gathered together, and them homeward bare:
Whylest euerie one with helping hands did striue
Amongst themselues, and did their labours
  share,
To helpe faire *Pastorella*, home to driue
Her fleecie flocke; but *Coridon* most helpe did
  giue.

16

But *Meliboe* (so hight that good old man)
Now seeing *Calidore* left all alone,
And night arriued hard at hand, began
Him to inuite vnto his simple home;
Which though it were a cottage clad with lome,
And all things therein meane, yet better so
To lodge, then in the saluage fields to rome.
The knight full gladly soone agreed thereto,
Being his harts owne wish, and home with him
  did go.

17

There he was welcom'd of that honest syre,
  And of his aged Beldame homely well;
Who him besought himselfe to disattyre,
  And rest himselfe, till supper time befell.
By which home came the fayrest *Pastorell*,
  After her flocke she in their fold had tyde,
  And supper readie dight, they to it fell
With small adoe, and nature satisfyde,
The which doth litle craue contented to abyde.

18

Tho when they had their hunger slaked well,
  And the fayre mayd the table ta'ne away,
The gentle knight, as he that did excell
  In courtesie, and well could doe and say,
For so great kindnesse as he found that day,
  Gan greatly thanke his host and his good wife;
  And drawing thence his speach another way,
Gan highly to commend the happie life,
Which Shepheards lead, without debate or bitter
  strife.

19

How much (sayd he) more happie is the state,
  In which ye father here doe dwell at ease,
Leading a life so free and fortunate,
  From all the tempests of these worldly seas,
Which tosse the rest in daungerous disease;
  Where warres, and wreckes, and wicked enmitie
  Doe them afflict, which no man can appease,
That certes I your happinesse enuie,
And wish my lot were plast in such felicitie.

20

Surely my sonne (then answer'd he againe)
  If happie, then it is in this intent,
That hauing small, yet doe I not complaine
  Of want, ne wish for more it to augment,
But doe my self, with that I haue, content;
  So taught of nature, which doth litle need
  Of forreine helpes to lifes due nourishment:
The fields my food, my flocke my rayment
  breed;
No better doe I weare, no better doe I feed.

21

Therefore I doe not any one enuy,
  Nor am enuyde of any one therefore;
They that haue much, feare much to loose
  thereby,
And store of cares doth follow riches store.
  The litle that I haue, growes dayly more
Without my care, but onely to attend it;
  My lambes doe euery yeare increase their score,
And my flockes father daily doth amend it.
What haue I, but to praise th'Almighty, that
  doth send it?

22

To them, that list, the worlds gay showes I leaue,
  And to great ones such follies doe forgiue,
Which oft through pride do their owne perill
  weaue,   [driue
And through ambition downe themselues doe
  To sad decay, that might contented liue.
Me no such cares nor combrous thoughts offend,
  Ne once my minds vnmoued quiet grieue,
But all the night in siluer sleepe I spend,
And all the day, to what I list, I doe attend.

23

Sometimes I hunt the Fox, the vowed foe
  Vnto my Lambes, and him dislodge away;
Sometime the fawne I practise from the Doe,
  Or from the Goat her kidde how to conuay;
Another while I baytes and nets display,
  The birds to catch, or fishes to beguyle:
And when I wearie am, I downe doe lay
  My limbes in euery shade, to rest from toyle,
And drinke of euery brooke, when thirst my throte
  doth boyle.

24

The time was once, in my first prime of yeares,
  When pride of youth forth pricked my desire,
That I disdain'd amongst mine equall peares
  To follow sheepe, and shepheards base attire:
For further fortune then I would inquire.
  And leauing home, to roiall court I sought;
Where I did sell my selfe for yearely hire,
  And in the Princes gardin daily wrought:
There I beheld such vainenesse, as I neuer
  thought.

25

With sight whereof soone cloyd, and long deluded
  With idle hopes, which them doe entertaine,
After I had ten yeares my selfe excluded
  From natiue home, and spent my youth in vaine,
I gan my follies to my selfe to plaine,
  And this sweet peace, whose lacke did then
    appeare.
Tho backe returning to my sheepe againe,
  I from thenceforth haue learn'd to loue more deare
This lowly quiet life, which I inherite here.

26

Whylest thus he talkt, the knight with greedy eare
  Hong still vpon his melting mouth attent;
Whose sensefull words empierst his hart so neare,
  That he was rapt with double rauishment,
Both of his speach that wrought him great
    content,
  And also of the obiect of his vew,
On which his hungry eye was alwayes bent;
  That twixt his pleasing tongue and her faire hew,
He lost himselfe, and like one halfe entraunced
  grew.

27

Yet to occasion meanes, to worke his mind,
And to insinuate his harts desire,
He thus replyde ; Now surely syre, I find,
That all this worlds gay showes, which we admire,
Be but vaine shadowes to this safe retyre
Of life, which here in lowlinesse ye lead,
Fearelesse of foes, or fortunes wrackfull yre,
Which tosseth states, and vnder foot doth tread
The mightie ones, affrayd of euery chaunges
    dread.

28

That euen I which daily doe behold
The glorie of the great, mongst whom I won,
And now haue prou'd, what happinesse ye hold
In this small plot of your dominion,
Now loath great Lordship and ambition ;
And wish the heauens so much had graced mee,
As graunt me liue in like condition ;
Or that my fortunes might transposed bee
From pitch of higher place, vnto this low degree.

29

In vaine (said then old *Meliboe*) doe men
The heauens of their fortunes fault accuse,
Sith they know best, what is the best for them :
For they to each such fortune doe diffuse,
As they doe know each can most aptly vse.
For not that, which men couet most, is best,
Nor that thing worst, which men do most
    refuse ;
But fittest is, that all contented rest
With that they hold : each hath his fortune in
    his brest.

30

It is the mynd, that maketh good or ill,
That maketh wretch or happie, rich or poore :
For some, that hath abundance at his will,
Hath not enough, but wants in greatest store ;
And other, that hath litle, askes no more,
But in that litle is both rich and wise.
For wisedome is most riches ; fooles therefore
They are, which fortunes doe by vowes deuize,
Sith each vnto himselfe his life may fortunize.

31

Since then in each mans self (said *Calidore*)
It is, to fashion his owne lyfes estate,
Giue leaue awhyle, good father, in this shore
To rest my barcke, which hath bene beaten late
With stormes of fortune and tempestuous fate,
In seas of troubles and of toylesome paine,
That whether quite from them for to retrate
I shall resolue, or backe to turne againe,
I may here with your selfe some small repose
    obtaine.

32

Not that the burden of so bold a guest
Shall chargefull be, or chaunge to you at all ;
For your meane food shall be my daily feast,
And this your cabin both my bowre and hall
Besides for recompence hereof, I shall
You well reward, and golden guerdon giue,
That may perhaps you better much withall,
And in this quiet make you safer liue.
So forth he drew much gold, and toward him it
    driue.

33

But the good man, nought tempted with the offer
Of his rich mould, did thrust it farre away,
And thus bespake ; Sir knight, your bounteous
    proffer
Be farre fro me, to whom ye ill display
That mucky masse, the cause of mens decay,
That mote empaire my peace with daungers
But if ye algates couet to assay   [dread.
This simple sort of life, that shepheards lead,
Be it your owne : our rudenesse to your selfe
    aread.

34

So there that night Sir *Calidore* did dwell,
And long while after, whilest him list remaine,
Dayly beholding the faire *Pastorell*,
And feeding on the bayt of his owne bane.
During which time he did her entertaine
With all kind courtesies, he could inuent ;
And euery day, her companie to gaine,
When to the field she went, he with her went :
So for to quench his fire, he did it more augment.

35

But she that neuer had acquainted beene
With such queint vsage, fit for Queenes and
    Kings,
Ne euer had such knightly seruice seene,
But being bred vnder base shepheards wings,
Had euer learn'd to loue the lowly things,
Did litle whit regard his courteous guize,
But cared more for *Colins* carolings
Then all that he could doe, or euer deuize :
His layes, his loues, his lookes she did them all
    despize.

36

Which *Calidore* perceiuing, thought it best
To chaunge the manner of his loftie looke ;
And doffing his bright armes, himselfe addrest
In shepheards weed, and in his hand he tooke,
In stead of steelehead speare, a shepheards
    hooke,
That who had seene him then, would haue
    bethought
On *Phrygian Paris* by *Plexippus* brooke,
When he the loue of fayre *Oenone* sought,
What time the golden apple was vnto him brought.

37

So being clad, vnto the fields he went
  With the faire *Pastorella* euery day,
  And kept her sheepe with diligent attent,
  Watching to driue the rauenous Wolfe away,
  The why lest at pleasure she mote sport and play;
  And euery euening helping them to fold :
  And otherwhiles for need, he did assay
In his strong hand their rugged teats to hold,
And out of them to presse the milke : loue so
    much could.

38

Which seeing *Coridon*, who her likewise
  Long time had lou'd, and hop'd her loue to
    gaine,
  He much was troubled at that straungers guize,
  And many gealous thoughts conceiu'd in vaine,
  That this of all his labour and long paine
  Should reap the haruest, ere it ripened were,
  That made him scoule, and pout, and oft com-
    plaine
Of *Pastorell* to all the shepheards there,
That she did loue a stranger swayne then him
    more dere.

39

And euer when he came in companie,
  Where *Calidore* was present, he would loure,
  And byte his lip, and euen for gealousie
  Was readie oft his owne hart to deuoure,
  Impatient of any paramoure :
  Who on the other side did seeme so farre
  From malicing, or grudging his good houre,
That all he could, he graced him with her,
Ne euer shewed signe of rancour or of iarre.

40

And oft, when *Coridon* vnto her brought
  Or litle sparrowes, stolen from their nest,
  Or wanton squirrels, in the woods farre sought,
  Or other daintie thing for her addrest,
  He would commend his guift, and make the
    best.
  Yet she no whit his presents did regard,
  Ne him could find to fancie in her brest :
This newcome shepheard had his market mard.
Old loue is litle worth when new is more prefard.

41

One day when as the shepheard swaynes together
  Were met, to make their sports and merrie glee,
  As they are wont in faire sunshynie weather,
  The whiles their flockes in shadowes shrouded
    bee,
  They fell to daunce : then did they all agree,
  That *Colin Clout* should pipe as one most fit ;
  And *Calidore* should lead the ring, as hee
That most in *Pastorellaes* grace did sit.
Thereat frown'd *Coridon*, and his lip closely bit.

42

But *Calidore* of courteous inclination
  Tooke *Coridon*, and set him in his place,
  That he should lead the daunce, as was his
    fashion ;
  For *Coridon* could daunce, and trimly trace.
  And when as *Pastorella*, him to grace,
  Her flowry garlond tooke from her owne head,
  And plast on his, he did it soone displace,
And did it put on *Coridons* in stead :
Then *Coridon* woxe frollicke, that earst seemed
    dead.

43

Another time, when as they did dispose
  To practise games, and maisteries to try,
  They for their Iudge did *Pastorella* chose ;
  A garland was the meed of victory.
  There *Coridon* forth stepping openly,
  Did chalenge *Calidore* to wrestling game :
  For he through long and perfect industry,
  Therein well practisd was, and in the same
Thought sure t'auenge his grudge, and worke
    his foe great shame.

44

But *Calidore* he greatly did mistake ;
  For he was strong and mightily stiffe pight,
  That with one fall his necke he almost brake,
  And had he not vpon him fallen light,
  His dearest ioynt he sure had broken quight.
  Then was the oaken crowne by *Pastorell*
  Giuen to *Calidore*, as his due right ;
But he, that did in courtesie excell,
Gaue it to *Coridon*, and said he wonne it well.

45

Thus did the gentle knight himselfe abeare
  Amongst that rusticke rout in all his deeds,
  That euen they, the which his riuals were,
  Could not maligne him, but commend him
    needs :
  For courtesie amongst the rudest breeds
  Good will and fauour. So it surely wrought
  With this faire Mayd, and in her mynde the
    seeds
Of perfect loue did sow, that last forth brought
The fruite of ioy and blisse, though long time
    dearely bought.

46

Thus *Calidore* continu'd there long time,
  To winne the loue of the faire *Pastorell* ;
  Which hauing got, he vsed without crime
  Or blamefull blot, but menaged so well,
  That he of all the rest, which there did dwell,
  Was fauoured, and to her grace commended.
  But what straunge fortunes vnto him befell,
Er° he attain'd the point by him intended,
Shall more conueniently in other place be ended.

Cant. X

∾∾∾∾∾∾∾∾∾∾∾∾∾∾∾∾∾

Calidore sees the Graces daunce,
To Colins melody :
The whiles his Pastorell is led,
Into captiuity.

∾∾∾∾∾∾∾∾∾∾∾∾∾∾∾∾∾

1

Who now does follow the foule *Blatant Beast*,
Whil∴st *Calidore* does follow that faire Mayd,
Vnmyndfull of his vow and high beheast,
Which by the Faery Queene was on him layd,
That he should neuer leaue, nor be delayd
From chacing him, till he had it attchieued ?
But now entrapt of loue, which him betrayd,
He mindeth more, how he may be relieued
With grace from her, whose loue his heart hath
    sore engrieued.

2

That from henceforth he meanes no more to sew
His former quest, so full of toile and paine ;
Another quest, another game in vew
He hath, the guerdon of his loue to gaine :
With whom he myndes for euer to remaine,
And set his rest amongst the rusticke sort,
Rather then hunt still after shadowes vaine
Of courtly fauour, fed with light report
Of euery blaste, and sayling alwaies in the port.

3

Ne certes mote he greatly blamed be,
From so high step to stoupe vnto so low.
For who had tasted once (as oft did he)
The happy peace, which there doth ouerflow,
And prou'd the perfect pleasures, which doe grow
Amongst poore hyndes, in hils, in woods, in dales,
Would neuer more delight in painted show
Of such false blisse, as there is set for stales,
T'entrap vnwary fooles in their eternall bales.

4

For what hath all that goodly glorious gaze
Like to one sight, which *Calidore* did vew ?
The glaunce whereof their dimmed eies would
    daze,
That neuer more they should endure the shew
Of that sunne-shine, that makes them looke
    askew.
Ne ought in all that world of beauties rare,
(Saue onely *Glorianaes* heauenly hew
To which what can compare ?) can it compare:
The which as commeth now, by course I will
    declare.

5

One day as he did raunge the fields abroad,
Whilest his faire *Pastorella* was elsewhere,
He chaunst to come, far from all peoples troad,
Vnto a place, whose pleasaunce did appere
To passe all others, on the earth which were :
For all that euer was by natures skill
Deuized to worke delight, was gathered there,
And there by her were poured forth at fill,
As if this to adorne, she all the rest did pill.

6

It was an hill plaste in an open plaine,
That round about was bordered with a wood
Of matchlesse hight, that seem'd th'earth to
    disdaine,
In which all trees of honour stately stood,
And did all winter as in sommer bud,
Spredding pauilions for the birds to bowre,
Which in their lower braunches sung aloud ;
And in their tops the soring hauke did towre,
Sitting like King of fowles in maiesty and powre.

7

And at the foote thereof, a gentle flud
His siluer waues did softly tumble downe,
Vnmard with ragged mosse or filthy mud,
Ne mote wylde beastes, ne mote the ruder
    clowne
Thereto approch, ne filth mote therein drowne:
But Nymphes and Faeries by the banckes did sit,
In the woods shade, which did the waters
    crowne,
Keeping all noysome things away from it,
And to the waters fall tuning their accents fit.

8

And on the top thereof a spacious plaine
Did spred it selfe, to serue to all delight,
Either to daunce, when they to daunce would
    faine,
Or else to course about their bases light ;
Ne ought there wanted, which for pleasure might
Desired be, or thence to banish bale :
So pleasauntly the hill with equall hight,
Did seeme to ouerlooke the lowly vale ;
Therefore it rightly cleeped was mount *Acidale.*

9

They say that *Venus*, when she did dispose
Her selfe to pleasaunce, vsed to resort
Vnto this place, and therein to repose
And rest her selfe, as in a gladsome port,
Or with the Graces there to play and sport ;
That euen her owne Cytheron, though in it
She vsed most to keepe her royall court,
And in her soueraine Maiesty to sit,
She in regard hereof refusde and thought vnfit.

10

Vnto this place when as the Elfin Knight
  Approcht, him seemed that the merry sound
  Of a shrill pipe he playing heard on hight,
  And many feete fast thumping th'hollow ground,
  That through the woods their Eccho did rebound.
  He nigher drew, to weete what mote it be ;
  There he a troupe of Ladies dauncing found
Full merrily, and making gladfull glee,
And in the midst a Shepheard piping he did see.

11

He durst not enter into th'open greene,
  For dread of them vnwares to be descryde,
  For breaking of their daunce, if he were seere ;
  But in the couert of the wood did byde,
  Beholding all, yet of them vnespyde.
  There he did see, that pleased much his sight,
  That euen he him selfe his eyes enuyde,
  An hundred naked maidens lilly white,
All raunged in a ring, and dauncing in delight.

12

All they without were raunged in a ring,
  And daunced round ; but in the midst of them
  Three other Ladies did both daunce and sing,
  The whilest the rest them round about did hemme,
  And like a girlond did in compasse stemme :
  And in the middest of those same three, was
    placed
  Another Damzell, as a precious gemme,
  Amidst a ring most richly well enchaced,
That with her goodly presence all the rest much
  graced.

13

Looke how the Crowne, which *Ariadne* wore
  Vpon her yuory forehead that same day,
  That *Theseus* her vnto his bridale bore,
  When the bold *Centaures* made that bloudy fray,
  With the fierce *Lapithes*, which did them dismay ;
  Being now placed in the firmament,
  Through the bright heauen doth her beams
    display,
  And is vnto the starres an ornament,
Which round about her moue in order excellent.

14

Such was the beauty of this goodly band,
  Whose sundry parts were here too long to tell:
  But she that in the midst of them did stand,
  Seem'd all the rest in beauty to excell,
  Crownd with a rosie girlond, that right well
  Did her beseeme   And euer, as the crew
  About her daunst, sweet flowres, that far did
    smell,
  And fragrant odours they vppon her threw ;
But most of all, those three did her with gifts
  endew.

15

Those were the Graces, daughters of delight,
  Handmaides of *Venus*, which are wont to haunt
  Vppon this hill, and daunce there day and night:
  Those three to men all gifts of grace do graunt,
  And all, that *Venus* in her selfe doth vaunt,
  Is borrowed of them. But that faire one,
  That in the midst was placed parauaunt,
  Was she to whom that shepheard pypt alone,
That made him pipe so merrily, as neuer none.

16

She was to weete that iolly Shepheards lasse,
  Which piped there vnto that merry rout,
  That iolly shepheard, which there piped, was
  Poore *Colin Clout* (who knowes not *Colin Clout?*)
  He pypt apace, whilest they him daunst about.
  Pype iolly shepheard, pype thou now apace
  Vnto thy loue, that made thee low to lout :
  Thy loue is present there with thee in place,
Thy loue is there aduaunst to be another Grace.

17

Much wondred *Calidore* at this straunge sight,
  Whose like before his eye had neuer seene,
  And standing long astonished in spright,
  And rapt with pleasaunce, wist not what to
    weene ;
  Whether it were the traine of beauties Queene,
  Or Nymphes, or Faeries, or enchaunted show,
  With which his eyes mote haue deluded beene.
  Therefore resoluing, what it was, to know,
Out of the wood he rose, and toward them did
  go.

18

But soone as he appeared to their vew,
  They vanisht all away out of his sight,
  And cleane were gone, which way he neuer knew;
  All saue the shepheard, who for fell despight
  Of that displeasure, broke his bag-pipe quight,
  And made great mone for that vnhappy turne.
  But *Calidore*, though no lesse sory wight,
  For that mishap, yet seeing him to mourne,
Drew neare, that he the truth of all by him mote
  learne.

19

And first him greeting, thus vnto him spake,
  Haile iolly shepheard, which thy ioyous dayes
  Here leadest in this goodly merry make,
  Frequented of these gentle Nymphes alwayes,
  Which to thee flocke, to heare thy louely layes ;
  Tell me, what mote these dainty Damzels be,
  Which here with thee doe make their pleasant
    playes ?
  Right happy thou, that mayst them freely see :
But why when I them saw, fled they away from
  me ?

20

Not I so happy, answerd then that swaine,
  As thou vnhappy, which them thence didst
    chace,
Whom by no meanes thou canst recall againe,
For being gone, none can them bring in place,
But whom they of them selues list so to grace.
  Right sory I, (saide then Sir *Calidore*,)
  That my ill fortune did them hence displace.
But since things passed none may now restore,
Tell me, what were they all, whose lacke thee
    grieues so sore.

21

Tho gan that shepheard thus for to dilate ;
  Then wote thou shepheard, whatsoeuer thou
    bee,
That all those Ladies, which thou sawest late,
Are *Venus* Damzels, all within her fee,
But differing in honour and degree :
  They all are Graces, which on her depend,
  Besides a thousand more, which ready bee
Her to adorne, when so she forth doth wend :
But those three in the midst, doe chiefe on her
    attend.

22

They are the daughters of sky-ruling Ioue,
  By him begot of faire *Eurynome*,
The Oceans daughter, in this pleasant groue,
As he this way comming from feastfull glee,
Of *Thetis* wedding with *Æacidee*,
  In sommers shade him selfe here rested weary.
  The first of them hight mylde *Euphrosyne*,
Next faire *Aglaia*, last *Thalia* merry :
Sweete Goddesses all three which me in mirth
    do cherry.

23

These three on men all gracious gifts bestow,
  Which decke the body or adorne the mynde,
To make them louely or well fauoured show,
As comely carriage, entertainement kynde,
Sweete semblaunt, friendly offices that bynde,
  And all the complements of curtesie :
  They teach vs, how to each degree and kynde
We should our selues demeane, to low, to hie ;
To friends, to foes, which skill men call Ciuility.

24

Therefore they alwaies smoothly seeme to smile,
  That we likewise should mylde and gentle be,
And also naked are, that without guile
Or false dissemblaunce all them plaine may see,
Simple and true from couert malice free :
  And eeke them selues so in their daunce they
    bore,
  That two of them still froward seem'd to bee,
But one still towards shew'd her selfe afore ;
That good should from vs goe, then come in
    greater store.

25

Such were those Goddesses, which ye did see ;
  But that fourth Mayd, which there amidst
    them traced,
Who can aread, what creature mote she bee,
Whether a creature, or a goddesse graced
With heauenly gifts from heuen first enraced ?
  But what so sure she was, she worthy was,
  To be the fourth with those three other placed :
Yet was she certes but a countrey lasse,
Yet she all other countrey lasses farre did passe.

26

So farre as doth the daughter of the day,
  All other lesser lights in light excell,
So farre doth she in beautyfull array,
Aboue all other lasses beare the bell,
Ne lesse in vertue that beseemes her well,
  Doth she exceede the rest of all her race,
  For which the Graces that here wont to dwell,
Haue for more honor brought her to this place,
And graced her so much to be another Grace.

27

Another Grace she well deserues to be,
  In whom so many Graces gathered are,
Excelling much the meane of her degree ;
Diuine resemblaunce, beauty soueraine rare,
Firme Chastity, that spight ne blemish dare ;
  All which she with such courtesie doth grace,
  That all her peres cannot with her compare,
But quite are dimmed, when she is in place.
She made me often pipe and now to pipe apace.

28

Sunne of the world, great glory of the sky,
  That all the earth doest lighten with thy rayes,
Great *Gloriana*, greatest Maiesty,
Pardon thy shepheard, mongst so many layes,
As he hath sung of thee in all his dayes,
  To make one minime of thy poore handmayd,
  And vnderneath thy feete to place her prayse,
That when thy glory shall be farre displayd
To future age of her this mention may be made.

29

When thus that shepherd ended had his speach,
  Sayd *Calidore* ; Now sure it yrketh mee,
That to thy blisse I made this luckelesse breach,
As now the author of thy bale to be,
Thus to bereaue thy loues deare sight from
    thee :
  But gentle Shepheard pardon thou my shame,
  Who rashly sought that, which I mote not see.
Thus did the courteous Knight excuse his
    blame,
And to recomfort him, all comely meanes did
    frame.

30

In such discourses they together spent
  Long time, as fit occasion forth them led ;
  With which the Knight him selfe did much
    content,
  And with delight his greedy fancy fed,
  Both of his words, which he with reason red ;
  And also of the place, whose pleasures rare
  With such regard his sences rauished,
  That thence, he had no will away to fare,
But wisht, that with that shepheard he mote
    dwelling share.

31

But that enuenimd sting, the which of yore,
  His poysnous point deepe fixed in his hart
  Had left, now gan afresh to rancle sore,
  And to renue the rigour of his smart :
  Which to recure, no skill of Leaches art
  Mote him auaile, but to returne againe
  To his wounds worker, that with louely dart
  Dinting his brest, had bred his restlesse paine,
Like as the wounded Whale to shore flies from
    the maine.

32

So taking leaue of that same gentle swaine,
  He backe returned to his rusticke wonne,
  Where his faire *Pastorella* did remaine :
  To whome in sort, as he at first begonne,
  He daily did apply him selfe to donne
  All dewfull seruice voide of thoughts impure :
  Ne any paines ne perill did he shonne,
  By which he might her to his loue allure,
And liking in her yet vntamed heart procure.

33

And euermore the shepheard *Coridon*,
  What euer thing he did her to aggrate,
  Did striue to match with strong contention,
  And all his paines did closely emulate ;
  Whether it were to caroll, as they sate
  Keeping their sheepe, or games to exercize,
  Or to present her with their labours late ;
  Through which if any grace chaunst to arize
To him, the Shepheard streight with iealousie did
    frize.

34

One day as they all three together went
  To the greene wood, to gather strawberies,
  There chaunst to them a dangerous accident;
  A Tigre forth out of the wood did rise,
  That with fell clawes full of fierce gour-
    mandize,
  And greedy mouth, wide gaping like hell gate,
  Did runne at *Pastorell* her to surprize :
  Whom she beholding, now all desolate
Gan cry to them aloud, to helpe her all too late

35

Which *Coridon* first hearing, ran in hast
  To reskue her, but when he saw the feend,
  Through cowherd feare he fled away as fast,
  Ne durst abide the daunger of the end ;
  His life he steemed dearer then his frend.
  But *Calidore* soone comming to her ayde,
  When he the beast saw ready now to rend
  His loues deare spoile, in which his heart was
    prayde,
He ran at him enraged in stead of being frayde.

36

He had no weapon, but his shepheards hooke,
  To serue the vengeaunce of his wrathfull will,
  With which so sternely he the monster strooke,
  That to the ground astonished he fell ;
  Whence ere he could recou'r, he did him quell,
  And hewing off his head, ⟨he⟩ it presented
  Before the feete of the faire *Pastorell* ;
  Who scarcely yet from former feare exempted,
A thousand times him thankt, that had her death
    preuented.

37

From that day forth she gan him to affect,
  And daily more her fauour to augment ;
  But *Coridon* for cowherdize reiect,
  Fit to keepe sheepe, vnfit for loues content :
  The gentle heart scornes base disparagement.
  Yet *Calidore* did not despise him quight,
  But vsde him friendly for further intent,
  That by his fellowship, he colour might
Both his estate, and loue from skill of any wight.

38

So well he wood her, and so well he wrought her,
  With humble seruice, and with daily sute,
  That at the last vnto his will he brought her ;
  Which he so wisely well did prosecute,
  That of his loue he reapt the timely frute,
  And ioyed long in close felicity :   [brute,
  Till fortune fraught with malice, blinde, and
  That enuies louers long prosperity,
Blew vp a bitter storme of foule aduersity.

39

It fortuned one day, when *Calidore*
  Was hunting in the woods (as was his trade)
  A lawlesse people, *Brigants* hight of yore,
  That neuer vsde to liue by plough nor spade,
  But fed on spoile and booty, which they made
  Vpon their neighbours, which did nigh them
    border,
  The dwelling of these shepheards did inuade,
  And spoyld their houses, and them selues did
    murder ;
And droue away their flocks, with other much
    disorder.

40

Amongst the rest, the which they then did pray,
  They spoyld old *Melibee* of all he had,
  And all his people captiue led away,
  Mongst which this lucklesse mayd away was lad,
  Faire *Pastorella*, sorrowfull and sad,
  Most sorrowfull, most sad, that euer sight,
  Now made the spoile of theeues and *Brigants* bad,
  Which was the conquest of the gentlest Knight,
That euer liu'd, and th'onely glory of his might.

41

With them also was taken *Coridon*,
  And carried captiue by those theeues away ;
  Who in the couert of the night, that none
  Mote them descry, nor reskue from their pray,
  Vnto their dwelling did them close conuay.
  Their dwelling in a little Island was,
  Couered with shrubby woods, in which no way
  Appeard for people in nor out to pas,
Nor any footing fynde for ouergrowen gras.

42

For vnderneath the ground their way was made,
  Through hollow caues, that no man mote
    discouer
  For the thicke shrubs, which did them alwaies
    shade
  From view of liuing wight, and couered ouer :
  But darkenesse dred and daily night did houer
  Through all the inner parts, wherein they dwelt,
  Ne lightned was with window, nor with louer,
  But with continuall candlelight, which delt
A doubtfull sense of things, not so well seene,
    as felt.

43

Hither those *Brigants* brought their present pray,
  And kept them with continuall watch and ward,
  Meaning so soone, as they conuenient may,
  For slaues to sell them, for no small reward,
  To merchants, which them kept in bondage
    hard,
  Or sold againe. Now when faire *Pastorell*
  Into this place was brought, and kept with gard
  Of griesly theeues, she thought her self in hell,
Where with such damned fiends she should in
    darkenesse dwell.

44

But for to tell the dolefull dreriment,
  And pittifull complaints, which there she made,
  Where day and night she nought did but lament
  Her wretched life, shut vp in deadly shade,
  And waste her goodly beauty, which did fade
  Like to a flowre, that feeles no heate of sunne,
  Which may her feeble leaues with comfort glade,
  But what befell her in that theeuish wonne,
Will in an other Canto better be begonne.

Cant. XI.

The theeues fall out for Pastorell,
  Whilest Melibee is slaine :
Her Calidore from them redeemes,
  And bringeth backe againe.

I

The ioyes of loue, if they should euer last,
  Without affliction or disquietnesse,
  That worldly chaunces doe amongst them cast,
  Would be on earth too great a blessednesse,
  Liker to heauen, then mortall wretchednesse.
  Therefore the winged God, to let men weet,
  That here on earth is no sure happinesse,
  A thousand sowres hath tempred with one
    sweet,
To make it seeme more deare and dainty, as is
    meet.

2

Like as is now befalne to this faire Mayd,
  Faire *Pastorell*, of whom is now my song,
  Who being now in dreadfull darkenesse layd,
  Amongst those theeues, which her in bondage
    strong
  Detaynd, yet Fortune not with all this wrong
  Contented, greater mischiefe on her threw,
  And sorrowes heapt on her in greater throng ;
  That who so heares her heauinesse, would rew
And pitty her sad plight, so chang'd from
    pleasaunt hew.

3

Whylest thus she in these hellish dens remayned,
  Wrapped in wretched cares and hearts vnrest,
  It so befell (as Fortune had ordayned)
  That he, which was their Capitaine profest,
  And had the chiefe commaund of all the rest,
  One day as he did all his prisoners vew,
  With lustfull eyes, beheld that louely guest,
  Faire *Pastorella*, whose sad mournefull hew
Like the faire Morning clad in misty fog did
    shew.

4

At sight whereof his barbarous heart was fired,
  And inly burnt with flames most raging whot,
  That her alone he for his part desired
  Of all the other pray, which they had got,
  And her in mynde did to him selfe allot.
  From that day forth he kyndnesse to her showed,
  And sought her loue, by all the meanes he mote ;
  With looks, with words, with gifts he oft her
    wowed ;
And mixed threats among, and much vnto her
    vowed.

5

But all that euer he could doe or say,
  Her constant mynd could not a whit remoue,
  Nor draw vnto the lure of his lewd lay,
  To graunt him fauour, or afford him loue.
  Yet ceast he not to sew and all waies proue,
  By which he mote accomplish his request,
  Saying and doing all that mote behoue ;
  Ne day nor night he suffred her to rest,
But her all night did watch, and all the day
  molest.

6

At last when him she so importune saw,
  Fearing least he at length the raines would lend
  Vnto his lust, and make his will his law,
  Sith in his powre she was to foe or frend,
  She thought it best, for shadow to pretend
  Some shew of fauour, by him gracing small,
  That she thereby mote either freely wend,
  Or at more ease continue there his thrall :
A little well is lent, that gaineth more withall.

7

So from thenceforth, when loue he to her made,
  With better tearmes she did him entertaine,
  Which gaue him hope, and did him halfe
    perswade,
  That he in time her ioyaunce should obtaine.
  But when she saw, through that small fauours
    gaine,
  That further, then she willing was, he prest,
  She found no meanes to barre him, but to faine
  A sodaine sickenesse, which her sore opprest,
And made vnfit to serue his lawlesse mindes
  behest.

8

By meanes whereof she would not him permit
  Once to approch to her in priuity,
  But onely mongst the rest by her to sit,
  Mourning the rigour of her malady,
  And seeking all things meete for remedy.
  But she resolu'd no remedy to fynde,
  Nor better cheare to shew in misery,
  Till Fortune would her captiue bonds vnbynde,
Her sickenesse was not of the body but the
  mynde.

9

During which space that she thus sicke did lie,
  It chaunst a sort of merchants, which were
    wount
  To skim those coastes, for bondmen there to buy,
  And by such trafficke after gaines to hunt,
  Arriued in this Isle though bare and blunt,
  T'inquire for slaues ; where being readie met
  By some of these same theeues at the instant
    brunt,
  Were brought vnto their Captaine, who was set
By his faire patients side with sorrowfull regret.

10

To whom they shewed, how those marchants were
  Arriu'd in place, their bondslaues for to buy,
  And therefore prayd, that those same captiues
    there
  Mote to them for their most commodity
  Be sold, and mongst them shared equally.
  This their request the Captaine much appalled ;
  Yet could he not their iust demaund deny,
  And willed streight the slaues should forth be
    called,
And sold for most aduantage not to be forstalled.

11

Then forth the good old *Meliboe* was brought,
  And *Coridon*, with many other moe,
  Whom they before in diuerse spoyles had caught:
  All which he to the marchants sale did showe.
  Till some, which did the sundry prisoners knowe,
  Gan to inquire for that faire shepherdesse,
  Which with the rest they tooke not long agoe,
  And gan her forme and feature to expresse,
The more t'augment her price, through praise of
  comlinesse.

12

To whom the Captaine in full angry wize
  Made answere, that the Mayd of whom they spake,
  Was his owne purchase and his onely prize,
  With which none had to doe, ne ought partake,
  But he himselfe, which did that conquest make :
  Litle for him to haue one silly lasse : [weake,
  Besides through sicknesse now so wan and
  That nothing meet in marchandise to passe.
So shew'd them her, to proue how pale and
  weake she was.

13

The sight of whom, though now decayd and mard,
  And eke but hardly seene by candle-light,
  Yet like a Diamond of rich regard,
  In doubtfull shadow of the darkesome night,
  With starrie beames about her shining bright,
  These marchants fixed eyes did so amaze,
  That what through wonder, and what through
  A while on her they greedily did gaze, [delight,
And did her greatly like, and did her greatly
  praize.

14

At last when all the rest them offred were,
  And prises to them placed at their pleasure,
  They all refused in regard of her,   [sure,
  Ne ought would buy, how euer prisd with mea-
  Withouten her, whose worth aboue all threasure
  They did esteeme, and offred store of gold.
  But then the Captaine fraught with more
    displeasure,
  Bad them be still, his loue should not be sold:
The rest take if they would, he her to him
  would hold.

15

Therewith some other of the chiefest theeues
Boldly him bad such iniurie forbeare ;
For that same mayd, how euer it him greeues,
Should with the rest be sold before him theare,
To make the prises of the rest more deare.
That with great rage he stoutly doth denay ;
And fiercely drawing forth his blade, doth sweare,
That who so hardie hand on her doth lay,
It dearely shall aby, and death for handsell pay.

16

Thus as they words amongst them multiply,
They fall to strokes, the frute of too much talke,
And the mad steele about doth fiercely fly,
Not sparing wight, ne leauing any balke,
But making way for death at large to walke :
Who in the horror of the griesly night,
In thousand dreadful shapes doth mongst them
    stalke,
And makes huge hauocke, whiles the candlelight
Out quenched, leaues no skill nor difference of
    wight.

17

Like as a sort of hungry dogs ymet
About some carcase by the common way,
Doe fall together, stryuing each to get
The greatest portion of the greedie pray ;
All on confused heapes themselues assay,
And snatch, and byte, and rend, and tug, and
    teare ;
That who them sees, would wonder at their fray,
And who sees not, would be affrayd to heare.
Such was the conflict of those cruell *Brigants*
    there.

18

But first of all, their captiues they doe kill,
Least they should ioyne against the weaker side,
Or rise against the remnant at their will ;
Old *Melibœ* is slaine, and him beside
His aged wife, with many others wide,
But *Coridon* escaping craftily,
Creepes forth of dores, whilst darknes him doth
    hide,
And flyes away as fast as he can hye,
Ne stayeth leaue to take, before his friends doe
    dye.

19

But *Pastorella*, wofull wretched Elfe,
Was by the Captaine all this while defended,
Who minding more her safety then himselfe,
His target alwayes ouer her pretended ;
By meanes whereof, that mote not be amended,
He at the length was slaine, and layd on ground,
Yet holding fast twixt both his armes extended
Fayre *Pastorell*, who with the selfe same wound
Launcht through the arme, fell down with him
    in drerie swound.

20

There lay she couered with confused preasse
Of carcases, which dying on her fell.
Tho when as he was dead, the fray gan ceasse,
And each to other calling, did compell
To stay their cruell hands from slaughter fell,
Sith they that were the cause of all, were gone.
Thereto they all attonce agreed well,
And lighting candles new, gan search anone,
How many of their friends were slaine, how
    many fone.

21

Their Captaine there they cruelly found kild,
And in his armes the dreary dying mayd,
Like a sweet Angell twixt two clouds vphild :
Her louely light was dimmed and decayd,
With cloud of death vpon her eyes displayd ;
Yet did the cloud make euen that dimmed
    light
Seeme much more louely in that darknesse
    layd,
And twixt the twinckling of her eye-lids bright,
To sparke out litle beames, like starres in foggie
    night.

22

But when they mou'd the carcases aside,
They found that life did yet in her remaine :
Then all their helpes they busily applyde,
To call the soule backe to her home againe ;
And wrought so well with labour and long
    paine,
That they to life recouered her at last.
Who sighing sore, as if her hart in twaine
Had riuen bene, and all her hart strings brast,
With drearie drouping eyne lookt vp like one
    aghast.

23

There she beheld, that sore her grieu'd to see,
Her father and her friends about her lying,
Her selfe sole left, a second spoyle to bee
Of those, that hauing saued her from dying,
Renew'd her death by timely death denying :
What now is left her, but to wayle and weepe,
Wringing her hands, and ruefully loud crying?
Ne cared she her wound in teares to steepe,
Albe with all their might those *Brigants* her
    did keepe.

24

But when they saw her now reliu'd againe,
They left her so, in charge of one the best
Of many worst, who with vnkind disdaine
And cruell rigour her did much molest ;
Scarse yeelding her due food, or timely rest,
And scarsely suffring her infestred wound,
That sore her payn'd, by any to be drest.
So leaue we her in wretched thraldome bound,
And turne we backe to *Calidore*, where we him
    found,

25

Who when he backe returned from the wood,
And saw his shepheards cottage spoyled quight,
And his loue reft away, he wexed wood,
And halfe enraged at that ruefull sight,
That euen his hart for very fell despight,
And his owne flesh he readie was to teare,
He chauft, he grieu'd, he fretted, and he sight,
And fared like a furious wyld Beare,
Whose whelpes are stolne away, she being
 otherwhere.

26

Ne wight he found, to whom he might complaine,
Ne wight he found, of whom he might inquire;
That more increast the anguish of his paine.
He sought the woods; but no man could see there:
He sought the plaines; but could no tydings
 heare.
The woods did nought but ecchoes vaine
 rebound;
The playnes all waste and emptie did appeare:
Where wont the shepheards oft their pypes
 resound,
And feed an hundred flocks, there now not one
 he found.

27

At last as there he romed vp and downe,
He chaunst one comming towards him to spy,
That seem'd to be some sorie simple clowne,
With ragged weedes, and lockes vpstaring hye,
As if he did from some late daunger fly,
And yet his feare did follow him behynd:
Who as he vnto him approched nye,
He mote perceiue by signes, which he did fynd,
That *Coridon* it was, the silly shepherds hynd.

28

Tho to him running fast, he did not stay
To greet him first, but askt where were the rest;
Where *Pastorell*? who full of fresh dismay,
And gushing forth in teares, was so opprest,
That he no word could speake, but smit his brest,
And vp to heauen his eyes fast streming threw.
Whereat the knight amaz'd, yet did not rest,
But askt againe, what ment that rufull hew;
Where was his *Pastorell*? where all the other
 crew?

29

Ah well away (sayd he then sighing sore)
That euer I did liue, this day to see,
This dismall day, and was not dead before,
Before I saw faire *Pastorella* dye.
Die? out alas! then *Calidore* did cry:
How could the death dare euer her to quell?
But read thou shepheard, read what destiny,
Or other dyrefull hap from heauen or hell
Hath wrought this wicked deed, doe feare away,
 and tell.

30

Tho when the shepheard breathed had a whyle,
He thus began: Where shall I then commence
This wofull tale? or how those *Brigants* vyle,
With cruell rage and dreadfull violence
Spoyld all our cots, and caried vs from hence?
Or how faire *Pastorell* should haue bene sold
To marchants, but was sau'd with strong
 defence?
Or how those theeues, whilest one sought her
 to hold,
Fell all at ods, and fought through fury fierce
 and bold.

31

In that same conflict (woe is me) befell
This fatall chaunce, this dolefull accident,
Whose heauy tydings now I haue to tell.
First all the captiues, which they here had hent,
Were by them slaine by generall consent;
Old *Meliboe* and his good wife withall
These eyes saw die, and dearely did lament:
But when the lot to *Pastorell* did fall,
Their Captaine long withstood, and did her
 death forstall.

32

But what could he gainst all them doe alone?
It could not boot, needs mote she die at last:
I onely scapt through great confusione
Of cryes and clamors, which amongst them
 past,
In dreadfull darknesse dreadfully aghast;
That better were with them to haue bene dead,
Then here to see all desolate and wast,
Despoyled of those ioyes and iollyhead,
Which with those gentle shepherds here I
 wont to lead.

33

When *Calidore* these ruefull newes had raught,
His hart quite deaded was with anguish great,
And all his wits with doole were nigh distraught,
That he his face, his head, his brest did beat,
And death it selfe vnto himselfe did threat;
Oft cursing th'heauens, that so cruell were
To her, whose name he often did repeat;
And wishing oft, that he were present there,
When she was slaine, or had bene to her succour
 nere.

34

But after griefe awhile had had his course,
And spent it selfe in mourning, he at last
Began to mitigate his swelling sourse,
And in his mind with better reason cast,
How he might saue her life, if life did last;
Or if that dead, how he her death might wreake,
Sith otherwise he could not mend thing past;
Or if it to reuenge he were too weake,
Then for to die with her, and his liues threed to
 breake.

35

Tho *Coridon* he prayd, sith he well knew
　The readie way vnto that theeuish wonne,
　To wend with him, and be his conduct trew
　Vnto the place, to see what should be donne.
　But he, whose hart through feare was late fordonne,
　Would not for ought be drawne to former drede,
　But by all meanes the daunger knowne did shonne:
　Yet *Calidore* so well him wrought with meed,
And faire bespoke with words, that he at last
　agreed.

36

So forth they goe together (God before)
　Both clad in shepheards weeds agreeably,
　And both with shepheards hookes: But *Calidore*
　Had vnderneath, him armed priuily.
　Tho to the place when they approched nye,
　They chaunst, vpon an hill not farre away,
　Some flockes of sheepe and shepheards to espy:
　To whom they both agreed to take their way,
In hope there newes to learne, how they mote
　best assay.

37

There did they find, that which they did not feare,
　The selfe same flocks, the which those theeues
　　had reft
　From *Meliboe* and from themselues whyleare,
　And certaine of the theeues there by them left,
　The which for want of heards themselues then
　　kept.
　Right well knew *Coridon* his owne late sheepe,
　And seeing them, for tender pittie wept:
　But when he saw the theeues, which did them
　　keepe,
His hart gan fayle, albe he saw them all asleepe.

38

But *Calidore* recomforting his griefe, [swade;
　Though not his feare; for nought may feare dis-
　Him hardly forward drew, whereas the thiefe
　Lay sleeping soundly in the bushes shade,
　Whom *Coridon* him counseld to inuade
　Now all vnwares, and take the spoyle away;
　But he, that in his mind had closely made
　A further purpose, would not so them slay,
But gently waking them, gaue them the time
　of day.

39

Tho sitting downe by them vpon the greene,
　Of sundrie things he purpose gan to faine;
　That he by them might certaine tydings weene
　Of *Pastorell*, were she aliue or slaine. [againe,
　Mongst which the theeues them questioned
　What mister men, and eke from whence they were.
　To whom they answer'd, as did appertaine,
　That they were poore heardgroomes, the which
　　whylere　　　　　　　　　　　[hyre elswhere.
Had from their maisters fled, and now sought

40

Whereof right glad they seem'd, and offer made
　To hyre them well, if they their flockes would
　　keepe :
　For they themselues were euill groomes, they
　　sayd,
　Vnwont with heards to watch, or pasture sheepe,
　But to forray the land, or scoure the deepe.
　Thereto they soone agreed, and earnest tooke,
　To keepe their flockes for litle hyre and chepe :
　For they for better hyre did shortly looke,
So there all day they bode, till light the sky
　forsooke.

41

Tho when as towards darksome night it drew,
　Vnto their hellish dens those theeues them
　　brought,
　Where shortly they in great acquaintance grew,
　And all the secrets of their entrayles sought.
　There did they find, contrarie to their thought,
　That *Pastorell* yet liu'd, but all the rest
　Were dead, right so as *Coridon* had taught :
　Whereof they both full glad and blyth did rest,
But chiefly *Calidore*, whom griefe had most
　possest.

42

At length when they occasion fittest found,
　In dead of night, when all the theeues did rest
　After a late forray, and slept full sound,
　Sir *Calidore* him arm'd, as he thought best,
　Hauing of late by diligent inquest,
　Prouided him a sword of meanest sort :
　With which he streight went to the Captaines
　　nest.
　But *Coridon* durst not with him consort,
Ne durst abide behind, for dread of worse effort.

43

When to the Caue they came, they found it fast:
　But *Calidore* with huge resistlesse might,
　The dores assayled, and the locks vpbrast.
　With noyse whereof the theefe awaking light,
　Vnto the entrance ran : where the bold knight
　Encountring him with small resistance slew ;
　The whiles faire *Pastorell* through great affright
　Was almost dead, misdoubting least of new
Some vprore were like that, which lately she did
　vew.

44

But when as *Calidore* was comen in,
　And gan aloud for *Pastorell* to call,
　Knowing his voice although not heard long sin,
　She sudden was reuiued therewithall,
　And wondrous ioy felt in her spirits thrall :
　Like him that being long in tempest tost,
　Looking each houre into deathes mouth to fall,
　At length espyes at hand the happie cost,
On which he safety hopes, that earst feard to be lost.

45

Her gentle hart, that now long season past
  Had neuer ioyance felt, nor chearefull thought,
  Began some smacke of comfort new to tast,
  Like lyfull heat to nummed senses brought,
  And life to feele, that long for death had
    sought ;
Ne lesse in hart reioyced *Calidore,*
  When he her found, but like to one distraught
  And robd of reason, towards her him bore,
A thousand times embrast, and kist a thousand
  more.

46

But now by this, with noyse of late vprore,
  The hue and cry was raysed all about ;
  And all the *Brigants* flocking in great store,
  Vnto the caue gan preasse, nought hauing dout
  Of that was doen, and entred in a rout.
But *Calidore* in th'entry close did stand,
  And entertayning them with courage stout,
  Still slew the formost, that came first to hand,
So long till all the entry was with bodies mand.

47

Tho when no more could nigh to him approch,
  He breath'd his sword, and rested him till day,
  Which when hespyde vpon the earth t'encroch,
  Through the dead carcases he made his way,
  Mongst which he found a sword of better say,
  With which he forth went into th'open light :
  Where all the rest for him did readie stay,
  And fierce assayling him, with all their might
Gan all vpon him lay : there gan a dreadfull
  fight.

48

How many flyes in whottest sommers day
  Doseize vpon some beast, whose flesh is bare,
  That all the place with swarmes do ouerlay,
  And with their litle stings right felly fare,
  So many theeues about him swarming are,
  All which do him assayle on euery side,
  And sore oppresse, ne any him doth spare :
  But he doth with his raging brond diuide
Their thickest troups, and round about him
  scattreth wide.

49

Like as a Lion mongst an heard of dere,
  Disperseth them to catch his choysest pray,
  So did he fly amongst them here and there,
  And all that nere him came, did hew and slay,
  Till he had strowd with bodies all the way ;
  That none his daunger daring to abide,
  Fled from his wrath, and did themselues conuay
  Into their caues, their heads from death to
    hide,
Ne any left, that victorie to him enuide.

50

Then backe returning to his dearest deare,
  He her gan to recomfort, all he might,
  With gladfull speaches, and with louely cheare,
  And forth her bringing to the ioyous light,
  Whereof she long had lackt the wishfull sight,
  Deuiz'd all goodly meanes, from her to driue
  The sad remembrance of her wretched plight.
So her vneath at last he did reuiue,
That long had lyen dead, and made againe
  aliue.

51

This doen, into those theeuish dens he went,
  And thence did all the spoyles and threasures
    take,
  Which they from many long had robd and rent,
  But fortune now the victors meed did make ;
  Of which the best he did his loue betake ;
  And also all those flockes, which they before
  Had reft from *Meliboe* and from his make,
  He did them all to *Coridon* restore.
So droue them all away, and his loue with him
  bore.

Cant. XII.

Fayre Pastorella by great hap
* her parents vnderstands,*
Calidore doth the Blatant beast
* subdew, and bynd in bands.*

1

Like as a ship, that through the Ocean wyde
  Directs her course vnto one certaine cost,
  Is met of many a counter winde and tyde,
  With which her winged speed is let and crost,
  And she her selfe in stormie surges tost ;
  Yet making many a borde, and many a bay,
  Still winneth way, ne hath her compasse lost :
  Right so it fares with me in this long way,
Whose course is often stayd, yet neuer is astray.

2

For all that hetherto hath long delayd
  This gentle knight, from sewing his first quest,
  Though out of course, yet hath not bene mis-
    sayd,
  To shew the courtesie by him profest,
  Euen vnto the lowest and the least.
  But now I come into my course againe,
  To his atchieuement of the *Blatant beast* ;
  Who all this while at will did range and raine,
Whilst none was him to stop, nor none him to
  restraine.

3

Sir *Calidore* when thus he now had raught
Faire *Pastorella* from those *Brigants* powre,
Vnto the Castle of *Belgard* her brought,
Whereof was Lord the good Sir *Bellamoure*;
Who whylome was in his youthes freshest flowre
A lustie knight, as euer wielded speare,
And had endured many a dreadfull stoure
In bloudy battell for a Ladie deare,
The fayrest Ladie then of all that liuing were.

4

Her name was *Claribell*, whose father hight
The Lord of *Many Ilands*, farre renound
For his great riches and his greater might.
He through the wealth, wherein he did abound,
This daughter thought in wedlocke to haue
    bound
Vnto the Prince of *Picteland* bordering nere,
But she whose sides before with secret wound
Of loue to *Bellamoure* empierced were,
By all meanes shund to match with any forrein
    fere.

5

And *Bellamour* againe so well her pleased,
With dayly seruice and attendance dew,
That of her loue he was entyrely seized,
And closely did her wed, but knowne to few.
Which when her father vnderstood, he grew
In so great rage, that them in dongeon deepe
Without compassion cruelly he threw;
Yet did so streightly them a sunder keepe,
That neither could to company of th'other creepe.

6

Nathlesse Sir *Bellamour*, whether through grace
Or secret guifts so with his keepers wrought,
That to his loue sometimes he came in place,
Whereof her wombe vnwist to wight was
    fraught,
And in dew time a mayden child forth brought.
Which she streight way for dread least, if her
    syre
Should know thereof, to slay he would haue
    sought,
Deliuered to her handmayd, that for hyre
She should it cause be fostred vnder straunge
    attyre.

7

The trustie damzell bearing it abrode
Into the emptie fields, where liuing wight
Mote not bewray the secret of her lode,
She forth gan lay vnto the open light
The litle babe, to take thereof a sight.
Whom why lest she did with watrie eyne behold,
Vpon the litle brest like christall bright,
She mote perceiue a litle purple mold,
That like a rose her silken leaues did faire vnfold.

8

Well she it markt, and pittied the more,
Yet could not remedie her wretched case,
But closing it againe like as before,
Bedeaw'd with teares there left it in the place·
Yet left not quite, but drew a litle space
Behind the bushes, where she her did hyde,
To weet what mortall hand, or heauens grace
Would for the wretched infants helpe prouyde,
For which it loudly cald, and pittifully cryde.

9

At length a Shepheard, which there by did
    keepe
His fleecie flocke vpon the playnes around,
Led with the infants cry, that loud did weepe,
Came to the place, where when he wrapped
    found
Th'abandond spoyle, he softly it vnbound;
And seeing there, that did him pittie sore,
He tooke it vp, and in his mantle wound;
So home vnto his honest wife it bore,
Who as her owne it nurst, and named euermore.

10

Thus long continu'd *Claribell* a thrall,
And *Bellamour* in bands, till that her syre
Departed life, and left vnto them all.
Then all the stormes of fortunes former yre
Were turnd, and they to freedome did retyre,
Thenceforth they ioy'd in happinesse together,
And liued long in peace and loue entyre,
Without disquiet or dislike of ether, [thether.
Till time that *Calidore* brought *Pastorella*

11

Both whom they goodly well did entertaine;
For *Bellamour* knew *Calidore* right well,
And loued for his prowesse, sith they twaine
Long since had fought in field. Als *Claribell*
No lesse did tender the faire *Pastorell*,
Seeing her weake and wan, through durance
    long.
There they a while together thus did dwell
In much delight, and many ioyes among,
Vntill the damzell gan to wex more sound and
    strong.

12

Tho gan Sir *Calidore* him to aduize
Of his first quest, which he had long forlore,
Asham'd to thinke, how he that enterprize,
The which the Faery Queene had long afore
Bequeath'd to him, forslacked had so sore;
That much he feared, least reprochfull blame
With foule dishonour him mote blot therefore;
Besides the losse of so much loos and fame,
As through the world thereby should glorifie his
    name.

13

Therefore resoluing to returne in hast
  Vnto so great atchieuement, he bethought
  To leaue his loue, now perill being past,
  With *Claribell*, whylest he that monster sought
  Throughout the world, and to destruction
    brought.
So taking leaue of his faire *Pastorell*,
  Whom to recomfort, all the meanes he wrought,
  With thanks to *Bellamour* and *Claribell*,
He went forth on his quest, and did, that him
    befell.

14

But first, ere I doe his aduentures tell,
  In this exploite, me needeth to declare,
  What did betide to the faire *Pastorell*,
  During his absence left in heauy care,
  Through daily mourning, and nightly misfare :
  Yet did that auncient matrone all she might,
  To cherish her with all things choice and rare ;
  And her owne handmayd, that *Melissa* hight,
Appointed to attend her dewly day and night.

15

Who in a morning, when this Mayden faire
  Was dighting her, hauing her snowy brest
  As yet not laced, nor her golden haire
  Into their comely tresses dewly drest,
  Chaunst to espy vpon her yuory chest
  The rosie marke, which she remembred well
  That litle Infant had, which forth she kest,
  The daughter of her Lady *Claribell*,
The which she bore, the whiles in prison she did
    dwell.

16

Which well auizing, streight she gan to cast
  In her conceiptfull mynd, that this faire Mayd
  Was that same infant, which so long sith past
  She in the open fields had loosely layd
  To fortunes spoile, vnable it to ayd :
  So full of ioy, streight forth she ran in hast
  Vnto her mistresse, being halfe dismayd,
  To tell her, how the heauens had her graste,
To saue her chylde, which in misfortunes mouth
    was plaste.

17

The sober mother seeing such her mood,
  Yet knowing not, what meant that sodaine
    thro,
  Askt her, how mote her words be vnderstood,
  And what the matter was, that mou'd her so.
  My liefe (sayd she) ye know, that long ygo,
  Whilest ye in durance dwelt, ye to me gaue
  A little mayde, the which ye chylded tho ;
  The same againe if now ye list to haue,
The same is yonder Lady, whom high God did
    saue.

18

Much was the Lady troubled at that speach,
  And gan to question streight how she it knew.
  Most certaine markes, (sayd she) do me it teach,
  For on her brest I with these eyes did vew
  The litle purple rose, which thereon grew,
  Whereof her name ye then to her did giue.
  Besides her countenaunce, and her likely hew,
  Matched with equall yeares, do surely prieue
That yond same is your daughter sure, which
    yet doth liue.

19

The matrone stayd no lenger to enquire,
  But forth in hast ran to the straunger Mayd ;
  Whom catching greedily for great desire,
  Rent vp her brest, and bosome open layd,
  In which that rose she plainely saw displayd.
  Then her embracing twixt her armes twaine,
  She long so held, and softly weeping sayd ;
  And liuest thou my daughter now againe ?
And art thou yet aliue, whom dead I long did
    faine ?

20

Tho further asking her of sundry things,
  And times comparing with their accidents,
  She found at last by very certaine signes,
  And speaking markes of passed monuments,
  That this young Mayd, whom chance to her
    presents
  Is her owne daughter, her owne infant deare,
  Tho wondring long at those so straunge euents,
  A thousand times she her embraced nere,
With many a ioyfull kisse, and many a melting
    teare.

21

Who euer is the mother of one chylde,
  Which hauing thought long dead, she fyndes
    aliue,
  Let her by proofe of that, which she hath fylde
  In her owne brest, this mothers ioy descriue :
  For other none such passion can contriue
  In perfect forme, as this good Lady felt,
  When she so faire a daughter saw suruiue,
  As *Pastorella* was, that nigh she swelt
For passing ioy, which did all into pitty melt.

22

Thence running forth vnto her loued Lord,
  She vnto him recounted, all that fell :
  Who ioyning ioy with her in one accord,
  Acknowledg'd for his owne faire *Pastorell*.
  There leaue we them in ioy, and let vs tell
  Of *Calidore*, who seeking all this while
  That monstrous Beast by finall force to quell,
  Through euery place, with restlesse paine and
    toile
Him follow'd, by the tract of his outragious
    spoile.

23

Through all estates he found that he had past,
  In which he many massacres had left,
  And to the Clergy now was come at last ;
  In which such spoile, such hauocke, and such theft
  He wrought, that thence all goodnesse he bereft,
  That endlesse were to tell. The Elfin Knight,
  Who now no place besides vnsought had left,
  At length into a Monastere did light,
Where he him found despoyling all with maine
  and might.

24

Into their cloysters now he broken had,
  Through which the Monckes he chaced here
  and there,
  And them pursu'd into their dortours sad,
  And searched all their cels and secrets neare ;
  In which what filth and ordure did appeare,
  Were yrkesome to report ; yet that foule Beast
  Nought sparing them, the more did tosse and
  teare,
  And ransacke all their dennes from most to least,
Regarding nought religion, nor their holy heast.

25

From thence into the sacred Church he broke,
  And robd the Chancell, and the deskes downe
  threw,
  And Altars fouled, and blasphemy spoke,
  And th'Images for all their goodly hew,
  Did cast to ground, whilest none was them to rew;
  So all confounded and disordered there.
  But seeing *Calidore*, away he flew,
  Knowing his fatall hand by former feare ;
But he him fast pursuing, soone approched
  neare.

26

Him in a narrow place he ouertooke,
  And fierce assailing forst him turne againe :
  Sternely he turnd againe, when he him strooke
  With his sharpe steele, and ran at him amaine
  With open mouth, that seemed to containe
  A full good pecke within the vtmost brim,
  All set with yron teeth in raunges twaine,
  That terrifide his foes, and armed him,
Appearing like the mouth of *Orcus* griesly grim.

27

And therein were a thousand tongs empight,
  Of sundry kindes, and sundry quality,
  Some were of dogs, that barked day and night,
  And some of cats, that wrawling still did cry,
  And some of Beares, that groynd continually,
  And some of Tygres, that did seeme to gren,
  And snar at all, that euer passed by :
  But most of them were tongues of mortall men,
Which spake reprochfully, not caring where
  nor when.

28

And them amongst were mingled here and there,
  The tongues of Serpents with three forked
  stings,
  That spat out poyson and gore bloudy gere
  At all, that came within his rauenings,
  And spake licentious words, and hatefull things
  Of good and bad alike, of low and hie ;
  Ne Kesars spared he a whit, nor Kings,
  But either blotted them with infamie,
Or bit them with his banefull teeth of iniury.

29

But *Calidore* thereof no whit afrayd,
  Rencountred him with so impetuous might,
  That th'outrage of his violence he stayd,
  And bet abacke, threatning in vaine to bite,
  And spitting forth the poyson of his spight,
  That fomed all about his bloody iawes.
  Tho rearing vp his former feete on hight,
  He rampt vpon him with his rauenous pawes,
As if he would haue rent him with his cruell
  clawes.

30

But he right well aware, his rage to ward,
  Did cast his shield atweene, and therewithall
  Putting his puissaunce forth, pursu'd so hard,
  That backeward he enforced him to fall,
  And being downe, ere he new helpe could call,
  His shield he on him threw, and fast downe
  held,
  Like as a bullocke, that in bloudy stall
  Of butchers balefull hand to ground is feld,
Is forcibly kept downe, till he be throughly queld.

31

Full cruelly the Beast did rage and rore,
  To be downe held, and maystred so with might,
  That he gan fret and fome out bloudy gore,
  Striuing in vaine to rere him selfe vpright.
  For still the more he stroue, the more the
  Knight
  Did him suppresse, and forcibly subdew ;
  That made him almost mad for fell despight.
  He grind, hee bit, he scratcht, he venim threw,
And fared like a feend, right horrible in hew.

32

Or like the hell-borne *Hydra*, which they faine
  That great *Alcides* whilome ouerthrew,
  After that he had labourd long in vaine,
  To crop his thousand heads, the which still new
  Forth budded, and in greater number grew,
  Such was the fury of this hellish Beast,
  Whilest *Calidore* him vnder him downe threw ;
  Who nathemore his heauy load releast,
But aye the more he rag'd, the more his powre
  increast.

33

Tho when the Beast saw, he mote nought auaile,
 By force, he gan his hundred tongues apply,
 And sharpely at him to reuile and raile,
 With bitter termes of shamefull infamy ;
 Oft interlacing many a forged lie,
 Whose like he neuer once did speake, nor heare,
 Nor euer thought thing so vnworthily :
 Yet did he nought for all that him forbeare,
But strained him so streightly, that he chokt
 him neare.

34

At last when as he found his force to shrincke,
 And rage to quaile, he tooke a muzzell strong
 Of surest yron, made with many a lincke ;
 Therewith he mured vp his mouth along,
 And therein shut vp his blasphemous tong,
 For neuer more defaming gentle Knight,
 Or vnto louely Lady doing wrong :
 And thereunto a great long chaine he tight,
With which he drew him forth, euen in his own
 despight.

35

Like as whylome that strong *Tirynthian* swaine,
 Brought forth with him the dreadfull dog of hell,
 Against his will fast bound in yron chaine,
 And roring horribly, did him compell
 To see the hatefull sunne, that he might tell
 To griesly *Pluto*, what on earth was donne,
 And to the other damned ghosts, which dwell
 For aye in darkenesse, which day light doth
 shonne.
So led this Knight his captyue with like con-
 quest wonne.

36

Yet greatly did the Beast repine at those
 Straunge bands, whose like till then he neuer
 Ne euer any durst till then impose,   [bore,
 And chauffed inly, seeing now no more
 Him liberty was left aloud to rore :   [stand
 Yet durst he not draw backe ; nor once with-
 The proued powre of noble *Calidore*,
 But trembled vnderneath his mighty hand,
And like a fearefull dog him followed through
 the land.

37

Him through all Faery land he follow'd so,
 As if he learned had obedience long,
 That all the people where so he did go,
 Out of their townes did round about him
 throng,
 To see him leade that Beast in bondage strong,
 And seeing it, much wondred at the sight ;
 And all such persons, as he earst did wrong,
 Reioyced much to see his captiue plight,
And much admyr'd the Beast, but more admyr'd
 the Knight.

38

Thus was this Monster by the maystring might
 Of doughty *Calidore*, supprest and tamed,
 That neuer more he mote endammadge wight
 With his vile tongue, which many had defamed,
 And many causelesse caused to be blamed :
 So did he eeke long after this remaine,
 Vntill that, whether wicked fate so framed,
 Or fault of men, he broke his yron chaine,
And got into the world at liberty againe.

39

Thenceforth more mischiefe and more scath he
 wrought
 To mortall men, then he had done before ;
 Ne euer could by any more be brought
 Into like bands, ne maystred any more :
 Albe that long time after *Calidore*,
 The good Sir *Pelleas* him tooke in hand,
 And after him Sir *Lamoracke* of yore,
 And all his brethren borne in Britaine land ;
Yet none of them could euer bring him into
 band.

40

So now he raungeth through the world againe,
 And rageth sore in each degree and state ;
 Ne any is, that may him now restraine,
 He growen is so great and strong of late,
 Barking and biting all that him doe bate,
 Albe they worthy blame, or cleare of crime :
 Ne spareth he most learned wits to rate,
 Ne spareth he the gentle Poets rime,
But rends without regard of person or of time.

41

Ne may this homely verse, of many meanest,
 Hope to escape his venemous despite,
 More then my former writs, all were they clearest
 From blamefull blot, and free from all that wite,
 With which some wicked tongues did it backebite,
 And bring into a mighty Peres displeasure,
 That neuer so deserued to endite.
 Therfore do you my rimes keep better measure,
 And seeke to please, that now is counted wisemens threasure.

FINIS.

TWO CANTOS
OF
MVTABILITIE:
Which, both for Forme and Matter, appeare
to be parcell of some following Booke of the
FAERIE QVEENE,
(∴)
VNDER THE LEGEND
OF
Constancie.
Neuer before imprinted.

Canto VI.

Proud Change *(not pleasd, in mortall things,*
beneath the Moone, to raigne)
Pretends, as well of Gods, as Men,
to be the Soueraine.

I

What man that sees the euer-whirling wheele
Of *Change,* the which all mortall things doth
sway,
But that therby doth find, and plainly
feele,
How *MVTABILITY* in them doth play
Her cruell sports, to many mens decay?
Which that to all may better yet appeare,
I will rehearse that whylome I heard say,
How she at first her selfe began to reare,
Gainst all the Gods, and th'empire sought from
them to beare.

2

But first, here falleth fittest to vnfold
Her antique race and linage ancient,
As I haue found it registred of old,
In *Faery* Land mongst records permanent:
She was, to weet, a daughter by descent
Of those old *Titans,* that did whylome
striue
With *Saturnes* sonne for heauens regiment.
Whom, though high *Ioue* of kingdome did
depriue,
Yet many of their stemme long after did suruiue.

3

And many of them, afterwards obtain'd
Great power of *Ioue,* and high authority;
As *Hecaté,* in whose almighty hand,
He plac't all rule and principality,
To be by her disposed diuersly,
To Gods, and men, as she them list diuide:
And drad *Bellona,* that doth sound on hie
Warres and allarums vnto Nations wide,
That makes both heauen and earth to tremble
at her pride.

4

So likewise did this *Titanesse* aspire,
Rule and dominion to her selfe to gaine ;
That as a Goddesse, men might her admire,
And heauenly honours yield, as to them twaine.
At first, on earth she sought it to obtaine ;
Where she such proofe and sad examples shewed
Of her great power, to many ones great paine,
That not men onely (whom she soone subdewed)
But eke all other creatures, her bad dooings
    rewed.

5

For, she the face of earthly things so changed,
That all which Nature had establisht first
In good estate, and in meet order ranged,
She did pervert, and all their statutes burst :
And all the worlds faire frame (which none yet
    durst
Of Gods or men to alter or misguide)
She alter'd quite, and made them all accurst
That God had blest ; and did at first prouide
In that still happy state for euer to abide

6

Ne shee the lawes of Nature onely brake,
But eke of Iustice, and of Policie ;
And wrong of right, and bad of good did make,
And death for life exchanged foolishlie :
Since which, all liuing wights haue learn'd to
    die,
And all this world is woxen daily worse.
O pittious worke of *MVTABILITIE* !
By which, we all are subiect to that curse,
And death in stead of life haue sucked from our
    Nurse.

7

And now, when all the earth she thus had
    brought
To her behest, and thralled to her might,
She gan to cast in her ambitious thought,
T'attempt the empire of the heauens hight,
And *Ioue* himselfe to shoulder from his right.
And first, she past the region of the ayre,
And of the fire, whose substance thin and slight,
Made no resistance, ne could her contraire,
But ready passage for her pleasure did prepaire.

8

Thence, to the Circle of the Moone she clambe,
Where *Cynthia* raignes in euerlasting glory,
To whose bright shining palace straight she
    came,
All fairely deckt with heauens goodly story ;
Whose siluer gates (by which there sate an hory
Old aged Sire, with hower-glasse in hand,
Hight *Tyme*) she entred, were he liefe or sory :
Ne staide till she the highest stage had scand,
Where *Cynthia* did sit, that neuer still did stand.

9

Her sitting on an Iuory throne shee found,
Drawne of two steeds, th'one black, the other
    white,
Environd with tenne thousand starres around,
That duly her attended day and night ;
And by her side, there ran her Page, that hight
Vesper, whom we the Euening-starre intend :
That with his Torche, still twinkling like twy light,
Her lightened all the way where she should wend,
And ioy to weary wandring trauailers did lend :

10

That when the hardy *Titanesse* beheld
The goodly building of her Palace bright,
Made of the heauens substance, and vp-held
With thousand Crystall pillors of huge hight,
Shee gan to burne in her ambitious spright,
And t'envie her that in such glorie raigned.
Eftsoones she cast by force and tortious might,
Her to displace ; and to her selfe to haue gained
The kingdome of the Night, and waters by her
    wained.

11

Boldly she bid the Goddesse downe descend,
And let her selfe into that Ivory throne ;
For, shee her selfe more worthy thereof wend,
And better able it to guide alone :
Whether to men, whose fall she did bemone,
Or vnto Gods, whose state she did maligne,
Or to th'infernall Powers, her need giue lone
Of her faire light, and bounty most benigne,
Her selfe of all that rule shee deemed most
    condigne.

12

But shee that had to her that soueraigne seat
By highest *Ioue* assign'd, therein to beare
Nights burning lamp, regarded not her threat,
Ne yielded ought for fauour or for feare ;
But with sterne countenaunce and disdainfull
    cheare,
Bending her horned browes, did put her back :
And boldly blaming her for comming there,
Bade her attonce from heauens coast to pack,
Or at her perill bide the wrathfull Thunders
    wrack.

13

Yet nathemore the *Giantesse* forbare :
But boldly preacing-on, raught forth her hand
To pluck her downe perforce from off her chaire ;
And there-with lifting vp her golden wand,
Threatned to strike her if she did with-stand.
Where-at the starres, which round about her
    blazed,   [stand,
And eke the Moones bright wagon, still did
All beeing with so bold attempt amazed,
And on her vncouth habit and sterne looke still
    gazed.

14

Meane-while, the lower World, which nothing
  knew
  Of all that chaunced here, was darkned quite;
  And eke the heauens, and all the heauenly crew
  Of happy wights, now vnpuruaide of light,
  Were much afraid, and wondred at that sight;
  Fearing least *Chaos* broken had his chaine,
  And brought againe on them eternall night:
  But chiefely *Mercury*, that next doth raigne,
Ran forth in haste, vnto the king of Gods to
  plaine.

15

All ran together with a great out-cry,
  To *Ioues* faire Palace, fixt in heauens hight ;
  And beating at his gates full earnestly,
  Gan call to him aloud with all their might,
  To know what meant that suddaine lack of
  light.
  The father of the Gods when this he heard,
  Was troubled much at their so strange affright,
  Doubting least *Typhon* were againe vprear'd,
Or other his old foes, that once him sorely fear'd.

16

Eftsoones the sonne of *Maia* forth he sent
  Downe to the Circle of the Moone, to knowe
  The cause of this so strange astonishment,
  And why shee did her wonted course forslowe ;
  And if that any were on earth belowe
  That did with charmes or Magick her molest,
  Him to attache, and downe to hell to throwe :
  But, if from heauen it were, then to arrest
The Author, and him bring before his presence
  prest.

17

The wingd-foot God, so fast his plumes did beat,
  That soone he came where-as the *Titanesse*
  Was striuing with faire *Cynthia* for her seat :
  At whose strange sight, and haughty hardinesse,
  He wondred much, and feared her no lesse.
  Yet laying feare aside to doe his charge,
  At last, he bade her (with bold stedfastnesse)
  Ceasse to molest the Moone to walke at large,
Or come before high *Ioue*, her dooings to dis-
  charge.

18

And there-with-all, he on her shoulder laid
  His snaky-wreathed Mace, whose awfull power
  Doth make both Gods and hellish fiends affraid:
  Where-at the *Titanesse* did sternely lower,
  And stoutly answer'd, that in euill hower
  He from his *Ioue* such message to her brought,
  To bid her leaue faire *Cynthias* siluer bower ;
  Sith shee his *Ioue* and him esteemed nought,
No more then *Cynthia's* selfe ; but all their
  kingdoms sought.

19

The Heauens Herald staid not to reply,
  But past away, his doings to relate
  Vnto his Lord ; who now in th'highest sky,
  Was placed in his principall Estate,
  With all the Gods about him congregate :
  To whom when *Hermes* had his message told,
  It did them all exceedingly amate,
  Saue *Ioue* ; who, changing nought his count'-
  nance bold,
Did vnto them at length these speeches wise
  vnfold ;

20

Harken to mee awhile yee heauenly Powers ;
  Ye may remember since th'Earths cursed seed
  Sought to assaile the heauens eternall towers,
  And to vs all exceeding feare did breed :
  But how we then defeated all their deed,
  Yee all doe knowe, and them destroied quite ;
  Yet not so quite, but that there did succeed
  An off-spring of their bloud, which did alite
Vpon the fruitfull earth, which doth vs yet
  despite.

21

Of that bad seed is this bold woman bred,
  That now with bold presumption doth aspire
  To thrust faire *Phœbe* from her siluer bed,
  And eke our selues from heauens high Empire,
  If that her might were match to her desire ;
  Wherefore, it now behoues vs to aduise
  What way is best to driue her to retire ;
  Whether by open force, or counsell wise,
Areed ye sonnes of God, as best ye can deuise.

22

So hauing said, he ceast ; and with his brow
  (His black eye-brow, whose doomefull dreaded
  beck
  Is wont to wield the world vnto his vow,
  And euen the highest Powers of heauen to check)
  Made signe to them in their degrees to speake :
  Who straight gan cast their counsell graue and
  wise.
  Meane-while, th'Earths daughter, thogh she
  nought did reck
  Of *Hermes* message ; yet gan now aduise,
What course were best to take in this hot bold
  emprize.

23

Eftsoones she thus resolv'd ; that whil'st the Gods
  (After returne of *Hermes* Embassie)
  Were troubled, and amongst themselues at ods,
  Before they could new counsels re-allie,
  To set vpon them in that extasie ;   [lend :
  And take what fortune time and place would
  So, forth she rose, and through the purest sky
  To *Ioues* high Palace straight cast to ascend,
To prosecute her plot: Good on-set boads good end.

24

Shee there arriuing, boldly in did pass ;
  Where all the Gods she found in counsell close,
  All quite vnarm'd, as then their manner was.
  At sight of her they suddaine all arose,
  In great amaze, ne wist what way to chose.
  But *Ioue*, all fearelesse, forc't them to aby ;
  And in his soueraine throne,gan straight dispose
Himselfe more full of grace and Maiestie,
Tnat mote encheare his friends, and foes mote
    terrifie.

25

That, when the haughty *Titanesse* beheld,
  All were she fraught with pride and impudence,
  Yet with the sight thereof was almost queld ;
  And inly quaking, seem'd as reft of sense,
  And voyd of speech in that drad audience ;
  Vntill that *Ioue* himselfe, her selfe bespake :
  Speake thou fraile woman, speake with con-
    fidence,
Whence art thou, and what doost thou here
    now make ?
What idle errand hast thou, earths mansion to
    forsake ?

26

Shee, halfe confused with his great commaund,
  Yet gathering spirit of her natures pride,
  Him boldly answer'd thus to his demaund :
  I am a daughter, by the mothers side,
  Of her that is Grand-mother magnifide
  Of all the Gods, great *Earth*, great *Chaos* child :
  But by the fathers (be it not envide)
I greater am in bloud (whereon I build)
Then all the Gods, though wrongfully from
    heauen exil'd.

27

For, *Titan* (as ye all acknowledge must)
  Was *Saturnes* elder brother by birth-right ;
  Both, sonnes of *Vranus* : but by vniust
  And guilefull meanes, through *Corybantes* slight,
  The younger thrust the elder from his right :
  Since which, thou *Ioue*, iniuriously hast held
  The Heauens rule from *Titans* sonnes by might ;
And them to hellish dungeons downe hast feld :
Witnesse ye Heauens the truth of all that I haue
    teld.

28

Whil'st she thus spake, the Gods that gaue good eare
  To her bold words, and marked well her grace,
  Beeing of stature tall as any there
  Of all the Gods, and beautifull of face,
  As any of the Goddesses in place,
  Stood all astonied, like a sort of Steeres ;
  Mongst whom, some beast of strange and
    forraine race,
Vnwares is chaunc't, far straying from his peeres :
So did their ghastly gaze bewray their hidden
    feares.

29

Till hauing pauz'd awhile, *Ioue* thus bespake ;
  Will neuer mortall thoughts ceasse to aspire,
  In this bold sort, to Heauen claime to make
  And touch celestiall seates with earthly mire ?
  I would haue thought, that bold *Procrustes* hire,
  Or *Typhons* fall, or proud *Ixions* paine,
  Or great *Prometheus*, tasting of our ire,
Would haue suffiz'd, the rest for to restraine ;
And warn'd all men by their example to refraine :

30

But now, this off-scum of that cursed fry,
  Dare to renew the like bold enterprize,
  And chalenge th'heritage of this our skie ;
  Whom what should hinder, but that we likewise
  Should handle as the rest of her allies,
  And thunder-driue to hell ? With that, he
    shooke
  His Nectar-deawed locks, with which the skyes
And all the world beneath for terror quooke,
And eft his burning leuin-brond in hand he
    tooke.

31

But, when he looked on her louely face,
  In which, faire beames of beauty did appeare,
  That could the greatest wrath soone turne to grace
  (Such sway doth beauty euen in Heauen beare)
  He staide his hand : and hauing chang'd his
    cheare,
  He thus againe in milder wise began ;
  But ah ! if Gods should striue with flesh yfere,
Then shortly should the progeny of Man
Be rooted out, if *Ioue* should doe still what he
    can :

32

But thee faire *Titans* child, I rather weene,
  Through some vaine errour or inducement light,
  To see that mortall eyes haue neuer seene ;
  Or through ensample of thy sisters might,
  Bellona ; whose great glory thou doost spight,
  Since thou hast seene her dreadfull power
    belowe,
  Mongst wretched men (dismaide with her
    affright)
To bandie Crownes, and Kingdomes to bestowe :
And sure thy worth, no lesse then hers doth seem
    to showe.

33

But wote thou this, thou hardy *Titanesse*,
  That not the worth of any liuing wight
  May challenge ought in Heauens interesse ;
  Much lesse the Title of old *Titans* Right :
  For, we by Conquest of our soueraine might,
  And by eternall doome of Fates decree,
  Haue wonne the Empire of the Heauens bright ;
Which to our selues we hold, and to whom wee
Shall worthy deeme partakers of our blisse to bee.

34

Then ceasse thy idle claime thou foolish gerle,
  And seeke by grace and goodnesse to obtaine
That place from which by folly *Titan* fell ;
  There-to thou maist perhaps, if so thou faine
Haue *Ioue* thy gratious Lord and Soueraigne.
  So, hauing said, she thus to him replide ;
Ceasse *Saturnes* sonne, to seeke by proffers vaine
  Of idle hopes t'allure mee to thy side,
For to betray my Right, before I haue it tride.

35

But thee, O *Ioue*, no equall Iudge I deeme
  Of my desert, or of my dewfull Right ;
That in thine owne behalfe maist partiall seeme:
  But to the highest him, that is behight
Father of Gods and men by equall might ;
  To weet, the God of Nature, I appeale.
There-at *Ioue* wexed wroth, and in his spright
  Did inly grudge, yet did it well conceale ;
And bade *Dan Phœbus* Scribe her Appellation
  seale.

36

Eftsoones the time and place appointed were,
  Where all, both heauenly Powers, and earthly
  wights,
Before great Natures presence should appeare,
  For triall of their Titles and best Rights :
That was, to weet, vpon the highest hights
  Of *Arlo-hill* (Who knowes not *Arlo-hill* ?)
That is the highest head (in all mens sights)
  Of my old father *Mole*, whom Shepheards quill
Renowmed hath with hymnes fit for a rurall
  skill.

37

And, were it not ill fitting for this file,
  To sing of hilles and woods, mongst warres
  and Knights,
I would abate the sternenesse of my stile,
  Mongst these sterne stounds to mingle soft
  delights ;
And tell how *Arlo* through *Dianaes* spights
  (Beeing of old the best and fairest Hill
That was in all this holy-Islands hights)
  Was made the most vnpleasant, and most ill.
Meane while, O *Clio*, lend *Calliope* thy quill.

38

Whylome, when *IRELAND* florished in fame
  Of wealths and goodnesse, far aboue the rest
Of all that beare the *British* Islands name,
  The Gods then vs'd (for pleasure and for rest)
Oft to resort there-to, when seem'd them best :
  But none of all there-in more pleasure found,
Then *Cynthia* ; that is soueraine Queene profest
  Of woods and forrests, which therein abound,
Sprinkled with wholsom waters, more then
  most on ground

39

But mongst them all, as fittest for her game,
  Either for chace of beasts with hound or boawe,
Or for to shroude in shade from *Phœbus* flame,
  Or bathe in fountaines that doe freshly flowe,
Or from high hilles, or from the dales belowe,
  She chose this *Arlo* ; where shee did resort
With all her Nymphes enranged on a rowe,
  With whom the woody Gods did oft consort :
For, with the Nymphes, the Satyres loue to play
  and sport.

40

Amongst the which, there was a Nymph that
  hight
Molanna ; daughter of old father *Mole*,
  And sister vnto *Mulla*, faire and bright :
Vnto whose bed false *Bregog* whylome stole,
  That Shepheard *Colin* dearely did condole,
And made her lucklesse loues wellknowne to be.
  But this *Molanna*, were she not so shole,
Were no lesse faire and beautifull then shee :
  Yet as she is, a fairer flood may no man see.

41

For, first, she springs out of two marble Rocks,
  On which, a groue of Oakes high mounted growes,
That as a girlond seemes to deck the locks
  Of som faire Bride, brought forth with pompous
  showes
Out of her bowre, that many flowers strowes :
  So, through the flowry Dales she tumbling
  downe,
Through many woods, and shady couerts flowes
  (That on each side her siluer channell crowne)
Till to the Plaine she come, whose Valleyes shee
  doth drowne.

42

In her sweet streames, *Diana* vsed oft
  (After her sweatie chace and toilesome play)
To bathe her selfe ; and after, on the soft
  And downy grasse, her dainty limbes to lay
In couert shade, where none behold her may :
  For, much she hated sight of liuing eye.
Foolish God *Faunus*, though full many a day
  He saw her clad, yet longed foolishly
To see her naked mongst her Nymphes in priuity.

43

No way he found to compasse his desire,
  But to corrupt *Molanna*, this her maid,
Her to discouer for some secret hire :
  So, her with flattering words he first assaid ;
And after, pleasing gifts for her puruaid,
  Queene-apples, and red Cherries from the tree,
With which he her allured and betraid,
  To tell what time he might her Lady see
When she her selfe did bathe, that he might
  secret bee.

44

There-to hee promist, if shee would him pleasure
With this small boone, to quit her with a better;
To weet, that where-as shee had out of measure
Long lov'd the *Fanchin*, who by nought did set her,
That he would vndertake, for this to get her
To be his Loue, and of him liked well:
Besides all which, he vow'd to be her debter
For many moe good turnes then he would tell;
The least of which, this little pleasure should excell.

45

The simple maid did yield to him anone;
And eft him placed where he close might view
That neuer any saw, saue onely one;
Who, for his hire to so foole-hardy dew,
Was of his hounds devour'd in Hunters hew.
Tho, as her manner was on sunny day,
Diana, with her Nymphes about her, drew
To this sweet spring; where, doffing her array,
She bath'd her louely limbes, for *Ioue* a likely pray.

46

There *Faunus* saw that pleased much his eye,
And made his hart to tickle in his brest,
That for great ioy of some-what he did spy,
He could him not containe in silent rest;
But breaking forth in laughter, loud profest
His foolish thought. A foolish *Faune* indeed,
That couldst not hold thy selfe so hidden blest,
But wouldest needs thine owne conceit areed.
Babblers vnworthy been of so diuine a meed.

47

The Goddesse, all abashed with that noise,
In haste forth started from the guilty brooke;
And running straight where-as she heard his voice,
Enclos'd the bush about, and there him tooke,
Like darred Larke; not daring vp to looke
On her whose sight before so much he sought.
Thence, forth they drew him by the hornes, and shooke
Nigh all to peeces, that they left him nought;
And then into the open light they forth him brought.

48

Like as an huswife, that with busie care
Thinks of her Dairie to make wondrous gaine,
Finding where-as some wicked beast vnware
That breakes into her Dayr'house, there doth draine
Her creaming pannes, and frustrate all her paine;
Hath in some snare or gin set close behind,
Entrapped him, and caught into her traine,
Then thinkes what punishment were best assign'd,   [mind:
And thousand deathes deuiseth in her vengefull

49

So did *Diana* and her maydens all
Vse silly *Faunus* now within their baile: [call;
They mocke and scorne him, and him foule mis-
Some by the nose him pluckt, some by the taile,
And by his goatish beard some did him haile:
Yet he (poore soule) with patience all did beare;
For, nought against their wils might counter-vaile:
Ne ought he said what euer he did heare;
But hanging downe his head, did like a Mome appeare.

50

At length, when they had flouted him their fill,
They gan to cast what penaunce him to giue.
Some would haue gelt him, but that same would spill
The Wood-gods breed, which must for euer liue:
Others would through the riuer him haue driue,
And ducked deepe: but that seem'd penaunce light;
But most agreed and did this sentence giue,
Him in Deares skin to clad; and in that plight,
To hunt him with their hounds, him selfe saue how hee might.

51

But *Cynthia*'s selfe, more angry then the rest,
Thought not enough, to punish him in sport,
And of her shame to make a gamesome iest;
But gan examine him in straighter sort,
Which of her Nymphes, or other close consort,
Him thither brought, and her to him betraid?
He, much affeard, to her confessed short,
That 'twas *Molanna* which her so bewraid.
Then all attonce their hands vpon *Molanna* laid.

52

But him (according as they had decreed)
With a Deeres-skin they couered, and then chast
With all their hounds that after him did speed;
But he more speedy, from them fled more fast
Then any Deere: so sore him dread aghast.
They after follow'd all with shrill out-cry,
Shouting as they the heauens would haue brast:
That all the woods and dales where he did flie,
Did ring againe, and loud reeccho to the skie.

53

So they him follow'd till they weary were;
When, back returning to *Molann'* againe,
They, by commaund'ment of *Diana*, there
Her whelm'd with stones. Yet *Faunus* (for her   [paine)
Of her beloued *Fanchin* did obtaine,
That her he would receiue vnto his bed.
So now her waues passe through a pleasant Plaine,
Till with the *Fanchin* she her selfe doe wed,
And (both combin'd) themselues in one faire riuer spred.

54

Nath'lesse, *Diana*, full of indignation,
Thence-forth abandond her delicious brooke ;
in whose sweet streame, before that bad occasion,
So much delight to bathe her limbes she tooke :
Ne onely her, but also quite forsooke
All those faire forrests about *Arlo* hid,
And all that Mountaine, which doth over-looke
The richest champian that may else be rid,
And the faire *Shure*, in which are thousand
    Salmons bred.

55

Them all, and all that she so deare did way,
Thence-forth she left; and parting from the place,
There-on an heauy haplesse curse did lay,
To weet, that Wolues, where she was wont to
    space,
Should harbour'd be, and al those Woods deface,
And Thieues should rob and spoile that Coast
    around.   [Chase,
Since which, those Woods, and all that goodly
Doth to this day with Wolues and Thieues
    abound :
Which too-too true that lands in-dwellers since
    haue found.

Canto VII.

Pealing, from Ioue, *to* Natur's *Bar,*
    bold Alteration *pleades*
Large Euidence : but Nature *soone*
    her righteous Doome areads.

1

Ah ! whither doost thou now thou greater Muse
Me from these woods and pleasing forrests bring?
And my fraile spirit (that dooth oft refuse
This too high flight, vnfit for her weake wing)
Lift vp aloft, to tell of heauens King
(Thy soueraine Sire) his fortunate successe,
And victory, in bigger noates to sing,
Which he obtain'd against that *Titanesse*,
That him of heauens Empire sought to dis-
    possesse.

2

Yet sith I needs must follow thy behest,
Doe thou my weaker wit with skill inspire,
Fit for this turne ; and in my feeble brest
Kindle fresh sparks of that immortall fire,
Which learned minds inflameth with desire
Of heauenly things : for, who but thou alone,
That art yborne of heauen and heauenly Sire,
Can tell things doen in heauen so long ygone ;
So farre past memory of man that may be knowne.

3

Now, at the time that was before agreed,
The Gods assembled all on *Arlo* hill ;
As well those that are sprung of heauenly seed,
As those that all the other world doe fill,
And rule both sea and land vnto their will :
Onely th'infernall Powers might not appeare ;
Aswell for horror of their count'naunce ill,
As for th'vnruly fiends which they did feare ;
Yet *Pluto* and *Proserpina* were present there.

4

And thither also came all other creatures,
What-euer life or motion doe retaine,
According to their sundry kinds of features ;
That *Arlo* scarsly could them all containe ;
So full they filled euery hill and Plaine :
And had not *Natures* Sergeant (that is *Order*)
Them well disposed by his busie paine,
And raunged farre abroad in euery border,
They would haue caused much confusion and
    disorder.

5

Then forth issewed (great goddesse) great dame
    Nature,
With goodly port and gracious Maiesty ;
Being far greater and more tall of stature
Then any of the gods or Powers on hie :
Yet certes by her face and physnomy,
Whether she man or woman inly were,
That could not any creature well descry :
For, with a veile that wimpled euery where,
Her head and face was hid, that mote to none
    appeare.

6

That some doe say was so by skill deuized,
To hide the terror of her vncouth hew,
From mortall eyes that should be sore agrized ;
For that her face did like a Lion shew,
That eye of wight could not indure to view :
But others tell that it so beautious was,
And round about such beames of splendor
    threw,
That it the Sunne a thousand times did pass,
Ne could be seene, but like an image in a glass.

7

That well may seemen true : for, well I weene
That this same day, when she on *Arlo* sat,
Her garment was so bright and wondrous sheene,
That my fraile wit cannot deuize to what
It to compare, nor finde like stuffe to that,
As those three sacred *Saints*, though else most
    wise,
Yet on mount *Thabor* quite their wits forgat,
When they their glorious Lord in strange disguise
Transfigur'd sawe ; his garments so did daze
    their eyes.

8

In a fayre Plaine vpon an equall Hill,
  She placed was in a pauilion ;
  Not such as Craftes-men by their idle skill
  Are wont for Princes states to fashion :
  But th'earth her self of her owne motion,
  Out of her fruitfull bosome made to growe
Most dainty trees ; that, shooting vp anon,
Did seeme to bow their bloosming heads full
    lowe,
For homage vnto her, and like a throne did shew.

9

So hard it is for any liuing wight,
  All her array and vestiments to tell,
  That old *Dan Geffrey* (in whose gentle spright
  The pure well head of Poesie did dwell)
  In his *Foules parley* durst not with it mel,
  But it transferd to *Alane*, who he thought
Had in his *Plaint of kindes* describ'd it well :
Which who will read set forth so as it ought,
Go seek he out that *Alane* where he may be
    sought.

10

And all the earth far vnderneath her feete
  Was dight with flowres, that voluntary grew
  Out of the ground, and sent forth odours sweet ;
  Tenne thousand mores of sundry sent and hew,
  That might delight the smell, or please the view :
  The which, the Nymphes, from all the brooks
    thereby
Had gathered, which they at her foot-stoole
    threw ;
That richer seem'd then any tapestry,
That Princes bowres adorne with painted
    imagery.

11

And *Mole* himselfe, to honour her the more,
  Did deck himself in freshest faire attire,
  And his high head, that seemeth alwaies hore
  With hardned frosts of former winters ire,
  He with an Oaken girlond now did tire,
  As if the loue of some new Nymph late seene,
Had in him kindled youthfull fresh desire,
And made him change his gray attire to greene :
Ah gentle *Mole* ! such ioyance hath thee well
    beseene.

12

Was neuer so great ioyance since the day,
  That all the gods whylome assembled were,
  On *Hæmus* hill in their diuine array,
  To celebrate the solemne bridall cheare,
  Twixt *Peleus*, and dame *Thetis* pointed there ;
  Where *Phœbus* self, that god of Poets hight,
They say did sing the spousall hymne full cleere,
That all the gods were rauisht with delight
Of his celestiall song, and Musicks wondrous
    might.

13

This great Grandmother of all creatures bred
  Great *Nature*, euer young yet full of eld,
  Still moouing, yet vnmoued from her sted ;
  Vnseene of any, yet of all beheld ;
  Thus sitting in her throne as I haue teld,
  Before her came dame *Mutabilitie* ;
And being lowe before her presence feld,
With meek obaysance and humilitie,
Thus gan her plaintif Plea, with words to
    amplifie ;

14

To thee O greatest goddesse, onely great,
  An humble suppliant loe, I lowely fly
  Seeking for Right, which I of thee entreat ;
  Who Right to all dost deale indifferently,
  Damning all Wrong and tortious Iniurie,
  Which any of thy creatures doe to other
(Oppressing them with power, vnequally)
Sith of them all thou art the equall mother,
And knittest each to each, as brother vnto
    brother.

15

To thee therefore of this same *Ioue* I plaine,
  And of his fellow gods that faine to be,
  That challenge to themselues the whole worlds
    raign ;
  Of which, the greatest part is due to me,
  And heauen it selfe by heritage in Fee :
  For, heauen and earth I both alike do deeme,
Sith heauen and earth are both alike to thee ;
And, gods no more then men thou doest esteeme :
For, euen the gods to thee, as men to gods do
    seeme.

16

Then weigh, O soueraigne goddesse, by what right
  These gods do claime the worlds whole soue-
    rainty ;
  And that is onely dew vnto thy might
  Arrogate to themselues ambitiously :
  As for the gods owne principality,
  Which *Ioue* vsurpes vniustly ; that to be
My heritage, *Ioue's* self cannot deny,
From my great Grandsire *Titan*, vnto mee,
Deriv'd by dew descent ; as is well knowen to
    thee.

17

Yet mauger *Ioue*, and all his gods beside,
  I doe possesse the worlds most regiment ;
  As, if ye please it into parts diuide,
  And euery parts inholders to conuent,
  Shall to your eyes appeare incontinent.
  And first, the Earth (great mother of vs all)
That only seems vnmov'd and permanent,
And vnto *Mutability* not thrall ;
Yet is she chang'd in part, and eeke in generall.

18

For, all that from her springs, and is ybredde,
　How-euer fayre it flourish for a time,
　Yet see we soone decay ; and, being dead,
　To turne again vnto their earthly slime :
　Yet, out of their decay and mortall crime,
　We daily see new creatures to arize ;
　And of their Winter spring another Prime,
Vnlike in forme, and chang'd by strange disguise :
So turne they still about, and change in restlesse
　wise.

19

As for her tenants ; that is, man and beasts,
　The beasts we daily see massacred dy,
　As thralls and vassalls vnto mens beheasts :
　And men themselues doe change continually,
　From youth to eld, from wealth to pouerty,
　From good to bad, from bad to worst of all.
　Ne doe their bodies only flit and fly :
But eeke their minds (which they immortall call)
Still change and vary thoughts, as new occasions
　fall.

20

Ne is the water in more constant case ;
　Whether those same on high, or these belowe.
　For, th'Ocean moueth stil, from place to place ;
　And euery Riuer still doth ebbe and flowe :
　Ne any Lake, that seems most still and slowe,
　Ne Poole so small, that can his smoothnesse
　　holde,
　When any winde doth vnder heauen blowe :
With which, the clouds are also tost and roll'd ;
Now like great Hills ; and, streight, like sluces,
　them vnfold.

21

So likewise are all watry liuing wights
　Still tost, and turned, with continuall change,
　Neuer abyding in their stedfast plights.
　The fish, still floting, doe at randon range,
　And neuer rest ; but euermore exchange
　Their dwelling places, as the streames them
　　carrie :
　Ne haue the watry foules a certaine grange,
Wherein to rest, ne in one stead do tarry ;
But flitting still doe flie, and still their places
　vary.

22

Next is the Ayre : which who feeles not by sense
　(For, of all sense it is the middle meane)
　To flit still ? and, with subtill influence
　Of his thin spirit, all creatures to maintaine,
　In state of life ? O weake life ! that does leane
　On thing so tickle as th'vnsteady ayre ;
　Which euery howre is chang'd, and altred cleane
With euery blast that bloweth fowle or faire :
The faire doth it prolong ; the fowle doth it impaire.

23

Therein the changes infinite beholde,
　Which to her creatures euery minute chaunce ;
　Now, boyling hot : streight, friezing deadly cold :
　Now, faire sun-shine, that makes all skip and
　　daunce :
　Streight, bitter storms and balefull countenance,
　That makes them all to shiuer and to shake :
　Rayne, hayle, and snowe do pay them sad
　　penance, 　　　　　　　　　　[quake)
And dreadfull thunder-claps (that make them
With flames and flashing lights that thousand
　changes make.

24

Last is the fire : which, though it liue for euer,
　Ne can be quenched quite ; yet, euery day,
　Wee see his parts, so soone as they do seuer,
　To lose their heat, and shortly to decay ;
　So, makes himself his owne consuming pray.
　Ne any liuing creatures doth he breed :
　But all, that are of others bredd, doth slay ;
And, with their death, his cruell life dooth feed ;
Nought leauing but their barren ashes, without
　seede.

25

Thus, all these fower (the which the ground-work
　　bee
　Of all the world, and of all liuing wights)
　To thousand sorts of *Change* we subiect see .
　Yet are they chang'd (by other wondrous slights)
　Into themselues, and lose their natiue mights ;
　The Fire to Aire, and th'Ayre to Water sheere,
　And Water into Earth : yet Water fights
With Fire, and Aire with Earth approaching
　neere :
Yet all are in one body, and as one appeare.

26

So, in them all raignes *Mutabilitie* ;
　How-euer these, that Gods themselues do call,
　Of them doe claime the rule and souerainty :
　As, *Vesta*, of the fire æthereall ;
　Vulcan, of this, with vs so vsuall ;
　Ops, of the earth ; and *Iuno* of the Ayre ;
　Neptune, of Seas ; and Nymphes, of Riuers all.
　For, all those Riuers to me subiect are :
And all the rest, which they vsurp, be all my
　share.

27

Which to approuen true, as I haue told,
　Vouchsafe, O goddesse, to thy presence call
　The rest which doe the world in being hold :
　As, times and seasons of the yeare that fall :
　Of all the which, demand in generall,
　Or iudge thy selfe, by verdit of thine eye,
　Whether to me they are not subiect all.
Nature did yeeld thereto ; and by-and-by,
Bade *Order* call them all, before her Maiesty.

28

So, forth issew'd the Seasons of the yeare ;
First, lusty *Spring*, all dight in leaues of flowres
That freshly budded and new bloosmes did beare
(In which a thousand birds had built their
    bowres
That sweetly sung, to call forth Paramours) :
And in his hand a iauelin he did beare,
And on his head (as fit for warlike stoures)
A guilt engrauen morion he did weare ;
That as some did him loue, so others did him
    feare.

29

Then came the iolly *Sommer*, being dight
In a thin silken cassock coloured greene,
That was vnlyned all, to be more light :
And on his head a girlond well beseene
He wore, from which as he had chauffed been
The sweat did drop ; and in his hand he bore
A boawe and shaftes, as he in forrest greene
Had hunted late the Libbard or the Bore,
And now would bathe his limbes, with labor
    heated sore.

30

Then came the *Autumne* all in yellow clad,
As though he ioyed in his plentious store,
Laden with fruits that made him laugh, full glad
That he had banisht hunger, which to-fore
Had by the belly oft him pinched sore.
Vpon his head a wreath that was enrold
With eares of corne, of euery sort he bore :
And in his hand a sickle he did holde,
To reape the ripened fruits the which the earth
    had yold.

31

Lastly, came *Winter* cloathed all in frize,
Chattering his teeth for cold that did him chill,
Whil'st on his hoary beard his breath did freese ;
And the dull drops that from his purpled bill
As from a limbeck did adown distill.
In his right hand a tipped staffe he held,
With which his feeble steps he stayed still :
For, he was faint with cold, and weak with eld ;
That scarse his loosed limbes he hable was to
    weld.

32

These, marching softly, thus in order went,
And after them, the Monthes all riding came ;
First, sturdy *March* with brows full sternly bent,
And armed strongly, rode vpon a Ram,
The same which ouer *Hellespontus* swam :
Yet in his hand a spade he also hent,
And in a bag all sorts of seeds ysame,
Which on the earth he strowed as he went,
And fild her womb with fruitfull hope of
    nourishment.

33

Next came fresh *Aprill* full of lustyhed,
And wanton as a Kid whose horne new buds :
Vpon a Bull he rode, the same which led
Europa floting through th'*Argolick* fluds :
His hornes were gilden all with golden studs
And garnished with garlonds goodly dight
Of all the fairest flowres and freshest buds
Which th'earth brings forth, and wet he seem'd
    in sight
With waues, through which he waded for his
    loues delight.

34

Then came faire *May*, the fayrest mayd on ground,
Deckt all with dainties of her seasons pryde,
And throwing flowres out of her lap around :
Vpon two brethrens shoulders she did ride,
The twinnes of *Leda* ; which on eyther side
Supported her like to their soueraine Queene.
Lord ! how all creatures laught, when her
    they spide,
And leapt and daunc't as they had rauisht beene !
And *Cupid* selfe about her fluttred all in greene.

35

And after her, came iolly *Iune*, arrayd
All in greene leaues, as he a Player were ;
Yet in his time, he wrought as well as playd,
That by his plough-yrons mote right well
    appeare :
Vpon a Crab he rode, that him did beare
With crooked crawling steps an vncouth pase,
And backward yode, as Bargemen wont to fare
Bending their force contrary to their face,
Like that vngracious crew which faines demurest
    grace.

36

Then came hot *Iuly* boyling like to fire,
That all his garments he had cast away :
Vpon a Lyon raging yet with ire
He boldly rode and made him to obay :
It was the beast that whylome did forray
The Nemæan forrest, till th'*Amphytrionide*
Him slew, and with his hide did him array ;
Behinde his back a sithe, and by his side
Vnder his belt he bore a sickle circling wide.

37

The sixt was *August*, being rich arrayd
In garment all of gold downe to the ground ·
Yet rode he not, but led a louely Mayd
Forth by the lilly hand, the which was cround
With eares of corne, and full her hand was found ;
That was the righteous Virgin, which of old
Liv'd here on earth, and plenty made abound ;
But, after Wrong was lov'd and Iustice solde,
She left th'vnrighteous world and was to heauen
    extold

38

Next him, *September* marched eeke on foote ;
Yet was he heauy laden with the spoyle
Of haruests riches, which he made his boot,
And him enricht with bounty of the soyle :
In his one hand, as fit for haruests toyle,
He held a knife-hook ; and in th'other hand
A paire of waights, with which he did assoyle
Both more and lesse, where it in doubt did
　　stand,
And equall gaue to each as Iustice duly scann'd.

39

Then came *October* full of merry glee :
For, yet his noule was totty of the must,
Which he was treading in the wine-fats see,
And of the ioyous oyle, whose gentle gust
Made him so frollick and so full of lust :
Vpon a dreadfull Scorpion he did ride,
The same which by *Dianaes* doom vniust
Slew great *Orion :* and eeke by his side
He had his ploughing share, and coulter ready
　　tyde.

40

Next was *Nouember*, he full grosse and fat,
As fed with lard, and that right well might
　　seeme ;
For, he had been a fatting hogs of late,
That yet his browes with sweat, did reek and
　　steem,
And yet the season was full sharp and breem ;
In planting eeke he took no small delight ;
Whereon he rode, not easie was to deeme ;
For it a dreadfull *Centaure* was in sight,
The seed of *Saturne*, and faire *Nais, Chiron*
　　hight.

41

And after him, came next the chill *December :*
Yet he through merry feasting which he made,
And great bonfires, did not the cold remember;
His Sauiours birth his mind so much did glad :
Vpon a shaggy-bearded Goat he rode,
The same wherewith *Dan Ioue* in tender yeares,
They say, was nourisht by th'*Idæan* mayd ;
And in his hand a broad deepe boawle he beares;
Of which, he freely drinks an health to all his
　　peeres.

42

Then came old *Ianuary*, wrapped well
In many weeds to keep the cold away ;
Yet did he quake and quiuer like to quell,
And blowe his nayles to warme them if he may :
For, they were numbd with holding all the day
An hatchet keene, with which he felled wood,
And from the trees did lop the needlesse spray :
Vpon an huge great Earth-pot steane he stood;
From whose wide mouth, there flowed forth the
　　Romane flood.

43

And lastly, came cold *February*, sitting
In an old wagon, for he could not ride ;
Drawne of two fishes for the season fitting,
Which through the flood before did softly slyde
And swim away : yet had he by his side
His plough and harnesse fit to till the ground,
And tooles to prune the trees, before the pride
Of hasting Prime did make them burgein
　　round :
So past the twelue Months forth, and their dew
　　places found.

44

And after these, there came the *Day*, and *Night*,
Riding together both with equall pase,
Th'one on a Palfrey blacke, the other white ;
But *Night* had couered her vncomely face
With a blacke veile, and held in hand a mace,
On top whereof the moon and stars were pight,
And sleep and darknesse round about did trace :
But *Day* did beare, vpon his scepters hight,
The goodly Sun, encompast all with beames
　　bright.

45

Then came the *Howres*, faire daughters of high
　　Ioue,
And timely *Night*, the which were all endewed
With wondrous beauty fit to kindle loue ;
But they were Virgins all, and loue eschewed,
That might forslack the charge to them fore-
　　shewed
By mighty *Ioue* ; who did them Porters make
Of heauens gate (whence all the gods issued)
Which they did dayly watch, and nightly wake
By euen turnes, ne euer did their charge forsake.

46

And after all came *Life*, and lastly *Death* ;
Death with most grim and griesly visage seene,
Yet is he nought but parting of the breath ;
Ne ought to see, but like a shade to weene,
Vnbodied, vnsoul'd, vnheard, vnseene.
But *Life* was like a faire young lusty boy,
Such as they faine *Dan Cupid* to haue beene,
Full of delightfull health and liuely ioy,
Deckt all with flowres, and wings of gold fit to
　　employ.

47

When these were past, thus gan the *Titanesse* ;
Lo, mighty mother, now be iudge and say,
Whether in all thy creatures more or lesse
CHANGE doth not raign and beare the great-
　　est sway :
For, who sees not, that *Time* on all doth pray ?
But *Times* do change and moue continually.
So nothing here long standeth in one stay :
Wherefore, this lower world who can deny
But to be subiect still to *Mutabilitie ?*

48

Then thus gan *Ioue* ; Right true it is, that these
And all things else that vnder heauen dwell
Are chaung'd of *Time*, who doth them all disseise
Of being : But, who is it (to me tell)
That *Time* himselfe doth moue and still compell
To keepe his course ? Is not that namely wee
Which poure that vertue from our heauenly cell,
That moues them all, and makes them changed
    be ?
So them we gods doe rule, and in them also thee.

49

To whom, thus *Mutability* : The things
Which we see not how they are mov'd and
    swayd,
Ye may attribute to your selues as Kings,
And say they by your secret powre are made :
But what we see not, who shall vs perswade ?
But were they so, as ye them faine to be,
Mov'd by your might, and ordred by your ayde;
Yet what if I can proue, that euen yee
Your selues are likewise chang'd, and subiect
    vnto mee ?

50

And first, concerning her that is the first,
Euen you faire *Cynthia*, whom so much ye make
Ioues dearest darling, she was bred and nurst
On *Cynthus* hill, whence she her name did take:
Then is she mortall borne, how-so ye crake ;
Besides, her face and countenance euery day
We changed see, and sundry forms partake,
Now hornd, now round, now bright, now
    brown and gray :
So that *as changefull as the Moone* men vse to
    say.

51

Next, *Mercury*, who though he lesse appeare
To change his hew, and alwayes seeme as one ;
Yet, he his course doth altar euery yeare,
And is of late far out of order gone :
So *Venus* eeke, that goodly Paragone,
Though faire all night, yet is she darke all day;
And *Phœbus* self, who lightsome is alone,
Yet is he oft eclipsed by the way,
And fills the darkned world with terror and
    dismay.

52

Now *Mars* that valiant man is changed most :
For, he some times so far runs out of square,
That he his way doth seem quite to haue lost,
And cleane without his vsuall sphere to fare ;
That euen these Star-gazers stonisht are
At sight thereof, and damne their lying bookes:
So likewise, grim Sir *Saturne* oft doth spare
His sterne aspect, and calme his crabbed lookes:
So many turning cranks these haue, so many
crookes.

53

But you *Dan Ioue*, that only constant are,
And King of all the rest, as ye do clame,
Are you not subiect eeke to this misfare ?
Then let me aske you this withouten blame,
Where were ye borne ? some say in *Crete* by
    name,
Others in *Thebes*, and others other-where ;
But wheresoeuer they comment the same,
They all consent that ye begotten were,
And borne here in this world, ne other can
    appeare.

54

Then are ye mortall borne, and thrall to me,
Vnlesse the kingdome of the sky yee make
Immortall, and vnchangeable to bee ;
Besides, that power and vertue which ye spake,
That ye here worke, doth many changes take,
And your owne natures change: for, each of you,
That vertue haue, or this, or that to make,
Is checkt and changed from his nature trew,
By others opposition or obliquid view.

55

Besides, the sundry motions of your Spheares,
So sundry waies and fashions as clerkes faine,
Some in short space, and some in longer yeares;
What is the same but alteration plaine ?
Onely the starrie skie doth still remaine :
Yet do the Starres and Signes therein still
    moue,
And euen it self is mov'd, as wizards saine.
But all that moueth, doth mutation loue :
Therefore both you and them to me I subiect
    proue.

56

Then since within this wide great *Vniuerse*
Nothing doth firme and permanent appeare,
But all things tost and turned by transuerse :
What then should let, but I aloft should reare
My Trophee, and from all, the triumph beare ?
Now iudge then (O thou greatest goddesse trew!)
According as thy selfe doest see and heare,
And vnto me addoom that is my dew ;
That is the rule of all, all being rul'd by you.

57

So hauing ended, silence long ensewed,
Ne *Nature* to or fro spake for a space,
But with firme eyes affixt, the ground still
    viewed.
Meane while, all creatures, looking in her face,
Expecting th'end of this so doubtfull case,
Did hang in long suspence what would ensew,
To whether side should fall the soueraigne place:
At length, she looking vp with chearefull view,
The silence brake, and gaue her doome in
    speeches few.

58

I well consider all that ye haue sayd,
 And find that all things stedfastnes doe hate
 And changed be : yet being rightly wayd
 They are not changed from their first estate ;
 But by their change their being doe dilate :
 And turning to themselues at length againe,
 Doe worke their owne perfection so by fate :
 Then ouer them Change doth not rule and
  raigne ;
 But they raigne ouer change, and doe their
  states maintaine.

59

Cease therefore daughter further to aspire,
 And thee content thus to be rul'd by me :
 For thy decay thou seekst by thy desire ;
 But time shall come that all shall changed bee,
 And from thenceforth, none no more change
  shall see.
 So was the *Titaness* put downe and whist,
 And *Ioue* confirm'd in his imperiall see.
 Then was that whole assembly quite dismist,
 And *Natur's* selfe did vanish, whither no man
  wist.

The VIII. Canto, vnperfite.

1

When I bethinke me on that speech whyleare,
 Of *Mutability*, and well it way :
 Me seemes, that though she all vnworthy were
 Of the Heav'ns Rule ; yet very sooth to say,
 In all things else she beares the greatest sway.
 Which makes me loath this state of life so
  tickle,
 And loue of things so vaine to cast away ;
 Whose flowring pride, so fading and so fickle,
 Short *Time* shall soon cut down with his con-
  suming sickle.

2

Then gin I thinke on that which Nature sayd,
 Of that same time when no more *Change* shall
  be,
 But stedfast rest of all things firmely stayd
 Vpon the pillours of Eternity,
 That is contrayr to *Mutabilitie* :
 For, all that moueth, doth in *Change* delight :
 But thence-forth all shall rest eternally
 With Him that is the God of Sabbaoth hight :
 O that great Sabbaoth God, graunt me that
  Sabaoths sight.

FINIS.

A

Letter of the Authors expounding his

whole intention in the course of this worke : which
for that it giueth great light to the Reader, for
the better vnderstanding is hereunto
annexed.

To the Right noble, and Valorous, Sir Walter Raleigh knight,
Lo. Wardein of the Stanneryes, and her Maiesties liefe-
tenaunt of the County of Cornewayll.

SIr knowing how doubtfully all Allegories may be construed, and this booke of mine, which I haue entituled the Faery Queene, being a continued Allegory, or darke conceit, I haue thought good aswell for auoyding of gealous opinions and mis-constructions, as also for your better light in reading therof, (being so by you commanded,) to discouer vnto you the general intention and meaning, which in the whole course thereof I haue fashioned, without expressing of any parti-cular purposes or by-accidents therein occa-sioned. The generall end therefore of all the booke is to fashion a gentleman or noble person in vertuous and gentle discipline: Which for that I conceiued shoulde be most plausible and pleasing, being coloured with an historicall fiction, the which the most part of men delight to read, rather for variety of matter, then for profite of the ensample : I chose the historye of king Arthure, as most fitte for the excellency of his person, being made famous by many mens former workes, and also furthest from the daunger of enuy, and suspition of present time. In which I haue followed all the antique Poets historicall, first Homere, who in the Persons of Agamemnon and Vlysses hath ensampled a good gouernour and a vertuous man, the one in his Ilias, the other in his Odysseis : then Virgil, whose like intention was to doe in the person of Aeneas : after him Ariosto comprised them both in his Orlando: and lately Tasso disseuered them againe, and formed both parts in two persons, namely that part which they in Philosophy call Ethice, or vertues of a priuate man, coloured in his Rinaldo: The other named Politice in his Godfredo. By ensample of which excellente Poets, I labour to pourtraict in Arthure, before he was king, the image of a braue knight, perfected in the twelue priuate morall vertues, as Aristotle hath de-uised, the which is the purpose of these first twelue bookes : which if I finde to be well accepted, I may be perhaps encoraged, to frame the other part of polliticke vertues in his person, after that hee came to be king. To some I know this Methode will seeme displeasaunt, which had rather haue good discipline deliuered plainly in way of pre-cepts, or sermoned at large, as they vse, then thus clowdily enwrapped in Allegoricall deuises. But such, me seeme, should be satisfide with the vse of these dayes, seeing all things accounted by their showes, and nothing esteemed of, that is not de-lightfull and pleasing to commune sence. For this cause is Xenophon preferred before Plato, for that the one in the exquisite depth of his iudgement, formed a Commune welth such as it should be, but the other in the person of Cyrus and the Persians fashioned a gouernement such as might best be : So much more profitable and gratious is doctrine by ensample, then by rule. So haue I laboured to doe in the person of Arthure : whome I conceiue after his long educa-tion by Timon, to whom he was by Merlin de-liuered to be brought vp, so soone as he was borne of the Lady Igrayne, to haue seene in a dream or vision the Faery Queen, with whose excellent beauty rauished, he awaking resolued to seeke her out, and so being by Merlin armed, and by Timon throughly instructed, he went to seeke her forth in Faerye land. In that Faery Queene I meane glory in my generall intention, but in my parti-cular I conceiue the most excellent and glorious person of our soueraine the Queene, and her kingdome in Faery land. And yet in some places els, I doe otherwise shadow her. For considering she beareth two persons, the one of a most royall Queene or Empresse, the other of a most vertuous and beautifull Lady, this latter part in some places I doe expresse in Belphoebe, fashioning her name according to your owne excellent conceipt of Cynthia, (Phoebe and Cynthia being both names of Diana.) So in the person of Prince Arthure I sette forth magnificence in particular, which vertue for that (according to Aristotle and the rest) it is the perfection of all the rest, and con-teineth in it them all, therefore in the whole course I mention the deedes of Arthure applyable to that vertue, which I write of in that booke. But of the xii. other vertues, I make xii. other knights the patrones, for the more variety of the history : Of which these three bookes contayn three, The first of the knight of the Redcrosse, in whome I expresse Holynes : The seconde of Sir Guyon, in *whome I sette forth Temperaunce: The third of Britomartis a Lady knight, in whome I picture Chastity. But because the beginning of the whole worke seemeth abrupte and as depending vpon other antecedents, it needs that ye know the occasion of these three knights seuerall aduentures. For the Methode of a Poet historical is not such, as of an Historiographer. For an Historiographer discourseth of affayres orderly as they were donne, accounting as well the times as the actions, but a Poet thrusteth into the middest, euen where it most concerneth him, and there recoursing to the thinges forepaste, and diuining of thinges to come, maketh a pleasing Analysis of all. The beginning therefore of my history, if it were to be told by an Historiographer, should be the twelfth booke, which is the last, where I deuise that the Faery Queene kept her Annuall feaste xii. dayes, vppon which xii. seuerall dayes, the occasions of the xii. seuerall aduentures hapned, which being vndertaken by xii. seuerall knights, are in these xii books seuerally handled and discoursed. The first was this. In the beginning of the feast, there presented him selfe a tall clownishe younge man, who falling before the Queen of Faries desired a boone (as the manner then was) which during that feast she might not refuse: which was that hee might haue the atchieuement of any aduenture, which during that feaste should happen, that being graunted, he rested him on the floore, vnfitte through his rusticity for a better place. Soone after entred a faire Ladye in mourning weedes, riding on a white Asse, with a dwarfe behind her leading a warlike steed, that bore the Armes of a knight, and his speare in the dwarfes hand. Shee falling before the Queene of Faeries, complayned that her father and mother an ancient King and Queene, had bene by an huge dragon many years shut vp in a brasen Castle, who thence suffred them not to yssew: and therefore besought the Faery Queene to assygne her some one of her knights to take on him that exployt. Presently that clownish person vpstarting, desired that aduenture: whereat the Queene much wondering, and the Lady much gainesaying, yet he earnestly importuned his desire. In the end the Lady told him that vnlesse that armour which she brought, would serue him (that is the armour of a Christian man specified by Saint Paul v. Ephes.) that*

he could not succeed in that enterprise, which being forthwith put vpon him with dewe furnitures thereunto, he seemed the goodliest man in al that company, and was well liked of the Lady. And eftesoones taking on him knighthood, and mounting on that straunge Courser, he went forth with her on that aduenture: where beginneth the first booke, vz.

A gentle knight was pricking on the playne. &c.

The second day ther came in a Palmer bearing an Infant with bloody hands, whose Parents he complained to haue bene slayn by an Enchaunteresse called Acrasia: and therfore craued of the Faery Queene, to appoint him some knight, to performe that aduenture, which being assigned to Sir Guyon, he presently went forth with that same Palmer: which is the beginning of the second booke and the whole subiect thereof. The third day there came in, a Groome who complained before the Faery Queene, that a vile Enchaunter called Busirane had in hand a most faire Lady called Amoretta, whom he kept in most grieuous torment, because she would not yield him the pleasure of her body. Whereupon Sir Scudamour the louer of that Lady presently tooke on him that aduenture. But being vnable to performe it by reason of the hard Enchauntments, after long sorrow, in the end met with Britomartis, who succoured him, and reskewed his loue.

But by occasion hereof, many other aduentures are intermedled, but rather as Accidents, then intendments. As the loue of Britomart, the ouerthrow of Marinell, the misery of Florimell, the vertuousnes of Belphœbe, the lasciuiousnes of Hellenora, and many the like.

Thus much Sir, I haue briefly ouerronne to direct your vnderstanding to the wel-head of the History, that from thence gathering the whole intention of the conceit, ye may as in a handfull gripe al the discourse, which otherwise may happily seeme tedious and confused. So humbly crauing the continuaunce of your honorable fauour towards me, and th'eternall establishment of your happines, I humbly take leaue.

23. Ianuary. 1589.

Yours most humbly affectionate.
Ed. Spenser.

¶ A Vision vpon this conceipt of the *Faery Queene.*

ME thought I saw the graue, where *Laura* lay,
Within that Temple, where the vestall flame
Was wont to burne, and passing by that way,
To see that buried dust of liuing fame,
Whose tombe faire loue, and fairer vertue kept,
All suddenly I saw the Faery Queene :
At whose approch the soule of *Petrarke* wept,

And from thenceforth those graces were not seene.
For they this Queene attended, in whose steed
Obliuion laid him downe on *Lauras* herse :
Hereat the hardest stones were seene to bleed,
And grones of buried ghostes the heauens did perse.
Where *Homers* spright did tremble all for griefe,
And curst th'accesse of that celestiall theife.

Another of the same.

THe prayse of meaner wits this worke like profit brings,
As doth the Cuckoes song delight when Philumena sings.
If thou hast formed right true vertues face herein :
Vertue her selfe can best discerne, to whom they written bin.
If thou hast beautie prays'd, let her sole lookes diuine
Iudge if ought therein be amis, and mend it by her eine.
If Chastitie want ought, or Temperance her dew,

Behold her Princely mind aright, and write thy Queene anew.
Meane while she shall perceiue, how farre her vertues sore
Aboue the reach of all that liue, or such as wrote of yore :
And thereby will excuse and fauour thy good will :
Whose vertue can not be exprest, but by an Angels quill.
Of me no lines are lou'd, nor letters are of price,
Of all which speake our English tongue, but those of thy deuice.

W. R.

To the learned Shepheard.

COllyn I see by thy new taken taske,
some sacred fury hath enricht thy braynes,
That leades thy muse in haughtie verse to maske,
and loath the layes that longs to lowly swaynes.
That lifts thy notes from Shepheardes vnto kings,
So like the liuely Larke that mounting sings.

Thy louely Rosolinde seemes now forlorne,
and all thy gentle flockes forgotten quight,
Thy chaunged hart now holdes thy pypes in scorne,
those prety pypes that did thy mates delight.
Those trustie mates, that loued thee so well,
Whom thou gau'st mirth : as they gaue thee the bell.

Yet as thou earst with thy sweete roundelayes,
didst stirre to glee our laddes in homely bowers :
So moughtst thou now in these refyned layes,
delight the dainty eares of higher powers.
And so mought they in their deepe skanning skill
Alow and grace our Collyns flowing quill.

And fare befall that Faerie Queene of thine,
in whose faire eyes loue linckt with vertue sits :
Enfusing by those bewties fiers deuyne,
such high conceites into thy humble wits,
As raised hath poore pastors oaten reede,
From rusticke tunes, to chaunt heroique deedes.

So mought thy Redcrosse knight with happy hand
victorious be in that faire Ilands right :
Which thou doest vaile in Type of Faery land
Elyzas blessed field, that Albion hight.
That shieldes her friends, and warres her mightie foes,
Yet still with people, peace, and plentie flowes.

But (iolly Shepheard) though with pleasing style,
thou feast the humour of the Courtly traine :
Let not conceipt thy setled sence beguile,
ne daunted be through enuy or disdaine.
Subiect thy dome to her Empyring spright,
From whence thy Muse, and all the world takes light.

Hobynoll.

FAyre *Thamis* streame, that from *Ludds* stately towne,
Runst paying tribute to the Ocean seas,
Let all thy Nymphes and Syrens of renowne
Be silent, whyle this Bryttane *Orpheus* playes :
Nere thy sweet bankes, there liues that sacred crowne,
Whose hand strowes Palme and neuer-dying bayes,
Let all at once, with thy soft murmuring sowne
Present her with this worthy Poets prayes.
For he hath taught hye drifts in shepeherdes weedes,
And deepe conceites now singes in *Faeries* deedes.

R. S.

GRaue Muses march in triumph and with prayses,
Our Goddesse here hath giuen you leaue to land :
And biddes this rare dispenser of your graces
Bow downe his brow vnto her sacred hand.
Desertes findes dew in that most princely doome,
In whose sweete brest are all the Muses bredde :
So did that great Augustus erst in Roome
With leaues of fame adorne his Poets hedde.
Faire be the guerdon of your Faery Queene,
Euen of the fairest that the world hath seene.

H. B.

WHen stout *Achilles* heard of *Helens* rape
And what reuenge the States of Greece deuisd:
Thinking by sleight the fatall warres to scape,
In womans weedes him selfe he then disguisde:
But this deuise *Vlysses* soone did spy,
And brought him forth, the chaunce of warre to try.

When *Spencer* saw the fame was spredd so large,
Through Faery land of their renowned Queene:
Loth that his Muse should take so great a charge,
As in such haughty matter to be seene,
To seeme a shepeheard then he made his choice,
But *Sydney* heard him sing, and knew his voice.

And as *Vlysses* brought faire *Thetis* sonne
From his retyred life to menage armes:
So *Spencer* was by *Sidneys* speaches wonne,
To blaze her fame not fearing future harmes:
For well he knew, his Muse would soone be tyred
In her high praise, that all the world admired.

Yet as *Achilles* in those warlike frayes,
Did win the palme from all the *Grecian* Peeres:
So *Spencer* now to his immortall prayse,
Hath wonne the Laurell quite from all his feres.
What though his taske exceed a humaine witt,
He is excus'd, sith *Sidney* thought it fitt.
W. L.

*T*O looke vpon a worke of rare deuise
The which a workman setteth out to view,
And not to yield it the deserued prise,
That vnto such a workmanship is dew,
Doth either proue the iudgement to be naught
Or els doth shew a mind with enuy fraught.

To labour to commend a peece of worke,
Which no man goes about to discommend,
Would raise a iealous doubt that there did lurke,
Some secret doubt, whereto the prayse did tend.
For when men know the goodnes of the wyne,
T'is needlesse for the hoast to haue a sygne.

Thus then to shew my iudgement to be such
As can discerne of colours blacke, and white,
As alls to free my minde from enuies tuch,
That neuer giues to any man his right,
I here pronounce this workmanship is such,
As that no pen can set it forth too much.

And thus I hang a garland at the dore,
Not for to shew the goodnes of the ware:
But such hath beene the custome heretofore,
And customes very hardly broken are.
And when your tast shall tell you this is trew,
Then looke you giue your hoast his vtmost dew.
Ignoto.

[DEDICATORY SONNETS.]

To the right honourable Sir Christopher Hatton,
Lord high Chauncelor of England. &c.

THose prudent heads, that with theire counsels wise
Whylom the Pillours of th'earth did sustaine,
And taught ambitious *Rome* to tyrannise,
And in the neck of all the world to rayne,
Oft from those graue affaires were wont abstaine,
With the sweet Lady Muses for to play:
So *Ennius* the elder Africane,
So *Maro* oft did *Cæsars* cares allay.
So you great Lord, that with your counsell sway
The burdeine of this kingdom mightily,
With like delightes sometimes may eke delay,
The rugged brow of carefull Policy:
And to these ydle rymes lend litle space,
Which for their titles sake may find more grace.

To the right honourable the Lo. Burleigh *Lo. high*
Threasurer of England.

TO you right noble Lord, whose carefull brest
To menage of most graue affaires is bent,
And on whose mightie shoulders most doth rest
The burdein of this kingdomes gouernement,
As the wide compasse of the firmament,
On *Atlas* mighty shoulders is vpstayd;
Vnfitly I these ydle rimes present,
The labor of lost time, and wit vnstayd:
Yet if their deeper sence be inly wayd,
And the dim vele, with which from comune vew
Their fairer parts are hid, aside be layd.
Perhaps not vaine they may appeare to you.
Such as they be, vouchsafe them to receaue,
And wipe their faults out of your censure graue.
E. S.

To the right Honourable the Earle of Oxenford,
Lord high Chamberlayne of England. &c.

REceiue most Noble Lord in gentle gree,
The vnripe fruit of an vnready wit:
Which by thy countenaunce doth craue to bee
Defended from foule Enuies poisnous bit.
Which so to doe may thee right well besit,
Sith th'antique glory of thine auncestry
Vnder a shady vele is therein writ,
And eke thine owne long liuing memory,
Succeeding them in true nobility:
And also for the loue, which thou doest beare
To th'*Heliconian* ymps, and they to thee,
They vnto thee, and thou to them most deare:
Deare as thou art vnto thy selfe, so loue
That loues and honours thee, as doth behoue.

To the right honourable the Earle of Northumberland.

THe sacred Muses haue made alwaies clame
  To be the Nourses of nobility,
  And Registres of euerlasting fame,
  To all that armes professe and cheualry.
Then by like right the noble Progeny,
  Which them succeed in fame and worth, are tyde
T'embrace the seruice of sweete Poetry,

By whose endeuours they are glorifide,
  And eke from all, of whom it is enuide,
  To patronize the authour of their praise,
  Which giues them life, that els would soone haue dide,
  And crownes their ashes with immortall baies
To thee therefore right noble Lord I send
  This present of my paines, it to defend.

To the right honourable the Earle of Cumberland.

REdoubted Lord, in whose corageous mind
  The flowre of cheualry now bloosming faire,
  Doth promise fruite worthy the noble kind,
  Which of their praises haue left you the haire;
To you this humble present I prepare,
  For loue of vertue and of Martiall praise,
  To which though nobly ye inclined are,
  As goodlie well ye shew'd in late assaies,

Yet braue ensample of long passed daies,
  In which trew honor yee may fashiond see,
  To like desire of honor may ye raise,
  And fill your mind with magnanimitee.
Receiue it Lord therefore as it was ment,
  For honor of your name and high descent.
                E. S.

To the most honourable and excellent Lo. the Earle of Essex. Great Maister of the Horse to her Highnesse, and knight of the Noble order of the Garter. &c.

MAgnificke Lord, whose vertues excellent
  Doe merit a most famous Poets witt,
  To be thy liuing praises instrument,
  Yet doe not sdeigne, to let thy name be writt
In this base Poeme, for thee far vnfitt.
  Nought is thy worth disparaged thereby,
  But when my Muse, whose fethers nothing flitt

Doe yet but flagg, and lowly learne to fly
With bolder wing shall dare alofte to sty
  To the last praises of this Faery Queene,
  Then shall it make more famous memory
  Of thine Heroicke parts, such as they beene:
Till then vouchsafe thy noble countenaunce,
  To these first labours needed furtheraunce.

To the right Honourable the Earle of Ormond and Ossory.

REceiue most noble Lord a simple taste
  Of the wilde fruit, which saluage soyl hath bred,
  Which being through long wars left almost waste,
  With brutish barbarisme is ouerspredd:
And in so faire a land, as may be redd,
  Not one Parnassus, nor one Helicone
  Left for sweete Muses to be harboured,

But where thy selfe hast thy braue mansione;
There in deede dwel faire Graces many one.
  And gentle Nymphes, delights of learned wits,
  And in thy person without Paragone
  All goodly bountie and true honour sits,
Such therefore, as that wasted soyl doth yield,
  Receiue dear Lord in worth, the fruit of barren field.

To the right honourable the Lo. Ch. Howard, Lo. high Admiral of England, knight of the noble order of the Garter, and one of her Maiesties priuie Counsel. &c.

ANd ye, braue Lord, whose goodly personage,
  And noble deeds each other garnishing,
  Make you ensample to the present age,
  Of th'old Heroes, whose famous ofspring
The antique Poets wont so much to sing,
  In this same Pageaunt haue a worthy place,
  Sith those huge castles of Castilian king,

That vainly threatned kingdomes to displace,
Like flying doues ye did before you chace;
  And that proud people woxen insolent
  Through many victories, didst first deface:
  Thy praises euerlasting monument
Is in this verse engrauen semblably,
  That it may liue to all posterity.

To the right honourable the Lord of Hunsdon, high Chamberlaine to her Maiesty.

REnowmed Lord, that for your worthinesse
And noble deeds haue your deserued place,
High in the fauour of that Emperesse,
The worlds sole glory and her sexes grace,
Here eke of right haue you a worthie place,
Both for your nearnes to that Faerie Queene,
And for your owne high merit in like cace,
Of which, apparaunt proofe was to be seene,
When that tumultuous rage and fearfull deene
Of Northerne rebels ye did pacify,
And their disloiall powre defaced clene,
The record of enduring memory.
Liue Lord for euer in this lasting verse,
That all posteritie thy honour may reherse.
E. S.

To the most renowmed and valiant Lord, the Lord Grey of Wilton, knight of the Noble order of the Garter, &c.

MOst Noble Lord the pillor of my life,
And Patrone of my Muses pupillage,
Through whose large bountie poured on me rife,
In the first season of my feeble age,
I now doe liue, bound yours by vassalage :
Sith nothing euer may redeeme, nor reaue
Out of your endlesse debt so sure a gage,
Vouchsafe in worth this small guift to receaue,
Which in your noble hands for pledge I leaue,
Of all the rest, that I am tyde t'account :
Rude rymes, the which a rustick Muse did weaue
In sauadge soyle, far from Parnasso mount,
And roughly wrought in an vnlearned Loome :
The which vouchsafe dear Lord your fauorable doome.

To the right honourable the Lord of Buckhurst, one of her Maiesties priuie Counsell.

IN vain I thinke right honourable Lord,
By this rude rime to memorize thy name ;
Whose learned Muse hath writ her owne record,
In golden verse, worthy immortal fame :
Thou much more fit (were leasure to the same)
Thy gracious Souerains praises to compile,
And her imperiall Maiestie to frame,
In loftie numbers and heroicke stile.
But sith thou maist not so, giue leaue a while
To baser wit his power therein to spend,
Whose grosse defaults thy daintie pen may file,
And vnaduised ouersights amend.
But euermore vouchsafe it to maintaine
Against vile Zoilus backbitings vaine.

To the right honourable Sir Fr. Walsingham knight, principall Secretary to her Maiesty, and of her honourable priuy Counsell.

THat Mantuane Poetes incompared spirit,
Whose girland now is set in highest place,
Had not Mecænas for his worthy merit,
It first aduaunst to great Augustus grace,
Might long perhaps haue lien in silence bace,
Ne bene so much admir'd of later age.
This lowly Muse, that learns like steps to trace,
Flies for like aide vnto your Patronage ;
That are the great Mecenas of this age,
As wel to al that ciuil artes professe
As those that are inspird with Martial rage,
Which if ye yield, perhaps ye may her rayse
In bigger tunes to sound your liuing prayse.
E. S.

To the right noble Lord and most valiaunt Captaine, Sir Iohn Norris knight, Lord president of Mounster.

WHo euer gaue more honourable prize
To the sweet Muse, then did the Martiall crew;
That their braue deeds she might immortalize
In her shril tromp, and sound their praises dew?
Who then ought more to fauour her, then you
Moste noble Lord, the honor of this age,
And Precedent of all that armes ensue?
Whose warlike prowesse and manly courage,
Tempred with reason and aduizement sage
Hath fild sad Belgicke with victorious spoile,
In Fraunce and Ireland left a famous gage,
And lately shakt the Lusitanian soile.
Sith then each where thou hast dispredd thy fame,
Loue him, that hath eternized your name.
E. S.

To the right noble and valorous knight, Sir Walter Raleigh, Lo. Wardein of the Stanneryes, and lieftenaunt of Cornewaile.

TO thee that art the sommers Nightingale,
* Thy soueraine Goddesses most deare delight,*
Why doe I send this rusticke Madrigale,
That may thy tunefull eare vnseason quite?
Thou onely fit this Argument to write,
* In whose high thoughts Pleasure hath built her*
* bowre,*
And dainty loue learnd sweetly to endite.
My rimes I know vnsauory and sowre,

To tast the streames, that like a golden showre
* Flow from thy fruitfull head, of thy loues*
* praise,*
Fitter perhaps to thonder Martiall stowre,
* When so thee list thy lofty Muse to raise:*
Yet till that thou thy Poeme wilt make knowne,
* Let thy faire Cinthias praises bee thus rudely*
* showne.*

E. S.

To the right honourable and most vertuous Lady, the Countesse of Penbroke.

REmembraunce of that most Heroicke spirit,
  The heuens pride, the glory of our daies,
Which now triumpheth through immortall merit
Of his braue vertues, crownd with lasting baies,
Of heuenlie blis and euerlasting praies;
  Who first my Muse did lift out of the flore,
To sing his sweet delights in lowlie laies;
Bids me most noble Lady to adore

His goodly image liuing euermore,
  In the diuine resemblaunce of your face;
  Which with your vertues ye embellish more,
  And natiue beauty deck with heuenlie grace:
For his, and for your owne especial sake,
  Vouchsafe from him this token in good worth to
  take.

E. S.

To the most vertuous, and beautifull Lady, *the Lady Carew.*

NE may I, without blot of endlesse blame,
  You fairest Lady leaue out of this place,
But with remembraunce of your gracious name,
Wherewith that courtly garlond most ye grace,
And deck the world, adorne these verses base:
  Not that these few lines can in them comprise
Those glorious ornaments of heuenly grace,
Wherewith ye triumph ouer feeble eyes,

And in subdued harts do tyranyse:
  For thereunto doth need a golden quill,
  And siluer leaues, them rightly to deuise,
  But to make humble present of good will:
Which whenas timely meanes it purchase may.
  In ampler wise it selfe will forth display.

E. S.

To all the gratious and beautifull Ladies in the Court.

THe Chian Peincter, when he was requirde
* To pourtraict Venus in her perfect hew,*
To make his worke more absolute, desird
Of all the fairest Maides to haue the vew.
Much more me needs to draw the semblant trew,
* Of beauties Queene, the worlds sole wonderment,*
To sharpe my sence with sundry beauties
* vew,*
And steale from each some part of ornament.

If all the world to seeke I ouerwent,
* A fairer crew yet no where could I see,*
Then that braue court doth to mine eie present,
That the worlds pride seemes gathered there
* to bee.*
Of each a part I stole by cunning thefte:
* Forgiue it me faire Dames, sith lesse ye haue*
* not lefte.*

E. S.

FINIS.

THE
Shepheardes Calender

Conteyning tvvelue Æglogues proportionable
to the twelue monethes.

Entitled
TO THE NOBLE AND VERTV-
ous Gentleman most worthy of all titles
both of learning and cheualrie M.
Philip Sidney.
(⋅∵⋅)

AT LONDON.
Printed by Hugh Singleton, dwelling in
Creede Lane neere vnto Ludgate at the
ſigne of the gylden Tunne, and
are there to be ſolde.
1579.

Goe little booke : thy selfe present,
As child whose parent is vnkent :
To him that is the president
Of noblesse and of cheualree,
And if that Enuie barke at thee,
As sure it will, for succoure flee
   Vnder the shadow of his wing,
And asked, who thee forth did bring,
A shepheards swaine saye did thee sing,
All as his straying flocke he fedde :   10

And when his honor has thee redde,
Craue pardon for my hardyhedde.
   But if that any aske thy name,
Say thou wert base begot with blame :
For thy thereof thou takest shame.
And when thou art past ieopardee,
Come tell me, what was sayd of mee
And I will send more after thee.

Immeritô.

¶ *To the most excellent and learned both*
Ⓞⓡⓐⓣⓞⓡ ⓐⓝⓓ ⓟⓞⓔⓣⓔ, Ⓜⓐⓨⓢⓣⓔⓡ Ⓖⓐⓑⓡⓘⓔⓛⓛ Ⓗⓐⓡⓤⓔⓨ, Ⓗⓘⓢ
verie special and singular good frend E. K. commendeth the good lyking of this his labour,
and the patronage of the
new Poete.

Vncouthe vnkiste, Sayde the olde famous Poete Chaucer : whom for his excellencie and wonderfull skil in making, his scholler Lidgate, a worthy scholler of so excellent a maister, calleth the Loadestarre of our Language : and whom our Colin clout in his Æglogue calleth Tityrus the God of shepheards, comparing hym to the worthiest of the Roman Tityrus Virgile. Which prouerbe, myne owne good friend Ma. Haruey, as in that good old Poete it serued well Pandares purpose, for the bolstering of his baudy brocage, so very well taketh place in this our new Poete, who for that he is vncouthe (as said Chaucer) is vnkist, and vnknown to most men, is regarded but of few. But I dout not, so soone as his name shall come into the knowledg of men, and his worthines be sounded in the tromp of fame, but that he shall be not onely kiste, but also beloued of all, embraced of the most, and wondred at of the best. No lesse I thinke, deserueth his wittinesse in deuising, his pithinesse in vttering, his complaints of loue so louely, his discourses of pleasure so pleasantly, his pastorall rudenesse, his morall wisenesse, his dewe obseruing of Decorum euerye where, in personages, in sea-

sons, in matter, in speach, and generally in al seemely simplycitie of handeling his matter, and framing his words : the which of many thinges which in him be straunge, I know will seeme the straungest, the words them selues being so auncient, the knitting of them so short and intricate, and the whole Periode and compasse of speache so delightsome for the roundnesse, and so graue for the straungenesse. And firste of the wordes to speake, I graunt they be something hard, and of most men vnused, yet both English, and also vsed of most excellent Authors and most famous Poetes. In whom whenas this our Poet hath bene much trauelled and throughly redd, how could it be, (as that worthy Oratour sayde) but that walking in the sonne although for other cause he walked, yet needes he mought be sunburnt ; and hauing the sound of those auncient Poetes still ringing in his eares, he mought needes in singing hit out some of theyr tunes. But whether he vseth them by such casualtye and custome, or of set purpose and choyse, as thinking them fittest for such rusticall rudenesse of shepheards, eyther for that theyr rough sounde would make his rymes more ragged and rustical, or els because such olde and obsolete wordes are most vsed of country folke, sure I think, and think I think not amisse, that they bring great grace and, as one would say, auctoritie to the verse. For albe amongst many other faultes it specially be obiected of Valla against Liuie, and of other against Saluste, that with ouer much studie they affect antiquitie, as coueting thereby credence and honor of elder yeeres, yet I am of opinion, and eke the best learned are of the lyke, that those auncient solemne wordes are a great ornament both in the one and in the other; the one labouring to set forth in hys worke an eternall image of antiquitie, and the other carefully discoursing matters of grauitie and importaunce. For if my memory fayle not, Tullie in that booke, wherein he endeuoureth to set forth the paterne of a perfect Oratour, sayth that ofttimes an auncient worde maketh the style seeme graue, and as it were reuerend: no otherwise then we honour and reuerence gray heares for a certein religious regard, which we haue of old age. Yet nether euery where must old words be stuffed in, nor the commen Dialecte and maner of speaking so corrupted therby, that as in old buildings it seme disorderly and ruinous. But all as in most exquisite pictures they vse to blaze and portraict not onely the daintie lineaments of beautye, but also rounde about it to shadow the rude thickets and craggy clifts, that by the basenesse of such parts, more excellency may accrew to the principall; for oftimes we fynde ourselues, I knowe not how, singularly delighted with the shewe of such naturall rudenesse, and take great pleasure in that disorderly order. Euen so doe those rough and harsh termes enlumine and make more clearly to appeare the brightnesse of braue and glorious words. So oftentimes a dischorde in Musick maketh a comely concordaunce: so great delight tooke the worthy Poete Alceus to behold a blemish in the ioynt of a wel shaped body. But if any will rashly blame such his purpose in choyse of old and vnwonted words, him may I more iustly blame and condemne, or of witlesse headinesse in iudging, or of heedelesse hardinesse in condemning for not marking the compasse of hys bent, he wil iudge of the length of his cast. For in my opinion it is one special prayse, of many whych are dew to this Poete, that he hath laboured to restore, as to theyr rightfull heritage such good and naturall English words, as haue ben long time out of vse and almost cleane disherited. Which is the

onely cause, that our Mother tonge, which truely of it self is both ful enough for prose and stately enough for verse, hath long time ben counted most bare and barrein of both. Which default when as some endeuoured to salue and recure, they patched vp the holes with peces and rags of other languages, borrowing here of the french, there of the Italian, euery where of the Latine, not weighing how il, those tongues accorde with themselues, but much worse with ours: So now they haue made our English tongue, a gallimaufray or hodgepodge of al other speches. Other some not so wel seene in the English tonge as perhaps in other languages, if they happen to here an olde word albeit very naturall and significant, crye out streight way, that we speak no English, but gibbrish, or rather such, as in old time Euanders mother spake. Whose first shame is, that they are not ashamed, in their own mother tonge straungers to be counted and alienes. The second shame no lesse then the first, that what so they vnderstand not, they streight way deeme to be sencelesse, and not at al to be vnderstode. Much like to the Mole in Æsopes fable, that being blynd her selfe, would in no wise be perswaded, that any beast could see. The last more shameful then both, that of their owne country and natural speach, which together with their Nources milk they sucked, they haue so base regard and bastard iudgement, that they will not onely themselues not labor to garnish and beautifie it, but also repine, that of other it shold be embellished. Like to the dogge in the maunger, that him selfe can eate no hay, and yet barketh at the hungry bullock, that so faine would feede: whose currish kind though it cannot be kept from barking, yet I conne them thanke that they refrain from byting.

Now for the knitting of sentences, whych they call the ioynts and members therof, and for al the compasse of the speach, it is round without roughnesse, and learned wythout hardnes, such indeede as may be perceiued of the leaste, vnderstoode of the moste, but iudged onely of the learned. For what in most English wryters vseth to be loose, and as it were vngyrt, in this Authour is well grounded, finely framed, and strongly trussed vp together. In regard wherof, I scorne and spue out the rakehellye route of our ragged rymers (for so themselues vse to hunt the letter) which without learning boste, without iudgement iangle, without reason rage and fome, as if some instinct of Poeticall spirite had newly rauished them

aboue the meanenesse of commen capacitie.
And being in the middest of all theyr brauery,
sodenly eyther for want of matter, or of ryme,
or hauing forgotten theyr former conceipt,
they seeme to be so pained and traueiled in
theyr remembrance, as it were a woman in
childebirth or as that same Pythia, when the
traunce came vpon her.

Os rabidum fera corda domans &c.

Nethelesse let them a Gods name feede on
theyr owne folly, so they seeke not to darken
the beames of others glory. As for Colin, vnder
whose person the Author selfe is shadowed,
how furre he is from such vaunted titles and
glorious showes, both him selfe sheweth, where
he sayth.

Of Muses Hobbin. I conne no skill. And,
Enough is me to paint out my vnrest, &c.

And also appeareth by the basenesse of the
name, wherein, it semeth, he chose rather to
vnfold great matter of argument couertly, then
professing it, not suffice thereto accordingly.
Which moued him rather in Æglogues, then
other wise to write, doubting perhaps his habili-
tie, which he little needed, or mynding to
furnish our tongue with this kinde, wherein it
faulteth, or following the example of the best
and most auncient Poetes, which deuised this
kind of wryting, being both so base for the
matter, and homely for the manner, at the
first to trye theyr habilities: and as young
birdes, that be newly crept out of the nest,
by little first to proue theyr tender wyngs,
before they make a greater flyght. So flew
Theocritus, as you may perceiue he was all
ready full fledged. So flew Virgile, as not yet
well feeling his winges. So flew Mantuane, as
being not full somd.   So Petrarque.   So
Boccace ;   So Marot, Sanazarus, and also
diuers other excellent both Italian and French
Poetes, whose foting this Author euery where
followeth, yet so as few, but they be wel sented
can trace him out. So finally flyeth this our
new Poete, as a bird, whose principals be scarce
growen out, but yet as that in time shall be
hable to keepe wing with the best.

Now as touching the generall dryft and purpose of his Æglogues, I mind not to say much,
him selfe labouring to conceale it. Onely this
appeareth, that his vnstayed yougth had long
wandred in the common Labyrinth of Loue, in
which time to mitigate and allay the heate of
his passion, or els to warne (as he sayth) the
young shepheards .s. his equalls and companions of his vnfortunate folly, he compiled

these xij. Æglogues, which for that they be
proportioned to the state of the xij. monethes,
he termeth the SHEPHEARDS CALENDAR,
applying an olde name to a new worke. Hereunto haue I added a certain Glosse or scholion
for thexposition of old wordes and harder
phrases : which maner of glosing and com-
menting, well I wote, wil seeme straunge and
rare in our tongue : yet for somuch as I knew
many excellent and proper deuises both in
wordes and matter would passe in the speedy
course of reading, either as vnknowen, or as
not marked, and that in this kind, as in other
we might be equal to the learned of other
nations, I thought good to take the paines
vpon me, the rather for that by meanes of
some familiar acquaintaunce I was made priuie
to his counsell and secret meaning in them, as
also in sundry other works of his. Which albeit
I know he nothing so much hateth, as to pro-
mulgate, yet thus much haue I aduentured
vpon his frendship, him selfe being for long
time furre estraunged, hoping that this will the
rather occasion him, to put forth diuers other
excellent works of his, which slepe in silence,
as his Dreames, his Legendes, his Court of
Cupide, and sondry others ; whose commendations to set out, were verye vayne ; the thinges
though worthy of many, yet being knowen to
few. These my present paynes if to any they
be pleasurable or profitable, be you iudge, mine
own good Maister Haruey, to whom I haue
both in respect of your worthinesse generally,
and otherwyse vpon some particular and special
considerations voued this my labour, and the
maydenhead of this our commen frends Poetrie,
himselfe hauing already in the beginning dedicated it to the Noble and worthy Gentleman,
the right worshipfull Ma. Phi. Sidney, a special
fauourer and maintainer of all kind of learning.
Whose cause I pray you Sir, yf Enuie shall stur
vp any wrongful accusasion, defend with your
mighty Rhetorick and other your rare gifts of
learning, as you can, and shield with your good
wil, as you ought, against the malice and
outrage of so many enemies, as I know wilbe
set on fire with the sparks of his kindled glory.
And thus recommending the Author vnto you,
as vnto his most special good frend, and my
selfe vnto you both, as one making singuler
account of two so very good and so choise
frends, I bid you both most hartely farwel,
and commit you and your most commendable
studies to the tuicion of the greatest.

                    Your owne assuredly to
                    be commaunded E. K.

Post scr

NOw I trust M. Haruey, that vpon sight of your speciall frends and fellow Poets doings, or els for enuie of so many vnworthy Quidams, which catch at the garlond, which to you alone is dewe, you will be perswaded to pluck out of the hateful darknesse, those so many excellent English poemes of yours, which lye hid, and bring them forth to eternall light. Trust me you doe both them great wrong, in depriuing them of the desired sonne, and also yourselfe, in smoothering your deserued prayses, and all men generally, in withholding from them so diuine pleasures, which they might conceiue of your gallant English verses, as they haue already doen of your Latine Poemes, which in my opinion both for inuention and Elocution are very delicate, and superexcellent. And thus againe, I take my leaue of my good Mayster Haruey. From my lodging at London thys 10. of Aprill. 1579.

The generall argument of

the whole booke.

LIttle I hope, needeth me at large to discourse the first Originall of Æglogues, hauing alreadie touched the same. But for the word Æglogues I know is vnknowen to most, and also mistaken of some the best learned (as they think) I wyll say somewhat thereof, being not at all impertinent to my present purpose.

They were first of the Greekes the inuentours of them called Æglogaj as it were αἴγον or αἰγονόμων. λόγοι. that is Goteheards tales. For although in Virgile and others the speakers be more shepheards, then Goteheards, yet Theocritus in whom is more ground of authoritie, then in Virgile, this specially from that deriuing, as from the first head and welspring the whole Inuention of his Æglogues, maketh Goteheards the persons and authors of his tales. This being, who seeth not the grossenesse of such as by colour of learning would make vs beleeue that they are more rightly termed Eclogai, as they would say, extraordinary discourses of vnnecessarie matter, which difinition albe in substaunce and meaning it agree with the nature of the thing, yet no whit answereth with the ἀνάλυσις and interpretation of the word. For they be not termed Eclogues, but Æglogues. Which sentence this authour very well obseruing, vpon good iudgement, though ndeede few Goteheards haue to doe herein, nethelesse doubteth not to cal them by the vsed and best knowen name. Other curious discourses hereof I reserue to greater occasion. These xij. Æclogues euery where answering to the seasons of the twelue monthes may be well deuided into three formes or ranckes. For eyther they be Plaintiue, as the first, the sixt, the eleuenth, and the twelfth, or recreatiue, such as al those be, which conceiue matter of loue, or commendation of special personages, or Moral : which for the most part be mixed with some Satyricall bitternesse, namely the second of reuerence dewe to old age, the fift of coloured deceipt, the seuenth and ninth of dissolute shepheards and pastours, the tenth of contempt of Poetrie and pleasaunt wits. And to this diuision may euery thing herein be reasonably applyed : A few onely except, whose speciall purpose and meaning I am not priuie to. And thus much generally of these xij. Æclogues. Now will we speake particularly of all, and first of the first. Which he calleth by the first monethes name Ianuarie : wherein to some he may seeme fowly to haue faulted, in that he erroniously beginneth with that moneth, which beginneth not the yeare. For it is wel known, and stoutely mainteyned with stronge reasons of the learned, that the yeare beginneth in March. For then the sonne reneweth his finished course, and the seasonable spring refresheth the earth, and the plesaunce thereof being buried in the sadnesse of the dead winter now worne away, reliueth. This opinion maynteine the olde Astrologers and Philosophers, namely the reuerend Andalo, and Macrobius in his holydayes of Saturne, which accoumpt also was generally obserued both of Grecians and Romans. But sauing the leaue of such learned heads, we mayntaine a custome of coumpting the seasons from the moneth Ianuary, vpon a more speciall cause, then the heathen Philosophers euer coulde conceiue, that is, for the incarnation of our mighty Sauiour and eternall redeemer the L. Christ, who as then renewing the state of the decayed world, and returning the compasse of expired yeres to theyr former date and first commencement, left to vs his heires a memoriall of his birth in the ende of the last yeere and beginning of the next. Which reckoning, beside that eternall monument of our saluation, leaneth also vppon good proofe of special iudgement. For albeit that in elder times, when as yet the coumpt of the yere was not perfected, as afterwarde it was by Iulius Cæsar, they began to tel the monethes from Marches beginning, and according to the same God (as is sayd in Scripture) comaunded the people of the Iewes to count the moneth Abib, that which we call March, for the first moneth, in remembraunce that in that moneth he brought them out of the land of Ægipt : yet according to tradition of latter times it hath bene otherwise obserued, both in gouernment of the church, and rule of Mightiest Realmes. For from Iulius Cæsar who first obserued the leape yeere which he called Bissextilem Annum, and brought in to a more certain course the odde wandring dayes which of the Greekes were called ὑπερβαίνοντες. Of the Romanes intercalares (for in such matter of learning I am forced to vse the termes of the learned) the monethes haue bene nombred xij. which in the first ordinaunce of Romulus were but tenne, counting but CCCiiij. dayes in euery

yeare, and beginning with March. But Numa Pompilius, who was the father of al the Romain ceremonies and religion, seeing that reckoning to agree neither with the course of the sonne, nor of the Moone, therevnto added two monethes, Ianuary and February : wherin it seemeth, that wise king minded vpon good reason to begin the yeare at Ianuarie, of him therefore so called tanquam Ianua anni the gate and entraunce of the yere, or of the name of the god Ianus, to which god for that the old Paynims attributed the byrth and beginning of all creatures new comming into the worlde, it seemeth that he therfore to him assigned the beginning and first entraunce of the yeare. Which account for the most part hath hetherto continued. Notwithstanding that the Ægiptians beginne theyr yeare at September, for that according to the opinion of the best Rabbins, and very purpose of the scripture selfe, God made the worlde in that Moneth, that is called of them Tisri. And therefore he commaunded them, to keepe the feast of Pauilions in the end of the yeare, in the xv. day of the seuenth moneth, which before that time was the first.

But our Authour respecting nether the subtiltie of thone parte, nor the antiquitie of thother, thinketh it fittest according to the simplicitie of commen vnderstanding, to begin with Ianuarie, wening it perhaps no decorum, that Shepheard should be seene in matter of so deepe insight, or canuase a case of so doubtful iudgment. So therefore beginneth he, and so continueth he throughout.

Januarye.

Ægloga prima.

ARGVMENT.

*IN this fyrst Æglogue Colin cloute a shep-
heardes boy complaineth him of his vnfortunate loue, being but newly (as semeth)
enamoured of a countrie lasse called* Rosalinde :
*with which strong affection being very sore
traueled, he compareth his carefull case to the
sadde season of the yeare, to the frostie ground,
to the frosen trees, and to his owne winterbeaten
flocke. And lastlye, fynding himselfe robbed of
all former pleasaunce and delights, hee breaketh
his Pipe in peeces and casteth him selfe to the
ground.*

COLIN CLOVTE.

A Shepeheards boye (no better doe him call)
　when Winters wastful spight was almost
　　spent,
All in a sunneshine day, as did befall,
Led forth his flock, that had bene long ypent.
So faynt they woxe, and feeble in the folde,
That now vnnethes their feete could them
　vphold.

All as the Sheepe, such was the shepeheards
　　looke,
For pale and wanne he was, (alas the while,)
May seeme he lovd, or els some care he tooke :
Well couth he tune his pipe, and frame his stile.
Tho to a hill his faynting flocke he ledde,   11
And thus him playnd, the while his shepe there
　　fedde.

Ye Gods of loue, that pitie louers payne,
(If any gods the paine of louers pitie :)
Looke from aboue, where you in ioyes remaine,
And bowe your eares vnto my dolefull dittie.
And *Pan* thou shepheards God, that once didst
　　loue,
Pitie the paines, that thou thy selfe didst proue.

Thou barrein ground, whome winters wrath
　　hath wasted,
Art made a myrrhour, to behold my plight :
Whilome thy fresh spring flowrd, and after
　　hasted   21
Thy sommer prowde with Daffadillies dight.
And now is come thy wynters stormy state,
Thy mantle mard, wherein thou maskedst late.

Such rage as winters, reigneth in my heart,
My life bloud friesing with vnkindly cold:
Such stormy stoures do breede my balefull smart,
As if my yeare were wast, and woxen old.
And yet alas, but now my spring begonne,
And yet alas, yt is already donne.   30

You naked trees, whose shady leaues are lost,
Wherein the byrds were wont to build their
    bowre:
And now are clothd with mosse and hoary frost,
Instede of bloosmes, wherwith your buds did
    flowre:
I see your teares, that from your boughes doe
    raine,
Whose drops in drery ysicles remaine.

All so my lustfull leafe is drye and sere,
My timely buds with wayling all are wasted:
The blossome, which my braunch of youth did
    beare,
With breathed sighes is blowne away, and
    blasted   40
And from mine eyes the drizling teares descend,
As on your boughes the ysicles depend.

Thou feeble flocke, whose fleece is rough and rent,
Whose knees are weake through fast and euill
    fare:
Mayst witnesse well by thy ill gouernement,
Thy maysters mind is ouercome with care.
Thou weake, I wanne: thou leane, I quite
    forlorne:
With mourning pyne I, you with pyning
    mourne.

A thousand sithes I curse that carefull hower,
Wherein I longd the neighbour towne to see:
And eke tenne thousand sithes I blesse the
    stoure,   51
Wherein I sawe so fayre a sight, as shee.

Yet all for naught: such sight hath bred my
    bane.
Ah God, that loue should breede both ioy and
    payne.

It is not *Hobbinol*, wherefore I plaine,
Albee my loue he seeke with dayly suit:
His clownish gifts and curtsies I disdaine,
His kiddes, his cracknelles, and his early fruit.
Ah foolish *Hobbinol*, thy gyfts bene vayne:
Colin them giues to *Rosalind* againe.   60

I loue thilke lasse, (alas why doe I loue?)
And am forlorne, (alas why am I lorne?)
Shee deignes not my good will, but doth
    reproue,
And of my rurall musick holdeth scorne.
Shepheards deuise she hateth as the snake,
And laughes the songes, that *Colin Clout* doth
    make.

Wherefore my pype, albee rude *Pan* thou
    please,
Yet for thou pleasest not, where most I would:
And thou vnlucky Muse, that wontst to ease
My musing mynd, yet canst not, when thou
    should: 70
Both pype and Muse, shall sore the while abye.
So broke his oaten pype, and downe dyd lye.

By that, the welked *Phœbus* gan availe,
His weary waine, and nowe the frosty *Night*
Her mantle black through heauen gan ouer-
    haile.
Which seene, the pensife boy halfe in despight
Arose, and homeward droue his sonned sheepe,
Whose hanging heads did seeme his carefull case
    to weepe.

Colins Embleme.
Anchôra speme.

GLOSSE.

COLIN CLOVTE) is a name not greatly vsed,
and yet haue I sene a Poesie of M. Skeltons
vnder that title. But indeede the word Colin is
Frenche, and vsed of the French Poete Marot
(if he be worthy of the name of a Poete) in
a certein Æglogue. Vnder which name this Poete
secretly shadoweth himself, as sometime did
Virgil vnder the name of Tityrus, thinking it
much fitter, then such Latine names, for the great
vnlikelyhoode of the language.
vnnethes) scarcely.
couthe) commeth of the verbe Conne, that is, to
know or to haue skill. As well interpreteth the
same the worthy Sir Tho. Smitth in his booke of
gouerment: wherof I haue a perfect copie in
wryting, lent me by his kinesman, and my verye

singular good freend, M. Gabriel Haruey: as
also of some other his most graue and excellent
wrytings.
Sythe) time.   Neighbour towne) the next towne:
expressing the Latine Vicina.
Stoure) a fitt.   Sere) withered.
His clownish gyfts) imitateth Virgils verse,
Rusticus es Corydon, nec munera curat Alexis.
Hobbinol) is a fained country name, whereby, it
being so commune and vsuall, seemeth to be
hidden the person of some his very speciall and
most familiar freend, whom he entirely and
extraordinarily beloued, as peraduenture shall
be more largely declared hereafter. In thys place
seemeth to be some sauour of disorderly loue,
which the learned call pæderastice: but it is

gathered beside his meaning. For who that hath red Plato his dialogue called Alcybiades, Xenophon and Maximus Tyrius of Socrates opinions, may easily perceiue, that such loue is muche to be alowed and liked of, specially so meant, as Socrates vsed it : who sayth, that in deede he loued Alcybiades extremely, yet not Alcybiades person, but hys soule, which is Alcybiades owne selfe. And so is pæderastice much to be præferred before gynerastice, that is the loue whiche enflameth men with lust toward woman kind. But yet let no man thinke, that herein I stand with Lucian or hys deuelish disciple Vnico Aretino, in defence of execrable and horrible sinnes of forbidden and vnlawful fleshlinesse. Whose abominable errour is fully confuted of Perionius, and others.

I loue) a prety Epanorthosis in these two verses, and withall a Paronomasia or playing with the word, where he sayth (I loue thilke lasse (alas &c.

Rosalinde) is also a feigned name, which being wel ordered, wil bewray the very name of hys

loue and mistresse, whom by that name he coloureth. So as Ouide shadoweth hys loue vnder the name of Corynna, which of some is supposed to be Iulia, themperor Augustus his daughter, and wyfe to Agryppa. So doth Aruntius Stella euery where call his Lady Asteris and Ianthis, albe it is wel knowen that her right name was Violantilla : as witnesseth Statius in his Epithalamium. And so the famous Paragone of Italy, Madonna Cœlia in her letters enuelopeth her selfe vnder the name of Zima : and Petrona vnder the name of Bellochia. And this generally hath bene a common custome of counterfeicting the names of secret Personages.

Auail) bring downe.

Embleme.

Ouerhaile) drawe ouer.

His Embleme or Poesye is here vnder added in Italian, Anchóra speme : the meaning wherof is, that notwithstande his extreme passion and lucklesse loue, yet leaning on hope, he is some what recomforted.

Februarie.

Ægloga Secunda.

ARGVMENT.

THis Æglogue is rather morall and generall, then bent to any secrete or particular purpose. It specially conteyneth a discourse of old age, in the persone of Thenot *an olde Shepheard, who for his crookednesse and vnlustinesse, is scorned of* Cuddie *an vnhappy Heardmans boye. The matter very well accordeth with the season of*

the moneth, the yeare now drouping, and as it were, drawing to his last age. For as in this time of yeare, so then in our bodies there is a dry and withering cold, which congealeth the crudled blood, and frieseth the wetherbeaten flesh, with stormes of Fortune, and hoare frosts of Care. To which purpose the olde man telleth a tale of the Oake and the Bryer, so liuely and so feelingly, as if the thing were set forth in some Picture before our eyes, more plainly could not appeare.

CVDDIE.   THENOT.

AH for pittie, wil rancke Winters rage,
   These bitter blasts neuer ginne tasswage?
The kene cold blowes through my beaten hyde,
All as I were through the body gryde.
My ragged rontes all shiver and shake,
As doen high Towers in an earthquake:
They wont in the wind wagge their wrigle tailes,
Perke as Peacock: but nowe it auales.

THENOT.

Lewdly complainest thou laesie ladde,
Of Winters wracke, for making thee sadde. 10
Must not the world wend in his commun course
From good to badd, and from badde to worse,
From worse vnto that is worst of all,
And then returne to his former fall?
Who will not suffer the stormy time,
Where will he liue tyll the lusty prime?
Selfe haue I worne out thrise threttie yeares,
Some in much ioy, many in many teares:
Yet neuer complained of cold nor heate,
Of Sommers flame, nor of Winters threat: 20
Ne euer was to Fortune foeman,
But gently tooke, that vngently came.
And euer my flocke was my chiefe care,
Winter or Sommer they mought well fare.

CVDDIE.

No marueile Thenot, if thou can beare
Cherefully the Winters wrathfull cheare:
For Age and Winter accord full nie,
This chill, that cold, this crooked, that wrye.
And as the lowring Wether lookes downe,
So semest thou like good fryday to frowne. 30
[..] my flowring youth is foe to frost,
My shippe vnwont in stormes to be tost.

THENOT.

The soueraigne of seas he blames in vaine,
That once seabeate, will to sea againe.
So loytring liue you little heardgroomes,
Keeping your beastes in the budded broomes:
And when the shining sunne laugheth once,
You deemen, the Spring is come attonce.
Tho gynne you, fond flyes, the cold to scorne,
And crowing in pypes made of greene corne,
You thinken to be Lords of the yeare. 41
But eft, when ye count you freed from feare,
Comes the breme winter with chamfred browes,
Full of wrinckles and frostie furrowes:
Drerily shooting his stormy darte,
Which cruddles the blood, and pricks the harte.
Then is your carelesse corage accoied,
Your carefull heards with cold bene annoied.
Then paye you the price of your surquedrie,
With weeping, and wayling, and misery. 50

CVDDIE.

Ah foolish old man, I scorne thy skill,
That wouldest me, my springing youngth to spil.
I deeme, thy braine emperished bee
Through rusty elde, that hath rotted thee:
Or sicker thy head veray tottie is,
So on thy corbe shoulder it leanes amisse.
Now thy selfe hast lost both lopp and topp,
Als my budding braunch thou wouldest cropp:
But were thy yeares greene, as now bene myne,
To other delights they would encline. 60
Tho wouldest thou learne to caroll of Loue,
And hery with hymnes thy lasses gloue.
Tho wouldest thou pype of Phyllis prayse:
But Phyllis is myne for many dayes:
I wonne her with a gyrdle of gelt,
Embost with buegle about the belt.
Such an one shepeheards woulde make fullfaine:
Such an one would make thee younge againe.

THENOT.

Thou art a fon, of thy loue to boste,
All that is lent to loue, wyll be lost. 70

CVDDIE.

Seest, howe brag yond Bullocke beares,
So smirke, so smoothe, his pricked eares?
His hornes bene as broade, as Rainebowe bent,
His dewelap as lythe, as lasse of Kent.
See howe he venteth into the wynd.
Weenest of loue is not his mynd?
Seemeth thy flocke thy counsell can,
So lustlesse bene they, so weake so wan,
Clothed with cold, and hoary wyth frost.
Thy flocks father his corage hath lost: 80
Thy Ewes, that wont to haue blowen bags,
Like wailefull widdowes hangen their crags:
The rather Lambes bene starued with cold,
All for their Maister is lustlesse and old.

THENOT.

Cuddie, I wote thou kenst little good,
So vainely taduaunce thy headlesse hood.
For Youngth is a bubble blown vp with breath,
Whose witt is weakenesse, whose wage is death,
Whose way is wildernesse, whose ynne Penaunce,
And stoopegallaunt Age the hoste of Greeu-
   aunce. 90
But shall I tel thee a tale of truth,
Which I cond of Tityrus in my youth,
Keeping his sheepe on the hils of Kent?

CVDDIE.

To nought more Thenot, my mind is bent,
Then to heare nouells of his deuise:
They bene so well thewed, and so wise,
What euer that good old man bespal[..].

THENOT.

Many meete tales of youth did he make,
And some of loue, and some of cheualrie :
But none fitter then this to applie. 100
Now listen a while, and hearken the end.

There grewe an aged Tree on the greene,
A goodly Oake sometime had it bene,
With armes full strong and largely displayd,
But of their leaues they were disarayde :
The bodie bigge, and mightely pight,
Throughly rooted, and of wonderous hight :
Whilome had bene the King of the field,
And mochell mast to the husband did yielde,
And with his nuts larded many swine. 110
But now the gray mosse marred his rine,
His bared boughes were beaten with stormes,
His toppe was bald, and wasted with wormes,
His honor decayed, his braunches sere.
Hard by his side grewe a bragging brere,
Which proudly thrust into Thelement,
And seemed to threat the Firmament.
Yt was embellisht with blossomes fayre,
And thereto aye wonned to repayre
The shepheards daughters, to gather flowres,
To peinct their girlonds with his colowres. 121
And in his small bushes vsed to shrowde
The sweete Nightingale singing so lowde :
Which made this foolish Brere wexe so bold,
That on a time he cast him to scold,
And snebbe the good Oake, for he was old.
Why standst there (quoth he) thou brutish
    blocke ?
Norforfruict, norforshadoweserues thy stocke :
Seest, how fresh my flowers bene spredde,
Dyed in Lilly white, and Cremsin redde, 130
With Leaues engrained in lusty greene,
Colours meete to clothe a mayden Queene.
Thy wast bignes but combers the grownd,
And dirks the beauty of my blossomes rownd.
The mouldie mosse, which thee accloieth,
My Sinamon smell too much annoieth.
Wherefore soone I rede thee, hence remoue,
Least thou the price of my displeasure proue.
So spake this bold brere with great disdaine :
Little him answered the Oake againe, 140
But yielded, with shame and greefe adawed,
That of a weede he was ouercrawed.

Yt chaunced after vpon a day,
The Hus-bandman selfe to come that way,
Of custome for to seruewe his grownd,
And his trees of state in compasse rownd.
Him when the spitefull brere had espyed,
Causlesse complained, and lowdly cryed
Vnto his Lord, stirring vp sterne strife :
O my liege Lord, the God of my life, 150

Pleaseth you ponder your Suppliants plaint,
Caused of wrong, and cruell constraint,
Which I your poore Vassall dayly endure ·
And but your goodnes the same recure,
Am like for desperate doole to dye,
Through felonous force of mine enemie.

Greatly aghast with this piteous plea,
Him rested the goodman on the lea,
And badde the Brere in his plaint proceede.
With painted words tho gan this proude weede,
(As most vsen Ambitious folke :) 161
His colowred crime with craft to cloke.

Ah my soueraigne, Lord of creatures all,
Thou placer of plants both humble and tall,
Was not I planted of thine owne hand,
To be the primrose of all thy land,
With flowring blossomes, to furnish the prime,
And scarlot berries in Sommer time ?
How falls it then, that this faded Oake,
Whose bodie is sere, whose braunches broke,
Whose naked Armes stretch vnto the fyre, 171
Vnto such tyrannie doth aspire :
Hindering with his shade my louely light,
And robbing me of the swete sonnes sight ?
So beate his old boughes my tender side,
That oft the bloud springeth from woundes wyde :
Vntimely my flowres forced to fall,
That bene the honor of your Coronall.
And oft he lets his cancker wormes light
Vpon my braunches, to worke me more spight :
And oft his hoarie locks downe doth cast, 181
Where with my fresh flowretts bene defast.
For this, and many more such outrage,
Crauing your goodlihead to aswage
The ranckorous rigour of his might,
Nought aske I, but onely to hold my right :
Submitting me to your good sufferance,
And praying to be garded from greeuance.

To this the Oake cast him to replie
Well as he couth : but his enemie 190
Had kindled such coles of displeasure,
That the good man noulde stay his leasure,
But home him hasted with furious heate,
Encreasing his wrath with many a threate.
His harmefull Hatchet he hent in hand,
(Alas, that it so ready should stand)
And to the field alone he speedeth.
(Ay little helpe to harme there needeth)
Anger nould let him speake to the tree,
Enaunter his rage mought cooled bee : 200
But to the roote bent his sturdy stroke,
And made many wounds in the wast Oake.
The Axes edge did oft turne againe,
As halfe vnwilling to cutte the graine :
Semed, the sencelesse yron dyd feare,
Or to wrong holy eld did forbeare.

For it had bene an auncient tree,
Sacred with many a mysteree,
And often crost with the priestes crewe,
And often halowed with holy water dewe. 210
But sike fancies weren foolerie,
And broughten this Oake to this miserye.
For nought mought they quitten him from decay:
For fiercely the good man at him did laye.
The blocke oft groned vnder the blow,
And sighed to see his neare ouerthrow.
In fine the steele had pierced his pitth,
Tho downe to the earth he fell forthwith :
His wonderous weight made the grounde to quake,
Thearth shronke vnder him, and seemed to
    shake. 220
There lyeth the Oake, pitied of none.
    Now stands the Brere like a Lord alone,
Puffed vp with pryde and vaine pleasaunce :
But all this glee had no continuaunce.
For eftsones Winter gan to approche,
The blustring Boreas did encroche,
And beate vpon the solitarie Brere :
For nowe no succoure was seene him nere.
Now gan he repent his pryde to late :
For naked left and disconsolate, 230

The byting frost nipt his stalke dead,
The watrie wette weighed downe his head,
And heaped snowe burdned him so sore,
That nowe vpright he can stand no more :
And being downe, is trodde in the durt
Of cattell, and brouzed, and sorely hurt.
Such was thend of this Ambitious brere,
For scorning Eld

CVDDIE.

Now I pray thee shepheard, tel it not forth :
Here is a long tale, and little worth. 240
So longe haue I listened to thy speche,
That graffed to the ground is my breche :
My hartblood is welnigh frorne I feele,
And my galage growne fast to my heele :
But little ease of thy lewd tale I tasted.
Hye thee home shepheard, the day is nigh
    wasted.

Thenots Embleme.

Iddio perche è vecchio,
Fa suoi al suo essempio.

Cuddies Embleme. 250

Niuno vecchio,
Spaventa Iddio.

GLOSSE.

Kene) sharpe.
Gride) perced : an olde word much vsed of Lidgate, but not found (that I know of) in Chaucer.
Ronts) young bullockes.
Wracke) ruine or Violence, whence commeth ship wracke : and not wreake, that is vengeaunce or wrath.
Foeman) a foe.
Thenot) the name of a shepheard in Marot his Æglogues.
The soueraigne of Seas) is Neptune the God of the seas. The saying is borowed of Mimus Publianus, which vsed this prouerb in a verse.

Improbè Neptunum accusat, qui iterum naufragium facit.

Heardgromes) Chaucers verse almost whole.
Fond Flyes) He compareth carelesse sluggardes or ill husbandmen to flyes, that so soone as the sunne shineth, or yt wexeth any thing warme, begin to flye abroade, when sodeinly they be ouertaken with cold.
But eft when) A verye excellent and liuely description of Winter, so as may bee indifferently taken, eyther for old Age, or for Winter season.
Breme) chill, bitter.
Chamfred) chapt, or wrinckled.
Accoied) plucked downe and daunted.
Surquedrie) pryde.   Elde) olde age.
Sicker) sure.   Tottie) wauering.
Corbe) crooked.   Herie) worshippe.
Phyllis) the name of some mayde vnknowen, whom Cuddie, whose person is secrete, loued. The name is vsuall in Theocritus, Virgile, and Mantuane.

Belte) a girdle or wast band.   A fon) a foole.
lythe) soft and gentile.
Venteth) snuffeth in the wind.
Thy flocks Father) the Ramme.   Crags) neckes.
Rather Lambes) that be ewed early in the beginning of the yeare.
Youth is) A verye moral and pitthy Allegorie of youth, and the lustes thereof, compared to a wearie wayfaring man.
Tityrus) I suppose he meane Chaucer, whose prayse for pleasaunt tales cannot dye, so long as the memorie of hys name shal liue, and the name of Poetrie shal endure.
Well thewed) that is, Bene moratæ, full of morall wisenesse.
There grew) This tale of the Oake and the Brere, he telleth as learned of Chaucer, but iti s cleane in another kind, and rather like to Æsopes fables. It is very excellente for pleasaunt descriptions, being altogether a certaine Icon or Hypotyposis of disdainfull younkers.
Embellisht) beautified and adorned.
To wonne) to haunt or frequent.   Sneb) checke.
Why standst) The speach is scorneful and very presumptuous.
Engrained) dyed in grain.
Accloieth) encombreth.
Adawed) daunted and confounded.
Trees of state) taller trees fitte for timber wood.
Sterne strife) said Chaucer . s. fell and sturdy.
O my liege) A maner of sui plication, wherein is kindly coloured the affection and speache of Ambitious men.
Coronall) Garlande.   Flourets) young blossomes.
The Primrose) The chiefe and worthiest.

Naked armes) metaphorically ment of the bare boughes, spoyled of leaues. This colourably he speaketh, as adiudging hym to the fyre.

The blood) spoken of a blocke, as it were of a liuing creature, figuratiuely, and (as they saye) κατ' εικασμόι.

Hoarie lockes) metaphorically for withered leaues.

Hent) caught.   Nould for would not.

Ay) euermore.   Wounds) gashes.

Enaunter) least that.

The priestes crewe) holy water pott, wherewith the popishe priest vsed to sprinckle and hallowe the trees from mischaunce. Such blindnesse was in those times, which the Poete supposeth, to haue bene the finall decay of this auncient Oake.

The blocke oft groned) A liuelye figure, whiche geueth sence and feeling to vnsensible creatures, as Virgile also sayeth: Saxa gemunt grauido &c.

Boreas) The Northerne wynd, that bringeth the moste stormie weather.

Glee) chere and iollitie.

For scorning Eld) And minding (as shoulde seme) to haue made ryme to the former verse, he is conningly cutte of by Cuddye, as disdayning to here any more.

Galage) a startuppe or clownish shoe.

Embleme.

This embleme is spoken of Thenot, as a moral of his former tale: namelye, that God, which is himselfe most aged, being before al ages, and without beginninge, maketh those, whom he loueth like to himselfe, in heaping yeares vnto theyre dayes, and blessing them wyth longe lyfe. For the blessing of age is not giuen to all, but vnto those, whome God will so blesse: and albeit that many euil men reache vnto such fulnesse of yeares, and some also wexe olde in myserie and thraldome, yet therefore is not age euer the lesse blessing. For euen to such euill men such number of yeares is added, that they may in their last dayes repent, and come to their first home. So the old man checketh the rashheaded boy, for despysing his gray and frostye heares. Whom Cuddye doth counterbuff with a byting and bitter prouerbe, spoken indeede at the first in contempt of old age generally. For it was an old opinion, and yet is continued in some mens conceipt, that men of yeares haue no feare of god at al, or not so much as younger folke. For that being rypened with long experience, and hauing passed many bitter brunts and blastes of vengeaunce, they dread no stormes of Fortune, nor wrathe of Gods, nor daunger of menne, as being eyther by longe and ripe wisedome armed against all mischaunces and aduersitie, or with much trouble hardened against all troublesome tydes: lyke vnto the Ape, of which is sayd in Æsops fables, that oftentimes meeting the Lyon, he was at first sore aghast and dismayed at the grimnes and austeritie of hys countenance, but at last being acquainted with his lookes, he was so furre from fearing him, that he would familiarly gybe and iest with him: Suche longe experience breedeth in some men securitie. Although it please Erasimus a great clerke and good old father, more fatherly and fauourablye to construe it in his Adages for his own behoofe, That by the prouerbe Nemo Senex metuit Iouem, is not meant, that old men haue no feare of God at al, but that they be furre from superstition and Idolatrous regard of false Gods, as is Iupiter. But his greate learning notwithstanding, it is to plaine, to be gainsayd, that olde men are muche more enclined to such fond fooleries, then younger heades.

March.

Ægloga Tertia.

ARGVMENT.

*I*N this Æglogue two shepheards boyes taking
occasion of the season, beginne to make
purpose of loue and other plesaunce, which to
springtime is most agreeable. The speciall meaning hereof is, to giue certaine markes and tokens,
to know Cupide the Poets God of Loue. But
more particularlye I thinke, in the person of
Thomalin is meant some secrete freend, who
scorned Loue and his knights so long, till at
length him selfe was entangled, and vnwares
wounded with the dart of some beautifull regard,
which is Cupides arrowe.

WILLYE.   THOMALIN.

*T*Homalin, why sytten we soe,
    As weren ouerwent with woe,
Vpon so fayre a morow ?
The ioyous time now nigheth fast,
That shall alegge this bitter blast,
    And slake the winters sorowe.

THOMALIN.

Sicker Willye, thou warnest well:
For Winters wrath beginnes to quell,

And pleasant spring appeareth.
The grasse nowe ginnes to be refresht,   10
The Swallow peepes out of her nest,
    And clowdie Welkin cleareth.

WILLYE.

Seest not thilke same Hawthorne studde,
How bragly it beginnes to budde,
    And vtter his tender head ?
Flora now calleth forth eche flower,
And bids make ready *Maias* bowre,
    That newe is vpryst from bedde.
Tho shall we sporten in delight,
And learne with Lettice to wexe light,   20
    That scornefully lookes askaunce,
Tho will we little Loue awake,
That nowe sleepeth in *Lethe* lake,
    And pray him leaden our daunce.

THOMALIN.

Willye, I wene thou bee assott :
For lustie Loue still sleepeth not,
    But is abroad at his game.

WILLYE.

How kenst thou, that he is awoke ?
Or hast thy selfe his slomber broke ?
    Or made preuie to the same ?   *3o*

THOMALIN.

No, but happely I hym spyde,
Where in a bush he did him hide,
  With winges of purple and blewe.
And were not, that my sheepe would stray,
The preuie marks I would bewray,
  Whereby by chaunce I him knewe.

WILLYE.

Thomalin, haue no care for thy,
My selfe will haue a double eye,
  Ylike to my flocke and thine :
For als at home I haue a syre,   40
A stepdame eke as whott as fyre,
  That dewly adayes counts mine.

THOMALIN.

Nay, but thy seeing will not serue,
My sheepe for that may chaunce to swerue,
  And fall into some mischiefe.
For sithens is but the third morowe,
That I chaunst to fall a sleepe with sorowe,
  And waked againe with griefe :
The while thilke same vnhappye Ewe,
Whose clouted legge her hurt doth shewe, 50
  Fell headlong into a dell.
And there vnioynted both her bones :
Mought her necke bene ioynted attones,
  She shoulde haue neede no more spell.
Thelf was so wanton and so wood,
(But now I trowe can better good)
  She mought ne gang on the greene.

WILLYE.

Let be, as may be, that is past :
That is to come, let be forecast.
  Now tell vs, what thou hast seene.   60

THOMALIN.

It was vpon a holiday,
When shepheardes groomes han leaue to playe,
  I cast to goe a shooting.
Long wandring vp and downe the land,
With bowe and bolts in either hand,
  For birds in bushes tooting :
At length within an Yuie todde
(There shrouded was the little God)
  I heard a busie bustling.
I bent my bolt against the bush,   70
Listening if any thing did rushe,
  But then heard no more rustling.
Tho peeping close into the thicke,
Might see the mouing of some quicke,

Whose shape appeared not :
But were it faerie, feend, or snake,
My courage earnd it to awake,
  And manfully thereat shotte.
With that sprong forth a naked swayne,
With spotted winges like Peacocks trayne, 80
  And laughing lope to a tree.
His gylden quiuer at his backe,
And siluer bowe, which was but slacke,
  Which lightly he bent at me.
That seeing, I leuelde againe,
And shott at him with might and maine,
  As thicke, as it had hayled.
So long I shott, that al was spent :
Tho pumie stones I hastly hent,
  And threwe : but nought auailed :   90
He was so wimble, and so wight,
From bough to bough he lepped light,
  And oft the pumies latched.
Therewith affrayd I ranne away :
But he, that earst seemd but to playe,
  A shaft in earnest snatched,
And hit me running in the heele :
For then I little smart did feele :
  But soone it sore encreased.
And now it ranckleth more and more,   100
And inwardly it festreth sore,
  Ne wote I, how to cease it.

WILLYE.

Thomalin, I pittie thy plight.
Perdie with loue thou diddest fight :
  I know him by a token.
For once I heard my father say,
How he him caught vpon a day,
  (Whereof he wilbe wroken)
Entangled in a fowling net,
Which he for carrion Crowes had set,   110
  That in our Peeretree haunted.
Tho sayd, he was a winged lad,
But bowe and shafts as then none had :
  Els had he sore be daunted.
But see the Welkin thicks apace,
And stouping *Phebus* steepes his face :
  Yts time to hast vs homeward.

Willyes Embleme.

To be wise and eke to loue,
Is graunted scarce to God aboue.   120

Thomalins Embleme.

Of Hony and of Gaule in loue there is store :
The Honye is much, but the Gaule is more.

GLOSS.

THIS Æglogue seemeth somewhat to resemble that same of Theocritus, wherein the boy likewise telling the old man, that he had shot at a winged boy in a tree, was by hym warned, to beware of mischiefe to come.

Ouer went) ouergone.

Alegge) to lessen or aswage.

To quell) to abate.   Welkin) the skie.

The swallow) which bird vseth to be counted the messenger, and as it were, the fore runner of springe.

Flora) the Goddesse of flowres, but indede (as saith Tacitus) a famous harlot, which with the abuse of her body hauing gotten great riches, made the people of Rome her heyre : who in remembraunce of so great beneficence, appointed a yearely feste for the memoriall of her, calling her, not as she was, nor as some doe think, Andronica, but Flora : making her the Goddesse of all floures, and doing yerely to her solemne sacrifice.

Maias bowre) that is the pleasant fielde, or rather the Maye bushes. Maia is a Goddes and the mother of Mercurie, in honour of whome the moneth of Maye is of her name so called, as sayth Macrobius.

Lettice) the name of some country lasse.

Ascaunce) askewe or asquint.

For thy) therefore.

Lethe) is a lake in hell, which the Poetes call the lake of forgetfulnes. For Lethe signifieth forgetfulnes. Wherein the soules being dipped, did forget the cares of their former lyfe. So that by loue sleeping in Lethe lake, he meaneth he was almost forgotten and out of knowledge, by reason of winters hardnesse, when al pleasures, as it were, sleepe and weare oute of mynde.

Assotte) to dote.

His slomber) To breake Loues slomber, is to exercise the delightes of Loue and wanton pleasures.

Winges of purple) so is he feyned of the Poetes.

For als) he imitateth Virgils verse.

Est mihi namque domi pater, est iniusta nouerca &c.

A dell) a hole in the ground.

Spell) is a kinde of verse or charme, that in elder tymes they vsed often to say ouer euery thing, that they would haue preserued, as the Nightspel for theeues, and the woodspell. And herehence I thinke is named the gospell. as it were Gods spell or worde. And so sayth Chaucer, Listeneth Lordings to my spell.

Gange) goe.   An Yuie todde) a thicke bushe.

Swaine) a boye : For so is he described of the Poetes, to be a boye .s. alwayes freshe and lustie : blindfolded, because he maketh no difference of Personages : wyth diuers coloured winges, .s. ful of flying fancies : with bowe and arrow, that is with glaunce of beautye, which prycketh as a forked arrowe. He is sayd also to haue

shafts, some leaden, some golden : that is, both pleasure for the gracious and loued, and sorow for the louer that is disdayned or forsaken. But who liste more at large to behold Cupids colours and furniture, let him reade ether Propertius, or Moschus his Idyllion of wandring loue, being now most excellently translated into Latine by the singuler learned man Angelus Politianus : whych worke I haue seene amongst other of thys Poets doings, very wel translated also into Englishe Rymes.

Wimble and wighte) Quicke and deliuer.

In the heele) is very Poetically spoken, and not without speciall iudgement. For I remember, that in Homer it is sayd of Thetis, that shee tooke her young babe Achilles being newely borne, and holding him by the heele, dipped him in the Riuer of Styx. The vertue whereof is, to defend and keepe the bodyes washed therein from any mortall wound. So Achilles being washed al ouer, saue onely his hele, by which his mother held, was in the rest invulnerable : therfore by Paris was feyned to bee shotte with a poysoned arrowe in the heele, whiles he was busie about the marying of Polyxena in the temple of Apollo. Which mysticall fable Eustathius vnfolding, sayth : that by wounding in the hele, is meant lustfull loue. For from the heele (as say the best Phisitions) to the preuie partes there passe certaine veines and slender synnewes, as also the like come from the head, and are carryed lyke little pypes behynd the eares : so that (as sayth Hipocrates) yf those veynes there be cut a sonder, the partie straighte becommeth cold and vnfruitefull. Which reason our Poete wel weighing, maketh this shepheards boye of purpose to be wounded by Loue in the heele.

Latched) caught.   Wroken) reuenged.

For once) In this tale is sette out the simplicitye of shepheards opinion of Loue.

Stouping Phæbus) Is a Periphrasis of the sunne setting.

Embleme.

Hereby is meant, that all the delights of Loue, wherein wanton youth walloweth, be but follye mixt with bitternesse, and sorow sawced with repentaunce. For besides that the very affection of Loue it selfe tormenteth the mynde, and vexeth the body many wayes, with vnrestfulnesse all night, and wearines all day, seeking for that we can not haue, and fynding that we would not haue : euen the selfe things which best before vs lyked, in course of time and chaung of ryper yeares, whiche also therewithall chaungeth our wonted lyking and former fantasies, will then seeme lothsome and breede vs annoyaunce, when yougthes flowre is withered, and we fynde our bodyes and wits aunswere not to suche vayne iollitie and lustful[1] pleasaunce.

Aprill.

Ægloga Quarta.

ARGVMENT.

THis Æglogue is purposely intended to the honor and prayse of our most gracious souereigne, Queene Elizabeth. The speakers herein be Hobbinoll and Thenott, two shep-heardes : the which Hobbinoll being before men-tioned, greatly to haue loued Colin, is here set forth more largely, complayning him of that boyes great misaduenture in Loue, whereby his mynd wa˜ alienate and with drawen not onely from him, who moste loued him, but also from all former delightes and studies, aswell in plea-saunt pyping, as conning ryming and singing, and other his laudable exercises. Whereby he taketh occasion, for proofe of his more excellencie and skill in poetrie, to recorde a songe, which the sayd Colin sometime made in honor of her Muestie, whom abruptely he termeth Elysa.

THENOT.　　　HOBBINOLL.

TEll me good Hobbinoll, what garres thee
　　greete?
What? hath some Wolfe thy tender Lambes
　　ytorne?
Or is thy Bagpype broke, that soundes so sweete?
Or art thou of thy loued lasse forlorne?

Or bene thine eyes attempred to the yeare,
Quenching the gasping furrowes thirst with
　　rayne?
Like April shoure, so stremes the trickling teares
Adowne thy cheeke, to quenche thy thristye
　　payne.

HOBBINOLL.

Nor thys, nor that, so muche doeth make me
　　mourne,
But for the ladde, whome long I lovd so deare,
Nowe loues a lasse, that all his loue doth
　　scorne:　　　　　　　　　　　　　　11
He plongd in payne, his tressed locks dooth
　　teare.

Shepheards delights he dooth them all for-
　　sweare,
Hys pleasant Pipe, whych made vs meriment,
He wylfully hath broke, and doth forbeare
His wonted songs, wherein he all outwent.

THENOT.

What is he for a Ladde, you so lament?
Ys loue such pinching payne to them, that
　　proue?
And hath he skill to make so excellent,
Yet hath so little skill to brydle loue?　　20

HOBBINOLL.

Colin thou kenst, the Southerne shepheardes
　　boye :
Him Loue hath wounded with a deadly darte.
Whilome on him was all my care and ioye,
Forcing with gyfts to winne his wanton heart.

But now from me hys madding mynd is starte,
And woes the Widdowes daughter of the glenne :
So nowe fayre *Rosalind* hath bredde hys smart,
So now his frend is chaunged for a frenne.

THENOT.

But if hys ditties bene so trimly dight,
I pray thee *Hobbinoll*, recorde some one :　30
The whiles our flockes doe graze about in sight,
And we close shrowded in thys shade alone.

HOBBINOL.

Contented I : then will I singe his laye
Of fayre *Eliza*, Queene of shepheardes all :
Which once he made, as by a spring he laye,
And tuned it vnto the Waters fall.

YE dayntye Nymphs, that in this blessed
　　Brooke
　doe bathe your brest,
Forsake your watry bowres, and hether looke,
　　at my request :　　　　　　　　　40
And eke you Virgins, that on *Parnasse* dwell,
Whence floweth *Helicon* the learned well,
　Helpe me to blaze
　Her worthy praise,
Which in her sexe doth all excell.

Of fayre *Elisa* be your siluer song,
　that blessed wight :
The flowre of Virgins, may shee florish long,
　In princely plight.
For shee is *Syrinx* daughter without spotte,　50
Which *Pan* the shepheards God of her begot :
　So sprong her grace
　Of heauenly race,
No mortall blemishe may her blotte.

See, where she sits vpon the grassie greene,
　(O seemely sight)
Yclad in Scarlot like a mayden Queene,
　And Ermines white.
Vpon her head a Cremosin coronet,
With Damaske roses and Daffadillies set :　60
　Bayleaues betweene,
　And Primroses greene
Embellish the sweete Violet.

Tell me, haue ye seene her angelick face,
　Like *Phœbe* fayre ?
Her heauenly haueour, her princely grace
　can you well compare ?

The Redde rose medled with the White yfere,
In either cheeke depeincten liuely chere.
　Her modest eye,　　　　　　　　　70
　Her Maiestie,
Where haue you seene the like, but there ?

I sawe *Phœbus* thrust out his golden hedde,
　vpon her to gaze :
But when he sawe, how broade her beames did
　　spredde,
　it did him amaze.
He blusht to see another Sunne belowe,
Ne durst againe his fyrye face out showe :
　Let him, if he dare,
　His brightnesse compare　　　　　　80
With hers, to haue the ouerthrowe.

Shewe thy selfe *Cynthia* with thy siluer rayes,
　and be not abasht :
When shee the beames of her beauty displayes,
　O how art thou dasht ?
But I will not match her with *Latonaes* seede,
Such follie great sorow to *Niobe* did breede.
　Now she is a stone,
　And makes dayly mone,
Warning all other to take heede.　　　　90

Pan may be proud, that euer he begot
　such a Bellibone,
And *Syrinx* reioyse, that euer was her lot
　to beare such an one.
Soone as my younglings cryen for the dam,
To her will I offer a milkwhite Lamb :
　Shee is my goddesse plaine,
　And I her shepherds swayne,
Albee forswonck and forswatt I am.

I see *Calliope* speede her to the place,　　100
　where my Goddesse shines :
And after her the other Muses trace,
　with their Violines.
Bene they not Bay braunches, which they do
　beare,
All for *Elisa* in her hand to weare ?
　So sweetely they play,
　And sing all the way,
That it a heauen is to heare.

Lo how finely the graces can it foote
　to the Instrument :　　　　　　　　110
They dauncen deffly, and singen soote,
　in their meriment.
Wants not a fourth grace, to make the daunce
　euen ?
Let that rowme to my Lady be yeuen :
　She shalbe a grace,
　To fyll the fourth place,
And reigne with the rest in heauen.

And whither rennes this beuie of Ladies bright,
  raunged in a rowe ?
They bene all Ladyes of the lake behight, 120
  that vnto her goe.
Chloris, that is the chiefest Nymph of al,
Of Oliue braunches beares a Coronall :
  Oliues bene for peace,
  When wars doe surcease :
Such for a Princesse bene principall.

Ye shepheards daughters, that dwell on the greene,
  hye you there apace :
Let none come there, but that Virgins bene,
  to adorne her grace.   130
And when you come, whereas shee is in place,
See, that your rudenesse doe not you disgrace :
  Binde your fillets faste,
  And gird in your waste,
For more finesse, with a tawdrie lace.

Bring hether the Pincke and purple Cullambine,
  With Gelliflowres :
Bring Coronations, and Sops in wine,
  worne of Paramoures.   39
Strowe me the ground with Daffadowndillies,
And Cowslips, and Kingcups, and loued Lillies :
  The pretie Pawnce,
  And the Cheuisaunce,
Shall match with the fayre flowre Delice.

Now ryse vp *Elisa*, decked as thou art,
  in royall aray :
And now ye daintie Damsells may depart
  echeone her way,
I feare, I haue troubled your troupes to longe :
Let dame *Eliza* thanke you for her song.   150
  And if you come hether,
  When Damsines I gether,
I will part them all you among.

THENOT.

And was thilk same song of *Colins* owne
  making ?
Ah foolish boy, that is with loue yblent :
Great pittie is, he be in such taking,
For naught caren, that bene so lewdly bent.

HOBBINOL.

Sicker I hold him, for a greater fon,
That loues the thing, he cannot purchase. 159
But let vs homeward : for night draweth on,
And twincling starres the daylight hence chase.

Thenots Embleme.

O quam te memorem virgo ?

Hobbinols Embleme.

O dea certe.

GLOSSE.

Gars thee greete) causeth thee weepe and complain.
Forlorne) left and forsaken.
Attempred to the yeare) agreeable to the season
  of the yeare, that is Aprill, which moneth is most
  bent to shoures and seasonable rayne : to quench,
  that is, to delaye the drought, caused through
  drynesse of March wyndes.
The Ladde) Colin Clout.   The Lasse) Rosalinda.
Tressed locks) wrethed and curled.
Is he for a ladde) A straunge manner of speaking
  .s. what maner of Ladde is he ?
To make) to rime and versifye. For in this word
  making, our olde Englishe Poetes were wont to
  comprehend all the skil of Poetrye, accoiding
  to the Greeke woorde ποιεῖν, to make, whence
  commeth the name of Poetes.
Colin thou kenst) knowest. Seemeth hereby that
  Colin perteyneth to some Southern noble man,
  and perhaps in Surrye or Kent, the rather
  bicause he so often nameth the Kentish downes,
  and before, As lythe as lasse of Kent.
The Widowes) He calleth Rosalind the Widowes
  daughter of the glenne, that is, of a country
  Hamlet or borough, which I thinke is rather
  sayde to coloure and concele the person, then
  simply spoken. For it is well knowen, euen in
  spighte of Colin and Hobbinoll, that shee is a
  Gentle woman of no meane house, nor endewed
  with anye vulgare and common gifts both of
  nature and manners : but suche indeede, as
  neede nether Colin be ashamed to haue her made
  knowne by his verses, nor Hobbinol be greued,

that so she should be commended to immortalitie
  for her rare and singular Vertues : Specially
  deseruing it no lesse, then eyther Myrto the most
  excellent Poete Theocritus his dearling, or Lau-
  retta the diuine Petrarches Goddesse, or Himera
  the worthye Poete Stesichorus hys Idole : Vpon
  whom he is sayd so much to haue doted, that in
  regard of her excellencie, he scorned and wrote
  against the beauty of Helena. For which his
  præsumptuous and vnheedie hardinesse, he is
  sayde by vengeaunce of the Gods, thereat being
  offended, to haue lost both his eyes.
Frenne) a straunger. The word I thinke was first
  poetically put, and afterwarde vsed in commen
  custome of speach for forenne.
Dight) adorned. Laye) a songe. As Roundelayes
  and Virelayes. In all this songe is not to be
  respected, what the worthinesse of her Maiestie
  deserueth, nor what to the highnes of a Prince is
  agreeable, but what is moste comely for the
  meanesse of a shepheards witte, or to conceiue,
  or to vtter. And therefore he calleth her Elysa,
  as through rudenesse tripping in her name : and
  a shepheards daughter, it being very vnfit, that
  a shepheards boy brought vp in the shepefold,
  should know, or euer seme to haue heard of a
  Queenes roialty.
Ye daintie) is, as it were an Exordium ad pre-
  parandos animos.
Virgins) the nine Muses, daughters of Apollo and
  Memorie, whose abode the Poets faine to be on
  Parnassus, a hill in Grece, for that in that

countrye specially florished the honor of all excellent studies.

Helicon) is both the name of a fountaine at the foote of Parnassus, and also of a mounteine in Bæotia, out of which floweth the famous Spring Castalius, dedicate also to the Muses: of which spring it is sayd, that when Pegasus the winged horse of Perseus (whereby is meant fame and flying renowme) strooke the grownde with his hoofe, sodenly thereout sprange a wel of moste cleare and pleasaunte water, which fro thence forth was consecrate to the Muses and Ladies of learning.

Your siluer song) seemeth to imitate the lyke in Hesiodus ἀργυρέον μέλος.

Syrinx) is the name of a Nymphe of Arcadie, whom when Pan being in loue pursued, she flying from him, of the Gods was turned into a reede. So that Pan catching at the Reedes in stede of the Damosell, and puffing hard (for he was almost out of wind) with hys breath made the Reedes to pype: which he seeing, tooke of them, and in remembraunce of his lost loue, made him a pype thereof. But here by Pan and Syrinx is not to bee thoughte, that the shephearde simplye meante those Poetical Gods: but rather supposing (as seemeth) her graces progenie to be diuine and immortàll (so as the Paynims were wont to iudge of all Kinges and Princes, according to Homeres saying.

Θυμὸς δὴ μέγας ἐστὶ διοτρεφέως βασιλήως,
τιμὴ δ' ἐκ διός ἐστι, φιλεῖ δε ὁ μητίετα Ζεύς.)

could deuise no parents in his iudgement so worthy for her, as Pan the shepheards God, and his best beloued Syrinx. So that by Pan is here meant the most famous and victorious King, her highnesse Father, late of worthy memorye K. Henry the eyght. And by that name, oftymes (as hereafter appeareth) be noted kings and mighty Potentates: And in some place Christ himselfe, who is the verye Pan and god of Shepheardes.

Cremosin coronet) he deuiseth her crowne to be of the finest and most delicate flowers, instede of perles and precious stones, wherewith Princes Diademes vse to bee adorned and embost.

Embellish) beautifye and set out.

Phebe) the Moone, whom the Poets faine to be sister vnto Phæbus, that is the Sunne.

Medled) mingled.

Yfere) together. By the mingling of the Redde rose and the White, is meant the vniting of the two principall houses of Lancaster and of Yorke: by whose longe discord and deadly debate, this realm many yeares was sore traueiled, and almost cleane decayed. Til the famous Henry the seuenth, of the line of Lancaster, taking to wife the most vertuous Princesse Elisabeth, daughter to the fourth Edward of the house of Yorke, begat the most royal Henry the eyght aforesayde, in whom was the firste vnion of the Whyte Rose and the Redde.

Calliope) one of the nine Muses: to whome they assigne the honor of all Poetical Inuention, and the firste glorye of the Heroicall verse. Other say, that shee is the Goddesse of Rhetorick: but by Virgile it is manifeste, that they mystake the thyng. For there in hys Epigrams, that arte semeth to be attributed to Polymnia, saying:

Signat cuncta manu, loquiturque Polymnia gestu.

which seemeth specially to be meant of Action and elocution, both special partes of Rhetorick: besyde that her name, which (as some construe it) importeth great remembraunce, conteineth another part. But I holde rather with them, which call her Polymnia or Polyhvmnia of her good singing.

Bay branches) be the signe of honor and victory, and therfore of myghty Conquerors worn in theyr triumphes, and eke of famous Poets, as saith Petrarch in hys Sonets.

Arbor vittoriosa triomphale,
Honor d' Imperadori & di Poëti, &c.

The Graces) be three sisters, the daughters of Iupiter, (whose names are Aglaia, Thalia, Euphrosyne, and Homer onely addeth a fourth .s. Pasithea) otherwise called Charites, that is thanks. Whom the Poetes feyned to be the Goddesses of al bountie and comelines, which therefore (as sayth Theodontius) they make three, to wete, that men first ought to be gracious and bountiful to other freely, then to receiue benefits at other mens hands curteously, and thirdly to requite them thankfully: which are three sundry Actions in liberalitye. And Boccace saith, that they be painted naked, (as they were indeede on the tombe of C. Iulius Cæsar) the one hauing her backe toward vs, and her face fromwarde, as proceeding from vs: the other two toward vs, noting double thanke to be due to vs for the benefit, we haue done.

Deaffly) Finelye and nimbly. Soote) Sweete.

Meriment) Mirth.

Beuie) A beauie of Ladyes, is spoken figuratiuely for a company or troupe. The terme is taken of Larkes. For they say a Beuie of Larkes, euen as a Couey of Partridge, or an eye of Pheasaunts.

Ladyes of the lake) be Nymphes. For it was an olde opinion amongste the Auncient Heathen, that of euery spring and fountaine was a goddesse the Soueraigne. Whiche opinion stucke in the myndes of men not manye yeares sithence, by meanes of certain fine fablers and lowd lyers, such as were the Authors of King Arthure the great and such like, who tell many an vnlawfull leasing of the Ladyes of the Lake, that is, the Nymphes. For the word Nymphe in Greeke signifieth Well water, or otherwise a Spouse or Bryde.

Behight) called or named.

Cloris) the name of a Nymph, and signifieth greenesse, of whome is sayd, that Zephyrus the Westerne wind being in loue with her, and coueting her to wyfe, gaue her for a dowrie, the chiefedome and soueraigntye of al flowres and greene herbes, growing on earth.

Oliues bene) The Oliue was wont to be the ensigne of Peace and quietnesse, eyther for that it cannot be planted and pruned, and so carefully looked to, as it ought, but in time of peace: or els for that the Oliue tree, they say, will not growe neare the Firre tree, which is dedicate to Mars the God of battaile, and vsed most for speares and other instruments of warre. Whereupon is finely feigned, that when Neptune and Minerua stroue for the naming of the citie of Athens, Neptune striking the ground with his mace, caused a horse to come forth, that importeth warre, but at Mineruaes stroke sprong out an Oliue, to note that it should be a nurse of learning, and such peaceable studies.

Binde your) Spoken rudely, and according to shepheardes simplicitye.

Bring) all these be names of flowers. Sops in wine a flowre in colour much like to a Coronation, but differing in smel and quantitye. Flowre delice, that which they vse to misterme, Flowre de luce, being in Latine called Flos delitiarum.

A Bellibone) or a Bonibell. Homely spoken for a fayre mayde or Bonilasse.

Forswonck and forswatt) ouerlaboured and sunneburnt.

I saw Phœbus) the sunne. A sensible Narration, and present view of the thing mentioned, which they call παρουσία.

Cynthia) the Moone so called of Cynthus a hyll, where she was honoured.

Latonaes seede) Was Apollo and Diana. Whom when as Niobe the wife of Amphion scorned, in respect of the noble fruict of her wombe, namely her seuen sonnes, and so many daughters, Latona being therewith displeased, commaunded her sonne Phœbus to slea al the sonnes, and Diana all the daughters: whereat the vnfortunate Niobe being sore dismayed, and lamenting out of measure, was feigned of the Poetes, to be turned into a stone vpon the sepulchre of her children. For which cause the shepheard sayth, he will not compare her to them, for feare of like mysfortune.

Now rise) is the conclusion. For hauing so decked her with prayses and comparisons, he returneth all the thanck of hys laboure to the excellencie of her Maiestie.

When Damsins) A base reward of a clownish giuer.

Yblent) Y, is a poeticall addition. Blent blinded.

Embleme.

This Poesye is taken out of Virgile, and there of him vsed in the person of Æneas to his mother Venus, appearing to him in likenesse of one of Dianaes damosells: being there most diuinely set forth. To which similitude of diuinitie Hobbinoll comparing the excelency of Elisa, and being through the worthynes of Colins song, as it were, ouercome with the hugenesse of his imagination, brusteth out in great admiration, (O quam te memorem virgo?) being otherwise vnhable, then by soddein silence, to expresse the worthinesse of his conceipt. Whom Thenot answereth with another part of the like verse, as confirming by his graunt and approuaunce, that Elisa is no whit inferiour to the Maiestie of her, of whome that Poete so boldly pronounced, O dea certe.

Maye.

Ægloga Quinta.

ARGVMENT.

In this fift Æglogue, vnder the persons of two shepheards Piers and Palinodie, be represented two formes of pastoures or Ministers, or the protestant and the Catholique: whose chiefe talke standeth in reasoning, whether the life of the one must be like the other. With whom hauing shewed, that it is daungerous to mainteine any felowship, or giue too much credit to their colourable and feyned goodwill, he telleth him a tale of the foxe, that by such a counterpoynt of craftines deceiued and deuoured the credulous kidde.

PALINODE.   PIERS.

IS not thilke the mery moneth of May,
  When loue lads masken in fresh aray?
How falles it then, we no merrier bene,
Ylike as others, girt in gawdy greene?
Our bloncket liueryes bene all to sadde,
For thilke same season, when all is ycladd
With pleasaunce: the grownd with grasse, the Woods
With greene leaues, the bushes with bloosming Buds.
Yougthes folke now flocken in euery where,
To gather may buskets and smelling brere: 10
And home they hasten the postes to dight,
And all the Kirke pillours eare day light,
With Hawthorne buds, and swete Eglantine,
And girlonds of roses and Sopps in wine.
Such merimake holy Saints doth queme,
But we here sytten as drownd in a dreme.

PIERS.

For Younkers *Palinode* such follies fitte,
But we tway bene men of elder witt.

PALINODE.

Sicker this morrowe, ne lenger agoe,
I sawe a shole of shepeheardes outgoe,   20
With singing, and shouting, and iolly chere:
Before them yode a lusty Tabrere,
That to the many a Horne pype playd,
Whereto they dauncen eche one with his mayd.
To see those folkes make such iouysaunce,
Made my heart after the pype to daunce.
Tho to the greene Wood they speeden hem all,
To fetchen home May with their musicall:
And home they bringen in a royall throne,
Crowned as king: and his Queene attone   30
Was Lady Flora, on whom did attend
A fayre flocke of Faeries, and a fresh bend
Of louely Nymphs. (O that I were there,
To helpen the Ladyes their Maybush beare)
Ah *Piers*, bene not thy teeth on edge, to thinke,
How great sport they gaynen with little swinck?

PIERS.

Perdie so farre am I from enuie,
That their fondnesse inly I pitie.
Those faytours little regarden their charge, 39
While they letting their sheepe runne at large,
Passen their time, that should be sparely spent,
In lustihede and wanton meryment.
Thilke same bene shepeheards for the Deuils stedde,
That playen, while their flockes be vnfedde.

Well is it seene, theyr sheepe bene not their owne,
That letten them runne at randon alone.
But they bene hyred for little pay
Of other, that caren as little as they,
What fallen the flocke, so they han the fleece
And get all the gayne, paying but a peece. 50
I muse, what account both these will make,
The one for the hire, which he doth take,
And thother for leauing his Lords taske,
When great *Pan* account of shepeherdes shall aske.

PALINODE.

Sicker now I see thou speakest of spight,
All for thou lackest somedele their delight.
I (as I am) had rather be enuied,
All were it of my foe, then fonly pitied:
And yet if neede were, pitied would be,
Rather, then other should scorne at me: 60
For pittied is mishappe, that nas remedie,
But scorned bene dedes of fond foolerie.
What shoulden shepeards other things tend,
Then sith their God his good does them send,
Reapen the fruite thereof, that is pleasure,
The while they here liuen, at ease and leasure?
For when they bene dead, their good is ygoe,
They sleepen in rest, well as other moe.
Tho with them wends, what they spent in cost,
But what they left behind them, is lost   70
Good is no good, but if it be spend:
God giueth good for none other end.

PIERS.

Ah *Palinodie*, thou art a worldes childe:
Who touches Pitch mought needes be defilde.
But shepheards (as Algrind vsed to say,)
Mought not liue ylike, as men of the laye:
With them it sits to care for their heire,
Enaunter their heritage doe impaire:
They must prouide for meanes of maintenaunce,
And to continue their wont countenaunce.   80
But shepheard must walke another way,
Sike worldly souenance he must foresay.
The sonne of his loines why should he regard
To leaue enriched with that he hath spard?
Should not thilke God, that gaue him that good,
Eke cherish his child, if in his wayes he stood?
For if he misliue in leudnes and lust,
Little bootes all the welth and the trust,
That his father left by inheritaunce: 89
All will be soone wasted with misgouernaunce.
But through this, and other their miscreaunce,
They maken many a wrong cheuisaunce,
Heaping vp waues of welth and woe,
The floddes whereof shall them ouerflowe.

Sike mens follie I cannot compare
Better, then to the Apes folish care,
That is so enamoured of her young one,
(And yet God wote, such cause hath she none)
That with her hard hold, and straight embrac-
ing,
She stoppeth the breath of her youngling. 100
So often times, when as good is meant,
Euil ensueth of wrong entent.

The time was once, and may againe retorne,
(For ought may happen, that hath bene
beforne)
When shepeheards had none inheritaunce,
Ne of land, nor fee in sufferaunce :
But what might arise of the bare sheepe,
(Were it more or lesse) which they did keepe.
Well ywis was it with shephearards thoe :
Nought hauing, nought feared they to forgoe.
For *Pan* himselfe was their inheritaunce, 111
And little them serued for their mayntenaunce.
The shepheards God so wel them guided,
That of nought they were vnprouided,
Butter enough, honye, milke, and whay,
And their flockes fleeces, them to araye.
But tract of time, and long prosperitie :
That nource of vice, this of insolencie,
Lull d the shepheards in such securitie,
That not content with loyall obeysaunce, 120
Some gan to gape for greedie gouernaunce,
And match them selfe with mighty potentates.
Louers of Lordship and troublers of states :
Tho gan shepheards swaines to looke a loft,
And leaue to liue hard, and learne to ligge soft :
Tho vnder colour of shepeheards, somewhile
There crept in Wolues, ful of fraude and guile,
That often deuoured their owne sheepe, 128
And often the shepheards, that did hem keepe.
This was the first sourse of shepheards sorowe,
That now nill be quitt with baile, nor borrowe.

PALINODE.

Three thinges to beare, bene very burdenous,
But the fourth to forbeare, is outragious.
Wemen that of Loues longing once lust,
Hardly forbearen, but haue it they must :
So when choler is inflamed with rage,
Wanting reuenge, is hard to asswage :
And who can counsell a thristie soule,
With patience to forbeare the offred bowle ?
But of all burdens, that a man can beare, 140
Moste is, a fooles talke to beare and to heare.
I wene the Geaunt has not such a weight,
That beares on his shoulders theheauens height.
Thou findest faulte, where nys to be found,
And buildest strong warke vpon a weake
ground :

Thou raylest on right withouten reason,
And blamest hem much, for small encheason.
How shoulden shepheardes liue, if not so ?
What ? should they pynen in payne and woe ?
Nay sayd I thereto, by my deare borrowe, 150
If I may rest, I nill liue in sorrowe.
Sorrowe ne neede be hastened on :
For he will come without calling anone.
While times enduren of tranquillitie,
Usen we freely our felicitie.
For when approchen the stormie stowres,
We mought with our shoulders beare of the
sharpe showres.
And sooth to sayne, nought seemeth sike strife,
That shepheardes so witen ech others life,
And layen her faults the world beforne, 160
The while their foes done eache of hem scorne.
Let none mislike of that may not be mended :
So conteck soone by concord mought be ended.

PIERS.

Shepheard, I list none accordaunce make
With shepheard, that does the right way forsake.
And of the twaine, if choice were to me,
Had leuer my foe, then my freend he be.
For what concord han light and darke sam ?
Or what peace has the Lion with the Lambe ?
Such faitors, when their false harts bene hidde.
Will doe, as did the Foxe by the Kidde. 171

PALINODE.

Now *Piers*, of felowship, tell vs that sayirg :
For the Ladde can keepe both our flocks from
straying.

PIERS.

THilke same Kidde (as I can well deuise)
Was too very foolish and vnwise.
For on a tyme in Sommer season,
The Gate her dame, that had good reason,
Yode forth abroade vnto the greene wood,
To brouze, or play, or what shee thought good.
But for she had a motherly care 180
Of her young sonne, and wit to beware,
Shee set her youngling before her knee,
That was both fresh and louely to see,
And full of fauour, as kidde mought be :
His Vellet head began to shoote out,
And his wrethed hornes gan newly sprout :
The blossomes of lust to bud did beginne,
And spring forth ranckly vnder his chinne.
My sonne (quoth she) (and with that gan
weepe :
For carefull thoughts in her heart did creepe)
God blesse thee poore Orphane, as he mought
me, 191
And send thee ioy of thy iollitee.

Thy father (that word she spake with payne:
For a sigh had nigh rent her heart in twaine)
Thy father, had he liued this day,
To see the braunche of his body displaie,
How would he haue ioyed at this sweete sight?
But ah false Fortune such ioy did him spight,
And cutte of hys dayes with vntimely woe,   200
Betraying him into the traines of hys foe.
Now I a wayfull widdowe behight,
Of my old age haue this one delight,
To see thee succeede in thy fathers steade,
And florish in flowres of lusty head.
For euen so thy father his head vpheld,
And so his hauty hornes did he weld.

Tho marking him with melting eyes,
A thrilling throbbe from her hart did aryse,
And interrupted all her other speache,
With some old sorowe, that made a newe
    breache: 210
Seemed shee sawe in the younglings face
The old lineaments of his fathers grace.
At last her solein silence she broke,
And gan his newe budded beard to stroke.

Kiddie (quoth shee) thou kenst the great care,
I haue of thy health and thy welfare,
Which many wyld beastes liggen in waite,
For to entrap in thy tender state:
But most the Foxe, maister of collusion:
For he has voued thy last confusion.   220
For thy my Kiddie be ruld by mee,
And neuer giue trust to his trecheree.
And if he chaunce come, when I am abroade,
Sperre the yate fast for feare of fraude:
Ne for all his worst, nor for his best,
Open the dore at his request.

So schooled the Gate her wanton sonne,
That answerd his mother, all should be done.
Tho went the pensife Damme out of dore,   229
And chaunst to stomble at the threshold flore:
Her stombling steppe some what her amazed,
(For such, as signes of ill luck bene dispraised)
Yet forth shee yode thereat halfe aghast:
And Kiddie the dore sperred after her fast.

It was not long, after shee was gone,
But the false Foxe came to the dore anone:
Not as a Foxe, for then he had be kend,
But all as a poore pedler he did wend,
Bearing a trusse of tryfles at hys backe,
As bells, and babes, and glasses in hys packe.
A Biggen he had got about his braine,   241
For in his headpeace he felt a sore payne.
His hinder heele was wrapt in a clout,
For with great cold he had gotte the gout.
There at the dore he cast me downe hys pack,
And layd him downe, and groned, Alack,
    Alack.

Ah deare Lord, and sweete Saint Charitee,
That some good body woulde once pitie mee.
    Well heard Kiddie al this sore constraint,
And lengd to know the cause of his com-
    plaint: 250
Tho creeping close behind the Wickets clinck,
Preuilie he peeped out through a chinck:
Yet not so preuilie, but the Foxe him spyed:
For deceifull meaning is double eyed.
    Ah good young maister (then gan he crye)
Iesus blesse that sweete face, I espye,
And keepe your corpse from the carefull
    stounds,
That in my carrion carcas abounds.
The Kidd pittying hys heauinesse,
Asked the cause of his great distresse,   260
And also who, and whence that he were.
Tho he, that had well ycond his lere,
Thus medled his talke with many a teare,
Sicke, sicke, alas, and little lack of dead,
But I be relieued by your beastlyhead.
I am a poore Sheépe, albe my coloure donne;
For with long traueile I am brent in the sonne.
And if that my Grandsire me sayd, be true,
Sicker I am very sybbe to you:
So be your goodlihead doe not disdayne   270
The base kinred of so simple swaine.
Of mercye and fauour then I you pray,
With your ayd to forstall my neere decay.
    Tho out of his packe a glasse he tooke:
Wherein while kiddie vnwares did looke,
He was so enamored with the newell,
That nought he deemed deare for the iewell.
Tho opened he the dore, and in came
The false Foxe, as he were starke lame.
His tayle he clapt betwixt his legs twayne,
Lest he should be descried by his trayne.   281
    Being within, the Kidde made him good glee,
All for the loue of the glasse he did see.
After his chere the Pedler can chat,
And tell many lesings of this, and that:
And how he could shewe many a fine knack.
Tho shewed his ware, and opened his packe,
All saue a bell, which he left behind
In the bas-ket for the Kidde to fynd.
Which when the Kidde stooped downe to
    catch,   290
He popt him in, and his basket did latch,
Ne stayed he once, the dore to make fast,
But ranne awaye with him in all hast.
Home when the doubtfull Damme had her hyde,
She mought see the dore stand open wyde.
All agast, lowdly she gan to cal
Her Kidde: but he nould answere at all.
Tho on the flore she sawe the merchandise,
Of which her sonne had sette to dere a prise.

What helpe? her Kidde shee knewe well was
gone : 300
Shee weeped,and wayled,and made great mone.
Such end had the Kidde, for he nould warned be
Of craft, coloured with simplicitie :
And such end perdie does all hem remayne,
That of such falsers freendship bene fayne.

PALINODIE.

Truly *Piers*, thou art beside thy wit,
Furthest fro the marke, weening it to hit,
Now I pray thee, lette me thy tale borrowe
For our sir Iohn, to say to morrowe
At the Kerke, when it is holliday : 310
For well he meanes, but little can say.

But and if Foxes bene so crafty, as so,
Much-needeth all shepheards hem to knowe.

PIERS.

Of their falshode more could I recount.
But now the bright Sunne gynneth to dis-
mount :
And for the deawie night now doth nye,
I hold it best for vs, home to hye.

Palinodes Embleme.

Πὰς μὲν ἄπιστος ἀπιστεῖ.

Piers his Embleme. 320

Τὶς δ' ἄρα πίστις ἀπίστω ;

GLOSSE.

Thilke) this same moneth. It is applyed to the season of the moneth, when all menne delight them selues with pleasaunce of fieldes, and gardens, and garments.
Bloncket liueries) gray coates.
Yclad) arrayed, Y, redoundeth, as before.
In euery where) a straunge, yet proper kind of speaking.
Buskets) a Diminutiue.s. little bushes of hauthorne.
Kirke) church. Queme) please.
A shole) a multitude; taken of fishe, whereof some going in great companies, are sayde to swimme in a shole.
Yode) went. Iouyssance) ioye.
Swinck) labour. Inly) entirely.
Faytours) vagabonds.
Great pan) is Christ, the very God of all shepheards, which calleth himselfe the greate and good shepherd. The name is most rightly (me thinkes) applyed to him, for Pan signifieth all or omnipotent, which is onely the Lord Iesus. And by that name (as I remember) he is called of Eusebius in his fifte booke de Preparat. Euang ; who thereof telleth a proper storye to that purpose. Which story is first recorded of Plutarch, in his booke of the ceasing of oracles, and of Lauetere translated, in his booke of walking sprightes. Who sayth, that about the same time, that our Lord suffered his most bitter passion for the redemtion of man, certein passengers sayling from Italy to Cyprus and passing by certain Iles called Paxæ, heard a voyce calling alowde Thamus, Thamus, (now Thamus was the name of an Ægyptian, which was Pilote of the ship,) who giuing eare to the cry, was bidden, when he came to Palodes, to tel, that the great Pan was dead: which he doubting to doe, yet for that when he came to Palodes, there sodeinly was such a calme of winde, that the shippe stoode still in the sea vnmoued, he was forced to cry alowd, that Pan was dead: wherewithall there was heard suche piteous outcryes and dreadfull shriking, as hath not bene the like. By whych Pan, though of some be vnderstoode the great Satanas, whose kingdome at that time was by Christ conquered, the gates of hell broken vp, and death by death deliuered to eternall death, (for at that time, as he sayth, all Oracles surceased, and enchaunted

spirits, that were wont to delude the people, thenceforth held theyr peace) and also at the demaund of the Emperoure Tiberius, who that Pan should be, answere was made him by the wisest and best learned, that it was the sonne of Mercurie and Penelope, yet I think it more properly meant of the death of Christ, the onely and very Pan, then suffering for his flock.
I as I am) seemeth to imitate the commen prouerb, Malim Inuidere mihi omnes quam miserescere.
Nas) a syncope, for ne has, or has not : as nould, for would not.
Tho with them) doth imitate the Epitaphe of the ryotous king Sardanapalus, whych caused to be written on his tombe in Greeke: which verses be thus translated by Tullie.

„ Hæc habui quæ edi, quæque exaturata libido
„ Hausit, at illa manent multa ac præclara
relicta.

which may thus be turned into English.

„ All that I eate did I ioye, and all that I
greedily gorged:
„ As for those many goodly matters left I for
others.

Much like the Epitaph of a good olde Erle of Deuonshire, which though much more wisedome bewraieth, then Sardanapalus, yet hath a smacke of his sensuall delights and beastlinesse. The rymes be these.

„ Ho, Ho, who lies here?
„ I the good Erle of Deuonshere,
„ And Maulde my wife, that was ful deare,
„ We liued together lv. yeare.
„ That we spent, we had :
„ That we gaue, we haue:
„ That we lefte, we lost.

Algrind) the name of a shepheard.
Men of the Lay) Lay men.
Enaunter) least that.
Souenaunce) remembraunce.
Miscreaunce) despeire or misbeliefe.
Cheuisaunce) sometime of Chaucer vsed for gaine : sometime of other for spoyle, or bootie, or enterprise, and sometime for chiefdome.
Pan himselfe, God. According as is sayd in Deuteronomie, That in diuision of the lande of Canaan, to the tribe of Leuie no portion of

heritage should bee allotted, for GOD himselfe was their inheritaunce.

Some gan) meant of the Pope, and his Antichristian prelates, which vsurpe a tyrannical dominion in the Churche, and with Peters counterfet keyes, open a wide gate to al wickednesse and insolent gouernment. Nought here spoken, as of purpose to deny fatherly rule and godly gouernaunce (as some malitiously of late haue done to the great vnreste and hinderaunce of the Churche) but to displaye the pride and disorder of such, as in steede of feeding their sheepe, indeede feede of theyr sheepe.

Sourse) welspring and originall.

Borrowe) pledge or suertie.

The Geaunte) is the greate Atlas, whom the poetes feign to be a huge giaunt, that beareth Heauen on his shoulders: being in deede a merueilous highe mountaine in Mauritania, that now is Barbarie, which to mans seeming perceth the cloudes, and seemeth to touch the heauens. Other thinke, and they not amisse, that this fable was meant of one Atlas king of the same countrye, (of whome may bee, that that hil had his denomination) brother to Prometheus who (as the Grekes say) did first fynd out the hidden courses of the starres, by an excellent imagination. Wherefore the poetes feigned, that he susteyned the firmament on hys shoulders. Many other coniectures needelesse be told hereof.

Warke) worke.   Encheason) cause, occasion.

Deare borow) that is our sauiour, the commen pledge of all mens deb s to death.

Wyten) blame.   Nought seemeth) is vnseemely.

Conteck) strife contention.

Her) theyr, as vseth Chaucer.

Han) for haue.   Sam) together.

This tale is much like to that in Æsops fables, but the Catastrophe and end is farre different. By the Kidde may be vnderstoode the simple sorte of the faythfull and true Christians. By hys dame Christe, that hath alreadie with carefull watchewords (as heere doth the gote) warned his little ones, to beware of such doubling deceit. By the Foxe, the false and faithlesse Papistes, to whom is no credit to be giuen, nor felowshippe to be vsed.

The gate) the Gote: Northernely spoken to turne O into A.

Yode) went.   Afforesayd.

She set) A figure called Fictio. Which vseth to attribute reasonable actions and speaches to vnreasonable creatures.

The bloosmes of lust) be the young and mossie heares, which then beginne to sproute and shoote foorth, when lustfull heate beginneth to kindle.

And with) A very Poeticall & c.

Orphane) A youngling or pupill, that needeth a Tutour and gouernour.

That word) A patheticall parenthesis, to encrease a carefull Hyperbaton.

The braunch) of the fathers body, is the child.

For euen so) Alluded to the saying of Andromache to Ascanius in Virgile.

Sic oculos, sic ille manus, sic ora ferebat.

A thrilling throb) a percing sighe.   Liggen) lye.

Maister of collusion) s. coloured guile, because the Foxe of al beasts is most wily and crafty.

Sperre the yate) shut the dore.

For such) The gotes stombling is here noted as an euill signe. The like to be marked in all histories: and that not the leaste of the Lorde Hastingues in king Rycharde the third his dayes. For beside his daungerous dreame (whiche was a shrewde prophecie of his mishap, that folowed) it is sayd that in the morning ryding toward the tower of London, to sitte vppon matters of counsell, his horse stombled twise or thrise by the way: which of some, that ryding with hym in his company, were priuie to his neere destenie, was secretly marked, and afterward noted for memorie of his great mishap, that ensewed. For being then as merye, as man might be, and least doubting any mortall daunger, he was within two howres after, of the Tyranne put to a shamefull deathe.

As belles) by such trifles are noted, the reliques and ragges of popish superstition, which put no smal religion in Belles: and Babies .s. Idoles: and glasses .s. Paxes, and such lyke trumperies.

Great cold) For they boast much of their outward patience, and voluntarye sufferaunce as a worke of merite and holy humblenesse.

Sweete S. Charitie. The Catholiques comen othe, and onely speache, to haue charitye alwayes in their mouth, and sometime in their outward Actions, but neuer inwardly in fayth and godly zeale.

Clincke.) a key hole. Whose diminutiue is clicket, vsed of Chaucer for a Key.

Stoundes) fittes: aforesayde.

His lere) his lesson.   Medled) mingled.

Bestlihead.) agreeing to the person of a beast.

Sibbe.) of kynne.   Newell) a newe thing.

To forestall) to præuent.

Glee) chere, afforesayde.

Deare a price.) his lyfe, which he lost for those toyes.

Such ende) is an Epiphonema, or rather the morall of the whole tale, whose purpose is to warne the protestaunt beware, howe he geueth credit to the vnfaythfull Catholique: whereof we haue dayly proofes sufficient, but one moste famous of all, practised of Late yeares in Fraunce by Charles the nynth.

Fayne) gladde or desyrous.

Our sir Iohn) a Popishe priest. A saying fit for the grosenesse of a shepheard, but spoken to taunte vnlearned Priestes.

Dismount) descende or set.   Nye) draweth nere.

Embleme.

Both these Emblemes make one whole Hexametre. The first spoken of Palinodie, as in reproche of them, that be distrustfull, is a peece of Theognis verse, intending, that who doth most mistrust is most false. For such experience in falsehod breedeth mistrust in the mynd, thinking no lesse guile to lurke in others, then in hymselfe. But Piers thereto strongly replyeth with another peece of the same verse, saying as in his former fable, what fayth then is there in the faythlesse. For if fayth be the ground of religion, which fayth they dayly false, what hold then is there of theyr religion. And thys is all that they saye.

Iune.

Ægloga sexta.

ARGVMENT.

THis Æglogue is wholly vowed to the com-
playning of Colins ill successe in his
loue. For being (as is aforesaid) enamoured of
a Country lasse Rosalind, and hauing (as seemeth)
founde place in her heart, he lamenteth to his
deare frend Hobbinoll, that he is nowe forsaken
vnfaithfully, and in his steede Menalcas, another
shepheard receiued disloyally. And this is the
whole Argument of this Æglogue.

HOBBINOL.   COLIN CLOVTE.

LO *Colin*, here the place, whose pleasaunt syte
From other shades hath weand my wan-
dring mynde.
Tell me, what wants me here, to worke delyte ?
The simple ayre, the gentle warbling wynde,
So calme, so coole, as no where else I fynde :
The grassye ground with daintye Daysies dight,
The Bramble bush, where Byrds of euery
kynde
To the waters fall their tunes attemper right.

COLLIN.

O happy *Hobbinoll*, I blesse thy state,
That Paradise hast found, whych *Adam* lost. 10
Here wander may thy flock early or late,
Withouten dreade of Wolues to bene ytost :

Thy louely layes here mayst thou freely boste.
But I vnhappy man, whom cruell fate,
And angry Gods pursue from coste to coste,
Can nowhere fynd, to shroude my lucklesse pate.

HOBBINOLL.

Then if by me, thou list aduised be,
Forsake the soyle, that so doth the bewitch :
Leaue me those hilles, where harbrough nis to
see,   19
Nor holybush, nor brere, nor winding witche :
And to the dales resort, where shepheards
ritch,
And fruictfull flocks bene euery where to see.
Here no night Rauens lodge more black then
pitche,
Nor eluish ghosts, nor gastly owlcs doe flee.

But frendly Faeries, met with many Graces,
And lightfote Nymphes can chace the lingring
night,
With Heydeguyes, and trimly trodden traces,
Whilst systers nyne, which dwell on *Parnasse*
hight,
Doe make them musick, for their more delight :
And *Pan* himselfe to kisse their christall faces,
Will pype and daunce, when *Phœbe* shineth
bright :   31
Such pierlesse pleasures haue we in those places.

COLLIN.

And I, whylst youth, and course of carelesse
    yeeres
Did let me walke withouten lincks of loue,
In such delights did ioy amongst my peeres :
But ryper age such pleasures doth reproue,
My fancye eke from former follies moue
To stayed steps : for time in passing weares
(As garments doen, which wexen old aboue)
And draweth newe delightes with hoary heares.

Tho couth I sing of loue, and tune my pype 41
Vnto my plaintiue pleas in verses made :
Tho would I seeke for Queene apples vnrype,
To giue my *Rosalind*, and in Sommer shade
Dight gaudy Girlonds, was my comen trade,
To crowne her golden locks, but yeeres more
    rype,
And losse of her, whose loue as lyfe I wayd,
Those weary wanton toyes away dyd wype.

HOBBINOLL.

Colin, to heare thy rymes and roundelayes,
Which thou were wont on wastfull hylls to
    singe,   50
I more delight, then larke in Sommer dayes :
Whose Echo made the neyghbour groues to ring,
And taught the byrds, which in the lower spring
Did shroude in shady leaues from sonny rayes,
Frame to thy songe their chereful cheriping,
Or hold theyr peace, for shame of thy swete
    layes.

I sawe *Calliope* wyth Muses moe,
Soone as thy oaten pype began to sound,
Theyr yuory Luyts and Tamburins forgoe ,
And from the fountaine, where they sat around,
Renne after hastely thy siluer sound.   61
But when they came, where thou thy skill didst
    showe,
They drewe abacke, as halfe with shame con-
    found,
Shepheard to see, them in theyr art outgoe.

COLLIN.

Of Muses *Hobbinol*, I conne no skill :
For they bene daughters of the hyghest *Ioue*,
And holden scorne of homely shepheards quill.
For sith I heard, that *Pan* with *Phœbus* stroue,
Which him to much rebuke and Daunger droue :
I neuer lyst presume to *Parnasse* hyll,   70
But pyping lowe in shade of lowly groue,
I play to please my selfe, all be it ill.

Nought weigh I, who my song doth prayse or
    blame,
Ne striue to winne renowne, or passe the rest :
With shepheard sittes not, followe flying fame :
But feede his flocke in fields, where falls hem best.

I wote my rymes bene rough, and rudely drest :
The fytter they, my carefull case to frame :
Enough is me to paint out my vnrest,
And poore my piteous plaints out in the same.

The God of shepheards *Tityrus* is dead,   81
Who taught me homely, as I can, to make.
He, whilst he liued, was the soueraigne head
Of shepheards all, that bene with loue ytake :
Well couth he wayle hys Woes, and lightly slake
The flames, which loue within his heart had bredd,
And tell vs mery tales, to keepe vs wake,
The while our sheepe about vs safely fedde.

Nowe dead he is, and lyeth wrapt in lead,
(O why should death on hym such outrage
    showe ?)   90
And all hys passing skil with him is fledde,
The fame whereof doth dayly greater growe.
But if on me some little drops would flowe,
Of that the spring was in his learned hedde,
I soone would learne these woods, to wayle my
    woe,
And teache the trees, their trickling teares to
    shedde.

Then should my plaints, causd of discurtesee,
As messengers of all my painfull plight,
Flye to my loue, where euer that she bee,
And pierce her heart with poynt of worthy
    wight :   100
As shee deserues, that wrought so deadly spight.
And thou *Menalcas*, that by trecheree
Didst vnderfong my lasse, to wexe so light,
Shouldest well be knowne for such thy villanee.

But since I am not, as I wish I were .
Ye gentle shepheards, which your flocks do feede,
Whether on hylls, or dales, or other where,
Beare witnesse all of thys so wicked deede :
And tell the lasse, whose flowre is woxe a weede,
And faultlesse fayth, is turned to faithlesse fere,
That she the truest shepheards hart made
    bleede,   111
That lyues on earth, and loued her most dere.

HOBBINOL.

O carefull *Colin*, I lament thy case,
Thy teares would make the hardest flint to flowe,
Ah faithlesse Rosalind, and voide of grace,
That art the roote of all this ruthfull woe.
But now is time, I gesse, homeward to goe :
Then ryse ye blessed flocks, and home apace,
Least night with stealing steppes doe you
    forsloe,
And wett your tender Lambes, that by you
    trace.   120

Colins Embleme.
Gia speme spenta.

GLOSSE.

Syte) situation and place.

Paradise) A Paradise in Greeke signifieth a Garden of pleasure, or place of delights. So he compareth the soile, wherin Hobbinoll made his abode, to that earthly Paradise, in scripture called Eden; wherein Adam in his first creation was placed. Which of the most learned is thought to be in Mesopotamia, the most fertile and pleasaunte country in the world (as may appeare by Diodorus Syculus description of it, in the hystorie of Alexanders conquest thereof) lying betweene the two famous Ryuers (which are sayd in scripture to flowe out of Paradise) Tygris and Euphrates, whereof it is so denominate.

Forsake the soyle) This is no poetical fiction, but vnfeynedly spoken of the Poete selfe, who for speciall occasion of priuate affayres (as I haue bene partly of himselfe informed) and for his more preferment remouing out of the Northparts came into the South, as Hobbinoll indeede aduised him priuately.

Those hylles) that is the North countrye, where he dwelt.

N'is) is not.

The Dales) The Southpartes, where he nowe abydeth, which thoughe they be full of hylles and woodes (for Kent is very hyllye and woodye; and therefore so called: for Kantsh in the Saxons tongue signifieth woodie) yet in respecte of the Northpartes they be called dales. For indede the North is counted the higher countrye.

Night Rauens &c.) by such hatefull byrdes, hee meaneth all misfortunes (Whereof they be tokens) flying euery where.

Frendly faeries) the opinion of Faeries and elfes is very old, and yet sticketh very religiously in the myndes of some. But to roote that rancke opinion of Elfes oute of mens hearts, the truth is, that there be no such thinges, nor yet the shadowes of the things, but onely by a sort of bald Friers and knauish shauelings so feigned; which as in all other things, so in that, soughte to nousell the comen people in ignorounce, least being once acquainted with the truth of things, they woulde in tyme smell out the vntruth of theyr packed pelfe and Massepenie religion. But the sooth is, that when all Italy was distraicte into the Factions of the Guelfes and the Gibelins, being two famous houses in Florence, the name began through their great mischiefes and many outrages, to be so odious or rather dreadfull in the peoples eares, that if theyr children at any time were frowarde and wanton, they would say to them that the Guelfe or the Gibeline came. Which words nowe from them (as many thinge els) be come into our vsage, and for Guelfes and Gibelines, we say Elfes and Goblins. No otherwise then the Frenchmen vsed to say of that valiaunt captain, the very scourge of Fraunce, the Lord Thalbot, afterward Erle of Shrewsbury; whose noblesse bred such a terrour in the hearts of the French, that oft times euen great armies were defaicted and put to flyght at the onely hearing of hys name. In somuch that the French wemen, to affray theyr chyldren, would tell them that the Talbot commeth.

Many Graces) though there be indeede but three Graces or Charites (as afore is sayd) or at the vtmost but foure, yet in respect of many gyftes of bounty, there may be sayde more. And so Musæus sayth, that in Heroes eyther eye there satte a hundred graces. And by that authoritye, thys same Poete in his Pageaunts sayth.

An hundred Graces on her eyeledde satte. &c.

Haydeguies) A country daunce or rownd. The conceipt is, that the Graces and Nymphes doe daunce vnto the Muses, and Pan his musicke all night by Moonelight. To signifie the pleasauntnesse of the soyle.

Peeres) Equalles and felow shepheards.

Queneapples vnripe) imitating Virgils verse.

Ipse ego cana legam tenera lanugine mala.

Neighbour groues) a straunge phrase in English, but word for word expressing the Latine vicina nemora.

Spring) not of water, but of young trees springing.

Calliope) afforesayde. Thys staffe is full of verie poetical inuention.

Tamburines) an olde kind of instrument, which of some is supposed to be the Clarion.

Pan with Phæbus) the tale is well knowne, howe that Pan and Apollo striuing for excellencye in musicke, chose Midas for their iudge. Who being corrupted wyth partiall affection, gaue the victorye to Pan vndeserued: for which Phæbus sette a payre of Asses eares vpon hys head &c.

Tityrus) That by Tityrus is meant Chaucer, hath bene already sufficiently sayde, and by thys more playne appeareth, that he sayth, he tolde merye tales. Such as be hys Canterburie tales. Whom he calleth the God of Poetes for hys excellencie, so as Tullie calleth Lentulus, Deum vitæ suæ .s. the God of hys lyfe.

To make) to versifie.

O why) A pretye Epanorthosis or correction.

Discurtesie) he meaneth the falsenesse of his louer Rosalinde, who forsaking hym, hadde chosen another.

Poynte of worthy wite) the pricke of deserued blame.

Menalcas) the name of a shephearde in Virgile; but here is meant a person vnknowne and secrete, agaynst whome he often bitterly inuayeth.

vnderfonge) vndermine and deceiue by false suggestion.

Embleme.

You remember, that in the fyrst Æglogue, Colins Poesie was Anchora speme: for that as then there was hope of fauour to be found in tyme. But nowe being cleane forlorne and reiected of her, as whose hope, that was, is cleane extinguished and turned into despeyre, he renounceth all comfort and hope of goodnesse to come. Which is all the meaning of thys Embleme.

Iulye.

Ægloga septima.

ARGVMENT.

*THis Æglogue is made in the honour and
commendation of good shepeheardes, and
to the shame and disprayse of proude and ambitious Pastours. Such as Morrell is here imagined
to bee.*

THOMALIN.	MORRELL.

IS not thilke same a goteheard prowde,
   that sittes on yonder bancke,
Whose straying heard them selfe doth shrowde
   emong the bushes rancke ?

MORRELL.

What ho, thou iollye shepheards swayne,
   come vp the hyll to me :
Better is, then the lowly playne,
   als for thy flocke, and thee.

THOMALIN.

Ah God shield, man, that I should clime,
   and learne to looke alofte,   10
This reede is ryfe, that oftentime
   great clymbers fall vnsoft.

In humble dales is footing fast,
   the trode is not so tickle :
And though one fall through heedlesse hast,
   yet is his misse not mickle.
And now the Sonne hath reared vp
   his fyriefooted teme,
Making his way betweene the Cuppe,
   and golden Diademe :   20
The rampant Lyon hunts he fast,
   with Dogge of noysome breath,
Whose balefull barking bringes in hast
   pyne, plagues, and dreery death.
Agaynst his cruell scortching heate
   where hast thou couerture ?
The wastefull hylls vnto his threate
   is a playne ouerture.
But if thee lust, to holden chat
   with seely shepherds swayne,   30
Come downe, and learne the little what,
   that Thomalin can sayne.

MORRELL.

Syker, thous but a laesie loord,
   and rekes much of thy swinck,
That with fond termes, and weetlesse words
   to blere myne eyes doest thinke.

In euill houre thou hentest in hond
  thus holy hylles to blame,
For sacred vnto saints they stond,
  and of them han theyr name.   40
S. Michels mount who does not know,
  that wardes the Westerne coste ?
And of S. Brigets bowre I trow,
  all Kent can rightly boaste :
And they that con of Muses skill,
  sayne most what, that they dwell
(As goteheards wont) vpon a hill,
  beside a larned well.
And wonned not the great God *Pan*,
  vpon mount *Oliuet* :   50
Feeding the blessed flocke of *Dan*,
  which dyd himselfe beget ?

THOMALIN.

O blessed sheepe, O shepheard great,
  that bought his flocke so deare,
And them did saue with bloudy sweat
  from Wolues, that would them teare.

MORREL.

Besyde, as holy fathers sayne,
  there is a hyllye place,
Where *Titan* ryseth from the mayne,
  to renne hys dayly race.   60
Vpon whose toppe the starres bene stayed,
  and all the skie doth leane,
There is the caue, where *Phebe* layed,
  the shepheard long to dreame.
Whilome there vsed shephcards all
  to feede theyr flocks at will,
Till by his foly one did fall,
  that all the rest did spill,
And sithens shepheardes bene foresayd
  from places of delight :   70
For thy I weene thou be affrayd,
  to clime this hills height.
Of *Synah* can I tell thee more,
  and of our Ladyes bowre :
But little needes to strow my store,
  suffice this hill of our.
Here han the holy *Faunes* resourse,
  and *Syluanes* haunten rathe.
Here has the salt Medway his sourse,
  wherein the Nymphes doe bathe.   80
The salt Medway, that trickling stremis
  adowne the dales of Kent :
Till with his elder brother Themis
  his brackish waues be meynt.
Here growes *Melampode* euery where,
  and *Teribinth* good for Gotes :
The one, my madding kiddes to smere,
  the next, to heale theyr throtes.

Hereto, the hills bene nigher heuen,
  and thence the passage ethe.   90
As well can proue the piercing leuin,
  that seeldome falls bynethe.

THOMALIN.

Syker thou speakes lyke a lewde lorrell,
  of Heauen to demen so :
How be I am but rude and borrell,
  yet nearer wayes I knowe.
To Kerke the narre, from God more farre,
  has bene an old sayd sawe.
And he that striues to touch the starres,
  oft stombles at a strawe,   100
Alsoone may shepheard clymbe to skye,
  that laddes in lowly dales,
As Gotcherd prowd that sitting hye,
  vpon the Mountaine sayles.
My seely sheepe like well belowe,
  they neede not *Melampode* :
For they bene hale enough, I trowe,
  and liken theyr abode.
But if they with thy Gotes should yede,
  they soone myght be corrupted :   110
Or like not of the frowie fede,
  or with the weedes be glutted.
The hylls, where dwelld holy saints,
  I reuerence and adore :
Not for themselfe, but for the sayncts,
  Which han be dead of yore.
And nowe they bene to heauen forewent,
  theyr good is with them goe :
Theyr sample onely to vs lent,
  that als we mought doe soe.   120
Shepheards then weren of the best,
  and liued in lowlye leas :
And sith theyr soules bene now at rest,
  why done we them disease ?
Such one he was, (as I haue heard
  old Algrind often sayne)
That whilome was the first shepheard,
  and liued with little gayne :
As meeke he was, as meeke mought be,
  simple, as simple sheepe,   130
Humble, and like in eche degree
  the flocke, which he did keepe.
Often he vsed of hys keepe
  a sacrifice to bring,
Nowe with a Kidde, now with a sheepe
  the Altars hallowing.
So lowted he vnto hys Lord,
  such fauour couth he fynd,
That sithens neuer was abhord,
  the simple shepheards kynd.   140
And such I weene the brethren were,
  that came from *Canaan* :

The brethren twelue, that kept yfere
  the flockes of mighty *Pan*.
But nothing such thilk shepharde was,
  whom *Ida* hyll dyd beare,
That left hys flocke, to fetch a lasse,
  whose loue he bought to deare :
For he was proude, that ill was payd,
  (no such mought shepheards bee)   150
And with lewde lust was ouerlayd :
  tway things doen ill agree :
But shepheard mought be meeke and mylde,
  well eyed, as *Argus* was,
With fleshly follyes vndefyled,
  and stoute as steede of brasse.
Sike one (sayd *Algrin*) *Moses* was,
  that sawe hys makers face,
His face more cleare, then Christall glasse,
  and spake to him in place.   160
This had a brother, (his name I knewe)
  the first of all his cote,
A shepheard trewe, yet not so true,
  as he that earst I hote.
Whilome all these were lowe, and lief,
  and loued their flocks to feede,
They neuer strouen to be chiefe,
  and simple was theyr weede :
But now (thanked be God therefore)
  the world is well amend,   170
Their weedes bene not so nighly wore,
  such simplesse mought them shend :
They bene yclad in purple and pall,
  so hath theyr god them blist,
They reigne and rul.n ouer all,
  and lord it, as they list :
Ygyrt with belts of glitterand gold,
  (mought they good sheepeheards bene)
Theyr Pan theyr sheepe to them has ~old,
  I saye as some haue seene.   180
For Palinode (if thou him ken)
  yode late on Pilgrimage
To Rome, (if such be Rome) and then
  he sawe thilke misusage.
For shepeheards (sayd he) there doen leade,
  as Lordes done other where,
Theyr sheepe han crustes, and they the bread :
  the chippes, and they the chere :
They han the fleece, and eke the flesh,
  (O seely sheepe the while)   190
The corne is theyrs, let other thresh,
  their hands they may not file.

They han great stores, and thriftye stockes,
  great freendes and feeble foes :
What neede hem caren for their flocks ?
  theyr boyes can looke to those.
These wisards weltre in welths waues,
  pampred in pleasures deepe,
They han fatte kernes, and leany knaues,
  their fasting flockes to keepe.   200
Sike mister men bene all misgone,
  they heapen hylles of wrath :
Sike syrlye shepheards han we none,
  they keepen all the path.

MORRELL.

Here is a great deale of good matter,
  lost for lacke of telling,
Now sicker I see, thou doest but clatter :
  harme may come of melling.
Thou medlest more, then shall haue thanke,
  to wyten shepheards welth :   210
When folke bene fat, and riches rancke,
  it is a signe of helth.
But say me, what is *Algrin* he,
  that is so oft bynempt.

THOMALIN.

He is a shepheard great in gree,
  but hath bene long ypent.
One daye he sat vpon a hyll,
  (as now thou wouldest me :
But I am taught by *Algrins* ill,
  to loue the lowe degree.)   220
For sitting so with bared scalpe,
  an Fagle sored hye,
That weening hys whyte head was chalke,
  a shell fish downe let flye :
She weend the shell fishe to haue broake,
  but therewith bruzd his brayne,
So now astonied with the stroke,
  he lyes in lingring payne.

MORRELL.

Ah good *Algrin*, his hap was ill,
  but shall be better in time.   230
Now farwell shepheard, sith thys hyll
  thou hast such doubt to climbe.

    Thomalins Embleme.
      In medio virtus.

    Morrells Embleme.
      In summo fœlicitas.

GLOSSE.

A Goteheard) By Gotes in scrypture be represented the wicked and reprobate, whose pastour
also must needes be such.

Banck) is the seate of honor.

Straying heard) which wander out of the waye of
truth.

Als) for also.

Clymbe) spoken of Ambition.

Great clymbers) according to Seneca his verse, Decidunt celsa grauiore lapsu.

Mickle) much.

The sonne) A reason, why he refuseth to dwell on Mountaines, because there is no shelter against the scortching sunne. According to the time of the yeare, whiche is the whotest moneth of all.

The Cupp and Diademe) Be two signes in the Firmament, through which the sonne maketh his course in the moneth of Iuly.

Lion) Thys is Poetically spoken, as if the Sunne did hunt a Lion with one Dogge. The meaning whereof is, that in Iuly the sonne is in Leo. At which tyme the Dogge starre, which is called Syrius or Canicula reigneth, with immoderate heate causing Pestilence, drougth, and many diseases.

Ouerture) an open place. The word is borrowed of the French, and vsed in good writers.

To holden chatt) to talke and prate.

A loorde) was wont among the old Britons to signifie a Lorde. And therefore the Danes, that long time vsurped theyr Tyrannie here in Brytanie, were called for more dreaa then dignitie, Lurdanes .s. Lord Danes. At which time it is sayd, that the insolencie and pryde of that nation was so outragious in thys Realme, that if it fortuned a Briton to be going ouer a bridge, and sawe the Dane set foote vpon the same, he muste retorne back, till the Dane were cleane ouer, or els abyde the pryce of his displeasure, which was no lesse, then present death. But being afterwarde expelled that name of Lurdane became so odious vnto the people, whom they had long oppressed, that euen at this daye they vse for more reproche, to call the Quartane ague the Feuer Lurdane.

Recks much of thy swinck) counts much of thy paynes.

Weetelesse) not vnderstoode.

S. Michels mount) is a promontorie in the West part of England.

A hill) Parnassus afforesayd. Pan Christ.

Dan) One trybe is put for the whole nation per Synecdochen.

Where Titan) the Sonne. Which story is to be redde in Diodorus Syc. of the hyl Ida; from whence he sayth, all night time is to bee seene a mightye fire, as if the skye burned, which toward morning beginneth to gather into a rownd forme, and thereof ryseth the sonne, whome the Poetes call Titan :

The Shepheard) is Endymion, whom the Poets fayne, to haue bene so beloued of Phœbe .s. the Moone, that he was by her kept a sleepe in a caue by the space of xxx. yeares, for to enioye his companye.

There) that is in Paradise, where through errour of shepheards vnderstanding, he sayth, that all shepheards did vse to feede theyr flocks, till one, (that is Adam) by hys follye and disobedience, made all the rest of hys ofspring be debarred and shutte out from thence.

Synah) a hill in Arabia, where God appeared.

Our Ladyes bowre) a place of pleasure so called.

Faunes or Syluanes) be of Poetes feigned to be Gods of the Woode.

Medway) the name of a Ryuer in Kent, which running by Rochester, meeteth with Thames; whom he calleth his elder brother, both because he is greater, and also falleth sooner into the Sea.

Meynt) mingled.

Melampode and Terebinth) be hearbes good to cure diseased Gotes. Of thone speaketh Mantuane, and of thother Theocritus.

τερμινθου τράγων ἔσχατον ἀκρέμονα.

Nigher heauen) Note the shepheards simplenesse, which supposeth that from the hylls is nearer waye to heauen.

Leuin) Lightning; which he taketh for an argument, to proue the nighnes to heauen, because the lightning doth comenly light on hygh mountaynes, according to the saying of the Poete. Feriuntque summos fulmina montes.

Lorrell) A losell.   A borell.) a playne fellowe.

Narre) nearer.   Hale) for hole.

Yede) goe.   Frowye) mustye or mossie.

Of yore) long agoe.   Forewente) gone afore.

The firste shepheard) was Abell the righteous, who (as scripture sayth) bent hys mind to keeping of sheepe, as did hys brother Cain to tilling the grownde.

His keepe) hys charge s. his flocke.

Lowted) did honour and reuerence.

The brethren) the twelue sonnes of Iacob, whych were shepemaisters, and lyued onelye thereupon.

Whom Ida) Paris, which being the sonne of Priamus king of Troy, for his mother Hecubas dreame, which being with child of hym, dreamed shee broughte forth a firebrand, that set all the towre of Ilium on fire, was cast forth on the hyll Ida; where being fostered of shepheards, he eke in time became a shepheard, and lastly came to knowledge of his parentage.

A lasse) Helena the wyfe of Menelaus king of Lacedemonia, was by Venus for the golden Aple to her geuen, then promised to Paris, who thereupon with a sorte of lustye Troyanes, stole her out of Lacedemonia, and kept her in Troye. Which was the cause of the tenne yeares warre in Troye, and the moste famous citye of all Asia most lamentably sacked and defaced.

Argus) was of the Poets deuised to be full of eyes, and therefore to hym was committed the keeping of the transformed Cow Io : So called because that in the print of a Cowes foote, there is figured an I in the middest of an O.

His name) he meaneth Aaron : whose name for more Decorum, the shephearde sayth he hath forgot, lest his remembraunce and skill in antiquities of holy writ should seeme to exceede the meanenesse of the Person.

Not so true) for Aaron in the absence of Moses started aside, and committed Idolatry.

In purple) Spoken of the Popes and Cardinalles, which vse such tyrannical colours and pompous paynting.

Belts) Girdles.

Glitterand) Glittering. A Participle vsed sometime in Chaucer, but altogether in I. Goore.

Theyr Pan) that is the Pope, whom they count theyr God and greatest shepheard.

Palinode) A shephearde, of whose report he seemeth to speake all thys.

Wisards) greate learned heads.

Welter) wallowe.

Kerne) a Churle or Farmer.

Sike mister men) such kinde of men

Surly) stately and prowde.

Melling) medling.

Bett) better.   Bynempte) name t.

Gree) for degree.

Algrin the name of a shepheard afforesayde, whose

myshap he alludeth to the chaunce, that happened to the Poet Æschylus, that was brayned with a shellfishe.

Embleme.

By thys poesye Thomalin confirmeth that, which in hys former speach by sondrye reasons he had proued. For being both hymselfe sequestred from all ambition and also abhorring it in others of hys cote, he taketh occasion to prayse the meane and lowly state, as that wherein is safetie without feare, and quiet without danger, according to the saying of olde Philosophers, that vertue dwelleth in the middest, being enuironed with two contrary vices: whereto Morrell replieth with continuaunce of the same Philosophers opinion, that albeit all bountye dwelleth in mediocritie, yet perfect felicitye dwelleth in supremacie. For they say, and most true it is, that happinesse is placed in the highest degree, so as if any thing be higher or better, then that streight way ceaseth to be perfect happines. Much like to that, which once I heard alleaged in defence of humilitve out of a great doctour, Suorum Christus humillimus: which saying a gentle man in the company taking at the rebownd, beate backe again with lyke saying of another Doctoure, as he sayde. Suorum deus altissimus.

August.

Ægloga octaua.

ARGVMENT.

IN this Æglogue is set forth a delectable controuersie, made in imitation of that in Theocritus: whereto also Virgile fashioned his third and seuenth Æglogue. They choose for vmpere of their strife, Cuddie a neatheards boye, who hauing ended their cause, reciteth also himselfe a proper song, whereof Colin he sayth was Authour.

WILLYE.   PERIGOT.   CVDDIE.

TEll me *Perigot*, what shalbe the game,
    Wherefore with myne thou dare thy
    musick matche?
Or bene thy Bagpypes renne farre out of frame?
Or hath the Crampe thy ioynts benomd with
    ache?

PERIGOT.

Ah *Willye*, when the hart is ill assayde,
How can Bagpipe, or ioynts be well apayd?

WILLYE.

What the foule euill hath thee so bestadde?
Whilom thou was peregall to the best,
And wont to make the iolly shepeheards gladde
With pyping and dauncing, didst passe the
    rest.   10

PERIGOT.

Ah *Willye* now I haue learnd a newe daunce:
My old musick mard by a newe mischaunce.

WILLYE.

Mischiefe mought to that newe mischaunce befall,
That so hath raft vs of our meriment.

But reede me, what payne doth thee so appall?
Or louest thou, or bene thy younglings miswent?

PERIGOT.

Loue hath misled both my younglings,and mee:
I pyne for payne, and they my payne to see.

WILLYE.

Perdie and wellawaye: ill may they thriue:
Neuer knewe I louers sheepe in good plight. 20
But and if in rymes with me thou dare striue,
Such fond fantsies shall soone be put to flight.

PERIGOT.

That shall I doe, though mochell worse I fared:
Neuer shall be sayde that *Perigot* was dared.

WILLYE.

Then loe *Perigot* the Pledge, which I plight:
A mazer ywrought of the Maple warre:
Wherein is enchased many a fayre sight
Of Beres and Tygres, that maken fiers warre:
And ouer them spred a goodly wild vine,
Entrailed with a wanton Yuie twine. 30

Thereby is a Lambe in the Wolues iawes:
But see, how fast renneth the shepheard swayne,
To saue the innocent from the beastes pawes:
And here with his shepehooke hath him slayne.
Tell me, such a cup hast thou euer sene?
Well mought it beseme any haruest Queene.

PERIGOT.

Thereto will I pawne yonder spotted Lambe,
Of all my flocke there nis sike another:
For I brought him vp without the Dambe.
But *Colin Clout* rafte me of his brother, 40
That he purchast of me in the playne field:
Sore against my will was I forst to yield.

WILLYE.

Sicker make like account of his brother.
But who shall iudge the wager wonne or lost?

PERIGOT.

That shall yonder heardgrome, and none other,
Which ouer the pousse hetherward doth post.

WILLYE.

But for the Sunnebeame so sore doth vs beate,
Were not better, to shunne the scortching heate?

PERIGOT.

Well agreed *Willy:* then sitte thee downe
swayne: 49
Sike a song neuer heardest thou, but *Colin* sing.

CVDDIE.

Gynne,when ye lyst, ye iolly shepheards twayne:
Sike a iudge, as *Cuddie*, were for a king.

SPENSER   Q

Perigot. IT fell vpon a holly eue,
Willye. Ihey ho hollidaye,
Per. When holly fathers wont to shrieue:
Wil. now gynneth this roundelay.
Per. Sitting vpon a hill so hye
Wil. hey ho the high hyll,
Per. The while my flocke did feede thereby,
Wil. the while the shepheard selfe did spill:
Per. I saw the bouncing Bellibone, 61
Wil. hey ho Bonibell,
Per. Tripping ouer the dale alone,
Wil. she can trippe it very well:
Per. Well decked in a frocke of gray,
Wil. hey ho gray is greete,
Per. And in a Kirtle of greene saye,
Wil. the greene is for maydens meete:
Per. A chapelet on her head she wore,
Wil. hey ho chapelet, 70
Per. Of sweete Violets therein was store,
Wil. she sweeter then the Violet.
Per. My sheepe did leaue theyr wonted foode,
Wil. hey ho seely sheepe,
Per. And gazd on her, as they were wood,
Wil. woode as he, that did them keepe.
Per. As the bonilasse passed bye,
Wil. hey ho bonilasse,
Per. She roude at me with glauncing eye,
Wil. as cleare as the christall glasse: 80
Per. All as the Sunnye beame so bright,
Wil. hey ho the Sunne beame,
Per. Glaunceth from *Phœbus* face forthright,
Wil. so loue into thy hart did streame:
Per. Or as the thonder cleaues the cloudes,
Wil. hey ho the Thonder,
Per. Wherein the lightsome leuin shroudes,
Wil. so cleaues thy soule a sonder:
Per. Or as Dame *Cynthias* siluer raye
Wil. hey ho the Moonelight, 90
Per. Vpon the glyttering waue doth playe:
Wil. such play is a pitteous plight.
Per. The glaunce into my heart did glide,
Wil. hey ho the glyder,
Per. Therewith my soule was sharply gryde,
Wil. such woundes soone wexen wider.
Per. Hasting to raunch the arrow out,
Wil. hey ho Perigot.
Per. I left the head in my hart roote:
Wil. it was a desperate shot. 100
Per. There it ranckleth ay more and more,
Wil. hey ho the arrowe,
Per. Ne can I find salue for my sore:
Wil. loue is a curelesse sorrowe.
Per. And though my bale with death I bought,
Wil. hey ho heauie cheere,
Per. Yet should thilk lasse not from my thought:
Wil. so you may buye gold to deare.

Per. But whether in paynefull loue I pyne,
Wil.   hey ho pinching payne,   110
Per. Or thriue in welth, she shalbe mine.
Wil.   but if thou can her obteine.
Per. And if for gracelesse greefe I dye,
Wil.   hey ho gracelesse griefe,
Per. Witnesse, shee slewe me with her eye :
Wil.   let thy follye be the priefe.
Per. And you, that sawe it, simple shepe,
Wil.   hey ho the fayre flocke,
Per. For priefe thereof, my death shall weepe,
Wil.   and mone with many a mocke.   120
Per. So learnd I loue on a hollye eue,
Wil.   hey ho holidaye,
Per. That euer since my hart did greue.
Wil.   now endeth our roundelay.

CVDDYE.

Sicker sike a roundle neuer heard I none.
Little lacketh *Perigot* of the best.
And *Willye* is not greatly ouergone,
So weren his vndersongs well addrest.

WILLYE.

Herdgrome, I feare me, thou haue a squint eye :
Areede vprightly, who has the victorye ?   130

CVDDIE.

Fayth of my soule, I deeme ech haue gayned.
For thy let the Lambe be *Willye* his owne :
And for *Perigot* so well hath hym payned,
To him be the wroughten mazer alone.

PERIGOT.

Perigot is well pleased with the doome :
Ne can *Willye* wite the witelesse herdgroome.

WILLYE.

Neuer dempt more right of beautye I weene,
The shepheard of *Ida*, that iudged beauties
    Queene.

CVDDIE.

But tell me shepherds, should it not yshend
Your roundels fresh, to heare a doolefull verse
Of Rosalend (who knowes not Rosalend ?) 141
That Colin made, ylke can I you rehearse.

PERIGOT.

Now say it *Cuddie*, as thou art a ladde :
With mery thing its good to medle sadde.

WILLY.

Fayth of my soule, thou shalt ycrouned be
In *Colins* stede, if thou this song areede :
For neuer thing on earth so pleaseth me,
As him to heare, or matter of his deede.

CVDDIE.

Then listneth ech vnto my heauy laye,
And tune your pypes as ruthful, as ye may. 150

YE wastefull woodes beare witnesse of my
    woe,
Wherein my plaints did oftentimes resound :
Ye carelesse byrds are priuie to my cryes,
    Which in your songs were wont to make a
    part :
Thou pleasaunt spring hast luld me oft a
    sleepe,
Whose streames my tricklinge teares did ofte
    augment.
Resort of people doth my greefs augment,
    The walled townes do worke my greater woe
    The forest wide is fitter to resound
    The hollow Echo of my carefull cryes,   160
    I hate the house, since thence my loue did
    part,
Whose waylefull want debarres myne eyes
    from sleepe.
Let stremes of teares supply the place of sleepe :
    Let all that sweete is, voyd : and all that
    may augment
My doole, drawe neare.   More meete to
    wayle my woe,
Bene the wild woddes my sorrowes to re-
    sound,
Then bedde, or bowre, both which I fill with
    cryes,
When I them see so waist, and fynd no part
Of pleasure past. Here will I dwell apart 169
    In gastfull groue therefore, till my last sleepe
    Doe close mine eyes : so shall I not augment
    With sight of such a chaunge my restlesse woe :
    Helpe me, ye banefull byrds, whose shriek-
    ing sound
Ys signe of dreery death, my deadly cryes
Most ruthfully to tune. And as my cryes
    (Which of my woe cannot bewray least part)
    You heare all night, when nature craueth
    sleepe,
Increase, so let your yrksome yells augment.
Thus all the night in plaints, the daye in woe
I vowed haue to wayst, till safe and sound
She home returne, whose voyces siluer sound 181
    To cheerefull songs can chaunge my chere-
    lesse cryes.
    Hence with the Nightingale will I take part,
    That blessed byrd, that spends her time of
    sleepe
    In songs and plaintiue pleas, the more taug-
    ment
    The memory of hys misdeede, that bred her
    woe :
And you that feele no woe, | when as the sound
    Of these my nightly cryes | ye heare apart,
    Let breake your sounder sleepe | and pitie
    augment.

PERIGOT.

O *Colin, Colin,* the shepheards ioye, 190
  How I admire ech turning of thy verse :
And *Cuddie,* fresh *Cuddie* the liefest boye,
  How dolefully his doole thou didst rehearse.

CUDDIE.

Then blowe your pypes shepheards, til you be
  at home :
The night nigheth fast, yts time to be gone.

Perigot his Embleme.
Vincenti gloria victi.

Willyes Embleme.
Vinto non vitto.

Cuddies Embleme. 200
Felice chi può.

GLOSSE.

Bestadde) disposed, ordered.
Peregall) equall.
Whilome) once.
Rafte) bereft, depriued.
Miswent) gon a straye.
Ill may) according to Virgile.

   Infelix o semper ouis pecus.

A mazer) So also do Theocritus and Virgile feigne
  pledges of their strife.
Enchased) engrauen. Such pretie descriptions
  euery where vseth Theocritus, to bring in his
  Idyllia. For which speciall cause indede he by
  that name termeth his Æglogues: for Idyllion
  in Greke signifieth the shape or picture of any
  thyng, wherof his booke is ful. And not, as
  I haue heard some fondly guesse, that they be
  called not Idyllia, but Hædilia, of the Goteheards in them.
Entrailed) wrought betwene.
Haruest Queene) The manner of country folke in
  haruest tyme.
Pousse.) Pease.
It fell vpon) Perigot maketh hys song in prayse of
  his loue, to whom Willy answereth euery vnder
  verse. By Perigot who is meant, I can not
  vprightly say. but if it be, who is supposed, his
  loue deserueth no lesse prayse, then he giueth her.

Greete) weeping and complaint.
Chaplet) a kind of Garlond lyke a crowne.
Leuen) Lightning.
Cynthia) was sayd to be the Moone.
Gryde) perced.
But if) not vnlesse.
Squint eye) partiall iudgement.
Ech haue) so saith Virgile.

   Et vitula tu dignus, et hic &c.

So by enterchaunge of gyfts Cuddie pleaseth
  both partes.
Doome) iudgement.
Dempt) for deemed, iudged.
Wite the witelesse) blame the blamelesse.
The shepherd of Ida) was sayd to be Paris.
Beauties Queene) Venus, to whome Paris adiudged
  the golden Apple, as the pryce of her beautie.

Embleme.

The meaning hereof is very ambiguous : for
  Perigot by his poesie claming the conquest, and
  Willye not yeelding, Cuddie the arbiter of theyr
  cause, and Patron of his own, semeth to chalenge
  it, as his dew, saying, that he, is happy which
  can. so abruptly ending but hee meaneth eyther
  him, that can win the beste, or moderate him
  selfe being best, and leaue of with the best.

September.

Ægloga Nona.

ARGVMENT.

*H*Erein Diggon Dauie is deuised to be
a shepheard, that in hope of more gayne,
droue his sheepe into a farre countrye. The
abuses whereof, and loose liuing of Popish prelates, by occasion of Hobbinols demaund, he
discourseth at large.

HOBBINOL.   DIGGON DAUIE.

DIggon Dauie, I bidde her god day :
Or Diggon her is, or I missaye.

DIGGON.

Her was her, while it was daye light,
But now her is a most wretched wight.
For day, that was, is wightly past,
And now at earst the dirke night doth hast.

HOBBINOLL.

Diggon areede, who has thee so dight ?
Neuer I wist thee in so poore a plight.
Where is the fayre flocke, thou was wont to
leade ?   9
Or bene they chaffred ? or at mischiefe dead ?

DIGGON.

Ah for loue of that, is to thee moste leefe,
Hobbinol, I pray thee gall not my old griefe :
Sike question ripeth vp cause of newe woe,
For one opened mote vnfolde many moe.

HOBBINOLL.

Nay, but sorrow close shrouded in hart
I know, to kepe, is a burdenous smart.
Eche thing imparted is more eath to beare :
When therayne is faln, the cloudes wexen clear .
And nowe sithence I sawe thy head last,   19
Thrise three Moones bene fully spent and past :
Since when thou hast measured much grownd,
And wandred I wene about the world rounde,
So as thou can many thinges relate :
But tell me first of thy flocks astate.

DIGGON.

My sheepe bene wasted, (wae is me therefore)
The iolly shepheard that was of yore,
Is nowe nor iollye, nor shepehearde more.
In forrein costes, men sayd, was plentye :
And so there is, but all of miserye.
I dempt there much to haue eeked my store, 30
But such eeking hath made my hart sore.
In tho countryes, whereas I haue bene,
No being for those, that truely mene,
But for such, as of guile maken gayne,
No such countrye, as there to remaine.
They setten to sale their shops of shame,
And maken a Mart of theyr good name.
The shepheards there robben one another,
And layen baytes to beguile her brother.

Or they will buy his sheepe out of the cote, 40
Or they will caruen the shepheards throte.
The shepheards swayne you cannot wel ken,
But it be by his pryde, from other men :
They looken bigge as Bulls, that bene bate,
And bearen the cragge so stiffe and so state
As cocke on his dunghill, crowing cranck.

HOBBINOLL.

Diggon, I am so stiffe, and so stanck,
That vneth may I stand any more :
And nowe the Westerne wind bloweth sore,
That nowe is in his chiefe souereigntee, 50
Beating the withered leafe from the tree.
Sitte we downe here vnder the hill :
Tho may we talke, and tellen our fill,
And make a mocke at the blustring blast.
Now say on Diggon, what euer thou hast.

DIGGON.

Hobbin, ah hobbin, I curse the stounde,
That euer I cast to haue lorne this grounde.
Wel-away the while I was so fonde,
To leaue the good, that I had in honde,
In hope of better, that was vncouth : 60
So lost the Dogge the flesh in his mouth.
My seely sheepe (ah seely sheepe)
That here by there I whilome vsd to keepe,
All were they lustye, as thou didst see,
Bene all sterued with pyne and penuree.
Hardly my selfe escaped thilke payne,
Driuen for neede to come home agayne.

HOBBINOLL.

Ah fon, now by thy losse art taught,
That seeldome chaunge the better brought.
Content who liues with tryed state, 70
Neede feare no chaunge of frowning fate :
But who will seeke for vnknowne gayne,
Oft liues by losse, and leaues with payne.

DIGGON.

I wote ne Hobbin how I was bewitcht
With vayne desyre, and hope to be enricht.
But sicker so it is, as the bright starre
Seemeth ay greater, when it is farre :
I thought the soyle would haue made me rich :
But nowe I wote, it is nothing sich. 79
For eyther the shepheards bene ydle and still,
And ledde of theyr sheepe, what way they wyll :
Or they bene false, and full of couetise,
And casten to compasse many wrong emprise.
But the more bene fraight with fraud and spight,
Ne in good nor goodnes taken delight :
But kindle coales of conteck and yre,
Wherewith they sette all the world on fire :
Which when they thinken agayne to quench
With holy water, they doen hem all drench.

They saye they con to heauen the high way,
But by my soule I dare vndersaye, 91
They neuer sette foote in that same troade,
But balk the right way, and strayen abroad.
They boast they han the deuill at commaund :
But aske hem therefore, what they han paund.
Marrie that great *Pan* bought with deare borrow,
To quite it from the blacke bowre of sorrowe.
But they han sold thilk same long agoe :
For thy woulden drawe with hem many moe.
But let hem gange alone a Gods name : 100
As they han brewed, so let hem beare blame.

HOBBINOLL.

Diggon, I praye thee speake not so dirke.
Such myster saying me seemeth to mirke.

DIGGON.

Then playnely to speake of shepheards most what,
Badde is the best (this english is flatt.)
Their ill hauiour garres men missay,
Both of their doctrine, and of their faye.
They sayne the world is much war then it wont,
All for her shepheards bene beastly and blont.
Other sayne, but how truely I note, 110
All for they holden shame of theyr cote.
Some sticke not to say, (who te cole on her tongue)
That sike mischiefe graseth hem emong,
All for they casten too much of worlds care,
To deck her Dame, and enrich her heyre :
For such encheason, If you goe nye,
Fewe chymneis reeking you shall espye :
The fatte Oxe, that wont ligge in the stal,
Is nowe fast stalled in her crumenall.
Thus chatten the people in theyr steads, 120
Ylike as a Monster of many heads.
But they that shooten neerest the pricke,
Sayne, other the fat from their beards doen lick.
For bigge Bulles *of Basan* brace hem about,
That with theyr hornes butten the more stoute:
But the leane soules treaden vnder foote.
And to seeke redresse mought little boote :
For liker bene they to pluck away more,
Then ought of the gotten good to restore.
For they bene like foule wagmoires ouergrast,
That if thy galage once sticketh fast, 131
The more to wind it out thou doest swinck,
Thou mought ay deeper and deeper sinck.
Yet better leaue of with a little losse,
Then by much wrestling to leese the grosse.

HOBBINOLL.

Nowe Diggon, I see thou speakest to plaine :
Better it were, a little to feyne,
And cleanly couer, that cannot be cured.
Such il, as is forced, mought nedes be endured.
But of sike pastoures howe done the flocks
creepe ? 140

DIGGON.

Sike as the shepheards, sike bene her sheepe,
For they nill listen to the shepheards voyce,
But if he call hem at theyr good choyce,
They wander at wil, and stray at pleasure,
And to theyr foldes yead at their owne leasure.
But they had be better come at their cal:
For many han into mischiefe fall,
And bene of rauenous Wolues yrent,
All for they nould be buxome and bent.

HOBBINOLL.

Fye on thee Diggon, and all thy foule leasing,
Well is knowne that sith the Saxon king, 151
Neuer was Woolfe seene many nor some,
Nor in all Kent, nor in Christendome:
But the fewer Wooliues (the soth to sayne,)
The more bene the Foxes that here remaine.

DIGGON.

Yes, but they gang in more secrete wise,
And with sheepes clothing doen hem disguise,
They walke not widely as they were wont
For feare of raungers, and the great hunt:
But priuely prolling two and froe, 160
Enaunter they mought be inly knowe.

HOBBINOL.

Or priuie or pert yf any bene,
We han great Bandogs will teare their skinne.

DIGGON.

Indeede thy ball is a bold bigge curre,
And could make a iolly hole in theyr furre.
But not good Dogges hem needeth to chace,
But heedy shepheards to discerne their face.
For all their craft is in their countenaunce,
They bene so graue and full of mayntenaunce.
But shall I tell thee what my selfe knowe, 170
Chaunced to Roffynn not long ygoe?

HOBBINOL.

Say it out Diggon, what euer it hight,
For not but well mought him betight,
He is so meeke, wise, and merciable,
And with his word his worke is conuenable.
Colin clout I wene be his selfe boye,
(Ah for Colin he whilome my ioye)
Shepheards sich, God mought vs many send,
That doen so carefully theyr flocks tend.

DIGGON.

Thilk same shepheard mought I well marke:
He has a Dogge to byte or to barke, 181
Neuer had shepheard so kene a kurre,
That waketh, and if but a leafe sturre.
Whilome there wonnéd a wicked Wolfe,
That with many a Lambe had glutted his gulfe.

And euer at night wont to repayre
Vnto the flocke, when the Welkin shone faire,
Ycladde in clothing of seely sheepe,
When the good old man vsed to sleepe.
Tho at midnight he would barke and ball, 190
(For he had eft learned a curres call.)
As if a Woolfe were emong the sheepe.
With that the shepheard would breake his sleepe,
And send out Lowder (for so his dog hote)
To raunge the fields with wide open throte.
Tho when as Lowder was farre awaye,
This Woluish sheepe would catchen his pray,
A Lambe, or a Kidde, or a weanell wast:
With that to the wood would he speede him fast.
Long time he vsed this slippery pranck, 200
Ere Roffy could for his laboure him thanck.
At end the shepheard his practise spyed,
(For Roffy is wise, and as Argus eyed)
And when at euen he came to the flocke,
Fast in theyr folds he did them locke,
And tooke out the Woolfe in his counterfect cote,
And let out the sheepes bloud at his throte.

HOBBINOLL.

Marry Diggon, what should him affraye,
To take his owne where euer it laye?
For had his wesand bene a little widder, 210
He would haue deuoured both hidder and shidder.

DIGGON.

Mischiefe light on him, and Gods great curse,
Too good for him had bene a great deale worse:
For it was a perilous beast aboue all,
And eke had he cond the shepherds call.
And oft in the night came to the shepecote,
And called Lowder, with a hollow throte,
As if it the old man selfe had bene.
The dog his maisters voice did it weene,
Yet halfe in doubt, he opened the dore, 220
And ranne out, as he was wont of yore.
No sooner was out, but swifter then thought,
Fast by the hyde the Wolfe lowder caught:
And had not Roffy renne to the steuen,
Lowder had be slaine thilke same euen.

HOBBINOLL.

God shield man, he should so ill haue thriue,
All for he did his deuoyr beliue.
If sike bene Wolues, as thou hast told,
How mought we Diggon, hem be-hold.

DIGGON.

How, but with heede and watchfulnesse, 230
Forstallen hem of their wilinesse?
For thy with shepheard sittes not playe,
Or sleepe, as some doen, all the long day:

But euer liggen in watch and ward,
From soddein force theyr flocks for to gard.

HOBBINOLL.

Ah Diggon, thilke same rule were too straight,
All the cold season to wach and waite.
We bene of fleshe, men as other bee.
Why should we be bound to such miseree?
What euer thing lacketh chaungeable rest, 240
Mought needes decay, when it is at best.

DIGGON.

Ah but Hobbinol, all this long tale,
Nought easeth the care, that doth me forhaile.
What shall I doe? what way shall I wend,
My piteous plight and losse to amend?
Ah good Hobbinol, mought I thee praye,
Of ayde or counsell in my decaye.

HOBBINOLL.

Now by my soule Diggon, I lament
The haplesse mischief, that has thee hent,
Nethel.sse thou seest my lowly saile, 250
That froward fortune doth euer auaile.
But were Hobbinoll, as God mought please,
Diggon should soone find fauour and ease.
But if to my cotage thou wilt resort,
So as I can, I wil thee comfort:
There mayst thou ligge in a vetchy bed,
Till fayrer Fortune shewe forth her head.

DIGGON.

Ah Hobbinol, God mought it thee requite.
Diggon on fewe such freends did euer lite.

Diggons Embleme. 260
Inopem me copia fecit.

GLOSSE.

The Dialecte and phrase of speache in this Dialogue, seemeth somewhat to differ from the comen. The cause whereof is supposed to be, by occasion of the party herein meant, who being very freend to the Author hereof, had bene long in forraine countryes, and there seene many disorders, which he here recounteth to Hobbinoll.

Bidde her) Bidde good morrow. For to bidde, is to praye, whereof commeth beades for prayers, and so they say, To bidde his beades. s. to saye his prayers.

Wightly) quicklye, or sodenlye.

Chaffred) solde.

Dead at mischiefe) an vnusuall speache, but much vsurped of Lidgate, and sometime of Chaucer.

Leefe) deare. Ethe) easie.

Thrice thre moones) nine monethes.

Measured) for traueled. Wae) woe Northernly.
Eeked) encreased. Caruen) cutte.
Kenne) know. Cragge) neck.
State) stoutely. Stanck) wearie or fainte.

And nowe) He applieth it to the tyme of the yeare, which is in thend of haruest, which they call the fall of the leafe: at which tyme the Westerne wynde beareth most swaye.

A mocke) Imitating Horace, Debes ludibrium ventis.

Lorne) lefte. Soote) swete.

Vncouthe) vnknowen.

Hereby there) here and there.

As the brighte) Translated out of Mantuane.

Emprise) for enterprise. Per Syncopen.

Contek) strife. Trode) path.

Marrie that) that is, their soules, which by pcpish Exorcismes and practises they damme to hell.

Blacke) hell. Gange) goe. Mister) maner.
Mirke) obscure. Warre) worse.
Crumenall) purse. Brace) compasse.

Encheson) occasion.

Ouergrast) ouergrowen with grasse.

Galage) shoe. The grosse) the whole.

Buxome and bent) meeke and obedient.

Saxon king) K. Edgare, that reigned here in Brytanye in the yeare of our Lorde. Which king caused all the Wolues, whereof then was store in thys countrye, by a proper policie to be destroyed. So as neuer since that time, there haue ben Wolues here founde, vnlesse they were brought from other countryes. And therefore Hobbinoll rebuketh him of vntruth, for saying there be Wolues in England.

Nor in Christendome) This saying seemeth to be strange and vnreasonable: but indede it was wont to be an olde prouerbe and comen phrase. The original whereof was, for that most part of England in the reigne of king Ethelbert was christened, Kent onely except, which remayned long after in mysbeliefe and vnchristened, So that Kent was counted no part of Christendome.

Great hunt) Executing of lawes and iustice.

Enaunter) least that.

Inly) inwardly. Afforesayde.

Priuie or pert) openly sayth Chaucer.

Roffy) The name of a shepehearde in Marot his Æglogue of Robin and the Kinge. Whome he here commendeth for greate care and wise gouernance of his flock.

Colin cloute) Nowe I thinke no man doubteth but by Colin is euer meante the Authour selfe. Whose especiall good freend Hobbinoll sayth he is, or more rightly Mayster Gabriel Haruey: of whose speciall commendation, aswell in Poetrye as Rhetorike and other choyce learning, we haue lately had a sufficient tryall in diuerse his workes, but specially in his Musarum Lachrymæ, and his late Gratulationum Valdinensium which boke in the progresse at Audley in Essex, he dedicated in writing to her Maiestie. Afterward presenting the same in print vnto her Highnesse at the worshipfull Maister Capells in Hertfordshire. Beside other his sundrye most rare and very notable writings, partely vnder vnknown Tytles, and partly vnder counterfayt names, as hys Tyrannomastix, his Ode Natalitia, his Rameidos, and esspecially that parte of Philomusus, his diuine Anticosmopolita, and diuers other of lyke importance. As also by the names of other shepheardes, he couereth the persons of diuers other his familiar freendes and best acquayntaunce.

This tale of Roffy seemeth to coloure some particular Action of his. But what, I certeinlye know not.

Wonned) haunted.   Welkin) skie.   Afforesaid.
A Weanell waste) a weaned youngling.
Hidder and shidder) He and she. Male and Female.
Steuen) Noyse.   Beliue) quickly.
What euer) Ouids verse translated.

    Quod caret alterna requie, durabile non est.

Forehaile) drawe or distresse.
Vetchie) of Pease strawe.

          Embleme.
This is the saying of Narcissus in Ouid. For when the foolishe boye by beholding hys face in the brooke, fell in loue with his owne likenesse: and not hable to content him selfe with much looking thereon, he cryed out, that plentye made him poore, meaning that much gazing had bereft him of sence. But our Diggon vseth it to other purpose, as who that by tryall of many wayes had founde the worst, and through greate plentye was fallen into greate penurie. This poesie I knowe, to haue bene much vsed of the author, and to suche like effecte, as fyrste Narcissus spake it.

October.

Ægloga decima.

ARGVMENT.

IN Cuddie is set out the perfecte paterne of a Poete, whiche finding no maintenaunce of his state and studies, complayneth of the contempte of Poetrie, and the causes thereof : Specially hauing bene in all ages, and euen amongst the most barbarous alwayes of singular accounpt and honor, and being indede so worthy and commendable an arte : or rather no arte, but a diuine gift and heauenly instinct not to bee gotten by laboure and learning, but adorned with both : and poured into the witte by a certaine ἐνθουσιασμός. and celestiall inspiration, as the Author hereof els where at large discourseth, in his booke called the English Poete, which booke being lately come to my hands, I mynde also by Gods grace vpon further aduisement to publish.

PIERCE.   CVDDIE.

CVddie, for shame hold vp thy heauye head,
    And let vs cast with what delight to chace,
And weary thys long lingring *Phœbus* race.
Whilome thou wont the shepheards laddes to leade,
In rymes, in ridles, and in bydding base :
Now they in thee, and thou in sleepe art dead.

CVDDYE.

Piers, I haue pyped erst so long with payne,
That all mine Oten reedes bene rent and wore:
And my poore Muse hath spent her spared store,
Yet little good hath got, and much lesse gayne.   10
Such pleasaunce makes the Grashopper so poore,
And ligge so layd, when Winter doth her straine.

The dapper ditties, that I wont deuise,
To feede youthes fancie, and the flocking fry,
Delighten much : what I the bett for thy ?
They han the pleasure, I a sclender prise.
I beate the bush, the byrds to them doe flye
What good thereof to Cuddie can arise ?

PIERS.

Cuddie, the prayse is better, then the price,
The glory eke much greater then the gayne :
O what an honor is it, to restraine 21
The lust of lawlesse youth with good aduice :
Or pricke them forth with pleasaunce of thy
vaine,
Whereto thou list their trayned willes entice.

Soone as thou gynst to sette thy notes in frame,
O how the rurall routes to thee doe cleaue :
Seemeth thou dost their soule of sence bereaue,
All as the shepheard, that did fetch his dame
From Plutoes balefull bowre withouten leaue :
His musicks might the hellish hound did tame.

CVDDIE.

So praysen babes the Peacoks spotted traine,
And wondren at bright Argus blazing eye :
But who rewards him ere the more for thy ?
Or feedes him once the fuller by a graine ?
Sike prayse is smoke, that sheddeth in the skye,
Sike wordsbene wynd,and wastensooneinvayne.

PIERS.

Abandon then the base and viler clowne,
Lyft vp thy selfe out of the lowly dust :
And sing of bloody Mars, of wars, of giusts, 39
Turne thee to those, that weld the awful crowne.
To doubted Knights, whose woundlesse armour
rusts,
And helmes vnbruzed wexen dayly browne.

There may thy Muse display her fluttryng wing,
And stretch herselfe at large from East to West:
Whither thou list in fayre Elisa rest,
Or if thee please in bigger notes to sing,
Aduaunce the worthy whome shee loueth best,
That first the white beare to the stake did bring.

And when the stubborne stroke of stronger
stounds,
Has somewhat slackt the tenor of thy string :
Of loue and lustihead tho mayst thou sing, 51
And carrol lowde, and leade the Myllers rownde,
All were Elisa one of thilke same ring.
So mought our Cuddies name to Heauen sownde.

CVDDYE.

Indeede the Romish Tityrus, I heare,
Through his Mecœnas left his Oaten reede,
Whereon he earst had taught his flocks to feede,
And laboured lands to yield the timely eare,

And eft did sing of warres and deadly drede,
So as the Heauens did quake his verse to here.

But ah Mecœnas is yclad in claye, 61
And great Augustus long ygoe is dead :
And all the worthies liggen wrapt in leade,
That matter made for Poets on to play :
For euer, who in derring doe were dreade,
The loftie verse of hem was loued aye.

But after vertue gan for age to stoupe,
And mighty manhode brought a bedde of ease.
The vaunting Poets found nought worth a pease,
To put in preace emong the learned troupe. 70
Tho gan the streames of flowing wittes to cease,
And sonnebright honour pend in shamefull
coupe.

And if that any buddes of Poesie,
Yet of the old stocke gan to shoote agayne :
Or it mens follies mote be forst to fayne,
And rolle with rest in rymes of rybaudrye :
Or as it sprong, it wither must agayne :
Tom Piper makes vs better melodie.

PIERS.

O pierlesse Poesye, where is then thy place ?
If nor in Princes pallace thou doe sitt : 80
(And yet is Princes pallace the most fitt)
Ne brest of baser birth doth thee embrace.
Then make thee winges of thine aspyring wit,
And, whence thou camst, flye backe to heauen
apace.

CVDDIE.

Ah Percy it is all to weake and wanne,
So high to sore, and make so large a flight :
Her peeced pyneons bene not so in plight,
For Colin fittes such famous flight to scanne :
He, were he not with loue so ill bedight,
Would mount as high, and sing as soote as
Swanne. 90

PIERS.

Ah fon, for loue does teach him climbe so hie,
And lyftes him vp out of the loathsome myre :
Such immortall mirrhor, as he doth admire,
Would rayse ones mynd aboue the starry skie.
And cause a caytiue corage to aspire,
For lofty loue doth loath a lowly eye.

CVDDIE.

All otherwise the state of Poet stands,
For lordly loue is such a Tyranne fell :
That where he rules, all power he doth expell.
The vaunted verse a vacant head demaundes,
Ne wont with crabbed care the Muses dwell.
Vnwisely weaues, that takes two webbes in
hand.

Who euer casts to compasse weightye prise,
And thinks to throwe out thondring words of
   threate:
Let powre in lauish cups and thriftie bitts of
   meate,
For *Bacchus* fruite is frend to *Phœbus* wise.
And when with Wine the braine begins to sweate,
The nombers flowe as fast as spring doth ryse.

Thou kenst not *Percie* howe the ryme should
   rage.
O if my temples were distaind with wine, 110
And girt in girlonds of wild Yuie twine,
How I could reare the Muse on stately stage,

And teache her tread aloft in bus-kin fine,
With queint *Bellona* in her equipage.

But ah my corage cooles ere it be warme,
For thy, content vs in thys humble shade:
Where no such troublous tydes han vs assayde,
Here we our slender pipes may safely charme.

PIRES.

And when my Gates shall han their bellies layd:
Cuddie shall haue a Kidde to store his farme.

Cuddies Embleme. 121
Agitante calescimus illo &c.

GLOSSE.

This Æglogue is made in imitation of Theocritus
his xvi. Idilion, wherein hee reproued the Tyranne
Hiero of Syracuse for his nigardise towarde
Poetes, in whome is the power to make men
immortal for theyr good dedes, or shameful for
their naughty lyfe. And the lyke also is in
Mantuane, The style hereof as also that in
Theocritus, is more loftye then the rest, and
applyed to the heighte of Poeticall witte.
Cuddie) I doubte whether by Cuddie be specified
the authour selfe, or some other. For in the
eyght Æglogue the same person was brought in,
singing a Cantion of Colins making, as he sayth.
So that some doubt, that the persons be different.
Whilome) sometime.   Oaten reedes) Auena.
Ligge so liyde) lye so faynt and vnlustye.
Dapper) pretye.
Frye) is a bold Metaphore, forced from the spawn-
ing fishes. For the multitude of young fish be
called the frye.
To restraine.) This place seemeth to conspyre with
Plato, who in his first booke de Legibus sayth,
that the first inuention of Poetry was of very
vertuous intent. For at what time an infinite
number of youth vsually came to theyr great
solemne feastes called Panegyrica, which they
vsed euery fiue yeere to hold, some learned man
being more hable then the rest, for speciall gyftes
of wytte and Musicke, would take vpon him to
sing fine verses to the people, in prayse eyther of
vertue or of victory or of immortality or such
like. At whose wonderful gyft al men being
astonied and as it were rauished, with delight,
thinking (as it was indeed) that he was inspired
from aboue, called him vatem: which kinde of
men afterwarde framing their verses to lighter
musick (as of musick be many kinds, some
sadder, some lighter, some martiall, some
heroical: and so diuersely eke affect the mynds
of men) found out lighter matter of Poesie also,
some playing wyth loue, some scorning at mens
fashions, some powred out in pleasures, and so
were called Poetes or makers.
Sence bereaue) what the secrete working of Musick
is in the myndes of men, aswell appeareth, hereby, that some of the auncient Philosophers, and
those the moste wise, as Plato and Pythagoras
held for opinion, that the mynd was made of
a certaine harmonie and musicall nombers, for
the great compassion and likenes of affection in
thone and in the other as also by that memorable

history of Alexander: to whom when as Timotheus
the great Musitian playd the Phrygian melodie,
it is said, that he was distraught with such
vnwonted fury, that streight way rysing from the
table in great rage, he caused himselfe to be
armed, as ready to goe to warre (for that musick
is very war like:) And immediatly whenas the
Musitian chaunged his stroke into the Lydian
and Ionique harmony, he was so furr from
warring, that he sat as styl, as if he had bene in
matters of counsell. Such might is in musick.
Wherefore Plato and Aristotle forbid the Arabian
Melodie from children and youth. For that
being altogither on the fyft and vii, tone, it is of
great force to molifie and quench the kindly
courage, which vseth to burne in yong brests.
So that it is not incredible which the Poete here
sayth, that Musick can bereaue the soule of
sence.
The shepheard that) Orpheus: of whom is sayd,
that by his excellent skil in Musick and Poetry,
he recouered his wife Eurydice from hell.
Argus eyes) of Argus is before said, that Iuno to
him committed hir husband Iupiter his Paragon
Iô, bicause he had an hundred eyes: but afterwarde Mercury wyth hys Musick lulling Argus
aslepe, slew him and brought Iô away, whose
eyes it is sayd that Iuno for his eternall memory
placed in her byrd the Peacocks tayle. For
those coloured spots indeede resemble eyes.
Woundlesse armour) vnwounded in warre, doe rust
through long peace.
Display) A poeticall metaphore: whereof the meaning is, that if the Poet list showe his skill in
matter of more dignitie, then is the homely
Æglogue, good occasion is him offered of higher
veyne and more Heroicall argument, in the
person of our most gratious soueraign, whom
(as before) he calleth Elisa. Or if mater of
knighthoode and cheualrie please him better,
that there be many Noble and valiaunt men, that
are both worthy of his payne in theyr deserued
prayses, and also fauourers of hys skil and
faculty.
The worthy) he meaneth (as I guesse) the most
honorable and renowmed the Erle of Leycester,
whom by his cognisance (although the same be
also proper to other) rather then by his name he
bewrayeth, being not likely, that the names of
noble princes be known to country clowne.
Slack) that is when thou chaungest thy verse from

stately discourse, to matter of more pleasaunce and delight.

The Millers) a kind of daunce.

Ring) company of dauncers.

The Romish Tityrus) wel knowen to be Virgile, who by Mecænas means was brought into the fauour of the Emperor Augustus, and by him moued to write in loftier kinde, then he erst had doen.

Whereon) in these three verses are the three seuerall workes of Virgile intended. For in teaching his flocks to feede, is meant his Æglogues. In labouring of lands, is hys Bucoliques. In singing of wars and deadly dreade, is his diuine Æneis figured.

In derring doe) In manhoode and cheualrie.

For euer) He sheweth the cause, why Poetes were wont be had in such honor of noble men ; that is, that by them their worthines and valor shold through theyr famous Posies be commended to al posterities. Wherfore it is sayd, that Achilles had neuer bene so famous, as he is, but for Homeres immortall verses. Which is the only aduantage, which he had of Hector. And also that Alexander the great comming to his tombe in Sigeus, with naturall teares blessed him, that euer was his hap to be honoured with so excellent a Poets work : as so renowmed and ennobled onely by hys meanes. Which being declared in a most eloquent Oration of Tullies, is of Petrarch no lesse worthely sette forth in a sonet

Giunto Alexandro a la famosa tomba
Del fero Achille sospirando disse
O fortunato che si chiara tromba. Trouasti &c.

And that such account hath bene alwayes made of Poetes, aswell sheweth this that the worthy Scipio in all his warres against Carthage and Numantia had euermore in his company, and that in a most familiar sort the good olde Poet Ennius: as also that Alexander destroying Thebes, when he was enformed that the famous Lyrick Poet Pindarus was borne in that citie, not onely commaunded streightly, that no man should vpon payne of death do any violence to that house by fire or otherwise : but also specially spared most, and some highly rewarded, that were of hys kinne. So fauoured he the only name of a Poete. Whych prayse otherwise was in the same man no lesse famous, that when he came to ransacking of king Darius coffers, whom he lately had ouerthrowen, he founde in a little coffer of siluer the two bookes of Homers works, as layd vp there for speciall iewells and richesse, which he taking thence, put one of them dayly in his bosome, and thother euery night layde vnder his pillowe. Such honor haue Poetes alwayes found in the sight of princes and noble men. Which this author here very well sheweth, as els where more notably.

But after) he sheweth the cause of contempt of Poetry to be idlenesse and basenesse of mynd.

Pent) shut vp in slouth, as in a coope or cage.

Tom piper) An Ironicall Sarcasmus, spoken in derision of these rude wits, whych make more account of a ryming rybaud, then of skill grounded vpon learning and iudgment.

Ne brest) the meaner sort of men.

Her peeced pineons) vnperfect skil. Spoken with humble modestie.

As soote as Swanne) The comparison seemeth to be strange : for the swanne hath euer wonne small commendation for her swete singing : but it is sayd of the learned that the swan a little before hir death, singeth most pleasantly, as prophecying by a secrete instinct her neere destinie As wel sayth the Poete elswhere in one of his sonetts.

The siluer swanne doth sing before her dying day
As shee that feeles the deepe delight that is in death &c.

Immortall myrrhour) Beauty, which is an excellent obiect of Poetica.l spirites, as appeareth by the worthy Petrachs saying.

Fiorir faceua il mio debile ingegno
A la sua ombra, et crescer ne gli affanni.

A caytiue corage) a base and abiect minde.

For lofty loue) I think this playing with the letter to be rather a fault then a figure, aswel in our English tongue, as it hath bene alwayes in the Latine, called Cacozelon.

A vacant) imitateth Mantuanes saying. vacuum curis diuina cerebrum Poscit.

Lauish cups) Resembleth that comen verse Fæcundi calices quem non fecere disert...m.

O if my) He seemeth here to be rauished with a Poetical furie. For (if one rightly mark) the numbers rise so ful, and the verse groweth so big, that it seemeth he hath forgot the meanenesse of shepheards state and stile.

Wild yuie) for it is dedicated to Bacchus and therefore it is sayd that the Mænades (that is Bacchus franticke priestes) vsed in theyr sacrifice to carry Thyrsos, which were pointed staues or Iauelins, wrapped about with yuie.

In buskin) it was the maner of Poetes and plaiers in tragedies to were buskins, as also in Comedies to vse stockes and light shoes. So that the buskin in Poetry is vsed for tragical matter, as is said in Virgile. Sola sophocleo tua carmina digna cothurno. And the like in Horace, Magnum loqui, nitique cothurno.

Queint) strange Bellona ; the goddesse of battaile. that is Pallas, which may therefore wel be called queint for that (as Lucian saith) when Iupiter hir father was in traueile of her, he caused his sonne Vulcane with his axe to hew his head. Out of which leaped forth lustely a valiant damsell armed at all poyntes, whom seeing Vulcane so faire and comely, lightly leaping to her, proferred her some cortesie, which the Lady disdeigning, shaked her speare at him, and threatned his saucinesse. Therefore such straungenesse is well applyed to her.

Æquipage.) order.   Tydes) seasons.

Charme) temper and order. For Charmes were wont to be made by verses as Ouid sayth.

Aut si carminibus.

Embleme.

Hereby is meant, as also in the whole course of this Æglogue, that Poetry is a diuine instinct and vnnatural rage passing the reache of comen reason. Whom Piers answereth Epiphonematicos as admiring the excellencye of the skyll whereof in Cuddie hee hadde alreadye hadde a taste.

Nouember.

Ægloga vndecima.

ARGVMENT.

*I*N this xi. Æglogue he bewayleth the death
of some mayden of greate bloud, whom he
calleth Dido. The personage is secrete, and to
me altogether vnknowne, albe of him selfe I often
required the same. This Æglogue is made in
imitation of Marot his song, which he made vpon
the death of Loys the frenche Queene. But farre
passing his reache, and in myne opinion all other
the Eglogues of this booke.

THENOT.   COLIN.

*C*Olin my deare, when shall it please thee
    sing,
As thou were wont songs of some iouisaunce?
Thy Muse to long slombreth in sorrowing,
Lulled a sleepe through loues misgouernaunce.
Now somewhat sing, whose endles souenaunce,
Emong the shepheards swaines may aye re-
    maine,
Whether thee list thy loued lasse aduaunce,
Or honor *Pan* with hymnes of higher vaine.

COLIN.

Thenot, now nis the time of merimake.
Nor *Pan* to herye, nor with loue to playe: 10
Sike myrth in May is meetest for to make,
Or summer shade vnder the cocked haye.

But nowe sadde Winter welked hath the day,
And *Phœbus* weary of his yerely taske,
Ystabled hath his steedes in lowlye laye,
And taken vp his ynne in *Fishes* haske.
Thilke sollein season sadder plight doth aske:
And loatheth sike delightes, as thou doest
    prayse:
The mornefull Muse in myrth now list ne maske,
As shee was wont in youngth and sommer
    dayes.   20
But if thou algate lust light virelayes,
And looser songs of loue to vnderfong
Who but thy selfe deserues sike Poetes prayse?
Relieue thy Oaten pypes, that sleepen long.

THENOT.

The Nightingale is souereigne of song,
Before him sits the Titmose silent bee:
And I vnfitte to thrust in skilfull thronge,
Should *Colin* make iudge of my fooleree.
Nay, better learne of hem, that learned bee,
And han be watered at the Muses well: 30
The kindlye dewe drops from the higher tree,
And wets the little plants that lowly dwell.
But if sadde winters wrathe and season chill,
Accorde not with thy Muses meriment:
To sadder times thou mayst attune thy quill,
And sing of sorrowe and deathes dreeriment.

For deade is Dido, dead alas and drent,
Dido the greate shepehearde his daughter
   sheene :
The fayrest May she was that euer went,
Her like shee has not left behinde I weene. 40
And if thou wilt bewayle my wofull tene :
I shall thee giue yond Cosset for thy payne :
And if thy rymes as rownd and rufull bene,
As those that did thy *Rosalind* complayne,
Much greater gyfts for guerdon thou shalt
   gayne,
Then Kidde or Cosset, which I thee bynempt :
Then vp I say, thou iolly shepheard swayne,
Let not my small demaund be so contempt.

     COLIN.

Thenot to that I choose, thou doest me tempt,
But ah to well I wote my humble vaine,   50
And howe my rymes bene rugged and vnkempt :
Yet as I conne, my conning I will strayne.

VP then *Melpomene* thou mournefulst Muse
   of nyne,
Such cause of mourning neuer hadst afore :
Vp grieslie ghostes and vp my rufull ryme,
Matter of myrth now shalt thou haue no more.
For dead shee is, that myrth thee made of yore.
   Dido my deare alas is dead,
   Dead and lyeth wrapt in lead :
     O heauie herse,   60
Let screaming teares be poured out in store :
     O carefull verse.

Shepheards, that by your flocks on Kentish
   downes abyde,
Waile ye this wofull waste of natures warke :
Waile we the wight, whose presence was our
   pryde :
Waile we the wight, whose absence is our carke.
The sonne of all the world is dimme and darke :
   The earth now lacks her wonted light,
   And all we dwell in deadly night,
     O heauie herse.   70
Breake we our pypes, that shrild as lowde as
   Larke,
     O carefull verse.

Why doe we longer liue, (ah why liue we so
   long)
Whose better dayes death hath shut vp in woe ?
   The fayrest floure our gyrlond all emong,
   Is faded quite and into dust ygoe.
Sing now ye shepheards daughters, sing no moe
   The songs that *Colin* made in her prayse,
   But into weeping turne your wanton layes,
     O heauie herse,   80
Now is time to dye. Nay time was long ygoe,
     O carefull verse.

Whence is it, that the flouret of the field doth
   fade,
And lyeth buryed long in Winters bale :
Yet soone as spring his mantle doth displaye,
It floureth fresh, as it should neuer fayle ?
But thing on earth that is of most availe,
   As vertues braunch and beauties budde,
   Reliuen not for any good.
     O heauie herse,   90
The braunch once dead, the budde eke needes
   must quaile,
     O carefull verse.

She while she was, (that was, a woful word to
   sayne)
For beauties prayse and plesaunce had no pere :
So well she couth the shepherds entertayne,
With cakes and cracknells and such country
   chere.
Ne would she scorne the simple shepheards
   swaine,
   For she would cal hem often heme
   And giue hem curds and clouted Creame.
     O heauie herse,   100
Als *Colin cloute* she would not once disdayne.
     O carefull verse.

But nowe sike happy cheere is turnd to heauie
   chaunce,
Such pleasaunce now displast by dolors dint :
All Musick sleepes, where death doth leade the
   daunce,
And shepherds wonted solace is extinct.
The blew in black, the greene in gray is tinct,
   The gaudie girlonds deck her graue,
   The faded flowres her corse embraue.
     O heauie herse,   110
Morne nowe my Muse, now morne with teares
   besprint.
     O carefull verse.

O thou greate shepheard *Lobbin*, how great is
   thy griefe,
Where bene the nosegayes that she dight for thee :
The colourd chaplets wrought with a chiefe,
The knotted rushrings, and gilte Rosemaree ?
For shee deemed nothing too deere for thee.
   Ah they bene all yclad in clay,
   One bitter blast blewe all away.
     O heauie herse,   120
Thereof nought remaynes but the memoree.
     O carefull verse.

Ay me that dreerie death should strike so
   mortall stroke,
That can vndoe Dame natures kindly course :
The faded lockes fall from the loftie oke,
The flouds do gaspe, for dryed is theyr sourse,

And flouds of teares flowe in theyr stead
    perforse.
  The mantled medowes mourne,
  Theyr sondry colours tourne.
        O heauie herse,   130
The heauens doe melt in teares without remorse.
        O carefull verse.

The feeble flocks in field refuse their former
    foode,
And hang theyr heads, as they would learne to
    weepe :
The beastes in forest wayle as they were woode,
Except the Wolues, that chase the wandring
    sheepe :
Now she is gon that safely did hem keepe,
  The Turtle on the bared braunch,
  Laments the wound, that death did launch.
        O heauie herse,   140
And *Philomele* her song with teares doth steepe.
        O carefull verse.

The water Nymphs, that wont with her to sing
    and daunce,
And for her girlond Oliue braunches beare,
Now balefull boughes of Cypres doen aduaunce:
The Muses, that were wont greene bayes to
    weare,
Now bringen bitter Eldre braunches seare,
  The fatall sisters eke repent,
  Her vitall threde so soone was spent.
        O heauie herse,   150
Morne now my Muse, now morne with heauie
    cheare.
        O carefull verse.

O trustlesse state of earthly things, and slipper
    hope
Of mortal men, that swincke and sweate for
    nought,
And shooting wide, doe misse the marked
    scope :
Now haue I learnd (a lesson derely bought)
That nys on earth assuraunce to be sought :
  For what might be in earthlie mould,
  That did her buried body hould,
        O heauie herse,   160
Yet saw I on the beare when it was brought
        O carefull verse.

But maugre death, and dreaded sisters deadly
    spight,
And gates of hel, and fyrie furies forse :
She hath the bonds broke of eternall night,
Her soule vnbodied of the burdenous corpse.

Why then weepes Lobbin so without remorse ?
  O Lobb, thy losse no longer lament,
  Dido nis dead, but into heauen hent.
        O happye herse,   170
Cease now my Muse, now cease thy sorrowes
    sourse,
        O ioyfull verse.

Why wayle we then ? why weary we the Gods
    with playnts,
As if some euill were to her betight ?
She raignes a goddesse now emong the saintes,
That whilome was the saynt of shepheards
    light :
And is enstalled nowe in heauens hight.
  I see thee blessed soule, I see,
  Walke in *Elisian* fieldes so free.
        O happy herse,   180
Might I once come to thee (O that I might)
        O ioyfull verse.

Vnwise and wretched men to weete whats good
    or ill,
We deeme of Death as doome of ill desert :
But knewe we fooles, what it vs bringes vntil,
Dye would we dayly, once it to expert.
No daunger there the shepheard can astert :
  Fayre fieldes and pleasaunt layes there benc,
  The fieldes ay fresh, the grasse ay greene :
        O happy herse,   190
Make hast ye shepheards, thether to reuert,
        O ioyfull verse.

Dido is gone afore (whose turne shall be the
    next ?)
There liues shee with the blessed Gods in blisse,
There drincks she *Nectar* with *Ambrosia* mixt,
And ioyes enioyes, that mortall men doe misse.
The honor now of highest gods she is,
  That whilome was poore shepheards pryde,
  While here on earth she did abyde.
        O happy herse,   200
Ceasse now my song, my woe now wasted is.
        O ioyfull verse.

THENOT.

Ay francke shepheard, how bene thy verses
    meint
With doolful pleasaunce, so as I ne wotte,
Whether reioyce or weepe for great constrainte?
Thyne be the cossette, well hast thow it gotte.
Vp *Colin* vp, ynough thou morned hast,
Now gynnes to mizzle, hye we homeward fast.

        Colins Embleme.
        La mort ry mord.   210

GLOSSE.

Iouisaunce) myrth.   Souenaunce) remembraunce.
Herie) honour.
Welked) shortned or empayred. As the Moone
being in the waine is sayde of Lidgate to welk.
In lowly lay) according to the season of the moneth
Nouember, when the sonne draweth low in the
South toward his Tropick or returne.
In fishes haske) the sonne, reigneth that is, in the
signe Pisces all Nouember. A haske is a wicker
pad, wherein they vse to cary fish.
Virelaies) a light kind of song.
Bee watred) For it is a saying of Poetes, that they
haue dronk of the Muses well Castalias, whereof
was before sufficiently sayd.
Dreriment) dreery and heauy cheere.
The great shepheard) is some man of high degree,
and not as some vainely suppose God Pan. The
person both of the shephearde and of Dido is
vnknowen and closely buried in the Authors
conceipt. But out of doubt I am, that it is not
Rosalind, as some imagin: for he speaketh soone
after of her also.
Shene) fayre and shining.   May) for mayde.
Tene) sorrow.   Guerdon) reward.
Bynempt) bequethed.
Cosset) a lambe brought vp without the dam.
Vnkempt) Incompti Not comed, that is rude and
vnhansome.
Melpomene) The sadde and waylefull Muse vsed
of Poets in honor of Tragedies: as saith Virgile
Melpomene Tragico proclamat mæsta boatu.
Vp griesly gosts) The maner of Tragicall Poetes,
to call for helpe of Furies and damned ghostes:
so is Hecuba of Euripides, and Tantalus brought
in of Seneca. And the rest of the rest.
Herse) is the solemne obsequie in funeralles.
Wast of) decay of so beautifull a peece.
Carke) care.
Ah why) an elegant Epanorthosis. As also soone
after. Nay time was long ago.
Flouret) a diminutiue for a little floure. This is
a notable and sententious comparison A minore
ad maius.
Reliuen not) liue not againe .s. not in theyr earthly
bodies: for in heauen they enioy their due
reward.
The braunch) He meaneth Dido, who being, as it
were the mayne braunch now withered the buddes
that is beautie (as he sayd afore) can no more
flourish.
With cakes) fit for shepheards bankets.
Heame) for home. After the northerne pro-
nouncing.
Tinct) deyed or stayned.
The gaudie) the meaning is, that the things, which
were the ornaments of her lyfe, are made the
honor of her funerall, as is vsed in buriálls.
Lobbin) the name of a shepherd, which seemeth to
haue bene the louer and deere frende of Dido.
Rushrings) agreeable for such base gyftes.
Faded lockes) dryed leaues. As if Nature her selfe
bewayled the death of the Mayde.
Sourse) spring.
Mantled medowes) for the sondry flowres are like
a Mantle or couerlet wrought with many colours.
Philomele) the Nightingale. Whome the Poetes
faine once to haue bene a Ladye of great beauty,
till being rauished by hir sisters husbande, she

desired to be turned into a byrd of her name.
Whose complaintes be very well set forth of
Ma. George Gaskin a wittie gentleman, and the
very chefe of our late rymers, who and if some
partes of learning wanted not (albee it is well
knowen he altogyther wanted not learning) no
doubt would haue attayned to the excellencye of
those famous Poets. For gifts of wit and
naturall promptnesse appeare in hym aboun-
dantly.
Cypresse) vsed of the old Paynims in the furnishing
of their funerall Pompe. And properly the signe
of all sorow and heauinesse.
The fatall sisters) Clotho Lachesis and Atropos,
daughters of Herebus and the Nighte, whom the
Poetes fayne to spinne the life of man, as it were
a long threde, which they drawe out in length,
till his fatal howre and timely death be come;
but if by other casualtie his dayes be abridged,
then one of them, that is Atropos, is sayde to
haue cut the threde in twain. Hereof commeth
a common verse.

Clotho colum baiulat, lachesis trahit, Atropos
occat.

O trustlesse) a gallant exclamation moralized with
great wisedom and passionate wyth great
affection.
Beare) a frame, wheron they vse to lay the dead
corse.
Furies) of Poetes be feyned to be three, Persephone
Alecto and Megera, which are sayd to be the
Authours of all euill and mischiefe.
Eternall might) Is death or darknesse of hell.
Betight) happened.
I see) A liuely Icon, or representation as if he saw
her in heauen present.
Elysian fieldes) be deuised of Poetes to be a place
of pleasure like Paradise, where the happye soules
doe rest in peace and eternal happynesse.
Dye would) The very expresse saying of Plato in
Phædone.
Astert) befall vnwares.
Nectar and Ambrosia) be feigned to be the drink
and foode of the gods: Ambrosia they liken to
Manna in scripture and Nectar to be white like
Creme, whereof is a proper tale of Hebe, that
spilt a cup of it, and stayned the heauens, as yet
appeareth. But I haue already discoursed that
at large in my Commentarye vpon the dreames
of the same Authour.
Meynt) Mingled.

Emblem.

Which is as much to say, as death biteth not. For
although by course of nature we be borne to dye,
and being ripened with age, as with a timely
haruest, we must be gathered in time, or els of
our selues we fall like rotted ripe fruite fro the
tree yet death is not to be counted for euil, nor
(as the Poete sayd a little before) as doome of ill
desert. For though the trespasse of the first man
brought death into the world, as the guerdon of
sinne, yet being ouercome by the death of one,
that dyed for al, it is now made (as Chaucer
sayth) the grene path way to lyfe. So that it
agreeth well with that was sayd, that Death
byteth not (that is) hurteth not at all.

December.

Ægloga Duodecima.

ARGVMENT.

THis Æglogue (euen as the first beganne) is ended with a complaynte of Colin to God Pan. Wherein as weary of his former wayes, he proportioneth his life to the foure seasons of the yeare, comparing hys youthe to the spring time, when he was fresh and free from loues follye. His manhoode to the sommer, which he sayth, was consumed with greate heate and excessiue drouth caused throughe a Comet or blasinge starre, by which hee meaneth loue, which passion is comenly compared to such flames and immoderate heate. His riper yeares hee resembleth to an vnseasonable harueste wherein the fruites fall ere they be rype. His latter age to winters chyll and frostie season, now drawing neare to his last ende.

THe gentle shepheard satte beside a springe,
All in the shadowe of a bushye brere,
That *Colin* hight, which wel could pype and singe,
For he of *Tityrus* his songs did lere.
　　There as he satte in secreate shade alone,
　　Thus gan he make of loue his piteous mone.

O soueraigne *Pan* thou God of shepheards all,
Which of our tender Lambkins takest keepe:
And when our flocks into mischaunce mought fall,
Doest saue from mischiefe the vnwary sheepe:

Als of their maisters hast no lesse regarde,
Then of the flocks, which thou doest watch and ward:

I thee beseche (so be thou deigne to heare,
Rude ditties tund to shepheards Oaten reede,
Or if I euer sonet song so cleare,
As it with pleasaunce mought thy fancie feede)
　　Hearken awhile from thy greene cabinet,
　　The rurall song of carefull Colinet.

Whilome in youth, when flowrd my ioyfull spring,
Like Swallow swift I wandred here and there:
For heate of heedlesse lust me so did sting, 21
That I of doubted daunger had no feare.
　　I went the wastefull woodes and forest wyde,
　　Withouten dreade of Wolues to bene espyed.

I wont to raunge amydde the mazie thickette,
And gather nuttes to make me Christmas game:
And ioyed oft to chace the trembling Pricket,
Or hunt the hartlesse hare, til shee were tame.
　　What wreaked I of wintrye ages waste,
　　Tho deemed I, my spring would euer laste.

How often haue I scaled the craggie Oke, 31
All to dislodge the Rauen of her neste:
Howe haue I wearied with many a stroke
The stately Walnut tree, the while the rest
　　Vnder the tree fell all for nuts at strife:
　　For ylike to me was libertee and lyfe.

And for I was in thilke same looser yeares,
(Whether the Muse so wrought me from my
birth,
Or I tomuch beleeued my shepherd peres)
Somedele ybent to song and musicks mirth.
  A good olde shephearde, *Wrenock* was his
  name, 41
  Made me by arte more cunning in the same.

Fro thence I durst in derring doe compare
With shepheards swayne, what euer fedde in
field :
And if that *Hobbinol* right iudgement bare,
To *Pan* his owne selfe pype I neede not yield.
  For if the flocking Nymphes did folow *Pan*,
  The wiser Muses after *Colin* ranne.

But ah such pryde at length was ill repayde,
The shepheards God (perdie God was he none)
My hurtlesse pleasaunce did me ill vpbraide,
My freedome lorne, my life he lefte to mone.
  Loue they him called, that gaue me check-
  mate,
  But better mought they haue behote him
  Hate.

Tho gan my louely Spring bid me farewel,
And Sommer season sped him to display
(For loue then in the Lyons house did dwell)
The raging fyre, that kindled at his ray.
  A comett stird vp that vnkindly heate,
  That reigned (as men sayd) in *Venus* seate.

Forth was I ledde, not as I wont afore, 61
When choise I had to choose my wandring waye:
But whether luck and loues vnbridled lore
Would leade me forth on Fancies bitte to playe,
  The bush my bedde, the bramble was my
  bowre,
  The Woodes can witnesse many a wofull
  stowre

Where I was wont to seeke the honey Bee,
Working her formall rowmes in Wexen frame :
The grieslie Todestoole growne there mought
  I see
And loathed Paddocks lording on the same.
  And where the chaunting birds luld me a
  sleepe, 71
  The ghastlie Owle her grieuous ynne doth
  keepe.

Then as the springe giues place to elder time,
And bringeth forth the fruite of sommers pryde:
All so my age now passed youngthly pryme,
To thinges of ryper reason selfe applyed.
  And learnd of lighter timber cotes to frame,
  Such as might saue my sheepe and me fro
  shame.

To make fine cages for the Nightingale,
And Baskets of bulrushes was my wont : 80
Who to entrappe the fish in winding sale
Was better seene, or hurtful beastes to hont ?
  I learned als the signes of heauen to ken,
  How *Phœbe* fayles, where *Venus* sittes and
  when.

And tryed time yet taught me greater thinges,
The sodain rysing of the raging seas :
The soothe of byrds by beating of their wings,
The power of herbs, both which can hurt and
  ease :
  And which be wont t'enrage the restlesse
  sheepe,
  And which be wont to worke eternall sleepe.

But ah vnwise and witlesse *Colin cloute*, 91
That kydst the hidden kinds of many a wede :
Yet kydst not ene to cure thy sore hart roote,
Whoseranckling wound as yet does rifelye
  bleede.
  Why liuest thou stil, and yet hast thy deathes
  wound ?
  Why dyest thou stil, and yet aliue art
  founde?

Thus is my sommer worne away and wasted,
Thus is my haruest hastened all to rathe :
The eare that budded faire, is burnt and
  blasted,
And all my hoped gaine is turnd to scathe. 100
  Of all the seede, that in my youth was sowne,
  Was nought but brakes and brambles to be
  mowne.

My boughes with bloosmes that crowned were
  at firste,
And promised of timely fruite such store,
Are left both bare and barrein now at erst
The flattring fruite is fallen to growned before;
  And rotted, ere they were halfe mellow ripe :
  My haruest wast, my hope away dyd wipe.

The fragrant flowres, that in my garden grewe,
Bene withered, as they had bene gathered
  long. 110
Theyr rootes bene dryed vp for lacke of dewe,
Yet dewed with teares they han be euer among.
  Ah who has wrought my *Rosalind* this spight
  To spil the flowres, that should her girlond
  dight ?

And I, that whilome wont to frame my pype,
Vnto the shifting of the shepheards foote :
Sike follies nowe haue gathered as too ripe
And cast hem out, as rotten and vnsoote.
  The loser Lasse I cast to please nomore,
  One if I please, enough is me therefore. 120

And thus of all my haruest hope I haue
Nought reaped but a weedye crop of care :
Which, when I thought haue thresht in swelling
   sheaue,
Cockel for corne, and chaffe for barley bare.
   Soone as the chaffe should in the fan be fynd,
   All was blowne away of the wauering wynd.

So now my yeare drawes to his latter terme,
My spring is spent, my sommer burnt vp quite :
My harueste hasts to stirre vp winter sterne,
And bids him clayme with rigorous rage hys
   right.   130
   So nowe he stormes with many a sturdy stoure,
   So now his blustring blast eche coste doth
   scoure.

The carefull cold hath nypt my rugged rynde,
And in my face deepe furrowes eld hath pight :
My head besprent with hoary frost I fynd,
And by myne eie the Crow his clawe dooth wright.
   Delight is layd abedde, and pleasure past,
   No sonne now shines, cloudes han all ouercast.

Now leaue ye shepheards boyes your merry glee,
My Muse is hoarse and weary of thys stounde :
Here will I hang my pype vpon this tree, 141
Was neuer pype of reede did better sounde.
   Winter is come, that blowes the bitter blaste,
   And after Winter dreerie death does hast.

Gather ye together my little flocke,
My little flock, that was to me so liefe :
Let me, ah lette me in your folds ye lock,
Ere the breme Winter breede you greater griefe.
   Winter is come, that blowes the balefull
   breath,
   And after Winter commeth timely death.

Adieu delightes, that lulled me asleepe,   151
Adieu my deare, whose loue I bought so deare :
Adieu my little Lambes and loued sheepe,
Adieu ye Woodes that oft my witnesse were :
   Adieu good *Hobbinol*, that was so true,
   Tell *Rosalind*, her *Colin* bids her adieu.

             Colins Embleme.

GLOSSE.

Tityrus) Chaucer, as hath bene oft sayd.
Lambkins) young lambes.
Als of their) Semeth to expresse Virgils verse

    Pan curat oues ouiumque magistros.

Deigne) voutchsafe.
Cabinet) Colinet) diminutiues.
Mazie) For they be like to a maze whence it is hard
   to get out agayne.
Peres) felowes and companions.
Musick) that is Poetry as Terence sayth Qui artem
   tractant musicam, speking of Poetes.
Derring doe) aforesayd.
Lions house) He imagineth simply that Cupid,
   which is loue, had his abode in the whote signe
   Leo, which is in middest of somer; a pretie
   allegory, whereof the meaning is, that loue in
   him wrought an extraordinarie heate of lust.
His ray) which is Cupides beame or flames of Loue.
A Comete) a blasing starre, meant of beautie,
   which was the cause of his whote loue.
Venus) the goddesse of beauty or pleasure. Also
   a signe in heauen, as it is here taken. So he
   meaneth that beautie, which hath alwayes aspect
   to Venus, was the cause of all his vnquietnes
   in loue.
Where I was) a fine discription of the chaunge of
   hys lyfe and liking; for all things nowe seemed
   to hym to haue altered their kindly course.
Lording) Spoken after the maner of Paddocks and
   Frogges sitting which is indeed Lordly, not
   remouing nor looking once a side, vnlesse they
   be sturred.
Then as) The second part. That is his manhoode.
Cotes) sheepecotes. For such be the exercises of
   shepheards.
Sale) or Salow a kind of woodde like Wyllow, fit
   to wreath and bynde in leapes to catch fish
   withall.
Phæbe fayles) The Eclipse of the Moone, which is

alwayes in **Cauda** or Capite Draconis, signes in
heauen.
Venus) .s. Venus starre otherwise called Hesperus
   and Vesper and Lucife, both because he seemeth
   to be one of the brightest starres, and also first
   ryseth and setteth last. All which skill in starres
   being conuenient for shepheardes to knowe as
   Theocritus and the rest vse.
Raging seaes) The cause of the swelling and ebbing
   of the sea commeth of the course of the Moone,
   sometime encreasing, sometime wayning and
   decreasing.
Sooth of byrdes) A kind of sooth saying vsed in
   elder tymes, which they gathered by the flying of
   byrds ; First (as is sayd) inuented by the
   Thuscanes, and from them deriued to the
   Romanes, who (as is sayd in Liuie) were so
   supersticiously rooted in the same, that they
   agreed that euery Nobleman should put his
   sonne to the Thuscanes, by them to be brought
   vp in that knowledge.
Of herbes) That wonderous thinges be wrought by
   herbes, aswell appeareth by the common working
   of them in our bodies, as also by the wonderful
   enchauntments and sorceries that haue bene
   wrought by them ; insomuch that it is sayde that
   Circe a famous sorceresse turned men into
   sondry kinds of beastes and Monsters, and onely
   by herbes : as the Poete sayth Dea sæua poten-
   tibus herbis &c.
Kidst) knewest.   Eare) of corne.
Scathe) losse hinderaunce.
Euer among) Euer and anone.
Thus is my) The thyrde parte wherein is set forth
   his ripe yeres as an vntimely haruest, that
   bringeth little fruite.
The flagraunt flowres) sundry studies and laudable
   partes of learning, wherein how our Poete is
   seene, be they witnesse which are priuie to his
   study.

So now my yeere) The last part, wherein is described
his age by comparison of wyntrye stormes.
Carefull cold) for care is sayd to coole the blood.
Glee) mirth.
Hoary frost) A metaphore of hoary heares scattred
lyke to a gray frost.
Breeme) sharpe and bitter.
Adiew delights) is a conclusion of all. Where in
sixe verses he comprehendeth briefly all that was
touched in this booke. In the first verse his
delights of youth generally. In the second, the
loue of Rosalind, in the thyrd, the keeping of
sheepe, which is the argument of all Æglogues.
In the fourth his complaints. And in the last two
his professed frendship and good will to his good
friend Hobbinoll.

Embleme.

The meaning wherof is that all thinges perish and
come to theyr last end, but workes of learned
wits and monuments of Poetry abide for euer.
And therefore Horace of his Odes a work though
ful indede of great wit and learning, yet of no so
great weight and importaunce boldly sayth.

> Exegi monimentum ære perennius,
> Quod nec imber nec aquilo vorax &c.

Therefore let not be enuied, that this Poete in his
Epilogue sayth he hath made a Calendar, that
shall endure as long as time &c. folowing the
ensample of Horace and Ouid in the like.

> Grande opus exegi quod nec Iouis ira nec ignis,
> Nec ferrum poterit nec edax abolere vetustas &c.

> *Loe I haue made a Calender for euery yeare,*
> *That steele in strength, and time in durance shall*
> *   outweare:*
> *And if I marked well the starres reuolution,*
> *   It shall continewe till the worlds dissolution.*
> *To teach the ruder shepheard how to feede his*
> *   sheepe,*
> *And from the falsers fraud his folded flocke to*
> *   keepe.*
> *Goe lytle Calender, thou hast a free passeporte,*
> *Goe but a lowly gate emongste the meaner sorte.*
> *Dare not to match thy pype with Tityrus hys style,*
> *   Nor with the Pilgrim that the Ploughman*
> *   playde a whyle:*
> *But followe them farre off, and their high steppes*
> *   adore,*
> *The better please, the worse despise, I aske nomore.*

> *Merce non mercede.*

Imprinted at London by Hugh
𝕾𝖎𝖓𝖌𝖑𝖊𝖙𝖔𝖓, 𝖉𝖜𝖊𝖑𝖑𝖎𝖓𝖌 𝖎𝖓 𝕮𝖗𝖊𝖊𝖉𝖊 𝖑𝖆𝖓𝖊
at the signe of the gylden
Tunn neere vnto
Ludgate

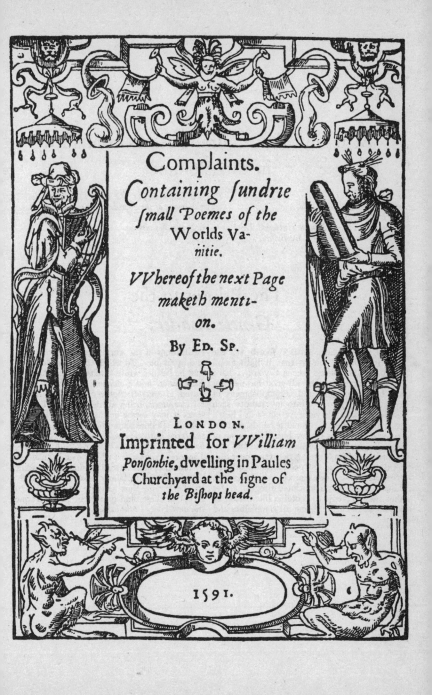

Complaints.

Containing sundrie small Poemes of the Worlds Vanitie.

Whereof the next Page maketh mention.

By Ed. Sp.

LONDON.

Imprinted for William Ponsonbie, dwelling in Paules Churchyard at the signe of the Bishops head.

1591.

A note of the sundrie Poemes contained in this Volume.

The Printer to the
Gentle Reader.

SINCE my late setting foorth of the *Faerie Queene*, finding that it hath found a fauourable passage amongst you ; I haue sithence endeuoured by all good meanes (for the better encrease and accomplishment of your delights,) to get into my handes such smale Poemes of the same Authors ; as I heard were disperst abroad in sundrie hands, and not easie to bee come by, by himselfe ; some of them hauing bene diuerslie imbeziled and purloyned from him, since his departure ouer Sea. Of the which I haue by good meanes gathered togeather these fewe parcels present, which I haue caused to bee imprinted altogeather, for that they al seeme to containe like matter of argument in them : being all complaints and meditations of the worlds vanitie, verie graue and profitable. To which effect I vnderstand that he besides wrote sundrie others, namelie *Ecclesiastes*, and *Canticum canticorum* translated, *A senights slumber, The hell of louers, his Purgatorie*, being all dedicated to Ladies ; so as it may seeme he ment them all to one volume. Besides some other Pamphlets looselie scattered abroad : as *The dying Pellican, The howers of the Lord, The sacrifice of a sinner, The seuen Psalmes, &c.* which when I can either by himselfe, or otherwise attaine too, I meane likewise for your fauour sake to set foorth. In the meane time praying you gentlie to accept of these, and graciouslie to entertaine the new Poet, *I take leaue.*

THE RVINE OF TIME.

Dedicated

To the right Noble and beauti-
full Ladie, the La. Marie
Countesse of Pembrooke.

*M*OST Honourable and bountifull Ladie, there bee long sithens deepe sowed in my brest, the seede of most entire loue and humble affection vnto that most braue Knight your noble brother deceased; which taking roote began in his life time somewhat to bud forth: and to shew themselues to him, as then in the weakenes of their first spring: And would in their riper strength (had it pleased high God till then to drawe out his daies) spired forth fruit of more perfection. But since God hath disdeigned the world of that most noble Spirit, which was the hope of all learned men, and the Patron of my young Muses; togeather with him both their hope of anie further fruit was cut off: and also the tender delight of those their first blossoms nipped and quite dead. Yet sithens my late cumming into England, some frends of mine (which might much preuaile with me, and indeede commaund me) knowing with howe straight bandes of duetie I was tied to him: as also bound vnto that noble house, (of which the chiefe hope then rested in him) haue sought to reuiue them by vpbraiding me: for that I haue not shewed anie thankefull remembrance towards him or any of them; but suffer their names to sleep in silence and forgetfulnesse. Whome chieflie to satisfie, or els to auoide that fowle blot of vnthankefulnesse, I haue conceiued this small Poeme, intituled by a generall name of the worlds Ruines: yet speciallie intended to the renowming of that noble race, from which both you and he sprong, and to the eternizing of some of the chiefe of them late deceased. The which I dedicate vnto your La. as whome it most speciallie concerneth: and to whome I acknowledge my selfe bounden, by manie singular fauours and great graces.
I pray for your Honourable happinesse: and so humblie kisse your handes.

Your Ladiships euer

humblie at commaund.

E. S.

The Ruines of Time.

*I*T chaunced me on day beside the shore
Of siluer streaming *Thamesis* to bee,
Nigh where the goodly *Verlame* stood of yore,
Of which there now remaines no memorie,
Nor anie little moniment to see,
By which the trauailer, that fares that way,
This once was she, may warned be to say.

There on the other side, I did behold
A Woman sitting sorrowfullie wailing,
Rending her yeolow locks, like wyrie golde, 10
About her shoulders carel. slie downe trailing,
And streames of teares from her faire eyes forth railing.
In her right hand a broken rod she held,
Which towards heauen shee seemd on high to weld.

Whether she were one of that Riuers Nymphes,
Which did the losse of some dere loue lament,

I doubt ; or one of those three fatall Impes,
Which draw the dayes of men forth in ext nt ;
Or th'auncient *Genius* of that Citie brent :
But seeing her so piteouslie perplexed,   20
I (to her calling) askt what her so vexed.

Ah what delight (quoth she) in earthlie thing,
Or comfort can I wretched creature haue ?
Whose happines the heauens enuying,
From highest staire to lowest step me draue,
And haue in mine owne bowels made my graue,
That of all Nations now I am forlorne,
The worlds sad spectacle, and fortunes scorne.

Much was I mooued at her piteous plaint,
And felt my heart nigh riuen in my brest 30
With tender ruth to see her sore constraint,
That shedding teares awhile I still did rest,
And after did her name of her request.
Name haue I none (quoth she) nor anie being,
Bereft of both by Fates vniust decreeing.

I was that Citie, which the garland wore
Of *Britaines* pride, deliuered vnto me
By *Romane* Victors, which it wonne of yore ;
Though nought at all but ruines now I bee,
And lye in mine owne ashes, as ye see :   40
Verlame I was ; what bootes it that I was
Sith now I am but weedes and wastfull gras ?

O vaine worlds glorie, and vnstedfast state
Of all that liues, on face of sinfull earth,
Which from their first vntill their vtmost
   date
Tast no one hower of happines or merth,
But like as at the ingate of their berth,
They crying creep out of their mothers woomb,
So wailing backe go to their wofull toomb.

Why then dooth flesh, a bubble glas of
   breath,   50
Hunt after honour and aduauncement vaine,
And reare a trophee for deuouring death,
With so great labour and long lasting paine,
As if his daies for euer should remaine ?
Sith all that in this world is great or gaie,
Doth as a vapour vanish, and decaie.

Looke backe, who list, vnto the former ages,
And call to count, what is of them become :
Where be those learned wits and antique Sages,
Which of all wisedome knew the perfect somme :
Where those great warriors, which did ouer-
   comme   61
The world with conquest of their might and
   maine,
And made one meare of th'earth and of their
   raine ?

What nowe is of th'*Assyrian* Lyonesse,
Of whome no footing now on earth appeares ?

What of the *Persian* Beares outragiousnesse,
Whose memorie is quite worne out with yeares?
Who of the *Grecian* Libbard now ought heares,
That ouerran the East with greedie powre, 69
And left his whelps their kingdomes to deuoure ?

And where is that same great seuen headded
   beast,
That made all nations vassals of her pride,
To fall before her feete at her beheast,
And in the necke of all the world did ride ?
Where doth she all that wondrous welth nowe
   hide ?
With her own weight down pressed now shee
   lies,
And by her heaps her hugenesse testifies.

O *Rome* thy ruine I lament and rue,
And in thy fall my fatall ouerthrowe,
That whilom was, whilst heauens with equall
   vewe   80
Deignd to behold me, and their gifts bestowe,
The picture of thy pride in pompous shew :
And of the whole world as thou wast the
   Empresse,
So I of this small Northerne world was Princesse.

To tell the beawtie of my buildings fayre,
Adornd with purest golde, and precious stone ;
To tell my riches, and endowments rare
That by my foes are now all spent and gone :
To tell my forces matchable to none,   89
Were but lost labour, that few would beleeue,
And with rehearsing would me more agreeue.

High towers, faire temples, goodly theaters,
Strong walls, rich porches, princelie pallaces,
Large streetes, braue houses, sacred sepulchers,
Sure gates, sweete gardens, stately galleries,
Wrought with faire pillours, and fine imageries,
All those (O pitie) now are turnd to dust,
And ouergrowen with blacke obliuions rust.

Thereto for warlike power, and peoples store,
In *Britannie* was none to match with mee, 100
That manie often did abie full sore :
Ne *Troynouant*, though elder sister shee,
With my great forces might compared bee ;
That stout *Pendragon* to his perill felt,
Who in a siege seauen yeres about me dwelt.

But long ere this *Bunduca* Britonnesse
Her mightie hoast against my bulwarkes
   brought,
Bunduca, that victorious conqueresse,
That lifting vp her braue heroick thought
Boue womens weaknes, with the *Romanes*
   fought,   110
Fought, and in field against them thrice pre-
   uailed :
Yet was she foyld, when as she me assailed.

And though at last by force I conquered were
Of hardie *Saxons,* and became their thrall ;
Yet was I with much bloodshed bought full
  deere,
And prizde with slaughter of their Generall :
The moniment of whose sad funerall,
For wonder of the world, long in me lasted ;
But now to nought through spoyle of time is
  wasted.

Wasted it is, as if it neuer were,   120
And all the rest that me so honord made,
And of the world admired eu'rie where,
Is turnd to smoake, that doth to nothing fade ;
And of that brightnes now appeares no shade,
But greislie shades, such as doo haunt in hell
With fearfull fiends, that in deep darknes dwell.

Where my high steeples whilom vsde to stand,
On which the lordly Faulcon wont to towre,
There now is but an heap of lyme and sand,
For the Shriche-owle to build her balefull
  bowre :   130
And where the Nightingale wont forth to powre
Her restles plaints, to comfort wakefull Louers,
There now haunt yelling Mewes and whining
  Plouers.

And where the christall *Thamis* wont to slide
In siluer channell, downe along the Lee,
About whose flowrie bankes on either side
A thousand Nymphes, with mirthfull iollitee
Were wont to play, from all annoyance free ;
There now no riuers course is to be seene, 139
But moorish fennes, and marshes euer greene.

Seemes, that that gentle Riuer for great griefe
Of my mishaps, which oft I to him plained ;
Or for to shunne the horrible mischiefe,
With which he saw my cruell foes me pained,
And his pure streames with guiltles blood oft
  stained,
From his vnhappie neighborhood farre fled,
And his sweete waters away with him led.

There also where the winged ships were seene
In liquid waues to cut their fomie waie,   149
And thousand Fishers numbred to haue been,
In that wide lake looking for plenteous praie
Of fish, which they with baits vsde to betraie,
Is now no lake, nor anie fishers store,
Nor euer ship shall saile there anie more.

They all are gone, and all with them is gone,
Ne ought to me remaines, but to lament
My long decay, which no man els doth mone,
And mourne my fall with dolefull dreriment.
Yet it is comfort in great languishment,
To be bemoned with compassion kinde,   160
And mitigates the anguish of the minde.

But me no man bewaileth, but in game,
Ne sheddeth teares from lamentable eie :
Nor anie liues that mentioneth my name
To be remembred of posteritie,
Saue One that maugre fortunes iniurie,
And times decay, and enuies cruell tort,
Hath writ my record in true-seeming sort.

Cambden the nourice of antiquitie,
And lanterne vnto late succeeding age,   170
To see the light of simple veritie,
Buried in ruines, through the great outrage
Of her owne people, led with warlike rage.
Cambden, though time all moniments obscure,
Yet thy iust labours euer shall endure.

But whie (vnhappie wight) doo I thus crie,
And grieue that my remembrance quite is raced
Out of the knowledge of posteritie,
And all my antique moniments defaced ?
Sith I doo dailie see things highest placed, 180
So soone as fates their vitall thred haue shorne,
Forgotten quite as they were neuer borne.

It is not long, since these two eyes beheld
A mightie Prince, of most renowmed race,
Whom *England* high in count of honour held,
And greatest ones did sue to gaine his grace
Of greatest ones he greatest in his place,
Sate in the bosome of his Soueraine,
And *Right and loyall* did his word maintaine.

I saw him die, I saw him die, as one   190
Of the meane people, and brought foorth on
  beare.
I saw him die, and no man left to mone
His dolefull fate, that late him loued deare .
Scarce anie left to close his eylids neare ;
Scarce anie left vpon his lips to laie
The sacred sod, or *Requiem* to saie.

O trustlesse state of miserable men,
That builde your blis on hope of earthly thing,
And vainly thinke your selues halfe happie then,
When painted faces with smooth flattering 200
Doo fawne on you, and your wide praises sing,
And when the courting masker louteth lowe,
Him true in heart and trustie to you trow.

All is but fained, and with oaker dide,
That euerie shower will wash and wipe away,
All things doo change that vnder heauen abide,
And after death all friendship doth decaie.
Therefore what euer man bearst worldlie sway,
Liuing, on God, and on thy selfe relie ;
For when thou diest, all shall with thee die. 210
He now is dead, and all is with him dead,
Saue what in heauens storehouse he vplaid :
His hope is faild, and come to passe his dread,
And euill men, now dead, his deeds vpbraid :
Spite bites the dead, that liuing neuer baid.

He now is gone, the whiles the Foxe is crept
Into the hole, the which the Badger swept.

He now is dead, and all his glorie gone,
And all his greatnes vapoured to nought,
That as a glasse vpon the water shone,   220
Which vanisht quite, so soone as it was sought.
His name is worne alreadie out of thought,
Ne anie Poet seekes him to reuiue;
Yet manie Poets honourd him aliue.

Ne doth his *Colin*, carelesse *Colin Cloute*,
Care now his idle bagpipe vp to raise,
Ne tell his sorrow to the listning rout
Of shepherd groomes, which wont his songs to
praise:
Praise who so list, yet I will him dispraise,
Vntill he quite him of this guiltie blame: 230
Wake shepheards boy, at length awake for
shame.

And who so els did goodnes by him gaine,
And who so els his bounteous minde did trie,
Whether he shepheard be, or shepheards swaine,
(For manie did, which doo it now denie)
Awake, and to his Song a part applie:
And I, the whilest you mourne for his decease,
Will with my mourning plaints your plaint
increase.

He dyde, and after him his brother dyde,   239
His brother Prince, his brother noble Peere,
That whilste he liued, was of none enuyde,
And dead is now, as liuing, counted deare,
Deare vnto all that true affection beare:
But vnto thee most deare, O dearest Dame,
His noble Spouse, and Paragon of fame.

He whilest he liued, happie was through thee,
And being dead is happie now much more;
Liuing, that lincked chaunst with thee to bee,
And dead, because him dead thou dost adore
As liuing, and thy lost deare loue deplore.   250
So whilst that thou, faire flower of chastitie,
Dost liue, by thee thy Lord shall neuer die.

Thy Lord shall neuer die, the whiles this verse
Shall liue, and surely it shall liue for euer:
For ever it shall liue, and shall rehearse
His worthie praise, and vertues dying neuer,
Though death his soule doo from his bodie seuer.
And thou thy selfe herein shalt also liue;
Such grace the heauens doo to my verses giue.

Ne shall his sister, ne thy father die,   260
Thy father, that good Earle of rare renowne,
And noble Patrone of weake pouertie;
Whose great good deeds in countrey and in towne
Haue purchast him in heauen an happie crowne;
Where he now liueth in eternall blis,
And left his sonne t'ensue those steps of his.

He noble bud, his Grandsires liuelie hayre,
Vnder the shadow of thy countenaunce
Now ginnes to shoote vp fast, and flourish fayre
In learned artes and goodlie gouernaunce,   270
That him to highest honour shall aduaunce.
Braue Impe of *Bedford*, grow apace in bountie,
And count of wisedome more than of thy
Countie.

Ne may I let thy husbands sister die,
That goodly Ladie, sith she eke did spring
Out of this stocke, and famous familie,
Whose praises I to future age doo sing,
And foorth out of her happie womb did bring
The sacred brood of learning and all honour;
In whom the heauens powrde all their gifts
vpon her.   280

Most gentle spirite breathed from aboue,
Out of the bosome of the makers blis,
In whom all bountie and all vertuous loue
Appeared in their natiue propertis,
And did enrich that noble breast of his,
With treasure passing all this worldes worth,
Worthie of heauen it selfe, which brought it
forth.

His blessed spirite full of power diuine
And influence of all celestiall grace,
Loathing this sinfull earth and earthlie slime,
Fled backe too soone vnto his natiue place,   291
Too soone for all that did his loue embrace,
Too soone for all this wretched world, whom he
Robd of all right and true nobilitie.

Yet ere his happie soule to heauen went
Out of this fleshlie goale, he did deuise
Vnto his heauenlie maker to present
His bodie, as a spotles sacrifise;
And chose, that guiltie hands of enemies
Should powre forth th'offring of his guiltles
blood: 300
So life exchanging for his countries good.

O noble spirite, liue there euer blessed,
The worlds late wonder, and the heauens
new ioy,
Liue euer there, and leaue me here distressed
With mortall cares, and cumbrous worlds anoy.
But where thou dost that happines enioy,
Bid me, O bid me quicklie come to thee,
That happie there I maie thee alwaies see.

Yet whilest the fates affoord me vitall breath,
I will it spend in speaking of thy praise,   310
And sing to thee, vntill that timelie death
By heauens doome doo end my earthlie daies:
Thereto doo thou my humble spirite raise,
And into me that sacred breath inspire,
Which thou there breathest perfect and entire.

Then will I sing : but who can better sing,
Than thine owne sister, peerles Ladie bright,
Which to thee sings with deep harts sorrowing,
Sorrowing tempered with deare delight.
That her to heare I feele my feeble spright 320
Robbed of sense, and rauished with ioy,
O sad ioy made of mourning and anoy.

Yet will I sing : but who can better sing,
Than thou thy selfe, thine owne selfes valiance,
That whilest thou liuedst, madest the forrests
  ring,
And fields resownd, and flockes to leap and
  daunce,
And shepheards leaue their lambs vnto mis-
  chaunce,
To runne thy shrill *Arcadian* Pipe to heare :
O happie were those dayes, thrice happie were.

But now more happie thou, and wretched wee,
Which want the wonted sweetnes of thy voice,
Whiles thou now in *Elisian* fields so free,
With *Orpheus*, and with *Linus*, and the choice
Of all that euer did in rimes reioyce,
Conuersest, and doost heare their heauenlie layes,
And they heare thine, and thine doo better
  praise.

So there thou liuest, singing euermore,
And here thou liuest, being euer song
Of vs, which liuing loued thee afore,
And now thee worship, mongst that blessed
  throng   340
Of heauenlie Poets and Heroes strong.
So thou both here and there immortall art,
And euerie where through excellent desart.

But such as neither of themselues can sing,
Nor yet are sung of others for reward,
Die in obscure obliuion, as the thing
Which neuer was, ne euer with regard
Their names shall of the later age be heard,
But shall in rustie darknes euer lie,
Vnles they mentioned be with infamie.   350

What booteth it to haue been rich aliue ?
What to be great ? what to be gracious ?
When after death no token doth suruiue,
Of former being in this mortall hous,
But sleepes in dust dead and inglorious,
Like beast, whose breath but in his nostrels is,
And hath no hope of happinesse or blis.

How manie great ones may remembred be,
Which in their daies most famouslie did florish ?
Of whome no word we heare, nor signe now see,
But as things wipt out with a sponge to perishe,
Because they liuing, cared not to cherishe
No gentle wits, through pride or couetize,
Which might their names for euer memorize.

Prouide therefore (ye Princes) whilst ye liue,
That of the *Muses* ye may friended bee,
Which vnto men eternitie do giue ;
For they be daughters of Dame memorie,
And *Ioue* the father of eternitie,
And do those men in golden thrones repose,
Whose merits they to glorifie do chose.   371

The seuen fold yron gates of grislie Hell,
And horrid house of sad *Proserpina*,
They able are with power of mightie spell
To breake, and thence the soules to bring awaie
Out of dread darkenesse, to eternall day,
And them immortall make, which els would die
In foule forgetfulnesse, and nameles lie.

So whilome raised they the puissant brood
Of golden girt *Alcmena*, for great mcrite,   380
Out of the dust, to which the *Oetæan* wood
Had him consum'd, and spent his vitall spirite :
To highest heauen, where now he doth inherite
All happinesse in *Hebes* siluer bowre,
Chosen to be her dearest Paramoure.

So raisde they eke faire *LeJaes* warlick twinnes,
And interchanged life vnto them lent,
That when th'one dies, th'other then beginnes
To shew in Heauen his brightnes orient ;
And they, for pittie of the sad wayment,   390
Which *Orpheus* for *Eurydice* did make,
Her back againe to life sent for his sake.

So happie are they, and so fortunate,
Whom the *Pierian* sacred sisters loue,
That freed from bands of impacable fate,
And power of death, they liue for aye aboue,
Where mortall wreakes their blis may not
  remoue :
But with the Gods, for former vertues meede,
On *Nectar* and *Ambrosia* do feede.

For deeds doe die, how euer noblie donne, 400
And thoughts of men do as themselues decay.
But wise wordes taught in numbers for to runne,
Recorded by the Muses, liue for ay ;
Ne may with storming showers be washt away
Ne bitter breathing windes with harmfull blast,
Nor age, nor enuie shall them euer wast.

In vaine doo earthly Princes then, in vaine
Seeke with Pyramides, to heauen aspired ;
Or huge Colosses, built with costlie paine ;
Or brasen Pillours, neuer to be fired,   410
Or Shrines, made of the mettall most desired ;
To make their memories for euer liue :
For how can mortall immortalitie giue ?

Such one *Mausolus* made, the worlds great wonder,
But now no remnant doth thereof remaine :
Such one *Marcellus*, but was torne with thunder :
Such one *Lisippus*, but is worne with raine :

Such one King _Edmond_, but was rent for gaine.
All such vaine moniments of earthlie masse,
Deuour'd of Time, in time to nought doo passe.

But fame with golden wings aloft doth flie,　421
Aboue the reach of ruinous decay,
And with braue plumes doth beate the azure skie,
Admir'd of base-borne men from farre away :
Then who so will with vertuous deeds assay
To mount to heauen, on _Pegasus_ must ride,
And with sweete Poets verse be glorifide.

For not to haue been dipt in _Lethe_ lake,
Could saue the sonne of _Thetis_ from to die ;
But that blinde bard did him immortall make
With verses, dipt in deaw of _Castalie :_　431
Which made the Easterne Conquerour to crie,
O fortunate yong-man, whose vertue found
So braue a Trompe, thy noble acts to sound.

Therefore in this halfe happie I doo read
Good _Melibæ_, that hath a Poet got,
To sing his liuing praises being dead,
Deseruing neuer here to be forgot,
In spight of enuie, that his deeds would spot :
Since whose decease, learning lies vnregarded,
And men of armes doo wander vnrewarded.

Those two be those two great calamities,
That long agoe did grieue the noble spright
Of _Salomon_ with great indignities ;
Who whilome was aliue the wisest wight.
But now his wisedome is disprooued quite ;
For he that now welds all things at his will,
Scorns th'one and th'other in his deeper skill.

O griefe of griefes, O gall of all good heartes,
To see that vertue should dispised bee　450
Of him, that first was raisde for vertuous parts,
And now broad spreading like an aged tree,
Lets none shoot vp, that nigh him planted bee :
O let the man, of whom the Muse is scorned,
Nor aliue, nor dead be of the Muse adorned.

O vile worlds trust, that with such vaine illusion
Hath so wise men bewitcht, and ouerkest,
That they see not the way of their confusion,
O vainesse to be added to the rest,
That do my soule with inward griefe infest :
Let them behold the piteous fall of mee :　461
And in my case their owne ensample see.

And who so els that sits in highest seate
Of this worlds glorie, worshipped of all,
Ne feareth change of time, nor fortunes threate,
Let him behold the horror of my fall,
And his owne end vnto remembrance call ;
That of like ruine he may warned bee,
And in himselfe be moou'd to pittie mee.

Thus hauing ended all her piteous plaint,　470
With dolefull shrikes shee vanished away,
That I through inward sorrowe wexen faint,
And all astonished with deepe dismay,
For her departure, had no word to say :
But sate long time in sencelesse sad affright,
Looking still, if I might of her haue sight.

Which when I missed, hauing looked long,
My thought returned greeued home againe,
Renewing her complaint with passion strong,
For ruth of that same womans piteous paine ;　480
Whose wordes recording in my troubled braine,
I felt such anguish wound my feeble heart,
That frosen horror ran through euerie part.

So inlie greeuing in my groning brest,
And deepelie muzing at her doubtfull speach,
Whose meaning much I labored foorth to wreste,
Being aboue my slender reasons reach ;
At length by demonstration me to teach,
Before mine eies strange sights presented were,
Like tragicke Pageants seeming to appeare.　490

1

I saw an Image, all of massie gold,
Placed on high vpon an Altare faire,
That all, which did the same from farre beholde,
Might worship it, and fall on lowest staire.
Not that great Idoll might with this compaire,
To which th'_Assyrian_ tyrant would haue made
The holie brethren, falslie to haue praid.

But th'Altare, on the which this Image staid,
Was (O great pitie) built of brickle clay,
That shortly the foundation decaid,　500
With showers of heauen and tempests worne away :
Then downe it fell, and low in ashes lay,
Scorned of euerie one, which by it went ;
That I it seing, dearelie did lament.

2

Next vnto this a statelie Towre appeared,
Built all of richest stone, that might bee found,
And nigh vnto the Heauens in height vprearcd,
But placed on a plot of sandie ground :
Not that great Towre, which is so much renownd
For tongues confusion in holie writ,　510
King _Ninus_ worke, might be compar'd to it.

But O vaine labours of terrestriall wit,
That buildes so stronglie on so frayle a soyle,
As with each storme does fall away, and flit,
And giues the fruit of all your trauailes toyle,
To be the pray of Tyme, and Fortunes spoyle :
I saw this Towre fall sodainlie to dust,
That nigh with griefe thereof my heart was brust.

3

Then did I see a pleasant Paradize,
Full of sweete flowres and daintiest delights, 520
Such as on earth man could not more deuize,
With pleasures choyce to feed his cheerefull
   sprights ;
Not that, which *Merlin* by his Magicke slights
Made for the gentle squire, to entertaine
His fayre *Belphœbe*, could this gardine staine.

But O short pleasure bought with lasting paine,
Why will hereafter anie flesh delight
In earthlie blis, and ioy in pleasures vaine,
Since that I sawe this gardine wasted quite,
That where it was scarce seemed anie sight ? 530
That I, which once that beautie did beholde,
Could not from teares my melting eyes with-
   holde. **4**

Soone after this a Giaunt came in place,
Of wondrous power, and of exceeding stature,
That none durst vewe the horror of his face,
Yet was he milde of speach, and meeke of nature.
Not he, which in despight of his Creatour
With railing tearmes defied the Iewish hoast,
Might with this mightie one in hugenes boast.

For from the one he could to th'other coast, 540
Stretch his strong thighes, and th'Occæan
   ouerstride,
And reatch his hand into his enemies hoast.
But see the end of pompe and fleshlie pride ;
One of his feete vnwares from him did slide,
That downe hee fell into the deepe Abisse,
Where drownd with him is all his earthlie blisse.

5

Then did I see a Bridge, made all of golde,
Ouer the Sea from one to other side,
Withouten prop or pillour it t'vpholde,
But like the coulored Rainbowe arched wide :
Not that great Arche, which *Traian* edifide, 551
To be a wonder to all age ensuing,
Was matchable to this in equall vewing.

But (ah) what bootes it to see earthlie thing
In glorie, or in greatnes to excell,
Sith time doth greatest things to ruine bring ?
This goodlie bridge, one foote not fastened well,
Gan faile, and all the rest downe shortlie fell,
Ne of so braue a building ought remained, 559
That griefe thereof my spirite greatly pained.

6

i saw two Beares, as white as anie milke,
Lying together in a mightie caue,
Of milde aspect, and haire as soft as silke,
That saluage nature seemed not to haue,
Nor after greedie spoyle of blood to craue :
Two fairer beasts might not elswhere be found,
Although the compast world were sought around.

But what can long abide aboue this ground
In state of blis, or stedfast happinesse ?
The Caue, in which these Beares lay sleeping
   sound, 570
Was but earth, and with her owne weightinesse
Vpon them fell, and did vnwares oppresse,
That for great sorrow of their sudden fate,
Henceforth all worlds felicitie I hate.

¶ Much was I troubled in my heauie spright,
At sight of these sad spectacles forepast,
That all my senses were bereaued quight,
And I in minde remained sore agast,
Distraught twixt feare and pitie ; when at last
I heard a voyce, which loudly to me called, 580
That with the suddein shrill I was appalled.

Behold (said it) and by ensample see,
That all is vanitie and griefe of minde,
Ne other comfort in this world can be,
But hope of heauen, and heart to God inclinde ;
For all the rest must needs be left behinde :
With that it bad me, to the other side
To cast mine eye, where other sights I spide.

1

¶ Vpon that famous Riuers further shore,
There stood a snowie Swan of heauenly hiew,
And gentle kinde, as euer Fowle afore ; 591
A fairer one in all the goodlie criew
Of white *Strimonian* brood might no man view :
There he most sweetly sung the prophecie
Of his owne death in dolefull Elegie.

At last, when all his mourning melodie
He ended had, that both the shores resounded,
Feeling the fit that him forewarnd to die,
With loftie flight aboue the earth he bounded,
And out of sight to highest heauen mounted : 600
Where now he is become an heauenly signe ;
There now the ioy is his, here sorrow mine.

2

Whilest thus I looked, loe adowne the *Lee*,
I sawe an Harpe stroong all with siluer twyne,
And made of golde and costlie yuorie,
Swimming, that whilome seemed to haue been
The harpe, on which *Dan Orpheus* was seene
Wylde beasts and forrests after him to lead,
But was th'Harpe of *Philisides* now dead.

At length out of the Riuer it was reard 610
And borne aboue the cloudes to be diuin'd,
Whilst all the way most heauenly noyse was
   heard
Of the strings, stirred with the warbling wind,
That wrought both ioy and sorrow in my mind :
So now in heauen a signe it doth appeare,
The Harpe well knowne beside the Northern
   Beare.

3

Soone after this I saw on th'other side,
A curious Coffer made of *Heben* wood,
That in it did most precious treasure hide,
Exceeding all this baser worldes good :   620
Yet through the ouerflowing of the flood
It almost drowned was, and done to nought,
That sight thereof much grieu'd my pensiue
   thought.

At length when most in perill it was brought,
Two Angels downe descending with swift flight,
Out of the swelling streame it lightly caught,
And twixt their blessed armes it carried quight
Aboue the reach of anie liuing sight :
So now it is transform'd into that starre,
In which all heauenly treasures locked are. 630

4

Looking aside I saw a stately Bed,
Adorned all with costly cloth of gold,
That might for anie Princes couche be red,
And deckt with daintie flowres, as if it shold
Be for some bride, her ioyous night to hold :
Therein a goodly Virgine sleeping lay ;
A fairer wight saw neuer summers day.

I heard a voyce that called farre away
And her awaking bad her quickly dight,
For lo her Bridegrome was in readie ray   640
To come to her, and seeke her loues delight :
With that she started vp with cherefull sight,
When suddeinly both bed and all was gone,
And I in languor left there all alone.

5

Still as I gazed, I beheld where stood
A Knight all arm'd, vpon a winged steed,
The same that was bred of *Medusaes* blood,
On which *Dan Perseus* borne of heauenly seed,
The faire *Andromeda* from perill freed :
Full mortally this Knight ywounded was,   650
That streames of blood foorth flowed on the
   gras.

Yet was he deckt (small ioy to him alas)
With manie garlands for his victories,
And with rich spoyles, which late he did purchas
Through braue atcheiuements from his enemies :
Fainting at last through long infirmities,
He smote his steed, that straight to heauen
   him bore,
And left me here his losse for to deplore.

6

Lastly I saw an Arke of purest golde
Vpon a brazen pillour standing hie,   660
Which th'ashes seem'd of some great Prince to
   hold,
Enclosde therein for endles memorie
Of him, whom all the world did glorifie :
Seemed the heauens with the earth did disagree,
Whether should of those ashes keeper bee.

At last me seem'd wing footed *Mercurie*,
From heauen descending to appease their strife,
The Arke did beare with him aboue the skie,
And to those ashes gaue a second life,
To liue in heauen, where happines is rife : 670
At which the earth did grieue exceedingly,
And I for dole was almost like to die.

L'Envoy.

Immortall spirite of *Philisides*,
Which now art made the heauens ornament,
That whilome wast the worlds chiefst riches :
Giue leaue to him that lou'de thee to lament
His losse, by lacke of thee to heauen hent,
And with last duties of this broken verse,
Broken with sighes, to decke thy sable Herse.

And ye faire Ladie th'honor of your daies, 680
And glorie of the world, your high thoughts
   scorne ;
Vouchsafe this moniment of his last praise,
With some few siluer dropping teares t'adorne :
And as ye be of heauenlie off spring borne,
So vnto heauen let your high minde aspire,
And loath this drosse of sinfull worlds desire.

FINIS.

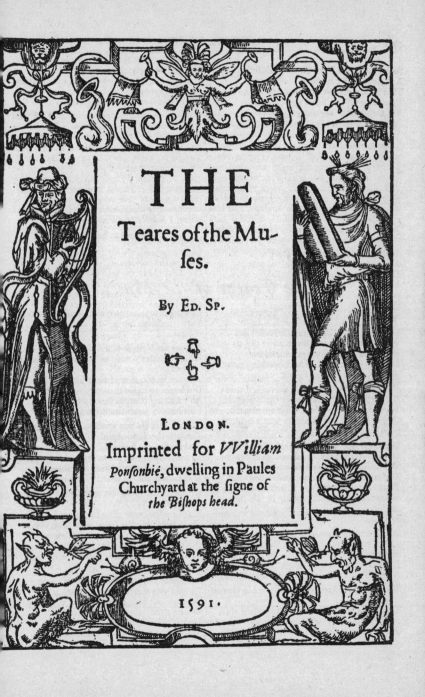

THE

Teares of the Mu-
ses.

By ED. SP.

LONDON.
Imprinted for *VVilliam
Ponsonbie*, dwelling in Paules
Churchyard at the signe of
the Bishops head.

1591.

TO THE RIGHT HONORABLE

the Ladie *Strange.*

MOst braue and noble Ladie, the things that make ye so much honored of the world as ye bee, are such, as (without my simple lines testimonie) are throughlie knowen to all men; namely, your excellent beautie, your vertuous behauior, and your noble match with that most honourable Lord the verie Paterne of right Nobilitie : But the causes for which ye haue thus deserued of me to be honoured (if honour it be at all) are, both your particular bounties, and also some priuate bands of affinitie, which it hath pleased your Ladiship to acknowledge. Of which whenas I found my selfe in no part worthie, I deuised this last slender meanes, both to inti-

mate my humble affection to your Ladiship and also to make the same vniuersallie knowen to the world; that by honouring you they might know me, and by knowing me they might honor you. Vouchsafe, noble Lady, to accept this simple remembrance, thogh not worthy of your self, yet such, as perhaps by good acceptance therof, ye may hereafter cull out a more meet and memorable euidence of your own excellent deserts. So recommending the same to your Ladiships good liking, I humbly take leaue.

Your La: humbly euer.

Ed. Sp.

The Teares of the Muses.

REhearse to me ye sacred Sisters nine,
The golden brood of great *Apollöes* wit,
Those piteous plaints and sorrowfull sad tine,
Which late ye powred forth as ye did sit
Beside the siluer Springs of *Helicone,*
Making your musick of hart-breaking mone.

For since the time that *Phœbus* foolish sonne
Ythundered through *Ioues* auengefull wrath,
For trauersing the charret of the Sunne
Beyond the compasse of his pointed path, 10
Of you his mournfull Sisters was lamented,
Such mournfull tunes were neuer since inuented.

Nor since that faire *Calliope* did lose
Her loued Twinnes, the dearlings of her ioy,
Her *Palici,* whom her vnkindly foes
The fatall Sisters, did for spight destroy,
Whom all the Muses did bewaile long space ;
Was euer heard such wayling in this place.

For all their groues, which with the heauenly noyses 19
Of their sweete instruments were wont to sound,
And th'hollow hills, from which their siluer voyces
Were wont redoubled Echoes to rebound,
Did now rebound with nought but rufull cries,
And yelling shrieks throwne vp into the skies

The trembling streames which wont in chanels cleare
To romble gently downe with murmur soft,
And were by them right tunefull taught to beare
A Bases part amongst their consorts oft ;

Now forst to ouerflowe with brackish teares,
With troublous noyse did dull their daintie eares. 30

The ioyous Nymphes and lightfoote Faeries
Which thether came to heare their musick sweet,
And to the measure of their melodies
Did learne to moue their nimble shifting feete ;
Now hearing them so heauily lament,
Like heauily lamenting from them went.

And all that els was wont to worke delight
Through the diuine infusion of their skill,
And all that els seemd faire and fresh in sight,
So made by nature for to serue their will, 40
Was turned now to dismall heauinesse,
Was turned now to dreadfull vglinesse.

Ay me, what thing on earth that all thing breeds,
Might be the cause of so impatient plight ?
What furie, or what feend with felon deeds
Hath stirred vp so mischieuous despight ?
Can griefe then enter into heauenly harts,
And pierce immortall breasts with mortall smarts ?

Vouchsafe ye then, whom onely it concernes,
To me those secret causes to display ; 50
For none but you, or who of you it learnes,
Can rightfully aread so dolefull lay.
Begin thou eldest Sister of the crew,
And let the rest in order thee ensew.

Clio.

Heare thou great Father of the Gods on hie
That most art dreaded for thy thunder darts:
And thou our Syre that raignst in *Castalie*
And mount *Parnasse*, the God of goodly Arts:
Heare and behold the miserable state
Of vs thy daughters, dolefull desolate. 60

Behold the fowle reproach and open shame,
The which is day by day vnto vs wrought
By such as hate the honour of our name,
The foes of learning, and each gentle thought;
They not contented vs themselues to scorne,
Doo seeke to make vs of the world forlorne.

Ne onely they that dwell in lowly dust,
The sonnes of darknes and of ignoraunce;
But they, whom thou great *Ioue* by doome
vniust
Didst to the type of honour earst aduaunce; 70
They now puft vp with sdeignfull insolence,
Despise the brood of blessed Sapience.

The sectaries of my celestiall skill,
That wont to be the worlds chiefe ornament,
And learned Impes that wont to shoote vp still,
And grow to hight of kingdomes gouernment
They vnderkeep, and with their spredding armes
Doo beat their buds, that perish through their
harmes.

It most behoues the honorable race
Of mightie Peeres, true wisedome to sustaine,
And with their noble countenaunce to grace 81
The learned forheads, without gifts or gaine:
Or rather learnd themselues behoues to bee;
That is the girlond of Nobilitie.

But (ah) all otherwise they doo esteeme
Of th'heauenly gift of wisdomes influence,
And to be learned it a base thing deeme;
Base minded they that want intelligence:
For God himselfe for wisedome most is praised,
And men to God thereby are nighest raised. 90

But they doo onely striue themselues to raise
Through pompous pride, and foolish vanitie;
In th'eyes of people they put all their praise,
And onely boast of Armes and Auncestrie:
But vertuous deeds, which did those Armes first
giue
To their Grandsyres, they care not to atchiue.

So I, that doo all noble feates professe
To register, and sound in trump of gold;
Through their bad dooings, or base slothful-
nesse,
Finde nothing worthie to be writ, or told: 100
For better farre it were to hide their names,
Than telling them to blazon out their blames.

So shall succeeding ages haue no light
Of things forepast, nor moniments of time,
And all that in this world is worthie hight
Shall die in darknesse, and lie hid in slime:
Therefore I mourne with deep harts sorrowing,
Because I nothing noble haue to sing.

With that she raynd such store of streaming
teares,
That could haue made a stonie heart to weep,
And all her Sisters rent their golden heares, 111
And their faire faces with salt humour steep.
So ended shee: and then the next anew,
Began her grieuous plaint as doth ensew.

Melpomene.

O who shall powre into my swollen eyes
A sea of teares that neuer may be dryde,
A brasen voice that may with shrilling cryes
Pierce the dull heauens and fill the ayer wide,
And yron sides that sighing may endure, 119
To waile the wretchednes of world impure?

Ah wretched world the den of wickednesse,
Deformd with filth and fowle iniquitie;
Ah wretched world the house of heauinesse
Fild with the wreaks of mortall miserie;
Ah wretched world, and all that is therein
The vassals of Gods wrath, and slaues of sin.

Most miserable creature vnder sky
Man without vnderstanding doth appeare;
For all this worlds affliction he thereby,
And Fortunes freakes is wisely taught to
beare: 130
Of wretched life the onely ioy shee is,
And th'only comfort in calamities.

She armes the brest with constant patience,
Against the bitter throwes of dolours darts.
She solaceth with rules of Sapience
The gentle minds, in midst of worldlie smarts:
When he is sad, shee seeks to make him merie,
And doth refresh his sprights when they be
werie.

But he that is of reasons skill bereft,
And wants the staffe of wisedome him to stay,
Is like a ship in midst of tempest left 141
Withouten helme or Pilot her to sway,
Full sad and dreadfull is that ships euent:
So is the man that wants intendiment.

Whie then doo foolish men so much despize
The precious store of this celestiall riches?
Why doo they banish vs, that patronize
The name of learning? Most vnhappie
wretches,
The which lie drowned in deep wretchednes,
Yet doo not see their owne vnhappines. 150

SPENSER   R

My part it is and my professed skill
The Stage with Tragick buskin to adorne,
And fill the Scene with plaint and outcries
   shril
Of wretched persons, to misfortune borne
But none more tragick matter I can finde
Than this, of men depriu'd of sense and minde.

For all mans life me seemes a Tragedy,
Full of sad sights and sore Catastrophees ;
First comming to the world with weeping eye,
Where all his dayes like dolorous Trophees, 160
Are heapt with spoyles of fortune and of feare,
And he at last laid forth on balefull beare.

So all with rufull spectacles is fild,
Fit for *Megera* or *Persephone* ;
But I that in true Tragedies am skild,
The flowre of wit, finde nought to busie me :
Therefore I mourne, and pitifully mone,
Because that mourning matter I haue none.

Then gan she wofully to waile, and wring
Her wretched hands in lamentable wise ;   170
And all her Sisters thereto answering,
Threw forth lowd shrieks and drerie dolefull
   cries.
So rested she : and then the next in rew,
Began her grieuous plaint as doth ensew.

Thalia.

Where be the sweete delights of learnings
   treasure,
That wont with Comick sock to beautefie
The painted Theaters, and fill with pleasure
The listners eyes, and eares with melodie ;
In which I late was wont to raine as Queene,
And maske in mirth with Graces well beseene ?

O all is gone, and all that goodly glee,   181
Which wont to be the glorie of gay wits
Is layd abed, and no where now to see ;
And in her roome vnseemly Sorrow sits,
With hollow browes and greisly countenaunce,
Marring my ioyous gentle dalliaunce.

And him beside sits vgly Barbarisme
And brutish Ignorance, ycrept of late
Out of dredd darknes of the deep Abysme,
Where being bredd, he light and heauen does
   hate   190
They in the mindes of men now tyrannize,
And the faire Scene with rudenes foule disguize.

All places they with follie haue possest,
And with vaine toyes the vulgare entertaine
But me haue banished, with all the rest
That whilome wont to wait vpon my traine,
Fine Counterfesaunce and vnhurtfull Sport,
Delight and Laughter deckt in seemly sort.

All these, and all that els the Comick Stage
With seasoned wit and goodly pleasance
   graced,   200
By which mans life in his likest image
Was limned forth, are wholly now defaced ;
And those sweete wits which wont the like to
   frame,
Are now despizd, and made a laughing game.

And he the man, whom Nature selfe had made
To mock her selfe, and Truth to imitate,
With kindly counter vnder Mimick shade,
Our pleasant *Willy*, ah is dead of late :
With whom all ioy and iolly meriment
Is also deaded, and in dolour drent.   210

In stead thereof scoffing Scurrilitie,
And scornfull Follie with Contempt is crept,
Rolling in rymes of shameles ribaudrie
Without regard, or due Decorum kept,
Each idle wit at will presumes to make,
And doth the Learneds taske vpon him take.

But that same gentle Spirit, from whose pen
Large streames of honnie and sweete Nectar
   flowe,
Scorning the boldnes of such base-borne men,
Which dare their follies forth so rashlie throwe ;
Doth rather choose to sit in idle Cell,   221
Than so himselfe to mockerie to sell.

So am I made the seruant of the manie,
And laughing stocke of all that list to scorne,
Not honored nor cared for of anie ;
But loath'd of losels as a thing forlorne :
Therefore I mourne and sorrow with the rest
Vntill my cause of sorrow be redrest.

Therewith she lowdly did lament and shrike,
Pouring forth streames of teares abundantly,
And all her Sisters with compassion like, 231
The breaches of her singults did supply.
So rested shee : and then the next in rew
Began her grieuous plaint, as doth ensew.

Euterpe.

Like as the dearling of the Summers pryde,
Faire *Philomele*, when winters stormie wrath
The goodly fields, that earst so gay were dyde
In colours diuers, quite despoyled hath,
All comfortlesse doth hide her chearlesse head
During the time of that her widowhead : 240

So we, that earst were wont in sweet accord
All places with our pleasant notes to fill,
Whilest fauourable times did vs afford
Free libertie to chaunt our charmes at will :
All comfortlesse vpon the bared bow,
Like wofull Culuers doo sit wayling now.

For far more bitter storme than winters stowre
The beautie of the world hath lately wasted,
And those fresh buds, which wont so faire to
   flowre,
Hath marred quite, and all their blossoms blasted:
And those yong plants, which wont with fruit
   t'abound,   251
Now without fruite or leaues are to be found.

A stonie coldnesse hath benumbd the sence
And liuelie spirits of each liuing wight,
And dimd with darknesse their intelligence,
Darknesse more than *Cymerians* daylie night?
And monstrous error flying in the ayre,
Hath mard the face of all that semed fayre.

Image of hellish horrour, Ignorance,
Borne in the bosome of the black *Abysse*, 260
And fed with furies milke, for sustenaunce
Of his weake infancie, begot amisse
By yawning Sloth on his owne mother Night;
So hee his sonnes both Syre and brother hight.

He armd with blindnesse and with boldnes stout,
(For blind is bold) hath our fayre light defaced;
And gathering vnto him a ragged rout
Of *Faunes* and *Satyres*, hath our dwellings raced
And our chast bowers, in which all vertue rained,
With brutishnesse and beastlie filth hath stained.

The sacred springs of horsefoot *Helicon*, 271
So oft bedeawed with our learned layes,
And speaking streames of pure *Castalion*,
The famous witnesse of our wonted praise,
They trampled haue with their fowle footings
   trade,
And like to troubled puddles haue them made.

Our pleasant groues, which planted were with
   paines,
That with our musick wont so oft to ring,
And arbors sweet, in which the Shepheards
   swaines
Were wont so oft their Pastoralls to sing, 280
They haue cut downe and all their pleasaunce
   mard,
That now no pastorall is to bee hard.

In stead of them fowle Goblins and Shriekowles,
With fearfull howling do all places fill;
And feeble *Eccho* now laments and howles,
The dreadfull accents of their outcries shrill.
So all is turned into wildernesse,
Whilest Ignorance the Muses doth oppresse.

And I whose ioy was earst with Spirit full
To teach the warbling pipe to sound aloft, 290
My spirits now dismayd with sorrow dull,
Doo mone my miserie in silence soft.
Therefore I mourne and waile incessantly,
Till please the heauens affoord me remedy.

Therewith shee wayled with exceeding woe
And pitious lamentation did make,
And all her sisters seeing her doo soe,
With equall plaints her sorrowe did partake.
So rested shee: and then the next in rew,
Began her grieuous plaint as doth ensew. 300

Terpsichore.

Who so hath in the lap of soft delight
Beene long time luld, and fed with pleasures
   sweet,
Feareles through his own fault or Fortunes
   spight,
To tumble into sorrow and regreet,
Yf chaunce him fall into calamitie,
Findes greater burthen of his miserie.

So wee that earst in ioyance did abound
And in the bosome of all blis did sit,
Like virgin Queenes with laurell garlands cround,
For vertues meed and ornament of wit, 310
Sith ignorance our kingdome did confound,
Bee now become most wretched wightes on
   ground:
And in our royall thrones which lately stood
In th'hearts of men to rule them carefully,
He now hath placed his accursed brood,
By him begotten of fowle infamy;
Blind Error, scornefull Follie, and base Spight,
Who hold by wrong, that wee should haue by
   right.

They to the vulgar sort now pipe and sing,
And make them merrie with their fooleries, 320
They cherelie chaunt and rymes at randon fling,
The fruitfull spawne of their ranke fantasies:
They feede the eares of fooles with flattery,
And good men blame, and losels magnify:
All places they doo with their toyes possesse,
And raigne in liking of the multitude,
The schooles they fill with fond new fanglenesse,
And sway in Court with pride and rashnes rude;
Mongst simple shepheards they do boast their
   skill,
And say their musicke matcheth *Phœbus* quill.

The noble hearts to pleasures they allure, 331
And tell their Prince that learning is but vaine,
Faire Ladies loues they spot with thoughts impure,
And gentle mindes with lewd delights distaine:
Clerks they to loathly idlenes entice,
And fill their bookes with discipline of vice.

So euery where they rule and tyrannize,
For their vsurped kingdomes maintenaunce,
The whiles we silly Maides, whom they dispize,
And with reprochfull scorne discountenaunce,
From our owne natiue heritage exilde, 341
Walk through the world of euery one reuilde.

Nor anie one doth care to call vs in,
Or once vouchsafeth vs to entertaine,
Vnlesse some one perhaps of gentle kin,
For pitties sake compassion our paine,
And yeeld vs some reliefe in this distresse :
Yet to be so relieu'd is wretchednesse.

So wander we all carefull comfortlesse,
Yet none doth care to comfort vs at all ;   350
So seeke we helpe our sorrow to redresse,
Yet none vouchsafes to answere to our call :
Therefore we mourne and pittilesse complaine,
Because none liuing pittieth our paine.

With that she wept and wofullie waymented,
That naught on earth her griefe might pacifie ;
And all the rest her dolefull din augmented,
With shrikes and groanes and grieuous agonie.
So ended shee : and then the next in rew,
Began her piteous plaint as doth ensew.   360

Erato

Ye gentle Spirits breathing from aboue,
Where ye in *Venus* siluer bowre were bred,
Thoughts halfe deuine, full of the fire of loue,
With beawtie kindled and with pleasure fed,
Which ye now in securitie possesse,
Forgetfull of your former heauinesse :

Now change the tenor of your ioyous layes,
With which ye vse your loues to deifie,
And blazon foorth an earthlie beauties praise,
Aboue the compasse of the arched skie :   370
Now change your praises into piteous cries,
And Eulogies turne into Elegies.

Such as ye wont whenas those bitter stounds
Of raging loue first gan you to torment,
And launch your hearts with lamentable wounds
Of secret sorrow and sad languishment,
Before your Loues did take you vnto grace ;
Those now renew as fitter for this place

For I that rule in measure moderate
The tempest of that stormie passion,   380
And vse to paint in rimes the troublous state
Of Louers life in likest fashion,
Am put from practise of my kindlie skill,
Banisht by those that Loue with leawdnes fill.

Loue wont to be schoolmaster of my skill
And the deuicefull matter of my song ;
Sweete Loue deuoyd of villanie or ill,
But pure and spotles, as at first he sprong
Out of th'Almighties bosome, where he nests ;
From thence infused into mortall brests.   390

Such high conceipt of that celestiall fire,
The base-borne brood of blindnes cannot gesse,
Ne euer dare their dunghill thoughts aspire
Vnto so loftie pitch of perfectnesse,

But rime at riot, and doo rage in loue ;
Yet little wote what doth thereto behoue.

Faire *Cytheree* the Mother of delight,
And Queene of beautie, now thou maist go pack ;
For lo thy Kingdome is defaced quight,
Thy scepter rent, and power put to wrack ;   400
And thy gay Sonne, that winged God of Loue,
May now goe prune his plumes like ruffed Doue.

And ye three Twins to light by *Venus* brought,
The sweete companions of the Muses late,
From whom what euer thing is goodly thought
Doth borrow grace, the fancie to aggrate ;
Go beg with vs, and be companions still
As heretofore of good, so now of ill.

For neither you nor we shall anie more
Finde entertainment, or in Court or Schoole :
For that which was accounted heretofore   411
The learneds meed, is now lent to the foole,
He sings of loue, and maketh louing layes,
And they him heare, and they him highly
  prayse.

With that she powred foorth a brackish flood
Of bitter teares, and made exceeding mone ;
And all her Sisters seeing her sad mood,
With lowd laments her answered all at one.
So ended she : and then the next in rew
Began her grieuous plaint, as doth ensew. 420

Calliope

To whom shall I my euill case complaine,
Or tell the anguish of my inward smart,
Sith none is left to remedie my paine,
Or deignes to pitie a perplexed hart ;
But rather seekes my sorrow to augment
With fowle reproach, and cruell banishment.

For they to whom I ysed to applie
The faithfull seruice of my learned skill,
The goodly off-spring of *Ioues* progenie,
That wont the world with famous acts to fill ;
Whose liuing praises in heroïck style,   431
It is my chiefe profession to compyle.

They all corrupted through the rust of time,
That doth all fairest things on earth deface,
Or through vnnoble sloth, or sinfull crime,
That doth degenerate the noble race ;
Haue both desire of worthie deeds forlorne,
And name of learning vtterly doo scorne.

Ne doo they care to haue the auncestrie
Of th'old Heroës memorizde anew,   440
Ne doo they care that late posteritie
Should know their names, or speak their praises
  dew :
But die forgot from whence at first they sprong,
As they themselues shalbe forgot ere long.

What bootes it then to come from glorious
Forefathers, or to haue been nobly bredd?
What oddes twixt *Irus* and old *Inachus*,
Twixt best and worst, when both alike are dedd;
If none of neither mention should make,
Nor out of dust their memories awake?   450
Or who would euer care to doo braue deed,
Or striue in vertue others to excell;
If none should yeeld him his deserued meed,
Due praise, that is the spur of dooing well?
For if good were not praised more than ill,
None would choose goodnes of his owne freewill.

Therefore the nurse of vertue I am hight,
And golden Trompet of eternitie,
That lowly thoughts lift vp to heauens hight,
And mortall men haue powre to deifie: 460
Bacchus and *Hercules* I raisd to heauen,
And *Charlemaine*, amongst the Starris seauen.

But now I will my golden Clarion rend,
And will henceforth immortalize no more:
Sith I no more finde worthie to commend
For prize of value, or for learned lore:
For noble Peeres whom I was wont to raise,
Now onely seeke for pleasure, nought for praise.

Their great reuenues all in sumptuous pride
They spend, that nought to learning they may
    spare;   470
And the rich fee which Poets wont diuide,
Now Parasites and Sycophants doo share:
Therefore I mourne and endlesse sorrow make,
Both for my selfe and for my Sisters sake.

With that she lowdly gan to waile and shrike,
And from her eyes a sea of teares did powre,
And all her sisters with compassion like,
Did more increase the sharpnes of her showre.
So ended she: and then the next in rew
Began her plaint, as doth herein ensew.   480

Vrania.

What wrath of Gods, or wicked influence
Of Starres conspiring wretched men t'afflict,
Hath powrd on earth this noyous pestilence,
That mortall mindes doth inwardly infect
With loue of blindnesse and of ignorance,
To dwell in darkenesse without souenance?

What difference twixt man and beast is left,
When th'heauenlie light of knowledge is put out,
And th'ornaments of wisdome are bereft?
Then wandreth he in error and in doubt,   490
Vnweeting of the danger hee is in,
Through fleshes frailtie and deceipt of sin.

In this wide world in which they wretches stray,
It is the onelie comfort which they haue,
It is their light, their loadstarre and their day;
But hell and darkenesse and the grislie graue

Is ignorance, the enemie of grace,
That mindes of men borne heauenlie doth
    debace.

Through knowledge we behold the worlds
    creation,
How in his cradle first he fostred was;   500
And iudge of Natures cunning operation,
How things she formed of a formelesse mas:
By knowledge wee do learne our selues to
    knowe,
And what to man, and what to God wee owe.

From hence wee mount aloft vnto the skie,
And looke into the Christall firmament,
There we behold the heauens great *Hierarchie*,
The Starres pure light, the Spheres swift moue-
    ment,
The Spirites and Intelligences fayre   509
And Angels waighting on th'Almighties chayre.

And there, with humble minde and high
    insight,
Th'eternall Makers maiestie wee viewe,
His loue, his truth, his glorie, and his might,
And mercie more than mortall men can vew.
O soueraigne Lord, O soueraigne happinesse
To see thee, and thy mercie measurelesse:

Such happines haue they, that doo embrace
The precepts of my heauenlie discipline;
But shame and sorrow and accursed case
Haue they, that scorne the schoole of arts
    diuine,   520
And banish me, which do professe the skill
To make men heauenly wise, through humbled
    will.

How euer yet they mee despise and spight,
I feede on sweet contentment of my thought,
And please my selfe with mine owne selfe-
    delight,
In contemplation of things heauenlie wrought:
So, loathing earth, I looke vp to the sky,
And being driuen hence, I thether fly.

Thence I behold the miserie of men,
Which want the blis that wisedom would them
    breed,   530
And like brute beasts doo lie in loathsome den,
Of ghostly darkenes, and of gastlie dreed:
For whom I mourne and for my selfe complaine,
And for my Sisters eake whom they disdaine.

With that shee wept and waild so pityouslie,
As if her eyes had beene two springing wells
And all the rest her sorrow to supplie,
Did throw forth shrieks and cries and dreery
    yells.
So ended shee, and then the next in rew,
Began her mournfull plaint as doth ensew.   540

Polyhymnia.

A dolefull case desires a dolefull song,
Without vaine art or curious complements,
And squallid Fortune into basenes flong,
Doth scorne the pride of wonted ornaments.
Then fittest are these ragged rimes for mee,
To tell my sorrowes that exceeding bee :

For the sweet numbers and melodious measures,
With which I wont the winged words to tie,
And make a tunefull Diapase of pleasures,
Now being let to runne at libertie   550
By those which haue no skill to rule them right,
Haue now quite lost their naturall delight.

Heapes of huge words vphoorded hideously,
With horrid sound though hauing little sence,
They thinke to be chiefe praise of Poëtry ;
And thereby wanting due intelligence,
Haue mard the face of goodly Poësie,
And made a monster of their fantasie :

Whilom in ages past none might professe   559
But Princes and high Priests that secret skill,
The sacred lawes therein they wont expresse,
And with deepe Oracles their verses fill :
Then was shee held in soueraigne dignitie,
And made the noursling of Nobilitie.

But now nor Prince nor Priest doth her main-
    tayne,
But suffer her prophaned for to bee
Of the base vulgar, that with hands vncleane
Dares to pollute her hidden mysterie.
And treadeth vnder foote hir holie things,
Which was the care of Kesars and of Kings.

One onelie liues, her ages ornament,   571
And myrrour of her Makers maiestie ;
That with rich bountie and deare cherishment,
Supports the praise of noble Poësie :
Ne onelie fauours them which it professe,
But is her selfe a peereles Poëtresse.

Most peereles Prince, most peereles Poëtresse,
The true *Pandora* of all heauenly graces,
Diuine *Elisa*, sacred Emperesse :
Liue she for euer, and her royall P'laces   580
Be fild with praises of diuinest wits,
That her eternize with their heauenlie writs.

Some few beside, this sacred skill esteme,
Admirers of her glorious excellence,
Which being lightned with her beawties beme,
Are thereby fild with happie influence :
And lifted vp aboue the worldes gaze,
To sing with Angels her immortall praize.

But all the rest as borne of saluage brood,
And hauing beene with Acorns alwaies fed,
Can no whit fauour this celestiall food,   591
But with base thoughts are into blindnesse led,
And kept from looking on the lightsome day :
For whome I waile and weepe all that I may.

Eftsoones such store of teares she forth did
    powre,
As if shee all to water would haue gone ;
And all her sisters seeing her sad stowre,
Did weep and waile and made exceeding
    mone,
And all their learned instruments did breake,
The rest, vntold, no louing tongue can speake.

FINIS.

Virgils Gnat.

Long since dedicated

To the most noble and excellent Lord,

the Earle of Leicester, late

deceased.

W Rong'd, yet not daring to expresse my
    paine,
To you (great Lord) the causer of my care,
In clowdie teares my case I thus complaine
Vnto your selfe, that onely priuie are :
    But if that any Oedipus vnware
Shall chaunce, through power of some diuining
    spright,

To reade the secrete of this riddle rare,
And know the purporte of my euill plight,
    Let him rest pleased with his owne insight.
Ne further seeke to glose vpon the text :
For griefe enough it is to grieued wight
To feele his fault, and not be further vext.
    But what so by my selfe may not be showen,
May by this Gnatts complaint be easily knowen.

Virgils Gnat.

WE now haue playde (*Augustus*) wantonly,
　Tuning our song vnto a tender Muse,
And like a cobweb weauing slenderly,
Haue onely playde : let thus much then excuse
This Gnats small Poeme, that th'whole history
Is but a iest, though enuie it abuse :
But who such sports and sweet delights doth blame,
Shall lighter seeme than this Gnats idle name.

Hereafter, when as season more secure
Shall bring forth fruit, this Muse shall speak to
　thee　　　　　　　　　　　　　　　　10
In bigger notes, that may thy sense allure,
And for thy worth frame some fit Poesie,
The golden offspring of *Latona* pure,
And ornament of great *Ioues* progenie,
Phœbus shall be the author of my song,
Playing on yuorie harp with siluer strong.

He shall inspire my verse with gentle mood
Of Poets Prince, whether he woon beside
Faire *Xanthus* sprincled with *Chimæras* blood ;
Or in the woods of *Astery* abide ;　　　20
Or whereas mount *Parnasse*, the Muses brood,
Doth his broad forhead like two hornes diuide,
And the sweete waues of sounding *Castaly*
With liquid foote doth slide downe easily.

Wherefore ye Sisters which the glorie bee
Of the *Pierian* streames, fayre *Naiades*,
Go too, and dauncing all in companie,
Adorne that God : and thou holie *Pales*,
To whome the honest care of husbandrie
Returneth by continuall successe,　　　30
Haue care for to pursue his footing light ;
Throgh the wide woods, and groues, with green
　leaues dight

Professing thee I lifted am aloft
Betwixt the forrest wide and starrie sky :
And thou most dread (*Octauius*) which oft
To learned wits giuest courage worthily,
O come (thou sacred childe) come sliding soft,
And fauour my beginnings graciously :
For not these leaues do sing that dreadfull stound,
When Giants bloud did staine *Phlegræan*
　ground.　　　　　　　　　　　　40
Nor how th'halfe horsy people, *Centaures* hight,
Fought with the bloudie *Lapithaes* at bord,
Nor how the East with tyranous despight
Burnt th'*Attick* towres, and people slew with
　sword ;
Nor how mount *Athos* through exceeding might
Was digged downe, nor yron bands abord
The *Pontick* sea by their huge Nauy cast,
My volume shall renowne, so long since past.

Nor *Hellespont* trampled with horses feete,　49
When flocking *Persians* did the *Greeks* affray ;
But my soft Muse, as for her power more meete,
Delights (with *Phœbus* friendly leaue) to play
An easie running verse with tender feete.
And thou (dread sacred child) to thee alway,
Let euerlasting lightsome glory striue,
Through the worlds endles ages to suruiue.

And let an happie roome remaine for thee
Mongst heauenly ranks, where blessed soules do
　rest ;
And let long lasting life with ioyous glee,
As thy due meede that thou deseruest best,　60
Hereafter many yeares remembred be
Amongst good men, of whom thou oft are blest ;
Liue thou for euer in all happinesse :
But let vs turne to our first businesse.

The fiery Sun was mounted now on hight
Vp to the heauenly towers, and shot each where
Out of his golden Charet glistering light ;
And fayre *Aurora* with her rosie heare,
The hatefull darknes now had put to flight,
When as the shepheard seeing day appeare,　70
His little Goats gan driue out of their stalls,
To feede abroad, where pasture best befalls.

To an high mountaines top he with them went,
Where thickest grasse did cloath the open hills :
They now amongst the woods and thickets
　ment,
Now in the valleies wandring at their wills,
Spread themselues farre abroad through each
　descent ;
Some on the soft greene grasse feeding their
　fills ;
Some clambring through the hollow cliffes on hy,
Nibble the bushie shrubs, which growe thereby.

Others the vtmost boughs of trees doe crop,
And brouze the woodbine twigges, that freshly
　bud ;　　　　　　　　　　　　　82
This with full bit doth catch the vtmost top
Of some soft Willow, or new growen stud ;
This with sharpe teeth the bramble leaues doth
　lop,
And chaw the tender prickles in her Cud ;
The whiles another high doth ouerlooke
Her owne like image in a christall brooke.

O the great happines, which shepheards haue,
Who so loathes not too much the poore estate,
With minde that ill vse doth before depraue,
Ne measures all things by the costly rate　92
Of riotise, and semblants outward braue ;
No such sad cares, as wont to macerate
And rend the greedie mindes of couetous men,
Do euer creepe into the shepheards den.

Ne cares he if the fleece, which him arayes,
Be not twice steeped in Assyrian dye,
Ne glistering of golde, which vnderlayes   99
The summer beames, doe blinde his gazing eye.
Ne pictures beautie, nor the glauncing rayes
Of precious stones, whence no good commeth by;
Ne yet his cup embost with Imagery
Of *Bætus* or of *Alcons* vanity.

Ne ought the whelky pearles esteemeth hee,
Which are from Indian seas brought far away:
But with pure brest from carefull sorrow free,
On the soft grasse his limbs doth oft display,
In sweete spring time, when flowres varietie
With sundrie colours paints the sprincled lay;
There lying all at ease, from guile or spight, 111
With pype of fennie reedes doth him delight.

There he, Lord of himselfe, with palme bedight,
His looser locks doth wrap in wreath of vine:
There his milk dropping Goats be his delight,
And fruitefull *Pales*, and the forrest greene,
And darkesome caues in pleasaunt vallies pight,
Whereas continuall shade is to be seene,
And where fresh springing wells, as christall neate,
Do alwayes flow, to quench his thirstie heate.

O who can lead then a more happie life,   121
Than he, that with cleane minde and heart sincere,
No greedy riches knowes nor bloudie strife,
No deadly fight of warlick fleete doth feare,
Ne runs in perill of foes cruell knife,
That in the sacred temples he may reare
A trophee of his glittering spoyles and treasure,
Or may abound in riches aboue measure.

Of him his God is worshipt with his sythe,
And not with skill of craftsman polished :   130
He ioyes in groues, and makes himselfe full
    blythe,
With sundrie flowers in wilde fieldes gathered ;
Ne frankincens he from *Panchæa* buyth,
Sweete quiet harbours in his harmeles head,
And perfect pleasure buildes her ioyous bowre,
Free from sad cares, that rich mens hearts
    deuowre.

This all his care, this all his whole indeuour
To this his minde and senses he doth bend,
How he may flow in quiets matchles treasour,
Content with any food that God doth send ;
And how his limbs, resolu'd through idle l.isour,
Vnto sweete sleepe he may securely lend,   142
In some coole shadow from the scorching heat,
The whiles his flock their chawed cuds do eate.

O flocks, O Faunes, and O ye pleasaunt springs
Of *Tempe*, where the countrey Nymphs are rife,
Through whose not costly care each shepheard
    sings
As merrie notes vpon his rusticke Fife,

As that *Ascræan* bard, whose fame now rings
Through the wide world, and leads as ioytulllife.
Free from all troubles and from worldly toyle,
In which fond men doe all their dayes turmoyle.

In such delights whilst thus his carelesse time
This shepheard driues, vpleaning on his batt,
And on shrill reedes chaunting his rustick rime,
Hyperion throwing foorth his beames full hott,
Into the highest top of heauen gan clime,
And the world parting by an equall lott,
Did shed his whirling flames on either side,
As the great *Ocean* doth himselfe diuide.   160

Then gan the shepheard gather into one
His stragling Goates, and draue them to a foord,
Whose cærule streame, rombling in Pible stone,
Crept vnder mosse as greene as any goord.
Now had the Sun halfe heauen ouergone,
When he his heard back from that water foord,
Draue from the force of *Phœbus* boyling ray,
Into thick shadowes, there themselues to lay.

Soone as he them plac'd in thy sacred wood
(O *Delian* Goddesse) saw, to which of yore
Came the bad daughter of old *Cadmus* brood,
Cruell *Agaue*, flying vengeance sore   172
Of king *Nictileus* for the guiltie blood,
Which she with cursed hands had shed before ;
There she halfe frantick hauing slaine her sonne,
Did shrowd her selfe like punishment to shonne.

Here also playing on the grassy greene,
Woodgods, and Satyres, and swift *Dryades*,
With many Fairies oft were dauncing seene.
Not so much did Dan *Orpheus* represse,   180
The streames of *Hebrus* with his songs I weene,
As that faire troupe of woodie Goddesses
Staied thee, (O *Peneus*) powring foorth to thee,
From cheerefull lookes, great mirth and glad-
    some glee.

The verie nature of the place, resounding
With gentle murmure of the breathing ayre,
A pleasant bowre with all delight abounding
In the fresh shadowe did for them prepayre,
To rest their limbs with wearines redounding.
For first the high Palme trees with braunches
    faire,   190
Out of the lowly vallies did arise,
And high shoote vp their heads into the skyes.

And them amongst the wicked Lotos grew,
Wicked, for holding guilefully away
Vlysses men, whom rapt with sweetenes new,
Taking to hoste, it quite from him did stay,
And eke those trees, in whose transformed hew
The Sunnes sad daughters waylde the rash decay
Of *Phaeton*, whose limbs with lightening rent,
They gathering vp, with sweete teares did
lament.   200

And that same tree, in which *Demophoon*,
By his disloyalty lamented sore,
Eternall hurte left vnto many one:
Whom als accompanied the Oke, of yore
Through fatall charmes transformd to such an
  one:
The Oke, whose Acornes were our foode, before
That *Ceres* seede of mortall men were knowne,
Which first *Triptoleme* taught how to be sowne.

Here also grew the rougher rinded Pine,
The great *Argoan* ships braue ornament 210
Whom golden Fleece did make an heauenly signe:
Which coueting, with his high tops extent,
To make the mountaines touch the starres diuine,
Decks all the forrest with embellishment,
And the blacke Holme that loues the watrie vale,
And the sweete Cypresse, signe of deadly bale.

Emongst the rest the clambring Yuie grew,
Knitting his wanton armes with grasping hold,
Least that the Poplar happely should rew
Her brothers strokes, whose boughes she doth
  enfold 220
With her lythe twigs, till they the top survew,
And paint with pallid greene her buds of gold.
Next did the Myrtle tree to her approach,
Not yet vnmindfull of her olde reproach.

But the small Birds in their wide boughs em-
  bowring,
Chaunted their sundrie tunes with sweete con-
  sent,
And vnder them a siluer Spring forth powring
His trickling streames, a gentle murmure sent;
Thereto the frogs, bred in the slimie scowring
Of the moist moores, their iarring voyces bent:
And shrill grashoppers chirped them around:
All which the ayrie Echo did resound. 232

In this so pleasant place this Shepheards flocke
Lay euerie where, their wearie limbs to rest,
On euerie bush, and euerie hollow rocke
Where breathe on them the whistling wind
  mote best;
The whiles the Shepheard self tending his stocke,
Sate by the fountaine side, in shade to rest,
Where gentle slumbring sleep oppressed him,
Displaid on ground, and seized euerie lim. 240

Of trecherie or traines nought tooke he keep,
But looslie on the grassie greene dispredd,
His dearest life did trust to careles sleep;
Which weighing down his drouping drowsie hedd,
In quiet rest his molten heart did steep,
Deuoid of care, and feare of all falshedd:
Had not inconstant fortune, bent to ill,
Bid strange mischance his quietnes to spill.

For at his wonted time in that same place 249
An huge great Serpent all with speckles pide,

To drench himselfe in moorish slime did trace,
There from the boyling heate himselfe to hide:
He passing by with rolling wreathed pace,
With brandisht tongue the emptie aire did gride,
And wrapt his scalie boughts with fell despight,
That all things seem'd appalled at his sight.

Now more and more hauing himselfe enrolde,
His glittering breast he lifteth vp on hie,
And with proud vaunt his head aloft doth holde;
His creste aboue spotted with purple die, 260
On euerie side did shine like scalie golde,
And his bright eyes glauncing full dreadfullie,
Did seeme to flame out flakes of flashing fyre,
And with sterne lookes to threaten kindled yre.

Thus wise long time he did himselfe dispace
There round about, when as at last he spide
Lying along before him in that place,
That flocks grand Captaine, and most trustie
  guide:
Eftsoones more fierce in visage, and in pace,
Throwing his firie eyes on euerie side, 270
He commeth on, and all things in his way
Full stearnly rends, that might his passage stay.

Much he disdaines, that anie one should dare
To come vnto his haunt; for which intent
He inly burns, and gins straight to prepare
The weapons, which Nature to him hath lent;
Fellie he hisseth, and doth fiercely stare,
And hath his iawes with angrie spirits rent,
That all his tract with bloudie drops is stained,
And all his foldes are now in length outstrained.

Whom thus at point prepared, to preuent,
A litle noursling of the humid ayre, 282
A Gnat vnto the sleepie Shepheard went,
And marking where his ey-lids twinckling rare,
Shewd the two pearles, which sight vnto him lent,
Through their thin couerings appearing fayre,
His little needle there infixing deep,
Warnd him awake, from death himselfe to keep.

Wherewith enrag'd, he fiercely gan vpstart,
And with his hand him rashly bruzing, slewe
As in auengement of his heedles smart, 291
That streight the spirite out of his senses flew,
And life out of his members did depart:
When suddenly casting aside his vew,
He spide his foe with felonous intent,
And feruent eyes to his destruction bent.

All suddenly dismaid, and hartles quight,
He fled abacke, and catching hastie holde
Of a yong alder hard beside him pight, 299
It rent, and streight about him gan beholde,
What God or Fortune would assist his might.
But whether God or Fortune made him bold
Its hard to read: yet hardie will he had
To ouercome, that made him lesse adrad.

The scalie backe of that most hideous snake
Enwrapped round, oft faining to retire,
And oft him to assaile, he fiercely strake
Whereas his temples did his creast-front tyre ;
And for he was but slowe, did slowth off shake,
And gazing ghastly on (for feare and yre   310
Had blent so much his sense, that lesse he feard ;)
Yet when he saw him slaine, himselfe he cheard.

By this the night forth from the darksome bowre
Of *Herebus* her teemed steedes gan call,
And laesie *Vesper* in his timely howre
From golden *Oeta* gan proceede withall ;
Whenas the Shepheard after this sharpe stowre,
Seing the doubled shadowes low to fall,
Gathering his straying flocke, does homeward
fare,
And vnto rest his wearie ioynts prepare.   320

Into whose sense so soone as lighter sleepe
Was entered, and now loosing euerie lim,
Sweete slumbring deaw in carelesnesse did
steepe,
The Image of that Gnat appeard to him,
And in sad tearmes gan sorrowfully weepe,
With greislie countenaunce and visage grim,
Wailing the wrong which he had done of late,
In steed of good hastning his cruell fate.

Said he, what haue I wretch deseru'd, that thus
Into this bitter bale I am outcast,   330
Whilest that thy life more deare and precious
Was than mine owne, so long as it did last ?
I now in lieu of paines so gracious,
Am tost in th'ayre with euerie windie blast :
Thou safe deliuered from sad decay,
Thy careles limbs in loose sleep dost display.

So liuest thou, but my poore wretched ghost
Is forst to ferrie ouer *Lethes* Riuer,
And spoyld of *Charon* too and fro am tost.
Seest thou, how all places quake and quiuer   340
Lightned with deadly lamps on euerie post ?
Tisiphone each where doth shake and shiuer
Her flaming fire brond, encountring me,
Whose lockes vncombed cruell adders be.

And *Cerberus*, whose many mouthes doo bay,
And barke out flames, as if on fire he fed ;
Adowne whose necke in terrible array,
Ten thousand snakes cralling about his hed
Doo hang in heapes, that horribly affray,
And bloodie eyes doo glister firie red ;   350
He oftentimes me dreadfullie doth threaten,
With painfull torments to be sorely beaten.

Ay me, that thankes so much should faile of meed,
For that I thee restor'd to life againe,
Euen from the doore of death and deadlie dreed.
Where then is now the guerdon of my paine ?

Where the reward ot my so piteous deed ?
The praise of pitie vanisht is in vaine,
And th'antique faith of Iustice long agone
Out of the land is fled away and gone.   360

I saw anothers fate approaching fast,
And left mine owne his safetie to tender ;
Into the same mishap I now am cast,
And shun'd destruction doth destruction render:
Not vnto him that neuer hath trespast,
But punishment is due to the offender.
Yet let destruction be the punishment,
So long as thankfull will may it relent.

I carried am into waste wildernesse,   369
Waste wildernes, amongst *Cymerian* shades,
Where endles paines and hideous heauinesse
Is round about me heapt in darksome glades.
For there huge *Othos* sits in sad distresse,
Fast bound with serpents that him oft inuades :
Far of beholding *Ephialtes* tide,
Which once assai'd to burne this world so wide.

And there is mournfull *Tityus* mindefull yet
Of thy displeasure, O *Latona* faire ;
Displeasure too implacable was it,
That made him meat for wild foules of the ayre :
Much do I feare among such fiends to sit ;   381
Much do I feare back to them to repayre,
To the black shadowes of the *Stygian* shore,
Where wretched ghosts sit wailing euermore.

There next the vtmost brinck doth he abide,
That did the bankets of the Gods bewray,
Whose throat through thirst to nought nigh
being dride
His sense to seeke for ease turnes euery way :
And he that in auengement of his pride,
For scorning to the sacred Gods to pray,   390
Against a mountaine rolls a mightie stone,
Calling in vaine for rest, and can haue none.

Go ye with them, go cursed damosells,
Whose bridale torches foule *Erynnis* tynde,
And *Hymen* at your Spousalls sad, foretells
Tydings of death and massacre vnkinde :
With them that cruell *Colchid* mother dwells,
The which conceiu'd in her reuengefull minde,
With bitter woundes her owne deere babes to
slay,
And murdred troupes vpon great heapes to lay.

There also those two *Pandionian* maides,   401
Calling on *Itis*, *Itis* euermore,
Whom wretched boy they slew with guiltie blades;
For whome the *Thracian* king lamenting sore,
Turn'd to a Lapwing, fowlie them vpbraydes,
And fluttering round about them still does sore:
There now they all eternally complaine
Of others wrong, and suffer endles paine.

But the two brethren borne of *Cadmus* blood,
Whilst each does for the Soueraignty contend,
Blinde through ambition, and with vengeance
  wood,   411
Each doth against the others bodie bend
His cursed steele, of neither well withstood,
And with wide wounds their carcases doth rend ;
That yet they both doe mortall foes remaine,
Sith each with brothers bloudie hand was slaine.

Ah (waladay) there is no end of paine,
Nor chaunge of labour may intreated bee :
Yet I beyond all these am carried faine,
Where other powers farre different I see,   420
And must passe ouer to th'*Elisian* plaine :
There grim *Persephone* encountring mee,
Doth vrge her fellow Furies earnestlie,
With their bright firebronds me to terrifie.

There chast *Alceste* liues inuiolate,
Free from all care, for that her husbands daies
She did prolong by changing fate for fate.
Lo there liues also the immortall praise
Of womankinde, most faithfull to her mate,
Penelope : and from her farre awayes   430
A rulesse rout of yongmen, which her woo'd
All slaine with darts, lie wallowed in their blood.

And sad *Eurydice* thence now no more
Must turne to life, but there detained bee,
For looking back, being forbid before :
Yet was the guilt thereof, *Orpheus,* in thee.
Bold sure he was, and worthie spirite bore,
That durst those lowest shadowes goe to see,
And could beleeue that anie thing could please
Fell *Cerberus,* or Stygian powres appease. 440

Ne feard the burning waues of *Phlegeton,*
Nor those same mournfull kingdomes, com-
  passed
With rustie horrour and fowle fashion,
And deep digd vawtes, and Tartar couered
With bloodie night, and darke confusion,
And iudgement seates, whose Iudge is deadlie
  dred.
A iudge, that after death doth punish sore
The faults, which life hath trespassed before.

But valiant fortune made *Dan Orpheus* bolde :
For the swift running riuers still did stand, 450
And the wilde beasts their furie did withhold,
To follow *Orpheus* musicke through the land :
And th'Okes deep grounded in the earthly molde
Did moue, as if they could him vnderstand ;
And the shrill woods, which were of sense
  bereau'd,
Through their hard barke his siluer sound
  receau'd.

And eke the Moone her hastie steedes did stay,
Drawing in teemes along the starrie skie,

And didst (O monthly Virgin) thou delay
Thy nightly course, to heare his melodie ? 460
The same was able with like louely lay
The Queene of hell to moue as easily,
To yeeld *Eurydice* vnto her fere,
Backe to be borne, though it vnlawfull were.

She (Ladie) hauing well before approoued,
The feends to be too cruell and seuere,
Obseru'd th'appointed way, as her behooued,
Ne euer did her ey-sight turne arere,
Ne euer spake, ne cause of speaking mooued :
But cruell *Orpheus,* thou much crueller,   470
Seeking to kisse her, brok'st the Gods decree,
And thereby mad'st her euer damn'd to be.

Ah but sweete loue of pardon worthie is,
And doth deserue to haue small faults remitted ;
If Hell at least things lightly done amis
Knew how to pardon, when ought is omitted :
Yet are ye both receiued into blis,
And to the seates of happie soules admitted.
And you, beside the honourable band
Of great Heroës, doo in order stand.   480

There be the two stout sonnes of *Aeacus,*
Fierce *Peleus,* and the hardie *Telamon,*
Both seeming now full glad and ioyeous
Through their Syres dreadfull iurisdiction,
Being the Iudge of all that horrid hous :
And both of them by strange occasion,
Renown'd in choyce of happie marriage
Through *Venus* grace, and vertues cariage.

For th'one was rauisht of his owne bondmaide,
The faire *Ixione* captiu'd from *Troy :*   490
But th'other was with *Thetis* loue assaid,
Great *Nereus* his daughter, and his ioy.
On this side them there is a yongman layd,
Their match in glorie, mightie, fierce and coy ;
That from th'Argolick ships, with furious yre,
Bett back the furie of the Troian fyre.

O who would not recount the strong diuorces
Of that great warre, which Troianes oft behelde,
And oft beheld the warlike Greekish forces, 499
When *Teucrian* soyle with bloodie riuers swelde,
And wide *Sigæan* shores were spred with corses,
And *Simois* and *Xanthus* blood outwelde,
Whilst *Hector* raged with outragious minde,
Flames, weapons, wounds in *Greeks* fleete to
  haue tynde.

For *Ida* selfe, in ayde of that fierce fight,
Out of her mountaines ministred supplies,
And like a kindly nourse, did yeeld (for spight)
Store of firebronds out of her nourseries,
Vnto her foster children, that they might
Inflame the Nauie of their enemies,   510
And all the *Rhetæan* shore to ashes turne,
Where lay the ships, which they did seeke to burne.

Gainst which the noble sonne of *Telamon*
Opposd' himselfe, and thwarting his huge shield,
Them battell bad, gainst whom appeard anon
Hector, the glorie of the *Troian* field :
Both fierce and furious in contention
Encountred, that their mightie strokes so shrild,
As the great clap of thunder, which doth ryue
The ratling heauens, and cloudes asunder dryue.

So th'one with fire and weapons did contend
To cut the ships, from turning home againe
To *Argos*, th'other stroue for to defend
The force of *Vulcane* with his might and maine.
Thus th'one *Aeacide* did his fame extend :
But th'other ioy'd, that on the *Phrygian* playne
Hauing the blood of vanquisht *Hector* shedd,
He compast *Troy* thrice with his bodie dedd.

Againe great dole on either partie grewe,
That him to death vnfaithfull *Paris* sent, 530
And also him that false *Vlysses* slewe,
Drawne into danger through close ambushment :
Therefore from him *Laërtes* sonne his vewe
Doth turne aside, and boasts his good euent
In working of *Strymonian Rhæsus* fall,
And efte in *Dolons* subtile surprysall.

Againe the dreadfull *Cycones* him dismay,
And blacke *Læstrigones*, a people stout :
Then greedie *Scilla*, vnder whom there bay
Manie great bandogs, which her gird about :
Then doo the *Aetnean* Cyclops him affray, 541
And deep *Charybdis* gulphing in and out :
Lastly the squalid lakes of *Tartarie*,
And griesly Feends of hell him terrifie.

There also goodly *Agamemnon* bosts,
The glorie of the stock of *Tantalus*,
And famous light of all the Greekish hosts,
Vnder whose conduct most victorious,
The *Dorick* flames consum'd the *Iliack* posts.
Ah but the *Greekes* themselues more dolorous,
To thee, O *Troy*, paid penaunce for thy fall,
In th'*Hellespont* being nigh drowned all. 552

Well may appeare by proofe of their mischaunce,
The chaungfull turning of mens slipperie state,
That none, whom fortune freely doth aduaunce,
Himselfe therefore to heauen should eleuate :
For loftie type of honour through the glaunce
Of enuies dart, is downe in dust prostrate ;
And all that vaunts in worldly vanitie,
Shall fall through fortunes mutabilitie. 560

Th'*Argolicke* power returning home againe,
Enricht with spoyles of th'*Erichthonian* towre,
Did happie winde and weather entertaine,
And with good speed the fomie billowes scowre :
No signe of storme, no feare of future paine,
Which soone ensued them with heauie stowre.

Nereïs to the Seas a token gaue,
The whiles their crooked keeles the surges claue.

Suddenly, whether through the Gods decree,
Or haplesse rising of some froward starre, 570
The heauens on euerie side enclowded bee :
Black stormes and fogs are blowen vp from farre,
That now the Pylote can no loadstarre see,
But skies and seas doo make most dreadfull
    warre ;
The billowes striuing to the heauens to reach,
And th'heauens striuing them for to impeach.

And in auengement of their bold attempt,
Both Sun and starres and all the heauenly
    powres
Conspire in one to wreake their rash contempt,
And downe on them to fall from highest towres :
The skie in pieces seeming to be rent, 581
Throwes lightning forth, and haile, and harmful
    showres,
That death on euerie side to them appeares
In thousand formes, to worke more ghastly
    feares.

Some in the greedie flouds are sunke and drent,
Some on the rocks of *Caphareus* are throwne ;
Some on th'*Euboick* Cliffs in pieces rent ;
Some scattred on the *Hercæan* shores vnknowne ;
And manie lost, of whom no moniment
Remaines, nor memorie is to be showne : 590
Whilst all the purchase of the *Phrigian* pray
Tost on salt billowes, round about doth stray.

Here manie other like Heroës bee,
Equall in honour to the former crue,
Whom ye in goodly seates may placed see,
Descended all from *Rome* by linage due,
From *Rome*, that holds the world in soueregntie,
And doth all Nations vnto her subdue :
Here *Fabij* and *Decij* doo dwell,
Horatij that in vertue did excell. 600

And here the antique fame of stout *Camill*
Doth euer liue, and constant *Curtius*,
Who stifly bent his vowed life to spill
For Countreyes health, a gulph most hideous
Amidst the Towne with his owne corps did fill,
T'appease the powers ; and prudent *Mutius*,
Who in his flesh endur'd the scorching flame,
To daunt his foe by ensample of the same.

And here wise *Curius*, companion
Of noble vertues, liues in endles rest ; 610
And stout *Flaminius*, whose deuotion
Taught him the fires scorn'd furie to detest ;
And here the praise of either *Scipion*
Abides in highest place aboue the best,
To whom the ruin'd walls of *Carthage* vow'd,
Trembling their forces, sound their praises lowd.

Liue they for euer through their lasting praise :
But I poore wretch am forced to retourne
To the sad lakes, that *Phœbus* sunnie rayes
Doo neuer see, where soules doo alwaies mourne,
And by the wayling shores to waste my dayes,
Where *Phlegeton* with quenchles flames doth
  burne ;   622
By which iust *Minos* righteous soules doth seuer
From wicked ones, to liue in blisse for euer.

Me therefore thus the cruell fiends of hell
Girt with long snakes, and thousand yron
  chaynes,
Through doome of that their cruell Iudge,
  compell
With bitter torture and impatient paines,
Cause of my death, and iust complaint to tell.
For thou art he, whom my poore ghost com-
  plaines   630
To be the author of her ill vnwares,
That careles hear'st my intollerable cares.

Them therefore as bequeathing to the winde,
I now depart, returning to thee neuer,
And leaue this lamentable plaint behinde.
But doo thou haunt the soft downe rolling riuer,
And wilde greene woods, and fruitful pastures
  minde,
And let the flitting aire my vaine words seuer.
Thus hauing said, he heauily departed   639
With piteous crie, that anie would haue smarted.

Now, when the sloathfull fit of lifes sweete rest
Had left the heauie Shepheard, wondrous cares
His inly grieued minde full sore opprest ;
That balefull sorrow he no longer beares,
For that Gnats death, which deeply was imprest :
But bends what euer power his aged yeares
Him lent, yet being such, as through their might
He lately slue his dreadfull foe in fight.

By that same Riuer lurking vnder greene,
Eftsoones he gins to fashion forth a place, 650
And squaring it in compasse well beseene,
There plotteth out a tombe by measured space :

His yron headed spade tho making cleene,
To dig vp sods out of the flowrie grasse,
His worke he shortly to good purpose
  brought,
Like as he had conceiu'd it in his thought.

An heape of earth he hoorded vp on hie,
Enclosing it with banks on euerie side,
And thereupon did raise full busily
A little mount, of greene turffs edifide ; 660
And on the top of all, that passers by
Might it behold, the toomb he did prouide
Of smoothest marble stone in order set,
That neuer might his luckie scape forget.

And round about he taught sweete flowres to
  growe,
The Rose engrained in pure scarlet die,
The Lilly fresh, and Violet belowe,
The Marigolde, and cherefull Rosemarie,
The *Spartan* Mirtle, whence sweet gumb does
  flowe,
The purple Hyacinthe, and fresh Costmarie,
And Saffron sought for in *Cilician* soyle, 671
And Lawrell th'ornament of *Phœbus* toyle.

Fresh *Rhododaphne*, and the *Sabine* flowre
Matching the wealth of th'auncient Frankin-
  cence,
And pallid Yuie building his owne bowre,
And Box yet mindfull of his olde offence,
Red *Amaranthus*, lucklesse Paramour,
Oxeye still greene, and bitter Patience ;
Ne wants there pale *Narcisse,* that in a well
Seeing his beautie, in loue with it fell : 680

And whatsoeuer other flowre of worth,
And whatso other hearb of louely hew
The ioyous Spring out of the ground brings
  forth,
To cloath her selfe in colours fresh and new ;
He planted there, and reard a mount of earth,
In whose high front was writ as doth ensue.

> To thee, small Gnat, in lieu of his life saued,
> The Shepheard hath thy deaths record engraued.

FINIS.

PROSOPOPOIA.
Or
Mother Hubberds Tale.

By ED. SP.

Dedicated to the right Honorable
the Ladie *Compton* and
Mountegle.

LONDON.

Imprinted for *William
Ponsonbie*, dwelling in Paules
Churchyard at the signe of
the Bishops head.

1591.

To the right Honourable, the Ladie *Compton* and *Mountegle*.

*M*Ost faire and vertuous Ladie; hauing often sought opportunitie by some good meanes to make known to your Ladiship, the humble affection and faithfull duetie, which I haue alwaies professed, and am bound to beare to that House, from whence yee spring, I haue at length found occasion to remember the same, by making a simple present to you of these my idle labours; which hauing long sithens composed in the raw conceipt of my youth, I lately amongst other papers lighted vpon, and was by others, which liked the same, mooued to set them foorth. Simple is the deuice, and the composition meane, yet carrieth some delight.

euen the rather because of the simplicitie and meannesse thus personated. The same I beseech your Ladiship take in good part, as a pledge of that profession which I haue made to you, and keepe with you vntill with some other more worthie labour, I do redeeme it out of your hands, and discharge my vtmost dutie. Till then wishing your Ladiship all increase of honour and happinesse, I humblie take leaue.

Your La : euer

humblie ;

Ed. Sp.

Prosopopoia : or *Mother Hubberds Tale.*

*I*T was the month, in which the righteous Maide,
That for disdaine of sinfull worlds vpbraide,
Fled back to heauen, whence she was first con-
ceiued,
Into her siluer bowre the Sunne receiued ;
And the hot *Syrian* Dog on him awayting,
After the chased Lyons cruell bayting,
Corrupted had th'ayre with his noysome breath,
And powr'd on th'earth plague, pestilence, and death.
Emongst the rest a wicked maladie
Raign'd emongst men, that manie did to die,
Depriu'd of sense and ordinarie reason ;   11
That it to Leaches seemed strange and geason.
My fortune was mongst manie others moe,
To be partaker of their common woe ;
And my weake bodie set on fire with griefe,
Was rob'd of rest, and naturall reliefe.
In this ill plight, there came to visite mee
Some friends, who sorie my sad case to see,
Began to comfort me in chearfull wise,
And meanes of gladsome solace to deuise.   20
But seeing kindly sleep refuse to doe
His office, and my feeble eyes forgoe,
They sought my troubled sense how to deceaue
With talke that might vnquiet fancies reaue ;

And sitting all in seates about me round,
With pleasant tales (fit for that idle stound)
They cast in course to waste the wearie howres :
Some tolde of Ladies, and their Paramoures ;
Some of braue Knights, and their renowned
Squires ;
Some of the Faeries and their strange attires ;
And some of Giaunts hard to be beleeued,   31
That the delight thereof me much releeued.
Amongst the rest a good old woman was,
Hight Mother *Hubberd*, who did farre surpas
The rest in honest mirth, that seem'd her well :
She when her turne was come her tale to tell,
Tolde of a strange aduenture, that betided
Betwixt the Foxe and th'Ape by him mis-
guided ;
The which for that my sense it greatly pleased,
All were my spirite heauie and diseased,   40
Ile write in termes, as she the same did say,
So well as I her words remember may.
No Muses aide me needes heretoo to call ;
Base is the style, and matter meane withall.
¶ Whilome (said she) before the world was
ciuill,
The Foxe and th'Ape disliking of their euill
And hard estate, determined to seeke
Their fortunes farre abroad, lyeke with his
lyeke :
For both were craftie and vnhappie witted ;
Two fellowes might no where be better fitted.
The Foxe, that first this cause of griefe did finde,
Gan first thus plaine his case with words vnkinde.

Neighbour Ape, and my Gossip eke beside,
(Both two sure bands in friendship to be tide,)
To whom may I more trustely complaine
The euill plight, that doth me sore constraine,
And hope thereof to finde due remedie ?
Heare then my paine and inward agonie.
Thus manie yeares I now haue spent and worne,
In meane regard, and basest fortunes scorne,
Dooing my Countrey seruice as I might,   61
No lesse I dare saie than the prowdest wight ;
And still I hoped to be vp aduaunced,
For my good parts ; but still it hath mis-
chaunced.
Now therefore that no lenger hope I see,
But froward fortune still to follow mee,
And losels lifted high, where I did looke,
I meane to turne the next leafe of the booke.
Yet ere that anie way I doo betake,
I meane my Gossip priuie first to make.   70
Ah my deare Gossip, (answer'd then the Ape,)
Deeply doo your sad words my wits awhape,
Both for because your griefe doth great
appeare,
And eke because my selfe am touched neare :
For I likewise haue wasted much good time,
Still wayting to preferment vp to clime,
Whilest others alwayes haue before me stept,
And from my beard the fat away haue swept ;
That now vnto despaire I gin to growe,
And meane for better winde about to throwe.
Therefore to me, my trustie friend, aread   81
Thy councell : two is better than one head.
Certes (said he) I meane me to disguize
In some straunge habit, after vncouth wize,
Or like a Pilgrime, or a Lymiter,
Or like a *Gipsen*, or a Iuggeler,
And so to wander to the worlds ende,
To seeke my fortune, where I may it mend
For worse than that I haue, I cannot meete.
Wide is the world I wote and euerie streete   90
Is full of fortunes, and aduentures straunge
Continuallie subiect vnto chaunge.
Say my faire brother now, if this deuice
Doth like you, or may you to like entice.
Surely (said th'Ape) it likes me wondrous well ;
And would ye not poore fellowship expell,
My selfe would offer you t'accompanie
In this aduentures chauncefull ieopardie.
For to wexe olde at home in idlenesse,
Is disaduentrous, and quite fortunelesse :   100
Abroad where change is, good may gotten bee.
The Foxe was glad, and quickly did agree :
So both resolu'd, the morrow next ensuing,
So soone as day appeard to peoples vewing,
On their intended iourney to proceede ;
And ouer night, whatso theretoo did neede,

Each did prepare, in readines to bee.
The morrow next, so soone as one might **see**
Light out of heauens windowes forth to looke,
Both their habiliments vnto them tooke,   110
And put themselues (a Gods name) on their way.
Whenas the Ape beginning well to wey
This hard aduenture, thus began t'aduise ;
Now read Sir Reynold, as ye be right wise,
What course ye weene is best for vs to take,
That for our selues we may a liuing make.
Whether shall we professe some trade or skill ?
Or shall we varie our deuice at will,
Euen as new occasion appeares ?
Or shall we tie our selues for certaine yeares
To anie seruice, or to anie place ?   121
For it behoues ere that into the race
We enter, to resolue first herevpon.
Now surely brother (said the Foxe anon)
Ye haue this matter motioned in season :
For euerie thing that is begun with reason
Will come by readie meanes vnto his end ;
But things miscounselld must needs miswend.
Thus therefore I aduize vpon the case,
That not to anie certaine trade or place,   130
Nor anie man we should our selues applie :
For why should he that is at libertie
Make himselfe bond ? sith then we are free
borne,
Let vs all seruile base subiection scorne ;
And as we bee sonnes of the world so wide,
Let vs our fathers heritage diuide,
And chalenge to our selues our portions dew
Of all the patrimonie, which a few
Now hold in hugger mugger in their hand,
And all the rest doo rob of good and land.   140
For now a few haue all and all haue nought,
Yet all be brethren ylike dearly bought :
There is no right in this partition,
Ne was it so by institution
Ordained first, ne by the law of Nature,
But that she gaue like blessing to each creture
As well of worldly liuelode as of life,
That there might be no difference nor strife,
Nor ought cald mine or thine : thrice happie
then
Was the condition of mortall men.   50
That was the golden age of *Saturne* old,
But this might better be the world of gold :
For without golde now nothing wilbe got.
Therefore (if please you) this shalbe our plot
We will not be of anie occupation,
Let such vile vassalls borne to base vocation
Drudge in the world, and for their liuing droyle
Which haue no wit to liue withouten toyle.
But we will walke about the world at pleasure
Like two free men, and make our ease a treasure.

Free men some beggers call, but they be free,
And they which call them so more beggers bee :
For they doo swinke and sweate to feed the
other,
Who liue like Lords of that which they doo
gather,
And yet doo neuer thanke them for the same,
But as their due by Nature doo it clame.
Such will we fashion both our selues to bee,
Lords of the world, and so will wander free
Where so we listeth, vncontrol'd of anie :
Hard is our hap, if we (emongst so manie) 170
Light not on some that may our state amend ;
Sildome but some good commeth ere the end.
Well seemd the Ape to like this ordinaunce :
Yet well considering of the circumstaunce,
As pausing in great doubt awhile he staid,
And afterwards with graue aduizement said ;
I cannot my lief brother like but well
The purpose of the complot which ye tell :
For well I wot (compar'd to all the rest
Of each degree) that Beggers life is best : 180
And they that thinke themselues the best of all,
Oft-times to begging are content to fall.
But this I wot withall that we shall ronne
Into great daunger like to bee vndonne,
Thus wildly to wander in the worlds eye,
Without pasport or good warrantie,
For feare least we like rogues should be
reputed,
And for eare marked beasts abroad be bruted :
Therefore I read, that we our counsells call,
How to preuent this mischiefe ere it fall, 190
And how we may with most securitie,
Beg amongst those that beggers doo defie.
Right well deere Gossip ye aduized haue,
(Said then the Foxe) but I this doubt will saue :
For ere we farther passe, I will deuise
A pasport for vs both in fittest wize,
And by the names of Souldiers vs protect ;
That now is thought a ciuile begging sect.
Be you the Souldier, for you likest are
For manly semblance, and small skill in warre :
I will but wayte on you, and as occasion 201
Falls out, my selfe fit for the same will fashion.
The Pasport ended, both they forward went,
The Ape clad Souldierlike, fit for th'intent,
In a blew iacket with a crosse of redd
And manie slits, as if that he had shedd
Much blood throgh many wounds therein
receaued,
Which had the vse of his right arme bereaued ;
Vpon his head an old Scotch cap he wore,
With a plume feather all to peeces tore : 210
His breeches were made after the new cut,
Al Portugese, loose like an emptie gut ;

And his hose broken high aboue the heeling,
And his shooes beaten out with traueling.
But neither sword nor dagger he did beare,
Seemes that no foes reuengement he did feare ;
In stead of them a handsome bat he held,
On which he leaned, as one farre in elde.
Shame light on him, that through so false
illusion,
Doth turne the name of Souldiers to abusion,
And that, which is the noblest mysterie, 221
Brings to reproach and common infamie.
Long they thus trauailed, yet neuer met
Aduenture, which might them a working set :
Yet manie waies they sought, and manie tryed :
Yet for their purposes none fit espyed.
At last they chaunst to meete vpon the way
A simple husbandman in garments gray ;
Yet though his vesture were but meane and bace,
A good yeoman he was of honest place, 230
And more for thrift did care than for gay
clothing :
Gay without good, is good hearts greatest
loathing.
The Foxe him spying, bad the Ape him dight
To play his part, for loe he was in sight,
That (if he er'd not) should them entertaine,
And yeeld them timely profite for their paine.
Eftsoones the Ape himselfe gan vp to reare,
And on his shoulders high his bat to beare,
As if good seruice he were fit to doo ;
But little thrift for him he did it too : 240
And stoutly forward he his steps did straine,
That like a handscme swaine it him became :
When as they nigh approached, that good man
Seeing them wander loosly, first began
T'enquire of custome, what and whence they
were ?
To whom the Ape, I am a Souldiere,
That late in warres haue spent my deerest
blood,
And in long seruice lost both limbs and good,
And now constrain'd that trade to ouergiue,
I driuen am to seeke some meanes to liue :
Which might it you in pitie please t'afford,
I would be readie both in deed and word, 252
To doo you faithfull seruice all my dayes.
This yron world (that same he weeping sayes)
Brings downe the stowtest hearts to lowest state:
For miserie doth brauest mindes abate,
And make them seeke for that they wont to
scorne,
Of fortune and of hope at once forlorne.
The honest man, that heard him thus complaine,
Was grieu'd, as he had felt part of his paine ;
And well disposd' him some reliefe to showe,
Askt if in husbandrie he ought did knowe,

To plough, to plant, to reap, to rake, to sowe,
To hedge, to ditch, to thrash, to thetch, to mowe;
Or to what labour els he was prepar'd?
For husbands life is labourous and hard.
Whenas the Ape him hard so much to talke
Of labour, that did from his liking balke,
He would haue slipt the coller handsomly,
And to him said ; good Sir, full glad am I, 270
To take what paines may anie liuing wight :
But my late maymed limbs lack wonted might
To doo their kindly seruices, as needeth :
Scarce this right hand the mouth with diet
  feedeth,
So that it may no painfull worke endure,
Ne to strong labour can it selfe enure.
But if that anie other place you haue,
Which askes small paines, but thriftines to saue,
Or care to ouerlooke, or trust to gather,
Ye may me trust as your owne ghostly father.
With that the husbandman gan him auize
That it for him were fittest exercise   282
Cattell to keep, or grounds to ouersee ;
And asked him, if he could willing bee
To keep his sheep, or to attend his swyne,
Or watch his mares, or take his charge of kyne?
Gladly (said he) what euer such like paine
Ye put on me, I will the same sustaine :
But gladliest I of your fleecie sheepe
(Might it you please) would take on me the
  keep.   290
For ere that vnto armes I me betooke,
Vnto my fathers sheepe I vsde to looke,
That yet the skill thereof I haue not loste :
Thereto right well this Curdog by my coste
(Meaning the Foxe) will serue, my sheepe to
  gather,
And driue to follow after their Belwether.
The Husbandman was meanly well content,
Triall to make of his endeuourment,
And home him leading, lent to him the charge
Of all his flocke, with libertie full large,   300
Giuing accompt of th'annuall increace
Both of their lambes, and of their woolley fleece.
Thus is this Ape become a shepheard swaine
And the false Foxe his dog (God giue them
  paine)
For ere the yeare haue halfe his course out-run,
And doo returne from whence he first begun,
They shall him make an ill accompt of thrift.
Now whenas Time flying with winges swift,
Expired had the terme, that these two iauels
Should render vp a reckning of their trauels
Vnto their master, which it of them sought,
Exceedingly they troubled were in thought,
Ne wist what answere vnto him to frame,
Ne how to scape great punishment, or shame,

For their false treason and vile theeuerie.
For not a lambe of all their flockes supply
Had they to shew : but euer as they bred,
They slue them, and vpon their fleshes fed :
For that disguised Dog lou'd blood to spill,
And drew the wicked Shepheard to his will.
So twixt them both they not a lambkin left,
And when lambes fail'd, the old sheepes liues
  they reft ;   322
That how t'acquite themselues vnto their Lord,
They were in doubt, and flatly set abord.
The Foxe then counsel'd th'Ape, for to require
Respite till morrow, t'answere his desire :
For times delay new hope of helpe still breeds.
The goodman granted, doubting nought their
  deeds,   328
And bad, next day that all should readie be.
But they more subtill meaning had than he :
For the next morrowes meed they closely ment,
For feare of afterclaps for to preuent.
And that same euening, when all shrowded were
In careles sleep, they without care or feare,
Cruelly fell vpon their flock in folde,
And of them slew at pleasure what they wolde :
Of which whenas they feasted had their fill,
For a full complement of all their ill,
They stole away, and tooke their hastie flight,
Carried in clowdes of all-concealing night.
So was the husbandman left to his losse,   341
And they vnto their fortunes change to tosse.
After which sort they wandered long while,
Abusing manie through their cloaked guile ;
That at the last they gan to be descryed
Of euerie one, and all their sleights espyed.
So as their begging now them failed quyte ;
For none would giue, but all men would them
  wyte :
Yet would they take no paines to get their
  liuing,   349
But seeke some other way to gaine by giuing,
Much like to begging but much better named ;
For manie beg, which are thereof ashamed.
And now the Foxe had gotten him a gowne,
And th'Ape a cassocke sidelong hanging downe ;
For they their occupation meant to change,
And now in other state abroad to range :
For since their souldiers pas no better spedd,
They forg'd another, as for Clerkes booke-redd.
Who passing foorth, as their aduentures fell,
Through manie haps, which needs not here to
  tell ;   360
At length chaunst with a formall Priest to
  meete,
Whom they in ciuill manner first did greete,
And after askt an almes for Gods deare loue.
The man straight way his choler vp did moue,

And with reproachfull tearmes gan them reuile,
For following that trade so base and vile ;
And askt what license, or what Pas they had ?
Ah (said the Ape as sighing wondrous sad)
Its an hard case, when men of good deseruing
Must either driuen be perforce to steruing,
Or asked for their pas by euerie squib,   371
That list at will them to reuile or snib :
And yet (God wote) small oddes I often see
Twixt them that aske, and them that asked bee.
Natheles because you shall not vs misdeeme,
But that we are as honest as we seeme,
Yee shall our pasport at your pleasure see,
And then ye will (I hope) well mooued bee.
Which when the Priest beheld, he vew'd it nere,
As if therein some text he studying were,   380
But little els (God wote) could thereof skill :
For read he could not euidence, nor will,
Ne tell a written word, ne write a letter,
Ne make one title worse, ne make one better :
Of such deep learning little had he neede,
Ne yet of Latine, ne of Greeke, that breede
Doubts mongst Diuines, and difference of texts,
From whence arise diuersitie of sects,
And hatefull heresies, of God abhor'd :   389
But this good Sir did follow the plaine word,
Ne medled with their controuersies vaine.
All his care was, his seruice well to saine,
And to read Homelies vpon holidayes :
When that was done, he might attend his playes;
An easie life, and fit high God to please.
He hauing ouerlookt their pas at ease,
Gan at the length them to rebuke againe,
That no good trade of life did entertaine,
But lost their time in wandring loose abroad,
Seeing the world, in which they bootles boad,
Had wayes enough for all therein to liue ;   401
Such grace did God vnto his creatures giue.
Said then the Foxe ; who hath the world not tride,
From the right way full eath may wander wide.
We are but Nouices, new come abroad,
We haue not yet the tract of anie troad,
Nor on vs taken anie state of life,
But readie are of anie to make preife.
Therefore might please you, which the world
    haue proued,   409
Vs to aduise, which forth but lately moued,
Of some good course, that we might vndertake ;
Ye shall for euer vs your bondmen make.
The Priest gan wexe halfe proud to be so praide,
And thereby willing to affoord them aide ;
It seemes (said he) right well that ye be Clerks,
Both by your wittie words, and by your werks.
Is not that name enough to make a liuing
To him that hath a whit of Natures giuing ?

How manie honest men see ye arize
Daylie thereby, and grow to goodly prize ?   420
To Deanes, to Archdeacons, to Commissaries,
To Lords, to Principalls, to Prebendaries ;
All iolly Prelates, worthie rule to beare,
Who euer them enuie : yet spite bites neare.
Why should ye doubt then, but that ye likewise
Might vnto some of those in time arise ?
In the meane time to liue in good estate,
Louing that loue, and hating those that hate ;
Being some honest Curate, or some Vicker
Content with little in condition sicker.   430
Ah but (said th'Ape) the charge is wondrous
    great,
To feed mens soules, and hath an heauie threat.
To feede mens soules (quoth he) is not in man :
For they must feed themselues, doo what
    we can.
We are but charg'd to lay the meate before :
Eate they that list, we need to doo no more.
But God it is that feedes them with his grace,
The bread of life powr'd downe from heauenly
    place.   438
Therefore said he, that with the budding rod
Did rule the Iewes, *All shalbe taught of God.*
That same hath Iesus Christ now to him raught,
By whom the **flock is** rightly fed, and taught :
He is the Shepheard, and the Priest is hee ;
We but his shepheard swaines ordain'd to bee.
Therefore herewith doo not your selfe dismay ;
Ne is the paines so great, but beare ye may ;
For not so great as it was wont of yore,
It's now a dayes, ne halfe so streight and sore :
They whilome vsed duly euerie day   449
Their seruice and their holie things to say,
At morne and euen, besides their Anthemes
    sweete,
Their penie Masses, and their Complynes meete,
Their Diriges, their Trentals, and their shrifts;
Their memories, their singings, and their gifts.
Now all those needlesse works are laid away :
Now once a weeke vpon the Sabbath day,
It is enough to doo our small deuotion,
And then to follow any merrie motion.
Ne are we tyde to fast, but when we list,
Ne to weare garments base of wollen twist,
But with the finest silkes vs to aray,   461
That before God we may appeare more gay,
Resembling *Aarons* glorie in his place :
For farre vnfit it is, that person bace
Should with vile cloaths approach Gods maiestie,
Whom no vncleannes may approachen nie :
Or that all men, which anie master serue,
Good garments for their seruice should deserue;
But he that serues the Lord of hoasts most high,
And that in highest place, t'approach him nigh,

And all the peoples prayers to present 471
Before his throne, as on ambassage sent
Both too and fro, should not deserue to weare
A garment better, than of wooll or heare.
Beside we may haue lying by our sides
Our louely Lasses, or bright shining Brides:
We be not tyde to wilfull chastitie,
But haue the Gospell of free libertie.
By that he ended had his ghostly sermon,
The Foxe was well induc'd to be a Parson ; 480
And of the Priest eftsoones gan to enquire,
How to a Benefice he might aspire.
Marie there (said the Priest) is arte indeed.
Much good deep learning one thereout may reed,
For that the ground worke is, and end of all,
How to obtaine a Beneficiall.
First therefore, when ye haue in handsome wise
Your selfe attyred, as you can deuise,
Then to some Noble man your selfe applye,
Or other great one in the worldes eye, 490
That hath a zealous disposition
To God, and so to his religion :
There must thou fashion eke a godly zeale,
Such as no carpers may contrayre reueale :
For each thing fained, ought more warie bee.
There thou must walke in sober grauitee,
And seeme as Saintlike as Saint *Radegund :*
Fast much, pray oft, looke lowly on the ground,
And vnto euerie one doo curtesie meeke :
These lookes (nought saying) doo a benefice
seeke, 500
And be thou sure one not to lacke or long.
But if thee list vnto the Court to throng,
And there to hunt after the hoped pray,
Then must thou thee dispose another way :
For there thou needs must learne, to laugh, to
lie,
To face, to forge, to scoffe, to companie,
To crouche, to please, to be a beetle stock
Of thy great Masters will, to scorne, or mock :
So maist thou chaunce mock out a Benefice,
Vnlesse thou canst one coniure by deuice,
Or cast a figure for a Bishoprick ; 511
And if one could, it were but a schoole-trick.
These be the wayes, by which without reward
Liuings in Court be gotten, though full hard.
For nothing there is done without a fee :
The Courtier needes must recompenced bee
With a Beneuolence, or haue in gage
The *Primitias* of your Parsonage :
Scarse can a Bishoprick forpas them by,
But that it must be gelt in priuitie. 520
Doo not thou therefore seeke a liuing there,
But of more priuate persons seeke elswhere,
Whereas thou maist compound a better penie,
Ne let thy learning question'd be of anie.

For some good Gentleman that hath the right
Vnto his Church for to present a wight,
Will cope with thee in reasonable wise ;
That if the liuing yerely doo arise
To fortie pound, that then his yongest sonne
Shall twentie haue, and twentie thou hast
wonne : 530
Thou hast it wonne, for it is of franke gift,
And he will care for all the rest to shift ;
Both that the Bishop may admit of thee,
And that therein thou maist maintained bee.
This is the way for one that is vnlern'd
Liuing to get, and not to be discern'd.
But they that are great Clerkes, haue nearer
wayes,
For learning sake to liuing them to raise :
Yet manie eke of them (God wote) are driuen,
T'accept a Benefice in peeces riuen. 540
How saist thou (friend) haue I not well dis-
courst
Vpon this Common place (though plaine, not
wourst) ?
Better a short tale, than a bad long shriuing.
Needes anie more to learne to get a liuing ?
Now sure and by my hallidome (quoth he)
Ye a great master are in your degree :
Great thankes I yeeld you for your discipline,
And doo not doubt, but duly to encline
My wits theretoo, as ye shall shortly heare.
The Priest him wisht good speed, and well to
fare. 550
So parted they, as eithers way them led.
But th'Ape and Foxe ere long so well them sped,
Through the Priests holesome counsell lately
tought,
And throgh their owne faire handling wisely
wroght,
That they a Benefice twixt them obtained ;
And craftie Reynold was a Priest ordained ;
And th'Ape his Parish Clarke procur'd to bee.
Then made they reuell route and goodly glee.
But ere long time had passed, they so ill
Did order their affaires, that th'euill will 560
Of all their Parishners they had constraind ;
Who to the Ordinarie of them complain'd,
How fowlie they their offices abusd',
And them of crimes and heresies accusd' ;
That Pursiuants he often for them sent :
But they neglected his commaundement.
So long persisted obstinate and bolde,
Till at the length he published to holde
A Visitation, and them cyted thether : 569
Then was high time their wits about to geather;
What did they then, but made a composition
With their next neighbor Priest for light con-
dition,

To whom their liuing they resigned quight
For a few pence, and ran away by night.
So passing through the Countrey in disguize,
They fled farre off, where none might them
surprize,
And after that long straied here and there,
Through euerie field and forrest farre and nere ;
Yet neuer found occasion for their tourne,
But almost steru'd, did much lament and
mourne.   580
At last they chaunst to meete vpon the way
The Mule, all deckt in goodly rich aray,
With bells and bosses, that full lowdly rung,
And costly trappings, that to ground downe
hung.
Lowly they him saluted in meeke wise,
But he through pride and fatnes gan despise
Their meanesse ; scarce vouchsafte them to
requite.
Whereat the Foxe deep groning in his sprite,
Said, Ah sir Mule, now blessed be the day,
That I see you so goodly and so gay   590
In your attyres, and eke your silken hyde
Fil'd with round flesh, that euerie bone doth
hide.
Seemes that in fruitfull pastures ye doo liue,
Or fortune doth you secret fauour giue.
Foolish Foxe (said the Mule) thy wretched need
Praiseth the thing that doth thy sorrow breed.
For well I weene, thou canst not but enuie
My wealth, compar'd to thine owne miserie,
That art so leane and meagre waxen late,
That scarse thy legs vphold thy feeble gate.
Ay me (said then the Foxe) whom euill hap
Vnworthy in such wretchednes doth wrap,
And makes the scorne of other beasts to bee :
But read (faire Sir, of grace) from whence come
yee ?
Or what of tidings you abroad doo heare ?
Newes may perhaps some good vnweeting beare.
From royall Court I lately came (said he)
Where all the brauerie that eye may see,
And all the happinesse that heart desire,
Is to be found ; he nothing can admire,   610
That hath not seene that heauens portracture :
But tidings there is none I you assure,
Saue that which common is, and knowne to all,
That Courtiers as the tide doo rise and fall.
But tell vs (said the Ape) we doo you pray,
Who now in Court doth beare the greatest sway.
That if such fortune doo to vs befall,
We may seeke fauour of the best of all.
Marie (said he) the highest now in grace,   619
Be the wilde beasts, that swiftest are in chace ;
For in their speedie course and nimble flight
The Lyon now doth take the most delight :

But chieflie, ioyes on foote them to beholde,
Enchaste with chaine and circulet of golde :
So wilde a beast so tame ytaught to bee,
And buxome to his bands, is ioy to see.
So well his golden Circlet him beseemeth :
But his late chayne his Liege vnmeete esteemeth;
For so braue beasts she loueth best to see,
In the wilde forrest raunging fresh and free.
Therefore if fortune thee in Court to liue,   631
In case thou euer there wilt hope to thriue,
To some of these thou must thy selfe apply :
Els as a thistle-downe in th'ayre doth flie,
So vainly shalt thou too and fro be tost,
And loose thy labour and thy fruitles cost.
And yet full few, which follow them I see,
For vertues bare regard aduaunced bee,
But either for some gainfull benefit,   639
Or that they may for their owne turnes be fit.
Nath'les perhaps ye things may handle soe,
That ye may better thriue than thousands moe.
But (said the Ape) how shall we first come in,
That after we may fauour seeke to win ?
How els (said he) but with a good bold face,
And with big words, and with a stately pace,
That men may thinke of you in generall,
That to be in you, which is not at all :
For not by that which is, the world now deemeth,
(As it was wont) but by that same that seemeth.
Ne do I doubt, but that ye well can fashion
Your selues theretoo, according to occasion :
So fare ye well, good Courtiers may ye bee ;
So proudlie neighing from them parted hee.
Then gan this craftie couple to deuize,
How for the Court themselues they might
aguize :
For thither they themselues meant to addresse,
In hope to finde there happier successe ;
So well they shifted, that the Ape anon
Himselfe had cloathed like a Gentleman,   660
And the slie Foxe, as like to be his groome,
That to the Court in seemly sort they come.
Where the fond Ape himselfe vprearing hy
Vpon his tiptoes, stalketh stately by,
As if he were some great *Magnifico*,
And boldlie doth amongst the boldest go.
And his man Reynold with fine counterfesaunce
Supports his credite and his countenaunce.
Then gan the Courtiers gaze on euerie side,
And stare on him, with big lookes basen wide,
Wondring what mister wight he was, and
whence :   671
For he was clad in strange accoustrements,
Fashion'd with queint deuises neuer seene
In Court before, yet there all fashions beene
Yet he them in newfanglenesse did pas :
But his behauiour altogether was

Alla Turchesca, much the more admyr'd,
And his lookes loftie, as if he aspyr'd   678
To dignitie, and sdeign'd the low degree ;
That all which did such strangenesse in him see,
By secrete meanes gan of his state enquire,
And priuily his seruant thereto hire :
Who throughly arm'd against such couerture,
Reported vnto all, that he was sure
A noble Gentleman of high regard,
Which through the world had with long trauel
far'd,
And seene the manners of all beasts on ground ;
Now here arriu'd, to see if like he found.   688
Thus did the Ape at first him credit gaine,
Which afterwards he wisely did maintaine
With gallant showe, and daylie more augment
Through his fine feates and Courtly complement;
For he could play, and daunce, and vaute, and
spring,
And all that els pertaines to reueling,
Onely through kindly aptnes of his ioynts.
Besides he could doo manie other poynts,
The which in Court him serued to good stead :
For he mongst Ladies could their fortunes read
Out of their hands, and merie leasings tell,
And iuggle finely, that became him well: 700
But he so light was at legier demaine,
That what he toucht, came not to light againe ;
Yet would he laugh it out, and proudly looke,
And tell them, that they greatly him mistooke.
So would he scoffe them out with mockerie,
For he therein had great felicitie ;
And with sharp quips ioy'd others to deface,
Thinking that their disgracing did him grace :
So whilst that other like vaine wits he pleased,
And made to laugh, his heart was greatly eased.
But the right gentle minde would bite his lip,
To heare the Iauell so good men to nip :   712
For though the vulgar yeeld an open eare,
And common Courtiers loue to gybe and fleare
At euerie thing, which they heare spoken ill,
And the best speaches with ill meaning spill ;
Yet the braue Courtier, in whose beauteous
thought
Regard of honour harbours more than ought,
Doth loath such base condition, to backbite
Anies good name for enuie or despite :   720
He stands on tearmes of honourable minde,
Ne will be carried with the common winde
Of Courts inconstant mutabilitie,
Ne after euerie tattling fable flie ;
But heares, and sees the follies of the rest,
And thereof gathers for himselfe the best :
He will not creepe, nor crouche with fained
face,
But walkes vpright with comely stedfast pace,

And vnto all doth yeeld due curtesie ;   729
But not with kissed hand belowe the knee,
As that same Apish crue is wont to doo :
For he disdaines himselfe t'embase theretoo.
He hates fowle leasings, and vile flatterie,
Two filthie blots in noble Gentrie ;
And lothefull idlenes he doth detest,
The canker worme of euerie gentle brest ;
The whicı ıo banish with faire exercise
Of knightly feates, he daylie doth deuise :
Now menaging the mouthes ot stubborne
steedes,   739
Now practising the proofe of warlike deedes,
Now his bright armes assaying, now his speare,
Now the nigh aymed ring away to beare ;
At other times he casts to sew the chace
Of swift wilde beasts, or runne on foote a race,
T'enlarge his breath (large breath in armes most
needfull)
Or els by wrestling to wex strong and heedfull,
Or his stiffe armes to stretch with Eughen bowe,
And manly legs, still passing too and fro,
Without a gowned beast him fast beside ;
A vaine ensample of the *Persian* pride,   750
Who after he had wonne th'*Assyrian* foe,
Did euer after scorne on foote to goe.
Thus when this Courtly Gentleman with toyle
Himselfe hath wearied, he doth recoyle
Vnto his rest, and there with sweete delight
Of Musicks skill reuiues his toyled spright,
Or els with Loues, and Ladies gentle sports,
The ioy of youth, himselfe he recomforts :
Or lastly, when the bodie list to pause,   759
His minde vnto the Muses he withdrawes ;
Sweete Ladie Muses, Ladies of delight,
Delights of life, and ornaments of light :
With whom he close confers with wise discourse,
Of Natures workes, of heauens continuall course,
Of forreine lands, of people different,
Of kingdomes change, of diuers gouernment,
Of dreadfull battailes of renowmed Knights ;
With which he kindleth his ambitious sprights
To like desire and praise of noble fame,
The onely vpshot whereto he doth ayme :
For all his minde on honour fixed is,   771
To which he leuels all his purposis,
And in his Princes seruice spends his dayes,
Not so much for to gaine, or for to raise
Himselfe to high degree, as for his grace,
And in his liking to winne worthie place ;
Through due deserts and comely carriage,
In whatso please employ his personage,
That may be matter meete to gaine him praise;
For he is fit to vse in all assayes,   780
Whether for Armes and warlike amenaunce,
Or else for wise and ciuill gouernaunce.

For he is practiz'd well in policie,
And thereto doth his Courting most applie :
To learne the enterdeale of Princes strange,
To marke th'intent of Counsells, and the change
Of states, and eke of priuate men somewhile,
Supplanted by fine falshood and faire guile ;
Of all the which he gathereth, what is fit
T'enrich the storehouse of his powerfull wit,
Which through wise speaches, and graue con-
    ference   791
He daylie eekes, and brings to excellence.
Such is the rightfull Courtier in his kinde :
But vnto such the Ape lent not his minde ;
Such were for him no fit companions,
Such would descrie his lewd conditions :
But the yong lustie gallants he did chose
To follow, meete to whom he might disclose
His witlesse pleasance, and ill pleasing vaine.
A thousand wayes he them could entertaine,
With all the thriftles games, that may be found
With mumming and with masking all around,
With dice, with cards, with balliards farre vnfit,
With shuttelcocks, misseeming manlie wit,
With courtizans, and costly riotize,
Whereof still somewhat to his share did rize :
Ne, them to pleasure, would he sometimes scorne
A Pandares coate (so basely was he borne) ;
Thereto he could fine louing verses frame,
And play the Poet oft.   But ah, for shame
Let not sweete Poets praise, whose onely pride
Is vertue to aduaunce, and vice deride,   812
Be with the worke of losels wit defamed,
Ne let such verses Poetrie be named :
Yet he the name on him would rashly take,
Maugre the sacred Muses, and it make
A seruant to the vile affection
Of such, as he depended most vpon,
And with the sugrie sweete thereof allure
Chast Ladies eares to fantasies impure.   820
To such delights the noble wits he led
Which him reliev'd, and their vaine humours
    fed
With fruitles follies, and vnsound delights.
But if perhaps into their noble sprights
Desire of honor, or braue thought of armes
Did euer creepe, then with his wicked charmes
And strong conceipts he would it driue away,
Ne suffer it to house there halfe a day.
And whenso loue of letters did inspire
Their gentle wits, and kindly wise desire,   830
That chieflie doth each noble minde adorne,
Then he would scoffe at learning, and eke scorne
The Sectaries thereof, as people base
And simple men, which neuer came in place
Of worlds affaires, but in darke corners mewd,
Muttred of matters, as their bookes them shewd,

Ne other knowledge euer did attaine,
But with their gownes their grauitie maintaine.
From them he would his impudent lewde speach
Against Gods holie Ministers oft reach,   840
And mocke Diuines and their profession :
What else then did he by progression,
But mocke high God himselfe, whom they pro-
    fesse ?
But what car'd he for God, or godlinesse ?
All his care was himselfe how to aduaunce,
And to vphold his courtly countenaunce
By all the cunning meanes he could deuise ;
Were it by honest wayes, or otherwise,
He made small choyce : yet sure his honestie
Got him small gaines, but shameles flatterie,
And filthie brocage, and vnseemly shifts,   851
And borowe base, and some good Ladies gifts :
But the best helpe, which chiefly him sustain'd,
Was his man Raynolds purchase which he gain'd.
For he was school'd by kinde in all the skill
Of close conueyance, and each practise ill
Of coosinage and cleanly knauerie,
Which oft maintain'd his masters brauerie.
Besides he vsde another slipprie slight,
In taking on himselfe in common sight,   860
False personages, fit for euerie sted,
With which he thousands cleanly coosined :
Now like a Merchant, Merchants to deceaue,
With whom his credite he did often leaue
In gage, for his gay Masters hopelesse dett :
Now like a Lawyer, when he land would lett,
Or sell fee-simples in his Masters name,
Which he had neuer, nor ought like the same :
Then would he be a Broker, and draw in   869
Both wares and money, by exchange to win :
Then would he seeme a Farmer, that would sell
Bargaines of woods, which he did lately fell,
Or corne, or cattle, or such other ware,
Thereby to coosin men not well aware ;
Of all the which there came a secret fee
To th'Ape, that he his countenaunce might bee.
Besides all this, he vsd' oft to beguile
Poore suters, that in Court did haunt some
    while :
For he would learne their busines secretly,
And then informe his Master hastely,   880
That he by meanes might cast them to preuent,
And beg the sute, the which the other ment.
Or otherwise false Reynold would abuse
The simple Suter, and wish him to chuse
His Master, being one of great regard
In Court, to compas anie sute not hard,
In case his paines were recompenst with reason :
So would he worke the silly man by treason
To buy his Masters friuolous good will,
That had not power to doo him good or ill.

So pitifull a thing is S ̄ters state. 891
Most miserable man, whom wicked fate
Hath brought to Court, to sue for had ywist,
That few haue found, and manie one hath mist;
Full little knowest thou that hast not tride,
What hell it is, in suing long to bide:
To loose good dayes, that might be better spent;
To wast long nights in pensiue discontent;
To speed to day, to be put back to morrow;
To feed on hope, to pine with feare and sorrow;
To haue thy Princes grace, yet want her Peeres;
To haue thy asking, yet waite manie yeeres;
To fret thy soule with crosses and with cares;
To eate thy heart through comfortlesse dispaires;
To fawne, to crowche, to waite, to ride, to
    ronne,
To spend, to giue, to want, to be vndonne.
Vnhappie wight, borne to desa ̄trous end,
That doth his life in so long tendance spend.
Who euer leaues sweete home, where meane
    estate
In safe assurance, without strife or hate, 910
Findes all things needfull for contentment
    meeke;
And will to Court for shadowes vaine to seeke,
Or hope to gaine, himselfe will a daw trie:
That curse God send vnto mine enemie.
For none but such as this bold Ape vnblest,
Can euer thriue in that vnluckie quest;
Or such as hath a Reynold to his man,
That by his shifts his Master furnish can.
But yet this Foxe could not so closely hide
His craftie feates, but that they were descride
At length, by such as sate in iustice seate, 921
Who for the same him fowlie did entreate;
And hauing worthily him punished,
Out of the Court for euer banished.
And now the Ape wanting his huckster man,
That wont prouide his necessaries, gan
To growe into great lacke, ne could vpholde
His countenaunce in those his garments olde:
Ne new ones could he easily prouide,
Though all men him vncased gan deride, 930
Like as a Puppit placed in a play,
Whose part once past all men bid take away:
So that he driuen was to great distresse,
And shortly brought to hopelesse wretchednesse.
Then closely as he might, he cast to leaue
The Court, not asking any passe or leaue;
But ran away in his rent rags by night,
Ne euer stayd in place, ne spake to wight,
Till that the Foxe his copesmate he had found,
To whome complaying his vnhappy stound,
At last againe with him in trauell ioynd, 941
And with him far'd some better chaunce to
    fynde.

So in the world long time they wandered,
And mickle want and hardnesse suffered;
That them repented much so foolishly
To come so farre to seeke for misery,
And leaue the sweetnes of contented home,
Though eating hipps, and drinking watry fome.
Thus as they them complayned too and fro,
Whilst through the forest rechlesse they did goe,
Lo where they spide, how in a gloomy glade,
The Lyon sleeping lay in secret shade, 952
His Crowne and Scepter lying him beside,
And hauing doft for heate his dreadfull hide:
Which when they sawe, the Ape was sore
    afrayde,
And would haue fled with terror all dismayde.
But him the Foxe with hardy words did stay,
And bad him put all cowardize away:
For now was time (if euer they would hope)
To ayme their counsels to the fairest scope,
And them for euer highly to aduaunce, 961
In case the good which their owne happie
    chaunce
Them freely offred, they would wisely take.
Scarse could the Ape yet speake, so did he quake,
Yet as he could, he askt how good might growe,
Where nought but dread and death do seeme in
    show.
Now (sayd he) whiles the Lyon sleepeth sound,
May we his Crowne and Mace take from the
    ground,
And eke his skinne the terror of the wood,
Wherewith we may our selues (if we thinke
    good) 970
Make Kings of Beasts, and Lords of forests all,
Subiect vnto that powre imperiall.
Ah but (sayd the Ape) who is so bold a wretch,
That dare his hardy hand to those outstretch:
When as he knowes his meede, if he be spide,
To be a thousand deathes, and shame beside?
Fond Ape (sayd then the Foxe) into whose brest
Neuer crept thought of honor, nor braue gest,
Who will not venture life a King to be,
And rather rule and raigne in soueraign see,
Than dwell in dust inglorious and bace, 981
Where none shall name the number of his place?
One ioyous houre in blisfull happines,
I chose before a life of wretchednes.
Be therefore counselled herein by me,
And shake off this vile harted cowardree.
If he awake, yet is not death the next,
For we may coulor it with some pretext
Of this, or that, that may excuse the cryme:
Else we may flye; thou to a tree mayst clyme,
And I creepe vnder ground; both from his
    reach: 991
Therefore be rul'd to doo as I doo teach.

The Ape, that earst did nought but chill and
  quake,
Now gan some courage vnto him to take,
And was content to attempt that enterprise,
Tickled with glorie and rash couetise.
But first gan question, whether should assay
Those royall ornaments to steale away?
Marie that shall your selfe (quoth he theretoo)
For ye be fine and nimble it to doo;   1000
Of all the beasts which in the forrests bee,
Is not a fitter for this turne than yee:
Therefore, mine owne deare brother take good
  hart,
And euer thinke a Kingdome is your part.
Loath was the Ape, though praised, to aduenter,
Yet faintly gan into his worke to enter,
Afraid of euerie leafe, that stir'd him by,
And euerie stick, that vnderneath did ly;
Vpon his tiptoes nicely he vp went,   1009
For making noyse, and still his eare he lent
To euerie sound, that vnder heauen blew,
Now went, now stept, now crept, now back-
  ward drew,
That it good sport had been him to haue eyde:
Yet at the last (so well he him applyde,)
Through his fine handling, and cleanly play,
He all those royall signes had stolne away,
And with the Foxes helpe them borne aside,
Into a secret corner vnespide.   1018
Whither whenas they came, they fell at words,
Whether of them should be the Lord of Lords:
For th'Ape was stryfull, and ambicious;
And the Foxe guilefull, and most couetous,
That neither pleased was, to haue the rayne
Twixt them diuided into euen twaine,
But either (algates) would be Lords alone:
For Loue and Lordship bide no paragone.
I am most worthie (said the Ape) sith I
For it did put my life in ieopardie;   1028
Thereto I am in person, and in stature
Most like a man, the Lord of euerie creature,
So that it seemeth I was made to raigne,
And borne to be a Kingly soueraigne.
Nay (said the Foxe) Sir Ape you are astray:
For though to steale the Diademe away
Were the worke of your nimble hand, yet I
Did first deuise the plot by pollicie;
So that it wholly springeth from my wit:
For which also I claime my selfe more fit
Than you, to rule: for gouernment of state
Will without wisedome soone be ruinate.
And where ye claime your selfe for outward
  shape   1041
Most like a man, Man is not like an Ape
In his chiefe parts, that is, in wit and spirite:
But I therein most like to him doo merite

For my slie wyles and subtill craftinesse,
The title of the Kingdome to possesse.
Nath'les (my brother) since we passed are
Vnto this point, we will appease our iarre,
And I with reason meete will rest content,
That ye shall haue both crowne and gouern-
  ment,   1050
Vpon condition, that ye ruled bee
In all affaires, and counselled by mee;
And that ye let none other euer drawe
Your minde from me, but keepe this as a lawe:
And herevpon an oath vnto me plight.
The Ape was glad to end the strife so light,
And thereto swore: for who would not oft
  sweare,
And oft vnsweare, a Diademe to beare?
Then freely vp those royall spoyles he tooke,
Yet at the Lyons skin he inly quooke;   1060
But it dissembled, and vpon his head
The Crowne, and on his backe the skin he did,
And the false Foxe him helped to array.
Then when he was all dight he tooke his way
Into the forest, that he might be seene
Of the wilde beasts in his new glory sheene.
There the two first, whome he encountred, were
The Sheepe and th'Asse, who striken both with
  feare
At sight of him, gan fast away to flye,
But vnto them the Foxe alowd did cry,   1070
And in the Kings name bad them both to stay,
Vpon the payne that thereof follow may.
Hardly naythles were they restrayned so,
Till that the Foxe forth toward them did goe,
And there disswaded them from needlesse feare,
For that the King did fauour to them beare;
And therefore dreadles bad them come to Corte:
For no wild beasts should do them any torte
There or abroad, ne would his maiestye   1079
Vse them but well, with gracious clemencye,
As whome he knew to him both fast and true;
So he perswaded them, with homage due
Themselues to humble to the Ape prostrate,
Who gently to them bowing in his gate,
Receyued them with chearefull entertayne.
Thenceforth proceeding with his princely trayne,
He shortly met the Tygre, and the Bore,
Which with the simple Camell raged sore
In bitter words, seeking to take occasion,
Vpon his fleshly corpse to make inuasion:
But soone as they this mock-King did espy,
Their troublous strife they stinted by and by,
Thinking indeed that it the Lyon was: 1093
He then to proue, whether his powre would pas
As currant, sent the Foxe to them streight way,
Commaunding them their cause of strife be-
  wray;

And if that wrong on eyther side there were,
That he should warne the wronger to appeare
The morrow next at Court, it to defend ;
In the meane time vpon the King t'attend.
The subtile Foxe so well his message sayd,
That the proud beasts him readily obayd :
Whereby the Ape in wondrous stomack woxe,
Strongly encorag'd by the crafty Foxe ;
That King indeed himselfe he shortly thought,
And all the Beasts him feared as they ought :
And followed vnto his palaice hye,
Where taking Conge, each one by and by
Departed to his home in dreadfull awe,   1109
Full of the feared sight, which late they sawe.
The Ape thus seized of the Regall throne,
Eftsones by counsell of the Foxe alone,
Gan to prouide for all things in assurance,
That so his rule might lenger haue endurance.
First to his Gate he pointed a strong gard,
That none might enter but with issue hard :
Then for the safegard of his personage,
He did appoint a warlike equipage   1118
Of forreine beasts, not in the forest bred,
But part by land, and part by water fed ;
For tyrannie is with strange ayde supported.
Then vnto him all monstrous beasts resorted
Bred of two kindes, as Griffons, Minotaures,
Crocodiles, Dragons, Beauers, and Centaures :
With those himselfe he strengthned mightelie,
That feare he neede no force of enemie.
Then gan he rule and tyrannize at will,
Like as the Foxe did guide his graceles skill,
And all wylde beasts made vassals of his
    pleasures,
And with their spoyles enlarg'd his priuate
    treasures.   1130
No care of iustice, nor no rule of reason,
No temperance, nor no regard of season
Did thenceforth euer enter in his minde,
But crueltie, the signe of currish· kinde,
And sdeignfull pride, and wilfull arrogaunce ;
Such followes those whom fortune doth ad-
    uaunce.
But the false Foxe most kindly plaid his part :
For whatsoeuer mother wit, or arte
Could worke, he put in proofe : no practise slie,
No counterpoint of cunning policie,   1140
No reach, no breach, that might him profit
    bring,
But he the same did to his purpose wring.
Nought suffered he the Ape to giue or graunt,
But through his hand must passe the Fiaunt.
All offices, all leases by him lept,
And of them all whatso he likte, he kept.
Iustice he solde iniustice for to buy,
And for to purchase for his progeny.

Ill might it prosper, that ill gotten was,
But so he got it, little did he pas.   1150
He fed his cubs with fat of all the soyle,
And with the sweete of others sweating toyle,
He crammed them with crumbs of Benefices,
And fild their mouthes with meeds of malefices,
He cloathed them with all colours saue white,
And loded them with lordships and with might,
So much as they were able well to beare,
That with the weight their backs nigh broken
    were ;
He chaffred Chayres in which Churchmen were
    set,
And breach of lawes to priuie ferme did let ;
No statute so established might bee,   1161
Nor ordinaunce so needfull, but that hee
Would violate, though not with violence,
Yet vnder colour of the confidence
The which the Ape repos'd in him alone,
And reckned him the kingdomes corner stone.
And euer when he ought would bring to pas,
His. long experience the platforme was :
And when he ought not pleasing would put by,
The cloke was care of thrift, and husbandry,
For to encrease the common treasures store ;
But his owne treasure he encreased more
And lifted vp his loftie towres thereby,
That they began to threat the neighbour sky ;
The whiles the Princes pallaces fell fast
To ruine : (for what thing can euer last ?)
And whilest the other Peeres for pouertie
Were forst their auncient houses to let lie,
And their olde Castles to the ground to fall,
Which their forefathers famous ouer all   1180
Had founded for the Kingdomes ornament,
And for their memories long moniment.
But he no count made of Nobilitie,
Nor the wilde beasts whom armes did glorifie,
The Realmes chiefe strength and girlond of the
    crowne,
All these through fained crimes he thrust adowne,
Or made them dwell in darknes of disgrace :
For none, but whom he list might come in place.
Of men of armes he had but small regard,
But kept them lowe, and streigned verie hard.
For men of learning little he esteemed ;   1191
His wisedome he aboue their learning deemed.
As for the rascall Commons least he cared ;
For not so common was his bountie shared ;
Let God (said he) if please, care for the manie,
I for my selfe must care before els anie :
So did he good to none, to manie ill,
So did he all the kingdome rob and pill,
Yet none durst speake, ne none durst of hun
    plaine ;
So great he was in grace, and rich through gaine.

Ne would he anie let to haue accesse 1201
Vnto the Prince, but by his owne addresse:
For all that els did come, were sure to faile,
Yet would he further none but for auaile.
For on a time the Sheepe, to whom of yore
The Foxe had promised of friendship store,
What time the Foxe the kingdome first did gaine,
Came to the Court, her case there to complaine,
How that the Wolfe her mortall enemie
Had sithence slaine her Lambe most cruellie;
And therefore crau'd to come vnto the King,
To let him knowe the order of the thing.
Soft Gooddie Sheepe (then said the Foxe) not soe:
Vnto the King so rash ye may not goe,
He is with greater matter busied, 1215
Than a Lambe, or the Lambes owne mothers hed.
Ne certes may I take it well in part,
That ye my cousin Wolfe so fowly thwart,
And seeke with slaunder his good name to blot:
For there was cause, els doo it he would not.
Therefore surcease good Dame, and hence depart.
So went the Sheepe away with heauie hart.
So manie moe, so euerie one was vsed,
That to giue largely to the boxe refused.
Now when high *Ioue*, in whose almightie hand
The care of Kings, and power of Empires stand,
Sitting one day within his turret hye,
From whence he vewes with his blacklidded eye,
Whatso the heauen in his wide vawte containes,
And all that in the deepest earth remaines,
The troubled kingdome of wilde beasts behelde,
Whom not their kindly Souereigne did welde,
But an vsurping Ape with guile suborn'd,
Had all subuerst, he sdeignfully it scorn'd
In his great heart, and hardly did refraine,
But that with thunder bolts he had him slaine,
And driuen downe to hell, his dewest meed:
But him auizing, he that dreadfull deed
Forbore, and rather chose with scornfull shame
Him to auenge, and blot his brutish name
Vnto the world, that neuer after anie 1241
Should of his race be voyd of infamie:
And his false counsellor, the cause of all,
To damne to death, or dole perpetuall,
From whence he neuer should be quit, nor stal'd.
Forthwith he *Mercurie* vnto him cal'd,
And bad him flie with neuer resting speed
Vnto the forrest, where wilde beasts doo breed,
And there enquiring priuily, to learne, 1249
What did of late chaunce to the Lyon stearne,
That he rul'd not the Empire, as he ought:
And whence were all those plaints vnto him brought
Of wrongs and spoyles, by saluage beasts committed;
Which done, he bad the Lyon be remitted

Into his seate, and those same treachours vile
Be punished for their presumptuous guile.
The Sonne of *Maia* soone as he receiu'd
That word, streight with his azure wings he cleau'd 1258
The liquid clowdes, and lucid firmament;
Ne staid, till that he came with steep descent
Vnto the place, where his prescript did showe.
There stouping like an arrowe from a bowe,
He soft arriued on the grassie plaine,
And fairly paced forth with easie paine,
Till that vnto the Pallace nigh he came.
Then gan he to himselfe new shape to frame,
And that faire face, and that Ambrosiall hew,
Which wonts to decke the Gods immortall crew,
And beautefie the shinie firmament, 1269
He doft, vnfit for that rude rabblement.
So standing by the gates in strange disguize,
He gan enquire of some in secret wize,
Both of the King, and of his gouernment,
And of the Foxe, and his false blandishment:
And euermore he heard each one complaine
Of foule abuses both in realme and raine.
Which yet to proue more true, he meant to see,
And an ey-witnes of each thing to bee.
Tho on his head his dreadfull hat he dight,
Which maketh him inuisible in sight, 1280
And mocketh th'eyes of all the lookers on,
Making them thinke it but a vision.
Through power of that, he runnes through enemies swerds;
Through power of that, he passeth through the herds
Of rauenous wilde beasts, and doth beguile
Their greedie mouthes of the expected spoyle;
Through power of that, his cunning theeueries
He wonts to worke, that none the same espies;
And through the power of that, he putteth on
What shape he list in apparition. 1290
That on his head he wore, and in his hand
He tooke *Caduceus* his snakie wand,
With which the damned ghosts he gouerneth,
And furies rules, and Tartare tempereth.
With that he causeth sleep to seize the eyes,
And feare the harts of all his enemyes;
And when him list, an vniuersall night
Throughout the world he makes on euerie wight; 1298
As when his Syre with *Alcumena* lay.
Thus dight, into the Court he tooke his way,
Both through the gard, which neuer did descride,
And through the watchmen, who him neuer spide:
Thenceforth he past into each secrete part,
Whereas he saw, that sorely grieu'd his hart.
Each place abounding with fowle iniuries,
And fild with treasure rackt with robberies:

Each place defilde with blood of guiltles beasts,
Which had been slaine, to serue the Apes beheasts ;
Gluttonie, malice, pride, and couetize,
And lawlesnes raigning with riotize ;　1310
Besides the infinite extortions,
Done through the Foxes great oppressions,
That the complaints thereof could not be tolde.
Which when he did with lothfull eyes beholde,
He would no more endure, but came his way,
And cast to seeke the Lion, where he may,
That he might worke the auengement for this shame,
On those two caytiues, which had bred him blame.
And seeking all the forrest busily,　1319
At last he found, where sleeping he did ly :
The wicked weed, which there the Foxe did lay,
From vnderneath his head he tooke away,
And then him waking, forced vp to rize.
The Lion looking vp gan him auize,
As one late in a traunce, what had of long
Become of him : for fantasie is strong.
Arise (said *Mercurie*) thou sluggish beast,
That here liest senseles, like the corpse deceast,
The whilste thy kingdome from thy head is rent,
And thy throne royall with dishonour blent :
Arise, and doo thy selfe redeeme from shame,
And be aueng'd on those that breed thy blame.
Thereat enraged, soone he gan vpstart,
Grinding his teeth, and grating his great hart,
And rouzing vp himselfe, for his rough hide
He gan to reach ; but no where it espide.
Therewith he gan full terribly to rore,
And chafte at that indignitie right sore.
But when his Crowne and scepter both he wanted,
Lord how he fum'd, and sweld, and rag'd, and panted ;　1340
And threatned death, and thousand deadly dolours
To them that had purloyn'd his Princely honours.
With that in hast, disroabed as he was,
He toward his owne Pallace forth did pas ;
And all the way he roared as he went,
That all the forrest with astonishment

Thereof did tremble, and the beasts therein
Fled fast away from that so dreadfull din.
At last he came vnto his mansion,　1349
Where all the gates he found fast lockt anon,
And manie warders round about them stood :
With that he roar'd alowd, as he were wood,
That all the Pallace quaked at the stound,
As if it quite were riuen from the ground,
And all within were dead and hartles left ;
And th'Ape himselfe, as one whose wits were reft,
Fled here and there, and euerie corner sought,
To hide himselfe from his owne feared thought.
But the false Foxe when he the Lion heard,
Fled closely forth, streightway of death afeard,
And to the Lion came, full lowly creeping,　1361
With fained face, and watrie eyne halfe weeping,
T'excuse his former treason and abusion,
And turning all vnto the Apes confusion :
Nath'les the royall Beast forbore beleeuing,
But bad him stay at ease till further preeuing.
Then when he saw no entrance to him graunted,
Roaring yet lowder that all harts it daunted,
Vpon those gates with force he fiercely flewe,
And rending them in pieces, felly slewe　1370
Those warders strange, and all that els he met.
But th'Ape still flying, he no where might get :
From rowme to rowme, from beame to beame he fled
All breathles, and for feare now almost ded :
Yet him at last the Lyon spide, and caught,
And forth with shame vnto his iudgement brought.
Then all the beasts he causd' assembled bee,
To heare their doome, and sad ensample see :
The Foxe, first Author of that treacherie,
He did vncase, and then away let flie.　1380
But th'Apes long taile (which then he had) he quight
Cut off, and both eares pared of their hight ;
Since which, all Apes but halfe their eares haue left,
And of their tailes are vtterlie bereft.
　So Mother *Hubberd* her discourse did end :
Which pardon me, if I amisse haue pend ;
For weake was my remembrance it to hold,
And bad her tongue that it so bluntly tolde.

FINIS.

Ruines of Rome: by Bellay.

1

YE heauenly spirites, whose ashie cinders lie
    Vnder deep ruines, with huge walls opprest,
But not your praise, the which shall neuer die
Through your faire verses, ne in ashes rest ;
    If so be shrilling voyce of wight aliue
May reach from hence to depth of darkest hell,
Then let those deep Abysses open riue,
That ye may vnderstand my shreiking yell.
    Thrice hauing seene vnder the heauens veale
Your toombs deuoted compasse ouer all,   10
Thrice vnto you with lowd voyce I appeale,
And for your antique furie here doo call,
    The whiles that I with sacred horror sing
    Your glorie, fairest of all earthly thing.

2

Great *Babylon* her haughtie walls will praise,
And sharped steeples high shot vp in ayre ;
Greece will the olde *Ephesian* buildings blaze ;
And *Nylus* nurslings their Pyramides faire ;
    The same yet vaunting *Greece* will tell the
      storie
Of *Ioues* great Image in *Olympus* placed,   20
Mausolus worke will be the *Carians* glorie,
And *Crete* will boast the Labyrinth, now raced ;
    The antique *Rhodian* will likewise set forth
The great Colosse, erect to Memorie ;
And what els in the world is of like worth,
Some greater learned wit will magnifie.
    But I will sing aboue all moniments
    Seuen *Romane* Hils, the worlds 7. wonder-
      ments.

3

Thou stranger, which for *Rome* in *Rome* here
    seekest,
And nought of *Rome* in *Rome* perceiu'st at all,
These same olde walls, olde arches, which thou
    seest,   31
Olde Palaces, is that which *Rome* men call.
    Behold what wreake, what ruine, and what
      wast,
And how that she, which with her mightie
     powre
Tam'd all the world, hath tam'd herselfe at last,
The pray of time, which all things doth deuowre.
    Rome now of *Rome* is th'onely funerall,
And onely *Rome* of *Rome* hath victorie ;
Ne ought saue *Tyber* hastning to his fall
Remaines of all : O worlds inconstancie.   40
    That which is firme doth flit and fall away,
    And that is flitting, doth abide and stay.

4

She, whose high top aboue the starres did sore,
One foote on *Thetis*, th'other on the Morning,
One hand on *Scythia*, th'other on the *Morè*,
Both heauen and earth in roundnesse com-
    passing,
    Ioue fearing, least if she should greater growe,
The old Giants should once againe vprise,
Her whelm'd with hills, these 7. hils, which be
    nowe
Tombes of her greatnes, which did threate the
    skies :   50
Vpon her head he heapt Mount *Saturnal*,
Vpon her bellie th'antique *Palatine*,
Vpon her stomacke laid Mount *Quirinal*,
On her left hand the noysome *Esquiline*,
    And *Cælian* on the right ; but both her feete
    Mount *Viminall* and *Aventine* doo meete.

5

Who lists to see, what euer nature, arte,
And heauen could doo, O *Rome*, thee let him see,
In case thy greatnes he can gesse in harte,
By that which but the picture is of thee.   60
    Rome is no more : but if the shade of *Rome*
May of the bodie yeeld a seeming sight,
It's like a corse drawne forth out of the tombe
By Magicke skill out of eternall night :
    The corpes of *Rome* in ashes is entombed,
And her great spirite reioyned to the spirite
Of this great masse, is in the same enwombed ;
But her braue writings, which her famous merite
    In spight of time, out of the dust doth reare,
    Doo make her Idole through the world
     appeare.   70

6

Such as the *Berecynthian* Goddesse bright
In her swift charret with high turrets crownde,
Proud that so manie Gods she brought to light ;
Such was this Citie in her good daies fownd :
    This Citie, more than that great *Phrygian*
     mother
Renowm'd for fruite of famous progenie,
Whose greatnes by the greatnes of none other,
But by her selfe her equall match could see :
    Rome onely might to *Rome* compared bee,
And onely *Rome* could make great *Rome* to
    tremble :   80
So did the Gods by heauenly doome decree,
That other earthlie power should not resemble
    Her that did match the whole earths puis-
     saunce,
    And did her courage to the heauens aduaunce.

7

Ye sacred ruines, and ye tragick sights,
Which onely doo the name of *Rome* retaine,
Olde moniments, which of so famous sprights
The honour yet in ashes doo maintaine :
    Triumphant Arcks, spyres neighbours to the
      skie,
That you to see doth th'heauen it selfe appall,
    Alas, by little ye to nothing flie,   91
The peoples fable, and the spoyle of all :
    And though your frames do for a time make
      warre
Gainst time, yet time in time shall ruinate
Your workes and names, and your last reliques
    marre.
My sad desires, rest therefore moderate :
    For if that time make ende of things so sure,
    It als will end the paine, which I endure.

8

Through armes and vassals *Rome* the world
    subdu'd,
That one would weene, that one sole Cities
    strength   100
Both land and sea in roundnes had suruew'd,
To be the measure of her bredth and length :
    This peoples vertue yet so fruitfull was
Of vertuous nephewes, that posteritie
Striuing in power their grandfathers to passe,
The lowest earth ioin'd to the heauen hie ;
    To th'end that hauing all parts in their power,
Nought from the Romane Empire might be
    quight,
And that though time doth Commonwealths
    deuowre,   109
Yet no time should so low embase their hight,
    That her head earth'd in her foundations deep,
    Should not her name and endles honour keep.

9

Ye cruell starres, and eke ye Gods vnkinde,
Heauen enuious, and bitter stepdame Nature,
Be it by fortune, or by course of kinde
That ye doo weld th'affaires of earthlie creature :
    Why haue your hands long sithence traueiled
To frame this world, that doth endure so long ?
Or why were not these Romane palaces   119
Made of some matter no lesse firme and strong?
    I say not, as the common voyce doth say,
That all things which beneath the Moone haue
    being
Are temporall, and subiect to decay :
But I say rather, though not all agreeing
    With some, that weene the contrarie in
      thought :
    That all this whole shall one day come to
    nought.

10

As that braue sonne of *Aeson*, which by
    charmes
Atcheiu'd the golden Fleece in *Colchid* land,
Out of the earth engendred men of armes
Of Dragons teeth, sowne in the sacred sand ;
    So this braue Towne, that in her youthlie
      daies   131
An *Hydra* was of warriours glorious,
Did fill with her renowmed nourslings praise
The firie sunnes both one and other hous :
    But they at last, there being then not liuing
An *Hercules*, so ranke seed to represse ;
Emongst themselues with cruell furie striuing,
Mow'd downe themselues with slaughter merci-
    lesse ;
    Renewing in themselues that rage vnkinde,
    Which whilom did those earthborn brethren
    blinde.   140

11

Mars shaming to haue giuen so great head
To his off-spring, that mortall puissaunce
Puft vp with pride of Romane hardie head,
Seem'd aboue heauens powre it selfe to ad-
    uaunce ;
    Cooling againe his former kindled heate,
With which he had those Romane spirits fild ;
Did blowe new fire, and with enflamed breath,
Into the Gothicke colde hot rage instil'd :
    Then gan that Nation, th'earths new Giant
      brood,
To dart abroad the thunder bolts of warre,
And beating downe these walls with furious
    mood   151
Into her mothers bosome, all did marre ;
    To th'end that none, all were it *Ioue* his sire
    Should boast himselfe of the Romane Empire.

12

Like as whilome the children of the earth
Heapt hils on hils, to scale the starrie skie,
And fight against the Gods of heauenly berth,
Whiles *Ioue* at them his thunderbolts let flie ;
    All suddenly with lightning ouerthrowne,
The furious squadrons downe to ground did
    fall,   160
That th'earth vnder her childrens weight did
    grone,
And th'heauens in glorie triumpht ouer all :
    So did that haughtie front which heaped was
On these seuen Romane hils, it selfe vpreare
Ouer the world, and lift her loftie face
Against the heauen, that gan her force to
    feare.
    But now these scorned fields bemone her fall,
    And Gods secure feare not her force at all.

13

Nor the swift furie of the flames aspiring,
Nor the deep wounds of victours raging blade,
Nor ruthlesse spoyle of souldiers blood-desiring,
The which so oft thee (*Rome*) their conquest
    made ;   172
Ne stroke on stroke of fortune variable,
Ne rust of age hating continuance,
Nor wrath of Gods, nor spight of men vnstable,
Nor thou opposd' against thine owne puissance;
    Nor th'horrible vprore of windes high blow-
      ing,
Nor swelling streames of that God snakie-paced,
Which hath so often with his overflowing
Thee drenched, haue thy pride so much abaced;
    But that this nothing, which they haue thee
      left,   181
    Makes the world wonder, what they from
      thee reft.

14

As men in Summer fearles passe the foord,
Which is in Winter lord of all the plaine,
And with his tumbling streames doth beare
      aboord
The ploughmans hope, and shepheards labour
      vaine :
And as the coward beasts vse to despise
The noble Lion after his liues end,
Whetting their teeth, and with vaine foolhardise
Daring the foe, that cannot him defend :   190
    And as at *Troy* most dastards of the Greekes
    Did braue about the corpes of *Hector* colde ;
    So those which whilome wont with pallid
      cheekes
    The Romane triumphs glorie to behold,
      Now on these ashie tombes shew boldnesse
        vaine,
      And conquer'd dare the Conquerour disdaine.

15

Ye pallid spirits, and ye ashie ghoasts,
Which ioying in the brightnes of your day,
Brought foorth those signes of your presump-
      tuous boasts   199
Which now their dusty reliques do bewray ;
    Tell me ye spirits (sith the darksome riuer
    Of *Styx*, not passable to soules returning,
    Enclosing you in thrice three wards for euer,
    Doo not restraine your images still mourning)
      Tell me then (for perhaps some one of you
      Yet here aboue him secretly doth hide)
    Doo ye not feele your torments to accrewe,
    When ye sometimes behold the ruin'd pride
      Of these old *Romane* works built with your
        hands,   209
      Now to become nought els, but heaped sands?

16

Like as ye see the wrathfull Sea from farre,
In a great mountaine heap't with hideous noyse,
Eftsoones of thousand billowes shouldred narre,
Against a Rocke to breake with dreadfull poyse :
Like as ye see fell *Boreas* with sharpe blast,
Tossing huge tempests through the troubled
      skie,
Eftsoones hauing his wide wings spent in wast,
To stop his wearie cariere suddenly :
    And as ye see huge flames spred diuerslie,
    Gathered in one vp to the heauens to spyre,
    Eftsoones consum'd to fall downe feebily :
    So whilom did this Monarchie aspyre   222
      As waues, as winde, as fire spred ouer all,
      Till it by fatall doome adowne did fall.

17

So long as *Ioues* great Bird did make his flight,
Bearing the fire with which heauen doth vs fray,
Heauen had not feare of that presumptuous
      might,
With which the Giaunts did the Gods assay.
    But all so soone, as scortching Sunne had
      brent   229
    His wings, which wont the earth to ouerspredd,
    The earth out of her massie wombe forth sent
    That antique horror, which made heauen adredd
      Then was the Germane Rauen in disguise
      That Romane Eagle seene to cleaue asunder,
      And towards heauen freshly to arise
    Out of these mountaines, now consum'd to
      pouder.
      In which the foule that serues to beare the
        lightning,
      Is now no more seen flying, nor alighting.

18

These heapes of stones, these old wals which
      ye see,   239
Were first enclosures but of saluage soyle ;
And these braue Pallaces which maystred bee
Of time, were shepheards cottages somewhile.
    Then tooke the shepheards Kingly ornaments
    And the stout hynde arm'd his right hand with
      steele :
    Eftsoones their rule of yearely Presidents
    Grew great, and sixe months greater a great
      deele ;
      Which made perpetuall, rose to so great might,
      That thence th'Imperiall Eagle rooting tooke,
      Till th'heauen it selfe opposing gainst her might,
      Her power to *Peters* successor betooke ; 250
        Who shepheardlike, (as fates the same fore-
          seeing)
        Doth shew, that all things turne to their first
          being.

19

All that is perfect, which th'heauen beaute-
fies ;
All that's imperfect, borne belowe the Moone ;
All that doth feede our spirits and our eies ;
And all that doth consume our pleasures soone ;
    All the mishap, the which our daies out-
weares,
All the good hap of th'oldest times afore,
Rome in the time of her great ancestors,
Like a *Pandora*, locked long in store.   260
    But destinie this huge *Chaos* turmoyling,
In which all good and euill was enclosed,
Their heauenly vertues from these woes assoyl-
ing,
Caried to heauen, from sinfull bondage losed :
    But their great sinnes, the causers of their
paine,
    Vnder these antique ruines yet remaine.

20

No otherwise than raynie cloud, first fed
With earthly vapours gathered in the ayre,
Eftsoones in compas arch't, to steepe his hed,
Doth plonge himselfe in *Tethys* bosome faire ;
    And mounting vp againe, from whence he
came,   271
With his great bellie spreds the dimmed world,
Till at the last dissoluing his moist frame,
In raine, or snowe, or haile he forth is horld ;
    This Citie, which was first but shepheards
shade,
Vprising by degrees, grewe to such height,
That Queene of land and sea her selfe she made.
At last not able to beare so great weight,
    Her power disperst, through all the world did
vade ;
    To shew that all in th'end to nought shall
fade.   280

21

The same which *Pyrrhus,* and the puissaunce
Of *Afrike* could not tame, that same braue Citie,
Which with stout courage arm'd against mis-
chaunce,
Sustein'd the shocke of common enmitie ;
    Long as her ship tost with so manie freakes,
Had all the world in armes against her bent,
Was neuer seene, that anie fortunes wreakes
Could breake her course begun with braue
intent.   288
    But when the obiect of her vertue failed,
Her power it selfe against it selfe did arme ;
As he that hauing long in tempest sailed,
Faine would ariue, but cannot for the storme,
    If too great winde against the port him driue,
    Doth in the port it selfe his vessell riue.

22

When that braue honour of the Latine
name,
Which mear'd her rule with *Africa*, and *Byze*,
With *Thames* inhabitants of noble fame,
And they which see the dawning day arize ;
    Her nourslings did with mutinous vprore
Harten against her selfe, her conquer'd spoile,
Which she had wonne from all the world afore,
Of all the world was spoyl'd within a while.
    So when the compast course of the vniuerse
In sixe and thirtie thousand yeares is ronne,
The bands of th'elements shall backe reuerse
To their first discord, and be quite vndonne :
    The seedes, of which all things at first were
bred,
    Shall in great *Chaos* wombe againe be hid.

23

O warie wisedome of the man, that would
That *Carthage* towres from spoile should be for-
borne,   310
To th'end that his victorious people should
With cancring laisure not be ouerworne ;
    He well foresaw, how that the Romane
courage,
Impatient of pleasures faint desires,
Through idlenes would turne to ciuill rage,
And be her selfe the matter of her fires.
    For in a people giuen all to ease,
Ambition is engendred easily ;
As in a vicious bodie, grose disease
Soone growes through humours superfluitie.
    That came to passe, when swolne with
plentis pride,   321
    Nor prince, nor peere, nor kin they would
abide.

24

If the blinde furie, which warres breedeth oft,
Wonts not t'enrage the hearts of equall
beasts,
Whether they fare on foote, or flie aloft,
Or armed be with clawes, or scalie creasts ;
    What fell *Erynnis* with hot burning tongs,
Did grype your hearts, with noysome rage
imbew'd,
That each to other working cruell wrongs,
Your blades in your owne bowels you em-
brew'd ?   330
    Was this (ye *Romanes*) your hard destinie ?
Or some old sinne, whose vnappeased guilt
Powr'd vengeance forth on you eternallie ?
Or brothers blood, the which at first was spilt
    Vpon your walls, that God might not endure,
    Vpon the same to set foundation sure ?

25

O that I had the *Thracian* Poets harpe,
For to awake out of th'infernall shade
Those antique *Cæsars*, sleeping long in darke,
The which this auncient Citie whilome made :
Or that I had *Amphions* instrument,   341
To quicken with his vitall notes accord,
The stonie ioynts of these old walls now rent,
By which th'*Ausonian* light might be restor'd :
Or that at least I could with pencill fine.
Fashion the pourtraicts of these Palacis,
By paterne of great *Virgils* spirit diuine ;
I would assay with that which in me is,
   To builde with leuell of my loftie style,   349
   That which no hands can euermore compyle.

26

Who list the Romane greatnes forth to
      figure,
Him needeth not to seeke for vsage right
Of line, or lead, or rule, or squaire, to measure
Her length, her breadth, her deepnes, or her
      hight :
But him behooues to vew in compasse round
All that the Ocean graspes in his long armes ;
Be it where the yerely starre doth scortch the
      ground,
Or where colde *Boreas* blowes his bitter stormes.
Rome was th'whole world, and al the world
      was *Rome*,
And if things nam'd their names doo equalize,
When land and sea ye name, then name ye
      Rome ;   361
And naming *Rome* ye land and sea comprize :
   For th'auncient Plot of *Rome* displayed
      plaine,
   The map of all the wide world doth containe.

27

Thou that at *Rome* astonisht dost behold
The antique pride, which menaced the skie,
These haughtie heapes, these palaces of olde,
These wals, these arcks, these baths, these
      temples hie ;   368
Iudge by these ample ruines vew, the rest
The which iniurious time hath quite outworne,
Since of all workmen helde in reckning best,
Yet these olde fragments are for paternes
      borne :
Then also marke, how Rome from day to day,
Repayring her decayed fashion,
Renewes herselfe with buildings rich and gay ;
That one would iudge, that the *Romaine
      Dæmon*
   Doth yet himselfe with fatall hand enforce,
   Againe on foote to reare her pouldred corse.

28

He that hath seene a great Oke drie and dead,
Yet clad with reliques of some Trophees olde,
Lifting to heauen her aged hoarie head,   381
Whose foote in ground hath left but feeble
      holde ;
But halfe disbowel'd lies aboue the ground,
Shewing her wreathed rootes, and naked armes,
And on her trunke all rotten and vnsound
Onely supports herselfe for meate of wormes ;
And though she owe her fall to the first winde,
Yet of the deuout people is ador'd,
And manie yong plants spring out of her rinde ;
Who such an Oke hath seene let him record   390
   That such this Cities honour was of yore,
   And mongst all Cities florished much more.

29

All that which *Aegypt* whilome did deuise,
All that which *Greece* their temples to embraue,
After th'Ionicke, Atticke, Doricke guise,
Or *Corinth* skil'd in curious workes to graue ;
All that *Lysippus* practike arte could forme,
Apelles wit, or *Phidias* his skill,
Was wont this auncient Citie to adorne,
And the heauen it selfe with her wide wonders
      fill ;   400
All that which *Athens* euer brought forth
      wise,
All that which *Afrike* euer brought forth strange,
All that which *Asie* euer had of prise,
Was here to see. O meruelous great change :
   Rome liuing, was the worlds sole ornament,
   And dead, is now the worlds sole moniment.

30

Like as the seeded field greene grasse first
      showes,
Then from greene grasse into a stalke doth
      spring,
And from a stalke into an eare forth-growes,
Which eare the frutefull graine doth shortly
      bring ;   410
And as in season due the husband mowes
The wauing lockes of those faire yeallow heares,
Which bound in sheaues, and layd in comely
      rowes,
Vpon the naked fields in stackes he reares :
   So grew the Romane Empire by degree,
   Till that Barbarian hands it quite did spill,
   And left of it but these olde markes to see,
   Of which all passers by doo somewhat pill :
   As they which gleane, the reliques vse to
      gather,
   Which th'husbandman behind him chanst to
      scater.   420

SPENSER   S

31

That same is now nought but a champian
  wide,
Where all this worlds pride once was situate.
No blame to thee, whosoeuer dost abide
By *Nyle*, or *Gange*, or *Tygre*, or *Euphrate*,
  Ne *Afrike* thereof guiltie is, nor *Spaine*,
Nor the bolde people by the *Thamis* brincks,
Nor the braue warlicke brood of *Alemaine*,
Nor the borne Souldier which *Rhine* running
  drinks:
  Thou onely cause, O Ciuill furie, art   429
Which sowing in th'*Aemathian* fields thy spight,
Didst arme thy hand against thy proper hart;
To th'end that when thou wast in greatest hight
  To greatnes growne, through long prosperitie,
  Thou then adowne might'st fall more horri-
  blie.

32

Hope ye my verses that posteritie
Of age ensuing shall you euer read ?
Hope ye that euer immortalitie
So meane Harpes worke may chalenge for her
  meed ?
  If vnder heauen anie endurance were,   439
These moniments, which not in paper writ,
But in Porphyre and Marble doo appeare,
Might well haue hop'd to haue obtained it.

Nath'les my Lute, whom *Phœbus* deignd to
  giue,
Cease not to sound these olde antiquities:
For if that time doo let thy glorie liue,
Well maist thou boast, how euer base thou
  bee,
  That thou art first, which of thy Nation
  song
Th'olde honour of the people gowned long.

L'Envoy.

Bellay, first garland of free Poësie
That *France* brought forth, though fruitfull of
  braue wits,   450
Well worthie thou of immortalitie,
That long hast traueld by thy learned writs,
  Olde *Rome* out of her ashes to reuiue,
And giue a second life to dead decayes:
Needes must he all eternitie suruiue,
That can to other giue eternall dayes.
  Thy dayes therefore are endles, and thy
  prayse
Excelling all, that euer went before ;
And after thee, gins *Bartas* hie to rayse
His heauenly Muse, th'Almightie to adore. 460
  Liue happie spirits, th'honour of your name,
  And fill the world with neuer dying fame.

FINIS.

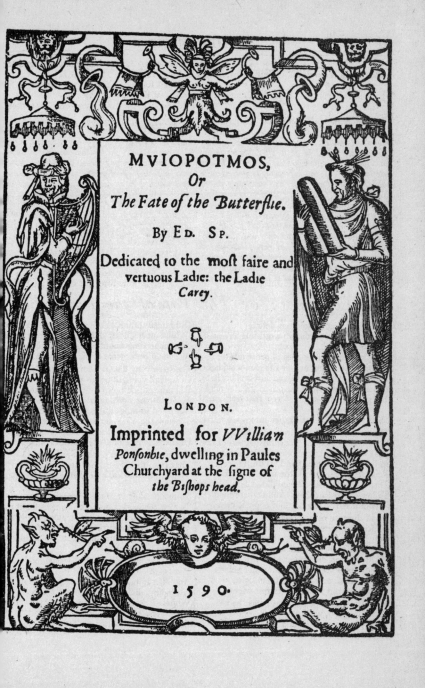

MVIOPOTMOS,
Or
The Fate of the Butterflie.

By E<small>D</small>. S<small>P</small>.

Dedicated to the most faire and
vertuous Ladie: the Ladie
Carey.

LONDON.

Imprinted for *William
Ponsonbie,* dwelling in Paules
Churchyard at the signe of
the Bishops head.

1590.

To the right worthy and vertuous Ladie; the La: *Carey*.

*M*Ost braue and bountifull La: for so excellent fauours as I haue receiued at your sweet handes, to offer these fewe leaues as in recompence, should be as to offer flowers to the Gods for their diuine benefites. Therefore I haue determined to giue my selfe wholy to you, as quite abandoned from my selfe, and absolutely vowed to your seruices: which in all right is euer held for full recompence of debt or damage to haue the person yeelded. My person I wot wel how little worth it is. But the faithfull minde and humble zeale which I beare vnto your La: may perhaps be more of price, as may please you to account and vse the poore seruice thereof; which taketh glory to aduance your excellent partes and noble vertues, and to spend it selfe in honouring you: not so much for your great bounty to my self, which yet may not be vnminded; nor for name or kindreds sake by you vouchsafed, beeing also regardable; as for that honorable name, which yee haue by your braue deserts purchast to your self, and spred in the mouths of al men: with which I haue also presumed to grace my verses, and vnder your name to commend to the world this smal Poëme, the which beseeching your La: to take in worth, and of all things therein according to your wonted graciousnes to make a milde construction, I humbly pray for your happines.

Your La: euer

humbly;

E. S.

Muiopotmos : or *The Fate of the Butterflie*.

I Sing of deadly dolorous debate,
Stir'd vp through wrathfull *Nemesis* despight,
Betwixt two mightie ones of great estate,
Drawne into armes, and proofe of mortall fight,
Through prowd ambition, and hartswelling hate,
Whilest neither could the others greater might
And sdeignfull scorne endure ; that from small iarre
Their wraths at length broke into open warre.

The roote whereof and tragicall effect,
Vouchsafe, O thou the mournfulst Muse of nyne,
That wontst the tragick stage for to direct,   11
In funerall complaints and waylfull tyne,
Reueale to me, and all the meanes detect,
Through which sad *Clarion* did at last declyne
To lowest wretchednes ; And is there then
Such rancour in the harts of mightie men ?

Of all the race of siluer-winged Flies
Which doo possesse the Empire of the aire,
Betwixt the centred earth, and azure skies,
Was none more fauourable, nor more faire,   20
Whilst heauen did fauour his felicities,
Then *Clarion*, the eldest sonne and haire
Of *Muscaroll*, and in his fathers sight
Of all aliue did seeme the fairest wight.

With fruitfull hope his aged breast he fed
Of future good, which his yong toward yeares,
Full of braue courage and bold hardyhed,
Aboue th'ensample of his equall peares,
Did largely promise, and to him forered   29
(Whilst oft his heart did melt in tender teares)
That he in time would sure proue such an one,
As should be worthie of his fathers throne.

The fresh yong flie, in whom the kindly fire
Of lustfull youngth began to kindle fast,
Did much disdaine to subiect his desire
To loathsome sloth, or houres in ease to wast,
But ioy'd to range abroad in fresh attire ;
Through the wide compas of the ayrie coast,
And with vnwearied wings each part t'inquire
Of the wide rule of his renowmed sire.   40

For he so swift and nimble was of flight,
That from this lower tract he dar'd to stie
Vp to the clowdes, and thence with pineons light,
To mount aloft vnto the Christall skie,
To vew the workmanship of heauens hight :
Whence downe descending he along would flie
Vpon the streaming riuers, sport to finde ;
And oft would dare to tempt the troublous winde.

So on a Summers day, when season milde
With gentle calme the world had quieted,   50
And high in heauen *Hyperions* fierie childe
Ascending, did his beames abroad dispred,
Whiles all the heauens on lower creatures smilde ;
Yong *Clarion* with vauntfull lustie head,
After his guize did cast abroad to fare ;
And theretoo gan his furnitures prepare.

His breastplate first, that was of substance
pure,
Before his noble heart he firmely bound,
That mought his life from yron death assure,
And ward his gentle corpes from cruell wound :
For it by arte was framed, to endure   61
The bit of balefull steele and bitter stownd,
No lesse than that, which *Vulcane* made to
sheild
Achilles life from fate of *Troyan* field.

And then about his shoulders broad he threw
An hairie hide of some wilde beast, whom hee
In saluage forrest by aduenture slew,
And reft the spoyle his ornament to bee :
Which spredding all his backe with dreadfull
vew,
Made all that him so horrible did see,   70
Thinke him *Alcides* with the Lyons skin,
When the *Nœmean* Conquest he did win.

Vpon his head his glistering Burganet,
The which was wrought by wonderous deuice,
And curiously engrauen, he did set :
The mettall was of rare and passing price ;
Not *Bilbo* steele, nor brasse from *Corinth* fet,
Nor costly *Oricalche* from strange *Phœnice* ;
But such as could both *Phœbus* arrowes ward,
And th'hayling darts of heauen beating hard.

Therein two deadly weapons fixt he bore,   81
Strongly outlaunced towards either side,
Like two sharpe speares, his enemies to gore :
Like as a warlike Brigandine, applyde
To fight, layes forth her threatfull pikes
afore,
The engines which in them sad death doo
hyde :
So did this flie outstretch his fearefull hornes,
Yet so as him their terrour more adornes.

Lastly his shinie wings as siluer bright,
Painted with thousand colours, passing farre
All Painters skill, he did about him dight :   91
Not halfe so manie sundrie colours arre
In *Iris* bowe, ne heauen doth shine so bright,
Distinguished with manie a twinckling starre,
Nor *Iunoes* Bird in her ey-spotted traine
So manie goodly colours doth containe.

Ne (may it be withouten perill spoken)
The Archer God, the sonne of *Cytheree*,
That ioyes on wretched louers to be wroken,
And heaped spoyles of bleeding harts to see,
Beares in his wings so manie a changefull token,
Ah my liege Lord, forgiue it vnto mee,
If ought against thine honour I haue tolde ;
Yet sure those wings were fairer manifolde.

Full manie a Ladie faire, in Court full oft
Beholding them, him secretly enuide,
And wisht that two such fannes, so silken soft,
And golden faire, her Loue would her prouide ;
Or that when them the gorgeous Flie had
doft,   109
Some one that would with grace be gratifide,
From him would steale them priuily away,
And bring to her so precious a pray.

Report is that dame *Venus* on a day,
In spring when flowres doo clothe the fruitful
ground,
Walking abroad with all her Nymphes to play,
Bad her faire damzels flocking her arownd,
To gather flowres, her forhead to array :
Emongst the rest a gentle Nymph was found,
Hight *Astery*, excelling all the crewe
In curteous vsage, and vnstained hewe.   120

Who being nimbler ioynted than the rest,
And more industrious, gathered more store
Of the fields honour, than the others best ;
Which they in secret harts enuying sore,
Tolde *Venus*, when her as the worthiest
She praisd', that *Cupide* (as they heard before)
Did lend her secret aide, in gathering
Into her lap the children of the spring.

Whereof the Goddesse gathering iealous feare,
Not yet vnmindfull, how not long agoe   130
Her sonne to *Psyche* secrete loue did beare,
And long it close conceal'd, till mickle woe
Thereof arose, and manie a rufull teare ;
Reason with sudden rage did ouergoe,
And giuing hastie credit to th'accuser,
Was led away of them that did abuse her.

Eftsoones that Damzel by her heauenly might,
She turn'd into a winged Butterflie,
In the wide aire to make her wandring flight ;
And all those flowres, with which so plen-
teouslie   140
Her lap she filled had, that bred her spight,
She placed in her wings, for memorie
Of her pretended crime, though crime none
were :
Since which that flie them in her wings doth
beare.

Thus the fresh *Clarion* being readie dight,
Vnto his iourney did himselfe addresse,
And with good speed began to take his flight :
Ouer the fields in his franke lustinesse,
And all the champion he soared light,   149
And all the countrey wide he did possesse,
Feeding vpon their pleasures bounteouslie,
That none gainsaid, nor none did him enuie.

The woods, the riuers, and the medowes green,
With his aire-cutting wings he measured wide,
Ne did he leaue the mountaines bare vnseene,
Nor the ranke grassie fennes delights vntride.
But none of these, how euer sweete they
    beene,
Mote please his fancie, nor him cause t'abide:
His choicefull sense with euerie change doth
    flit.
No common things may please a wauering wit.

To the gay gardins his vnstaid desire   161
Him wholly caried, to refresh his sprights:
There lauish Nature in her best attire,
Powres forth sweete odors, and alluring sights ;
And Arte with her contending, doth aspire
T'excell the naturall, with made delights:
And all that faire or pleasant may be found,
In riotous excesse doth there abound.

There he arriuing, round about doth flie,
From bed to bed, from one to other border,
And takes suruey with curious busie eye,   171
Of euerie flowre and herbe there set in order ;
Now this, now that he tasteth tenderly,
Yet none of them he rudely doth disorder,
Ne with his feete their silken leaues deface ;
But pastures on the pleasures of each place.

And euermore with most varietie,
And change of sweetnesse (for all change is
    sweete)
He casts his glutton sense to satisfie,   179
Now sucking of the sap of herbe most meete,
Or of the deaw, which yet on them does lie,
Now in the same bathing his tender feete:
And then he pearcheth on some braunch
    thereby,
To weather him, and his moyst wings to dry.

And then againe he turneth to his play,
To spoyle the pleasures of that Paradise :
The wholsome Saulge, and Lauender still gray,
Ranke smelling Rue, and Cummin good for
    eyes,
The Roses raigning in the pride of May,   189
Sharpe Isope, good for greene wounds remedies,
Faire Marigoldes, and Bees alluring Thime,
Sweete Marioram, and Daysies decking prime.

Coole Violets, and Orpine growing still,
Embathed Balme, and chearfull Galingale,
Fresh Costmarie, and breathfull Camomill,
Dull Poppie, and drink-quickning Setuale,
Veyne-healing Veruen, and hed-purging Dill,
Sound Sauorie, and Bazill hartie-hale,
Fat Colworts, and comforting Perseline,
Colde Lettuce, and refreshing Rosmarine. 200

And whatso else of vertue good or ill
Grewe in this Gardin, fetcht from farre away,
Of euerie one he takes, and tastes at will,
And on their pleasures greedily doth pray.
Then when he hath both plaid, and fed
    his fill,
In the warme Sunne he doth himselfe embay,
And there him rests in riotous suffisaunce
Of all his gladfulnes, and kingly ioyaunce.

What more felicitie can fall to creature,
Than to enioy delight with libertie,   210
And to be Lord of all the workes of Nature,
To raine in th'aire from earth to highest skie,
To feed on flowres, and weeds of glorious
    feature,
To take what euer thing doth please the eie ?
Who rests not pleased with such happines,
Well worthie he to taste of wretchednes.

But what on earth can long abide in state ?
Or who can him assure of happie day ;
Sith morning faire may bring fowle euening
    late,
And least mishap the most blisse alter may ?
For thousand perills lie in close awaite   221
About vs daylie, to worke our decay ;
That none, except a God, or God him guide,
May them auoyde, or remedie prouide.

And whatso heauens in their secret doome
Ordained haue, how can fraile fleshly wight
Forecast, but it must needs to issue come ?
The sea, the aire, the fire, the day, the night,
And th'armies of their creatures all and some
Do serue to them, and with importune might
Warre against vs the vassals of their will. 231
Who then can saue, what they dispose to spill ?

Not thou, O *Clarion*, though fairest thou
Of all thy kinde, vnhappie happie Flie,
Whose cruell fate is wouen euen now
Of *Ioues* owne hand, to worke thy miserie :
Ne may thee helpe the manie hartie vow,
Which thy olde Sire with sacred pietie
Hath powred forth for thee, and th'altars
    sprent :
Nought may thee saue from heauens auenge-
    ment.   240

It fortuned (as heauens had behight)
That in this gardin, where yong *Clarion*
Was wont to solace him, a wicked wight
The foe of faire things, th'author of confusion,
The shame of Nature, the bondslaue of spight,
Had lately built his hatefull mansion,
And lurking closely, in awayte now lay,
How he might anie in his trap betray.

But when he spide the ioyous Butterflie
In this faire plot dispacing too and fro,   250
Fearles of foes and hidden ieopardie,
Lord how he gan for to bestirre him tho,
And to his wicked worke each part applie :
His heart did earne against his hated ioe,
And bowels so with ranckling poyson swelde,
That scarce the skin the strong contagion
    helde.

The cause why he this Flie so maliced,
Was (as in stories it is written found)
For that his mother which him bore and bred,
The most fine-fingred workwoman on ground,
Arachne, by his meanes was vanquished   261
Of Pallas, and in her owne skill confound,
When she with her for excellence contended,
That wrought her shame, and sorrow neuer
    ended.

For the Tritonian Goddesse hauing hard
Her blazed fame, which all the world had fil'd,
Came downe to proue the truth, and due reward
For her prais-worthie workmanship to yeild
But the presumptuous Damzel rashly dar'd
The Goddesse selfe to chalenge to the field,
And to compare with her in curious skill   271
Of workes with loome, with needle, and with
    quill.

Minerua did the chalenge not refuse,
But deign'd with her the paragon to make :
So to their worke they sit, and each doth chuse
What storie she will for her tapet take.
Arachne figur'd how Ioue did abuse
Europa like a Bull, and on his backe   278
Her through the sea did beare ; so liuely seene,
That it true Sea, and true Bull ye would weene.

She seem'd still backe vnto the land to looke,
And her play-fellowes aide to call, and feare
The dashing of the waues, that vp she tooke
Her daintie feete, and garments gathered
    neare :
But (Lord) how she in euerie member shooke,
When as the land she saw no more appeare,
But a wilde wildernes of waters deepe :
Then gan she greatly to lament and weepe.

Before the Bull she pictur'd winged Loue,
With his yong brother Sport, light fluttering
Vpon the waues, as each had been a Doue ;
The one his bowe and shafts, the other Spring
A burning Teade about his head did moue,
As in their Syres new loue both triumphing :
And manie Nymphes about them flocking round,
And manie Tritons, which their hornes did
    sound.

And round about, her worke she did empale
With a faire border wrought of sundrie flowres,
Enwouen with an Yuie winding trayle :   299
A goodly worke, full fit for Kingly bowres,
Such as Dame Pallas, such as Enuie pale,
That al good things with venemous tooth
    deuowres,
Could not accuse. Then gan the Goddesse
    bright
Her selfe likewise vnto her worke to dight.

She made the storie of the olde debate,
Which she with Neptune did for Athens trie :
Twelue Gods doo sit around in royall state,
And Ioue in midst with awfull Maiestie,
To iudge the strife betweene them stirred late :
Each of the Gods by his like visnomie   310
Eathe to be knowen ; but Ioue aboue them all,
By his great lookes and power Imperiall.

Before them stands the God of Seas in place,
Clayming that sea-coast Citie as his right,
And strikes the rockes with his three-forked
    mace :
Whenceforth issues a warlike steed in sight,
The signe by which he chalengeth the place,
That all the Gods, which saw his wondrous
    might
Did surely deeme the victorie his due :   319
But seldome seene, foreiudgement proueth true.

Then to her selfe she giues her Aegide shield,
And steelhed speare, and morion on her hedd,
Such as she oft is seene in warlicke field :
Then sets she forth, how with her weapon dredd
She smote the ground, the which streight foorth
    did yield
A fruitfull Olyue tree, with berries spredd,
That all the Gods admir'd ; then all the storie
She compast with a wreathe of Olyues hoarie.

Emongst those leaues she made a Butterflie,
With excellent deuice and wondrous slight,
Fluttring among the Oliues wantonly,   331
That seem'd to liue, so like it was in sight ·
The veluet nap which on his wings doth lie,
The silken downe with which his backe is dight,
His broad outstretched hornes, his hayrie thies,
His glorious colours, and his glistering eies.

Which when Arachne saw, as ouerlaid,
And mastered with workmanship so rare,
She stood astonied long, ne ought gainesaid,
And with fast fixed eyes on her did stare,   340
And by her silence, signe of one dismaid,
The victorie did yeeld her as her share :
Yet did she inly fret, and felly burne,
And all her blood to poysonous rancor turne.

That shortly from the shape of womanhed
Such as she was, when *Pallas* she attempted,
She grew to hideous shape of dryrihed,
Pined with griefe of follie late repented :
Eftsoones her white streight legs were altered
To crooked crawling shankes, of marrowe
   empted,   350
And her faire face to fowle and loathsome hewe,
And her fine corpes to a bag of venim grewe.

This cursed creature, mindfull of that olde
Enfestred grudge, the which his mother felt,
So soone as *Clarion* he did beholde,
His heart with vengefull malice inly swelt,
And weauing straight a net with manie a folde
About the caue, in which he lurking dwelt,
With fine small cords about it stretched wide,
So finely sponne, that scarce they could be spide.

Not anie damzell, which her vaunteth most
In skilfull knitting of soft silken twyne ; 362
Nor anie weauer, which his worke doth boast
In dieper, in damaske, or in lyne ;
Nor anie skil'd in workmanship embost ;
Nor anie skil'd in loupes of fingring fine,
Might in their diuers cunning euer dare,
With this so curious networke to compare.

Ne doo I thinke, that that same subtil gin,
The which the *Lemnian* God framde craftilie,
Mars sleeping with his wife to compasse in,
That all the Gods with common mockerie 372
Might laugh at them, and scorne their shame-
   full sin,
Was like to this. This same he did applie,
For to entrap the careles *Clarion*,
That rang'd each where without suspition.

Suspition of friend, nor feare of foe,
That hazarded his health, had he at all,
But walkt at will, and wandred too and fro,
In the pride of his freedome principall : 380
Litle wist he his fatall future woe,
But was secure, the liker he to fall.
He likest is to fall into mischaunce,
That is regardles of his gouernaunce.

Yet still *Aragnoll* (so his foe was hight)
Lay lurking couertly him to surprise,
And all his gins that him entangle might,
Drest in good order as he could deuise.
At length the foolish Flie without foresight,
As he that did all daunger quite despise, 390
Toward those parts came flying careleslie,
Where hidden was his hatefull enemie.

Who seeing him, with secrete ioy therefore
Did tickle inwardly in euerie vaine,
And his false hart fraught with all treasons
   store,
Was fil'd with hope, his purpose to obtaine :
Himselfe he close vpgathered more and more
Into his den, that his deceiptfull traine
By his there being might not be bewraid,
Ne anie noyse, ne anie motion made. 400

Like as a wily Foxe, that hauing spide,
Where on a sunnie banke the Lambes doo play,
Full closely creeping by the hinder side,
Lyes in ambushment of his hoped pray,
Ne stirreth limbe, till seeing readie tide,
He rusheth forth, and snatcheth quite away
One of the litle yonglings vnawares :
So to his worke *Aragnoll* him prepares.

Who now shall giue vnto my heauie eyes
A well of teares, that all may ouerflow ? 410
Or where shall I finde lamentable cryes,
And mournfull tunes enough my griefe to
   show ?
Helpe O thou Tragick Muse, me to deuise
Notes sad enough, t'expresse this bitter throw :
For loe, the drerie stownd is now arriued,
That of all happines hath vs depriued.

The luckles *Clarion*, whether cruell Fate,
Or wicked Fortune faultles him misled,
Or some vngracious blast out of the gate
Of *Aeoles* raine perforce him droue on hed,
Was (O sad hap and howre vnfortunate) 421
With violent swift flight forth caried
Into the cursed cobweb, which his foe
Had framed for his finall ouerthroe.

There the fond Flie entangled, strugled long,
Himselfe to free thereout ; but all in vaine.
For striuing more, the more in laces strong
Himselfe he tide, and wrapt his winges twaine
In lymie snares the subtill loupes among ;
That in the ende he breathelesse did remaine,
And all his yougthly forces idly spent, 431
Him to the mercie of th'auenger lent.

Which when the greisly tyrant did espie,
Like a grimme Lyon rushing with fierce might
Out of his den, he seized greedelie
On the resistles pray, and with fell spight,
Vnder the left wing stroke his weapon slie
Into his heart, that his deepe groning spright
In bloodie streames foorth fled into the aire,
His bodie left the spectacle of care. 440

FINIS.

Visions of the worlds vanitie.

1

ONe day, whiles that my daylie cares did
   sleepe,
My spirit, shaking off her earthly prison,
Began to enter into meditation deepe
Of things exceeding reach of common reason ;
  Such as this age, in which all good is geason,
  And all that humble is and meane debaced,
  Hath brought forth in her last declining season,
  Griefe of good mindes, to see goodnesse disgraced.
    On which when as my thought was throghly
     placed,   9
    Vnto my eyes strange showes presented were,
    Picturing that, which I in minde embraced,
    That yet those sights empassion me full nere.
      Such as they were (faire Ladie) take in worth,
      That when time serues, may bring things
       better forth.

2

In Summers day, when *Phœbus* fairly shone,
I saw a Bull as white as driuen snowe,
With gilden hornes embowed like the Moone,
In a fresh flowring meadow lying lowe :
  Vp to his eares the verdant grasse did growe,
  And the gay floures did offer to be eaten ;   20
  But he with fatnes so did ouerflowe,
  That he all wallowed in the weedes downe beaten,
    Ne car'd with them his daintie lips to sweeten :
    Till that a Brize, a scorned little creature,
    Through his faire hide his angrie sting did
     threaten,
And vext so sore, that all his goodly feature,
    And all his plenteous pasture nought him
     pleased :
    So by the small the great is oft diseased.

3

Beside the fruitfull shore of muddie *Nile*,
Vpon a sunnie banke outstretched lay   30
In monstrous length, a mightie Crocodile,
That cram'd with guiltles blood, and greedie pray
Of wretched people trauailing that way,
Thought all things lesse than his disdainful
  pride.
I saw a little Bird, cal'd *Tedula*,
The least of thousands which on earth abide,
  That forst this hideous beast to open wide
The greisly gates of his deuouring hell,
And let him feede, as Nature doth prouide,
Vpon his iawes, that with blacke venime swell.
  Why then should greatest things the least
   disdaine,   41
   Sith that so small so mightie can constraine ?

4

The kingly Bird, that beares *Ioues* thunder-
  clap,
One day did scorne the simple Scarabee,
Proud of his highest seruice, and good hap,
That made all other Foules his thralls to bee :
  The silly Flie, that no redresse did see,
  Spide where the Eagle built his towring nest,
  And kindling fire within the hollow tree,
  Burnt vp his yong ones, and himselfe distrest ;
    Ne suffred him in anie place to rest,   51
    But droue in *Ioues* owne lap his egs to lay ;
    Where gathering also filth him to infest,
    Forst with the filth his egs to fling away :
      For which when as the Foule was wroth,
      said *Ioue*,
      Lo how the least the greatest may reproue.

5

Toward the sea turning my troubled eye,
I saw the fish (if fish I may it cleepe)
That makes the sea before his face to flye,   59
And with his flaggie finnes doth seeme to sweepe
  The fomie waues out of the dreadfull deep,
  The huge *Leuiathan*, dame Natures wonder,
  Making his sport, that manie makes to weep :
  A sword-fish small him from the rest did sunder,
    That in his throat him pricking softly vnder,
    His wide Abysse him forced forth to spewe,
    That all the sea did roare like heauens thunder,
    And all the waues were stain'd with filthie hewe.
      Hereby I learned haue, not to despise,
      What euer thing seemes small in common
      eyes.   70

6

An hideous Dragon, dreadfull to behold,
Whose backe was arm'd against the dint of
  speare
With shields of brasse, that shone like burnisht
  golde,
And forkhed sting, that death in it did beare,
  Stroue with a Spider his vnequall peare :
And bad defiance to his enemie.
The subtill vermin creeping closely neare,
Did in his drinke shed poyson priuilie ;
  Which through his entrailes spredding
   diuersly,
Made him to swell, that nigh his bowells brust,
And him enforst to yeeld the victorie,
That did so much in his owne greatnesse trust.
  O how great vainnesse is it then to scorne
  The weake, that hath the strong so oft for-
  lorne.

7

High on a hill a goodly Cedar grewe,
Of wondrous length, and streight proportion,
That farre abroad her daintie odours threwe ;
Mongst all the daughters of proud *Libanon*,
  Her match in beautie was not anie one.
Shortly within her inmost pith there bred   90
A litle wicked worme, perceiu'd of none,
That on her sap and vitall moysture fed :
  Thenceforth her garland so much honoured
Began to die, (O great ruth for the same)
And her faire lockes fell from her loftie head,
That shortly balde, and bared she became.
  I, which this sight beheld, was much dis-
    mayed,
  To see so goodly thing so soone decayed.

8

Soone after this I saw an Elephant,
Adorn'd with bells and bosses gorgeouslie, 100
That on his backe did beare (as batteilant)
A gilden towre, which shone exceedinglie ;
  That he himselfe through foolish vanitie,
Both for his rich attire, and goodly forme,
Was puffed vp with passing surquedrie,
And shortly gan all other beasts to scorne,
  Till that a little Ant, a silly worme,
Into his nosthrils creeping, so him pained,
That casting downe his towres, he did deforme
Both borrowed pride, and natiue beautie
    stained.   110
  Let therefore nought that great is, therein
    glorie,
  Sith so small thing his happines may varie.

9

Looking far foorth into the Ocean wide,
A goodly ship with banners brauely dight,
And flag in her top-gallant I espide,
Through the maine sea making her merry
    flight :
  Faire blew the winde into her bosome right ;
And th'heauens looked louely all the while,
That she did seeme to daunce, as in delight,
And at her owne felicitie did smile.   120
  All sodainely there cloue vnto her keele
A little fish, that men call *Remora*,
Which stopt her course, and held her by the
    heele,
  That winde nor tide could moue her thence
    away.
  Straunge thing me seemeth, that so small a
    thing
  Should able be so great an one to wring.

10

A mighty Lyon, Lord of all the wood,
Hauing his hunger throughly satisfide,
With pray of beasts, and spoyle of liuing blood,
Safe in his dreadles den him thought to hide :
  His sternesse was his prayse, his strength his
    pride,   131
And all his glory in his cruell clawes.
I saw a wasp, that fiercely him defide,
And bad him battaile euen to his iawes ;
  Sore he him stong, that it the blood forth
    drawes,
And his proude heart is fild with fretting ire :
In vaine he threats his teeth, his tayle, his
    pawes,
And from his bloodie eyes doth sparkle fire :
  That dead himselfe he wisheth for despight.
  So weakest may anoy the most of might.

11

What time the Romaine Empire bore the
    raine   141
Of all the world, and florist most in might,
The nations gan their soueraigntie disdaine,
And cast to quitt them from their bondage
    quight :
  So when all shrouded were in silent night,
The *Galles* were, by corrupting of a mayde,
Possest nigh of the Capitol through slight,
Had not a Goose the treachery bewrayde.
  If then a Goose great *Rome* from ruine stayde,
And *Ioue* himselfe, the patron of the place,
Preserud from being to his foes betrayde,   151
Why do vaine men mean things so much deface,
  And in their might repose their most assur-
    ance,
  Sith nought on earth can chalenge long
    endurance ?

12

When these sad sights were ouerpast and
    gone,
My spright was greatly moued in her rest,
With inward ruth and deare affection,
To see so great things by so small distrest :
  Thenceforth I gan in my engrieued brest
To scorne all difference of great and small, 160
Sith that the greatest often are opprest,
And vnawares doe into daunger fall.
  And ye, that read these ruines tragicall
Learne by their losse to loue the low degree,
And if that fortune chaunce you vp to call
To honours seat, forget not what you be :
  For he that of himselfe is most secure,
  Shall finde his state most fickle and vnsure.

FINIS.

The Visions of Bellay.

1

IT was the time, when rest soft sliding downe
From heauens hight into mens heauy eyes,
In the forgetfulnes of sleepe doth drowne
The carefull thoughts of mortall miseries :
  Then did a Ghost before mine eyes appeare,
On that great riuers banck, that runnes by
    Rome,
Which calling me by name, bad me to reare
My lookes to heauen whence all good gifts do
    come,
  And crying lowd, loe now beholde (quoth hee)
What vnder this great temple placed is : 10
Lo all is nought but flying vanitee.
So I that know this worlds inconstancies,
  Sith onely God surmounts all times decay,
  In God alone my confidence do stay.

2

On high hills top I saw a stately frame,
An hundred cubits high by iust assize,
With hundreth pillours fronting faire the
    same,
All wrought with Diamond after Dorick wize :
  Nor brick, nor marble was the wall in view,
But shining Christall, which from top to base
Out of her womb a thousand rayons threw,
On hundred steps of *Afrike* golds enchase :
  Golde was the parget, and the seeling bright
Did shine all scaly with great plates of golde ;
The floore of *Iasp* and *Emeraude* was dight.
O worlds vainesse. Whiles thus I did behold,
  An earthquake shooke the hill from lowest
    seat,
  And ouerthrew this frame with ruine great.

3

Then did a sharped spyre of Diamond
    bright,
Ten feete each way in square, appeare to mee,
Iustly proportion'd vp vnto his hight,   31
So far as Archer might his leuel see :
  The top thereof a pot did seeme to beare,
Made of the mettall, which we most do honour,
And in this golden vessell couched weare
The ashes of a mightie Emperour :
  Vpon foure corners of the base were pight,
To beare the frame, foure great Lyons of gold ;
A worthy tombe for such a worthy wight.
Alas this world doth nought but grieuance
    hold.   40
I saw a tempest from the heauen descend,
  Which this braue monument with flash did
    rend.

4

I saw raysde vp on yuorie pilloures tall,
Whose bases were of richest mettalls warke,
The chapters Alablaster, the fryses christall,
The double front of a triumphall Arke :
  On each side purtraid was a Victorie,
Clad like a Nimph, that wings of siluer weares,
And in triumphant chayre was set on hie,
The auncient glory of the Romaine Peares. 50
  No worke it seem'd of earthly craftsmans wit,
But rather wrought by his owne industry,
That thunder-dartes for *Ioue* his syre doth fit,
Let me no more see faire thing vnder sky,
  Sith that mine eyes haue seene so faire a sight
  With sodain fall to dust consumed quight.

5

Then was the faire *Dodonian* tree far seene,
Vpon seauen hills to spread his gladsome
    gleame,
And conquerours bedecked with his greene,
Along the bancks of the *Ausonian* streame :
  There many an auncient Trophee was
    addrest,   61
And many a spoyle, and many a goodly show,
Which that braue races greatnes did attest,
That whilome from the *Troyan* blood did flow.
  Rauisht I was so rare a thing to vew,
When lo a barbarous troupe of clownish fone
The honour of these noble boughs down threw,
Vnder the wedge I heard the tronck to grone ;
  And since I saw the roote in great disdaine
  A twinne of forked trees send forth againe.

6

I saw a Wolfe vnder a rockie caue   71
Noursing two whelpes ; I saw her litle ones
In wanton dalliance the teate to craue,
While she her neck wreath'd from them for the
    nones :
  I saw her raunge abroad to seeke her food,
And roming through the field with greedie rage
T'embrew her teeth and clawes with lukewarm
    blood
Of the small heards, her thirst for to asswage.
  I saw a thousand huntsmen, which descended
Downe from the mountaines bordring *Lom-*
    bardie,   80
That with an hundred speares her flank wide
    rended.
I saw her on the plaine outstretched lie,
  Throwing out thousand throbs in her owne
    soyle :
  Soone on a tree vphang'd I saw her spoyle.

7

I saw the Bird that can the Sun endure,
With feeble wings assay to mount on hight,
By more and more she gan her wings t'assure,
Following th'ensample of her mothers sight:
  I saw her rise, and with a larger flight
To pierce the cloudes, and with wide pinneons
To measure the most haughtie mountaines
        hight,   91
Vntill she raught the Gods owne mansions:
  There was she lost, when suddaine I behelde,
Where tumbling through the ayre in firie fold;
All flaming downe she on the plaine was felde,
And soone her bodie turn'd to ashes colde.
  I saw the foule that doth the light dispise,
Out of her dust like to a worme arise

8

I saw a riuer swift, whose fomy billowes
Did wash the ground work of an old great
        wall;   100
I saw it couer'd all with griesly shadowes,
That with black horror did the ayre appall.
  Thereout a strange beast with seuen heads
        arose,
That townes and castles vnder her brest did
        coure,
And seem'd both milder beasts and fiercer foes
Alike with equall rauine to deuoure.
  Much was I mazde, to see this monsters kinde
In hundred formes to change his fearefull hew,
When as at length I saw the wrathfull winde,
Which blows cold storms, burst out of Scithian
        mew,   110
  That sperst these cloudes, and in so short as
        thought,
This dreadfull shape was vanished to nought.

9

Then all astonied with this mighty ghoast,
An hideous bodie big and strong I sawe,
With side long beard, and locks down hanging
        loast,
Sterne face, and front full of Saturnlike awe;
  Who leaning on the belly of a pot,
Pourd foorth a water, whose out gushing flood
Ran bathing all the creakie shore aflot,   119
Whereon the Troyan prince spilt Turnus blood;
  And at his feete a bitch wolfe suck did yeeld
To two young babes: his left the Palme tree
        stout,
His right hand did the peacefull Oliue wield,
And head with Lawrell garnisht was about.
  Sudden both Palme and Oliue fell away,
  And faire greene Lawrell branch did quite
        decay.

10

Hard by a riuers side a virgin faire,
Folding her armes to heauen with thousand
        throbs,
And outraging her cheekes and golden haire,
To falling riuers sound thus tun'd her sobs.
  Where is (quoth she) this whilom honoured
        face?   131
Where the great glorie and the auncient praise,
In which all worlds felicitie had place,
When Gods and men my honour vp did raise?
  Suffisd' it not that ciuill warres me made
The whole worldsspoile, but that this Hydra new,
Of hundred Hercules to be assaide,
With seuen heads, budding monstrous crimes
        anew,
  So many Neroes and Caligulaes
  Out of these crooked shores must dayly
        rayse?   140

11

Vpon an hill a bright flame I did see,
Wauing aloft with triple point to skie,
Which like incense of precious Cedar tree,
With balmie odours fil'd th'ayre farre and nie.
  A Bird all white, well feathered on each wing,
Hereout vp to the throne of Gods did flie,
And all the way most pleasant notes did sing,
Whilst in the smoake she vnto heauen did stie.
  Of this faire fire the scattered rayes forth
        threw   149
On euerie side a thousand shining beames:
When sudden dropping of a siluer dew
(O grieuous chance) gan quench those precious
        flames;
  That it which earst so pleasant sent did yeld,
  Of nothing now but noyous sulphure smeld.

12

I saw a spring out of a rocke forth rayle,
As cleare as Christall gainst the Sunnie beames,
The bottome yeallow, like the golden grayle
That bright Pactolus washeth with his streames;
  It seem'd that Art and Nature had assembled
All pleasure there, for which mans hart could
        long;   160
And there a noyse alluring sleepe soft trembled,
Of manie accords more sweete than Mermaids
        song:
  The seates and benches shone as yuorie,
And hundred Nymphes sate side by side about;
When from nigh hills with hideous outcrie,
A troupe of Satyres in the place did rout,
  Which with their villeine feete the streame
        did ray,
  Threw down the seats, and droue the Nymphs
        away.

13

. Much richer then that vessell seem'd to bee,
Which did to that sad *Florentine* appeare, 170
Casting mine eyes farre off, I chaunst to see,
Vpon the *Latine* Coast herselfe to reare :
  But suddenly arose a tempest great,
Bearing close enuie to these riches rare,
Which gan assaile this ship with dreadfull
    threat,
This ship, to which none other might compare.
  And finally the storme impetuous
Sunke vp these riches, second vnto none,
Within the gulfe of greedie *Nereus*.
I saw both ship and mariners each one, 180
  And all that treasure drowned in the
    maine :
  But I the ship saw after raisd' againe.

14

  Long hauing deeply gron'd these visions sad,
I saw a Citie like vnto that same,
Which saw the messenger of tidings glad ;
But that on sand was built the goodly frame :
  It seem'd her top the firmament did rayse,
And no lesse rich than faire, right worthie
    sure
(If ought here worthie) of immortall dayes,
Or if ought vnder heauen might firme endure.

Much wondred I to see so faire a wall : 191
When from the Northerne coast a storme
    arose,
Which breathing furie from his inward gall
On all, which did against his course oppose,
  Into a clowde of dust sperst in the aire
  The weake foundations of this Citie faire.

15

  At length, euen at the time when *Morpheus*
Most trulie doth vnto our eyes appeare,
Wearie to see the heauens still wauering thus,
I saw *Typhœus* sister comming neare ; 200
  Whose head full brauely with a morion
    hidd,
Did seeme to match the Gods in Maiestie.
She by a riuers bancke that swift downe
    slidd,
Ouer all the world did raise a Trophee hie ;
  An hundred vanquisht Kings vnder her lay,
With armes bound at their backs in shamefull
    wize ;
Whilst I thus mazed was with great affray,
I saw the heauens in warre against her rize :
  Then downe she stricken fell with clap of
    thonder,
  That with great noyse I wakte in sudden
    wonder. 210

FINIS.

The Visions of Petrarch.

formerly translated.

1

BEing one day at my window all alone,
  So manie strange things happened me
    to see,
As much it grieueth me to thinke thereon.
At my right hand a Hynde appear'd to mee,
  So faire as mote the greatest God delite ;
Two eager dogs did her pursue in chace,
Of which the one was blacke, the other
    white :
With deadly force so in their cruell race
  They pincht the haunches of that gentle
    beast,
That at the last, and in short time I spide, 10
Vnder a Rocke where she was opprest.
Fell to the ground, and there vntimely dide.
  Cruell death vanquishing so noble beautie,
  Oft makes me wayle so hard a destenie.

2

  After at sea a tall ship did appeare,
Made all of Heben and white Yuorie,
The sailes of golde, of silke the tackle were,
Milde was the winde, calme seem'd the sea to
    bee,
  The skie eachwhere did show full bright and
    faire ;
With rich treasures this gay ship fraighted
    was : 20
But sudden storme did so turmoyle the aire,
And tumbled vp the sea, that she (alas)
  Strake on a rock, that vnder water lay,
And perished past all recouerie.
O how great ruth and sorrowfull assay,
Doth vex my spirite with perplexitie,
  Thus in a moment to see lost and drown'd,
  So great riches, as like cannot be found.

3

Then heauenly branches did I see arise
Out of the fresh and lustie Lawrell tree, 30
Amidst the yong greene wood : of Paradise
Some noble plant I thought my selfe to see :
   Such store of birds therein yshrowded were,
Chaunting in shade their sundrie melodie,
That with their sweetnes I was rauish't nere.
   While on this Lawrell fixed was mine eie,
The skie gan euerie where to ouercast,
And darkned was the welkin all about, 38
When sudden flash of heauens fire out brast,
And rent this royall tree quite by the roote,
   Which makes me much and euer to complaine:
   For no such shadow shalbe had againe.

4

Within this wood, out of a rocke did rise
A spring of water, mildly rumbling downe,
Whereto approched not in anie wise
The homely shepheard, nor the ruder clowne ;
   But manie Muses, and the Nymphes withall,
That sweetly in accord did tune their voyce
To the soft sounding of the waters fall, 45
That my glad hart thereat did much reioyce.
   But while herein I tooke my chiefe delight,
I saw (alas) the gaping earth deuoure
The spring, the place, and all cleane out of
   sight.
Which yet aggreeues my hart euen to this
   houre,
   And wounds my soule with rufull memorie,
   To see such pleasures gon so suddenly.

5

I saw a Phœnix in the wood alone,
With purple wings, and crest of golden hewe ;
Strange bird he was, whereby I thought anone,
That of some heauenly wight I had the vewe ;
   Vntill he came vnto the broken tree, 61
And to the spring, that late deuoured was.
What say I more ? each thing at last we see
Doth passe away : the Phœnix there alas

Spying the tree destroid, the water dride,
Himselfe smote with his beake, as in disdaine,
And so foorthwith in great despight he dide :
That yet my heart burnes in exceeding paine,
   For ruth and pitie of so haples plight.
   O let mine eyes no more see such a sight. 70

6

At last so faire a Ladie did I spie,
That thinking yet on her I burne and quake ;
On hearbs and flowres she walked pensiuely,
Milde, but yet loue she proudly did forsake :
   White seem'd her robes, yet wouen so they
      were,
As snow and golde together had been wrought.
Aboue the wast a darke clowde shrouded her,
A stinging Serpent by the heele her caught ;
   Wherewith she languisht as the gathered
      floure,
And well assur'd she mounted vp to ioy. 80
Alas, on earth so nothing doth endure,
But bitter griefe and sorrowfull annoy :
   Which make this life wretched and miserable,
   Tossed with stormes of fortune variable.

7

When I behold this tickle trustles state
Of vaine worlds glorie, flitting too and fro,
And mortall men tossed by troublous fate
In restles seas of wretchednes and woe,
   I wish I might this wearie life forgoe,
And shortly turne vnto my happie rest, 90
Where my free spirite might not anie moe
Be vext with sights, that doo her peace molest.
   And ye faire Ladie, in whose bounteous brest
All heauenly grace and vertue shrined is,
When ye these rythmes doo read, and vew the
   rest,
Loath this base world, and thinke of heauens
   blis :
   And though ye be the fairest of Gods creatures,
   Yet thinke, that death shall spoyle your goodly
      features.

FINIS.

Daphnaïda.

An Elegie vpon the

death of the noble and vertuous
Douglas Howard, *Daughter and*
heire of *Henry* Lord *Howard*, Vis-
count *Byndon*, *and wife of* Arthure Gorges *Esquier.*

Dedicated to the Right honorable the Lady
Helena, Marquesse of *Northampton.*

By Ed. Sp.

AT LONDON
Printed for VVilliam Ponsonby, *dwelling in*
Paules Churchyard at the signe of the
Bishops head 1591.

TO THE RIGHT
HONORABLE AND VER-
tuous Lady *Helena Marquesse* of North-hampton.

I Haue the rather presumed humbly to offer vnto your Honour the dedication of this little Poëme, for that the noble and vertuous Gentlewoman of whom it is written, was by match neere alied, and in affection greatly deuoted vnto your Ladiship. The occasion why I wrote the same, was aswell the great good fame which I heard of her deceassed, as the particular goodwill which I beare vnto her husband Master Arthur Gorges, a louer of learning and vertue, whose house, as your Ladiship by mariage hath honoured, so doe I find the name of them by many notable records, to be of great antiquitie in this Realme ; and such as haue euer borne themselues with honourable reputation to the world, and vnspotted loyaltie to their Prince and Countrey : besides so lineally are they descended from the Howards, as that the Lady Anne Howard, eldest daughter to Iohn Duke of Norfolke, was wife to Sir Edmund, mother to Sir Edward, and grandmother to Sir William and Sir Thomas Gorges Knightes. And therefore I doe assure my selfe, that no due honour done to the white Lyon but will be most gratefull to your Ladiship, whose husband and children do so neerely participate with the bloud of that noble family. So in all dutie I recommende this Pamphlet, and the good acceptance thereof, to your honourable fauour and protection. London this first of Ianuarie. 1591.

Your Honours humbly euer.

Ed. Sp.

Daphnaïda.

WHat euer man he be, whose heauie minde
With griefe of mournefull great mishap opprest,
Fit matter for his cares increase would finde :
Let reade the rufull plaint herein exprest
Of one (I weene) the wofulst man aliue ;
Euen sad *Alcyon*, whose empierced brest
Sharpe sorrowe did in thousand peeces riue.

But who so else in pleasure findeth sense,
Or in this wretched life dooth take delight,
Let him be banisht farre away from hence :
Ne let the sacred Sisters here be hight,   11
Though they of sorrowe heauilie can sing ;
For euen their heauie song would breede delight :
But here no tunes, saue sobs and grones shall ring.

In stead of them, and their sweete harmonie,
Let those three fatall Sisters, whose sad hands
Doo weaue the direfull threds of destinie,
And in their wrath breake off the vitall bands,
Approach hereto : and let the dreadfull Queene
Of darkenes deepe come from the Stygian strands,   20
And grisly Ghosts to heare this dolefull teene.

In gloomie euening, when the wearie Sun
After his dayes long labour drew to rest,
And sweatie steeds now hauing ouer run
The compast skie, gan water in the west,
I walkt abroad to breath the freshing ayre
In open fields, whose flowring pride opprest
With early frosts, had lost their beautie faire.

There came vnto my minde a troublous thought,
Which dayly dooth my weaker wit possesse,
Ne lets it rest, vntill it forth haue brought   31
Her long borne Infant, fruit of heauinesse,
Which she conceiued hath through meditation
Of this worlds vainnesse and lifes wretchednesse,
That yet my soule it deepely doth empassion.

So as I muzed on the miserie,
In which men liue, and I of many most,
Most miserable man ; I did espie
Where towards me a sory wight did cost,
Clad all in black, that mourning did bewray :
And *Iaakob* staffe in hand deuoutlie crost,   41
Like to some Pilgrim come from farre away.

His carelesse locks, vncombed and vnshorne,
Hong long adowne, and beard all ouer growne,
That well he seemd to be sum wight forlorne ;
Downe to the earth his heauie eyes were throwne
As loathing light : and euer as he went,
He sighed soft, and inly deepe did grone,
As if his heart in peeces would haue rent.

Approaching nigh, his face I vewed nere,   50
And by the semblant of his countenance,
Me seemd I had his person seene elsewhere,
Most like *Alcyon* seeming at a glaunce ;
Alcyon he, the iollie Shepheard swaine,
That wont full merrilie to pipe and daunce,
And fill with pleasance euery wood and plaine.

Yet halfe in doubt because of his disguize,
I softlie sayd *Alcyon ?* There with all
He lookt a side as in disdainefull wise,
Yet stayed not : till I againe did call.   60
Then turning back he saide with hollow sound,
Who is it, that dooth name me, wofull thrall,
The wretchedst man that treades this day on
    ground ?

One, whome like wofulnesse impressed deepe,
Hath made fit mate thy wretched case to heare,
And giuen like cause with thee to waile and
    weepe :
Griefe findes some ease by him that like does
    beare.
Then stay *Alcyon,* gentle shepheard stay,
(Quoth I) till thou haue to my trustie eare
Committed, what thee dooth so ill apay.   70

Cease foolish man (saide he halfe wrothfully)
To seeke to heare that which cannot be told :
For the huge anguish, which dooth multiplie
My dying paines, no tongue can well vnfold :
Ne doo I care, that any should bemone
My hard mishap, or any weepe that would,
But seeke alone to weepe, and dye alone.

Then be it so (quoth I) that thou art bent
To die alone, vnpitied, vnplained,
Yet ere thou die, it were conuenient   80
To tell the cause, which thee theretoo con-
    strained :
Least that the world thee dead accuse of guilt,
And say, when thou of none shalt be maintained,
That thou for secret crime thy blood hast spilt.

Who life dooes loath, and longs to bee vnbound
From the strong shackles of fraile flesh (quoth he)
Nought cares at all, what they that liue on
    ground
Deeme the occasion of his death to bee :
Rather desires to be forgotten quight,
Than question made of his calamitie,   90
For harts deep sorrow hates both life and light.

Yet since so much thou seemst to rue my griefe,
And carest for one that for himselfe cares nought,
(Signe of thy loue, though nought for my reliefe:
For my reliefe exceedeth liuing thought).
I will to thee this heauie case relate.
Then harken well till it to ende be brought,
For neuer didst thou heare more haplesse fate.

Whilome I vsde (as thou right well doest know)
My little flocke on westerne downes to keepe,
Not far from whence *Sabrinaes* streame doth
    flow,   101
And flowrie bancks with siluer liquor steepe :
Nought carde I then for worldly change or
    chaunce,
For all my ioy was on my gentle sheepe,
And to my pype to caroll and to daunce.

It there befell, as I the fields did range
Fearelesse and free, a faire young Lionesse,
White as the natiue Rose before the chaunge,
Which *Venus* blood did in her leaues impresse,
I spied playing on the grassie playne   110
Her youthfull sports and kindlie wantonnesse,
That did all other Beasts in beawtie staine.

Much was I moued at so goodly sight ;
Whose like before mine eye had seldome seene,
And gan to cast, how I her compasse might,
And bring to hand, that yet had neuer beene :
So well I wrought with mildnes and with paine,
That I her caught disporting on the grene,
And brought away fast bound with siluer chaine.

And afterwards I handled her so fayre,   120
That though by kind shee stout and saluage
    were,
For being borne an auncient Lions haire,
And of the race, that all wild beastes do feare ;
Yet I her fram'd and wan so to my bent,
That shee became so meeke and milde of cheare,
As the least lamb in all my flock that went.

For shee in field, where euer I did wend,
Would wend with me, and waite by me all day :
And all the night that I in watch did spend,
If cause requir'd, or els in sleepe, if nay,   130
Shee would all night by mee or watch, or sleepe ;
And euermore when I did sleepe or play,
She of my flock would take full warie keepe.

Safe then and safest were my sillie sheepe,
Ne fear'd the Wolfe, ne fear'd the wildest beast :
All were I drown'd in carelesse quiet deepe :
My louelie Lionesse without beheast
So carefull was for them and for my good,
That when I waked, neither most nor least
I found miscaried or in plaine or wood.   140

Oft did the Shepeheards, which my hap did
    heare,
And oft their lasses which my luck enuide,
Daylie resort to me from farre and neare,
To see my Lyonesse, whose praises wide
Were spred abroad ; and when her worthinesse
Much greater than the rude report they tri'de,
They her did praise, and my good fortune blesse.

Long thus I ioyed in my happinesse,   148
And well did hope my ioy would haue no end :
But oh fond man, that in worlds ficklenesse
Reposedst hope, or weenedst her thy frend,
That glories most in mortall miseries,
And daylie doth her changefull counsels bend
To make new matter fit for Tragedies.

For whilest I was thus without dread or dout,
A cruell *Satyre* with his murdrous dart,
Greedie of mischiefe ranging all about,
Gaue her the fatall wound of deadlie smart :
And reft fro me my sweete companion,
And reft fro me my loue, my life, my hart :
My Lyonesse (ah woe is mee) is gon.   161

Out of the world thus was she reft awaie,
Out of the world, vnworthie such a spoyle ;
And borne to heauen, for heauen a fitter pray :
Much fitter than the Lyon, which with toyle
Alcides slew, and fixt in firmament ;
Her now I seek throughout this earthlie soyle,
And seeking misse, and missing doe lament.

Therewith he gan afresh to waile and weepe,
That I for pittie of his heauie plight,   170
Could not abstaine mine eyes with teares to
      steepe :
But when I saw the anguish of his spright
Some deale alaid, I him bespake againe.
Certes *Alcyon*, painfull is thy plight,
That it in me breeds almost equall paine.

Yet doth not my dull wit well vnderstand
The riddle of thy loued Lionesse ;
For rare it seemes in reason to be skand
That man, who doth the whole worlds rule
      possesse,
Should to a beast his noble hart embase,   180
And be the vassall of his vassalesse :
Therefore more plaine aread this doubtfull case.

Then sighing sore, *Daphne* thou knewest (quoth
      he)
She now is dead ; ne more endured to say :
But fell to ground for great extreamitie,
That I beholding it, with deepe dismay
Was much appald, and lightlie him vprearing,
Reuoked life that would haue fled away,
All were my self through griefe in deadly
      drearing.

Then gan I him to comfort all my best,   190
And with milde counsaile stroue to mitigate
The stormie passion of his troubled brest ;
But he thereby was more empassionate :
As stubborne steed, that is with curb restrained,
Becomes more fierce and feruent in his gate ;
And breaking foorth at last, thus dearnelie
      plained.

I
What man henceforth, that breatheth vitall ayre,
Will honour heauen, or heauenlie powers adore?
Which so vniustlie doe their iudgments share ;
Mongst earthlie wightes, as to afflict so sore
The innocent, as those which do transgresse,
And do not spare the best or fayrest, more
Than worst or fowlest, but doe both oppresse.

If this be right, why did they then create
The world so fayre, sith fairenesse is neglected?
Or whie be they themselues immaculate,
If purest things be not by them respected ?
She faire, shee pure, most faire most pure shee
      was,
Yet was by them as thing impure reiected :
Yet shee in purenesse, heauen it selfe did pas.

In purenesse and in all celestiall grace,   211
That men admire in goodlie womankinde,
Shee did excell, and seem'd of Angels race,
Liuing on earth like Angell new diuinde,
Adorn'd with wisedome and with chastitie :
And all the dowries of a noble mind,.
Which did her beautie much more beautifie.

No age hath bred (since fayre *Astræa* left
The sinfull world) more vertue in a wight,
And when she parted hence, with her she reft
Great hope ; and robd her race of bountie
      quight :   221
Well may the shepheard lasses now lament,
For dubble losse by her hath on them light ;
To loose both her and bounties ornament.

Ne let *Elisa* royall Shepheardesse
The praises of my parted loue enuy,
For she hath praises in all plenteousnesse
Powr'd vpon her like showers of *Castaly*
By her own Shepheard, *Colin* her owne Shepherd,
That her with heauenly hymnes doth deifie,
Of rustick muse full hardly to be betterd.   231

She is the Rose, the glorie of the day,
And mine the Primrose in the lowly shade,
Mine, ah not mine ; amisse I mine did say :
Not mine but his, which mine awhile her made :
Mine to be his, with him to liue for ay :
O that so faire a flower so soone should fade,
And through vntimely tempest fall away.

She fell away in her first ages spring,
Whil'st yet her leafe was greene, and fresh her
      rinde,   240
And whil'st her braunch faire blossomes foorth
      did bring,
She fell away against all course of kinde :
For age to dye is right, but youth is wrong ;
She fel away like fruit blowne downe with winde:
Weepe Shepheard weepe to make my vndersong.

2

What hart so stony hard, but that would weepe,
And poure foorth fountaines of incessant
    teares ?
What *Timon*, but would let compassion creepe
Into his brest, and pierce his frosen eares ?
In stead of teares, whose brackish bitter well
I wasted haue, my heart blood dropping weares,
To thinke to ground how that faire blossome
    fell.   252

Yet fell she not, as one enforst to dye,
Ne dyde with dread and grudging discontent,
But as one toyld with trauaile downe doth lye,
So lay she downe, as if to sleepe she went,
And closde her eyes with carelesse quietnesse ;
The whiles soft death away her spirit hent,
And soule assoyld from sinfull fleshlinesse.

Yet ere that life her lodging did forsake,   260
She all resolu'd and ready to remoue,
Calling to me (ay me) this wise bespake ;
Alcyon, ah my first and latest loue,
Ah why does my *Alcyon* weepe and mourne,
And grieue my ghost, that ill mote him behoue,
As if to me had chanst some euill tourne ?

I, since the messenger is come for mee,
That summons soules vnto the bridale feast
Of his great Lord, must needes depart from
    thee,
And straight obay his soueraine beheast :   270
Why should *Alcyon* then so sore lament,
That I from miserie shall be releast,
And freed from wretched long imprisonment ?

Our daies are full of dolor and disease,
Our life afflicted with incessant paine,
That nought on earth may lessen or appease.
Why then should I desire here to remaine ?
Or why should he that loues me, sorie bee
For my deliuerance, or at all complaine
My good to heare, and toward ioyes to see ?

I goe, and long desired haue to goe,   281
I goe with gladnesse to my wished rest,
Whereas no worlds sad care, nor wasting woe
May come their happie quiet to molest,
But Saints and Angels in celestiall thrones
Eternally him praise, that hath them blest ;
There shall I be amongst those blessed ones.

Yet ere I goe, a pledge I leaue with thee
Of the late loue, the which betwixt vs past,
My yong *Ambrosia*, in lieu of mee   290
Loue her : so shall our loue for euer last.
Thus deare adieu, whom I expect ere long :
So hauing said, away she softly past :
Weep Shepheard weep, to make mine vnder-
    song.

3

So oft as I record those piercing words,
Which yet are deepe engrauen in my brest,
And those last deadly accents, which like swords
Did wound my heart and rend my bleeding chest,
With those sweet sugred speaches doo compare,
The which my soule first conquerd and possest,
The first beginners of my endles care ;   301

And when those pallid cheekes and ashy hew,
In which sad death his pourtraicture had writ,
And when those hollow eyes and deadly view,
On which the clowde of ghastly night did sit,
I match with that sweet smile and chearful
    brow,
Which all the world subdued vnto it ;
How happie was I then, and wretched now ?

How happie was I, when I saw her leade   309
The Shepheards daughters dauncing in a rownd ?
How trimly would she trace and softly tread
The tender grasse with rosie garland crownd ?
And when she list aduance her heauenly voyce,
Both Nimphs and Muses nigh she made astownd,
And flocks and shepheards caused to reioyce.

But now ye Shepheard lasses, who shall lead
Your wandring troupes, or sing your virelayes ?
Or who shall dight your bowres, sith she is dead
That was the Lady of your holy dayes ?
Let now your blisse be turned into bale,   320
And into plaints conuert your ioyous playes,
And with the same fill euery hill and dale.

Let Bagpipe neuer more be heard to shrill,
That may allure the senses to delight ;
Ne euer Shepheard sound his Oaten quill
Vnto the many, that prouoke them might
To idle pleasance : but let ghastlinesse
And drery horror dim the chearfull light,
To make the image of true heauinesse.

Let birds be silent on the naked spray,   330
And shady woods resound with dreadfull yells :
Let streaming floods their hastie courses stay,
And parching drougth drie vp the christall
    wells ;
Let th'earth be barren and bring foorth no
    flowres,
And th'ayre be fild with noyse of dolefull knells,
And wandring spirits walke vntimely howres.

And Nature nurse of euery liuing thing,
Let rest her selfe from her long wearinesse,
And cease henceforth things kindly forth to
    bring,
But hideous monsters full of vglinesse :   340
For she it is, that hath me done this wrong,
No nurse, but Stepdame, cruell, mercilesse,
Weepe Shepheard weepe to make my vnder song.

4

My little flocke, whom earst I lou'd so well,
And wont to feede with finest grasse that grew,
Feede ye hencefoorth on bitter *Astrofell*,
And stinking Smallage, and vnsauerie Rew ;
And when your mawes are with those weeds
      corrupted,
Be ye the pray of Wolues : ne will I rew,
That with your carkasses wild beasts be glutted.

Ne worse to you my sillie sheepe I pray, 351
Ne sorer vengeance wish on you to fall
Than to my selfe, for whose confusde decay
To carelesse heauens I doo daylie call :
But heauens refuse to heare a wretches cry,
And cruell death doth scorne to come at call,
Or graunt his boone that most desires to dye.

The good and righteous he away doth take,
To plague th'vnrighteous which aliue remaine :
But the vngodly ones he doth forsake,   360
By liuing long to multiplie their paine :
Els surely death should be no punishment,
As the great Iudge at first did it ordaine,
But rather riddance from long languishment.

Therefore my *Daphne* they haue tane away ;
For worthie of a better place was she :
But me vnworthie willed here to stay,
That with her lacke I might tormented be.
Sith then they so haue ordred, I will pay
Penance to her according their decree,   370
And to her ghost doo seruice day by day.

For I will walke this wandring pilgrimage
Throughout the world from one to other end,
And in affliction wast my better age.
My bread shall be the anguish of my mind,
My drink the teares which fro mine eyes do
      raine,
My bed the ground that hardest I may finde ;
So will I wilfully increase my paine.

And she my loue that was, my Saint that is,
When she beholds from her celestiall throne,
(In which shee ioyeth in eternall blis)   381
My bitter penance, will my case bemoane,
And pitie me that liuing thus doo die :
For heauenly spirits haue compassion
On mortall men, and rue their miserie.

So when I haue with sorowe satisfide
Th'importune fates, which vengeance on me
      seeke,
And th'heauens with long languor pacifide,
She for pure pitie of my sufferance meeke,
Will send for me ; for which I daylie long, 390
And will till then my painfull penance eeke :
Weep Shepheard, weep to make my vnder song.

5

Hencefoorth I hate what euer Nature made,
And in her workmanship no pleasure finde :
For they be all but vaine, and quickly fade,
So soone as on them blowes the Northern winde,
They tarrie not, but flit and fall away,
Leauing behind them nought but griefe of
      minde,
And mocking such as thinke they long will stay.

I hate the heauen, because it doth withhold
Me from my loue, and eke my loue from me ;
I hate the earth, because it is the mold   402
Of fleshly slime and fraile mortalitie ;
I hate the fire, because to nought it flyes,
I hate the Ayre, because sighes of it be,
I hate the Sea, because it teares supplyes.

I hate the day, because it lendeth light
To see all things, and not my loue to see ;
I hate the darknesse and the drery night,
Because they breed sad balefulnesse in mee :
I hate all times, because all times doo flye 411
So fast away, and may not stayed bee,
But as a speedie post that passeth by.

I hate to speake, my voyce is spent with crying:
I hate to heare, lowd plaints haue duld mine
      eares :
I hate to tast, for food withholds my dying :
I hate to see, mine eyes are dimd with teares :
I hate to smell, no sweet on earth is left :
I hate to feele, my flesh is numbd with feares:
So all my senses from me are bereft.   420

I hate all men, and shun all womankinde ;
The one, because as I they wretched are,
The other, for because I doo not finde
My loue with them, that wont to be their
      Starre :
And life I hate, because it will not last,
And death I hate, because it life doth marre,
And all I hate, that is to come or past.

So all the world, and all in it I hate,
Because it changeth euer too and fro,
And neuer standeth in one certaine state, 430
But still vnstedfast round about doth goe,
Like a Mill wheele, in midst of miserie,
Driuen with streames of wretchednesse and woe,
That dying liues, and liuing still does dye.

So doo I liue, so doo I daylie die,
And pine away in selfe-consuming paine,
Sith she that did my vitall powres supplie,
And feeble spirits in their force maintaine
Is fetcht fro me, why seeke I to prolong
My wearie daies in dolor and disdaine ?   440
Weep Shepheard weep to make my vnder song,

6

Why doo I longer liue in lifes despight?
And doo not dye then in despight of death:
Why doo I longer see this loathsome light,
And doo in darknesse not abridge my breath,
Sith all my sorrow should haue end thereby,
And cares finde quiet; is it so vneath
To leaue this life, or dolorous to dye?

To liue I finde it deadly dolorous;   449
For life drawes care, and care continuall woe:
Therefore to dye must needes be ioyeous,
And wishfull thing this sad life to forgoe.
But I must stay; I may it not amend,
My *Daphne* hence departing bad me so,
She bad me stay, till she for me did send.

Yet whilest I in this wretched vale doo stay,
My wearie feete shall euer wandring be,
That still I may be readie on my way,
When as her messenger doth come for me:
Ne will I rest my feete for feeblenesse,   460
Ne will I rest my limmes for fraïltie,
Ne will I rest mine eyes for heauinesse.

But as the mother of the Gods, that sought
For faire *Eurydice* her daughter deere
Throughout the world, with wofull heauie
      thought;
So will I trauell whilest I tarrie heere,
Ne will I lodge, ne will I euer lin,
Ne when as drouping *Titan* draweth neere
To loose his teeme, will I take vp my Inne.

Ne sleepe (the harbenger of wearie wights)
Shall euer lodge vpon mine ey-lids more;   471
Ne shall with rest refresh my fainting sprights,
Nor failing force to former strength restore:
But I will wake and sorrow all the night
With *Philumene*, my fortune to deplore,
With *Philumene*, the partner of my plight.

And euer as I see the starres to fall,
And vnder ground to goe, to giue them light
Which dwell in darknes, I to minde will call,
How my faire Starre (that shinde on me so
      bright)   480
Fell sodainly, and faded vnder ground;
Since whose departure, day is turnd to night,
And night without a *Venus* starre is found.

But soone as day doth shew his deawie face,
And calls foorth men vnto their toylsome trade,
I will withdraw me to some darksome place,
Or some deepe caue, or solitarie shade;
There will I sigh and sorrow all day long,
And the huge burden of my cares vnlade: 489
Weep Shepheard, weep, to make my vndersong.

7

Henceefoorth mine eyes shall neuer more behold
Faire thing on earth, ne feed on false delight
Of ought that framed is of mortall moulde,
Sith that my fairest flower is faded quight:
For all I see is vaine and transitorie,
Ne will be helde in anie stedfast plight,
But in a moment loose their grace and glorie.

And ye fond men on fortunes wheele that ride,
Or in ought vnder heauen repose assurance,
Be it riches, beautie, or honors pride: 500
Be sure that they shall haue no long endurance,
But ere ye be aware will flit away;
For nought of them is yours, but th'onely vsance
Of a small time, which none ascertaine may.

And ye true Louers, whom desastrous chaunce
Hath farre exiled from your Ladies grace,
To mourne in sorrow and sad sufferaunce,
When ye doo heare me in that desert place
Lamenting lowde my *Daphnes* Elegie,
Helpe me to wayle my miserable case,   510
And when life parts, vouchsafe to close mine eye.

And ye more happie Louers, which enioy
The presence of your dearest loues delight,
When ye doo heare my sorrowfull annoy,
Yet pittie me in your empassiond spright,
And thinke that such mishap, as chaunst to me,
May happen vnto the most happiest wight;
For all mens states alike vnstedfast be.

And ye my fellow Shepheards, which do feed
Your carelesse flocks on hils and open plaines,
With better fortune, than did me succeed,   521
Remember yet my vndeserued paines;
And when ye heare, that I am dead or slaine,
Lament my lot, and tell your fellow swaines
That sad *Alcyon* dyde in lifes disdaine.

And ye faire Damsels, Shepheards dere delights,
That with your loues do their rude hearts
      possesse,
When as my hearse shall happen to your sightes,
Vouchsafe to deck the same with Cyparesse;
And euer sprinckle brackish teares among, 530
In pitie of my vndeseru'd distresse,
The which I wretch, endured haue thus long.

And ye poore Pilgrimes, that with restlesse toyle
Wearie your selues in wandring desert wayes,
Till that you come, where ye your vowes
      assoyle,
When passing by ye read these wofull layes
On my graue written, rue my *Daphnes* wrong,
And mourne for me that languish out my dayes:
Cease Shepheard, cease, and end thy vndersong.

Thus when he ended had his heauie plaint,
  The heauiest plaint that euer I heard
    sound,   541
His cheekes wext pale, and sprights began to
  faint,
As if againe he would haue fallen to ground ;
Which when I saw, I (stepping to him light)
Amooued him out of his stonie swound,
And gan him to recomfort as I might.

But he no waie recomforted would be,
Nor suffer solace to approach him nie,
But casting vp a sdeinfull eie at me,   549
That in his traunce I would not let him lie,
Did rend his haire, and beat his blubbred face
As one disposed wilfullie to die,
That I sore grieu'd to see his wretched case.

Tho when the pang was somewhat ouerpast,
And the outragious passion nigh appeased,
I him desirde, sith daie was ouercast,
And darke night fast approched, to be pleased
To turne aside vnto my Cabinet,
And staie with me, till he were better eased
Of that strong stownd, which him so sore
  beset.   560

But by no meanes I could him win thereto,
Ne longer him intreate with me to staie,
But without taking leaue, he foorth did goe
With staggring pace and dismall lookes
  dismay,
As if that death he in the face had seene,
Or heilish hags had met vpon the way :
But what of him became I cannot weene.

FINIS.

COLIN. CLOVTS
Come home againe.

By Ed. Spencer.

LONDON
Printed for William Ponsonbie.
1595.

TO THE RIGHT
worthy and noble Knight
Sir *Walter Raleigh*, Captaine of her Maiesties
Guard, Lord Wardein of the Stanneries,
*and Lieutenant of the Countie of
Cornwall.*

(∴)

*S*IR, *that you may see that I am not
alwaies ydle as yee thinke, though not
greatly well occupied, nor altogither vndutifull,
though not precisely officious, I make you present
of this simple pastorall, vnworthie of your higher
conceipt for the meanesse of the stile, but agreeing
with the truth in circumstance and matter. The
which I humbly beseech you to accept in part of
paiment of the infinite debt in which I acknowledge my selfe bounden vnto you, for your singular*
*fauours and sundrie good turnes shewed to me at
my late being in England, and with your good
countenance protect against the malice of euill
mouthes, which are alwaies wide open to carpe
at and misconstrue my simple meaning. I pray
continually for your happinesse. From my house
of* Kilcolman *the* 27. *of December.* 1591.

Yours euer humbly.

Ed. Sp.

COLIN CLOVTS
come home againe.

*T*He shepheards boy (best knowen by that
name)
That after *Tityrus* first sung his lay,
Laies of sweet loue, without rebuke or blame,
Sate (as his custome was) vpon a day,
Charming his oaten pipe vnto his peres,
The shepheard swaines that did about him
play:
Who all the while with greedie listfull eares,
Did stand astonisht at his curious skill,
Like hartlesse deare, dismayd with thunders
sound.
At last when as he piped had his fill,   10
He rested him: and sitting then around,
One of those groomes (a iolly groome was he,
As euer piped on an oaten reed,
And lou'd this shepheard dearest in degree,
Hight *Hobbinol*) gan thus to him areed.
    Colin my liefe, my life, how great a losse
Had all the shepheards nation by thy lacke?
And I poore swaine of many greatest crosse:
That sith thy *Muse* first since thy turning
backe

Was heard to sound as she was wont on hye,
Hast made vs all so blessed and so blythe. 21
Whilest thou wast hence, all dead in dole did lie:
The woods were heard to waile full many a
sythe,
And all their birds with silence to complaine:
The fields with faded flowers did seem to mourne,
And all their flocks from feeding to refraine:
The running waters wept for thy returne,
And all their fish with languour did lament:
But now both woods and fields, and floods
reviue,
Sith thou art come, their cause of meriment, 30
That vs late dead, hast made againe aliue:
But were it not too painfull to repeat
The passed fortunes, which to thee befell
In thy late voyage, we thee would entreat,
Now at thy leisure them to vs to tell.
    To whom the shepheard gently answered
thus,
Hobbin thou temptest me to that I couet:
For of good passed newly to discus,
By dubble vsurie doth twise renew it.

And since I saw that Angels blessed eie,   40
Her worlds bright sun, her heauens fairest
   light,
My mind full of my thoughts satietie,
Doth feed on sweet contentment of that sight:
Since that same day in nought I take delight,
Ne feeling haue in any earthly pleasure,
But in remembrance of that glorious bright,
My lifes sole blisse, my hearts eternall threasure.
Wake then my pipe, my sleepie *Muse* awake,
Till I haue told her praises lasting long:
Hobbin desires, thou maist it not forsake,   50
Harke then ye iolly shepheards to my song.

   With that they all gan throng about him
      neare,
With hungrie eares to heare his harmonie:
The whiles their flocks deuoyd of dangers feare,
Did round about them feed at libertie.

   One day (quoth he) I sat, (as was my trade)
Vnder the foote of *Mole* that mountaine hore,
Keeping my sheepe amongst the cooly shade,
Of the greene alders by the *Mullaes* shore:
There a straunge shepheard chaunst to find me
   out,   60
Whether allured with my pipes delight,
Whose pleasing sound yshrilled far about,
Or thither led by chaunce, I know not right:
Whom when I asked from what place he came,
And how he hight, himselfe he did ycleepe,
The shepheard of the Ocean by name,
And said he came far from the main-sea
   deepe.

He sitting me beside in that same shade,
Prouoked me to plaie some pleasant fit,
And when he heard the musicke which I made,
He found himselfe full greatly pleasd at it: 71
Yet æmuling my pipe, he tooke in hond
My pipe before that æmuled of many,
And plaid theron ; (for well that skill he cond)
Himselfe as skilfull in that art as any.
He pip'd, I sung ; and when he sung, I piped,
By chaunge of turnes, each making other mery,
Neither enuying other, nor enuied,
So piped we, vntill we both were weary.

   There interrupting him, a bonie swaine,   80
That *Cuddy* hight, him thus atweene bespake:
And should it not thy readie course restraine,
I would request thee *Colin*, for my sake,
To tell what thou didst sing, when he did plaie.
For well I weene it worth recounting was,
Whether it were some hymne, or morall laie,
Or carol made to praise thy loued lasse.

   Nor of my loue, nor of my losse (quoth he).
I then did sing, as then occasion fell:
For loue had me forlorne, forlorne of me,   90
That made me in that desart chose to dwell.

But of my riuer *Bregogs* loue I soong,
Which to the shiny *Mulla* he did beare,
And yet doth beare, and euer will, so long
As water doth within his bancks appeare.
   Of fellow ship (said then that bony Boy)
Record to vs that louely lay againe:
The staie whereof, shall nought these eares
   annoy,
Who all that *Colin* makes, do couet faine.

   Heare then (quoth he) the tenor of my tale,
In sort as I it to that shepheard told: 101
No leasing new, nor Grandams fable stale,
But auncient truth confirm'd with credence old.
   Old father *Mole*, (*Mole* hight that mountaine
      gray
That walls the Northside of *Armulla* dale)
He had a daughter fresh as floure of May,
Which gaue that name vnto that pleasant vale ;
Mulla the daughter of old *Mole*, so hight
The Nimph, which of that water course has
   charge,
That springing out of *Mole*, doth run downe
   right   110
To *Butteuant*, where spreading forth at large,
It giueth name vnto that auncient Cittie,
Which *Kilnemullah* cleped is of old :
Whose ragged ruines breed great ruth and
   pittie,
To trauailers, which it from far behold.
Full faine she lou'd, and was belou'd full faine,
Of her owne brother riuer, *Bregog* hight,
So hight because of this deceitfull traine,
Which he with *Mulla* wrought to win delight.
But her old sire more carefull of her good,   120
And meaning her much better to preferre,
Did thinke to match her with the neighbour
   flood,
Which *Allo* hight, Broad water called farre :
And wrought so well with his continuall paine,
That he that riuer for his daughter wonne :
The dowre agreed, the day assigned plaine,
The place appointed where it should be doone.
Nath lesse the Nymph her former liking held ;
For loue will not be drawne, but must be
   ledde,
And *Bregog* did so well her fancie weld,   130
That her good will he got her first to wedde.
But for her father sitting still on hie,
Did warily still watch which way she went,
And eke from far obseru'd with iealous eie,
Which way his course the wanton *Bregog* bent,
Him to deceiue for all his watchfull ward,
The wily louer did deuise this slight :
First into many parts his streame he shar'd,
That whilest the one was watcht, the other
   might

Passe vnespide to meete her by the way ; 140
And then besides, those little streames so
   broken
He vnder ground so closely did conuay,
That of their passage doth appeare no token,
Till they into the *Mullaes* water slide
So secretly did he his loue enioy :
Yet not so secret, but it was descride,
And told her father by a shepheards boy.
Who wondrous wroth for that so foule despight,
In great auenge did roll downe from his hill
Huge mightie stones, the which encomber might
His passage, and his water-courses spill. 151
So of a Riuer, which he was of old,
He none was made, but scattred all to nought,
And lost emong those rocks into him rold,
Did lose his name : so deare his loue he bought.

   Which hauing said, him *Thestylis* bespake,
Now by my life this was a mery lay :
Worthie of *Colin* selfe, that did it make.
But read now eke of friendship I thee pray,
What dittie did that other shepheard sing ?
For I do couet most the same to heare, 161
As men vse most to couet forreine thing.
That shall I eke (quoth he) to you declare.
His song was all a lamentable lay,
Of great vnkindnesse, and of vsage hard,
Of *Cynthia* the Ladie of the sea,
Which from her presence faultlesse him debard.
And euer and anon with singults rife,
He cryed out, to make his vndersong
Ah my loues queene, and goddesse of my life,
Who shall me pittie, when thou doest me
   wrong ? 171

   Then gan a gentle bony lasse to speake,
That *Marin* hight, Right well he sure did
   plaine :
That could great *Cynthiaes* sore displeasure
   breake,
And moue to take him to her grace againe.
But tell on further *Colin*, as befell
Twixt him and thee, that thee did hence dis-
   suade.

   When thus our pipes we both had wearied
   well,
(Quoth he) and each an end of singing made,
He gan to cast great lyking to my lore, 180
And great dislyking to my lucklesse lot :
That banisht had my selfe, like wight forlore,
Into that waste, where I was quite forgot.
The which to leaue, thenceforth he counseld
   mee,
Vnmeet for man, in whom was ought regardfull,
And wend with him, his *Cynthia* to see :
Whose grace was great, and bounty most
   rewardfull.

Besides her peerlesse skill in making well
And all the ornaments of wondrous wit,
Such as all womankynd did far excell : 190
Such as the world admyr'd and praised it :
So what with hope of good, and hate of ill,
He me perswaded forth with him to fare :
Nought tooke I with me, but mine oaten quill :
Small needments else need shepheard to prepare.
So to the sea we came ; the sea ? that is
A world of waters heaped vp on hie,
Rolling like mountaines in wide wildernesse,
Horrible, hideous, roaring with hoarse crie.

   And is the sea (quoth *Coridon*) so fearfull ?
   Fearful much more (quoth he) then hart can
   fear : 201
Thousand wyld beasts with deep mouthes gap-
   ing direfull
Therin stil wait poore passengers to teare.
Who life doth loath, and longs death to behold,
Before he die, alreadie dead with feare,
And yet would liue with heart halfe stonie
   cold,
Let him to sea, and he shall see it there.
And yet as ghastly dreadfull, as it seemes,
Bold men presuming life for gaine to sell,
Dare tempt that gulf, and in those wandring
   stremes 210
Seek waies vnknowne, waies leading down to
   hell.
For as we stood there waiting on the strond,
Behold an huge great vessell to vs came,
Dauncing vpon the waters back to lond,
As if it scornd the daunger of the same,
Yet was it but a wooden frame and fraile,
Glewed togither with some subtile matter,
Yet had it armes and wings, and head and taile,
And life to moue it selfe vpon the water.
Strange thing, how bold and swift the monster
   was, 220
That neither car'd for wynd, nor haile, nor
   raine,
Nor swelling waues, but thorough them did
   passe
So proudly, that she made them roare againe.
The same aboord vs gently did receaue,
And without harme vs farre away did beare,
So farre that land our mother vs did leaue,
And nought but sea and heauen to vs appeare.
Then hartlesse quite and full of inward feare,
That shepheard I besought to me to tell, 229
Vnder what skie, or in what world we were,
In which I saw no liuing people dwell.
Who me recomforting all that he might,
Told me that that same was the Regiment
Of a great shepheardesse, that *Cynthia* hight,
His liege his Ladie, and his lifes Regent

If then (quoth I) a shepheardesse she bee,
Where be the flockes and heards, which she doth
    keep ?   237
And where may I the hills and pastures see,
On which she vseth for to feed her sheepe ?
These be the hills (quoth he) the surges hie,
On which faire *Cynthia* her heards doth feed :
Her heards be thousand fishes with their frie,
Which in the bosome of the billowes breed.
Of them the shepheard which hath charge in
    chief,
Is *Triton* blowing loud his wreathed horne :
At sound whereof, they all for their relief
Wend too and fro at euening and at morne.
And *Proteus* eke with him does driue his heard
Of stinking Seales and Porcpisces together,
With hoary head and deawy dropping beard,
Compelling them which way he list, and
    whether.   251
And I among the rest of many least,
Haue in the Ocean charge to me assignd :
Where I will liue or die at her beheast,
And serue and honour her with faithfull mind.
Besides an hundred Nymphs all heauenly
    borne,
And of immortall race, doo still attend
To wash faire *Cynthiaes* sheep, when they be
    shorne,
And fold them vp, when they haue made an end.
Those be the shepheards which my *Cynthia*
    serue,   260
At sea, beside a thousand moe at land :
For land and sea my *Cynthia* doth deserue
To haue in her commandement at hand.
Thereat I wondred much, till wondring more
And more, at length we land far off descryde :
Which sight much gladed me ; for much afore
I feard, least land we neuer should haue eyde :
Thereto our ship her course directly bent,
As if the way she perfectly had knowne.   269
We *Lunday* passe ; by that same name is ment
An Island, which the first to west was showne.
From thence another world of land we kend,
Floting amid the sea in ieopardie,
And round about with mightie white rocks
    hemd,
Against the seas encroching crueltie.
Those same the shepheard told me, were the
    fields
In which dame *Cynthia* her landheards fed,
Faire goodly fields, then which *Armulla* yields
None fairer, nor more fruitfull to be red.
The first to which we nigh approched, was
An high headland thrust far into the sea,   281
Like to an horne, whereof the name it has,
Yet seemed to be a goodly pleasant lea :

There did a loftie mount at first vs greet,
Which did a stately heape of stones vpreare,
That seemd amid the surges for to fleet,
Much greater then that frame, which vs did
    beare :
There did our ship her fruitfull wombe vnlade,
And put vs all ashore on *Cynthias* land.
    What land is that thou meanst (then *Cuddy*
        sayd)   290
And is there other, then whereon we stand ?
Ah *Cuddy* (then quoth *Colin*) thous a fon,
That hast not seene least part of natures worke :
Much more there is vnkend, then thou doest
    kon,
And much more that does from mens know-
    ledge lurke.
For that same land much larger is then this,
And other men and beasts and birds doth feed :
There fruitfull corne, faire trees, fresh herbage is
And all things else that liuing creatures need.
Besides most goodly riuers there appeare, 300
No whit inferiour to thy *Funchins* praise,
Or vnto *Allo* or to *Mulla* cleare :
Nought hast thou foolish boy seene in thy daies.
But if that land be there (quoth he) as here,
And is theyr heauen likewise there all one ?
And if like heauen, be heauenly graces there,
Like as in this same world where we do wone ?
    Both heauen and heauenly graces do much
        more
(Quoth he) abound in that same land, then this.
For there all happie peace and plenteous store
Conspire in one to make contented blisse : 311
No wayling there nor wretchednesse is heard,
No bloodie issues nor no leprosies,
No griesly famine, nor no raging sweard,
No nightly bodrags, nor no hue and cries ;
The shepheards there abroad may safely lie,
On hills and downes, withouten dread or
    daunger :
No rauenous wolues the good mans hope
    destroy,
Nor outlawes fell affray the forest raunger.
There learned arts do florish in great honor,
And Poets wits are had in peerlesse price : 321
Religion hath lay powre to rest vpon her,
Aduancing vertue and suppressing vice.
For end, all good, all grace there freely growes,
Had people grace it gratefully to vse :
For God his gifts there plenteously bestowes
But gracelesse men them greatly do abuse.
    But say on further, then said *Corylas*,
The rest of thine aduentures, that betyded.
    Foorth on our voyage we by land did passe,
(Quoth he) as that same shepheard still vs
    guyded,   331

Vntill that we to *Cynthiaes* presence came:
Whose glorie, greater then my simple thought,
I found much greater then the former fame;
Such greatnes I cannot compare to ought:
But if I her like ought on earth might read,
I would her lyken to a crowne of lillies,
Vpon a virgin brydes adorned head,
With Roses dight and Goolds and Daffadillies;
Or like the circlet of a Turtle true,   340
In which all colours of the rainbow bee;
Or like faire *Phebes* garlond shining new,
In which all pure perfection one may see.
But vaine it is to thinke by paragone
Of earthly things, to iudge of things diuine:
Her power, her mercy, and her wisedome, none
Can deeme, but who the Godhead can define.
Why then do I base shepheard bold and blind,
Presume the things so sacred to prophane?
More fit it is t'adore with humble mind,   350
The image of the heauens in shape humane.

With that *Alexis* broke his tale asunder,
Saying, By wondring at thy *Cynthiaes* praise,
Colin, thy selfe thou mak'st vs more to wonder,
And her vpraising, doest thy selfe vpraise.
But let vs heare what grace she shewed thee,
And how that shepheard strange, thy cause
  aduanced?

The shepheard of the Ocean (quoth he)
Vnto that Goddesse grace me first enhanced,   360
And to mine oaten pipe enclin'd her eare,
That she thenceforth therein gan take delight,
And it desir'd at timely houres to heare,
All were my notes but rude and roughly
  dight.
For not by measure of her owne great mynd,
And wondrous worth she mott my simple song,
But ioyd that country shepheard ought could
  fynd
Worth harkening to, emongst the learned
  throng.

Why? (said *Alexis* then) what needeth shee
That is so great a shepheardesse her selfe,   370
And hath so many shepheards in her fee,
To heare thee sing, a simple silly Elfe?
Or be the shepheards which do serue her laesie,
That they list not their mery pipes applie?
Or be their pipes vntunable and craesie,
That they cannot her honour worthylie?

Ah nay (said *Colin*) neither so, nor so:
For better shepheards be not vnder skie,
Nor better hable, when they list to blow
Their pipes aloud, her name to glorifie.
There is good *Harpalus*, now woxen aged 380
In faithfull seruice of faire *Cynthia*:
And there is *Corydon* though meanly waged,
Yet hablest wit of most I know this day.

And there is sad *Alcyon* bent to mourne,
Though fit to frame an euerlasting dittie,
Whose gentle spright for *Daphnes* death doth
  tourn
Sweet layes of loue to endlesse plaints of pittie.
Ah pensiue boy pursue that braue conceipt,
In thy sweet Eglantine of *Meriflure*,
Lift vp thy notes vnto their wonted height, 390
That may thy *Muse* and mates to mirth allure.
There eke is *Palin* worthie of great praise,
Albe he enuie at my rustick quill:
And there is pleasing *Alcon*, could he raise
His tunes from laies to matter of more skill.
And there is old *Palemon* free from spight,
Whose carefull pipe may make the hearer rew:
Yet he himselfe may rewed be more right,
That sung so long vntill quite hoarse he grew.
And there is *Alabaster* throughly taught, 400
In all this skill, though knowen yet to few:
Yet were he knowne to *Cynthia* as he ought,
His Eliseïs would be redde anew.
Who liues that can match that heroick song,
Which he hath of that mightie Princesse made?
O dreaded Dread, do not thy selfe that
  wrong,
To let thy fame lie so in hidden shade:
But call it forth, O call him forth to thee,
To end thy glorie which he hath begun:
That when he finisht hath as it should be, 410
No brauer Poeme can be vnder Sun.
Nor *Po* nor *Tyburs* swans so much renowned,
Nor all the brood of *Greece* so highly praised,
Can match that *Muse* when it with bayes is
  crowned,
And to the pitch of her perfection raised.
And there is a new shepheard late vp sprong,
The which doth all afore him far surpasse:
Appearing well in that well tuned song,
Which late he sung vnto a scornfull lasse.
Yet doth his trembling *Muse* but lowly flie,
As daring not too rashly mount on hight, 421
And doth her tender plumes as yet but trie,
In loues soft laies and looser thoughts delight.
Then rouze thy feathers quickly *Daniell*,
And to what course thou please thy selfe
  aduance:
But most me seemes, thy accent will excell,
In Tragick plaints and passionate mischance.
And there that shepheard of the Ocean is,
That spends his wit in loues consuming smart:
Full sweetly tempred is that *Muse* of his 430
That can empierce a Princes mightie hart.
There also is (ah no, he is not now)
But since I said he is, he quite is gone,
Amyntas quite is gone and lies full low,
Hauing his *Amaryllis* left to mone.

Helpe, O ye shepheards helpe ye all in this,
Helpe *Amaryllis* this her losse to mourne:
Her losse is yours, your losse *Amyntas* is,
Amyntas floure of shepheards pride forlorne:
He whilest he liued was the noblest swaine,
That euer piped in an oaten quill: 441
Both did he other, which could pipe, maintaine,
And eke could pipe himselfe with passing skill.
And there though last not least is *Aetion*,
A gentler shepheard may no where be found:
Whose *Muse* full of high thoughts inuention,
Doth like himselfe Heroically sound.
All these, and many others mo remaine,
Now after *Astrofell* is dead and gone:
But while as *Astrofell* did liue and raine,   450
Amongst all these was none his Paragone.
All these do florish in their sundry kynd,
And do their *Cynthia* immortall make:
Yet found I lyking in her royall mynd,
Not for my skill, but for that shepheards sake.
  Then spake a louely lasse, hight *Lucida*,
Shepheard, enough of shepheards thou hast
        told,
Which fauour thee, and honour *Cynthia :*
But of so many Nymphs which she doth hold
In her retinew, thou hast nothing sayd;   460
That seems, with none of them thou fauor
        foundest,
Or art ingratefull to each gentle mayd,
That none of all their due deserts resoundest.
  Ah far be it (quoth *Colin Clout*) fro me,
That I of gentle Mayds should ill deserue:
For that my selfe I do professe to be
Vassall to one, whom all my dayes I serue;
The beame of beautie sparkled from aboue,
The floure of vertue and pure chastitie,
The blossome of sweet ioy and perfect loue, 470
The pearle of peerlesse grace and modestie:
To her my thoughts I daily dedicate,
To her my heart I nightly martyrize:
To her my loue I lowly do prostrate,
To her my life I wholly sacrifice:
My thought, my heart, my loue, my life is
        shee,
And I hers euer onely, euer one:
One euer I all vowed hers to bee,
One euer I, and others neuer none.
  Then thus *Melissa* said; Thrise happie Mayd,
Whom thou doest so enforce to deifie: 481
That woods, and hills, and valleyes thou hast
        made
Her name to eccho vnto heauen hie.
But say, who else vouchsafed thee of grace?
  They all (quoth he) me graced goodly well,
That all I praise, but in the highest place,
Vrania, sister vnto *Astrofell,*

In whose braue mynd, as in a golden cofer,
All heauenly gifts and riches locked are:
More rich then pearles of *Ynde,* or gold of *Opher,*
And in her sex more wonderfull and rare.   491
Ne lesse praise worthie I *Theana* read,
Whose goodly beames though they be ouer
        dight
With mourning stole of carefull wydowhead,
Yet through that darksome vale do glister
        bright;
She is the well of bountie and braue mynd,
Excelling most in glorie and great light:
She is the ornament of womankind,
And Courts chief garlond with all vertues dight.
Therefore great *Cynthia* her in chiefest grace
Doth hold, and next vnto her selfe aduance,   502
Well worthie of so honourable place,
For her great worth and noble gouernance.
Ne lesse praise worthie is her sister deare,
Faire *Marian,* the *Muses* onely darling:
Whose beautie shyneth as the morning cleare,
With siluer deaw vpon the roses pearling.
Ne lesse praise worthie is *Mansilia,*
Best knowne by bearing vp great *Cynthiaes*
        traine:
That same is she to whom *Daphnaida*   510
Vpon her neeces death I did complaine.
She is the paterne of true womanhead,
And onely mirrhor of feminitie:
Worthie next after *Cynthia* to tread,
As she is next her in nobilitie.
Ne lesse praise worthie *Galathea* seemes,
Then best of all that honourable crew,
Faire *Galathea* with bright shining beames,
Inflaming feeble eyes that her do view.
She there then waited vpon *Cynthia,*   520
Yet there is not her won, but here with vs
About the borders of our rich *Coshma,*
Now made of *Maa* the Nymph delitious.
Ne lesse praisworthie faire *Neæra* is,
Neæra ours, not theirs, though there she be,
For of the famous Shure, the Nymph she is,
For high desert, aduaunst to that degree.
She is the blosome of grace and curtesie,
Adorned with all honourable parts:
She is the braunch of true nobilitie,   530
Belou'd of high and low with faithfull harts.
Ne lesse praisworthie *Stella* do I read,
Though nought my praises of her needed arre,
Whom verse of noblest shepheard lately dead
Hath prais'd and rais'd aboue each other
        starre.
Ne lesse praisworthie are the sisters three,
The honor of the noble familie:
Of which I meanest boast my selfe to be,
And most that vnto them I am so nie.

Phyllis, Charillis, and sweet Amaryllis,	540
Phillis the faire, is eldest of the three :
The next to her, is bountifull Charillis.
But th'youngest is the highest in degree.
Phyllis the floure of rare perfection,
Faire spreading forth her leaues with fresh
    delight,
That with their beauties amorous reflexion,
Bereaue of sence each rash beholders sight.
But sweet Charillis is the Paragone
Of peerlesse price, and ornament of praise,
Admyr'd of all, yet enuied of none,	550
Through the myld temperance of her goodly
    raies.
Thrice happie do I hold thee noble swaine,
The which art of so rich a spoile possest,
And it embracing deare without disdaine,
Hast sole possession in so chaste a brest :
Of all the shepheards daughters which there bee,
(And yet there be the fairest vnder skie,
Or that elsewhere I euer yet did see)
A fairer Nymph yet neuer saw mine eie :
She is the pride and primrose of the rest,	560
Made by the maker selfe to be admired :
And like a goodly beacon high addrest,
That is with sparks of heauenle beautie fired.
But Amaryllis, whether fortunate,
Or else vnfortunate may I aread,
That freed is from Cupids yoke by fate,
Since which she doth new bands aduenture
    dread.
Shepheard what euer thou hast heard to be
In this or that praysd diuersly apart,	569
In her thou maist them all assembled see,
And seald vp in the threasure of her hart.
Ne thee lesse worthie gentle Flauia,
For thy chaste life and vertue I esteeme :
Ne thee lesse worthie curteous Candida,
For thy true loue and loyaltie I deeme.
Besides yet many mo that Cynthia serue,
Right noble Nymphs, and high to be com-
    mended :
But if I all should praise as they deserue,
This sun would faile me ere I halfe had ended.
Therefore in closure of a thankfull mynd,	580
I deeme it best to hold eternally,
Their bounteous deeds and noble fauours shrynd,
Then by discourse them to indignifie.
    So hauing said, Aglaura him bespake :
Colin, well worthie were those goodly fauours
Bestowd on thee, that so of them doest make,
And them requitest with thy thankfull labours.
But of great Cynthiaes goodnesse and high grace,
Finish the storie which thou hast begunne.
    More eath (quoth he) it is in such a case	590
How to begin, then know how to haue donne.

For euerie gift and euerie goodly meed,
Which she on me bestowd, demaunds a day ;
And euerie day, in which she did a deed,
Demaunds a yeare it duly to display.
Her words were like a streame of honny fleeting,
The which doth softly trickle from the hiue :
Hable to melt the hearers heart vnsweeting,
And eke to make the dead againe aliue.	599
Her deeds were like great clusters of ripe grapes,
Which load the braunches of the fruitfull vine :
Offring to fall into each mouth that gapes,
And fill the same with store of timely wine.
Her lookes were like beames of the morning Sun,
Forth looking through the windowes of the East :
When first the fleecie cattell haue begun
Vpon the perled grasse to make their feast.
Her thoughts are like the fume of Franckin-
    cence,
Which from a golden Censer forth doth rise :
And throwing forth sweet odours mounts fro
    thence	610
In rolling globes vp to the vauted skies.
There she beholds with high aspiring thought,
The cradle of her owne creation :
Emongst the seats of Angels heauenly wrought,
Much like an Angell in all forme and fashion.
    Colin (said Cuddy then) thou hast forgot
Thy selfe, me seemes, too much, to mount so hie :
Such loftie flight, base shepheard seemeth not,
From flocks and fields, to Angels and to skie.
    True (answered he) her great excellence,
Lifts me aboue the measure of my might :	621
That being fild with furious insolence,
I feele my selfe like one yrapt in spright.
For when I thinke of her, as oft I ought,
Then want I words to speake it fitly forth :
And when I speake of her what I haue thought,
I cannot thinke according to her worth.
Yet will I thinke of her, yet will I speake,
So long as life my limbs doth hold together,
And when as death these vitall bands shall
    breake,	630
Her name recorded I will leaue for euer.
Her name in euery tree I will endosse,
That as the trees do grow, her name may grow :
And in the ground each where will it engrosse,
And fill with stones, that all men may it know.
The speaking woods and murmuring waters fall,
Her name Ile teach in knowen termes to frame :
And eke my lambs when for their dams they call,
Ile teach to call for Cynthia by name.
And long while after I am dead and rotten :
Amongst the shepheards daughters dancing
    rownd,	641
My layes made of her shall not be forgotten.
But sung by them with flowry gyrlonds crownd,

And ye, who so ye be, that shall surviue:
When as ye heare her memory renewed,
Be witnesse of her bountie here aliue,
Which she to *Colin* her poore shepheard shewed.

  Much was the whole assembly of those heards,
Moov'd at his speech, so feelingly he spake:
And stood awhile astonisht at his words,   650
Till *Thestylis* at last their silence brake,
Saying, Why *Colin*, since thou foundst such grace
With *Cynthia* and all her noble crew:
Why didst thou euer leaue that happie place,
In which such wealth might vnto thee accrew?
And back returnedst to this barrein soyle,
Where cold and care and penury do dwell:
Here to keep sheepe, with hunger and with toyle,
Most wretched he, that is and cannot tell.

  Happie indeed (said *Colin*) I him hold,   660
That may that blessed presence still enioy,
Of fortune and of enuy vncomptrold,
Which still are wont most happie states t'annoy:
But I by that which little while I prooued:
Some part of those enormities did see,
The which in Court continually hooued,
And followd those which happie seemd to bee.
Therefore I silly man, whose former dayes
Had in rude fields bene altogether spent,   669
Durst not aduenture such vnknowen wayes,
Nor trust the guile of fortunes blandishment,
But rather chose back to my sheep to tourne,
Whose vtmost hardnesse I before had tryde,
Then hauing learnd repentance late, to mourne
Emongst those wretches which I there descryde.

  Shepheard (said *Thestylis*) it seemes of spight
Thou speakest thus gainst their felicitie, ·
Which thou enuiest, rather then of right
That ought in them blameworthie thou doest spie.   679

  Cause haue I none (quoth he) of cancred will
To quite them ill, that me demeand so well:
But selfe-regard of priuate good or ill,
Moues me of each, so as I found, to tell,
And eke to warne yong shepheards wandring wit,
Which through report of that liues painted blisse,
Abandon quiet home, to seeke for it,
And leaue their lambes to losse, misled amisse.
For sooth to say, it is no sort of life,
For shepheard fit to lead in that same place,
Where each one seeks with malice and with strife,   690
To thrust downe other into foule disgrace,
Himselfe to raise: and he doth soonest rise
That best can handle his deceitfull wit,
In subtil shifts, and finest sleights deuise,

Either by slaundring his well deemed name,
Through leasings lewd, and fained forgerie:
Or else by breeding him some blot of blame,
By creeping close into his secrecie;
To which him needs a guilefull hollow hart,
Masked with faire dissembling curtesie,   700
A filed toung furnisht with tearmes of art,
No art of schoole, but Courtiers schoolery.
For arts of schoole haue there small countenance,
Counted but toyes to busie ydle braines,
And there professours find small maintenance,
But to be instruments of others gaines.
Ne is there place for any gentle wit,
Vnlesse to please, it selfe it can applie:
But shouldred is, or out of doore quite shit,
As base, or blunt, vnmeet for melodie.   710
For each mans worth is measured by his weed,
As harts by hornes, or asses by their eares:
Yet asses been not all whose eares exceed,
Nor yet all harts, that hornes the highest beares.
For highest lookes haue not the highest mynd,
Nor haughtie words most full of highest thoughts:
But are like bladders blowen vp with wynd,
That being prickt do vanish into noughts.
Euen such is all their vaunted vanitie,
Nought else but smoke, that fumeth soone away;
Such is their glorie that in simple eie   721
Seeme greatest, when their garments are most gay.
So they themselues for praise of fooles do sell,
And all their wealth for painting on a wall;
With price whereof, they buy a golden bell,
And purchace highest rowmes in bowre and hall:
Whiles single Truth and simple honestie
Do wander vp and downe despys'd of all;
Their plaine attire such glorious gallantry   729
Disdaines so much, that none them in doth call.

  Ah *Colin* (then said *Hobbinol*) the blame
Which thou imputest, is too generall,
As if not any gentle wit of name,
Nor honest mynd might there be found at all.
For well I wot, sith I my selfe was there,
To wait on *Lobbin* (*Lobbin* well thou knewest)
Full many worthie ones then waiting were,
As euer else in Princes Court thou vewest:
Of which, among you many yet remaine,   739
Whose names I cannot readily now ghesse:
Those that poore Sutors papers do retaine,
And those that skill of medicine professe.
And those that do to *Cynthia* expound
The ledden of straunge languages in charge:
For *Cynthia* doth in sciences abound,
And giues to their professors stipends large.

Therefore vniustly thou doest wyte them all,
For that which thou mislikedst in a few.

Blame is (quoth he) more blamelesse generall,
Then that which priuate errours doth pursew :
For well I wot, that there amongst them bee,
Full many persons of right worthie parts,   752
Both for report of spotlesse honestie,
And for profession of all learned arts,
Whose praise hereby no whit impaired is,
Though blame do light on those that faultie bee,
For all the rest do most-what fare amis,
And yet their owne misfaring will not see :
For either they be puffed vp with pride,
Or fraught with enuie that their galls do swell,
Or they their dayes to ydlenesse diuide,   761
Or drownded lie in pleasures wastefull well,
In which like Moldwarps nousling still they
    lurke,
Vnmyndfull of chiefe parts of manlinesse,
And do themselues for want of other worke,
Vaine votaries of laesie loue professe,
Whose seruice high so basely they ensew,
That Cupid selfe of them ashamed is,
And mustring all his men in Venus vew,
Denies them quite for seruitors of his.   770

And is loue then (said Corylas) once knowne
In Court, and his sweet lore professed there ?
I weened sure he was our God alone :
And only woond in fields and forests here.

Not so (quoth he) loue most aboundeth
    there.
For all the walls and windows there are writ,
All full of loue, and loue, and loue my deare,
And all their talke and studie is of it.
Ne any there doth braue or valiant seeme,
Vnlesse that some gay Mistresse badge he
    beares :   780
Ne any one himselfe doth ought esteeme,
Vnlesse he swim in loue vp to the eares.
But they of loue and of his sacred lere,
(As it should be) all otherwise deuise,
Then we poore shepheards are accustomd here,
And him do sue and serue all otherwise.
For with lewd speeches and licentious deeds,
His mightie mysteries they do prophane,
And vse his ydle name to other needs,
But as a complement for courting vaine.   790
So him they do not serue as they professe,
But make him serue to them for sordid vses,
Ah my dread Lord, that doest liege hearts
    possesse,
Auenge thy selfe on them for their abuses.
But we poore shepheards, whether rightly so,
Or through our rudenesse into errour led,
Do make religion how we rashly go,
To serue that God, that is so greatly dred ;

For him the greatest of the Gods we deeme,
Borne without Syre or couples, of one kynd,
For Venus selfe doth soly couples seeme,   801
Both male and female, through commixture ioynd,
So pure and spotlesse Cupid forth she brought,
And in the gardens of Adonis nurst :
Where growing, he his owne perfection wrought,
And shortly was of all the Gods the first.
Then got he bow and shafts of gold and lead,
In which so fell and puissant he grew,
That Ioue himselfe his powre began to dread,
And taking vp to heauen, him godded new.
From thence he shootes his arrowes euery where
Into the world, at randon as he will,   812
On vs fraile men, his wretched vassals here,
Like as himselfe vs pleaseth, saue or spill.
So we him worship, so we him adore
With humble hearts to heauen vplifted hie,
That to true loues he may vs euermore
Preferre, and of their grace vs dignifie :
Ne is there shepheard, ne yet shepheardsswaine,
What euer feeds in forest or in field,   820
That dare with euil deed or leasing vaine
Blaspheme his powre, or termes vnworthie yield.

Shepheard it seemes that some celestiall rage
Of loue (quoth Cuddy) is breath'd into thy brest,
That powreth forth these oracles so sage,
Of that high powre, wherewith thou art possest.
But neuer wist I till this present day
Albe of loue I alwayes humbly deemed,
That he was such an one, as thou doest say,
And so religiously to be esteemed.   830
Well may it seeme by this thy deep insight,
That of that God the Priest thou shouldest bee :
So well thou wot'st the mysterie of his might,
As if his godhead thou didst present see.

Of loues perfection perfectly to speake,
Or of his nature rightly to define,
Indeed (said Colin) passeth reasons reach,
And needs his priest t'expresse his powre diuine.
For long before the world he was y'bore
And bred aboue in Venus bosome deare :   840
For by his powre the world was made of yore,
And all that therein wondrous doth appeare.
For how should else things so far from attone
And so great enemies as of them bee,
Be euer drawne together into one,
And taught in such accordance to agree ?
Through him the cold began to couet heat,
And water fire ; the light to mount on hie,
And th'heauie downe to peize ; the hungry t'eat
And voydnesse to seeke full satietie.   850
So being former foes, they wexed friends,
And gan by litle learne to loue each other :
So being knit, they brought forth other kynds
Out of the fruitfull wombe of their great mother.

Then first gan heauen out of darknesse dread
For to appeare, and brought forth chearfull day:
Next gan the earth to shew her naked head,
Out of deep waters which her drownd alway.
And shortly after, euerie liuing wight   859
Crept forth like wormes out of her slimie nature,
Soone as on them the Suns life giuing light,
Had powred kindly heat and formall feature,
Thenceforth they gan each one his like to loue,
And like himselfe desire for to beget,
The Lyon chose his mate, the Turtle Doue
Her deare, the Dolphin his owne Dolphinet:
But man that had the sparke of reasons might,
More then the rest to rule his passion,
Chose for his loue the fairest in his sight,
Like as himselfe was fairest by creation.   870
For beautie is the bayt which with delight
Doth man allure, for to enlarge his kynd,
Beautie the burning lamp of heauens light,
Darting her beames into each feeble mynd:
Against whose powre, nor God nor man can fynd,
Defence, ne ward the daunger of the wound,
But being hurt, seeke to be medicynd
Of her that first did stir that mortall stownd.
Then do they cry and call to loue apace,
With praiers lowd importuning the skie,   880
Whence he them heares, and when he list shew
     grace,
Does graunt them grace that otherwise would die.
So loue is Lord of all the world by right,
And rules the creatures by his powrfull saw:
All being made the vassalls of his might,
Through secret sence which therto doth them
     draw.
Thus ought all louers of their lord to deeme:
And with chaste heart to honor him alway:
But who so else doth otherwise esteeme,
Are outlawes, and his lore do disobay.   890
For their desire is base, and doth not merit,
The name of loue, but of disloyall lust:
Ne mongst true louers they shall place inherit,
But as Exuls out of his court be thrust.

So hauing said, *Melissa* spake at will,
Colin, thou now full deeply hast divynd:
Of loue and beautie, and with wondrous skill,
Hast *Cupid* selfe depainted in his kynd.
To thee are all true louers greatly bound,   899
That doest their cause so mightily defend:
But most, all wemen are thy debtors found,
That doest their bountie still so much commend.

That ill (said *Hobbinol*) they him requite,
For hauing loued euer one most deare:
He is repayd with scorne and foule despite,
That yrkes each gentle heart which it doth
     heare.

Indeed (said *Lucid*) I haue often heard
Faire *Rosalind* of diuers fowly blamed:
For being to that swaine too cruell hard,
That her bright glorie else hath much defamed.
But who can tell what cause had that faire
     Mayd   911
To vse him so that vsed her so well:
Or who with blame can iustly her vpbrayd,
For louing not? for who can loue compell?
And sooth to say, it is foolhardie thing,
Rashly to wyten creatures so diuine,
For demigods they be and first did spring
From heauen, though graft in frailnesse
     feminine.
And well I wote, that oft I heard it spoken,
How one that fairest *Helene* did reuile: 920
Through iudgement of the Gods to been
     ywroken
Lost both his eyes and so remaynd long while,
Till he recanted had his wicked rimes,
And made amends to her with treble praise:
Beware therefore, ye groomes, I read betimes,
How rashly blame of *Rosalind* ye raise.

Ah shepheards (then said *Colin*) ye ne weet
How great a guilt vpon your heads ye draw:
To make so bold a doome with words vnmeet,
Of thing celestiall which ye neuer saw.   930
For she is not like as the other crew
Of shepheards daughters which emongst you
     bee,
But of diuine regard and heauenly hew,
Excelling all that euer ye did see.
Not then to her that scorned thing so base,
But to my selfe the blame that lookt so hie:
So hie her thoughts as she her selfe haue place,
And loath each lowly thing with loftie eie.
Yet so much grace let her vouchsafe to grant
To simple swaine, sith her I may not loue:
Yet that I may her honour parauant,   941
And praise her worth, though far my wit aboue.
Such grace shall be some guerdon for the griefe,
And long affliction which I haue endured:
Such grace sometimes shall giue me some
     reliefe,
And ease of paine which cannot be recured.
And ye my fellow shepheards which do see
And heare the languours of my too long dying,
Vnto the world for euer witnesse bee,
That hers I die, nought to the world denying,
This simple trophe of her great conquest.   951

So hauing ended, he from ground did rise,
And after him vprose eke all the rest:
All loth to part, but that the glooming skies
Warnd them to draw their bleating flocks to
     rest.

FINIS.

SPENSER

T

ASTROPHEL.

A Paſtorall Elegie vpon

the death of the moſt Noble and valorous
Knight, Sir *Philip Sidney.*

Dedicated

*To the moſt beautifull and vertuous Ladie, the Counteſſe
of* Eſſex.

Astrophel.

SHepheards that wont on pipes of oaten reed,
  Oft times to plaine your loues concealed smart:
And with your piteous layes haue learnd to breed
Compassion in a countrey lasses hart.
Hearken ye gentle shepheards to my song,
And place my dolefull plaint your plaints emong.

To you alone I sing this mournfull verse,
The mournfulst verse that euer man heard tell:
To you whose softened hearts it may empierse,
With dolours dart for death of Astrophel.   10
To you I sing and to none other wight,
For well I wot my rymes bene rudely dight.

Yet as they been, if any nycer wit
Shall hap to heare, or couet them to read:
Thinke he, that such are for such ones most fit,
Made not to please the liuing but the dead.
And if in him found pity euer place,
Let him be moov'd to pity such a case.

A Gentle Shepheard borne in Arcady,
  Of gentlest race that euer shepheard bore:
About the grassie bancks of Hæmony,
Did keepe his sheep, his litle stock and store.
Full carefully he kept them day and night,
In fairest fields, and Astrophel he hight.

Young Astrophel the pride of shepheards praise,
Young Astrophel the rusticke lasses loue:
Far passing all the pastors of his daies,
In all that seemly shepheard might behoue.   10
In one thing onely fayling of the best,
That he was not so happie as the rest.

For from the time that first the Nymph his
  mother
Him forth did bring, and taught her lambs to
  feed,
A sclender swaine excelling far each other,
In comely shape, like her that did him breed,
He grew vp fast in goodnesse and in grace,
And doubly faire wox both in mynd and face.

Which daily more and more he did augment,
With gentle vsage and demeanure myld: 20
That all mens hearts with secret rauishment
He stole away, and weetingly beguyld.
Ne spight it selfe that all good things doth spill,
Found ought in him, that she could say was ill.

His sports were faire, his ioyance innocent,
Sweet without sowre, and honny without gall:
And he himselfe seemd made for meriment,
Merily masking both in bowre and hall.
There was no pleasure nor delightfull play,
When Astrophel so euer was away.   30

For he could pipe and daunce, and caroll sweet,
Emongst the shepheards in their shearing feast:
As Somers larke that with her song doth greet
The dawning day forth comming from the East.
And layes of loue he also could compose.
Thrise happie she, whom he to praise did chose.

Full many Maydens often did him woo,
Them to vouchsafe emongst his rimes to name,
Or make for them as he was wont to doo,
For her that did his heart with loue inflame.
For which they promised to dight, for him,   41
Gay chapelets of flowers and gyrlonds trim.

And many a Nymph both of the wood and brooke,
Soone as his oaten pipe began to shrill:
Both christall wells and shadie groues forsooke,
To heare the charmes of his enchanting skill.
And brought him presents, flowers if it were
  prime,
Or mellow fruit if it were haruest time.

But he for none of them did care a whit,
Yet wood Gods for them often sighed sore: 50
Ne for their gifts vnworthie of his wit,
Yet not vnworthie of the countries store.
For one alone he cared, for one he sight,
His lifes desire, and his deare loues delight.

Stella the faire, the fairest star in skie,
As faire as Venus or the fairest faire:
A fairer star saw neuer liuing eie,
Shot her sharp pointed beames through purest aire.
Her he did loue, her he alone did honor,
His thoughts, his rimes, his songs were all vpon
  her.   60

To her he vowd the seruice of his daies,
On her he spent the riches of his wit:
For her he made hymnes of immortall praise,
Of onely her he sung, he thought, he writ.
Her, and but her, of loue he worthie deemed,
For all the rest but litle he esteemed.

Ne her with ydle words alone he wowed,
And verses vaine (yet verses are not vaine)
But with braue deeds to her sole seruice vowed,
And bold atchieuements her did entertaine. 70
For both in deeds and words he nourtred was,
Both wise and hardie (too hardie alas).

In wrestling nimble, and in renning swift,
In shooting steddie, and in swimming strong:
Well made to strike, to throw, to leape to lift,
And all the sports that shepheards are emong.
In euery one he vanquisht euery one,
He vanquisht all, and vanquisht was of none.

Besides, in hunting, such felicitie,
Or rather infelicitie he found :   80
That euery field and forest far away,
He sought, where saluage beasts do most
    abound.
No beast so saluage but he could it kill,
No chace so hard, but he therein had skill.

Such skill matcht with such courage as he had,
Did prick him foorth with proud desire of
    praise :
To seek abroad, of daunger nought y'drad,
His mistresse name, and his owne fame to raise.
What needeth perill to be sought abroad,
Since round about vs, it doth make aboad ?

It fortuned, as he that perilous game   91
In forreine soyle pursued far away :
Into a forest wide and waste he came
Where store he heard to be of saluage pray.
So wide a forest and so waste as this,
Nor famous *Ardeyn*, nor fowle *Arlo* is.

There his welwouen toyles and subtil traines
He laid, the brutish nation to enwrap :
So well he wrought with practise and with
    paines,   99
That he of them great troups did soone entrap.
Full happie man (misweening much) was hee,
So rich a spoile within his power to see.

Eftsoones all heedlesse of his dearest hale,
Full greedily into the heard he thrust :
To slaughter them, and worke their finall bale,
Least that his toyle should of their troups be
    brust.
Wide wounds emongst them many one he made,
Now with his sharp borespear, now with his
    blade.

His care was all how he them all might kill,
That none might scape (so partiall vnto none)
Ill mynd so much to mynd anothers ill,   111
As to become vnmyndfull of his owne.
But pardon that vnto the cruell skies,
That from himselfe to them withdrew his eies.

So as he rag'd emongst that beastly rout,
A cruell beast of most accursed brood
Vpon him turnd (despeyre makes cowards stout)
And with fell tooth accustomed to blood,   118
Launched his thigh with so mischieuous might,
That it both bone and muscles ryued quight.

So deadly was the dint and deep the wound,
And so huge streames of blood thereout did flow,
That he endured not the direfull stound,
But on the cold deare earth himselfe did throw.
The whiles the captiue heard his nets did rend,
And hauing none to let, to wood did wend.

Ah where were ye this while his shepheard peares,
To whom aliue was nought so deare as hee :
And ye faire Mayds the matches of his yeares,
Which in his grace did boast you most to bee ?
Ah where were ye, when he of you had need,
To stop his wound that wondrously did bleed ?

Ah wretched boy the shape of dreryhead,
And sad ensample of mans suddein end :
Full litle faileth but thou shalt be dead,
Vnpitied, vnplaynd, of foe or frend.
Whilest none is nigh, thine eylids vp to close,
And kisse thy lips like faded leaues of rose.

A sort of shepheards sewing of the chace,
As they the forest raunged on a day :   140
By fate or fortune came vnto the place,
Where as the lucklesse boy yet bleeding lay.
Yet bleeding lay, and yet would still haue bled,
Had not good hap those shepheards thether led.

They stopt his wound (too late to stop it was)
And in their armes then softly did him reare :
Tho (as he wild) vnto his loued lasse,
His dearest loue him dolefully did beare.
The dolefulst beare that euer man did see,
Was *Astrophel*, but dearest vnto mee.   150

She when she saw her loue in such a plight,
With crudled blood and filthie gore deformed :
That wont to be with flowers and gyrlonds dight,
And her deare fauours dearly well adorned,
Her face, the fairest face, that eye mote see,
She likewise did deforme like him to bee.

Her yellow locks that shone so bright and long,
As Sunny beames in fairest somers day
She fiersly tore, and with outragious wrong
From her red cheeks the roses rent away.   160
And her faire brest the threasury of ioy,
She spoyld thereof, and filled with annoy.

His palled face impictured with death,
She bathed oft with teares and dried oft :
And with sweet kisses suckt the wasting breath,
Out of his lips like lillies pale and soft.
And oft she cald to him, who answerd nought,
But onely by his lookes did tell his thought.

The rest of her impatient regret,
And piteous mone the which she for him made,
No toong can tell, nor any forth can set,   171
But he whose heart like sorrow did inuade.
At last when paine his vitall powres had spent,
His wasted life her weary lodge forwent.

Which when she saw, she staied not a whit,
But after him did make vntimely haste :
Forth with her ghost out of her corps did flit,
And followed her make like Turtle chaste.
To proue that death their hearts cannot diuide,
Which liuing were in loue so firmly tide.   180

The Gods which all things see, this same beheld,
And pittying this paire of louers trew,
Transformed them there lying on the field,
Into one flowre that is both red and blew.
It first growes red, and then to blew doth fade,
Like *Astrophel*, which thereinto was made.

And in the midst thereof a star appeares,
As fairly formd as any star in skyes :
Resembling *Stella* in her freshest yeares,
Forth darting beames of beautie from her eyes,
And all the day it standeth full of deow, 191
Which is the teares, that from her eyes did flow.

That hearbe of some, Starlight is cald by name,
Of others *Penthia*, though not so well
But thou where euer thou doest finde the same,
From this day forth do call it *Astrophel*.
And when so euer thou it vp doest take,
Do pluck it softly for that shepheards sake.

Hereof when tydings far abroad did passe,
The shepheards all which loued him full deare,
And sure full deare of all he loued was, 201
Did thether flock to see what they did heare.
And when that pitteous spectacle they vewed,
The same with bitter teares they all bedewed.

And euery one did make exceeding mone,
With inward anguish and great griefe opprest :
And euery one did weep and waile, and mone,
And meanes deviz'd to shew his sorrow best.
That from that houre since first on grassie greene
Shepheards kept sheep, was not like mourning seen. 210

But first his sister that *Clorinda* hight,
The gentlest shepheardesse that liues this day :
And most resembling both in shape and spright
Her brother deare, began this dolefull lay.
Which least I marre the sweetnesse of the vearse,
In sort as she it sung, I will rehearse.

A Y me, to whom shall I my case complaine,
That may compassion my impatient griefe ?
Or where shall I enfold my inward paine,
That my enriuen heart may find reliefe ?
Shall I vnto the heauenly powres it show ?
Or vnto earthly men that dwell below ?

To heauens ? ah they alas the authors were,
And workers of my vnremedied wo :
For they foresee what to vs happens here,
And they foresaw, yet suffred this be so. 10
  From them comes good, from them comes also il,
  That which they made, who can them warne to spill.

To men ? ah they alas like wretched bee,
And subiect to the heauens ordinance :
Bound to abide what euer they decree,
Their best redresse, is their best sufferance.
  How then can they, like wretched, comfort mee,
  The which no lesse, need comforted to bee ?

Then to my selfe will I my sorrow mourne,
Sith none aliue like sorrowfull remaines : 20
And to my selfe my plaints shall back retourne,
To pay their vsury with doubled paines.
  The woods, the hills, the riuers shall resound
  The mournfull accent of my sorrowes ground.

Woods, hills and riuers, now are desolate,
Sith he is gone the which them all did grace :
And all the fields do waile their widow state,
Sith death their fairest flowre did late deface.
  The fairest flowre in field that euer grew,
  Was *Astrophel* ; that was, we all may rew,

What cruell hand of cursed foe vnknowne, 31
Hath cropt the stalke which bore so faire a flowre ?
Vntimely cropt, before it well were growne,
And cleane defaced in vntimely howre.
  Great losse to all that euer him did see,
  Great losse to all, but greatest losse to mee.

Breake now your gyrlonds, O ye shepheards lasses,
Sith the faire flowre, which them adornd, is gon :
The flowre, which them adornd, is gone to ashes,
Neuer againe let lasse put gyrlond on. 40
  In stead of gyrlond, weare sad Cypres nowe,
  And bitter Elder, broken from the bowe.

Ne euer sing the loue-layes which he made,
Who euer made such layes of loue as hee ?
Ne euer read the riddles, which he sayd
Vnto your selues, to make you mery glee.
  Your mery glee is now laid all abed,
  Your mery maker now alasse is dead.

Death the deuourer of all worlds delight,
Hath robbed you and reft fro me my ioy : 50
Both you and me, and all the world he quight
Hath robd of ioyance, and left sad annoy.
  Ioy of the world, and shepheards pride was hee,
  Shepheards hope neuer like againe to see.

Oh death that hast vs of such riches reft,
Tell vs at least, what hast thou with it done ?
What is become of him whose flowre here left
Is but the shadow of his likenesse gone.
  Scarse like the shadow of that which he was,
  Nought like, but that he like a shade did pas. 60

But that immortall spirit, which was deckt
With all the dowries of celestiall grace:
By soueraine choyce from th'heuenly quires
 select,
And lineally deriv'd from Angels race,
 O what is now of it become, aread.
  Ay me, can so diuine a thing be dead ?

Ah no : it is not dead, ne can it die,
But liues for aie, in blisfull Paradise :
Where like a new-borne babe it soft doth lie.
In bed of lillies wrapt in tender wise.   70
 And compast all about with roses sweet,
 And daintie violets from head to feet.

There thousand birds all of celestiall brood,
To him do sweetly caroll day and night :
And with straunge notes, of him well vnderstood,
Lull him a sleep in Angelick delight ;
 Whilest in sweet dreame to him presented bee
 Immortall beauties, which no eye may see.

But he them sees and takes exceeding pleasure
Of their diuine aspects, appearing plaine,   80
And kindling loue in him aboue all measure,
Sweet loue still ioyous, neuer feeling paine.
 For what so goodly forme he there doth see,
 He may enioy from iealous rancor free.

There liueth he in euerlasting blis,
Sweet spirit neuer fearing more to die :
Ne dreading harme from any foes of his,
Ne fearing saluage beasts more crueltie.
 Whilest we here wretches waile his priuate lack,
 And with vaine vowes do often call him back.

But liue thou there still happie, happie spirit,
And giue vs leaue thee here thus to lament :
Not thee that doest thy heauens ioy inherit,
But our owne selues that here in dole are drent.
 Thus do we weep and waile, and wear our eies,
 Mourning in others, our owne miseries.

Which when she ended had, another swaine
Of gentle wit and daintie sweet deuice :
Whom *Astrophel* full deare did entertaine,   99
Whilest here he liv'd, and held in passing price,
Hight *Thestylis*, began his mournfull tourne,
And made the *Muses* in his song to mourne.

And after him full many other moe,
As euerie one in order lov'd him best,
Gan dight themselues t'expresse their inward
          woe,
With dolefull layes vnto the time addrest,
The which I here in order will rehearse,
As fittest flowres to deck his mournfull hearse.

The mourning Muse *of* Thestylis.

Come forth ye Nymphes come forth, forsake your watry bowres,
 Forsake your mossy caues, and help me to lament :
Help me to tune my dolefull notes to gurgling sound
Of *Liffies* tumbling streames : Come let salt teares of ours,
Mix with his waters fresh.   O come, let one consent
Ioyne vs to mourne with wailfull plaints the deadly wound
Which fatall clap hath made ; decreed by higher powres.
The dreery day in which they haue from vs yrent
The noblest plant that might from East to West be found.
Mourne, mourne, great *Philips* fall, mourn we his wofull end,   10
Whom spitefull death hath pluct vntimely from the tree,
Whiles yet his yeares in flowre, did promise worthie frute.
 Ah dreadfull *Mars* why didst thou not thy knight defend ?
What wrathfull mood, what fault of ours hath moued thee
Of such a shining light to leaue vs destitute ?
Thou with benigne aspect sometime didst vs behold,
Thou hast in Britons valour tane delight of old,
And with thy presence oft vouchsaft to attribute
Fame and renowme to vs for glorious martiall deeds.
But now thy ireful bemes haue chill'd our harts with cold ;   20
Thou hast estrang'd thy self, and deignest not our land :
Farre off to others now, thy fauour honour breeds,
And high disdaine doth cause thee shun our clime (I feare)
For hadst thou not bene wroth, or that time neare at hand,
Thou wouldst haue heard the cry that woful England made,
Eke *Zelands* piteous plaints, and *Hollands* toren heare

Would haply haue appeas'd thy diuine angry mynd:
Thou shouldst haue seen the trees refuse to yeeld their shade,
And wailing to let fall the honor of their head,
And birds in mournfull tunes lamenting in their kinde: 30
Vp from his tombe the mightie *Corineus* rose,
Who cursing oft the fates that this mishap had bred,
His hoary locks he tare, calling the heauens vnkinde.
The *Thames* was heard to roare, the *Reyne* and eke the *Mose*,
The *Schald*, the *Danow* selfe this great mischance did rue,
With torment and with grief; their fountains pure and cleere
Were troubled, and with swelling flouds declar'd their woes.
The *Muses* comfortles, the Nymphs with paled hue,
The *Siluan* Gods likewise came running farre and neere,
And all with teares bedeawd, and eyes cast vp on hie,   40
O help, O help ye Gods, they ghastly gan to crie.
O chaunge the cruell fate of this so rare a wight,
And graunt that natures course may measure out his age.
The beasts their foode forsooke, and trembling fearfully,
Each sought his caue or den, this cry did them so fright.
Out from amid the waues, by storme then stirr'd to rage
This crie did cause to rise th'old father *Ocean* hoare,
Who graue with eld, and full of maiestie in sight,
Spake in this wise. Refrain (quoth he) your teares and plaints,
Cease these your idle words, make vaine requests no more.   50
No humble speech nor mone, may moue the fixed stint
Of destinie or death: Such is his will that paints
The earth with colours fresh; the darkest skies with store
Of starry lights: And though your teares a hart of flint
Might tender make, yet nought herein they will preuaile.
   Whiles thus he said, the noble knight, who gan to feele
His vitall force to faint, and death with cruell dint
Of direfull dart his mortall bodie to assaile,
With eyes lift vp to heau'n, and courage franke as steele,
With cheerfull face, where valour liuely was exprest,   60
But humble mynd he said. O Lord if ought this fraile
And earthly carcasse haue thy seruice sought t'aduaunce,
If my desire haue bene still to relieue th'opprest:
If Iustice to maintaine that valour I haue spent
Which thou me gau'st; or if henceforth I might aduaunce
Thy name, thy truth, then spare me (Lord) if thou think best;
Forbeare these vnripe yeares. But if thy will be bent,
If that prefixed time be come which thou hast set,
Through pure and feruent faith, I hope now to be plast,
In th'euerlasting blis, which with thy precious blood   70
Thou purchase didst for vs. With that a sigh he fet,
And straight a cloudie mist his sences ouercast,
His lips waxt pale and wan, like damaske roses bud
Cast from the stalke, or like in field to purple flowre,
Which languisheth being shred by culter as it past.
A trembling chilly cold ran throgh their veines, which were
With eies brimfull of teares to see his fatall howre,
Whose blustring sighes at first their sorrow did declare,
Next, murmuring ensude; at last they not forbeare
Plaine outcries, all against the heau'ns that enuiously   80
Depriv'd vs of a spright so perfect and so rare.
The Sun his lightsom beames did shrowd, and hide his face

For griefe, whereby the earth feard night eternally:
The mountaines eachwhere shooke, the riuers turn'd their streames,
And th'aire gan winterlike to rage and fret apace:
And grisly ghosts by night were seene, and fierie gleames,
Amid the clouds with claps of thunder, that did seeme
To rent the skies, and made both man and beast afeard:
The birds of ill presage this lucklesse chance foretold,
By dernfull noise, and dogs with howling made man deeme   90
Some mischief was at hand: for such they do esteeme
As tokens of mishap, and so haue done of old.

   Ah that thou hadst but heard his louely *Stella* plaine
Her greeuous losse, or seene her heauie mourning cheere,
While she with woe opprest, her sorrowes did vnfold.
Her haire hung lose neglect, about her shoulders twaine,
And from those two bright starres, to him sometime so deere,
Her heart sent drops of pearle, which fell in foyson downe
Twixt lilly and the rose.   She wroong her hands with paine,
And piteously gan say, My true and faithfull pheere,   100
Alas and woe is me, why should my fortune frowne
On me thus frowardly to rob me of my ioy?
What cruell enuious hand hath taken thee away,
And with thee my content, my comfort and my stay?
Thou onelie wast the ease of trouble and annoy:
When they did me assaile, in thee my hopes did rest.
Alas what now is left but grief, that night and day
Afflicts this wofull life, and with continuall rage
Torments ten thousand waies my miserable brest?
O greedie enuious heau'n what needed thee to haue   110
Enricht with such a Iewell this vnhappie age,
To take it back againe so soone? Alas when shall
Mine eies see ought that may content them, since thy graue
My onely treasure hides the ioyes of my poore hart?
As here with thee on earth I liv'd, euen so equall
Methinkes it were with thee in heau'n I did abide:
And as our troubles all we here on earth did part,
So reason would that there of thy most happie state
I had my share. Alas if thou my trustie guide
Were wont to be, how canst thou leaue me thus alone   120
In darknesse and astray; weake, wearie, desolate,
Plung'd in a world of woe, refusing for to take
Me with thee, to the place of rest where thou art gone.
This said, she held her peace, for sorrow tide her toong;
And insteed of more words, seemd that her eies a lake
Of teares had bene, they flow'd so plenteously therefro:
And with her sobs and sighs, th'aire round about her roong.

   If *Venus* when she waild her deare *Adonis* slaine,
Ought moov'd in thy fiers hart compassion of her woe,
His noble sisters plaints, her sighes and teares emong,   130
Would sure haue made thee milde, and inly rue her paine:
Aurora halfe so faire, her selfe did neuer show,
When from old *Tithons* bed, shee weeping did arise.
The blinded archer-boy, like larke in showre of raine
Sat bathing of his wings, and glad the time did spend
Vnder those cristall drops, which fell from her faire eies,
And at their brightest beames him proynd in louely wise.
Yet sorie for her grief, which he could not amend,

The gentle boy gan wipe her eies, and clear those lights,
Those lights through which, his glory and his conquests shine. 140
The Graces tuckt her hair, which hung like threds of gold,
Along her yuorie brest the treasure of delights.
All things witn her to weep, it seemed, did encline,
The trees, the hills, the dales, the caues, the stones so cold.
The aire did help them mourne, with dark clouds, raine and mist,
Forbearing many a day to cleare it selfe againe,
Which made them eftsoones feare the daies of *Pirrha* shold,
Of creatures spoile the earth, their fatall threds vntwist.
For *Phœbus* gladsome raies were wished for in vaine,
And with her quiuering light *Latonas* daughter faire, 150
And *Charles-waine* eke refus'd to be the shipmans guide.
On *Neptune* warre was made by *Aeolus* and his traine,
Who letting loose the winds, tost and tormented th'aire,
So that on eu'ry coast men shipwrack did abide,
Or else were swallowed vp in open sea with waues,
And such as came to shoare, were beaten with despaire.
The Medwaies siluer streames, that wont so still to slide,
Were troubled now and wrothe : whose hidden hollow caues
Along his banks with fog then shrowded from mans eye,
Ay *Phillip* did resownd, aie *Phillip* they did crie. 160
His Nimphs were seen no more (thogh custom stil it craues)
With haire spred to the wynd themselues to bath or sport,
Or with the hooke or net, barefooted wantonly
The pleasant daintie fish to entangle or deceiue.
The shepheards left their wonted places of resort,
Their bagpipes now were still ; their louing mery layes
Were quite forgot ; and now their flocks, men might perceiue
To wander and to straie, all carelesly neglect.
And in the stead of mirth and pleasure, nights and dayes,
Nought els was to be heard, but woes, complaints and mone. 170
　But thou (O blessed soule) doest haply not respect,
These teares we shead, though full of louing pure affect,
Hauing affixt thine eyes on that most glorious throne,
Where full of maiestie the high creator reignes.
In whose bright shining face thy ioyes are all complete,
Whose loue kindles thy spright, where happie alwaies one,
Thou liu'st in blis that earthly passion neuer staines ;
Where from the purest spring the sacred *Nectar* sweete
Is thy continuall drinke : where thou doest gather now
Of well emploied life, th'inestimable gaines. 180
There *Venus* on thee smiles, *Apollo* giues thee place,
And *Mars* in reuerent wise doth to thy vertue bow,
And decks his fiery sphere, to do thee honour most.
In highest part whereof, thy valour for to grace,
A chaire of gold he setts to thee, and there doth tell
Thy noble acts arew, whereby euen they that boast
Themselues of auncient fame, as *Pirrhus, Hanniball,*
Scipio and *Cæsar*, with the rest that did excell
In martiall prowesse, high thy glorie do admire.
　Aíl haile therefore O worthie *Phillip* immortall, 190
The flowre of *Sydneyes* race, the honour of thy name,
Whose worthie praise to sing, my *Muses* not aspire,
But sorrowfull and sad these teares to thee let fall,
Yet with their verses might so farre and wide thy fame
Extend, that enuies rage, nor time might end the same.

A pastorall Aeglogue vpon the death of Sir Phillip Sidney Knight, &c.

Lycon.   Colin.

Olin, well fits thy sad cheare this sad
    stownd,
This wofull stownd, wherein all things complaine
This great mishap, this greeuous losse of owres.
Hear'st thou the *Orown?* how with hollow
    sownd
He slides away, and murmuring doth plaine,
And seemes to say vnto the fading flowres,
Along his bankes, vnto the bared trees;
Phillisides is dead. Vp iolly swaine,
Thou that with skill canst tune a dolefull lay,
Help him to mourn. My hart with grief doth
    freese,   10
Hoarse is my voice with crying, else a part
Sure would I beare, though rude: But as I may,
With sobs and sighes I second will thy song,
And so expresse the sorrowes of my hart.
    Colin. Ah *Lycon*, *Lycon*, what need skill, to
        teach
A grieued mynd powre forth his plaints? how
    long
Hath the pore Turtle gon to school (weenest
    thou)
To learne to mourne her lost make? No, no,
    each
Creature by nature can tell how to waile.
Seest not these flocks, how sad they wander
    now?   20
Seemeth their leaders bell their bleating tunes
In dolefull sound. Like him, not one doth faile
With hanging head to shew a heauie cheare.
What bird (I pray thee) hast thou seen, that
    prunes
Himselfe of late? did any cheerfull note
Come to thine eares, or gladsome sight appeare
Vnto thine eies, since that same fatall howre?
Hath not the aire put on his mourning coat,
And testified his grief with flowing teares?
Sith then, it seemeth each thing to his powre
Doth vs inuite to make a sad consort;   31
Come let vs ioyne our mournfull song with
    theirs.
Griefe will endite, and sorrow will enforce
Thy voice, and *Eccho* will our words report.
    Lyc. Though my rude rymes, ill with thy
        verses frame,
That others farre excell, yet will I force
My selfe to answere thee the best I can,
And honor my base words with his high name.

But if my plaints annoy thee where thou sit
In secret shade or cave; vouchsafe (O *Pan*)
To pardon me, and here this hard constraint
With patience while I sing, and pittie it.   42
And eke ye rurall *Muses*, that do dwell
In these wilde woods; If euer piteous plaint
We did endite, or taught a wofull minde
With words of pure affect, his griefe to tell,
Instruct me now. Now *Colin* then goe on,
And I will follow thee, though farre behinde.
    Colin. *Phillisides* is dead. O harmfull death,
O deadly harme. Vnhappie *Albion*   50
When shalt thou see emong thy shepheards all,
Any so sage, so perfect? Whom vneath
Enuie could touch for vertuous life and skill;
Curteous, valiant, and liberall.
Behold the sacred *Pales*, where with haire
Vntrust she sitts, in shade of yonder hill.
And her faire face bent sadly downe, doth send
A floud of teares to bathe the earth; and there
Doth call the heau'ns despightfull, enuious,
Cruell his fate, that made so short an end   60
Of that same life, well worthie to haue bene
Prolongd with many yeares, happie and
    famous.
The Nymphs and *Oreades* her round about
Do sit lamenting on the grassie grene;
And with shrill cries, beating their whitest
    brests,
Accuse the direfull dart that death sent out
To giue the fatall stroke. The starres they
    blame,
That deafe or carelesse seeme at their request.
The pleasant shade of stately groues they shun;
They leaue their cristall springs, where they
    wont frame   70
Sweet bowres of Myrtel twigs and Lawrel faire,
To sport themselues free from the scorching
    Sun.
And now the hollow caues where horror darke
Doth dwell, whence banisht is the gladsome aire
They seeke; and there in mourning spend
    their time
With wailfull tunes, whiles wolues do howle
    and barke,
And seem to beare a bourdon to their plaint.
    Lyc. *Phillisides* is dead. O dolefull ryme.
Why should my toong expresse thee? who is
    left   79
Now to vphold thy hopes, when they do faint,

Lycon vnfortunate? What spitefull fate,
What lucklesse destinie hath thee bereft
Of thy chief comfort; of thy onely stay?
Where is become thy wonted happie state,
(Alas) wherein through many a hill and dale,
Through pleasant woods, and many an vn-
   knowne way,
Along the bankes of many siluer streames,
Thou with him yodest; and with him didst
   scale
The craggie rocks of th'Alpes and *Appenine?*
Still with the *Muses* sporting, while those beames
Of vertue kindled in his noble brest,   91
Which after did so gloriously forth shine?
But (woe is me) they now yquenched are
All suddeinly, and death hath them opprest.
Loe father *Neptune,* with sad countenance,
How he sitts mourning on the strond now bare,
Yonder, where th'Ocean with his rolling waues
The white feete washeth (wailing this mis-
   chance)
Of *Douer* cliffes. His sacred skirt about   99
The sea-gods all are set; from their moist caues
All for his comfort gathered there they be.
The *Thamis* rich, the *Humber* rough and stout,
The fruitfull *Seuerne,* with the rest are come
To helpe their Lord to mourne, and eke to see
The dolefull sight, and sad pomp funerall
Of the dead corps passing through his king-
   dome.
And all their heads with Cypres gyrlonds
   crown'd
With wofull shrikes salute him great and small.
Eke wailfull *Eccho,* forgetting her deare   109
Narcissus, their last accents, doth resownd.
   Col. Phillisides is dead. O lucklesse age;
O widow world; O brookes and fountains cleere;
O hills, O dales, O woods that oft haue rong
With his sweet caroling, which could asswage
The fiercest wrath of Tygre or of Beare.
Ye Siluans, Fawnes, and Satyres, that emong
These thickets oft haue daunst after his pipe,
Ye Nymphs and *Nayades* with golden heare,
That oft haue left your purest cristall springs
To harken to his layes, that coulden wipe   120
Away all griefe and sorrow from your harts.
Alas who now is left that like him sings?
When shall you heare againe like harmonie?
So sweet a sownd, who to you now imparts?
Loe where engraued by his hand yet liues
The name of *Stella,* in yonder bay tree.

Happie name, happie tree; faire may you grow,
And spred your sacred branch, which honor
   giues,
To famous Emperours, and Poets crowne.
Vnhappie flock that wander scattred now, 130
What maruell if through grief ye woxen leane,
Forsake your food, and hang your heads
   adowne?
For such a shepheard neuer shall you guide,
Whose parting, hath of weale bereft you cleane.
   Lyc. Phillisides is dead. O happie sprite,
That now in heau'n with blessed soules doest
   bide:
Looke down a while from where thou sitst
   aboue,
And see how busie shepheards be to endite
Sad songs of grief, their sorrowes to declare,
And gratefull memory of their kynd loue.   140
Behold my selfe with *Colin,* gentle swaine
(Whose lerned *Muse* thou cherisht most why-
   leare)
Where we thy name recording, seeke to ease
The inward torment and tormenting paine,
That thy departure to vs both hath bred;
Ne can each others sorrow yet appease.
Behold the fountains now left desolate,
And withred grasse with cypres boughes be
   spred,
Behold these floures which on thy graue we
   strew;
Which faded, shew the giuers faded state,   150
(Though eke they shew their feruent zeale and
   pure)
Whose onely comfort on thy welfare grew.
Whose praiers importune shall the heau'ns for
   ay,
That to thy ashes, rest they may assure:
That learnedst shepheards honor may thy name
With yeerly praises, and the Nymphs alway
Thy tomb may deck with fresh and sweetest
   flowres;
And that for euer may endure thy fame.
   Colin. The Sun (lo) hastned hath his face to
   steep
In western waues: and th'aire with stormy
   showres   160
Warnes vs to driue homewards our silly sheep,
Lycon, lett's rise, and take of them good keep.

Virtule summa : cætera fortuna.

L. B.

An Elegie, or friends pas-
sion, for his *Astrophill*.

Written vpon the death of the right Honourable sir
Phillip Sidney Knight, Lord gouernour
of Flushing.

AS then, no winde at all there blew,
  No swelling cloude, accloid the aire,
The skie like glasse of watchet hew,
Reflected Phœbus golden haire,
  The garnisht tree, no pendant st.rd,
  No voice was heard of anie bird.

There might you see the burly Beare
The Lion king, the Elephant,
The maiden Vnicorne was the⁻
So was *Acteons* horned plant,   10
  And what of wilde or tame are found,
  Were couckt in order on the ground.

Alcides speckled poplar tree,
The palme that Monarchs do obtaine,
With Loue iuice staind the mulberie,
The fruit that dewes the Poets braine,
  And Phillis philbert there away,
  Comparde with mirtle and the bay.

The tree that coffins doth adorne,
With stately height threatning the skie,   20
And for the bed of Loue forlorne,
The blacke and dolefull Ebonie,
  All in a circle compast were,
  Like to an Amphitheater.

Vpon the branches of those trees,
The airie winged people sat,
Distinguished in od degrees,
One sort in this, another that,
  Here *Philomell*, that knowes full well,
  What force and wit in loue doth dwell.   30

The skiebred Egle roiall bird,
Percht there vpon an oke aboue,
The Turtle by him neuer stird,
Example of immortall loue.
  The swan that sings about to dy,
  Leauing *Meander*, stood thereby.

And that which was of woonder most,
The Phœnix left sweet *Arabie* :
And on a Cædar in this coast,
Built vp her tombe of spicerie,   40
  As I coniecture by the same,
  Preparde to take her dying flame.

In midst and center of this plot,
I saw one groueling on the grasse :
A man or stone, I knew not what.
No stone, of man ;he figure was,
  And yet I could not count him one,
  More than the image made of stone.

At length I might perceiue him reare
His bodie on his elbow end :   50
Earthly and pale with gastly cheare,
Vpon his knees he vpward tend,
  Seeming like one in vncouth stound,
  To be ascending out the ground.

A grieuous sigh forthwith he throwes,
As might haue torne the vitall strings,
Then down his cheeks the teares so flows,
As doth the streame of many springs.
  So thunder rends the cloud in twaine,
  And makes a passage for the raine.   60

Incontinent with trembling sound,
He wofully gan to complaine,
Such were the accents as might wound,
And teare a diamond rocke in twaine.
  After his throbs did somewhat stay,
  Thus heauily he gan to say.

O sunne (said he) seeing the sunne,
On wretched me why dost thou shine,
My star is falne, my comfort done,
Out is the apple of my eine,   70
  Shine vpon those possesse delight,
  And let me liue in endlesse night.

O griefe that liest vpon my soule,
As heauie as a mount of lead,
The remnant of my life controll,
Consort me quickly with the dead,
  Halfe of this hart, this sprite and will,
  Di'de in the brest of *Astrophill*.

And you compassionate of my wo,
Gentle birds, beasts and shadie trees,   80
I am assurde ye long to kno,
What be the sorrowes me agreeu's,
  Listen ye then to that insu'th,
  And heare a tale of teares and ruthe.

You knew, who knew not *Astrophill*,
(That I should liue to say I knew,
And haue not in possession still)
Things knowne permit me to renew,
  Of him you know his merit such,
  I cannot say, you heare too much. 90

Within these woods of *Arcadie*,
He chiefe delight and pleasure tooke,
And on the mountaine *Parthenie*,
Vpon the chrystall liquid brooke,
  The Muses met him eu'ry day,
  That taught him sing, to write, and say.

When he descended downe the mount,
His personage seemed most diuine,
A thousand graces one might count,
Vpon his louely cheerfull eine. 100
  To heare him speake and sweetly smile,
  You were in Paradise the while.

A sweet attractiue kinde of grace,
A full assurance giuen by lookes,
Continuall comfort in a face,
The lineaments of Gospell bookes,
  I trowe that countenance cannot lie,
  Whose thoughts are legible in the eie.

Was neuer eie, did see that face,
Was neuer eare, did heare that tong, 110
Was neuer minde, did minde his grace,
That euer thought the trauell long,
  But eies, and eares, and eu'ry thought,
  Were with his sweete perfections caught.

O God, that such a worthy man,
In whom so rare desarts did raigne,
Desired thus, must leaue vs than,
And we to wish for him in vaine,
  O could the stars that bred that wit,
  In force no longer fixed sit. 120

Then being fild with learned dew,
The Muses willed him to loue,
That instrument can aptly shew,
How finely our conceits will moue,
  As *Bacchus* opes dissembled harts,
  So loue sets out our better parts.

Stella, a Nymph within this wood,
Most rare and rich of heauenly blis,
The highest in his fancie stood,
And she could well demerite this, 130
  Tis likely they acquainted soone,
  He was a Sun, and she a Moone.

Our *Astrophill* did *Stella* loue,
O *Stella* vaunt of *Astrophill*,
Albeit thy graces gods may moue,
Where wilt thou finde an *Astrophill*,
  The rose and lillie haue their prime,
  And so hath beautie but a time.

Although thy beautie do exceed,
In common sight of eu'ry eie, 140
Yet in his Poesies when we reede,
It is apparant more thereby,
  He that hath loue and iudgement too,
  Sees more than any other doo.

Then *Astrophill* hath honord thee,
For when thy bodie is extinct,
Thy graces shall eternall be,
And liue by vertue of his inke,
  For by his verses he doth giue,
  To short liude beautie aye to liue. 150

Aboue all others this is hee,
Which erst approoued in his song,
That loue and honor might agree,
And that pure loue will do no wrong,
  Sweet saints, it is no sinne nor blame,
  To loue a man of vertuous name.

Did neuer loue so sweetly breath
In any mortall brest before,
Did neuer Muse inspire beneath,
A Poets braine with finer store: 160
  He wrote of loue with high conceit,
  And beautie reard aboue her height.

Then *Pallas* afterward attyrde,
Our *Astrophill* with her deuice,
Whom in his armor heauen admyrde,
As of the nation of the skies,
  He sparkled in his armes afarrs,
  As he were dight with fierie starrs.

The blaze whereof when *Mars* beheld,
(An enuious eie doth see afar) 170
Such maiestie (quoth he) is seeld,
Such maiestie my mart may mar,
  Perhaps this may a suter be,
  To set *Mars* by his deitie.

In this surmize he made with speede,
An iron cane wherein he put,
The thunder that in cloudes do breede
The flame and bolt togither shut,
  With priuie force burst out againe,
  And so our *Astrophill* was slaine. 180

This word (was slaine) straightway did moue,
And natures inward life strings twitch,
The skie immediately aboue,
Was dimd with hideous clouds of pitch,
  The wrastling winds from out the ground,
  Fild all the aire with ratling sound.

The bending trees exprest a grone,
And sigh'd the sorrow of his fall,
The forrest beasts made ruthfull mone,
The birds did tune their mourning call, 190
  And *Philomell* for *Astrophill*,
  Vnto her notes annext a phill.

The Turtle doue with tunes of ruthe,
Shewd feeling passion of his death,
Me thought she said I tell thee truthe,
Was neuer he that drew in breath,
  Vnto his loue more trustie found,
  Than he for whom our griefs abound.

The swan that was in presence heere,
Began his funerall dirge to sing,   200
Good things (quoth he) may scarce appeere,
But passe away with speedie wing.
  This mortall life as death is tride,
  And death giues life, and so he di'de.

The generall sorrow that was made,
Among the creatures of kinde,
Fired the Phœnix where she laide,
Her ashes flying with the winde,
  So as I might with reason see,
  That such a Phœnix nere should bee.   210

Haply the cinders driuen about,
May breede an offspring neere that kinde,
But hardly a peere to that I doubt,
It cannot sinke into my minde,
  That vnder branches ere can bee,
  Of worth and value as the tree.

The Egle markt with pearcing sight,
The mournfull habite of the place,
And parted thence with mounting flight,
To signifie to *Ioue* the case,   220
  What sorrow nature doth sustaine,
  For *Astrophill* by enuie slaine.

And while I followed with mine eie,
The flight the Egle vpward tooke,
And things did vanish by and by,
And disappeared from my looke,
  The trees, beasts, birds, and groue was
    gone,
  So was the friend that made this mone.

This spectacle had firmly wrought,
A deepe compassion in my spright,   230
My molting hart issude, me thought,
In streames forth at mine eies aright,
  And here my pen is forst to shrinke,
  My teares discollors so mine inke.

An Epitaph vpon the right Honourable sir Phillip Sidney knight : Lord gouernor of Flushing.

TO praise thy life, or waile thy worthie
    death,
And want thy wit, thy wit high, pure, diuine,
Is far beyond the powre of mortall line,
Nor any one hath worth that draweth breath.

Yet rich in zeale, though poore in learnings lore,
And friendly care obscurde in secret brest,
And loue that enuie in thy life supprest,
Thy deere life done, and death, hath doubled
    more.

And I, that in thy time and liuing state,   9
Did onely praise thy vertues in my thought,
As one that seeld the rising sun hath sought,
With words and teares now waile thy timelesse
    fate.

Drawne was thy race, aright from princely line,
Nor lesse than such, (by gifts that nature gaue,
The common mother that all creatures haue,)
Doth vertue shew and princely linage shine.

A king gaue thee thy name a kingly minde,
That God thee gaue, who found it now too deere
For this base world, and hath resumde it neere,
To sit in skies, and sort with powres diuine. 20

Kent thy birth daies, and Oxford held thy
    youth,
The heauens made hast, and staid nor yeers,
    nor time,
The fruits of age grew ripe in thy first prime,
Thy will, thy words : thy words the seales of
    truth.

Great gifts and wisedom rare imployd thee
    thence,
To treat from kings, with those more great
    than kings,
Such hope men had to lay the highest things,
On thy wise youth, to be transported hence.

Whence to sharpe wars sweet honor did thee
    call,   29
Thy countries loue, religion, and thy friends :
Of worthy men, the marks, the liues and ends,
And her defence, for whom we labor all.

There didst thou vanquish shame and tedious
    age,
Griefe, sorrow, sicknes, and base fortunes might :
Thy rising day, saw neuer wofull night,
But past with praise, from of this worldly stage.

Back to the campe, by thee that day was
  brought,
First thine owne death, and after thy long fame;
Teares to the soldiers, the proud Castilians
  shame ;
Vertue exprest, and honor truly taught.   40

What hath he lost, that such great grace hath
  woon,
Yoong yeeres, for endles yeeres, and hope vnsure
Of fortunes gifts, for wealth that still shall dure,
Oh happie race with so great praises run.

England doth hold thy lims that bred the same,
Flaunders thy valure where it last was tried,
The Campe thy sorrow where thy bodie died,
Thy friends, thy want ; the world, thy vertues
  fame.

Nations thy wit, our mindes lay vp thy loue,
Letters thy learning, thy losse, yeeres long to
  come,   50
In worthy harts sorrow hath made thy tombe,
Thy soule and spright enrich the heauens
  aboue.

Thy liberall hart imbalmd in gratefull teares,
Yoong sighs, sweet sighes, sage sighes, bewaile
  thy fall,
Enuie her sting, and spite hath left her gall,
Malice her selfe, a mourning garment weares.

That day their *Hanniball* died, our *Scipio* fell,
Scipio, *Cicero*, and *Petrarch* of our time,
Whose vertues wounded by my worthlesse
  rime,   59
Let Angels speake, and heauen thy praises tell.

Another of the same.

SIlence augmenteth grief, writing encreaseth
  rage,
Stald are my thoughts, which lou'd, and lost,
  the wonder of our age :
Yet quickned now with fire, though dead with
  frost ere now,
Enrag'd I write, I know not what : dead, quick,
  I know not how.

Hard harted mindes relent, and rigors teares
  abound,
And enuie strangely rues his end, in whom no
  fault she found,
Knowledge her light hath lost, valor hath slaine
  her knight,
Sidney is dead, dead is my friend, dead is the
  worlds delight.

Place pensiue wailes his fall, whose presence
  was her pride,
Time crieth out, my ebbe is come : his life was
  my spring tide,   10
Fame mournes in that she lost the ground of
  her reports,
Ech liuing wight laments his lacke, and all in
  sundry sorts.

He was (wo worth that word) to ech well thinking minde,
A spotlesse friend, a matchles man, whose
  vertue euer shinde,
Declaring in his thoughts, his life, and that he
  writ,
Highest conceits, longest foresights, and deepest
  works of wit.

He onely like himselfe, was second vnto none,
Whose deth (though life) we rue, and wrong,
  and al in vain do mone,
Their losse, not him waile they, that fill the
  world with cries,
Death slue not him, but he made death his
  ladder to the skies.   20

Now sinke of sorrow I, who liue, the more the
  wrong,
Who wishing death, whom deth denies, whose
  thred is al to long,
Who tied to wretched life, who lookes for no
  reliefe,
Must spend my euer dying daies, in neuer ending griefe.

Harts ease and onely I, like parallels run on,
Whose equall length, keep equall bredth, and
  neuer meet in one,
Yet for not wronging him, my thoughts, my
  sorrowes cell,
Shall not run out, though leake they will, for
  liking him so well.

Farewell to you my hopes, my wonted waking
  dreames,
Farewell sometimes enioyed ioy, eclipsed are
  thy beames,   30
Farewell selfe pleasing thoughts, which quietnes brings foorth,
And farewel friendships sacred league, vniting
  minds of woorth.

And farewell mery hart, the gift of guiltlesse
   mindes,
And all sports, which for liues restore, var.etie
   assignes,
Let all that sweete is voyd ; in me no mirth
   may dwell,
Phillip, the cause of all this woe, my liues content, farewell.

Now rime, the sonne of rage, which art no kin
   to skill,
And endles griefe, which deads my life, yet
   knowes not how to kill,
Go seeke that haples tombe, which if ye hap to
   finde,
Salute the stones, that keep the lims, that held
   so good a minde.

FINIS.

LONDON
Printed by T. C. for William Ponsonbie.
1 5 9 5.

AMORETTI
AND
Epithalamion.

Written not long since
by Edmunde
Spenser.

Printed for William
Ponsonby. 1595.

To the Right Worship-
full Sir Robart Need-
ham Knight.

SIr, to gratulate your safe return from Ireland, I had nothing so readie, nor thought any thing so meete, as these sweete conceited Sonets, the deede of that wel deseruing gentleman, maister Edmond Spenser: whose name sufficiently warranting the worthinesse of the work: I do more confidently presume to publish it in his absence, vnder your name to whom (in my poore opinion) the patronage therof, doth in some respectes properly appertaine. For, besides your iudgement and delighte in learned poesie: This gentle Muse for her former perfection long wished for in Englande, nowe at the length crossing the Seas in your happy companye, (though to your selfe vnknowne) seemeth to make choyse of you, as meetest to giue her deserued countenaunce, after her retourne: entertaine her, then, (Right worshipfull) in sorte best beseeming your gentle minde, and her merite, and take in worth my good will herein, who seeke no more, but to shew my selfe yours in all dutifull affection.

W. P.

G: W. senior, to the Author

DArke is the day, when *Phœbus* face is shrowded,
and weaker sights may wander soone astray:
but when they see his glorious raies vn-
clowded,
with steddy steps they keepe the perfect way:
So while this Muse in forraine landes doth stay,
inuention weepes, and pens are cast aside,
the time like night, depriud of chearefull day,
and few do write, but (ah) too soone may slide.
Then, hie thee home, that art our perfect guide,
and with thy wit illustrate Englands fame,
dawnting thereby our neighbors auncient pride,
that do for poesie, challendge cheefest name.
So we that liue and ages that succeede.
With great applause thy learned works shall reede.

Ah Colin, whether on the lowly plaine,
pyping to shepherds thy sweete roundelaies:
or whether singing in some lofty vaine,
heroick deedes, of past, or present daies.
Or whether in thy louely mistris praise,
thou list to exercise thy learned quill,
thy muse hath got such grace, and power to please,
with rare inuention bewtified by skill.
As who therein can euer ioy their fill!
O therefore let that happy muse proceede
to clime the height of vertues sacred hill,
where endles honor shall be made thy meede.
Because no malice of succeeding daies,
can rase those records of thy lasting praise.

G. W. I.

SONNET. I.

HAppy ye leaues when as those lilly hands,
which hold my life in their dead doing might,
shall handle you and hold in loues soft bands,
lyke captiues trembling at the victors sight.
And happy lines, on which with starry light,
those lamping eyes will deigne sometimes to look
and reade the sorrowes of my dying spright,
written with teares in harts close bleeding book.
And happy rymes bath'd in the sacred brooke,
of *Helicon* whence she deriued is,
when ye behold that Angels blessed looke,
my soules long lacked foode, my heauens blis.
Leaues, lines, and rymes, seeke her to please alone,
whom if ye please, I care for other none.

SONNET. II.

VNquiet thought, whom at the first I bred,
Of th'inward bale of my loue pined hart:
and sithens haue with sighes and sorrowes fed,
till greater then my wombe thou woxen art.
Breake forth at length out of the inner part,
in which thou lurkest lyke to vipers brood:
and seeke some succour both to ease my smart
and also to sustayne thy selfe with food.
But if in presence of that fayrest proud
thou chance to come, fall lowly at her feet:
and with meeke humblesse and afflicted mood,
pardon for thee, and grace for me intreat.
Which if she graunt, then liue, and my loue cherish,
if not, die soone, and I with thee will perish.

SONNET. III.

THe souerayne beauty which I doo admyre,
    witnesse the world how worthy to be
        prayzed :
    the light wherof hath kindled heauenly fyre,
    in my fraile spirit by her from basenesse
        raysed.
That being now with her huge brightnesse dazed,
    base thing I can no more endure to view :
    but looking still on her I stand amazed,
    at wondrous sight of so celestiall hew.
So when my toung would speak her praises dew,
    it stopped is with thoughts astonishment :
    and when my pen would write her titles true,
    it rauisht is with fancies wonderment :
Yet in my hart I then both speake and write
    the wonder that my wit cannot endite.

SONNET. IIII.

NEw yeare forth looking out of Ianus gate,
    Doth seeme to promise hope of new delight :
    and bidding th'old Adieu, his passed date
    bids all old thoughts to die in dumpish spright.
And calling forth out of sad Winters night,
    fresh loue, that long hath slept in cheerlesse
        bower :
    wils him awake, and soone about him dight
    his wanton wings and darts of deadly power.
For lusty spring now in his timely howre,
    is ready to come forth him to receiue :
    and warnes the Earth with diuers colord
        flowre,
    to decke hir selfe, and her faire mantle weaue.
Then you faire flowre, in whom fresh youth
        doth raine,
    prepare your selfe new loue to entertaine.

SONNET. V.

RVdely thou wrongest my deare harts desire,
    In finding fault with her too portly pride :
    the thing which I doo most in her admire,
    is of the world vnworthy most enuide.
For in those lofty lookes is close implide,
    scorn of base things, and sdeigne of foule dis-
        honor :
    thretning rash eies which gaze on her so wide,
    that loosely they ne dare to looke vpon her.
Such pride is praise, such portlinesse is honor,
    that boldned innocence beares in hir eies :
    and her faire countenance like a goodly
        banner,
    spreds in defiaunce of all enemies.
Was neuer in this world ought worthy tride,
    without some spark of such self-pleasing
        pride.

SONNET. VI.

BE nought dismayd that her vnmoued mind
    doth still persist in her rebellious pride :
    such loue not lyke to lusts of baser kynd,
    the harder wonne, the firmer will abide.
The durefull Oake, whose sap is not yet dride,
    is long ere it conceiue the kindling fyre :
    but when it once doth burne, it doth diuide,
    great heat, and makes his flames to heauen
        aspire.
So hard it is to kindle new desire,
    in gentle brest that shall endure for euer :
    deepe is the wound, that dints the parts entire
    with chast affects, that naught but death
        can seuer.
Then thinke not long in taking litle paine,
    to knit the knot, that euer shall remaine.

SONNET. VII.

FAyre eyes, the myrrour of my mazed hart,
    what wondrous vertue is contaynd in you,
    the which both lyfe and death forth from you
        dart
    into the obiect of your mighty view ?
For when ye mildly looke with louely hew,
    then is my soule with life and loue inspired
    but when ye lowre, or looke on me askew,
    then doe I die, as one with lightning fyred.
But since that lyfe is more then death desyred,
    looke euer louely, as becomes you best,
    that your bright beams of my weak eies
        admyred,
    may kindle liuing fire within my brest.
Such life should be the honor of your light,
    such death the sad ensample of your might.

SONNET. VIII.

MOre then most faire, full of the liuing fire,
    Kindled aboue vnto the maker neere :
    no eies but ioyes, in which al powers conspire,
    that to the world naught else be counted deare.
Thrugh your bright beames doth not the
        blinded guest,
    shoot out his darts to base affections wound :
    but Angels come to lead fraile mindes to rest
    in chast desires on heauenly beauty bound.
You frame my thoughts and fashion me within,
    you stop my toung, and teach my hart to
        speake,
    you calme the storme that passion did begin,
    strong thrugh your cause, but by your vertue
        weak.
Dark is the world, where your light shined
        neuer ;
    well is he borne, that may behold you euer.

SONNET. IX.

Long-while I sought to what I might compare
those powrefull eies, which lighten my dark
spright,
yet find I nought on earth to which I dare
resemble th'ymage of their goodly light.
Not to the Sun : for they doo shine by night ;
nor to the Moone : for they are changed
neuer ;
nor to the Starres: for they haue purer sight;
nor to the fire : for they consume not euer ;
Nor to the lightning : for they still perseuer ;
nor to the Diamond : for they are more
tender ;
nor vnto Christall : for nought may them
seuer ;
nor vnto glasse : such basenesse mought
offend her ;
Then to the Maker selfe they likest be,
whose light doth lighten all that here we see.

SONNET. X.

VNrighteous Lord of loue, what law is this,
That me thou makest thus tormented be :
the whiles she lordeth in licentious blisse
of her freewill, scorning both thee and me.
See how the Tyrannesse doth ioy to see
the huge massacres which her eyes do make :
and humbled harts brings captiues vnto thee,
that thou of them mayst mightie vengeance
take.
But her proud hart doe thou a little shake
and that high look, with which she doth
comptroll
all this worlds pride, bow to a baser make,
and al her faults in thy black booke enroll.
That I may laugh at her in equall sort,
as she doth laugh at me and makes my pain
her sport.

SONNET. XI.

DAyly when I do seeke and sew for peace,
And hostages doe offer for my truth :
she cruell warriour doth her selfe addresse
to battell, and the weary war renew'th.
Ne wilbe moou'd with reason or with rewth,
to graunt small respit to my restlesse toile :
but greedily her fell intent poursewth,
Of my poore life to make vnpittied spoile.
Yet my poore life, all sorrowes to assoyle,
I would her yield, her wrath to pacify :
but then she seekes with torment and turmoyle,
to force me liue, and will not let me dy.
All paine hath end and euery war hath peace,
but mine no price nor prayer may surcease.

SONNET. XII.

ONe day I sought with her hart-thrilling eies
to make a truce, and termes to entertaine :
all fearelesse then of so false enimies,
which sought me to entrap in treasons traine.
So as I then disarmed did remaine,
a wicked ambush which lay hidden long
in the close couert of her guilefull eyen,
thence breaking forth did thick about me
throng.
Too feeble I t'abide the brunt so strong,
was forst to yeeld my selfe into their hands :
who me captiuing streight with rigorous
wrong,
haue euer since me kept in cruell bands.
So Ladie, now to you I doo complaine,
against your eies that iustice I may gaine.

SONNET. XIII.

IN that proud port, which her so goodly
graceth,
whiles her faire face she reares vp to the skie :
and to the ground her eie lids low embaseth,
most goodly temperature ye may descry.
Myld humblesse mixt with awfull maiesty.
For looking on the earth whence she was borne,
her minde remembreth her mortalitie,
what so is fayrest shall to earth returne.
But that same lofty countenance seemes to
scorne
base thing, and thinke how she to heauen
may clime :
treading downe earth as lothsome and forlorne,
that hinders heauenly thoughts with drossy
slime.
Yet lowly still vouchsafe to looke on me,
such lowlinesse shall make you lofty be.

SONNET. XIIII.

REtourne agayne my forces late dismayd,
Vnto the siege by you abandon'd quite,
great shame it is to leaue like one afrayd,
so fayre a peece for one repulse so light.
Gaynst such strong castles needeth greater
might,
then those small forts which ye were wont
belay :
such haughty mynds enur'd to hardy fight,
disdayne to yield vnto the first assay.
Bring therefore all the forces that ye may,
and lay incessant battery to her heart,
playnts, prayers, vowes, ruth, sorrow, and
dismay,
those engins can the proudest loue conuert.
And if those fayle, fall downe and dy before her,
so dying liue, and liuing do adore her.

SONNET. XV.

YE tradefull Merchants, that with weary
toyle,
  do seeke most pretious things to make your
  gain ;
  and both the Indias of their treasures spoile,
  what needeth you to seeke so farre in vaine ?
For loe my loue doth in her selfe containe
  all this worlds riches that may farre be found,
  if Saphyres, loe her eies be Saphyres plaine,
  if Rubies, loe hir lips be Rubies sound :
If Pearles, hir teeth be pearles both pure and
  round ;
  if Yuorie, her forhead yuory weene ;
  if Gold, her locks are finest gold on ground ;
  if siluer, her faire hands are siluer sheene.
But that which fairest is, but few behold,
  her mind adornd with vertues manifold.

SONNET. XVI.

ONe day as I vnwarily did gaze
  on those fayre eyes my loues immortall
  light :
  the whiles my stonisht hart stood in amaze,
  through sweet illusion of her lookes delight.
I mote perceiue how in her glauncing sight,
  legions of loues with little wings did fly :
  darting their deadly arrowes fyry bright,
  at euery rash beholder passing by.
One of those archers closely I did spy,
  ayming his arrow at my very hart :
  when suddenly with twincle of her eye,
  the Damzell broke his misintended dart.
Had she not so doon, sure I had bene slayne,
  yet as it was, I hardly scap't with paine.

SONNET. XVII.

THe glorious pourtraict of that Angels face,
  Made to amaze weake mens confused skil :
  and this worlds worthlesse glory to embase,
  what pen, what pencill can expresse her fill ?
For though he colours could deuize at will,
  and eke his learned hand at pleasure guide,
  least trembling it his workmanship should
  spill,
  yet many wondrous things there are beside.
The sweet eye-glaunces, that like arrowes glide,
  the charming smiles, that rob sence from the
  hart :
  the louely pleasance and the lofty pride,
  cannot expressed be by any art.
A greater craftesmans hand thereto doth neede,
  that can expresse the life of things indeed.

SONNET. XVIII.

THe rolling wheele that runneth often round,
  The hardest steele in tract of time doth
  teare :
  and drizling drops that often doe redound,
  the firmest flint doth in continuance weare.
Yet cannot I, with many a dropping teare,
  and long intreaty, soften her hard hart :
  that she will once vouchsafe my plaint to heare,
  or looke with pitty on my payneful smart.
But when I pleade, she bids me play my part,
  and when I weep, she sayes teares are but
  water :
  and when I sigh, she sayes I know the art,
  and when I waile she turnes hir selfe to
  laughter.
So doe I weepe, and wayle, and pleade in vaine,
  whiles she as steele and flint doth still remayne.

SONNET. XIX.

THe merry Cuckow, messenger of Spring,
  His trompet shrill hath thrise already
  sounded :
  that warnes al louers wayt vpon their king,
  who now is comming forth with girland
  crouned.
With noyse whereof the quyre of Byrds resounded
  their anthemes sweet deuized of loues prayse,
  that all the woods theyr ecchoes back re-
  bounded,
  as if they knew the meaning of their layes.
But mongst them all, which did Loues honor rayse
  no word was heard of her that most it ought,
  but she his precept proudly disobayes,
  and doth his ydle message set at nought.
Therefore O loue, vnlesse she turne to thee
  ere Cuckow end, let her a rebell be.

SONNET. XX.

IN vaine I seeke and sew to her for grace,
  and doe myne humbled hart before her poure
  the whiles her foot she in my necke doth place,
  and tread my life downe in the lowly floure.
And yet the Lyon that is Lord of power,
  and reigneth ouer euery beast in field,
  in his most pride disdeigneth to deuoure
  the silly lambe that to his might doth yield.
But she more cruell and more saluage wylde,
  then either Lyon or the Lyonesse :
  shames not to be with guiltlesse bloud defylde,
  but taketh glory in her cruelnesse.
Fayrer then fayrest, let none euer say,
  that ye were blooded in a yeelded pray.

SONNET. XXI.

WAs it the worke of nature or of Art,
  which tempred so the feature of her face,
that pride and meeknesse mixt by equall part,
doe both appeare t'adorne her beauties grace?
For with mild pleasance, which doth pride
    displace,
  she to her loue doth lookers eyes allure:
  and with sterne countenance back again doth
    chace
  their looser lookes that stir vp lustes impure.
With such strange termes her eyes she doth
    inure,
  that with one looke she doth my life dismay:
  and with another doth it streight recure,
  her smile me drawes, her frowne me driues
    away.
Thus doth she traine and teach me with her
    lookes,
  such art of eyes I neuer read in bookes.

SONNET. XXII.

THis holy season fit to fast and pray,
  Men to deuotion ought to be inclynd:
therefore, I lykewise on so holy day,
  for my sweet Saynt some seruice fit will find.
Her temple fayre is built within my mind,
  in which her glorious ymage placed is,
  on which my thoughts doo day and night
    attend
  lyke sacred priests that neuer thinke amisse.
There I to her as th'author of my blisse,
  will builde an altar to appease her yre:
  and on the same my hart will sacrifise,
  burning in flames of pure and chast desyre:
The which vouchsafe O goddesse to accept,
  amongst thy deerest relicks to be kept.

SONNET. XXIII.

PEnelope for her Vlisses sake,
  Deuiz'd a Web her wooers to deceaue:
in which the worke that she all day did make
  the same at night she did againe vnreaue.
Such subtile craft my Damzell doth conceaue,
  th'importune suit of my desire to shonne:
  for all that I in many dayes doo weaue,
  in one short houre I find by her vndonne.
So when I thinke to end that I begonne,
  I must begin and neuer bring to end:
  for with one looke she spils that long I sponne,
  and with one word my whole yeares work
    doth rend.
Such labour like the Spyders web I fynd,
  whose fruitlesse worke is broken with least
    wynd.

SONNET. XXIIII.

WHen I behold that beauties wonderment,
  And rare perfection of each goodly part:
of natures skill the onely complement,
  I honor and admire the makers art.
But when I feele the bitter balefull smart,
  which her fayre eyes vnwares doe worke in
    mee:
  that death out of theyr shiny beames doe
    dart,
  I thinke that I a new Pandora see;
Whom all the Gods in councell did agree,
  into this sinfull world from heauen to send:
  that she to wicked men a scourge should bee,
  for all their faults with which they did offend.
But since ye are my scourge I will intreat,
  that for my faults ye will me gently beat.

SONNET. XXV.

HOw long shall this lyke dying lyfe endure,
  And know no end of her owne mysery:
but wast and weare away in termes vnsure,
  twixt feare and hope depending doubtfully.
Yet better were attonce to let me die,
  and shew the last ensample of your pride:
  then to torment me thus with cruelty,
  to proue your powre, which I too wel haue
    tride.
But yet if in your hardned brest ye hide,
  a close intent at last to shew me grace:
  then all the woes and wrecks which I abide,
  as meanes of blisse I gladly wil embrace.
And wish that more and greater they might be,
  that greater meede at last may turne to mee.

SONNET. XXVI.

SWeet is the Rose, but growes vpon a brere;
  Sweet is the Iunipere, but sharpe his bough;
  sweet is the Eglantine, but pricketh nere;
  sweet is the firbloome, but his braunches
    rough.
Sweet is the Cypresse, but his rynd is tough,
  sweet is the nut, but bitter is his pill;
  sweet is the broome-flowre, but yet sowre
    enough;
  and sweet is Moly, but his root is ill.
So euery sweet with soure is tempred still,
  that maketh it be coueted the more:
  for easie things that may be got at will,
  most sorts of men doe set but little store.
Why then should I accoumpt of little paine,
  that endlesse pleasure shall vnto me gaine.

SONNET. XXVII.

FAire proud now tell me why should faire be
proud,
   Sith all worlds glorie is but drosse vncleane :
   and in the shade of death it selfe shall shroud,
   how euer now thereof ye little weene.
That goodly Idoll now so gay beseene,
   shall doffe her fleshes borowd fayre attyre :
   and be forgot as it had neuer beene,
   that many now much worship and admire.
Ne any then shall after it inquire,
   ne any mention shall thereof remaine :
   but what this verse, that neuer shall expyre,
   shall to you purchas with her thankles paine.
Faire be no lenger proud of that shall perish,
   but that which shal you make immortall,
   cherish.

SONNET. XXVIII.

THe laurell leafe, which you this day doe
weare,
   giues me great hope of your relenting mynd :
   for since it is the badg which I doe beare,
   ye bearing it doe seeme to me inclind :
The powre thereof, which ofte in me I find,
   let it lykewise your gentle brest inspire
   with sweet infusion, and put you in mind
   of that proud mayd, whom now those leaues
   attyre :
Proud *Daphne* scorning Phæbus louely fyre,
   on the Thessalian shore from him did flie :
   for which the gods in theyr reuengefull yre
   did her transforme into a laurell tree.
Then fly no more fayre loue from Phebus chace,
   but in your brest his leafe and loue embrace.

SONNET. XXIX.

SEe how the stubborne damzell doth depraue
  my simple meaning with disdaynfull scorne :
   and by the bay which I vnto her gaue,
   accoumpts my selfe her captiue quite forlorne.
The bay (quoth she) is of the victours borne,
   yielded them by the vanquisht as theyr meeds,
   and they therewith doe poetes heads adorne,
   to sing the glory of their famous deedes.
But sith she will the conquest challeng needs,
   let her accept me as her faithfull thrall,
   that her great triumph which my skill exceeds,
   I may in trump of fame blaze ouer all.
Then would I decke her head with glorious
bayes,
   and fill the world with her victorious prayse.

SONNET. XXX.

MY loue is lyke to yse, and I to fyre ;
  how comes it then that this her cold so
   great
   is not dissolu'd through my so hot desyre,
   but harder growes the more I her intreat ?
Or how comes it that my exceeding heat
   is not delayd by her hart frosen cold :
   but that I burne much more in boyling sweat,
   and feele my flames augmented manifold ?
What more miraculous thing may be told
   that fire which all thing melts, should harden
   yse :
   and yse which is congeald with sencelesse cold
   should kindle fyre by wonderfull deuyse ?
Such is the powre of loue in gentle mind,
   that it can alter all the course of kynd.

SONNET. XXXI.

AH why hath nature to so hard a hart
  giuen so goodly giftes of beauties grace ?
   whose pryde depraues each other better part,
   and all those pretious ornaments deface.
Sith to all other beastes of bloody race,
   a dreadfull countenaunce she giuen hath :
   that with theyr terrour al the rest may chace,
   and warne to shun the daunger of theyr
   wrath.
But my proud one doth worke the greater scath,
   through sweet allurement of her louely hew :
   that she the better may in bloody bath
   of such poore thralls her cruell hands embrew.
But did she know how ill these two accord,
   such cruelty she would haue soone abhord.

SONNET. XXXII.

THe paynefull smith with force of feruent
heat,
   the hardest yron soone doth mollify :
   that with his heauy sledge he can it beat,
   and fashion to what he it list apply.
Yet cannot all these flames in which I fry,
   her hart more harde then yron soft awhit :
   ne all the playnts and prayers with which I
   doe beat on th'anduyle of her stubberne wit :
But still the more she feruent sees my fit,
   the more she frieseth in her wilfull pryde :
   and harder growes the harder she is smit,
   with all the playnts which to her be applyde.
What then remaines but I to ashes burne,
   and she to stones at length all frosen turne ?

SONNET. XXXIII.

Great wrong I doe, I can it not deny,
 to that most sacred Empresse my dear
  dred,
not finishing her Queene of faëry,
 that mote enlarge her liuing prayses dead:
But lodwick, this of grace to me aread:
 doe ye not thinck th'accomplishment of it,
 sufficient worke for one mans simple head,
 all were it as the rest but rudely writ.
How then should I without another wit,
 thinck euer to endure so tædious toyle,
 sins that this one is tost with troublous fit,
 of a proud loue, that doth my spirite spoyle.
Ceasse then, till she vouchsafe to grawnt me rest,
 or lend you me another liuing brest.

SONNET. XXXIIII.

Lyke as a ship that through the Ocean wyde,
 by conduct of some star doth make her way,
 whenas a storme hath dimd her trusty guyde,
 out of her course doth wander far astray.
So I whose star, that wont with her bright ray,
 me to direct, with cloudes is ouercast,
 doe wander now in darknesse and dismay,
 through hidden perils round about me plast.
Yet hope I well, that when this storme is past
 my *Helice* the lodestar of my lyfe
 will shine again, and looke on me at last,
 with louely light to cleare my cloudy grief.
Till then I wander carefull comfortlesse,
 in secret sorow and sad pensiuenesse.

SONNET. XXXV.

My hungry eyes through greedy couetize,
 still to behold the obiect of their paine,
 with no contentment can themselues suffize:
 but hauing pine and hauing not complaine.
For lacking it they cannot lyfe sustayne,
 and hauing it they gaze on it the more:
 in their amazement lyke *Narcissus* vaine
 whose eyes him staru'd: so plenty makes me
  poore.
Yet are mine eyes so filled with the store
 of that faire sight, that nothing else they
  brooke,
 but lothe the things which they did like
  before,
 and can no more endure on them to looke.
Ail this worlds glory seemeth vayne to me,
 and all their showes but shadowes, sauing she.

SONNET. XXXVI.

Tell me when shall these wearie woes haue
 end,
 Or shall their ruthlesse torment neuer cease:
 but al my dayes in pining languor spend,
 without hope of aswagement or release.
Is there no meanes for me to purchace peace,
 or make agreement with her thrilling eyes:
 but that their cruelty doth still increace,
 and dayly more augment my miseryes.
But when ye haue shewed all extremityes,
 then thinke how litle glory ye haue gayned:
 by slaying him, whose lyfe though ye despyse,
 mote haue your life in honour long main-
  tayned.
But by his death which some perhaps will mone,
 ye shall condemned be of many a one.

SONNET. XXXVII.

What guyle is this, that those her golden
 tresses,
 She doth attyre vnder a net of gold:
 and with sly skill so cunningly them dresses,
 that which is gold or heare, may scarse be
  told?
Is it that mens frayle eyes, which gaze too bold,
 she may entangle in that golden snare:
 and being caught may craftily enfold,
 theyr weaker harts, which are not wel aware?
Take heed therefore, myne eyes, how ye doe
 stare
 henceforth too rashly on that guilefull net,
 in which if euer ye entrapped are,
 out of her bands ye by no meanes shall get.
Fondnesse it were for any being free,
 to couet fetters, though they golden bee.

SONNET. XXXVIII.

Arion, when through tempests cruel wracke,
 He forth was thrown into the greedy seas:
 through the sweet musick which his harp did
  make
allu'rd a Dolphin him from death to ease.
But my rude musick, which was wont to please
 some dainty eares, cannot with any skill,
 the dreadfull tempest of her wrath appease,
 nor moue the Dolphin from her stubborne will.
But in her pride she dooth perseuer still,
 all carelesse how my life for her decayse:
 yet with one word she can it saue or spill,
 to spill were pitty, but to saue were prayse.
Chose rather to be praysd for dooing good,
 then to be blam'd for spilling guiltlesse blood.

SONNET. XXXIX.

SWeet smile, the daughter of the Queene of
loue,
  Expressing all thy mothers powrefull art:
  with which she wonts to temper angry Ioue,
  when all the gods he threats with thundring
    dart.
Sweet is thy vertue as thy selfe sweet art,
  for when on me thou shinedst late in sadnesse,
  a melting pleasance ran through euery part,
  and me reuiued with hart robbing gladnesse.
Whylest rapt with ioy resembling heauenly
    madnes,
  my soule was rauisht quite as in a traunce:
  and feeling thence no more her sorowes sad-
    nesse,
  fed on the fulnesse of that chearefull glaunce,
More sweet than Nectar or Ambrosiall meat,
  seemd euery bit, which thenceforth I did eat.

SONNET. XL.

MArk when she smiles with amiable cheare,
  And tell me whereto can ye lyken it:
  when on each eyelid sweetly doe appeare
  an hundred Graces as in shade to sit.
Lykest it seemeth in my simple wit
  vnto the fayre sunshine in somers day:
  that when a dreadfull storme away is flit,
  thrugh the broad world doth spred his goodly
    ray:
At sight whereof each bird that sits on spray,
  and euery beast that to his den was fled
  comes forth afresh out of their late dismay,
  and to the light lift vp theyr drouping hed.
So my storme beaten hart likewise is cheared,
  with that sunshine when cloudy looks are
    cleared.

SONNET. XLI.

IS it her nature or is it her will,
  to be so cruell to an humbled foe?
  if nature, then she may it mend with skill,
  if will, then she at will may will forgoe.
But if her nature and her wil be so,
  that she will plague the man that loues her
    most:
  and take delight t'encrease a wretches woe,
  then all her natures goodly guifts are lost.
And that same glorious beauties ydle boast,
  is but a bayt such wretches to beguile:
  as being long in her loues tempest tost,
  she meanes at last to make her piteous spoyle.
O fayrest fayre let neuer it be named,
  that so fayre beauty was so fowly shamed.

SONNET. XLII.

THe loue which me so cruelly tormenteth,
  So pleasing is in my extreamest paine:
  that all the more my sorrow it augmenteth,
  the more I loue and doe embrace my bane.
Ne doe I wish (for wishing were but vaine)
  to be acquit fro my continuall smart:
  but ioy her thrall for euer to remayne,
  and yield for pledge my poore captyued hart;
The which that it from her may neuer start,
  let her, yf please her, bynd with adamant
    chayne:
  and from all wandring loues which mote
    peruart,
  his safe assurance strongly it restrayne.
Onely let her abstaine from cruelty,
  and doe me not before my time to dy.

SONNET. XLIII.

SHall I then silent be or shall I speake?
  And if I speake, her wrath renew I shall:
  and if I silent be, my hart will breake,
  or choked be with ouerflowing gall.
What tyranny is this both my hart to thrall,
  and eke my toung with proud restraint to tie?
  that nether I may speake nor thinke at all,
  but like a stupid stock in silence die.
Yet I my hart with silence secretly
  will teach to speak, and my iust cause to
    plead:
  and eke mine eies with meeke humility,
  loue learned letters to her eyes to read.
Which her deep wit, that true harts thought
    can spel,
  will soone conceiue, and learne to construe
    well.

SONNET. XLIIII.

WHen those renoumed noble Peres of
  Greece,
  thrugh stubborn pride amongst themselues
    did iar
  forgetfull of the famous golden fleece,
  then Orpheus with his harp theyr strife did bar.
But this continuall cruell ciuill warre,
  the which my selfe against my selfe doe make:
  whilest my weak powres of passions warreid
    arre,
  no skill can stint nor reason can aslake.
But when in hand my tunelesse harp I take,
  then doe I more augment my foes despight:
  and griefe renew, and passions doe awake
  to battaile, fresh against my selfe to fight.
Mongst whome the more I seeke to settle peace,
  the more I fynd their malice to increace.

SONNET. XLV.

LEaue lady in your glasse of christall clene,
  Your goodly selfe for euermore to vew:
and in my selfe, my inward selfe I meane,
most liuely lyke behold your semblant trew.
Within my hart, though hardly it can shew
  thing so diuine to vew of earthly eye,
  the fayre Idea of your celestiall hew,
  and euery part remaines immortally:
And were it not that through your cruelty,
  with sorrow dimmed and deformd it were:
  the goodly ymage of your visnomy,
  clearer then christall would therein appere.
But if your selfe in me ye playne will see,
  remoue the cause by which your fayre
    beames darkned be.

SONNET. XLVI.

WHen my abodes prefixed time is spent,
  My cruell fayre streight bids me wend
    my way:
but then from heauen most hideous stormes
    are sent
as willing me against her will to stay.
Whom then shall I or heauen or her obay?
  the heauens know best what is the best for me:
  but as she will, whose will my life doth sway,
  my lower heauen, so it perforce must be.
But ye high heuens, that all this sorowe see,
  sith all your tempests cannot hold me backe:
  aswage your stormes, or else both you and she,
  will both together me too sorely wrack.
Enough it is for one man to sustaine
  the stormes, which she alone on me doth
    raine.

SONNET. XLVII.

TRust not the treason of those smyling
    lookes,
  vntill ye haue theyr guylefull traynes well
    tryde:
  for they are lyke but vnto golden hookes,
  that from the foolish fish theyr bayts doe hyde:
So she with flattring smyles weake harts doth
    guyde
  vnto her loue, and tempte to theyr decay,
  whome being caught she kills with cruell pryde,
  and feeds at pleasure on the wretched pray:
Yet euen whylst her bloody hands them slay,
  her eyes looke louely and vpon them smyle:
  that they take pleasure in her cruell play,
  and dying doe them selues of payne beguyle.
O mighty charm which makes men loue theyr
    bane,
  and thinck they dy with pleasure, liue with
    payne.

SONNET. XLVIII.

INnocent paper, whom too cruell hand
  Did make the matter to auenge her yre:
and ere she could thy cause wel vnderstand,
did sacrifize vnto the greedy fyre.
Well worthy thou to haue found better hyre,
  then so bad end for hereticks ordayned:
  yet heresy nor treason didst conspire,
  but plead thy maisters cause vniustly payned.
Whom she all carelesse of his griefe constrayned
  to vtter forth the anguish of his hart:
  and would not heare, when he to her com-
    playned,
  the piteous passion of his dying smart.
Yet liue for ever, though against her will,
  and speake her good, though she requite
    it ill.

SONNET. XLIX.

FAyre cruell, why are ye so fierce and cruell?
  Is it because your eyes haue powre to kill?
then know, that mercy is the mighties iewell,
and greater glory thinke to saue, then spill.
But if it be your pleasure and proud will,
  to shew the powre of your imperious eyes:
  then not on him that neuer thought you ill,
  but bend your force against your enemyes.
Let them feele th'utmost of your crueltyes,
  and kill with looks, as Cockatrices doo:
  but him that at your footstoole humbled
    lies,
  with mercifull regard, giue mercy too.
Such mercy shal you make admyred to be,
  so shall you liue by giuing life to me.

SONNET. L.

LOng languishing in double malady,
  of my harts wound and of my bodies griefe,
there came to me a leach that would apply
fit medicines for my bodies best reliefe.
Vayne man (quod I) that hast but little priefe
  in deep discouery of the mynds disease,
  is not the hart of all the body chiefe?
  and rules the members as it selfe doth please.
Then with some cordialls seeke first to appease
  the inward languour of my wounded hart,
  and then my body shall haue shortly ease:
  but such sweet cordialls passe Physitions
    art,
Then my lyfes Leach doe you your skill reueale,
  and with one salue both hart and body heale.

SONNET. LI.

DOe I not see that fayrest ymages
  Of hardest Marble are of purpose made?
for that they should endure through many
  ages,
ne let theyr famous moniments to fade.
Why then doe I, vntrainde in louers trade,
  her hardnes blame which I should more com-
    mend?
sith neuer ought was excellent assayde,
  which was not hard t'atchiue and bring to
    end.
Ne ought so hard, but he that would attend,
  mote soften it and to his will allure:
so doe I hope her stubborne hart to bend,
  and that it then more stedfast will endure.
Onely my paines wil be the more to get her,
  but hauing her, my ioy wil be the greater.

SONNET. LII.

SO oft as homeward I from her depart,
  I goe lyke one that hauing lost the field,
is prisoner led away with heauy hart,
  despoyld of warlike armes and knowen shield.
So doe I now my selfe a prisoner yeeld,
  to sorrow and to solitary paine:
from presence of my dearest deare exylde,
  longwhile alone in languor to remaine.
There let no thought of ioy or pleasure vaine,
  dare to approch, that may my solace breed:
but sudden dumps and drery sad disdayne,
  of all worlds gladnesse more my torment feed.
So I her absens will my penaunce make,
  that of her presens I my meed may take.

SONNET. LIII.

THe Panther knowing that his spotted hyde
  Doth please all beasts, but that his looks
    them fray,
within a bush his dreadfull head doth hide,
  to let them gaze whylest he on them may
    pray.
Right so my cruell fayre with me doth play,
  for with the goodly semblant of her hew
she doth allure me to mine owne decay,
  and then no mercy will vnto me shew.
Great shame it is, thing so diuine in view,
  made for to be the worlds most ornament,
to make the bayte her gazers to embrew,
  good shames to be to ill an instrument.
But mercy doth with beautie best agree,
  as in theyr maker ye them best may see.

SONNET. LIIII.

OF this worlds Theatre in which we stay,
  My loue lyke the Spectator ydly sits
beholding me that all the pageants play,
  disguysing diuersly my troub!ed wits.
Sometimes I ioy when glad occasion fits,
  and mask in myrth lyke to a Comedy:
soone after when my ioy to sorrow flits,
  I waile and make my woes a Tragedy.
Yet she beholding me with constant eye,
  delights not in my merth nor rues my smart:
but when I laugh she mocks, and when
    I cry
she laughes, and hardens euermore her hart.
What then can moue her? if nor merth nor
    mone,
  she is no woman, but a sencelesse stone.

SONNET. LV.

SO oft as I her beauty doe behold,
  And therewith doe her cruelty compare,
I maruaile of what substance was the mould
  the which her made attonce so cruell faire.
Not earth; for her high thoghts more heauenly
    are,
not water; for her loue doth burne like fyre:
not ayre; for she is not so light or rare,
  not fyre; for she doth friese with faint desire.
Then needs another Element inquire
  whereof she mote be made; that is the skye.
for to the heauen her haughty lookes aspire:
  and eke her mind is pure immortall hye.
Then sith to heauen ye lykened are the best,
  be lyke in mercy as in all the rest:

SONNET. LVI.

FAyre ye be sure, but cruell and vnkind,
  As is a Tygre that with greedinesse
hunts after bloud, when he by chance doth
    find
a feeble beast, doth felly him oppresse.
Fayre be ye sure, but proud and pittilesse,
  as is a storme, that all things doth prostrate:
finding a tree alone all comfortlesse,
  beats on it strongly it to ruinate.
Fayre be ye sure, but hard and obstinate,
  as is a rocke amidst the raging floods:
gaynst which a ship of succour desolate,
  doth suffer wreck both of her selfe and goods.
That ship, that tree, and that same beast
    am I,
  whom ye doe wreck, doe ruine, and destroy.

SONNET. LVII.

SWeet warriour when shall I haue peace
　　with you?
High time it is, this warre now ended were:
　which I no lenger can endure to sue,
　ne your incessant battry more to beare:
So weake my powres, so sore my wounds
　　appeare,
　that wonder is how I should liue a iot,
　seeing my hart through launched euery where
　with thousand arrowes, which your eies haue
　　shot:
Yet shoot ye sharpely still, and spare me not,
　but glory thinke to make these cruel stoures.
　ye cruell one, what glory can be got,
　in slaying him that would liue gladly yours?
Make peace therefore, and graunt me timely grace.
　that al my wounds wil heale in little space.

SONNET. LVIII.

By her that is most assured to her selfe.

WEake is th'assurance that weake flesh
　　reposeth
In her owne powre, and scorneth others ayde:
　that soonest fals when as she most supposeth
　her selfe assurd, and is of nought affrayd.
All flesh is frayle, and all her strength vnstayd,
　like a vaine bubble blowen vp with ayre:
　deuouring tyme and changeful chance haue
　　prayd
　her glories pride that none may it repayre.
Ne none so rich or wise, so strong or fayre,
　but fayleth trusting on his owne assurance:
　and he that standeth on the hyghest stayre
　fals lowest: for on earth nought hath endur-
　　aunce.
Why then doe ye proud fayre, misdeeme so farre,
　that to your selfe ye most assured arre.

SONNET. LIX.

THrise happie she, that is so well assured
　Vnto her selfe and setled so in hart:
　that nether will for better be allured,
　ne feard with worse to any chaunce to start:
But like a steddy ship doth strongly part
　the raging waues and keepes her course
　　aright:
　ne ought for tempest doth from it depart,
　ne ought for fayrer weathers false delight.
Such selfe assurance need not feare the spight
　of grudging foes, ne fauour seek of friends:
　but in the stay of her owne stedfast might,
　nether to one her selfe nor other bends.
Most happy she that most assured doth rest,
　but he most happy who such one loues best.

SONNET. LX.

THey that in course of heauenly spheares
　are skild,
To euery planet point his sundry yeare:
　in which her circles voyage is fulfild,
　as Mars in three score yeares doth run his
　　spheare.
So since the winged God his planet cleare,
　began in me to moue, one yeare is spent:
　the which doth longer vnto me appeare,
　then al those fourty which my life outwent.
Then by that count, which louers books inuent,
　the spheare of Cupid fourty yeares containes:
　which I haue wasted in long languishment,
　that seemd the longer for my greater paines.
But let my loues fayre Planet short her wayes
　this yeare ensuing, or else short my dayes.

SONNET. LXI.

THe glorious image of the makers beautie,
　My souerayne saynt, the Idoll of my
　　thought,
　dare not henceforth aboue the bounds of
　　dewtie,
　t'accuse of pride, or rashly blame for ought.
For being as she is diuinely wrought,
　and of the brood of Angels heuenly borne:
　and with the crew of blessed Saynts vpbrought,
　each of which did her with theyr guifts
　　adorne;
The bud of ioy, the blossome of the morne,
　the beame of light, whom mortal eyes
　　admyre:
　what reason is it then but she should scorne
　base things, that to her loue too bold aspire?
Such heauenly formes ought rather worshipt be,
　then dare be lou'd by men of meane degree.

SONNET. LXII.

THe weary yeare his race now hauing run,
　The new begins his compast course anew:
　with shew of morning mylde he hath begun,
　betokening peace and plenty to ensew.
So let vs, which this chaunge of weather vew,
　chaunge eeke our mynds and former liues
　　amend,
　the old yeares sinnes forepast let vs eschew,
　and fly the faults with which we did offend.
Then shall the new yeares ioy forth freshly send,
　into the glooming world his gladsome ray:
　and all these stormes which now his beauty
　　blend,
　shall turne to caulmes and tymely cleare away.
So likewise loue cheare you your heauy spright,
　and chaunge old yeares annoy to new delight.

SONNET. LXIII.

AFter long stormes and tempests sad assay,
    Which hardly I endured heretofore :
in dread of death and daungerous dismay,
    with which my silly barke was tossed sore :
I doe at length descry the happy shore,
    in which I hope ere long for to arryue ;
fayre soyle it seemes from far and fraught
        with store
    of all that deare and daynty is alyue.
Most happy he that can at last atchyue
    the ioyous safety of so sweet a rest :
whose least delight sufficeth to depriue
    remembrance of all paines which him opprest.
All paines are nothing in respect of this,
    all sorrowes short that gaine eternall blisse.

SONNET. LXIIII.

COmming to kisse her lyps, (such grace I
        found)
    Me seemd I smelt a gardin of sweet flowres :
that dainty odours from them threw around
    for damzels fit to decke their louers bowres.
Her lips did smell lyke vnto Gillyflowers,
    her ruddy cheekes lyke vnto Roses red :
her snowy browes lyke budded Bellamoures,
    her louely eyes lyke Pincks but newly spred.
Her goodly bosome lyke a Strawberry bed,
    her neck lyke to a bounch of Cullambynes :
her brest lyke lillyes, ere theyr leaues be shed,
    her nipples lyke yong blossomd Iessemynes.
Such fragrant flowres doe giue most odorous
        smell,
    but her sweet odour did them all excell.

SONNET. LXV.

THe doubt which ye misdeeme, fayre loue,
        is vaine,
    That fondly feare to loose your liberty,
when loosing one, two liberties ye gayne,
    and make him bond that bondage earst dyd fly.
Sweet be the bands, the which true loue doth tye,
    without constraynt or dread of any ill :
the gentle birde feeles no captiuity
    within her cage, but singes and feeds her fill.
There pride dare not approch, nor discord spill
    the league twixt them, that loyal loue hath
        bound :
but simple truth and mutuall good will,
    seekes with sweet peace to salue each others
        wound :
There fayth doth fearlesse dwell in brasen
        towre,
    and spotlesse pleasure builds her sacred
        bowre.

SONNET. LXVI.

TO all those happy blessings which ye haue,
    with plenteous hand by heauen vpon you
        thrown,
this one disparagement they to you gaue,
    that ye your loue lent to so meane a one.
Yee whose high worths surpassing paragon,
    could not on earth haue found one fit for
        mate,
    ne but in heauen matchable to none,
    why did ye stoup vnto so lowly state ?
But ye thereby much greater glory gate,
    then had ye sorted with a princes pere :
for now your light doth more it selfe dilate,
    and in my darknesse greater doth appeare.
Yet since your light hath once enlumind me,
    with my reflex yours shall encreased be.

SONNET. LXVII.

LYke as a huntsman after weary chace,
    Seeing the game from him escapt away,
sits downe to rest him in some shady place,
    with panting hounds beguiled of their pray :
So after long pursuit and vaine assay,
    when I all weary had the chace forsooke,
the gentle deare returnd the selfe-same way,
    thinking to quench her thirst at the next
        brooke.
There she beholding me with mylder looke,
    sought not to fly, but fearelesse still did bide :
till I in hand her yet halfe trembling tooke,
    and with her owne goodwill hir fyrmely tyde.
Strange thing me seemd to see a beast so wyld,
    so goodly wonne with her owne will beguyld.

SONNET. LXVIII.

MOst glorious Lord of lyfe, that on this
        day,
    Didst make thy triumph ouer death and sin :
and hauing harrowd hell, didst bring away
    captiuity thence captiue vs to win :
This ioyous day, deare Lord, with ioy begin,
    and grant that we for whom thou diddest dye
being with thy deare blood clene washt from
        sin,
    may liue for euer in felicity.
And that thy loue we weighing worthily,
    may likewise loue thee for the same againe :
and for thy sake that all lyke deare didst buy,
    with loue may one another entertayne.
So let vs loue, deare loue, lyke as we ought,
    loue is the lesson which the Lord vs taught.

SONNET. LXIX.

THe famous warriors of the anticke world,
  Vsed Trophees to erect in stately wize :
in which they would the records haue enrold,
of theyr great deeds and valarous emprize.
What trophee then shall I most fit deuize,
  in which I may record the memory
  of my loues conquest, peerelesse beauties
    prise,
  adorn'd with honour, loue, and chastity.
Euen this verse vowd to eternity,
  shall be thereof immortall moniment :
  and tell her prayse to all posterity,
  that may admire such worlds rare wonder-
    ment.
The happy purchase of my glorious spoile,
  gotten at last with labour and long toyle.

SONNET. LXX.

FResh spring the herald of loues mighty
    king,
  In whose cote armour richly are displayd
  all sorts of flowers the which on earth do
    spring
  in goodly colours gloriously arrayd.
Goe to my loue, where she is carelesse layd,
  yet in her winters bowre not well awake :
  tell her the ioyous time wil not be staid
  vnlesse she doe him by the forelock take.
Bid her therefore her selfe soone ready make,
  to wayt on loue amongst his louely crew :
  where euery one that misseth then her make,
  shall be by him amearst with penance dew.
Make hast therefore sweet loue, whilest it is
    prime,
  for none can call againe the passed time.

SONNET. LXXI.

I Ioy to see how in your drawen work,
  Your selfe vnto the Bee ye doe compare ;
and me vnto the Spyder that doth lurke,
in close awayt to catch her vnaware.
Right so your selfe were caught in cunning snare
  of a deare foe, and thralled to his loue :
  in whose streight bands ye now captiued are
  so firmely, that ye neuer may remoue.
But as your worke is wouen all aboue,
  with woodbynd flowers and fragrant Eglan-
    tine :
  so sweet your prison you in time shall proue,
  with many deare delights bedecked fyne.
And all thensforth eternall peace shall see,
  betweene the Spyder and the gentle Bee.

SONNET. LXXII.

OFt when my spirit doth spred her bolder
    winges,
  In mind to mount vp to the purest sky :
  it down is weighd with thoght of earthly
    things
  and clogd with burden of mortality,
Where when that souerayne beauty it doth spy,
  resembling heauens glory in her light :
  drawne with sweet pleasures bayt, it back
    doth fly,
  and vnto heauen forgets her former flight.
There my fraile fancy fed with full delight,
  doth bath in blisse and mantleth most at ease :
  ne thinks of other heauen, but how it might
  her harts desire with most contentment please.
Hart need not with none other happinesse,
  but here on earth to haue such heuens blisse.

SONNET. LXXIII.

BEing my selfe captyued here in care,
  My hart, whom none with seruile bands
    can tye,
  but the fayre tresses of your golden hayre,
  breaking his prison forth to you doth fly.
Lyke as a byrd that in ones hand doth spy
  desired food, to it doth make his flight :
  euen so my hart, that wont on your fayre eye
  to feed his fill, flyes backe vnto your sight.
Doe you him take, and in your bosome bright,
  gently encage, that he may be your thrall :
  perhaps he there may learne with rare
    delight,
  to sing your name and prayses ouer all.
That it hereafter may you not repent,
  him lodging in your bosome to haue lent.

SONNET. LXXIIII.

MOst happy letters fram'd by skilfull
    trade,
  with which that happy name was first
    desynd :
  the which three times thrise happy hath me
    made,
  with guifts of body, fortune and of mind.
The first my being to me gaue by kind,
  from mothers womb deriu'd by dew descent,
  the second is my souereigne Queene most kind,
  that honour and large richesse to me lent.
The third my loue, my liues last ornament,
  by whom my spirit out of dust was raysed :
  to speake her prayse and glory excellent,
  of all aliue most worthy to be praysed.
Ye three Elizabeths for euer liue,
  that three such graces did vnto me giue.

SONNET. LXXV.

ONe day I wrote her name vpon the strand,
　but came the waues and washed it away :
agayne I wrote it with a second hand,
　but came the tyde, and made my paynes his
　　pray.
Vayne man, sayd she, that doest in vaine assay,
　a mortall thing so to immortalize,
for I my selue shall lyke to this decay,
　and eek my name bee wyped out lykewize.
Not so, (quod I) let baser things deuize
　to dy in dust, but you shall liue by fame :
my verse your vertues rare shall eternize,
　and in the heuens wryte your glorious name.
Where whenas death shall all the world subdew,
　our loue shall liue, and later life renew.

SONNET. LXXVI.

FAyre bosome fraught with vertues richest
　tresure,
The neast of loue, the lodging of delight :
　the bowre of blisse, the paradice of pleasure,
　the sacred harbour of that heuenly spright.
How was I rauisht with your louely sight,
　and my frayle thoughts too rashly led astray?
whiles diuing deepe through amorous insight,
　on the sweet spoyle of beautie they did
　　pray.
And twixt her paps like early fruit in May,
　whose haruest seemd to hasten now apace :
they loosely did theyr wanton winges display,
　and there to rest themselues did boldly place.
Sweet thoughts I enuy your so happy rest,
　which oft I wisht, yet neuer was so blest.

SONNET. LXXVII.

WAs it a dreame, or did I see it playne,
　a goodly table of pure yvory :
all spred with iuncats, fit to entertayne
　the greatest Prince with pompous roialty.
Mongst which there in a siluer dish did ly
　twoo golden apples of vnualewd price :
far passing those which Hercules came by,
　or those which Atalanta did entice.
Exceeding sweet, yet voyd of sinfull vice,
　That many sought yet none could euer taste,
　sweet fruit of pleasure brought from para-
　　dice
by loue himselfe, and in his garden plaste.
Her brest that table was so richly spredd,
　my thoughts the guests, which would thereon
　　haue fedd.

SONNET. LXXVIII.

LAckyng my loue I go from place to place,
　lyke a young fawne that late hath lost the
　　hynd :
and seeke each where, where last I sawe her
　　face,
　whose ymage yet I carry fresh in mynd.
I seeke the fields with her late footing synd,
　I seeke her bowre with her late presence deckt,
yet nor in field nor bowre I her can fynd :
　yet field and bowre are full of her aspect.
But when myne eyes I thereunto direct,
　they ydly back returne to me agayne,
and when I hope to see theyr trew obiect,
　I fynd my selfe but fed with fancies vayne.
Ceasse then myne eyes, to seeke her selfe to see,
　and let my thoughts behold her selfe in mee.

SONNET. LXXIX.

MEn call you fayre, and you doe credit it,
　For that your selfe ye dayly such doe see :
but the trew fayre, that is the gentle wit,
　and vertuous mind, is much more praysd of
　　me.
For all the rest, how euer fayre it be,
　shall turne to nought and loose that glorious
　　hew :
　but onely that is permanent and free
　from frayle corruption, that doth flesh ensew.
That is true beautie : that doth argue you
　to be diuine and borne of heauenly seed :
　deriu'd from that fayre Spirit, from whom al
　　true
　and perfect beauty did at first proceed.
He onely fayre, and what he fayre hath made,
　all other fayre lyke flowres vntymely fade.

SONNET. LXXX.

AFter so long a race as I haue run
　Through Faery land, which those six
　　books compile,
giue leaue to rest me being halfe fordonne,
　and gather to my selfe new breath awhile.
Then as a steed refreshed after toyle,
　out of my prison I will breake anew :
　and stoutly will that second worke assoyle,
　with strong endeuour and attention dew.
Till then giue leaue to me in pleasant mew,
　to sport my muse and sing my loues sweet
　　praise :
　the contemplation of whose heauenly hew,
　my spirit to an higher pitch will rayse.
But let her prayses yet be low and meane,
　fit for the handmayd of the Faery Queene.

SONNET. LXXXI.

FAyre is my loue, when her fayre golden
heares,
with the loose wynd ye wauing chance to
marke :
fayre when the rose in her red cheekes
appeares,
or in her eyes the fyre of loue does sparke.
Fayre when her brest lyke a rich laden barke,
with pretious merchandize she forth doth lay:
fayre when that cloud of pryde, which oft
doth dark
her goodly light with smiles she driues away.
But fayrest she, when so she doth display,
the gate with pearles and rubyes richly dight:
throgh which her words so wise do make their
way
to beare the message of her gentle spright.
The rest be works of natures wonderment,
but this the worke of harts astonishment.

SONNET. LXXXII.

IOy of my life, full oft for louing you
I blesse my lot, that was so lucky placed :
but then the more your owne mishap I rew,
that are so much by so meane loue embased.
For had the equall heuens so much you graced
in this as in the rest, ye mote inuent
som heuenly wit, whose verse could haue
enchased
your glorious name in golden moniment.
But since ye deignd so goodly to relent
to me your thrall, in whom is little worth,
that little that I am, shall all be spent,
in setting your immortall prayses forth.
Whose lofty argument vplifting me,
shall lift you vp vnto an high degree.

SONNET. LXXXIII.

MY hungry eyes, through greedy couetize,
still to behold the obiect of theyr payne:
with no contentment can themselues suffize,
but hauing pine, and hauing not complayne.
For lacking it, they cannot lyfe sustayne,
and seeing it, they gaze on it the more :
in theyr amazement lyke Narcissus vayne
whose eyes him staru'd : so plenty makes me
pore.
Yet are myne eyes so filled with the store
of that fayre sight, that nothing else they
brooke :
but loath the things which they did like before,
and can no more endure on them to looke.
All this worlds glory seemeth vayne to me,
and all theyr shewes but shadowes, sauing she.

SONNET. LXXXIIII.

LEt not one sparke of filthy lustfull fyre
breake out, that may her sacred peace
molest :
ne one light glance of sensuall desyre
Attempt to work her gentle mindes vnrest.
But pure affections bred in spotlesse brest,
and modest thoughts breathd from wel
tempred sprites
goe visit her in her chast bowre of rest,
accompanyde with angelick delightes.
There fill your selfe with those most ioyous
sights,
the which my selfe could neuer yet attayne :
but speake no word to her of these sad plights,
which her too constant stiffenesse doth con-
strayn.
Onely behold her rare perfection,
and blesse your fortunes fayre election.

SONNET. LXXXV.

THe world that cannot deeme of worthy
things,
when I doe praise her, say I doe but flatter :
so does the Cuckow, when the Mauis sings,
begin his witlesse note apace to clatter.
But they that skill not of so heauenly matter,
all that they know not, enuy or admyre,
rather then enuy let them wonder at her,
but not to deeme of her desert aspyre.
Deepe in the closet of my parts entyre,
her worth is written with a golden quill :
that me with heauenly fury doth inspire,
and my glad mouth with her sweet prayses fill.
Which when as fame in her shrill trump shal
thunder
let the world chose to enuy or to wonder.

SONNET. LXXXVI.

VEnemous toung, tipt with vile adders sting,
Of that selfe kynd with which the Furies fell
theyr snaky heads doe combe, from which
a spring
of poysoned words and spitefull speeches well.
Let all the plagues and horrid paines of hell,
vpon thee fall for thine accursed hyre :
that with false forged lyes, which thou didst tel,
in my true loue did stirre vp coles of yre,
The sparkes whereof let kindle thine own fyre,
and catching hold on thine owne wicked hed
consume thee quite, that didst with guile
conspire
in my sweet peace such breaches to haue bred
Shame be thy meed, and mischiefe thy reward,
dew to thy selfe that it for me prepard.

SONNET. LXXXVII.

SInce I did leaue the presence of my loue,
　Many long weary dayes I haue outworne:
and many nights, that slowly seemd to moue
theyr sad protract from euening vntill morne.
For when as day the heauen doth adorne,
　I wish that night the noyous day would end:
and when as night hath vs of light forlorne,
　I wish that day would shortly reascend.
Thus I the time with expectation spend,
　and faine my griefe with chaunges to beguile,
that further seemes his terme still to extend,
　and maketh euery minute seeme a myle.
So sorrow still doth seeme too long to last,
　but ioyous houres doo fly away too fast.

SONNET. LXXXVIII.

SInce I haue lackt the comfort of that light,
　The which was wont to lead my thoughts
　　astray:
I wander as in darkenesse of the night,
　affrayd of euery dangers least dismay.
Ne ought I see, though in the clearest day,
　when others gaze vpon theyr shadowes vayne:
but th'onely image of that heauenly ray,
　whereof some glance doth in mine eie re-
　　mayne.
Of which beholding the Idæa playne,
　through contemplation of my purest part:
with light thereof I doe my selfe sustayne,
　and thereon feed my loue-affamisht hart.
But with such brightnesse whylest I fill my
　mind,
I starue my body and mine eyes doe blynd.

SONNET. LXXXIX.

LYke as the Culuer on the bared bough,
　Sits mourning for the absence of her mate:
and in her songs sends many a wishfull vow,
　for his returne that seemes to linger late.
So I alone now left disconsolate,
　mourne to my selfe the absence of my loue:
and wandring here and there all desolate,
　seek with my playnts to match that mourn-
　　ful doue:
Ne ioy of ought that vnder heauen doth houe,
　can comfort me, but her owne ioyous sight:
whose sweet aspect both God and man can
　moue,
　in her vnspotted pleasauns to delight.
Dark is my day, whyles her fayre light I mis,
　and dead my life that wants such liuely blis.

SPENSER　　　　　　　　U

IN youth before I waxed old,
　The blynd boy Venus baby,
For want of cunning made me bold,
　In bitter hyue to grope for honny.
　　But when he saw me stung and cry,　5
　　He tooke his wings and away did fly.

AS Diane hunted on a day,
　She chaunst to come where Cupid lay,
　his quiuer by his head:
One of his shafts she stole away,
And one of hers did close conuay,　5
　into the others stead:
　　With that loue wounded my loues hart,
　　but Diane beasts with Cupids dart.

I Saw in secret to my Dame,
　How little Cupid humbly came:
　and sayd to her All hayle my mother.
But when he saw me laugh, for shame
His face with bashfull blood did flame,　5
　not knowing Venus from the other,
Then neuer blush Cupid (quoth I)
　for many haue err'd in this beauty.

VPon a day as loue lay sweetly slumbring,
　all in his mothers lap:
A gentle Bee with his loud trumpet murm'ring,
　about him flew by hap.
Whereof when he was wakened with the noyse,
　and saw the beast so small:
Whats this (quoth he) that giues so great a
　voyce,
　that wakens men withall?
In angry wize he flyes about,
　and threatens all with corage stout.　10

To whom his mother closely smiling sayd,
　twixt earnest and twixt game:
See thou thy selfe likewise art lyttle made,
　if thou regard the same.
And yet thou suffrest neyther gods in sky,
　nor men in earth to rest:
But when thou art disposed cruelly,
　theyr sleepe thou doost molest.
Then eyther change thy cruelty,
　or giue lyke leaue vnto the fly.　20

Nathlesse the cruell boy not so content,
 would needs the fly pursue :
And in his hand with heedlesse hardiment,
 him caught for to subdue.
But when on it he hasty hand did lay,
 the Bee him stung therefore :
Now out alasse (he cryde) and welaway,
 I wounded am full sore :
The fly that I so much did scorne,
 hath hurt me with his little horne.   30

Vnto his mother straight he weeping came,
 and of his griefe complayned :
Who could not chose but laugh at his fond
 game,
 though sad to see him pained.
Think now (quod she) my sonne how great the
 smart
 of those whom thou dost wound :
Full many thou hast pricked to the hart,
 that pitty neuer found :
Therefore henceforth some pitty take,
 when thou doest spoyle of louers make.   40

She tooke him streight full pitiously lamenting,
 and wrapt him in her smock :
She wrapt him softly, all the while repenting,
 that he the fly did mock.
She drest his wound and it embaulmed wel
 with salue of soueraigne might :
And then she bath'd him in a dainty well
 the well of deare delight
Who would not oft be stung as this
 to be so bath'd in Venus blis ?   50

The wanton boy was shortly wel recured,
 of that his malady
But he soone after fresh againe enured,
 his former cruelty.
And since that time he wounded hath my
 selfe
 with his sharpe dart of loue :
And now forgets the cruell carelesse elte
 his mothers heast to proue.
So now I languish, till he please
 my pining anguish to appease.   60

FINIS.

Epithalamion.

YE learned sisters which haue oftentimes
    Beene to me ayding, others to adorne:
Whom ye thought worthy of your gracefull
    rymes,
That euen the greatest did not greatly scorne
To heare theyr names sung in your simple layes,
But ioyed in theyr prayse.
And when ye list your owne mishaps to mourne,
Which death, or loue, or fortunes wreck did
    rayse,
Your string could soone to sadder tenor turne,
And teach the woods and waters to lament
Your dolefull dreriment.   11
Now lay those sorrowfull complaints aside,
And hauing all your heads with girland crownd,
Helpe me mine owne loues prayses to resound,
Ne let the same of any be enuide:
So Orpheus did for his owne bride,
So I vnto my selfe alone will sing,
The woods shall to me answer and my Eccho
    ring.

EArly before the worlds light giuing lampe,
    His golden beame vpon the hils doth spred,
Hauing disperst the nights vnchearefull dampe,
Doe ye awake, and with fresh lusty hed,
Go to the bowre of my beloued loue,
My truest turtle doue,
Bid her awake; for Hymen is awake,
And long since ready forth his maske to moue,
With his bright Tead that flames with many a
    flake,
And many a bachelor to waite on him,
In theyr fresh garments trim.
Bid her awake therefore and soone her dight,
For lo the wished day is come at last,   31
That shall for al the paynes and sorrowes past,
Pay to her vsury of long delight:
And whylest she doth her dight,
Doe ye to her of ioy and solace sing,
That all the woods may answer and your eccho
    ring.

BRing with you all the Nymphes that you
    can heare
Both of the riuers and the forrests greene:
And of the sea that neighbours to her neare,
Al with gay girlands goodly wel beseene.   40
And let them also with them bring in hand,
Another gay girland
For my fayre loue of lillyes and of roses,
Bound trueloue wize with a blew silke riband.
And let them make great store of bridale poses,
And let them eeke bring store of other flowers
To deck the bridale bowers.

And let the ground whereas her foot shall tread,
For feare the stones her tender foot should
    wrong
Be strewed with fragrant flowers all along,   50
And diapred lyke the discolored mead.
Which done, doe at her chamber dore awayt,
For she will waken strayt,
The whiles doe ye this song vnto her sing,
The woods shall to you answer and your Eccho
    ring.

YE Nymphes of Mulla which with carefull
    heed,
The siluer scaly trouts doe tend full well,
And greedy pikes which vse therein to feed,
(Those trouts and pikes all others doo excell)
And ye likewise which keepe the rushy lake,
Where none doo fishes take,   61
Bynd vp the locks the which hang scatterd
    light,
And in his waters which your mirror make,
Behold your faces as the christall bright,
That when you come whereas my loue doth lie,
No blemish she may spie.
And eke ye lightfoot mayds which keepe the
    deere,
That on the hoary mountayne vse to towre,
And the wylde wolues which seeke them to
    deuoure,
With your steele darts doo chace from com-
    ming neer   70
Be also present heere,
To helpe to decke her and to help to sing,
That all the woods may answer and your eccho
    ring.

WAke, now my loue, awake; for it is time,
    The Rosy Morne long since left Tithones
    bed,
All ready to her siluer coche to clyme,
And Phœbus gins to shew his glorious hed.
Hark how the cheerefull birds do chaunt theyr
    laies
And carroll of loues praise.
The merry Larke hir mattins sings aloft,   80
The thrush replyes, the Mauis descant playes,
The Ouzell shrills, the Ruddock warbles soft,
So goodly all agree with sweet consent,
To this dayes merriment.
Ah my deere loue why doe ye sleepe thus long
When meeter were that ye should now awake
T'awayt the comming of your ioyous make,
And hearken to the birds louelearned song,
The deawy leaues among.
For they of ioy and pleasance to you sing,   90
That all the woods them answer and theyr
    eccho ring.

MY loue is now awake out of her dreame,
And her fayre eyes like stars that
    dimmed were
With darksome cloud, now shew theyr goodly
    beams
More bright then Hesperus his head doth rere.
Come now ye damzels, daughters of delight,
Helpe quickly her to dight,
But first come ye fayre houres which were begot
In Ioues sweet paradice, of Day and Night,
Which doe the seasons of the yeare allot,   100
And al that euer in this world is fayre
Doe make and still repayre.
And ye three handmayds of the Cyprian Queene,
The which doe still adorne her beauties pride,
Helpe to addorne my beautifullest bride :
And as ye her array, still throw betweene
Some graces to be seene,
And as ye vse to Venus, to her sing,
The whiles the woods shal answer and your
    eccho ring.

NOw is my loue all ready forth to come,
Let all the virgins therefore well awayt,
And ye fresh boyes that tend vpon her groome
Prepare your selues ; for he is comming strayt.
Set all your things in seemely good aray
Fit for so ioyfull day,
The ioyfulst day that euer sunne did see.
Faire Sun, shew forth thy fauourable ray,
And let thy lifull heat not feruent be
For feare of burning her sunshyny face,
Her beauty to disgrace.   120
O fayrest Phœbus, father of the Muse,
If euer I did honour thee aright,
Or sing the thing, that mote thy mind delight,
Doe not thy seruants simple boone refuse,
But let this day let this one day be myne,
Let all the rest be thine.
Then I thy souerayne prayses loud wil sing,
That all the woods shal answer and theyr eccho
    ring.

HArke how the Minstrels gin to shrill aloud
Their merry Musick that resounds from
    far,   130
The pipe, the tabor, and the trembling Croud,
That well agree withouten breach or iar.
But most of all the Damzels doe delite,
When they their tymbrels smyte,
And thereunto doe daunce and carrol sweet,
That all the sences they doe rauish quite,
The whyles the boyes run vp and downe the
    street,

Crying aloud with strong confused noyce,
As if it were one voyce.
Hymen io Hymen, Hymen they do shout,   140
That euen to the heauens theyr shouting shrill
Doth reach, and all the firmament doth fill,
To which the people standing all about,
As in approuance doe thereto applaud
And loud aduaunce her laud,
And euermore they Hymen Hymen sing,
That al the woods them answer and theyr eccho
    ring.

LOe where she comes along with portly pace
Lyke Phœbe from her chamber of the East,
Arysing forth to run her mighty race,   150
Clad all in white, that seemes a virgin best.
So well it her beseemes that ye would weene
Some angell she had beene.
Her long loose yellow locks lyke golden wyre,
Sprinckled with perle, and perling flowres a
    tweene,
Doe lyke a golden mantle her attyre,
And being crowned with a girland greene,
Seeme lyke some mayden Queene.
Her modest eyes abashed to behold
So many gazers, as on her do stare,   160
Vpon the lowly ground affixed are.
Ne dare lift vp her countenance too bold,
But blush to heare her prayses sung so loud,
So farre from being proud.
Nathlesse doe ye still loud her prayses sing,
That all the woods may answer and your eccho
    ring.

TEll me ye merchants daughters did ye see
So fayre a creature in your towne before,
So sweet, so louely, and so mild as she,   169
Adornd with beautyes grace and vertues store,
Her goodly eyes lyke Saphyres shining bright,
Her forehead yuory white,
Her cheekes lyke apples which the sun hath
    rudded,
Her lips lyke cherryes charming men to byte,
Her brest like to a bowle of creame vncrudded,
Her paps lyke lyllies budded,
Her snowie necke lyke to a marble towre,
And all her body like a pallace fayre,
Ascending vppe with many a stately stayre,
To honors seat and chastities sweet bowre.
Why stand ye still ye virgins in amaze,   181
Vpon her so to gaze,
Whiles ye forget your former lay to sing,
To which the woods did answer and your eccho
    ring.

BVt if ye saw that which no eyes can
　　see,
The inward beauty of her liuely spright,
Garnisht with heauenly guifts of high degree,
Much more then would ye wonder at that
　　sight,
And stand astonisht lyke to those which red
Medusaes mazeful hed.　　　　　　　190
There dwels sweet loue and constant chastity,
Vnspotted fayth and comely womanhood,
Regard of honour and mild modesty,
There vertue raynes as Queene in royal throne,
And giueth lawes alone.
The which the base affections doe obay,
And yeeld theyr seruices vnto her will,
Ne thought of thing vncomely euer may
Thereto approch to tempt her mind to ill.
Had ye once seene these her celestial threa-
　　sures,　　　　　　　　　　　　　　200
And vnreuealed pleasures,
Then would ye wonder and her prayses sing,
That al the woods should answer and your echo
　　ring.

OPen the temple gates vnto my loue,
　　Open them wide that she may enter in,
And all the postes adorne as doth behoue,
And all the pillours deck with girlands trim,
For to recyue this Saynt with honour dew,
That commeth in to you.　　　　　　　209
With trembling steps and humble reuerence,
She commeth in, before th'almighties vew,
Of her ye virgins learne obedience,
When so ye come into those holy places,
To humble your proud faces :
Bring her vp to th'high altar, that she may
The sacred ceremonies there partake,
The which do endlesse matrimony make,
And let the roring Organs loudly play
The praises of the Lord in liuely notes,
The whiles with hollow throates　　　　220
The Choristers the ioyous Antheme sing,
That al the woods may answere and their eccho
　　ring.

Behold whiles she before the altar stands
　　Hearing the holy priest that to her speakes
And blesseth her with his two happy hands,
How the red roses flush vp in her cheekes,
And the pure snow with goodly vermill stayne,
Like crimsin dyde in grayne,
That euen th'Angels which continually,
About the sacred Altare doe remaine,　　230

Forget their seruice and about her fly,
Ofte peeping in her face that seemes more
　　fayre,
The more they on it stare.
But her sad eyes still fastened on the ground,
Are gouerned with goodly modesty,
That suffers not one looke to glaunce awry,
Which may let in a little thought vnsownd.
Why blush ye loue to giue to me your hand,
The pledge of all our band ?
Sing ye sweet Angels, Alleluya sing,　　240
That all the woods may answere and your eccho
　　ring.

NOwalisdone; bring home the bride againe,
　　Bring home the triumph of our victory,
Bring home with you the glory of her gaine,
With ioyance bring her and with iollity.
Neuer had man more ioyfull day then this,
Whom heauen would heape with blis.
Make feast therefore now all this liue long
　　day,
This day for euer to me holy is,
Poure out the wine without restraint or stay,
Poure not by cups, but by the belly full,　251
Poure out to all that wull,
And sprinkle all the postes and wals with wine,
That they may sweat, and drunken be withall.
Crowne ye God Bacchus with a coronall,
And Hymen also crowne with wreathes of vine,
And let the Graces daunce vnto the rest ;
For they can doo it best :
The whiles the maydens doe theyr carroll sing,
To which the woods shal answer and theyr
　　eccho ring.　　　　　　　　　　　　260

RIng ye the bels, ye yong men of the towne,
　　And leaue your wonted labors for this day:
This day is holy ; doe ye write it downe,
That ye for euer it remember may.
This day the sunne is in his chiefest hight,
With Barnaby the bright,
From whence declining daily by degrees,
He somewhat loseth of his heat and light,
When once the Crab behind his back he sees.
But for this time it ill ordained was,　　270
To chose the longest day in all the yeare,
And shortest night, when longest fitter weare :
Yet neuer day so long, but late would passe.
Ring ye the bels, to make it weare away,
And bonefiers make all day,
And daunce about them, and about them sing :
that all the woods may answer, and your eccho
　　ring.

AH when will this long weary day haue end,
And lende me leaue to come vnto my loue?
How slowly do the houres theyr numbers spend?
How slowly does sad Time his feathers moue ?
Hast thee O fayrest Planet to thy home
Within the Westerne fome :
Thy tyred steedes long since haue need of rest.
Long though it be, at last I see it gloome,
And the bright euening star with golden creast
Appeare out of the East.
Fayre childe of beauty, glorious lampe of loue
That all the host of heauen in rankes doost lead,
And guydest louers through the nightes dread,
How chearefully thou lookest from aboue, 291
And seemst to laugh atweene thy twinkling light
As ioying in the sight
Of these glad many which for ioy doe sing,
That all the woods them answer and their echo
ring.

Now ceasse ye damsers your delights forepast;
Enough is it, that all the day was youres:
Now day is doen, and night is nighing fast :
Now bring the Bryde into the brydall boures.
Now night is come, now soone her disaray,
And in her bed her lay ; 301
Lay her in lillies and in violets,
And silken courteins ouer her display,
And odourd sheetes, and Arras couerlets.
Behold how goodly my faire loue does ly
In proud humility ;
Like vnto Maia, when as Ioue her tooke,
In Tempe, lying on the flowry gras,
Twixt sleepe and wake, after she weary was,
With bathing in the Acidalian brooke. 310
Now it is night, ye damsels may be gon,
And leaue my loue alone,
And leaue likewise your former lay to sing :
The woods no more shal answere, nor your echo
ring.

Now welcome night, thou night so long
expected,
That long daies labour doest at last defray,
And all my cares, which cruell loue collected,
Hast sumd in one, and cancelled for aye :
Spread thy broad wing ouer my loue and me,
That no man may vs see, 320
And in thy sable mantle vs enwrap,
From feare of perrill and foule horror free.
Let no false treason seeke vs to entrap,
Nor any dread disquiet once annoy
The safety of our ioy :

But let the night be calme and quietsome,
Without tempestuous storms or sad afray :
Lyke as when Ioue with fayre Alcmena lay,
When he begot the great Tirynthian groome :
Or lyke as when he with thy selfe did lie, 330
And begot Maiesty.
And let the mayds and yongmen cease to sing :
Ne let the woods them answer, nor theyr eccho
ring.

Let no lamenting cryes, nor dolefull teares,
Be heard all night within nor yet without:
Ne let false whispers, breeding hidden feares,
Breake gentle sleepe with misconceiued dout.
Let no deluding dreames, nor dreadful sights
Make sudden sad affrights ;
Ne let housefyres, nor lightnings helpelesse
harmes, 340
Ne let the Pouke, nor other euill sprights,
Ne let mischiuous witches with theyr charmes,
Ne let hob Goblins, names whose sence we see
not,
Fray vs with things that be not.
Let not the shriech Oule, nor the Storke be
heard :
Nor the night Rauen that still deadly yels,
Nor damned ghosts cald vp with mighty spels,
Nor griesly vultures make vs once affeard :
Ne let th'unpleasant Quyre of Frogs still crok-
ing
Make vs to wish theyr choking. 350
Let none of these theyr drery accents sing ;
Ne let the woods them answer, nor theyr eccho
ring.

But let stil Silence trew night watches keepe,
That sacred peace may in assurance rayne,
And tymely sleep, when it is tyme to sleepe,
May poure his limbs forth on your pleasant
playne,
The whiles an hundred little winged loues,
Like diuers fethered doues,
Shall fly and flutter round about your bed,
And in the secret darke, that none reproues,
Their prety stealthes shal worke, and snares
shal spread 361
To filch away sweet snatches of delight,
Conceald through couert night.
Ye sonnes of Venus, play your sports at will,
For greedy pleasure, carelesse of your toyes,
Thinks more vpon her paradise of ioyes,
Then what ye do, albe it good or ill.
All night therefore attend your merry play,
For it will soone be day :
Now none doth hinder you, that say or sing,
Ne will the woods now answer, nor your Eccho
ring. 371

WHo is the same, which at my window
  peepes?
Or whose is that faire face, that shines so
  bright,
Is it not Cinthia, she that neuer sleepes,
But walkes about high heauen al the night?
O fayrest goddesse, do thou not enuy
My loue with me to spy:
For thou likewise didst loue, though now
  vnthought,
And for a fleece of woll, which priuily,
The Latmian shephard once vnto thee brought,
Ilis pleasures with thee wrought. 381
Therefore to vs be fauorable now;
And sith of wemens labours thou hast charge,
And generation goodly dost enlarge,
Encline thy will t'effect our wishfull vow,
And the chast wombe informe with timely seed,
That may our comfort breed:
Till which we cease our hopefull hap to sing,
Ne let the woods vs answere, nor our Eccho
  ring.

ANd thou great Iuno, which with awful
  might 390
The lawes of wedlock still dost patronize,
And the religion of the faith first plight
With sacred rites hast taught to solemnize:
And eeke for comfort often called art
Of women in their smart,
Eternally bind thou this louely band,
And all thy blessings vnto vs impart.
And thou glad Genius, in whose gentle hand,
The bridale bowre and geniall bed remaine,
Without blemish or staine, 400
And the sweet pleasures of theyr loues delight
With secret ayde doest succour and supply,
Till they bring forth the fruitfull progeny,
Send vs the timely fruit of this same night.

And thou fayre Hebe, and thou Hymen free,
Grant that it may so be.
Til which we cease your further prayse to
  sing,
Ne any woods shal answer, nor your Eccho
  ring.

ANd ye high heauens, the temple of the gods,
  In which a thousand torches flaming bright
Doe burne, that to vs wretched earthly clods,
In dreadfull darknesse lend desired light;
And all ye powers which in the same remayne,
More then we men can fayne,
Poure out your blessing on vs plentiously,
And happy influence vpon vs raine,
That we may raise a large posterity,
Which from the earth, which they may long
  possesse,
With lasting happinesse,
Vp to your haughty pallaces may mount, 420
And for the guerdon of theyr glorious merit
May heauenly tabernacles there inherit,
Of blessed Saints for to increase the count.
So let vs rest, sweet loue, in hope of this,
And cease till then our tymely ioyes to sing,
The woods no more vs answer, nor our eccho
  ring.

SOng made in lieu of many ornaments,
  With which my loue should duly haue bene
  dect,
Which cutting off through hasty accidents,
Ye would not stay your dew time to expect,
But promist both to recompens, 431
Be vnto her a goodly ornament,
And for short time an endlesse moniment.

FINIS

Imprinted by P. S. for Wil-
liam Ponsonby.

Fowre Hymnes,

MADE BY
EDM. SPENSER.

LONDON,
Printed for William Ponsonby.
1596.

TO THE RIGHT HO-
NORABLE AND MOST VER-
tuous Ladies, the Ladie Margaret Countesse
of Cumberland, and the Ladie Marie
Countesse of Warwicke.

HAuing in the greener times of my youth, composed these former two Hymnes in the praise of Loue and beautie, and finding that the same too much pleased those of like age and dis-position, which being too vehemently caried with that kind of affection, do rather sucke out poyson to their strong passion, then hony to their honest delight, I was moued by the one of you two most excellent Ladies, to call in the same. But being vnable so to doe, by reason that many copies thereof were formerly scattered abroad, I resolued at least to amend, and by way of retractation to reforme them, making in stead of those two Hymnes of earthly or naturall love and beautie, two others of heauenly and celestiall. The which I doe dedicate ioyntly vnto you two honorable

sisters, as to the most excellent and rare orna-ments of all true loue and beautie, both in the one and the other kinde, humbly beseeching you to vouchsafe the patronage of them, and to accept this my humble seruice, in lieu of the great graces and honourable fauours which ye dayly shew vnto me, vntill such time as I may by better meanes yeeld you some more notable testimonie of my thankfull mind and dutifull deuotion.

And euen so I pray for your happinesse.
Greenwich this first of September.
1596.

Your Honors most bounden euer
in all humble seruice.

Ed. Sp.

AN HYMNE IN
HONOVR OF
LOVE.

LOue, that long since hast to thy mighty powre,
  Perforce subdude my poore captiued hart,
And raging now therein with restlesse stowre,
Doest tyrannize in eueric weaker part ;
Faine would I seeke to ease my bitter smart,
By any seruice I might do to thee,
Or ought that else might to thee pleasing bee.

And now t'asswage the force of this new flame,
And make thee more propitious in my need,
I meane to sing the praises of thy name,   10
And thy victorious conquests to areed ;
By which thou madest many harts to bleed
Of mighty Victors, with wyde wounds em-
  brewed,
And by thy cruell darts to thee subdewed.

Onely I feare my wits enfeebled late,
Through the sharpe sorrowes, which thou hast
  me bred,
Should faint, and words should faile me, to relate
The wondrous triumphs of thy great godhed.
But if thou wouldst vouchsafe to ouerspred
Me with the shadow of thy gentle wing,   20
I should enabled be thy actes to sing.

Come then, O come, thou mightie God of loue,
Out of thy siluer bowres and secret blisse,
Where thou doest sit in *Venus* lap aboue,
Bathing thy wings in her ambrosiall kisse,
That sweeter farre then any Nectar is ;
Come softly, and my feeble breast inspire
With gentle furie, kindled of thy fire.

And ye sweet Muses, which haue often proued
The piercing points of his auengefull darts ;
And ye faire Nimphs, which oftentimes haue
  loued   31
The cruell worker of your kindly smarts,
Prepare your selues, and open wide your harts,
For to receiue the triumph of your glorie,
That made you merie oft, when ye were sorie.

And ye faire blossomes of youths wanton breed,
Which in the conquests of your beautie bost,
Wherewith your louers feeble eyes you feed,
But sterue their harts, that needeth nourture
  most,   39
Prepare your selues, to march amongst his host,
And all the way this sacred hymne do sing,
Made in the honor of your Soueraigne king.

Great god of might, that reignest in the
   mynd,
And all the bodie to thy hest doest frame,
Victor of gods, subduer of mankynd,
That doest the Lions and fell Tigers tame,
Making their cruell rage thy scornefull game,
And in their roring taking great delight ;
Who can expresse the glorie of thy might ?

Or who aliue can perfectly declare,   50
The wondrous cradle of thine infancie ?
When thy great mother *Venus* first thee bare,
Begot of Plentie and of Penurie,
Though elder then thine owne natiuitie ;
And yet a chyld, renewing still thy yeares
And yet the eldest of the heauenly Peares.

For ere this worlds still mouing mightie masse,
Out of great *Chaos* vgly prison crept,
In which his goodly face long hidden was
From heauens view, and in deepe darknesse
   kept,   60
Loue, that had now long time securely slept
In *Venus* lap, vnarmed then and naked,
Gan reare his head, by *Clotho* being waked.

And taking to him wings of his owne heate,
Kindled at first from heauens life-giuing fyre,
He gan to moue out of his idle seate,
Weakely at first, but after with desyre
Lifted aloft, he gan to mount vp hyre,
And like fresh Eagle, make his hardie flight
Through all that great wide wast, yet wanting
   light.   70

Yet wanting light to guide his wandring way,
His owne faire mother, for all creatures sake,
Did lend him light from her owne goodly ray :
Then through the world his way he gan to take,
The world that was not till he did it make ;
Whose sundrie parts he from them selues did
   seuer,
The which before had lyen confused euer.

The earth, the ayre, the water, and the fyre,
Then gan to raunge them selues in huge array,
And with contrary forces to conspyre   80
Each against other, by all meanes they may,
Threatning their owne confusion and decay :
Ayre hated earth, and water hated fyre,
Till Loue relented their rebellious yre.

He then them tooke, and tempering goodly well
Their contrary dislikes with loued meanes,
Did place them all in order, and compell
To keepe them selues within their sundrie raines,
Together linkt with Adamantine chaines ;
Yet so, as that in euery liuing wight   90
They mixe themselues, and shew their kindly
   might.

So euer since they firmely haue remained,
And duly well obserued his beheast ;
Through which now all these things that are
   contained
Within this goodly cope, both most and least
Their being haue, and dayly are increast,
Through secret sparks of his infused fyre,
Which in the barraine cold he doth inspyre.

Thereby they all do liue, and moued are
To multiply the likenesse of their kynd,   100
Whilest they seeke onely, without further care,
To quench the flame, which they in burning
   fynd :
But man, that breathes a more immortall mynd,
Not for lusts sake, but for eternitie,
Seekes to enlarge his lasting progenie.

For hauing yet in his deducted spright,
Some sparks remaining of that heauenly fyre,
He is enlumind with that goodly light,
Vnto like goodly semblant to aspyre :
Therefore in choice of loue, he doth desyre
That seemes on earth most heauenly, to em-
   brace,   111
That same is Beautie, borne of heauenly race.

For sure of all, that in this mortall frame
Contained is, nought more diuine doth seeme,
Or that resembleth more th'immortall flame
Of heauenly light, then Beauties glorious beame.
What wonder then, if with such rage extreme
Fraile men, whose eyes seek heauenly things to
   see,
At sight thereof so much enrauisht bee ?   119

Which well perceiuing, that imperious boy,
Doth therwith tip his sharp empoisned darts;
Which glancing through the eyes with coun-
   tenance coy,
Rest not, till they haue pierst the trembling
   harts,
And kindled flame in all their inner parts,
Which suckes the blood, and drinketh vp the
   lyfe
Of carefull wretches with consuming griefe.

Thenceforth they playne, and make ful piteous
   mone
Vnto the author of their balefull bane ;
The daies they waste, the nights they grieue
   and grone,
Their liues they loath, and heauens light dis-
   daine ;   130
No light but that, whose lampe doth yet
   remaine
Fresh burning in the image of their eye,
They deigne to see, and seeing it still dye.

The whylst thou tyrant Loue doest laugh and
    scorne
At their complaints, making their paine thy
    play ;
Whylest they lye languishing like thrals for-
    lorne,
The whyles thou doest triumph in their decay,
And otherwhyles, their dying to delay,
Thou doest emmarble the proud hart of her,
Whose loue before their life they doe prefer.

So hast thou often done (ay me the more) 141
To me thy vassall, whose yet bleeding hart,
With thousand wounds thou mangled hast so
    sore
That whole remaines scarse any little part,
Yet to augment the anguish of my smart,
Thou hast enfrosen her disdainefull brest,
That no one drop of pitie there doth rest.

Why then do I this honor vnto thee,
Thus to ennoble thy victorious name,   149
Since thou doest shew no fauour vnto mee,
Ne once moue ruth in that rebellious Dame,
Somewhat to slacke the rigour of my flame ?
Certes small glory doest thou winne hereby,
To let her liue thus free, and me to dy.

But if thou be indeede, as men thee call,
The worlds great Parent, the most kind
    preseruer
Of liuing wights, the soueraine Lord of all,
How falles it then, that with thy furious
    feruour,
Thou doest afflict as well the not deseruer, 159
As him that doeth thy louely heasts despize,
And on thy subjects most doest tyrannize ?

Yet herein eke thy glory seemeth more,
By so hard handling those which best thee
    serue,
That ere thou doest them vnto grace restore,
Thou mayest well trie if they will euer swerue,
And mayest them make it better to deserue ;
And hauing got it, may it more esteeme.
For things hard gotten, men more dearely
    deeme.

So hard those heauenly beauties be enfyred,
As things diuine, least passions doe impresse,
The more of stedfast mynds to be admyred,
The more they stayed be on stedfastnesse :
But baseborne mynds such lamps regard the
    lesse,
Which at first blowing take not hastie fyre,
Such fancies feele no loue, but loose desyre.

For loue is Lord of truth and loialtie,
Lifting himselfe out of the lowly dust,
On golden plumes vp to the purest skie,
Aboue the reach of loathly sinfull lust,   179
Whose base affect through cowardly distrust
Of his weake wings, dare not to heauen fly,
But like a moldwarpe in the earth doth ly.

His dunghill thoughts, which do themselues
    enure
To dirtie drosse, no higher dare aspyre,
Ne can his feeble earthly eyes endure
The flaming light of that celestiall fyre,
Which kindleth loue in generous desyre,
And makes him mount aboue the natiue might
Of heauie earth, vp to the heauens hight.

Such is the powre of that sweet passion,   190
That it all sordid basenesse doth expell,
And the refyned mynd doth newly fashion
Vnto a fairer forme, which now doth dwell
In his high thought, that would it selfe excell ;
Which he beholding still with constant sight,
Admires the mirrour of so heauenly light.

Whose image printing in his deepest wit,
He thereon feeds his hungrie fantasy,
Still full, yet neuer satisfyde with it,
Like *Tantale*, that in store doth sterued ly :
So doth he pine in most satiety,   201
For nought may quench his infinite desyre,
Once kindled through that first conceiued fyre.

Thereon his mynd affixed wholly is,
Ne thinks on ought, but how it to attaine ;
His care, his ioy, his hope is all on this,
That seemes in it all blisses to containe,
In sight whereof, all other blisse seemes vaine.
Thrise happie man, might he the same possesse ;
He faines himselfe, and doth his fortune blesse.

And though he do not win his wish to end,
Yet thus farre happie he him selfe doth weene,
That heauens such happie grace did to him lend,
As thing on earth so heauenly, to haue seene,
His harts enshrined saint, his heauens queene,
Fairer then fairest, in his fayning eye,
Whose sole aspect he counts felicitye.

Then forth he casts in his vnquiet thought,
What he may do, her fauour to obtaine ;
What braue exploit, what perill hardly wrought,
What puissant conquest, what aduenturous
    paine,   221
May please her best, and grace vnto him gaine :
He dreads no danger, nor misfortune feares,
His faith, his fortune, in his breast he beares

Thou art his god, thou art his mightie guyde,
Thou being blind, letst him not see his feares,
But cariest him to that which he hath eyde,
Through seas, through flames, through thousand
    swords and speares :
Ne ought so strong that may his force with-
    stand,
With which thou armest his resistlesse hand.

Witnesse *Leander*, in the Euxine waues,   231
And stout *Æneas* in the Troiane fyre,
Achilles preassing through the Phrygian glaiues,
And *Orpheus* daring to prouoke the yre
Of damned fiends, to get his loue retyre :
For both through heauen and hell thou makest
    way,
To win them worship which to thee obay.

And if by all these perils and these paynes,
He may but purchase lyking in her eye,
What heauens of ioy, then to himselfe he faynes,
Eftsoones he wypes quite out of memory,   241
What euer ill before he did aby :
Had it bene death, yet would he die againe,
To liue thus happie as her grace to gaine.

Yet when he hath found fauour to his will,
He nathemore can so contented rest,
But forceth further on, and striueth still
T'approch more neare, till in her inmost brest,
He may embosomd bee, and loued best ;
And yet not best, but to be lou'd alone :   250
For loue can not endure a Paragone.

The feare whereof, O how doth it torment
His troubled mynd with more then hellish
    paine !
And to his fayning fansie represent
Sights neuer seene, and thousand shadowes
    vaine,
To breake his sleepe, and waste his ydle braine;
Thou that hast neuer lou'd canst not beleeue,
Least part of th'euils which poore louers greeue.

The gnawing enuie, the hart-fretting feare,
The vaine surmizes, the distrustfull showes,
The false reports that flying tales doe beare,
The doubts, the daungers, the delayes, the woes,
The fayned friends, the vnassured foes,
With thousands more then any tongue can tell,
Doe make a louers life a wretches hell.

Yet is there one more cursed then they all,
That cancker worme, that monster Gelosie,
Which eates the hart, and feedes vpon the gall,
Turning all loues delight to miserie,
Through feare of loosing his felicitie.   270
Ah Gods, that euer ye that monster placed
In gentle loue, that all his ioyes defaced.

By these, O Loue, thou doest thy entrance
    make,
Vnto thy heauen, and doest the more endeere,
Thy pleasures vnto those which them partake,
As after stormes when clouds begin to cleare,
The Sunne more bright and glorious doth
    appeare ;
So thou thy folke, through paines of Purgatorie,
Dost beare vnto thy blisse, and heauens glorie.

There thou them placest in a Paradize   280
Of all delight, and ioyous happie rest,
Where they doe feede on Nectar heauenly wize,
With *Hercules* and *Hebe*, and the rest
Of *Venus* dearlings, through her bountie blest,
And lie like Gods in yuorie beds arayd,
With rose and lillies ouer them displayd.

There with thy daughter *Pleasure* they doe play
Their hurtlesse sports, without rebuke or blame,
And in her snowy bosome boldly lay   289
Their quiet heads, deuoyd of guilty shame,
After full ioyance of their gentle game,
Then her they crowne their Goddesse and their
    Queene,
And decke with floures thy altars well beseene.

Ay me, deare Lord, that euer I might hope,
For all the paines and woes that I endure,
To come at length vnto the wished scope
Of my desire ; or might my selfe assure,
That happie port for euer to recure.
Then would I thinke these paines no paines at
    all,
And all my woes to be but penance small.   300

Then would I sing of thine immortall praise
An heauenly Hymne, such as the Angels sing,
And thy triumphant name then would I raise
Boue all the gods, thee onely honoring,
My guide, my God, my victor, and my king ;
Till then, dread Lord, vouchsafe to take of me
This simple song, thus fram'd in praise of thee.

FINIS.

AN HYMNE IN
HONOVR OF
BEAVTIE.

AH whither, Loue, wilt thou now carrie mee?
    What wontlesse fury dost thou now inspire
Into my feeble breast, too full of thee ?
Whylest seeking to aslake thy raging fyre,
Thou in me kindlest much more great desyre,
And vp aloft aboue my strength doest rayse
The wondrous matter of my fyre to prayse.

That as I earst in praise of thine owne name,
So now in honour of thy Mother deare,   9
An honourable Hymne I eke should frame ;
And with the brightnesse of her beautie cleare,
The rauisht harts of gazefull men might reare,
To admiration of that heauenly light,
From whence proceeds such soule enchaunting
   might.

Therto do thou great Goddesse, queene of
   Beauty,
Mother of loue, and of all worlds delight,
Without whose souerayne grace and kindly
   dewty,
Nothing on earth seemes fayre to fleshly sight,
Doe thou vouchsafe with thy loue-kindling
   light,
T'illuminate my dim and dulled eyne,   20
And beautifie this sacred hymne of thyne.

That both to thee, to whom I meane it most,
And eke to her, whose faire immortall beame,
Hath darted fyre into my feeble ghost,
That now it wasted is with woes extreame,
It may so please that she at length will streame
Some deaw of grace, into my withered hart,
After long sorrow and consuming smart.

WHat time this worlds great workmaister
   did cast
To make al things, such as we now behold, 30
It seemes that he before his eyes had plast
A goodly Paterne, to whose perfect mould
He fashiond them as comely as he could ;
That now so faire and seemely they appeare,
As nought may be amended any wheare.

That wondrous Paterne wheresoere it bee,
Whether in earth layd vp in secret store,
Or else in heauen, that no man may it see
With sinfull eyes, for feare it to deflore,
Is perfect Beautie which all men adore,   40
Whose face and feature doth so much excell
All mortal sence, that none the same may tell.

Thereof as euery earthly thing partakes,
Or more or lesse by influence diuine,
So it more faire accordingly it makes,
And the grosse matter of this earthly myne,
Which clotheth it, thereafter doth refyne,
Doing away the drosse which dims the light
Of that faire beame, which therein is empight.

For through infusion of celestiall powre,   50
The duller earth it quickneth with delight,
And life-full spirits priuily doth powre
Through all the parts, that to the lookers sight
They seeme to please. That is thy soueraine
   might,
O *Cyprian* Queene, which flowing from the beame
Of thy bright starre, thou into them doest
   streame.

Tʌat is the thing which giueth pleasant grace
To all things faire, that kindleth liuely fyre,
Light of thy lampe, which shyning in the face,
Thence to the soule darts amorous desyre,   60
And robs the harts of those which it admyre,
Therewith thou pointest thy Sons poysned
   arrow,
That wounds the life, and wastes the inmost
   marrow.

How vainely then doe ydle wits inuent,
That beautie is nought else, but mixture made
Of colours faire, and goodly temp'rament
Of pure complexions, that shall quickly fade
And passe away, like to a sommers shade,
Or that it is but comely composition   69
Of parts well measurd, with meet disposition.

Hath white and red in it such wondrous powre,
That it can pierce through th'eyes vnto the
   hart,
And therein stirre such rage and restlesse
   stowre,
As nought but death can stint his dolours
   smart ?
Or can proportion of the outward part,
Moue such affection in the inward mynd,
That it can rob both sense and reason blynd ?

Why doe not then the blossomes of the field,
Which are arayd with much more orient hew,
And to the sense most daintie odours yield, 80
Worke like impression in the lookers vew ?
Or why doe not faire pictures like powre shew,
In which oftimes, we Nature see of Art
Exceld, in perfect limming euery part.

But ah, beleeue me, there is more then so
That workes such wonders in the minds of men.
I that haue often prou'd, too well it know ;
And who so list the like assayes to ken,
Shall find by tryall, and confesse it then,   89
That Beautie is not, as fond men misdeeme,
An outward shew of things, that onely seeme.

For that same goodly hew of white and red,
With which the cheekes are sprinckled, shal
    decay,
And those sweete rosy leaues so fairely spred
Vpon the lips, shall fade and fall away
To that they were, euen to corrupted clay.
That golden wyre, those sparckling stars so
    bright
Shall turne to dust, and loose their goodly light.

But that faire lampe, from whose celestiall ray
That light proceedes, which kindleth louers fire,
Shall neuer be extinguisht nor decay   101
But when the vitall spirits doe expyre,
Vnto her natiue planet shall retyre,
For it is heauenly borne and can not die,
Being a parcell of the purest skie.

For when the soule, the which deriued was
At first, out of that great immortall Spright,
By whom all liue to loue, whilome did pas
Downe from the top of purest heauens hight,
To be embodied here, it then tooke light   110
And liuely spirits from that fayrest starre,
Which lights the world forth from his firie carre.

Which powre retayning still or more or lesse,
When she in fleshly seede is eft enraced,
Through euery part she doth the same im-
    presse,
According as the heauens haue her graced,
And frames her house, in which she will be
    placed,
Fit for her selfe, adorning it with spoyle
Of th'heauenly riches, which she robd erewhyle.

Therof it comes, that these faire soules, which
    haue   120
The most resemblance of that heauenly light,
Frame to themselues most beautifull and braue
Their fleshly bowre, most fit for their delight,
And the grosse matter by a soueraine might
Tempers so trim, that it may well be seene,
A pallace fit for such a virgin Queene.

So euery spirit, as it is most pure,
And hath in it the more of heauenly light,
So it the fairer bodie doth procure
To habit in, and it more fairely dight   130
With chearefull grace and amiable sight.
For of the soule the bodie forme doth take :
For soule is forme, and doth the bodie make.

Therefore where euer that thou doest behold
A comely corpse, with beautie faire endewed,
Know this for certaine, that the same doth hold
A beauteous soule, with faire conditions thewed,
Fit to receiue the seede of vertue strewed,
For all that faire is, is by nature good ;
That is a signe to know the gentle blood.   140

Yet oft it falles, that many a gentle mynd
Dwels in deformed tabernacle drownd,
Either by chaunce, against the course of kynd,
Or through vnaptnesse in the substance fownd,
Which it assumed of some stubborne grownd,
That will not yield vnto her formes direction,
But is perform'd with some foule imperfection.

And oft it falles (ay me the more to rew)
That goodly beautie, albe heauenly borne,
Is foule abusd, and that celestiall hew,   150
Which doth the world with her delight adorne,
Made but the bait of sinne, and sinners scorne ;
Whilest euery one doth seeke and sew to haue it,
But euery one doth seeke, but to depraue it.

Yet nathemore is that faire beauties blame,
But theirs that do abuse it vnto ill :
Nothing so good, but that through guilty shame
May be corrupt, and wrested vnto will.
Nathelesse the soule is faire and beauteous still,
How euer fleshes fault it filthy make :   160
For things immortall no corruption take.

But ye faire Dames, the worlds deare orna-
    ments,
And liuely images of heauens light,
Let not your beames with such disparagements
Be dimd, and your bright glorie darkned quight:
But mindfull still of your first countries sight,
Doe still preserue your first informed grace,
Whose shadow yet shynes in your beauteous
    face.

Loath that foule blot, that hellish fierbrand,
Disloiall lust, faire beauties foulest blame,   170
That base affections, which your eares would
    bland,
Commend to you by loues abused name ;
But is indeede the bondslaue of defame,
Which will the garland of your glorie marre,
And quench the light of your bright shyning
    starre.

But gentle Loue, that loiall is and trew,
Will more illumine your resplendent ray,
And adde more brightnesse to your goodly hew,
From light of his pure fire, which by like way
Kindled of yours, your likenesse doth display,
Like as two mirrours by opposd reflexion,   181
Doe both expresse the faces first impression.

Therefore to make your beautie more appeare,
It you behoues to loue, and forth to lay
That heauenly riches, which in you ye beare,
That men the more admyre their fountaine may,
For else what booteth that celestiall ray,
If it in darknesse be enshrined euer,
That it of louing eyes be vewed neuer ?

But in your choice of Loues, this well aduize,
That likest to your selues ye them select,   191
The which your forms first sourse may sym-
  pathize,
And with like beauties parts be inly deckt :
For if you loosely loue without respect,
It is no loue, but a discordant warre,
Whose vnlike parts amongst themselues do
  iarre.

For Loue is a celestiall harmonie,
Of likely harts composd of starres concent,
Which ioyne together in sweete sympathie,
To worke ech others ioy and true content,
Which they haue harbourd since their first
  descent   201
Out of their heauenly bowres, where they did
  see
And know ech other here belou'd to bee.

Then wrong it were that any other twaine
Should in loues gentle band combyned bee,
But those whom heauen did at first ordaine,
And made out of one mould the more t'agree :
For all that like the beautie which they see,
Streight do not loue : for loue is not so light,
As streight to burne at first beholders sight.

But they which loue indeede, looke otherwise,
With pure regard and spotlesse true intent,
Drawing out of the obiect of their eyes,
A more refyned forme, which they present
Vnto their mind, voide of all blemishment ;
Which it reducing to her first perfection,
Beholdeth free from fleshes frayle infection.

And then conforming it vnto the light,
Which in it selfe it hath remaining still
Of that first Sunne, yet sparckling in his sight,
Thereof he fashions in his higher skill,   221
An heauenly beautie to his fancies will,
And it embracing in his mind entyre,
The mirrour of his owne thought doth admyre.

Which seeing now so inly faire to be,
As outward it appeareth to the eye,
And with his spirits proportion to agree,
He thereon fixeth all his fantasie,
And fully setteth his felicitie,

Counting it fairer, then it is indeede,   230
And yet indeede her fairenesse doth exceede.

For louers eyes more sharply sighted bee
Then other mens, and in deare loues delight
See more then any other eyes can see,
Through mutuall receipt of beames bright,
Which carrie priuie message to the spright,
And to their eyes that inmost faire display,
As plaine as light discouers dawning day.

Therein they see through amorous eye-glaunces,
Armies of loues still flying too and fro,   240
Which dart at them their litle fierie launces,
Whom hauing wounded, backe againe they go,
Carrying compassion to their louely foe ;
Who seeing her faire eyes so sharpe effect,
Cures all their sorrowes with one sweete aspect.

In which how many wonders doe they reede
To their conceipt, that others neuer see,
Now of her smiles, with which their soules they
  feede,
Like Gods with Nectar in their bankets free,
Now of her lookes, which like to Cordials bee ;
But when her words embassade forth she sends,
Lord how sweete musicke that vnto them lends.

Sometimes vpon her forhead they behold
A thousand Graces masking in delight,
Sometimes within her eye-lids they vnfold
Ten thousand sweet belgards, which to their
  sight
Doe seeme like twinckling starres in frostie
  night :
But on her lips, like rosy buds in May,
So many millions of chaste pleasures play.

All those, O Cytherea, and thousands more   260
Thy handmaides be, which do on thee attend
To decke thy beautie with their dainties store,
That may it more to mortall eyes commend,
And make it more admyr'd of foe and frend ;
That in mens harts thou mayst thy throne
  enstall
And spred thy louely kingdome ouer all.

Then Iö tryumph, O great beauties Queene,
Aduance the banner of thy conquest hie,
That all this world, the which thy vassals beene,
May draw to thee, and with dew fealtie,   270
Adore the powre of thy great Maiestie,
Singing this Hymne in honour of thy name,
Compyld by me, which thy poore liegeman am.

In lieu whereof graunt, O great Soueraine,
That she whose conquering beautie doth cap-
  tiue
My trembling hart in her eternall chaine,
One drop of grace at length will to me giue,
That I her bounden thrall by her may liue,
And this same life, which first fro me she
  reaued,
May owe to her, of whom I it receaued.   280

And you faire *Venus* dearling, my deare dread,
Fresh flowre of grace, great Goddesse of my life,
When your faire eyes these fearefull lines shal
  read,
Deigne to let fall one drop of dew reliefe,
That may recure my harts long pyning griefe,
And shew what wondrous powre your beauty
  hath,
That can restore a damned wight from death.

FINIS

AN HYMNE OF
HEAVENLY
LOVE.

LOue, lift me vp vpon thy golden wings,
  From this base world vnto thy heauens
    hight,
Where I may see those admirable things,
Which there thou workest by thy soueraine
    might,
Farre aboue feeble reach of earthly sight,
That I thereof an heauenly Hymne may sing
Vnto the god of Loue, high heauens king.

Many lewd layes (ah woe is me the more)
In praise of that mad fit, which fooles call
    loue,
I haue in th'heat of youth made heretofore,
That in light wits did loose affection moue. 11
But all those follies now I do reproue,
And turned haue the tenor of my string,
The heauenly prayses of true loue to sing.

And ye that wont with greedy vaine desire
To reade my fault, and wondring at my flame,
To warme your selues at my wide sparckling
    fire,
Sith now that heat is quenched, quench my
    blame,
And in her ashes shrowd my dying shame :
For who my passed follies now pursewes,   20
Beginnes his owne, and my old fault renewes.

BEfore this worlds great frame, in which al
    things
Are now containd, found any being place
Ere flitting Time could wag his eyas wings
About that mightie bound, which doth embrace
The rolling Spheres, and parts their houres by
    space,
That high eternall powre, which now doth moue
In all these things, mou'd in it selfe by loue.

It lou'd it selfe, because it selfe was faire ;
(For faire is lou'd ;) and of it selfe begot   30
Like to it selfe his eldest sonne and heire,
Eternall, pure, and voide of sinfull blot,
The firstling of his ioy, in whom no iot
Of loues dislike, or pride was to be found,
Whom he therefore with equall honour crownd.

With him he raignd, before all time prescribed,
In endlesse glorie and immortall might,
Together with that third from them deriued,
Most wise, most holy, most almightie Spright,
Whose kingdomes throne no thought of earthly
    wight   40
Can comprehend, much lesse my trembling verse
With equall words can hope it to reherse.

Yet O most blessed Spirit, pure lampe of light,
Eternall spring of grace and wisedome trew,
Vouchsafe to shed into my barren spright,
Some little drop of thy celestiall dew,
That may my rymes with sweet infuse embrew,
And giue me words equall vnto my thought,
To tell the marueiles by thy mercie wrought.

Yet being pregnant still with powrefull grace,
And full of fruitfull loue, that loues to get 51
Things like himselfe, and to enlarge his race,
His second brood though not in powre so great,
Yet full of beautie, next he did beget
An infinite increase of Angels bright,
All glistring glorious in their Makers light.

To them the heauens illimitable hight,
Not this round heauen, which we from hence behold,
Adornd with thousand lamps of burning light,
And with ten thousand gemmes of shyning gold,
He gaue as their inheritance to hold,   61
That they might serue him in eternall blis,
And be partakers of those ioyes of his.

There they in their trinall triplicities
About him wait, and on his will depend,
Either with nimble wings to cut the skies,
When he them on his messages doth send,
Or on his owne dread presence to attend,
Where they behold the glorie of his light,
And caroll Hymnes of loue both day and night.

Both day and night is vnto them all one, 71
For he his beames doth still to them extend,
That darknesse there appeareth neuer none,
Ne hath their day, ne hath their blisse an end,
But there their termelesse time in pleasure
    spend,
Ne euer should their happinesse decay,
Had not they dar'd their Lord to disobay.

But pride impatient of long resting peace,
Did puffe them vp with greedy bold ambition,
That they gan cast their state how to increase
Aboue the fortune of their first condition, 81
And sit in Gods owne seat without commission:
The brightest Angell, euen the Child of light,
Drew millions more against their God to fight.

Th'Almighty seeing their so bold assay,
Kindled the flame of his consuming yre,
And with his onely breath them blew away
From heauens hight, to which they did aspyre,
To deepest hell, and lake of damned fyre;
Where they in darknesse and dread horror
    dwell,   90
Hating the happie light from which they fell.

So that next off-spring of the Makers loue,
Next to himselfe in glorious degree,
Degendering to hate, fell from aboue
Through pride; (for pride and loue may ill
    agree)
And now of sinne to all ensample bee:
How then can sinfull flesh it selfe assure,
Sith purest Angels fell to be impure?

But that eternall fount of loue and grace,
Still flowing forth his goodnesse vnto all, 100
Now seeing left a waste and emptie place
In his wyde Pallace, through those Angels fall,
Cast to supply the same, and to enstall
A new vnknowen Colony therein,
Whose root from earths base groundworke
    shold begin.

Therefore of clay, base, vile, and next to nought,
Yet form'd by wondrous skill, and by his might:
According to an heauenly patterne wrought,
Which he had fashiond in his wise foresight,
He man did make, and breathd a liuing spright
Into his face most beautifull and fayre, 111
Endewd with wisedomes riches, heauenly, rare.

Such he him made, that he resemble might
Himselfe, as mortall thing immortall could;
Him to be Lord of euery liuing wight,
He made by loue out of his owne like mould,
In whom he might his mightie selfe behould:
For loue doth loue the thing belou'd to see,
That like it selfe in louely shape may bee.

But man forgetfull of his makers grace, 120
No lesse then Angels, whom he did ensew,
Fell from the hope of promist heauenly place,
Into the mouth of death, to sinners dew,
And all his off-spring into thraldome threw:
Where they for euer should in bonds remaine,
Of neuer dead, yet euer dying paine.

Till that great Lord of Loue, which him at first
Made of meere loue, and after liked well,
Seeing him lie like creature long accurst,
In that deepe horror of despeyred hell, 130
Him wretch in doole would let no lenger dwell,
But cast out of that bondage to redeeme,
And pay the price, all were his debt extreeme.

Out of the bosome of eternall blisse,
In which he reigned with his glorious syre,
He downe descended, like a most demisse
And abiect thrall, in fleshes fraile attyre,
That he for him might pay sinnes deadly hyre,
And him restore vnto that happie state,
In which he stood before his haplesse fate. 140

In flesh at first the guilt committed was,
Therefore in flesh it must be satisfyde:
Nor spirit, nor Angell, though they man surpas,
Could make amends to God for mans misguyde,
But onely man himselfe, who selfe did slyde.
So taking flesh of sacred virgins wombe,
For mans deare sake he did a man become.

And that most blessed bodie, which was borne
Without all blemish or reprochfull blame,
He freely gaue to be both rent and torne 150
Of cruell hands, who with despightfull shame
Reuyling him, that them most vile became,
At length him nayled on a gallow tree,
And slew the iust, by most vniust decree.

O huge and most vnspeakeable impression
Of loues deepe wound, that pierst the piteous
    hart
Of that deare Lord with so entyre affection,
And sharply launching euery inner part,
Dolours of death into his soule did dart;
Doing him die, that neuer it deserued, 160
To free his foes, that from his heast had
    swerued.

What hart can feele least touch of so sore
  launch,
Or thought can think the depth of so deare
  wound ?
Whose bleeding sourse their streames yet neuer
  staunch,
But stil do flow, and freshly still redound,
To heale the sores of sinfull soules vnsound,
And clense the guilt of that infected cryme,
Which was enrooted in all fleshly slyme.

O blessed well of loue, O floure of grace,
O glorious Morning starre, O lampe of light,
Most liuely image of thy fathers face,   171
Eternall King of glorie, Lord of might,
Meeke lambe of God before all worlds behight,
How can we thee requite for all this good ?
Or what can prize that thy most precious blood?

Yet nought thou ask'st in lieu of all this loue,
But loue of vs for guerdon of thy paine.
Ay me ; what can vs lesse then that behoue ?
Had he required life of vs againe,
Had it beene wrong to aske his owne with gaine?
He gaue vs life, he it restored lost ;   181
Then life were least, that vs so litle cost.

But he our life hath left vnto vs free,
Free that was thrall, and blessed that was band;
Ne ought demaunds, but that we louing bee,
As he himselfe hath lou'd vs afore hand,
And bound therto with an eternall band,
Him first to loue, that vs so dearely bought,
And next, our brethren to his image wrought.

Him first to loue, great right and reason is,
Who first to vs our life and being gaue ;   191
And after when we fared had amisse,
Vs wretches from the second death did saue ;
And last the food of life, which now we haue,
Euen himselfe in his deare sacrament,
To feede our hungry soules vnto vs lent.

Then next to loue our brethren, that were made
Of that selfe mould, and that selfe makers hand,
That we, and to the same againe shall fade,
Where they shall haue like heritage of land,
How euer here on higher steps we stand ;   201
Which also were with selfe same price re-
  deemed
That we, how euer of vs light esteemed.

And were they not, yet since that louing Lord
Commaunded vs to loue them for his sake,
Euen for his sake, and for his sacred word,
Which in his last bequest he to vs spake,
We should them loue, and with their needs
  partake ;
Knowing that whatsoere to them we giue,
We giue to him, by whom we all doe liue.   210

Such mercy he by his most holy reede
Vnto vs taught, and to approue it trew,
Ensampled it by his most righteous deede,
Shewing vs mercie, miserable crew,
That we the like should to the wretches shew,
And loue our brethren ; thereby to approue,
How much himselfe that loued vs, we loue.

Then rouze thy selfe, O earth, out of thy soyle,
In which thou wallowest like to filthy swyne
And doest thy mynd in durty pleasures moyle,
Vnmindfull of that dearest Lord of thyne ; 221
Lift vp to him thy heauie clouded eyne,
That thou his soueraine bountie mayst behold,
And read through loue his mercies manifold.

Beginne from first, where he encradled was
In simple cratch, wrapt in a wad of hay,
Betweene the toylefull Oxe and humble Asse,
And in what rags, and in how base aray,
The glory of our heauenly riches lay,   229
When him the silly Shepheards came to see,
Whom greatest Princes sought on lowest knee.

From thence reade on the storie of his life,
His humble carriage, his vnfaulty wayes,
His cancred foes, his fights, his toyle, his strife,
His paines, his pouertie, his sharpe assayes,
Through which he past his miserable dayes,
Offending none, and doing good to all,
Yet being malist both of great and small.

And looke at last how of most wretched wights,
He taken was, betrayd, and false accused, 240
How with most scornefull taunts, and fell
  despights
He was reuyld, disgrast, and foule abused,
How scourgd, how crownd, how bufleted, how
  brused ;
And lastly how twixt robbers crucifyde,
With bitter wounds through hands, through
  feet and syde.

Then let thy flinty hart that feeles no paine,
Empierced be with pittifull remorse,
And let thy bowels bleede in euery vaine,
At sight of his most sacred heauenly corse,
So torne and mangled with malicious forse,
And let thy soule, whose sins his sorrows
  wrought,   251
Melt into teares, and grone in grieued thought.

With sence whereof whilest so thy softened
  spirit
Is inly toucht, and humbled with meeke zeale,
Through meditation of his endlesse merit,
Lift vp thy mind to th'author of thy weale,
And to his soueraine mercie doe appeale ;
Learne him to loue, that loued thee so deare,
And in thy brest his blessed image beare.   259

With all thy hart, with all thy soule and
    mind,
Thou must him loue, and his beheasts em-
    brace;
All other loues, with which the world doth
    blind
Weake fancies, and stirre vp affections base,
Thou must renounce, and vtterly displace,
And giue thy selfe vnto him full and free,
That full and freely gaue himselfe to thee.

Then shalt thou feele thy spirit so possest,
And rauisht with deuouring great desire
Of his deare selfe, that shall thy feeble brest
Inflame with loue, and set thee all on fire   270
With burning zeale, through euery part entire,
That in no earthly thing thou shalt delight,
But in his sweet and amiable sight.

Thenceforth all worlds desire will in thee dye,
And all earthes glorie on which men do gaze,
Seeme durt and drosse in thy pure sighted eye,
Compar'd to that celestiall beauties blaze,
Whose glorious beames all fleshly sense doth
    daze
With admiration of their passing light,
Blinding the eyes and lumining the spright.

Then shall thy rauisht soule inspired bee   281
With heauenly thoughts, farre aboue humane
    skil,
And thy bright radiant eyes shall plainely see
Th'Idee of his pure glorie, present still
Before thy face, that all thy spirits shall fill
With sweete enragement of celestiall loue,
Kindled through sight of those faire things
    aboue.

FINIS.

AN HYMNE OF
HEAVENLY
BEAVTIE.

RApt with the rage of mine own rauisht
    thought,
Through contemplation of those goodly sights,
And glorious images in heauen wrought,
Whose wondrous beauty breathing sweet
    delights,
Do kindle loue in high conceipted sprights:
I faine to tell the things that I behold,
But feele my wits to faile, and tongue to fold.

Vouchsafe then, O thou most almightie Spright,
From whom all guifts of wit and knowledge
    flow,
To shed into my breast some sparkling light
Of thine eternall Truth, that I may show   11
Some litle beames to mortall eyes below,
Of that immortall beautie, there with thee,
Which in my weake distraughted mynd I see.

That with the glorie of so goodly sight,
The hearts of men, which fondly here admyre
Faire seeming shewes, and feed on vaine delight,
Transported with celestiall desyre
Of those faire formes, may lift themselues vp
    hyer,   19
And learne to loue with zealous humble dewty
Th'eternall fountaine of that heauenly beauty.

Beginning then below, with th'easie yew
Of this base world, subiect to fleshly eye,
From thence to mount aloft by order dew,
To contemplation of th'immortall sky,
Of the soare faulcon so I learne to fly,
That flags awhile her fluttering wings beneath,
Till she her selfe for stronger flight can breath.

Then looke who list, thy gazefull eyes to feed
With sight of that is faire, looke on the frame
Of this wyde *vniuerse*, and therein reed   31
The endlesse kinds of creatures, which by name
Thou canst not count, much lesse their natures
    aime:
All which are made with wondrous wise respect,
And all with admirable beautie deckt.

First th'Earth, on adamantine pillers founded,
Amid the Sea engirt with brasen bands;
Then th'Aire still flitting, but yet firmely
    bounded
On euerie side, with pyles of flaming brands,
Neuer consum'd nor quencht with mortall
    hands;   40
And last, that mightie shining christall wall,
Wherewith he hath encompassed this All.

By view whereof, it plainly may appeare,
That still as euery thing doth vpward tend,
And further is from earth, so still more cleare
And faire it growes, till to his perfect end
Of purest beautie, it at last ascend :
Ayre more then water, fire much more then ayre,
And heauen then fire appeares more pure and
    fayre.

Looke thou no further, but affixe thine eye 50
On that bright shynie round still mouing Masse,
The house of blessed Gods, which men call *Skye*,
All sowd with glistring stars more thicke then
    grasse,
Whereof each other doth in brightnesse passe ;
But those two most, which ruling night and day,
As King and Queene, the heauens Empire sway.

And tell me then, what hast thou euer seene,
That to their beautie may compared bee,
Or can the sight that is most sharpe and keene,
Endure their Captains flaming head to see ? 60
How much lesse those, much higher in degree,
And so much fairer, and much more then these,
As these are fairer then the land and seas ?

For farre aboue these heauens which here we see,
Be others farre exceeding these in light,
Not bounded, not corrupt, as these same bee,
But infinite in largenesse and in hight,
Vnmouing, vncorrupt, and spotlesse bright,
That need no Sunne t'illuminate their spheres,
But their owne natiue light farre passing theirs.

And as these heauens still by degrees arize, 71
Vntill they come to their first Mouers bound,
That in his mightie compasse doth comprize,
And carrie all the rest with him around,
So those likewise doe by degrees redound,
And rise more faire, till they at last ariue
To the most faire, whereto they all do striue.

Faire is the heauen, where happy soules haue
    place,
In full enioyment of felicitie,
Whence they doe still behold the glorious face
Of the diuine eternall Maiestie ; 81
More faire is that, where those *Idees* on hie,
Enraunged be, which *Plato* so admyred,
And pure *Intelligences* from God inspyred.

Yet fairer is that heauen, in which doe raine
The soueraine *Powres* and mightie *Potentates*,
Which in their high protections doe containe
All mortall Princes, and imperiall States ;
And fayrer yet, whereas the royall Seates
And heauenly *Dominations* are set, 90
From whom all earthly gouernance is fet

Yet farre more faire be those bright *Cherubins*,
Which all with golden wings are ouerdight,
And those eternall burning *Seraphins*,
Which from their faces dart out fierie light ;
Yet fairer then they both, and much more bright
Be th'Angels and Archangels, which attend
On Gods owne person, without rest or end.

These thus in faire each other farre excelling,
As to the Highest they approch more neare,
Yet is that Highest farre beyond all telling,
Fairer then all the rest which there appeare,
Though all their beauties ioynd together were :
How then can mortall tongue hope to expresse,
The image of such endlesse perfectnesse ?

Cease then my tongue, and lend vnto my mynd
Leaue to bethinke how great that beautie is,
Whose vtmost parts so beautifull I fynd :
How much more those essentiall parts of his,
His truth, his loue, his wisedome, and his blis,
His grace, his doome, his mercy and his might,
By which he lends vs of himselfe a sight.

Those vnto all he daily doth display,
And shew himselfe in th'image of his grace,
As in a looking glasse, through which he may
Be seene, of all his creatures vile and base,
That are vnable else to see his face,
His glorious face which glistereth else so bright,
That th'Angels selues can not endure his sight.

But we fraile wights, whose sight cannot sus-
    taine   120
The Suns bright beames, when he on vs doth
    shyne,
But that their points rebutted backe againe
Are duld, how can we see with feeble eyne,
The glory of that Maiestie diuine,
In sight of whom both Sun and Moone are
    darke,
Compared to his least resplendent sparke ?

The meanes therefore which vnto vs is lent,
Him to behold, is on his workes to looke,
Which he hath made in beauty excellent,
And in the same, as in a brasen booke, 130
To reade enregistred in euery nooke
His goodnesse, which his beautie doth declare.
For all thats good, is beautifull and faire.

Thence gathering plumes of perfect speculation,
To impe the wings of thy high flying mynd,
Mount vp aloft through heauenly contemplation,
From this darke world, whose damps the soule
    do blynd,
And like the natiue brood of Eagles kynd,
On that bright Sunne of glorie fixe thine eyes,
Clear'd from grosse mists of fraile infirmities.

Humbled with feare and awfull reuerence, 141
Before the footestoole of his Maiestie,
Throw thy selfe downe with trembling inno-
    cence,
Ne dare looke vp with corruptible eye
On the dred face of that great *Deity*,
For feare, lest if he chaunce to looke on thee,
Thou turne to nought, and quite confounded be.

But lowly fall before his mercie seate,
Close couered with the Lambes integrity, 149
From the iust wrath of his auengefull threate,
That sits vpon the righteous throne on hy :
His throne is built vpon Eternity,
More firme and durable then steele or brasse,
Or the hard diamond, which them both doth
    passe.

His scepter is the rod of Righteousnesse,
With which he bruseth all his foes to dust,
And the great Dragon strongly doth represse,
Vnder the rigour of his iudgement iust ;
His seate is Truth, to which the faithfull trust ;
From whence proceed her beames so pure and
    bright,   160
That all about him sheddeth glorious light.

Light farre exceeding that bright blazing sparke,
Which darted is from *Titans* flaming head,
That with his beames enlumineth the darke
And dampish aire, wherby al things are red :
Whose nature yet so much is maruelled
Of mortall wits, that it doth much amaze
The greatest wisards, which thereon do gaze.

But that immortall light which there doth shine,
Is many thousand times more bright, more
    cleare,   170
More excellent, more glorious, more diuine,
Through which to God all mortall actions here,
And euen the thoughts of men, do plaine
    appeare
For from th'eternall Truth it doth proceed,
Through heauenly vertue, which her beames
    doe breed.

With the great glorie of that wondrous light,
His throne is all encompassed around,
And hid in his owne brightnesse from the sight
Of all that looke thereon with eyes vnsound :
And vnderneath his feet are to be found   180
Thunder, and lightning, and tempestuous fyre,
The instruments of his auenging yre.

There in his bosome *Sapience* doth sit,
The soueraine dearling of the *Deity*,
Clad like a Queene in royall robes, most fit
For so great powre and peerelesse maiesty.
And all with gemmes and iewels gorgeously
Adornd, that brighter then the starres appeare,
And make her natiue brightnes seem more cleare.

And on her head a crowne of purest gold   190
Is set, in signe of highest soueraignty,
And in her hand a scepter she doth hold,
With which she rules the house of God on hy,
And menageth the euer-mouing sky,
And in the same these lower creatures all,
Subiected to her powre imperiall.

Both heauen and earth obey vnto her will,
And all the creatures which they both containe :
For of her fulnesse which the world doth fill,
They all partake, and do in state remaine, 200
As their great Maker did at first ordaine,
Through obseruation of her high beheast,
By which they first were made, and still in-
    creast.

The fairenesse of her face no tongue can tell,
For she the daughters of all wemens race,
And Angels eke, in beautie doth excell,
Sparkled on her from Gods owne glorious face,
And more increast by her owne goodly grace,
That it doth farre exceed all humane thought,
Ne can on earth compared be to ought.   210

Ne could that Painter (had he liued yet)
Which pictured *Venus* with so curious quill,
That all posteritie admyred it,
Haue purtrayd this, for all his maistring skill ;
Ne she her selfe, had she remained still,
And were as faire, as fabling wits do fayne,
Could once come neare this beauty so. uerayne.

But had those wits the wonders of their dayes
Or that sweete *Teian* Poet which did spend
His plenteous vaine in setting forth her prayse,
Seene but a glims of this, which I pretend,
How wondrously would he her face commend,
Aboue that Idole of his fayning thought,
That all the world shold with his rimes be
    fraught ?

How then dare I, the nouice of his Art,
Presume to picture so diuine a wight,
Or hope t'expresse her least perfections part,
Whose beautie filles the heauens with her light,
And darkes the earth with shadow of her sight?
Ah gentle Muse thou art too weake and faint,
The pourtraict of so heauenly hew to paint.

Let Angels which her goodly face behold
And see at will, her soueraigne praises sing,
And those most sacred mysteries vnfold,
Of that faire loue of mightie heauens king.
Enough is me t'admyre so heauenly thing,
And being thus with her huge loue possest,
In th'only wonder of her selfe to rest.

But who so may, thrise happie man him hold,
Of all on earth, whom God so much doth grace,
And lets his owne Beloued to behold: 241
For in the view of her celestiall face,
All ioy, all blisse, all happinesse haue place,
Ne ought on earth can want vnto the wight,
Who of her selfe can win the wishfull sight.

For she out of her secret threasury,
Plentie of riches forth on him will powre,
Euen heauenly riches, which there hidden ly
Within the closet of her chastest bowre,
Th'eternall portion of her precious dowre, 250
Which mighty God giuen to her free,
And to all those which thereof worthy bee.

None thereof worthy be, but those whom shee
Vouchsafeth to her presence to receaue,
And letteth them her louely face to see,
Wherof such wondrous pleasures they conceaue,
And sweete contentment, that it doth bereaue
Their soule of sense, through infinite delight,
And them transport from flesh into the spright.

In which they see such admirable things, 260
As carries them into an extasy,
And heare such heauenly notes, and carolings,
Of Gods high praise, that filles the brasen sky,
And feele such ioy and pleasure inwardly,
That maketh them all worldly cares forget,
And onely thinke on that before them set.

Ne from thenceforth doth any fleshly sense,
Or idle thought of earthly things remaine:
But all that earst seemd sweet, seemes now
    offense,   269
And all that pleased earst, now seemes to paine.
Their ioy, their comfort, their desire, their gaine,
Is fixed all on that which now they see,
All other sights but fayned shadowes bee

And that faire lampe, which vseth to enflame
The hearts of men with selfe consuming fyre,
Thenceforth seemes fowle, and full of sinfull
    blame ;
And all that pompe, to which proud minds
    aspyre
By name of honor, and so much desyre,
Seemes to them basenesse, and all riches drosse,
And all mirth sadnesse, and all lucre losse. 280

So full their eyes are of that glorious sight,
And senses fraught with such satietie,
That in nought else on earth they can de-
    light,
But in th'aspect of that felicitie,
Which they haue written in their inward ey ;
On which they feed, and in their fastened
    mynd
All happie ioy and full contentment fynd.

Ah then my hungry soule, which long hast fed
On idle fancies of thy foolish thought,   289
And with false beauties flattring bait misled,
Hast after vaine deceiptfull shadowes sought,
Which all are fled, and now haue left thee
    nought,
But late repentance through thy follies prief ;
Ah ceasse to gaze on matter of thy grief.

And looke at last vp to that soueraine light,
From whose pure beams al perfect beauty
    springs,
That kindleth loue in euery godly spright,
Euen the loue of God, which loathing brings
Of this vile world, and these gay seeming
    things ;
With whose sweete pleasures being so possest,
Thy straying thoughts henceforth for euer
    rest.   301

Prothalamion

Or

A Spousall Verse made by
Edm. Spenser.

IN HONOVR OF THE DOV-
ble mariage of the two Honorable & vertuous
Ladies,the Ladie Elizabeth *and the Ladie* Katherine
Somerset , Daughters to the Right Honourable the
Earle of *Worcester* and espoused to the two worthie
Gentlemen M. *Henry Gilford*, and
M. *William Peter* Esquyers.

AT LONDON.
Printed for *William Ponsonby.*
1596.

Prothalamion.

1

CAlme was the day, and through the trem-
  bling ayre,
Sweete breathing *Zephyrus* did softly play
A gentle spirit, that lightly did delay
Hot *Titans* beames, which then did glyster fayre:
When I whom sullein care,
Through discontent of my long fruitlesse stay
In Princes Court, and expectation vayne
Of idle hopes, which still doe fly away,
Like empty shaddowes, did aflict my brayne,
Walkt forth to ease my payne   10
Along the shoare of siluer streaming *Themmes*,
Whose rutty Bancke, the which his Riuer hemmes,
Was paynted all with variable flowers,
And all the meades adornd with daintie gemmes,
Fit to decke maydens bowres,
And crowne their Paramours,
Against the Brydale day, which is not long :
  Sweete *Themmes* runne softly, till I end my
  Song.

2

There, in a Meadow, by the Riuers side,
A Flocke of *Nymphes* I chaunced to espy,   20
All louely Daughters of the Flood thereby,
With goodly greenish locks all loose vntyde,
As each had bene a Bryde,
And each one had a little wicker basket,
Made of fine twigs entrayled curiously,
In which they gathered flowers to fill their flasket:
And with fine Fingers, cropt full feateously
The tender stalkes on hye.
Of euery sort, which in that Meadow grew,
They gathered some ; the Violet pallid blew,
The little Dazie, that at euening closes,   31
The virgin Lillie, and the Primrose trew,
With store of vermeil Roses,
To decke their Bridegromes posies,
Against the Brydale day, which was not long :
  Sweete *Themmes* runne softly, till I end my
  Song.

3

With that, I saw two Swannes of goodly hewe,
Come softly swimming downe along the Lee ;
Two fairer Birds I yet did neuer see :
The snow which doth the top of *Pindus* strew,
Did neuer whiter shew,   41
Nor *Ioue* himselfe when he a Swan would be
For loue of *Leda*, whiter did appeare :
Yet *Leda* was they say as white as he,
Yet not so white as these, nor nothing neare ;
So purely white they were,
That euen the gentle streame, the which them
  bare,

Seem'd foule to them, and bad his billowes spare
To wet their silken feathers, least they might
Soyle their fayre plumes with water not so fayre,
And marre their beauties bright,   51
That shone as heauens light,
Against their Brydale day, which was not long:
  Sweete *Themmes* runne softly, till I end my
  Song.

4

Eftsoones the *Nymphes*, which now had
  Flowers their fill,
Ran all in haste, to see that siluer brood,
As they came floating on the Christal Flood.
Whom when they sawe, they stood amazed still,
Their wondring eyes to fill,   59
Them seem'd they neuer saw a sight so fayre,
Of Fowles so louely, that they sure did deeme
Them heauenly borne, or to be that same payre
Which through the Skie draw *Venus* siluer
  Teeme,
For sure they did not seeme
To be begot of any earthly Seede,
But rather Angels or of Angels breede :
Yet were they bred of *Somers-heat* they say,
In sweetest Season, when each Flower and weede
The earth did fresh aray,
So fresh they seem'd as day,   70
Euen as their Brydale day, which was not long:
  Sweete *Themmes* runne softly, till I end my
  Song.

5

Then forth they all out of their baskets drew,
Great store of Flowers, the honour of the field,
That to the sense did fragrant odours yeild,
All which vpon those goodly Birds they threw,
And all the Waues did strew,
That like old *Peneus* Waters they did seeme,
When downe along by pleasant *Tempes* shore
Scattred with Flowres, through *Thessaly* they
  streeme,   80
That they appeare through Lillies plenteous store,
Like a Brydes Chamber flore :
Two of those *Nymphes*, meane while, two Gar-
  lands bound,
Of freshest Flowres which in that Mead they
  found,
The which presenting all in trim Array,
Their snowie Foreheads therewithall they
  crownd,
Whil'st one did sing this Lay,
Prepar'd against that Day,
Against their Brydale day, which was not long:
  Sweete *Themmes* runne softly, till I end my
  Song.   90

6

Ye gentle Birdes, the worlds faire ornament,
And heauens glorie, whom this happie hower
Doth leade vnto your louers blisfull bower,
Ioy may you haue and gentle hearts content
Of your loues couplement :
And let faire *Venus*, that is Queene of loue,
With her heart-quelling Sonne vpon you smile,
Whose smile they say, hath vertue to remoue
All Loues dislike, and friendships faultie guile
For euer to assoile.   100
Let endlesse Peace your steadfast hearts accord,
And blessed Plentie wait vpon your bord,
And let your bed with pleasures chast abound,
That fruitfull issue may to you afford,
Which may your foes confound,
And make your ioyes redound,
Vpon your Brydale day, which is not long :
  Sweete *Themmes* run softlie, till I end my
  Song.

7

So ended she ; and all the rest around
To her redoubled that her vndersong,   110
Which said, their bridale daye should not be
  long.
And gentle Eccho from the neighbour ground,
Their accents did resound.
So forth those ioyous Birdes did passe along,
Adowne the Lee, that to them murmurde low,
As he would speake, but that he lackt a tong
Yeat did by signes his glad affection show,
Making his streame run slow.
And all the foule which in his flood did dwell
Gan flock about these twaine, that did excell
The rest, so far, as *Cynthia* doth shend   121
The lesser starres. So they enranged well,
Did on those two attend,
And their best seruice lend,
Against their wedding day, which was not long :
  Sweete *Themmes* run softly, till I end my song.

8

At length they all to mery *London* came,
To mery London, my most kyndly Nurse,
That to me gaue this Lifes first natiue sourse :
Though from another place I take my name,
An house of auncient fame.   131
There when they came, whereas those bricky
  towres,
The which on *Themmes* brode aged backe doe ryde,
Where now the studious Lawyers haue their
  bowers
There whylome wont the Templer Knights to
  byde,
Till they decayd through pride :

Next whereunto there standes a stately place,
Where oft I gayned giftes and goodly grace
Of that great Lord, which therein wont to dwell,
Whose want too well now feeles my freendles
  case :   140
But Ah here fits not well
Olde woes but ioyes to tell
Against the bridale daye, which is not long :
  Sweete *Themmes* runne softly, till I end my
  Song.

9

Yet therein now doth lodge a noble Peer,
Great *Englands* glory and the Worlds wide
  wonder,
Whose dreadfull name, late through all *Spaine*
  did thunder,
And *Hercules* two pillors standing neere,
Did make to quake and feare :   149
Faire branch of Honor, flower of Cheualrie,
That fillest *England* with thy triumphs fame,
Ioy haue thou of thy noble victorie,
And endlesse happinesse of thine owne name
That promiseth the same :
That through thy prowesse and victorious armes,
Thy country may be freed from forraine harmes :
And great *Elisaes* glorious name may ring
Through al the world, fil'd with thy wide Alarmes,
Which some braue muse may sing
To ages following,   160
Vpon the Brydale day, which is not long :
  Sweete *Themmes* runne softly, till I end my
  Song.

10

From those high Towers, this noble Lord issu-
  ing,
Like Radiant *Hesper* when his golden hayre
In th'*Ocean* billowes he hath Bathed fayre,
Descended to the Riuers open vewing,
With a great traine ensuing.
Aboue the rest were goodly to bee seene
Two gentle Knights of louely face and feature
Beseeming well the bower of anie Queene, 170
With gifts of wit and ornaments of nature,
Fit for so goodly stature :
That like the twins of *Ioue* they seem'd in sight,
Which decke the Bauldricke of the Heauens
  bright.
They two forth pacing to the Riuers side,
Receiued those two faire Brides, their Loues
  delight,
Which at th'appointed tyde,
Each one did make his Bryde,
Against their Brydale day, which is not long :
  Sweete *Themmes* runne softly, till I end my
  Song.   180

FINIS.

MISCELLANEOVS SONNETS.

I

To the right worshipfull my singular good Frend, M. Gabriell Haruey, Doctor of the Lawes.

HAruey, the happy aboue happiest men,
I read; that, sitting like a looker-on
Of this worldes stage, doest note, with critique pen,
The sharpe dislikes of each condition;
And, as one carelesse of suspition,
Ne fawnest for the fauour of the great,
Ne fearest foolish reprehension
Of faulty men, which daunger to thee threat:
But freely doest of what thee list entreat,
Like a great lord of peerelesse liberty;
Lifting the good up to high Honours seat,
And the euill damning euermore to dy;
  For Life, and Death, is in thy doomefull writing!
  So thy renowme liues euer by endighting.

Dublin, this xviij. of July, 1586.

Your deuoted frend during life,
EDMVND SPENCER.

II

Prefixed to *Nennio, or A Treatise of Nobility*, &c.

WHo so wil seeke by right desertst'attaine,
Vnto the type of true Nobility,
And not by painted shewes and titles vaine,
Deriued farre from famous Auncestrie:
Behold them both in their right visnomy
Here truly pourtrayt, as they ought to be,
And striuing both for termes of dignitie,
To be aduanced highest in degree.
And, when thou doost with equall insight see
The ods twixt both, of both them deem aright,
And chuse the better of them both to thee:
But thanks to him that it deserues, behight;
  To Nenna first, that first this worke created,
  And next to Jones, that truely it translated.

ED. SPENSER.

III

Upon the Historie of George Castriot, alias Scanderbeg, king of the Epirots, translated into English.

WHerefore doth vaine antiquitie so vaunt
Her ancient monuments of mightie peeres,
And old Heroes, which their world did daunt
With their great deedes, and fild their childrens eares?
Who, rapt with wonder of their famous praise,
Admire their statues, their Colossoes great,
Their rich triumphall Arcks which they did raise,
Their huge Pyramids, which do heauen threat
Lo one, whom later age hath brought to light,
Matchable to the greatest of those great;
Great both by name, and great in power and might,
And meriting a meere triumphant seate.
  The scourge of Turkes, and plague of infidels,
  Thy acts, O Scanderbeg, this volume tels.

ED. SPENSER

IV

Prefixed to *The Commonwealth and Government of Venice*.

THe antique *Babel*, Empresse of the East,
    Vpreard her buildinges to the threatned
        skie :
And second *Babell*, tyrant of the West,
Her ayry Towers upraised much more high.
But with the weight of their own surquedry,
They both are fallen, that all the earth did
    feare,
And buried now in their own ashes ly,
Yet shewing by their heapes how great they
    were.
But in their place doth now a third appeare,
Fayre *Venice*, flower of the last worlds delight,
And next to them in beauty draweth neare,
But farre exceedes in policie of right.
    Yet not so fayre her buildinges to behold
    As *Lewkenors* stile that hath her beautie told.

                                        EDM. SPENCER.

APPENDIX

OF EPIGRAMS AND SONNETS

FROM :

A THEATRE

wherein be repre-
sented as wel the miseries & calamities that follow the voluptuous Worldlings,

*As also the greate ioyes and
plesures which the faith-
full do enioy.*

An Argument both profitable and
delectable, to all that sincerely
loue the word of God.

*Deuised by S. Iohn van-
der Noodt.*

Seene and allowed according
to the order appointed.

¶ Imprinted at London by
Henry Bynneman.
Anno Domini. 1569.

CVM PRIVILEGIO.

Epigrams.

BEing one day at my window all alone,
So many strange things hapned me to see,
As much it grieueth me to thinke thereon.
At my right hande, a Hinde appearde to me,
So faire as mought the greatest God delite :
Two egre Dogs dyd hir pursue in chace,
Of which the one was black, the other white.
With deadly force so in their cruell race
They pinchte the haunches of this gentle beast,
That at the last, and in shorte time, I spied,
Vnder a rocke, where she (alas) opprest,
Fell to the grounde, and there vntimely dide.
Cruell death vanquishing so noble beautie,
Oft makes me waile so harde a destinie.

AFter at Sea a tall Ship dyd appere,
Made all of Heben and white Iuorie,
The sailes of Golde, of Silke the tackle were :
Milde was the winde, calme seemed the sea to be :
The Skie eche where did shew full bright and faire.
With riche treasures this gay ship fraighted was.
But sodaine storme did so turmoyle the aire,
And tombled vp the sea, that she, alas,
Strake on a rocke that vnder water lay.
O great misfortune, O great griefe, I say,
Thus in one moment to see lost and drownde
So great riches, as lyke can not be founde.

THen heauenly branches did I see arise,
Out of a fresh and lusty Laurell tree
Amidde the yong grene wood. Of Paradise
Some noble plant I thought my selfe to see,
Suche store of birdes therein yshrouded were,
Chaunting in shade their sundry melodie.
My sprites were rauisht with these pleasures there.
While on this Laurell fixed was mine eye,
The Skie gan euery where to ouercast,
And darkned was the welkin all aboute,
When sodaine flash of heauens fire outbrast,
And rent this royall tree quite by the roote.
Which makes me much and euer to complaine,
For no such shadow shal be had againe.

WIthin this wood, out of the rocke did rise
A Spring of water mildely romblyng downe,
Whereto approched not in any wise
The homely Shepherde, nor the ruder cloune,
But many Muses, and the Nymphes withall,
That sweetely in accorde did tune their voice
Vnto the gentle sounding of the waters fall.
The sight wherof dyd make my heart reioyce.
But while I toke herein my chiefe delight,
I sawe (alas) the gaping earth deuoure
The Spring, the place, and all cleane out of sight.
Whiche yet agreues my heart euen to this houre.

I Saw a Phœnix in the wood alone,
With purple wings and crest of golden hew,
Straunge birde he was, wherby I thought anone,
That of some heauenly wight I had the vew :
Vntill he came vnto the broken tree
And to the spring that late deuoured was.
What say I more ? Eche thing at length we see
Doth passe away : the Phœnix there, alas,
Spying the tree destroyde, the water dride,
Himselfe smote with his beake, as in disdaine,
And so forthwith in great despite he dide.
For pitie and loue my heart yet burnes in paine.

AT last so faire a Ladie did I spie,
That in thinking on hir I burne and quake,
On herbes and floures she walked pensiuely.
Milde, but yet loue she proudely did forsake.
White seemed hir robes, yet wouen so they were,
As snowe and golde together had bene wrought.
Aboue the waste a darke cloude shrouded hir,
A stinging Serpent by the heele hir caught,
Wherewith she languisht as the gathered floure :
And well assurde she mounted vp to joy.
Alas in earth so nothing doth endure
But bitter griefe that dothe our hearts anoy.

MY Song thus now in thy Conclusions,
Say boldly that these same six visions
Do yelde vnto thy lorde a sweete request,
Ere it be long within the earth to rest.

Sonets.

IT was the time when rest the gift of Gods
Sweetely sliding into the eyes of men,
Doth drowne in the forgetfulnesse of slepe,
The carefull trauailes of the painefull day :
Then did a ghost appeare before mine eyes
On that great riuers banke that runnes by Rome,
And calling me then by my propre name,

He bade me vpwarde vnto heauen looke.
He cride to me, and loe (quod he) beholde,
What vnder this great Temple is containde,
Loe all is nought but flying vanitie.
So I knowing the worldes vnstedfastnesse,
Sith onely God surmountes the force of tyme,
In God alone do stay my confidence.

*O*N hill, a frame an hundred cubites hie
  I sawe, an hundred pillers eke about,
All of fine Diamant decking the front,
And fashiond were they all in Dorike wise.
Of bricke, ne yet of marble was the wall,
But shining Christall, which from top to base
Out of deepe vaute threw forth a thousand rayes
Vpon an hundred steps of purest golde.
Golde was the parget : and the sielyng eke
Did shine all scaly with fine golden plates.
The floore was Iaspis, and of Emeraude.
O worldes vainenesse. A sodein earthquake loe,
Shaking the hill euen from the bottome deepe,
Threwe downe this building to the lowest stone.

*T*Hen did appeare to me a sharped spire
  Of diamant, ten feete eche way in square,
Iustly proportionde vp vnto his height,
So hie as mought an Archer reache with sight.
Vpon the top therof was set a pot
Made of the mettall that we honour most.
And in this golden vessell couched were
The ashes of a mightie Emperour.
Vpon foure corners of the base there lay
To beare the frame, foure great Lions of golde.
A worthie tombe for such a worthie corps.
Alas, nought in this worlde but griefe endures
A sodaine tempest from the heauen, I saw,
With flushe stroke downe this noble monument.

*I*Saw raisde vp on pillers of Iuorie,
  Whereof the bases were of richest golde,
The chapters Alabaster, Christall frises,
The double front of a triumphall arke.
On eche side portraide was a victorie.
With golden wings in habite of a Nymph.
And set on hie vpon triumphing chaire,
The auncient glorie of the Romane lordes.
The worke did shewe it selfe not wrought by man,
But rather made by his owne skilfull hande
That forgeth thunder dartes for Ioue his sire.
Let me no more see faire thing vnder heauen,
Sith I haue seene so faire a thing as this,
With sodaine falling broken all to dust.

*T*Hen I behelde the faire Dodonian tree,
  Vpon seuen hilles throw forth his gladsome
      shade,
And Conquerers bedecked with his leaues
Along the bankes of the Italian streame.
There many auncient Trophees were erect,
Many a spoile, and many goodly signes,
To shewe the greatnesse of the stately race,
That erst descended from the Troian bloud.

Rauisht I was to see so rare a thing,
When barbarous villaines in disordred heape,
Outraged the honour of these noble bowes.
I hearde the tronke to grone vnder the wedge.
And since I saw the roote in hie disdaine
Sende forth againe a twinne of forked trees.

*I*Saw the birde that dares beholde the Sunne,
  With feeble flight venture to mount to heauen.
By more and more she gan to trust hir wings,
Still folowing th'example of hir damme :
I saw hir rise, and with a larger flight
Surmount the toppes euen of the hiest hilles,
And pierce the cloudes, and with hir wings to reache
The place where is the temple of the Gods,
There was she lost, and sodenly I saw
Where tombling through the aire in lompe of fire,
All flaming downe she fell vpon the plaine.
I saw hir bodie turned all to dust,
And saw the foule that shunnes the cherefull light
Out of hir ashes as a worme arise.

*T*Hen all astonned with this nightly ghost,
  I saw an hideous body big and strong,
Long was his beard, and side did hang his hair,
A grisly forehed and Saturnelike face.
Leaning against the belly of a pot
He shed a water, whose outgushing streame
Ran flowing all along the creekie shoare
Where once the Troyan Duke with Turnus fought.
And at his feete a bitch Wolfe did giue sucke
To two yong babes. In his right hand he bare
The tree of peace, in left the conquering Palme,
His head was garnisht with the Laurel bow.
Then sodenly the Palme and Oliue fell,
And faire greene Laurel witherd vp and dide.

*H*Ard by a riuers side, a wailing Nimphe,
  Folding hir armes with thousand sighs to
      heauen
Did tune hir plaint to falling riuers sound,
Renting hir faire visage and golden haire,
Where is (quod she) this whilome honored face ?
Where is thy glory and the auncient praise,
Where all worldes hap was reposed,
When erst of Gods and man I worshipt was ?
Alas, suffisde it not that ciuile bate
Made me the spoile and bootie of the world
But this new Hydra mete to be assailde
Euen by an hundred such as Hercules,
With seuen springing heds of monstrous crimes,
So many Neroes and Caligulaes
Must still bring forth to rule this croked shore.

*V*Pon a hill I saw a kindled flame,
   Mounting like waues with triple point to
     heauen,
Which of incense of precious Ceder tree
With Balmelike odor did perfume the aire.
A bird all white, well fetherd on hir winges
Hereout did flie vp to the throne of Gods,
And singing with most plesant melodie
She climbed vp to heauen in the smoke.
Of this faire fire the faire dispersed rayes
Threw forth abrode a thousand shining leames,
When sodain dropping of a golden shoure
Gan quench the glystering flame. O greuous
   chaunge !
That which erstwhile so pleasaunt scent did yelde,
Of Sulphure now did breathe corrupted smel.

I Saw a fresh spring rise out of a rocke,
   Clere as Christall against the Sunny beames,
The bottome yellow like the shining land,
That golden Pactol driues vpon the plaine.
It seemed that arte and nature striued to ioyne
There in one place all pleasures of the eye.
There was to heare a noise alluring slepe
Of many accordes more swete than Mermaids
   song,
The seates and benches shone as Iuorie,
An hundred Nymphes sate side by side about,
When from nie hilles a naked rout of Faunes
With hideous cry assembled on the place,
Which with their feete vncleane the water fouled,
Threw down the seats, and droue the Nimphs to
   flight.

*A*T length, euen at the time when Morpheus
   Most truely doth appeare vnto our eyes,
Wearie to see th'inconstance of the heauens :
I saw the great Typhæus sister come,
Hir head full brauely with a morian armed,
In maiestie she seemde to matche the Gods.
And on the shore, harde by a violent streame,
She raisde a Trophee ouer all the worlde.
An hundred vanquisht kings groäte at hir feete,
Their armes in shamefull wise bounde at their
   backes.
While I was with so dreadfull sight afrayde,
I saw the heauens warre against hir tho,
And seing hir striken fall with clap of thunder,
With so great noyse I start in sodaine wonder.

I Saw an vgly beast come from the sea,
   That seuen heads, ten crounes, ten hornes did
     beare,
Hauing theron the vile blaspheming name.
The cruell Leopard she resembled much :
Feete of a beare, a Lions throte she had.

The mightie Dragon gaue to hir his power.
One of hir heads yet there I did espie,
Still freshly bleeding of a grieuous wounde.
One cride aloude. What one is like (quod he)
This honoured Dragon, or may him withstande ?
And then came from the sea a sauage beast,
With Dragons speche, and shewde his force by fire,
With wondrous signes to make all wights adore
The beast, in setting of hir image vp.

I Saw a Woman sitting on a beast
   Before mine eyes, of Orenge colour hew :
Horrour and dreadfull name of blasphemie
Filde hir with pride. And seuen heads I saw,
Ten hornes also the stately beast did beare.
She seemde with glorie of the scarlet faire,
And with fine perle and golde puft vp in heart.
The wine of hooredome in a cup she bare.
The name of Mysterie writ in hir face.
The bloud of Martyrs dere were hir delite.
Most fierce and fell this woman seemde to me.
An Angell then descending downe from Heauen,
With thondring voice cride out aloude, and sayd,
Now for a truth great Babylon is fallen.

*T*Hen might I see vpon a white horse set
   The faithfull man with flaming counte-
     naunce,
His head did shine with crounes set therupon.
The worde of God made him a noble name.
His precious robe I saw embrued with bloud.
Then saw I from the heauen on horses white,
A puissant armie come the selfe same way.
Then cried a shining Angell as me thought,
That birdes from aire descending downe on earth
Should warre vpon the kings, and eate their flesh.
Then did I see the beast and Kings also
Ioinyng their force to slea the faithfull man.
But this fierce hatefull beast and all hir traine,
Is pitilesse throwne downe in pit of fire.

I Saw new Earth, new Heauen, sayde Saint
   Iohn.
And loe, the sea (quod he) is now no more.
The holy Citie of the Lorde, from hye
Descendeth garnisht as a loued spouse.
A voice then sayde, beholde the bright abode
Of God and men. For he shall be their God.
And all their teares he shall wipe cleane away.
Hir brightnesse greater was than can be founde.
Square was this Citie, and twelue gates it had.
Eche gate was of an orient perfect pearle,
The houses golde, the pauement precious stone.
A liuely streame, more cleere than Christall is,
Ranne through the mid, sprong from triumphant
   seat.
There growes lifes fruite vnto the Churches good.

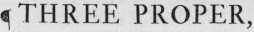

¶ THREE PROPER,
and wittie, familiar Letters:
lately paſſed betvvene tvvo V-
niuerſitie men : touching the Earthquake in Aprill laſt, and our Engliſh
refourmed Verſifying.

With the Preface of a wellwiller
to them both.

IMPRINTED AT LON-
don, by H.Bynneman, dvvelling
in Thames ſtreate, neere vnto
Baynardes Caſtell.

Anno Domini. 1580.

Cum gratia & priuilegio Regiæ Maieſtatis

x

¶TO THE CVRTEOVS
Buyer, by a VVelwiller of
the tvvo Authours.

CVrteous Buyer, (for I write not to the enuious Carper) it was my good happe, as I inter-
preate it, nowe lately at the fourthe or fifte hande, to bee made acquainted wyth the *three
Letters following*, by meanes of a faithfull friende, who with muche entreaty had procured the
copying of them oute, at *Immeritos* handes. And I praye you, interprete it for your good
happe, so soone after to come so easilye by them, throughe my meanes, who am onely to craue
these twoo things at your handes, to thinke friendely of my friendly meaning, and to take
them of me wyth this Presumption, *In exiguo quandoque cespite latet lepus :* and many pretious stones, thoughe in quantitie small, yet in qualitie and valewe are esteemed for great.
The first, for a good familiar and sensible Letter, sure liketh me verye well, and gyueth some
hope of good mettall in the Author, in whome I knowe myselfe to be very good partes
otherwise. But shewe me, or *Immerito*, two Englyshe Letters in Printe, in all pointes equall
to the other twoo, both for the matter it selfe, and also for the manner of handling, and saye,
wee neuer sawe good Englishe Letter in our liues. And yet I am credibly certified by the
foresaide faithfull and honest friende, that himselfe hathe written manye of the same stampe
bothe to Courtiers and others, and some of them discoursing vppon matter of great waight
and importance, wherein he is said, to be fully as sufficient and hable, as in these schollerly
pointes of Learning. The whiche Letters and Discourses I would very gladly see in Writing,
but more gladly in Printe, if it might be obtayned. And at this time to speake my conscience
in a worde of *these two following*, I esteeme them for twoo of the rarest, and finest Treaties,
as wel for ingenious deuising, as also for significant vttering, and cleanly conueying of his matter,
that euer I read in this Tongue : and I hartily thanke God for bestowing vppon vs some such
proper and hable men with their penne, as I hartily thanke the Author himselfe, for vsing
his pleasaunte, and witty Talente, with so muche discretion, and with so little harme, contrarye to the veine of moste, whych haue thys singular conceyted grace in writing. If they
had bene of their owne setting forth, I graunt you they might haue beene more curious,
but beeyng so well, and so sufficiently done, as they are, in my simple iudgement,
and hauing so many notable things in them, togither with so greate varietie of
Learning, worth the reading, to pleasure you, and to helpe to garnish our
Tongue, I feare their displeasure the lesse. And yet, if they thinke I
haue made them a faulte, in not making them priuy to the Publi-
cation : I shall be alwayes readye to make them the beste
amendes I can, any other friendly waye. Surely, I wishe
them bothe hartilye wel in the Lord, and betake
you and them to his mercifull gouernemente,
hoping, that he will at his pleasure con-
uerte suche good and diuine giftes as
these, to the setting out of his
own glory, and the bene-
fite of his Churche.
This XIX. of
Iune. 1580.
(∵)

Your, and their vnfayned
friend, in the Lorde.

Three proper wittie fami-
liar Letters, lately passed be-
tvvene tvvo Vniuersitie men, touching the Earthquake in April last,
and our English reformed Versifying.

To my long approoued and singular
good friende, Master *G. H.*

Good Master *H.* I doubt not but you haue some great important matter in hande, which al this while restraineth youre Penne, and wonted readinesse in prouoking me vnto that, wherein your selfe nowe faulte. If there bee any such thing in hatching, I pray you hartily, lette vs knowe, before al the worlde see it. But if happly you dwell altogither in *Iustinians* Courte, and giue your selfe to be deuoured of secreate Studies, as of all likelyhood you doe : yet at least imparte some your olde, or newe, Latine, or Englishe, Eloquent and Gallant Poesies to vs, from whose eyes, you saye, you keepe in a manner nothing hidden. Little newes is here stirred : but that olde greate matter still depending. His Honoure neuer better. I thinke the *Earthquake* was also there wyth you (which I would gladly learne) as it was here with vs : ouerthrowing diuers old buildings, and peeces of Churches. Sure verye straunge to be hearde of in these Countries, and yet I heare some saye (I knowe not howe truely) that they haue knowne the like before in their dayes. *Sed quid vobis videtur magnis Philosophis?* I like your late Englishe Hexameters so exceedingly well, that I also enure my Penne sometime in that kinde : whyche I fynd indeede, as I haue heard you often defende in worde, neither so harde, nor so harshe, that it will easily and fairely, yeelde it selfe to oure Moother tongue. For the onely, or chiefest hardnesse, whych seemeth, is in the Accente : whyche sometime gapeth, and as it were yawneth ilfauouredly, comming shorte of that it should, and sometime exceeding the measure of the Number, as in *Carpenter*, the middle sillable being vsed shorte in speache, when it shall be read long in Verse, seemeth like *a lame Gosling, that draweth one legge after hir :* and *Heauen*, beeing vsed shorte as one sillable, when it is in Verse, stretched out with a *Diastole*, is like *a lame Dogge that holdes up one legge.* But it is to be wonne with Custome, and rough words must be subdued with Use. For, why a Gods name may not we, as else the Greekes, haue the kingdome of oure owne Language, and measure our Accentes, by the sounde, reseruing the Quantitie to the Verse : Loe here I let you see my olde vse of toying in Rymes, turned into your artificial straightnesse of Verse, by this *Tetrasticon.* I beseech you tell me your fancie, without parcialitie.

See yee the blinde foulded pretie God, that feathered Archer,
  Of Louers Miseries which maketh his bloodie Game?
Wote ye why, his Moother with a Veale hath coouered his Face?
  Trust me, least he my Looue happely chaunce to beholde.

Seeme they comparable to those two, which I translated you *ex tempore* in bed, the last time we lay togither in Westminster?

That which I eate, did I ioy, and that which I greedily gorged,
  As for those many goodly matters leaft I for others.

I would hartily wish, you would either send me the Rules and Precepts of Arte, which you obserue in Quantities, or else followe mine, that M. *Philip Sidney* gaue me, being the very same which M. *Drant* deuised, but enlarged with M. *Sidneys* own iudgement, and augmented with my Obseruations, that we might both accorde and agree in one: leaste we ouerthrowe one an other, and be ouerthrown of the rest. Truste me, you will hardly beleeue what greate good liking and estimation Maister *Dyer* had of youre *Satyricall Verses*, and I, since the viewe thereof, hauing before of my selfe had speciall liking of *Englishe Versifying*, am euen nowe aboute to giue you some token, what, and howe well therein I am able to doe: for, to tell you trueth, I minde shortely at conuenient leysure, to sette forth a Booke in this kinde, whyche I entitle, *Epithalamion Thamesis*, whyche Booke I dare vndertake wil be very profitable for the knowledge, and rare for the Inuention, and manner of handling. For in setting forth the marriage of the Thames: I shewe his first beginning, and offspring, and all the Countrey, that he passeth thorough, and also describe all the Riuers throughout Englande, whyche came to this Wedding, and their righte names, and right passage, &c. A worke beleeue me, of much labour, wherein notwith-

standing Master *Holinshed* hath muche furthered and aduantaged me, who therein hath bestowed singular paines, in searching oute their firste heades, and sourses: and also in tracing, and dogging out all their Course, til they fall into the Sea.

> *O Tite, siquid, ego,*
> *Ecquid erit pretij?*

But of that more hereafter. Nowe, my *Dreames*, and *dying Pellicane*, being fully finished (as I partelye signified in my laste Letters) and presentlye to bee imprinted, I wil in hande forthwith with my *Faery Queene*, whyche I praye you hartily send me with al expedition: and your frendly Letters, and long expected Iudgement wythal, whyche let not be shorte, but in all pointes suche, as you ordinarilye vse, and I extraordinarily desire. *Multum vale. Westminster. Quarto Nonas Aprilis* 1580. *Sed, amabò te, Meum Corculum tibi se ex animo commendat plurimùm: iamdiu mirata, te nihil ad literas suas responsi dedisse. Vide quæso, ne id tibi Capitale sit: Mihi certè quidem erit, neque tibi hercle impunè, vt opinor, Iterum vale, et quàm voles sæpè.*

Yours alwayes to commaunde

IMMERITO.

Postscripte.

I take best my *Dreames* shoulde come forth alone, being growen by meanes of the Glosse, (running continually in maner of a Paraphrase) full as great as my *Calendar*. Therin be some things excellently, and many things wittily discoursed of *E. K.* and the Pictures so singularly set forth, and purtrayed, as if *Michael Angelo* were there, he could (I think) nor amende the best, nor reprehende the worst. I know you

woulde lyke them passing wel. Of my *Stemmata Dudleiana*, and especially of the sundry Apostrophes therein, addressed you knowe to whome, muste more aduisement be had, th..ii so lightly to sende them abroade: howbeit, trust me (though I doe neuer very well,) yet in my owne fancie, I neuer dyd better: *Veruntamen te sequor solùm: nunquam verò assequar.*

A Pleasant and pitthy fami-
liar discourse, of the Earthquake
in Aprill last.

To my loouing frende, *M. Immerito.*

Ignor Immerito, after as many gentle God-morrowes, as your self, and your sweete Harte listeth: May it please your Maister-shippe to dispense with a poore Oratour of yours, for breaking one principall graund Rule of our olde inuiolable Rules of Rhetorick, in shewing himselfe somewhat too pleasurably disposed in a sad matter: (of purpose, to meete with *A coople of shrewde wittie new marryed Gentlewomen*, which were more In-quisitiue, than Capable of Natures works) I will report you a prettie conceited *discourse*, that I had with them no longer agoe, than yester-night, in a Gentlemans house, here in *Essex.* Where being in the company of certaine cur-teous Gentlemen, and those two Gentlewomen, it was my chaunce to be well occupied, I war-rant you, at Cardes, (which I dare saye I scarcely handled a whole tweluemoonth before) at that very instant, that the Earth vnder vs quaked, and the house shaked aboue: besides the moouing, and ratling of the Table, and fourmes, where wee sat. Wherevpon, the two Gentlewomen hauing continually beene wrang-ling with all the rest, and especially with my selfe, and euen at that same very moment, making a great loude noyse, and much a doo: Good Lorde, quoth I, is it not woonderful straunge that the delicate voyces of two so propper fine Gentlewoomen, shoulde make such a suddayne terrible Earthquake? Imagining in good fayth, nothing in the worlde lesse, than that it shoulde be any Earthquake in deede, and imputing that shaking to the suddayne sturring, and remoouing of some cumberous thing or other, in the vpper Chamber ouer our Heades: which onely in effect most of vs noted, scarcely perceyuing the rest, beeing so closely and eagerly set at our game, and some of vs taking on, as they did. But beholde, all on the suddayne there commeth stumbling into the Parlour, the Gentleman of the house, somewhat straungely affrighted, and in a manner all agast, and telleth vs, as well as his Head and Tongue woulde giue him leaue, what a woonderous violent motion, and shaking there was of all things in his Hall: sensibly and visibly seene, as well of his owne selfe, as of many of his Seruauntes, and Neighbours there. I straite wayes beginnyng to thinke somewhat more seriously of the matter: Then I pray you, good Syr, quoth I, send presently one of your seruauntes farther into the Towne, to enquire, if the like hath happened there, as most likely is, and then must it needes be some Earthquake. Whereat the good fearefull Gentleman being a little reccmforted, (as mis-doubting, and dreading before, I knowe not what in his owne House, as many others did) and immediately dispatching his man into the Towne, wee had by and by certayne woord, that it was generall ouer all the Towne, and within lesse than a quarter of an howre after, that the very like behappened the next Towne too, being a farre greater and goodlyer Towne. The Gentlewoomens hartes nothing acquaynted with any such Accidentes, were maruellously daunted: and they, that immediately before were so eagerly, and greedily praying on vs, began nowe forsooth, very demurely, and deuoutely to pray vnto God, and the one especially, that was euen nowe in the House toppe, I beseeche you hartily quoth shee, let vs leaue off playing, and fall a praying. By my truely, I was neuer so scared in my lyfe, Me thinkes it maruellous straunge. What good Partener? Cannot you pray to your selfe, quoth one of the Gentlemen, but all the House must heare you, and ring All-in to our Ladyes Mattins? I see woomen are euery way vehe-ment, and affectionate. Your selfe was liker euen nowe, to make a fraye, than to pray: and will you nowe needes in all hast bee on both your knees? Let vs, and you say it, first dispute the matter, what daunger, and terror it carryeth with it. God be praysed, it is already ceased, and heere be some present, that are able cunningly, and clearkly to argue the case. I beseeche you master, or mystresse, your zealous and deuoute Passion a while. And with that turning to me, and smiling a little at the first: Nowe I pray you, Master *H*. what say you Philosophers, quoth he, to this suddayne Earthquake? May there not be some sensible Naturall cause therof, in the concauities of the Earth it self, as some forcible and violent Eruption of wynde, or the like? Yes no doubt, ir, may there, quoth I, as well, as an Intelligible Supernaturall: and peraduenture the great aboundaunce and superfluitie of waters, that fell shortly after Michaelmas last, beeyng not as yet dryed, or drawen vp with the heate of the Sunne, which hath not yet recouered his full attractiue strength and power, might minister some occasion thereof, as might easily be discoursed by Naturall Philosophie, in what sorte the poores, and ventes, and crannies of the Earth being so stopped, and fylled vp euery where with moysture, that the windie Exhal a- tions, and Vapors, pent vp as it were in the bowels thereof, could not otherwise get out, and ascende to their Naturall Originall place. But the Termes of Arte, and verye Natures of things themselues so vtterly vnknowen, as they are to most heere, it were a peece of woorke to laye open the Reason to euery ones Capacitie.

I know well, it is we that you meane, quoth one of the Gentlewomen (whom for distinction sake, and bicause I imagine they would be loath to be named, I will hereafter call, Mystresse *Inquisitiua*, and the other, Madame *Incredula*:) now I beseeche you, learned Syr, try our wittes a little, and let vs heare a peece of your deepe Uniuersitie Cunning. Seeing you Gentlewomen will allgates haue it so, with a good will, quoth I: and then forsooth, very solemnly pawsing a whyle, most grauely, and doctorally proceeded, as followeth.

The Earth you knowe, is a mightie great huge body, and consisteth of many diuers, and contrarie members, and vaines, and arteries, and concauities, wherein to auoide the absurditie of *Vacuum*, most necessarily, be very great store of substantiall matter, and sundry Accidentall humours, and fumes, and spirites, either good, or bad, or mixte. Good they cannot possibly all be, whereout is ingendred so much bad, as namely so many poysonfull, and vene-

mous Hearbes, and Beastes, besides a thousand infectiue, and contagious thinges else. If they be bad, bad you must needes graunt is subiect to bad, and then can there not, I warrant you, want an Obiect, for bad to worke vpon. If mixt, which seemeth most probable, yet is it impossible, that there should be such an equall, and proportionable Temperature, in all, and singular respectes, but sometime the Euill (in the diuels name,) will as it were interchaungeably haue his naturall Predominaunt Course, and issue one way, or other. Which euill working vehemently in the partes, and malitiously encountering the good, forcibly tosseth, and cruelly disturbeth the whole: Which conflict indureth so long, and is fostred with aboundaunce of corrupt putrified Humors, and ylfauoured grosse infected matter, that it must needes (as well, or rather as ill, as in mens and womens bodyes) brust out in the ende into one perillous disease or other, and sometime, for want of Naturall voyding such feuerous, and flatuous Spirites, as lurke within, into such a violent chill shiuering shaking Ague, as euen nowe you see the Earth haue. Which Ague, or rather euery fitte thereof, we schollers call grossely, and homely, *Terræ motus*, a moouing, or sturring of the Earth, you Gentlewomen, that be learned, somewhat more finely, and daintily, *Terræ metus*, a feare, and agony of the Earth: we being onely mooued, and not terrified, you being onely in a manner terrified, and scarcely mooued therewith. Nowe here, (and it please you) lyeth the poynt, and quidditie of the controuersie, whether our *Motus*, or your *Metus*, be the better, and more consonant to the Principles and Maximes of Philosophy? the one being manly, and deuoyde of dreade, the other woomannish, and most wofully quiuering, and shiuering for very feare. In sooth, I vse not to dissemble with Gentlewoomen: I am flatly of Opinion, the Earth whereof man was immediately made, and not wooman, is in all proportions and similitudes liker vs than you, and when it fortuneth to be distempered, and disseased, either in part, or in whole, I am persuaded, and I beleeue Reason, and Philosophy will beare me out in it, it only moooueth with the very impulsiue force of the malady, and not trembleth, or quaketh for dastardly feare.

Nowe, I beseeche you, what thinke ye, Gentlewomen, by this Reason? Reason, quoth Madame *Incredula*: By my truly, I can neither picke out Rime, nor Reason, out of any thing I haue hearde yet. And yet me thinkes all should be Gospell, that commeth from you

Doctors of Cambridge. But I see well, all is not Gould, that glistereth. In deede, quoth Mistresse *Inquisitiua*, heere is much adooe, I trowe, and little helpe. But it pleaseth Master *H.* (to delight himselfe, and these Gentlemen) to tell vs a trim goodly Tale of Robinhood, I knowe not what. Or suer if this be Gospell, I dowte, I am not in a good beleefe. Trust me truly, Syr your Eloquence farre passeth my Intelligence. Did I not teil you aforehand, quoth I, as muche? And yet would you needes presume of your Capacities in such profound mysteries of Philosophie, and Priuities of Nature, as these be? The very thinking whereof, (vnlesse happily it be *per fidem implicitam*, in beleeuing, as the learned beleeue, And saying, It is so, bycause it is so) is nighe enough, to caste you both into a fitte, or two, of a daungerous shaking feauer, vnlesse you presently seeke some remedie to preuent it. And in earnest, if ye wyll giue me leaue, vpon that small skill I haue in Extrinsecall, and Intrinsecall Physiognomie, and so foorth, I will wager all the money in my poore purse to a pottle of Hyppocrase, you shall both this night, within somwhat lesse than two howers and a halfe, after ye be layed, *Dreame* of terrible straunge Agues, and Agonyes as well in your owne prettie bodyes, as in the mightie great body of the Earth. You are very merily disposed, God be praysed, quoth Mistresse *Inquisitiua*, I am glad to see you so pleasurable. No doubt, but you are maruellous priuie to our dreames. But I pray you now in a little good earnest, doo you Schollers thinke, that it is the very reason in deede, which you spake of euen now? There be many of vs, good Mistresse, quoth I, of that opinion: wherin I am content to appeale to the knowledge of these learned Gentlemen here. And some againe, of our finest conceited heades defend this Position, (a very straunge Paradox in my fancie:) that the Earth hauing taken in too much drinke, and as it were ouer lauish Cups, (as it hath sensibly done in a maner all this Winter past) now staggereth, and reeleth, and tottereth, this way and that way, vp and downe, like a drunken man, or wooman (when their Alebench Rhetorick comes vpon them, and specially the moouing Pathetically figure *Pottypósis*), and therefore in this forcible sort, you lately sawe, payneth it selfe to vomit vp againe, that so disordereth, and disquieteth the whole body within. And, forsoothe, a fewe new Contradictorie fellowes make no more of it, but a certaine vehement, and passionate

neesing, or scbbing, or coffing, wherewithall they say, and as they say, say with great Physicall, and Naturall Reason, The Earth in some place, or other, euer lightly after any great, and suddayne alteration of weather, or diet, is exceedingly troubled, and payned, as namely this very Time of the yeare, after the extreeme pynching colde of Winter, and agayne in Autumne, after the extreeme parching heate of Sommer. But shall I tell you, Mistresse *Inquisitiua*? The soundest Philosophers in deede, and very deepest Secretaries of Nature, holde, if it please you, an other Assertion, and maintayne this for truth: (which at the leastwise, of all other seemeth maruellous reasonable, and is questionlesse farthest off from Heresie:) That as the Earth, vpponit, hath many stately, and boysterous and fierce Creatures, as namely, Men and Women, and diuers Beastes, wherof some one is in maner continually at variaunce and fewde with an other, euermore seeking to be reuenged vpon his enimie, which eft soones breaketh forth into professed and open Hostilitie: and then consequently followe set battels, and mortall warres: wherin the one partie bendeth all the force of his Ordinance and other Martiall furniture against the other: so likewise within it too, it hath also some, as vengibly and frowardly bent, as for Example, Woormes, and Moules, and Cunnyes, and such other valiauntly highminded Creatures, the Sonnes and daughters of *Mars*, and *Bellona* that nurrish ciuill debate, and contrarie factions amongst them selues: which are seldome, or neuer ended too, without miserable bloudshed, and deadly warre: and then go me their Gunnes lustily off, and the one dischargeth his Peece couragiously at the other: and there is suche a Generall dub a dubbe amongst them, and such horrible Thundering on euery syde, and suche a monstrous cruell shaking of one an others Fortes and Castels, that the whole Earth agayne, or at the least, so muche of the Earth, as is ouer, or neere them, is terribly hoysed, and ———— No more Ands, or Ifs, for Gods sake, quoth the Madame, and this be your great Doctorly learning. Wee haue euen Enoughe alreadie for our Money: and if you shoulde goe a little farther, I feare mee, you woulde make vs nyghe as cunning as your selfe: and that woulde bee a great disgrace to the Uniuersitie. Not a whitte, gentle Madame, quoth I, there be of vs, that haue greater store in our bowgets, than we can well occupie our selues, and therefore we are glad as you see, when by the fauourable, and gratious aspect of some blessed Planet, and specially our *Mercury*, or your *Venus*, it is our good Fortune, to lighte on such good friendes, as you, and some other good Gentlewoomen be, that take pleasure, and comfort in such good things. Wherat Mistresse *Inquisitiua*, laughing right out, and beginning to demaunde I know not what, (me thought, shee made, as if it shoulde haue been some goodly plausible Jest, wherat shee is, and takes her selfe prettily good :) Well, well, Master *H.* quoth the Gentleman of the house, now you haue playde your part so cunningly with the Gentlewoomen, (as I warrant you shall be re-membred of *Inquisitiua*, when you are gone, and may happely forget her : which I hope, Mistresse *Incredula* will do sometyme too, by hir leaue :) I pray you in earnest, let vs men learne some thing of you too : and especially I would gladly heare your Iudgement, and resolution, whether you counte of Earthquakes. as Naturall, or Supernaturall motions. But the shorter, all the better. To whom I made answere, in effect, as followeth :

Master Hˢ. short, but sharpe, and learned Iudgement of Earthquakes.

TRuely Syr, vnder correction, and in my fancie : The Earthquakes themselues I would saye are Naturall: as I veryly beleeue the Internall Causes thereof, are : I meane those two Causes, which the Logicians call, the Materiall, and the Formall : Marry, the Externall Causes, which are the Efficient and Finall, I take rather of the two, to be supernaturall. I must craue a little leaue to laye open the matter.

The Materiall Cause of Earthquakes, (as was superficially touched in the beginning of our speache, and is sufficiently prooued by *Aristotle* in the seconde Booke of his *Meteors*) is no doubt great aboundance of wynde, or stoare of grosse and drye vapors, and spirites, fast shut vp, and as a man would saye, emprysoned in the Caues, and Dungeons of the Earth : which winde, or vapors, seeking to be set at libertie, and to get them home to their Naturall lodgings, in a great fume, violently rush out, and as it were, breake prison, which forcible Eruption, and strong breath, causeth an Earthquake. As is excellently, and very liuely expressed of *Ouid*, as I remember, thus :

> *Vis fera ventorum cœcis inclusa cauernis,*
> *Exspirare aliquò cupiens, luctataque frustra*
> *Liberiore frui cœlo, cùm carcere Rima*
> *Nulla foret, toto nec peruia flatibus esset,*
> *Extentam tumefecit humum, ceu spiritus oris,*
> *Tendere vesicam solet,* and so foorth.

The formall Cause, is nothing but the very manner of this same Motion, and shaking of the Earth without : and the violent kinde of striuing, and wrastling of the windes, and Exhalations within : which is, and must needes be done in this, or that sort, after one fashion, or other. Nowe, syr, touching the other two Causes, which I named Externall : The first immediate Efficient, out of all Question, is God himselfe, the Creatour, and Continuer, and Corrector of Nature, and therefore Supernaturall : whose onely voyce carrieth such a reuerend and terrible Maiestie with it, that the very Earth againe, and highest Mountaines quake and tremble at the sounde and noyse thereof : the text is rife in euery mans mouth : *Locutus est Dominus et contremuit Terra :* howbeit, it is not to be gainesayd, that is holden of all the auncient Naturall Philosophers, and Astronomers, for the principall, or rather sole Efficient, that the Influence, and heate of the Sunne, and Starres, and specially of the three superior Planets, *Saturne, Iupiter,* and *Mars,* is a secondarie Instrumentall Efficient of such motions.

The finall, not onely that the wynde shoulde recouer his Naturall place, than which a naturall reasonable man goeth no farther, no not our excellentest profoundest Philosophers themselues : but sometime also, I graunt, to testifie and denounce the secrete wrathe, and indignation of God, or his sensible punishment vppon notorious malefactours, or, a threatning Caueat, and forewarning for the inhabitantes, or the like, depending vppon a supernaturall Efficient Cause, and tending to a supernaturall Morall End.

Which End, (for that I knowe is the very poynt, whereon you stande) albeit it be acknowledged Supernaturall and purposed, as I sayd, of a supernaturall Cause, to whom nothing at all is impossible, and that can worke supernaturally, and myraculously without ordinarie meanes, and inferiour causes : yet neuerthelesse is, we see, commonly performed, by the qualifying, and conforming of Nature, and Naturall things, to the accomplishment of his Diuine and incomprehensible determination. For being, as the olde Philosophers call him, very Nature seife, or as it hath pleased our later schoolemen to terme him, by way of distinction, *Natura Naturans*, he hath all these secondarie inferiour thinges, the foure Elementes, all sensible, and vnsensible, reasonable, and vnreasonable Creatures, the whole worlde, and what soeuer is contayned in the Compas of the worlde, being the workmanship of his owne hands, and, as they call them, *Natura naturata*, euer pliable and flexible Instrumentes at his Commaundement: to put in execution such Effectes, either ordinarie or extraordinarie, as shall seeme most requisite to his eternall Prouidence: and now in these latter dayes, very seldome, or in manner neuer worketh any thing so myraculously, and extraordinarily, but it may sensibly appeare, he vseth the seruice and Ministerie of his Creatures, in the atcheeuing thereof. I denie not, but Ɣarthquakes (as well as many other fearefull Accidentes in the same Number,) are terrible signes, and, as it were certaine manacing forerunners, and forewarners of the great latter day; and therefore out of controuersie the more reuerendly to be considered vppon: and I acknowledge considering the Euentes, and sequeles, according to the collection and discourse of mans Reason, they haue seemed to Prognosticate, and threaten to this, and that Citie, vtter ruyne and destruction: to such a Country, a generall plague and pestilence: to an other place, the death of some mightie Potentate or great Prince: to some other Realme or Kingdome, some cruell imminent warres: and sundry the like dreadfull and particular Incidentes, as is notoriously euident by many olde and newe, very famous and notable Histories to that effect. Which of all other the auncient Romaines, long before the Natiuitie of Christ, did most religiously or rather superstitiously obserue, not without a number of solemne Ceremonies, and Hollydayes for the nonce, euer after any Earthquake, making full account of some such great rufull casualtie or other, as otherwhyles fell out in very deede: and namely, as I remember, the yeare *Ante bellum Sociale*, which was one of the lamentablest, and myserablest warres, that *Italy* euer sawe: and *Plinie*, or I knowe not well who, hath such a saying: *Roma nunquam tremuit, vt non futurus aliquis portenderetur insignis Euentus.*

But yet, notwithstanding, dare not I aforehand presume thus farre, or arrogate so much vnto my selfe, as to determine precisely and peremptorily of this, or euery the like singular Earthquake, to be necessarily, and vndoubtedly a supernaturall, and immediate fatall Action of God, for this, or that singular intent, when as I am sure, there may be a sufficient Naturall, eyther necessarie or contingent Cause in the very Earth it selfe: and there is no question, but the selfe same Operation in *Genere*, or in *specie*, may at one tyme, proceeding of one Cause, and referred to one End, be preternaturall, or supernaturall: at another tyme, proceeding of an other, or the same Cause, and referred to an other End, but Ordinarie, and Naturall. To make shorte, I cannot see, and would gladly learne, howe a man on Earth, should be of so great authoritie, and so familiar acquaintance with God in Heauen, (vnlesse haply for the nonce he hath lately intertained some few choice singular ones of his priuie Counsell) as to be able in such specialties, without any iustifyable certificate, or warrant to reueale hys inccmprehensible mysteries, and definitiuely to giue sentence of his Maiesties secret and inscrutable purposes. As if they had a key for all the lockes in Heauen, or as if it were as cleare and resolute a case, as the Eclipse of the Sunne, that darkened all the Earth, or at the least all the Earth in those Countries, at Christes Passion, happening altogether prodigiously and Metaphysically in *Plenilunio*, not according to the perpetuall course of Nature, in *Nouilunio*: in so much that *Dionisius Areopagita*, or scme other graunde Philosopher, vpon the suddayne contemplation thereof, is reported in a certaine Patheticall Ecstasie to haue cryed out, *Aut rerum Natura patitur, aut Mundi machina destruetur :* as my minde giueth me, some of the simpler, and vnskilfuller sort, will goe nye to doe vpon the present sight, and agony of this Earthquake. Marry the Errour I graunt, is the more tollerable, thcugh perhappes it be otherwhiles, (and why not euen nowe,) a very presumptuous Errour in deede, standing only vpon these two weake and deceitfull grcundes, Credulitie and Ignoraunce : if so be inwardly (not onely in Externall shewe, after an Hypocriticall, and Pharisaicall manner) it certainly doo vs good for our reformation, and amendment, and seeme to preache vnto vs, *Pænitentiam agite*, (as in scme respect euery suche straunge and rare Accident may seeme ·) how Ordinarie, and Naturall so euer the Cause shall appeare otherwise to the best learned: especially, as the Earthquake shall be knowne to endure a longer, or a shorter Tyme, or to be more or lesse generall, in more, or fewer places. Which two differences, touching the quantitie of Tyme, and Place, after I had a little more fully prosecuted, alledging certaine particuler Examples thereof, howe in some places huge Castels, in some Townes, in some great and mightie Cities, in some Shires and Seigniories, and Prouinces, in some whole Countryes, and Regions haue been perillously mooued and shaken therewith: in one place, a long time together: in an other place, not so long, or at seuerall and parted times: in another, very short, as, God be thanked here euen nowe: and finally by the way, shewing a thirde and most notable difference of all, (as well for the present or imminent terrour and daunger, as otherwise) by the sundry *species*, and formes which *Aristotle*, *Plinie*, and other Meteorologicians haue set downe of Experience, as they haue heard, or read, or seen the earth to quake, to sturre, and hoyse vp Houses, Walles, Towers, Castelles, Churches, Minsters, whole Townes, whole Cities, whole Prouinces, without farther harme: to ruinate and ouerthrowe, and destroy some: to yawne and gape, and open lyke a graue, and consequently to swallow vp and deuour other: and sometime also to drinke vp whole riuers, and mightie bigge running waters withall, or to chaunge and alter their common woonted course some other way: to sinke and fall downewardes: to cast out and vomitte vp either huge vaste heapes, as it were Mountaines of Earth, or large Ilandes in the mayne Sea, neuer remembred, or seen before: or great ouerflowing waters, and fountaynes: or hotte scalding sulphurous lakes: or burning sparkles and flames of fire: to make a horrible hissing, gnashing, ratling, or some like woonderfull straunge noyse, (which all Effectes are credibly reported, and constantly auouched, of our most famous and best allowed Philosophers) a fewe such particularities, and distinctions, compendiously and familiarly coursed ouer. The good Gentleman gaue me hartily, as appeared, very great thankes, and tolde me plainly, he neuer either read, or heard halfe so much of Earthquakes before: confessing withall, that he yeelded resolutely to my opinion: that an Earthquake might as well be supposed a Naturall Motion of the Earth, as a preternaturall, or supernaturall ominous worke of God: and that he thought it hard,

and almost impossible, for any man, either by Philosophie, or Diuinitie, euermore to determine flatly the very certaintie either way. Which also in conclusion was the verdit, and finall resolution of the greater and sager part of the Gentlemen present: and namely of an auncient learned common Lawyer, that had been Graduate, and fellow of a Colledge in Cambridge, in Queene *Maries* dayes. Who tooke vpon him, to knit vp the matter, and as he said, determine the controuersie, with the authoritie of all the naturall Philosophers, old or newe, Heathen or Christian, Catholique or Protestant, that euer he read, or heard tell of. There Physickes quoth he, are in euery mans hands: they are olde enough to speake for them selues, and wee are young enough to turne our Bookes. They that haue Eyes and Tongues, let them see, and reade. But what say you nowe, quoth I, to the staying and quieting of the Earthe, beeing once a moouing? May it not seeme a more myraculous woorke, and greater woonderment, that it shoulde so suddainely staye againe, being mooued, than that it shoulde so suddainely mooue, beyng quiet and still? Mooue or turne, or shake me a thing in lyke order, be it neuer so small, and lesse than a pynnes Head, in comparison of the great mightie circuite of the Earth, and see if you shall not haue much more a doo to staye it presently, beeing once sturred, than to sturre it at the very first. Whereat the Gentleman smyling, and looking merrily on the Gentlewoomen, heere is a schoole poynt, quoth he, that by your leaues, I beleeue will poase the better scholler of you both. But is it not more than tyme, thynke ye, wee were at Supper? And if you be a hungered, Maister *H*. you shall thanke no body but your selfe, that haue holden vs so long with your profounde and clerkly discourses, whereas our manner is to suppe at the least a long howre before this tyme. Beyng set, and newe occasion of speeche ministered, our Supper put the Earthquake in manner out of our myndes, or at the leastwise, out of our Tongues: sauing that the Gentlewoomen, nowe and then pleasauntly tyhyhing betweene them selues, especially Mystresse *Inquisitiua*, (whose minde did still runne of the drinking, and Neesing of the Earth,) repeated here, and there, a broken peece of that, which had been already sayde before Supper. With deepe iudgement no doubt, and to maruellous great purpose, I warrant you after the manner of women Philosophers, and Diuines.

And this summarily in Effect was our yester-nyghtes graue Meteorologicall Conference, touching our Earthquake here in the Country : which being in so many neighbour Townes, and Villages about vs, as I heare say of this morning, maketh me presuppose, the like was wyth you also at London, and elsewhere farther of. And then forsoothe, must I desire Maister *Immerito*, to send me within a weeke or two, some odde fresh paulting threehalfepennie Pamphlet for newes : or some Balductum Tragicall Ballet in Ryme, and without Reason, setting out the right myserable, and most wofull estate of the wicked, and damnable worlde at these perillous dayes, after the deuisers best manner : or whatsoeuer else shall first take some of your braue London Eldertons in the Head. In earnest, I could wishe some learned, and well aduized Uniuersitie man, woulde vndertake the matter, and bestow some paynes in deede vppon so famous and materiall an argument. The generall Nature of Earthquakes by definition, and the speciall diuersitie of them by diuision, beyng perfectly knowen : (a thing soone done) and a complete Induction of many credible and autenticall, both olde and newe, diuine and prophane, Greeke, Lattine, and other Examples, (with discretion, and iudgement, compyled and compared togither) being considerately and exactly made, (a thing not so easily done) much no doubt myght be alledged too or fro, to terrifie or pacifie vs, more or lesse. If it appeare by generall Experience, and the foresayde Historicall Induction of particulars, that Earthquakes, *sine omni exceptione*, are ominous, and significatiue Effectes, as they saye of Comets, and carrie euer some Tragicall and horrible matter with or after them : as eyther destruction of Townes and Cities, or decay of some mightie Prince, or some particular, or generall plague, warre, or the lyke, *(vt supra)* whatsoeuer the Materiall, or Formall cause be, Natural, or supernaturall, (howbeit for myne owne part I am resolued, as wel for the one, as for the other, that these two I speake of, both Matter and Fourme, are rather Naturall in both, than otherwise) it concerneth vs, vpon the vewe of so Effectuall and substanciall euidence, to conceiue seriously, and reuerently of the other two Causes : the first, supreme Efficient, whose Omnipotent Maiestie hath nature self, and all naturall Creatures at commaundement : and the last finall, which we are to iudge of as aduisedly, and prouidently, as possibly we can, by the consideration, and

comparison of Circumstances, the tyme when : the place where ? the qualities, and dispositions of the persons, amongst whom such, and such an Ominous token is giuen. Least happily through ouer great credulitie, and rashnesse, we mistake *Non causam pro causa*, and sophistically be entrapped *Elencho Finium*. Truely, I suppose, he had neede be an excellent Philosopher, a reasonable good Historian, a learned Diuine, a wise discrete man, and generally, such a one as our Doctor *Still*, and Doctor *Byng* are in Cambridge, that shoulde shew himselfe accordingly in this argument, and to the iudgement and contentation of the wisest, perfourme it exactly. My selfe remember nothing to the contrarie, either in Philosophie, or in Histories, or in Diuinitie either, why I may not safely and lawfully subscribe to the iudgement of the noble *Italian* Philosopher, and most famous learned Gentleman, whilest he liued, Lord of *Mirandola*, and Erle of *Concordia*, Counte *Ioannes Franciscus Picus*, in my opinion, very considerately, and partly Philosophically, partly Theologically set downe, in the sixt Chapter of his sixt Booke, against Cogging deceitfull Astrologers, and Southsayers, *De rerum Prænotione, pro veritate Relligionis, contra Superstitiosas vanitates*. In which Chapter, (if happely you haue not read it already,) you shall finde many, but specially these three notable places, most effectuall and directly pertinent to the very purpose. The first more vniuersall. *Naturæ opere fieri non potest, vt Ostentis, vt Monstris magni illi, seu dextri, seu sinistri euentus portendantur, et ab aliqua pendeant proxima causa, quæ et futura etiam proferat. Impostura Dæmonum, vt id fiat, videri potest. Sed et plæraque non monstrosa, non prodigiosa per sese, pro monstris tamen, et portentis, haberi possunt, et solent à quibusdam, quibus Rerum Natura non satis comperta est, causarum enim ignoratio, noua in re Admirationem parit. Propter quam, philosophari homines cæpisse, in exordijs primæ philosophiæ scribit Aristoteles.* Wherein those two seuerall points, *Impostura Dæmonum*, and *Ignoratio causarum*, are no doubt maruellous probable, and moste worthy bothe presentlye to bee noted nowe, and more fully to be discussed hereafter : appearing vnto me the verie right principall Causes of so manye erroneous opinions, and fantasticall superstitious dreames in this, and the like behalfe.

The seconde more speciall, as it were hitting the white in deede, and cleauing the Pinne in sunder.

Idem in Terræ motibus etiam, quod in ful-guribus, fulminibusque interpretandis, obseruauit Antiquitas. Cuius Rei liber, Græco eloquio, nuper ad manus peruenit, in Orpheum relatus Autorem : sed per absurdum nimis, vt quod frequentissimè fit, pro vario terræ anhelitu, pro ventorum violentia, vaporumque conductione, (marke you that?) *ex eo rerum futurarum significationem petere, quorum nec effectus esse possunt, nec causa, præterquam forte mortis inferendæ illis, qui fulmen exceperit, aut qui terrarum hiatu perierit. Sed nec ab eadem proxima deduci causa possunt, à qua et futuræ pendeant res, vt supra deductum est.*

And then shortly after, the thirde, moste agreeable to the seconde, as flatlye determining on my side, and as directlye concluding the same position as may be.

Nec sanè Orpheus ille, si tamen Orpheus fuit, vllam affert omninò causam, cur quispiam ex terræ motibus, vrbium, hominum, regionum euenta præsagire possit. Soliùm vano narrat arbitrio : si terræ contigerit motus noctu, si æstate, si hyeme, si aurora, si interdiu, quid portendatur : Quæ certè, et saniore possunt arbitrio refelli, et Experientiæ testimonio, vt arbitror, non secus irrideri, ac supra Tagis portenta irrisimus, Haruspicinæ Autoris.

A moste excellent sounde Iudgement in my conceit : and ful wel beseeming so Honorable and admirable a Witte, as out of Question, *Picus Mirandula* had: who being yet scarcely thirty yeres of age, for his singularitie in al kind of knowleege, as wel diuine as prophane, was in Italy and France, as *Paulus Iouius* reporteth, surnamed *Phœnix*, as the odde, and in effecte the onely singular learned man of Europe : and to make shorte : suche a one, in moste respectes, as I woulde wishe nowe to be tempering with this newe notorious incident : staying my selfe in the meane while vpon this probable and reasonable *Interim* of his : and preferring it before at the friuolous coniecturall Allegations, and surmises, that oure counterfaite, and reasonlesse *Orphei* oppose to the contrarye. But, Iesu, what is all this to Master *Immerito*? Forsoothe I knowe not by what mischaunce, these miserable balde odious three halfepenny fellowes, alas, a company of silly beetleheaded Asses, came into my minde, that wil needes be sturring, and taking on in euerye suche rare and vnaccustomed euent, as if they sawe farther in a Milstone, than all the worlde besides, whereas euerie man, that hathe but halfe an eye in his head, seeth them to be more blinde, than anye Buzzarde, or Bayarde,

Scribimus indocti, doctique Poemata passim, and surely, as the worlde goeth nowe in Englande, rather the firste, for aught I see, than the laste. *O interim miseras Musas, et miserabiles :* Where the faulte shoulde rest, *viderint Oculi, atque capita Reip. Mihi quidem isthic, neque seritur admodum, neque metitur. Non valdè mea nouos Bibliothecæ libros desiderat, seipsa, id est, quos habet, veteribus contenta est. Quid plura? Tu vale, mi Immerito, atque ita tibi persuade, Aliquid esse eum, qui istorum longè est dissimillimus, quos Typographi nostri habent venales maximè.* Commende mee to thine owne good selfe, and tell thy dying Pellicane, and thy Dreames from me, I wil nowe leaue dreaming any longer of them, til with these eyes I see them forth indeede : And then againe, I imagine your *Magnificenza*, will holde vs in suspense as long for your nine Englishe *Commœdies*, and your Latine *Stemmata Dudleiana :* whiche two shal go for my money, when all is done : especiallye if you woulde but bestow one seuennights pollishing and trimming vppon eyther. Whiche I praye thee hartily doe, for my pleasure, if not for their sake, nor thine owne profite. My *Schollers Loue*, of *Reconcilement of contraries*, is shrunke in the wetting : I hadde purposed to haue dispatched you a Coppie thereof, long ere this : but, no remedie, hitherto it hath alwayes gone thus with me : Some newe occasion, or other, euer carrieth me from one matter to another, and will neuer suffer me to finishe eyther one or other. And truly, *Experto crede*, it is as true a Verse as euer was made, since the first Verse, that euer was made : *Pluribus intentus minor est ad singula sensus :* whiche my *Anticosmopolita*, thoughe it greeue him, can beste testifye, remayning still as we saye, *in statu, quo*, and neither an inche more forward, nor packewarde, than he was fully a tweluemonth since in the Courte, at his laste attendaunce vpon my Lorde there. But the Birde that will not sing in Aprill, nor in May, maye peraduenture sing in September : and yet me thinkes, *Sat citò, si sat bene*, if I coulde steale but one poore fortnight, to peruse him ouer afreshe, and coppy him out anewe. Whiche I hope in God to compasse shortly. But I beseech you, what Newes al this while at Cambridge? That was wont to be euer one great Question. What? *Det mihi Mater ipsa bonam veniam, eius vt aliqua mihi liceat Secreta, vni cuidam de eodem gremio obsequentissimo filio, reuelare : et sic paucis habeto. Nam aliàs fortasse pluribus : nunc non placet, non vacat. molestum esset.*

Tully, and *Demosthenes* nothing so much studyed, as they were wonte : *Liuie*, and *Salust* possiblye rather more, than lesse : *Lucian* neuer so much : *Aristotle* muche named, but little read : *Xenophon* and *Plato*, reckned amongest Discoursers, and conceited Superficiall fellowes : much verball and sophisticall iangling : little subtile and effectual disputing : noble and royall Eloquence, the best and persuasiblest Eloquence : no such Orators againe, as redheadded Angelles : An exceeding greate difference, betweene the countenaunces, and portes of those, that are braue and gallaunt, and of those, that are basely, or meanly apparelled : betwene the learned, and vnlearned, *Tully*, and *Tom Tooly*, in effect none at all.

Matchiauell a great man : *Castilio* of no small reputation : *Petrach*, and *Boccace* in euery mans mouth : *Galateo*, and *Guazzo* neuer so happy : ouer many acquainted with *Vnico Aretino* : The *French* and *Italian* when so highlye regarded of Schollers ? The *Latine* and *Greeke*, when so lightly ? The *Queene mother* at the beginning, or ende of euerye conference : many bargaines of *Mounsieur : Shymeirs* a noble gallant fellowe : all inquisitiue after Newes, newe Bookes, newe Fashions, newe Lawes, newe Officers, and some after newe Elementes, and some after newe Heauens, and Helles to. *Turkishe affaires* familiarly knowen : Castels builded in the Ayre : muche adoe, and little helpe : *Iacke* would faine be a Gentlemanne : in no age so little so muche made of, euery one highly in his owne fauour, thinking no mans penny, so good siluer as his own : Something made of Nothing, in spite of Nature : Numbers made of Ciphars, in spite of Arte : Geometricall Proportion seldome, or neuer vsed, Arithmeticall ouermuch abused : Oxen and Asses (notwithstanding the absurditie it seemed to *Plautus*) draw both togither in one, and the same Yoke : *Conclusio ferè sequitur deteriorem partem*. The *Gospell* taughte, not learned : Charitie key colde : nothing good, but by Imputation : the *Ceremoniall* Lawe, in worde abrogated : the *Iudiciall* in effecte disanulled : the *Morall* indeede abandoned : the *Lighte*, the *Lighte* in euery mans Lippes, but marke me their eyes, and tell me, if they looke not liker Howlets, or Battes, than Egles : as of olde Bookes, so of auntient Vertue, Honestie, Fidelitie, Equitie, newe Abridgementes : euery

day freshe span newe Opinions : Heresie in Diuinitie, in Philosophie, in Humanitie, in Manners, grounded muche vpon heresay : *Doctors* contemned : the *Text* knowen of moste, vnderstood of fewe, magnified of all, practised of none : the *Diuell* not so hated, as the *Pope :* many Inuectiues, small amendment : Skill they say controlled of Will : and Goodnesse mastered of Goods : but Agent, and Patient muche alike, neither Barrell greatly better Herring : No more adoe aboute *Cappes* and *Surplesses :* Maister *Cartwright* nighe forgotten : The man you wot of, conformable, with his square Cappe on his rounde heade : and *Non resident* at pleasure : and yet *Non-residents* neuer better bayted, but not one the fewer, either I beleeue in Acte, or I beleeue, in Purpose. A number of our preachers sibbe to *French Souldiors*, at the first, more than Men, in the end, lesse than Women. Some of our pregnantest and soonest ripe Wits, of *Hermogenes* mettall for al the world : Olde men and Counsailours amongst Children : Children amongst Counsailours, and olde men : Not a fewe dubble faced *Iani*, and chaungeable *Camelions* : ouer-manye Clawbackes, and Pickethanks : Reedes shaken of euerie Wind : Iackes of bothe sides : Aspen leaues : painted Sheathes, and Sepulchres : Asses in Lions skins : Dunglecockes : slipperye Eles : Dormise : I blush to thinke of some, that weene themselues as fledge as the reste, being, God wot, as kallowe as the rest : euery yonker to speake of as politique, and as great a Commonwealths man as Bishoppe *Gardner*, or Doctor *Wutton* at the least : as if euerie man nowe adayes hauing the framing of his own *Horoscope*, were borne in *decimo cœli domicilio*, and had al the Wit, Wisedome, and Worshippe in the world at commaundement. *Sed heus in aurem : Meministin' quod ait Varro ? Omnes videmur nobis esse belli, festiui, saperdæ, cùm sumus* [1] *Canopi : Dauid, Vlisses*, and *Solon,* fayned themselues fooles and madmen : our fooles and madmen faine themselues *Dauids, Vlisses*, and *Solons* : and would goe nigh to deceiue the cunningest, and best experienced *Metaposcopus* in a country : It is pity faire weather should euer do hurt, but I know what peace and quietnes hath done with some melancholy pickstrawes in the world : as good vnspoken as vnamended. And wil you needes haue my Testimoniall of youre olde Controllers

---

[1] In Nonius Marcellus *de Compendiosa Doctrina* s.v. *saperdae.* The true reading is *cum simus σαπροί*, but the first edition (*c.* 1470) gives *canopi* (possibly a misreading of CAΠPOI); corrected to *canopitici* in the editions of 1471 and 1483.

new behauior? A busy and dizy heade, a brazen forehead: a ledden braine: a woodden wit: a copper face: a stony breast: a factious and eluish hearte: a founder of nouelties: a confounder of his owne, and his friends good gifts: a morning bookeworm, an afternoone maltworm: a right Iuggler, as ful of his sleights, wyles, fetches, casts of Legerdemaine, toyes to mocke Apes withall, odde shiftes, and knauish practizes, as his skin can holde. He often telleth me, he looueth me as himselfe, but out lyar out, thou lyest abhominably in thy throate. Iesu, I had nigh hand forgotten one thing, that ywis somtime I think often ynough vpon: Many *Pupils*, Iackemates, and Hayle fellowes wel met, with their *Tutors*, and by your leaue, some too, because forsooth they be Gentlemen, or great heires, or a little neater and gayer than their fellowes, (shall I say it for shame? beleeue me, tis too true) their very own Tutors. *Ah mala* Licentia, *ab initio non fuit sic. Stulta est omnis iuuenilis* Doctrina, *sine virili quadam* Disciplina. *Quasi verò pauperioribus duntaxat pueris, ac non multò magis generosæ, atque nobili Iuuentuti conueniat, pristinæ illius Institutionis, atque Educationis seueritas, et ingenuæ, et prudentis, et eruditæ, et cum Tutoris personæ, tum pupillo, etiam ipsi perquam accomodatæ. Vsquequaque* sapere oportet: *id erit telum acerrimum. Cætera ferè, vt olim: Bellum inter Capita, et membra continuatum: δοχοσοφία publicis defensa scholis, priuatis confirmata parietibus,*

omnibus locis ostentata, Scire tuum *nihil est, nisi te scire, hoc sciat alter. Plurimi passim fit* Pecunia, Pudor *parui penditur: Nihil habentur* Literæ: *Mihi crede,* credendum nulli: *O amice,* amicus nemo. *Quid tu interim? Quomodo te inquies, geris? Quomodo? Optimum est aliena frui insania. Video: taceo, rideo: Dixi. Et tamen addam, quod ait Satyricus ille:*

> *Viuendum est rectè, tum propter plurima, tum his*
> *Præcipuè causis, vt linguas Mancipiorum Contemnas.*

E meo municipio, Postridie quàm superiores de Terræmotu *sermones haberentur, id est, ni fallor, Aprilis septimo, Vesperi.* With as manye gentle Goodnightes, as be letters in this tedious Letter.

Nosti manum tanquam tuam.

POSTSCRIPTE.

This Letter may only be shewed to the two odde Gentlemen you wot of. Marry I would haue those two to see it, as sone as you may conueniently.

Non multis dormio: non multis scribo: non cupio placere multis: Alij *alios numeros laudant, præferunt, venerantur: Ego ferè apud nos, ferè apud vos* Trinitatem.

Verbum sapienti sat: nosti cætera: et tres Charites habes ad vnguem

A Gallant familiar Letter, containing
an Ansvvere to that of M. Immerito, vvith
sundry proper examples, and some Precepts
of our Englishe reformed Versifying.

To my very friend *M. Immerito.*

Signor Immerito, to passe ouer youre neede-lesse complaint, wyth the residue of your preamble (for of the *Earthquake* I presuppose you haue ere this receyued my goodly dis-course) and withall to let my late Englishe Hexametres goe as lightlye as they came : I cannot choose, but thanke and honour the good Aungell, (whether it were *Gabriell* or some other) that put so good a motion into the heads of those two excellent Gentlemen *M. Sidney,* and *M. Dyer,* the two very Dia-mondes of hir Maiesties Courte for many speciall and rare qualities : as to helpe for-warde our new famous enterprise for the Ex-changing of Barbarous and Balductum Rymes with Artificiall Verses : the one being in manner of pure and fine Goulde, the other but counterfet, and base ylfauoured Copper. I doubt not but their liuelie example, and Prac-tise, wil preuaile a thousand times more in short space, than the dead Aduertizement, and persuasion of *M. Ascham* to the same Effecte : whose *Scholemaister* notwithstanding I reuerence in respect of so learned a Motiue. I would gladly be acquainted with *M. Drants* Prosodye, and I beseeche you, commende me to good *M. Sidneys* iudgement, and gentle *M. Immeritos* Obseruations. I hope your nexte Letters, which I daily exspect, wil bring me in farther familiaritie and acquaintance with al three. Mine owne Rules and Precepts of Arte, I beleeue wil fal out not greatly repugnant, though peraduenture somewhat different : and yet am I not so resolute, but I can be content to reserue the Coppying out and publishing therof, vntil I haue a little better consulted with my pillowe, and taken some farther aduize of *Madame Sperienza.* In the meane, take this for a general Caueat, and say I haue reuealed one great mysterie vnto you : I am of Opinion, there is no one more regular and iustifiable direction, eyther for the assured, and infallible Certaintie of our English Artificiall Prosodye particularly, or generally to bring our Lan-guage into Arte, and to frame a Grammer or Rhetorike thereof : than first of all vniuersally to agree vpon *one and the same Ortographie,* in all pointes conformable and proportionate to *our Common Natural Prosodye :* whether *Sir Thomas Smithes* in that respect be the most perfit, as surely it must needes be very good : or else some other of profounder Learning, and longer Experience, than *Sir Thomas* was, shewing by necessarie demonstration, wherin he is defectiue, wil vndertake shortely to sup-plie his wantes, and make him more absolute. My selfe dare not hope to hoppe after him, til I see something or other, too, or fro, publickely and autentically established, as it were by a generall Counsel, or acte of Parliament : and then peraduenture, standing vppon firmer grounde, for Companie sake, I may aduenture to do as other do. *Interim,* credit me, I dare geue no Preceptes, nor set downe any *Certaine General Arte :* and yet see my boldenesse, I am not greatly squaimishe of my *Particular Examples,* whereas he that can but reasonably skil of the one, wil giue easily a shreude gesse at the other : considering that the one fetcheth his original and offspring from the other. In which respecte, to say troth, *we Beginners* haue the start, and aduauntage of our Followers, who are to frame and conforme both their Examples, and Precepts, according to that President which they haue of vs: as no doubt *Homer* or some other in *Greeke*, and *Ennius*, or I know not who else in *Latine*, did preiudice, and ouer-rule those, that followed them, as well for the quantities of syllables, as number of feete, and the like: their onely Examples going for current payment, and standing in steade of Lawes, and Rules with the posteritie. In so much that it seemed a sufficient warrant (as still it doth in our Common Grammer schooles) to make τί in τιμὴ, and υ, in *Vnus* long, because the one hath τιμὴ δ᾽ ἐκ Διός ἐστι, and the other, *Vnus homo nobis*, and so consequently in the rest. But to let this by-disputation passe, which is already so throughly discoursed and canuassed of the best Philosophers, and namely *Aristotle*, that poynt vs, as it were with the forefinger, to the *very fountaines and head springs* of Artes, and Artificiall preceptes, in the *Analitiques*, and *Metaphysikes* : most excellently set downe in these *foure Golden Termes*, the famoussest Termes to speake of in all *Logique* and *Philosophie*, ἐμπειρία, ἱστορία, αἴσθησις, ἐπαγωγή : shall I nowe by the way sende you a *Ianuarie* gift in *Aprill*: and as it were shewe you a *Christmas Gambowlde* after *Easter* ? Were the manner so very fine, as the matter is very good, I durst presume of an other kinde of *Plaudite* and *Gramercie*, than now I will: but being as it is, I beseeche you set parcialitie aside, and tell me your maister-ships fancie.

A Nevv yeeres Gift to my old friend Maister

George Bilchaunger : In commendation of three most precious
Accidentes, *Vertue, Fame*, and *Wealth* : and finally of
the fourth, *A Good Tongue.*

VErtue *sendeth a man to* Renowne, Fame *lendeth* Aboundaunce,
Fame *with Aboundaunce maketh a man thrise blessed and happie.*
So *the Rewarde of Famous Vertue makes many wealthy,*
And *the Regard of Wealthie Vertue makes many blessed :*
O *blessed Vertue, blessed Fame, blessed Aboundaunce.*
O *that I had you three, with the losse of thirtie Comencementes.*
Nowe *farewell* Mistresse, *whom lately I loued aboue all,*
These *be my three bonny lasses, these be my three bonny Ladyes,*
Not *the like* Trinitie *againe, saue onely the* Trinitie *aboue all :*
Worship *and Honour, first to the one, and then to the other.*
A *thousand good leaues be for euer graunted* Agrippa.
For *squibbing and declayming against many fruitlesse*
Artes, *and Craftes, deuisde by the* Diuls *and* Sprites, *for a torment,*
And *for a plague to the world : as both* Pandora, Prometheus,
And *that cursed* good bad Tree, *can testifie at all times.* [*these.*
Meere *Gewgawes and Bables, in comparison of* Toyes *to mock Apes, and Woodcockes, in comparison of these.*
Iugling *castes, and knicknackes, in comparison of these.*
Yet *behinde there is one thing, worth a prayer at all tymes,*
A *good* Tongue, *in a mans Head,* A *good* Tongue *in a woomans.*
And *what so precious matter, and foode for a good* Tongue,
As *blessed* Vertue, *blessed* Fame, *blessed Aboundaunce.*

L'Enuoy.

Maruell *not, what I meane to send these Verses at Euensong :*
On Neweyeeres Euen, *and* Oldyeeres End, *as a* Memento :
Trust *me, I know not a richter* Iewell, *newish or oldish,*
Than *blessed* Vertue, *blessed* Fame, *blessed Abundaunce,*
O *blessed* Vertue, *blessed* Fame, *blessed Aboundaunce,*
O *that you had these three, with the losse of* Fortie Valetes,

He *that wisheth, you may liue to see a hundreth Good Newe yeeres, euery one happier, and merrier, than other.*

Now to requite your *Blindfolded pretie God*, (wherin by the way I woulde gladly learne, why, *Thē*, in the first, *Yē* in the first, and thirde, *Hē*, and *My*, in the last, being shorte, *Mē*, alone should be made longer in the very same) Imagin me to come into a goodly Kentishe *Garden* of your old Lords, or some other Noble man, and spying a florishing Bay Tree there, to demaunde *ex tempore*, as followeth : Thinke vppon *Petrarches*

Arbor vittoriosa, triomfale,
Onor d' Imperadori, e di Poete :

and perhappes it will aduaunce the wynges of your Imagination a degree higher : at the least if any thing can be added to the loftinesse of his conceite, whom gentle *Mistresse Rosalinde*, once reported to haue all the *Intelligences* at commaundement, and an other time, Christened her *Segnior Pegaso*.

Encomium Lauri.

WHat might I call this Tree ? A Laurell ?
  O bonny Laurell :
Needes to thy bowes will I bow this knee, and
  vayle my bonetto :
Who, but thou, the renowne of Prince, and
  Princely Poeta :
Th'one for Crowne, for Garland th'other thanketh
  Apollo.
Thrice happy Daphne : *that turned was to the*
  Bay Tree,
Whom such seruauntes serue, as challenge seruice
  of all men.
Who chiefe Lorde, and King of Kings, but
  *th'*Emperour only ?
*And Poet of right stampe, ouerawith th'*Emperour himselfe.
Who, but knowes Aretyne, *was he not halfe*
  Prince to the Princes.
And many a one there liues, as nobly minded at
  all poyntes.
Now Farewell Bay Tree, *very Queene, and*
  Goddesse of all trees,
Ritchest perle to the Crowne, and fayrest Floure
  to the Garland.
Faine wod I craue, might I so presume, some
  farther acquaintaunce,
O that I might ? but I may not : woe to my
  destinie therefore.
Trust me, not one more loyall seruaunt longes to
  thy Personage,
But what sayes Daphne ? *Non omni dormio,*
  worse lucke :

Yet Farewell, Farewell, the Reward of those,
  that I honour :
Glory to Garden : *Glory to* Muses : *Glory to*
  Vertue.

Partim Ioui, et Palladi,
Partim Apollini et Musis.

But seeing I must needes bewray my store, and set open my shoppe wyndowes, nowe I pray thee, and coniure thee by all thy amorous Regardes, and Exorcismes of Loue, call a Parliament of thy Sensible, and Intelligible powers together, and tell me, in Tom Trothes earnest, what *Il secondo, et famoso Poeta, Messer Immerito*, sayth to this bolde Satyri[c]all Libell lately deuised at the irstaunce of a certayne worshipfull Hartefordshyre Gentleman, of myne olde acquayntaunce : *in Gratiam quorundam Illustrium Anglofrancitalorum, hic et vbique apud nos volitantium. Agedum verò, nosti homines, tanquam tuam ipsius cutem.*

Speculum Tuscanismi.

Since Galateo *came in, and* Tuscanisme *gan vsurpe,*
Vanitie aboue all : Villanie next her, Statelynes Empresse.
No man, but Minion, Stowte, Lowte, Plaine, swayne, quoth a Lording :
No wordes but valorous, no workes but woomanish onely.
For life Magnificoes, not a beck but glorious in shew,
In deede most friuolous, not a looke but Tuscanish alwayes.
His cringing side necke, Eyes glauncing, Fisnamie smirking,
With forefinger kisse, and braue embrace to the footewarde.
Largebelled Kodpeasd Dublet, vnkodpeased halfe hose,
Straite to the dock, like a shirte, and close to the britch. like a diueling.
A little Apish Hatte, cowched fast to the pate, like an Oyster,
French Camarick Ruffes, deepe with a witnesse, starched to the purpose.
Euery one A *per se* A, *his termes, and braueries in Print,*
Delicate in speach, queynte in araye : conceited in all poyntes :
In Courtly guyles, a passing singular odde man,
For Gallantes a braue Myrrour, a Primerose of Honour,

A Diamond for nonce, a fellowe perelesse in England.

Not the like Discourser for Tongue, and head to be found out :

Not the like resolute Man, for great and serious affayres,

Not the like Lynx, to spie out secretes, and priuities of States.

Eyed, like to Argus, Earde, like to Midas, Nosd, like to Naso,

Wingd, like to Mercury, fittst of a Thousand for to be employde,

This, nay more than this doth practise of Italy in one yeare.

None doe I name, but some doe I know, that a peece of a tweluemonth :

Hath so perfited outly, and inly, both body, both soule,

That none for sense, and senses, halfe matchable with them.

A Vulturs smelling, Apes tasting, sight of an Eagle,

A spiders touching, Hartes hearing, might of a Lyon.

Compoundes of wisedome, witte, prowes, bountie, behauiour,

All gallant Vertues, all qualities of body and soule :

O thrice tenne hundreth thousand times blessed and happy,

Blessed and happy Trauaile, Trauailer most blessed and happy.

Penatibus Hetruscis laribusque nostris Inquilinis :

Tell me in good sooth, doth it not too euidently appeare, that this English Poet wanted but *a good patterne* before his eyes, as it might be some delicate, and choyce elegant Poesie of good *M. Sidneys*, or *M. Dyers*, (ouer very *Castor*, and *Pollux* for such and many greater matters) when this trimme geere was in hatching : Much like some *Gentlewooman*, I coulde name in England, who by all Phisick and Physiognomie too, might as well haue brought forth all goodly faire children, as they haue now some ylfauored and deformed, had they at the tyme of their *Conception*, had in sight, the amiable and gallant beautifull Pictures of *Adonis, Cupido, Ganymedes*, or the like, which no doubt would haue wrought such deepe impression in their fantasies, and imaginations, as their children, and perhappes their Childrens children too, myght haue thanked them for, as long as they shall haue Tongues in their heades.

But myne owne leysure fayleth me : and to say troth, I am lately become a maruellous great straunger at myne olde *Mistresse Poetries*, being newly entertayned, and dayly employed in our Emperour *Iustinians seruice* (sauing that I haue alreadie addressed a certaine pleasurable, and Morall Politique Naturall mixte deuise, to his most Honourable Lordshippe, in the same kynde, wherevnto my next Letter, if you please mee well, may perchaunce make you priuie :) marrie nowe, if it lyke you in the meane while, for varietie sake, to see howe I taske a young Brother of myne, (whom of playne *Iohn*, our *Italian* Maister hath Cristened his *Picciolo Giouannibattista*,) Lo here (and God will) a peece of hollydayes exercise. In the morning I gaue him this *Theame* out of *Ouid*, to translate, and varie after his best fashion.

Dum fueris fœlix, multos numerabis Amicos,
    Tempora si fuerint nubila, solus eris.
Aspicis, vt veniant ad candida tecta columbæ?
    Accipiat nullas sordida Turris Aues?

His translation, or rather Paraphrase before dinner, wus first this :

1.

Whilst your Bearnes are fatte, whilst Cofers stuffd with aboundaunce,
Freendes will abound : If bearne waxe bare, then adieu sir a Goddes name.
See ye the Dooues? they breede, and feede in gorgeous Houses :
Scarce one Dooue doth loue to remaine in ruinous Houses,

And then forsooth this : to make proofe of his facultie in Pentameters too, affecting a certaine *Rithmus* withall.

2.

Whilst your Ritches abound, your friends will play the Placeboes,
    If your wealth doe decay, friend, like a feend, will away,
Dooues light, and delight in goodly faire tyled houses ;
    If your House be but olde, Dooue to remoue be ye bolde.

And the last and largest of all, this :

3.

If so be goods encrease, then dayly encreaseth a goods friend.
If so be goods decrease, then straite decreaseth a goods friend.
Then God night goods friend, who seldome prooueth a good friend,

*Giue me the goods, and giue me the good friend,
take ye the goods friend.*

*Douehouse, and Louehouse, in writing differ
a letter :*

*In deede scarcely so much, so resembleth an other
an other.*

*Tyle me the Doouehouse trimly, and gallant,
where the like storehouse ?*

*Fyle me the Doouehouse : leaue it vnhansome,
where the like poorehouse ?*

*Looke to the Louehouse : where the resort is,
there is a gaye showe :*

*Gynne port, and mony fayle : straight sports and
Companie faileth.*

Beleeue me, I am not to be charged with
aboue one, or two of the Verses : and a foure
or fiue wordes in the rest. His afternoones
Theame was borrowed out of him, whom one in
your Coate, they say, is as much beholding
vnto, as any Planet, or Starre in Heauen is
vnto the Sunne : and is quoted as your self
best remember, in the Close of your *October.*

> *Giunto Alessandro a la famosa tomba
> Del fero Achille, sospirando disse,
> O fortunato, che si chiara tromba
> Trouasti.*

Within an houre, or there aboutes, he
brought me these foure lustie Hexameters,
altered since not past in a worde, or two.

Noble Alexander, *when he came to the tombe of
Achilles,
Sighing spake with a bigge voyce; O thrice
blessed Achilles,
That such a Trump, so great, so loude, so glorious
hast found,
As the renowned, and surprizing, Archpoet
Homer.*

Vppon the viewe whereof, Ah my Syrrha,
quoth I here is a gallant exercise for you in
deede : we haue had a little prettie triall of
you⟨r⟩ *Latin,* and *Italian* Translation : Let me
see now I pray, what you can doo in your
owne Tongue : And with that, reaching
a certaine famous Booke, called the newe *Shep-
hardes Calender :* I turned to *Willyes,* and
Thomalins Emblemes, in *Marche :* and bad
him make them eyther better, or worse in
English verse. I gaue him an other howres
respite : but before I looked for him, he suddainely rushed vpon me, and gaue me his
deuise, thus formally set downe in a faire
peece of Paper.

1. *Thomalins Embleme.*

*Of Honny, and of Gaule, in Loue there is store,
The Honny is much, but the Gaule is more.*

2. *Willyes Embleme.*

*To be wize, and eke to Loue,
Is graunted scarce to God aboue.*

3. *Both combined in one.*

*Loue is a thing more fell, than full of Gaule, than
of Honny,
And to be wize, and Loue, is a worke for a God,
or a Goddes peere.*

With a small voluntarie Supplement of his
owne, on the other side, in commendation of
hir most gratious, and thrice excellent Maiestie :
*Not the like Virgin againe, in Asia, or Afric, or
Europe,
For Royall Vertues, for Maiestie, Bountie, Behauiour*

Raptim, vti vides.

In both not passing a worde, or two, corrected
by mee. Something more I haue of his, partly
that very day begun, and partly continued
since : but yet not so perfitly finished, that
I dare committe the viewe, and examination
thereof, to *Messer Immeritoes* Censure, whom
after those same two incomparable and myraculous *Gemini, Omni exceptione maiores,* I
recount, and chaulk vppe in the Catalogue of
our very principall Englishe *Aristarchi.* Howbeit, I am nigh halfe perswaded, that in tyme
(siquidem vltima primis respondeant) for length,
bredth, and depth, it will not come far behinde
your *Epithalamion Thamesis :* the rather, hauing so fayre a president, and patterne before
his Eyes, as I warrant him, and he presumeth
to haue of that : both *Master Collinshead,* and
M.Holli⟨n⟩shead too, being togither therein. But
euer, and euer, me thinkes your great *Catoes,
Ecquid erit pretij,* and our little *Catoes, Res age
quæ prosunt,* make suche a buzzing, and ringing
in my head, that I haue little ioy to animate,
and encourage either you, or him to goe forward,
vnlesse ye might make account of some certaine
ordinarie wages, at [at] the leastwise haue your
meate, and drinke for your dayes workes. As
for my selfe, howsoeuer I haue toyed, and
trifled heretofore, I am nowe taught, and I
trust I shall shortly learne, (no remedie, I must
of meere necessitie giue you ouer in the playne
fielde) to employ my trauayle, and tyme wholly

or chiefely on those studies and practizes, that carrie as they saye, meate in their mouth, hauing euermore their eye vppon the *Title De pane lucrando*, and their hand vpon their halfpenny. For, I pray now, what faith *M. Cuddie*, *alias* you know who, in the tenth Æglogue of the foresaid famous new Calender ?

Piers, I haue piped erst so long with payne,
That all myne Oten reedes been rent, and wore,
And my poore Muse hath spent hir spared store,
Yet litle good hath got, and much lesse gayne.
Such pleasaunce makes the Grashopper so poore,
And ligge so layde, when winter doth her strayne.

The Dapper Ditties, that I woont deuize,
To feede youthes fancie, and the flocking fry,
Delighten much : what 1 the bett for thy ?
They han the pleasure, I a sclender prize.
I beate the bushe, the birdes to them doe flye,
What good thereof to Cuddy can arise ?

But Master *Collin Cloute* is not euery body, and albeit his olde Companions, *Master Cuddy*, and *Master Hobbinoll* be as little beholding to their *Mistresse Poetrie*, as euer you wilt : yet he peraduenture, by the meanes of hir special fauour, and some personall priuiledge, may happely liue by *dying Pellicanes*, and purchase great landes, and Lordshippes, with the monev, which his *Calendar* and *Dreames* haue, and will affourde him. *Extra iocum*, I like your *Dreames* passingly well : and the rather, bicause they fauour of that singular extraordinarie veine and inuention, whiche I euer fancied moste, and, in a manner admired onelye in *Lucian*, *Petrarche*, *Aretine*, *Pasquill*, and all the most delicate, and fine conceited Grecians and Italians : (for the Romanes to speake of, are but verye Ciphars in this kinde :) whose chiefest endeuour, and drifte was, to haue nothing vulgare, but in some respecte or other, and especially in *liuely Hyperbolicall Amplifications*, rare, queint, and odde in euery pointe, and as a man woulde saye, a degree or two at the leaste, aboue the reache, and compasse of a common Schollers capacitie. In whiche respecte notwithstanding, as well for the singularitie of the manner, as the Diuinitie of the matter, I hearde once a Diuine, preferre *Saint lohns Reuelation* before al the veriest *Metaphysicall Visions*, and iollyest conceited *Dreames* or *Extasies*, that euer were deuised by one or other, howe admirable, or superexcellent soeuer they seemed otherwise to the worlde. And truely I am so confirmed in this opinion, that when I bethinke me of the verie notablest, and moste wonderful Propheticall, or Poetical

Vision, that euer I read, or hearde, me seemeth the proportion is so vnequall, that there hardly appeareth anye semblaunce of Comparison : no more in a manner (specially for Poets) than doth betweene the incomprehensible Wisedome of God, and the sensible Wit of Man. But what needeth this digression betweene you and me ? I dare saye you wyll holde your selfe reasonably wel satisfied, if youre *Dreames* be but as well esteemed of in Englande, as *Petrarches Visions* be in Italy : whiche I assure you, is the very worst I wish you. But, see, how I haue the Arte *Memoratiue* at commaundement. In good faith I had once againe nigh forgotten your *Faerie Queene* : howbeit by good chaunce, I haue nowe sent hir home at the laste, neither in better nor worse case, than I founde hir. And must you of necessitie haue my Iudgement of hir in deede ? To be plaine, I am voyde of al iudgement, if your *Nine Comœdies*, whervnto in imitation of *Herodotus*, you giue the names of the *Nine Muses*, (and in one mans fansie not vnworthily) come not neerer *Ariostoes Comœdies*, eyther for the finenesse of plausible Elocution, or the rarenesse of Poetical Inuention, than that *Eluish Queene* doth to his *Orlando Furioso*, which notwithstanding, you wil needes seeme to emulate, and hope to ouergo, as you flatly professed your self in one of your last Letters. Besides that you know, it hath bene the vsual practise of the most exquisite and odde wittes in all nations, and specially in *Italie*, rather to shewe, and aduaunce themselues that way, than any other : as namely, those three notorious dyscoursing heads, *Bibiena*, *Machiauel*, and *Aretine* did, (to let *Bembo* and *Ariosto* passe) with the great admiration, and wonderment of the whole countrey : being in deede reputed matchable in all points, both for conceyt of Witte, and eloquent decyphering of matters, either with *Aristophanes* and *Menander* in Greek, or with *Plautus* and *Terence* in Latin, or with any other, in any other tong. But I wil not stand greatly with you in your owne matters. If so be the *Faerye Queene* be fairer in your eie than the *Nine Muses*, and *Hobgoblin* runne away with the Garland from *Apollo* : Marke what I saye, and yet I will not say that I thought, but there an End for this once, and fare you well, till God or some good Aungell putte you in a better minde.

And yet, bicause you charge me somewhat suspitiouslye with an olde promise, to deliuer you of that iealousie, I am so farre from hyding mine owne matters from you, that loe, I muste needes be reuealing my friendes secreates, now an honest Countrey Gentleman, sometimes a Scholler: At whose request, I bestowed this pawlting bongrely Rime vpon him, to present his Maistresse withall. The parties shall bee namelesse: sauing, that the Gentlewomans true, or counterfaite Christen name, must necessarily be bewrayed.

¶ To my good Mistresse *Anne*: the
very lyfe of my lyfe, and onely
beloued Mystresse.

*G*Entle Mistresse Anne, *I am plaine by nature :*
I was neuer so farre in loue with any creature.
Happy were your seruant, if hee coulde bee so Anned,
   And you not vnhappy, if you shoulde be so manned.
I loue not to gloze, where I loue indeede,
   Nowe God, and good Saint Anne, sende me good speede.
Suche goodly Vertues, suche amiable Grace,
   But I must not fall a praysing : I wante Time, and Place.
Oh, that I had mine olde Wittes at commaundement :
   I knowe, what I coulde say without controlement :
But let this suffice : thy desertes are suche :
   That no one in this worlde can loue thee too muche.
My selfe moste vnworthy of any suche fœlicitie,
   But by imputation of thy gratious Curtesie.
I leaue to loue the Muses, since I loued thee,
   Alas, what are they, when I thee see ?

Adieu, adieu pleasures, and profits all :
   My Hart, and my Soule, but at one bodyes call.
Woulde God, I might saye to hir : My hart-roote is thine :
   And, (ô Pleasure of Pleasures) Thy sweete hartroote mine.
Nowe I beseeche thee by whatsoeuer thou louest beste,
   Let it be, as I haue saide, and, Soule, take thy reste.
By the faith of true Loue, and by my truest Truely,
   Thou shalt neuer putte forth thy Loue to greater Vsurie.
And for other odde necessaries, take no care,
   Your seruaunts Dæmonium shall ridde you of that feare.
I serue but two Saints, Saint Penny, and Saint Anne,
   Commende this I muste, commaunde that I canne.
Nowe, shall I be plaine ? I praye thee euen most hartily,
   Requite Loue, with Loue : and farewell most hartily.

Postscripte.

I But once loued before, and shee forsooth was *a Susanne :*
   But the Heart of a Susanne, not worth the Haire of an Anne :
A Sus to Anne, if you can any Latine, or Pewter :
   Shee Flesh, hir, Mother Fish, hir Father a verye Newter.
I woulde once, and might after, haue spedde a Gods name :
   But, if she coye it once, she is none of my Dame.
Nowe I praye thee moste hartily, Thricegentle Mistresse Anne,
Looke for no long seruice of so plaine a manne.

And yet I assure thee, thou shalt neuer want any seruice,
If my selfe, or my S. Penny may performe thy wishe.
And thus once againe, (full loath) I take my leaue of thy sweete harte,
With as many louing Farewels, as be louing pangs in my heart.
      He that longeth to be thine owne
      inseparably, for euer and euer.

God helpe vs, you and I are wisely employed, (are wee not ?) when our Pen and Inke, and Time, and Wit, and all runneth away in this goodly yonkerly veine: as if the world had

nothing else for vs to do : or we were borne to
be the only *Nonproficients* and *Nihilagents* of
the world. *Cuiusmodi tu nugis, atque naeniis
nisi vnâ mecum (qui solemni quodam iureiuran-
do, atque voto obstringor, relicto isto amoris
Poculo, iuris Poculum primo quoque tempore
exhaurire) iam tandem aliquando valedicas,
(quod tamen, vnum tibi, credo, τῶν ἀδυνάτων
videbitur) nihil dicam amplius, Valeas. E meo
municipio. Nono Calendas Maias.*

But hoe I pray you, gentle sirra, a word
with you more. In good sooth, and by the
faith I beare to the Muses, you shal neuer haue
my subscription or consent (though you should
charge me wyth the authoritie of fiue hundreth
Maister *Drants*,) to make your *Carpēnter* our
Carpŏnter, an inche longer, or bigger, than God
and his Englishe people haue made him. Is
there no other Pollicie to pull downe Ryming,
and set vppe Versifying, but you must needes
correcte *Magnificat :* and against all order of
Lawe, and in despite of Custome, forcibly
vsurpe, and tyrannize vppon a quiet companye
of wordes, that so farre beyonde the memorie
of man, haue so peaceably enioyed their seueral
Priuiledges and Liberties, without any disturbance, or the leaste controlement ? What ?
Is *Horaces Ars Poëtica* so quite out of our
Englishe Poets head, that he muste haue his
Remembrancer, to pull hym by the sleeue, and
put him in mind, of, *Penes vsum, et ius, et
norma loquendi ?* Indeed I remember, who
was wont in a certaine brauerie, to call our
M. Valanger Noble *M. Valanger.* Else neuer
heard I any, that durst presume so much ouer
the Englishe, (excepting a fewe suche stam-
merers, as haue not the masterie of their owne
Tongues) as to alter the Quantitie of any one
sillable, otherwise, than oure common speache,
and generall receyued Custome woulde beare
them oute. Woulde not I laughe, thinke you,
to heare *Messer Immerito* come in baldely with
his *Maiēstie, Royāltie, Honēstie, Sciēnces, Facúl-
ties, Excēllent, Tauērnour, Manfully, Faith-
fúlly,* and a thousande the like : in steade of
Maiēstie, Royāltie, Honēstie, and so forth ?
And trowe you anye coulde forbeare the byting
of his Lippe, or smyling in his Sleeue, if a iolly
fellowe, and greate Clarke, (as it mighte be
youre selfe,) reading a fewe Verses vnto him,
for his own credite and commendation, should
nowe and then, tell him of, *bargaĩneth, follw-
ing, harrŵwing, thoroŭghly, Trauaĩlers,* or the
like, in steade of, *bargaĩneth, follŵwing, harrŵwing,* and the reste ? Or will *Segnior Immerito,*
bycause, may happe, he hathe a fat-bellyed

Archedeacon on his side, take vppon him to
controll Maister Doctor *Watson* for his *All
Trauaĩlers,* in a Verse so highly extolled of
Master *Ascham ?* or Maister *Ascham* himselfe,
for abusing *Homer,* and corrupting our Tongue,
in that he saith :

*Quite throŭghe a Doore flĕwe a shafte with a
brasse head ?*

Nay, haue we not somtime, by your leaue,
both the Position of the firste, and Dipthong
of the seconde, concurring in one, and the same
sillable, which neuerthelesse is commonly and
ought necessarily to be pronounced short ?
I haue nowe small time, to bethink me of
many examples. But what say you to the
second in *Merchaũndise ?* to the third in
Couenaũnteth ? and to the fourth in *Appurten-
aũnces ?* Durst you aduenture to make any
of them long, either in Prose, or in Verse ?
I assure you I knowe who dareth not, and
suddaĩnly feareth the displeasure of all true
Englishmen if he should. Say you *suddaĩnly,* if
you liste : by my *certaĩnly,* and *certaĩnty* I wil
not. You may preceiue by the *Premisses,* (which
very worde I woulde haue you note by the waye
to) the Latine is no rule for vs : or imagine aforehande, (bycause you are like to proue a great
Purchaser, and leaue suche store of money,
and possessions behinde you) your *Execũtors*
wil deale *fraudulẽntly,* or *violẽntly* with your
succẽssour, (whiche in a maner is euery mans
case) and it will fall oute a resolute pointe :
the third in *Execũtores, fraudulẽter, violẽter,*
and the seconde in *Succẽssor,* being long in the
one, and shorte in the other : as in seauen
hundreth more : suche as, *discĩple, recĩted,
excĩted : tenĕment, orãtour, laudible :* and a number of their fellowes are long in English, short
in Latine : long in Latine, short in English.
Howbeit, in my fancy, such words, as *violently,
diligently, magnificently, indifferently,* seeme in
a manner reasonably indifferent, and tollerable
either waye, neither woulde I greatly stande
with him, that translated the Verse.

*Cur mittis violas ? vt me violentiùs vras ?
Why send you violets ? to burne my poore hart
violẽntly.*

Marry so, that being left common for verse,
they are to be pronounced shorte in Prose, after
the maner of the Latines, in suche wordes as
these, *Cathedra, Volŭcres, mediocres, Celebres.*

And thus farre of your *Carpēnter,* and his
fellowes, wherin we are to be moderated, and
ouerruled by the vsuall, and common receiued

sounde, and not to deuise any counterfaite fantasticall Accent of oure owne, as manye, otherwise not vnlearned haue corruptely and ridiculouslye done in the Greeke.

Nowe for your *Heauen, Seauen, Eleauen,* or the like, I am likewise of the same opinion: as generally in all words else: we are not to goe a little farthei, either for the *Prosody,* or the *Orthography,* (and therefore your Imaginarie *Diastole* nothing worthe) then we are licenced and authorized by the ordinarie vse, and custome, and proprietie, and Idiome, and, as it were, Maiestie of our speach: whiche I accounte the only infallible, and soueraigne Rule of all Rules. And therefore hauing respecte therevnto, and reputing it Petty Treason to reuolt therefro: dare hardly eyther in the *Prosodie,* or in the *Orthography* either, allowe them two sillables in steade of one, but woulde as well in Writing, as in Speaking, haue them vsed, as *Monosyllaba,* thus: *heavn, seavn, a leavn,* as Maister *Ascham* in his *Toxophilus* doth *Yrne,* commonly written *Yron:*

Vp to the pap his string did he pull, his shafte to the harde yrne.

Especially the difference so manifestly appearing by the Pronunciation, betweene these twoo, *a leavn a clocke* and *a leaven of Dowe,* whyche *lea-ven* admitteth the *Diastole,* you speake of. But see, what absurdities thys yl-fauoured *Orthographye,* or rather *Pseudography,* hathe ingendred: and howe one errour still breedeth and begetteth an other. Haue wee not, *Mooneth,* for *Moonthe: sithence,* for *since: whilest,* for *whilste: phantasie,* for *phansie: euen,* for *evn: Diuel,* for *Divl: God hys wrath,* for *Goddes wrath:* and a thousande of the same stampe: wherein the corrupte *Orthography* in the moste, hathe beene the sole, or principall cause of corrupte *Prosodye* in ouer many?

Marry, I confesse some wordes we haue indeede, as for example, *fayer,* either for beautifull, or for a *Marte: ayer,* bothe *pro aere,* and *pro hærede,* for we say not *Heire,* but plaine *Aire* for him to, (or else *Scoggins Aier* were a poore iest) whiche are commonly, and maye indifferently be vsed eyther wayes. For you shal as well, and as ordinarily heare *fayer,* as *faire,* and *Aier,* as *Aire,* and bothe alike: not onely of diuers and sundrye persons, but often of the very same: otherwhiles vsing the one, otherwhiles the other: and so *died,* or *dyde: spied,* or *spide: tryed,* or *tride: fyer,* or *fyre: myer,* or *myre:* wyth an infinyte companye of

the same sorte: sometime *Monosyllaba,* sometime *Polysyllaba.*

To conclude both pointes in one, I dare sweare priuately to your selfe, and will defende publiquely againste any, it is neither Heresie, nor Paradox, to sette downe, and stande vppon this assertion, (notwithstanding all the Preiudices and Presumptions to the contrarie, if they were tenne times as manye moe) that it is not, either Position, or Dipthong, or Diastole, or anye like Grammer Schoole Deuice, that doeth, or can indeede, either make long or short, or encrease, or diminish the number of Sillables, but onely the common allowed, and receiued *Prosodye:* taken vp by an vniuersall consent of all, and continued by a generall vse, and Custome of all. Wherein neuerthelesse I grant, after long aduise, and diligent obseruation of particulars, a certain Uniform Analogie, and Concordance, being in processe of time espyed out. Sometime this, sometime that, hath been noted by good wits in their *Analyses,* to fall out generally alyke? and as a man woulde saye, regularly in all, or moste wordes: as Position, Dipthong, and the like: not as firste, and essentiall causes of this, or that effecte, (here lyeth the point) but as Secundarie and Accidentall Signes, of this, or that Qualitie.

It is the vulgare, and naturall Mother *Prosodye,* that alone worketh the feate, as the onely supreame Foundresse, and Reformer of Position, Dipthong, Orthographie, or whatsoeuer else: whose Affirmatiues are nothing worth, if she once conclude the Negatiue: and whose *secundæ intentiones* muste haue their whole allowance and warrante from hir *primæ.* And therefore in shorte, this is the verie shorte, and the long: Position neither maketh shorte, nor long in oure Tongue, but so farre as we can get hir good leaue. Peraduenture, vppon the diligent suruewe, and examination of Particulars, some the like Analogie and Uniformity, might be founde oute in some other respecte, that shoulde as vniuersally and Canonically holde amongst vs, as Position doeth with the Latines and Greekes. I saye, (peraduenture,) bycause, hauing not yet made anye speciall Obseruation, I dare not precisely affirme any generall certaintie: albeit I presume, so good and sensible a Tongue, as ours is, beeyng wythall so like itselfe, as it is, cannot but haue something equipollent, and counteruaileable to the beste Tongues, in some one such kinde of conformitie, or other. And this forsooth is all the Artificial Rules and Precepts, you are like to borrowe of one man at this time.

Sed amabo ite, ad Corculi tui delicatissimas Literas, propediem, quam potero, accuratissimè : tot interim illam exquisitissimis salutibus, atque salutationibus impertiens, quot habet in Capitulo, capillos semiaureos, semiargenteos, semigemmeos. Quid quæris? Per tuam Venerem altera Rosalindula est : eamque non alter, sed idem ille, (tua, vt ante, bona cum gratia) copiosè amat Hobbinolus. O mea Domina Immerito, mea bellissima Collina Clouta, multo plus plurimùm salue, atque vale.

You knowe my ordinarie *Postscripte :* you may communicate as much, or as little, as you list, of these Patcheries, and fragments, with the two Gentlemen : but there a straw, and you loue me : not with any else, friend or foe, one, or other : vnlesse haply you have a special desire to imparte some parte hereof, to my good friend *M. Daniel Rogers :* whose curtesies are also registred in my Marble booke. You know my meaning.

Nosti manum et stylum.

G.

¶ TVVO OTHER,
very commendable Let-
ters, of the ſame mens vvri-
ting : both touching the foreſaid
Artificiall Verſifying, and certain other Particulars :

More lately deliuered vnto the
Printer.

IMPRINTED AT LON-
don, by H. Bynneman, dvvelling
in Thames ſtreate, neere vnto
Baynardes Caſtell.

Anno Domini. 1 5 8 0.

Cum gratia & priuilegio Regiæ Maieſtatis.

¶ To the VVorshipfull his very singular good friend, Maister G. H. Fellovv of Trinitie Hall in Cambridge.

Good Master *G.* I perceiue by your most curteous and frendly Letters your good will to be no lesse in deed, than I alwayes esteemed. In recompence wherof, think I beseech you, that I wil spare neither speech, nor wryting, nor aught else, whensoeuer, and wheresoeuer occasion shal be offred me: yea, I will not stay, till it be offred, but will seeke it, in al that possibly I may. And that you may perceiue how much your Counsel in al things preuaileth with me, and how altogither I am ruled and ouer-ruled thereby : I am now determined to alter mine owne former purpose, and to subscribe to your aduizement : being notwithstanding resolued stil, to abide your farther resolution. My principal doubts are these. First, I was minded for a while to haue intermitted the vttering of my writings : leaste by ouer-much cloying their noble eares, I should gather a contempt of my self, or else seeme rather for gaine and commoditie to doe it, for some sweetnesse that I haue already tasted. Then also me seemeth the work too base for his excellent Lordship, being made in Honour of a priuate Personage vnknowne, which of some yl-willers might be vpbraided, not to be so worthie, as you knowe she is : or the matter not so weightie, that it should be offred to so weightie a Personage : or the like. The selfe former Title stil liketh me well ynough, and your fine Addition no lesse. If these, and the like doubtes, maye be of importaunce in your seeming, to frustrate any parte of your aduice, I beeseeche you, without the leaste selfe loue of your own purpose, councell me for the beste : and the rather doe it faithfullye, and carefully, for that, in all things I attribute so muche to your iudgement, that I am euermore content to adnihilate mine owne determinations, in respecte thereof. And indeede for your selfe to, it sitteth with you now, to call your wits, and senses togither, (which are alwaies at call) when occasion is so fairely offered of Estimation and Preferment. For, whiles the yron is hote, it is good striking, and minds of Nobles varie, as their Estates. *Verùm ne quid durius.*

I pray you bethinke you well hereof, good Maister *G.* and forthwith write me those two or three special points and caueats for the nonce, *De quibus in superioribus illis mellitissimis, longissimisque Litteris tuis.* Your desire to heare of my late beeing with hir Maiestie, muste dye in it selfe. As for the twoo worthy Gentlemen, Master *Sidney*, and Master *Dyer*, they haue me, I thanke them, in some vse of familiarity : of whom, and to whome, what speache passeth for youre credite and estimation, I leaue your selfe to conceiue, hauing alwayes so well conceiued of my vnfained affection, and zeale towardes you. And nowe they haue proclaimed in their ἀριίῳ πάγῳ, a generall surceasing and silence of balde Rymers, and also of the verie beste to : in steade whereof, they haue by autho(ri)tie of their whole Senate, prescribed certaine Lawes and rules of Quantities of English sillables, for English Verse : hauing had thereof already greate practise, and drawen mee to their faction. Newe Bookes I heare of none, but only of one, that writing a certaine Booke, called *The Schoole of Abuse*, and dedicating it to Maister *Sidney*, was for hys labor scorned : if at leaste it be in the goodnesse of that nature to scorne. Suche follie is it, not to regarde aforehande the inclination and qualitie of him, to whome wee dedicate oure Bookes. Suche mighte I happily incurre, entituling *My Slomber*, and the other Pamphlets, vnto his honor. I meant them rather to *Maister Dyer.* But I am, of late, more in loue wyth my Englishe Versifying, than with Ryming : whyche I should haue done long since, if I would then haue followed your councell. *Sed te solum iam tum suspicabar cum Aschamo sapere : nunc Aulam video egregios alere Poëtas Anglicos.* Maister *E. K.* hartily desireth to be commended vnto your Worshippe : of whome, what accompte he maketh, youre selfe shall hereafter perceiue, by hys paynefull and dutifull Verses of your selfe.

Thus muche was written at Westminster yesternight : but comming this morning, beeyng the sixteenth of October, to Mystresse *Kerkes*, to haue it deliuered to the Carrier, I receyued youre letter, sente me the laste weeke : whereby I perceiue you other whiles continue your old exercise of Versifying in English : whych glorie I had now thought shoulde haue bene onely ours heere at London, and the Court.

Truste me, your Verses I like passingly well, and enuye your hidden paines in this kinde, or rather maligne, and grudge at your selfe, that woulde not once imparte so muche to me. But once, or twice, you make a breache in Maister *Drants* Rules : *quod tamen condonabimus tanto*

Poëtæ, tuæquae ipsius maximæ in his rebus autoritati. You shall see when we meete in London, (whiche, when it shall be, certifye vs) howe fast I haue followed after you, in that Course : beware, leaste in time I ouertake you. *Veruntamen te solùm sequar, (vt sæpenumerò sum professus,) nunquam sanè assequar, dum viuam.* And nowe requite I you with the like, not with the verye beste, but with the verye shortest, namely with a fewe *Iambickes :* I dare warrant, they be precisely perfect for the feete (as you can easily iudge) and varie not one inch from the Rule. I will imparte yours to Maister *Sidney*, and Maister *Dyer*, at my nexte going to the Courte. I praye you, keepe mine close to your selfe, or your verie entire friendes, Maister *Preston*, Maister *Still*, and the reste.

Iambicum Trimetrum.

*V*Nhappie Verse, the witnesse of my vnhappie state,
   Make thy selfe fluttring wings of thy fast flying
   Thought, and fly forth vnto my Loue, whersoeuer she be :
Whether lying reastlesse in heauy bedde, or else
   Sitting so cheerelesse at the cheerfull boorde, or else
   Playing alone carelesse on hir heauenlie Virginals.
If in Bed, tell hir, that my eyes can take no reste :
   If at Boorde, tell hir, that my mouth can eate no meate :
   If at hir Virginals, tel hir, I can heare no mirth.
Asked why ? say : Waking Loue suffereth no sleepe :
   Say, that raging Loue dothe appall the weake stomacke :
   Say, that lamenting Loue marreth the Musicall.
Tell hir, that hir pleasures were wonte to lull me asleepe :
   Tell hir, that hir beautie was wonte to feede mine eyes :
   Tell hir, that hir sweete Tongue was wonte to make me mirth.
Nowe doe I nightly waste, wanting my kindely reste :
   Nowe doe I dayly starue, wanting my liuely foode :
   Nowe doe I always dye, wanting thy timely mirth.
And if I waste, who will bewaile my heauy chaunce ?
   And if I starue, who will record my cursed end ?
   And if I dye, who will saye : this was, Immerito ?

I thought once agayne here to haue made an ende, with a heartie *Vale*, of the best fashion : but loe, an ylfauoured myschaunce. My last farewell, whereof I made great accompt, and muche maruelled you shoulde make no mention thereof, I am nowe tolde, (in the Diuels name) was thorough one mans negligence quite forgotten, but shoulde nowe vndoubtedly haue beene sent, whether I hadde come, or no. Seing it can now be no otherwise, I pray

you take all togither, wyth all their faultes : and nowe I hope, you will vouchsafe mee an answeare of the largest size, or else I tell you true, you shall bee verye deepe in my debte : notwythstandyng, thys other sweete, but shorte letter, and fine, but fewe Verses. But I woulde rather I might yet see youre owne good selfe, and receiue a Reciprocall farewell from your owne sweete mouth.

[1]*Ad Ornatissimum virum, multis iamdiu*
nominibus clarissimum, G. H. Immerito
sui, mox in Gallias nauigaturi,
εὐτυχεῖν.

Sic malus egregium, sic non inimicus Ami-
  cum:
Sicque nouus veterem iubet ipse Poëta Poëtam,
Saluere, ac cœlo post secula multa secundo
Iam reducem, cœlo mage, quàm nunc ipse,
  secundo
Vtier. Ecce Deus, (modò sit Deus ille, renixum
Qui vocet in scelus, et iuratos perdat amores)
Ecce Deus mihi clara dedit modò signa Marinus,
Et sua veligero lenis parat Æquora Ligno,
Mox sulcanda, suas etiam pater Æolus Iras
Ponit, et ingentes animos Aquilonis———
Cuncta vijs sic apta meis: ego solus ineptus.
Nam mihi nescio quo mens saucia vulnere,
  dudum
Fluctuat ancipiti Pelago, dum Nauita proram
Inualidam validus rapit huc Amor, et rapit illuc.
Consilijs Ratio melioribus vsa, decusque
Immortale leui diffessa Cupidinis Arcu.
Angimur hoc dubio, et portu vexamur in ipso.
Magne pharetrati nunc tu contemptor Amoris,
(Id tibi Dij nomen precor haud impune remittant)
Hos modos exsolue, et eris mihi magnus Apollo.
Spiritus ad summos, scio, te generosus Honores
Exstimulat, maiusque docet spirare Poëtam,
Quàm leuis est Amor, et tamen haud leuis est
  Amor omnis.

Ergo nihil laudi reputas æquale perenni,
Præque sacrosancta splendoris imagine tanti,
Cætera, quæ vecors, vti Numina, vulgus adorat,
Prædia, Amicitias, vrbana peculia, Nummos,
Quæque placent oculis, formas, spectacula,
  Amores
Conculcare soles, vt humum, et ludibria sensus.
Digna meo certè Harueio sententia, digna
Oratore amplo, et generoso pectore, quam non
Stoica formidet veterum Sapientia vinclis
Sancire æternis: sapor haud tamen omnibus
  idem,
Dicitur effæti proles facunda Laërtæ,
Quamlibet ignoti iactata per æquora Cœli,
Inque procelloso longùm exsul gurgite ponto,
Præ tamen amplexu lachrymosæ Coniugis, Ortus

Cælestes Diuûmque thoros spreuisse beatos.
Tantùm Amor, et Mulier, vel Amore potentior.
  Illum
Tu tamen illudis: tua Magnificentia tanta est:
Præque subumbrata Splendoris Imagine tanti,
Præque illo Meritis famosis nomine parto,
Cætera, quæ Vecors, vti Numina, vulgus adorat,
Prædia, Amicitias, armenta, peculia, nummos,
Quæque placent oculis, formas, spectacula,
  Amores,
Quæque placent ori, quæque auribus, omnia
  temnis.
Næ tu grande sapis, Sapor at sapientia non est:
Omnis et in paruis benè qui scit desipuisse,
Sæpe supercilijs palmam sapientibus aufert.
Ludit Aristippum modo tetrica Turba Sophorum,
Mitia purpureo moderantem verba Tyranno:
Ludit Aristippus dictamina vana Sophorum,
Quos leuis emensi male torquet Culicis vmbra:
Et quisquis placuisse studet Heroibus altis,
Desipuisse studet, sic gratia crescit ineptis.
Denique Laurigeris quisquis sua tempora vittis
Insignire volet, Populoque placere fauenti,
Desipere insanus discit, turpemque pudendæ
Stultitiæ laudem quærit. Pater Ennius vnus
Dictus in innumeris sapiens: laudatur at ipse
Carmina vesano fudisse liquentia vino.
Nec tu pace tua, nostri Cato Maxime sæcli,
Nomen honorati sacrum mereare Poëtæ,
Quantamuis illustre canas, et nobile Carmen,
Ni stultire velis, sic Stultorum omnia plena.
Tuta sed in medio superest via gurgite, nam Qui
Nec reliquis nimiùm vult desipuisse videri,
Nec sapuisse nimis, Sapientem dixeris vnum.
Hinc te merserit vnda, illinc combusserit Ignis.
Nec tu delicias nimis aspernare fluentes,
Nec serò Dominam venientem in vota, nec
  Aurum
Si sapis, ablatum, (Curijs ea, Fabricijsque
Linque viris miseris miseranda Sophismata
  quondam
Grande sui decus ij. nostri sed dedecus æui:)
Nec sectare nimis. Res vtraque crimine plena.

---

[1] [An Enclosure with the previous letter. This is the 'last farewell' there referred to, written on
5 Oct. 1579, but not forwarded owing to some one's negligence, now recovered by Spenser, and
enclosed with his *later* letter of 15th and 16th Oct.]

Hoc bene qui callet, (si quis tamen hoc bene
  callet)
Scribe, vel invito sapientem hunc Socrate solum.
Vis facit vna pios : Iustos facit altera : et altra
Egregiè cordata, ac fortia pectora : verùm
Omne tulit punctum, qui miscuit vtile dulci.
Dij mihi, dulce diu dederant : verùm vtile nun-
  quam :
Vtile nunc etiam,ò vtinamquoque dulce dedissent.
Dij mihi, (quippe Dijs æquiualia maxima
  paruis)
Ni nimis inuideant mortalibus esse beatis,
Dulce simul tribuisse queant, simul vtile : tanta
Sed Fortuna tua est : pariter quæque vtile,
  quæque
Dulce dat ad placitum : sæuo nos sydere nati
Quæsitum imus eam per inhospita Caucasa
  longè,
Perque Pyrenæos montes, Babilonaque turpem,
Quòd si quæsitum nec ibi invenerimus, ingens
Æquor inexhaustis permensi erroribus, vltrâ
Fluctibus in medijs socij quæremus Vlyssis.
Passibus inde Deam fessis comitabimur ægram,
Nobile cui furtum quærenti defuit orbis.
Namque sinu pudet in patrio, tenebrisque pu-
  dendis
Non nimis ingenio Iuuenem infœlice, virentes
Officijs frustra deperdere vilibus Annos,
Frugibus et vacuas speratis cernere spicas.
Ibimus ergo statim : (quis eunti fausta prece-
  tur ?)
Et pede Clivosas fesso calcabimus Alpes.
Quis dabit interea conditas rore Britanno,
Quis tibi Litterulas ? quis carmen amore petul-
  cum ?
Musa sub Oebalij desueta cacumine montis,
Flebit inexhausto tam longa silentia blanctu,
Lugebitque sacrum lachrymis Helicona tacentem.
Haruetiusque bonus, (charus licet omnibus idem,
Idque suo merito, prope suauior omnibus vnus,)
Angelus et Gabriel, (quamuis comitatus amicis
Innumeris, geniûmque choro stipatus amæno)
Immerito tamen vnum absentem sæpe requiret,
Optabitque, Vtinam meus hïc Edmundus adesset,
Qui noua scripsisset, nec Amores conticuisset
Ipse suos, et sæpe animo, verbisque benignis

Fausta precaretur : Deus illum aliquando re-
  ducat, etc.

  Plura vellem per Charites, sed non licet per
    Musas.
  Vale, Vale plurimùm, Mi amabilissime
  Harueie, meo cordi, meorum omnium longè
  charissime.

I was minded also to haue sent you some
English verses : or Rymes, for a farewell : but
by my Troth, I haue no spare time in the world,
to thinke on such Toyes, that you knowe will
demaund a freer head, than mine is presently.
I beseeche you by all your Curtesies,and Graces,
let me be answered, ere I goe : which will be,
(I hope, I feare, I thinke) the next weeke, if
I can be dispatched of my Lorde. I goe thither,
as sent by him, and maintained what most of
him : and there am to employ my time, my
body, my minde, to his Honours seruice. Thus
with many superhartie Commendations, and
Recommendations to your selfe, and all my
friendes with you, I ende my last Farewell, not
thinking any more to write vnto you, before
I goe : and withall committing to your faithfull Credence the eternall Memorie of our euerlasting friendship, the inuiolable Memorie of
our vnspotted friendshippe, the sacred Memorie
of our vowed friendship : which I beseech you
Continue with vsuall writings, as you may, and
of all things let me heare some Newes from
you. As gentle M. Sidney, I thanke his good
Worship, hath required of me, and so promised
to doe againe. Qui monet, vt facias, quod iam
facis, you knowe the rest. You may alwayes
send them most safely to me by Mistress
Kerke, and by none other. Soonce againe,
and yet once more, Farewell most hartily,
mine owne good Master H. and loue me, as
I loue you, and thinke vpon poore Immerito,
as he thinketh vppon you.

  Leycester House. This. 5. of October. 1579.

    Per mare, per terras,
    Viuus, mortuusque.
    Tuus Immerito.

To my verie Friende,
M. Immerito.

*L*iberalissimo *Signor Immerito*, in good soothe my poore Storehouse will presently affourd me nothing, either to recompence, or counteruaile your gentle Masterships, long, large, lauish, Luxurious, Laxatiue Letters withall, (now a Gods name, when did I euer in my life, hunt the Letter before? but, belike, theres no remedie, I must needes be euen with you once in my dayes,) but only forsoothe, a fewe Millions of Recommendations, and a running Coppie of the Verses enclosed. Which Verses, (*extra iocum*) are so well done in *Lattin* by two Doctors, and so well Translated into English by one odde Gentleman, and generally so well allowed of all, that chaunced to haue the perusing of them: that trust mee, *G. H.* was at the first hardly intreated, to shame himselfe, and truely, now blusheth, to see the first Letters of his name, stande so neere their Names, as of necessitie they must. You know the *Greeke* prouerb, πορφύρα ποτὶ πορφύραν διακριτία, and many colours, (as in a manner euery thing else) that seuerally by themselues, seeme reasonably good, and freshe ynough, beyng compared, and ouermatched wyth their betters, are maruellously disgraced, and as it were, dashed quite oute of Countenaunce. I am at this instant, very busilye, and hotly employed in certaine greate and serious affayres: whereof, notwithstanding (for all youre vowed, and long experimented secrecie) you are not like to heare a worde more at the moste, till I my selfe see a World more at the leaste. And therefore, for this once I beseech you (notwithstanding your greate expectation of I knowe not what Volumes for an aunsweare) content your good selfe, with these Presentes, (pardon me, I came lately out of a Scriueners shop) and in lieu of many gentle Farewels, and goodly Godbewyes, at your departure: gyue me once againe leaue, to playe the Counsaylour a while, if it be but to iustifie your liberall Mastershippes, *Nostri Cato maxime sæcli :* and I coniure you by the Contents of the Verses, and Rymes enclosed, and by al the good, and bad Spirites, that attende vpon the Authors themselues, immediatly vpon the contemplation thereof, to abandon all other fooleries, and honour Vertue, the onely immortall and suruiuing Accident amongst so manye mortall, and euer-perishing Substaunces. As I strongly presume, so good a Texte, so clearkly handeled, by three so famous Doctours, as olde *Maister Wythipole*, and the other two bee, may easily, and will fully perswade you, howsoeuer you tush at the fourths vnsutable Paraphrase. But a worde or two, to your large, lauishe, laxatiue Letters, and then for thys time, *Adieu*. Of my credite, youre doubtes are not so redoubted, as youre selfe ouer suspiciously imagine: as I purpose shortely to aduize you more at large. Your hotte yron, is so hotte, that it striketh mee to the hearte, I dare not come neare to strike it : The Tyde tarryeth no manne, but manye a good manne is fayne to tarry the Tyde. And I knowe some, whyche coulde be content to bee theyr own Garners, that are gladde to thanke other for theyr courtesie: But Beggars, they saye, muste be no choosers.

Your new-founded ἄριιον πάγον I honoure more, than you will or can suppose: and make greater accompte of the twoo worthy Gentlemenne, than of two hundreth *Dionisii Areopagitæ*, or the verye notablest Senatours, that euer *Athens* dydde affourde of that number.

Your Englishe *Trimetra* I lyke better, than perhappes you will easily beleeue: and am to requite them wyth better, or worse, at more conuenient leysure. Marry, you must pardon me, I finde not your warrant so sufficiently good, and substauntiall in Lawe, that it can persuade me, they are all, so precisely perfect for the Feete, as your selfe ouer-partially weene, and ouer-confidently auouche: especiallye the thirde, whyche hathe a foote more than a Lowce (a wonderous deformitie in a righte and pure *Senarie*) and the sixte, whiche is also in the same Predicament, vnlesse happly one of the feete be sawed off wyth a payre of *Syncopes :* and then shoulde the Orthographie haue testified so muche: and in steade of H⁵auᵉnlⁱ *Virgⁱnãls*, you should haue written, Heaᵘnlⁱ *Virgnãls :* and *Virgnãls* againe in the ninth, and should haue made a Curtoll of *Immᵉrⁱtⁱ* in the laste: being all notwithstandyng vsuall, and tollerable ynoughe, in a mixte, and licentious *Iambicke :* and of two euilles, better (no doubte) the fyrste, than the laste : a thyrde superfluous sillable, than a dull *Spondee-*

Then me thinketh, you haue in my fancie somewhat too many *Spondees* beside : and whereas *Trochee* sometyme presumeth in the firste place, as namely in the second Verse, *Make thy*, whyche *thy*, by youre Maistershippes owne authoritie muste needes be shorte, I shall be faine to supplye the office of the Arte Memoratiue, and putte you in minde of a pretty Fable in *Abstemio* the Italian, implying thus much, or rather thus little in effect.

A certaine lame man beyng inuited to a solempne Nuptiall Feaste, made no more adoe, but sate me hym roundlye downe foremoste at the hyghest ende of the Table. The Master of the feast, suddainly spying his presumption, and hansomely remoouing him from thence, placed me this haulting Gentleman belowe at the nether end of the bourd : alledging for his defence the common verse : *Sedes nulla datur, prælerquam sexta Trochæo :* and pleasantly alluding to this foote, which standing vppon two syllables, the one long, the other short, (much like, of a like, his guestes feete) is always thrust downe to the last place, in a true Hexameter, and quite thrust out of doores in a pure, and iust *Senarie*. Nowe Syr, what thinke you, I began to thinke with my selfe, when I began to reade your warrant first : so boldly, and venterously set downe in so formall, and autentique wordes, as these, *Precisely perfit, and not an inch from the Rule?* Ah Syrrha, and Iesu Lord, thought I, haue we at the last gotten one, of whom his olde friendes and Companions may iustly glory, *In eo solùm peccat, quòd nihil peccat :* and that is yet more exacte, and precise in his English Comicall Iambickes, than euer *M. Watson* himselfe was in his *Lattin* Tragicall Iambickes, of whom *M. Ascham* reporteth, that he would neuer to this day suffer his famous *Absolon* to come abrode, onely because *Anapæstus in Locis paribus,* is twice, or thrice vsed in steade of *Iambus?* A small fault, ywisse, and such a one in *M. Aschams* owne opinion, as perchaunce woulde neuer haue beene espyed, no neither in *Italy,* nor in *Fraunce.* But when I came to the curious scanning, and fingering of euery foote, and syllable : Lo here, quoth I, *M. Watsons Anapæstus* for all the worlde. A good horse, that trippeth not once in a iourney : and *M. Immerito* doth, but as *M. Watson,* and in a manner all other *Iambici* haue done before him : marry he might haue spared his preface, or at the least, that same restrictiue, and streightlaced terme, *Precisely,* and all had been well enough : and I assure

you, of my selfe, I beleeue, no peece of a fault marked at all. But this is the Effect of warrantes, and perhappes the Errour may rather proceede of his Master, *M. Drantes* Rule, than of himselfe. Howsoeuer it is, the matter is not great, and I alwayes was, and will euer continue of this Opinion, *Pauca multis condonanda vitia Virtutibus,* especially these being no *Vitia* neither, in a common and licencious *Iambicke. Verùm ista obiter, non quidem contradicendi animo, aut etiam corrigendi mihi crede : sed nostro illo Academico, pristinoque more ratiocinandi.* And to saye trueth, partly too, to requite your gentle courtesie in beginning to me, and noting I knowe not what breache in your gorbellyed Maisters Rules : which Rules go for good, I perceiue, and keepe a Rule, where there be no better in presence. My selfe neither sawe them, nor heard of them before : and therefore will neither praise them, nor dispraise them nowe : but vppon the suruiewe of them, and farther conference, (both which I desire) you shall soone heare one mans opinion too or fro. Youre selfe remember, I was wonte to haue some preiudice of the man : and I still remaine a fauourer of his deserued, and iust commendation. Marry in these poyntes, you knowe, *Partialitie* in no case, may haue a foote : and you remember mine olde Stoicall exclamation : *Fie on childish affection, in the discoursing, and deciding of schoole matters.* This I say, because you charge me with an vnknowne authoritie : which for aught I know yet, may as wel be either vnsufficient, or faultie, as otherwise : and I dare more than halfe promise, (I dare not saye, warrant) you shall alwayes in these kinde of controuersies, finde me nighe hande answerable in mine owne defence. *Reliqua omnia, quæ de hac supersunt Anglicorum versuum ratione, in aliud tempus reseruabimus, ociosum magis.* Youre Latine Farewell is a goodly braue yonkerly peece of work, and Goddilge yee, I am alwayes maruellously beholding vnto you, for your bountifull Titles : I hope by that time I haue been resident a yeare or twoo in *Italy,* I shall be better qualifyed in this kind, and more able to requite your lauishe, and magnificent liberalitie that way. But to let Titles and Tittles passe, and come to the very pointe in deede, which so neare toucheth my lusty Trauayler to the quicke, and is one of the *prædominant humors* that raigne in our common Youths : *Heus mi tu, bone proce, magne muliercularum amator, egregie Pamphile, eum aliquando tandem, qui te manet, qui mulierosos omnes, qui vniuersam Fœministarum sectam, Respice finem.* And I shal then be content to appeale to your owne learned experience, whether it be, or be not, too too true: *quod dici solet à me sæpe: à te ipso nonnunquam: ab expertis cmnibus quotidie: Amare amarum: Nec deus, vt perhibent, Amor est, sed amaror, et error: et quicquid in eandem solet sententiam Empiricos aggregari. Ac scite mihi quidem Agrippa Ouidianam illam, de Arte Amandi, ἀ-γ-εαφὴν videtur correxisse, meritoque, de Arte Meretricandi, inscripsisse. Nec verò ineptè alius, Amatores Alchumistis comparauit, aureos, argenteosque montes, atque fontes lepidè somniantibus, sed interim miserè immanibus Caronum fumis propemodum occæcatis, atque etiam suffocatis: præterquam celebratum illum Adami Paradisum, alium esse quendam præ-licauit, stultorum quoque Amatorumque mirabilem Paradisum: illum verè, hunc phantasticè, fanaticeque beatorum. Sed hæc alias, fortassis oberiùs.* Credite me, I will neuer linne baityng at you, til I haue rid you quite of this yonkerly, and womanly humor. And as for your speedy and hasty traueil: me thinks I dare stil wager al the Books and writings in my study, which you know, I esteeme of greater value, than al the golde and siluer in my purse, or chest, that you wil not, (and yet I muste take heede, how I make my bargaine with so subtile and in-ricate a Sophister) that you shall not, I saye, see gone ouer Sea, for al your saying, neither the next nor the nexte weeke. And then per-duenture I may personally performe your request, and bestowe the sweetest Farewell, vpon your sweetmouthed Mastershippe, that so vnsweete a Tong, and so sowre a paire of lippes can affoorde. And, thinke you I will eaue my *Il Pellegrino* so? No I trowe. My Lords Honor, the expectation of his

friendes, his owne credite and preferment, tell me, he mustè haue a moste speciall care, and good regarde of employing his trauaile to the best. And therfore I am studying all this fortnight, to reade him suche a Lecture in *Homers Odysses,* and *Virgils Æneads,* that I dare vndertake he shall not neede any further instruction, in *Maister Turlers Trauayler,* or *Maister Zuingers Methodus Apodemica:* but in his whole trauaile abroade, and euer after at home, shall shewe himselfe a verie liuelye and absolute picture of *Vlysses* and *Æneas.* Wherof I haue the stronger hope he muste needes proue a most capable and apt subiecte (I speake to a Logician) hauing the selfe same Goddesses and Graces attendant vpon his body and mind, that euermore guided them, and their actions: especially the ones *Minerua,* and the others *Venus:* that is (as one Doctor ex-poundeth it) the pollitique head, and wise gouernement of the one: and the amiable behauiour, and gratious courtesie of the other: the two verye principall, and moste singular Companions, of a right Trauailer: and as per-haps one of oure subtile Logicians woulde saye, the two inseparable, and indivisible accidents of the foresaide Subiects. *De quibus ipsis, cæterisque omnibus artificis Apodemici instrumentis: inprimisque de Homerica illa, diuinaque herba μῶλυ δί μιν καλίουσι θιοὶ qua Vlissem suum Mercurius, aduersus Cyrcca et pocula, et carmina, et venena, morbosque omnes præmuniuit: et coram, vti spero, breui: et longe, vti soleo, copiosius: et fortasse etiam, aliquantò, quàm soleo, cum subtilius cum verò Polliticè, Pragmaticeque magis. Interim tribus eris syllabis contentus, ac valebis. Trinitie Hall,* stil in my Gallerie. 23. Octob. 1579. In haste.

Yours, as you knowe. *G.H.*

Certaine Latin Verses, of the frailtie and
mutabilitie of all things, sauing onely Ver-
tue : made by M. Doctor Norton, for the right
Worshipfull, M. Thomas Sackford, Master of
Requestes vnto hir Maiestie.

ακροsιχα.

Th.   *Tempora furtiuo morsu laniantur amœna,*
S   *Sensim florescunt, occubitura breui.*
A *Anni vere salit, Senio mox conficiendus,*
C   *Cura, labor ditant, non eademque premunt?*
F *Fallax, vel vigili studio Sapientia parta :*
O   *Oh, et magnatum gloria sæpe iacet,*
R *Res inter varias fluimus, ruimusque gradatim :*
D.   *Dulcia Virtutis præmia sola manent.*

The same paraphrastically varied by M.
Doctor Gouldingam, at the request of olde
M. Wythipoll of Ipswiche

T. *Tempora furtiuo labuntur dulcia cursu,*
S   *Subsiduntque breui, quæ viguere diu.*
A *Autumno capitur, quicquid nouus educat annus :*
C   *Curta Iuuentutis gaudia, Fata secant.*
F *Fallax Ambitio est, atque anxia cura tenendi,*
O   *Obscurum decus, et nomen inane Sophi.*
R *Res Fors humanas incerto turbine voluit,*
D.   *Dulcia Virtutis præmia sola manent.*

Olde Maister Wythipols
owne Translation.

OVr merry dayes, by theeuish bit are pluckt, and torne away,
  And euery lustie growing thing, in short time doth decay.
The pleasaunt Spring times ioy, how soone it groweth olde ?
And wealth that gotten is with care, doth noy as much, be bolde.
No wisedome had with Trauaile great, is for to trust in deede,
For great Mens state we see decay, and fall downe like a weede.
Thus by degrees we fleete, and sinke in worldly things full fast,
But Vertues sweete and due rewardes stande sure in euery blast.

The same Paraphrastically varied by
Master G. H. at M. Peter Wythipolles
request, for his Father.

THese pleasant dayes, and Monthes, and yeares, by stelth do passe apace,
  And do not things, that florish most, soone fade, and lose their grace ?
Iesu, how soone the Spring of yeare, and Spring of youthfull rage,
Is come, and gone, and ouercome, and ouergone with age ?
In paine is gaine, but doth not paine as much detract from health,
As it doth adde vnto our store, when most we roll in wealth ?
Wisedome hir selfe must haue hir doome, and grauest must to graue,
And mightiest power sib to a flower : what then remaines to craue ?
Nowe vp, now downe, we flowe, and rowe in seas of worldly cares,
Vertue alone eternall is, and shee the Laurell weares.

L'Enuoy.

Soone said, soone writ, soone learnd : soone trimly done in prose, or verse ;
Beleeud of some, practizd of fewe, from Cradle to their Herse.
Virtuti, non tibi Feci.

M. Peter Wythipoll.

Et Virtuti, et mihi :
Virtuti, ad laudem :
Mihi, ad vsum.

FINIS.

CRITICAL APPENDIX.

THE FAERIE QVEENE.

BIBLIOGRAPHY.

The first three books of *F. Q.* were originally published in 1590. Books IV–VI, with a second edition of Books I–III, appeared in 1596. The fragmentary Book VII appeared first in the Folio of 1609. Except for this fragment, the text here printed is based on 1596. Some printers' errors have been corrected by reference to *1590*, with its valuable list of *Faults Escaped*, cited in these notes as *F.E.* The authority of *1609* has been preferred in half a dozen places. The later folios of 1611-12-13, 1617, and 1679, have no independent authority. Spenser's poetical works were subsequently edited by J. Hughes, 1715; H. J. Todd, 1805; F. J. Child, 1855; J. P. Collier, 1862; R. Morris, 1869; A. B. Grosart, 1882–4; R. E. Neil Dodge, 1908. The *F. Q.* was also edited separately by J. Upton, 1758, R. Church, 1758–9, and Kate M. Warren, 1897-1900. J. Jortin's *Remarks on Spenser's Poems* (1734) contain some good emendations.

DEDICATION. *The words ' and of Virginia' and ' to live with the eternitie of her fame' were added in* 1596.

BOOK I.

Proem iv. 5. my] mine *1590.*

I. ii. 1. But] And *1590. The 'But' of 1596 marks the contrast between the Knight's 'jolly' appearance and his dedicated purpose.*

v. 1. an innocent] and innocent *1590*: an Innocent *1609.*

ix. 6. sweete bleeding] sweet, bleeding *1609. But* 'sweete' *is probably adverbial.*

ix. 9. seeldom] sildom *1609 passim. See on* IV. xxiii. 5 *below.*

xii. 5. your hardy stroke *1590, &c.*: corr. *F.E. The corrections of F.E. are frequently ignored by 1596.*

xv. 6. poisonous] poisnous *1590. Spenser was more tolerant of resolved feet by 1596.*

xx. 4. vildly] vilely *1609 passim. The spelling* ' vild ' *is rare after 1600.*

xxi. 5. spring] ebbe *1590, &c.*: corr. *F.E.* to auale] t'auale *1590*: corr. *F.E. See note on* I. xii. 5 *above. The correction of* ' t'auale ' *was obviously made by 1596 independently.*

xxii. 3. longer] lenger *1590. But cf.* I. xxvi. 8.

xxviii. 8. passed] passeth *1596, 1609.*

xxx. 9. sits] fits *1609. But see Glossary.*

xxxi. 6. you] thee *1590.*

xlviii. 9. with *om.* *1596, 1609. 1609 made little use of 1590.*

l. 3. thought haue] thought t'haue *1609.*

liii. 6. since no'vntruth] sith n'vntruth *1609. In the quartos* ' sith ' *and* ' since ' *are used indifferently: 1609 tries to confine* ' sith' *to the causal,* ' since ' *to the temporal sense.*

II. xi. 3, 4. anon: shield, *1590, 1596*: corr. *1609. The punctuation of 1609 is more logical than that of the quartos.*

xvi. 8. idely, *1590, 1596* : idlely *1609.*

xvii. 5. cruell spies] cruelties *1590, &c.*: corr. *F.E.*

xxii. 5. your] thy *1590. Cf.* I. xxxi. 6 *above.*

xxvii. 9. so dainty] so, Dainty *1609—to show that Spenser is quoting the proverb* ' Quae rara, cara '.

xxix. 2. shade him] shade *1596*: shadow *1609, supplying the omission by conjecture. See note on* I. xlviii. 9 *above.*

xxix. 3. ymounted] that mounted *1590, &c.*: corr. *F.E.*

xxxii. 9. ruefull plaints] tuefull plants *1590. F.E. corrects* 'tuefull', *but not* ' plants '.

xl. 1, xli. 5. Thens forth] Then forth *1590, 1596*: corr. *F.E.*

III. xi. 1. To whom] Whom *1596.*

xxv. 7. inquere] inquire *1596. The rhyme favours 1590.*

xxxii. 9. Who told her all that fell] told *1609—taking the words to mean* ' Who told all that befell her '. *We should perhaps read* ' all that her fell '.

xxxiv. 9. spurnd] spurd *1590*.

xxxvi. 7. mourning] morning *1596*.

xxxviii. 7. the] that *F.E., referring probably to this line.* (*The references in F.E. are to pages only.*)

IV. xii. 2. a *om. 1596*. 7. Realmes] Realme *1590*.

xvi. 3. hurtlen] hurlen *1609; and so at* Bk. I, IV. xl. 1, *and* Bk. II, V. viii. 7. 9. glitterand] glitter and *1596, 1609*.

xx. 3. From] For *1596, 1609*.

xxiii. 5. seldome] seeldome *1590*, sildom *1609*. 7. dry dropsie] dire dropsie *conj. Upton, after Horace s* 'dirus hydrops'.

xxxii. 9. fifte] first *1590, &c.: corr. F.E.*

xxxvii. 6. *Lucifera*] Lucifer' *1590. See note on* I. xv. 6 *above.*

xlv. 4. *Sans ioy*] Sans ioy *1590*. 6. cause of my new ioy] cause of new ioy *1590, 1596 : corr. F.E.*

V. i. 9. he *om. 1596*.

ii. *This stanza is imitated in Peele's David and Bethsabe, written probably before 1590*.

ii. 5. hurld] hurls *1590, 1596*: hurles *1609 : corr. F.E.*

vii. 9. helmets hewen deepe] hewen helmets deepe *1590*.

xv. 2. thirstie] thristy *1590*. 3. bath] bathe *1590, 1609*.

xvii. 5. can] gan *1590. For* 'can' = ' did' *see Glossary.*

xxiii. 8. *Nightes* children] *Nights* drad children *1609, not observing that* '*Nightes*' *is dissyllabic.*

xxiv. 9. for] and *1596, 1609*.

xxvi. 6. am] ame *1590. Otherwise eye-rhymes are common in both quartos.*

xxxviii. 6. cliffs] clifts *1590, &c.: corr. F.E. So at* Bk. I, IX. xxxiv. 6. *But Spenser found that he needed* 'clift' *for the rhyme in* Bk. I, VIII. xxii. 5.

xli. 2. nigh] high *1596, 1609*.

xlv. 4. woundes] woundez *1609, observing the dissyllable.*

li. 5. that] the *1590, &c.: corr. F.E.*

VI. i. 5. in] it *1590, &c.: corr. F.E.*

v. 5. win] with *1596, 1609*.

viii. 7. misshapen] mishappen *1590*: mishapen *1596*.

xiv. 2. doubled] double *1609*.

xv. 2. Or] Of *1596, 1609* : If *conj. Hughes.*

xxiii. 8. noursled] nousled *1590 passim. 1596 uses* 'nousle' *as* = 'nuzzle'.

xxvi. 5. fierce and fell] swifte and cruell

1590 : corr. F.E. 9. as a tyrans law] as tyrans law *1596* : as proud tyrans law *1609*.

xxxix. 7. quoth he] qd. she *1590*.

xliv. 1. fell] full *1590*.

xlvii. 8. So they to fight] So they two fight *1596, 1609*.

VII. v. 9. did] do *1590*.

xx. 3. the] that *1590*.

xxii. 9. sight *om. 1590*.

xxxii. 8. Whose] Her *1590. This stanza is imitated in 2 Tamburlaine, iv. 4, acted some years before 1590*.

xxxvii. 7. trample] amble *1590. This is clearly an author's, not a printer's, change.*

xlii. 6. inquire] inquere *1590*.

xliii. 4. whilest] whiles *1590*. 6. runne] come *1590*: ronne *F.E.* 9. *Gehons*] Gebons *1596, 1609*.

xlviii. 9. haue you] haue yee *1590*.

VIII. Arg. 3. *the Gyant*] that Gyaunt *1590, &c.: corr. F.E.*

i. 6. through] thorough *1590*.

iii. 1. the] his *1590*.

x. 3. auantage] aduantage *1590*.

xi. 5–9. *Imitated in 2 Tamburlaine, iv. 3 ; see note on* VII. xxxii *above.* 9. murmur ring] murmuring *1590, &c.: corr. F.E.*

xxi. 5. their] his *Grosart—after Church. But* 'their' *may mean* '*Orgoglio's* and *Duessa's*'.

xxiv. 6. his] her *1590*.

xxvii. 7. eyes] eye *1590*.

xxxiii. 5. sits] fits *1596, 1609. But see* I. xxx. 9 *above and Glossary.*

xli. 7. and *om. 1596*.

xliv. 4. delight] dislike *conj. Jortin : others* despight. *As* 'delight' *is repeated from l. 3, the form of the error is no guide.*

IX. ix. 3. the] that *1590*. 5. *Timons*] Cleons *1590 : corr. F.E.*

xi. 4. vnwares] vnwares *1596*.

xii. 9. on] at *1590, 1596 : corr. F.E. and 1609*.

xv. 8. vow] vowd *1590, perhaps rightly.*

xviii. 9. as] the *1596, 1609*.

xxiv. 4. aspide] espide *1609*.

xxxi. 5. mealt'th] mealt'h *1590, &c.: corr. ed. after* Bk. II, II. iv. 5.

xxxii. 7. nor glee] nor fee *conj. Church ; cf.* Bk. I, x. xliii. 6. *Against this cf.* Bk. VI, v. xxxix. 3 ; VII. xlix. 9.

xxxiii. 3. ypight] yplight *1590*.

xxxiv. 6. cliffs] clifts *1590, &c.: corr. F.E. See on* V. xxxviii. 6 *above.*

CRITICAL APPENDIX.

lii. 1. saw] heard *1590*.   3. reliu'd] reliu'd *1609*.

liii. 1. feeble] seely *1596*: silly *1609*. *Comparison with* VII. vi. 5, xi. 8 *of this Book, where* 'feeble' *and* 'fraile' *occur together in lines which this was meant to recall, make it certain that* 'seely' (=feelie) *is a misprint for* 'feeble'.

X. vii. 8. simple true. *Cf. note on* I. ix. 6 *above.*

xv. 4. well] for *1590*.   gan] can *1609*. *See note on* V. xvii. 5 *above.*

xvi. 8. be] her *1590, &c.: corr. F.E.*

xx. 5. om. *1590, 1596* : add. *1609. This is one of the places which lead us to assign some independent authority to* 1609.

xxvii. 6. His bodie in salt water smarting sore] His blamefull body in salt water sore *1590*. *Another clear case of author's correction, designed to remove ambiguity.*

xxxiv. 8. worldes] worlds *1609. See on* v. xxiii. 8 *and* xlv. 4 *above.*

xxxvi. 6. Their *1609* : There *1590, 1596*. 9. call in commers-by] call in-commers by *1590, 1596*.

xxxix. 4. clothes] clothez *1609. See on* v. xlv. 4 *above.*

lii. 6. Brings] Bring *1590, 1596*.

lvii. 5. pretious] piteous *1590, &c.: corr. F.E.*

lix. 2. frame] fame *1590, &c.: corr. F.E.*

lxii. 4. (Quoth he) as wretched, and liu'd in like paine] As wretched men, and liued in like paine *1590*.   8. and battailes none are to be fought] and bitter battaile all are fought *1590*.   9. As for loose loues are vaine] As for loose loues they are vaine *1590. But cf.* Bk. V, III. xxii. 5 *and* 6.

lxiv. 7. doen nominate] doen then nominate *1596*.

lxv. 3. place] face *1590*.

XI. iii. *This stanza appears for the first time in* 1596.

v. 1. his] this *1590, &c.: corr. F.E.*

vi. 9. scared] feared *1590, &c.: corr. F.E.*

viii. 7. vast] vaste *1590* : wast *1596*.

xi. 5. as] all *1590, &c.: corr. F.E.*

xxvi. 6. swinged] singed *1609 needlessly : the form* 'swinge' *is still common in dialect.*

xxvii. 2. vaunt] daunt *1596, 1609*.

xxx. 5. one] it *1590, &c.: corr. F.E.*

xxxvii. 2. yelled] yelded *1590, 1596*. *But elsewhere* 'yelled' *in F.Q. Cf., however,*

'drownded' *in the quarto of Colin Clout* 762. *The true reading may be* 'yelped'.

xxxix. 4, 7. sting *and* string *transposed in 1596, 1609.*

xli. 4. Nor *1609* : For *1590, 1596. Spenser may have written* 'For'. *Negatives are similarly confused in* Bk. V, VI. xxvi. 5 *and* 6.

li. 7, 8. *The early editions have a semi-colon at* 'spred' *and a comma at* 'darke', *making l. 8 refer to the lark.*

XII. iii. 5. fond] found *1596, 1609*.

vii. 3. sung] song *1590—an eye-rhyme but ambiguous.*

xi. 5. talants] talents *1590, &c.: corr. F.E.*

xvi. 1. pleasure] pleasures *1596, 1609.*

xvii. 1. that] the *1596, 1609*.   4. note] no'te *1609, 1611.*

xxi. 7. To tell that dawning day is drawing neare] To tell the dawning day is dawning neare *1596, 1609.*

xxvii. 7. of] and *1596, 1609.*

xxviii. 7. her] his *1596, 1609. Cf.* xl. 9 *below.*

xxxviii. 3. frankencense *1596, 1609— possibly a deliberate achaism.* 1590 *has* frankincense. *Cf. note on* Bk. II, VII. iv. 8.

xl. 9. His] Her *1596, 1609.*

BOOK II.

Proem v. 4. else] elles *1590*.   beames] beamez *1609*.

I. i. 7. caytiues hands] caytiue hands *1609* : 'caytiue bands' *has been conjectured.*

ii. 7. natiue] natiues *1596, 1609.*

iii. 9. be] he *1609*.

iv. 6, 7. *These lines are transposed in* 1596, 1609.

viii. 5. with faire] with a faire *1596*.

xvi. 1. liefe] life *1590*.

xviii. 6. did he] he did *1590*.

xxxi. 2. handling] handing *1596*.

xxxiii. 8. thrise] these *1590, &c.: corr. F.E.*

xxxix. 4. dolour] labour *1596, 1609*.

xl. 4. gore] gold *1596, 1609*.

xliv. 6. reuenging] auenging *1590*.

xlix. 9. Mordant] Mortdant *1590, 1596* ; *but cf.* Argument.

lviii. 4. fry] frieze *or* frize *conj. Church.* 'Frize' (=freeze) *gives the contrast desired : the spelling* 'fryze' *would explain the corruption better.*

lix. 1. equall] euill *1596, 1609*.

THE FAERIE QVEENE. 647

II. iv. 3. in lieu of] in loue of *conj. Church.*

vii. 7. chace] *The rhyme requires* 'pray', *and so Collier suggested. Spenser has this error—the substitution for a rhyming word of a metrically equivalent synonym which does not rhyme—in nine places in F.Q.*

ix. 1. whose] those *1596, 1609.*

xxi. 1. cald] calth *1596, 1609—owing to the following* ' forth '.

xxiii. 2. boldly] bloudy *1596* : boldy *1609.*

xxviii. 2. both their champions] both her champions *1590* : both their champion *1596, 1609.*

xxix. 2. *The quartos omit the comma after* ' Erinnys ', *and insert it after* ' harts '.

xxx. 1. there] their *1590, 1596.*

xxxiv. 9. thought their] though ther *1590* : ? ' thought her ' ?

xxxvii. 1. Fast] First *1590, &c. : corr. F.E.*

xl. 5. peaceably] peaceable *1596, 1609.*

xlii. 6. make] *The rhyme requires* ' hold '. *See on* II. vii. 7 *above.*

xliv. 4. introld] entrold *1590* : enrold *conj. edd.*

III. iv. 5. A pleasing vaine of glory vaine did find] A pleasing vaine of glory he did find *1590. The reading of 1596 gives a play on words that is quite Spenserian.*

ix. 7. From] For *1596.*

xviii. 6. deuice] aduise *1596, 1609.*

xx. 5. As ghastly bug their haire on end does reare] As ghastly bug does vnto them affeare *1590* : ' vnto ' *corr. to* ' greatly ' *F.E. Spenser may have originally written* ' appeare '.

xxv. 1. Vpon her eyelids many Graces sate]. *In his Glosse on June in S.C., E.K. quotes from Spenser's Pageaunts the line* ' An hundred Graces on her eyeledde satte '.

xxviii. 7. play] *The rhyme requires* ' sport '. *See on* II. vii. 7 *above.*

xxxviii. 4. haue I] I haue *1590—transposed in 1596 for euphony.*

xlv. 4. one foot] on foot *1590, 1596.*

xlvi. 9. erne] yerne *1609. In the sixteenth century these two forms are both used to mean either* ' long ' *or* ' grieve '.

IV. Arg. 3. Phedon] Phaon *1590.*

x. 4. He is not] He is no *1590, &c. : corr. F.E.*

xvii. 6. one] wretch *1590.* 8. occasion] her guilful trech *1590.* 9. light vpon]

wandring ketch *1590. These corrections all hang together, and are clearly Spenser's.*

xxxv. *This stanza was quoted by Abraham Fraunce in his Arcadian Rhetorike two years before F.Q. was published. Fraunce quotes it as from the* ' Fairie Queene, 2 booke, cant. 4 ', *showing that by 1588 this part of the poem had been arranged as we have it.*

xxxvi. 2. into] vnto *1596.*

xli. 2. Pyrrochles *1590, &c., passim : corr. F.E.*

xlv. 5. thus to fight] that did fight *1590.*

V. Arg. *And Furors chayne vntyes*
Who him sore wounds, whiles Atin to
Gymochles for ayd flyes. 1590.

v. 9. do not much me faile] doe me not much fayl *1590.*

viii. 7. hurtle] hurle *1596* : hurlen *1609.*

xii. 8, 9. *The meaning seems to be* ' Nor judge of thy might by fortune's unjust judgement, that hath (curse on her spite) thus laid me low '. For ' maugre ' *see Glossary.*

xix. 4. shee] hee *1590, 1596.* 7. do] garre *1590—rejected as a provincialism perhaps : not elsewhere in F.Q., though used in S.C.*

xxvii. 3. her] his *1596.*

xxix. 5. pricking] prickling *1590.*

xxxi. 5. Gaynd in Nemea] In Netmus gaynd *1590* : Nemus *F.E.*

xxxiv. 8. So, them deceiues] So, he them deceiues *1590, 1596.*

VI. i. 7. restraine] abstaine *1590.* 8. their] her *1590.*

iii. 4. that nigh her breth was gone] as merry as Pope Ione *1590.* 6. might to her] to her might *1590.*

v. 6. cut away] ? cut a way ?

xii. 9. her sweet smels throw] throwe her sweete smels *1590.*

xiv. 9. a loud lay] a loue lay *1590.*

xviii. 7. griesly] griesy *1590 : cf.* v. xxix. 5 *above.*

xxvii. 9. there] their *1590, 1596.*

xxix. 2. importune] importance *1596* : important *1609.*

xxxviii. 8. There by] Thereby *1590, 1596.*

xliii. 7. lent this cursed light] lent but this his cursed light *1590.*

xlv. 3. Burning] But *1596.*

VII. iv. 4. yet] it *1596, 1609.* 8. vpsidowne] vpside downe *1590. This looks like a deliberate return to an archaic form.*

vii. 3. heapes] hils *1590*.

xii. 9. as] in *1590*.

xviii. 2. that *om.* 1596.

xxi. 5. infernall] internall *1590*.

xxiv. 7. ought] nought *1590*.

xxxvii. 1. as] an *1590*. 5. came] cam *1590*.

xl. 5. that] the *1590, &c.: corr. F.E.*
7. But] And *1590*. golden] yron *1590*.

xli. 3. his] to *1596, 1609*.

lii. 6. With which] Which with *1590, 1596:*
Which-with *1609*.

lx. 4. intemperate] more temperate *1590*.

VIII. iii. 8. Come hither, come hither]
Come hither, hither *1609*.

xxv. 1. his cruell] same *1590, 1596 : corr.
F.E. :* Which those same foes that doen
awaite hereby *1609*.

xxix. 7. vpreare] *The rhyme requires
'vpheaue'. See on* II. vii. *7 above.*

xl. 4. so wisely as it ought] so well, as he
it ought *1590, i.e. so well as he who owned it.
Perhaps a correction of the printer, who mis-
understood* 'ought'.

xliv. 8. but bit no more] but bit not thore
1590—'thore' *being probably=*'there', *on
the analogy of* ' tho '=' then '.

xlviii. 8. Prince *Arthur*] Sir *Guyon 1590,
1596.*

IX. vii. 5. Now hath] Seuen times *1590.*
6. Walkt round] Hath walkte *1590.* *Cf.*
Bk. I, IX. xv.

ix. 1. weete] wote *1590, &c.*

xv. 3. Capitaine] Captaine *1590, 1596.*
. i. 8. with *om. 1596.*

xxi. 1. them] him *1596.*

xxxvii. 8. you loue] your loue *1590,1596.*

xxxviii. 2. mood] word *1590 &c.: corr.
Drayton teste Collier.* (*Collier professed to
have a copy of the 1611 folio that had belonged
to Drayton and had corrections in his hand.*)
9. twelue moneths] three years *1590. See
on* IX. vii. 5 *above.*

xlix. 4. reason] season *Drayton teste Collier.*

X. vi. 6. safeties sake] safety *1590—a
trisyllable.*

vii. 7. liued then] liueden *1590.*

xv. 9. munifence] munificence *1590, 1609.
One of the few places in which 1590 and 1609
combine against 1596.*

xix. 5. in that impatient stoure] vpon the
present floure *1590.*

xxiv. 8. *Scuith guiridh om. 1590.* 9. *Extant copies of 1590 in Bodl. and B.M. have
only* ' But ' ; *but F.E.* ' Seuith Scuith' *shows*

that some copies of 1590 had ' Seuith', *and
Church, Upton, and Todd had copies with the
line in full.*

xxxiv. 6. Then] Till *1596 :* When *1609.*

xxxvii. 3. with] vp *1596.*

xxxviii. 2. of] or *1596, 1609.*

xliii. 1. *Sisillus*] Sifillus *1590, &c. The
correct spelling is given by Geoffrey of Monmouth.*

xlix. 8. defrayd] did defray *1596, 1609—
mistaking the rhyme-scheme.*

li. 7. Both in his armes, and croune] Both
in armes, and crowne *1596 :* In armes, and
eke in croune *1609.*

lxv. 9. enforst] haue forst *1590.*

lxvii. 2. *Ambrose*] Ambrise *1596, 1609 :*
' Ambrose' *in Geoffrey of Monmouth.*

XI. ix. 9. they that Bulwarke sorely rent]
they against that Bulwarke lent *1590.*

x. 2. dessignment] assignment *1590.*

xi. 4. dismayd] mismayd (*i.e.* mismade)
conj. Jortin.

xiii. 5. assayled] assayed *1590.*

xxiii. 8. support] disport *1596, 1609.*

xxvii. 5. Who] But *1590.*

xxx. 9. suruiue] reuiue *1590 &c.: corr. F.E.*

xxxii. 5. vnrest] infest *1590.*

XII. Arg. 1. by] *through 1590 passing
through*] *through passing 1590.*

xiii. 9. honor] temple *1590.*

xx. 8. their] the *1596, 1609.*

xxi. 1. heedfull] earnest *1590.*

xxiii. 9. *Monoceros*] Monoceroses Child after
Jortin ; but the accentuation 'immeasured'
is paralleled by 'treasures' *in Visions of
Petrach,* ii. 6.

xxxix. 8. vpstarting] vpstaring *1590.*

xliii. 5. Nought feared their force] Nought
feared they force *conj. Church. i.e.* ' they had
no fear of force'. *With* 'their', 'feared'
must be taken to mean 'frightened'.

li. 1. Thereto] Therewith *1590.*

lxi. 8. tenderly] fearefully *1590.*

lxxxi. 4. the same] that same *1590.*

lxxxiii. 7. spoyle] spoyld *1596, 1609.*

BOOK III.

Proem iv. 2. Your selfe you] Thy selfe thou
1590.

I. xli. 8. lightly] highly *1590, 1596—
evidently a misprint.*

xlvii. 7. which] that *1590—changed because
of* 'that' *in the next line.*

lvi. 8. *Basciomani*] *Bascimano 1590*. ' *Basciomani* ' *was perhaps coined as a substantive
from* ' *bascio le mani* '.

lx. 8. wary] weary *1596, 1609*.

II. iv. 1. *Guyon*] *should be Redcrosse*.

viii. 5. Which I to proue] Which to proue, I
1590.

xxx. 5. in her warme bed her dight] her in
her warme bed dight *1590*.

xxxvi. 1. others] other *1590*.

xlix. 7. a earthen Pot] an earthen Pot
*1609. Spenser may have intended to pro-
nounce* ' yearthen '.

III. iv. 8. protense] pretence *1596, 1609*.

xxxv. 1. thy] the *1596, 1609*.

xliv. 5. yeares *om. 1596, 1609* : shall be
full supplide *1609*.   6 to] vnto their *1590*
—*making a hexameter*.

l. 9. ⟨as earst⟩ *om. 1590, 1596 : add. 1609*.

liii. 3. (whom need new strength shall
teach)] (need makes good schollers) teach
1590.

IV. viii. 9. these] thy *1590*.

xv. 6. speare] speares *1590, 1596*.

xxxiii. 4. raynes] traines *1596, 1609*.

xxxix. 9. sith we no more shall meet] till
we againe may meet *1590. Spenser has
remembered that Cymoent is a heathen goddess*.

lix. 5. Dayes dearest children] The children
of day *1590*.

V. v. 5. A] And *1596, 1609—perhaps due
to* ' And ' *in the next line*.

xi. 1. ye] you *1596, 1609*.

xxi. 9. bloud] flood *1590*.

xxxvii. 2. Had vndertaken after her,
arriu'd] Had undertaken, after her arriu'd
1609. 1596 has no point.   6. follow]
followd *1590, perhaps rightly*.

xxxix. 9. his] their *1590*.

xl. 4. loues sweet teene] sweet loues teene
1590.   9. liuing] liking *1590*.

lii. 6. admire :] admire *1590, 1596—con-
necting it with* ' In gentle Ladies brest '.

liii. 3. Realmes] Reames *1590. But cf.*
Bk. V, VII. xxiii. 6, 8, 9.

VI. iii. 9. was] were *1590*

vi. 5. his beames] his hot beames *1609*.

xii. 4. beautie] beauties *1596, 1609*.

xxv. 4. Which as a fountaine from her
sweet lips went] From which, &c., *1590,
1596 : corr. 1609*. Of which *conj.* Church.

xxvi. 4. both farre and nere *om. 1590*.

xxviii. 6. thence] hence *1596, 1609*.

xxxix. 1. and to all] and all *1611—to
avoid the trisyllabic foot*.

xl. 6. spyde] *The rhyme requires* ' saw '.
See on II. vii. 7 *above*.

xliii. 5. heauy] heauenly *1590*.

xlv. 4. And dearest loue, *om. 1590, 1596 :
add. 1609. See on* Bk. I, x. xx. 5.

VII. ix. 3. two] to *conj.* Hughes.

xiii. 6. had gazed]. *Todd and Morris
imply that some copies of 1596 read* ' hath '.

xviii. 5. be by] by *1590* : be *1596, 1609*.
that] by *1590*.

xxii. 5. Monstrous mishapt] Monstrous,
mishapt *1590. See on* Bk. I, I. ix. 6.

xxxiv. 2. enclose]. *The rhyme requires*
' containe '. *See on* II. vii. 7 *above*.

xliii. 7. saw, with great remorse] saw with
great remorse, *1590, 1596*.

xlv. 1. the *om. 1596, 1609*.   wake]
awake *1609*.

xlviii. 4. And many hath to foule confusion
brought] Till him Chylde *Thopas* to confusion
brought *1590*.

l. 2. thrust] thurst *1596, 1609*.

VIII. ii. 7. broken] golden *1590*.

v. 1. aduise] deuice *1590*.

vii. 4. a womans] to womans *1590*.

xxiii. 8. the same] this same *1590*.

xxx. 3. frory] frowy *1590, 1596. But
see* xxxv. 2 *below, and Glossary under*
' frowie '.

IX. iv. 5. her] his *1609*.

xiii. 9. And so defide them each] And
defide them each *1596* : And them defied
each *1609*.

xiv. 7. to kenell] in kenell *1590*.

xxii. 1. *Minerua*] Bellona *1590*.

xxiv. 5. most *om. 1596*.

xxvii. 5. that] with *1590*.

xlviii. 6. to sea] to the sea *1596*.

X. viii. 9. To take to his new loue] To take
with his new loue *1590*.

xiii. 8. would beare] did beare *1590*.

xviii. 4. Then] So *1590*.

xxxi. 3. with thy rudenesse beare] that
with rudenesse beare *1590*.   7. vertues]
vertuous *1590*.

xl. 3. wastefull] faithfull *1590*.

xlvi. 6. th' Earthes] the Earthes *1609—,
not observing the dissyllable*.

XI. ii. 3. golden] golding *1590, 1596*.

iv. 4. that I did euer] all, that I euer *1590*. ç. him did] did him *1590*.

ix. 6. Or hast thou, Lord,] Or hast, thou Lord, *1590, 1596*.

xii. 1. singultes] singulfes *1590, 1596*. *There is the same misspelling in F.Q. Bk. V,* VI. *xiii, C.C. 168, and Tears of the Muses,* 232.

xix. 9. death] life *conj. Jortin, which gives the sense required.*

xxii. 8. Foolhardy as th' Earthes children, the which made] Foolhardy as the Earthes children, which made *1590*.

xxvi. 8. and with imperious sway] and imperious sway *1596*: and his imperious sway *1609*.

xxvii. 7. entred] decked *1590*.

xxviii. 8. Like a] Like to a *1590*.

xxxix. 6. each] his *1590*.   8. Stag *conj. Jortin*: Hag *1590, &c. Jortin's conjecture is demonstrated by comparison with Natalis Comes, Mythologia,* iv. 10, *on which Spenser drew for this Canto.*

xlvii. 9. heauen bright] heuens hight *conj. Church.*

XII. v. 7. concent] consent *1596*.

ix. 3. other] others *1590, 1596*.

xii. 6. wingyheeld] winged heeld *1590*.

xvii. 6. a firebrand she did tosse] a fier-brand she tost *conj. Church.*

xviii. 8. an hony-lady Bee] an hony-laden *conj. Upton.*

xxi. 7. fading] failing *conj. Church.*

xxiii. 5. hand *om. 1590, 1596*: *corr. F.E.*

xxvi. 7. with that Damozell] by the Damozell *1590—which makes the Damozell Brito-mart.*

xxvii. 3. and bore all away] nothing did remayne *1590*.

xxxiii. 3. her selfe] the next *1590*.

xxxiv. 4. her] him *1590, 1596. Cf. next note.*

xlii. 2. She] He *1590*.   4. She] He *1590: corr. F.E.*   5. her] him *1590: corr. F.E. Spenser seems momentarily to have forgotten Britomart's sex.*

BOOK IV.

Title 5. TELAMOND] *Triamond in* II. xxxi. 8, *&c.*

Proem v. 5. thereof] whereof *1609*.

I. xi. 6. then] and *1609*.

xvi. 7. none] one *1609*.

II. iii. 5. As] And *1609*.

xxi. 7. knowen] known *1609*.

xxii. 7. aduizing] avising *1609*. *See Glossary under* 'aduize'.

III. ix. 6. n'ote] not *1596*.   9. of] at *1609*.

xviii. 2. so deadly it was ment] so deadly was it ment *1609*.

xix. 5, 6. The warie fowle that spies him toward bend
His dreadfull souse, auoydes it shunning light.]
The warie fowle that spies him toward bend,
His dreadfull souse auoydes, it shunning light *1609*.

xliii. 5. quiet age] quiet-age, *suggested to Jortin by a friend, is adopted by Morris. Not elsewhere in F.Q.*

l. 3. To] Too *1596*.

lii. 1. feast] feasts *1609*.

IV. i. 4. minds] liues *16(11)–12–13*. (*No genuine 1611 copy of Books IV–VI is known to the editors. Morris reports* liues *1609: not so in our copies.*)

ii. 3. els] als *1609*. 'Els' *separates,* 'als' *joins the two comparisons.*   4. Scudamour] Blandamour *1679 rightly.*

viii. 2. Ferrau] Ferrat *1596*: Ferraugh *in* II. iv *below.*

x. 5. worse] worst *1596*.

xvii. 4. maiden-headed] satyr-headed *conj. Church, comparing Bk.* III, VII. xxx. 6. *Perhaps* 'maiden-headed' = 'belonging to one of the Knights of Maidenhead'.

xix. 7. an heap] a heap *1609*.

xxiv. 1. beamlike] brauelike *1596. But Upton reports* 'beamlike' *from one of his copies of 1596*.

xlv. 1. t' auenge] t' euenge *1596*.

V. iv. 4. *Lemno*] *Lemnos 16(11)–12–13.*

viii. 1. that] the *1609*.

ix. 8. Then] The *1609*.

xvi. 1. that] the *1609*.

xxv. 5. one] once *1596*.

xxxi. 3. his] her *1596*.

VI. xxiv. 8. his *om. 1609, to avoid the trisyllabic foot.*

xxviii. 6. He] Her *1596*: Him *conj. Upton.*

xliv. 4. in the morrow] on the morrow *1609*.

xlvi. 5. who she had left behind] whom *16(11)–12–13, but not in our copies of 1609*.

VII. i. 1. dart] darts *1609*.

iv. 6. snatched vp from ground] snatcht vp from the ground *1609*.

x. 9. ouersight] ore-sight *1609*.

xii. 1. caytiue] captiue *Collier, &c. But cf.* Bk. I, VII. xix. 3.

xxii. 1. Nor] For *Collier*.

xxv. 1. Which] With *1596*.

xxxii. 7. oft] eft *conj. Hughes, for the rhyme.*

xxxiii. 1. Thence forth she past] Thenceforth she past *1596*.

xxxiv. 1. the sad Æmylia] the said Æmylia *1596*.

xli. 6. euer] neuer *1609*.

VIII. x. 4. ribbands] ribband *1609*.

xii. 3. him] her *conj. Church.*

lxiv. 1. this] his *(1611)–12–13, but not our copies of 1609.*

IX. Arg. 2. *Pæana*] *Æmylia conj. Church rightly.*

i. 8. vertuous] vertues *1596*.

iii. 3. these] this *1609*.

xi. 9. him] them *conj. Hughes.*

xvii. 5. quest] guest *1596, 1609*.

xxvi. 1. There] Their *1596* : Then *conj. Church.*

xxx. 8. repayed] repayred *1596*.

xxxvii. 2. Knight] Knights *conj. Upton.*

xxxix. 8. a wretch and] a wretch I and *1596*.

X. viii. 8. *his*] *Upton reports* 'this' *from one of his quartos.*

ix. 1. earne] yearne *1609 passim.*

xvii. 5. adward] award *1609*.

xix. 1. meanest] nearest *1596*.

xxiii. 2, 8. ghesse *and* bee *are transposed in all but two of our copies.*

xxvii. 1. Hylas] *Hyllus 1596* : *Hylus 1609. But cf.* Bk. III, XII. vii. 9.

xxxv. 6. and hell them quight]. *The meaning is either* ' And hell requite them ' *or* ' And cover them (i.e. the lands) quite '. *But* ' hell ' =cover *is not elsewhere in F.Q., though* ' vnhele ' =uncover *occurs in* Bk. II, XII. lxiv. 8. *Hence* ' mell ' =confuse *has been suggested. But even so there is a difficult parenthesis.*

xlii. 6. eldest] elder *1609*.

li. 9. girlonds] gardians *conj. Church* : guerdons *conj. Collier.*

lv. 8. warie] wearie *conj. Upton.*

lvi. 4. To laugh at me] To laugh on me *1609*.

XI. iv. 6. seuen] three *occurs in two copies of 1596, and in all of 1609.*

xvii. 6. times]. *The rhyme requires* ' age '. *But see on* Bk. II, II. vii. 7 *above.*

xxx. 5. none] one *1609*.

xxxiv. 5. Grant] Guant *1596, 1609* : *corr. Child after Upton. The* ' Grant ' *is the* Granta, *i.e. the* Cam.

xliv. 4. deuided] diuided *1609 passim.*

xlv. 1. louely] louing *1609*.

xlviii. 8. *Eudore*] *Endore 1596, 1609* : *corr. Child.*

lii. 7. but] both *conj. edd., needlessly* : ' floods and fountaines, *though derived from* Ocean, *are akin to sky and sun.*

XII. iv. 9. disauentrous] disaduentrous *1609*.

x. 4. shall] should *1609*.

xiii. 1, 2. Thus whilst his stony heart with tender ruth
Was toucht, and mighty courage mollifide]
Thus whilst his stony heart was toucht with tender ruth,
And mighty courage something mollifide *1609*.
Spenser probably altered the text, meaning to omit ' tender '.

xxx. 4. t'adward] t'award *1609*.

BOOK V.

Proem ii. 2. at earst] as earst *16(11)–12–13. But cf.* Bk.VI, III. viii. 7.

vii. 8. thirtie] thirteen *conj. Child, which is said to be astronomically correct.*

xi. 2. stead] place *1596. The rhyme requires* ' stead '—*see on* Bk. II, II. vii. 7 *above. This is the only correction of this nature in 1609, and has been accepted as Spenserian.* 9. *Artegall*] *Arthegall 1609 passim; and so generally in* Bk. III.

II. Arg. 3. *Munera*] *Momera 1596, 1609* : *corr. Hughes.*

ii. 7. As] And *1596*.

iv. 1. hee] she *1596*.

xi. 4. Who] Tho *conj. Church* : When *Morris. No correction is needed.*

xxxii. 4. earth] eare *1596*.

xxxviii. 1. these] those *1609*.

xlvi. 9. way] lay *1609, to avoid the identical rhyme.*

III. xi. 7, 9. the other] th' other *1596, 1609*.

xl. 6. we] were *1596*.

IV. i. 3. Had need haue] Had neede of *16(11)–12-13.* —

xxii. 2. pinnoed] pinnioned *16(11)–12-13.*

xxvi. 1. *Terpine*] *Turpine 1596.*

xxxvi. 1. watchmen] watchman *1609.*
8. their Queene her selfe, halfe like a man] their Queene her selfe halfe, like a man *1596:* their Queene her self, arm'd like a man *1609—perhaps rightly.*

xxxvii. 1. neare] newe *conj. Church.* **3.** so few] to feare *conj. Collier. One or other correction seems needed for the rhyme : Church's is the better.*

xxxix. 3. doale] doile *1596.* diuide] dauide *1596. Probably 'a' and 'i' interchanged. For* 'doale' = portion *see Glossary.*

xlviii. 3. *Clarin*] *Clarind' 1609 passim.* yesterday] yeester day *1596 ; but Spenser has* 'yester' *elsewhere.*

V. xx. 8. a napron] an apron *1609.*

xxxviii. 8. And, though (vnlike) they should for euer last] And, though vnlike, they should for euer last *1596. The meaning of 1609 is* 'Though—which is unlikely—they should last, &c.'

xli. 2. he] she *1609.*

VI. iv. 7. from] for *1609.*

v. 6, 7. For houres but dayes ; for weekes, that passed were,
She told but moneths, to make them seeme more few *1596, 1609.*
Church would transpose ' houres' *and* ' dayes', 'weekes' *and* 'moneths'. *Spenser perhaps means that she said* 'three months' *for* 'twelve weeks' *and then ignored the noun.*

xvi. 7. That this is things compacte] thing *conj. Church.*

xvii. 5. Heard] Here *1596.*

xxiv. 1. their] her *1609.*

xxv. 7. Your nights want] your Knight's want *conj. Church.*

xxvi. 5. Ne lesse]. *Sense requires* 'Ne more', *but no authority for this. Spenser probably meant at first to turn the sentence differently.*

xxxiii. 7. auenge] reuenge *16(11)–12-13— Morris and Grosart report* 'reuenge' *1609 ; not so our copies.*

xxxiv. 7. their] that *1609.*

VII. vi. 9. her wreathed taile] his wreathed taile *conj. Church—cf. stanza* xv *below.*

xxxviii. 5. bad] sad *1609.*

VIII. xl. 6. knowen] knowne *1596.*

IX. xxvi. 4. FONT] FONS *1596, 1609.*

xliv. 1. appose] oppose *1609.*

X. iii. 6. *Americke*] *Americke conj. Todd, very plausibly ; otherwise* '*Armericke*' *can only mean* 'Armoric'.

vi. 4. and of her Peares] and her Peares *1609, to avoid the trisyllabic foot.*

viii. 4. Idols] Idol *conj. Church.*

xxiv. 5. farewell open field] well fare *conj. edd. needlessly* : ' farewell' *here* =welcome.

xxvi. 3. so now ruinate] now so ruinate *conj. Church.*

xxxvii. 6. hard preased] had preased *1609.*

XI. xxiv. 7. And Eagles wings] An Eagles wings *1609.*

xl. 6. She death shall by] She death shall sure aby *16(11)–12-13, to complete the pentameter.*

xli. 6. know] knew *1596, 1609 : corr. Hughes.*

li. 1. this] his *1609.*

liv. 9. corruptfull] corrupted *16(11)–12-13 ; Morris and Grosart report* 'corrupted' *1609 ; not so our copies.*

lx. 2. had] haue *1609.*

lxi. 7. meed]. *The rhyme requires* ' hyre'. *But see on* Bk. II, II. vii. 7. **8.** froward] forward *1596. See Glossary.*

XII. i. 9. enduren] endure *1596.*

xiv. 8. steale] steele *1609. But see Glossary.*

xvii. 5. such] sure *1609.*

BOOK VI.

I. viii. 7. wretched] wicked *16(11)–12-13.*

xxviii. 6. Ere he] Ere thou *1596.*

xl. 9. yearne] earne *1609.*

II. iii. 2. deed and word] act and deed *1596.* **3, 4.** eyes . . . eares] eares . . . eyes *corr. edd. ; but there is no evidence that the error is not Spenser's own.*

xxxix. 2. implements] ornaments *1609—probably an editorial improvement.*

III. x. 2. Would to no bed] Would not to bed *1609.*

xxi. 8. default] assault *conj. Collier with much plausibility.*

xxiii. 2. *Serena*] *Crispina 1596 Bodl.—corr. at press.*

xxiv. 5. in vaine *om. 16(11)–12-13, to reduce the line to a pentameter.*

xxviii. 6. soft footing) softing foot *1596*, *1609*: corr. *1679*.

xxxv. 3. which] That *1596 Bodl.—corr. at press*.

xxxvii. 9. did for her] for her did *1596 Bodl.—corr. at press*.

xliii. 4. approue] reproue *1596*.   7. re-proue] approue *1596*.

IV. iv. 7. stroke] strokes *1609*.

v. 7. He stayed not t' aduize] He stayd not to aduize *1609*.

xiii. 8. Where] There *1596*.

xvi. 8. hurts] hurt *16(11)–12–13, for the sake of the grammar*.

xxx. 5. these] those *1609*.

xxxiii. 2. sides] side *1609*.

V. Arg. 1. *Matilda*] *Serena corr. Hughes, rightly*.

xxviii. 2. liue] liues *1609*.

xxxix. 3. glee] gree *1609. For* 'gree' *cf.* Bk. V, VI. xxi. 7 ; *for* 'glee', Bk. I, IX. xxxii. 7.

xli. 2. there] their *1596*.

VI. Arg. 3. '*He*' *refers to Prince Arthur, but no correction is possible*.

xvii. 7. *Calidore*] *Calepine corr. Hughes, rightly*.

xxxv. 6. fight] right *1596*.

xxxvi. 1. thy] this *1609*.

VII. i. 1. the] a *1609*.

xxxv. 8. there] their *1609*.

xlix. 9. Words] Swords *conj. Church, plausibly*.

VIII. xvii. 6. From] For *1596*.

xlv. 9. a loud] aloud *1609*.

xlvii. 3. toyles] toyle *1609*.   6. lost] tost *Drayton teste Collier*.

l. 4. what they ought] what shee ought *1609, taking* 'ought' = owned.

IX. iv. 9. time] tine *conj. Church*.

vi. 5. him] them *1596*.

xxvi. 1. eare] care *1609*.

xxviii. 6. the heauens] th' heauens *1596*, *1609*.

xxxvi. 8. *Oenone*] *Benone 1596, 1609 : corr. Hughes*.

xlv. 9. bought] sought *conj. Church*.

xlvi. 5. which there did dwell] which there did well *1596*, *1609 : corr. 16(11)–12–13*.

X. ii. 9. in the port] on the port *1596. The reading of 1609 recalls* 'in portu nauigare ',

but that means 'to be out of danger '. *Possibly 1596 preserves some lost nautical phrase*.

xxiv. 7. froward] forward *1596, 1609 : corr. 16(11)–12–13. Cf. Glossary on S.C. for April :* '. . . they (the Graces) be painted naked, . . . the one hauing her backe toward us, and her face fromwarde.'

xxxiv. 9. to helpe her all too late] to helpe ere all too late *Drayton teste Collier*.

xxxvi. 6. And hewing off her head, ⟨he⟩ it presented] ⟨he⟩ om. *1596, 1609*.

xliv. 3–7.] *1609 marks a parenthesis and reads* ' And ' *for* ' But ' *in* l. 8.

XI. xi. 6. that] the *1609*.

xix. 4. pretended] protended *conj. Collier*.

xxiv. 1. reliu'd] reuiv'd *1609*

XII. xii. 8. loos] praise *1609—possibly Spenser's own correction, because of the preceding* ' losse ' ; *or the editor of 1609 did not recognize* ' loos '.

xl. 7. learned] gentle *1609—from the next line*.

xli. 3. clearest] cleanest *conj. Hughes, perhaps rightly*.

BOOK VII.

VI. x. 1. That] Tho *Hughes*.

xxii. 9. hot] her *Hughes*.

xxxviii. 2. wealths] wealth *Hughes, &c., perhaps rightly*.

xliv. 4. *Fanchin*] *called Funchin in C.C. 301. The Funschin is a tributary of the Blackwater. Here Spenser perhaps intended an etymological connexion with Faunus*.

VII. ii. 3. feeble] sable *1609 : corr. Hughes*.

ix. 7. *Plaint of kindes*] *Plaint of kinde Upton after Chaucer, Parlement of Foules 316*.

x. 4. mores] more *Hughes, &c.: others explain* 'mores' *as* = roots ; *see Glossary*.

xvi. 3. thy] my *16(11)–12–13*.

lv. 7. saine] faine *16(11)–12–13*.

VIII. ii. 9. Sabaoths] Sabbath's *Upton and Church, distinguishing between* ' Sabaoth ' = hosts *and* ' Sabbath ' = rest. *But this seems to spoil the point of the stanza*.

LETTER TO RALEIGH.

l. 16. *by-accidents*] by accidents *1590*

THE SHEPHEARDES CALENDER.

Five Quarto editions of the *Shep. Cal.* appeared in the poet's lifetime—in 1579, 1581, 1586, 1591, and 1597. They are referred to below as *Qq 1-5* respectively. An exhaustive collation of these editions proves conclusively that though some of the corrections may have been made at Spenser's instigation, he cannot be regarded as in any way responsible for the general form of the text after *Q 1*. Each *Q* was printed from its predecessor, and the first Folio, 1611 (*F*), from *Q 5*. Each edition corrects a few errors, reproduces many, and initiates others. The present text, therefore, is printed from *Q 1*, and the following notes record departures from *Q 1*, adding a few characteristic readings from other copies to illustrate their relation with one another.

EPISTLE.

p. 417, l. 41. oftentimes *Qq 2-5*: ofentimes *Q*.

p. 417, A56. cleane *Qq 3-5*, *F*: cleare *Q 1*: clean *Q 2*.

p. 417, B14. not ... seene *Qq 3-5*, *F*: no ... seme *Qq 1, 2*.

p. 417, B38. though it cannot *Qq 3-5*, *F*: though cannot *Qq 1, 2*.

p. 418, A32. habilities: *Qq 3-5*, *F*: habilities? *Qq 1, 2*.

GENERALL ARGVMENT.

p. 419, A12. more Shepherds, then Goatheards *Q 5*, *F*: most shepheards, and Goteheards *Qq 1-4*.

p. 419, A16. inuention *Qq 2-5*, *F*: inuericion *Q 1*.

p. 420, A20. Abib *F*: Abil *Qq 1-5*.

p. 420, B32. Shepheard *Q 2*: Sepheard *Q 1*: shepheards *Qq 3-5*, *F*.

JANVARY.

49. hower, *Qq 2-5*, *F*: hower. *Q 1*.

FEBRVARY.

137. Wherefore I rede thee hence to remove *F*.

142. ouercrawed *Qq 3-5*, *F*: ouerawed *Qq 1, 2*; *overcrawed is the northern form of* overcrowed. Cf. *Hamlet*, v. ii. 368.

151. ponder *Qq 1-3*: pond *Qq 4, 5, F*.

This error of Qq 4, 5, and F led to the inclusion of 'pond' in Johnson's Dictionary as a genuine Spenserian form.

176. woundes *Qq 2-4*: wounds *Qq 1, 5, F*.

218. earth *Qq 1-5*: ground *F*.

229-30. late: For ... disconsolate, *Qq 1-3*: late: Yor (*sic*) ... disconsolate, *Q 4*: late, Yore ... disconsolate. *Q 5, F*.

MARCH.

4. nigheth *F*: nighest *Qq 1-5*. *Morris suggests* 'nighës'.

57. greene. *Qq 3-5, F*: greene, *Qq 1, 2*.

85. seeing, I *Q 5, F*: seeing I, *Qq 1-4*.

Gloss to 23. by loue sleeping *Qq 1, 2*: by our sleeping *Qq 3, 4*: by sleeping *Q 5, F*.

Gloss to 23. pleasures, *Q 5, F*: pleasures *Qq 1-4*.

Gloss to 79. wandring *Qq 1-3*: wingdring *Q 4*: winged *Q 5, F*. *A good example of the gradual corruption of the text, and its emendation by the printer without reference to earlier Qq.*

APRILL.

39. Forsake *Qq 2-5, F*: For sake *Q 1*.

64. angelick *Q 1*: angelike *Q 2*: angellike *Qq 3-5*: angel-like *F*.

113. not not *Qq 1, 2*.

135. finesse, *Qq 1-4*: finenesse, *Q 5, F*.

Gloss to 50. simplye *Qq 1-4*: plainly *Q 2, F*.

Gloss to 63. Embellish) beautifye *Qq 1, 2*: Emblemish) beautifie *Q 3*: Emblemish) beautified *Q 4*: Emblemisht) beautified *Q 5*: embellisht, beautified *F*.

Gloss to 120. *Behight F*: Bedight *Qq 1-5*.

MAYE.

ARG. 1. fift *Q 5, F*: firste *Qq 1-4*.

7, 8. woods ... buds *Q 5, F*: Wods ... Buds *Qq 1-3*: Woods ... Boods *Q 4*.

8. bloosming *Qq 1-3*: blossoming *Qq 4, 5, F*.

36. swinke? *Q 5, F*: swinck. *Qq 1-4*.

54. great *Q 5, F*: gread *Qq 1-4*.

82. worldly *Qq 2-5, F*: wordly *Q 1*.

113. shepheards *Qq 2-5, F*: shephears *Q 1*.

177. reason, *Q 5, F*: reason. *Qq 1-4*.

187. blossomes *Qq, F*; *it is probable, however, that Spenser wrote* 'bloosmes', *for*

'bloosmes' *is the form given in the Gloss upon this passage.* Cf. *also Jan.* 34, *Dec.* 103.

192. jollitee.] *Qq 1–5, F omit full stop.*

214. stroke.] *Qq 1–5, F omit full stop.*

261. were. *Q 5, F* : were, *Qq 1–4.*

Gloss to 75. Algrind *Q 5, F* : Algrim *Qq 1–4.*

Gloss to 189. πάθος.] παφός *Q 1* : Pathos *Qq 2, 3, 5, F* : Patdos *Q 4.*

IVNE.

16. shroud *F* : shouder *Qq 1–5.*

21. shipheardes *Q 1.*

23. Rauens *F* : Rauene *Qq 1, 2* : Rauen *Qq 3–5.*

38. steps : *F* : steps *Qq 1–5.*

89. Now dead he is, &c. *This stanza is omitted from Q 5 and F.*

Gloss to 57. is is *Q 1.*

Gloss to 103. undermine *Q 5, F* : undermynde *Qq 1, 2* : underminde *Qq 3, 4.*

IVLYE.

14. tickle *Q 5, F* : trickle *Qq 1–4.*

99. the starres *Qq 1–5* : a starre *F.*

177. glitterand *Q 1* : glitter and *Qq 2–5, F.* gold, *Qq 4, 5, F* : gold. *Qq 1–3.*

208. melling. *Qq 2–5, F* : melling, *Q 1.*

215. gree, *Q 3–5, F* : gree. *Qq 1, 2.*

219. ill, *Qq 2–5, F* : ill. *Q 1.*

233. *Thomalins* (conj., v. 340) : Palinodes *Qq 1–5, F.*

Gloss to 8. Seneneca (sic) *Q 1.* lapsu *Qq 3–5, F* : lapsus *Qq 1, 2.*

Gloss to 33. then *Qq 3–5, F* : and *Qq 1, 2.*

AVGVST.

16 a. PERIGOR (sic) *Q 1.*

84. thy *F* : my *Qq 1–5.*

104. curelesse *conj. Collier* : carelesse *Qq, F.*

105. bought, *Qq 2–5, F* : bought. *Q 1.*

134. hm *Q 1.*

148. deede. *Qq 3–5, F* : deede, *Qq 1, 2.*

154. a part *Qq 3–5* : apart *Qq 1, 2, F.*

SEPTEMBER.

59. hond *Qq 3–5, F* : hande *Qq 1, 2.*

139. endured *Qq 3–5, F* : endured *Qq 1, 2.*

145. yead *F* : yeeld *Qq 1–5.*

153. Chrisiendome *Q 1.*

163. priuie *Qq 4, 5, F* : priue *Qq 1–3.*

165. theyr *Qq 2, 3* : thoyr *Q 1* : their *Qq 4, 5, F.*

169. They *Q 5, F* : The *Qq 1–4.*

196. away, *Qq 3–5, F* : awaye. *Qq 1, 2.*

201. thanck. *Q 5, F* : thanck *Qq 1–4.*

207 a. Hobbinoll *Qq 2–5* : Diggon *Q 1.*

255. can. *Qq 3–5, F* : can : *Qq 1, 2.*

Gloss to 20. Thrice *F* : These *Qq 1–5.*

Gloss to 96. practtises *Q 1.*

Gloss to 151. *Date omitted Qq, F.*

Gloss to 162. Privy *F* : Preuely *Qq.*

Gloss to Emblem, p. 456, B4. looking *Q 1.*

Gloss to Emblem, p. 456, B5. poore, *Qq 2–5, F* : poore. *Q 1.*

OCTOBER.

ARG. 1. whishe *Q 1.*

2. chace, *Q 5, F* : chace : *Qq 1–4.*

6. dead. *Q 5, F* : dead ? *Qq 1–4.*

76. rybaudrye : *Qq 4, 5, F* : rybaudrye. *Qq 1–3.*

79. thy *Qq 3–5, F* : the *Qq 1, 2.*

96 a. CVDDIE. *Qq 3–5, F* : om. *Qq 1, 2.*

Gloss to 27. mattes *Q 1.*

Gloss to 27. Arabian *Qq 3–5, F* : Aradian *Qq 1, 2.*

Gloss to 78. Sarcasmus *Qq 3–5, F* : Sacrasmus *Qq 1. 2.*

NOVEMBER.

4. misgouernaunce *F* : misgouernaunce, *Qq 1–5.*

14. taske, *F* : taske : *Qq 1–5.*

85. doth display. *So Qq, F. Hughes corrects to* hath display'd, *for the sake of rime, and that was doubtless Spenser's intention.*

115. colourd. *So Q 1. Spenser intended the reader to dwell upon the* '1', *so as almost to give the word the metrical value of a trisyllable.*

128–9. mourne, . . . tourne, *Qq 2–5. F* : morune, . . . torune. *Q 1.*

132. carsefull *Q 1.*

159. hould. *Qq 4, 5, F* : hould. *Qq 1–3.*

Gloss to 30. Castalias *Qq 3–5. F* : Castlias *Qq 1, 2.*

Gloss to 83. diminutiue *Qq 3–5, F* : dimumtine *Qq 1, 2.*

Gloss to 107. Tinct *Qq 3–5, F* : Tuict *Qq 1, 2.*

Gloss to 145. the signe of *Qq 3–5, F* : the of *Qq 1, 2.*

Gloss to 158. Atropos, daughters *Qq 3–5, F* : Atropodas, ughters *Qq 1, 2.*

Gloss to 158. Atropos *Qq 3–5, F* : Atrhops *Qq 1, 2.*

Gloss to 186. express *Oq 3–5, F ·* epresse *Qq 1, 2.*

DECEMBER.

33. stroke *Q 5* : stroke, *Qq 1-4, F.*
38. Muse, *F 2* : Muse *Qq 1-5, F.*
43. derring doe (v. Gloss, p. 120, l. 1)] derring to *Qq, F.*
64. playe,] playe. *Qq 1, 2* : play. *Qq 3-5, F.*
69. see *Qq 2-5, F* : se *Q 1.*
89. t'enrage *Q 5, F* : to tenrage *Qq 1, 2* : tenrage *Qq 3, 4.*
106. before, *Qq 4, 5, F* : before. *Qq 1-3.*
113. *Rolalind Q 1.*
114. dight ? *Qq 3-5, F* : dight, *Qq 1, 2.*

Colins Embleme.] *All Qq and Ff fail to give the Embleme to December. It is first found in Hughes (1715)—Vivitur ingenio : caetera mortis erunt. It is possible that Hughes found it in some copy of a Q or F, but more likely that he supplied it himself.*
Gloss to 17. Cabinet *Qq 3-5, F* : Eabinet *Qq 1, 2.*
Gloss to Emblem. quod *Qq 3-5, F* : quæ *Qq 1, 2.*
Gloss to Emblem. ferrum *Qq 3-5, F* : ferum *Qq 1, 2*

COMPLAINTS. 1591.

The text is based on the *Q* of 1591, the only edition of *Complaints* published in the lifetime of Spenser. Different extant copies of this *Q* supply for a few passages different readings. Our text is printed from the Bodleian copy, and variants are quoted from the Huth *Q.* At the British Museum, among the *Harleian MSS,* is a transcript of *Complaints* dating from 1596, which supplies a few variants. These are quoted as *Harl. MS. F* also in places enables us to correct the text, and in places gives new readings. The more important of these are recorded below, but where *F* merely corrects the punctuation of *Q* the change has not been recorded unless it seems peculiarly significant and interesting.

THE RVINES OF TIME.

316, 323. I sing : *F* : I sing, *Q.*
333. and with *Linus, Huth Q* : and with *Linus Q* : with *Linus, F.*
363. couetize *F* : couertize *Q.*
413. give. *Q, F.*
414. *Mausolus F* : Mansolus *Q.*
447-8. For such as now have most the world at will, Scorn . . . their *F.*
451. such as first were *F.*
453. him *Q* : them *F.*
454. O ! let not those, *F.*
455. Aliue nor dead, *F.*
551. which *F* : with *Q.*
571. Was but of earth, and with her weightinesse *F.*
574. worlds *F* : words *Q.*

THE TEARES OF THE MVSES.

113. anew *Q, F* : in rew *conj. Collier, v. ll.* 177, 233, &c.

232. singults *F* : singulfs *Q* ; *v. F.Q.* III. xi. 12. 1 *note.*
288. Ignorance *cf. l.* 259 : ignorance *Q, F.*
310. wit. *Q, F.*
399. defaced *F* : defacd *Q.*
486. souenaunce *Harl. MS.* : souerance *Q, F.*
566. be *F* : beee *Q.*
600. louing *Q* : living *F.*

VIRGILS GNAT.

122. heart] hear *Q* : hart *F.*
149. *Ascræan corr. Jortin* : Astræan *Q, F.*
233. Shepheards *F* : Speheards *Q.*
308. creast-front tyre *F* : creast front-tyre *Q.*
340. Seest thou not, *F.*
387. throat *F* : threat *Q.*
406. fluttering *F* : flattering *Q.*
536. subtile *F* : slye *Q.*
575. billowes *Harl. MS.* : billowe *Q, F.*

MOTHER HVBBERDS TALE.

[*In all F copies that I have examined M.H.T. is dated either 1611 or 1612.*]

53. Gossip *F* : Goship *Q.*
67. high *F* : up on high *Q.*
87. worlds *Q, giving a syllabic value to the* ' r ' : worldes *F.*
185. Wildly to wander thus *F.*
308. winges *Hughes* : wings *Q, Ff.*
453. Diriges *F* : Dirges *Q.*
626. bands *Q, F.*
648. at all, *F, Harl. MS.* : all *Q.*
830. kindly wise desire *Q, F* : kindle wise desire *Drayton teste Collier.*
913. will a daw trie *Q* : a daw will try *F,*

i.e. will prove himself a fool. Grosart quoted a manuscript in his possession reading one day will cry, *but the emendation is unnecessary.*

1108. Conge *F* : Couge *Q*.

1224. boxe *Q, F, Harl. MS. Grosart quoted a manuscript reading* foxe, *but the change is unnecessary. ' boxe ' =' exchequer, treasury', a ' porter's box ' for gratuities.*

1231. The *conj. J. C. Smith* : And *Q, F*

1289. on] on, *Q, F.*

RVINES OF ROME.

21. *Mausolus F* : Mansolus *Q*.   glorie. *Q, F.*

32. Palaces, is that] Palaces is that, *Q* : Palaces, is that, *F*.

48. The old Giants *Huth Q* : Th'old Giants *Q* : The Giants old *F*.

56. *Viminall Huth Q, F* : Vimnial *Q*.

145-6. heate ; . . . fild *Q, F*.

210. Now to become *F* : To become *Q*.

243. ornaments] ornament *Q, F.*

414. stackes *F* : stalkes *Q*.

435. verses *F* : yerses *Q*.

MVIOPOTMOS.

(Dated 1590 in *Complaints*, and printed separately from the rest of the volume.)

149. champion he *Q* : champaine o're he *F*.

196. *Huth Q* omits Dull.

250. dispacing *Q* : displacing *Huth Q, F*.

354. Enfestred *Q* : Enfested *Huth Q, F*.

370. framde craftilie *Huth Q, F* : did slily frame *Q*.

391. thoss *Q*.

VISIONS OF THE WORLDS VANITIE

110. natiue *Huth Q, F* : natures *Q*.

THE VISIONS OF BELLAY.

For the *1569* version of *The Visions of Bellay* and *The Visions of Petrarch*, v. Appendix.

12. inconstancies,] inconstancies. *Q, F*.

22. On *Morris conj.* : One *Q, F*.   Afrike golds *Q, F* : Afrikes gold *Morris conj.*

38. great Lyons *Q* : Lyons great *F*.

43. pillers *1569* : pillowes *Q, F.*

113. astonied *F* : astoined *Q*.

THE VISIONS OF PETRARCH.

27. monent *Q*.

29. Then *1569* : The *Q, F*.

Q omits 7 *above this sonnet.*

85. behold *Morris* : beheld *Q, Ff.*

DAPHNAIDA. 1591.

Q 1 =1591.   *Q 2* =1596. The text printed from *Q 1* ; obvious errors of punctuation silently corrected from *Q 2* and *F* ; all other changes recorded below.

The dedicatory letter is missing in B.M. copy of Q 1.

13. honourable *F* : honoarable *Q*.

388. th' heauens *F* : th'eauens *Qq*.

391. till *Hughes 1715* : tell *Qq, F*.

422-3. one, . . . other, *Q 2* : one . . . other *Q 1*.

477. starres *Q 1* : starre *Q 2, F*.

487. deepe *Q 1* : deere *Q 2, F*.

549. a sdeinfull *F* : asdeinfull *Qq*.

COLIN CLOVTS COME HOME AGAINE. 1595.

Published with *Astrophel*, &c., in 1595. Our text follows *Q*, but is in places emended from *F*. These emendations, except in slight matters of punctuation, are recorded below. Of the non-Spenserian poems some (pp. 556-60) had already appeared in a Miscellany entitled *The Phoenix Nest* (1593). The text found therein gives some slight variants, which are quoted below as *1593*.

COLIN CLOVT.

1. knowen *F* : knowne *Q*.

168. singults *F* : singulfs *Q*.

380. *Harpalus, . . . aged*] Harpalus . . . aged, *Q* : Harpalus, . . . aged, *F*.

382. Corydon *F* : a Corydon *Q*.

487. *Vrania F* : Vriana *Q*.

600. clusters *F* : glusters *Q*.

601. braunches] *Collier* : bunches *Q, F*
670. Durst *F* : Darest *Q.*
699. needs *Todd* : needs, *Q, F*
757. fare *F* : far *Q.*
861. life giuing *F 2* : like giuing *Q, F.*
884. the *F* : their *Q.*

ASTROPHEL.

50. often *F* : oft *Q.*
89. needeth *F* : need *Q.*
116. brood] brood : *Q, F.*
158. day] day : *Q, F.*
200. deare,] deare : *Q.*
The Lay of Clorinda] 17. wetched *Q.*
35. did see *F* : see *Q.*

THE MOVRNING MVSE OF THESTYLIS.

The Mourning Muse] *Each line of Q is printed in F as two short lines, the second without capital letter.*
1. your *F* : you *Q.*
16. Thou *F* : Tho *Q.*
20 thy *Hughes 1715* : their *Q, Ff.*
80. heau'ns *F* : heau's *Q.*
129. testified *F* : testfied *Q.*
153. heau'ns *F* : heau's *Q.*

AN ELEGIE, OR FRIENDS PASSION, FOR HIS *ASTROPHILL.*

2. glasse *P.N.* (1593) *F 2* : grasse *Q, F.*
24. Ampitheater *Q, F.*
29. in *P.N.* : is *Q, F.*
36. *Meander, F* : Meander *Q, P.N.*
45. what.] that, *Q, P.N.* : that. *F.*
72. night *F* : might *Q, P.N.*
97. the mount *P.N* , *F* : to the mount *Q.*
109. neuer *P.N., F* : euer *Q.*
134. *Astrophill P.N., F* : *Astrophrill Q.*
181. This *P.N., F* : His *Q.*
195. thee truthe *Q, P.N.* : the truth *F.*

AN EPITAPH, &c.

36. of *Q, P.N.* : off *F.*
Another of the same] *P.N. adds* excellently written by a most worthy Gentleman. *F divides into two each line of Q.*
2. age : *F* : age, *Q, P.N.*
25. parallels *F* : parables *Q, P.N.*
39. seeke *P.N., F* : seekes *Q.*

AMORETTI AND EPITHALAMION. 1595.

First published in 1595, in a small 18° volume, the text of which is reproduced in this volume. The punctuation, which is very faulty, has been corrected chiefly from *F*. Other emendations are recorded below.

AMORETTI.

11. neighbors *F* : neighoures *18°.*
2. roundelaies *F* : roudelaies *18°.*
VII. 2. you,] you *18°, F.*
VIII. 5. the *F* : *printed* ỹ *18°.*
X. 11. pride,] pride *F, 18°.*
XI. 8. vnpitteid *18°.*
XIII. 6. borne, *F* : borne : *18°.*
XVII. 7. workmanship *F* : wormanship *18°.*
XIX. 4. crouned, *18°, F.*
XXI. 6. loue *F* : loues *18°.*
8. impure, *18°, F.*
XXIII. 4. unreaue, *18°, F.*
XXVIII. 2. giues *F* : guies *18°.*
XXIX. 4. forlorne, *18°, F.*
XXXII. 9. fit : *18°, F.*
XXXIII. 9. wit,] wit : *18°* : wit ? *F.*

XXXVIII. 8. will, *18°, F.*
XLV. 6. eye : *18°, F.*
XLVIII. 10. the *F* : th' *18°.*
L. 2. griefe, *F* : greife : *18°.*
LIII. 1-2. hyde ... beasts, ... 'fray,] hyde, ... beasts ... fray : *18°* : hyde ... beasts, ... fray : *F.*
6. semblant *18°* : semblance *F.*
10. ornament : *18°, F.*
LVI. 5. sure *18°, F.*
LVIII. 3. supposeth, *18°, F.*
7. prayd, *18°, F.*
LIX. 4. start, *18°, F.*
LX. 4. spheare. *F* : spheare *18°.*
LXII. 4. ensew, *18°, F.*
LXIII. 9, 11. atchyue, . . . depriue, *18°, F.*
LXIIII. 8. spred, *18°, F.*
12. Iessemynes, *18°, F.*
LXV. 1. vaine *18°, F.*
LXVIII. 3. hell, *F* : hell *18°.*
4. away, *18°, F.*
6. thou *F* : tbou *18°.*
LXXI. 9. aboue,] about, *18°, F.*
LXXIII. 2. tye,] tye : *18°, F.*

LXXV. 2. away *F* : a way *18°*.
LXXVII. 11. paradice] paradice : *18°* :
Paradyse : *F*.
LXXXVIII. 9. the Idæa *F* : th'Idæa *18°*.
LXXXIX. 3. vow *F 2* : vew *18°*, *F*.

EPITHALAMION
61. take,] take. *18°*, *F*.

67. deere] dore *18°*, *F*.
218. play] play ; *18°*, *F*.
239. band *?*] band, *18°* : band. *F*.
290. nightes dread] nights dread *18°* : nights
sad dread *F*. *Cf. F.Q.* I. v. 23 *note*.
341. Pouke] Ponke *18°*, *F*.
356. poure *F* : ponre *18°*.
385. thy *F* : they *18°*.

FOURE HYMNES. 1596.

First published in 1596 (*Q*). The text
follows *Q* with some emendations of punctuation from *F*.

AN HYMNE OF LOVE.
83. hated *F* : hate *Q*.

AN HYMNE IN HONOVR OF BEAVTIE.
14. soule *F 3* (1679) : foule *Q*, *F*.
47. clotheth *Q* : closeth *F*.

AN HYMNE OF HEAVENLY LOVE.
214. mercie, miserable crew,] mercie
miserable crew, *Q* : mercy (miserable crew) *F*.
245. feet & syde *Q* : feet, throgh side *F*.
266. to thee *Q* : for thee *F*.

AN HYMNE OF HEAVENLY BEAVTIE.
50. eye] eye, *Q*, *F*.
121. Suns bright *Q* : Sun-bright *F*.
165. And dampish] The dark & dampish
Q : The darke damp *F*.
170. more bright, *F* : *Q omits*.
270. to paine.] to paine, *Q* : a paine. *F*.
294. on *F* : no *Q*.
298. the loue *Q* : the true loue *F*.

PROTHALAMION. 1596.

First published in 1596 (*Q*). The text follows *Q*, with some emendations of punctuation
from *F*.
102. your *F* : you *Q*.

MISCELLANEOUS SONNETS.

Printed from copies of the volumes in
which they originally appeared.
I. From *Foure Letters, and Certaine
Sonnets : Especially touching Robert Greene,
and other parties, by him abused, &c.* London.
Imprinted by John Wolfe, 4to, 1592.
II. From *Nennio, Or a Treatise of
Nobility, &c. Written in Italian by that
famous Doctor and worthy Knight, Sir John
Baptista Nenna of Bari. Done into English
by William Jones, Gent., Q, 1595*.
III. From *Historie of George Castriot, sur-*

named *Scanderbeg, King of Albanie and
Containing his famous actes, &c. Newly
translated out of French into English by Z. I.
Gentleman. Imprinted for W. Ponsonby,
1596, F*.
IV. From *The Commonwealth and Govern-
ment of Venice. Written by the Cardinal
Gasper Contareno, and translated out of the
Italian into English by Lewis Lewkenor,
Esquire.* London. *Imprinted by John
Windet for Edmund Mattes, &c., 1599*.

III. 1. vaunt] vaunt, *1596*.

GLOSSARY.

The Faerie Queene is referred to by book, canto, and stanza, thus: III. iv. 41.

Cross-references are not as a rule given to variant spellings showing the following interchanges of letters: *i, y*: *e, ee, ea*; *o, oa, oo*; *u, w*; *s, z*; *c, s*.

A

a, in : *a Gods name* p. 418, *S. C. Sept.* 100, *Hubberd* 111, *Three Lett.* pp. 611, 626, 629, *Two Lett.* p. 639.

aband, to abandon, II. x. 65.

abase, to lower, II. i. 26, IV. vi. 3, VI. vi. 31, viii. 5.

abashed, *pa. part.* astonished, I. xii. 29; discomfited, II. iv. 8.

abashment, fear, astonishment, III. viii. 16, 34.

abate, to diminish, decrease, *tr.*, I. iii. 7, II. ii. 19, v. ix. 35; to depress, *Hubberd* 256.

abeare, *refl.* to comport oneself, v. xii. 19, VI. ix. 45.

abet, *sb.* instigation, abetment, IV. iii. 11.

abet, *vb.* to support, uphold, I. x. 64, IV. iii. 6, VI. v. 22.

abide, to attend, I. v. 17; to await, remain, rest, stop, III. v. 11, v. viii. 5, *Two Lett.* p. 635; *pret.* (1) **abid**, III. iv. 32, (2) **abode**, III. xii. 37; to abide by, accept, v. i. 25; to endure, suffer, II. i. 20, *Thest.* 154.

abie, *see* **aby**.

abiect, to cast down, throw down (with idea of degradation), III. xi. 13, v. ix. 9.

abode, *sb.* delay, III. viii. 19; stay, II. i. 1.

abolish, to annul, destroy, II. iv. 45.

abord, aboord, alongside, III. x. 6; abroad, adrift, astray, *Hubberd* 324, *R. R.* 185; abroad, across, *Gnat* 46.

abouts, about, I. ix. 36.

aboue, upstairs, IV. xii. 20.

abray, *for* **abrayd** (see next), to awake (*intr.*), IV. vi. 36.

abrade, abrayd, *pret.* **abrayd**, to awake, arouse, startle, III. i. 61, x. 50, xi. 8, IV. iv. 22.

abridge, to cut off, cut short, *Daphn.* 445.

abridgement, cutting short, III. viii. 2.

abuse, *sb.* injury, wrong, II. v. 21.

abuse, *vb.* to deceive, I. i. 46, II. i. Arg. 19, *Muiop.* 277; to ill-treat, misuse, VI. i. 22.

abusion, deception, II. xi. 11, IV. i. 7, v. xii. 40, *Hubberd* 1363; disgrace, discredit, *Hubberd* 220.

aby, abie [1], to pay the penalty for, expiate, II. iv. 40, viii. 33, IV. vi. 8; to endure, suffer, III. iv. 38, *R. T.* 101; to endure, to remain, III. vii. 3, x. 3, VII. vi. 24.

aby [2], *for* **abide** (q.v.), abide by, submit to VI. ii. 19.

abysse, gulf, interior, *Worlds Vanitie* 66.

accident, attribute, *Two Lett.* p. 639.

accloy, to clog, choke; to encumber, render heavy, II. vii. 15, *S. C. Feb.* 135; **accloid**, *pa. part.*, *Elegie* 2.

accompt, accoumpt, *sb.* account, VI. viii. 22, p. 419, *Hubberd* 307, *S. C. Oct.* Arg. 7.

accompted, *pa. part.* accounted, considered, I. x. 6.

accord, *sb.* consent, agreement, II. iv. 21, ix. 2.

accord, *vb.* to agree, *S. C. Feb.* Arg. 7; *pa. part.* IV. ix. 40; to reconcile, IV. v. 25.

accordaunce, agreement, III. iii. 30, v. viii. 14.

according, according to, I. x. 50, xii. 15, II. iv. 26, xi. 11; accordingly, II. x. 71.

accoste, accoaste, to adjoin, border on, v. xi. 42; to fly near to or skim along the ground, VI. ii. 32.

accoumpt, *vb.* to take into account, consideration, *Amor. Son.* 26.

accouráge, accóurage, to encourage, II. ii. 38, III. viii. 34.

accourting, *pres. part.* entertaining (courteously), II. ii. 16.

accoustrement, apparel, *Hubberd* 672.

accoy, *pa. part.* **accoyd, accoied**, to appease, soothe, IV. viii. 59; to daunt, subdue, *S. C. Feb.* 47.

accoyl, to gather together, assemble, II. ix. 30.

accrew, to collect, combine, IV. vi. 18; to increase, v. v. 7, *R. R.* 207; to come as an addition or increase, *S. C.* p. 417, *Clout* 655.

accusement, accusation, v. ix. 47.

accustom, to be used, wont, III. i. 13.

achates, provisions, II. ix. 31.

acquainted, *pret.* became acquainted, *Elegie* 131.

acquit, to free, release, deliver, v. iv. 39, viii. 6; *pa. part.* (1) **acquit**, I. vii. 52, *Amor. Son.* 42; (2) **acquight**, II. xii. 3; to perform, act, *refl.* VI. vi. 24.

adamant, diamond (*fig.*), crystal, IV. xi. 31.

adamant rocke, hard rock, I. vii. 33.

adaw, to daunt, subdue, III. vii. 13, v. ix. 35, *S. C. Feb.* 141; to become subdued, IV. vi. 26;

adawed, adaw'd, *pa. part.* daunted, terrified, v. v. 45, *S. C. Feb.* 141.

adayes, daily, *S. C. March* 42.

addeeme, to award, adjudge, v. iii. 15, vi. viii. 22.

addoom, to adjudge, vii. vii. 56.

addresse, skill, dexterity, *Hubberd* 1202.

addresse, *vb.* to prepare, direct (*refl.*), i. v. 6, iv. viii. 10, v. iii. 4; to direct one's course (*refl.*), iii. iv. 6, x. 40, *Hubberd* 657; to clothe (*refl.*), vi. ix, 36. addrest, *pa. part.* prepared, ready, set up, iv. iii. 14, vi. ix. 40, *S. C. Aug.* 128, *Bellay* 61, *Clout* 562, *Past. Elegie* 106, p. 550; arrayed, clothed, equipped, armed, i. ii. 11, iii. vi. 39.

adioyned, *pret.* approached, drew near, iii. vii. 42.

admirable, wonderful, i. vii. 36.

admiraunce, admiration, v. x. 39.

admire, to wonder, wonder at, ii. Prol. 4, iv. v. 38, vi. viii. 27.

adnihilate, to annihilate, destroy, *Two Lett.* p. 635.

adore, to adorn, iv. xi. 46.

adorne, adornment, iii. xii. 20.

adowne, *adv.* down, i. vii. 24, vi. viii. 49, *Past. Aeglogue* 132, *Hubberd* 118); *prep.* i. vii. 31.

adrad, adred(de), *pa. part.* frightened, i:i. i. 62, iv.iii. 25, viii. 47, *Gnat* 304, *R. R.* 232; adrad, *pret.* was afraid, v. i. 22.

aduantaged, *pret.* benefited, *Three Lett.* p. 612.

aduaunce, to extol, praise, i. v. 16, *S. C. Oct.* 47, *Nov.* 7; to claim, ii. iv. 36; aduaunst, *pa. part.* moved, impelled, ii. i. 20.

aduenture, *sb.* enterprise, i. ix. 6; chance, accident, iv. ii. 20, iii. 20, v. viii. 15.

aduenture, aduenter, *vb.* to attempt, venture, v. iv. 31, *Hubberd* 1005, *Three Lett.* p. 623.

aduewed, *pa. part.* viewed, surveyed, v. iii. 20.

aduise, auise, -ze, to perceive, view, notice, look at, i. v. 40, ii. ix. 38, 59, xii. 66, iii. ix. 23, xii. 10, iv. ii. 22, iv. 25, vi. xii. 16; to consider, bethink oneself, remember (often *refl.*), i. i. 33, iii. 19, viii. 15, ii. Prol. 2, vi. 27, iii. i. 18, ii. 22, iii. 6, 59, iv. xii. 28, vi. xii. 12, vii. vi. 21, *Hubberd* 1238; to advise, iv. viii. 58.

aduizement, advice, counsel, consideration, i. iv. 12, ii. v. 13, ix. 9, p. 412, *S. C. Oct.* Arg. 16, *Hubberd* 176, *Two Lett.* p. 635.

adward, *sb.* award, iv. x. 17.

adward, *vb.* to award, iv. xii. 30.

aegide shield, the aegis or shield of Minerva, *Muiop.* 321.

æmule, to emulate, rival, *Clout* 72, 73.

aerie, aerial, in the air, ii. iii. 19.

Aetion, *pseudonym* = Drayton, *Clout* 444.

Aetn', Etna, volcano, iii. ii. 32.

afarrs, afar, *Elegie* 167.

afeared, affeard, *ppl. adj.* frightened, afraid, ii. iii. 45, iii. x. 52, iv. i. 50.

affami..ht, *ppl. adj.* hungry: *loue-affamisht*, *Amor.* Son. 88.

affeare, to frighten, ii. iii. 20.

affect, *sb.* kind feeling, affection, passion, vi. i. 45, v. 24, *Past. Aegl gue* 46, *Amor.* Son. 6; imitation, counterfeit, *Love* 180.

affect, *vb.* to like, have a preference for, vi. vi. 7, x. 37.

affection, passion, ii. iv. 34, xi. 1, iii. iii. 1, vi. vi. 7.

affectionate, *pa. part.*: *well a.* = having become very affectionate, well beloved, iii. iii. 62.

affiance, betrothal, ii. iv. 21.

affide, *see* affy.

affixed, fixed, set, iii. ii. 11.

afflicted, *ppl. adj.* cast down, humble, *Amor.* Son. 2.

afford, affoord, to bestow, give, ii. viii. 19, vi. i. 26; to consent, ii. vi. 19.

affrap, to strike, ii. i. 26, iii. ii. 6.

affray, *sb.* fear, terror, v. x. 19.

affray, *vb.* to frighten, terrify, iii. v. 27, *S. C. June* (*Glosse*, p. 443).

affray, *pa. part.*, frightened, afraid, v. ix. 24.

affrended, *pa. part.* made friends, reconciled, iv. iii. 50.

affret, encounter, onslaught, iii. ix. 16, iv. ii. 15, iii. 6, 11.

affright, *sb.* fear, fright, ii. iii. 19, xi. 16.

affright, *pa. part.* frightened, ii. v. 37.

affront, to face, confront, oppose, attack, i. viii. 13, iii. iv. 7, iv. iii. 22.

affy, to betroth, espouse, vi. iii. 7; affide, -yde, *pa. part.* iv. viii. 53, v. iii. 2, vi. iii. 49; entrusted, v. v. 53.

aflot, in a state of overflow or submersion, *Bellay* 119.

afore, before, beforehand, in front, i. xii. 1, iv. vii. 7, v. v. 3, xii. 6, *R. R.* 258.

afore hand, formerly, *H. Love* 186.

afterclaps, unexpected strokes or events, *Hubberd* 332.

after-send, to pursue, send after, i. v. 10.

agast, aghast, *pret.* frightened, terrified, i. ix. 21, iii. v. 3, vii. vi. 52.

age, iv. iii. 43. *See quiet age.*

agent, one who acts, *Three Lett.* p. 621.

aggrace, *sb.* favour, goodwill, II. viii. 56.

aggrace, agrace, *vb.* to favour; **agrast,** *pret.*, I. x. 18; to add grace to, II. xii. 58.

aggrate, to please, gratify, II. v. 33, ix. 34, xii. 42, III. vi. 50, viii. 36, v. xi. 19, VI. x. 33, *Teares* 406. *intr.* IV. ii. 23.

aglet, aygulet, tag, spangle, II. iii. 26, VI. ii. 5.

agonyes, strifes, contentions, which were held to be due to Saturn's influence, II. ix. 52.

agraste, *see* aggrace.

agree, to settle, II. iv. 3.

agreeable, in accord, similar, *Three Lett.* p. 620.

agreeably, similarly, VI. vii. 3.

agreeue, to cause to grieve, *R. T.* 91, *Elegie* 82.

agrise, agrize, to cause to shudder, horrify, II. vi. 46, III. ii. 24, VII. vii. 6; *Impers.* v. x. 28; **agryz'd,** *ppl. adj.* of horrible appearance, IV. viii. 12.

aguise, aguize, to array, deck, equip, fashion, II. i. 21, 31, vi. 7, III. ii. 18, v. iii. 4, *Hubberd* 656.

a hungered, hungry, *Three Lett.* p. 618.

aime, to guess, conjecture, *H. Beautie* 33.

Alabaster, *pseudonym, Clout* 400.

alablaster, alabaster, III. ii. 42, VI. viii. 42, *Bellay* 45.

alaid, *pa. part.* allayed, *Daphn.* 173.

Albanese-wyse, after the manner of the Albanese (Albanians?), III. xii. 10.

albe, albee, although, I. x. 44, *S. C. Jan.* 67, *Apr.* 99; in spite of, v. viii. 3, *S. C. May* 265.

Alcon, *pseudonym, Clout* 394.

Alcyon, *pseudonym, Clout* 384.

alegge, allegge, alleviate, assuage, III. ii. 15, *S. C. March* 5.

aleggeaunce, alleviation, III. v. 42.

alew = halloo; lamentation, v. vi. 13.

algate, algates, entirely, altogether, always, II. i. 2, III. iv. 26, IV. vi. 13, 44; by any means, *Hubberd* 1025; at all, in any way, III. viii. 9; nevertheless, v. viii. 5, *S. C. Nov.* 21.

Algrin, *pseudonym, S. C. July* 213.

alienate, *pa. part.* alienated, withdrawn, *S. C. Apr.* Arg. 9.

all, though, although, II. xii. 57, III. i. 21, vi. 47, vii. 9, 43, *S. C. June* 72; *all were it* = although it were, *S. C. May* 58. **all and some,** entirely, altogether, III. xii. 30. **all as,** as if, *S. C. Feb.* 4. **all for,** just because, *S. C. Sept.* 109, 111, 114.

Alla Turchesca, in the Turkish fashion, *Hubberd* 677.

almner, almoner, I. x. 38.

almóst, v. v. 10.

alone, only, IV. v. 25.

along, without interruption, throughout, III. iv. 3.

alow, *vb.* to praise, p. 409.

alow, *adv.* below, VI. viii. 13.

Al Portugese, in the Portuguese fashion, *Hubberd* 212.

als, alls, also, II. i. 7, IV. iv. 2, xi. 31, VI. xii. 11, p. 410, *S. C. March* 40; both (*als . . . . and*), *S. C. July* 8.

alsoone, as soon, *S. C. July* 101.

altogether, without exception, *S. C. July,* p. 447.

alwáy, always, v. ix. 24, *Clout* 888.

amain, amayne, at once, hastily, I. vi. 41; with force, violently, III. xi. 41, IV. iii. 47, v. 38, VI. vi. 27, viii. 27.

amarous, lovely, II. xii. 64.

Amaryllis, a shepherdess, *Clout* 435, 540.

amate[1], to dismay, daunt, cast down, I. i. 51, III. iv. 27, vii. 35, xi. 21, VII. vi. 19. **amated,** *pa. part.* dismayed, overwhelmed, II. ii. 5, v. xi. 64.

amate[2], to keep company with, II. ix. 34.

amaze, amazement, III. vii. 7, IV. ii. 17, v. vii. 25, *Amor.* Son. 16, *Epith.* 181.

ambássage, embassy, *Hubberd* 472.

ambúshment, ambush, IV. x. 30, *Gnat* 532.

amearst, *pa. part.* punished, amerced, *Amor.* Son. 70.

ámenage, to domesticate, control, II. iv. 11.

amenance, amenaunce, bearing, conduct, behaviour, II. viii. 17, ix. 5, III. i. 41, IV. iii. 5, *Hu'berd* 781.

amend, to retrieve, restore, III. iii. 23.

amendment, amends, II. i. 20.

ámiáole, IV. x. 31, 56.

amis[1], hood, cape (orig. an article of costume of the religious orders, made of, or lined with, grey fur), I. iv. 18.

amis[2], misdeed, fault, II. i. 19.

amisse, wrongly, in mistake, *Daphn.* 234.

amounted, *pret.* mounted, ascended, I. ix. 54.

amoue, ammoue, to move, stir, cause emotion, I. iv. 45, ix. 18, III. ix. 24; to touch, III. xi. 13; to arouse (from sleep, &c.), *Daphn.* 545.

Amyntas, *pseudonym, Clout* 434.

and, if, *Three Lett.* p. 632.

anduile, anduyle, anvil, I. xi. 42, IV. iv. 23, *Amor.* Son. 32.

ángelick, angelic, *Astrophel,* p. 550 l. 76.

annexe, to add, IV. viii. 35.

annoy, anoy, grief, annoyance, I. vi. 17, II. ii. 43, ix. 35, *R. T.* 305, 322, *Petrarch* 82, *Daphn.* 514, *Amor.* Son. 62.

anon, anone, again, v. viii. 9; at once, immediately, v. xi. 37.

answer, aunswere, to make a responsive sound, re-echo, II. xii. 33; to repeat (correspondingly), IV. v. 33; to return, requite, v. i. 24.

ánticke, *sb.* antique, relic; ancient or strange figures or designs, II. iii. 27, vii. 4, III. xi. 51.

ánticke, ántique, *adj.* former, ancient, olden, *R. R.* 232, 266, *Amor.* Son. 69.

apace, copiously, IV. xi. 11; fast, v. viii 5.

apay, appay, *pa. part.* **apaid, apayd,** to please, satisfy, II. xii. 28, IV. ix. 40, *S. C. Aug.* 6, *Daphn.* 70; to repay, requite, v. v. 33; *ill apaid* = ill requited, II. ix. 37, v. xi. 64.

appall, to check, quell, weaken, II. ii. 32, III. 44, III. i. 46; to fail, falter, IV. vi. 26.

apparaunce, appearance, III. i. 52.

apparition, appearance, semblance, *Hubberd* 1290.

appeach, to accuse, be an accusation to, II. viii. 44, xi. 40, v. v. 37, ix. 47.

appeale, appele: *praiers to a.* = to say prayers, III. ii. 48; to remind, v. ix. 39.

appease, to check, cease, I. iii. 29.

appellation, appeal, VII. vi. 35.

apply, *pa. part.* **applide, applyde,** to employ, use, I. i. 38; to ply, follow, I. x. 46; to steer, direct, II. v. 10 (*refl.*), vi. 5, vii. 1, v. iv. 21, xi. 6; to administer, II. xii. 32; to prepare, make ready, *Muiop.* 84.

appose, to examine, question, v. ix. 44.

approuance, approval, II. xii. 76, *Epith.* 144.

approue, approuen, to prove, demonstrate, test, I. vi. 26, ix. 37, III. i. 27, IV. x. 1, v. x. 5, VI. viii. 14, *Elegie* 152; to commend, approve, III. i. 26. **approved** *ppl. adj.* tested, II. v. 8.

arboret, small tree, shrub, II. vi. 12.

arck, arke, box, chest, IV. iv. 15; arch, *R. R.* 89, 368, *Bellay* 46, *Misc. Sonn.* iii, *Epigrams* p. 607.

aread, areed, *pa. part.* **ared,** to counsel, advise, teach, I. Prol. 1; to tell, make known, proclaim, describe, show, I. viii. 31, 33, ix. 23, 28, x. 17, II. iii. 14, III. iv. 59, v. xii. 9, VII. vi. 46, *Love* 11, *Clout* 15; to divine, guess, discover, detect, understand, II. i. 7, IV. v. 15, v. iii. 35, xii. 9, VI. vii. 10; to decide, adjudge, VII. vii. Arg.; to take, assume, VI. ix. 33.

areare, arere, back, backward, behind, behindhand, II. xi. 36, III. vii. 24, x. 23, VI. iv. 5, *Gnat* 468.

aret, *see* arret.

arew, in a row, v. xii. 29; in order, consecutively, *Thest.* 186.

argument, theme, subject, III. ix. 1; proof, token, manifestation, VI. vii. 1.

aright, rightly, VI. vii. 31; direct, *Epitaph* (i) 13.

a rights, aright, rightly, v. x. 4.

arise, to rise, *Hubberd* 419, 426.

arming: *a. sword* = sword forming part of arms or armour, II. vi. 47.

armorie, armour, I. i. 27, III. iii. 59.

arras, tapestry, I. iv. 6, III. xi. 39.

arraught, *pret.* of *arreach,* to seize, II. x. 34.

array, aray, to afflict, v. ii. 25, VI. ii. 42.

arreare, to raise, VI. viii. 23.

arret, aret, to entrust, deliver, consign, II. viii. 8, xi. 7, III. viii. 7, IV. v. 21.

as, as if, as though, I. viii. 23 l. 9, xi. 21 i. 4, II. ix. 11, III. vii. 36, *S. C. Dec.* 110. **as that,** in such a manner as ..., I. i. 30. **as then,** till then, v. iv. 36.

ascértaine, *Daphn.* 504.

askaunce, sideways (with idea of disfavour), II. vii. 7, III. i. 41, *S. C. March* 21.

askew, askewe, sidelong (cf. **askaunce**), asquint, angrily, III. x. 29, v. xii. 29, *S. C. Mar. Glosse,* *Amor.* Son. 7.

aslake, to assuage, appease, I. iii. 36, *Amor.* Son. 44, *Beautie* 4.

aslombering, *pres. part.* slumbering, II. xii. 72.

aslope, aslant (*fig.*), III. iv. 52.

aspéct, II. xii. 53, III. vi. 12, vii. 22, xii. 7, 14, iv. x. 39.

aspire, *pa. part.* **aspyred,** to inspire, IV. x. 26; to desire, aim at, v. ix. 41; to ascend, rise up, *R. T.* 408.

assaile, to attack, I. vii. 6.

assay, *sb.* value, quality, I. ii. 13, III. iv. 18, v. viii. 37; tribulation, affliction, i. vii. 27, *Petrarch* 25; trial, attempt, assault, attack, II. iii. 12, 15, v. iv. 23, v. 52, *Beautie* 88; *to all assayes* = at every juncture, on every occasion, v. ix. 39.

assay, *vb.,* *pa. part.* **assaid,** to try, test, touch, I. iv. 8, viii. 2, II. iii. 4, VI. ix. 33; to assail, assault, afflict, I. ii. 24, vi. 11, IV. ix. 30, *Gnat* 491; to affect, v. xi. 64, *S. C. Aug.* 5.

assemblaunce, assembly, v. iv. 21.

assieged, besieged, II. xi. 15.

assignment, design, II. xi. 10.

assize, measure, *Bellay* 16.

assot, to befool, besot, bewilder, beguile, II. x. 8. *pa. part.* **assott,** *S. C. Mar.* 25; **assotted** III. viii. 22.

assoyle, assoile, to absolve, free, release, I. x. 52, II. v. 19, III. viii. 32, VI. v. 37, viii. 6, *R. R.* 263, *Daphn.* 259; to dispel, III. i. 58, IV. v. 30.

Amor. Son. 11, *Proth.* 100; to expiate, IV. vi. 25; to determine, VII. vii. 38; to discharge, acquit oneself of, *Daphn.* 535, *Amor.* Son. 80.

assurance, certainty, III. iv. 9; security, v. xi. 35.

assure, to secure, keep safe (also *fig.*), II. viii. 30, III. ii. 23, v. xii. 2; to be sure, assert, II. x. 8; to make sure of, have confidence in, *Bellay* 87.

assynd, *pret.* pointed out, I. vii. 28.

astart, astert, to start up, III. ii. 29; to happen to, befall, *S. C. Nov.* 187.

astate, state, condition, *S. C. Sept.* 24.

astond, astound, *ppl. adj.* stunned, amazed, I. ii. 31, vii. 7, *Daphn.* 314.

astonied, *ppl. adj. = pa. part.* of *astony*, stunned, I. ii. 15, *S. C. July* 227; astonished, *Bellay* 113.

astonish, to stun, IV. viii. 43.

astonying, *ppl. adj.* causing amazement, confounding, v. ii. 54.

astound, *pret.* struck, IV. vii. 9.

astrofell, astrophel, a bitter substance, perhaps *astrophyllum* star-leaf, or *Aster Tripolium*: *Daphn.* 346, *Past Elegie* 196.

Astrofell, *pseudonym* = Sir Philip Sidney, *Clout* 449, 45C.

atchieuen, to finish, conclude (successfully), I. v. 1.

atonce, attonce, immediately, I. iii. 5, xi. 13; together, III. iii. 40, x. 17; already, *S. C. Feb.* 38.

atone, attone, together, II. i. 42, III. ix. 2, IV. iv. 14, ix. 30, v. xi. 43, *S. C. May* 30, *Teares* 418; agreed, united, II. i. 19; agreement, *Clout* 843; at once, immediately, IV. xii. 9.

attach, *pret., pa. part.* **attacht**, -ed, to seize, IV. ix. 6, v. v. 18, VI. vii. 35, 36; to attack, III. viii. 33, VI. iii. 10.

attaine, to reach, manage, IV. vii. 27, VI. viii. 15.

attaint, to sully, stain, I. vii. 34, IV. i. 5.

attemper, to moderate, regulate, II. ii. 39, xiii. 51; to attune, bring into harmony, II. xii. 71, *S. C. Apr.* 5, *June* 8.

attempted, tempted, v. xi. 63.

attendement, intention, VI. vi. 18.

attent, *sb.* attention, III. ix. 52, VI. ix. 37.

attent, *ppl. adj.* attentive, intent, VI. ix. 26.

attone, *see* **atone**.

attonement, agreement, concord, reconciliation, v. viii. 21.

attones, together, *S. C. March* 53.

attrapt, furnished, dressed (of a horse), IV. iv. 39.

áttribute, *vb.* v. iv. 28.

atweene, *adv.* in between, *Clout* 81, *Epith.* 155.

atweene, atwene, *prep.* between, II. i. 58, VI. vi. 37.

atwixt, *adv.* in between, at intervals, III. xii. 2.

aumayld, *pa. part.* enamelled, II. iii. 27.

autenticall, authentic, IV. xii. 32.

autentique, authentic, *Two Lett.* p. 640.

authór, III. vi. 9.

auaile, *sb.* value, proñt, benefit, v. v. 49, *S. C. Nov.* 87, *Hubberd* 1204.

auaile, auale, *vb.* to fall, sink, descend, lower, I. i. 21, IV. iii. 46, *S. C. Jan.* 73, *Feb.* 8, *Sept.* 251; to dismount, alight, II. ix. 10.

auaunt, to advance, II. iii. 6; to depart, be off, VI. vi. 21.

auauntage, advantage, II. v. 9.

auenge, revenge, IV. i. 52, ii. 15.

auengement, vengeance, I. iv. 34, II. iv. 6, III. v. 24, *Hubberd* 1317.

auentre, to push, thrust forward, III. i. 28, IV. iii. 9, vi. 11.

auise, auize, &c., *see* **aduise**.

auisefull, attentive, observant, IV. vi. 26.

auoided, *pa. part.* emptied, II. ix. 32; departed, withdrawn, III. i. 58.

auouche, to prove, establish, I. x. 64; to state, maintain, *Two Lett.* pp. 618, 639.

auoure, avowal: *to make a.* = to answer for, VI. iii. 48.

auow, to vow, III. iv. 10.

awaite, *sb.* watch, ambush, IV. x. 14, v. ix 9.

aware, wary, alert, v. xi. 13.

awarned, *pa. part.* warned, III. x. 46.

awayes, away, *Gnat* 430.

awhape, to terrify, IV. vii. 5, v. xi. 32, *Hubberd* 72.

ay, ever, II. i. 60, III. xi. 41, *S. C. Feb.* 198.

ayer, air, *Teares* 118.

aygulet, *see* **aglet**.

ayme, *sb.* intention, design, II. vi. 10.

aymed, *ppl. adj.* intended, desired, II. iv. 46, III. vii. 40.

ayrie, airy, v. viii. 34. Cf. **ayer**.

B

babe, doll, *S. C. May* 240.

bable, bauble, toy, *Three Lett.* p. 624.

bace, *sb.* prisoner's base, v. viii. 5; *to bid bace* = to challenge, III. xi. 5; *bydding base* = prisoner's base, *S. C. Oct.* 5.

bace, *adj.* low, deep, I. v. 31, II. xii. 8, III. ii 50.

backbite, to slander, *Hubberd* 719.

backstarting, starting back, v. xi. 61.

baffuld, disgraced as a perjured knight, v. iii. 37, vi. vii. Arg. 27.

baid, *see* bay.

baile, *sb.* charge, custody, vii. vi. 49; pledge, security, *S. C. May* 131.

baile, *vb.* to deliver, liberate, iv. ix. 7.

bait, bayt, to bait (a bull, &c.), i. xii. 35, ii. viii. 42, vi. v. 19.

baite, to feed on a journey, i. i. 32.

balductum, trashy, rubbishy, *Three Lett.* pp. 619, 623.

bale[1] (*for* **baile,** q.v.), release, *S. C. Aug.* 105.

bale[2], injury, fatal influence, i. i. 16, *S. C. Nov.* 84; sorrow, grief, i. vii. 28, ix. 29, ii. ii. 45, vi. x. 3, 8.

bale[3], fire (cf. **bale**[2]), i. ix. 16.

balefull, harmful, injurious, deadly, i. ii. 2, iii. iii. 8; *subjectively,* full of pain, painful, *S. C. Jan.* 27.

balefulnesse, distress, sorrow, ii. xii. 83.

balke, *sb.* (*fig.*), omission, exception; *lit.* ridge or piece of land left unploughed by accident, vi. xi. 16.

balke, *vb.* to quibble, bandy words, iii. ii. 12; to stop short, refrain, iv. x. 25; to miss, stray from, *S. C. Sept.* 93; to lie out of the way, *Hubberd* 268.

ball, to bawl, howl, *S. C. Sept.* 190.

ballance : *paire of b.* = balances, scales, v. i. 11, ii. 30.

balleardes, billiards, *Hubberd* 803.

ban, banne, *vb.* to curse, iv. ix. 9, v. viii. 28, 39, vi. ii. 21. *pret.* **band,** v. ii. 18, xi. 12; *pa. part.* **band,** *H. Love* 184.

band, *sb.* bond, vi. xii. 36; pledge, vi. i. 31; captivity, bondage (also *plur.*), iv. xi. 1, vi. xii. 39.

band, *vb.*[1] to assemble, i. iv. 36.

band, *vb.*[2] to ban, banish, iii. ii. 41.

bandog, mastiff, bloodhound, *S. C. Sept.* 163, *Gnat* 540.

bane, destruction, death, ii. xi. 29.

banes, banns, i. xii. 36.

banket, bancket, banquet, i. xi. 2, iii. vi. 22, iv. vii. 20.

banne, *sb.* curse, iii. vii. 39.

bannerall, small streamer attached to lance of knight, vi. vii. 26.

barbes, armour of war-horse, ii. ii. 11.

barbican, watch-tower, ii. ix. 25.

bard, adorned with bars, ii. iii. 27.

bare, *pret.* bore, ii. vii. 5, v. Prol. 1, *S. C. Dec.* 124.

basciomani, kissing of the hand, iii. i. 56.

base[1], lower part, v. ix. 16; pedestal, *Bellay* 44.

base[2], bass voice, low, deep sound, ii. xii. 33; a bass singer, *T. M.* 28.

basen, basin : *b. wide* = as wide as a basin, *Hubberd* 670.

basenesse, low estate, condition, vi. iii. 1.

basenet, a steel headpiece, vi. i. 31.

bases[1], a plaited skirt appended to the doublet, reaching from the waist to the knee, v. v. 20.

bases[2] : *bases light* = sportive races, vi. x. 3.

bash, to be abashed, daunted, ii. iv. 37.

bastard, base, i. vi. 24, ii. iii. 42.

baste, to sew, stitch, v. v. 3.

bate[1], to abate, diminish, v. ix. 35, *Epigrams* p. 607.

bate[2], *pret.* bit. ii. v. 7.

bate[3], *pa. part.* fed (cf. **baite**), *S. C. Sept.* 44.

bate[4], to bait (cf. **bait**), vi. vii. 40.

batt, bat, stick, club, *Gnat* 154, *Hubberd* 217.

battailous, ready for battle, warlike, pugnacious, i. v. 2, ii. vii. 37, iii. iii. 47, v. v. 21, vi. vii. 41.

batteilant, engaged in battle, combatant, *Worlds Vanitie* 101.

battill, to become fat, vi. viii. 38.

batton, club, baton, vi. vii. 46.

bauldrick, baudricke, belt, girdle, i. vii. 29, ii. iii. 29, *Proh.* 174; the zodiac, viewed as a gem-studded belt, v. i. 11.

bay, *sb.* extremity, vi. i. 12 : *at, unto a b.* = at close quarters, iii. i. 22, iv. vi. 41.

bay, *vb.* to bay, bark, i. v. 30, *Gnat* 345. *pret.* baid, *R. T.* 215.

baye, to bathe (cf. **embay,** i. ix. 13, &c.), i. vii. 3.

bayes, baies, laurels (*fig.*), iv. i. 47, vi. vi. 4.

baylieffe errant, a sheriff's officer going about the country executing writs, &c., vi. vii. 35.

bayt, *sb.* bait, enticement, artifice, ii. v. 9, vii. 10, vi. ix. 23.

bayt, *vb.*[1] to abate, let rest (*see* **bate**[1]), ii. xii. 29.

bayt, *vb.*[2] to speak gently or with bated breath, iii. x. 6.

bayted, *pa. part.* fed, *Three Lett.* 621.

bazil, a genus of aromatic, shrubby plants (*Ocymum,* N. O. *Labiatæ*), *Muiop.* 188.

be, bee, been, *pa. part.* iv. iii. 21, *S. C. Sept.* 146.

beades, bedes, prayers : *bidding his b.* = saying his prayers, i. i. 30, x. 3.

bead-men, men of prayer, i. x. 36.

beadroll, list, iv. ii. 32.

beame[1], gleam, glitter (*fig.*), i. xii. 23, ii. vii. 45 ; ray, glance (*fig.*), *Clout* 493, 518.

beame[2], spear, shaft, III. vii. 40.

bear, to take (as a companion), I. iv. 2 (*pa. part.* **borne**); *beare up* = to put the helm 'up', I. xii. 1.

beare, bere, bier, II. xii. 36, VI. ii. 48, iii. 4, *R. T.* 191; *transf.* tomb, sepulchre, III. iii. 11; *transf.* corpse, burden, *Past. Elegie* 149.

bearne, barn, granary, *Three Lett.* p. 626.

beastly, *adj.* animal, I. iii. 44.

beastly, *adv.* in a disgusting manner, III. viii. 26.

beastlyhead, beasthood, beastliness; *your b.* = your 'beastly' self, your personality as a beast, *S. C. May* 265.

beat, to overcome, v. i. 1.

beath'd, heated, IV. vii. 7.

beaupere, companion, III. i. 35.

beck, nod, *Three Lett.* p. 625.

becke, beak, II. xi. 8.

become, to come to, go to, I. x. 16, III. iv. 1; to suit, be becoming to, I. x. 66, II. ii. 14, viii. 23; to happen, III. ix. 32.

bed, to order, command, I. ix. 41; to pray (cf. **bid**), VI. v. 35.

bedide, *pret.* dyed, IV. iv. 24.

bedight, to equip, VI. v. 7. **bedight**, *pa. part.* adorned, equipped, III. vi. 43, IV. iv. 39, *Gnat* 113; afflicted, II. vi. 50; *ill b.* = (1) stricken, II. i. 14, *S. C. Oct.* 89; (2) disfigured, II. vii. 3.

beduck, to dip, dive, II. vi. 42.

beetle stock, the stock or handle of a beetle. *Hubberd* 507.

befall, to be fitting, I. x. 14; to occur, happen to be, *Gnat* 72. **befeld**, *pa. part.*, IV. iii. 50.

beforne, *adv.* before, *S. C. May* 104. *prep., May* 160.

begin, beginning, III. iii. 21.

begor'd, stained with gore, IV. xi. 3.

beguile, to deprive, II. ii. 46, *Hubberd* 1285; *pa. part.* disappointed, foiled, I. xi. 25.

behalfe : *in this b.* = in this matter or respect, *Three Lett.* p. 619.

behalue, behalf, IV. iv. 27.

behappen, to happen, v. xi. 52.

behaue, to conduct, regulate, II. iii. 40.

beheast, behest, command, bidding, I. vi. Arg., II. ii. 32, III. iii. 31, IV. ix. 31, *R. T.* 73, *Daphn.* 137, 270, *Hubberd* 1308, *Love* 93.

behight, *pa. part.* behight, to deliver, grant, entrust, I. x. 50, II. viii. 9, IV. xi. 6; to call, name, I. x. 64, III. vii. 47, *S. C. Apr.* 120, *May* 201; to speak, address, IV. ii. 23, vi. 38, v. iv. 25; to adjudge, pronounce, consider, IV. i. 44, iii. 31, v. 7; to ordain, decide. II. iii. 1, *Muiop.* 241, *H. Love* 173; to command, II. iv. 43. **behot, behote**, *pret., pa.*

part. held out hope, I. xi. 38, IV. iv. 40; called, *S. C. Dec.* 54.

be-hold, to hold, retain, capture, *S. C. Sept.* 229.

behoofe, advantage, profit, IV. vii. 37.

behot, *see* **behight**.

behoue, to be proper, fitting; to be incumbent, necessary, IV. ix. 31, VI. v. 20. **be-hooued**, *pa. part., Gnat* 467.

belaccoyle, greeting, welcome, IV. vi. 25.

belamoure, lover, II. vi. 16; a flower (unidentified), *Amor.* Son. 64.

belamy, lover, II. vii. 52.

belay, to besiege, encompass, *Amor.* xiv. **belayd**, *pa. part.* adorned, VI. ii. 5.

beldame, form of address to an aged woman, III. ii. 43.

belgard, kind, loving look, II. iii. 25, III. ix. 52, *Beautie* 256.

beliue, biliue, byliue, forthwith, quickly, immediately, I. v. 32, ix. 4, II. viii. 18, III. i. 18, v. 16, x. 10, *S. C. Sept.* 227.

bell : *to bear the b.* = to obtain the prize, gain the victory, IV. iv. 25, v. 13.

bellibone, fair maid, bonny lass, *S. C. Apr.* 92, *Aug.* 61.

belyde, *pret.* counterfeited, III. x. 7.

bend, band, II. iii. 27, vii. 30, v. v. 3, *S. C. May* 32.

bene, beene, are, I. i. 10, III. i. 26, x. 16, IV. i. 24, ii. 24, *S. C. Apr.* 124, *Oct.* 87, *Past. Elegie* Introd. 12, *Beautie* 269.

beneficiall, a letter presenting to a benefice, *Hubberd* 486.

beneuolence, gift, *Hubberd* 517.

bent, *sb.* aim, purpose, intention, *S. C. Epistle* p. 417.

bent, *adj.* obedient, *S. C. Sept.* 149.

bents, stalks of reed-like grass, VI. iv. 4.

bequeathed, *ppl. adj.* committed, entrusted, I. x. 63.

bere[1], *see* **beare**.

bere[2], to bear, carry, IV. xii. 15.

bereaue, to deprive of, I. i. 52; to take away, remove, destroy, get rid of, II. vii. 19, v. iv. 10, vi. 2. **beraft**, *pa. part.* bereft, robbed, IV. ii. 10. **bereaued**, *pa. part.* stolen, carried off, v. iii. 30; taken away, *Hubberd* 208.

berobbed, *pa. part.* robbed, I. viii. 42, v. viii. 46.

beseeke, to beseech, IV. iii. 47.

beseme, beseem, to befit, become, seem, be seemly, I. viii. 32, II. ix. 26, 37, III. i. 55, IV. ix. 20, v. v. 38, *S. C. Aug.* 36. **beseeming**, *ppl. adj.; Three Lett.* 620.

beseene, *pa. part.* provided, treated, v. x. 17,

vii. vii. 11. **well** b. = of good appearance, good looking, i. xii. 8, iii. iii. 58, *Gnat* 651; accomplished, versed, read, *Teares* 180. **gay** b. = gaily apparelled, adorned, *Amor.* xxvii.

besit, to become, befit, ii. vii. 10. **besitting**, *ppl. adj.* iv. ii. 19.

bespake, *pret.* addressed, v. iv. 50.

bespredd, *pa. part.* adorned, iii. x. 44.

besprint, *ppl. adj.*, *S. C. Nov.* 111. **besprent**, *pa. part.*, *S. C. Dec.* 135, besprinkled.

bestaine, to stain, iv. vii. 27.

bested, bestad, *pa. part.* situated, placed, iii. x. 54. **bestadde**, disposed, ordered, *S. C. Aug.* 7. *ill, sore, sorely* b. = hard pressed, placed in a dangerous situation, i. i. 24. ii. i. 30, 52, iv. vii. 46, v. i. 22, vi. i. 4, vi. 18; *ill bestedded*, iv. i. 3. **bestedde, bestad**, *pret.* beset, iii. v. 22, iv. iii. 25.

bestow, to place, arrange, ii. ix. 28.

bestrad, *pret.* bestrode, v. ii. 13.

bet, *pret.* beat, i. iii. 19, ii. ii. 22, xii. 63. *pa. part.* beaten, i. vii. 28; *storme-bet*, ii. xii. 32.

betake, to betake oneself, i. v. 28, ix. 44; to deliver, give to, vi. xi. 51. **betooke**, *pret.* to entrust, iii. vi. 28.

beteeme, to grant, give, ii. viii. 19.

bethinke, to make up one's mind, i. vi. 16.

bethrall, to make captive, i. viii. 28.

betide, to befall, happen, ii. i. 35, iii. v. 11. **betided**, *pret.*, *Hubberd* 37, *Clout* 329. **betid**, *pret.* ii. viii. 24, iv. xii. 4, v. iii. 10, xii. 32. **betight**, *pa. part.*, *S. C. Sept.* 173, *Nov.* 174. **betidde**, *pa. part.* ii. i. 26.

bett, better, *S. C. Oct.* 15.

beuer, the lower part of a helmet, i. vii. 31, ii. i. 29, iv. vi. 25.

beuy, company (of ladies), ii. ix. 34, v. ix. 31, *S. C. Apr.* 118, *Glosse* p. 434.

bewaile, to mourn? (*perh. an error*), i. vi. 1.

bewray, to disclose, reveal, betray, i. iv. 39, v. 30, iii. iii. Arg., v. iii. 25, vi. iii. 1, *Worlds Vanitie* 148, *S. C. Jan. Glosse, March* 35, *Hubberd* 1096. **bewraide**, *pret.* iii. iv. 61; perceived, iv. ix. 28.

bickerment, strife, bickering, v. iv. 6.

bid, to pray, i. i. 30. *See* beades.

bide, byde[1], to endure, i. iii. 31; to remain, abide, i. x. 66, ii. ii. 9, vi. 19, iv. i. 24.

bide[2], to bid, offer, iii. viii. 16.

biggen, cap (of a child), *S. C. May* 241.

bight, to bite, i. xi. 16.

Bilbo, Bilbao, noted for its swords, *Muiop.* 77.

biliue, *see* beliue.

bil, bill, a sword, weapon, v. xi. 58 : *forrest* b. = a digging or pruning implement, iii. v. 21.

bin, *pa. part.* been, i. i. 33; *pres.* are, v. i. 13.

birchen, of a birch-tree, v. xi. 58.

bit, bite, v. viii. 49.

bittur, bittern, ii. viii. 50.

blacksmith, iv. v. 33.

blame, *sb.* injury, hurt, i. ii. 18, iii. i. 9; fault, *Beautie* 155.

blame, *vb.* to find fault with, *S. C. July* 38; to bring into discredit, vi. iii. 11.

blanck, entirely confounded, discomfited, iii. iii. 17.

bland, to sooth, flatter, cajole, *Beautie* 171.

blandishment, cajolery, flattery, i. ix. 14, *Hubberd* 1274.

blasphémous, iii. vii. 39, v. ii. 19.

blasphémy, vi. xii. 25.

blast, to wither, iii. v. 48.

blaze, to proclaim, describe, depict, portray, extol, i. xi. 7, v. iii. 2, ix. 25, p. 410, *S. C.* p. 417, *Apr.* 43, *Muiop.* 266; to shine, i. iv. 16. **blazed**, *pa. part.* emblazoned, v. iii. 14.

blazer, one who proclaims, extols, 'trumpeter,' ii. ix. 25.

blazon (*broade, out*), to make known, proclaim, describe, i. Prol. 1, *Teares* 102.

blemishment, blemish, iv. ii. 36.

blend, *vb.*[1] to blind, dazzle, ii. xii. 80, iv. iii. 35. **blent**, *pa. part.* ii. iv. 7, *Gnat* 311.

blend, *vb.*[2] to mix, mingle, defile, obscure, blemish, ii. vii. 10, iii. ix. 1. **blent**, *pa. part.* i. vi. 42, ii. iv. 26, v. 5, xii. 7, iii. ix. 33, xii. 29, v. iii. 37, vi. 13, *Hubberd* 1330.

blere, to deceive, *S. C. July* 36.

blesse, *sb.* bliss, i. x. Arg., iv. x. 23.

bless, *vb.*[1] to preserve, protect, guard, i. ii. 18, vii. 12, iv. vi. 13.

blesse, *vb.*[2] to wave, brandish, i. v. 6, viii. 22.

blin, to cease from, stop, iii. v. 22.

blincked, affected with a blink, iii. ix. 5.

blind, dark, without openings, iv. xi. 2.

blist, *pret.*[1] blessed, iv. vii. 46, *S. C. July* 174.

blist, *pret.*[2] brandished, vi. viii. 13. cf **blesse**, *vb.*[2]

blith, joyfully, i. xi. 4.

bliue, forthwith, ii. iii. 18. Cf. **beliue**.

bloncket, grey : b. *liveryes* = grey coats, *S. C. May* 5.

blont, rough, rude, unpolished, *S. C. Sept.* 109. Cf. **blunt**.

blooded, *pa. part.* wet or smeared with blood, *Amor. Son.* 20.

bloodshéd, ii. vi. 34.

bloosme, blossom, bloom, iv. viii. 2, vi. Prol. 4, *S. C. Jan.* 34.

bloosming, *ppl. adj. S. C. May* 8; *pres. part.* p. 411 : blossoming, flowering.

blot, *sb.* blemish, disgrace, VI. xii. 41, *Clout* 697.

blot, blotten, *vb.* to sully, defame, blemish, IV. i. 4, 51, V. ix. 38, VI. xii. 28.

blubbred, *ppl. adj.* tear-stained, -swollen, I. vi. 9, II. i. 13, V. i. 13, *Daphn.* 551.

blunt, uncultivated, VI. xi. 9.

boad¹, to bode, indicate, VII. vi. 23.

boad, bode², *pret.* sojourned, dwelt, abode, v. xi. 60, *Hubberd* 400. Cf. **bide¹.**

bodrag, bo(r)draging, hostile incursion, raid, II. x. 63, *Clout* 315.

bollet, bullet, I. vii. 13.

bolt, arrow, *S. C. March* 70.

bond, *pa. part.* bound, I. i. 3, IV. viii. 21, *Hubberd* 133.

bondáge, II. xi. 1.

bone, leg, *S. C. March* 52.

bonefier, bonfire, *Epith.* 275.

bonetto, bonnet, cap, *Three Lett.* p. 625.

bongrely, bungling, slovenly, *Three Lett.* p. 629.

bonie, bony, comely, beautiful, *Clout* 80, 96, 172.

bonilasse, a beautiful girl, *S. C. Aug.* 77-8.

booke-redd, *ppl. adj.* educated, *Hubberd* 358.

boone, petition, prayer, III. vii. 34. IV. ii. 50, V. ix. 34.

boorde, *see* **bord.**

boot, gain, advantage, profit, III. xi. 9, V. ix. 10; booty, VII. vii. 38.

boote, *vb.* to avail, profit, I. iii. 20, II. i. 16, V. 3, III. xi. 16, IV. xii. 25, *S. C. Sept.* 127.

bootelesse, unprofitable, useless, I. ii. 2; *adv. Hubberd* 400.

bord, boord, *sb.* table, III. x. 6, *Two Lett.* p. 636; conversation, intercourse, IV. iv. 13; coast, VI. xii. 1; *at b.* = against, alongside, *Gnat* 42.

bord, boord, *vb.* to speak, address, accost, II. ii. 5, IV. 24, ix. 2, xii. 16, III. iii. 19; to border on, approach, IV. xi. 43.

bordraging, *see* **bodrag.**

bore, *pa. part.* borne, IV. iv. 4.

borrell, rude, rustic, *S. C. July* 95.

borrow, borowe, pledge, security, *S. C. May* 131, *Sept.* 96, *Hubberd* 852 : *by my dear b.* = by our Saviour (Glosse), *S. C. May* 150.

bosome, IV. xi. 43.

bosse, projection in centre of shield, I. ii. 13, v. xi. 53, *Worlds Vanitie* 150.

bouget, bow-, leathern pouch, III. x. 29, *Three Lett.* p. 615.

bought, coil, fold, knot, I. i. 15, xi. 11, *Gnat* 255.

boult, to sift, II. iv. 24.

bound, to go, lead, I. x. 67.

bounse, to beat, thump, III. xi. 27.

bounteous, virtuous, III. i. 49, ii. 10, xi. 10.

bountie, -y, goodness, virtue, II. iii. 4, 24, III. i. 49, ix. 4.

bountiest, most virtuous, III. v. 8.

bountihed, bountyhed, generosity, II. x. 2, III. i. 41, iii. 47.

bourdon, burden, accompaniment (of a song), *Past. Aeglogue* 77.

bourne, boundary, II. vi. 10.

bout, about, VI. v. 11.

bouzing, *ppl. adj.* drinking, tippling, I. iv. 22.

boue, above, IV. iv. 37, *R. T.* 110.

bow-bent, bent like a bow, V. Prol. 6.

bowr, muscle, I. viii. 41.

bowre, *sb.* bower, inner room, chamber, I. i. 55, III. i. 58.

bowre, *vb.* to lodge, shelter, VI. Prol. 4, VI. x. 6.

boystrous, rough, rude, rude, I. viii. 10.

brace, to encompass, *S. C. Sept.* 124.

brag, proudly, boastfully, *S. C. Feb.* 71.

bragging, proud, boastful, *S. C. Feb.* 115.

bragly, ostentatiously, boastfully, *S. C. March* 14.

brake, fern, bracken, II. xi. 22, *S. C. Dec.* 102.

brame, longing, III. ii. 52.

bransle, dance, III. x. 8.

brast, *pret.* burst, I. v. 31, viii. 4, III. vii. 40, IV. iii. 12, V. viii. 8, xi. 28, *Petrarch* 39.

braue, splendidly, finely, I. iv. 8; beautiful, fair, II. iii. 24, xii. 83, *R. T.* 94.

brauely, gaily, splendidly, II. vi. 13.

brauery, finery, *S. C. Epistle* p. 418, *Hubberd* 608, 858, *Three Lett.* p. 625.

brawned, brawny, well-developed, I. viii. 41.

bray, braie, to resound, cry out, gasp out, utter, give forth, I. vi. 7, viii. 11, II. i. 38, V. xi. 20.

braynepan, skull, VI. vi. 30.

breach, breaking, injury, I. viii. 34, II. xii. 56; gap, fissure, fracture, II. vii. 28; *sobbing breaches* = sobs which break out intermittingly, III. iv. 35; violation, VI. ii. 42, *Hubberd* 1141.

breaded, braided, plaited, II. ii. 15, III. ii. 50.

breare, briar, I. x. 35, III. xi. 37. *See also* **brere.**

breath'd, *pret.* rested, VI. xi. 47.

breathfull, full of breath, IV. v. 38.

breche, breech, breeches, V. ix. 10, *S. C. Feb.* 242.

breed, to cause, produce, I. vii. 17, III. i. 37, *Clout* 697.

breme, breem, cold, chill, rough, harsh, VII. vii. 40, *S. C. Feb.* 43, *Dec.* 148.

bren, brenne, to burn, III. iii. 34. **brent,** *pret.* I. ix. 10, III. i. 47 ; *pa. part. S. C. May* 267 ; *ppl. adj.* I. xi. 28, *R. T.* 19.

brere, briar, III. i. 46, *S. C. May* 10, *Amor. Son.* 26.

brickle, fragile, brittle, IV. x. 39, *R. T.* 499.

bridale, wedding, wedding feast, IV. xi. 9, v. ii. 3, *Proth.* 17.

brigandine, a small, light vessel for fighting, IV. ii. 16, *Muiop.* 84.

brigant, brigand, VI. x. 39.

brim, edge (of shield), IV. iii. 34; edge (of horizon), v. ix. 35 ; edge, limit, VI. xii. 26.

brimstón, II. x. 26.

britch, breeches, *Three Lett.* p. 625. cf. **breche.**

brize, bryze, gadfly (*mod.* breeze), VI. i. 24, *Worlds Vanitie* 24.

broad-blazed, widespread, widely proclaimed, I. x. 11.

brocage, pimping, procuration, *S. C.* p. 416, *Hubberd* 851.

broch, to begin, commence, III. i. 64.

brode, abroad, afar, I. iv. 16, IV. iii. 5.

brond, brand (of lightning), I. viii. 21 ; sword, brand, I. iv. 33, II. viii. 22, 37. *bronds* = embers, brands, II. vii. 36.

brondiron, sword, III. xii. 24, IV. iv. 32, VI. viii. 10.

brood, parentage, extraction, lineage, race, I. iii. 8, x. 64, II. vii. 8 ?, v. vii. 21.

brooding, breeding, v. xi. 23.

brooke, to endure, bear, remain, III. iv. 44, IV. ii. 40, VI. iv. 21.

broome, broom (plant), VI. ix. 5.

brouze, twig, III. x. 45.

brouzed, *pa. part.* eaten (by cattle), *S. C. Feb.* 236.

brunt, stroke, assault, II. viii. 37, v. xi. 59, *S. C.* p. 427, *Amor.* xii. *at the instant b.* = suddenly, at starting, VI. xi. 9.

brusd, to, *see* **tobrusd.**

brust, to burst, *S. C.* p. 435 ; *pret.* III. i. 48 viii. 25, v. viii. 22, *Worlds Vanitie* 80 ; *pa. part.* broken, burst, IV. iv. 41, v. xi. 31, *Past. Elegie* 106 ; *pres. part.* brusting, III. iii. 19.

bruted, bruited, noised abroad, *Hubberd* 188.

brutenesse, brutishnesse, brutality, stupidity, II. viii. 12, IV. vii. 45, *Teares* 270.

bubble glas, glass as thin as a bubble, *R. T.* 50.

buckle, to make ready, gird oneself (in armour), v. xi. 10; *refl.* v. xii. 16, VI. viii. 12.

buegle, glass beads, *S. C. Feb.* 66.

buffe, blow, stroke, I. ii. 17, xi. 24, II. ii. 23.

bug, apparition, goblin (cf. *mod.* bugbear), II. iii. 20, xii. 25.

bugle, wild ox or buffalo, I. viii. 3.

bulke, hull or hold of a ship, v. xi. 29.

bullion, solid gold or silver, III. i. 32.

Bunduca, Boadicea, II. x. 54.

burdenous, heavy, severe, v. xii. 19, *S. C. May* 132.

burganet, steel cap used by infantry, especially pikemen, II. viii. 45, III. v. 31, *Muiop.* 73.

burgein, to bud, VII. vii. 43.

busket, small bush, *S. C. May* 10.

buskin, high boot, I. vi. 16 ; = tragedy, *S. C. Oct.* 113.

busse, a kiss, III. x. 46.

but, unless, *S. C. May* 265 ; only, *S. C. Aug.* 112. *but if* = unless, III. iii. 16, IV. viii. 23, *S. C. Sept.* 143.

buxome, yielding, unresisting, obedient, I. xi. 37, III. ii. 23, VI. viii. 12, *S. C. Sept.* 149, *Hubberd* 626.

by-, *see* **bi-.**

by-accident, side issue, p. 407.

by and by, immediately, I. x. 1, II. vii. 20, viii. 4, *Hubberd* 1092 ; in succession, one by one ?, VII. vii. 27.

bydding base, *see* **bace** *sb.*

by-disputation, incidental argument, *Three Lett.* p. 624.

bynempt, named, mentioned, *S. C. July* 214; declared, uttered (on oath), promised, II. i. 60, *S. C. Nov.* 46 (*Glosse* bequethed).

byte, to eat, I. i. 23.

Byze, Byzantium, *R. R.* 296.

C

cabinet, arbour, bower, II. xii. 83, *S. C. Dec.* 17 ; cottage, dwelling, *Daphn.* 558.

cœrule, deep blue, azure, *Gnat* 163.

caitiue, caytiue, *sb.* villain, wretch, II. i. 1, viii. 37.

caitiue, caytiue, *adj.* captive, I. vii. 19, ix. 11 ; mean, base, II. iii. 35, III. vii. 16.

calamint, an aromatic herb of the genus *Calamintha,* III. ii. 49.

call, *sb.* netted cap or head-dress, I. viii. 46.

camphora, a tree or plant which yields camphor, III. ii. 49.

carmariok, cambric, *Three Lett.* p. 625.

camus, camis, a light, loose dress of silk; a chemise, shirt, tunic, II. iii. 26, v. v. 2.

can, knows, *S. C. Feb.* 77.

can, *for* gan, did, i. i. 8, x¹. 39, iv. iii. 20, iv. 29, vi. 3.

canapee, canopy, i. v. 5.

cancred, venomous, corrupt, i. iv. 30, ii. i. 1; malignant, ill-tempered, envious, iii. ix. 3, *Clout* 680.

cancker worme, caterpillar or insect larva which destroys plants, *S. C. Feb.* 179.

Candida, *pseudonym, Clout* 574.

canon bitt, a smooth, round bit, i. vii. 37.

cantion, song, *S. C.* p. 458.

canuase, to discuss, *S. C.* p. 420.

capias, writ of arrest, vi. vii. 35.

capitayn, captain, ii. xi. 14.

capon, a term of reproach, coward, iii. viii. 15.

caprifole, honeysuckle or woodbine, iii. vi. 44.

captiuaunce, captiuance, captivity, iii. vii. 45, v. vi. 17.

captiue, to capture, v. viii. 2. **captiud,** *pret.* ii. iv. 16. **captiued, captiu'd,** *pa. part.* iii. i. 2, v. vi. 11, vi. viii. 13, *Gnat* 490.

capuccio, hood of a cloak, iii. xii. 10.

card, chart, map, ii. vii. 1, iii. ii. 7.

care, object or matter of concern, ii. x. 37; trouble, sorrow, grief, iv. viii. 5, v. xi. 13, vi. iii. 24.

carefull, full of care, sad, sorrowful, i. i. 44, vi. 6, viii. 15, iii. i. 58, iv. vii. 41, *S. C. Jan.* Arg. 49, 78, *May* 190, *Nov.* 61.

carelesse, unconscious, free from care, i. ii. 45, *Daphn.* 137; untended, uncared for, iv. iv. 38.

cáriere, career, course, *R. R.* 218.

carke, sorrow, grief, i. i. 44, *S C. Nov.* 66.

carle, churl, base fellow, i. ix. 54, ii. xi. 16, iii. ix. 3, iv. v. 44, vi. iii. 34.

carol, carroll, *sb.* song, *Clout* 87, *Epith.* 259.

carol, carroll, *vb.: tr.* to sing, vi. ix. 9; *intr.* to sing a lively or joyous strain, vi. ix. 5, *S C. Feb.* 61, *Oct.* 52; (of birds) *Epith.* 79.

caroling, *sb.* singing, vi. ix. 35, *H. Beautie* 262.

carriage, cariage, burden, vi. iii. 34; action, conduct, *Gnat* 488; behaviour, demeanour, *Hubberd* 777.

carrol, *see* carol.

caruen, to cut, *S. C. Sept.* 41.

caruer, (tree) used for carving work, i. i. 9.

case, condition, plight, iv. viii. 38, *Proth.* 140.

cast, *sb.* bout, iii. x. 35 l. 4; couple (of falcons), vi. vii. 9; time, opportunity, vi. viii. 51; throw, *S. C. Epistle* p. 417; trick, *Three Lett.* p. 622 l. 8. *nere their utmost c.* = almost dead, vi. v. 9.

cast, *vb.* to resolve, purpose, plan, i. x. 2, x

63 (*refl.*), xi. 28, iii. vii. 38, vi. v. 17, *S. C. Mar.* 63, *Oct.* 2; to attempt, *S. C. Feb.* 189, *Oct.* 103, *Hubberd* 27; to consider, *S. C. Sept.* 114.

castory, colour (red or pink), extracted from *castoreum,* ii. ix. 41.

casualtye, chance, haphazardness, *S. C.* p. 416.

causen, to explain, iii. ix. 26.

caue, to make into a cave, iv. v. 33.

cease, to stop, check, v. iv. 20.

cemitare, scimitar, v. v. 3.

centonel, sentinel, i. ix. 41, iv. ii. 36.

certes, certainly, i. vii. 52, iii. ii. 9, vii. 58.

certifye, to notify, *Two Lett.* p. 636.

cesse, to cease, iv. ix. 1.

cesure, stop, interruption, interval, ii. x. 68.

chaffar : *to c. words* = to bandy words, ii. v. 2. **chaffred,** *pa. part.* sold, exchanged, *S. C. Sept.* 10; *pret. Hubberd* 1159.

chaire, dear, iii. v. 51.

chalenge, challenge, *sb.* claim, ii. viii. 27; accusation, iv. ix. 36.

chalenge, *vb.* to claim, i. iv. 20, iv. i. 35, ii. 28, iv. in. 8, v. 23, *Hubberd* 137; to track (the quarry), ii. i. 12.

chamelot, camlet (an Eastern fabric): *water c.* = camlet with a wavy or watered surface, iv. xi. 45.

chamfred, furrowed, wrinkled, *S C. Feb.* 43.

champian, champion, open country, plain, v. ii. 15, vii. vi. 54, *R. R.* 421, *Muiop.* 149. *plaine c.* = open country, vi. iv. 26.

championesse, female champion, warrior, iii. xii. 41.

chappellane, chaplain, confessor, iii. vii. 58.

chapter, capital of a column, *Bellay* 45, *Epigrams* p. 607.

character, image, form, v. vi. 2.

chargefull, onerous, vi. ix. 32.

Charillis, *pseudonym, Clout* 540.

charet, charret, chariot, i. v. 38, iii. vii. 41, *Teares* 9.

charme, *sb.* song, *Teares* 244.

charme, *vb.* to play, tune, v. ix. 13, *S. C. Oct.* 118, *Clout* 5.

chast, pure, stainless, i. v. 38.

chaufe, chauff, *sb.* rage, passion, v. ii. 15, vi. ii. 21, v. 19.

chaufe, *vb.* to rub, i. vii. 21, vii. vii. 29; to chafe, become angry, i. vii. 37, ii. iv. 32, vi. xii. 36; to rage, ii. iii. 46. iv. iv. 29.

chauffed, *ppl. adj.* heated, rubbed, chafed, i. iii. 33; irritated, i. iii. 42, xi. 15.

chauncefull, risky, hazardous, *Hubberd* 98.

chaunge, to cause a change, vi. ix. 32.

chaw, *sb.* jaw, i. iv. 30.

chaw, *vb.* to chew, i. iv. 30, iii. x. 18, v. vi. 19, xii. 39, *Gnat* 86; to meditate on, ii. iv. 29.

chayre, throne, *Teares* 510.

chearen, to become cheered up, courageous, i. x. 2; to encourage, i. iii. 34; *pa. part.* entertained, regaled, iii. i. 42.

cheere, chere, cheare, countenance, i. i. 2, ii. 42, iv. i. 50; aspect, *S. C. Feb.* 26; food, *S. C. July* 188; mood, iv. ii. 51, *S. C. Apr.* 69, *Nov.* 151, *Past. Aeglogue* 23.

checked, chequered, ii. xii. 18.

checklaton, ciclaton, a stuff of silk or cloth of gold, vi. vii. 43.

chepe, *sb.* price, charge, vi. xi. 40.

cherelie, cheerfully, cheerily, *Teares* 321.

cheriping, *vbl. sb.* chirping, *S. C. June* 55.

cherishment, tenderness, cherishing, *Teares* 576.

cherry, to cheer, delight, vi. x. 22.

cheuisaunce, enterprise, ii. ix. 8, iii. vii. 45, xi. 24, *S. C. May* 92.

cheuisaunce, a flower (wall-flower?), *S. C. Apr.* 143.

chickens: *faithlesse chickens*, heathen brood, iii. iii. 46.

chiefe, head, top, *S. C. Nov.* 115.

chill, to shiver (with cold), *Hubberd* 993.

chimney, fireplace, ii. ix. 29.

chine, back, vi. iii. 3.

chippes, parings of bread-crust, *S. C. July* 188.

chorle, churl, iii. vii. 15.

chyld, to give birth to, vi. xii. 17.

chynd, *pret.* split asunder, broke, iv. vi. 13.

ciuil, civilized, *Hubberd* 45.

ciuilite, civilization, vi. Prol. 4; courtesy, chivalry, iii. i. 44, vi. i. 26.

clad, to clothe, vi. iv. 4.

clambe, *pret.* climbed, vii. vi. 8.

clame, to call, shout, iv. x. 11.

clap, *sb.* stroke, iv. x. 9, *Gnat* 519.

clap, *vb.* to shut, slam, iii. xii. 3.

clark, clerk, scholar, v. x. 1, *Teares* 335.

claue, *pret.* cleaved, *Gnat* 568.

clawbacke, sycophant, toady, *Three Lett.* p. 621.

cleane, clene, cleene, entirely; *adv.* i. i. 50, iv. vii. 13, v. x. 25, vii. vii. 52, *S. C.* pp. 426, 443, 447; *adj.* pure, i. x. 58.

cleanly, *adj.* artful, *Hubberd* 857; *adv.* artfully, *Hubberd* 862.

clearkly, learnedly, *Three Lett.* p. 614.

cleep, clepe, to call, name, ii. iii. 8, ix. 58, iv. x. 34, vi. x. 8, *Worlds Vanitie* 58, *Clout* 113.

clemence, clemency, v. vii. 22.

clew, plot—*lit.* a ball of thread, ii. i. 8; ball (of silk), iii. xii. 14.

clieffe, cliff, iv. xii. 5.

clift¹, cliff, i. viii. 22, ii. xii. 4, 7, 8, iii. iv. 7.

clift², chink, opening, crack, iv. ix. 27.

clim, to climb, iii. iv. 42.

clinck, chink, keyhole, *S. C. May* 251.

clipping, *pres. part.* clasping, embracing, iii. viii. 10.

clogd, encumbered, burdened, iii. x. 35.

clombe, *pret.* mounted, climbed, i. x. 49, iii. iii. 61, iv. v. 46.

close, secret, hidden, iii. i. 56, iv. iv. 16, *Bellay* 174, *Amor.* Son. 25.

closely, secretly, i. vi. 32, iii. ii. 28, vi. 16, *Hubberd* 331.

clouch, clutch, iii. x. 20, v. ix. 11.

clout, shred, rag, i. ix. 36; cloth, *S. C. May* 242.

clouted¹, *ppl. adj.* covered with a clout or cloth, *S. C. Mar.* 50.

clouted² (cream), *ppl. adj.* clotted, *S. C. Nov.* 99.

cloue, *pret.* cleaved, ii. ii. 3, vi. 31. clouen, *pa. part.* i. v. 12.

cloyd, *pret.* pierced, gored, iii. vi. 48.

clyme, to climb, mount, i. iv. 17.

coast¹, quarter, region, iii. iii. 6.

coast²: *on even c.* = on equal terms, ii. iii. 17. cf. cost.

coasted, *pret.* approached, v. ii. 29.

cooh, coach, iv. iii. 46.

cockatrice, serpent, identified with the basilisk, fabulously said to kill by its mere glance, *Amor.* Son. 49.

cock-bote, a small, light boat, iii. viii. 24.

cocked (hay), heaped up, made into haycocks, *S. C. Nov.* 12.

cockel, cockle, a weed which grows in corn-fields, *S. C. Dec.* 124.

cognizaunce, recognition, ii. i. 31.

colled, *pret.* embraced, iii. ii. 34.

colour, *vb.* to disguise, hide, vi. x. 37.

colourable, specious, plausible, deceptive, iii. iii. 19, *S. C. May* Arg. 9.

colourably, with a hidden meaning, metaphorically, *S. C.* p. 427.

coloure, *sb.* pretence, *S. C.* p. 455.

coloured, *ppl. adj.* disguised, hidden, *S. C. Feb.* 162.

colt wood, leaves, &c. of coltsfoot, iii. ii. 49.

colwort, plant of the cabbage kind (genus *Brassica*), *Muiop.* 200.

comber, to encumber, *S. C. Feb.* 133. combred, *ppl. adj.* hindered, impeded, i. viii. 10.

combrous, cumbrous, harassing, i. i. 23, ii. ix. 17.

combyned, joined, fastened, iv. x. 40, *Beautie* 205.

comen, common, usual, *S. C. June* 45.

commandement, command, control, *Clout* 263.

commen, common, to converse, ii. ix. 41, v. ix. 4.

comment, to devise, invent (of a false statement), vii. vii. 53.

commixtion, copulation, vi. vi. 12.

commixture, mingling, mixture, vi. i. 8; copulation, *Clout* 802.

commodity, -ie, advantage, vi. xi. 10, *Two Lett.* p. 635.

commonly, familiarly, in intimate union, i. x. 56.

compacte, agreed, arranged, v. vi. 16.

compacted, close, iii. i. 23.

compacture, compact structure, ii. ix. 24.

companie, *sb.* companion, iv. i. 38.

companie, *vb.* to be a gay companion, *Hubberd* 506.

compare, compaire[1] (with), to vie with, rival, ii. v. 29, *Muiop.* 271, *Elegie* 18.

compare[2], to acquire, i. iv. 28.

compasse, proportion, ii. ix. 24; extent, range, iii. ix. 46. *in compas* = around, iii. iii. 10.

compassion, *vb.* to pity, *Clorinda* 2.

compast, *ppl. adj.* round, circular, iv. iv. 30.

compást, *pa. part.* contrived, iii. vii. 18; arranged (in a circle), *Elegie* 23.

compel, to force to come, ii. i. 5; to force, constrain, i. vi. 26.

compile, compyle, to build, iii. iii. 10; to heap up, produce, iii. ii. 12, vi. i. 2; to compose (of a song), iv. viii. 4, *Beautie* 273; to compose, settle, iv. ix. 17.

complaine, -playne, to lament, *S. C. Nov.* 44; to compose as a complaint, *Clout* 511.

complement, completeness, iii. v. 55; politeness, courtesy, vi. x. 23, *Hubberd* 692; accomplishment, consummation, *Hubberd* 338; (mock) courtesy, civility, *Clout* 790.

complexion, quality, character, 'humour,' 'temperament,' ii. iii. 22, iii. vi. 8, vi. 38.

complish, to accomplish, fulfil, v. xi. 41.

complot, conspiracy, plot, *Hubberd* 178.

complyne, the last service of the day in the Catholic ritual, *Hubberd* 452.

comportance, bearing, behaviour, ii. i. 29.

composition, agreement, v. x. 27; agreement (to pay money), vi. i. 43.

compound, to settle, compose, iii. iii. 23; to settle, agree (as to terms), v. xii. 4.

comprehend, to contain, iv. i. 27.

comprize, to perceive, comprehend, ii. ix. 49;

to draw together, iii. vi. 19; to contain, vi. viii. 18.

comprouinciall, of the same province, iii. iii. 32.

con, to know, *S. C. July* 45, *Sept.* 90.

conceipt, conceit, idea, v. vii. 38; conception, pp. 407, 409, 435, *Elegie* 124; opinion, judgement, estimation, *S. C.* p. 427, *Clout* p. 536.

conceiptfull, clever, vi. xii. 16.

conceiue, to perceive, v. v. 31, 35.

concent, *sb.* harmony, iii. xii. 5, *Beautie* 199.

concent, *vb.* to harmonize, iv. ii. 2.

concrew, to grow into a mass, iv. vii. 40.

concurring, combining, *Three Lett.* p. 630.

cond, *pret.* learned, *S. C. Feb.* 92, *Clout* 74.

condigne, worthy, vii. vi. 11.

condiscend, to consent, v. i. 25.

conditions, qualities, iii. ix. 4, *Beautie* 137.

conduct[1], management, ii. ii. 25.

conduct[2], guide, vi. xi. 35.

conference, conversation, *Two Lett.* p. 640.

confound, confounded, *Muiop.* 262.

confusion, destruction, *S. C. May* 219.

congé, leave, farewell, ii. i. 34, iii. 2, iii. i. 1, *Hubberd* 1109.

congregate, *pa. part.* congregated, assembled, vii. vi. 19.

coniúre, to entreat, i. xii. 27; to conspire, v. x. 26.

conne, can, *S. C. Epistle* p. 417; to know, *S. C. June* 65.

consent[1], wish, opinion, iv. viii. 50.

consent[2], harmony, *Gnat* 226. Cf. concent.

consórt, *sb.*[1] companion, vii. vi. 51.

consórt, *sb.*[2] accord, i. xii. 4; harmony, singing together, iii. i. 40, *Past. Aeglogue* 31.

consort, *vb.* to combine, unite, ii. xii. 70, *Elegie* 76.

conspyre, to agree, *S. C.* p. 458.

constraine, to bring about by force, v. vi. 19; to incur, *Hubberd* 561.

constraint, force, i. vii. 34; confinement, i. x. 2; distress, ii. ii. 8, *S. C. May* 249.

contagion, contagious quality or influence, v. vii. 11, *Muiop.* 256.

containe, to restrain, control, iii. ix. 7, v. xii. 1, vi. vi. 7.

conteck, strife, discord, iii. i. 64, *S. C. May* 163, *Sept.* 86.

contempt, contemned, despised, *S. C. Nov.* 48.

contentation, satisfaction, *Three Lett.* p. 619.

continent, land, earth, iii. iv. 30, v. 25.

continuaunce, stay, delay, vi. iii. 19.

contráct, *pa. part.* contracted, iii. ix. 42.

contraire, to oppose, hinder, VII. vi. 7.

contráry, contrárie, II. ii. 24, XI. 6, III. ii. 40, IV. i. 42, iii. 27.

contriue, to pass, spend (time), II. ix. 48.

controlement, control, restraint, *Three Lett.* p. 629.

controuerse, controversy, dispute, IV. v. 2.

conuaid, *pa. part.* removed, I. ii. 24.

conuenable, in agreement, conformable, *S. C. Sept.* 175.

conuent, to summon together, VII. vii. 17.

conuert, *refl.* to turn one's attention, v. ix. 37.

conueyance, underhand dealing, *Hubberd* 856.

conuince, to conquer, III. ii. 21.

coosen, *sb.* kinsman, III. iii. 13.

coosen, *adj.* kindred, III. iv. 12.

coosin, *vb.* to cozen, cheat, *Hubberd* 874.

coosinage, fraud, *Hubberd* 857.

coosined, *pret.* defrauded, *Hubberd* 862.

cope, *sb.* canopy, *Love* 95.

cope, *vb.* to make an exchange, *Hubberd* 527.

copesmate, partner, accomplice, *Hubberd* 939.

coportion, joint portion, VI. ii. 47.

corage, mind, nature, I. v. 1, III. ii. 10 ; anger, wrath, III. x. 30.

corbe, *sb.* corbel, IV. x. 6.

corbe, *adj.* bent. crooked, *S. C. Feb.* 56.

cordwayne, -waine, Spanish leather made originally at Cordova, II. iii. 27, VI. ii. 6.

cormoyrant, cormorant, II. xii. 8.

coronall, circlet for head, coronet, III. v. 53 ; wreath, garland, *S. C. Feb.* 178, *Epith.* 255.

coronation, carnation, *S. C. Apr.* 138.

corpse, body (living), form, *S. C. Nov.* 168, *Beautie* 135. **corps**, body (dead), I. v. 38.

corse, body (dead), I. i. 24, ii. 24 ; body (living), I. viii. 40, II. v. 23 ; stature, form, I. iii. 42.

corsiue, *sb.* corrosive (grief, annoyance), IV. ix. 14.

Corydon, *pseudonym, Clout* 382.

Coshma, *pseudonym, Clout* 522.

cosset, hand-reared lamb, *S. C. Nov.* 42, 46, 206.

cost, coste, *sb.* point (of compass), direction, VI. xii. 1 ; side, *Hubberd* 294. *on equall cost* = on equal ground, on equal terms, IV. iii. 24.

cost, *vb.* to approach (cf. **coast**), *Daphn.* 39.

costmarie, an aromatic perennial plant allied to the pansy, *Gnat* 670, *Muiop.* 195.

cot, boat, II. vi. 9.

cote, house, *S. C. July* 162 ; profession, *S. C. Sept.* 111.

couch, to crouch, stoop, III. i. 4. **couched**, *pa. part.* set, placed, arranged, I. xi. 9, *Bellay* 35 ; **coucht**, *Elegie* 12. **couched**, *ppl. adj.* lowered, I. iii. 34.

couchant, lying with the body rested on the legs and the head lifted up (*herald.*), III. ii. 25.

could, knew, VI. v. 36.

count, consideration, esteem, IV. x. 18. *care and c.* = important consideration, v. x. 16.

countenance, *sb.* demeanour, I. iv. 15, IV. i. 5 ; position, standing, v. ix. 38, *S. C. May* 80.

countenance, *vb.* to make a show of, pretend, II. ii. 16.

counter, *sb.* encounter, *Teares* 207.

counter, *adj.* opposing, VI. xii. 1.

counterbuff, to rebuff, *S. C.* p. 427.

counter-cast, antagonistic artifice, VI. iii. 16.

counterchaunge, requital, III. ix. 16.

counterfect, false, counterfeit, *S. C. Sept.* 206.

counterfesaunce, -feisance, counterfeiting, deception, I. viii. 49, III. viii. 8, IV. iv. 27, *Teares* 197, *Hubberd* 667.

counterpeise, to counterbalance, v. ii. 46.

counterpoint, counter-stroke, *Hubberd* 1140.

counterpoynt, app. plot, trick, stratagem, *S. C. May* Arg. p. 435.

counterpoys, to counterbalance, v. ii. 30.

counteruailable, to be matched or set up as equivalent, *Three Lett.* p. 631.

counteruaile, to resist, II. vi. 29, VII. vi. 49 ; to reciprocate, *Two Lett.* p. 639.

countie, domain of a count, earldom, *R. T.* 273.

coupe, coop, cage, prison, *S. C. Oct.* 72.

couplement, union (of two), IV. iii. 52, *Proth.* 95 ; couple, VI. v. 24.

courd, *pret.* covered, protected, II. viii. 9.

courst, *pret.* ran a course (in a tournament), IV. iv. 30 ; chased, v. iv. 44, ix. 16. *coursed (over)* = recounted quickly, *Three Lett.* p. 618.

court, to pay court to, make love to, II. ix. 34 *absol.* II. ii. 15. **courting**, *ppl. adj., R. T.* 202.

courting, frequenting the court, practice of a courtier, *Hubberd* 784.

couth, could, II. vii. 58, *S. C. Jan.* 10, *Feb.* 190, *June* 41.

couert, concealing, II. Prol. 5 ; covered, secret, IV. viii. 9.

couerture, shelter, *S. C. July* 26 ; dissimulation, deceit, *Hubberd* 683.

couet, to desire (*with inf.*), I. xii. 20, II. xii. 20

couetise, -ize, covetousness, I. iv. 29, III. iv 7, *S. C. Sept.* 82, *Hubberd* 996, 1309.

cowardree, cowardice, *Hubberd* 986.

cowched, laid down, placed, *Three Lett.* p 625.

cowheard, cowardly, v. viii. 50, x. 15.

cowherdize, cowardice, vi. x. 37.

coy, adj. hidden, secluded, iv. x. 22.

coye, vb. to act coyly, affect reserve, *Three Lett.* p. 629.

cracknelle, light, crisp biscuit, *S.C. Jan.* 58, *Nov.* 95.

craesie, cracked, *Clout* 374.

crag, cragge, neck, *S. C. Feb.* 82, *Sept.* 45.

craggy, rugged, rough, iv. vii. 25.

crake, sb. boasting, ii. xi. 10.

crake, vb. to boast, brag, v. iii. 16, vii. vii. 50.

crall, to crawl, i. i. 2, iii. iii. 26.

cranck, adv. boldly, lustily, *S. C. Sept.* 46.

crank, sb. winding, vii. vii. 52.

craple, grapple, claw, v. viii. 40.

crased, ppl. adj. impaired, iii. ix. 26.

cratch, manger, *H. Love* 226.

creakie, full of creeks, *Bellay* 119.

creast, helmet, vi. iv. 30. creast-front = front of excrescence on dragon's head, *Gnat* 308.

creasted, crested, adorned, iv. i. 13.

cremosin, ii. xi. 3, *S.C. Apr.* 59; cremsin, *S. C. Feb.* 130, crimson.

crew, sb.[1] company, band, iii. vii. 11, vii. vi. 14, *Clout* 931.

crewe, sb.[2] pot, *S. C. Feb.* 209.

crime, wrongdoing, sin (collect.), ii. xii. 75, vii. vii. 18; (criminal) cause, i. xi. 46; accusation, *S. C. Feb.* 162.

crisped, ppl. adj. curled, ii. iii. 30.

critique, critical, *Misc. Sonn.* i.

crocke, pot, jar, v. ii. 33.

crooke, gallows (cross), v. v. 18; bending (of a path), vii. vii. 52.

croscut, to cut across, iii. x. 59.

croslet, small cross, i. vi. 36.

croud, fiddle or viol, *Epith.* 131.

crouper, crupper, iii. i. 6.

cruddle, to curdle, *S. C. Feb.* 46.

cruddy, curdled, i. v. 29, iii. iii. 47, iv. 34.

crudled, ppl. adj. curdled, i. vii. 6, ix. 52, *S. C. Feb.* Arg. 11, *Past. Elegie* 152.

cruell, cruelly, iv. vii. 30, *Clout* 909.

crumenall, purse, pouch, *S. C. Sept.* 119.

cud, inside of throat; place where cud is chewed?, *Gnat* 86.

cuffling, striking (= scuffling ?), iv. iv. 29.

cull (out), to select, *Teares* p. 480.

cullambyne, Columbine (name of flower), *Amor. Son.* 64.

culter, ploughshare, *Thest.* 75.

culuer, dove, ii. vii. 34, *Teares* 246, *Amor. Son.* 89.

culuering, culverin, a kind of cannon, v. x. 34.

cumbrous, troublesome, i. i. 23, *R. T.* 305.

cunnye, cony, rabbit, *Three Lett.* p. 615.

curat, curiet, cuirass, v. v. 20, v. viii. 34, vi. v. 8.

cure, care, charge, i. v. 44.

curelesse, incurable, irremediable, iii. x. 59, vi. vi. 2, *S. C. Aug.* 104.

curious, inquisitive, prying, iii. ix. 26; elaborate, *Teares* 542; ingenious, *Clout* 8; adv. carefully, iv. x. 22.

cursed, ill-fated, v. viii. 43.

curtaxe, cutlass, iv. ii. 42.

curtoll, abbreviation, *Two Lett.* p. 639.

custome: of c. = as was usual, *Hubberd* 245.

cut, fashion, shape, *Hubberd* 211.

cypher, letter, character, iii. ii. 25, 45.

D

dædale, skilful, iii. Prol. 2; fertile, iv. x. 45.

daffadillies, -downdillies, daffodils, iii. iv. 29, xi. 32, *S.C. Jan.* 22, *Apr.* 140.

daint, choice, dainty, i. x. 2, iii. Prol. 2, iv. i. 5. dayntiest (superl.), ii. xii. 42.

dainty, daintiness, fastidiousness, i. ii. 27.

dalliaunce, amorous talk or play, i. viii. 5, ii. ii. 35, *Teares* 186.

dallie, to trifle, iv. i. 36.

damb, dam (mill-d.), v. xi. 31.

dambe, dam (of a lamb), *S. C. Aug.* 39.

dame, lady, ii. vi. 22.

damme, mother (of a bird), *Epigrams* p. 607.

damn, damne, to condemn, v. x. 4, *Hubberd* 1244, *Misc. Sonn.* i.

damnifyde, pa. part. injured, i. xi. 52, ii. vi. 43.

damozell, damsel, ii. i. 19.

Dan, a title; Master, Sir, iii. viii. 21, iv. ii. 32.

Danisk, Danish, iv. x. 31.

Daphne, pseudonym, *Clout* 386.

dapper, neat, pretty, *S. C. Oct.* 13.

dared, pa. part. afraid, *S. C. Aug.* 24.

darksom, dark, iii. iii. 12, 15.

darraine, darrayne, to set troops in array, prepare, for battle, i. iv. 40, vii. 11, ii. ii. 26, iii. i. 20, iv. iv. 26, v. 24, v. ii. 15, xii. 9; to order, arrange (a battle), iv. ix. 4.

darre, to dare, iii. Prol. 2.

darred, ppl. adj. frightened, terrified (cf. dared), vii. vi. 47.

daw (jackdaw), fool, *Hubberd* 913.

dayes-man, mediator, judge, ii. viii. 28.

dayr'house, dairy, vii. vi. 48.

daze, to bewilder, iii. vii. 7. dazd, dazed, pa. part. dazzled, bewildered, i. i. 18. viii. 20, iii. vii. 13. *Amor. Son.* 3; ppl. adj. i. viii. 21.

dead, to deaden, deprive of force, vigour, *Epitaph* (2) 38. **deaded,** *pa. part.* IV. x.i. 20, VI. vii. 25, xi. 33.

dead-doing, death-dealing, murderous, II. iii. 8, *Amor.* Son. 1.

deadly, death-like, I. iii. 11 ; mortal, fatal, I. vii. 23, xi. 49; *adv.* III. i. 38.

dealth, bestows, IV. i. 6.

deare, *sb.* injury, harm, I. vii. 48.

deare, *adj.*[1] valuable, III. iv. 23; (as *sb.*) darling, I. vii. 16.

deare, *adj.*[2] sore. grievous, II. v. 38, xi. 34; hard, *Past. Elegie* 124.

dearely, boldly, resolutely, II. viii. 11 ; grievously, at great cost, I. iv. 42, v. iii. 36, *R. T.* 504.

dearling, *sb.* lover, IV. viii. 54; darling, *Teares* 14.

dearling, *adj.* darling, IV. Prol. 5.

dearnelie, dearnly, sorrowfully, dismally II. i. 35, *Daphn.* 196. *See also* **dernely.**

deaw, *sb.* dew, I. i. 36, 39.

deaw, *vb.* to bedew, sprinkle, I. xi. 48, II. ii. 6, v. xii. 13.

deawy, -ie, dewy, I. ii. 7, v. 2.

debard, *pa. part.* stopped, v. ix. 36.

debate, *sb.* struggle, battle, strife, contest, II. viii. 54, x. 58, IV. Prol. 1, VI. iii. 22, viii. 13, *Muiop.* 305.

debate, *vb.* to strive, contend, II. i. 6, III. ix. 14, VI. iv. 30.

debatement, strife, contention, II. vi. 39.

debonaire, gracious, courteous, I. ii. 23, III. i. 26, v. 8.

Debóra, III. iv. 2.

decay, *sb.* destruction, death, I. ii. 41, vi. 48, II. iii. 15, viii. 51, xi. 41, III. vii. 41, xi. 52, v. viii. 40, ix. 31, xii. 12. **decayes,** ruins, *R. R.* 454.

decayd, *vb. pret.* became weaker, VI. i. 21 ; *pa. part.* destroyed, III. viii. 4.

deceaved, *pa. part.* taken away by deceit, v. iii. 30.

deceipt, deceit, *S. C.* p. 419, *Teares* 492.

decesse, death, v. x. 11.

decreed, *pa. part.* resolved on, determined, IV. vi. 8.

lecrewed, *pret.* decreased, IV. vi. 18.

deducted, *ppl. adj.* reduced, weakened, *Love* 106.

deeme, deemen, to think, consider, III. viii. 3, *S. C. Feb.* 38, *Clout* 575; to judge, IV. iii. 4, v. 6, v. i. 28; to discern, distinguish, v. i. 8; to judge of, estimate, *Love* 168; to imagine, *Amor.* Son. 85. *d. his payne* = adjudge his punishment, IV. xii. 11. **dempt,**

pa. part. considered, III. xi. 23; judged, *pret.* II. viii. 55, *S. C. Aug.* 137.

deene, din, noise (*fig.*), p. 412.

deface, to abash, put out of countenance, II. iv. 25, *Hubberd* 707; to destroy, extinguish, II. viii. 25, *Worlds Vanitie* 152, *Amor.* Son. 31. **defaced,** *pa. part.* destroyed, *Teares* 399. *See also* **defaste.**

defaicted, *pa. part.* defeated, *S. C.* p. 443.

defame, disgrace, dishonour, II. v. 26, III. i. 27, v. i. 28, iii. 38, ix. 43, VI. v. 15.

defaste, *pa. part.* of 'deface', destroyed, II. iv. 14, III. ii. 28. **defast,** broken (law), II. viii. 31.

defeasance, defeat, I. xii. 12.

defeature, undoing, ruin, IV. vi. 17.

defend, to ward off, II. xii. 63, IV. iii. 32, *Gnat* 523.

deffly, deftly, skilfully, *S. C. Apr.* 111.

define, to decide, settle, IV. iii. 3.

deflore, to deflower, desecrate, *Beautie* 39.

deforme, hideous, deformed, I. xii. 20, II. xii. 24.

deformed, *pa. part.* rendered hideous, disfigured, II. v. 22.

deformed, *ppl. adj.* (*fig.*), hateful, I. ix. 48.

defray, to settle (*fig.*), appease, I. v. 42, IV. v. 31. **defraide, defrayd,** *pa. part.* discharged, paid (*fig.*), v. xi. 41, VI. viii. 24.

degendered, *pa. part.* degenerated, v. Prol. 2.

degendering, *pres. part.* degenerating, *H. Love* 94.

degenerate, to cause to degenerate, *Teares* 436.

degree : *in faire d.* = in a pleasant manner, III. xii. 18 ; *by d.* = according to rank, v. ix. 27 ; *dearest in d.* = as dearly as possible, *Clout* 14.

deign, to notice (favourably), *Thest.* 21 ; to condescend to accept, *S. C. Jan.* 63.

delay, to weaken, temper, II. iv. 35, ix. 30, IV. viii. 1. **delayd,** *pa. part.* quenched, III. xii. 42.

delice, deluce, *see* **flowre delice.**

délices, delights, pleasures, II. v. 28, IV. x. 6, v. iii. 40.

delight, charm, IV. xi. 6.

dell, hole, *S. C. March* 51.

delue, cave, pit, den, II. vii. Arg., viii. 4, III. iii. 7, IV. i. 20.

demaine, demeanour, bearing, II. viii. 23.

demeane, *sb.* demeanour, behaviour, II. ix. 40, v. v. 51 ; treatment, VI. vi. 18.

demeane, *vb.* to ill-treat, abuse, VI. vii. 39.

demeand, *pret.* behaved to, treated (well), *Clout* 681.

demeanure, III. i. 40, IV. vi. 5, *Past. Elegie* 20;

demeasnure, III. ix. 27 : demeanour, behaviour.

demerite, to merit, deserve, *Elegie* 130.

demisse, submissive, base, *H. Love* 136.

dempt, *see* **deeme.**

denay, to deny, III. xi. 11, VI. xi. 15. **denayd,** *pret.* III. vii. 57 ; *pa. part.* IV. xii. 28.

denominate, *pa. part.* called, *S. C.* p. 443.

dent, stroke, blow, IV. vi. 15.

deowe, deow, dew, III. xii. 13, *Past. Elegie* 191. Cf. **deaw.**

depainted, *pa. part.* depicted, II. v. 11 ; described, *Clout* 898.

depart, *sb.* departure, III. vii. 20.

depart, to divide, separate, II. x. 14 ; to remove, III. iv. 6.

depasturing, consuming, feeding on (*fig.*), II. xii. 73.

depeincten, to depict, *S. C. Apr.* 69. **depeincted,** *pa. part.* III. xi. 7.

dependant, attached, hanging, III. xii. 10.

depend, to hang, *S. C. Jan.* 42. **depending,** *pres. part.* II. xii. 4, *Amor.* Son. 25 (*fig.* = wavering). **depended,** *pret.* (*fig.*), IV. ix. 24.

depraue, to defame, pervert, v. vii. 32, xii. 34, *Amor.* Son. 29.

der-doing, doing of daring deeds, I. vii. 10.

dernely, dismally, grievously, III. i. 14, xii. 34.

dernfull, mournful, *Thest.* 90.

derring do, doe, daring deeds, II. iv. 42, VI. v. 37, *S. C. Oct.* 65, *Dec.* 43.

derring dooer, daring doer, IV. ii. 38.

derth, scarcity, I. ii. 27.

deryue, to obtain, appropriate, v. ix. 41. **deriued,** *pa. part.* taken away, I. iii. 2 ; carried across, IV. iii. 13.

descant, melody sung extempore upon a plainsong, ground, or bass, to which it forms the air, *Epith.* 81.

descriue, to describe, II. iii. 25, VI. xii. 21.

descry, descrie, to perceive, discover, II. iv. 37, xii. 34, v. iii. 32 ; to reveal, IV. i. 32, VI. vii. 12. **describe, -yde,** *pret.* perceived, *Hubberd* 1301, *Clout* 675 ; revealed, I. x. 34 ; *pa. part.* seen, revealed, VI. iii. 2 ; *ppl. adj.* perceived, II. xii. 35.

desine, to indicate, IV. iii. 37, v. vii. 8, *Amor.* Son. 74.

despairefull, hopeless, II. xii. 8.

desperate, despairing, IV. iii. 25.

despight, anger, I. i. 50, *S. C. Jan.* 76 ; wrong, injury, II. i. 14, III. i. 24, IV. i. 52 ; spite, malice, III. i. 65, *Teares* 46 ; defiance, v. iii. 31, *Daphn.* 442. *in despite of* = in spite of, *Daphn.* 443 ; *in my d.* = in spite of me, III. iv. 14.

despightfull, malicious, spiteful, II. i. 15.

despiteous, malicious, II. vii. 62.

despoile, to undress, disrobe, I. x. 17, II. xi. 49.

desse, dais, IV. x. 50.

desynde, *pa. part.* destined, IV. vii. 30.

detaine, *sb.* detention, v. vi. 15.

detect, to expose, accuse, v. ix. 48 ; to reveal, *Muiop.* 13.

détestable, II. xii. 8.

detter, debtor, v. v. 37.

deuicefull, full of devices, ingenuity, ingenious, v. iii. 3, x. 1, *Teares* 385.

deuise, deuize, to talk, converse, discourse, I. x. 12, xii. 17, IV. vi. 10 ; to describe, recount, III. i. 42, IV. viii. 3, *S. C. Jan.* 65 ; to guess, II. ix. 42, III. x. 21 ; to plan, contrive, VI. ix. 30, 35, *R. T.* 295 ; to consider, VI. iv. 34, vii. 6. **deuized,** *pa. part.* designed, drawn, II. i. 31.

deuoyd, empty, I. ix. 15.

déuoyr, duty, *S. C. Sept.* 227.

dew, due, II. viii. 55 ; duly, v. v. 22.

dewelap, dewlap, fold of loose skin hanging from throat of cattle, *S. C. Feb.* 74.

dewest, most deserved, appropriate, *Hubberd* 1237.

dewfull, duefull, due, IV. xi. 44, VII. vi. 35.

diapase, diapason, II. ix. 22, *Teares* 549.

diapred, *pa. part.* variegated (with flowers), *Epith.* 51.

dide : *bloudie d.,* dyed with blood, II. xi. 21.

dieper, diaper ; a textile fabric (cf. **diapred**), *Muiop.* 364.

differd, *pret.* deferred, postponed, IV. iv. 36.

difference, variation, II. xii. 71 ; alteration, II. xii. 87.

diffused, *ppl. adj.* dispersed, scattered, v. xi. 47.

dight, to deck, adorn, I. iv. 14, *S. C. May* 11 ; to put on, I. vii. 8, *Muiop.* 91, *Hubberd* 1279 ; to prepare, make (*trans.*), II. xi. 2, *Past. Elegie* 41 ; to prepare (*refl.*), VI. ii. 18, v. 40, *Hubberd* 233 ; to direct oneself, repair, go (*refl.*), IV. i. 16, v. iv. 43 ; to perform, do, v. ii. 18 ; to dress, VI. xii. 15. **dight,** *pa. part.* decked, equipped, adorned, I. iv. 6, II. xii. 53, IV. x. 38, *S. C. Jan.* 22 ; dressed, IV. x. 38 ; placed, set, III. i. 39 ; made, fashioned, *S. C. Apr.* 29.

dilate, *trans.* to spread out, II. xii. 53 ; *refl.*, *Amor.* Son. 66 ; to relate, enlarge upon, III. iii. 62, v. vi. 17 ; to expand, extend, VII. vii. 58.

dill, an umbelliferous annual plant with yellow flowers, III. ii. 49, *Muiop.* 197.

dint, *sb.* mark, dent, I. i. 1 ; blow, v. i. 10 ; stroke, *Thest.* 58. *dolors d.* = pang of grief, *S. C. Nov.* 104.

dinting, *pres. part.* striking, VI. x. 30.

dirige, dirge, *Hubberd* 453.

dirk, to darken, *S. C. Feb.* 134.

dirke, *adj.* dark, *S. C. Sept.* 6.

dirke, *adv.* darkly (*fig.*), *S. C. Sept.* 102.

disaccord, to refuse assent, vi. iii. 7.

disaduaunce, to draw back, lower, iv. iii. 8, iv. 7.

disaduentrous, disastrous, *Hubberd* 100.

disaray, *sb.* disorderly undress, ii. iv. 40.

disarayd, *pa. part.* stript, disrobed, i. v. 41; despoiled, *S. C. Feb.* 105; *pret.* stript, i. viii. 46.

disattyre, to undress, vi. ix. 17.

disauaunce, to hinder, iii. xi. 24.

disauentrous, unfortunate, disastrous, i. vii. 48, ix. 11, iv. viii. 51, xii. 4, v. xi. 55.

disauenture, mishap, misfortune, i. ix. 45, vi. iii. 15.

disboweld, *ppl. adj.* disembowelled, *R. R.* 383.

disburdned, *pret.* unloaded, ii. vi. 11.

discarded, *pret.* cast or forced away (*Spens.*), v. v. 8.

discided, *pa. part.* cut (in two) *fig.*, iv. i. 27.

discipled, *pa. part.* taught, disciplined, iv. Prol. i.

discipline, teaching, advice, *Hubberd* 547.

disclame, to renounce, iii. x. 15, iv. v. 25.

disclost, *pa. part.* revealed, recounted, iii. iv. 13. **disclos'd**, unfastened, iv. v. 16. **disclosing**, *pres. part.* unfolding.

discolour'd, *ppl. adj.* variously coloured, i. iv. 31, iii. x. 21, xi. 47, *Epith.* 51.

discomfited, *ppl. adj.* disconcerted, iii. i. 43.

discommended, *pret.* spoke disparagingly of, v. v. 57.

discordfull, quarrelsome, iv. ii. 30, iv. 3.

discounselled, *pret.* dissuaded, ii. xii. 34, iii. i. 11.

discountenaunce, to show disapprobation of, *Teares* 340.

discoure, to discover, iii. ii. 20; to reveal, iii. iii. 50, p. 407. **discouer**, to tell, reveal, iv. vi. 4. **discouered**, *pa. part.* uncovered, i. ii. 7. **discure**, to reveal, ii. ix. 42.

discouerie, disclosure, v. v. 33.

discourse, course of arms or combat, vi. viii. 14.

discourteise, discourteous, iii. i. 55.

discreet, becoming, suitable, moderate, ii. xii. 71.

discust, *pa. part.* shaken off (*fig.*), iii. i. 48.

disdeigned, *pret.* thought unworthy, *R. T.* p. 471.

disease, *sb.* trouble, distress, iii. v. 19, vi. v. 40, ix. 19.

disease, *vb.* to incommode, trouble, i. xi. 38, ii. ii. 12, 24, *S. C. July* 124, *Worlds Vanitie* 28. **diseased**, *ppl. adj.* troubled, afflicted, vi. iii. 22, *Hubberd* 40.

disentrayle, to draw forth from the entrails or inward parts, iv. vi. 16, v. ix. 19. **disentrayled**, *ppl. adj.* iv. iii. 28.

disgrace, ill-favouredness, v. xii. 28.

disguizement, disguise, iii. vii. 14, iv. v. 29.

dishabled, *pret.* disparaged, ii. v. 21.

disherited, *pa. part.* dispossessed, banished from its rightful domain, *S. C. Epistle* p. 417.

disinherit, to prevent from taking possession (*fig.*), v. v. 36.

disleall, disloyal, ii. v. 5.

dislikefull, distasteful, iv. ix. 40.

disloignd, *pa. part.* distant, removed, iv. x. 24.

dismall day, one of the *dies mali* or unpropitious days, ii. vii. 26, viii. 51.

dismay, *sb.* faintheartedness, terror, ii. xi. 41; ruin, v. ii. 50; dismaying influence, *Amor. Son.* 88.

dismay, *vb.* to defeat, ii. v. 38, iii. iv. 25, v. ii. 8, vi. x. 13; to grieve (*refl.*), iv. i. 40. **dismayd**, **-id**, *pa. part.* defeated, iii. i. 29; grieved, iv. i. 37; daunted, v. xi. 26.

dismayd, *ppl. adj.* ill-made, misshapen, ii. xi. 11.

dismayfull, appalling, v. xi. 26.

dismayfully, in dismay, v. viii. 38.

dismayld, *pret.* stript the mail of, ii. vi. 29.

dispace, to walk or move about, *Gnat* 265 (*refl.*). **dispacing**, *pres. part.*, *Muiop.* 250.

disparage, *sb.* misalliance, unequal match, iv. viii. 50.

disparaged, *pa. part.* cast down, ii. x. 2.

disparagement, disgrace of a misalliance, iii. viii. 12; low rank, iv. vii. 16.

dispart, to part asunder, cleave, i. x. 53, iii. xii 38, iv. ix. 1.

dispatcht, *pret.* freed, relieved, vi. iii. 10.

dispence, *sb.* dispensing or bestowing liberally, liberality, hospitality, ii. ix. 29, xii. 42, v. xi. 45.

dispence, *vb.* to make amends, i. iii. 30, v. xi. 45.

dispiteous, unpitying, i. ii. 15.

display, to stretch out, spread out, ii. v. 30, x. 15, iii. ii. 47, *Epith.* 303; *intr.*, *S. C. May* 196; to descry, discover, ii. xii. 76; to expose, ii. xii. 66. **displaid, -yed**, *pa. part.* spread out, stretched out, i. i. 16, ii. v. 32, *Gnat* 240, *Love* 286.

disple, to subject to penance, i. x. 27.

displeasance, displeasure, ii. x. 28, iv. vi. 4.

displease, to annoy, III. v. 19.

disport, entertainment, amusement, sport, pleasure, I. ii. 14, II. vi. 26, III. i. 40.

disporting, *pres. part.* sporting, frolicking, *Daphn.* 118.

dispraise, -ze, to disparage, depreciate, VI. viii. 26, *R. T.* 229.

dispred, **dispredden**, to spread out, abroad, I. iv. 17, II. ii. 40, III. v. 51, v. xii. 13; (*intr.*) IV. vii. 40. **disprad**, *pa. part.* v. xii. 36. **dispred**, -dd, *pa. part.* and *ppl. adj.* II. iii. 30, p. 412 (*fig.*), *Gnat* 242.

disprofesse, to renounce the profession of, III. xi. 20.

dispuruayance, want of provisions, III. x. 10.

disquietnesse, trouble, unrest, II. vii. 12.

disseise, -ze, to deprive, dispossess, I. xi. 20, VII. vii. 48.

disshiuered, *ppl. adj.* shattered to pieces, IV. i. 21.

dissolute, enfeebled, weak, I. vii. 51; wanton, III. viii. 14.

distaine, to stain, III. iv. 17. **distaind**, -ynd, *pa. part.* stained, I. xi. 23, III. viii. 49, *S. C. Oct.* 110; sullied, defiled (*fig.*), II. iv. 22.

distent, *pa. part.* extended, beaten out, II. vii. 5.

disthronize, to dethrone, II. x. 44.

distinct, *pa. part.* marked, VI. iii. 23.

distort, *ppl. adj.* distorted, wry, awry, IV. i. 28, v. xii. 36.

distraine, to oppress, afflict, I. vii. 38; to pull off, tear asunder, II. xii. 82.

distraught, *pa. part.* distracted, distressed, I. ix. 38, IV. iii. 48, *R. T.* 579; pulled asunder, drawn in different directions, IV. vii. 31, v. v. 2.

distraughted, *ppl. adj.* distracted, *H. Beautie* 14.

distroubled, *ppl. adj.* greatly troubled, III. iv. 12.

dit, ditty, II. vi. 13.

dites (*for* **dights**), lifts, raises, I. viii. 18.

diueling, young devil, imp, *Three Lett.* p. 625.

diuers, *adv.* differently, IV. v. 11.

diuerse, diverting, distracting, I. i. 10, 44, II. ii. 3, IV. i. 5.

diuersly, in different ways, v. v. 2.

diuerst, *pret.* turned aside, III. iii. 62.

diuide, to perform with 'divisions'; to descant, I. v. 17, III. i. 40; to penetrate, I. xi. 18; to dispense, v. Prol. 9; to allocate, *Clout* 761; to give forth in various directions, *Amor.* Son. 6.

diuin'd, *pa. part. R. T.* 611: **diuinde**, *ppl.*

adj. Daphn. 214: rendered divine. **diuynd**, *pa. part.*, *Clout* 896: described.

diuorced, *pa. part.* separated, I. iii. 2.

do, **doe**, to cause, make, I. vii. 14, II. vi. 7, III. ii. 34, iii. 39, v. 50, vii. 32, ix. 17, v. ix. 35, VI. v. 28. **doen**, *inf. arch.* to do, cause, make, I. xii. 19, II. iii. 12, III. iv. 22. **done**, *inf.* III. i. 28, ii. 23. **donne**, *inf.* III. vii. 12, VI. x. 32. **doen**, *pa. part.* I. iii. 14, 39, III. x. 32; *doen* (*done*) *be dead, to dye* = put to death, *pa. part.*, v. iv. 29, VI. viii. 29. **donne**, *pa. part.* IV. vi. 5. **doen**, *3rd pers. plur. arch.* I. iii. 36, II. i. 29, III. iv. 1, *S. C. Feb.* 6; *to doe away* = to banish, remove, I. iii. 39, III. ii. 33, VI. xi. 29; *for nothing good to donne* = good-for-nothing, III. vii. 12; *hardly doen* = done with difficulty, I. iii. 14; *well to donne* = well-doing, I. x. 33. **doon**, *pa. part.*, *Amor.* Son. 16.

doale, distribution, dealing (of blows), v. iv. 39.

dock, buttocks (*lit.* tail), *Three Lett.* p. 625.

doctorally, in the manner of a doctor, learnedly, *Three Lett.* p. 614.

document, instruction, teaching, I. x. 19.

doffing, *pres. part.* taking off. **dofte**, *pret.* III. iv. 5, ix. 21.

dole, IV. vii. Arg., v. xi. 14, *Hubberd* 1244, *Clout* 22. **doole**, grief, sorrow, II. xii. 20, III. x. 17, xi. 7, v. xi. 25, VI. vii. 39, *S. C. Feb.* 155, *Aug.* 165; mourning, lamentation, IV. viii. 3.

dolor, **dolour**, grief, III. ii. 17, IV. viii. 3, *S. C. Nov.* 104.

Dolphinet, *pseudonym*, *Clout* 866.

don, to put on, wear, III. vi. 38, VI. viii. 24.

donne, dun, dark, *S. C. May* 265.

doome, decree, I. ix. 41; judgement, II. v. 12, vii. 62, IV. iv. 36, *S. C. Aug.* 135; opinion, IV. x. 21; fate, v. iv. 39. **dome**, punishment, IV. xi. 38.

doomefull, fateful, VI. vi. 22, *Misc. Sonn.* 1.

dooue, dove, *Three Lett.* p. 626.

dortour, sleeping-room, VI. xii. 24.

doted, stupid, I. viii. 34.

doubt, *sb.* fear, III. v. 12, VI. ii. 29, viii. 32; danger, risk, v. xi. 47.

doubt, *vb.* to fear, v. xi. 2, VI. iv. 27.

doubted, redoubted, *S. C. Oct.* 41.

doubtful, fearful, apprehensive, I. vi. 12, VI. ii. 29, *S. C. May* 294; awful, II. i. 22; *adv.* II. vii. 6.

doucepere, one of the twelve peers of Charlemagne celebrated in mediaeval romances, III. x. 31.

dout, fear, III. xii. 37, v. xi. 18; doubt, IV. i. 11, 14.

douehouse, dovecot, *Three Lett.* p. 627.

dowe, dough, *Three Lett*. p. 631.

drad, *pret*. dreaded, feared, II. i. 45, III. xii. 18, v. vii. 38, x. 18; *pa. part*. II. iv. 42; *ppl. adj.* VII. vi. 3, 25.

draft, attraction, IV. ii. 10.

drapet, cloth, II. ix. 27.

draught, plot, artifice, II. x. 51; drawing, stroke, IV. vii. 31.

draue, *pret*. drove, *Gnat* 162.

dread, fury, II. v. 16.

dreadfull, fearful, apprehensive, III. i. 37; awe-inspiring, v. vii. 40.

dreadlesse, fearless, v. iii. 11.

dreare, *sb*. fall, IV. viii. 42; grief, sadness, v. x. 35; stroke, v. xii. 20; mishap, misfortune, VI. ii. 46, iii. 4. **drere**, dreariness, sadness, gloom, I. viii. 40, II. xii. 36.

dreare, *adj*. dreadful, II. xi. 8.

drearing, sorrow, grief, *Daphn*. 189.

dred, *sb*. I. Prol. 4, IV. viii. 17; dread, III. ii. 30; **dreed**, I. vi. 2 : object of reverence, attention. **dreed**, injury, II. xii. 26.

dreddest, most dreadful, IV. ii. 32.

drenched, *pa. part*. drowned, IV. xi. 38, (*fig.*) VI. iii. 10.

drent, *pa. part*. drowned, II. vi. 49, vii. 61, xii. 6, *S. C. Nov*. 37, *Gnat* 585; (*fig.*) *Teares* 210, *Clorinda* 94.

drerihed, drearyhead, dreariness, grief, III. i. 16, 62, ii. 30, *Past. Elegie* 133; dismalness, gloom, III. xii. 17, *Muiop*. 347.

dreriment, dreeriment, dreariness, grief, sorrow, I. ii. 44, viii. 9, III. iv 30, *S. C. Nov.* 36, *R. T*. 158, *Epith*. 11.

ᵈˢ .. y, bloody, gory, I. vi. 45.

dresse, to arrange, prepare, III. xi. 20. **drest**, *pret*. I. ix. 54; carried on, IV. x. 54.

dreuill, a dirty or foul person (*orig*. a slave), IV. ii. 3.

drift, impetus, I. viii. 22; plan, plot, I. ii. 9, II. xii. 69; aim, object, III. x. 6, v. ix. 42, p. 409.

driue, to pass, spend, *Gnat* 154. **driue**, *pret*. drove, struck, v. xi. 5. **driuen**, *pa. part*. smelted, II. vii. 5.

drizling, falling in fine drops (of tears, water), I. iii. 6, *S. C. Jan*. 41, *Amor*. Son. 18.

dromedare, dromedary, IV. viii. 38.

droome, drum, I. ix. 41.

drouping, drooping, fading, I. i. 36, II. x. 30.

drouth, drought, thirst, II. vii. 57.

drouer, boat (used for fishing), III. viii. 22.

drowsy-hed, drowsiness, I. ii. 7.

droyle, to drudge, slave, *Hubberd* 157.

drugs, medicine, II. i. 54.

dryrihed, *see* drerihed.

dub adubbe, scuffle, fight, *Three Lett*. p. 615.

duefull, *see* dewfull.

dumpish, dull, heavy, sad, IV. ii. 5, *Amor*. Son. 4.

dumps, depression, *Amor*. Son. 52.

dunglecocke, dunghill cock, i. e. coward, *Three Lett*. p. 621

duraunce, captivity, III. v. 42.

durefull, lasting, enduring, IV. x. 39, *Amor*. Son. 6.

duresse, confinement, constraint, IV. viii. 19, xii. 10.

dye, hazard, I. ii. 36.

E

each where, everywhere, I. x. 54, *Muiop*. 376, *Thest*. 84, *Clout* 634.

earne, to yearn, long, I. i. 3, VI. 25, ix. 18, II. iii. 46, III. x. 21, *S. C. March* 77 ; to be grieved, IV. xii. 24 ; to become angry, *Muiop*. 254.

earnest, pledge, VI. xi. 40.

earst, erst, formerly, a short time ago, lately, I. v. 9, xi. 27, III. ii. 27, viii. 2, 3, VI. iii. 8, *S. C. Oct.* 7. **at earst, erst** = at first, formerly, II. i. 29, iv. 39, VI. iii. 8 ; at length, now, II. vi. 49, v. Prol. 2, VI. iii. 8, *S. C. Dec.* 105 ; at once, *S. C. Sept.* 6.

easement, relief, VI. iv. 15.

Easterlings, inhabitants of eastern countries, such as Eastern Germany and the Baltic coasts, II. x 63.

eath, ethe, easy, II. iii. 40, IV. xi. 53, *S. C. July* 90, *Sept.* 17, *Muiop*. 311 ; ready, susceptible, IV. vi. 40 ; easily, *Hubberd* 404.

edgd, *pret*. stimulated, IV. ii. 17.

edifyde, -ide, built, I. i. 34 (*pa. part.*), *Gnat* 660 ; III. i. 14 (*ppl. adj.*); *R. T*. 551 (*pret.*).

eeke, eke, *vb*. to augment, increase, I. v. 42, III. ii. 35, VI. 22, vii. 55, v. xii. 35. **eekt**, *pa. part*. lengthened, IV. ii. 53 ; **eeked**, increased *S. C. Sept.* 30.

eeking, *vbl. sb*. increasing, *S. C. Sept.* 31.

effierced, *pa. part*. rendered fierce, maddened, III. xi. 27. Cf. **enfierced**.

efforce, to violate by force, I. vi. 4 ; to force out, III. ii. 15, v. ix. 47 ; to force open, III. ix. 9, xii. 27. **efforced**, *ppl. adj*. uttered with effort, forced out, II. viii. 4. **efforst**, *pa. part*. compelled by force, III. xii. 43.

effórt, III. i. 52, xi. 46, v. ii. 5.

effraide, *ppl. adj*. frightened, I. i. 16.

eft, afterwards, II. iv. 18, viii. 41, *S. C. Feb.* 42 ; again, IV. iii. 21, VI. ix. 1, *Beautie* 114 ; also, *S. C. Sept.* 191, *Gnat* 536.

eftsoones, forthwith, I. i. 11, III. i. 31, v. viii. 45.

eide, *pa. part.* kept in view, aimed at, II. iv. 7; seen, IV. iv. 7.

eie, aye, ever, II. iii. 19.

eine, eyes, p. 409, *Elegie* 64. Cf. eyen.

eke, *adv.* also, II. i. 21, p. 411, *S. C. Jan.* 51, *May* 86, p. 434.

eld, old age, age, I. viii. 47, x. 7, II. iii. 16, IV. ii. 33, xi. 24, VII. vii. 13, 31, *S. C. Feb.* 54, 206, *Dec.* 134.

elect, *ppl. adj.* chosen, III. vii. 22.

election, choice, v. v. 26, *Amor.* Son. 84.

elfe, (1) name applied to a knight, I. i. 17, v. 2, II. vii. 7; (2) a masculine supernatural creature, II. x. 71, III. iii. 26; (3) creature, IV. v. 34.

elfin, elfish, I. iv. 42, x. 65; elf, I. x. 60.

Eliseïs, *pseudonym, Clout* 403.

ellope, to run away, v. v. 9.

elocution, literary style, *S. C. Epistle* p. 419.

els, else, already, formerly, I. v. 43; or else, II. viii. 33, *S. C. March* 114; otherwise, elsewhere, II. ix. 8, III. vi. 16, IV. v. 28, *Hubberd* 1203.

embace, -se, to humble, humiliate, III. vii. 15, VI. i. 3, vi. 20 (*refl.*), *R. R.* 110; to lower, *Daphn.* 180, *Amor.* Son. 13. embased, *pa. part.* degraded, *Amor.* Son. 82. embaste, *pret.* dishonoured, III. i. 12; *pa. part.* III. ix. 33.

embard, *pa. part.* confined, imprisoned, I. ii. 31, vii. 44, III. xi. 16.

embase, embaste, *see* embace.

embássade, *quasi-adv.* on an embassy, *Beautie* 251.

embássage, message, III. ix. 28.

embathed, *ppl. adj.* fragrant (*ellipt. for* embathed in perfume), *Muiop.* 194.

embatteld, -eild, *ppl. adj.* armed for battle, II. v. 2, v. viii. 34.

embaulm'd, *pa. part.* anointed, IV. vii. 40.

embay, to bathe, I. x. 27, II. i. 40, xii. 60 (*refl.*); to bask, *Muiop.* 206. embayd, *pret.* bathed (*fig.*), pervaded, suffused, I. ix. 13, III. vi. 7; *pa. part.* II. viii. 55, III. xii. 21.

embayed, *ppl. adj.* furnished with a bay, IV. xi. 44.

embayld, *pa. part.* enclosed, II. iii. 27.

embellisht, *pa. part.* adorned, *S. C. Feb.* 118.

embosome, to cherish, embrace (*fig.*), II. iv. 25; to plunge, implant (*fig.*), II. xii. 29.

embosse [1], *pa. part.* embost, adorned, III. i. 32, IV. iv. 15, *S. C. Feb.* 66.

embosse [2], *pa. part.* embost, driven to extremity, hard pressed (of a hunted animal), III. i. 22, xii. 17; *embost with bale* = exhausted (cf. embosse [5]), I. ix. 29.

embosse [3], to plunge, I. xi. 20; to cover, encase, III. i. 64 (cf. embosse [1]). embost, *pa. part.* covered, encased (in armour), I. iii. 24; *in ease embost* = 'wrapped' in ease, VI. iv. 40.

embowd, *pa. part.* encircled, I. ix. 19. embowed, *ppl. adj.*, *Worlds Vanitie* 17.

embowelled, *pa. part.* disembowelled, III. vii. 29; thrust into the bowels (*fig.*), VI. viii. 15.

embowring, *pres. part.* sheltering (*intr.*), *Gnat* 225.

emboyled, *ppl. adj.* agitated, I. xi. 28; *pres. part.* II. iv. 9, v. 18, boiling (with anger).

embrace [1], to fasten, buckle on (arms), II. i. 26.

embrace [2], to protect, III. viii. 29; to love, VI. i. 3. embraste, *pret.* grasped, II. iv. 14.

embracement, embrace, II. iv. 26, III. viii. 10.

embraue, to adorn, II. i. 60, *S. C. Nov.* 109, *R. R.* 394.

embreaded, *pa. part.* plaited, braided, III. vi. 18.

embrew, to plunge, I. xi. 36, II. i. 37, III. xii. 32, *R. R.* 330; to pour, emit moisture, II. v. 33; to stain (with blood), VI. viii. 40, *Bellay* 77; to imbue, *H. Love* 47. embrewed, *ppl. adj.* blood-stained, III. vi. 17.

embrodered, *ppl. adj.* embroidered, III. xii. 9 v. iii. 33.

embusied, *pa. part.* occupied, IV. vii. 29.

eme, uncle, II. x. 47.

emeraude, emerald, II. xii. 54.

emmarble, to convert into marble (*fig.*), *Love* 139.

emmoue, to move (*fig.*), I. ii. 21, II. i. 50. emmoued, *pa. part.* II. vii. 51, III. xi. 4, xii. 2; enmoued, I. vii. 38, ix. 48.

emong, among, II. xii. 10.

emongst, amongst, I. Prol. 1, viii. 37, III. i. 39, iii. 47.

empaire, I. vii. 41, II. x. 30, v. iv. 40, xi. 48 (to injure); empare, I. x. 63: to diminish, impair.

empale, to encircle, border, *Muiop.* 297.

emparlance, -aunce, treaty, parleying, IV. ix. 31, v. iv. 50.

empart, to assign, IV. vi. 32.

empassion, to excite deeply, *Worlds Vanitie* 12, *Daphn.* 35. *pa. part.* empassioned, I. iii. 2, III. ix. 38, xi. 18, *Daphn.* 515; empassionate, v. ix. 46, *Daphn.* 193: stirred, excited by passion.

empeach, *sb.* injury, detriment, II. xii. 56.

empeach, *vb.* to hinder, I. viii. 34, II. vii. 15, III. iii. 53, xi. 12, VI. ii. 42, IV. 11, 19.

empeopled, *pa. part.* established as the population, I. x. 56.

emperill, to imperil, endanger, IV. iv. 10.

emperisht, -ed, *pa. part.* enfeebled, III. vii. 20, *S. C. Feb.* 53.

empierce, to penetrate (*fig.*), *Clout* 431.
pret. **emperced** (*fig.*), II. ii. 1 ; **empierst**,
I. xi. 53, II. viii. 45, IV. xii. 19 (*fig.*) ; **empierced**, III. v. 19, xi. 41. **empierst**, *pa.
part.* (*fig.*), III. ix. 39. **empierced**, *ppl. adj.*
(*fig.*), *Daphn.* 6.

empight, fixed in, implanted, penetrated : *pret.*
II. iv. 46, III. v. 20, IV. iii. 10, v. x. 32 ; *pa.
part.* VI. xii. 27, *Beautie* 49.

empíre, VII. vi. 21.

emplonged, *pa. part.* plunged, III. x. 17.

empoysned, *pa. part.* III. v. 49 ; *ppl. adj.* III.
vi. 13 : poisoned.

emprize, -se, enterprise, undertaking (of a
chivalrous nature), I. ix. 1, xii. 18, II. iv. 12,
vii. 39, v. iii. 15, iv. 2, vi. iv. 33 ; *plur.*, *S. C.
Sept.* 83.

empurpled, *pa. part.* made purple, reddened,
II. xii. 54, III. vii. 17, IV. vii. 6 ; *pret.* III. xii.
33.

empyring, *ppl. adj.* ruling, p. 409.

enaunter, in case, lest by chance, *S. C. Feb.*
200, *May* 78, *Sept.* 161.

enbracement, embrace, I. ii. 5.

enbrewd, *pa. part.* stained, I. vii. 17. *See*
embrew.

enchace, to set, serve as a setting for, I. xii.
23 (*fig.*), v. i. 11 ; to depict, IV. v. 12 ; to en-
grave (*fig.*), VI. iv. 35. *pa. part.* **enchaced**,
-sed, IV. x. 8, *S. C. Aug.* 27 ; to close in,
enclose, v. x. 34. *pa. part.* **enchaste**,
Hubberd 624. **enchaced**, -sed, *pa. part.*
adorned, II. ix. 24, *Amor.* Son. 82.

encheare, to cheer, encourage, VII. vi. 24.

encheason, occasion, cause, II. i. 30, *S. C.
May* 147, *Sept.* 116.

enclynd, *pret.* assented, VI. vii. 37.

encomberment, disturbance, VI. viii. 38.

encroch, to come on, advance, VI. xi. 47, *S. C.
Feb.* 226.

endamadge, to injure, II. iii. 18 ; *pret.* v.
viii. 14 ; *pa. part.* VI. xii. 38.

endangerment, danger, v. ii. 20.

endeuourment, endeavour, *Hubberd* 298.

endew, to endow, I. iv. 51, v. i. 2, VI. x. 14,
VII. vii. 45, *S. C.* p. 433, *Beautie* 135.

endighting, *vbl. sb.* inditing, composing,
Sonnets p. 603.

endite[1], to censure, VI. xii. 41.

endite[2], to give a literary form to, *Past.
Aeglogue* 33.

endlong, from end to end, III. ix. 51, x. 19.

endosse, to inscribe, portray (on the back), v.
xi. 53, *Clout* 632.

endur'd, *pret.* hardened, strengthened, IV. viii.
27.

ene, even, *S. C. Dec.* 93.

enfelon'd, *ppl. adj.* infuriated, v. viii. 48.

enfierced, *pa. part.* rendered fierce, II. iv. 8.
Cf. **efflerced.**

enforce, to drive with force, IV. iv. 35 ; to
emphasize, v. ix. 43 ; to strive, attempt, *Clout*
481.

enforme, to affect, inspire, VI. vi. 3.

enfouldred, *ppl. adj.* like a thunder-cloud, I.
xi. 40.

enfrosen, *pa. part.* frozen (*fig.*), *Love* 146.

enfyre, to harden by fire, *Love* 169.

engine, trick, plot, II. i. 23, iv. 27 ; *plur.*
wiles, III. i. 57, x. 7, *Amor.* Son. 14.

engirt, *pa. part.* girt, surrounded, IV. vii. 7,
H. Beautie 37.

englut, to glut, fill (*fig.*), II. ii. 23.

engore, to goad, infuriate (*fig.*), II. viii. 42;
to wound deeply (*refl.*), VI. vii. 9. **engored**,
pa. part. gored, wounded, III. i. 38, v. 28;
ppl. adj. IV. ix. 31

engorge, to swallow up (*fig.*), II. xii. 3. **engorged**, *ppl. adj.* devoured (*fig.*), I. xi. 40.

engraffed, *ppl. adj.* III. ii. 17 ; **engraft**, *pa.
part.* IV. ii. 10 : implanted.

engrained, *pa. part.* dyed, *S. C. Feb.* 131,
Gnat 666.

engrasped, *pret.* II. viii. 49 ; *pa. part.* II. v.
20 : grasped, seized.

engraue[1], to bury, I. x. 42, II. i. 60.

engraue[2], to make (wounds) by incision, III.
vii. 32 ; to cut into, III. viii. 37.

engrieved, *ppl. adj.* II. iv. 23 (ee), III. i. 59,
IV. viii. 7, VI. viii. 34, *Worlds Vanitie* 159;
pa. part. III. vi. 21 : grieved.

engrosse, to take possession of, III. iv. 38 ; to
write in large letters, *Clout* 634. **engrost**,
pa. part. thickened, rendered gross, dense, II.
vi. 46, III. iv. 13.

enhaunse, to raise, lift, I. i. 17, v. 47 (*fig.*), II.
vi. 31; to exalt, *Clout* 359. **enhaunced**,
ppl. adj. lifted.

enlarge, -en, to set free, I. viii. 37, II. v. 18,
viii. 61, ix. 13. **enlargd**, *pa. part.* II. v. 19.

enlumine, to illuminate, shed lustre on, II. ix.
4, v. Prol. 7, *S. C.* p. 417; *pa. part. Amor.*
Son. 66 (*fig.*), *Love* 108 (*fig.*).

enmoued, *see* **emmoue.**

enrace, to implant, III. v. 52 ; *pa. part.* VI. x.
25, *Beautie* 114.

euragement, rapture, *H. Love* 286.

enranckled, *pa. part.* enraged, III. viii. 2.

enraunged, -anged, *pa. part.* placed in a row,
rank, arranged, I. xi. 13, xii. 7, III. vi. 35, xii. 5,
H. Beautie 83, *Proth.* 122. **enraunging**,
pres. part. ranging, rambling in, VI. ii. 9.

enriuen, *ppl. adj.* torn, v. viii. 34, *Clorinda* 4 (*fig.*).

enrold, *pa. part.* enfolded, wrapped up, II. xii. 25, IV. iii. 41 ; coiled, VI. vi. 11, *Gnat* 257 ; formed into a roll, VII. vii. 30.

ensample, imitation, p. 407 ; warning, *R. T.* 462.

enseam, to contain, IV. xi. 35.

ensew, ensewen, to follow, I. iv. 40, v. 25, III. i. 45, v. iv. 15, *Teares* 54. ensew'd, *pret.* VI. iii. 50; to pursue, III. xi. 5,(a profession) IV. ii. 46. ensue, to result from, I. iv. 34 ; to follow, II. iii. 2 ; to pursue (a profession), p. 412; *pres. part.* IV. ix. 5. ensude, *pa. part.* imitated, II. xii. 59.

ensnarle, to catch, ensnare, v. ix. 9.

entayl, *vb.* to penetrate, cut, II. vi. 29 ; entayld, *pa. part.* carved, II. iii. 27.

entayle, *sb.* carving, ornamentation, II. vii. 4.

entent, intent, intention, *S. C. May* 102. Cf. intent.

enterdeale, negotiation, v. viii. 21; intercourse, *Hubberd* 785.

enterprise, -ze, *sb.* attempt, undertaking, I. viii. 15, v. x. Arg.

enterpris, -se, -ze, *vb.* to entertain, II. ii. 14 ; to attempt, undertake, II. i. 19, v. viii. 11, VI. viii. 18 ; to attempt to obtain, procure, IV. xii. 28. enterprizd, *pa. part.* undertaken, I. vii. 45. enterprised, *ppl. adj.* attempted, III. xi. 24.

entertaine, to treat, I. iii. 43 ; to accept, receive (pay), II. ix. 6 ; to show hospitality to, receive as a guest, v. xii. 10, *Hubberd* 235 ; to take (a way), VI. iv. 24; to encounter, meet with, VI. xi. 34, *Gnat* 563; to treat of, *Amor.* Son. 12 ; to engage in, *Hubberd* 398.

entertainment, provisions, hospitality, I. x. 37, II. ii. 35.

entertake, to entertain, v. ix. 35.

entertayne, hospitality, IV. viii. 27, v. ix. 37 ; reception, welcome, *Hubberd* 1085.

entire, *adj.* fresh, I. vi. 44 ; all of one piece, I. vii. 33 ; perfect, genuine, sincere, I. viii. 40, III. ii. 44, vii. 16, IV. v. 4, ix. 13, v. xi. 61, vI. v. 38, viii. 3, *H. Love* 157 ; strong, III. i. 47. *parts entire* = inward, internal parts, IV. viii. 23, 48, v. vii. 37, *Amor.* Son. 6, 85, *H. Love* 271 ; *mind e.*, *Beautie* 223.

entire, *adv.* entirely, altogether, II. v. 8, viii. 15, vI. viii. 15; sincerely, earnestly, vI. v. 23.

entirely, earnestly, I. xi. 32, III. ix. 51, vI. vii. 22.

entitled, *pa. part.* dedicated, p. 415.

entraile, twisting, coil, I. i. 16.

entrailed, entrayld, entrayled, *pa. part.* entwined, interlaced, II. iii. 27, v. 29, III. vi. 44, xi. 46, IV. iii. 42, *S. C. Aug.* 30, *Proth.* 25.

entrall, -e, interior, II. xii. 6, 25.

entrayle, mind, thought, vI. xi. 41.

entreat, to occupy oneself in, II. vii. 53; to treat, deal with, IV. x. 10, vI. i. 40, *Hubberd* 922, *Misc. Sonn.* 1 ; to treat of, describe, v. i. 1.

entrenchéd, *pa. part.* pierced, III. xii. 20.

enure, to make use of, IV. ii. 29; to exercise, *Amor.* p. 578, *Three Lett.* p. 611. enur'd, *pa. part.* inured, accustomed, IV. viii. 27, vI. viii. 14 ; committed, v. ix. 39.

énuíe, *sb.* emulation, III. i. 18. énuy, envy, III. iv. 47, v. 54, ix. 38.

enuíe, *vb.* to have malevolent feelings, be angry, II. ii. 19. *pret.* enuýde, IV. iv. 44. enuý, to grudge, I. ix. 1, III. v. 50, vI. viii. 4.

enwallowed, *pa. part.* rolled, III. iv. 34, v. xi. 14.

enwombed, *pa. part.* pregnant, II. i. 50, x. 50, v. vii. 16 ; contained (as in a womb), *R. R.* 67.

enwrap, to capture (as in a fold), *Past. Elegie* 98. enwrapt, *pret.* wrapped, I. xi. 23.

epiphonema, sentence or reflection concluding a discourse, *S. C.* p. 440. epiphonematicos, in the form of an epiphonema, *S. C.* p. 459.

equal, equitable, impartial, vII. vi. 35 l. 1.

equalise, to equal, III. ix. 44.

equipage, *sb.* equipment, retinue, I. xi. 6, IV. xi. 17, *S. C. Oct.* 114.

equipaged, *pa. part.* arrayed, equipped, II. ix. 17.

equipollent, equivalent, *Three Lett.* p. 631.

ere, ever, *S. C. Oct.* 33.

ere many yeares, many years ago, v. iv. 7.

erect, to set up, establish, vI. vi. 34.

erewhile, before, formerly, IV. xi. 2.

ermelin, ermine (animal) ; stoat, III. ii. 25.

ermine, fur of ermine, III. i. 59.

erne, *see* earne.

errant, wandering, I. x. 10, III. viii. 6, vI. v. 11.

erst, *see* earst.

eschew, to escape, IV. viii. 56, vI. viii. 50 ; to avoid, *Amor.* Son. 62. eschewd, *pa. part.* untroubled, avoided, II. x. 13.

esloyne (*refl.*), to withdraw, I. iv. 20.

espiall, sight, glimpse, IV. x. 17 ; appearance, v. iv. 15.

essoyne, exemption, I. iv. 20.

estate, state, condition, I. iii. 7, IV. ii. 20; rank, vI. ii. 27.

estraunged, *pa. part.* removed abroad, *S. C. Epistle* p. 418.

eterne, eternal, III. vi. 37, 47.

etérnize, to render eternal, immortal, *Teares* 582; *pa. part.* I. x. 59. **éternize,** *Amor.* Son. 75.

ethe, *see* eath.

eugh, yew, I. i. 9.

euzhen, ewghen, of yew, I. xi. 19, *Hubberd* 747

Eúphrates, IV. xi. 21.

euangely, gospel, II. x. 53.

euent, fate, *Teares* 143; fortune, *Gnat* 534.

euill, poor, unskilful, VI. xi. 40.

ewfte, eft, newt, V. x. 23.

exanimate, *ppl. adj.* lifeless, II. xii. 7.

excheat, gain, I. v. 25; personal property, which fell by escheat (*fig.*), III. viii. 16.

excrement, overflow, IV. xi. 35.

expell, to discharge (an arrow), II. xi. 24.

experiment, *sb.* experience, practice, II. vii. 1, v. ii. 17.

experimented, *ppl. adj.* experienced, practised, proved, *Two Lett.* p. 639.

expért, *vb.* to experience, *S. C. Nov.* 186.

expért, *adj.* or *pa. part.* experienced, tried, II. vii. 1, IV. xi. 19, V. ii. 16, VI. i. 36.

expire, to fulfil a term, I. vii. 9; to breathe out, I. xi. 45; to bring to an end, IV. i. 54; to continue for, IV. vi. 43.

exprest, *pret.* expelled, ejected, II. x. 43; *pa. part.* crushed out, II. xi. 42.

extasie, astonishment, VII. vi. 23.

extent, *pa. part.* stretched out, II. vii. 61.

extirpe, to root out, I. x. 25.

extold, *pa. part.* raised, VII. vii. 37.

extort, *pa. part.* extorted, V. ii. 5, III. 30, X. 25.

extract, *pa. part.* descended, III. ix. 38.

extreamitie, extreme suffering, *Daphn.* 185

extreate, extraction, V. x. i.

extrinsecall, external, *Three Lett.* p. 615.

exul, exile, *Clout* 894.

eyas (*attrib.*), a young newly-fledged or -trained hawk, I. xi. 34, *H. Love* 24 (*fig.*).

eyde, *pa. part.* perceived, caught sight of, *Clout* 267. Cf. eide.

eye, a brood (of pheasants), *S. C.* p. 434.

eyen, -ne, eyes, I. ii. 27, iv. 9, 21, x. 47, III. vii. 9, VI. xi. 22.

F

face, to maintain a false appearance, V. ix. 5.

fact, deed, I. iv. 34, ix. 37, III. viii. 32, ix. 38, v. ix. 43.

fail, to deceive, II. v. 11, III. xi. 46, IV. xii. 23.

fain. -e, *adj.* eager, I. i. 6, IV. vi. 33; apt, wont, IV. viii. 37; glad, I. vi. 12, VI. iv. 16,

S. C. Feb. 67, *May* 305; *adv.* gladly, with pleasure, I. iv. 10, V. xii. 10.

fain, fayne, *vb.*[1] to delight, rejoice, V. xii. 36.

fain'd, *pret.* desired, III. ix. 24, VI. iii. 9.

fayning, *ppl. adj.* longing, wistful, *Love* 216.

faine, fayne, feyne, feign, *vb.*[2] to feign, pretend, I. vii. 38, xii. 35, II. i. 9, IV. iv. 47, *S. C. Sept.* 137; to disguise, hide, II. iii. 20; to mistake, IV. vii. 15; to fashion, form, VI. viii. 44; to imagine wrongly, VI. xii. 19; *refl.* to imagine, *Love* 210. **fained, fayned,** *pret.* were anxious, V. viii. 24; *ppl. adj.* pretended, I. i. 50, ii. 39; disguised, I. xii. 10, IV. i 7; imaginary, III. xii. 43.

faire, *adv.* gently, I. vii. 29; cleverly, I. viii. 7.

fairely, completely, entirely, IV. vi. 13; gently, II. vi. 40.

faitor, faytor, -our, vagabond, villain, impostor, I. iv. 47, xii. 35, IV. i. 44, iii. 11, VI. i. 18, iv. 1, *S. C. May* 39, 170.

fall, fallen, to befall, II. xii. 68, IV. i. 44, *S. C. May* 50, *June* 76; *fall with* = to make (land), V. xii. 4.

false, *adj.* weak, insecure, I. xi. 54.

false, *vb.* to be false to, betray, deceive, *S. C.* p. 440; *ppl. adj.* I. ii. 30, II. xii. 44, III. i. 47; *falsed his blowes* = made a feint, II. v. 9.

falser, deceiver, *S. C. May* 305, *Dec.* p. 467.

falses, *sb.* falsehoods, V. ii. 48.

fancie, imagination, *Beautie* 222.

fantasy, -zy, fancy, II. xii. 42, *S. C. Aug.* 22; apprehension, VI. ix. 12.

fare, *sb.* departure, journey, V. x. 16; food, *S. C. Jan.* 44.

fare, *vb.* to go, proceed, I. i. 11, iii. 16, II. i. 4, ii. 12, V. x. 17; to act, proceed, IV. ix. 27, VI. xi. 48, xii. 31; *far'd with* = employed, used, IV. vi. 41.

farre forth, farforth, far, III. Prol. 3, IX. 53.

fast, *ppl. adj.* having a face, II. xi. 12.

fastned, *pret.* attached herself, III. ii. 26; took hold, V. iv. 15; *ppl. adj.* settled, confirmed, *H. Beautie* 286.

fastnesse, security, safety, V. ix. 5, x. 18.

fatal, ordained by fate, III. iii. 2, ix. 49.

fate, destined term of life, III. viii. 2.

faulchin, falchion; a broadsword, V. vii. 29.

fault, to do wrong, offend, II. xi. 9, *S. C.* p. 419; to lack, be deficient in, *S. C.* p. 418, *Three Lett.* p. 611.

faund, *pret.* fawned, II. ix. 35.

fauour, face, feature, V. vii. 39.

fay[1], fairy, II. x. 71, IV. iii. 2.

fay[2], faye, faith, V. viii. 19, *S. C. Sept.* 107.

feare, *sb.* companion, VI. viii. 25; *to f.* = together, II. x. 64. *See* **fere.**

fearefull, timid, VI. xii. 36.

fearen, to frighten, II. xii. 25, III. iv. 15, VI. viii. 47, VII. vi. 15.

feastfull, festival (*adj.*), VI. x. 22.

feat, action, deed, II. ix. 6, V. v. 7.

feateously, dexterously, *Proth.* 27.

feature, form, I. viii. 49, III. ix. 21; character, IV. ii. 44.

feculent, foul, II. vii. 61.

fee, tenure, II. ii. 13; wealth, property, II. vii. 56, IV. i. 35, ix. 13, v. vii. 43, *S. C. May* 106; service, VI. x 21, *Clout* 370.

feebled, *pa. part.* weakened, I. viii. 23.

feeblesse, weakness, IV. viii. 37.

feld, *pa. part.* broken, I. viii. 47; overthrown, IV. i. 34, iv. 18; prostrated, VII. vii. 13; *pret.* cast, II. vi. 32.

fell, *sb.* gall, rancour, III. xi. 2.

fell, *adj.* fierce, savage, I. ii. 10, III. xi. 27, IV. iii. 8, ix. 20, v. ix. 1, *Clout* 808.

fell, *vb. pret.* befell, IV. iv. 23.

fellonest, most fierce, IV. ii. 32.

felly, fiercely, cruelly, I. v. 34, II. xi. 24, VI. xi. 48, *Muiop.* 343, *Gnat* 277, *Amor.* Son. 56.

felnesse, cruelty, fierceness, II. viii. 37, IV. viii. 23, V. xii. 32.

felonous, fierce, fell, III. i. 65.

feminitee, -ie, womanhood, III. vi. 51, *Clout* 513.

fensible, strong, fortified, II. ix. 21, III. x. 10.

feood, feud, enmity, IV. i. 26.

fere, feare, companion, mate, I. x. 4, IV. iii. 52, x. 27, v. iii. 22, VI. ii. 31, xii. 4, p. 410.

ferme, enclosure, habitation (*fig.*), III. v. 23; rent, *Hubberd* 1160.

ferry, ferry-boat, II. vi. 19.

fet, to fetch, II. ix. 58; *pret.* v. iii. 11, rescued; *Thest.* 71, drew forth; *pa. part.* H. *Beautie* 91, derived.

fetch, *vb.* to reach, II. xii. 21. **fetcht,** *pa. part.* = taken, *Daphn.* 439.

fetche, trick, *Three Lett.* p. 622.

feutre, fewter, to put a spear into the 'fewter' or rest, IV. iv. 45, vi. 10.

fiaunt, a warrant addressed to the Irish Chancery for a grant under the great seal. Used gen. = warrant, *Hubberd* 1144.

field, (*her.*) the surface of an escutcheon or shield on which the 'charge' is displayed, II. i. 18.

file, *sb.* catalogue, recital, VII. vi. 37.

file, fyle, *vb.*[1] to render smooth, polish, I. i.

35 (*fig.*), III. ii. 12 (*fig.*), p. 412. **filed,** *ppl. adj.* polished (*fig.*), II. i. 3, *Clout* 701.

file, *vb.*[2] to defile, *S. C. July* 192. **filed,** *ppl. adj.* III. i. 62.

fill: *at f.* = in abundance, VI. x. 5.

fillet, ribbon for the head, I. iii. 4.

fine, end, II. xii. 59, IV. iii. 37; *in fine* = finally, at last, *S. C. Feb.* 217.

fingring, work done with the fingers, *Muiop.* 366.

firme, to fasten, fix, II. vii. 1.

fisnamie, physiognomy, face, *Three Lett.* p. 625. Cf. **physnomy.**

fit, fitt, *sb.*[1] attack (of illness, &c.), condition, I. i. 40, ii. 18, iv. 45, xi. 27, II. xii. 44, III. ii. 5; mortal crisis, feeling of impending death, I. vi. 37, II. vii. 66, *R. T.* 598; painful experience, sorrow, III. i. 1, IV. vi. 30; access of rage, v. iv. 39; **fitte,** paroxysm, *Three Lett.* p. 614.

fit, *sb.*[2] strain of music, I. xi. 7, *Clout* 69.

fit, fitte, *vb.* to be fitting, II. ii. 11, *S. C. Oct.* 88. **fitted,** *pa. part.* suited, IV. i. 12.

flagg, to move feebly (of a bird's wings), p. 411.

flaggy, -ie, drooping, I. xi. 10, III. iv. 33, VI. 39, *Worlds Vanitie* 60.

flake, flash (of lightning, flame), III. ii. 5, *Epith.* 27.

flamed, *ppl. adj.* inflamed, II. vi. 8.

flaring, *ppl. adj.* spreading, v. xii. 38.

flasht, *pret.* dashed, splashed, II. vi. 42.

flasket, a long shallow basket, *Proth.* 26.

flatling, with the flat side (of a sword), v. v. 18.

flatly, plainly, absolutely, *Hubberd* 324.

flatt, plain, *S. C. Sept.* 105.

flatuous, full of air or wind, *Three Lett.* p. 614.

Flauia, pseudonym, *Clout* 572.

flaw, rush, onset, v. v. 6.

fleare, to jeer, mock, *Hubberd* 714.

fledge, fledged, fully developed, *Three Lett.* p. 621.

fleet, to float, II. vii. 14, xii. 14, IV. ix. 33, *Clout* 286, 596; to fly, flit, III. ix. 7.

fleshlinesse, lust, *S. C.* p. 423.

flesht, *pa. part.* incited, VI. viii. 9.

flex, flax, III. i. 47.

flit, *vb.* to give way, I. iv. 5, *R. T.* 514; to depart, II. vii. 66; to flutter, III. xi. 42. **flitted,** *pa. part.* I. ii. 19; *ppl. adj.* I. vii. 21. **flit,** *ppl. adj.* departed, II. xii. 44. **fitting,** *ppl. adj.* fleeting, changing, I. xi. 18, II. viii. 2.

flit, flitt, *adj.* swift, fleet, II. iv. 38, vi. 20, III. xi. 39, p. 411; fleeting, changing, III. i. 56; light, III. x. 57.

flong, *pa. part.* flung, *Teares* 543.

flore, ground, II. x. 10, VI. ii. 40.

flote, to be flooded, III. vii. 34.

flouret, flowrett, little flower, II. vi. 7, *S. C. Feb.* 182, *Nov.* 83.

flout, to mock, deride, VI. viii. 11 ; *pa. part.* VII. vi. 50.

flowre, ground, VI. vii. 8. *See* flore.

flowre, floure, -deluce, -delice, flower of a plant of the genus *Iris*, II. vi. 16, IV. i. 31, *S. C. Apr.* 144.

flud, flood, VII. vii. 33.

flush, *sb.* a flight of birds suddenly started up, v. ii. 54.

flushing, *ppl. adj.* rushing, flowing quickly, IV. vi. 29.

foen, *see* fone.

foile, a thin sheet of metal, I. iv. 4.

fold : *twise so many fold* = twice as many, II. viii. 41.

folded, *ppl. adj.* shut in a fold (of sheep), *S. C.* p. 467.

folke-mote, assembly, IV. iv. 6.

foltring, *ppl. adj.* faltering, I. vii. 24, III. xi. 12.

foming, *pres. part.* giving forth as foam, I. v. 28; *ppl. adj.* covered with foam, I. i. 1.

fon, fool, *S. C. Feb.* 69, *Apr.* 158, *Sept.* 68, *Oct.* 91, *Clout* 292.

fond, fonde, *adj.* foolish, I. ix. 39, III. i. 10, ii. 44, xii. 25, *S. C. Sept.* 58, *Teares* 327, *Gnat* 152, *Daphn.* 498.

fond, *vb.*[1] *pret.* I. x. 66; *pa. part.* II. xii. 57 ; found.

fond, *vb.*[2] *pret.* tried, III. vii. 26.

fondling, fool, VI. vi. 42.

fondly, foolishly, III. xi. 38, v. iv. 26.

fondnesse, folly, *S. C. May* 38, *Amor.* Son. 37.

fone, I. ii. 23, II. viii. 21, III. iii. 33, IV, v. 26, v. iii. 12, ii. 37, VI. xi. 20, *Bellay* 66; foen, II. iii. 13 : foes.

fonly, foolishly, *S. C. May* 58.

food, feud, I. viii. 9, II. i. 3.

foole-happie, lucky, I. vi. 1.

foole-hardize, -ize, folly, foolhardiness, II. ii. 17, iv. 42, *R. R.* 189.

footewarde, towards the foot, *Three Lett.* p. 625.

footing, *pres. part.* stepping, walking, I. xi. 8, VI. iii. 28.

footpace : *on f.* = on foot, IV. viii. 34.

for, notwithstanding, III. iv. 18; *what is he for a* . . . = what kind of a . . . is he, *S. C. Apr.* 17.

for end, finally, in short, *Clout* 324.

for that, because, v. xi. 54.

for then, at the time, *S. C. March* 98.

for thy, therefore, because, II. i. 14, vii. 65, ix. 49, III. iv. 26, *S. C. July* 71.

for why, because, IV. xii. 15.

forbeare, to give up, forth, II. i. 53 ; to leave alone, III. i. 22; to refrain from, cease, *S. C. Apr.* 15. forborne, *pa. part.* refrained from using, v. xi. 52; spared, *R. R.* 310. forbore, *pa. part.* v. xi. 54.

forby, by, v. xi. 17. foreby, near, close by, I. vi. 39, VII. 2, III. v. 17, v. ii. 54; close by, past, III. i. 15.

fordoo, to destroy, v. xii. 3. fordonne, *pa. part.* ruined, undone, I. x. 60, II. i. 51, III. vii. 34, IV. ix. 28; IV. v. 7 *(auxiliary omitted)*; *ppl. adj.* exhausted, ruined, overcome, I. v. 41, x. 47, III. iii. 34, IV. iv. 38, *Amor.* Son. 80.

forecast, to contrive, plan, I. iv. 45. forecast, *pa. part.* determined beforehand, III. xii. 29.

foredamned, *ppl. adj.* utterly damned, III. x. 56.

foregoe, to go before, precede, III. v. 6. forewent, *pa. part. S. C. July* 117.

forelay, *pret.* lay before, II. iii. 29.

forelent, *pa. part.* given up or resigned beforehand, IV. iii. 6.

forelifting, lifting up in front, I. xi. 15.

forepast, *ppl. adj.* bygone, past, IV. i. 21, v. iii. 40, *Amor.* Son. 62 ; former, IV. iii. 44.

forered, *pret.* betokened, *Muiop.* 29.

foresay, to renounce, *S. C. May* 82. foresayd, *pa. part.* excluded, *S. C. July* 69.

foreshewed, *pa. part.* ordained, VII. vii. 45.

foreside, front, upper side *(fig.)*, v. iii. 39.

foresight, III. iii. 2, IV. Prol. 1, viii. 44, x. 20, *Muiop.* 389.

forestall, to prevent (by anticipation), I. ix. 45, II. ix. 11. forestalled, *ppl. adj.* taken beforehand, II. iv. 39.

foretaught, *ppl. adj.* previously taught, I. vii. 18.

forewent, *see* foregoe.

forgat, *pret.* forgot, VII. vii. 7.

forged, false, I. ii. 36, VI. xii. 33, *Amor.* Son. 86.

forgerie, -y, -ye, deceit, artifice, II. xii. 28, III. i. 53, v. xi. 56, *Clout* 696 ; counterfeit, IV. iii. 39.

forgiue, to give, leave, VI. ix. 22.

forgo, to give up, VI. iii. 39. forgon, -e, *pa. part.* relinquished, II. iii. 12 ; allowed to go, v. viii. 9.

forhaile, to distract *(fig.)*, *S. C. Sept.* 243.

for-hent, *pa. part.* seized, overtaken, III. iv. 49.

forlent, *pret.* gave up, III. iv. 47.

forlore, *ppl. adj.* forlorn, destroyed, lost, deserted, I. viii. 39, III. v. 50, *Clout* 182; *pa. part.* forsaken, abandoned, II. iii. 31, III. vi. 53, v. viii. 39, vi. xii. 12 ; *pret.* deserted, abandoned, II. xii. 52, III. iv. 34, ix. 52.

forlore, *adj.* abandoned, depraved, v. xi. 61.

forlorne, *ppl. adj.* forlorn, ruined, abandoned, I. vii. 10, III. iii. 42 ; *pa. part.* abandoned, deserted, IV. viii. 15, *Clout* 90; led astray, *Worlds Vanitie* 84 ; bereft, deprived, *S. C. Apr.* 4.

formall, regular, *S. C. Dec.* 68, *Hubberd* 361, *Clout* 862.

formally, expressly, II. xii. 81.

formerlie, -ly, a little time before, II. xii. 67 ; first, beforehand, VI. i. 38, iii. 38.

forpas, to pass by, *Hubberd* 519 ; *pret.* III. x. 20.

forpined, *ppl. adj.* wasted away, III. x. 57.

forráy, *sb.* raid, III. iii. 58, VI. xi. 42.

forráy, *vb.* to ravage, raid, VI. xi. 40, VIII. vii. 36 ; *pret.* I. xii. 3.

forrést, III. x. 41.

forsake, to avoid, I. xi. 24 ; to renounce, II. vi. 21.

forslack, to neglect, VII. vii. 45. **forslackt, -ed,** *pa. part.* v. xii. 3, VI. xii. 12.

forslow, -sloe, to delay, hinder, IV. x. 15, VII. vi. 16, *S. C. June* 119.

forspent, fore-, *pa. part.* utterly wasted, I. ix. 43, IV. v. 34.

forstall, forstallen, to prevent, impede, III. i. 46, v. xii. 4, *S. C. May* 273.

forswatt, *ppl. adj.* covered with sweat, *S. C. April* 99.

forswonk, *ppl. adj.* tired with hard work, *S. C. April* 99. See **swink.**

forthinke, to renounce, IV. xii. 14 ; to regret, vi. iv. 32.

forthright, straightway, immediately, II. vii. 35 ; straight forward, II. xi. 4, VI. vii. 7, *S. C. Aug.* 83.

fortilage, a small fort, II. xii. 43.

Fortune, *sb.* IV. iv. 37, V. iv. 6.

fortúne, *vb.* to happen, I. iii. 5, vi. 20, III. ii. 22, v. 18, vi. vii. 14, *S. C.* p. 447, *Hubberd* 631.

fortunelesse, unfortunate, IV. viii. 27.

fortunize, to make fortunate, VI. ix. 30.

forwandring, *pres. part.* wandering astray, I. vi. 34. **forwandred,** *ppl. adj.* wandered astray, III. xi. 20.

forward, far, III. ix. 11.

forwarned, *pa. part.* prevented, I. ii. 18.

forwasted, *pret.* I. i. 5, II. x. 52; *ppl. adj.* I. xi. 1 : laid utterly waste, ravaged.

forwearied, *ppl. adj.* I. i. 32, ix. 13, xi. 45; *pa. part.* v. v. 50: utterly wearied.

forwent, *pret. of* forgo, left, III. v. 10, IV. vi. 11, *Past. Elegie* 174.

forworne, *ppl. adj.* worn out, I. vi. 35.

foster, forester, III. i. 17, iv. 45, 50, v. 13.

fouldring, *ppl. adj.* thundering, II. ii. 20.

foule, bird, *Bellay* 97, *Sonnets* p. 607.

fowle, *adv.* foully, IV. vii. 16.

foy, allegiance, II. x. 41.

foyle, *sb.*[1] repulse, II. iii. 13.

foyle, *sb.*[2] a thin layer (*fig.*), IV. ii. 29.

foyle, *vb.* to defeat, overthrow, II. x. 48, v. xi. 33.

foynd, *pret.* lunged, thrust, II. v. 9, viii. 47, IV. iii. 25, v. v. 6.

foyson, abundance, profusion, *Thest.* 98.

fraight, *ppl. adj.* fraught, I. xii. 35, *S. C. Sept.* 84.

frame, *sb.* structure, construction, I. x. 59, II. ii. 12, III. i. 31, *Clout* 287 ; web (*spiders f.*), IV. ii. 50; *in, out of f.* = in, out of condition, order, *S. C. Aug.* 3, *Oct.* 25,

frame, *vb.* to make, form, I. ii. 30, xii. 13, III. i. 24, iii. 12, *Teares* 203, *Muiop.* 370 ; to support, I. viii. 30 ; to direct, II. i. 20 ; tc set on the way, VI. v. 40 ; to plan, III. x. 16 ; *refl.* to direct, prepare, VI. vi. 25.

franchise, privilege, IV. ix. 37.

franchisement, deliverance, v. xi. 36.

francker, *comp.* more free, forward, II. ii. 37 ; frank, free, *Hubberd* 531.

francklin, franklin, freeman, I. x. 6.

franion, a loose woman, II. ii. 37, v. iii. 22.

fraught, *ppl. adj.* filled (*fig.*), v. xi. 8, 20.

fray, *vb.* to frighten, terrify, I. i. 38, 52, iii. 19, xii. 11, II. viii. 46, xii. 40, III. iii. 12, v. xii. 15.

fraye, *sb.* battle, affray, IV. i. 47.

frayle, tender, III. viii. 31 ; weak (*transf.*), IV. vi. 22.

frend : *with God to f.* = with God as help, I. i. 28 ; *with love to f.,* III. iii. 14.

frenne, stranger, enemy, *S. C. Apr.* 28.

fresh, to freshen, revive, v. v. 45.

fret, *sb.* a carved border, IV. xi. 27.

fret, frett, *vb.* to devour, destroy, I. vi. 44, II. ii. 34.

fretted, *pa. part.* adorned, II. ix. 37, III. iii. 58.

friend, to befriend, help, IV. ii. 7, x. 57.

frigot, a light, swift vessel, frigate, II. vi. 7, xii. 10.

frise, fryse, frieze, decoration on a column, *Bellay* 45, *Sonnets* p. 607.

friske, sb. caper, gambol, IV. x. 46.

frize, sb. frieze, coarse woollen cloth, VII. vii. 31.

frize, vb. to freeze (*fig.*), VI. x. 33.

fro, from, I. iii. 28, VI. ix. 33.

frolicke, vb. to rejoice, be merry, VI. iii. 9.

frollick, -e, adj. joyful, merry, VI. ix. 42, VII. vii. 39.

fromwarde, adv. turned away from, *S. C.* p. 434.

front, sb. forehead, I. ii. 16.

fronting, *pres. part.* serving as a front to, *Bellay* 17.

frorne, pa. part. frozen, *S. C. Feb.* 243.

frory, frosty, frozen, III. viii. 30.

froth-fomy, foaming, I. xi. 23.

frounce, to gather in folds, I. iv. 14.

froward, adj. perverse, II. ii. 26, III. v. 7, *Hubberd* 66; adv. = fromward, away, VI. x. 24.

frowie, musty, stale, *S. C. July* 111.

fruict, offspring, *S. C.* p. 435; fruit, *S. C. Feb.* 128.

fry, sb. swarm, I. xii. 7, *S. C. Oct.* 14. **frie,** spawn, young fish, *Clout* 242.

fry, frie, vb. intr. to boil, seethe (of water), II. xii. 45, v. ii. 15.

fryse, see frise.

fulfill, to fill, occupy, II. xii. 30.

fulmined, pa. part. fulminated, sent forth, III. ii. 5.

fume, sb.: *in a great f.* = at great pressure (of vapour), *Three Lett.* p. 616.

fume, vb. to pass away, *Clout* 720.

funerall, death, destruction, II. v. 25, *R. T.* 117; grave, monument, *R. R.* 37.

furniment, furnishing, fittings, IV. iii. 38.

furniture, gear, equipment, III. i. 11, vii. 18, *S. C.* p. 430, *Muiop.* 56 (plur.), *Three Lett.* p. 615.

furre, furr, far, *S. C.* pp. 418, 427, 458.

furst, first, III. xi. 1.

fylde, pa. part. felt, VI. xii. 21.

fyled, pa. part. filed, registered, VI. vii. 33.

fynd, pa. part. made fine, driven off (of chaff), *S. C. Dec.* 125.

G

gagd, pa. part. pledged, risked, II. iii. 14.

gage, sb. pledge, I. iv. 39, xi. 41, p. 412, *Hubberd* 517, 865.

gainesay, sb. contradiction, III. ii. 15.

gain-, gainestriue, to resist, strive against, II. iv. 14, IV. vii. 12.

gainsaying, *pres. part.* protesting, p. 408. **gainsaid, -sayd,** pret. opposed, II. ii. 28; pa. part. denied, *S. C.* p. 427.

galage, a wooden shoe (galoshe), *S. C. Feb.* 244, *Sept.* 131.

Galathea, pseudonym, *Clout* 516.

galingale, an aromatic East Indian plant, or English species of sedge, *Muiop.* 194.

gall, bile, gall-bladder, I. i. 19, ii. 6.

gallimaufray, jumble, medley, *S. C.* p. 417.

gallow tree, gallows, *H. Love* 153.

game, joke, I. xii. 8.

gamesom, -e, sportive, III. iv. 30, VII. vi. 51.

gan, did (*properly* began), I. ii. 2, II. vi. 39, viii. 8, III. viii. 45, 48; *with* to, v. xi. 2, *Daphn.* 115. Cf. gin.

gang, -e, to go, *S. C. March* 57, *Sept.* 100, 155.

gard, protection, care, III. ii. 21.

garish, to cure, III. v. 41. Cf. guarish.

garland, chief ornament, ' glory ', *R. R.* 449.

garre, to make, cause, II. v. 19, *S. C. April* 1, *Sept.* 106.

gasp, to gasp (*fig.*), *S. C. Nov.* 126. **gasping,** *ppl. adj.* gaping, gasping (*fig.*), *S. C. Apr.* 6.

gastfull, fearful, *S. C. Aug.* 170.

gat, pret. got, III. v. 7.

gate, sb.[1] manner of going, gait, I. viii. 12, III. iv. 32, v. xii. 14, *S. C.* p. 467, *Daphn.* 195; way, path, II. xii. 17.

gate, sb.[2] goat, *S. C. May* 177.

gate, vb. pret. got, obtained, *Amor.* Son. 66.

gaule, gall, bitterness, *Three Lett.* p. 627.

gawdy green, green dyed with weld, yellowish green; *S. C. May* 4.

gaze: *at g.* = astonished, bewildered, II. ii. 5.

gazefull, gazing intently, IV. x. 28, *H. Beautie* 29.

gazement, observation, v. iii. 17.

gealosy, gelosy, -ie, jealousy, I. xii. 41, II. iv. 34, *Love* 267.

geare, sb. dress, apparel, II. iv. 26; fashion, IV. xi. 45; equipment, apparatus, v. ii. 50, VI. viii. 16; affair, matter, business, v. viii. 30, VI. iii. 6.

geare, vb. to jeer, II. vi. 21.

geason, uncommon, extraordinary, VI. iv. 37, *Hubberd* 12, *Worlds Vanitie* 5.

geere, matter, ' stuff,' *Three Lett.* p. 626. Cf. geare.

gelly, congealed, III. iv. 40.

gelt, sb.[1] lunatic, IV. vii. 21.

gelt, sb.[2] gold, *S. C. Feb.* 65.

gelt, pa. part. gelded, VII. vi. 50, *Hubberd* 520 (*fig.*).

gent, gentle, I. ix. 6, 27, II. i. 30, xi. 17, III. i. 44, iv. 45, 49, vii. 3.

gentlesse, gentleness, vi. iv. 3.

gere, foul matter, vi. xii. 28. Cf. geare.

german, brother, i. v. 10, 13, ii. viii. 46.

gerne, to grin, v. xii. 15. Cf. gren.

gesse, to deem, think, iv. i. 7.

gest[1], seat of arms, exploit, i. x. 15, ii. ix. 53, iv. iv. 36, x. 4, *Hubberd* 978.

gest[2], gesture, sign, ii. ix. 26 ; countenance, mien, bearing, iii. ii. 24, viii. 8, vi. iv. 14.

gether, to gather, *S. C. Apr.* 152.

ghastlinesse, terribleness, terror, ii. iii. 44, *Daphn.* 327.

ghastly, full of fear, iii. i. 62 ; terrible, iii. ii. 29.

ghesse, to guess ; to deem, judge, i. vi. 13, iv. v. 45, vi. ii. 45. ghest, *pa. part.* i. vi. 40.

ghost, spirit, soul, i. vii. 21, ii. i. 42, iv. iii. 13, vii. 41 ; person, creature, ii. viii. 26. ghoast, apparition, vision, *Bellay* 113.

ghostly, spiritual, *Hubberd* 280, 479.

giambeux, leg-armour, greaves, ii. vi. 29.

gieft, gift, v. x. 14.

gilden, *ppl. adj.* gilded, iii. iv. 17, vi. ii. 44 ; *pa. part.* vii. vii. 33.

gillyflower, clove-scented pink, *Amor.* Son. 64.

gin, *sb.* instrument of torture, rack, i. v. 35 ; stratagem, plot, ii. iii. 13, iii. vii. 7 ; snare, net, *Muiop.* 369, 387.

gin, ginne, gynne, *vb.* to begin, i. i. 21, vi. 9, 17, xi. 21, iii. iii. 36, viii. 51, *S. C. Feb.* 2, 39, *March* 10, *Oct.* 25.

gipsen, gipsy, *Hubberd* 86.

girland, -lond, gyrl-, band, vi. ix. 8; ' glory,' *Hubberd* 1185; garland, *Past. Elegie* 153. Cf. garland.

giust, *sb.* joust, tournament, i. i. 1, *S. C. Oct.* 39.

giust, *vb.* to joust, tilt, iii. x. 35, iv. i. 11.

glade, to gladden, vi. x. 44; *pret., Clout* 266.

gladfull, joyful, iv. vi. 34, v. iii. 34, 40, viii. 6.

gladfulnes, joyfulness, *Muiop.* 208.

gladsome, cheerful, pleasant, *Hubberd* 20.

glaue, iv. vii. 28 ; glayue, v. xi. 58 ; glaiue, iv. x. 19, *Love* 233 : sword.

glee, coupled with *gold*, app. = glitter, i. ix. 32, v. xi. 63 ; joy, mirth, happiness, iv. ix. 13, vi. iii. 43 ; exaltation, prosperity, *S. C. Feb.* 224; *take in g.* = gladly accept, vi. v. 39.

glenne, glen, valley, *S. C. Apr.* 26.

glib, a thick mass of matted hair on the forehead and over the eyes, iv. viii. 12.

glims, a momentary shining, glimpse, v. vi. 29, vi. viii. 48, *H. Beautie* 221.

glister, to glitter, shine, iii. i. 41, v. ix. 21, *Clout* 495. glistring, *ppl. adj.* i. i. 14, iv. 8, vii. 34, iii. xi. 52 ; glyster, *Proth.* 4.

glitterand, *ppl. adj.* glittering, shining, i. iv. 16, vii. 29, ii. xi. 17, *S. C. July* 177.

glode, *pret.* glided, passed, iv. iv. 23.

gloome, to gloom, become dusk, *Epith.* 284.

glose, -ze, to comment upon, interpret, *Gnat* p. 486 ; to flatter, talk speciously, *Three Lett.* p. 629. glozing, *ppl. adj.* flattering, deceitful, iii. viii. 14.

glow, to be red as with glowing heat, iv. vii. 6.

glutted, *pa. part.* filled, *S. C. Sept.* 185.

gnarre, to snarl, growl, i. v. 34.

gobbeline, goblin, ii. x. 73.

gobbet, piece (of flesh), lump (of food), i. i. 20, x. 13, v. xii. 39.

Godbewye, good-bye, *Two Lett.* p. 639.

godded, *pret.* deified, *Clout* 810.

Goddilge ye, God yield you = God bless you, *Two Lett.* p. 640.

godhead, divinity, *Clout* 834.

goe, *pa. part.* gone, *S. C. July* 118.

gondelay, gondola, ii. vi. 2, 11.

good, goods, property, v. i. 33 ; *knew his g.* = knew how to behave, i. x. 7.

goodly, *adv.* courteously, i. v. 15 ; beautifully, well, ii. vii. 53, iv. ix. 14.

goodlyhed, -lihead : *thy, your g.* = the personality of one who is goodly (a form of address), ii. iii. 33, *S. C. Feb.* 184, *May* 270; goodly appearance, beauty, iii. ii. 38, vi. ii. 25.

goold, marigold, *Clout* 339.

gorbellyed, *lit.* corpulent ; inflated, unwieldy, *Two Lett.* p. 640.

gore, to pierce, wound, ii. vii. 13, iii. ii. 65. gored, *ppl. adj.* i. iii. 35, v. 9.

gore bloud, clotted blood, ii. i. 39.

gorge, throat (internal), i. i. 19, vi. iv. 22; maw, i. xi. 13.

gorget, armour for the throat, iv. iii. 12.

goshauke, a large short-winged hawk, v. iv. 42.

gossip, relative, friend, i. xii. 11, *Hubberd* 53, 193.

got, *pa. part.* won, iv. i. 50 ; *was got* = had betaken herself, iv. xi. 42.

gourmandize, gur-, greediness, vi. viii. 38, x. 34.

gouernall, management, ii. xii. 48.

gouernance, -aunce, conduct, demeanour, ii. i. 29, *Muiop.* 384, *Clout* 503; restraint, ii. iv. 7.

gouerning, *pres. part.* supporting, i. vi. 14 ; *vbl. sb.* conduct, i. viii. 28.

gouernment, management (of body), i. ix. 10; conduct, demeanour, iv. v. 20, v. viii. 3; guidance, v. iv. 4.

grace, kindness, mercy, iii. vii. 59 ; favour, *Love* 244, *Clout* 484, 500; *graces* = pleasing qualities, *Epith.* 107.

grace, *vb.* to favour, I. x. 64, VI. xi. 6, *Clout* 485. **graced**, *ppl. adj.* favoured, embellished, VI. ix. 8.

gracelesse, unfortunate, unlucky, IV. iii. 8; cruel, merciless, V. xii. 18, *S. C. Aug.* 113.

graffed, *pa. part.* grafted, firmly fixed, *S. C. Feb.* 242.

graft, *pa. part., graft in* = engrafted upon, *Clout* 918.

graile, -yle, gravel, I. vii. 6, V. ix. 19, *Bellay* 157.

graine: *died in g.* = dyed thoroughly (*orig.* in scarlet), I. vii. 1.

gramercy, -ie, thank you, thanks, II. vii. 50 ; *sb., Three Lett.* p. 624.

grange, dwelling-place, VII. vii. 21.

graple, *sb.* an instrument for grasping, V. viii. 42.

graplement, clutch, grasp, II. xi. 29.

grapling, *pres. part.* gripping, wrestling, IV. iv. 29.

grase (*fig.*), to move on devouring, to grow, be prevalent, *S. C. Sept.* 113.

graste, *pa. part.* graced, favoured, VI. xii. 16.

grate, to fret, harass, I. i. 19, II. i. 56, III. ix. 14, *Hubberd* 1334.

gratulate, to greet, welcome, *Amor.* Ded. 1.

grayle [1], grail ; holy vessel said to have been used at the Last Supper, II. x. 53.

grayle [2], *see* graile.

greaue, grove, thicket, III. x. 42, VI. ii. 43.

gree [1], station, rank, degree, *S. C. July* 215.

gree [2], favour, goodwill, I. v. 16, II. iii. 5 ; *in gree* = with favour, p. 410 ; *to take it well in g.* = to take in good part, to consent, V. vi. 21.

greedie, -y (*transf.*), greedily pursued, V. iv. 42, VI. xi. 17.

greet, to congratulate, I. i. 27, V. iii. 14, 15, xi. 15.

greete, *sb.* weeping, lamentation, *S. C. Aug.* 66.

greete, *vb.* to weep, *S. C. Apr.* 1.

gren, to grin, VI. xi. 27. **grenning**, *pres. part.* I. vi. 11 ; *ppl. adj.* IV. vii. 24.

gride, -yde, to pierce (*lit.* and *fig.*), II. viii. 36, III. i. 62, ix. 29, IV. vi. 1, *Gnat* 254. **gride, -yde**, *pa. part.* III. ii. 37, *S. C. Feb.* 4, *Aug.* 95.

griefull, -ff-, sorrowful, IV. i. 16, VI. viii. 40.

griesie, gryesy, grey, grizzled, I. ix. 35, III. i. 67.

griesly, -isely, -lie, *adj.* horrible, grim, ghastly, I. i. 37, v. 20, 30, ix. 21, II. i. 39, vi. 18, ix. 29, xii. 6, III. i. 14, iv. 52, vi. 37, xii. 11, IV. iii. 13, *S. C. Nov.* 55, *Dec.* 68 ; *adv.* IV. vii. 40.

grieuaunce, hurt, pain, IV. iv. 26.

grieued, *ppl. adj.* injured, I. viii. 17.

grin, to gnash (the teeth), V. iv. 37.

gripe, grype, *sb.* grasp, V. xi. 27, VI. iv. 7.

gripe, *vb.* to grasp, understand, p. 408. **griped**, *ppl. adj.* I. xi. 41 ; **grypt**, *pa. part.* VI. iii. 28 : grasped.

griple, *sb.* grasp, V. ii. 14; *adj.* grasping, greedy, I. iv. 31 ; tenacious, VI. iv. 6.

gronefull, full of groans, mournful, II. xi. 42.

groome, young man, IV. v. 36, V. i. 12, VI. iv. 42, ix. 5 ; shepherd, *Clout* 12.

grosse, *adj.* heavy, I. xi. 20; *sb.* the whole, *S. C. Sept.* 135.

grossenesse, stupidity, *S. C.* p. 419.

ground, reason, cause, *Clorinda* 24.

grounded, *ppl. adj.: ill g. seeds* = seeds planted in bad soil, IV. iv. 1 ; *pa. part.* based, *Three Lett.* p. 621.

groundhold, anchors of a vessel, VI. iv. 1.

groueling, prone, having the face towards the ground, flat, II. i. 45, viii. 32, xi. 34, iii. i. 38, iv. 17, v. 23, VI. i. 39.

groynd, *pret.* growled, VI. xii. 27.

grudge, *sb.* ill will, resentment, III. iv. 61, IV. ix. 32.

grudgeing, *vb.* to complain, murmur, V. vii. 37; *pres. part.* murmuring, II. i. 42 ; *ppl. adj.* complaining, repining, I. ii. 19, V. x. 37.

grutch, to murmur, complain, II. ii. 34.

gryfon, -phon, griffin, vulture, I. v. 8, II. xi. 8.

gryping, *vbl. sb.* grip, grasp, I. xi. 20. Cf. **gripe**.

grysie, horrible, grim, grisly, II. xi. 12, III. xii. 19.

guarisht, *pret.* healed, IV. iii. 29. Cf. **garish**.

guerdon, reward, I. x. 59, IV. iii. 16, V. iii. 14, *S. C. Nov.* 45, *Clout* 943.

guilen, to beguile, deceive, III. ix. 7.

guiler, deceiver, II. vii. 64, III. x. 37.

guilt, gilded, VII. vii. 28.

guise, -ze, -yse, mode (of life), behaviour, I. iv. 20, vi. 25, V. xi. 19, VI. v. 2; custom, mode, fashion, III. i. 39, IV. x. 6, 49, VI. ii. 6; condition, VI. vi. 32.

gulfe, voracious appetite; 'maw,' *S. C. Sept.* 185.

gurmandize, *see* gourmandize.

gust, taste, flavour, VII. vii. 39.

gut, stomach, *Hubberd* 212.

gybe, to jibe, jeer, *S. C.* p. 427, *Hubberd* 714.

gyeld, meeting-place of a guild, guild-house, II. vii. 43.

gynne, gynst, *see* gin.

gyre, whirl, revolution, II. v. 8 ; ring, circle, III. i. 23.

gyu'd, *pa. part.* bound, fettered, V. iv. 35.

H

haberjeon, -geon, a sleeveless coat of mail, II. vi. 29, III. iii. 57, v. v. 2.

habiliment, *sing.* I. vi. 30; *plur.* I. iii. 17, xii. 5, II. i. 22, vi. iv. 4, *Hubberd* 110: equipment, dress, clothes.

hability, ability, vi. iii. 7.

habitaunce, dwelling, II. vii. 7.

hable, able, powerful, I. xi. 19, vii. vii. 31.

hacqueton, a stuffed jacket worn under the mail, II. viii. 38.

had ywist (*lit.* had I known) = a vain regret, *Hubberd* 893.

hagard, wild, untamed, I. xi. 19.

hale, *sb.* well-being, welfare, *Past. Elegie* 103.

hale, hayle, *vb.* to drag, pull, II. iv. 8, 14, III. iv. 31, v. ii. 26, vi. i. 17.

halfen, half : *halfen eye* = half sight, one eye, III. x. 5.

halfendeale, *adv.* half, III. ix. 53.

hallidome, only in asseveration : *by my h.*, *Hubberd* 545.

hallow, to consecrate, III. iv. 10; *pa. part.*, *S. C. Feb.* 210.

hallowing, *pres. part.* shouting, hallooing,, vi. viii. 40.

ham, thigh, II. iii. 27, v. v. 2.

han, *pl.* have, *S. C. March* 62, *May* 49, 168, *July* 40, 203, *Sept.* 163, *Oct.* 16, 117, *Dec.* 112.

hand : *out of h.* = at once, III. v. 3, v. iv. 42.

handeled, *pret.* used, III. i. 11.

handsell, reward, vi. xi. 15.

handsome, handy, suitable, III. vii. 60.

hap, *sb.* lot, fortune, fate, I iv. 49, II. iv. 43, iv. ii. 43, vi. iv. 36, *Worlds Vanitie* 45, *Epigrams* p. 607 ; *by hap* = by chance, *Amor.* p. 577

haplesse, bearing misfortune, iv. iv. 21.

happily, -ely, by chance, II. Prol. 3, iv. iv. 6, xi. 52, xii. 32, *S. C. March* 31.

happy, successful, II. i. 10.

harbenger, host, entertainer, *Daphn.* 470.

harbour, -brough, shelter, I. i. 7, *S. C. June* 18.

hard, *pret.* heard, III. ii. 21, *Hubberd* 267 ; *pa. part.* II. ix. 25.

hardiment, courage, boldness, audacity, I. i. 14, ix. 12, II. i. 27, ii. 37, III. i. 2, v. 10, v. viii. 23, *Amor.* p. 577 ; daring exploit, III. ix. 53.

hardnesse, rudeness, iv. viii. 60.

hardyhedde, -hed, boldness, audacity, courage, p. 416, I. iv. 38, *R. R.* 143 (hardie head), *Muiop.* 27.

harnesse, arms, weapons, v. iv. 36 ; *harnesse-bearing* = armour-bearing, II. xi. 43.

Harpalus, *pseudonym, Clout* 380.

harrow, *interj.* a cry of distress or alarm, II. vi. 43, 49, viii. 46.

harrowd, *pret.* harried, I. x. 40.

harten, to incite, encourage, *R. R.* 300 ; *pa. part.* IV. ix. 34.

hartie, courageous, I. ix. 25.

hartie-hale, healthy, *Muiop.* 188.

hartlesse, -les, timid, without courage, disheartened, II. ii. 7, *Hubberd* 1355, *Clout* 9, 228.

hart roote, depth of the heart, *S. C. Dec.* 93.

hart sore, cause of grief, II. i. 2.

harts ease, tranquility, peace of mind, *Epitaph* (2) 25.

haske, rush or wicker basket, *S. C. Nov.* 16.

hatching, *vbl. sb.* process of production, *Three Lett.* p. 611.

hauberque, -berk, -bergh, coat of mail, II. viii. 44, III. iv. 16, xi. 52, iv. ix. 27.

haught, noble, I. vi. 29.

haulst, *pret.* embraced, iv. iii. 49.

hault, haughty, vi. ii. 23.

haulting, *ppl. adj.* halt, lame, *Two Lett.* p. 640.

haunt, haunten, to frequent, visit, I. xi. 2, *S. C. March* 111, *July* 78 ; to pursue, molest (*fig.*,) I. xi. 27.

haueour, -iour, bearing, deportment, behaviour, II. ii. 15, III. vi. 52, xii. 3, *S. C. Apr.* 66.

hayling, hayld, *see* hale.

haynous, heinous, hateful, vi. i. 18.

hazarded, *pret.* endangered, *Muiop.* 378.

hazardize, perilous position, condition, II. xii. 19.

hazardry, venturesomeness, II. v. 13 ; gaming, playing at dice, III. i. 57.

headinesse, hastiness, rashness, *S. C.* p. 417.

headlesse hood, *lit.* hood without a head ; hence, perh. = brainless head, *S. C. Feb.* 86.

headpeace, head, *S. C. May* 242.

heape, *sb.* multitude, troop, I. iv. 16.

heaped, *ppl. adj.* profuse, v. viii. 23.

heard¹, herd, III. iii. 1, iv. iv. 35.

heard², keeper of a herd of cattle, vi. ix. 4, 10, 12.

heardgroome, herdsman, vi. xi. 39, *S. C. Feb.* 35, *Aug.* 45.

heardman, herdsman, *S. C. Feb.* Arg.

heare, *sb.* hair, I. viii. 32, II. ix. 13, III. xii. 17, *Thest.* 26, *Past. Aeglogue* 118.

heare, *vb.* to be spoken of, I. v. 23.

hearie, -y, hairy, III. i. 16, iv. viii. 12.

heast, hest, bidding, command, behest, I. vii. 18, iv. iii. 39, v. v. 25, 43, *H. Love* 161, *Amor.* p. 578 ; vow, vi. xii. 24 ; name, iv. xi. 50.

heben, -e, *sb.* ebony-tree, II. vii. 52 ; ebony-wood, *Petrarch* 16; *adj.* of ebony wood, I. Prol. 3, vii. 37, iv. v. 8.

hedded, *ppl. adj.* : *ill h.* = with the head affected by wine, iv. i. 3.

hedstall, the part of a bridle that fits round the head, v. iii. 33.

heed, *sb.* care, caution, v. x.i. 18.

heed, *vb.* to notice, perceive, v. viii. 4.

heedfull, careful, v. viii. 32.

heedinesse, heedfulness, caution, v. vi. 34; attentiveness, vi. vi. 26.

heedy, heedie, careful, v. ix. 13, *S. C. Sept.* 167.

heeling, heel-piece of a stocking, *Hubberd* 213.

heft, *pret.* raised, i. xi. 39 ; threw, iv. iii. 12.

helme, helmet, iv. ii. 17.

helpless, inevitable, that cannot be helped, i. iv. 49, vii. 39; affording no help, from which rescue is impossible, ii. xii. 4.

hem, them, *S. C. May* 129, 304, 313, *June* 76, *Sept.* 113, 157.

heme (1597 heame), *adv.* home, *S. C. Nov.* 98.

hend, to seize, grasp, v. xi. 27.

henge, axis (of earth), i. xi. 21.

hent, *pret.* took, seized, ii. ii. I, iv. 12, xi. 17, vii. vii. 32, *S. C. Feb.* 195, *March* 89. *hent, hentest, in hand* = undertook, iii. vii. 61, *S. C. July* 37. hent, *pa. part.* taken, seized, ii. vi. 49, vi. xi. 31, *R. T.* 677.

hept, *pret.* heaped, dealt in large quantities, iii. vii. 33. Cf. heaped.

her [1], their, *S. C. May* 160, *Sept.* 39.

her [2], he, him, *S. C. Sept.* 1, 2, 3, 4.

herbar, herb-garden, ii. ix. 46.

here by there, here and there, *S. C. Sept.* 63.

herneshaw, heron, vi. vii. 9.

hersall, rehearsal, iii. xi. 18.

herse, ceremonial, iii. ii. 48 ; the solemn obsequy in a funeral, *S. C. Nov.* 60, 70, &c., 200.

hery, -ye, to praise, glorify, *S. C. Feb.* 62, *Nov.* 10. herried, heried, *pa. part.* honoured, praised, ii. xii. 13, iii. i. 43.

hest, *see* heast.

hether, hither, i.x. 43, vi. viii. 46, *S. C. Apr.* 151.

hetherto, hitherto, *S. C.* p. 420.

hetherward, hither, *S. C. Aug.* 46.

hew [1], form, shape, condition (hue), i. i. 46, ii. 40, iii. 11, ix. 20, iii. vi. 33, 35.

hew [2], hacking, slaughter, vi. viii. 49.

heydeguye, a kind of country dance, *S. C. June* 27.

hidder, a young male sheep, *S. C. Sept.* 211.

hide, *see* hye.

hight, *sb.* : *on h.* = aloud, vi. vi. 24.

hight, *vb.* to designate, choose, name, vi. vii.

31 ; *pres.* means, purports, *S. C. Sept.* 172 ; is called, p. 409; *pret.* was called, ii. ii. 35, iii. i. 24, iv. xi. 50 ; *pa. part.* committed, entrusted, i. iv. 6, iv. x. 38 ; called, ii. iv. 41, ix. 59 ; appointed, designated, iv. vii. 17 ; a-signed, ordained, iv. viii. 54, v. iv. 9 ; meant, directed, v. xi. 8 ; destined, vi. iv. 36 ; called, summoned, *Daphn.* 11.

hild, *pret.* held, iv. iii. 42, xi. 17.

hinder, *adj.* back, at the back, i. iv. 5, iii. vi. 32, *S. C. May* 243, *Muiop.* 403.

hipp, fruit of the wild rose, *Hubberd* 948.

hippodame, sea-horse, ii. ix. 50, iii. xi. 40.

hire, hyre, *sb.* wages, vi. xii. 6 ; reward, bribe, vii. vi. 43, 45.

hire, *vb.* to bribe, *Hubberd* 682.

hoare, hore, frosty, ii. xii. 10, iv. xi. 46 ; grey, i. iii. 10, *Clout* 57; ancient, ii. vii. *Arg.*

hoarie, hoary, grey, *Muiop.* 328 ; *h. frost* = hoar-frost, i. x. 48, *S. C. Jan.* 33.

hodgepodge, mixture, medley, *S. C.* p. 417.

hold, *sb.* refuge, shelter, ii. ii. 44.

hole, whole, well, better (of a wound), iii. v. 43. xii. 38.

holme, holm-oak, *Gnat* 215.

holpen, *pa. part.* helped, vi. viii. 25.

homely, *adv.* kindly, vi. ix. 17 ; familiarly, *Three Lett.* p. 614.

hong, *pa. part.* hung, iii. vi. 18.

hont, to hunt, *S. C. Dec.* 32.

hood, state, condition, v. vii. 21.

hoord, *vb.* to conceal, iv. xi. 43, vi. iv. 29 ; *pret.* piled, *Gnat* 657; *ppl. adj.* stored up, treasured, iv. ix. 12.

hooued, *pret.* waited, lingered, *Clout* 666. Cf. houing, *vb.* [2]

hopelesse, unhoped for, unexpected, iii. v. 34.

hore, *see* hoare.

horld, *pa. part.* hurled, *R. R.* 274.

horrid, bristling, rough, i. vii. 31, iii. xi. 44.

horror, roughness, i. vi. 11.

horsefoot Helicon, *Hippocrene H.* (so called because it was fabled to have been produced by a stroke of Pegasus' hoof), *Teares* 271.

hospitage, position of a guest ; guestship, iii. x. 6.

host, hoste, *vb.* to entertain, receive as a guest, iii. ix. *Arg.*; iv. viii. 27 ; to be a guest, lodge, vi. ix. *Arg.* *to h* = to be guests, *Gnat* 196.

hoste, *sb.* army, v. xi. 42.

hostlesse, inhospitable, iii. xi. 3.

hostry, lodging, shelter, v. x. 23.

hot, hote, *pret.* was called, i. xi. 29, iv. iv. 40, *S. C. Sept.* 194; named, mentioned, *S. C. July* 164. Cf. hight, *vb.*

houre, howre, time, II. iii. 34; *plur.* VI. v.
35 = the seven daily offices of the church;
good h. = good fortune, VI. ix. 39.

housling, sacramental (*transf.*), I. xii. 37.

houe, *vb.*[1] to rise, I. ii. 31.

houing, *vb.*[2] *pres. part.* floating, III. vii. 27.

houed, *pret.* waited, lingered, III. x. 20. Cf.
hooued.

how be, although, *S. C. July* 95.

howlet, owl, owlet, *Three Lett.* p. 621.

hoye, a small vessel, II. x. 64.

hoyse, to raise up, *Three Lett.* pp. 615, 618.

hububs, shouts, noise, III. x. 43.

huckster: *h. man* = man who bargains, *Hubberd* 925.

hugger mugger, concealment, secrecy, *Hubberd* 139.

humáne, human, IV. ii. 51, *Clout* 351.

humblesse, humbleness, humility, I. ii. 21, iii.
26, xii. 8, *Amor. Son.* 2.

humors, -ours, fluids in the body which were
supposed to affect or determine a person's temperament, *R. R.* 320; *proud h.* = pride, I. x.
26; *sad h.* = sadness, IV. x. 50; sleep, I. i. 36.

hurly-burly, commotion, tumult, v. iii. 30.

hurtle, hurtlen, to rush, dash, I. iv. 16, 40,
viii. 17, IV. iv. 29; to brandish, wave, II.
vii. 42.

hurtlesse, harmless, I. vi. 31.

husband, farmer, husbandman, IV. iii. 29,
Hubberd 266; *husband farme* = farm, IV. iv.
35.

husher, usher, I. iv. 13.

hy, hye, high, I. i. 8, *Proth.* 28.

hyacine, hyacinth (precious stone), II. xii. 54.

hydra, -dre, a fabulous many-headed snake,
supposed to have been killed by Hercules, II.
xii. 23, VI. xii. 32.

hye, hie, to hasten, IV. xi. 6, *S. C. Apr.* 128,
May 317. **hide,** *pret.* hastened, II. xi. 25.

hylding, base, worthless, VI. v. 25.

hynd, hynde, servant, rustic labourer, VI. viii.
12, x. 3, xi. 27, *R. R.* 244.

hyppocrase, a cordial made of wine flavoured
with spices, *Three Lett.* p. 615.

I

idee, idea, conception, *H. Love* 284.

idle, ydle, causeless, baseless, I. xii. 9, III. vi.
54; empty, I. v. 8.

idole, image, counterpart, imitation, II. ii. 41,
IV. v. 15.

ill-faste, evil-faced, ugly, II. xii. 36.

ilfauouredly, in a bad or unpleasing way,
Three Lett. p. 611. Cf. **fauoured.**

ill fauored, *ppl. adj.* evil-looking, I. i. 15.

illude, to elude, evade, II. v. 9.

illústrate, to render illustrious, *Amor.* p. 562.

imáge, *Teares* 201.

imbeziled, *pa. part.* taken away, stolen, *R. T.*
p. 470.

imbrast, *pa. part.* embraced, IV. viii. 59.

imbrew, to thrust, I. vi. 38; to stain, VI. v.
5; *pa. part.* spilt, III. iii. 38. Cf. **embrew.**

immeasurd, -ed, unmeasured, enormous, II.
x. 8, xii. 23.

immixing, *pres. part.* mingling, IV. iii. 47.

imp, ymp, -e, *sb.* scion, child, offspring (*lit.
and fig.*), I. Prol. 3, III. v. 53, xii. 7, IV. xi. 10,
VI. ii. 38, p. 410, *R. T.* 272; young shoot,
scion, IV. xi. 26, v. xi. 16, *Teares* 75.

impacáble, inappeasable, implacable, IV. ix.
22, *R. T.* 395.

impart, to allow, grant, III. ii. 1.

impe (a wing), *vb.* to engraft feathers in a
wing so as to improve the powers of flight,
H. Beautie 135. **ympt,** *pa. part.* (*transf.*),
fastened, IV. ix. 4.

impeach, to hinder, prevent, *Gnat* 576. Cf.
empeach.

imperceáble, not pierceable, I. xi. 17.

impertinent, irrelevant, *S. C.* p. 419.

impictured, *pa. part.* impressed as with a
picture, *Past. Elegie* 163.

implacáble, III. vii. 35.

implore, entreaty, II. v. 37.

imployd, *pret.* found employment for, *Epitaph* (I) 25.

implye, to enfold, I. iv. 31, vi. 6; to entangle.
I. xi. 23; to contain, III. vi. 34.

importable, unbearable, II. viii. 35.

importune, *adj.* heavy, severe, grievous, I. xi.
53, xii. 16, II. vi. 29, viii. 38, xi. 7, VI. i. 20,
Muiop. 230; troublesome, III. iii. 44, *Daphn.*
387; persistent, pertinacious, VI. xi. 6.

importune, *vb.* to portend, import, III. i. 16.

importunely, importunately, urgently, II. viii.
4.

impresse, to affect, influence, *Love* 170.

imprest, *pret.* stamped, marked, II. xi. 5;
produced by pressure, imprinted, IV. iii. 34;
pa. part. imprinted, III. xii. 33.

improuided, unforeseen, I. xii. 34.

in, inne, abode, lodging, dwelling (*lit.* and
fig.), I. i. 33, II. xii. 32, III. iii. 30, *Daphn.*
469.

inburning, *ppl. adj.* burning internally, III. i.
53, IV. viii. 17.

incénse, *sb., Bellay* 143, *Epigrams* p. 608.

incessantly, immediately, without pausing, VI.
iv. 2.

incline, to apply oneself, vi. iii. 3.

incontinent, forthwith, immediately, i. vi. 8, iv. iii.18, v. ix. 18, vii. vii. 17, *Elegie* 61.

indew, to put on, iii. vi. 35. **indewed**, *pret.* took in, 'inwardly digested,' iii. x. 9. **indewd**, *pa. part.* invested, ii. ii. 6, iii. iii. 38. Cf. **endew**.

indifferent, fair, just, iii. ii. 1; impartial, v. ix. 36.

indifferently, impartially, vii. vii. 14.

indignaunce, indignation, iii. xi. 13.

indigne, unworthy, iv. i. 30.

indignifie, to dishonour, treat with indignity, *Clout* 583. **-fyde**, *pret.* vi. i. 30.

indited, *pa. part.* indicted, vi. vii. 35.

infant, a youth of noble or gentle birth, ii. viii. 56, xi. 25, v. viii. 41, vi. viii. 25.

inferd, *pa. part.* inflicted, vi. viii. 31.

infest, *adj.* hostile, vi. iv. 5, vi. 41.

infest, *vb.* to attack, assail (*fig.*), i. xi. 6, *Worlds Vanitie* 53.

infestred, *ppl. adj.* festered, vi. xi. 24.

infinite, ii. ix. 50, iii. vi. 35.

inflame, to set on fire, *Gnat* 510.

influence, an ethereal fluid supposed to flow from the stars or heaven and affect the destiny of men, i. viii. 42.

inforcement, compulsion, v. xi. 52.

informed, *pa. part.* formed, fashioned, iii. vi. 8.

infuse, infusion, *H. Love* 47.

ingate, entrance, iv. x. 12, *R. T.* 47.

ingenerate, *ppl. adj.* innate, iii. vi. 3.

ingoe, ingot, mass of cast metal, ii. vii. 5.

inherite, to receive as one's lot, vi. ix. 25.

inholder, tenant, vii. vii. 17.

inly, inwardly, ii. xi. 21, xii. 28, iii. i. 55, ii. 11, xi. 27, vi. v. 38, vii. vi. 25, *S. C. May* 38 (*Glosse* entirely), *Gnat* 275, *Muiop.* 343, *Three Lett.* p. 628; thoroughly, *S. C. Sept.* 161.

inquere, to inquire, seek information, i. i. 31.

inquést, quest, search, knightly expedition, iii. ii. 4, v. i. 13, vi. xi. 42.

inquire, **-quyre**, to call, name, ii. x. 12; to seek, request, v. xi. 58.

insight, iii. iii. 11, v. ix. 39.

insolence, pride, *Teares* 72; exultation, *Clout* 622.

insolencie, pride, *S. C. May* 118.

insolent, rude, barbarous, iii. iv. 50.

inspyre, to breathe, blow, ii. iii. 30.

insu'th, follows, *Elegie* 83. Cf. **ensue**.

intend, to call, name, vii. vi. 9; *fret. refl.* directed, ii. iv. 46; *ppl. adj.* outstretched, i. ix. 38; directed, iv. i. 27.

intendiment, attention attentive considera-

tion, i. xii. 31; knowledge, understanding, iii. v. 32, xii. 5, *Teares* 144.

intendment, intention, design, p. 408.

intent, purpose, intention, ii. i. 22, vi. viii. 15, *Gnat* 274, *R. R.* 288, *Amor.* Son. 25; quest, v. viii. 3. *in this i.* = in this respect, vi. ix. 20.

intentive, attentive, v. ix. 14.

interesse, interest, vii. vi. 33.

interlace, to intermingle, cross each other intricately, v. iii. 23 (*intr.*); *pres. part.* interspersing, vi. xii. 33.

intermedled, *pa. part.* intermixed, p. 408.

intermitted, *pa. part.* suspended, left off, *Two Lett.* p. 635.

intimate, to communicate, iii. ix. 30, vi. iii. 12.

intire, sincere, genuine, v. viii. 12. Cf. **entire**.

intreat, to prevail upon, induce, ii. ii. 35; to describe, treat of, v. i. 1. Cf. **entreat**.

intreatfull, supplicating, full of entreaty, v. x. 6.

intrinsecall, interior, internal, *Three Lett.* p. 615.

introld, obscure reading in ii. ii. 44 (v. ll. *entrold*, *enrold*).

intuse, bruise, iii. v. 33.

inure, to practise, exercise, *Amor.* Son. 21. Cf. **enure**.

inuade, to go, enter, ii. x. 6, iii. vi. 37; to intrude upon, attack, vi. iii. 8.

inuent, to find, discover, i. vi. 15, iii. v. 10, v. ii. 20, *Amor.* Son. 82.

inuest, to put on, iv. v. 18.

irke, to weary, vi. vii. 15.

irkesome, **yrkesome**, tired, i. i. 55, ii. 6.

irrenowmed, unrenowned, ii. i. 23.

isope, hyssop, *Muiop.* 190.

issew, *sb.* issue, iii. ix. 15, xii. 43.

isséwed, **-'d**, iii. vii. 19, ix. 15, xii. 3, 5, 27, iv. vi. 3, v. iii. 20; **issúing**, v. iv. 50; **issú'd**, v. iii. 4; **issúde**, *Elegie* 231: issue.

J (I)

iacke of both sides, a person who sides first with one side and then with another, a trimmer, *Three Lett.* p. 621.

iackemate, companion, *Three Lett.* p. 622.

Iacobs, **Iaakob staffe**, a pilgrim's staff, i. vi. 35, *Daphn.* 41.

iade, contemptuous name for a horse, hack, iii. i. 17, vi. vii. 40; term of reprobation applied to a woman, ii. xi. 31.

iane, small silver coin of Genoa introduced into England towards the end of the fourteenth century, III. vii. 58.

iarre, discord, dissension, quarrelling, II. ii. 26, iv. 41, v. 16.

iasp, jasper, *Bellay* 25.

iauel, -ell, rascal, *Hubberd* 309, 712.

ieopardee, -ie, danger, peril, *Hubberd* 98; *in his i.* = into danger at his hands, II. iv. 43.

iessemyne, jasmine, *Amor.* Son. 64.

iesses, straps of leather, silk, &c., fastened round the legs of hawks, VI. iv. 19.

iollity, -ee, revelry, II. xii. 60, III. i. 40, *S. C. May* 192.

iolly, -ie, gallant, brave, fine, I. i. 1, ii. 11, III. i. 45, IV. i. 32; cheerful, *Hubberd* 422; big, *S. C. Sept.* 165.

iollyhead, jollity, merriment, VI. xi. 32.

iollyment, mirth, enjoyment, joyfulness, II. vi. 3, IV. xi. 12, VI. ii. 16.

iott, least portion, I. x. 26.

iournall, daily, diurnal, I. xi. 31, p. 210.

iouysaunce, -isaunce, merriment, mirth, *S. C. May* 25, *Nov.* 2.

iouial, under the influence of the planet Jupiter, regarded as the source of joy and happiness, II, xii. 51.

ioy, to enjoy. ioyed, ioyd, *pret.* I. iv. 46, II. x. 53, III. i. 37. ioying, *pres. part. trans.* deriving enjoyment from, III. vi. 48; to rejoice, delight, I. vi. 1, 17, *Muiop.* 99. ioy'd, *pret.*, *Hubberd*, 707. ioying, *pres. part.*, *R. R.* 198.

ioyance, -aunce, enjoyment, mirth, joy, I. iv. 37, III. xii. 18, *Muiop.* 208, *Past. Elegie* 25; enjoyment (of a person), VI. xi. 7.

ioynted, *pret.* disjointed, dismembered, v. xi. 29.

iuncats, -ates, sweetmeats, delicacies (junkets), v. iv. 49, *Amor.* Son. 77.

K

kaies, keys, IV. x. 18.

keasars, *see* kesars.

keep, keepe, *sb.* heed, care; *to take k.* = (1) to take heed, notice, I. i. 40, III. x. 38, v. ix. 13, xii. 42, *Gnat* 241; (2) to take care (of), *S. C. Dec.* 8; that which is kept, a charge, *S. C. July* 133; keeping, care, charge, *Hubberd* 290.

keepe, *vb.* to tend, guard, *S. C. May* 129, *July* 200, *Dec.* 137.

keeping: *bee at your k.* = be on your guard, I. xi. 2.

keight, *pret.* caught, III. ii. 30, v vi. 29.

kemd, *pa. part.* combed, v. vii. 4.

ken, to ascertain, discover, *Beautie* 88. kend, *pa. part.* known, I. xii. 1; ascertained, discovered, II. viii. 19; recognized, *S. C. May* 237. kent, kend, *pret.* discovered, III. vii. 19; recognized, IV. x. 14; knew, v. xi. 20; caught sight of, descried, v. xi. 43, *Clout* 272. kenst = knowest, *S. C. Feb.* 85, *March* 28, *Apr.* 21, *May* 215.

kernes, rustics, peasants, *S. C. July* 199.

kerue, to pierce, cut, IV. i. 4.

kesars, keasars, kaisers, emperors, II. vii. 5, IV. vii. 1, *Teares* 570.

kest, *pa. part.* I. xi. 31; *pret.* II. xi. 42, VI. xii. 15: cast.

kestrell, *lit.* a small hawk; applied as a contemptuous designation; base, II. iii. 4.

ketch, to catch, II. i. 4, III. vi. 37.

key colde, cold as a key (*fig.*), *Three Lett.* p. 621.

kight, kite, II. viii. 16.

kind, kynd, -e, nature, I. ii. 43, iii. 44, II. ii. 36, v. 28, III. ii. 40, vi. 8; fashion, manner, II. iii. 40, III. xii. 22; sex, III, ii. 4; family kin, p. 411; respect, manner, *S. C.* p. 418.

kindly, -ely, natural, innate, I. iii. 28, viii. 11, x. 47, III. ix. 33, *Two Lett.* p. 636.

kinred, kindred, II. x. 35, *S. C. May* 271.

kirtle, a tunic, originally a garment reaching to the knees or lower, I. iv. 31, *S. C. Aug.* 67.

knack, trinket, knick-knack, *S. C. May* 286.

knee, projection, crag, I. ix. 34.

knife, sword, II. v. 9.

knowe, *pa. part.* known, *S. C. Sept.* 161.

kodpeasd, *ppl. adj.* furnished with a *cod-piece* or bagged appendage to the front of the close-fitting hose or breeches worn by men from the fifteenth to the seventeenth century, *Three Lett.* p. 625.

kon, to know, *Clout* 294. kond, *pret.* v. vi. 35. Cf. con.

kurre, dog, cur, *S. C. Sept.* 182.

kydst, *pret.* knewest, *S. C. Dec.* 92.

kynded, *pa. part.* begotten, v. v. 40.

L

L., Lord, *S. C.* p. 420.

lace, thread, III. ii. 50.

lacke, loss, absence, *Epitaph* (2) 12.

lackey, to act as a lackey, run as a footman, VI. ii. 15.

lad, *pret.* led, II. xii. 84, III. xii. 16, IV. viii. 2, v. xii. 37.

lade, to load, v. v. 54.

laesie, -y, lazy, idle, I. iv. 36, III. vii. 12, S. C. Fe*b*. 9, *July* 33, *Clout* 372, 766.

laire, resting-place (of a corpse); grave, IV. viii. 51.

lamentable, lamenting, mournful, VI. iv. 29, viii. 3.

lamping, *ppl. adj.* flashing, resplendent, III. iii. 1, *Amor. Son.* 1.

lanck, slim, slender, III. vi. 18, ix. 21.

landheards, flocks, *Clout* 277.

langourous, sorrowful, II. i. 9.

languishment, suffering, trouble, IV. viii. 16, xii. 23, *R. T.* 159.

lap, to fold, wrap up, II. iii. 30, III. v. 51; *pa. part.* lapped in, enfolded, surrounded with (*fig.*). v. vi. 6.

larded, *pret.* fattened, *S. C. Feb.* 110.

lare, pasture, IV. viii. 29.

large, *at l.* = at length, IV. vii. 34.

largebelled, *ppl. adj.* adorned with large bells, *Three Lett.* p. 625.

larumbell, alarm bell, II. ix. 25.

latched, *vb.*[1] *pret.* caught, *S. C. March* 93.

latch, *vb.*[2] to fasten, *S. C. May* 291.

later, recent, last, I. i. 32.

latest, last, *Daphn.* 263.

lattice, screen, III. xii. 15.

launce, scale, balance, III. vii. 4.

launch, to pierce, VI. ii. 6, viii. 48. launcht, *pret.* I. iii. 42. launched, *pret.* darted, II. vi. 20. launcht, *pa. part.* I. iv. 46, VI. vi. 40, x. I. launched, II. i. 38, III. ii. 37, VI. 52, *Amor. Son.* 57. launchedst, IV. vii. 1.

lauer, basin, II. xii. 62.

lawnds, open spaces among woods, glades, IV. x. 24.

laxatiue, profuse, copious, *Two Lett.* p. 639.

lay, laye, *sb.*[1] song, I. x. 54, II. x. 59, p. 409; 'strain,' II. i. 35, VI. xi. 5, *Clout* 423.

lay, *sb.*[2] = lea, III. viii. 15, x. 23, *Gnat* 110.

lay, *vb.*: *lay on load, lode* = to deal heavy blows, II. xi. 29, IV. iv. 23, ix. 22, 33; to deposit, II. xii. 3. layd, *pa. part.* brought down, reduced (of a swelling), *S. C. Oct.* 119; *ppl. adj.* subdued, *S. C. Oct.* 12.

laye[1], ? place of rest, III. xii. 44; *pl., S. C. Nov.* 15.

laye[2], laity, *S. C. May* 76.

laye[3], law, II. x. 42.

lay-stall, dung-heap, refuse-heap, I. v. 53.

lazars, lepers, I. iv. 3.

lea, open ground, meadow land, plain, *S. C. Feb.* 158, *July* 122; *the watry l.* = the water, IV. ii. 16.

leach, doctor, I. v. 17, III. iii. 18, iv. 41, IV. vi. 1.

leach-craft, medicine, III. iii. 17.

leachour, lecher, debauchee, I. iii. *Arg.*

leade, to live, pass one's life, *S. C. July* 102, 185.

leafe, trust, faith: *l. and love, Amor. Son.* 28.

leake, leaky, I. v. 35, VI. viii. 24.

leames, gleams, rays, *Epigrams* p. 608.

leaneth, depends, *S. C.* p. 420.

leany, lean, thin, *S. C. July* 199.

leapes, baskets in which to catch or keep fish, *S. C.* p. 466.

leare, lore, 'art', III. xi. 16, IV. iii. 40, VI. iv. 4. *leares* = lessons, III. vii. 21.

learnd, *pa. part.* taught, I. vi. 12.

leasing, lesing, lie, falsehood, I. vi. 48, II. ix. 51, xi. 10, IV. viii. 24, v. ii. 33, *S. C. May* 285, *Hubberd* 699, 733, *Clout* 696; lying, falsehood, *S. C. Sept.* 150, *Clout* 102.

least, *conj.* lest, III. viii. 24, v. xi. 26, VI. viii. 1, xi. 43.

least, *adv.*: *at l.* = at last, II. x. 68.

leau'd, *pret.* raised, II. x. 31.

leauy, leafy, IV. x. 45.

ledden, speech, IV. xi. 19, *Clout* 744.

lee, river, v. ii. 19, *R. T.* 603.

leese, to lose, *S. C. Sept.* 135.

lefte, *pret.* lifted, II. iii. 34.

legierdemaine, sleight of hand, v. ix. 13, *Hubberd* 701.

leman, lemman, lover, I. i. 6, vii. 14, II. v. 28, III. ii. 20, viii. 40, IV. i. 9, v. viii. 2.

lend, to give, II. ix. 58; to cause, IV. xii 21; *pret.* gave, dealt, II. v. 6, v. i. 21; *pa. part.* granted, given, v. xi. 42.

lengd, *pret.* tarried, remained, *S. C. May* 250.

lenger, longer, I. i. 22, iii. 19.

lere, *sb.* lesson, *S. C. May* 262; instruction, lore, *Clout* 783; *plur.* VI. ii. 31.

lere, *vb.* to learn, *S. C. Dec.* 4.

lessoned, *pret.* instructed, III. vi. 51.

lest, to listen, VI. i. 17.

let, *sb.* hindrance, obstacle, I. viii. 13, II. xi. 31, IV. i. 12; hesitation, VI. vi. 20.

let, *vb.*[1] to leave, II. vi. 16. *let be* (*imper.*) = cease from, II. iii. 16.

let, *vb.*[2] to hinder, prevent, I. vii. 20, II. i. 47, viii. 28, III. v. 17, v. ii. 4, ix. 7, *Past Elegie* 126. let, *pa. part.* VI. xii. 1.

leuell, to direct, III. ix. 1. leueled, *pret.* II. xii. 34.

leuer, rather, I. ix. 32, III. ii. 6. *me l. were* = I would rather, III. v. 7. Cf. liefe, liefer.

leuin, lightning, III. v. 48, v. vi. 40, *S. C. July* 91, *Aug.* 87. *levin-brond* = flash of lightning, VII. vi. 30.

lewd, poor, 'sorry,' *S. C. Feb.* 245; foolish, *H. Love* 8.

lewdly, wickedly, basely, IV. viii. 24, VI. vi. 17, *S. C. Feb.* 9.

lewdnesse, -nes, wickedness, III. iv. 58, v. iii. 38.

libbard, leopard, I. vi. 25, II. iii. 28, VII. vii. 29.

lich, like, III. vii. 29.

lidge, ledge, v. vi. 36.

lief, liefe, *sb.* and *adj.* dear, beloved, I. iii. 28, ix. 17, II. i. 16, ix. 4, III. i. 24, ii. 33, IV. iii. 52, VI. xii. 17, *S. C. July* 16ζ, *Clout* 16; agreeable, III. viii. 42; *liefe or loth,* III. ix. 13, VI. i. 44; *l. or sory,* VII. vi. 8 = willing or unwilling. liefer (*comp.*), preferable, II. iv. 28, III. i. 24. liefest (*superl.*), dearest, II. i. 52, III. ii. 33, x. 15, *S. C. Aug.* 192.

liege, *sb.* lord; superior to whom one owes allegiance and service, II. iii. 8, ix. 4 (*fig.*), VI. vii. 23.

liege, *adj.* loyal, faithful, *Clout* 793.

liegeman, a vassal sworn to the service and support of his superior lord, II. iii. 9; *plur.* III. i. 30.

lien, lyen, *pa. part.* lain, IV. ix. 4, p. 412.

lifull, lyfull, giving or bestowing life, VI. xi. 45, *Epith.* 118.

lig, ligge, liggen, to lie, VI. iv. 40, *S. C. May* 125, 217, *Sept.* 118, *Oct.* 12, 63.

light, *vb.* to relieve, unload, I. xii. 42; to remove, III. v. 31; to happen, befall, V. xi. 55.

light, *pa. part.* lit, I. v. 19, III. i. 58.

light, *adv.* easily, quickly, I. viii. 10, *Hubberd* 1056.

lightly, easily, III. v. 25, viii. 19.

lightsome, -som, radiant, I. vii. 23, III. vii. 48, VII. vii. 51, *S. C. Aug.* 87, *Thest.* 82.

lignage, lineage, I. vi. 20.

like, to please, *Hubberd* 945; likt, *pret.* II. vii. 27; *to like well* = to thrive, *S. C. July* 105.

like as, as if, V. v. 2.

likely, similar, alike, *Beautie* 198.

likelynesse, likeness, resemblance, V. vii. 39.

liker, more like, V. x. 21.

lilled, *pret.* put out (the tongue), I. V. 34.

limbeck, alembic, retort, VII. vii. 31.

limehound, bloodhound, V. ii. 25.

limming, *vbl. sb.* painting, *Beautie* 84.

limned, *pa. part.* depicted, *Teares* 202.

lin, I. i. 24, v. 35, III. iii. 22, 30, viii. 24, *Daphn.* 467; linne, *Two Lett.* p. 641: to cease, desist.

line, lyne, linen, v. vii. 6, *Muiop.* 364.

list, to wish, desire, choose, *pres.* II. ix. 1, III.

ix. 7, *S. C. May* 164, *June* 17; *pret.* I. ii. 22, III. ii. 15; *him, thee, me,* &c., *list* (*impers.*) = it pleased him, &c., he liked, I. vii. 35, II. vii. 18, 19, IV. ix. 35.

listfull, attentive, V. i. 25, *Clout* 7.

lite, lyte, *vb.* to fall (of a blow), I. viii. 18, II. viii. 38; to befall, VI. vi. 17; to alight, VI. vii. 40; to come across, discover, *S. C. Sept.* 259; *lite in* = to deal with, treat of, III. ii. 3. Cf. light, *vb.*

lites, lungs, VI. iii. 26.

liuelihead, -hed, inheritance, II. ii. 2 (cf. liuelod), living original, II. ix. 3; life, liveliness, VI. vii. 20.

liuelod, livelihood, income, prosperity, v. iv. 9, *Hubberd* 147.

liuelood, vigour, VI. iii. 7.

liuely, living, lifelike, I. ii. 24, vii. 20, II. ix. 2, III. i. 38, viii. 5, 6, *H. Love* 171; *adv.* in a lifelike way, III. xi. 39.

liuerey : *l. and seisin* = the delivery of property into the corporal possession of a person by handing over a token, VI. iv. 37.

liues end, death, *R. R.* 188.

load, blows, II. ii. 23. See lay, *vb.*

loast, *ppl. adj.* loosened, unfastened, *Bellay* 115. Cf. lose.

loathfulnesse, reluctance, IV. xii. 32.

loathly, loathsome, IV. i. 27, V. xi. 31, *Teares* 335.

Lobbin, *pseudonym, Clout* 736.

lodge, dwelling (*fig.*), II. viii. 32.

lodgings, bedrooms, sleeping quarters, I. i. 36.

loft, sky, upper region, I. i. 41 ; ceiling or flooring of a room, V. vi. 27.

lome, loam, clay, mud, VI. ix. 16.

lompe, mass, *Epigrams* p. 607.

lompish, low-spirited, dejected, III. xii. 18. Cf. lumpish.

long, to belong, I. iv. 48, III. iii. 58, VI. ii. 8, p. 409, *Three Lett.* p. 625.

loord, lout, III. vii. 12, *S. C. July* 33.

loos, praise, renown, VI. xii. 12.

loose [1], to loosen, I. viii. 19; to solve, V. xi. 25.

loose [2], to lose, I. iv. 39.

lope, *pret.* leapt, *S. C. March* 81.

lopp, smaller branches and twigs of trees, such as are not measured for timber; *l. and topp,* *S. C. Feb.* 57 (*fig.*).

lord, to rule, domineer, *S. C. July* 176 ; *pres. part., S. C. Dec.* 70.

lordings, lords, V. ii. 38.

lore, *sb.* teaching, doctrine, I. i. 5, II. iii. 2; advice, III. xi. 18; learning, IV. iii. 42; story, language, IV. xi. 23; speech, V. xi. 61.

lore, *pret.* left, lost, III. xii. 44, v. x. 38.

lorne, *pa. part.* left, deserted, I. iv. 2, *S. C. Sept.* 57; forlorn, *S. C. Jan.* 62.

loring, *vbl. sb.* instruction, v. vii. 42.

lorrell, rogue, blackguard, *S. C. July* 93. Cf. losell.

lose, losen, to loosen, unfasten, II. xii. 67, III. viii. 51, xii. 2; to release, free, III. vi. 48, VI. viii. 29. losed, *pa. part.* released, *R. R.* 264. lo'st, *pa. part.* released, set free, III. iv. 13.

losell, -zell, profligate, scoundrel, II. iii. 4, v. iii. 20, VI. iv. 10, *S. C.* p. 447, *Hubberd* 67, 813, *Teares* 226, 324. Cf. lorrell.

losse, destruction, I. vii. 10.

lot, division, II. vii. 19; share, IV. iv. 33; fate, VI. i. 39.

lothfull, lothe-, unpleasant, III. iv. 52; hateful, loathsome, *Hubberd* 735; reluctant, bashful, *Hubberd* 1314.

loup, loop, loophole, II. ix. 10.

loupes, loop (in needlework), *Muiop.* 366.

lout, lowt, to bow, I. i. 30, x. 44, II. iii. 13, ix. 26, III. x. 23, IV. ii. 23, iii. 5, *S. C. July* 137, *R. T.* 202.

loue-affamisht, *Amor.* Son. 88. *See* affamisht.

louely, *adj.* affectionate, loving, friendly, I. iii. 30, IV. ii. 30, iii. 42; of love, IV. vi. 40, VI. vii. 28.

louely, *adv.* lovingly, II. xii. 51, IV. iii. 49.

louer, louvre; a domed turret-like erection with lateral openings for the passage of smoke or the admission of light, VI. x. 42.

lowce, louse, *Two Lett.* p. 639.

lowe, humble, meek, *S. C. July* 165.

lowre, loure, to lour, scowl (*lit.* and *fig.*), I. ii. 22, III. xii. 24, IV. v. 19, 24.

lugs, poles, perches (measure of land), II. x. 11.

lumining, *pres. part.* illumining, *H. Love* 280.

lumpish, heavy, clumsy, dull, I. i. 43, III. iv. 61.

lurdane · *feuer l.* = fever-lurdan, laziness, *S. C.* p. 447.

luskishnesse, laziness, slothfulness, VI. i. 35.

lust, desire, II. ii. 39, IV. i. 34, iv. 44, xi. 51; pleasure, v. xi. 31.

lust, *vb., pres.* to please, choose, II. vii. 11; to desire, wish for, *S. C. Nov.* 21. lust, *pret.* wished, v. iii. 6, viii. 22. Cf. list.

luster, lustre, brightness, v. xi. 58.

lustfull, vigorous, lusty, *S. C. Jan.* 37.

lustihede, -head, -yhed, lustie head, lustfulness, libidinousness, pleasure, I. ii. 3, *S. C. May* 42, 204, *Oct.* 51; lustiness,

energy, vigour, III. x. 45, VII. vii. 33, *Muiop.* 54, *Epith.* 22.

lustlesse, feeble, listless, I. iv. 20, III. iv. 56, VI. i. 35, *S. C. Feb.* 78.

lusty, beautiful, pleasant, *S. C. Feb.* 131.

lybicke, Libyan; belonging to Libya. the ancient name of a large country in North Africa, II. ii. 22.

lymiter, a friar licensed to beg within certain limits, *Hubberd* 85.

lynage, lineage, I. i. 5. Cf. lignage.

lynce, lynx, II. xi. 8.

lythe, pliant, supple, *S. C. Feb.* 74, *Gnat* 221.

M

Maa, *pseudonym, Clout* 523.

mace, sceptre, II. x. 4.

macerate, to fret, vex, *Gnat* 94.

madding, *ppl. adj.* foolish, frenzied, *S. C. Apr.* 25, *July* 87.

made, *ppl. adj.* artificial, *Muiop.* 166.

mage, magician, III. iii. 14.

magnes stone, magnet, II. xii. 4.

magnificke, renowned, glorious, v. Prol. 11, p. 410.

magnify, to become greater (*refl.*), v. viii. 17; to praise, *Teares* 324. magnifide, *pret.* glorified, III. vii. 31; *pa. part.* VII. vi. 26.

Mahoune, Mahomet, IV. viii. 44.

maiden-headed, bearing a representation of the Virgin Mary, IV. iv. 17.

mailes, mail-armour (composed of interlaced rings or overlapping plates), IV. ii. 17, v. v. 3.

maine, mayne, *sb.* force, I. vii. 11, viii. 7, II. xi. 15, IV. iv. 18, 44; ocean, III. vii. 34, viii. 51; *adj.,* ocean *m.* = ocean, IV. v. 45.

mainly, maynly, strongly, violently, I. vii. 12, III. i. 21.

mainsheat, mainsail, v. xii. 18.

maintaine, maíntaine, to uphold (a quarrel); to back up, VI. vi. 35.

main-, mayntenaunce, condition of life or subsistence, III. vii. 59; deportment, behaviour, *S. C. Sept.* 169.

maisterdome, mayster-, masterful behaviour, IV. i. 46; mastery, victory, v. ii. 15.

maisterie, superior force, III. i. 25; *plur.* feats of strength, VI. ix. 43; *shewes maysteries* = performs wonderful feats, II. vi. 1.

maistring, mayst-, *ppl. adj.* controlling, II. v. 2, III. vii. 2, IV. ix. 2; superior, v. xii. 38, *H. Beautie* 214.

make, *sb.* companion, mate, I. vii. 7, III. xi. 2, xii. 40, IV. ii. 30, VI. viii. 33, *Past. Aeglogue* 18, *Past. Elegie* 178, *Epith.* 87.

make, *vb.* to compose verses, *S. C. Apr.* 19, *June* 82. **making**, *vbl. sb.* poetic composition, *S. C.* p. 416, *Clout* 188.

malefices, evil deeds, *Hubberd* 1154.

malengine, deceit, III. i. 53.

malicing, *pres. part.* VI. x. 39; **maliced**, *pret.*, *Muiop.* 257; **malist**, *pa. part.*, *H. Love* 238: to regard with malice, to envy.

maligne, to grudge, envy, III. iv. 39, v. viii. 18; to speak evil of, VI. ix. 45.

mall, *sb.* a (wooden) club, mallet, I. vii. 51, IV. v. 42.

mall, *vb.* to knock down, v. xi. 8.

maltalent, ill will, malevolence, III. iv. 61.

mand, *pa. part.* filled up with men, VI. xi. 46.

manner, custom, behaviour, VI. i. 27; *all m.* = all kinds of, IV. x. 7.

Mansilia, *pseudonym*, *Clout* 508.

mantle, to spread one wing and then the other over the corresponding outstretched leg for exercise, VI. ii. 32, *Amor.* Son. 72 (*fig.*).

many, **manie**, multitude, company, I. xii. 9, III. ix. 11, xii. 23, IV. x.i. 18, v. xi. 3, 65, *S. C. May* 23, *Hubberd* 1194.

mard, *pret.* marred, destroyed, III. i. 30; *pa. part.* spoilt, III. x. 31, *S. C. Jan.* 24.

marge, margin, edge, II. v. 6, IV. viii. 61.

margent, margin, edge, II. xii. 63, III. iv. 34, v. x. 3.

Marian, *pseudonym*, *Clout* 505.

marishes, marshes, v. x. 23.

marke, a coin value 13s. 4d., IV. iv. 15.

markewhite, bull's-eye of a target (*fig.*), v. v. 35.

marle, earth, II. xi. 33.

Mart [1], Mars, I. Prol. 3.

mart [2], traffic, profit, *S. C. Sept.* 37; *mar one's mart*, lit. spoil one's trade, ruin one, I. iii. Arg., *Elegie* 172.

martelled, *pret.* hammered, III. vii. 42.

martyrest, tormentest, afflictest, IV. vii. 2.

martyrize, to make a martyr of (*transf.*), *Clout* 473.

maruaile, to wonder, marvel, VI. vi. 9.

maske, to disguise oneself, itself (as with a mask), I. vi. 1, *S. C. Jan.* 24, *Nov.* 19; to conceal, III. iii. 51; to take part in a masque (*fig.*), *Teares* 180. **masking**, *ppl. adj.* as if forming a masque, III. xii. 26.

masker, one who takes part in a masque, III. xii. 6; *transf.* deceiver, *R. T.* 202.

massácre, *sb.* and *vb.* III. iii. 35, xi. 29, VII. vii. 19, *Amor.* Son. 10.

masse, wealth, III. ix. 4; plastic substance, IV. x. 39.

massepenie, *lit.* an offering of money made at Mass, *S. C.* p. 443 (*attrib.*).

massy, **-ie**, heavy, solid, III. iii. 57.

mast, fruit of trees used as food for swine, *S. C. Feb.* 109.

matchlesse, odd, not a pair, IV. i. 28.

mate, *sb.* fellow, II. ii. 8.

mate, *vb.* to overcome, confound, IV. viii. 17; *pa. part.* I. ix. 12. Cf. *amate*.

mattins, morning song (of a bird), *Epith.* 80.

maugre, **maulgre**, **mauger**, in spite of, IV. i. 48, VII. vii. 17, *S. C. Nov.* 163, *Hubberd* 816; unwillingly, reluctantly, III. v. 7, xi. 27, v. i. 29; a curse upon! II. v. 12, III. iv. 39.

mauis, thrush, *Amor.* Son. 85, *Epith.* 81.

may, maiden, *S. C. Nov.* 39.

maydenhead, firstfruits, *S. C.* p. 418.

may-game, laughing-stock, object of ridicule, v. vii. 40.

mazd, **mazed**, **mazde**, *pret.* wondered, IV. ix. 11; *pa. part.* stupefied, bewildered, IV. i. 43, *Bellay* 107; *ppl. adj.* IV. vi. 37, v. viii. 38.

maze, bewilderment, stupor, IV. iv. 18.

mazeful, bewildering, confounding, *Epith.* 190.

mazer, (1) a hard wood (properly maple) used as a material for drinking cups : *mazer bowle*, II. xii. 49; (2) a bowl or drinking-cup made of such wood, *S. C. Aug.* 26.

mazie, like a maze, *S. C. Dec.* 25.

mealt'th, melteth, I. ix. 31.

meane, *sb.* medium, average, middling condition, II. vii. 16, VI. ix. 11, x. 27, *H. Love* 86; middle part in a musical composition, alto or tenor (*fig.*), II. xii. 33; means, III. xii. 40; *in the m.* = in the meantime, II. i. 58; *middle m.* = medium, VII. vii. 22; *by meanes* = because of, on account of, VI. viii. 25.

meane, *adj.* ordinary, middling, III. i. 33.

meanesse, **-nesse**, humble birth, IV. vii. 16, VI. iii. 7.

meaner, one who intends or purposes, III. v. 25.

meaneth, intendeth, IV. vi. 6.

meanly, fairly, moderately, *Hubberd* 297.

mear'd, *pret.* bounded, *R. R.* 296.

meare, *sb.* boundary, III. ix. 46 (2) (*lit.* and *fig.*), *R. T.* 63.

meare, *adj.* pure, II. xi. 34.

measure [1], moderation, VI. viii. 43, xi. 14.

measure [2], song, melody, *Teares* 547.

measured, *pret.* proportioned, adjusted, II. xii. 33.

measurelesse, boundless, *Teares* 516.

meawes, sea-gulls, II. xii. 8.

medæwart, meadow-sweet (*Spiræa Ulmaria*), II. viii. 20.

medicynd, *pa. part.* cured, healed, *Clout* 877.

medle, to mix, mingle, *S. C. Aug.* 144. **medling**, *pres. part.* II. i. 61. **medled**, *pret.*, *S. C. May* 263; *pa. part.*, *S. C. Apr.* 68.

meed, -e, reward, gain, I. ii. 37, vii. 23, v. Prol. 3, xi. 61, *R. T.* 398; booty, gain, I. vii. 14; requital, v. ix. 42, *Hubberd* 331.

meere, perfect, *Misc. Sonn* III. Cf. *meare*, *adj.*

meet, *vb.* to be in accord, blend, II. xii. 71.

meet, *adj.* proper, I. xii. 39, II. xii. 71.

meiger, thin, IV. viii. 12.

meint; **meynt**, *pa. part.* joined in marriage, III. xi. 36; mingled, mixed, *S. C. Nov.* 203; *pret.* mingled, *S. C. July* 84. Cf. *ment*[2].

melampode, black hellebore, *S. C. July* 85, 106.

melánicholicke, v. vi. 19.

melánicholie, -y, IV. vi. 2, vii. 38, v. vii. 17.

mell, to meddle, I. i. 30, VII. vii. 9; to mix together (*intr.*), v. ix. 1. **melling**, *vbl. sb.* interference, meddling, v. xii. 35, *S. C. July* 208.

member, limb, III. iv. 37.

memories, services for the dead, *Hubberd* 454.

menage, *sb.* handling, control, III. xii. 22, p. 410.

menage, *vb.* to handle (a horse), I. vii. 37; (a rod, weapons), II. ii. 18, iv. 8, ix. 27; to control, VI. ix. 46, *H. Beautie* 194.

mendes, amends, reparation, II. i. 20.

mene, *sb.* means, v. ix. 42, VI. vi. 9. Cf. *meane*, *sb.*

ment[1], intended, purposed, meant, *pret.* II. iii. 11, III. xii. 33, v. ix. 10, VI. vii. 29; *pa. part.* v. ix. 7.

ment[2], *pa. part.* joined, mixed, mingled, I. ii. 5, v. v. 12, VI. vi. 27.

merciable, merciful, *S. C. Sept.* 174.

mercie, -y, pardon, II. i. 27; favour, II. v. 18.

mercifide, *pa. part.* pitied, VI. vii. 32.

mercilesse, obtaining no mercy, IV. viii. 64.

Meriflure, pseudonym, *Clout* 389.

merimake, **merry-**, merry-making, festivity, II. vi. 21, v. x. 19, *S. C. May* 15, *Nov.* 9.

meriment, joy, merry-making, III. i. 57, IV. ii. 5, *Clout* 30.

meruaile, *vb.* to marvel, wonder, IV. vi. 30.

mery, pleasant, delightful, charming, I. x. 61, *Proth.* 128; sweet, having a pleasant voice, II. v. 31.

mesprise, -**prize**[1], contempt, scorn, insolence, II. vii. 39, III. ix. 9, IV. iv. 11.

mesprize[2], mistake, II. xii. 19.

met, meet, fitting, VI. viii. 45.

Metaposcopus, *Three Lett.* p. 621.

mettall, metile, quality, *Three Lett.* p. 610.

mew, -e, *sb.* den, secret place, I. v. 20, II. vii. 19, v. ix. 14, *Amor.* Son. 80; prison, place of confinement, II. v. 27, *Bellay* 110.

mew, *vb.* to shut up, confine, III. ix. 5; *pa. part.* II. iii. 34.

mickle, much, great, II. i. 6, iv. 7, III. iv. 20, ix. 53, *S. C. July* 16, *Hubberd* 944.

mid, middle, midst, IV. ii. 48.

middest, *adj.* most central, in the middle, I. iv. 15, II. ii. 13; *sb.* midst, middle, IV. iv. 44, VI. iii. 25, p. 408.

mieue, to move, affect, IV. xii. 26.

militant, engaged in warfare, II. viii. 2.

mincing, *ppl. adj.* affected, II. ii. 37.

mind, to bring to mind, II. ii. 10; to intend, contemplate, wish, II. iv. 40, *S. C.* p. 420.

mineon, mistress, paramour, II. ii. 37.

minime, a musical note, minim (*transf.*), VI. x. 28.

miniments, things with which a person is provided, articles, IV. viii. 6.

minisht, *ppl. adj.* diminished, I. xi. 43.

minister, to provide, furnish, III. vi. 9. **ministered**, *pret.*, *Gnat* 505.

mirke, dark, obscure, *S. C. Sept.* 103.

mirkesome, dark, obscure, I. v. 28.

mirrhour, mirror, I. iv. 10.

mis, to lack, II. iii. 39; to go wrong, err, II. iii. 40, III. ix. 2.

misauised, *ppl. adj.* ill-advised, III. ii. 9.

misaymed, *ppl. adj.* badly aimed, I. viii. 8.

miscall, to revile, abuse, IV. viii. 24.

mischalenge, wrong challenge, IV. iii. 11.

mischance, unhappiness, *Clout* 427.

mischíefe, **míschiefe**, misfortune, III. x. 18, v. viii. 7.

mischíeuous, III. vi. 14, IV. vi. 2, v. vi. 31.

misconceipt, misconception, IV. vi. 2.

miscounselled, *ppl. adj.* ill-advised, *Hubberd* 128.

miscreant, -aunt, wretch, villain, I. v. 13, vi. 41.

miscreate, *pa. part.* wrongly created, II. x. 38. **miscreated**, *ppl. adj.* misshapen, mis-formed, II. vii. 42.

miscreaunce, false faith, II. viii. 51, *S. C. May* 91.

misdeeme, to form an unfavourable judgement of, think evil of, I. vii. 49; **misdempt**, *pa. part.* III. x. 29; to have a wrong opinion about, misjudge, I. xi. 55, VI. Prol. 4, *Hubberd* 375. **misdeeming**, *ppl. adj.* dark, suspicious, I. ii. 3; *vbl. sb.* misjudging, I. iv. 2.

misdesert, undeservingness, vi. i. 12.

misdid, *pret.* did wrong, iv. iv. 27.

misdiet, improper feeding, i. iv. 23, ii. xi. 12.

misdight, *pa. part.* ill-clothed (*fig.*), v. vii. 37.

misdonne, *inf.* to misdo, do wrong, iii. ix. 7.

misdoubting, *pres. part.* fearing, suspecting, vi. iv. 47, xi. 43.

miser, wretch, ii. i. 8, iii. 8.

misfare, mishap, misfortune, iv. v. 30, vi. 2, viii. 5, 27, xii. 12, v. xi. 48, vi. iii. 24, xii. 24.

misfaring, *vbl. sb.* wrongdoing, *Clout* 758.

misfeigning, feigning with an evil intention, i. iii. 40.

misgone, *pa. part.* gone astray, *S. C. July* 201.

misgotten, *ppl. adj.* ill-gotten, vi. i. 18.

misgouernaunce, mismanagement, misuse, *S. C. May* 90; misbehaviour, *S. C. Nov.* 4.

misguyde, *sb.* wrongdoing, trespass, *H. Love* 144.

misguyde, *vb.* to misdirect, vi. iii. 47.

mishappen, to happen amiss, i. iii. 20.

mishapt, *ppl. adj.* misshapen, iii. vii. 22.

misintended, *ppl. adj.* maliciously aimed, *Amor.* Son. 16.

misleeke, to dislike, v. ii. 49.

mislike, to disapprove of, *S. C. May* 162; to be ill-pleasing to, iii. viii. 51.

misliue, to live a bad life, *S. C. May* 87.

misregard, lack of care, iv. viii. 29.

missay, -e, to speak wrongly, say what is wrong, *S. C. Sept.* 2; *pa. part.* **missayd**, vi. xii. 2; to speak evil of, abuse, *S. C. Sept.* 106; *pa. part.* **missayd**, iv. vi. 27.

misseeme, to misbecome, iii. iii. 53, viii. 26, *Hubberd* 804.

misseeming, *ppl. adj.* unseemly, i. ix. 23, ii. ii. 31; *vbl. sb.* false show, i. vii. 50.

mis-shape, deformity, v. xii. 29.

misshapen, *ppl. adj.* deformed, ii. xi. 8.

missing, *pres. part.* failing, iv. xi. 2.

mistake, to imagine erroneously, iv. viii. 55; *pret.* **mistooke**, iii. xi. 13; **mistooke**, *pret.* fell upon grievously, v. viii. 8.

mister, myster, (what, such) kind or sort of, i. ix. 23, iii. v. 5, iv. vii. 10, xii. 22, vi. xi. 39, *S. C. July* 201, *Sept.* 103.

misthought, wrong opinion, iv. viii. 58.

mis-trayned, *pa. part.* misled, v. xi. 54.

mistreth, is necessary, iii. vii. 51.

misusage, abuse, *S. C. July* 184.

miswandred, *ppl. adj.* gone astray, iii. vii. 18.

misweene, to have a wrong opinion, think wrongly, ii. Prol. 3, *Past. Elegie* 101. **misween'd**, *pa. part.* mistaken, v. viii. 46.

misweening, *vbl. sb.* misjudgement, i. iv. 1.

miswend, to go astray (*fig.*), *Hubberd* 128.

miswent, *ppl. adj.* iv. v. 30.

mizzle, to rain in fine drops, to drizzle, *S. C. Nov.* 208.

mo, moe, more, i. ix. 44, iii. xi. 45, iv. i. 24; *other m.* = many others, *S. C. May* 68.

mochell, much, *S. C. Feb.* 109, *Aug.* 23. Cf. **muchell**.

mocke, act of derision, *S. C. Aug.* 120; *mockes and mowes* = derisive gestures, vi. vii. 49.

mode, wrath, iv. iv. 5.

mold [1], mole, spot on the skin, vi. xii. 7.

mold [2], *see* **mould**.

moldwarpe, -e, mole, *Clout* 763, *Love* 182.

mollify, to melt, soften (*lit.*), *Amor.* Son. 32; *pa. part.* **mollifide**, iii. vi. 7. **mollifide**, *pa. part.* rendered less obdurate, iv. xii. 13.

molt, *pret.* melted, ii. v. 8, **molten**, *ppl. adj.* 'dissolved' in emotion, *Gnat* 245.

moly, a herb of the liliaceous genus *Allium*, *Amor.* Son. 26.

mome, blockhead, vii. vi. 49.

monastere, monastery, vi. xii. 23.

mone, *sb.* plea, iii. ix. 12; grief, vi. v. 4; lamentation, *S. C. Apr.* 89 (*makes m.*), *Teares* 6.

mone, *vb.* to bewail, bemoan, i. iv. 49, *Teares* 292.

moniment, trace, something serving to identify, i. v. 38, v. viii. 43, *Gnat* 589; mark, figure, ii. vii. 5, xii. 80; record, ii. ix. 59; token, memorial, v. viii. 45.

monoceros, a fish with a 'horn', as a saw-fish, sword-fish, or narwhal, ii. xii. 23.

moralize, to supply with a moral, i. Prol. 1.

mores [1], roots, plants, vii. vii. 10.

Mores [2], Moors, vi. vii. 43.

morion, -an, a kind of helmet, without beaver or visor, worn by soldiers in the 16th and 17th c., vii. vii. 28, *Muiop.* 322, *Bellay* 201, *Epigrams* p. 608.

morish, moorish, swampy, marshy, iv. xi. 29, *Gnat* 251.

morrow, morow, -e, morning, iii. xii. 28, v iii. 7, *S. C. March* 3, 46, *May* 19.

mortality, mortal existence; the estate of mortal man, i. x. 1.

mortall, deadly, ii. iii. 22.

most, greatest, iv. xi. 9, vii. vii. 17; *most what* = for the most part, *S. C. July* 46, *Sept.* 104, *Clout* 757.

mot, mote, *pres.* may, ii. i. 33, vi. viii. 46, x. 3, *Daphn.* 265; *pret. sing.* might, could, i. ii. 29, ii. iii. 18, iv. ii. 8, vii. 47, v. viii. 26; **moten**, *plur.* iii. vi. 31; must, iii. x. 7, v. viii. 5.

motioned, *pa. part.* proposed, suggested, *Hubberd* 125.

mott, *pret.* measured, appraised, *Clout* 365.

mought¹, *pret.* might, could, I. i. 42, III. x. 18, v. ix. 34, *S. C. March* 53.

mought², must, *S. C.* p. 416, *May* 74, 157, *July* 153, *Sept.* 133.

mould, *sb.*¹ dross, VI. ix. 33.

mould, mold, *sb.*² form, shape, I. ii. 39, vii. 26, III. ii. 25, IV. ii. 41 ; structure, I. iv. 5, vii. 33; bodily shape, body, II. vii. 42 ; stature, IV. x. 10.

mould, *vb.* to moulder (*fig.*), II. iii. 41.

mount, mound, *Gnat* 660, 686, *Clout* 284.

mountenance, space, distance, extent, III. viii. 18, xi. 20, v. vi. 36.

mouth'd, *ppl. adj.* having a mouth, II. xi. 12.

moue, to attempt, propose, IV. ix. 31 ; *moued speech* = spoke, VI. iii. 14.

mowes, grimaces, VI. vii. 49.

moyity, half, II. xii. 31.

moyle, to defile, *H. Love* 220.

moystie, damp, VI. ix. 13.

muchell, much, great, I. iv. 46, vi. 20, III. vii. 32, x. 31. Cf. mickle.

mum, not a word, IV. vii. 44.

mumming, *vbl. sb.* masking, *Hubberd* 802.

munifience, fortification, defence, II. x. 15.

mured, *pret.* blocked up, closed, VI. xii. 34.

murrins, plagues, diseases, III. iii. 40.

murther, to kill, murder, VI. vi. 26.

muse, *sb.* wonderment, I. xii. 29.

muse, *vb.* to wonder, II. i. 19.

musicall, music, *S. C. May* 28.

must, new wine, VII. vii. 39.

mysterie, trade, profession, *Hubberd* 221.

N

name, quality, reputation, I. xii. 13.

namely, particularly, above all, VII. vii. 48.

napron, apron, v. v. 20.

narre, nearer, *S. C. July* 97; near, close, *R. R.* 213.

nas, has not, *S. C. May* 61.

nathemoe, II. iv. 8 ; nathemore, I. viii. 13, ix. 25, II. v. 8, III. v. 22, IV. v. 20, VI. xii. 32 : never the more.

nathlesse, nathe-, -les, naytheles, nevertheless, none the less, II. i. 5, 22, v. 6, III. i. 55, IV. v. 20, VI. 38, *Hubberd* 375, 1073, *Beautie* 159.

nation, class, kind (of animals), II. xii. 36 ; *brutish nation* = animal creation, *Past. Elegie* 98.

natiue, natural, II. iv. 1, v. vi. 27.

natúre, VI. viii. 41.

nay: *if nay* = if not, *Daphn.* 130.

naythles, *see* nathlesse.

ne, nor, not, I. i. 22, VI. 1, III. iv. 56, p. 413, *S. C. May* 152, *Nov.* 19; *ne . . . ne* = neither . . . nor, I. vi. 11.

Neæra, *pseudonym, Clout* 524.

neat, cattle, VI. ix. 4.

neate, clear, bright, *Gnat* 119.

neatheard, one who looks after cattle, *S. C. Aug.* Arg. 5.

needments, necessaries, I. i. 6, vi. 35, *Clout* 195.

neesing, *vbl. sb.* sneezing, *Three Lett.* p. 615 ; (*fig.*) p. 618.

neglect, *pa. part.* neglected, *Thest.* 96.

nempt, *pa. part.* named, called, III. x. 29.

nephew, descendant, grandchild, I. v. 22, II. viii. 29, III. iv. 22, *R. R.* 104.

nest, lodging, retreat, IV. v. 32, VI. xi. 42.

net, pure, clean, III. xii. 20, VI. viii. 45. Cf. neate.

nethelesse, nevertheless, *S. C.* pp. 418, 419. Cf nathlesse.

nether, no one, v. vi. 35.

new, anew, again, v. ii. 36; *of new* = over again, afresh, VI. xi. 43.

newell, novelty, *S. C. May* 276.

newfanglenesse, novelty of fashion, innovation, I. iv. 25, *Hubberd* 675.

nice, fastidious, particular, IV. x. 22, VI. ix. 7 ; *nicer* = too fastidious, I. viii. 40.

nicely, cautiously, gently, III. xii. 10.

nicenesse, luxury, effeminacy, IV. viii. 27.

nicetie, -itee, reserve, coyness, I. x. 7, II. ii. 3.

nigardise, niggardliness, meanness, IV. viii. 15, *S. C.* p. 458.

nigheth, approaches, *S. C. March* 4. Cf. nye.

nighly, niggardly, sparingly, *S. C. July* 171.

ni'll, nill, will not, I. ix. 15, II. vii. 32, III. v, 11, xi. 14, *S. C. May* 131, 151; *will or nill* = willing or unwilling, I. iii. 43. willed or nilled, *pret.* were willing or unwilling, IV. vii. 16.

nimblesse, nimbleness, v. ix. 29.

nip, to slander, *Hubberd* 712.

nis, nys, is not, *S. C. May* 144, *June* 19, *Aug.* 38, *Nov.* 9.

noblesse, nobility, I. viii. 26.

nominate, to name, designate, I. x. 64.

nonce, nones : *for (the) n.* = for the purpose, but used as a metrical tag or stop-gap, *Bellay* 74, *Three Lett.* p. 626.

noriture, nour-, nurture, upbringing, I. ix. 5, II. iii. 2.

Norueyses, Norwegians, III. iii. 33.

nosethrill, nostril, I. xi. 22, III. ix. 22, xi. 41.

note, no'te, know not, I. xii. 7, *S. C. Sept.* 110; cannot, II. Prol. 4; could, might not,

GLOSSARY.

703

II. iv. 4, 13, vii. 39, III. iii. 50, vi. 40, xii. 26, IV. xii. 20, v. iii. 7.

nothing, *adv.* not at all, I. iv. 4, II. vi. 15.

notifide, *pa. part.* proclaimed, known, III. iii. 44.

nought, *adj.* bad, useless, II. ix. 32.

nould, -e, would not, I. vi. 17, v. viii. 41, vi. iii. 26, vii. 36, *S. C. Feb.* 192, 199.

noule, head, VII. vii. 39.

nource, -ice, nurse (*fig.*), *S. C. May* 118, *R. T.* 169.

noursle, to train, foster, rear, vi. iv. 35 ; *pret.* I. vi. 23, v. i. 6.

noursling, nursling ; object of a nurse's care (*transf.*), II. viii. 20, *Teares* 564, *Gnat* 282, *R. R.* 299.

nourtred, *pa. part.* trained, skilled, *Past. Elegie* 71.

nousell, to train, foster (*fig.*), *S. C.* p. 443. Cf. **noursle.**

nousling, *pres. part.,* *Clout* 763 ; *ppl. adj.* IV. xi. 32 : burrowing.

nouells, news, *S. C. Feb.* 95.

noy, to annoy, vex, grieve, *Two Lett.* p. 643. **noyd,** *pret.* I. x. 24, xi. 45.

noyance, annoyance, noxiousness, I. i. 23, iii. xii. 2.

Noyes, Noah's, II. x. 15.

noyous, troublesome, harmful, noxious, I. v. 45, viii. 40, xi. 50, II. ix. 32, III. i. 43, *Teares* 483.

noysome, harmful, noxious, vi. x. 7, *S. C. July* 22, *R. R.* 54.

nye, to draw near, *S. C. May* 316.

O

oaker, ocher, *R. T.* 204.

object, to reproach, accuse, vi. vii. 26.

óblique, II. ix. 52.

obliquid, directed obliquely, VII. vii. 54.

obsequy, funeral rites, II. i. 60.

occasions, reasons, II. v. 21 ; pretexts, IV. x. 13.

oddes, difference, v. Prol. 1 ; advantage, vi. ii. 18.

of, by, I. ii. 5, iv. 17, v. 8, 23, II. vii. 2, ix. 18, xii. 31, IV. xi. 25, v. viii. 16 ; off, *S. C. May* 199; on, IV. iv. I l. 4.

offal, dregs, scum (*fig.*), II. iii. 8.

offend, to harm, injure, II. viii. 8, xii. 63, III. x. I, vi. iv. 25, ix. 6.

offer, attempt, v. viii. 42.

off-scum, scum, refuse (*fig.*), VII. vi. 30.

off-shakt, *pa. part.* shaken off, II. xi. 33.

ofspring, origin, source, II. x. 69.

on, one, *R. T.* I,

onely, alone, I. vii. 13, xii. 29, IV. vi. 46, v. xi. 30, *Daphn.* 503 ; singly, IV. viii. 28.

on hed, ahead, *Muiop.* 420.

ope, open, IV. iii. 46, vi. vi. 19.

opprest, *pa. part.* fallen upon, taken by surprise, II. xii. 81.

or, before, ere, *Hubberd* 501 ; *or . . . or=* whether . . . or, I. vi. 15.

ordaind, *ppl. adj.* arrayed, drawn up (of a battle), II. x. 18 ; set up, v. ii. 19.

order, *sb.* usage, practice, vi. viii. 36 ; *plur.* ranks, II. ix. 15.

order, *vb.* to prepare, arrange, II. ix. 31, III. ix. 11 ; *pa. part.* determined, *S. C.* p. 423.

ordinarie, archbishop or bishop ; one who has jurisdiction in ecclesiastical cases, *Hubberd* 562.

ordinance, -aunce, arrangement, II. ix. 30, *Hubberd* 173 ; ordnance, artillery, II. xi. 14 ; equipment, furniture, III. xi. 53; decree, *Hubberd* 1162.

oricalche, yellow ore or alloy of copper, *Muiop.* 78.

orifis, opening of a wound, IV. xii. 22.

origane, plant of the genus *Origanum,* probably Wild Marjoram, I. ii. 40.

orpine, a succulent herbaceous plant, *Sedum Telephium, Muiop.* 193.

other, one of the two; left (hand, leg), II. iv. 4, v. xii. 36; *other some* = some others, *S. C.* p. 417; *otherwhere, other where* = elsewhere, II. xii. 45, vi. xi. 25 ; *otherwhiles, other whiles* = at times, sometimes, III. x. 8, vi. vii. 49; *other . . . other* = some . . . other, IV. i. 7.

ought, *pret.* owned, I. iv. 39, II. viii. 40, vi. vii. 16 ; owed, III. i. 44.

out alasse, excl. of grief, *Amor.* p. 577.

outbarre, to bar out, II. x. 63.

out find, to discover, IV. xii. 25.

outgoe, to exceed, surpass, IV. v. 11.

outhyred, *pa. part.* let out for hire, v. Prol. 3.

outlaunched, *pa. part.* thrust out, *Muiop.* 82. Cf. **launce, -ch.**

outlearne, to find out, elicit, IV. viii. 22.

outly, outwardly, externally, *Three Lett.* p. 626.

outrage, violent outcry, clamour, I. xi. 40; want of moderation, excess, II. ii. 38.

outragious, violent, v. xi. 29.

outraigned, *pa. part.* reigned to the end of, II. x. 45.

outstrained, *pa. part.* stretched out tightly, *Gnat* 280.

out ward, to ward off, keep out, v. i. 10.

outweare, to wear out, away (*fig.*), IV. ii. 33.

outwore, *pret.,* **-worne** *pa. part.* spent, passed

(time), III. xii. 29, *Amor.* Son. 87; to wear longer than, *S. C.* p. 467.

outwell, to pour forth, I. i. 21. **outwelde**, *pret., Gnat* 502.

outwent, *pret.* outstripped, v. viii. 4; surpassed, *S. C. Apr.* 16. Cf. **outgo.**

out win, to get out of, IV. i. 20.

outwind, to disentangle, extricate, v. iii. 9.

outwrest, to draw out, extract (*fig.*), II. iv. 23.

outwrought, *pa. part.* completed, II. vii. 65.

ouzell, blackbird, *Epith.* 82.

ouer all, in every part, all over, I. xi. 9, *Amor.* Son. 29; everywhere, I. xi. 46, *Hubberd* 1180.

ouerbore, *pret.* overthrew, IV. iv. 40.

ouercame, *pret.* covered, spread over, III. vii. 4.

ouercast, *pa. part.* covered over, II. i. 24. Cf. **ouerkest.**

ouercaught, *pret.* overtook, IV. vii. 31.

ouercraw, to exult over, I. ix. 50; *pa. part. S. C. Feb.* 142.

overdight, over dight, *pa. part.* overspread, covered over, II. vii. 53, IV. viii. 34, *Clout* 493, *H. Beautie* 93.

ouer-giue, ouergiue, to give, hand over, III. iii. 41; to give up, *Hubberd* 249.

ouergo, to overcome, v. ii. 7. **ouergone**, *pa. part.* excelled, *S. C. Aug.* 128.

ouergrast, *pa. part.* overgrown with grass, *S. C. Sept.* 130.

ouerhaile, to draw over, *S. C. Jan.* 75.

ouerhent, *pret.* overtook, II. x. 18, III. v. 25, v. iii. 11, x. 36; *pa. part.* overtaken, III. vii. 19, v. viii. 4.

ouerkest, *pret.* III. vi. 10; *pa. part., R. T.* 457: covered, overspread. Cf. **overcast.**

ouerlade, to overwhelm, v. xii. 19.

ouerlay, to overwhelm, v. xi. 51.

ouerlooke, to look over, peruse, III. xii. 36; to look after, oversee, *Hubberd* 279. **ouerlookt**, *pa. part.* considered, *Hubberd* 396.

ouerpasse, to cause to pass, alleviate, VI. iii. 14. **ouerpast**, *pa. part.* passed over, I. ii. 32.

ouerplast, *ppl.* overhanging, I. i. 24.

ouer raught, *pa. part.* extended over, v. xii. 30; *pret.* overtook, VI. iii. 50.

ouer-red, *pret.* read over, III. xi. 50.

ouerren, to oppress, v. ii. 19; *pret.* **ouerran**, v. iv. 44. **ouerrun**, *pa. part.* crushed, run down, v. xi. 6.

ouersee, to overlook, fail to see, II. ix. 44; to overlook, look down upon, IV. x. 30; to overlook, look after, *Hubberd* 283.

ouerset, *ppl. adj.* oppressed, VI. v. 22.

ouer side, over the side of, v. vi. 39.

ouersight, escape, I. vi. 1.

ouerstrooke, *pret.* struck above, v. xi. 13.

ouerswim, to swim over, III. iii. 33.

ouert, open, III. ix. 46.

ouerthwart, opposite, IV. x. 51.

ouerture, open or exposed place, *S. C. July* 28.

ouerwent, ouer-went, *pret.* went over, traversed, III. iv. 18, p. 413; *pa. part.* overcome, overwhelmed, v. viii. 7, *S. C. March* 2.

owches, gems, jewels, I. ii. 13, x. 31, III. iv. 23.

owe: *owe her fall* = is bound to fall, *R. R.* 387.

owre, ore, II. vii. 5, III. iv. 18.

oystriges, ostriches, II. xi. 12.

P

pace, step, I. iv. 3; place through which one passes, tract, III. i. 19.

pack, *vb.* to go away, depart, VII. vi. 12; *go pack, Teares* 398.

packe, *sb.* burden, VI. ii. 21.

packed, *ppl. adj.* heaped up, amassed, *S. C.* p. 443.

paddocks, toads, *S. C. Dec.* 70.

paine, payne, *sb.* pains, care, I. vi. 33, II. xi. 15; punishment, II. vii. 21.

paine, payne, *vb. refl.* to take pains, exert oneself, I. iv. 15, v. xii. 10. **paynd**, *pret.* IV. vi. 40.

painefull, payne-, troublesome, laborious, VI. vii. 35; careful, painstaking, *Two Lett.* p. 636.

paint out, to depict, *S. C. June* 79.

paire, to impair, I. vii. 41.

Palemon = Thomas Churchyard, *Clout* 396.

paled [1], *ppl. adj.*: *paled part per part* = furnished or marked with (vertical) stripes; in heraldry *paly*, VI. ii. 6.

paled [2], *ppl. adj.* fenced in with pales, I. v. 5.

Palin, *pseudonym, Clout* 392.

pall, *sb.* robe, cloak (esp. of rich material), II. ix. 37, v. v. 24, *S. C. July* 173.

pall, *vb.* to subdue, daunt, IV. iv. 5. **palled**, *ppl. adj.* enfeebled, *Past. Elegie* 163.

palled, ? pallid, *Past. Elegie* 163.

panachæa, a reputed herb of healing virtue; all-heal, III. v. 32.

pance, paunce, pawnce, pansy, III. i. 36, xi. 37, *S. C. Apr.* 142.

pangues, pangs, III. xi. 44.

pannikell, brain-pan, skull, iii. v. 23.

paragon, equal, match, III. ii. 13, IV. ix. 11, VI. ix. 11, *Clout* 451; emulation, comparison, III. iii. 54, ix. 2, IV. v. 9, v. iii. 24, *Muiop.* 274, *Clout* 344, *Amor.* Son. 66; mate, companion, IV. i. 33, *S. C.* p. 458; consort in marriage, IV.

x. 43 ; pattern or model of supreme excellence,
vi. i. 1, *Clout* 548 ; rival, competitor, *Hubberd*
1026.

paramour, lover, i. i, 9 (*fig.*), iv. v. 5, *S. C.
Apr.* 139, *Gnat* 678 ; rival, vi. ix. 39.

parauaunt, -ant, before, iii. ii. 16 ; in front,
vi. x. 15 ; pre-eminently, *Clout* 941.

parbreake, vomit, i. i. 20.

parcell, part, *H. Beautie* 105.

pardale, panther or leopard, i. vi. 26.

parentage, parent, ii. x. 27.

parget, ornamental work in plaster on a wall,
ceiling, &c., *Bellay* 23, *Epigrams* p. 607.

part, *sb.* side, v. vii. 3, vi. viii. 40 ; *plur.* conduct, habits, v. ix. 2, vi. v. 33 ; *part per part*,
vi. ii. 6 (*see* paled).

part, *vb.* to share, divide, iii. ix. 43, *S. C. Apr.*
153. **parted**, *pret.* departed, i. iii. 22.

partake, to share (a thing) *with* another,
v. xi. 32 ; to make a sharer *of*, ii. iv. 20 ;
? to carry through (a purpose), iii. iii. 25, v. i.
(pertake).

particularities, particulars, *Three Lett.* p. 618.

parture, departure, iii. viii. 46.

party, side, iv. iv. 20, vi. i. 19.

pas, passe, to surpass, excel, i. iv. 11, ii. vi. 25,
iii. iv. 23, ix. 50, iv. ii. 2, v. iii. 17, x. 3, vi. x.
5, *S. C. June* 74, *Aug.* 10 ; to disregard, take
no notice, ii. vi. 37 ; to care, reck, *Hubberd*
1150 ; *pas by* = care about, regard ; to be beyond, *Clout* 837 ; *pres. part.* surpassing, *H.
Beautie* 70 ; *ppl. adj.* i. x. 24, 31, *Clorinda*
100.

passant, (*her.*) walking, looking towards the
dexter side, with three paws on the ground and
the dexter fore-paw raised, iii. i. 4.

passion, sorrow, grief, i. ii. 26, iv. viii. 3.

passionate, *adj.* that moves to compassion,
pitiful, *Clout* 427.

passionate, *vb.* to express with feeling, i. xii. 16.

passioned, *pa. part.* expressed with feeling, iii.
xii. 4.

pastor, -oure, shepherd, *S. C. Sept.* 140, *Past.
Elegie* 9, p. 409.

pasture, food, iii. x. 59.

patcheries, things made of patches or fragments (*fig.*), *Three Lett.* p. 632.

patience, a species of dock, called by old her-
balists *Patientia* (= *Rumex Patientia*, Linn.),
Gnat 678.

patronage, defence, ii. viii. 26.

patronesse, female protector, i. x. 44.

paulting, paw-, trifling, paltry, *Three Lett.*
pp. 619, 629.

paund, pawnd, *pa. part.* pawned, pledged,
iv. iii. 3, *S. C. Sept.* 95.

pauilions, tents, tabernacles, *S. C.* p. 420.

pauone, peacock, iii. xi. 47.

pawnce, *see* pance.

paynim, pagan, i. iv. 41.

paysd, *pa. part.* poised, ii. x. 5. Cf. peise.

pealing, *pres. part.* appealing, vii. vii. Arg.

peare, pere, peer, equal, ii. iv. 18 ; companion, v. i. 6, vi. ii. 31 ; rival, *Worlds Vanitie* 75.

pearling, pere-, *pres. part.* forming pearl-
like drops, *Clout* 507 ; *ppl. adj.*, *Epith.* 155.

peasant, *attrib.* base, vi. iii. 31.

pease, pea ; *not worth a pease* = of no value,
S. C. Oct. 69.

peaze, blow, iii. ii. 20. Cf. peise.

peece, piece of work, structure, i. x. 59 ; (of a
fortress, or stronghold), ii. xi. 14, iii. x. 10, v.
ii. 21 ; (of a sea-vessel), ii. xii. 44.

peeced, *ppl. adj.* pieced, imperfect, *S. C. Oct.*
87.

peeretree, pear-tree, *S. C. March* 111.

peeuishnesse, folly, perverse conduct, vi. vii.
37.

peinct, to paint, *S. C. Feb.* 121.

peise, -ze, to balance, weigh, v. ii. 46 ; to press
downwards by its weight, *Clout* 849.

pele, peal, v. ix. 39.

pelfe, wealth, ii. vii. 7, iii. ix. 4, *S. C.* p. 443.

pen, to restrain, confine, v. ii. 19. **pend**, *pa.
part.*, *S. C. Oct.* 72. Cf. pent.

pendant, something hanging (said of foliage
or fruit), *Elegie* 5 ; *plur.* ornaments hanging
down from a vault or roof, iv. x. 6.

penie masses, masses at which offerings are
made, *Hubberd* 452. Cf. masse penie.

pennes, feathers, i. xi. 10.

pensifenesse, anxious thought, iv. v. 38.

pent, *pa. part.* enclosed, v. ix. 10.

penurie, lack of food, i. ix. 35, v. v. 22.

penurious, poverty-stricken, destitute, v. v. 46.

perceable, penetrable, i. i. 7.

percen, to pierce, i. vii. 33.

perdie, -y, indeed, verily, truly, certainly,
interj. i. vi. 42, ii. iii. 18, iii. x. 7, 39, xi. 24,
S. C. May 37, *Aug.* 19 ; *adv.* iii. ii. 27, *S. C.
March* 104.

peregall, equal, *S. C. Aug.* 8.

péremptórie, -y, iii. viii. 16, v. ix. 44.

perfit, perfect, *Two Lett.* p. 640.

perfited, *pa. part.* perfected, *Three Lett.* p.
626.

perforce, -forse, of necessity, ii. iii. 3, *S. C.
Nov.* 127.

perke, pert, *S. C. Feb.* 8.

perlous, perilous, dangerous, ii. ix. 17, iii. i. 19,
vii. 28, xii. 42, iv. x. 28.

persant, piercing, i. x. 47, ii. iii. 23 ; that is pierced, iii. ix. 20.

perse, to pierce, i. ix. 48. **perst**, *pa. part.* i. iii. 1.

perseline, parsley, *Muiop.* 199.

perséuer, to continue, *Amor.* Son. 9. **perséuered, -uer'd**, *pret.* iii. xii. 2, iv. x. ii.

personable, handsome, well-made, iii. iv. 5.

personage, representation of a person ; image, ii. iii. 5, iii. ii. 26.

pérsue, track, iii. v. 28.

perswade, persuasion, v. x. 25.

pert, unconcealed, open, *S. C. Sept.* 162.

pertake, to endure, iv. viii. 9.

pheere, companion, *Thest.* 100. *See* **fere**.

philbert, filbert-tree, *Elegie* 17.

phill, the last syllable of 'Astrophill', *Elegie* 192.

Philomele, *S. C. Nov.* 141 ; **Philumene**, *Daphn.* 475 : the nightingale.

Phyllis, *pseudonym, Clout* 540.

physnomy, countenance, vii. vii. 5.

pible stone, pebbles, *Gnat* 163.

pickethanks, flatterers, sycophants, *Three Lett.* p. 621.

pickstrawes, triflers, *Three Lett.* p. 621.

picturals, pictures, ii. ix. 53.

pide, particoloured, dappled, *Gnat* 250.

pight, *pret.* placed, i. ii. 42 ; pitched, alighted, v. viii. 8 ; *pa. part.* fixed, placed, set, i. viii. 37, x. 43, xii. 25, iii. v. 40, vi. ix. 44, *S. C. Feb.* 106, *Dec.* 134.

pill, pil, to rob, plunder, v. ii. 6, vi. x. 5, *Hubberd* 1198, *R. R.* 418.

pilloures, pillars, *Bellay* 43.

pillów, iii. iv. 53.

pinckt, *pa. part.* ornamented, vi. ii. 6.

pine, pyne, *sb.* suffering, grief, i. ix. 35, v. v. 22 ; famine, hunger, *S. C. July* 24.

pine, *vb.* pined, pyn'd, *pret.* languished, iv. xii. 19. *ppl. adj.* i. viii. 40, iii. iii. 52, iv. vii. 41, *pa. part.* i. x. 48 ; exhausted or wasted by suffering or hunger. *done to pine* = caused to die, vi. v. 28.

pinnoed, *pa. part.* bound, pinioned, v. iv. 22.

pitch, *sb.* altitude, elevation, i. xi. 31 ; extent, v. ii. 34.

pitcht, *pret.* fixed, fastened, v. ii. 19. Cf. **pight**.

piteously, compassionately, vi. viii. 37.

pitifull, compassionate, merciful, ii. v. 24.

pitteous, compassionate, pitiful, ii. x. 44.

pittie, to move to pity, grieve, vi. xii. 9.

place, rank, i v. viii. 14, v. ix. 38 ; *in p.* = on the spot, i. v. 36 ; *come in p.* = be present, iii. ix. 26 ; *to take p.* = to find acceptance, iii. ix. 26.

plaine, to complain, complain of, ii. iii. 13, viii. 19, iii. v. 39, xi. 16, vi. viii. 21. **playned**,

playnd, *pret.* i. i. 47, iii. v. 44, xi. 23, *S. C. Jan.* 12.

plaintiffe, plaintive, v. iv. 40.

platane, the oriental plane-tree, i. i. 9.

plaudite, applause, *Three Lett.* p. 624.

pleasaunce, -auns, ples-, courtesy, pleasing behaviour, i. ii. 30 ; pleasantness, i. iv. 38 ; joy, pleasure, enjoyment, *S. C. Jan.* Arg. 10 *S. C. Feb.* 223, *Mar.* Arg. 3, *Amor.* Son. 17, 21, 89 ; delightful things, *S. C. May* 7 ; part of a garden laid out ornamentally (*plur.*), ii. xii. 50.

pled, *pret.* pleaded, v. ix. 43.

plesh, puddle, pool, ii. viii. 36.

plight, *sb.* fold, pleat, ii. iii. 26, ix. 40, v. ix. 28 ; condition, iii. i. 1, iv. i. 38, v. xii. 16, *S. C. Apr.* 49, *Oct.* 87 ; health, good condition, iii. vii. 21, ix. 19 ; attire, array, iii. xii. 8.

plight, *vb.*[1] plighted, pledged, *pa. part.* v. xi. 62 *pret. S. C. Aug.* 25.

plight, *vb.*[2] *pa. part.* plaited, woven, ii. vi. 7, vi. vii. 43 ; *ppl. adj.* pleated, iii. ix. 21.

plot, map, chart, *R. R.* 363.

plough-yrons, coulter and share of a plough vii. vii. 35.

ply, to apply (*refl.*), iii. vii. 12 ; to move towards, iv. i. 38.

poase, to puzzle, *Three Lett.* p. 618.

poesie, poesye, poem ; motto or short inscription, *S. C.* pp. 422, 423, 435.

poëtresse, poetess, *Teares* 576.

point, *sb.* : *full p.* = full stop, ii. x. 68 ; *t point* = completely, fully, i. i. 16, ii. 12 exactly, iii. ii. 16.

point, *vb.* to appoint, i. ix. 41 ; *pret.* iv. vi. 1 51, v. xii. 9, *Hubberd* 1115 ; *pa. part.* vii vii. 12.

poise, poyse, force, i. xi. 54, v. xii. 21 *R. R.* 214 ; weight, v. ii. 31.

poke, bag, pouch, iv. vii. 6.

pollicy, statecraft, i. iv. 12, ii. ix. 48, 53, x. 39, vii. vi. 6, p. 410.

pols, levies a tax upon, v. ii. 6.

polygony, plant of the genus *Polygonum* Snakewood, iii. v. 32.

poore, to pour, *S. C. June* 80.

porcpisces, porpoises, *Clout* 249.

porphyre, porphyry ; a beautiful hard rock often used poetically to mean granite or marble, *R. R.* 441.

port, carriage, bearing, ii. iii. 28, iii. viii. 44 *Amor.* Son. 13, *Three Lett.* p. 621 (*plur.*) station, rank, iii. vii. 15, xi. 46.

portance, -aunce, carriage, bearing, demeanour, ii. iii. 5, 21, vii. 41, iii. ii. 27, vi. v. 11 vii. 6.

portend, to signify, v. vii. 4.

portesse, portable breviary, I. iv. 19.

portlinesse, stateliness, dignity, *Amor. Son.* 5.

portly, stately, dignified, *Amor. Son.* 5, *Epith.* 148.

possesse, to accomplish, obtain, III. iii. 51 ; to occupy, *Muiop.* 150.

post : *in p.* = in haste, at express speed, VI. vii. 35.

potshares, potsherds, broken pieces of earthenware, VI. i. 37.

pottle, measure equal to two quarts, *Three Lett.* p. 615.

Pouke, Puck ; an evil spirit or goblin, also called Robin Goodfellow and Hobgoblin, *Epith.* 341.

pouldred, *pa. part.* crushed, powdered, I. vii. 12 ; *ppl. adj.* spotted, III. ii. 25 ; reduced to powder, *R. R.* 378.

pounce, claw or talon of a bird of prey, I. xi. 19, v. iv. 42.

pounching, *pres. part.* poking, prodding, VI. ii. 22.

pound : *in p.* = in a balance, v. ii. 36.

pourtrahed, *pa. part.* drawn, portrayed, I. viii. 33, II. ix. 33, III. i. 34.

pourtraict, *sb.* image, representation, likeness, II. iii. 22, xii. 23, III. Prol. 1, IV. v. 13, *R. R.* 346.

pourtraict, por-, *vb.* to portray, IV. v. 12, p. 407, *S. C.* p. 417.

pourtraiture, -acture, -aicture, image, portrait, representation, I. iv. 17, *Hubberd* 611, *Daphn.* 303.

pousse, pulse, pease, *S. C. Aug.* 46.

powre, to pour, *R. T.* 131.

poynant, poin-, sharp, piercing, I. vii. 19, II. viii. 36, III. i. 5, IV. iii. 9.

practick, -e, crafty, cunning, artful, I. xii. 34, II. i. 3, iii. 9 ; skilful, IV. iii. 7, v. vii. 29, VI. i. 36.

practise, actions, conduct, III. iii. 28, v. vi. 31 ; artifice, stratagem, *Hubberd* 856.

practiz'd, *ppl. adj.* skilled, IV. ii. 10. práctiz'd, *pa. part.* plotted, schemed, v. ix. 41.

prancke, *vb.*[1] to fold, plait, I. iv. 14.

prancke, *vb.*[2] to dress, deck (*refl.*), II. ii. 36 ; to show off, II. iii. 6.

pranke, *sb.* evil deed, v. i. 15.

pray, to take possession of, make prey of, v. iv. 14. prayde, *pa. part.* captured as booty (*fig.*), VI. x. 34.

preace, -se, -sse, *sb.* multitude, press, crowd, I. iii. 3, II. vii. 46, III. i. 23, IV. iii. 4. iv. 34 ; *to put in preace* = to exercise, put in practice, *S. C. Oct.* 70.

preace, *vb.* to press, strive, contend, I. xii. 19 ;

pret. pressed, thronged, II. vii. 44 ; *pres. part.* advancing, IV. x. 10, VII. vi. 10.

precedent, pattern, model, p. 412.

preeuing, *vbl. sb.* trial, probation, *Hubberd* 1366.

preferre, to promote, *Clout* 818. prefard, *pret.* preferred, liked, III. viii. 14 ; *pa. part.* proferred, IV. ii. 27.

prefixt, *pa. part.* fixed, settled (beforehand), v. xi. 40.

preife, *see* priefe.

preiudice, *vb.* to influence, *Three Lett.* p. 624.

preiudize, *sb.* prognostication, presaging, II. ix. 49.

prepense, to consider, III. xi. 14.

prescript, command, instruction, *Hubberd* 1261.

present, immediate, instant, *S. C.* p. 447.

president, precedent, example, v. iv. 2, *Three Lett.* p. 623.

prest, *adj.* ready ; at hand, II. viii. 28 ; prepared, IV. iii. 22 ; *adv.* quickly, immediately, VII. vi. 16.

pretence, design, intention, II. iv. 1, v. v. 33, viii. 10.

pretend, to attempt, II. xi. 15 ; *pa. part.* portended, VI. iv. 10 ; stretched out, VI. xi. 19.

preuent, to forestall, anticipate, *pres. part.* IV. i. 41, VI. viii. 15 ; *pret.* VI. i. 38.

preuie, preuelie, *see* priuie, priuely.

price, *sb.* value, I. x. 31, *Clorinda* 100.

price, -ze, *vb.* to pay the price for, pay for, I. v. 26, ix. 37, *H. Love* 175. prizde, *pa. part.* revenged, paid for, *R. T.* 116.

prick, *vb.* to spur, ride fast, *pres. part.* I. i. 1 ; *pret.* II. i. 50, v. i. 19.

pricke, *sb.* point, pitch, II. xii. 1 ; target, bull's-eye, *S. C. Sept.* 122.

pricket, a buck in its second year, *S. C. Dec.* 27.

priefe, experience, I. viii. 43, II. i. 48, iv. 28 ; test, trial, I. ix. 17, VI. iv. 34 ; proved or tested power, I. x. 24 ; proof, *S. C. Aug.* 116. preife, trial, *Hubberd* 408. Cf. proofe.

prieue, to prove, VI. xii. 18 ; *pa. part.* v. iv. 33. Cf. proue.

prime, spring, spring-time, I. ii. 40, VI. 13, II. xii. 75, III. vi. 42, VII. vii. 18, 43, *S. C. Feb.* 16, 167, *Past. Elegie* 47 ; sunrise, morning, II. ix. 25.

primitias, first fruits, *Hubberd* 518.

primrose, best, finest, *S. C. Feb.* 166, *Clout* 560.

principals, the two principal feathers in each wing (*falconry*), *S. C.* p. 418.

principle, beginning, x. xi. 2.

prisd, *ppl. adj.* with the price fixed, vi. xi. 14.

prise, *sb.*[1] price, vi. xi. 14; worth, value, *R. R.* 403. Cf. **price,** *sb.*

prise, *sb.*[2] contest, enterprise, vi. viii. 25.

priuate, personal, particular, *Clorinda* 89.

priuely, priuily, -lie, preu-, secretly, i. v. 4, v. vii. 14, *S. C. May* 252, *Sept.* 160, *Worlds Vanitie* 78.

priuie, preuie, priue, *adj.* secret, *S. C. March* 35, *H. Beautie* 236; secret, hidden, concealed, vi. v. 24, *Elegie* 179, *S. C. Sept.* 162; *to make priuie* = to make cognizant, familiar, *S. C. March* 30, *Hubberd* 70, *Three Lett.* p. 626.

priuitie, -y, design, plan, iv. v. 1; secret thoughts, iv. ix. 19.

prize, prizde, *see* **price,** *vb.*

procure, to endeavour to cause, ii. ii. 32, xii. 48, v. ix. 39; to cause, v. viii. 1; *pret.* iv. xii. 23; *pa. part.* urged, pressed, iii. i. 1; *pret.* induced, prevailed upon, vi. viii. 29.

prodigious, ominous, portentous, iv. i. 13.

professe, to indicate, vi. vi. 10.

proffer, offer, vi. ix. 33.

progrésse, journey, iii. xi. 20.

proiect, to throw, cast, vi. i. 45.

prolling, *pres. part.* prowling, *S. C. Sept.* 160.

prolong, to postpone, iv. iv. 12; to delay, v. xi. 1.

prone, yielding, iii. ii. 23.

proofe, experience, iv. vii. 37, viii. 44; effect v. ix. 42; *arm'd to p.* = with tested weapons; *put in p.* = tried, *Hubberd* 1252.

proper, own, iii. ii. 1, v. iv. 24, *R. R.* 431; *proper good* = private property, v. i. 23.

propertis, characteristics, ii. ix. 58.

protense, extension, duration, iii. iii. 4.

protract, duration, length, *Amor.* Son. 87.

proue, prooue, to try, test, i. i. 50, iii. xii. 31, iv. vi. 4, vi. xi. 5, *Amor.* p. 578; *pret.* iii. i. 60, v. ii. 46; to experience, endure, feel, iv. vi. 34, viii. 3, ix. 31; *pret. Clout,* 664.

prouokement, provocation, iv. iv. 4.

prow, brave, iii. iii. 28; **prowest** (*superl.*), i. iv. 41, v. 14, ii. iii. 15, viii. 18, iii. iii. 24.

prowes, prowess, i. ix. 17.

proynd, *pret.* preened, *Thest.* 137.

prune, to trim or dress the feathers with the beak, to preen, ii. iii. 36, *Teares* 402; *refl. Past. Aeglogue* 24.

pryse, to pay for, iv. xi. 5. Cf. **price,** *vb.*

puddle, foul, muddy water, iv. v. 33.

puissant (2 syll.), mighty, powerful, i. vi. 45, iv. xi. 15.

púissa(u)nce (3 syll.), power, i. ii. 17, iii. xi. 4.

pumy, pumie stones, pumice stones, ii. v. 30, iii. v. 39, *S. C. March* 89. **pumies,** *plur.* pieces of pumice stone.

pupillage, minority, ii. x. 64, (*fig.*) p. 412.

purchase, *sb.* acquisition, i. iii. 16; booty, vi. xi. 12, *Hubberd* 854, *Gnat* 591.

purchase, *vb.* to obtain, ii. iii. 18; to acquire, win, v. x. 24. **purchast,** *pret.* won, v. viii. 25, 26.

purfled, *pa. part.* decorated with an ornamental border, i. ii. 13, ii. iii. 26.

purport, outward bearing, iii. i. 52.

purpos, -e, *sb.* intention, i. ii. 30; discourse, conversation, i. vii. 38, xii. 13, iii. ii. 4, viii. 14, iv. i. 7; *S. C. March.* Arg. 3; *plur.* riddles, games, iii. x. 8; *to purpose* = to the purpose, ii. iv. 39; *p. was moved* = it was suggested, iii. ix. 32.

purpose, *vb.* to discourse, ii. xii. 16.

pursuiuant, -siuant, follower, attendant, ii. viii. 2; warrant-officer, *Hubberd* 565.

puruay, to provide, ii. iii. 15 (of), v. xii. 10.

purueyance, provision, i. xii. 13; preparation, management, iii. i. 11; equipment, iii. i. 33, xi. 53.

puttock, kite or buzzard, ii. xi. 11, v. v. 15, xii. 30.

pyonings, *vbl. sb.* diggings, excavations, ii. x. 63.

Q

quadrate, rectangle, ii. ix. 22.

quaile, to become dismayed, i. ix. 49; to become feeble, fail, iii. ii. 27; to fade, wither, *S. C. Nov.* 91, **quayld, quaild,** *pa. part.* subdued, overpowered, ii. iv. 14, iii. viii. 34.

quaint, queint, fastidious, iii. vii. 10; artful, iv. i. 5; pretty, iv. x. 22; strange, iv. viii. 45, *S. C. Oct.* 114; fine, elegant, vi. ix. 35; *adv.* strangely, iii. vii. 22.

qualifyde, *pa. part.* modified, moderated, ii. vi. 51.

quarrell, quar'le, square-headed arrow, ii. xi. 24, 33.

quarrey, -ie, the bird flown at or killed by a bird of prey, ii. xi. 43, iii. vii. 39, v. iv. 42.

quart, quarter, region, ii. x. 14.

quartred, *pret.* divided into quarters (*her.*), ii. i. 18.

quayd, *pa. part.* for **quayld,** daunted, subdued, i. viii. 14.

queane, a worthless woman, iv. viii. 28.

queint, *adj.* *See* **quaint.**

queint, *pa. part.* extinguished, ii. v. 11.

quell, *trans.* to frighten, daunt, v. iii. 16;

queld, *pa. part.* v. iii. 26, xii. 16; to overcome, kill, vi. x. 36; *pa. part.* ii. vii. 40, vi. xii. 30; *intr.* to perish, vii. vii. 42; to abate, *S. C. March* 8.

queme, to please, *S. C. May* 15.

quest, expedition, search, iii. viii. 53, iv. vi. 42.

quick, *vb.* to stir, v. ix. 33.

quicke, *adj.* alive, ii. i. 3 ; *sb.* living thing, *S. C. March* 74.

quidams, somebodies, certain persons, *S. C.* p. 419.

quidditie, essence, *Three Lett.* p. 614.

quiet age, tranquillity, quietness, iv. iii. 43.

quight, *adj.* free, *R. R.* 108.

quight, *vb.* to release, set free, i. viii. 10; to requite, repay, i. x. 67, iii. v. 45, x. 35. Cf. **quit**.

quight, *adv.* quite, i. i. 45, iii. v. 41, v. xi. 60, &c.

quip, *vb.* to jeer, vi. vii. 44.

quips, *sb.* sneers, taunts, *Hubberd* 707.

quire, company, vi. viii. 48. **quire**, **quyre**, a company of singers, ii. vi. 24, *Clorinda* 63, *Amor.* Son. 19.

quit, **quite**, **quyte**, to return (a salutation), i. x. 15; **quited**, *pret.* i. i. 30; to return, repay, requite, i. ii. 17, viii. 26, vi. vi. 44, *Clout* 681; to free, release, i. vi. 6, vi. viii. Arg., *S. C. Feb.* 213; *pa. part.* **quitt**, i. v. 11, x. 63; **quitted**, *pa. part.* taken away, iv. i. 12; **quit**, *inf. refl.* to clear oneself of, ii. i. 20.

quite clame, to release, discharge, vi. ii. 14.

quod, quoth, said, *Amor.* Son. 50, *Amor.* p. 578, *Epigrams* p. 606-7.

quooke, *pret.* quaked, iii. x. 24, v. viii. 9, vi. vii. 24, vii. vi. 30. *Hubberd* 1060.

R

rab(b)lement, rabble, mob, i. vi. 8, ii. xi. 17, iii. xi. 46, *Hubberd* 1270; confusion, tumult, i. xii. 9.

race, *sb.* act of riding rapidly on horseback; onset, rush, iv. vi. 3, v. x. 34.

race, *vb.*[1] to raze, destroy, ii. xii. 83, iii. iii. 34, v. ii. Arg. **raced**, *pret.* v. ii. 28; *pa. part.*, *R. R.* 22; **raced**, *pa. part.* erased, v. ix. 26.

raced, *vb.*[2], *pa. part.* cut away, v. v. 11.

rackt, *pa. part.* extorted, *Hubberd* 1306.

rad[1], *pret.* rode, v. ii. 13.

rad[2], *see* **read**, *vb.*[2]

raft, *pret.* cut away, i. i. 24; *pa. part.* deprived, *S. C. Aug.* 14. Cf. **reave**, **reft**.

rag'd, ragged, torn, v. xii. 28.

ragged, rugged, i. v. 3[8], vi. iv. 21, *Clout* 114; rough, *S. C. Feb.* 5.

raid, *pa. part.* smeared, soiled, iii. viii. 32. Cf. **ray**, *vb.*

raile, **rayle**, to flow, gush, i. vi. 43, ii. viii. 37, iii. xi. 46, iv. ii. 18, *Bellay* 155; **rayling**, *ppl. adj.* iii. iv. 57; **railing**, *pres. part.*, *R. T.* 12.

rain, **-e**, *vb.* to reign, i. v. 40, *Amor.* Son. 4.

raine, **rayne**, **raign**, *sb.* kingdom, rule, domain, ii. vii. 21, iii. iv. 49, iv. iii. 27, v. xi. 35, vi. ii. 9, vii. vii. 15, *R. T.* 63.

rakehell, rascal, scoundrelly, v. xi. 44.

rakehellye, worthless, rascally, *S. C.* p. 417.

ramp, to rage, i. iii. 41, v. 28; **ramping**, *ppl. adj.* i. iii. 5. **rampt**, *pret.* seized, vi. xii. 29.

rancke, **ranke**, *sb.* row, iv. v. 33, v. xi. 9; series, *S. C.* p. 419.

rancke, *adj.* violent, fierce, *S. C. Feb.* 1; thick, dense, *S. C. July* 4.

rancke, **ranke**, *adv.* fiercely, violently, ii. iii. 6, iv. v. 33.

ranckorous, bitter, sharp, *S. C. Feb.* 185.

randon, random, ii. iv. 7, iii. viii. 20, *Clout* 812.

rape, *sb.* robbery, iv. vii. 5.

rape, *vb.* to carry off, iii. x. Arg.

rapt, *pa. part.* carried off, seized, i. iv. 9, v. viii. 43.

rase, to erase, destroy, *Amor.* G. W. to Author; to graze, iii. i. 65. **rast**, *pa. part.* ii. xii. 80, iii. iii. 43, iv. i. 21. Cf. **race**, *vb.*[1]

rash, to cut, slash, iv. ii. 17, v. iii. 8.

rashly, hastily, quickly, iii. i. 62, xii. 33; suddenly, iv. ii. 17.

raskall, base, worthless, i. xii. 9, ii. xi. 19, iii. xi. 46.

rate, *sb.* amount, allowance, iv. viii. 19; manner, iv. x. 52.

rate, *vb.* to reprove angrily, iii. ix. 14; to drive away by rating, iv. ix. 31.

rathe, soon, iii. iii. 28, *S. C. Dec.* 98; swiftly, *S. C. July* 78. **rather**, *comp.* earlier (born), *S. C. Feb.* 83.

raught, *pret.* and *pa. part.* reached, i. vi. 29, ii. ix. 19, v. i. 6, 8, vi. xi. 33; handed, i. ix. 51, ii. iv. 5; took, took away, iii. i. 5, iv. iv. 20, vi. xii. 3; granted, *Hubberd* 441.

raunch, to pull, pluck, *S. C. Aug.* 97.

raunge, row, vi. xii. 26; fire-grate, ii. vii. 35.

rauin, **-e**, plunder, booty, prey, i. v. 8, xi. 12, iv. vii. 5; voracity, v. xi. 24.

rauishment, ecstasy, vi. ix. 26.

raw-bone, raw-boned, showing the bone, i. ix. 35.

ray, *sb.* array, equipment, v, ii. 50, *R. T.* 640; order, v. xi. 34.

ray, *vb.* to soil, defile, II. i. 40, VI. iv. 23, *Bellay* 167. *See* raid.

rayle, *sb.* abuse, IV. i. 43.

rayle, *vb.* to utter abusive language, complain, *S. C. May* 146; *pa. part.* II. iv. Arg. railing, *ppl. adj.* abusive, *R. T.* 538.

rayons, rays, *Bellay* 21.

reach, *sb.* penetration, v. ix. 39; device, scheme, *Hubberd* 1141.

reach, *vb.* to give, yield, IV. ii. 12; to launch, direct, aim, *Hubberd* 840.

read, reed, -e, *sb.* saying, motto, IV. x. 10, *S. C. July* 11; speech, IV. x. 34; counsel, advice, IV. xii. 27, v. Prol. 11, i. 26, VI. ii. 30, vi. 5.

read, rede, *vb.*[1] to counsel, advise, I. i. 13, *S. C. Feb.* 137, *Hubberd* 114, *Clout* 925; red, *pa. part.* VI. ii. 30.

read, -e, reed, -e, *vb.*[2] to see, discern, distinguish, perceive, I. i. 21, *H. Love* 16; *pret.* rad, VI. i. 4; red, *Epith.* 189; *pa. part.* read, I. vi. 36, viii. 33, III. i. 33, *H. Beautie* 165; rad, III. ix. 2, IV. vii. 24, v. xii. 29; read, v. xii. 39; redd, p. 411;—to discover, guess, perceive, II. xii. 70, IV. iv. 39, v. xii. 18, VI. v. 10, *Clout* 336; *pa. part.* red, IV. vii. 40, *Clout* 279; rad, v. vi. 10;—to tell, say, declare, II. i. 17, 18, vii. 7, III. ii. 14, iii. 25, VI. xi. 29, *Hubberd* 604; *pret.* red, III. x. 44, IV. xii. 25, v. ix. 43, VI. x. 30; *pa. part.* red, I. x. 67, v. viii. 13;—to call, name: red, *pret.* III. vi. 28; *pa. part.* I. vii. 46; II. vi. 9;—to deem, think, imagine, take to be, II. vii. 2, 7, 12, v. iii. 21, VI. ii. 25, iii. 31, viii. 31, *Misc. Sonn.* i.; red, *pa. part.*, v. Prol. 2, *R. T.* 633. readen, to describe, III. xii. 26; redd, *pa. part.* II. vii. 51. red, *pa. part.* counted, IV. xii. 2; to foresee, predict, *Hubberd* 698.

reædifye, to rebuild, II. x. 46.

re-allie, to form again, VII. vi. 23.

reame, realm, IV. viii. 45.

reare, rearen, to raise, I. v. 13, vi. 37, viii. 10, 40, x. 35, II. xi. 17, III. x. 52, IV. iv. 41, vi. 25, VI. ii. 42; to arouse, cause, bring about, II. iv. 5, vi. 21, xii. 22, III. i. 9, IV. i. 34; to take away, III. viii. 19, x. 12, IV. vi. 6; to gather, collect, v. xii. 6; *refl.* to rise up, *Hubberd* 237.

reason, ratio, proportion, II. ii. 15; a reasonable amount, *Hubberd* 887.

reaue, to take away, I. iii. 36, xi. 41, II. i. 17, xi. 19, III. viii. 14, v. xi. 27, *Hubberd* 24; reaued, *pret. Beautie* 279; to deprive, II. viii. 15; to release, p. 412.

rebuke, shame, disgrace, III. i. 55.

rebut, to recoil, I. ii. 15; to repel, drive

back, II. ii. 23; rebutted, *pret.* I. xi. 53, III. viii. 10; *pa. part.* IV. iv. 18; rebutting, *pres. part.* v. x. 35.

rechlesse, reckless, *Hubberd* 950.

reclame, *sb.* recall, bringing back, III. x. 16.

reclame, -ayme, *vb.* to recall, v. xii. 9; to recant, VI. iii. 43.

recomfort, to refresh, recreate (*refl.*), *Hubberd* 758.

recomfortlesse, without comfort, v. vi. 24.

record, -e, to call to mind, meditate on, IV. xii. 19; to sing, *S. C. Apr.* 30.

recourse, *sb.* retiring (to rest), III. ix. 26; flow, IV. vi. 2); *had recourse* = came back, v. ii. 2.

recoursing, *pres. part.* recurring, p. 408.

recower, -coure, to recover, IV. iii. 20, ix. 25.

recoyle, to retire, retreat, I. x. 17, v. ix. 9, *Hubberd* 754. recule, -cuile, to recoil, v. xi. 47, VI. i. 20.

recure, to restore (to health), I. v. 44, ix. 2, II. i. 54, *Amor.* Son. 21; to recover, III. v. 34, IV. iv. 37, viii. 45, VI. v. 12; to remedy, II. x. 23, v. x. 26, *S. C. Feb.* 154, p. 417; to cure, heal, VI. vi. 1, 15, *Amor.* p. 578.

redisbourse, to pay back again, IV. iii. 27.

redoubted, *ppl. adj.* reverenced, III. ix. 1; dreaded, feared, v. i. 3.

redound, to flow, overflow, I. vi. 30 (*fig.*), v. ix. 33, *Amor.* Son. 18, *H. Love* 165, *H. Beautie* 75; to result, arise, III. ii. 26; to be redundant, in excess, IV. x. 1. redounding, *ppl. adj.* overflowing, I. iii. 8; *pres. part.* filled, *Gnat* 189.

redresse, to cure, repair, put right again, I. v. 36; to put in order, IV. v. 10. redrest, *pa. part.* relieved, IV. v. 39.

reduce, to bring back, restore, VI. vi. 3.

reeking, *pres. part.* smoking, *S. C. Sept.* 117.

reele, to roll, I. v. 35; *pret.* staggered, III. vii. 42.

refection, refreshment, IV. xii. 34.

reflex, reflection, *Amor.* Son. 66.

reformed, *pret.* punished, chastised, v. i. 21.

refraine, to restrain, IV. ix. 3.

reft, *pret.* took away, IV. ii. 4, v. iii. 37; cut off, IV. iii. 20, v. xii. 23; *pa. part.* seized, taken away, I. iii. 41, ix. 26, II. xii. 67, IV. iii. 21, iv. 8; bereaved, deprived, III. iv. 36. Cf. raft, reave.

refúge, VI. iii. 49.

regalitie, sovereignty, II. i. 57.

regard, *plur.* interests, objects of care, II. vii. 33; considerations, v. ix. 43; *sing.* value, VI. xi. 13; *in r.* = in comparison, VI. x. 9; on account of, VI. xi. 14.

GLOSSARY

regardfull, heedful, IV. vii. 22 ; worthy of regard or esteem, *Clout* 185.

regiment, kingdom, domain, II. ix. 59, *Clout* 233 ; office of a ruler, II. x. 30 ; rule, power, III. iii. 40, IV. viii. 30, v. viii. 30, VII. vi. 2.

regret, -greet, sorrow, pain, II. viii. 45, VI. ii. 23, *Teares* 304.

rehearse, to relate, recount, *R. T.* 255, *Teares* 1, *Past. Elegie* 216.

reincreast, *pa. part.* increased again, VI. vi. 15.

rekes, recks, cares, *S. C. July* 34.

relate, to bring back, III. viii. 51.

release, -ce, to revoke, remit, II. i. 60; to give up, IV. ii. 19 ; to withdraw, VI. i. 43. *pret.* **relest,** transferred, IV. iv. 36 ; **releast,** relaxed, VI. i. 36.

relent, *sb.* delay, v. vii. 24.

relent, *vb.* to slow, slacken, abate, II. xi. 27, III. iv. 49, vii. 2, IV. ii. 18, iii. 26 ; to repent, regret, III. vi. 25 ; to soften, cause to relent, III. vi. 39, 40; to be gentle, *Amor.* Son. 82.

relide, *pret.* rallied, IV. ix. 26.

reliques, remains, II. x. 57.

reliue, -en, to come to life again, *S. C.* p. 419, *Nov.* 88. **reliu'd,** *pa. part.* revived, restored to life, I. ix. 52, III. iv. 35, viii. 3, VI. xi. 24.

remaine : *in r.* = as an inheritance, III. ix. 37.

remeasure, to retrace, III. vii. 18.

remédilesse, without hope of rescue, or cure, I. v. 36, III. xii. 34.

remercied, *pret.* thanked, II. xi. 16.

remitted, *pa. part.* put back, reinstated, *Hubberd* 1254.

remorse, pity, II. iv. 6, III. vii. 43; biting or cutting force, IV. ii. 15 ; *without r.* = without mitigation, *S. C. Nov.* 131.

remoue, to conceal, II. iv. 27 ; to change, III. viii. 42. **remoud,** *pret.* went away, III. ix. 43.

rencounter, *sb.* encounter, III. i. 9.

rencountring, *pres. part.* engaging in battle, I. iv. 39.

renfierst, *pa. part.* rendered fierce, II. viii. 45.

renforst, *pret.* made a strong effort, II. iv. 14 ; *pa. part.* forced again, II. x. 48.

renne, to run, *S. C. Apr.* 118, *July* 60; *pa. part., S. C. Aug.* 3 ; **renning,** *vbl. sb., Past. Elegie* 73.

renowmd, -ed, *pa. part.* renowned, *F. Q.* Dedic. p. 2, II. iv. 41.

renowning, *vbl. sb.* making famous, glorification, *R. T.* p. 471.

rent, to propel violently, v. x. 34.

renuerst, *pret.* v. iii. 37 ; *pa. part.* I. iv. 41 : reversed.

repaire, to draw back, v. xi. 13.

repast, refreshment, repose, I. ii. 4, v. iii. 40.

Repent, *sb.* Repentance, III. xii. 24.

repent, *vb.* to grieve, mourn, III. viii. 47.

repine, to grumble, complain, IV. ii. 51 ; to fret or murmur at, VI. vii. 26.

repining, *ppl. adj.* angry, I. ii. 17.

repleuie, to recover for, or restore to, the owner by replevin, i.e. upon his giving security to have the matter tried in a court of justice and to return the goods if the case is decided against him, IV. xii. 31.

report, to convey (news), II. i. 33, x. 3.

repriefe, reproof, reproach, I. ix. 29, II. iv. 28, III. iii. 5, IV. ii, viii. 1.

repriue, to rescue, II. i. 55, v. iv. Arg. ; to reprieve, IV. xii. 31.

reprize, to take again, II. xi. 44, IV. iv. 8.

requere, to demand, I. iii. 12, VI. 27, VI. i. 43. **require,** to request, ask, demand, IV. i. 12, v. i. 21, ii. 2, 11, VI. v. 11, *S. C. Nov.* Arg., *Hubberd* 325.

requests, demands, II. ii. 32.

requight, -quite, to pay back, revenge, I. iv. 42 ; to salute in return, I. x. 49, *Hubberd* 587 ; *pret.* **requit,** IV. iii. 47. **requit,** *pret.* repayed, v. vii. 33.

reseized, *pa. part.* restored, replaced, II. x. 45.

resemblance, -aunce, demonstration of affection, III. vii. 16 ; appearance, v. ix. 22.

resiant, resident, IV. xi. 28.

resolu'd, *pa. part.* relaxed, slackened, *Gnat* 141.

resort, visiting, frequenting of a person's company, III. ix. 5.

respect, care, attention, v. xii. 21.

respire, -yre, to take breath, rest, I. vi. 44, ix. 8, xi. 28, III. iii. 36, xii. 45 ; to breathe, II. iv, 16.

respondence, answer, response, II. xii. 71.

rest [1] : *set his r.* = took up his abode, VI. x. 2.

rest [2], a contrivance to hold a lance or spear, v. viii. 5, 9.

restore, *sb.* restitution, III. v. 19 ; restoration, *Epitaph* (2) 34.

restore, *vb.* to reward, I. viii. 27.

resty, restive, v. viii. 39.

retourned, -turnd, *pret.* turned (back), II. iii. 19, III. viii. 18.

retrate, *sb.*[1] retiring, retreat, IV. x. 57.

retrate, *sb.*[2], **-ait,** portrait, picture, II. iii. 25, ix. 4.

retrate, *vb.* to retreat, I. i. 13, viii. 12, IV. iii. 26.

retyre, retirement, VI. ix. 27.

reuell rout, uproarious revelry, *Hubberd* 558.

reuengement, revenge, *Hubberd* 216.

reuénue, v. ii. 9.

reuerse, to bring back, i. ix. 48 ; to remove, divert, iii. ii. 48 ; to return, iii. iv. 1, *R. R.* 305.

reuest, to clothe, ii. i. 22.

reuoke, to check, restrain, ii. ii. 28 ; to withdraw, ii. viii. 39, iii. xi. 21.

reuolt, to turn back, iii. xi. 25.

reuyld, *pret.* scolded, i. xii. 11.

rew, *sb.*[1] row, order, iii. vi. 17, 35, v. v. 22 ; *in r.* = in turn, older, *Teares* 173, 233, &c.

rew, *sb.*[2] rue, a perennial evergreen shrub, iii. ii. 49.

rew, *vb.* to pity, i. i. 51, vi. 31, iii. v. 30 ; to repent, lament, be sorry, i. i. 53, v. 42, ii. i. 25, v. xi. 30. Cf. rue.

reynold, reynard, fox, *Hubberd* 556.

ribaudrie, rybaudrye, ribaldry, obscenity, *S. C. Oct.* 76, *Teares* 213.

ribauld, a wicked, dissolute person, ii. i. 10 ; an obscene composition, *S. C.* p. 459.

richesse, riches, i. iv. 28, ii. vii. 24.

rid[1], *pret.* ride, v. iii. 10, vi. iii. 37.

rid[2], *pa. part.* (*for* red), seen, perceived, vii. vi. 54. *See* read, reed, *vb.*[2]

riddes, dispatches, i. i. 36.

ridling, *ppl. adj.* that can expound riddles ; divining, iii.·xi. 54.

rife, ryfe, *adj.* strong, deep, ii. ii. 32 ; abundant, *Gnat* 146 ; common, *S. C. July* 11 ; *adv.* deeply, strongly, abundantly, i. ix. 44, 52, iii. v. 31, iv. iii. 12, v. ix. 48, vi. v. 5.

rifelye, copiously, abundantly, *S. C. Dec.* 94.

rift, *sb.* split, fissure, i. ii. 30 ; fragment, ii. ·ii· 4.

rift, *pa. part.* rent asunder, i. xi. 54, ii. vii 23.

right, territory, domain, v. viii. 26.

rigorous, violent, fierce, i. xi. 16, iii. xii. 27.

rigour, violence, force, i. viii. 18, iii. v. 23, v. viii. 32.

rine, rinde, bark, rind, *S. C. Feb.* 111, *R. R.* 389.

ring, to encircle, vi. Prol. 7.

riotise, -ize, riotous life, conduct, expenditure ; extravagance, i. iv. 20, iii. i. 33, xii. 25, *Hubberd* 805, 1310.

rip up, to open up, iv. ix. 37, *S. C. Sept.* 13.

riuage, bank, shore, iv. vi. 20.

riue, ryue, to split, tear, pierce, i. ii. 19, v. ii. 50, *Gnat* 519 ; ryu'd, *pret.* iii. v. 37 ; *pa. part.* riu'd, ryued, iii. i. 6, viii. 3, iv. iii. 18, *Past. Elegie* 120 ; riuen, *Hubberd* 540.

rize, to come to hand, ii. ix. 59 ; to accrue, *Hubberd* 806.

rocke, distaff, iv. ii. 48.

rode, roadstead, i. xii. 42 ; raid, vi. viii. 35.

rong, *pret.* rang, iii. i. 62.

ronte, ox or cow of a small breed or size, *S. C. Feb.* 5.

roode, cross, crucifix, vi. v. 35.

roome, place, position, ii. x. 60.

rosiere, rose-tree, ii. ix. 19.

rosmarine[1], rosemary, *Muiop.* 200.

rosmarines[2], walruses, ii. xii. 24.

rote, a mediaeval musical instrument, probably of the violin class, ii. x. 3, iv. ix. 6.

roules, rolls, records, vi. vii. 33.

rounded, *pret.* whispered, iii. x. 30.

roundelay, a short simple song with a refrain, *S. C. June* 49, *Aug.* 56.

roundell, circle, iii. iv. 33. roundle, rondeau, rondel, short poem, *S. C. Aug.* 125.

rout, crowd, troop, i. iv. 36, v. 51, ii. ix. 15, v. ii. 51, v. 5, vi. ix. 8, *S. C. Oct.* 26, *Hubberd* 558.

rouze, rowze, to shake, ruffle, i. xi. 9, ii. iii. 35 ; rouzed, *ppl. adj.* i. xi. 9.

roue, to shoot with arrows (*fig.*), i. Prol. 3, iii. i. 50 ; rou'd, roude, -ed, *pret.* iii. ix. 28, v. v. 35, *S. C. Aug.* 79.

rowels, knobs on a horse's bit, i. vii. 37.

rowme, place, space, room, i. iv. 13, *S. C. Apr.* 114, *S. C. Dec.* 68.

royne, to roar, growl, v. ix. 33.

rubin, -e, ruby, ii. iii. 24. xii. 54.

rudded, *pa. part.* reddened, *Epith.* 173.

ruddock, redbreast, robin, *Epith.* 82.

rudenesse, uncouthness, *S. C.* p. 416.

rue, to cause to pity, i. ii. 21. ruing, *pres. part.* pitying, v. x. 4. Cf. rew, *vb.*

ruefull, pitifull, ii. xii. 36.

ruefully, pitiably, iii. viii. 30.

ruefulnesse, dismalness, pathos, i. iv. 25.

ruffed, *pa. part.* iii. ii. 27 ; *ppl. adj.*, *Teares* 402 : ruffled. ruffing, *pres. part.* ruffling, iii. xi. 32.

ruffin, *sb.* the ruff, *Acerina cernua*, iv. xi. 33.

ruffin, *adj.* ruffian, disorderly, i. iv. 34.

ruinate, to ruin, ii. xii. 7, iii. viii 28, *R. R.* 94 ; *pa. part.* v. x. 26, *Hubberd* 1040.

rulesse, lawless, *Gnat* 431.

rushrings, rings of rush, *S. C. Nov.* 116.

ruth, pity, grief, i. i. 50, iii. v. 7, v. ix. 50, *R. T.* 480.

ruthfull, piteous, grievous, *S. C. June* 116.

rutty, full of ruts, *Proth.* 12.

S

.s. = *scilicet*, *S. C.* pp. 418, 447.

sacrament, solemn oath or engagement, v. i. 25.

sacred, accursed, I. viii. 35, II. xii. 37, v. xii. 1.

sad, grave, serious, I. i. 29, II. ii. 28; dark-coloured, sober-coloured, I. x. 7, xii. 5; grievous, II. i. 38; heavy, II. i. 45, viii. 30; constant, III. xi. 45.

safe, save, except, III. vii. 60.

safegard, safety, III. ix. 41.

saine, sayne, to say, 3rd pers. plur. pres. III. ix. 40, VII. vii. 55; inf., S. C. May 158, Sept. 108, 110, 123, Nov. 93.

sake, cause, I. i. 52; regard, consideration, I. v. 12.

sale, net made out of sallow or willow branches, S. C. Dec. 81.

salewd, pret. saluted, greeted, IV. vi. 25. Cf. salued.

saliaunce, assault, sally, II. i. 29.

saluage, adj. savage, wild, I. iii. 5 (transf.), III. iii. 45, x. 39, IV. iv. 42, VI. i. 9, v. 27, p. 411, R. T. 564, Teares 589; sb. VI. v. 41.

salued, pret. saluted, greeted, II. viii. 23.

salue, sb. remedy, I. v. 40, III. iv. 43, v. 50, S. C. Aug. 103, Amor. Son. 50.

salue, vb.¹ to remedy, IV. iv. 27, p. 417; pret. remedied, made amends for, II. x. 21.

salue, vb.² to save, v. v. 43; to arrange, contrive, IV. i. 11; to preserve unblemished, IV. iv. 27.

saluing, vbl. sb. restoration, vindication, II. i. 20.

sam, together, I. x. 57, S. C. May 168.

samite, rich silk fabric, III. xii. 13.

sample, example, S. C. July 119.

sanguine, blood-red colour, II. i. 39, III. viii. 6.

sans, without; in the names Sans foy faithless, Sans joy joyless, Sans loy lawless, I. ii. 25.

sardonian, sardonic, v. ix. 12.

saufgard, guard, defence, II. v. 8.

saulge, sage, Muiop. 187.

saue, to meet or overcome (a doubt), Hubberd 194.

sauegard, to guard, protect, III. viii. 46.

sauine, small bushy evergreen shrub, Juniperus Sabina, bearing a small, round, bluish-purple berry, III. ii. 49.

sauing, without, in default of, S. C. p. 419.

sauorie, plant of the genus Satureia, used for flavouring, Muiop. 198.

saw, decree, command, Clout 884.

say, saye ¹, a cloth of fine texture resembling serge; in the 16th c. sometimes partly of silk, subsequently woollen, I. iv. 31, III. xii. 8, S. C. Aug. 66.

say ², temper, VI. xi. 47.

scald, a scabby disease, I. viii. 47.

scalp, crown of the head, skull, v. ii. 6.

scand, pa. part. examined, v. ix. 37; climbed, VII. vi. 8.

scanne, to attempt (a high ascent), S. C. Oct. 88.

scape, sb. escape, deliverance, Gnat 664.

scape, vb. to escape, I. iv. 3, III. xi. 34.

scarabee, beetle, Worlds Vanitie 44.

scarmoges, skirmishes, II. vi. 34.

scath, harm, damage, injury, loss, I. iv. 35, xii. 34, II. v. 18, III. i. 37, x. 11, S. C. Dec. 100, Amor. Son. 31; harmful nature, v. viii. 49.

scattered, pa. part. dropped, II. ii. 2.

scatterlings, vagrants, II. x. 63.

scene, stage, Teares 192.

scerne, to discern, III. x. 22.

schoolery, education, Clout 702.

sclaunder, slander, v. ix. 26.

sclaue, slave, II. vii. 33.

sclender, slender, thin, III. i. 47, vii. 36, v. vii. 7.

scolopendraes, a kind of fabulous sea-fishes, II. xii. 23.

scope, object of desire or pursuit, III. iv. 52; extent, space, III. ix. 46; mark for shooting at (lit. and fig.), VI. iii. 5, S. C. Nov. 155, Hubberd 960.

score, number, VI. ix. 21.

scorse, sb. exchange, II. ix. 55.

scorse, vb.¹ to exchange, III. ix. 16.

scorsed, vb.² pret. chased, VI. ix. 3.

scould, pret. scowled, II. ii. 35.

scowre, to run, pursue, I. ii. 20, Gnat 564.

scowring, vbl. sb. dirt or scum, Gnat 229.

scriene, screen, doorway, v. ix. 25.

scrike, to shriek, VI. iv. 18.

scrine, scryne, chest for the safe keeping of books and documents, I. Prol. 2, II. ix. 56.

scrip, bag, wallet, I. vi. 35.

scruze, to squeeze, III. v. 33; scruzd, pret. II. xii. 56; pa. part. II. xii. 46.

scryde, pa. part. descried, perceived, v. xii. 38.

scuchin, scutchin, -ion, escutcheon, shield, coat of arms, III. iv. 16, IV. i. 34, iii. 5, v. xi. 54.

scuith guiridh (Welsh), green shield; y scuith gogh, the red shield, II. x. 24.

sdaine, sdeigne, sb. disdain, v. v. 51, Amor. Son. 5.

sdeigne, vb. to disdain, III. i. 55, p. 411; pret. sdeigned, III. i. 40, Hubberd 679; pa. part. sdayned, v. v. 44.

sdeignfull, s'deign-, sdein-, disdainful, III. vii. 10, v. ii. 33, Teares 71, Daphn. 549.

sdeignfully, disdainfully, Hubberd 1234.

seabeate, pa. part. beaten by the sea, weather-beaten, S. C. Feb. 34.

seard, pret. burned, I. xi. 26.

seare, *adj.* burning, 1. xi. 13 ; sere, withered, *S. C. Nov.* 147.

sea-satyre, some kind of maritime monster, 11. xii. 24.

sease, to reach, attain, 111. v. 19. **seasd**, *pret.* penetrated, 1. xi. 38. Cf. **seize**.

sea-shouldring, *ppl. adj.* with shoulders that displace the sea, 11. xii. 23.

seasure : *made s.* = took possession, 1v. ix. 12.

seat, to lie down, v1. ix. 4.

Secretaries of nature, men acquainted with the secrets of nature, *Three Lett.* p. 615.

sectaries, disciples, *Teares* 73, *Hubberd* 833.

secure, free from apprehension, careless, v1. v. 16, *Muiop.* 382.

securitie, carelessness, *S. C.* p. 427.

see, seat, throne, 111. vi. 2 ; dwelling-place, abode, 1v. x. 30.

seeld, *adj.* rare, uncommon, *Elegie* 171.

seeld, *adv.* seldom, *Epitaph* (1) 11.

seeled, *pa. part.* made blind, 1. vii. 23.

seeling, ceiling, *Bellay* 23.

seely, simple, innocent, 1. vi. 10, 11. iii. 6, *S. C. July* 30. Cf. **silly**.

seem, to be seemly, becoming, *S. C. May* 158, *Hubberd* 35, *Clout* 618.

seemelesse, unseemly, shameful, v. ii. 25.

seemely, comely, handsome, 11. xii. 27, 111. xii. 19, v. iv. 4.

seeming, *vbl. sb.* opinion, *Two Lett.* p. 635.

seemlyhed, a becoming appearance, 1v. viii. 14.

seene, *ppl. adj.* : *well s.* = well-versed, skilled, 1v. ii. 35, v. iii. 5, *S. C.* p. 417.

seisin, v1. iv. 37. *See* **liverey**.

seize, **seise**, to fasten upon, 1. iii. 19, viii. 15, v. iv. 40 ; to arrive at, attain, 1. xii. 17 ; to penetrate, 11. viii. 38, 111. vii. 40. **seized of**, *pa. part.* = possessed of, v1. iv. 30, xii. 5, *Hubberd* 1111.

selcouth, strange, 1v. viii. 14.

select, *pa. part.* chosen, *Clorinda* 63.

selfe, himself, 1v. v. 34, vi. 17, *H. Love* 145 ; herself, 1v. i. 2, *Gnat* 505 ; itself, 1v. vii. 36.

sell, saddle, 11. ii. 11, iii. 12, viii. 31, 111. i. 6, iii. 60, 1v. iv. 30, vi. 13.

semblably, similarly, p. 411.

semblance, -aunce, demeanour, expression, 111. vii. 16 ; joyous, *faire s.*, 1v. vii. 44, v1. iv. 14.

semblant, -aunt, likeness, resemblance, 1. ii. 12, p. 413, *Amor.* Son. 45 ; outward appearance, 11. i. 21, ix. 2, 111. ii. 38, 40 ; false appearance, pretence, 11. xii. 49, 111. iv. 54, *Gnat* 93 ; demeanour, 1v. x. 31, v1. x. 23 ; signs, appearance, v1. v. 4 ; *fair s.* = favour, v. v. 56.

seminarie, seed-plot, 111. vi. 30.

senarie, verse consisting of six feet, each of which is either an iambus or some foot which the law of the verse allows to be substituted, *Two Lett.* p. 640.

sencelesse, insensible, unfeeling, *Amor.* Son. 30, 54.

senight, week, *R. T.* p. 470.

sens, since, ago, 1v. v. 23.

sense, sence, perception, 1. i. 50 ; senses, feelings, 1v. vi. 21 1. 7, *Gnat* 11.

sensefull, sensible, v1. iv. 37, ix. 26.

sensibly, feelingly, sensitively, 1v. viii. 4.

sent, perception, 1. i. 43 ; scent, 111. vii. 23.

sented : *well s.* = gifted with keen perception, *S. C.* p. 418.

sere, withered, *S. C. Jan.* 37.

seru'd, brought into action, 11. x. 55.

seruewe, to examine, survey, *S. C. Feb.* 145.

set : *set by* = make much of, esteem, 1v. vi. 46 ; *set* (a person) *by* = deprive him of, *Elegie* 174.

setuale, zedoary, East Indian plant having aromatic and medicinal properties, *Muiop.* 196.

seuerall, *adj.* diverse, 1. iii. 16 ; *adv.* separately, in different directions, v1. i. 10.

sew, to follow, pursue (*lit.* and *fig.*), 11. ii. 17, 111. iv. 50, x. 9, 1v. ix. 26, v1. ix. 2, x. 2, xi. 5, *Hubberd* 743 ; *serve and sew*, 11. vii. 9, 111. v. 47 ; *seeke and sew*, *Beautie* 153 ; to solicit, plead, 1v. xii. 29.

shade, to shadow, represent, v. vii. 3 ; to hide, disguise, v. viii. 14, ix. 12.

shadow, dissimulation, pretence, v1. xi. 6 ; shade, *Gnat* 143.

shagged, *pret.* hung in a shaggy mass, v. ix. 10.

shaires, parts, divisions, 11. x. 37.

shallop, sloop, a light boat, 111. vii. 27.

shallowes, 111. iv. 9.

shame, to feel ashamed, 11. xii. 23, v. iv. 24.

shamefast, modest, bashful, 1. x. 15, v. v. 25.

shamefastnesse, modesty, v. iii. 23.

shard, bourn, boundary, 11. vi. 38.

share, *sb.* piece, portion, 1. ii. 18.

share, *vb.* to cut, pierce, 1v. ii. 17 ; *pret.* **shard, shared**, 1v. vi. 19, v. i. 10, v. 9 ; divided, *Clout* 138.

sharpe, to sharpen, p. 413 ; **sharped**, *ppl. adj.* sharpened, tapering, *R. R.* 16.

shaume, musical instrument of the oboe class, 1. xii. 13, v. v. 4.

shauelings, rascals, *S. C.* p. 443.

sheare, sheere, *adj.* clear, bright, 111. xi. 7, vii. vii. 25.

sheare, shere, *vb.* to cut, divide, cleave, 11. vi. 5, 111. iv. 33, 42, 1v. v. 34. **sheard**, *pret.* 11. vi. 31.

sheares, wings (as if made to cut the air), II. viii. 5.

shed, to pour out, emit, *S. C. Oct.* 35, *Worlds Vanitie* 78; *pa. part.* II. vii. 30.

sheene, shene, bright, beautiful, fair, II. i. 10, ii. 40, III. i. 65, iv. 51, v. viii. 29, x. 25, *S. C. Nov.* 38.

shend, to disgrace, I. i. 53, II. vi. 35, viii. 12, III. ix. 1, iv. i. 51, *S. C. July* 172; to use injuriously, v. iv. 24, to surpass, *Proth.* 121.

shent, *pret.* reproached, reproved, II. v. 5; disgraced, v. iii. 37; *pa. part.* disgraced, II. i. 11, 27, III. ix. 33, v. viii. 23; injured, III. iv. 50, 58.

shere, bright, clear, III. ii. 44, iv. vi. 20. Cf. **sheare,** *adj.*

shew, sheow, sign, I. i. 46, III. vii. 29; sign, trace, I. iii. 10.

shidder, young female sheep, *S. C. Sept.* 211. Cf. **hidder.**

shield : *God s.* = God forbid, *S. C. July* 9.

shift, movement, III. i. 61; artifice, *Clout* 694.

shifted, *pret.* succeeded, *Hubberd* 659.

shine, bright, iv. iii. 3.

shinie-beame, glittering ray, v. iv. 45.

shit, *pa. part.* shut, *Clout* 709.

shiuering, *ppl. adj.* quivering, iv. i. 49, ii. 14.

shole, troop, band, *S. C. May* 20.

shole, *adj.* shallow, vii. vi. 40.

shonne, to shun, avoid, III. i. 52, vi. xii. 35, *Gnat* 176.

shope, *pret.* framed, shaped, v. v. 39.

shot, advanced (in years), v. vi. 19.

shouldred, *pa. part.* pushed, buffeted, *Clout* 709.

shred, *pa. part.* cut, *Thest.* 75.

shrieches, shrieks, vi. iv. 18.

shriech oule, scrich-, shriekowle, screech-owl, *R. T.* 130, *Teares* 283, *Epith.* 345.

shrieue, to question, iv. xii. 26; to confess, *S. C. Aug.* 55.

shrifts, confessions, *Hubberd* 453.

shright, *sb.* shriek, II. vii. 57, vi. iv. 2.

shright, *pret.* shrieked, III. viii. 32.

shrike, *sb.* shriek, cry, *R. T.* 471, *Teares* 358, *Past. Aeglogue* 108.

shrike, *vb.* to shriek, iv. v. 41, *Teares* 229.

shrill, *sb.* shrill sound, *R. T.* 581.

shrill, *vb.* to give forth a shrill sound, resound, vi. viii. 46, *Daphn.* 323, *Past. Elegie* 44; **shrild,** *pret.*, *S. C. Nov.* 71, *Gnat* 518.

shrilling, *ppl. adj.* shrill, resounding, III. viii. 29, iv. ii. 32.

shriuing, confession, *Hubberd* 543.

shrowd, -e, to take shelter, hide, I. i. 6, *S. C. Feb.* 122, *Gnat* 176. **shrouded, shrowded,** *pa. part.* hidden, sheltered, *S. C. Mar.* 68, *Apr.* 32.

shyne, brightness, I. x. 67.

sib, sibbe, sybbe, akin, related, III. iii. 26, vi. vii. 41, *S. C. May* 269; *transf., Three Lett.* p. 621, *Two Lett.* p. 643.

sich, such, III. vii. 29, *S. C. Sept.* 79, 165.

sicker, *adv.* certainly, surely, assuredly, *S. C. Feb.* 55, *March* 7, *Apr.* 158, *May* 19, 55, *Aug.* 43, *Sept.* 76; *adj.* secure, *Hubberd* 430.

sickernesse, safety, security, III. vii. 26, xi. 55.

side, *adv.* at the sides, *Epigrams* p. 607.

siege, seat, throne, II. ii. 39, vii. 44.

sield, *pa. part.* 'ceiled', adorned on the walls and ceiling, v. v. 21.

sielyng, ceiling, *Epigrams* p. 607.

sient, scion, v. i. 1.

sight, *pret.* sighed, II. i. 47, vi. xi. 25.

signe, emblem, ensign, iv. i. 22; *plur.* insignia, *Hubberd* 1016.

sike, such, *S. C. Feb.* 211, *May* 82, *July* 201, 203, *Aug.* 50, 52, *Sept.* 13, 113, 140, *Nov.* 11, 18.

silly, simple, innocent, harmless, I. i. 30, ii. 21, vi. 35, II. iii. 36, III. vii. 8, x. 45, *Teares* 339.

simplesse, simplicity, *S. C. July* 172.

sin, since, vi. xi. 44.

sinamon, cinnamon, *S. C. Feb.* 136.

singled, *pret.* separated, emerged, iv. iv. 17.

singular, eminent, noble, *Misc. Sonn.* 1.

singults, -es, sobs, III. xi. 12, v. vi. 13, *Teares* 232, *Clout* 168.

sited, *pa. part.* III. vi. 31; **site,** p. 210: situated, set.

sith, *conj.* since, II. i. 22, iii. 3, viii. 52, p. 411, *Muiop.* 219; *sith that* = since, I. v. 43; *adv., sith of late* = since, recently, III. viii. 36.

sith, sithes, *sb. plur.* times; *thousand s.,* III. x. 33, *S. C. Jan.* 49.

sithens, -ce, *adv.* since, *R. T.* p. 471, *Hubberd* 1210, *R. R.* 117, *Amor. Son.* 3; ago, *S. C. March* 46; *conj.* I. iv. 51, ix. 8, I. vi. 48.

sitte, sittes, is becoming, behoves, I. i. 30, *S. C. May* 77, *June* 75, *Nov.* 26.

situate, *pa. part.* situated, II. xii. 42.

skand, *pa. part.* understood, *Daphn.* 178.

skanning, *ppl. adj.* understanding, p. 409. Cf. **scand.**

skill, *sb.* sense of what is right and fitting, II. i. 54; process of discrimination, v. iv. 1.

skill, *vb.* to care, III. i. 50, vi. iv. 38; to avail, matter, v. iv. 14; to have perception of, *Three Lett.* 623.

skilful, having a good knowledge of, vi. v. 16.

skippet, small boat or skiff, ii. xii. 14.

skreene, entrance door, v. x. 37. Cf. scriene.

skyen, skies, i. iv. 9.

sky-threating, towering up to the sky, v. x. 23. See threat.

slacke, remiss, iii. vi. 19.

slake, to slacken, neglect, iii. iii. 10 ; to abate, moderate, v. vii. 5; *pa. part.* relieved, rendered less acute, i. vii. 28.

slauered, *pret.* slabbered, v. xii. 29.

sledge, hammer, ii. ii. 22.

sleight, slight, device, artifice, trickery, i. iii. 17, xii. Arg., iv. i. 44, vi. v. 13, vii. vi. 27, vii. 25, *Hubberd* 346, *Worlds Vanitie* 147 ; trick, v. ix. 13 ; design, pattern, i. vii. 30.

slipper, slippery, unstable, *S. C. Nov.* 153.

slipt the coller (*fig.*), drawn back, *Hubberd* 269.

slombred, *ppl. adj.* unconscious, i. vii. 15.

slombry, sleepy, iii. vi. 26.

slouth, sloth, idleness, i. v. 35, ii. i. 23.

slug, to idle, live idly, ii. i. 23, iii. vii. 12.

sly, wise, clever, ii. viii. 47 ; cleverly made, ii. ix. 46.

small, *sb.* little, vi. ix. 20.

smallage, wild celery, *Daphn.* 347.

smight, to smite, strike, ii. ii. 23. smit, *pret.* i. ii. 18, v. xi. 7, vi. xi. 28 ; *pa. part.* iii. 1. 34, ii. 13. 35, xi. 12, iv. i. 14. smot, *pret.* iii. i. 28 ; *pa. part.* iii. ii. 46.

smirke, neat, trim, *S. C. Feb.* 72.

smoothering, smothering, i. xi. 13.

smouldring, *ppl. adj.* suffocating, ii. v. 3.

smouldry, suffocating, i. vii. 13, iii. xi. 21.

snaggy, jagged, knotty, i. vii. 10.

snags, knots, stumps, ii. xi. 23, iv. vii. 7

snakie-paced, moving like a snake, *R. R.* 178.

snaky-wreathed, wrapped round with a snake or snakes, vii. vi. 18.

snar, to snarl, growl, vi. xii. 27.

snarled, *ppl. adj.* twisted, tangled, iii. xii. 17.

snebbe, snib, to reprove, chide, *S. C. Feb.* 126, *Hubberd* 372.

snubbes, knobby protuberances, snags, i. viii. 7.

so, provided that, *Hubberd* 1150.

so that, as if, iii. ii. 19.

soare faulcon, a falcon of the first year, *H. Beautie* 26.

sock, light shoe worn by the ancient actors of comedy ; *hence* comedy, *Teares* 176.

softly, gentle, vi. viii. 6.

sold, *sb.* pay, remuneration, ii. ix. 6.

sold, *pa. part.* given, iv. x. 54.

sole, foot, i. x. 9 ; lowest part, v. ii. 28.

solein, sad, *S. C. May* 213.

solemnize, *sb.* solemnization, i. x. 4.

sólemniz'd, *pa. part.* celebrated, renowned, iii. ii. 18 ; solémniz'd, v. ii. 3.

soly, alone, iv. ix. 18, *Clout* 801.

somd, *pa. part.* properly of a hawk, having the full complement of feathers (*fig.*), *S. C.* p. 418.

somedele, somewhat, *S. C. May* 56, *Dec.* 40.

sometime, formerly, *Thest.* 16.

somewhat, something, *S. C. Nov.* 4.

somme, sum, whole, v. vi. 8.

sondry, separate, iii. vi. 35.

sonet, song, *S. C. Dec.* 15.

song, *pret.* sang, ii. vi. 3, iii. v. 40, *S. C. Dec.* 15.

sonned, *ppl. adj.* exposed to the sun, *S. C. Jan.* 77.

soote, *adv.* sweetly, *S. C. Apr.* 111, *Oct.* 90.

sooth, soth, truth, *S. C. May* 158, p. 443, *Sept.* 154; *adv.* truly, iii. iii. 13, 54, iv. ix. 27, v. x. 9, vi. ii. 9.

soothlich, iii. ii. 14; soothly, v. x. 8, vi. ii. 13 : truly.

soothsay, prediction, prophecy, ii. ix. 51, iv. ii. 35 ; omen, portent, iii. viii. 50.

sopps in wine, the common garden pink, *Dianthus plumarius*, *S. C. Apr.* 138, *May* 14.

sorrow, to cause sorrow to, to grieve, iv. ix. 38.

sort, *sb.* manner, fashion, i. iv. 37, iv. ii. 29, vii. vi. 29, *Teares* 198, 319, *Hubberd* 662 ; company, iii. i. 40, vi. ix. 5, x. 2, xi. 9, *Past. Elegie* 139 ; swarm, flock, v. iv. 36, vii. vi. 28. *in sort as* = the same as, i. xii. 20, v. vi. 17, vi. x. 32, *Past. Elegie* 216 ; *in equall sort* = in the same way, *Amor.* Son. 10.

sort, *vb.* to consort, *Epitaph* (1) 20, *Amor.* Son. 66.

souce, -se, sowse, *vb.* to strike, i. v. 8 ; *pret.* soust, iv. iii. 25 ; sowst, iv. iv. 30; soused, iv. v. 36; to descend, swoop, iii. iv. 16. soust, *pa. part.* thrown down, iv. vii. 9 ; steeped, dipped, i. iii. 31.

souldan, sultan, v. viii. 24.

souse, sowce, *sb.* swoop, pounce (of a hawk), ii. xi. 36, iv. iii. 19, v. iv. 42 ; blow, stroke, iv. viii. 44, v. iv. 24, xii. 23.

sout, soot, ii. viii. 3.

southsayes, prophecies, omens, iv. xi. 13. Cf. soothsay.

souenaunce, remembrance, care, ii. vi. 8, viii. 51, *S. C. May* 82, *Nov.* 5.

sownd, *sb.* swoon, iii. v. Arg. Cf. swound.

sownd, *vb.* ? to wield, I. xii. 5.

sowne, sound, I. i. 41, II. v. 30, vi. 47, p. 409.

soyle, dirt, III. viii. 32; body, IV. iii. 16, *Bellay* 83.

space, to move, walk, roam, IV. ii. 44, viii. 54, v. i. 11, VII. vi. 55.

spalles, shoulders, II. vi. 29.

span, *pret.* IV. ii. 49; *ppl. adj., Three Lett.* p. 621: spun.

spangs, spangles, IV. xi. 45.

sparckle, to emit sparklingly, III. i. 32.

spare, *sb.* niggardliness, sparing, III. i. 51.

spare, *vb.* to restrain, IV. viii. 37. **spard,** *pa. part.* IV. vii. 6, *S. C. May* 84; spared, *ppl. adj., S. C. Oct.* 9: saved.

sparely, sparingly, *S. C. May* 41.

sparke, to emit sparklingly, VI. xi. 21.

sparkle, spark; beam of light, I. iv. 33, *Three Lett.* p. 618.

sparre, bar, bolt, V. xi. 4.

spect, *pa. part.* specked, spotted, III. vii. 22.

spectácle, III. v. 22.

speculation, seeing, vision, *H. Beautie* 134.

speed, *sb.* fortune, success, III. viii. 50, IV. v. 22.

speed, *vb.* to succeed, III. viii. 51, *Hubberd* 899; *pret.* spedd, *Hubberd* 357.

spell, verse used as charm, *S. C. March* 54.

spend, *pa. part.* spent, used, *S. C. May* 71.

sperre, to bolt, bar, v. x. 37, *S. C. May* 224, 233. Cf. **sparre**.

spersed, *ppl. adj.* I. i. 39; **sperst,** *pa. part.* I. iv. 48, *Bellay* 195; **sperst,** *pret.* V. iii. 37, *Bellay* 111: dispersed, scattered.

spials, spies, watchers, II. i. 4.

spiceree, -y, **spyc-,** spices, II. xi. 49, III. i. 42; aromatic effluence, III. vi. 46, *Elegie* 40.

spies, spyes, glances, looks, I. ii. 17, VI. viii. 43; eyes, III. i. 36.

spight, *sb.* spite, disgrace, injury, I. i. 53, II. v. 12, *S. C. Jan.* 2, *Feb.* 180.

spight, *vb.* to grudge, envy, bear ill will to, III. v. 7, v. v. 29, VI. iii. 20, VII. vi. 32, *S. C. May* 198.

spill, to destroy, I. iii. 43, III. vii. 54, v. xii. 36, VII. vi. 50, *Clorinda* 12, *Amor.* Son. 23.; to spoil, injure, II. ix. 37, III. viii. 26, v. vi. 1, viii. 19, *S. C. Feb.* 52, *July* 68, *Gnat* 248, *Hubberd* 716, *Amor.* Son. 17.

spilt, *pa. part.* ? lavishly adorned, IV. x. 5.

spire, to cause to shoot, send forth, III. v. 52; *a. part.* produced, *R. T.* p. 471.

spoile, to ravage, carry off, II. VII. 25, v. viii. 18; *refl.* to rid oneself, II. ii. 33. **spoild, spoyled,** *pa. part.* deprived, bereft, I. ii. 24, *S. C.* p. 427.

spoilefull, rapacious, II. x. 63.

sponne, *pret.* spurted, gushed, IV. ix. 27.

sporten, to play, frolic, *S. C. March* 19.

spot, to blame, III. vi. 13.

spousall, I. II. 23; *plur.* v. iii. Arg.: marriage.

spousd, *ppl. adj.* betrothed, I. x. 4.

spoyle, injury, III. viii. 32.

sprad, *pa. part.* spread, v. ix. 25, VI. ii. 5.

spray, branch, VII. vii. 42, *Daphn.* 330, *Amor.* Son. 40.

spred, spredden, to spread over, cover, III. i. 20, *R. R.* 272.

sprent, *pa. part.* sprinkled, II. xii. 45, IV. ii. 18, *Muiop.* 239.

spright, spirit, I. i. 55, vii. 40, 52, p. 409, III. i. 59, *Clout* 623; breath, VI. i. 4, iii. 26.

sprinckle: *holy water* s. = aspergillum or brush for sprinkling holy water, III. xii. 13.

spring = springal, *Muiop.* 292.

springals, youths, striplings, v. x. 6.

spring-headed, *ppl. adj.* having heads that spring afresh, II. xii. 23.

sprites, spirits, I. viii. 36.

sprong, *pret.* sprang, iii. i. 62, iv. 3.

spurne, to spur, III. i. 5.

squaimishe, squeamish, fastidious, *Three Lett.* p. 623.

square: *out of* s. = out of its course, out of order, v. Prol. I, VII. vii. 52; *in* s. = square, *Bellay* 30.

squib, a paltry trifling fellow, *Hubberd* 371.

squire, square, carpenter's rule, II. i. 58.

stablish, to establish, arrange, II. ii. 32.

stablishment, establishment, v. viii. 21.

stadle, prop, staff, I. vi. 14.

staid, constant, fixed, I. vii. 41.

staie, duration, *Clout* 98.

staine, to dim, deface, II. iv. 15; to eclipse, excel, *R. T.* 525, *Daphn.* 112.

staire, step, III. v. 54.

stald, stalled, *pa. part.* confined (*lit.* and *fig.*), *S. C. Sept.* 120, *Epitaph* (2) 2.

stal'd, rescued, released, *Hubberd* 1245.

stales, snares, baits, II. i. 4, VI. x. 3.

stalke, stride, II. vii. 26.

stanck, weary, exhausted, *S.C. Sept.* 47.

stare, to shine, glitter, III. vii. 39; *pret.* stood stiffly on end, III. xii. 36.

starke, *adj.* stiff, strong, I. i. 44, II. i. 42; *adv., s. lame* = quite lame, *S. C. May* 279.

star-read, knowledge of the stars, astronomy, v. Prol. 8.

start, *pret.* started, rose, I. ii. 5. **starte,** *pa. part.* gone away, *S. C. Apr.* 25.

startuppe, rustic half-boot or buskin, described

in the 16th c. as laced above the ankle, *S. C.* p. 427.

state, *sb.* v. xi. 3.

state, *adj.* stately, *S. C. Sept.* 45.

state, *adv.* stately, *S. C. Sept.* 45.

stay, *sb.* restraint, *Epith.* 250.

stay, *vb.* to support, hold up, i. vi. 35, vii. 10, iii. xi. 23; to hinder, cause to stay, i. ix. 25, x. 45, ii. ix. 8, vi. iii. 6; to place, fix, *Bellay* 14, *Epigrams* p. 606; to stop, cease, *Elegie* 65; **stayed,** *ppl. adj.* constant, steady, resolute, ii. v. 1, xii. 29, vi. v. 36. Cf. **staid.**

stead, sted, -dd, -dde, *sb.* place, situation, i. viii. 17, ix, 41, xi. 46, ii. ii. 21, iv. 42, iii. ii. 16, xi. 50, iv. vii. 7, vi. i. 42, vii. vii. 13, *S. C. May* 43, *Hubberd* 861; condition, plight, v. xii. 23; while, space of time, vi. vii. 40.

stead, *vb.* to assist, avail, ii. ix. 9.

steale, handle, stale, v. xii. 14.

steane, stone, vii. vii. 42.

steare, steer, iii. xi. 42, iv. vi. 37, vi. viii. 12.

stearne, stern, *Hubberd* 1250.

steedie, steady, ii. i. 34.

steely, of steel, v. i. 9.

steemed, *pa. part.* iv. iv. 3; *pret.* vi. x. 35: esteemed.

steep, to dye, **stain,** iii. i. 65.

Stella, *pseudonym, Clout* 532.

stelths, thefts, i. iii. 16.

steme, to exhale, ii. vi. 27.

stemme, *sb.* stock, race, vii. vi. 2.

stemme, *vb.*[1] to dash against, iv. ii. 16.

stemme, *vb.*[2] to encircle, vi. x. 12.

stent, to cease, stop, ii. iv. 12. Cf. **stint,** *vb.*

sterue, to die, ii. vi. 34, iv. i. 4, 26; to starve, *Hubberd* 580, *Love* 200.

steuen, cry, voice, *S. C. Sept.* 224.

stew, a hot, steaming place, i. xi. 44.

stile, title, v. xi. 55; composition, *S. C. Jan.* 10.

still, to drop, trickle, iii. ii. 29; **stild,** *pret.* iv. vii. 35.

stint, *sb.* limit, bound, *Thest.* 51.

stint, *vb.* to stop, cease, ii. ii. 22, iii. iv. 8, iv. iii. 18, ix. Arg., 15.

stire, styre, to stir, move, incite, ii. i. 7, v. 2, ix. 30, iii. vii. 45.

stocke, flock, *Gnat* 237.

stockes, stockings, socks, *S. C.* p. 459.

stole, mantle, i. i. 4, 45, xii. 22.

stomachous, resentful, angry, ii. viii. 23.

stomacke, temper, ii. vii. 41; courage, spirit, *Hubberd* 1103.

stonds, stands, defences, ii. xi. 15.

stonied, *pa. part.* astonished, alarmed, v. xi. 30.

stonisht, *ppl. adj.* astonisht, alarmed, v. xi. 29; *pa. part.* vii. vii. 52.

stoopegallaunt, (?), *S. C. Feb.* 90.

stop, obstruction, obstacle, i. viii. 13.

store : *in s.* = at hand, iv. i. 9.

stound, stownd, -e, *sb.*[1] moment, i. viii. 38; *in the s.,* ? at this moment, vi. viii. 16; time, i. xi. 36, iii. v. 29, vi. i. 42, *S. C. Sept.* 56, *Hubberd* 26.

stound, stownd, *sb.*[2] stroke, blow, ii. viii. 32, v. iii. 22, *S. C. Oct.* 49, *Muiop.* 62; force of a blow, iv. vi. 37; attack, assault, affray, iii. i. 21, 63, vii. vi. 37; peril, vi. iii. 10; noise, *S. C. Dec.* 140, *Hubberd* 1353; ? violence, virulence, vii. vi. 5.

stound, stownd, *sb.*[3] amazement, bewilderment, iv. vi. 12, vi. iii. 30, *Elegie* 53; trouble, sorrow, i. viii. 25, viii. 25, iii. ii. 26, vi. ii. 41, v. 6, 28, *S. C. May* 257, *Daphn.* 560, *Hubberd* 940.

stound, *vb. pret.* stunned, bewildered, i. vii. 12; *pa. part.* v. xi. 29.

stoupe, *sb.* concession, v. ix. 34.

stoupe, *vb.* to stoop, i. v. 12; to swoop, ii. xi. 43.

stoure, stowre, tumult, disturbance; conflict, encounter, i. ii. 7, v. 51, ii. x. 19, iii. i. 34, ii. 6, iv. 13, iv. iii. 15, v. 25, ix. 22, 39, v. iii. 21, vi. vii. 8, p. 413, *S. C. Jan.* 27, 51, *May* 156, *Teares* 597, *Beautie* 73; peril, i. iii. 30, iv. 46, vii. 12, ii. viii. 35, iii. ix. 13, iv. xii. 19, v. v. 18; crisis, ii. iii. 34; fit, paroxysm, iii. ii. 5, iii. 50.

stout, bold, brave, doughty, i. vi. 39, iii. iii. 54, iv. i. 11, ii. 27, vi. 26, *Past. Elegie* 117.

stowte, *sb.* a bold man, *Three Lett.* p. 625.

straine, *sb.* lineage, iv. viii. 33.

straine, strayne, *vb.* to wield, stretch forth, ii. vii. 21, iii. v. 21, vi. iv. 22; to constrain, force, *S. C. Oct.* 12.

straint, strain, v. ii. 14.

strait, a narrow passage, ii. vii. 40.

strake, *pret.* struck, ii. iii. 32, iii. vii. 44, v. iii. 33, vi. vii. 11, *Gnat* 307, *Petrarch* 23.

strakes, streaks, ii. iv. 15.

straunge, added, borrowed, iii. xii. 11.

strawen, of straw, v. v. 50.

strayne, to put into verse, *S. C. Nov.* 52.

streight, close, iv. viii. 63; strict, strait, narrow, v. v. 33, xii. 10, *Amor.* Son. 71.

streightly, strictly, ii. viii. 29, *S. C.* p. 459; closely, iii. ii. 34.

streightnesse, straitness, v. vi. 2.

streigned, *pa. part.* restrained, *Hubberd* 1190.

strene, strain, race, v. ix. 32, vi. vi. 9.

stresse, *sb.* distress, iii. xi. 18.

stressed, *ppl. adj.* distressful, II. x. 37.

strew, *pret.* strewed, scattered, II. xi. 28.

strich, screech-owl, II. xii. 36.

strifull, stry-, strife-, full of strife, contentions, II. ii. 13, III. ii. 12, IV. iii. 16, v. 24, 30, *Hubberd* 1021.

stripe, blow, stroke, v. xi. 27.

stroke, strooke, *pret.* II. xii. 86, v. ii. 53, v. 10, 11, viii. 9; **stroken,** *pa. part.* vi. ii. 7: struck.

strond, strand, shore, II. vi. 19, III. vii. 26.

strong, *pa. part.* strung, *Gnat* 16.

strow, to scatter, v. vi. 40; **strowd,** *pret.* I. i. 35; to display, *S. C. July* 75.

stubs, stumps of trees, I. ix. 34.

studde, trunk, stem, *S. C. March* 13. **stud,** tree, shrub, *Gnat* 84.

sturre, *sb.* disturbance, tumult, I. iv. 40.

sturre, *vb.* to stir, *S. C. Sept.* 183.

sty, -e, stie, to ascend, mount, I. xi. 25, II. vii. 46, IV. ix. 33, p. 411, *Bellay* 148.

subiect, *ppl. adj.* I. xi. 19; *pa. part.* III. vii. 4 : situated beneath.

submisse, submissive, humble, IV. x. 51.

subtile, delicate, finely-spun, II. xii. 77.

subuerst, *ppl. adj.* III. xii. 42; *pa. part.*, *Hubberd* 1234: subverted.

succeed, to approach, vi. iv. 8.

successe, succession, II. x. 45, *Gnat* 30; issue, result, IV. ix. 24.

sude, *pa. part.* wooed, vi. viii. 20. Cf. **sew.**

sufferance, -aunce, patience, endurance, I. i. 50, II. viii. 47, IV. i. 54, viii. 1. *see in s. =* property retained after the title to it has ceased, *S. C. May* 106.

suffisaunce, abundance, *Muiop.* 207.

suffised, *ppl. adj.* satisfied, I. ii. 43.

sugred, *ppl. adj.* sweet, II. v. 33.

suit, -e, pursuit, II. vii. 10, III. xi. 5, v. viii. 3. *suit and service =* service as followers, vi. vii. 34. Cf. **sew.**

sunder: *in s. =* asunder, *Three Lett.* p. 619.

sundry, different, distinct, *Epitaph* (2) 12; *sundry way =* parting of the way, II. xi. 35.

sunneshine, sunshiny, *S. C. Jan.* 3.

suppled, *pret.* made supple, III. v. 33.

supplie, to reinforce, *Teares* 537. **supplyde,** *pa. part.* made up for, vi. viii. 9.

suppress, to keep down, overcome, vi. viii. 18, xii. 31. **supprest,** *pa. part.* I. vi. 40.

surbate, to bruise, batter, III. iv. 34. **surbet,** *pa. part.* II. ii. 22.

surceasse, -cease, to leave off, refrain finally, stop, cause to stop, III. i. 23, IV. ii. 19, vi. vi. 43, *S. C. Apr.* 125, *Hubberd* 1221, *Amor. Son.* 11. **surceast,** *pret.* III. iv. 31; *pa. part.*

v. ii. 37. **surceasing,** *vbl. sb.* stoppage, *Three Lett.* p. 635.

surcharged, *pret.* charged with renewed vigour, IV. ix. 30; *pa. part.* overladen, IV. vii. 32.

sure, surely, v. ix. 38.

surplusage, excess, II. vii. 18.

surprize, to seize suddenly, vi. x. 34.

surprysall, capture, surprising, *Gnat* 536.

surquedry, -ie, presumption, arrogance, II. xii. 31, 39, III. i. 13, iii. 46, iv. 7, x. 2, v. ii. 30, *S. C. Feb.* 49, *Worlds Vanitie* 105.

suruew, -e, to survey, *S. C. Feb.* 145, *R. R.* 101; to overlook, II. ix. 45, *Gnat* 221.

suruiewe, survey, examination, *Two Lett.* p. 640.

suspect, suspicion, I. vi. 13, III. xii. 14, v. vii. 38, vi. iii. 23.

suspence, in doubt, IV. vi. 34.

suspition, suspicion, *Muiop.* 376.

swaine, swayne, boy, youth, man, I. ii. 4, II. xi. 28, vi. vii. 22, *S. C. March* 79, *R. T.* 234; labourer, rustic, *Hubberd* 303, *Daph.* 524.

sware, *pret.* swore, I. iii. 16.

swart, dark, swarthy, II. x. 15.

swarue, to swerve, turn, retreat, I. x. 14, II. iii. 43, viii. 30, 36, III. i. 11.

swat, *pret.* sweated, III. v. 3, v. ii. 46.

sway, *sb.* swing, rapid motion, blow, I. viii. 8, II. viii. 38, xii. 20; force, II. xi. 36, v. v. 9, vi. viii. 11.

sway, *vb.* to brandish, wield, strike, II. viii. 46, III. i. 66; to advance, attack, II. x. 49.

sweard, sword, IV. iii. 31, 33, *Clout* 314.

sweathbands, swaddling-bands, vi. iv. 23.

sweld, *pret.* swelled (with anger), *Hubberd* 1340.

swelt [1], *pret.* swelled, raged, I. vii. 6, III. xi. 27.

swelt [2], *pret.* swooned, fainted, IV. vii. 9, v. xii. 21.

swet, *pret.* sweated, IV. x. 38.

swinck, *sb.* toil, labour, *S. C. May* 36. *July* 34.

swinck, swinke, *vb.* to toil, labour, II. vii. 8, vi. iv. 32, *S. C. Sept.* 132.

swinged, *pret.* singed, I. xi. 6.

swound, swownd, swowne, *sb.* swoon, I. i. 41, v. 19, x. 52, II. xi. 35, III. vi. 7, IV. vii. 9, vi. iii. 10, v. 6, *Daphn.* 545.

swowned, *pa. part.* sunk, drowned (as in a swoon), v. v. 36.

syker, surely, *S. C. July* 33, 93. Cf. **sicker.**

sympathize, to agree, or harmonize with, *H. Beautie* 192.

synd, *pa. part.* signed, *Amor. Son.* 78.

syrlye, surly, *S. C. July* 203.

sythe, time, *Clout* 23. Cf. **sith.**

T

table, picture, i. ix. 59; tablet, iii. iv. 10.

tabrere, player on the tabor or drum, *S. C. May* 22.

tackles, tackle; equipment of a ship, i. xii. 42.

taduaunce, to advance, *S. C. Feb.* 86.

taking, plight, condition, *S. C. Apr.* 156.

talaunts, -ants, claws, i. viii. 48, xi. 41, xii. 11.

tamburins, small tabors or drums, *S. C. June* 59.

tane, *pa. part.* taken, *Daphn.* 365, *Thest.* 17.

tapet, tapestry, figured cloth, iii. xi. 29, *Muiop.* 276.

targe, shield, ii. v. 6, iv. xii. 14, vi. ii. 44.

tarras, terrace, v. ix. 21.

Tartar, -e, Tartarus; the infernal regions, ii. xii. 6, *Gnat* 444, *Hubberd* 1294.

tassell gent, tercel, a male falcon or goshawk, iii. iv. 49.

tasswage, to assuage, *S. C. Nov.* 2.

tawdrie lace, a silk 'lace' or necktie, originally lace sold at fairs during the festival of St. Audrey (Ethelreda), *S. C. Apr.* 135.

teade, -e, torch, i. xii. 37, *Muiop.* 293, *Epith.* 27.

tedula, trochilus or crocodile-bird, *Worlds Vanitie* 35.

teemed, *ppl. adj.* harnessed in a team, *Gnat* 314.

teene, tene, *sb.* affliction, grief, sorrow, i. ix. 34, ii. i. 58, iii. v. 40, *S. C. Nov.* 41, *Daphn.* 21; injury, hurt, i. xii. 18.

teene, *vb.* to appoint, allot, ii. i. 59.

tell, to count, ii. vii. 19. teld, *pret.* told, vi. i. 44; *pa. part.* vii. vi. 27, vii. 13.

teme, team, i. v. 28.

temed, *ppl. adj.* yoked in a team, iii. iv. 34. Cf. teemed.

temewise, in a team, iii. xi. 40.

temper, to govern, control, *Hubberd* 1294.
tempring, *pres. part.* restraining himself, ii. vi. 26; tempred, *pret.* iv. x. 33.

temperature, proportion, combination, *Amor.* Son. 13.

tend, *vb.* to attend, v. vii. 9; ? to be suitable or opportune, v. iii. 40; *pret.*, ? directed his way, *Elegie* 52.

tendance, waiting in expectation, *Hubberd* 908.

tender, to cherish, foster, treat with tenderness, iii. v. 51, vi. 51, vi. xii. 11; to hold precious, v. vii. 45, vi. iii. 11.

tenor, manner or fashion of behaviour, conduct, iv. vii. 47; *second tenor*, countertenor or second part in a musical composition; hence, lower tone or strain, i. xi. 7.

teribinth, the turpentine tree, *Pistacia Terebinthus*, *S. C. July* 86.

terme, terms, v. xi. 56; condition, *Amor.* Son. 21.

termelesse, boundless, endless, *H. Love* 75.

Theana, *pseudonym, Clout* 492.

théatre, iii. xii. 3; théatre, iv. iii. 37.

thee, to prosper, thrive, ii. i. 33.

theeuerie, -y, theft, iii. xi. 45, *Hubberd* 315, 1287.

thelement, the elements, *S. C. Feb.* 116.

then, than, i. vi. 3, 45, ii. iv. 15, p. 407 &c.

thend, the end, *S. C. Feb.* 237.

thereout, thence, *Hubberd* 484.

therewithal, with that, vi. vii. 35.

thetch, to thatch, *Hubberd* 264.

thether, thither, vi. ix. 4.

thewed, trained, instructed in morals and manners: *ppl. adj.* ii. vi. 26; *pa. part.*, *S. C. Feb.* 96, *Beautie* 137.

thelf, the elf, *S. C. March* 55.

thewes, manners, habits, i. ix. 3, x. 4, ii. i. 33, x. 59, iv. ix. 14, vi. ii. 2, 31, iv. 38.

thicke, dense part of a wood, thicket, ii. i. 39, *S. C. March* 73.

thilk(e), this, *S. C. Jan.* 61, *March* 13, 49, *Apr.* 154, *May* 6, *July* 1, *Sept.* 66, 98, *Oct.* 53.

tho(e), then, thereupon, i. i. 18, 50, iii. i. 23, *S. C. Jan.* 11, *Feb.* 218, *March* 73; *adv.* then, iii. v. 6, *S. C. Feb.* 160, *March* 19, 22, *May* 109.

tho, *pron.* those, *S. C. Sept.* 32.

thone, the one, *S. C. p.* 420.

thorough, through, i. i. 32.

thother, the other, *S. C. p.* 420.

thous, thou art, *S. C. July* 33, *Clout* 292.

thraldome, subjection, captivity, iii. xi. 16, iv. i. 8, v. v. 32.

thrall, *sb.* slave, i. v. 51, vii. vii. 19, *R. T.* 114, *Amor.* Son. 82; *adj.* subject, enslaved, captive, i. vii. 44, iv. xi. 7, vii. vii. 17, 54, *H. Love* 184.

thrall, *vb.* to make captive, enslave, v. v. 29 (*fig.*); thrald, thralled, *pa. part.* ii. i. 54. iii. xi. 15, vi. viii. 7, 11, vii. vi. 7; ? to dominate (*intr.*), vi. xi. 44.

threasure, treasure, ii. vii. Arg.

threasury, store of treasure, ii. vii. 4.

threat, to threaten, iv. vii. 37, v. xii. 18: to move threateningly, vi. v. 19.

threatfull, threatening, iii. xii. 37, iv. vi. 10, *Muiop.* 85.

three-square, with three equal sides, I. vi. 41, III. i. 4, iv. 16.

thresh, to thrash, strike, III. vii. 32.

thresher, instrument for thrashing or striking, v. vi. 29.

threttie, thirty, *S. C. Feb.* 17.

thrid, thread, IV. ii. 48, 50.

thrill, to pierce, penetrate (*lit.* and *fig.*), III. v. 20; **thrild, thrilled**, *pret.* I. vi. 37, II. xii. 78, IV. vii. 31; *pa. part.* I. viii. 39, III. v. 21, IV. vii. 36; *ppl. adj.* III. ii. 32; **thrilling**, *ppl. adj.* I. iii. 42, *S. C. May* 208.

thrillant, piercing, penetrating, I. xi. 20, II. iv. 46.

thrise, by a great deal, III. viii. 7.

thrist, *sb.* thirst, II. vi. 17.

thristed, *pret.* thirsted, I. vi. 38.

thristy, -ie, thirsty, I. x. 38, II. v. 30, *S. C. May* 138.

throng, to press, crush, III. ix. 45.

throughly, thoroughly, II. vii. 58, IV. xii. 22, 23, v. iii. 17, p. 407.

throw[1], time, instant, III. iv. 53.

throw[2], **thro**, pang, throe, I. x. 41, VI. xii. 17, *Muiop.* 414.

throw[3], **throe**, thrust, throw (of a weapon), II. v. 9, viii. 41, III. v. 21, IV. iii. 26, 33, v. viii. 35, *Teares* 134.

thrust, *sb.* thirst, III. vii. 50.

thrust, *vb.* to thirst, II. ii. 29.

thwart, athwart, across, III. vii. 43.

thwarting, *pres. part.* laying across, *Gnat* 514.

tickle, unstable, inconstant, uncertain, III. iv. 28, VI. iii. 5, VII. vii. 22, viii. 1, *S.C. July* 14, *Petrarch* 85.

tickle, *vb. intr.* to tingle, thrill, VII. vi. 46, *Muiop.* 394.

tide, tyde, time, opportunity, I. ii. 29, III. vi. 21, ix. 32, IV. vi. 47, vii. 47, *Muiop.* 405, *Proth.* 177.

tight, *pret.* tied, VI. xii. 34.

timbered, massive, v. ii. 50.

timelesse, untimely, *Epitaph* (1) 12.

timely, passing (of time), I. iv. 4; keeping time, I. v. 3; seasonable, *S. C. Jan.* 38.

tinct, tinged, *C. S. Nov.* 107.

tind, tynd, tynde, *pret.* II. viii. 11, III. iii. 57, IV. vii. 30 (?), *Gnat* 344; *fa. part.* III. vii. 15, x. 13, *Gnat* 504: kindled.

tine, tyne, *sb.* pain, sorrow, affliction, I. ix. 15, IV. iii. 37, xii. 34, XI. viii. 33, *Teares* 3, *Muiop.* 12; hate, anger, III. xi. 1. Cf. *teen, sb.*

tine, *vb.* to grieve, suffer, II. xi. 21.

tire, *sb.*[1] train, series, i. iv. 35.

tire, tyre, *sb.*[2] attire, dress, I. viii. 46, II. i. 57, ii. 36, ix. 40, IV. x. 31.

tire, tyre, *vb.* to attire, array, VII. vii. 11, *Gnat* 308.

titmose, tit, tomtit, *S. C. Nov.* 26.

to, as, for: *to name, friend*, I. i. 28, v. ix. 43.

tobrusd, *ppl. adj.* completely battered, v. viii. 44.

todde, thick bush, *S. C. March* 67.

tofore, before, IV. iv. 7, v. vii. 38, VI. vi. 9.

tonnell, opening of a chimney, flue, II. ix. 29.

too, very, *S. C. Feb.* 136; *too-too, too very* = exceedingly, VII. vi. 55, *S. C. May* 175; *too or fro* = for or against, *Two Lett.* p. 640.

tooles, weapons, II. iii. 37.

tooting, *pres. part.* spying out, searching, *S. C. March* 66.

top, head, I. vii. 29.

topside turuey, topsy-turvy, v. viii. 42.

to rent, *pa. part.* torn asunder, IV. vii. 8, v. viii. 4.

tort, -e, wrong, injury, I. xii. 4, II. v. 17, III. ii. 12, IV. viii. 31, *R. T.* 167, *Hubberd* 1078.

tortious, wrong, wicked, injurious, II. ii. 18, IV. ix. 12, v. viii. 30, 51, VII. vi. 10.

tosse, to agitate, I. vii. 27.

tossen, to brandish, wield, III. ii. 6.

to torne, *pa. part.* torn to pieces, v. ix. 10.

totty, -ie, unsteady, dizzy, VII. vii. 39, *S. C. Feb.* 55.

touch, touchstone : *true as t.* = absolutely true, I. iii. 2.

tourney, *sb.* encounter, III. ii. 9.

tourney, *vb.* to joust, tilt, II. i. 6.

touzd, *pa. part.* harassed, worried, II. xi. 33.

toward, approaching, near at hand, II. iv. 22, III. i. 9, *Daphn.* 280 ; promising, *Muiop.* 26.

towards, forward, II. i. 26, iii. 34.

to worne, *pa. part.* worn out, v. ix. 10.

toy, *sb.* play, amorous sport, II. vi. 37, xii. 60.

toy, *vb. intr.* to play, II. ix. 35.

toyles, nets, snares, *Past. Elegie* 97.

trace, *sb.* path, track, VI. i. 6, *S. C. June* 27.

trace, *vb.* to walk, I. viii. 31, *Gnat* 251 ; to travel, go forward, IV. vii. 28, viii. 34, v. ix. 7, VI. i. 7, iii. 29; to track, III. vii. 23; to step, pace, dance, VI. ix. 42.

tract, *sb.*[1] course, process (of time), v. iv. 8, *S. C. May* 117, *Amor.* Son. 18.

tract, *sb.*[2] trace, track, footprint, I. i. 11, II. iii. 19, VI. iv. 24, xii. 22, *Gnat* 279, *Hubberd* 406.

tract, *vb.* to trace, track, II. i. 12, VI. vii. 3; **tracted**, *fa. part.* II. vi. 39.

trade, tread, track, II. vi. 39, *Teares* 275;

occupation, ii. xii. 30, *S. C. June* 45 ; conduct, iii. i. 67.

tradefull, busy in traffic, *Amor.* Son. 15.

traduction, transfer, iv. iii. 13.

traine, trayne, artifice, wile, snare, i. vi. 3, vii. 1, ix. 31, xii. 36, iii. iii. 11, x. 11, iv. viii. 31, v. viii. 2, 19, xii. 40, *Gnat* 241, *Muiop.* 398, *Clout* 118, *Past. Elegie* 97 ; trail, track, v. ii. 15 ; assembly, v. ii. 33.

tramels, nets (for the hair), ii. ii. 15, iii. ix. 20.

transfard, *pret.* transformed, iii. xi. 31.

translated, transferred, v. vii. 29.

transmew, to transform, transmute, i. vii. 35, ii. iii. 37, iii. i. 38.

transmoue, to transform, iii. xi. 43.

transuerse : *by t.* = in a haphazard way, vii. vii. 56.

trap, to furnish with trappings, ii. viii. 16.

trap fals, trap-doors so made as to give way beneath the feet, pitfalls, v. ii. 7.

trast, *pret.* moved, ran, v. viii. 37. Cf. trace, *vb.*

trauayler, worker, *Two Lett.* p. 640.

traueled, -eiled, *pa. part.* troubled, *S. C. Jan.* Arg. 6 ; laboured, *R. R.* 117.

trauell, *sb.* toil, travail, vi. vii. 19, ix. 2.

trauell, *vb.* to travail, labour (in childbirth) (*fig.*), iv. ix. 17.

trayle, *sb.* woven pattern, *Muiop.* 299.

trayled, *pa. part.* interwoven with a pattern, v. v. 2.

trayned, *pa. part.* vi. vi. 39 ; *pret.* vi. vi. 42: allured.

treachetour, traitor, ii. x. 51, vi. viii. 7.

treachour, traitor, cheat, i. iv. 41, ix. 32, ii. i. 12, iv. 27, *Hubberd* 1255.

treague, truce, ii. ii. 33.

treat, *sb.* parley, iii. viii. 17.

treat, -en, *vb.* to speak, talk (of), i. vii. 40, viii. 43, iv. i. 16.

treaty, arrangement, iii. i. 11.

treen, of trees, i. ii. 39, vii. 26.

trenchand, -ant, sharp, piercing, i. i. 17, xi. 24, v. v. 9.

trentals, services of thirty masses for the dead on as many successive days, *Hubberd* 453.

trespassed, *pa. part.* committed, *Gnat* 448.

trild, *pret.* flowed, trickled, ii. xii. 78.

trim, neat, well-formed, iii. i. 36, *Past. Elegie* 42 ; pleasing, iii. i. 40.

trimly, neatly, *S. C. Apr.* 29.

trinall, threefold, i. xii. 39, *H. Love* 64.

triplicities, trinities, triads, i. xii. 39, *H. Love* 64.

triúmph, triúmphing, iv. ii. 24, iv. 28.

trode, troad, -e, footstep, trace, track, path,

iii. ix. 49, vi. x. 5, *S. C. July* 14, *Sept.* 92, *Hubberd* 406.

tromp(e), trumpet, iii. iii. 3, p. 412 ; trumpeter, herald, *R. T.* 434.

troncheon, headless spear, cudgel, ii. viii. 38, iv. iii. 12.

troth, truth, ii. i. 11, ii. 34.

troublous, agitated, disturbed, ii. ii. 24 ; restless, ii. iii. 4.

trow(e), to believe, think, ii. v. 13, v. ii. 34, *S. C. March* 56, *July* 107.

trump, trumpet, *Amor.* Son. 29, 85. Cf. tromp.

truncked, *ppl. adj.* truncated, beheaded, i. viii. 10, ii. v. 4.

trusse, *sb.* bundle, *S. C. May* 239.

trusse, *vb.* to seize and carry off, i. xi. 19, iv. vii. 18 ; to pack up, iii. x. 46.

trustily, -ely, faithfully, vi. iii. 19 ; with confidence, *Hubberd* 55.

truth, trust, care, i. vi. 12, ii. iii. 2.

try(e), trie, *vb.* to experience, iv. vii. 11, *R. T.* 233 ; tride, *pret.* iv. vii. 2 ; tryde, *pa. part.* vi. iii. 2 ; to prove (oneself), *Hubberd* 913. tryde, *pa. part.* purified, ii. ii. 9. tride, *ppl. adj.* firm, faithful, vi. viii. 33.

trye, *adj.* choice, select, v. ii. 26.

tunes, tones, strains, *Elegie* 193.

turmoýle, *sb.* trouble, agitation, *Amor.* Son. 11.

turmoýle, *vb. intr.* to labour amid trouble, *Gnat* 152 ; *tr.* to disturb, agitate, *R. R.* 261, *Petrarch* 21. turmoíld, *pa. part.* troubled, iv. ix. 39.

turney, *sb.* tournament, encounter, iv. vi. 6, ix. 36. Cf. tourney.

turney, *vb.* to joust, tilt, iv. v. 7, v. iii. Arg. Cf. tourney.

turribant, turban, iv. xi. 28.

twaine : *into even t.* = into two even portions. *Hubberd* 1024.

tway, two, twain, i. vii. 27, ii. vi. 31, iii. xi. 11, iv. ii. 13, v. iv. 35, *S. C. July* 152.

twight, to twit, v. vi. 12.

twine, twyne, *sb.* coil, band, i. vi. 14, *S. C. Aug.* 30, *Oct.* 111.

twine, *vb.* to twist, iv. ii. 51.

twinne, pair, couple, *Bellay* 70, *Epigrams* p. 607.

twist, fabric made with a double and hence heavy thread, coarse cloth, *Hubberd* 460.

twyfold, twofold, i. v. 28.

tyhyhing, *pres. part.* tittering, *Three Lett.* p. 618.

tyned, *pret.* were lost, perished, iv. xi. 36.

type, emblem, pattern, model, *Teares* 70, *Gnat* 557.

tyranne, tyrant, *S. C. Oct.* 98.

tyrannesse, female tyrant, I. v. 46.

tyrannical : *t. colours, S. C.* p. 447.

tyranning, tyrannizing, IV. vii. 1.

tyre, head-dress, I. x. 31. Cf. tire, *sb.*[2]

tyreling, tired, fatigued, III. i. 17, VI. vii. 40.

U

vgly, horrible, I. ix. 48.

vmbriere, a defence for the face, attached to a helmet, III. i. 42, IV. iv. 44.

vnacquainted, strange, unknown, I. x. 29.

vnaduised, *ppl. adj.* unperceived, p. 412.

vnawares, suddenly, unexpected, IV. viii. 7. Cf. vnwares.

vnbid, *ppl. adj.* not prayed for, I. ix. 54.

vnblest, *ppl. adj.* unwounded, v. ii. 12.

vnbrace, to unfasten, II. iv. 9.

vncase, to strip, *Hubberd* 1380 ; *pa. part.* revealed, v. iii. Arg., 39, *Hubberd* 930.

vnchearefull, cheerless, depressing, *Epith.* 21.

vncivile, uncivilized, wild, II. vii. 3.

vncomely, unbecoming, VI. viii. 51.

vncomptrold, uncontrolled, *Clout* 662.

úncouth, strange, unusual, I. i. 15, II. v. 20, VI. 43, III. x. 34, IV. vii. 45, x. 45, V. v. 37, VII. vii. 6, 35 ; unknown, *S. C. S pt.* 60.

vncrudded, uncurdled, *Epith.* 175.

vndefide, unchallenged, II. viii. 31.

únderfong, to ensnare, entrap, deceive, v. ii. 7, *S. C. June* 103; to undertake, *S. C. Nov.* 22.

vnder hand, secretly, IV. xi. 34.

vnderkeep, to keep under, subdue, oppress, III. vii. 33, *Teares* 77.

vnderlay, to overpower, surpass, *Gnat* 99.

vnderminde, to undermine, deceive, v. vi. 32.

vndersaye, to say in contradiction, *S. C. Sept.* 91.

vndersong, burden of a song, refrain, *S. C. Aug.* 127, *Daphn.* 245, 294, *Clout* 168, *Proth.* 110.

vndertake, to hear, understand, v. iii. 34.

vndertane, *pa. part.* promised, v. viii. 3.

vndertime, the time of the midday meal (undern), III. vii. 13.

vnderuerse, following or second verse, *S. C.* p. 451.

vndight, to take off, III. v. 31, ix. 19, v. viii. 2 ; *pret.* I. iii. 4; *pa. part.* VI. vii. 19 ; *pa. part.* unloosened, II. xii. 15, III. vi. 18.

vneasy, uncomfortable, disagreeable, I. v. 36.

vneath, -eth, vnneath, *adj.* difficult, I. x. 31, III. v. 17, IV. vii. 40, *Daphn.* 447 ; *adv.* with difficulty, uneasily, I. ix. 38, xi. 4, II. i. 56, III.

i. 33, x. 2, IV. ix. 25, *S. C. Sept.* 48, *Past. Aeglogue* 52. **vneathes, vnnethes,** *adv.* with difficulty, II. vi. 1, *S. C. Jan.* 6.

vnespyde, *pa. part.* unseen, III. i. 37.

vneuen, ill-matched, VI. v. 9.

vnfilde, *ppl. adj.* unpolished, III. vii. 30.

vngentle, discourteous, rude, III. i. 67.

vngentlenesse, harshness, discourtesy, III. v. 2.

vnguilty, innocent, III. ii. 26.

vnhable, unable, incapable, I. iv. 23, VI. i. 16, iii. 46.

vnhappy, -ie, unfortunate, inauspicious, II. vi. 44 ; unsuccessful, VI. iv. 31 ; *unhappie witted* = with minds full of tricks, *Hubberd* 49.

vnhastie, slow, I. iii. 4.

vnheale, -hele, to disclose, uncover, II. xii. 64, IV. v. 10.

vnherst, *pret.* removed from a hearse or monument, v. iii. 37.

vnhurtfull, doing no harm, *Teares* 197.

vnkempt, rough, unpolished (*fig.*), III. x. 29, *S. C. Nov.* 51.

vnkend, -t, unknown, IV. xi. 13, p. 416.

vnkinds, unnatural, III. ii. 43, *Hubberd* 52.

vnkindly, unnatural, II. x. 9, *S. C. Jan.* 26.

vnkodpeased, *ppl. adj.* without a cod-piece, *Three Lett.* p. 625. *See* kodpeasd.

vnlast, *pa. part.* unlaced, VI. i. 39.

vnlich, unlike, I. v. 28.

vnlike, unlikely, v. v. 38.

vnlustye, feeble, *S. C.* p. 458.

vnnethes, *see* vneath.

vnmanurd, *ppl. adj.* untilled, uncultivated, II. x. 5.

vnmard, *pa. part.* unspoiled, VI. x. 7.

vnmeete, unfit, unsuitable, unbecoming, unseemly, III. vi. 50, IV. i. 27, VI. iv. 37, viii. 22.

vnmercifully, extremely, v. vii. 31.

vnnoble, ignoble, base, *Teares* 435.

vnplained, -playnd, *ppl. adj.* not bewailed or lamented, *Daphn.* 79; *pa. part., Past. Elegie* 136.

vnproued, *ppl. adj.* not tested, untried, I. vii. 47.

vnpuruaide, *pa. part.* deprived, VII. vi. 14.

vnreaue, to disentangle, take to pieces, *Amor. Son.* 23.

vnred, *ppl. adj.* untold, IV. xii. 2.

vnredrest, *ppl. adj.* without redress, IV. viii. 41.

vnremédied (cf. **remédilesse**), *Clorinda* 8.

vnreproued, *ppl. adj.* blameless, II. vii. 16.

vnrestfulnesse, restlessness, uneasiness, *S. C.* p. 430.

vnruliment, unruliness, IV. ix. 23.

vnruly, unrestrained, excessive, VI. vi. 5.

vnseason, to strike or affect disagreeably, p. 413.

vnseene, unrevealed, incognito, IV. iv. 3.

vnshed, ppl. adj. unparted, IV. vii. 40.

vnsoote, not sweet, S. C. Dec. 118.

vnspide, pa. part. unseen, III. vi. 7.

vnstayd, unsteady, VI. i. 20.

vnstedfastnesse, instability, Epigrams p. 606.

vnthrifty, wicked, I. iv. 35.

vnthriftyhed, -ihead, unthriftiness, II. xii. 18, III. xii. 25.

vntill, -til, unto, towards, I. xi. 4, S. C. Nov. 185.

vntimely, unfortunately, V. v. 29.

vntitled, ppl. adj. without a title, claim, v. ix. 42.

vntride, ppl. adj. not felt, experienced, IV. vii. 11. Cf. try, vb.

vntrust, ppl. adj. unbound, Past. Aeglogue 56.

vnualewd, ppl. adj. inestimable, Amor. Son. 77.

vnwares, unexpectedly, suddenly, I. v. 18, III. i. 37, IV. iv. 31, S. C. March Arg., May 275 ; unknown, IV. iv. 27 ; unknowingly, Gnat 631.

vnwarie, unexpected, I. xii. 25.

vnweeting, adj. not knowing, unconscious, I. iii 65, x. 65, 66, II. xii. 22 ; unknown, III. iii. 57; adv. unwittingly, I. ii. 40, Hubberd 606.

vnweetingly, unwittingly, v. viii. 15.

vnweldy, adj. unwieldy, I. viii. 24 ; adv. in an unwieldy manner, VI. viii. 28.

vnwist, unknown, III. ii. 26, ix. 21, IV. iv. 27, V. i. 9, 22.

vnwont, unaccustomed, VI. xi. 40, S. C. Feb. 32.

vnworthy, undeserved, VI. iv. 34.

vnwreaked, pa. part. unrevenged, III. xi 9.

vpblowing, pres. part. blowing up, III. iv. 13

vp-blowne, pa. part. inflated, I. iv. 21.

vpbounden, pa. part. bound up, tied, III. ix. 20.

vpbraide, reproach, abuse, IV. ix. 24, 28, v. xi. 41, Hubberd 2.

vpbrast, pret. burst asunder, VI. xi. 43.

vpbray, vb. to bring reproach on, II. iv. 45 , to upbraid, IV. i. 42.

vpbrayes, upbraidings, reproaches, III. vi. 50.

vpbrought, pret. brought up, reared, VI. iv. 38.

vpcheard, pret. encouraged, VI. i. 44.

vpfild, pa. part. filled up, IV. iii. 42.

vpheld, pa. part. upheld, VI. xi. 21.

vphoorded, ppl. adj. hoarded up, Teares 553.

vpknit, to explain, sum up, IV. vi. 30.

vpleaning, pres. part. leaning upon, Gnat 154.

vprear, -e, to raise up, I. xi. 15, II. i. 29, III iii. 45, IV. i. 55, VI. i. 19, 31, Daphn. 187.

vprightly, honestly, really, S. C. p. 451.

vpryst, pa. part. risen up, S. C. March 18.

vpstaring, pres. part. bristling, standing up, I. ix. 22.

vpstart, adj. starting up, bristling, III. x. 54.

vpstart, vb. to start, rise up, II. iv. 9, viii. 18, VI. viii. 40; vpstarting, ppl. adj. II. xii. 39.

vpstayd, pret. supported, III. xii. 21, IV. i. 37.

vptyde, pa. part. tied up, wound up, II. ii. 1, VI. iv. 24.

vp-wound, pa. part. coiled up, I. i. 15.

Vrania, pseudonym, Clout 487.

vrchins, hedgehogs, II. xi. 13.

vsage, behaviour, conduct, IV. vii. 45, Muiop. 120.

vsaunce, -ance, use, II. vii. 7, Daphn. 503.

vse, sb. habit, conduct, II. v. 19, III. xi. 4.

vse, vb. to be wont, accustomed, IV. v. 3, v. viii. 17; to practise, IV. v. 3; did vse = used, IV. viii. 5.

vsurped, pa. part. used, affected, S. C. Sept. p. 455.

vsury, -ie, interest, VI. viii. 9, Clout 39, Clorinda 22.

vtmost, last, II. i. 49; most outward, II. xii. 20, 21, VI. xii. 26; uttermost, III. xi. 25, H. Love 108; furthest, II. x. 12.

vtter, adj. outer, II. ii. 34, IV. x. 11.

vtter, vb. to put out or forth, S. C. March 15.

V

vade, to vanish, depart, III. ix. 20, v. ii. 40, R. R. 279.

vaile, vayle[1], to let down, III. ix. 20, Three Lett. p. 625.

vaile[2], to veil, conceal, p. 409.

vaine, sb. poetic vein, S. C. Oct. 23 ; humour, disposition, Hubberd 799.

vaine, adj. weak, frail, IV. ii. 48.

vainesse, vanity, R. T. 459, Bellay 26 ; folly, Worlds Vanitie 83.

valiaunce, valour, II. iii. 14, viii. 51, III. iii. 28.

valorous, brave, valiant, II. iv. 1, xi. 34.

value, valour, II. iv. 29, III. xi. 14.

valure, valour, Epitaph (1) 46.

variable, various, III. v. 1, Proth. 13.

varlet, young man, II. iv. 37.

vauncing, *pres. part.* advancing, IV. iv. 17.

vaunt, to display, exhibit, III. ii. 16; **vaunted**, *ppl. adj.* IV. iv. 7.

vauntage, advantage, opportunity, III. vii. 51.

vauntfull, boastful, *Muiop.* 54.

vaut, vawte, *sb.* vault, II. vii. 28, ix. 29, *Gnat* 444, *Hubberd* 1229.

vaute, *vb.* to vault, jump, leap, *Hubberd* 693.

vauted, *pa. part.* IV. iv. 43; *ppl. adj., Clout* 611 : vaulted, arched.

veale, IV. v. 10, *Three Lett.* p. 611; **vele**, I. i. 4, viii. 19, II. Prol. 5, III. i. 59 : veil (*lit. and fig.*).

vellenage, slavery (*fig.*), II. xi. 1.

vellet, velvet, *S. C. May* 185.

venery, hunting (*fig.*), I. vi. 22.

vengeable, eager for vengeance, II. iv. 30.

vengement, revenge, IV. vii. 30, VI. iii. 18.

venger, avenger, I. iii. 20.

venim(e), venom, poison, *Muiop.* 352, *Worlds Vanitie* 39.

vent, to snuff, *S. C. Feb.* 75. **vented**, *pret.* lifted up so as to give air, III. i. 42.

ventayle, -taile, movable front or mouthpiece of a helmet, which may be raised to admit fresh air, III. ii. 24, IV. vi. 19, v. viii. 12.

venterously, daringly, *Two Lett.* p. 640.

ventred, *pret.* ventured, IV. vii. 31.

ventrous, venturous, daring, adventurous, II. xii. 44, IV. ii. 27, vi. 4, V. x. 30.

verdit, judgement, opinion, decision, VII. vii. 27, *Three Lett.* p. 618.

vere, to turn, shift, I. xii. 1, V. xii. 18.

vermell, -eill, *sb.* II. x. 24; *adj.* III. i. 46, IV. ix. 27, *Proth.* 33 : vermilion.

vermily, *sb.* vermilion, III. viii. 6.

vermin, (a noxious) insect, *Worlds Vanitie* 77.

vertue, power, worth, V. i. 10.

vertuous, potent, powerful, II. xii. 86.

Veruen, vervain ; one of several weedy plants of the genus *Verbena*, which formerly had sacred associations, *Muiop.* 197.

vestiment, vestment, garment, I. iii. 17, III. xii. 29, V. ix. 10.

vetchy, of vetch, *S. C. Sept.* 256.

vild, vylde, *adj.* vile, I. iii. Arg., vi. 3, III. vii. 15, V. xi. 18; *adv.* vilely, VI. i. Arg.

vildly, vilely, I. i. 20, iii. 43.

virelayes, a short light song or poem written to an old French measure, III. x. 8, *S. C. Nov.* 21, *Daphn.* 317.

virginals, keyed instrument of the harpsichord class, *Two Lett.* p. 636.

visnomie, -y, visage, countenance, v. iv. 11,

Muiop. 310, *Amor.* Son. 45, *Misc. Sonn.* II. Cf. **physnomy**.

visour, mask, disguise, I. vii. 1.

vitall, necessary to life, life-giving, II. i. 2, *R. R.* 342, *Daphn.* 197.

voide, voyd, to avoid, turn aside, IV. vi. 3 ; *pa. part.* turned aside, removed, VI. vii. 43 ; cleared, removed, v. iv. 46 ; to go, depart, *S. C. Aug.* 164, *Epitaph* (2) 35.

voydnesse, emptiness, *Clout* 850.

vow, will, wish, VII. vi. 22

vulgar, -e, the common people, I. v. 8, III. xii. 4, v. ii. 33, *Teares* 194.

W

wad, bundle, *H. Love* 226.

wade, to go, pass, I. i. 12.

wae, woe, *S. C. Sept.* 25.

wag, to move, IV. iv. 18, v. i. 22.

wage, *sb.* pledge, I. iv. 39.

wage, *vb.* to let out for pay, II. vii. 18 **waged**, *ppl. adj.* paid, *Clout* 382.

wagmoires, quagmires, *S. C. Sept.* 130.

waide, *pa. part.* weighed, proved, IV. ix. 38. Cf. **way**.

waift, waif, a thing blown by the wind or carried in by the sea, IV. xii. 31. Cf. **weft**, *sb.*

waild, *pret.* bewailed, *Thest.* 128. Cf. **wayle**.

wailefull, wayl-, mournful, III. iv. 38, v. vi. 26, *S. C. Feb.* 82, *May* 201, *Muiop.* 12.

waine, wayne, wagon, I. iv. 19, v. 41, III. iv. 60.

wained, *pa. part.* carried along, moved, VII. vi. 10.

wait, -e, wayt, *vb.* to watch for, II. iv. 17 ; to await, I. v. 3, v. xii. 12 ; to watch, III. xi. 21.

wakefull, watchful, III. ix. 7.

waladay, *interj.* alas! *Gnat* 417.

walke, to move, wag, II. iv. 5. **walkt**, *pret.* rolled, III. xii. 12.

wallowed, *ppl. adj.* grovelling, III. xi. 7.

wan, *adj.* pale, faint, II. vi. 41 ; sorrowful, sad, *S. C. Oct.* 85. **wanne**, feeble, *S. C. Jan.* 47.

wan, *vb. pret.* won, gained, II. ii. 17, vi. 41, VII. 54.

wand, bough, branch, v. ix. 17.

wanton, playful, I. xii. 7 ; wild, III. vi. 22.

war, worse, *S. C. Sept.* 108.

ward, *sb.* guard, garrison, II. xi. 15.

ward, *vb.* to guard, I. viii. 3. v. ix. 22, *S. C. July* 42 ; to ward off, repel, I. ix. 10.

ware, *adj.* wary, sharp, I. vii. 1 ; aware, III. ix. 28.

ware, *vb. pret.* wore, I. iv. 47.

warelesse, unaware ; unawares, IV. ii. 3, v. v.

52; heedless, unwary, IV. x. 20, v. v. 17; unperceived, v. i. 22.

warely, carefully, warily, I. xii. 36.

war-hable, fit for war, II. x. 62.

wariment, caution, IV. iii. 17.

warke, work, II. i. 32, *S. C. May* 145, *Nov.* 65, *Bellay* 4¼.

war-monger, a mercenary soldier, III. x. 29.

warne, to deny, forbid, prevent, *Clorinda* 12.

warrant, rule, licence, *Two Lett.* pp. 639, 640.

warrayd, **-eyd**, **-eid**, *pret.* waged war on, attacked, I. v. 48, II. x. 21, 50; *intr.* struggled, warred (*fig.*), III. v. 48; *pa. part.* assailed, *Amor.* Son. 44.

warre, *sb.* knob or protuberance on a tree, *S. C. Aug.* 26.

warre, *adv.* in a worse manner, IV. viii. 31. Cf. **war**.

warriouresse, female warrior, V. vii. 27.

wasserman, male sea-monster of human form, II. xii. 24.

wast, *sb.* waist. II. xi. 12, V. x. 8.

wast(e), *adj.* idle, useless, wasted, I. i. 42, *S. C. Feb.* 133; stray, deserted, *S. C. Sept.* 198.

wast, *vb.* to lay waste, devastate, IV. i. 45; **wasted**, *pa. part.*, *S. C. Jan.* 19.

wast(e)full, desolate, waste, barren, I. iii. 3, II. vii. 2, xii. 8, III. xi. 53, IV. viii. 8, *S. C. June* 50; devastating, *S. C. Jan.* 2.

wastnesse, wilderness, I. iii. 3.

watchet, light or pale-blue colour, III. iv. 40, IV. xi. 27, *Elegie* 3.

water-sprinkles, drops, splashes of water, IV. iii. 25.

wav'd, *pa. part.* watered, having a sort of pattern on which there is a changeable play of light, IV. xi. 45.

wawes, waves, II. xii. 4.

waxe, to grow, become, II. x. 30; **waxen**, *pa. part.*, *Hubberd* 599. Cf. **wex**, **wox**(en).

way, to weigh, V. ii. 46, 49; to consider, esteem, VII. vi. 55; to weigh (*fig.*), consider, VII. viii. 1; **wayd**, *pret.* I. x. 40; *pa. part.* VII. vii. 58; *ta. part.* weighed, determined, IV. i, 7.

way'd, *pret.* journeyed, IV. ii. 12.

wayle, to bewail, lament, mourn, *Daphn.* 510; **wayld**, *pa. part.* I. v. 23.

wayment, *sb.* lamentation, III. iv. 35, *R. T.* 390.

wayment, *vb.* to lament, II. i. 16, *Teares* 355.

weale, happiness, *Past. Aeglogue* 134.

weanell, weanling, a lamb or kid newly weaned, *S. C. Sept.* 198.

weare, to pass, spend (time), I. i. 31.

wearish, wizened, withered, IV. v. 34.

weasand pipe, windpipe, IV. iii. 12. Cf. **wesand**.

weather, to expose to the air, V. iv. 42, *Muiop.* 184.

weaued, *fret.* wavered, V. iv. 10.

weed, undergrowth, IV. vii. 4.

weed(e), weeds, clothes, dress, attire, I. Prol. 1, vii. 19, II. iii. 27, iv. 29, viii. 16, p. 409, *S. C. July* 168, *Hubberd* 1321, *Clout* 711.

weeke, wick, III. x. 30.

weeldlesse, unwieldy, IV. iii. 19.

ween(e), **-en**, to expect, suppose, think, I. i. 10, x. 58, II. iv. 28, viii. 26, III. ii. 13, vi. 54, v. ii. 25; to tell, IV. xi. 27.

weet(e), **-on¹**, to know, learn, perceive, discover, I. iii. 6, vi. 34, vii. 11, II. iii. 11, III. i. 19, ii. 6, v. 31, IV. i. 41, 43, VI. ii. 30; *to w.* = to wit, I. iii. 17, III. vi. 54, IV. iv. 40, xi. 28, v. x. 1, VI. iii. 3.

weet², to wet, IV. ix. 33.

weeting, knowledge, V. x. 39.

weetingly, wittingly, knowingly, VI. iii. 11, *Past. Elegie* 22.

weetlesse, unconscious, ignorant, thoughtless, III. ii. 26, ix. 41, VI. viii. 47, *S. C. July* 35.

weft, *sb.* = **waift**, III. x. 36, IV. ii. 4, v. iii. 27, VI. i. 18.

weft, *vb.*: *ta. part.* wafted, carried, II. vi. 18, VI. v. 23; waived, avoided, III. iv. 36.

weighing, *pres. part.* considering, *S C.* p. 417. Cf. **way**.

welaway, excl. of distress, *Amor.* p. 577.

welaway the while, alas the time! *S. C. Sept.* 58.

weld(e), to wield, I. xi. 28, *S. C. May* 206; to govern, manage, control, IV. Prol. 1, v. ix. 11, VI. viii. 11, *R. T.* 447, *Hubberd* 1232, *Clout* 130; to bear, *S. C. Oct.* 40; *intr.* to exert oneself, IV. i. 37.

wele, weal, V. xi. 16.

welfare, may (it) prosper, III. ii. 42.

welhead, **-hed**, well head, source, fountain (*lit.* and *fig.*), II. ii. 6, vii. 15, V. ix. 26.

welke, to fade, wane, I. i. 23; **welked**, *tpl. adj.*, *S. C. Jan.* 73; *pa. part.*, *S. C. Nov.* 13.

welkin, sky, heaven, I. iv. 9 (*attrib.*), III. ix. 11, *S. C. Sept.* 187.

well, *sb.* weal, happiness, I. ii. 43.

well, *vb.* to pour forth (*lit.* and *fig.*), II. x. 26, VI. Prol. 7.

well away, **wel-**, **wellawaye**, *interj.* alas! II. vi. 43, viii. 46, v. i. 15, *S. C. Aug.* 19.

well to donne, welldoing, I. x. 33.

weltre, to roll, wallow, *S. C. July* 197.

wend¹, to turn, go, I. i. 28, IV. viii. 50.

wend², *pret.* thought, VII. vi. 11. Cf. **ween**.

wene, to think, *S. C. March* 25. Cf. ween.

went, course, journey, iv. v. 46; resort, haunt, iv. ii. 47; turning, veering, vi. vi. 3.

wesand, windpipe, v. ii. 14, *S. C. Sept.* 210.

west, to set (of the sun), v. Prol. 8.

wex, *sb.* wax, iii. viii. 6.

wex(e), *vb.* to wax, grow, become, i. ii. 4, iv. 30, ii. iii. 9, x. 20, iii. i. 47, vii. 24, ix. 13, vi. i. Arg., xii. 11, *S. C. Feb.* 124, *June* 103, *Clout* 851; wexen, 3rd pers. plur. pres., *S. C. Aug.* 96, *Oct.* 42; *pa. part., R. T.* 472. wext, *pa. part.* increased, iv. ii. 52.

wexen, waxen, *S. C. Dec.* 68.

wey, to weigh, consider, *Hubberd* 112. Cf. way.

whally, having a greenish tinge, i. iv. 24.

what, fare, things, vi. ix. 7.

what (is he) for a (ladde), what kind of (a lad is he), *S. C. Apr.* 17.

wheare, place, iii. iv. 19.

whelky, knobby, rounded, *Gnat* 105.

whelmd, *pa. part.* ii. ii. 43; *pret.* vii. vi. 53: overwhelmed, crushed. whelming, *ppl. adj.* ii. iv. 17.

whenas, when, i. ii. 32, ii. ix. 10, 14, p. 413.

whereas, where-as, where, ii. xii. 42, vii. vi. 17, 47, 48.

whet, *pa. part.* whetted, sharpened, vi. viii. 45.

whether, *pron., adj.* which (of two), i. ii. 37, iv. iii. 37, ix. 1, 10, v. ii. 17, vii. vii. 57, *Hubberd* 997.

whether, *adv.* whither, v. viii. 48, *Clout* 251.

whight, white, ii. iii. 26.

while, time, iv. i. 7, *S. C. Jan.* 8; *the whyles* = while, vi. vi. 44.

whilere, whyl-, -eare, erewhile, lately, formerly, i. ix. 28, iii. vi. 26, x. 17, iv. v. 8, *Past. Aeglogue* 142; already, iii. ix. 13.

whiles, while, ii. iv. 34.

whilom, -e, whyl-, formerly, once, i. Prol. 1, iii. vii. 47. p. 410, *S. C. Apr.* 23.

whirlpooles, sea-monsters of the whale kind, ii. xii. 23.

whist, *pa. part.* silenced, vii. vii. 59.

whistler, ? plover or pewit, ii. xii. 36.

whit : *no w.* = nothing at all, not at all, ii. viii. 54, vii. vii. 44.

white, mark, *Three Lett.* p. 619.

whot, whott(e), hot, i. x. 26, ii. i. 58, viii. 11, ix. 29, iii. viii. 49, *S. C. March* 41, *Sept.* 112. whotest, hottest, *S. C.* p. 447.

wicked, baneful, cruel, iii. xi. 24.

widder, wider, *S. C. Sept.* 210.

wide, wyde, round about, vi. xi. 18; away, i. i. 34, xi. 5, ii. viii. 36.

widow, bereaved, *Past. Aeglogue* 112.

widowhead, widowhood, *Teares* 240.

wield, to sway, influence, v. x. 24.

wight, *sb.*[1] creature, person, human being, i. ii. 30, 42, v. 36, ix. 23, ii. xi. 8, iii. iii. 60, ix. 21, iv. vii. 10, xii. 19, v. Prol. 9, *S. C. Apr.* 47.

wight, *sb.*[2] blame, *S. C. June* 100. Cf. wite, *sb.*

wight, *adj.* nimble, active, *S. C. March* 91.

wightly, quickly, *S. C. Sept.* 5.

wildings, crab-apples, iii. vii. 17.

wile, wyle, to beguile, iii. x. 5.

will, *sb.* desire, *Beautie* 158.

will, *vb.* to wish, request, v. xii. 8, 9. wild, *pret.* ordered, vi. vii. 35. *will or nill* = willy nilly, i. iii. 43.

wimble, nimble, *S. C. March* 91.

wimple, covering of linen worn by women on the head, cheeks, and neck, i. xii. 22.

wimpled, *pa. part.* i. i. 4; *pret.* vii. vii. 5 : laid, lay in plaits or folds.

win, to reach, get to, vi. i. 23.

winde, to perceive or follow by the scent, v. ii. 25.

wine-fats, vats of wine, vii. vii. 39.

wisards, sages, wise men, wizards, i. iv. 12, ii. ix. 53, v. Prol. 8.

wise, wize, manner, guise, i:i. i. 55, ii. 24, vi. ix. 6, vii. viii. 18, *Teares* 170.

wishful, desirable, v. ix. 10.

wist, *pret.* knew, i. ii. 40, iii. ii. 23, iv. i. 7, xii. 17. Cf. wot.

wit, witt, knowledge, intelligence, ii. xii. 44, iii. i. 12, iv. iv. 39; mind, *Clout* 707.

witche, witch-elm, *S. C. June* 20.

wite, *sb.* blame, censure, vi. iii. 16, xii. 41.

wite, witen, wyte, *vb.* to blame, reproach, censure, ii. xii. 16, iii. iv. 52, iv. Prol. 1, v. xi. 57, *S. C. May* 159, *July* 210, *Aug.* 136, *Hubberd* 348, *Clout* 749, 916.

witelesse, blameless, *S. C. Aug.* 136.

withdraw, to carry off, iii. xi. 30.

with-hault, *pret.* withheld, ii. xi. 9.

without, outside, vii. vii. 52.

withouten, without, ii. viii. 47, iv. vii. 2, v. xii. 39, vii. vii. 53, *S. C. Oct.* 29, *Hubberd* 158, 186.

witnesse, a rough edge (as in the leaves of books), *Three Lett.* p. 625.

wittily, wisely, sensibly, ii. ix. 53.

wiuehood, state of being a wife, iv. v. 3.

wiuely, wifelike, iv. v. 3.

wo, woe, sad, ii. viii. 53, iv. i. 38.

womanhead, -hed, womanhood, womankind, ii. xii. 55, v. ix. 45, *Muiop.* 345; womanliness, vi. ii. 15, *Clout* 512. womanhood, womanly feeling, vi. viii. 51.

won, wonne, *sb.* abode, dwelling-place, retreat, ii. vii. 20, xii. 11, iii. iii. 7, viii. 37,

iv. viii. 22, v. ix. 8, vi. iii. 37, xi. 35, *Clout* 521.

won, *vb.*[1]: *did won* = was wont, used, iii. ix. 21. **wonned**, *pret.* was wont, *S. C. Feb.* 119. **wonst**, is wont, *Muiop.* 11.

wondred, wonderful, ii. xii. 44, iv. xi. 49.

won(e), wonne, *vb.*[2] to dwell, live, abide, i. vi. 39, ii. i. 51, iii. 18, vii. 49, xii. 69, iii. i. 3, ii. 14, iii. 26, v. 27, iv. vi. 5, xi. 37, vi. ii. 25, *S. C. Feb.* 184, *Clout* 307.

wonne, *vb.*[3] : *pret.* i. vi. 39 (*intr.*) ; *pa. part.*, *Hubberd* 751 (*tr.*) : conquered.

wonning, dwelling-place, vi. iv. 13.

wont, *ppl. adj.* wonted, accustomed, v. iii. 1. Cf. **won**, *vb.*

wont, *pret.* was, were accustomed, iv. vii. 6, 40 ; used to be, *S. C. Feb.* 108. **wontes**, **wonts**, is accustomed, ii. ii. 42, *Amor.* Son. 39. Cf. **won**, *vb.*

wontlesse, unaccustomed, *Beautie* 2.

wood, mad, furious, i. iv. 34, v. 20, ii. iv. 11, iv. ix. 29, *S. C. March* 55, *Aug.* 75, *Hubberd* 1352

woodnesse, madness, iii. xi. 27.

wooe, to obtain by solicitation, iv. x. 57.

woon, to dwell, *Gnat* 18, *Clout* 774. Cf. **won**, *vb.*[2]

word, motto, iv. iv. 39.

wore, *pret.* passed, iv. ix. 19. Cf. **weare**.

world : *worlds pride* = earthly magnificence, *R. R.* 422.

worship, glory, honour, i. i. 3, iii. ii. 8.

worth, *sb.*: *in w.*, *in good w.* = in good part, pp. 411, 412, 413.

worth, *vb.* : *wo worth* = woe betide, ii. vi. 32, *Epitaph* (2) 13.

worthy, deserved, i. i. 26, *S. C. June* 100.

wot, wote, to know, i. i. 13, 32, ii. 18, ix. 43, ii. iii. 16, iii. ix. 7, vii. vi. 33, *S. C. Feb.* 85, *March* 102.

wound, *pa. part.* weaved, ii. xii. 82.

woundlesse, unwounded, *S. C. Oct.* 41.

wowed, *pret.* wooed, vi. xi. 4, *Past. Elegie* 67.

wox(e), *pret.* waxed, became, grew, ii. viii. 9, 47, x. 17, xii. 22, iii. iii. 17, iv. 52, iv. viii. 31, v. ix. 46, *S. C. Jan.* 5, *Hubberd* 1103. **woxen**, *pa. part.* become, grown, i iv. 34, x. 29, iii. v. 29, x. 60, vii. vi. 6, p. 411, *Past. Aeglogue* 112.

wrack(e), wreck, destruction, i. vi. 1, iv. ix. 25, *Teares* 400 ; violence, *S. C. Feb.* 10.

wrackfull, avenging, destructive, vi. ix. 27.

wrast, to wrest, v. xii. 21.

wrastling, wrestling, *Three Lett.* p. 616.

wrate, *pret.* wrote, iii. xii. 31.

wrawling, *pres. part.* mewing (as a cat), vi. xii. 27.

wreake, *sb.* revenge, punishment, i. viii. 43, xii. 16 ; destruction, ruin, iii. vii. 48 ; wreck, *Teares* 124, *R. R.* 33.

wreak, -e, *vb.* to avenge, i. iv. Arg., ii. iii. 14, iv. i. 39, 52, vi. 38 (*intr.*), *Gnat* 579.

wreakfull, avenging, v. i. 8.

wreath, to turn, twist, ii. i. 56, *Bellay* 74. **wreathed**, *ppl. adj.* writhing, *Gnat* 253 ; twisted, *Clout* 245.

wrecke, to avenge, v. iv. 24.

wreckfull, destructive, vi. viii. 36.

wrest, *vb.* to wrench, twist, turn, ii. xii. 81, v. xii. 34, *Beautie* 158.

wrest[1], wrist, i. v. 6, ii. ii. 21, viii. 22, iii. vii. 2, iv. xi. 51.

wrest[2], wrench, ii. xi. 42.

wretch, wretched, vi. ix. 30.

wrethed, *ppl. adj.* twisted, coiled, i. i. 18.

wrigle, wriggling, *S. C. Feb.* 7.

wring, to distress, i. xi. 39 ; to turn, twist, vi. vii. 9 ; to turn or divert the course of, to affect, *Worlds Vanitie* 126.

writ, written document, i. xii. 25. **writs**, *plur.* writings, iii. ii. 1, iv. ii. 33, vi. xii. 41, *Teares* 582.

wrizled, *ppl. adj.* wrinkled, shrivelled, i. viii. 47.

wroke, ii. v. 21, iv. vii. 26; **wroken**, iv. ii. 21, vi. ii. 7, *S. C. March* 108, *Muiop.* 99 ; *pa. part.* avenged.

wrought, *pa. part.* app. released, freed, v. v. Arg.

wrye, awry, *S. C. Feb.* 28.

wull, will, *Epith.* 252.

wynd, to extricate, vi. iv. 26.

Y

y-, archaic prefix used to form the past participle, e. g. **ybrought**, brought, i. v. 5. **ymounted**, mounted, i. ii. 29.

yate, gate, *S. C. May* 224.

ybent, turned, iii. iv. 47.

ybet, beaten, iv. iv. 9.

yblent, blinded, dazzled, i. ii. 5, ii. vii. 1, *S. C. Apr.* 155.

ybore, born, iii. iv. 21.

ybrent, burnt out, iii. ix. 53.

yclad, ycled, clothed, i. i. 1, iv. 38.

ycleepe, to call, *Clout* 65.

ycleped, called, named, iii. v. 8.

ycond, learnt, *S. C. May* 262.

ydlesse, idleness, vi. ii. 31.

ydrad, dreaded, i. i. 2, v. xi. 3, xii. 37.

yearne, to earn, vi. i. 40, vii. 15.

yede, yeed, yead, to go, i. xi. 5, ii. iv. 2, *S. C. July* 109, *Sept.* 145.

yeeld, to admit, grant, ii. ix. 38.

yeuen, given, *S. C. April* 114.

yfere, together, in company with, I. ix. 1, II. i. 35, ix. 2, III. vii. 48, ix. 13, x. 16, VII. vi. 31, *S. C. Apr.* 68, *July* 143.

yglaunst, *pret.* glanced, glided, II. vi. 31.

ygoe, *pa. part.* gone, *S. C. May* 67, *Nov.* 76.

ygoe, *adv.* ago, I. ii. 18, III. v. 9, xii. 41, *S. C. Nov.* 81; *late y.* = lately, II. i. 2.

yield, to admit, grant, II. Prol. 4.

yirk, to lash, VI. vii. 44.

ylike, alike, I. iv. 27; *y. as* = like, *S. C. May* 76.

ylke, that (same), *S. C. Aug.* 142.

ymolt, melted, III. xi. 25.

ympt, *see* impe, *vb.*

Ynd, India, I. v. 4, vi. 2.

ynne, inn, abode, *S. C. Feb.* 89, *Nov.* 16.

yod, yode, *pret.* went, I. x. 53, II. vii. 2, III. i. 1, 4, viii. 19, 45, IV. viii. 34, VII. vii. 35, *S. C. May* 22, 178, *July* 182; yodest, *Past. Aeglogue* 88. *See* yede.

yold, *pret.* III. xi. 25; *pa. part.* III. xi. 17 (2), VII. vii. 30: yielded.

yond, *adj.* mad, furious, II. viii. 40, III. vii. 26.

yond, *adv.* yonder, IV. i. 33, 35, VI. xii. 18.

yongmen, young men, *Gnat* 431.

yongth, yongthly, v.ll. for *yougth*, *yougthly*.

yonker, younker, young man, youngster, IV. i. 11, *S. C.* p. 426, *Three Lett.* p. 621.

yonkerly, youthful, *Three Lett.* pp. 629, 641.

yougthes folke, young people, *S. C. May* 9.

yougthly, youthful, *Muiop.* 431.

youngling, young of man or beast, I. x. 57, v. viii. 46, *S. C. May* 100, 182, 211, *Aug.* 17.

youngth, youth, *S. C. Feb.* 52, 87, *Nov.* 20, *Muiop.* 34.

youthly, *adj.* youthful, I. v. 7, II. iii. 38, III. ix. 48, IV. ii. 45, VI. vii. 5.

youthly, *adv.* youthfully, I. xi. 34.

ypent, pent up, *S. C. Jan.* 4, *July* 216.

ypight, placed, set, I. ix. 33.

yplast, placed, I. iv. 28.

yplight, pledged, II. iii. 1.

yrapt, rapt, *Clout* 623.

yrent, torn to pieces, IV. vii. 15, *S. C. Sept.* 148.

yriu'd, torn, IV. vi. 15.

yrke, to trouble, III. viii. 48, VI. x. 29.

yron braced, iron sinewed, II. v. 7.

ysame, together, VII. vii. 32.

yse, ice, *Amor.* Son. 30.

yshend, to disgrace, spoil, *S. C. Aug.* 139. cf. shend.

yshrilled, *pret.* sounded shrill, *Clout* 62.

yssew, to get out, p. 408.

ythundered, *pa. part.* struck by a thunderbolt, *Teares* 8.

ytost, disturbed, *S. C. June* 12.

ywis, -sse, certainly, II. i. 19, III. vii. 53, *S. C. May* 109, *Two Lett.* p. 640.

ywrake, ywroke, ywroken, avenged, revenged, IV. vi. 23, viii. 14, xi. 5, VI. vi. 18, *Clout* 921.

INDEX OF FIRST LINES

OF MINOR POEMS.